national STATISTICS

Economic Trends

Annual Supplement

2000 Edition

No. 26

Editor: Paul Dickman

London: The Stationery Office

ISBN 0 11 621208 X
ISSN 0308-1133

Contact points

For enquiries about this publication, contact the Editor, Paul Dickman:
Tel: 020 7533 5914
E-mail: paul.dickman@ons.gov.uk

To order this publication, call The Stationery Office on **0870 600 5522.** See also back cover.

For general enquiries, contact the National Statistics Public Enquiry Service on **0845 601 3034**
(minicom: 01633 812399)
E-mail: info@statistics.gov.uk
Fax: 01633 652747
Letters: Room DG/18, 1 Drummond Gate,
London SW1V 2QQ

You can also find National Statistics on the internet - go to **www.statistics.gov.uk**

About the Office for National Statistics

The Office for National Statistics (ONS) is the government agency responsible for compiling, analysing and disseminating many of the United Kingdom's economic, social and demographic statistics, including the retail prices index, trade figures and labour market data, as well as the periodic census of the population and health statistics. The Director of ONS is also the National Statistician and the Registrar General for England and Wales, and the agency administers the statutory registration of births, marriages and deaths there.

A National Statistics publication

Official statistics bearing the National Statistics logo are produced to high professional standards set out in the National Statistics Code of Practice. They undergo regular quality assurance reviews to ensure that they meet customer needs. They are produced free from any political interference.

Contents

Introduction

The *Economic Trends Annual Supplement* provides a notes and definitions supplement to the monthly *Economic Trends* and also contains long runs of up to fifty years data for some of the main economic indicators.

National accounts data comparable with the 2000 edition of *UK National Accounts* (the National Statistics *Blue Book*) is included. This includes annual data to 1999 and quarterly data to 2000 quarter 2. Some 2000 quarter 3 is included in other tables, where available.

The tables relate fairly closely to those included in the monthly *Economic Trends* but with very long runs of annual and quarterly data. For ease of reference, the table numbers of *Economic Trends* are shown on the contents page. In many cases it has been possible to show both unadjusted and seasonally adjusted data. The aim has been to provide, for the most useful periodicities, as balanced a collection of economic series as possible within the confines of the size of the publication. In some instances it has seemed appropriate to include slightly different series to those shown in the monthly publication.

The notes and definitions section gives definitions of items and units employed both in *Economic Trends* and in this supplement in more detail than is possible in the headings and footnotes of the tables themselves. The definitions and table numbers relate to the tables as they appear in issue No. 564 of *Economic Trends* for November 2000 and in this issue of the *Annual Supplement*. If further new series are added or changes are made in *Economic Trends* before the next issue of the *Annual Supplement,* additional definitions will be given where necessary in the footnotes to the tables in the monthly publication.

Readers requiring figures for years earlier than shown in this *Annual Supplement* may wish to consult *Economic Statistics 1900–1983* (Economist Publications 1985) or *The British Economy: Key Statistics 1900 –1970*, published by Times Newspapers Ltd for the London and Cambridge Economic Service. The latter is now out of print but should still be available for consultation in many libraries. These publications contain annual estimates, back to 1900 in most cases, for many important economic series. However, care should be taken, to allow for any discontinuities or differences in definition when using series from them, to extend backwards the series in the *Annual Supplement*.

Any enquiries about the data shown in this publication should be directed to the appropriate telephone number shown at the foot of each table. General enquiries about National Statistics data can be directed to the Public Enquiry Service on 0845 601 3034.

If you have any comments or suggestions about the *Economic Trends Annual Supplement* or any of the other National Statistics macro-economic publications (see chart on page 6), contact Paul Dickman, ONS, Zone D4/19, 1 Drummond Gate, London, SW1V 2QQ or e-mail paul.dickman@ons.gov.uk.

We would like to acknowledge the help and advice given by government departments and other bodies in preparing this issue.

Notes on tables

1. Statistics relate mainly to the United Kingdom; where figures are for Great Britain only, this is shown on the table.

2. Rounding may lead to inconsistencies between the sum of constituent parts and the total in some tables.

3. A line drawn across a column between two consecutive figures indicates that the figures above and below the line have been compiled on different bases and are not strictly comparable. In each case a footnote explains the difference.

4. Symbols used:
   .. not available
   - nil or less than half the final digit shown.

Office for National Statistics
1 Drummond Gate
London, SW1V 2QQ

November 2000

Data in computer readable form

This publication is available in electronic format via the National Statistics DataBank Service and StatBase®.

The DataBank Service provides electronic versions of various National Statistics business and economic publications and press notices on diskette, or as files downloadable via the internet. A DataBank catalogue can be downloaded from the DataBank web-page *(http://www.statistics.gov.uk/databank/dbcatalogue.asp)* which is hosted on the National Statistics web-site *(http://www.statistics.gov.uk/).*

StatBase® provides on-line access to individual and groups of time series, cross sectional data and metadata. StatBase® is also held on the National Statistics web-site: *http://www.statistics.gov.uk/statbase/mainmenu.asp.*

For more details of these services please contact:
Online Services Branch
Room B1/12
1 Drummond Gate
LONDON SW1V 2QQ
(Tel: 020 7533 5675 Fax: 020 7533 5688 E-mail *on-line.services.branch@statistics.gov.uk*).

United Kingdom Macro-Economic Statistics Publications

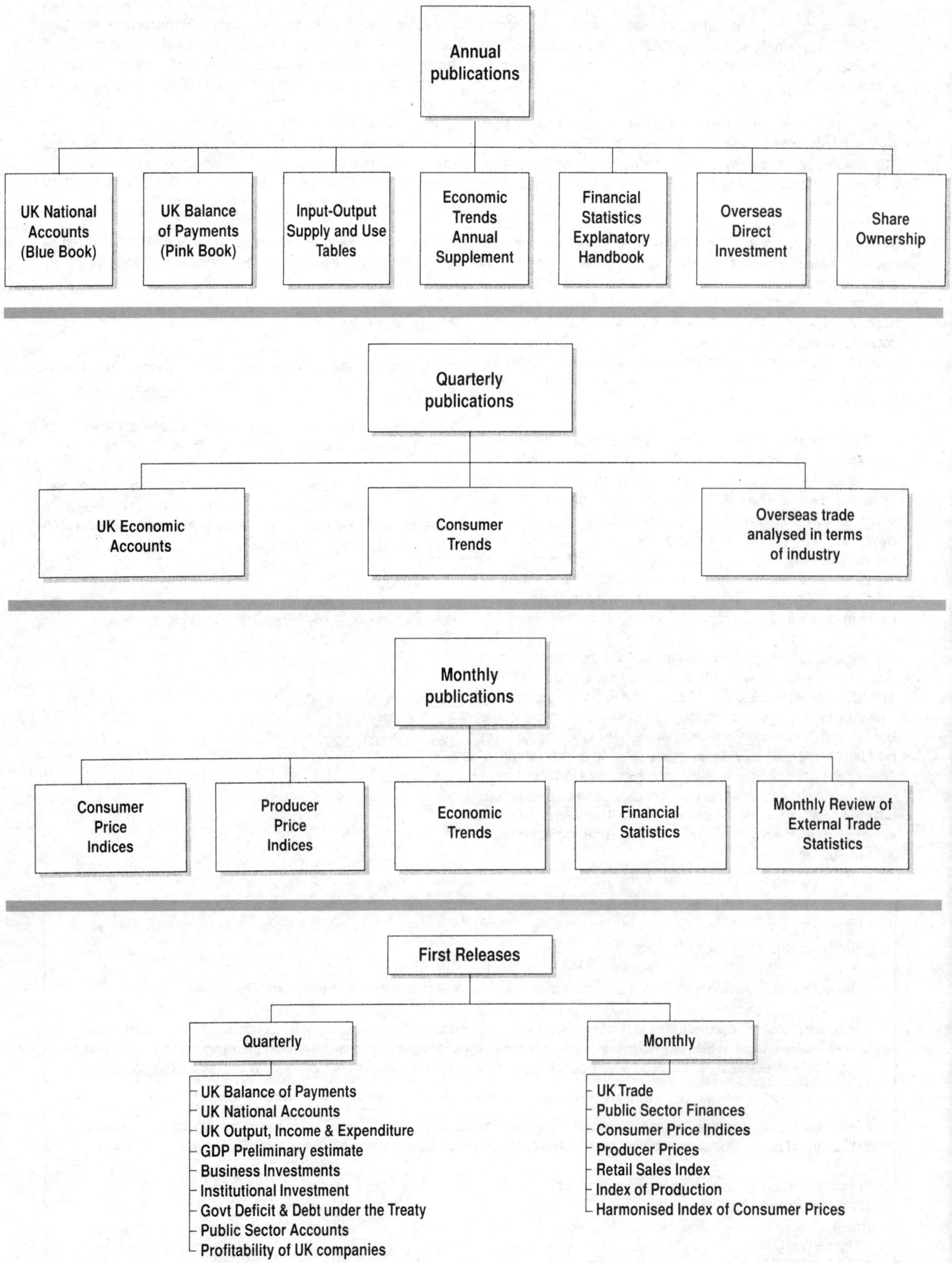

Other publications: - *Retail Prices 1914-1990 - Labour Market Trends - National Accounts Concepts, Sources and Methods - Sector Classification Guide for the National Accounts*

UK Economic Accounts

1.1 National accounts aggregates
Index numbers[1]

1995=100

	Value indices at current prices		Volume indices at 1995 prices			Implied deflators[2]	
	Gross domestic product at market prices	Gross value added (GVA)at basic prices	Gross national disposable income at market prices	Gross domestic product at market prices	Gross value added (GVA)at basic prices	GDP at market prices	GVA at basic prices
	YBEU	YBEX	YBFP	YBEZ	CGCE	YBGB	CGBV
1948	1.7	1.7	32.4	31.5	31.6	5.2	5.3
1949	1.8	1.8	33.2	32.6	32.9	5.4	5.5
1950	1.8	1.9	34.4	33.6	33.8	5.5	5.5
1951	2.0	2.1	34.7	34.5	34.6	5.9	6.0
1952	2.2	2.3	35.2	34.7	34.9	6.4	6.5
1953	2.4	2.4	36.6	36.0	36.2	6.6	6.7
1954	2.5	2.6	37.9	37.5	37.8	6.7	6.8
1955	2.7	2.7	38.8	38.7	38.9	6.9	7.0
1956	2.9	3.0	39.4	39.1	39.4	7.4	7.5
1957	3.0	3.1	40.1	39.8	40.1	7.6	7.8
1958	3.2	3.3	40.5	39.9	40.2	7.9	8.1
1959	3.4	3.5	42.2	41.6	41.8	8.0	8.3
1960	3.6	3.7	44.3	43.9	44.1	8.1	8.4
1961	3.8	3.9	45.5	45.0	45.3	8.4	8.7
1962	4.0	4.1	46.3	45.5	46.0	8.7	8.9
1963	4.2	4.4	48.4	47.7	48.3	8.9	9.1
1964	4.6	4.8	50.9	50.3	50.9	9.2	9.4
1965	5.0	5.2	52.3	51.5	52.3	9.7	9.9
1966	5.3	5.5	53.3	52.5	53.3	10.1	10.3
1967	5.6	5.8	54.6	53.8	54.4	10.4	10.6
1968	6.1	6.2	56.5	56.0	56.7	10.9	11.0
1969	6.6	6.6	57.9	57.1	57.9	11.5	11.4
1970	7.2	7.3	59.5	58.5	59.2	12.3	12.3
1971	8.0	8.2	60.7	59.6	60.5	13.5	13.6
1972	9.0	9.3	63.0	61.8	62.6	14.6	14.8
1973	10.4	10.8	66.7	66.3	66.7	15.6	16.2
1974	11.7	12.4	64.0	65.2	65.8	18.0	18.9
1975	14.8	15.7	63.6	64.8	65.5	22.8	24.0
1976	17.5	18.5	65.5	66.6	67.1	26.3	27.6
1977	20.4	21.3	66.5	68.1	68.6	29.9	31.0
1978	23.5	24.5	69.4	70.5	70.5	33.4	34.7
1979	27.7	28.3	71.8	72.4	71.9	38.2	39.4
1980	32.3	33.0	70.4	70.8	70.5	45.6	46.8
1981	35.5	36.0	70.1	69.9	69.8	50.7	51.6
1982	38.8	39.3	71.3	71.2	71.3	54.5	55.2
1983	42.4	43.1	74.5	73.9	73.9	57.4	58.3
1984	45.4	46.3	76.4	75.7	75.5	60.0	61.2
1985	49.8	50.7	78.7	78.5	78.7	63.4	64.4
1986	53.5	54.0	81.8	81.8	81.6	65.4	66.1
1987	58.7	59.3	85.2	85.5	85.1	68.8	69.7
1988	65.5	66.0	89.8	89.9	89.2	72.9	74.0
1989	71.9	72.7	91.7	91.8	91.1	78.3	79.8
1990	77.9	78.9	92.1	92.4	92.0	84.3	85.8
1991	81.9	82.3	91.4	91.0	90.9	90.0	90.6
1992	85.2	85.8	91.9	91.1	91.1	93.5	94.2
1993	89.5	90.2	94.0	93.2	93.2	96.1	96.8
1994	94.9	95.3	98.5	97.3	97.4	97.5	97.9
1995	100.0	100.0	100.0	100.0	100.0	100.0	100.0
1996	105.9	106.1	103.4	102.6	102.5	103.3	103.4
1997	112.8	112.5	108.6	106.2	106.0	106.3	106.2
1998	119.3	118.9	112.2	109.0	109.1	109.5	108.9
1999	124.8	123.9	114.5	111.3	111.4	112.2	111.2

1 These estimates are given to one decimal place but this does not imply that they can be regarded as accurate to the last digit shown. Estimates at current market prices are affected by the abolition of domestic rates and the introduction of the community charge.

2 Derived from expenditure components.

Source: Office for National Statistics; Enquiries 020 7533 5944

1.1 National accounts aggregates Index numbers[1]

continued

1995=100, seasonally adjusted

	Value indices at current prices		Volume indices at 1995 prices			Implied deflators[2]	
	Gross domestic product at market prices	Gross value added (GVA)at basic prices	Gross national disposable income at market prices	Gross domestic product at market prices	Gross value added (GVA)at basic prices	GDP at market prices	GVA at basic prices
	YBEU	YBEX	YBFP	YBEZ	CGCE	YBGB	CGBV
1955 Q1	2.6	2.7	38.6	38.5	38.9	6.8	6.9
Q2	2.6	2.7	38.6	38.4	38.7	6.8	7.0
Q3	2.7	2.8	39.2	39.0	39.1	7.0	7.1
Q4	2.8	2.8	38.7	38.8	39.0	7.1	7.3
1956 Q1	2.8	2.9	39.4	39.1	39.3	7.2	7.4
Q2	2.9	2.9	39.3	39.1	39.4	7.3	7.4
Q3	2.9	3.0	39.3	39.0	39.4	7.4	7.5
Q4	3.0	3.0	39.5	39.1	39.4	7.5	7.7
1957 Q1	3.0	3.0	40.0	39.9	40.2	7.4	7.6
Q2	3.0	3.1	40.1	39.9	40.3	7.5	7.7
Q3	3.1	3.2	40.1	39.7	40.0	7.7	7.9
Q4	3.1	3.2	40.1	39.6	40.0	7.9	8.0
1958 Q1	3.2	3.3	40.9	40.2	40.6	7.9	8.1
Q2	3.1	3.2	39.8	39.3	39.5	7.9	8.1
Q3	3.2	3.3	40.7	40.0	40.3	7.9	8.1
Q4	3.2	3.3	40.7	40.1	40.3	8.0	8.2
1959 Q1	3.2	3.3	41.0	40.5	40.8	8.0	8.1
Q2	3.3	3.5	42.1	41.2	41.3	8.1	8.3
Q3	3.4	3.5	42.5	41.9	42.1	8.0	8.2
Q4	3.5	3.6	43.3	42.9	43.0	8.1	8.3
1960 Q1	3.5	3.6	44.2	43.8	44.0	8.0	8.3
Q2	3.5	3.7	43.9	43.4	43.7	8.1	8.4
Q3	3.6	3.7	44.4	44.0	44.3	8.1	8.4
Q4	3.7	3.8	44.8	44.2	44.5	8.3	8.5
1961 Q1	3.7	3.9	45.6	45.0	45.3	8.3	8.6
Q2	3.7	3.9	45.5	45.1	45.4	8.3	8.5
Q3	3.9	4.0	45.7	45.0	45.4	8.6	8.8
Q4	3.8	4.0	45.3	44.8	45.2	8.5	8.7
1962 Q1	3.9	4.0	45.9	45.1	45.6	8.6	8.8
Q2	4.0	4.1	46.4	45.6	46.0	8.7	8.9
Q3	4.0	4.1	46.6	45.8	46.2	8.7	9.0
Q4	4.0	4.2	46.3	45.6	46.0	8.8	9.1
1963 Q1	4.0	4.2	46.4	45.8	46.6	8.8	9.0
Q2	4.2	4.4	48.6	47.9	48.5	8.8	9.1
Q3	4.3	4.5	49.0	48.1	48.6	8.9	9.1
Q4	4.4	4.6	49.6	48.8	49.4	9.0	9.3
1964 Q1	4.4	4.6	49.9	49.4	50.3	9.0	9.2
Q2	4.6	4.8	50.8	50.1	50.7	9.1	9.4
Q3	4.7	4.8	51.0	50.3	50.8	9.3	9.5
Q4	4.8	5.0	52.0	51.3	51.7	9.4	9.6
1965 Q1	4.9	5.0	51.7	51.2	51.8	9.6	9.7
Q2	4.9	5.1	51.9	51.2	52.0	9.6	9.8
Q3	5.1	5.2	52.5	51.7	52.4	9.8	10.0
Q4	5.2	5.3	53.2	52.2	52.9	9.9	10.1
1966 Q1	5.2	5.4	52.9	52.2	53.0	10.0	10.1
Q2	5.3	5.4	53.4	52.5	53.2	10.1	10.2
Q3	5.4	5.5	53.6	52.8	53.5	10.2	10.3
Q4	5.4	5.6	53.4	52.7	53.5	10.3	10.4
1967 Q1	5.5	5.6	54.0	53.3	54.0	10.3	10.4
Q2	5.6	5.8	54.6	53.8	54.4	10.4	10.6
Q3	5.6	5.8	54.8	53.9	54.5	10.5	10.6
Q4	5.7	5.9	54.9	54.0	54.7	10.6	10.7
1968 Q1	5.9	6.1	56.3	55.8	56.4	10.6	10.8
Q2	6.0	6.1	55.9	55.3	56.2	10.8	10.9
Q3	6.2	6.3	56.9	56.2	57.0	10.9	11.0
Q4	6.3	6.4	57.0	56.5	57.1	11.1	11.2
1969 Q1	6.4	6.4	57.5	56.4	57.3	11.3	11.3
Q2	6.5	6.5	57.6	57.0	57.7	11.4	11.3
Q3	6.6	6.6	58.1	57.4	58.1	11.5	11.4
Q4	6.7	6.8	58.3	57.6	58.5	11.7	11.6

See footnotes on page 7.

Source: Office for National Statistics; Enquiries 020 7533 5944

1.1 National accounts aggregates Index numbers[1]

continued

1995=100, seasonally adjusted

	Value indices at current prices		Volume indices at 1995 prices			Implied deflators[2]	
	Gross domestic product at market prices	Gross value added (GVA)at basic prices	Gross national disposable income at market prices	Gross domestic product at market prices	Gross value added (GVA)at basic prices	GDP at market prices	GVA at basic prices
	YBEU	YBEX	YBFP	YBEZ	CGCE	YBGB	CGBV
1970 Q1	6.8	6.9	58.2	57.2	58.0	11.9	11.8
Q2	7.1	7.2	59.4	58.4	59.1	12.2	12.1
Q3	7.3	7.4	60.0	58.9	59.4	12.4	12.4
Q4	7.6	7.7	60.3	59.3	60.3	12.8	12.7
1971 Q1	7.6	7.8	59.7	58.6	59.5	13.1	13.0
Q2	7.9	8.0	60.4	59.4	60.2	13.3	13.3
Q3	8.2	8.4	61.5	60.3	61.1	13.6	13.7
Q4	8.4	8.7	61.4	60.3	61.3	13.9	14.1
1972 Q1	8.5	8.8	61.3	60.1	60.8	14.2	14.4
Q2	8.9	9.2	63.2	61.8	62.4	14.4	14.7
Q3	9.1	9.4	63.1	62.0	62.9	14.6	14.9
Q4	9.6	9.9	64.4	63.3	64.4	15.1	15.4
1973 Q1	10.2	10.5	66.9	66.5	66.9	15.3	15.7
Q2	10.1	10.6	67.0	66.4	66.8	15.3	15.9
Q3	10.4	10.8	66.9	66.6	67.0	15.6	16.2
Q4	10.7	11.3	66.1	65.8	66.1	16.3	17.0
1974 Q1	10.6	11.2	63.2	64.2	64.7	16.5	17.3
Q2	11.4	12.0	64.2	65.5	65.8	17.5	18.3
Q3	12.1	12.9	64.8	66.1	66.9	18.3	19.3
Q4	12.7	13.6	63.7	65.1	65.7	19.5	20.6
1975 Q1	13.7	14.7	64.0	65.3	66.0	21.0	22.3
Q2	14.4	15.4	63.1	64.3	65.0	22.4	23.6
Q3	15.1	16.0	63.4	64.4	65.0	23.4	24.6
Q4	15.9	16.9	64.0	65.0	65.8	24.4	25.7
1976 Q1	16.7	17.6	65.4	66.3	67.0	25.2	26.2
Q2	17.0	18.1	64.7	65.8	66.3	25.9	27.3
Q3	17.6	18.6	65.4	66.5	67.0	26.5	27.8
Q4	18.7	19.7	66.4	67.8	68.2	27.6	28.9
1977 Q1	19.3	20.4	66.1	67.8	68.5	28.5	29.8
Q2	20.0	20.8	65.9	67.6	68.0	29.6	30.7
Q3	20.6	21.5	66.4	68.2	68.5	30.3	31.3
Q4	21.5	22.4	67.7	69.1	69.3	31.1	32.2
1978 Q1	22.4	23.4	68.3	69.5	69.8	32.2	33.5
Q2	23.2	24.2	69.7	70.2	70.2	33.1	34.5
Q3	23.8	24.9	69.9	70.9	70.8	33.6	35.1
Q4	24.6	25.5	69.7	71.3	71.1	34.5	35.9
1979 Q1	25.3	26.1	70.4	70.9	70.6	35.6	36.9
Q2	27.1	27.9	72.6	73.8	73.2	36.7	38.2
Q3	28.4	29.0	72.3	72.2	71.9	39.4	40.3
Q4	29.8	30.4	71.9	72.7	72.1	41.0	42.1
1980 Q1	30.9	31.3	71.5	72.2	71.4	42.8	43.8
Q2	31.7	32.5	70.0	70.8	70.7	44.8	45.9
Q3	32.8	33.6	70.2	70.5	70.4	46.5	47.7
Q4	33.6	34.5	70.0	69.7	69.3	48.3	49.7
1981 Q1	34.3	35.0	70.3	69.4	69.1	49.4	50.7
Q2	34.9	35.4	69.5	69.5	69.4	50.2	50.9
Q3	35.9	36.4	70.2	70.5	70.4	50.9	51.7
Q4	36.8	37.4	70.4	70.4	70.4	52.3	53.1
1982 Q1	37.6	37.9	70.9	70.4	70.4	53.4	53.9
Q2	38.4	39.0	70.8	71.2	71.4	53.9	54.6
Q3	39.0	39.7	71.3	71.3	71.5	54.7	55.5
Q4	40.1	40.7	72.2	71.7	71.8	55.9	56.7
1983 Q1	41.5	42.1	74.2	73.2	73.4	56.7	57.4
Q2	41.6	42.2	73.2	73.3	73.2	56.7	57.6
Q3	42.7	43.5	75.0	74.0	74.1	57.7	58.7
Q4	43.8	44.5	75.6	74.9	74.9	58.4	59.4
1984 Q1	44.3	45.0	76.4	75.6	75.6	58.5	59.5
Q2	45.2	46.0	75.9	75.4	75.1	59.9	61.3
Q3	45.5	46.3	75.6	75.4	75.2	60.4	61.6
Q4	46.7	47.7	77.6	76.2	76.2	61.3	62.6

See footnotes on page 7.

Source: Office for National Statistics; Enquiries 020 7533 5944

1.1 National accounts aggregates Index numbers[1]

continued

1995=100, seasonally adjusted

	Value indices at current prices		Volume indices at 1995 prices			Implied deflators[2]	
	Gross domestic product at market prices	Gross value added (GVA)at basic prices	Gross national disposable income at market prices	Gross domestic product at market prices	Gross value added (GVA)at basic prices	GDP at market prices	GVA at basic prices
	YBEU	YBEX	YBFP	YBEZ	CGCE	YBGB	CGBV
1985 Q1	47.9	48.9	77.4	77.5	77.5	61.9	63.1
Q2	49.7	50.7	79.0	78.7	79.1	63.1	64.1
Q3	50.3	51.1	78.9	78.7	78.8	63.9	64.8
Q4	51.2	52.0	79.7	79.2	79.2	64.7	65.6
1986 Q1	52.0	52.5	80.7	80.4	80.1	64.7	65.5
Q2	52.9	53.6	81.6	81.4	81.3	65.1	65.9
Q3	53.8	54.3	81.8	82.2	82.0	65.4	66.2
Q4	55.2	55.6	83.0	83.3	83.1	66.3	66.9
1987 Q1	56.5	57.0	83.6	83.6	83.3	67.5	68.4
Q2	57.7	58.6	84.6	84.6	84.5	68.2	69.3
Q3	59.7	60.1	86.1	86.3	86.0	69.2	70.0
Q4	61.1	61.5	86.5	87.3	86.8	70.0	70.9
1988 Q1	62.8	63.3	88.0	88.6	88.1	70.9	71.8
Q2	64.2	64.6	89.2	89.2	88.5	72.0	73.0
Q3	66.5	66.9	90.9	90.5	89.8	73.4	74.5
Q4	68.6	69.2	91.3	91.3	90.6	75.2	76.4
1989 Q1	69.8	70.6	91.5	91.3	90.7	76.5	77.9
Q2	70.9	71.6	91.9	91.8	91.1	77.3	78.6
Q3	72.6	73.4	91.4	92.0	91.2	79.0	80.5
Q4	74.2	75.1	91.8	92.0	91.6	80.6	82.1
1990 Q1	75.8	76.5	92.1	92.7	92.2	81.7	83.0
Q2	77.9	78.8	92.7	93.2	92.6	83.6	85.2
Q3	79.0	80.1	92.5	92.0	91.7	85.8	87.3
Q4	78.9	80.2	91.4	91.5	91.4	86.2	87.8
1991 Q1	80.4	81.2	91.7	91.4	91.1	87.9	89.1
Q2	81.3	81.8	91.8	90.9	90.9	89.5	90.0
Q3	82.3	82.5	90.7	90.8	90.8	90.6	90.9
Q4	83.6	83.8	91.6	90.9	90.9	91.9	92.3
1992 Q1	84.2	84.6	91.6	90.9	90.8	92.7	93.2
Q2	85.0	85.8	91.5	90.7	90.7	93.7	94.6
Q3	85.5	86.4	92.2	91.2	91.2	93.7	94.7
Q4	86.1	86.5	92.3	91.6	91.7	94.0	94.4
1993 Q1	87.6	88.3	92.5	92.1	92.2	95.1	95.8
Q2	88.6	89.4	93.2	92.6	92.7	95.6	96.5
Q3	90.4	91.0	94.5	93.5	93.6	96.6	97.2
Q4	91.7	92.2	95.5	94.5	94.3	97.0	97.7
1994 Q1	92.9	93.3	96.8	95.5	95.5	97.2	97.8
Q2	94.0	94.4	97.8	96.7	96.9	97.2	97.4
Q3	95.3	95.8	98.9	98.1	98.1	97.2	97.6
Q4	97.4	97.8	100.6	98.9	99.0	98.5	98.8
1995 Q1	98.3	98.5	99.8	99.3	99.4	99.0	99.0
Q2	99.4	99.2	99.4	99.7	99.7	99.7	99.5
Q3	100.4	100.5	99.9	100.2	100.2	100.2	100.3
Q4	101.9	101.8	100.9	100.8	100.7	101.1	101.1
1996 Q1	103.8	103.9	102.1	101.6	101.6	102.2	102.2
Q2	105.1	105.4	103.0	102.1	102.1	102.9	103.2
Q3	106.7	106.9	103.4	102.8	102.8	103.8	104.0
Q4	108.0	108.2	104.9	103.7	103.6	104.2	104.4
1997 Q1	110.3	110.3	107.0	104.8	104.6	105.3	105.4
Q2	111.6	111.2	108.0	105.7	105.5	105.6	105.5
Q3	113.6	113.3	109.9	106.8	106.5	106.3	106.4
Q4	115.7	115.3	109.4	107.3	107.2	107.8	107.5
1998 Q1	117.0	117.0	110.3	108.1	108.1	108.2	108.2
Q2	118.7	118.4	111.7	108.8	109.1	109.0	108.6
Q3	120.2	119.5	114.1	109.4	109.6	109.9	109.1
Q4	121.2	120.4	112.9	109.5	109.7	110.7	109.7
1999 Q1	121.7	120.9	112.5	109.9	110.1	110.8	109.8
Q2	123.8	123.1	113.6	110.7	110.8	111.8	111.1
Q3	126.1	125.2	114.9	111.8	111.9	112.8	111.8
Q4	127.5	126.4	117.0	112.6	112.8	113.3	112.1
2000 Q1	128.8	127.5	116.0	113.2	113.3	113.8	112.6

See footnotes on page 7.

Source: Office for National Statistics; Enquiries 020 7533 5944

1.2 Gross domestic product and Gross national income

£ million

	At current prices					Revalued at 1995 prices			
	Gross national income at market prices	Net income from abroad[1]	Gross domestic product at market prices	*less* Basic price adjustment[2]	Gross value added at basic prices	Gross domestic product at market prices	*less* Basic price adjustment[1]	Gross value added at basic prices	Gross value added at factor cost
	ABMZ	CAES	YBHA	NTAP	ABML	ABMI	NTAO	ABMM	YBHH
1948	12 029	232	11 797	1 049	10 748	224 733	23 303	201 096	199 485
1949	12 747	214	12 533	1 045	11 488	232 596	23 306	208 768	206 795
1950	13 477	405	13 072	1 160	11 912	239 743	24 457	214 842	213 233
1951	14 903	344	14 559	1 345	13 214	246 379	26 002	220 109	218 741
1952	16 011	243	15 768	1 386	14 382	247 437	25 308	221 685	220 322
1953	17 096	213	16 883	1 476	15 407	256 993	26 279	230 252	228 847
1954	18 103	234	17 869	1 493	16 376	268 024	26 904	240 528	238 516
1955	19 255	148	19 107	1 678	17 429	276 319	28 556	247 331	245 725
1956	20 748	207	20 541	1 789	18 752	279 042	28 219	250 253	248 862
1957	21 896	225	21 671	1 799	19 872	283 930	28 075	255 136	253 235
1958	22 844	259	22 585	1 858	20 727	284 957	29 225	255 238	253 096
1959	24 102	225	23 877	1 969	21 908	297 306	31 527	265 514	263 288
1960	25 692	198	25 494	1 967	23 527	313 213	32 335	280 386	277 611
1961	27 190	219	26 971	2 044	24 927	320 997	32 467	287 864	284 835
1962	28 567	297	28 270	2 174	26 096	324 988	32 073	292 047	288 761
1963	30 583	360	30 223	2 230	27 993	340 297	32 241	306 823	295 368
1964	33 407	371	33 036	2 589	30 448	358 896	34 147	323 439	311 685
1965	36 189	416	35 773	2 911	32 862	368 001	34 536	332 154	320 970
1966	38 429	363	38 066	3 253	34 813	375 180	35 180	338 665	327 344
1967	40 456	362	40 094	3 461	36 633	383 790	36 647	345 733	334 712
1968	43 761	311	43 450	3 989	39 461	399 487	37 872	360 166	349 312
1969	47 263	484	46 779	4 786	41 993	407 657	38 120	368 094	357 938
1970	51 972	540	51 432	5 195	46 237	417 403	39 598	376 289	365 590
1971	57 857	490	57 367	5 167	52 200	425 770	39 669	384 603	371 936
1972	64 801	542	64 259	5 169	59 090	441 210	41 630	397 993	382 733
1973	75 194	1 201	73 993	5 393	68 600	473 478	47 695	423 875	411 229
1974	84 922	1 309	83 613	4 617	78 996	465 525	44 524	418 032	405 447
1975	106 251	752	105 499	5 545	99 954	462 374	42 829	415 953	402 772
1976	126 048	1 129	124 919	7 372	117 547	475 342	45 924	426 599	413 584
1977	144 989	–490	145 479	10 371	135 108	486 576	48 542	435 855	424 195
1978	167 818	9	167 809	12 161	155 648	503 136	55 209	447 987	435 601
1979	196 876	–543	197 419	17 264	180 155	516 956	60 739	457 215	447 303
1980	228 910	–1 619	230 529	21 086	209 443	505 691	58 782	447 737	438 338
1981	252 910	–342	253 252	24 282	228 970	499 259	55 979	443 619	433 539
1982	276 209	–728	276 937	27 004	249 933	508 239	55 275	452 910	441 629
1983	303 435	815	302 620	28 943	273 677	527 288	57 809	469 531	458 206
1984	326 049	1 900	324 149	30 200	293 949	540 202	60 436	480 000	468 117
1985	354 511	–837	355 348	33 279	322 069	560 639	60 726	499 857	486 779
1986	383 107	1 284	381 823	38 625	343 198	584 239	65 693	518 848	505 737
1987	417 073	–2 388	419 461	42 606	376 855	610 110	69 538	541 032	526 815
1988	465 903	–1 859	467 762	48 283	419 479	641 637	75 373	567 096	553 741
1989	509 047	–4 231	513 278	51 353	461 925	655 174	76 969	579 055	565 816
1990	550 521	–5 696	556 217	54 744	501 473	659 486	75 493	584 542	570 833
1991	579 071	–5 465	584 536	61 399	523 137	649 815	72 335	577 704	562 457
1992	606 027	–2 138	608 165	62 678	545 487	650 288	71 524	578 854	563 241
1993	635 531	–3 825	639 356	65 979	573 377	665 427	73 383	592 166	577 375
1994	682 301	4 707	677 594	71 874	605 720	694 616	75 775	618 841	603 047
1995	715 029	1 049	713 980	78 482	635 498	713 980	78 482	635 498	620 321
1996	760 281	4 223	756 058	82 029	674 029	732 203	80 538	651 665	636 015
1997	813 974	8 572	805 402	90 275	715 127	757 921	84 543	673 378	658 005
1998	862 462	10 808	851 654	96 357	755 297	777 937	84 379	693 558	678 476
1999	896 257	5 151	891 106	103 720	787 386	794 366	86 407	707 959	692 566

1 Includes employment, entrepreneurial and property income.
2 Taxes on products *less* subsidies on products.

Sources: Office for National Statistics; Enquiries Columns 1-3, 5,6, 8,9 020 7533 5944; Columns 4,7 020 7533 5986

1.2 Gross domestic product and Gross national income

continued

£ million, seasonally adjusted

	At current prices					Revalued at 1995 prices			
	Gross national income at market prices	Net income from abroad[1]	Gross domestic product at market prices	*less* Basic price adjustment[2]	Gross value added at basic prices	Gross domestic product at market prices	*less* Basic price adjustment[1]	Gross value added at basic prices	Gross value added at factor cost
	ABMZ	CAES	YBHA	NTAP	ABML	ABMI	NTAO	ABMM	YBHH
1955 Q1	4 691	48	4 643	398	4 245	68 710	6 788	61 747	61 321
Q2	4 727	45	4 682	411	4 271	68 626	7 083	61 434	61 045
Q3	4 893	44	4 849	441	4 408	69 675	7 458	62 164	61 777
Q4	4 944	11	4 933	428	4 505	69 308	7 227	61 986	61 582
1956 Q1	5 078	46	5 032	438	4 594	69 787	7 230	62 452	62 164
Q2	5 132	47	5 085	441	4 644	69 737	6 939	62 631	62 271
Q3	5 196	46	5 150	452	4 698	69 642	6 899	62 569	62 220
Q4	5 342	68	5 274	458	4 816	69 876	7 151	62 601	62 207
1957 Q1	5 324	45	5 279	448	4 831	71 138	7 086	63 883	63 418
Q2	5 412	53	5 359	449	4 910	71 248	6 950	64 097	63 651
Q3	5 519	54	5 465	452	5 013	70 778	7 054	63 557	63 067
Q4	5 641	73	5 568	450	5 118	70 766	6 985	63 599	63 099
1958 Q1	5 729	77	5 652	459	5 193	71 791	7 141	64 472	63 927
Q2	5 603	41	5 562	461	5 101	70 165	7 344	62 735	62 224
Q3	5 734	78	5 656	463	5 193	71 386	7 287	63 967	63 419
Q4	5 778	63	5 715	475	5 240	71 615	7 453	64 064	63 526
1959 Q1	5 797	34	5 763	493	5 270	72 354	7 488	64 757	64 261
Q2	6 043	82	5 961	492	5 469	73 571	7 992	65 559	65 022
Q3	6 030	62	5 968	482	5 486	74 866	7 822	66 949	66 344
Q4	6 232	47	6 185	502	5 683	76 515	8 225	68 249	67 661
1960 Q1	6 315	38	6 277	504	5 773	78 245	8 284	69 888	69 271
Q2	6 358	47	6 311	487	5 824	77 555	8 096	69 359	68 673
Q3	6 428	40	6 388	492	5 896	78 576	8 034	70 400	69 695
Q4	6 591	73	6 518	484	6 034	78 837	7 921	70 739	69 972
1961 Q1	6 729	66	6 663	502	6 161	80 239	8 188	71 902	71 154
Q2	6 687	44	6 643	516	6 127	80 502	8 228	72 128	71 389
Q3	6 928	62	6 866	495	6 371	80 236	7 980	72 057	71 247
Q4	6 846	47	6 799	531	6 268	80 020	8 071	71 777	71 045
1962 Q1	6 974	75	6 899	526	6 373	80 551	7 873	72 444	71 622
Q2	7 151	81	7 070	549	6 521	81 306	8 017	73 070	72 265
Q3	7 204	70	7 134	559	6 575	81 819	8 166	73 457	72 662
Q4	7 238	71	7 167	540	6 627	81 312	8 017	73 076	72 212
1963 Q1	7 242	72	7 170	521	6 650	81 735	7 434	74 026	70 954
Q2	7 616	81	7 535	540	6 996	85 455	8 121	77 023	74 167
Q3	7 735	98	7 637	583	7 054	85 938	8 381	77 229	74 623
Q4	7 990	109	7 881	586	7 293	87 169	8 305	78 545	75 624
1964 Q1	8 055	129	7 926	605	7 321	88 138	7 895	79 954	76 733
Q2	8 286	100	8 186	647	7 539	89 499	8 583	80 585	77 879
Q3	8 412	76	8 336	651	7 685	89 752	8 694	80 720	78 107
Q4	8 654	66	8 588	686	7 903	91 507	8 975	82 180	78 966
1965 Q1	8 851	106	8 745	743	8 002	91 322	8 745	82 240	79 350
Q2	8 923	112	8 811	706	8 105	91 338	8 370	82 656	80 010
Q3	9 121	101	9 020	719	8 301	92 204	8 664	83 211	80 527
Q4	9 294	97	9 197	743	8 454	93 137	8 757	84 047	81 083
1966 Q1	9 401	91	9 310	789	8 521	93 261	8 786	84 140	81 135
Q2	9 567	114	9 453	797	8 656	93 768	8 972	84 450	81 676
Q3	9 691	88	9 603	809	8 794	94 158	8 754	85 074	82 311
Q4	9 770	70	9 700	858	8 842	93 993	8 668	85 001	82 222
1967 Q1	9 878	86	9 792	855	8 937	95 052	8 985	85 724	82 857
Q2	10 119	77	10 042	875	9 167	96 113	9 333	86 416	83 894
Q3	10 163	85	10 078	875	9 203	96 156	9 188	86 614	83 977
Q4	10 296	114	10 182	856	9 326	96 469	9 141	86 979	83 984
1968 Q1	10 667	78	10 589	929	9 660	99 685	9 697	89 610	86 580
Q2	10 757	108	10 649	949	9 700	98 637	9 003	89 300	86 805
Q3	11 072	90	10 982	1 013	9 969	100 358	9 411	90 590	88 013
Q4	11 265	35	11 230	1 098	10 132	100 807	9 761	90 666	87 914
1969 Q1	11 561	153	11 408	1 161	10 247	100 752	9 404	90 992	88 550
Q2	11 678	127	11 551	1 171	10 380	101 662	9 568	91 730	89 293
Q3	11 865	90	11 775	1 219	10 556	102 373	9 633	92 373	89 899
Q4	12 159	114	12 045	1 235	10 810	102 870	9 515	92 999	90 196

See footnotes on page 11.

Sources: Office for National Statistics; Enquiries Columns 1-3,5,6,8,9 020 7533 5944;
Columns 4,7 020 7533 5986

1.2 Gross domestic product and Gross national income

continued

£ million, seasonally adjusted

	At current prices					Revalued at 1995 prices			
	Gross national income at market prices	Net income from abroad[1]	Gross domestic product at market prices	*less* Basic price adjustment[2]	Gross value added at basic prices	Gross domestic product at market prices	*less* Basic price adjustment[1]	Gross value added at basic prices	Gross value added at factor cost
	ABMZ	CAES	YBHA	NTAP	ABML	ABMI	NTAO	ABMM	YBHH
1970 Q1	12 327	141	12 186	1 278	10 908	102 150	9 594	92 191	89 537
Q2	12 834	156	12 678	1 274	11 404	104 203	9 929	93 893	91 298
Q3	13 181	114	13 067	1 348	11 719	105 199	10 403	94 385	91 815
Q4	13 630	129	13 501	1 295	12 206	105 851	9 672	95 820	92 940
1971 Q1	13 788	143	13 645	1 318	12 327	104 529	9 693	94 471	91 766
Q2	14 256	137	14 119	1 346	12 773	106 036	9 976	95 680	92 768
Q3	14 725	113	14 612	1 273	13 339	107 592	10 132	97 074	93 786
Q4	15 088	97	14 991	1 230	13 761	107 613	9 868	97 378	93 616
1972 Q1	15 323	145	15 178	1 273	13 905	107 258	10 243	96 621	93 151
Q2	16 016	153	15 863	1 311	14 552	110 251	10 682	99 153	95 348
Q3	16 299	133	16 166	1 247	14 919	110 658	10 306	99 963	96 181
Q4	17 163	111	17 052	1 338	15 714	113 043	10 399	102 256	98 053
1973 Q1	18 320	151	18 169	1 486	16 683	118 646	11 835	106 279	103 114
Q2	18 422	343	18 079	1 252	16 827	118 544	11 996	106 096	102 760
Q3	18 831	270	18 561	1 361	17 200	118 845	11 918	106 423	103 233
Q4	19 621	437	19 184	1 294	17 890	117 443	11 946	105 077	102 122
1974 Q1	19 312	384	18 928	1 087	17 841	114 510	10 908	102 851	99 329
Q2	20 782	369	20 413	1 318	19 095	116 858	11 836	104 581	101 511
Q3	21 868	274	21 594	1 081	20 513	118 037	10 830	106 242	103 070
Q4	22 960	282	22 678	1 131	21 547	116 120	10 950	104 358	101 537
1975 Q1	24 676	237	24 439	1 075	23 364	116 548	10 703	104 897	101 675
Q2	25 923	143	25 780	1 389	24 391	114 842	10 606	103 329	100 012
Q3	27 071	163	26 908	1 542	25 366	114 892	10 833	103 255	99 883
Q4	28 581	209	28 372	1 539	26 833	116 092	10 687	104 472	101 202
1976 Q1	29 992	247	29 745	1 826	27 919	118 265	10 889	106 427	103 025
Q2	30 685	311	30 374	1 648	28 726	117 464	11 416	105 383	102 248
Q3	31 746	291	31 455	1 831	29 624	118 638	11 478	106 464	103 210
Q4	33 625	280	33 345	2 067	31 278	120 975	12 141	108 325	105 101
1977 Q1	34 519	−6	34 525	2 138	32 387	121 004	11 209	108 855	105 688
Q2	35 569	−167	35 736	2 630	33 106	120 642	12 155	108 002	105 299
Q3	36 676	−177	36 853	2 759	34 094	121 667	12 380	108 854	106 038
Q4	38 225	−140	38 365	2 844	35 521	123 263	12 798	110 144	107 170
1978 Q1	39 817	−97	39 914	2 769	37 145	124 140	13 096	110 936	107 610
Q2	41 459	42	41 417	2 970	38 447	125 262	13 811	111 481	108 392
Q3	42 584	33	42 551	3 029	39 522	126 546	14 070	112 534	109 377
Q4	43 958	31	43 927	3 393	40 534	127 188	14 232	113 036	110 222
1979 Q1	45 135	16	45 119	3 703	41 416	126 581	14 635	112 135	109 349
Q2	48 056	−252	48 308	3 936	44 372	131 780	15 895	116 235	113 286
Q3	50 795	15	50 780	4 703	46 077	128 811	14 729	114 236	112 120
Q4	52 890	−322	53 212	4 922	48 290	129 784	15 480	114 609	112 548
1980 Q1	54 831	−407	55 238	5 517	49 721	128 918	15 965	113 393	111 344
Q2	56 118	−543	56 661	5 097	51 564	126 388	14 180	112 296	110 081
Q3	58 150	−418	58 568	5 151	53 417	125 913	14 113	111 884	109 247
Q4	59 811	−251	60 062	5 321	54 741	124 472	14 524	110 164	107 666
1981 Q1	61 166	−90	61 256	5 594	55 662	123 906	14 363	109 737	107 217
Q2	62 199	−60	62 259	6 093	56 166	123 990	13 749	110 289	108 021
Q3	63 814	−195	64 009	6 240	57 769	125 772	14 050	111 795	109 077
Q4	65 731	3	65 728	6 355	59 373	125 591	13 817	111 798	109 224
1982 Q1	66 801	−401	67 202	6 972	60 230	125 735	13 951	111 835	109 217
Q2	68 314	−159	68 473	6 507	61 966	127 129	13 690	113 394	110 573
Q3	69 493	−194	69 687	6 654	63 033	127 344	13 628	113 651	110 707
Q4	71 601	26	71 575	6 871	64 704	128 031	14 006	114 030	111 132
1983 Q1	74 343	272	74 071	7 126	66 945	130 627	14 016	116 578	113 469
Q2	74 093	−131	74 224	7 243	66 981	130 840	14 654	116 245	113 758
Q3	76 766	557	76 209	7 176	69 033	132 165	14 527	117 656	114 872
Q4	78 233	117	78 116	7 398	70 718	133 656	14 612	119 052	116 107
1984 Q1	79 499	509	78 990	7 505	71 485	135 019	14 860	120 181	117 366
Q2	80 606	15	80 591	7 509	73 082	134 566	15 422	119 257	116 407
Q3	81 591	374	81 217	7 635	73 582	134 575	15 193	119 461	116 536
Q4	84 353	1 002	83 351	7 551	75 800	136 042	14 961	121 101	117 808

See footnotes on page 11.

Sources: Office for National Statistics; Enquiries Columns 1-3,5,6,8,9 020 7533 5914; Columns 4,7 020 7533 5986

1.2 Gross domestic product and Gross national income

continued

£ million, seasonally adjusted

	At current prices					Revalued at 1995 prices			
	Gross national income at market prices	Net income from abroad[1]	Gross domestic product at market prices	*less* Basic price adjust-ment[2]	Gross value added at basic prices	Gross domestic product at market prices	*less* Basic price adjust-ment[1]	Gross value added at basic prices	Gross value added at factor cost
	ABMZ	CAES	YBHA	NTAP	ABML	ABMI	NTAO	ABMM	YBHH
1985 Q1	85 839	301	85 538	7 843	77 695	138 292	15 272	123 050	119 978
Q2	88 260	–368	88 628	8 048	80 580	140 496	14 672	125 728	122 186
Q3	89 419	–290	89 709	8 512	81 197	140 430	15 181	125 231	121 819
Q4	90 993	–480	91 473	8 876	82 597	141 421	15 601	125 848	122 796
1986 Q1	93 141	364	92 777	9 373	83 404	143 467	16 234	127 323	123 830
Q2	94 829	347	94 482	9 284	85 198	145 242	16 092	129 188	125 883
Q3	96 132	132	96 000	9 761	86 239	146 785	16 540	130 326	127 173
Q4	99 005	441	98 564	10 207	88 357	148 745	16 827	132 011	128 851
1987 Q1	100 796	–2	100 798	10 276	90 522	149 242	17 030	132 328	128 684
Q2	102 454	–517	102 971	9 931	93 040	150 950	16 769	134 228	130 439
Q3	105 908	–645	106 553	10 993	95 560	154 027	17 532	136 608	133 129
Q4	107 915	–1 224	109 139	11 406	97 733	155 891	18 207	137 868	134 563
1988 Q1	111 364	–721	112 085	11 564	100 521	158 103	18 324	139 946	136 457
Q2	114 289	–320	114 609	11 960	102 649	159 135	18 755	140 596	137 375
Q3	118 484	–134	118 618	12 309	106 309	161 496	19 050	142 668	139 446
Q4	121 766	–684	122 450	12 450	110 000	162 903	19 244	143 886	140 463
1989 Q1	124 311	–330	124 641	12 414	112 227	162 938	19 113	144 032	140 688
Q2	125 709	–823	126 532	12 836	113 696	163 779	19 350	144 659	141 291
Q3	128 156	–1 458	129 614	12 975	116 639	164 161	19 506	144 902	141 718
Q4	130 871	–1 620	132 491	13 128	119 363	164 296	19 000	145 462	142 119
1990 Q1	133 635	–1 659	135 294	13 745	121 549	165 538	19 184	146 528	143 391
Q2	137 508	–1 613	139 121	13 854	125 267	166 335	19 425	147 108	143 800
Q3	140 017	–929	140 946	13 726	127 220	164 254	18 640	145 726	142 114
Q4	139 361	–1 495	140 856	13 419	127 437	163 359	18 244	145 180	141 528
1991 Q1	141 603	–1 853	143 456	14 490	128 966	163 233	18 689	144 680	141 198
Q2	143 599	–1 520	145 119	15 226	129 893	162 223	17 847	144 399	140 603
Q3	145 169	–1 650	146 819	15 730	131 089	162 025	17 786	144 256	140 272
Q4	148 700	–442	149 142	15 953	133 189	162 334	18 013	144 369	140 384
1992 Q1	149 622	–709	150 331	15 892	134 439	162 231	18 085	144 206	140 310
Q2	150 675	–957	151 632	15 255	136 377	161 818	17 669	144 152	140 024
Q3	152 238	–313	152 551	15 348	137 203	162 730	17 867	144 881	140 847
Q4	153 492	–159	153 651	16 183	137 468	163 509	17 903	145 615	142 060
1993 Q1	154 845	–1 446	156 291	15 998	140 293	164 383	17 962	146 426	142 308
Q2	157 008	–1 053	158 061	15 956	142 105	165 315	18 079	147 243	143 567
Q3	160 433	–945	161 378	16 846	144 532	166 978	18 357	148 643	144 863
Q4	163 245	–381	163 626	17 179	146 447	168 751	18 985	149 854	146 637
1994 Q1	167 146	1 403	165 743	17 491	148 252	170 433	18 784	151 649	147 922
Q2	168 172	425	167 747	17 806	149 941	172 586	18 604	153 982	150 176
Q3	171 118	924	170 194	18 027	152 167	175 051	19 133	155 918	151 853
Q4	175 865	1 955	173 910	18 550	155 360	176 546	19 254	157 292	153 096
1995 Q1	175 806	312	175 494	19 009	156 485	177 304	19 306	157 998	154 541
Q2	176 785	–598	177 383	19 747	157 636	177 964	19 592	158 372	154 635
Q3	179 874	633	179 241	19 558	159 683	178 795	19 654	159 141	155 131
Q4	182 564	702	181 862	20 168	161 694	179 917	19 930	159 987	156 014
1996 Q1	186 186	890	185 296	20 278	165 018	181 356	19 899	161 457	157 650
Q2	189 431	1 910	187 521	20 118	167 403	182 296	20 030	162 266	158 391
Q3	190 578	194	190 384	20 625	169 759	183 448	20 149	163 299	159 297
Q4	194 086	1 229	192 857	21 008	171 849	185 103	20 460	164 643	160 677
1997 Q1	199 128	2 174	196 954	21 767	175 187	187 037	20 855	166 182	162 331
Q2	201 565	2 287	199 278	22 550	176 728	188 670	21 097	167 573	163 734
Q3	205 486	2 772	202 714	22 678	180 036	190 611	21 333	169 278	165 514
Q4	207 795	1 339	206 456	23 280	183 176	191 603	21 258	170 345	166 426
1998 Q1	210 489	1 651	208 838	22 911	185 927	192 981	21 178	171 803	167 778
Q2	213 525	1 709	211 816	23 638	188 178	194 289	20 995	173 294	169 331
Q3	219 069	4 462	214 607	24 683	189 924	195 186	21 052	174 134	170 557
Q4	219 379	2 986	216 393	25 125	191 268	195 481	21 154	174 327	170 810
1999 Q1	217 829	523	217 306	25 204	192 102	196 111	21 183	174 928	171 178
Q2	221 742	685	221 057	25 475	195 582	197 644	21 609	176 035	172 455
Q3	225 536	421	225 115	26 210	198 905	199 621	21 772	177 849	173 920
Q4	231 150	3 522	227 628	26 831	200 797	200 990	21 843	179 147	175 013
2000 Q1	229 876	–85	229 961	27 368	202 593	201 993	22 024	179 969	175 856

See footnotes on page 11.

Sources: Office for National Statistics; Enquiries Columns 1-3,5,6,8,9 020 7533 5944; Columns 4,7 020 7533 5986

1.3 Gross domestic product: by category of expenditure[1]

£ million, current prices

	Domestic expenditure on goods and services at market prices											
	Final consumption expenditure			Gross capital formation								
	Households	Non-profit institutions[2]	General government	Gross fixed capital formation	Changes in inventories[3]	Acquisitions less disposals of valuables	Total	Total exports	Gross final expenditure	*less* Total Imports	Statistical discrepancy (expenditure)[4]	Gross domestic product at market prices[4]
	ABPB	ABNV	NMRK	NPQX	ABMP	NPJO	YBIJ	KTMW	ABMD	KTMX	GIXM	YBHA
1946	..	–	2 316	..	..	–	..	1 425	..	1 800	..	..
1947	..	–	1 783	..	..	–	..	1 647	..	2 202	..	..
1948	8 417	48	1 810	1 502	175	–	11 952	2 191	14 143	2 407	61	11 797
1949	8 771	52	2 034	1 662	65	–	12 584	2 489	15 073	2 669	129	12 533
1950	9 257	57	2 125	1 799	–210	–	13 028	2 988	16 016	3 046	102	13 072
1951	9 998	62	2 491	2 011	575	–	15 137	3 639	18 776	4 299	82	14 559
1952	10 526	68	2 956	2 265	50	–	15 865	3 750	19 615	3 899	52	15 768
1953	11 226	74	3 088	2 540	125	–	17 053	3 677	20 730	3 798	–49	16 883
1954	11 906	81	3 167	2 741	56	–	17 951	3 827	21 778	3 922	13	17 869
1955	12 832	88	3 235	3 026	300	–	19 481	4 166	23 647	4 439	–101	19 107
1956	13 494	96	3 491	3 315	259	–	20 655	4 586	25 241	4 510	–190	20 541
1957	14 227	105	3 650	3 600	238	–	21 820	4 823	26 643	4 731	–241	21 671
1958	15 013	112	3 722	3 724	111	–	22 682	4 688	27 370	4 535	–250	22 585
1959	15 802	123	3 970	3 980	178	–	24 053	4 836	28 889	4 834	–178	23 877
1960	16 573	137	4 205	4 368	562	–	25 845	5 134	30 979	5 499	14	25 494
1961	17 422	148	4 542	4 889	279	–	27 280	5 366	32 646	5 459	–216	26 971
1962	18 438	173	4 868	5 049	–8	–	28 520	5 500	34 020	5 554	–196	28 270
1963	19 565	261	5 127	5 295	161	–	30 409	5 852	36 261	5 971	–67	30 223
1964	20 868	288	5 458	6 279	700	–	33 593	6 183	39 776	6 768	28	33 036
1965	22 151	381	6 156	6 804	461	–	35 953	6 596	42 549	6 925	149	35 773
1966	23 391	421	6 700	7 261	288	–	38 061	7 148	45 209	7 215	72	38 066
1967	24 579	453	7 395	7 945	286	–	40 658	7 370	48 028	7 814	–120	40 094
1968	26 451	502	7 859	8 728	452	–	43 992	8 962	52 954	9 329	–175	43 450
1969	28 054	556	8 228	9 066	537	–	46 441	10 064	56 505	9 886	160	46 779
1970	30 547	661	9 278	10 036	382	–	50 904	11 489	62 393	11 052	91	51 432
1971	34 250	741	10 560	11 243	114	–	56 908	12 890	69 798	12 095	–336	57 367
1972	38 780	848	12 022	12 347	25	–	64 022	13 587	77 609	13 658	308	64 259
1973	44 360	1 000	13 766	15 227	1 529	–	75 882	17 027	92 909	18 840	–76	73 993
1974	51 126	1 182	17 114	18 134	1 045	–	88 601	22 831	111 432	27 007	–812	83 613
1975	62 881	1 487	23 611	21 856	–1 354	–	108 481	26 803	135 284	28 655	–1 130	105 499
1976	73 060	1 811	27 666	25 516	901	–	128 954	35 018	163 972	36 483	–2 570	124 919
1977	83 504	1 996	30 176	28 201	1 824	–	145 701	43 210	188 911	42 262	–1 170	145 479
1978	96 368	2 225	34 150	32 208	1 804	–	166 755	47 379	214 134	45 234	–1 091	167 809
1979	114 458	2 538	39 591	38 211	2 162	–	196 960	54 804	251 764	54 165	–180	197 419
1980	132 663	3 162	49 767	43 238	–2 572	–	226 258	62 495	288 753	57 449	–775	230 529
1981	147 120	3 676	56 272	43 331	–2 768	–	247 631	67 315	314 946	60 243	–1 451	253 252
1982	160 997	4 116	61 259	47 394	–1 188	–	272 578	72 579	345 157	67 631	–589	276 937
1983	176 881	4 597	66 593	51 490	1 465	–	301 026	79 751	380 777	77 428	–729	302 620
1984	189 244	5 133	70 479	58 698	1 296	–	324 850	91 509	416 359	92 577	367	324 149
1985	206 600	5 820	74 441	64 463	821	–	352 145	101 926	454 071	98 723	–	355 348
1986	228 848	6 719	79 992	68 718	682	–24	384 935	97 781	482 716	100 893	–	381 823
1987	251 143	7 526	85 784	78 924	1 228	–132	424 473	106 437	530 910	111 449	–	419 461
1988	283 425	8 763	92 339	96 076	4 333	49	484 985	107 434	592 419	124 657	–	467 762
1989	310 493	9 986	99 887	111 033	2 677	9	534 085	121 883	655 968	142 690	–	513 278
1990	336 492	11 401	110 620	114 314	–1 800	–113	570 914	133 501	704 415	148 198	–	556 217
1991	357 785	11 096	121 740	104 680	–4 927	–86	590 288	135 365	725 653	141 117	–	584 536
1992	377 147	10 806	129 211	100 278	–1 937	36	615 541	143 291	758 832	150 667	–	608 165
1993	399 108	13 981	131 413	101 230	329	–9	646 052	162 078	808 130	168 774	–	639 356
1994	419 262	15 287	136 374	107 390	3 708	136	682 157	178 767	860 924	183 330	–	677 594
1995	438 453	16 481	141 075	116 360	4 512	–92	716 789	202 412	919 201	205 221	–	713 980
1996	467 841	18 385	146 760	125 675	1 771	–185	760 247	220 303	980 550	224 492	–	756 058
1997	498 307	19 602	148 409	134 153	4 388	39	804 898	229 326	1 034 224	228 822	–	805 402
1998	530 851	20 972	154 767	148 071	4 461	487	859 609	225 474	1 085 083	233 429	–	851 654
1999	564 369	22 537	163 121	158 372	–1 946	346	906 799	229 649	1 136 448	244 878	–464	891 106

1 Estimates are given to the nearest £ million, but cannot be regarded as accurate to this degree.
2 Non-profit institutions serving households.
3 Quarterly alignment adjustment included in this series.
4 Gross Domestic Product is estimated in seasonally adjusted form only, no equivalent unadjusted estimates exist.

Sources: Office for National Statistics; Enquiries Column 1,2 020 7533 5998; Columns 4,6, 020 7533 5926; Column 3 020 7533 5990; Column 5 020 7533 6009; Columns 7,9,11 020 7533 5944; Columns 8,10 020 7533 6078

1.3 Gross domestic product: by category of expenditure[1]

continued

£ million, current prices, not seasonally adjusted

	Domestic expenditure on goods and services at market prices											
	Final consumption expenditure			Gross capital formation								
	Households	Non-profit institutions[2]	General government	Gross fixed capital formation	Changes in inventories[3]	Acquisitions less disposals of valuables	Total	Total exports	Gross final expenditure	*less* Total Imports	Statistical discrepancy (expenditure)[4]	Gross domestic product at market prices[4]
	ABPB	ABNV	NMRK	NPQX	ABMP	NPJO	YBIJ	KTMW	ABMD	KTMX		
1955 Q1	2 923	21	818	701	165	–	4 628	1 052	5 680	1 134		
Q2	3 154	22	796	721	–23	–	4 670	971	5 641	1 039		
Q3	3 253	22	808	766	147	–	4 996	1 054	6 050	1 144		
Q4	3 502	23	813	838	11	–	5 187	1 089	6 276	1 122		
1956 Q1	3 102	23	841	787	123	–	4 876	1 130	6 006	1 134		
Q2	3 360	24	869	799	91	–	5 143	1 179	6 322	1 136		
Q3	3 386	24	877	823	48	–	5 158	1 099	6 257	1 122		
Q4	3 646	25	904	906	–3	–	5 478	1 178	6 656	1 118		
1957 Q1	3 242	25	924	866	149	–	5 206	1 219	6 425	1 215		
Q2	3 517	26	902	876	103	–	5 424	1 232	6 656	1 192		
Q3	3 602	27	906	889	58	–	5 482	1 179	6 661	1 195		
Q4	3 866	27	918	969	–72	–	5 708	1 193	6 901	1 129		
1958 Q1	3 467	27	926	921	92	–	5 433	1 191	6 624	1 110		
Q2	3 714	28	929	903	30	–	5 604	1 145	6 749	1 095		
Q3	3 762	28	920	915	68	–	5 693	1 176	6 869	1 173		
Q4	4 070	29	947	985	–79	–	5 952	1 176	7 128	1 157		
1959 Q1	3 639	29	979	921	18	–	5 586	1 159	6 745	1 128		
Q2	3 928	30	998	971	84	–	6 011	1 220	7 231	1 198		
Q3	3 949	31	982	983	73	–	6 018	1 188	7 206	1 233		
Q4	4 286	33	1 011	1 105	3	–	6 438	1 269	7 707	1 275		
1960 Q1	3 869	33	1 027	1 038	146	–	6 113	1 294	7 407	1 350		
Q2	4 163	34	1 046	1 040	141	–	6 424	1 289	7 713	1 372		
Q3	4 150	35	1 038	1 102	164	–	6 489	1 253	7 742	1 406		
Q4	4 391	35	1 094	1 188	111	–	6 819	1 298	8 117	1 371		
1961 Q1	4 033	36	1 135	1 164	157	–	6 525	1 353	7 878	1 391		
Q2	4 353	36	1 126	1 189	53	–	6 757	1 353	8 110	1 392		
Q3	4 410	37	1 130	1 257	132	–	6 966	1 318	8 284	1 361		
Q4	4 626	39	1 151	1 279	–63	–	7 032	1 342	8 374	1 315		
1962 Q1	4 252	40	1 206	1 228	–30	–	6 696	1 342	8 038	1 368		
Q2	4 681	42	1 207	1 245	18	–	7 193	1 411	8 604	1 391		
Q3	4 634	44	1 212	1 277	53	–	7 220	1 352	8 572	1 421		
Q4	4 871	47	1 243	1 299	–49	–	7 411	1 395	8 806	1 374		
1963 Q1	4 456	64	1 259	1 169	–19	–	6 930	1 425	8 355	1 398		
Q2	4 936	64	1 265	1 292	81	–	7 639	1 474	9 113	1 475		
Q3	4 984	66	1 279	1 368	–3	–	7 694	1 449	9 143	1 558		
Q4	5 189	67	1 324	1 466	102	–	8 146	1 504	9 650	1 540		
1964 Q1	4 791	68	1 338	1 508	90	–	7 794	1 524	9 318	1 650		
Q2	5 212	70	1 354	1 507	232	–	8 374	1 572	9 946	1 691		
Q3	5 303	73	1 363	1 586	172	–	8 497	1 502	9 999	1 727		
Q4	5 562	77	1 403	1 678	206	–	8 928	1 585	10 513	1 700		
1965 Q1	5 131	87	1 465	1 697	119	–	8 499	1 560	10 059	1 641		
Q2	5 516	94	1 536	1 619	141	–	8 906	1 673	10 579	1 739		
Q3	5 646	99	1 546	1 673	170	–	9 134	1 642	10 776	1 802		
Q4	5 858	101	1 609	1 815	31	–	9 414	1 721	11 135	1 743		
1966 Q1	5 456	104	1 615	1 803	78	–	9 056	1 750	10 806	1 803		
Q2	5 914	104	1 656	1 713	126	–	9 513	1 723	11 236	1 803		
Q3	5 912	105	1 679	1 821	156	–	9 673	1 777	11 450	1 908		
Q4	6 109	108	1 750	1 924	–72	–	9 819	1 898	11 717	1 701		
1967 Q1	5 661	108	1 828	1 980	61	–	9 638	1 857	11 495	1 874		
Q2	6 082	112	1 810	1 945	142	–	10 091	1 888	11 979	1 947		
Q3	6 262	115	1 833	1 981	92	–	10 283	1 840	12 123	1 958		
Q4	6 574	118	1 924	2 039	–9	–	10 646	1 785	12 431	2 035		
1968 Q1	6 256	121	1 976	2 151	–92	–	10 412	2 135	12 547	2 302		
Q2	6 418	124	1 929	2 029	212	–	10 712	2 186	12 898	2 295		
Q3	6 689	127	1 962	2 158	238	–	11 174	2 295	13 469	2 396		
Q4	7 088	130	1 992	2 390	94	–	11 694	2 346	14 040	2 336		
1969 Q1	6 498	133	2 044	2 190	110	–	10 975	2 305	13 280	2 410		
Q2	6 909	137	2 001	2 121	222	–	11 390	2 544	13 934	2 470		
Q3	7 081	140	2 045	2 295	142	–	11 703	2 588	14 291	2 495		
Q4	7 566	146	2 138	2 460	63	–	12 373	2 627	15 000	2 511		

See footnotes on page 15.

Sources: Office for National Statistics; Enquiries Column 1,2 020 7533 5998; Columns 4,6 020 7533 5926; Column 3 020 7533 5990; Column 5 020 7533 6009; Columns 7,9,11 020 7533 5944; Columns 8,10 020 7533 6078

1.3 Gross domestic product: by category of expenditure[1]

continued

£ million, current prices, not seasonally adjusted

	Domestic expenditure on goods and services at market prices											
	Final consumption expenditure			Gross capital formation								
	Households	Non-profit institutions[2]	General government	Gross fixed capital formation	Changes in inventories[3]	Acquisitions less disposals of valuables	Total	Total exports	Gross final expenditure	*less* Total Imports	Statistical discrepancy (expenditure)[4]	Gross domestic product at market prices[4]
	ABPB	ABNV	NMRK	NPQX	ABMP	NPJO	YBIJ	KTMW	ABMD	KTMX		
1970 Q1	6 929	158	2 177	2 349	–76	–	11 537	2 690	14 227	2 524		
Q2	7 468	164	2 278	2 390	208	–	12 508	2 871	15 379	2 812		
Q3	7 807	168	2 363	2 523	214	–	13 075	2 813	15 888	2 808		
Q4	8 343	171	2 460	2 774	36	–	13 784	3 115	16 899	2 908		
1971 Q1	7 663	177	2 506	2 664	26	–	13 036	2 896	15 932	2 931		
Q2	8 414	184	2 587	2 676	2	–	13 863	3 319	17 182	3 075		
Q3	8 800	188	2 685	2 847	47	–	14 567	3 333	17 900	3 037		
Q4	9 373	192	2 782	3 056	39	–	15 442	3 342	18 784	3 052		
1972 Q1	8 729	199	2 935	2 978	–144	–	14 697	3 190	17 887	3 248		
Q2	9 419	208	2 863	2 934	97	–	15 521	3 442	18 963	3 309		
Q3	9 918	216	3 028	3 077	38	–	16 277	3 120	19 397	3 316		
Q4	10 714	225	3 196	3 358	34	–	17 527	3 835	21 362	3 785		
1973 Q1	10 211	237	3 361	3 739	427	–	17 975	3 773	21 748	4 197		
Q2	10 722	245	3 287	3 528	322	–	18 104	4 166	22 270	4 416		
Q3	11 277	255	3 494	3 748	478	–	19 252	4 377	23 629	4 823		
Q4	12 150	263	3 624	4 212	302	–	20 551	4 711	25 262	5 404		
1974 Q1	11 181	275	3 863	4 432	–167	–	19 584	4 988	24 572	6 128		
Q2	12 256	287	3 939	4 109	640	–	21 231	5 759	26 990	6 933		
Q3	13 136	302	4 420	4 532	601	–	22 991	6 015	29 006	6 922		
Q4	14 553	318	4 892	5 061	–29	–	24 795	6 069	30 864	7 024		
1975 Q1	13 854	337	5 630	5 249	–583	–	24 487	6 111	30 598	6 786		
Q2	15 363	359	5 621	5 095	–366	–	26 072	6 605	32 677	6 986		
Q3	16 189	382	6 012	5 628	–227	–	27 984	6 783	34 767	7 374		
Q4	17 475	409	6 348	5 884	–178	–	29 938	7 304	37 242	7 509		
1976 Q1	16 539	427	6 639	6 413	–209	–	29 809	7 625	37 434	7 756		
Q2	17 549	448	6 889	5 921	34	–	30 841	8 549	39 390	9 106		
Q3	18 581	463	6 982	6 350	457	–	32 833	9 077	41 910	9 469		
Q4	20 391	473	7 156	6 832	619	–	35 471	9 767	45 238	10 152		
1977 Q1	19 078	485	7 258	6 762	583	–	34 166	9 927	44 093	10 368		
Q2	20 132	493	7 523	6 623	712	–	35 483	10 737	46 220	10 939		
Q3	21 240	502	7 606	7 045	114	–	36 507	11 568	48 075	10 665		
Q4	23 054	516	7 789	7 771	415	–	39 545	10 978	50 523	10 290		
1978 Q1	22 172	528	8 234	8 028	208	–	39 170	10 887	50 057	10 783		
Q2	23 151	548	8 401	7 549	766	–	40 415	12 016	52 431	11 519		
Q3	24 735	566	8 593	8 036	475	–	42 405	12 187	54 592	11 484		
Q4	26 310	583	8 922	8 595	355	–	44 765	12 289	57 054	11 448		
1979 Q1	25 287	597	9 124	8 833	766	–	44 607	11 464	56 071	12 223		
Q2	27 914	613	9 645	8 717	458	–	47 347	14 127	61 474	13 935		
Q3	29 403	642	10 177	9 642	1 054	–	50 918	14 215	65 133	13 544		
Q4	31 854	686	10 645	11 019	–116	–	54 088	14 998	69 086	14 463		
1980 Q1	31 065	734	11 477	10 754	–366	–	53 664	15 381	69 045	15 161		
Q2	31 930	774	12 019	10 057	–37	–	54 743	15 541	70 284	15 165		
Q3	34 050	811	12 829	10 739	–366	–	58 063	15 819	73 882	13 959		
Q4	35 618	843	13 442	11 688	–1 803	–	59 788	15 754	75 542	13 164		
1981 Q1	34 041	874	13 621	10 755	–951	–	58 340	15 276	73 616	12 720		
Q2	35 630	905	13 927	10 242	–946	–	59 758	16 214	75 972	14 375		
Q3	37 721	936	14 285	10 862	61	–	63 865	17 600	81 465	16 710		
Q4	39 728	961	14 439	11 472	–932	–	65 668	18 225	83 893	16 438		
1982 Q1	37 433	986	15 000	11 383	699	–	65 501	17 130	82 631	16 093		
Q2	38 739	1 013	15 287	11 044	436	–	66 519	17 968	84 487	17 528		
Q3	41 126	1 044	15 282	12 002	–324	–	69 130	18 337	87 467	17 240		
Q4	43 699	1 073	15 690	12 965	–1 999	–	71 428	19 144	90 572	16 770		
1983 Q1	41 323	1 099	16 646	12 816	544	–	72 428	18 943	91 371	18 237		
Q2	42 542	1 133	16 572	11 647	526	–	72 420	19 292	91 712	19 457		
Q3	45 481	1 165	16 448	12 729	1 005	–	76 828	20 339	97 167	19 761		
Q4	47 535	1 200	16 927	14 298	–610	–	79 350	21 177	100 527	19 973		
1984 Q1	44 305	1 228	17 673	14 348	443	–	77 997	21 544	99 541	21 068		
Q2	46 155	1 263	17 167	13 419	187	–	78 191	21 869	100 060	22 856		
Q3	47 676	1 300	17 494	14 806	557	–	81 833	22 822	104 655	23 523		
Q4	51 108	1 342	18 145	16 125	109	–	86 829	25 274	112 103	25 130		

See footnotes on page 15.

Sources: Office for National Statistics; Enquiries Column 1,2 020 7533 5998; Columns 4,6 020 7533 5926; Column 3 020 7533 5990; Column 5 020 7533 6009; Columns7,9,11 020 7533 5944; Columns 8,10 020 7533 6078

1.3 Gross domestic product: by category of expenditure[1]

continued

£ million, current prices, not seasonally adjusted

	Domestic expenditure on goods and services at market prices											
	Final consumption expenditure			Gross capital formation								
	Households	Non-profit institutions[2]	General government	Gross fixed capital formation	Changes in inventories[3]	Acquisitions less disposals of valuables	Total	Total exports	Gross final expenditure	*less* Total Imports	Statistical discrepancy (expenditure)[4]	Gross domestic product at market prices[4]
	ABPB	ABNV	NMRK	NPQX	ABMP	NPJO	YBIJ	KTMW	ABMD	KTMX		
1985 Q1	48 056	1 382	19 262	16 872	159	–	85 731	25 361	111 092	25 985		
Q2	49 702	1 428	18 095	14 384	857	–	84 466	26 061	110 527	25 227		
Q3	52 582	1 479	18 232	15 995	690	–	88 978	24 808	113 786	23 772		
Q4	56 260	1 531	18 852	17 212	–885	–	92 970	25 696	118 666	23 739		
1986 Q1	52 732	1 601	20 427	17 424	415	–21	92 578	23 205	115 783	23 454		
Q2	55 307	1 654	19 683	15 027	563	38	92 272	24 296	116 568	25 243		
Q3	58 842	1 707	19 639	17 449	–103	–61	97 473	23 905	121 378	25 678		
Q4	61 967	1 757	20 243	18 818	–193	20	102 612	26 375	128 987	26 518		
1987 Q1	57 778	1 784	21 335	18 481	11	–55	99 334	25 430	124 764	25 637		
Q2	60 018	1 845	20 997	17 448	712	96	101 116	25 971	127 087	27 460		
Q3	64 514	1 912	21 332	20 631	1 282	–213	109 458	27 423	136 881	29 407		
Q4	68 833	1 985	22 120	22 364	–777	40	114 565	27 613	142 178	28 945		
1988 Q1	64 653	2 105	23 074	23 243	706	–25	113 756	25 261	139 017	28 543		
Q2	67 637	2 169	22 573	22 146	1 511	87	116 123	26 671	142 794	30 777		
Q3	73 876	2 223	22 649	24 682	691	–138	123 983	27 651	151 634	32 845		
Q4	77 259	2 266	24 043	26 005	1 425	125	131 123	27 851	158 974	32 492		
1989 Q1	71 745	2 253	24 655	27 878	844	9	127 384	27 800	155 184	33 146		
Q2	75 070	2 517	24 161	25 743	1 629	80	129 200	30 062	159 262	36 227		
Q3	80 099	2 574	25 088	28 164	723	–126	136 522	30 803	167 325	37 414		
Q4	83 579	2 642	25 983	29 248	–519	46	140 979	33 218	174 197	35 903		
1990 Q1	77 627	2 794	26 773	30 463	148	–26	137 779	32 035	169 814	37 040		
Q2	81 975	2 829	27 109	26 599	732	55	139 299	33 491	172 790	38 497		
Q3	86 812	2 876	28 011	28 278	–41	–170	145 766	32 780	178 546	37 136		
Q4	90 078	2 902	28 727	28 974	–2 639	28	148 070	35 195	183 265	35 525		
1991 Q1	83 027	2 880	29 273	28 305	–1 457	–67	141 961	30 664	172 625	33 189		
Q2	86 703	2 724	30 573	24 286	–808	161	143 639	34 178	177 817	35 710		
Q3	92 328	2 740	30 903	25 425	–339	–101	150 956	34 485	185 441	36 735		
Q4	95 727	2 752	30 991	26 664	–2 323	–79	153 732	36 038	189 770	35 483		
1992 Q1	88 365	2 739	31 750	27 056	–872	–111	148 927	33 664	182 591	35 448		
Q2	91 922	2 711	32 222	23 373	–106	77	150 199	35 619	185 818	37 814		
Q3	97 086	2 735	32 415	24 732	278	–68	157 178	35 201	192 379	38 122		
Q4	99 774	2 621	32 824	25 117	–1 237	138	159 237	38 807	198 044	39 283		
1993 Q1	93 511	2 888	33 056	26 522	–1 465	25	154 537	39 200	193 737	40 499		
Q2	96 369	3 738	32 569	23 051	1 137	125	156 989	39 264	196 253	42 503		
Q3	103 274	3 722	32 604	25 164	468	–107	165 125	40 922	206 047	43 432		
Q4	105 954	3 633	33 184	26 493	189	–52	169 401	42 692	212 093	42 340		
1994 Q1	99 005	3 691	33 442	28 146	–323	–23	163 938	41 912	205 850	42 937		
Q2	101 502	3 693	34 142	24 298	2 765	28	166 428	43 834	210 262	46 282		
Q3	108 054	3 942	34 163	26 674	690	–71	173 452	45 621	219 073	46 838		
Q4	110 701	3 961	34 627	28 272	576	202	178 339	47 400	225 739	47 273		
1995 Q1	103 558	3 566	35 302	29 526	–1 399	34	170 587	48 935	219 522	47 016		
Q2	106 289	4 090	34 979	26 987	3 216	118	175 679	49 202	224 881	52 099		
Q3	112 690	4 633	34 896	29 257	1 445	–147	182 774	51 082	233 856	53 664		
Q4	115 916	4 192	35 898	30 590	1 250	–97	187 749	53 193	240 942	52 442		
1996 Q1	110 023	4 153	37 047	32 061	–966	–64	182 254	53 554	235 808	54 342		
Q2	113 046	4 718	36 352	29 799	1 964	14	185 893	54 229	240 122	57 497		
Q3	120 548	4 818	36 303	31 373	–103	–97	192 842	55 335	248 177	56 957		
Q4	124 224	4 696	37 058	32 442	876	–38	199 258	57 185	256 443	55 696		
1997 Q1	116 475	4 970	36 827	33 163	261	–17	191 679	55 037	246 716	53 712		
Q2	120 848	4 757	36 833	31 515	2 934	57	196 944	57 088	254 032	58 432		
Q3	128 738	4 954	36 755	33 304	869	7	204 627	58 141	262 768	58 476		
Q4	132 246	4 921	37 994	36 171	324	–8	211 648	59 060	270 708	58 202		
1998 Q1	124 171	5 218	37 910	37 245	585	166	205 295	55 212	260 507	56 108		
Q2	129 487	5 140	38 278	35 404	1 707	61	210 077	56 408	266 485	59 076		
Q3	136 429	5 270	38 947	36 643	959	124	218 372	57 103	275 475	59 817		
Q4	140 764	5 344	39 632	38 779	1 210	136	225 865	56 751	282 616	58 428		
1999 Q1	132 785	5 179	39 992	39 664	–1 777	65	215 908	53 607	269 515	57 896		
Q2	138 512	5 570	40 634	37 709	–998	162	221 589	55 785	277 374	59 250		
Q3	143 213	5 701	41 071	39 373	1 642	–59	230 941	60 189	291 130	64 649		
Q4	149 859	6 087	41 424	41 626	–813	178	238 361	60 068	298 429	63 083		
2000 Q1	139 693	6 223	41 102	40 470	2 157	67	229 712	59 624	289 336	63 033		

See footnotes on page 15.

Sources: Office for National Statistics; Enquiries Column 1,2 020 7533 5998; Columns 4,6, 020 7533 5926; Column 3 020 7533 5990; Column 5 020 7533 6009; Columns7,9,11 020 7533 5944; Columns 8,10 020 7533 6078

1.3 Gross domestic product: by category of expenditure[1]

continued

£ million, current prices, seasonally adjusted

	Domestic expenditure on goods and services at market prices											
	Final consumption expenditure			Gross capital formation								
	Households	Non-profit institutions[2]	General government	Gross fixed capital formation	Changes in inventories[3]	Acquisitions less disposals of valuables	Total	Total Exports	Gross final expenditure	*less* Total Imports	Statistical discrepancy (expenditure)[4]	Gross domestic product at market prices[4]
	ABJQ	HAYE	NMRP	NPQS	CAEX	NPJQ	YBIL	IKBH	ABMF	IKBI	GIXM	YBHA
1955 Q1	3 130	21	814	715	89	–	4 769	1 053	5 822	1 128	–51	4 643
Q2	3 161	22	792	740	–16	–	4 699	962	5 661	1 031	52	4 682
Q3	3 243	22	813	778	115	–	4 971	1 068	6 039	1 144	–46	4 849
Q4	3 298	23	816	793	112	–	5 042	1 083	6 125	1 136	–56	4 933
1956 Q1	3 315	23	836	802	100	–	5 076	1 126	6 202	1 126	–44	5 032
Q2	3 374	24	865	820	16	–	5 099	1 158	6 257	1 123	–49	5 085
Q3	3 379	24	883	835	44	–	5 165	1 140	6 305	1 130	–25	5 150
Q4	3 426	25	907	858	99	–	5 315	1 162	6 477	1 131	–72	5 274
1957 Q1	3 464	25	919	883	77	–	5 368	1 221	6 589	1 216	–94	5 279
Q2	3 514	26	898	899	70	–	5 407	1 206	6 613	1 192	–62	5 359
Q3	3 599	27	912	901	48	–	5 487	1 204	6 691	1 187	–39	5 465
Q4	3 650	27	921	917	43	–	5 558	1 192	6 750	1 136	–46	5 568
1958 Q1	3 694	27	921	939	58	–	5 639	1 189	6 828	1 115	–61	5 652
Q2	3 704	28	925	927	3	–	5 587	1 121	6 708	1 094	–52	5 562
Q3	3 761	28	926	923	66	–	5 704	1 203	6 907	1 169	–82	5 656
Q4	3 854	29	950	935	–16	–	5 752	1 175	6 927	1 157	–55	5 715
1959 Q1	3 870	29	974	939	–32	–	5 780	1 159	6 939	1 149	–27	5 763
Q2	3 919	30	993	999	48	–	5 989	1 194	7 183	1 186	–36	5 961
Q3	3 945	31	988	988	51	–	6 003	1 217	7 220	1 207	–45	5 968
Q4	4 068	33	1 015	1 054	111	–	6 281	1 266	7 547	1 292	–70	6 185
1960 Q1	4 118	33	1 022	1 059	104	–	6 336	1 296	7 632	1 342	–13	6 277
Q2	4 125	34	1 040	1 069	109	–	6 377	1 261	7 638	1 370	43	6 311
Q3	4 148	35	1 046	1 101	145	–	6 475	1 279	7 754	1 389	23	6 388
Q4	4 182	35	1 097	1 139	204	–	6 657	1 298	7 955	1 398	–39	6 518
1961 Q1	4 284	36	1 128	1 185	131	–	6 764	1 355	8 119	1 401	–55	6 663
Q2	4 325	36	1 127	1 221	24	–	6 733	1 328	8 061	1 378	–40	6 643
Q3	4 395	37	1 136	1 251	118	–	6 937	1 344	8 281	1 337	–78	6 866
Q4	4 418	39	1 151	1 232	6	–	6 846	1 339	8 185	1 343	–43	6 799
1962 Q1	4 509	40	1 203	1 243	–60	–	6 935	1 348	8 283	1 365	–19	6 899
Q2	4 647	42	1 209	1 278	–17	–	7 159	1 386	8 545	1 389	–86	7 070
Q3	4 612	44	1 216	1 271	35	–	7 178	1 378	8 556	1 403	–19	7 134
Q4	4 670	47	1 240	1 257	34	–	7 248	1 388	8 636	1 397	–72	7 167
1963 Q1	4 722	64	1 256	1 176	–2	–	7 216	1 426	8 643	1 415	–57	7 170
Q2	4 889	64	1 265	1 330	42	–	7 590	1 447	9 038	1 471	–31	7 535
Q3	4 948	66	1 292	1 366	–17	–	7 655	1 476	9 131	1 516	22	7 637
Q4	5 006	67	1 314	1 423	138	–	7 948	1 503	9 449	1 569	–1	7 881
1964 Q1	5 083	68	1 321	1 506	111	–	8 089	1 522	9 610	1 681	–4	7 926
Q2	5 158	70	1 355	1 555	188	–	8 326	1 549	9 874	1 663	–26	8 186
Q3	5 252	73	1 384	1 590	150	–	8 449	1 535	9 984	1 688	40	8 336
Q4	5 375	77	1 398	1 628	251	–	8 729	1 577	10 308	1 736	18	8 588
1965 Q1	5 428	87	1 449	1 661	147	–	8 772	1 596	10 368	1 666	43	8 745
Q2	5 476	94	1 539	1 681	94	–	8 884	1 629	10 513	1 725	23	8 811
Q3	5 584	99	1 564	1 697	135	–	9 079	1 660	10 739	1 751	32	9 020
Q4	5 663	101	1 604	1 765	85	–	9 218	1 711	10 929	1 783	51	9 197
1966 Q1	5 761	104	1 597	1 764	107	–	9 333	1 737	11 070	1 828	68	9 310
Q2	5 879	104	1 661	1 780	77	–	9 501	1 722	11 223	1 788	18	9 453
Q3	5 841	105	1 700	1 849	114	–	9 609	1 803	11 412	1 848	39	9 603
Q4	5 910	108	1 742	1 868	–10	–	9 618	1 886	11 504	1 751	–53	9 700
1967 Q1	5 962	108	1 808	1 928	97	–	9 903	1 891	11 794	1 895	–107	9 792
Q2	6 063	112	1 816	2 036	88	–	10 115	1 839	11 954	1 903	–9	10 042
Q3	6 216	115	1 855	2 005	40	–	10 231	1 863	12 094	1 924	–92	10 078
Q4	6 338	118	1 916	1 976	61	–	10 409	1 777	12 186	2 092	88	10 182
1968 Q1	6 599	121	1 954	2 109	–45	–	10 738	2 159	12 897	2 297	–11	10 589
Q2	6 444	124	1 938	2 124	149	–	10 779	2 146	12 925	2 282	6	10 649
Q3	6 634	127	1 979	2 184	185	–	11 109	2 311	13 420	2 369	–69	10 982
Q4	6 774	130	1 988	2 311	163	–	11 366	2 346	13 712	2 381	–101	11 230
1969 Q1	6 866	133	2 021	2 168	174	–	11 362	2 369	13 731	2 437	114	11 408
Q2	6 955	137	2 012	2 214	146	–	11 464	2 482	13 946	2 447	52	11 551
Q3	7 022	140	2 062	2 320	96	–	11 640	2 591	14 231	2 450	–6	11 775
Q4	7 211	146	2 133	2 364	121	–	11 975	2 622	14 597	2 552	–	12 045

1 Estimates are given to the nearest £ million, but cannot be regarded as accurate to this degree.

2 Non-profit institutions serving households.

3 Quarterly alignment adjustment included in this series. For description of adjustment see notes in the article on "UK National Accounts, second quarter 1992", *Economic Trends* No.468, October 1992.

4 Gross Domestic Product is estimated in seasonally adjusted form only. No equivalent unadjusted estimates exist.

Sources: Office for National Statistics; Enquiries Column 1,2 020 7533 5998; Columns 4,6, 020 7533 5926; Column 3 020 7533 5990; Column 5 020 7533 6009; Columns 7,9,11 020 7533 5944; Columns 8,10 020 7533 6078

1.3 Gross domestic product: by category of expenditure[1]

continued

£ million, current prices, seasonally adjusted

	Domestic expenditure on goods and services at market prices											
	Final consumption expenditure			Gross capital formation								
	Households	Non-profit institutions 2	General government	Gross fixed capital formation	Changes in inventories3	Acquisitions less disposals of valuables	Total	Total Exports	Gross final expenditure	*less* Total Imports	Statistical discrepancy (expenditure)4	Gross domestic product at market prices4
	ABJQ	HAYE	NMRP	NPQS	CAEX	NPJQ	YBIL	IKBH	ABMF	IKBI	GIXM	YBHA
1970 Q1	7 325	158	2 145	2 315	1	–	11 944	2 806	14 750	2 586	22	12 186
Q2	7 524	164	2 301	2 512	119	–	12 620	2 786	15 406	2 738	10	12 678
Q3	7 752	168	2 375	2 551	169	–	13 015	2 800	15 815	2 777	29	13 067
Q4	7 946	171	2 457	2 658	93	–	13 325	3 097	16 422	2 951	30	13 501
1971 Q1	8 106	177	2 471	2 608	106	–	13 468	3 006	16 474	2 906	77	13 645
Q2	8 474	184	2 612	2 780	–44	–	14 006	3 242	17 248	3 065	–64	14 119
Q3	8 734	188	2 701	2 887	10	–	14 520	3 318	17 838	3 021	–205	14 612
Q4	8 936	192	2 776	2 968	42	–	14 914	3 324	18 238	3 103	–144	14 991
1972 Q1	9 219	199	2 907	2 908	–62	–	15 171	3 286	18 457	3 220	–59	15 178
Q2	9 508	208	2 885	3 042	59	–	15 702	3 332	19 034	3 254	83	15 863
Q3	9 842	216	3 049	3 125	–21	–	16 211	3 138	19 349	3 318	135	16 166
Q4	10 211	225	3 181	3 272	49	–	16 938	3 831	20 769	3 866	149	17 052
1973 Q1	10 797	237	3 305	3 637	523	–	18 499	3 881	22 380	4 137	–74	18 169
Q2	10 871	245	3 327	3 669	278	–	18 390	4 090	22 480	4 387	–14	18 079
Q3	11 161	255	3 506	3 827	355	–	19 104	4 373	23 477	4 869	–47	18 561
Q4	11 531	263	3 628	4 094	373	–	19 889	4 683	24 572	5 447	59	19 184
1974 Q1	11 845	275	3 820	4 277	–79	–	20 138	5 133	25 271	6 141	–202	18 928
Q2	12 430	287	3 983	4 328	599	–	21 627	5 698	27 325	6 852	–60	20 413
Q3	13 044	302	4 425	4 620	463	–	22 854	5 968	28 822	6 965	–263	21 594
Q4	13 807	318	4 886	4 909	62	–	23 982	6 032	30 014	7 049	–287	22 678
1975 Q1	14 664	337	5 564	5 020	–488	–	25 097	6 442	31 539	6 993	–107	24 439
Q2	15 592	359	5 645	5 390	–415	–	26 571	6 407	32 978	6 734	–464	25 780
Q3	16 028	382	6 049	5 697	–349	–	27 807	6 678	34 485	7 385	–192	26 908
Q4	16 597	409	6 353	5 749	–102	–	29 006	7 276	36 282	7 543	–367	28 372
1976 Q1	17 296	427	6 576	6 108	–84	–	30 323	7 772	38 095	7 715	–635	29 745
Q2	17 837	448	6 895	6 293	–55	–	31 418	8 512	39 930	9 005	–551	30 374
Q3	18 476	463	7 039	6 436	333	–	32 747	8 958	41 705	9 539	–711	31 455
Q4	19 451	473	7 156	6 679	707	–	34 466	9 776	44 242	10 224	–673	33 345
1977 Q1	19 895	485	7 186	6 513	738	–	34 817	10 176	44 993	10 382	–86	34 525
Q2	20 482	493	7 518	6 979	556	–	36 028	10 745	46 773	10 828	–209	35 736
Q3	21 180	502	7 680	7 158	–41	–	36 479	11 305	47 784	10 651	–280	36 853
Q4	21 947	516	7 792	7 551	571	–	38 377	10 984	49 361	10 401	–595	38 365
1978 Q1	23 101	528	8 193	7 796	355	–	39 973	11 298	51 271	10 974	–383	39 914
Q2	23 560	548	8 371	7 967	553	–	40 999	11 780	52 779	11 102	–260	41 417
Q3	24 574	566	8 642	8 144	248	–	42 174	12 022	54 196	11 562	–83	42 551
Q4	25 133	583	8 944	8 301	648	–	43 609	12 279	55 888	11 596	–365	43 927
1979 Q1	26 182	597	9 117	8 632	862	–	45 390	11 673	57 063	12 214	270	45 119
Q2	28 449	613	9 651	9 272	189	–	48 174	14 163	62 337	13 766	–263	48 308
Q3	29 109	642	10 166	9 810	724	–	50 451	14 091	64 542	13 620	–142	50 780
Q4	30 718	686	10 657	10 497	387	–	52 945	14 877	67 822	14 565	–45	53 212
1980 Q1	32 327	734	11 388	10 437	–354	–	54 532	15 720	70 252	15 235	221	55 238
Q2	32 607	774	12 026	10 761	–360	–	55 808	15 661	71 469	15 044	236	56 661
Q3	33 606	811	12 916	10 963	–726	–	57 570	15 523	73 093	13 729	–796	58 568
Q4	34 123	843	13 437	11 077	–1 132	–	58 348	15 591	73 939	13 441	–436	60 062
1981 Q1	35 455	874	13 561	10 555	–1 043	–	59 402	15 709	75 111	12 955	–900	61 256
Q2	36 365	905	13 985	10 775	–1 265	–	60 765	16 273	77 038	14 155	–624	62 259
Q3	37 144	936	14 334	10 936	–356	–	62 994	17 476	80 470	16 547	86	64 009
Q4	38 156	961	14 392	11 065	–104	–	64 470	17 857	82 327	16 586	–13	65 728
1982 Q1	38 860	986	14 962	11 089	505	–	66 402	17 596	83 998	16 358	–438	67 202
Q2	39 515	1 013	15 333	11 703	137	–	67 701	18 117	85 818	17 316	–29	68 473
Q3	40 654	1 044	15 330	12 126	–753	–	68 401	18 103	86 504	16 917	100	69 687
Q4	41 968	1 073	15 634	12 476	–1 077	–	70 074	18 763	88 837	17 040	–222	71 575
1983 Q1	42 892	1 099	16 541	12 587	435	–	73 554	19 196	92 750	18 399	–280	74 071
Q2	43 650	1 133	16 600	12 444	336	–	74 163	19 465	93 628	19 183	–221	74 224
Q3	44 959	1 165	16 518	12 811	64	–	75 517	20 302	95 819	19 478	–132	76 209
Q4	45 380	1 200	16 934	13 648	630	–	77 792	20 788	98 580	20 368	–96	78 116
1984 Q1	46 114	1 228	16 925	13 985	68	–	78 320	21 651	99 971	21 028	47	78 990
Q2	47 225	1 263	17 439	14 545	512	–	80 984	22 203	103 187	22 659	63	80 591
Q3	47 300	1 300	17 893	14 898	151	–	81 542	23 197	104 739	23 643	121	81 217
Q4	48 605	1 342	18 222	15 270	565	–	84 004	24 458	108 462	25 247	136	83 351

See footnotes on page 19.

Sources: Office for National Statistics; Enquiries Column 1,2 020 7533 5998; Columns 4,6 020 7533 5926; Column 3 020 7533 5990; Column 5 020 7533 6009; Columns 7,9,11 020 7533 5944; Columns 8,10 020 7533 6078

1.3 Gross domestic product: by category of expenditure[1]

continued

£ million, current prices, seasonally adjusted

	Domestic expenditure on goods and services at market prices											
	Final consumption expenditure			Gross capital formation								
	Households	Non-profit institutions [2]	General government	Gross fixed capital formation	Changes in inventories[3]	Acquisitions less disposals of valuables	Total	Total Exports	Gross final expenditure	*less* Total Imports	Statistical discrepancy (expenditure)[4]	Gross domestic product at market prices[4]
	ABJQ	HAYE	NMRP	NPQS	CAEX	NPJQ	YBIL	IKBH	ABMF	IKBI	GIXM	YBHA
1985 Q1	49 977	1 382	18 552	16 488	–233	–	86 166	25 711	111 877	26 339	–	85 538
Q2	50 923	1 428	18 346	15 583	850	–	87 130	26 515	113 645	25 017	–	88 628
Q3	52 272	1 479	18 653	16 053	–15	–	88 442	24 881	113 323	23 614	–	89 709
Q4	53 428	1 531	18 890	16 339	219	–	90 407	24 819	115 226	23 753	–	91 473
1986 Q1	55 127	1 613	19 576	16 728	–513	–10	92 521	24 477	116 998	24 221	–	92 777
Q2	56 947	1 649	19 962	16 424	216	–15	95 183	24 029	119 212	24 730	–	94 482
Q3	57 977	1 700	20 072	17 512	158	14	97 433	23 846	121 279	25 279	–	96 000
Q4	58 797	1 757	20 382	18 054	821	–13	99 798	25 429	125 227	26 663	–	98 564
1987 Q1	60 490	1 788	20 831	17 829	–73	–38	100 827	26 339	127 166	26 368	–	100 798
Q2	61 697	1 842	21 287	18 852	352	32	104 062	26 175	130 237	27 266	–	102 971
Q3	63 446	1 908	21 645	20 669	398	–116	107 950	27 347	135 297	28 744	–	106 553
Q4	65 510	1 988	22 021	21 574	551	–10	111 634	26 576	138 210	29 071	–	109 139
1988 Q1	67 874	2 105	22 605	22 773	–93	–5	115 259	25 884	141 143	29 058	–	112 085
Q2	69 472	2 168	22 858	23 581	226	13	118 318	26 815	145 133	30 524	–	114 609
Q3	72 185	2 220	22 925	24 589	1 274	–24	123 169	27 577	150 746	32 128	–	118 618
Q4	73 894	2 270	23 951	25 133	2 926	65	128 239	27 158	155 397	32 947	–	122 450
1989 Q1	75 512	2 247	24 298	27 162	899	34	130 152	28 911	159 063	34 422	–	124 641
Q2	76 987	2 521	24 425	27 363	753	–5	132 044	29 787	161 831	35 299	–	126 532
Q3	77 949	2 570	25 281	28 156	1 403	–11	135 348	30 931	166 279	36 665	–	129 614
Q4	80 045	2 648	25 883	28 352	–378	–9	136 541	32 254	168 795	36 304	–	132 491
1990 Q1	81 532	2 777	26 522	28 913	394	4	140 142	33 124	173 266	37 972	–	135 294
Q2	83 927	2 839	27 290	28 608	974	–40	143 598	33 607	177 205	38 084	–	139 121
Q3	84 861	2 865	28 146	28 576	–359	–55	144 034	33 097	177 131	36 185	–	140 946
Q4	86 172	2 920	28 662	28 217	–2 809	–22	143 140	33 673	176 813	35 957	–	140 856
1991 Q1	87 143	2 861	29 143	26 958	–426	–33	145 646	32 269	177 915	34 459	–	143 456
Q2	88 873	2 734	30 252	26 241	–2 227	57	145 930	34 077	180 007	34 888	–	145 119
Q3	90 487	2 723	31 001	25 553	–1 820	7	147 951	34 747	182 698	35 879	–	146 819
Q4	91 282	2 778	31 344	25 928	–454	–117	150 761	34 272	185 033	35 891	–	149 142
1992 Q1	92 197	2 729	31 758	25 524	–390	–81	151 737	34 871	186 608	36 277	–	150 331
Q2	94 044	2 718	32 123	25 303	–1 071	–22	153 095	35 824	188 919	37 287	–	151 632
Q3	94 905	2 705	32 548	24 897	–651	32	154 436	35 306	189 742	37 191	–	152 551
Q4	96 001	2 654	32 782	24 554	175	107	156 273	37 290	193 563	39 912	–	153 651
1993 Q1	97 436	2 938	32 937	25 007	–154	50	158 214	39 993	198 207	41 916	–	156 291
Q2	98 710	3 743	32 395	24 956	37	28	159 869	39 591	199 460	41 399	–	158 061
Q3	100 789	3 606	32 868	25 364	160	–13	162 774	40 803	203 577	42 199	–	161 378
Q4	102 173	3 694	33 213	25 903	286	–74	165 195	41 691	206 886	43 260	–	163 626
1994 Q1	103 065	3 689	33 648	26 740	192	–16	167 318	42 606	209 924	44 181	–	165 743
Q2	104 188	3 792	33 684	25 925	1 429	–53	168 965	43 974	212 939	45 192	–	167 747
Q3	105 253	3 840	34 389	27 013	327	20	170 842	45 300	216 142	45 948	–	170 194
Q4	106 756	3 966	34 653	27 712	1 760	185	175 032	46 887	221 919	48 009	–	173 910
1995 Q1	107 797	3 952	35 152	28 285	–520	18	174 684	49 129	223 813	48 319	–	175 494
Q2	109 083	4 098	34 808	28 610	2 194	51	178 844	49 378	228 222	50 839	–	177 383
Q3	109 939	4 147	35 204	29 574	2 044	–66	180 842	51 176	232 018	52 777	–	179 241
Q4	111 634	4 284	35 911	29 891	794	–95	182 419	52 729	235 148	53 286	–	181 862
1996 Q1	114 535	4 452	36 669	30 995	476	–80	187 047	54 000	241 047	55 751	–	185 296
Q2	115 978	4 579	36 354	31 386	789	–49	189 037	54 824	243 861	56 340	–	187 521
Q3	117 663	4 621	36 688	31 674	644	–20	191 270	55 235	246 505	56 121	–	190 384
Q4	119 665	4 733	37 049	31 620	–138	–36	192 893	56 244	249 137	56 280	–	192 857
1997 Q1	121 169	5 050	36 552	32 149	1 253	–7	196 166	56 592	252 758	55 804	–	196 954
Q2	123 470	4 718	37 091	33 145	755	–5	199 174	57 222	256 396	57 118	–	199 278
Q3	125 696	4 895	37 184	33 555	939	55	202 324	57 638	259 962	57 248	–	202 714
Q4	127 972	4 939	37 582	35 304	1 441	–4	207 234	57 874	265 108	58 652	–	206 456
1998 Q1	129 795	5 218	37 891	36 425	840	177	210 346	56 310	266 656	57 818	–	208 838
Q2	132 016	5 140	38 445	36 672	883	–49	213 107	57 088	270 195	58 379	–	211 816
Q3	133 576	5 270	39 057	37 270	1 127	291	216 591	56 569	273 160	58 553	–	214 607
Q4	135 464	5 344	39 374	37 704	1 611	68	219 565	55 507	275 072	58 679	–	216 393
1999 Q1	138 174	5 179	40 094	38 730	20	65	222 262	54 874	277 136	59 728	–102	217 306
Q2	140 102	5 570	40 708	39 338	–1 604	162	224 276	56 425	280 701	59 516	–128	221 057
Q3	141 735	5 701	41 057	40 010	–562	–59	227 882	59 665	287 547	62 300	–132	225 115
Q4	144 358	6 087	41 262	40 294	200	178	232 379	58 685	291 064	63 334	–102	227 628
2000 Q1	145 491	6 223	41 280	39 939	1 056	67	234 056	60 281	294 337	64 328	–48	229 961

See footnotes on page 19.

Sources: Office for National Statistics; Enquiries Column 1,2 020 7533 5998; Columns 4,6 020 7533 5926; Column 3 020 7533 5990; Column 5 020 7533 6009; Columns 7,9,11 020 7533 5944; Columns 8,10 020 7533 6078

1.3 Gross domestic product: by category of expenditure[1]

continued

£ million, 1995 prices[2]

	Domestic expenditure on goods and services at market prices											
	Final consumption expenditure			Gross capital formation								
	Households	Non-profit institutions[3]	General government	Gross fixed capital formation	Changes in inventories[4]	Acquisitions less disposals of valuables	Total	Total Exports	Gross final expenditure	*less* Total Imports	Statistical discrepancy (expenditure)[5]	Gross domestic product at market prices[5]
	ABPF	ABNU	NMRU	NPQR	ABMQ	NPJP	YBIK	KTMZ	ABME	KTNB	GIXS	ABMI
1948	142 958	959	63 059	23 396	1 671	–	227 956	26 479	247 844	28 860	1 162	224 733
1949	145 251	1 007	66 732	25 465	601	–	233 643	29 381	257 092	31 125	2 394	232 596
1950	149 082	1 080	66 661	26 838	–1 842	–	235 583	33 563	264 613	31 386	1 871	239 743
1951	147 049	1 067	71 530	27 145	4 125	–	246 441	33 228	274 235	33 590	1 388	246 379
1952	147 017	1 117	78 413	27 596	441	–	245 440	32 554	272 384	31 084	816	247 437
1953	153 393	1 186	80 466	30 613	902	–	258 192	33 914	286 083	33 539	–746	256 993
1954	159 716	1 274	80 216	33 124	427	–	267 313	35 824	297 163	34 763	195	268 024
1955	166 245	1 339	78 256	34 864	2 472	–	278 668	38 296	311 085	38 209	–1 441	276 319
1956	167 041	1 389	77 475	36 457	1 923	–	280 157	40 045	314 859	38 344	–2 561	279 042
1957	170 434	1 468	76 437	38 257	1 974	–	285 554	41 073	321 276	39 296	–3 167	283 930
1958	175 182	1 525	74 482	38 570	875	–	288 147	40 427	322 800	39 723	–3 155	284 957
1959	182 697	1 662	75 823	41 474	1 642	–	301 665	41 529	336 919	42 351	–2 214	297 306
1960	189 586	1 824	77 348	45 191	5 126	–	318 928	43 895	356 186	47 468	178	313 213
1961	193 663	1 906	80 158	49 457	2 467	–	327 164	45 296	365 729	47 143	–2 565	320 997
1962	197 837	2 169	82 667	49 801	81	–	331 147	46 068	370 465	48 141	–2 246	324 988
1963	206 304	3 365	84 020	50 566	1 501	–	344 699	48 324	386 105	50 163	–765	340 297
1964	212 644	3 494	85 517	58 648	6 169	–	367 129	49 914	409 297	55 543	305	358 896
1965	215 002	4 172	87 907	61 707	4 013	–	372 993	52 052	417 501	56 103	1 531	368 001
1966	218 707	4 404	90 509	63 376	2 542	–	379 277	54 781	426 836	57 528	729	375 180
1967	223 851	4 586	95 598	69 065	2 013	–	394 542	55 128	441 707	61 563	–1 169	383 790
1968	230 135	4 812	96 134	73 040	3 207	–	407 609	62 043	462 661	66 203	–1 585	399 487
1969	231 201	5 083	94 593	72 628	3 550	–	407 734	68 119	470 330	68 481	1 412	407 657
1970	237 739	5 465	96 345	74 751	2 645	–	417 673	71 746	484 239	71 779	735	417 403
1971	245 429	5 466	99 344	76 242	841	–	427 691	76 710	499 884	75 640	–2 434	425 770
1972	261 277	5 629	103 876	76 212	–10	–	447 139	77 535	519 305	83 142	2 072	441 210
1973	275 705	5 897	107 722	81 198	9 186	–	481 962	86 769	563 720	92 416	–515	473 478
1974	271 228	5 871	109 876	79 614	4 150	–	471 317	93 131	561 254	93 346	–4 473	465 525
1975	270 421	6 000	116 138	78 108	–4 739	–	463 442	90 428	550 493	87 191	–4 899	462 374
1976	271 477	6 249	118 229	79 457	2 259	–	476 725	98 665	573 080	91 689	–9 779	475 342
1977	270 434	6 210	116 574	78 240	4 758	–	475 805	105 426	580 358	93 452	–3 843	486 576
1978	284 901	6 602	118 672	80 206	3 993	–	493 828	107 375	599 876	96 939	–3 281	503 136
1979	297 453	6 739	120 591	82 307	4 635	–	511 299	111 440	621 413	106 289	–430	516 956
1980	297 256	6 830	122 471	78 398	–4 694	–	496 913	111 146	607 289	102 541	–1 573	505 691
1981	297 237	7 209	122 682	71 451	–4 457	–	489 339	110 333	599 075	99 709	–2 919	499 259
1982	299 810	7 716	123 454	75 666	–1 784	–	501 387	111 265	611 714	104 617	–1 088	508 239
1983	313 648	8 105	126 010	79 489	1 890	–	526 677	113 235	638 262	111 491	–1 277	527 288
1984	319 357	8 571	127 489	86 912	1 510	–	542 106	120 693	661 944	122 551	608	540 202
1985	331 404	9 229	127 259	90 421	1 143	–	557 995	127 901	685 763	125 647	–	560 639
1986	353 831	9 283	129 244	92 330	1 384	–68	585 146	133 664	718 576	134 262	–	584 239
1987	372 601	9 928	129 251	100 520	1 907	–216	613 690	141 558	755 019	144 842	–	610 110
1988	400 427	10 971	129 281	115 362	5 883	38	662 991	142 426	805 058	163 373	–	641 637
1989	413 498	11 202	130 324	122 158	3 123	–8	681 721	149 323	830 708	175 511	–	655 174
1990	415 788	12 079	133 620	119 368	–2 079	–130	679 494	156 640	835 887	176 377	–	659 486
1991	408 309	12 217	137 541	109 000	–5 349	–90	661 163	156 362	817 330	167 472	–	649 815
1992	410 026	12 445	138 209	108 246	–1 962	39	666 495	162 819	829 176	178 879	–	650 288
1993	420 081	14 723	137 037	109 127	360	–9	680 925	169 225	850 039	184 607	–	665 427
1994	431 462	15 900	138 914	113 042	4 836	140	704 294	184 873	889 167	194 551	–	694 616
1995	438 453	16 481	141 075	116 360	4 512	–92	716 789	202 412	919 201	205 221	–	713 980
1996	454 686	16 691	143 501	122 042	1 830	–186	738 564	217 600	956 164	223 961	–	732 203
1997	472 701	17 055	141 495	131 246	3 762	14	766 273	236 283	1 002 556	244 635	–	757 921
1998	491 378	18 112	143 053	144 437	4 229	457	801 666	242 498	1 044 164	266 227	–	777 937
1999	512 864	18 552	147 313	153 272	–1 386	323	830 938	250 429	1 081 367	286 587	–414	794 366

1 Estimates are given up to the nearest £ million, but cannot be regarded as accurate to this degree.
2 For years up to and including 1993,totals differ from the sum of the components because of the method used to rebase on 1995 prices.
3 Non-profit institutions serving households.
4 Quarterly alignment adjustment included in this series.
5 Gross Domestic Product is estimated in seasonally adjusted form only. No equivalent unadjusted estimates exist.

Sources: Office for National Statistics; Enquiries Column 1,2 020 7533 5998; Columns 4,6 020 7533 5926; Column 3 020 7533 5990; Column 5 020 7533 6009; Columns 7,9,11 020 7533 5944; Columns 8,10 020 7533 6078

1.3 Gross domestic product: by category of expenditure[1]

continued

£ million, 1995 prices, not seasonally adjusted [2]

	Domestic expenditure on goods and services at market prices											
	Final consumption expenditure			Gross capital formation								
	Households	Non-profit institutions [3]	General government	Gross fixed capital formation	Changes in inventories[4]	Acquisitions less disposals of valuables	Total	Total Exports	Gross final expenditure	*less* Total Imports	Statistical discrepancy (expenditure)[5]	Gross domestic product at market prices[5]
	ABPF	ABNU	NMRU	NPQR	ABMQ	NPJP	YBIK	KTMZ	ABME	KTNB		
1955 Q1	38 798	334	19 856	8 309	1 385	–	67 581	9 926	76 316	9 766		
Q2	41 214	341	19 558	8 405	–208	–	67 579	8 872	74 873	8 992		
Q3	42 313	330	19 448	8 689	1 162	–	71 251	9 526	79 176	9 701		
Q4	43 920	334	19 394	9 461	133	–	72 257	9 972	80 720	9 750		
1956 Q1	39 476	336	19 330	8 819	1 042	–	68 060	9 996	76 857	9 864		
Q2	41 503	340	19 262	8 837	976	–	70 143	10 174	79 034	9 679		
Q3	41 878	347	19 363	8 972	305	–	69 705	9 485	77 685	9 332		
Q4	44 184	366	19 520	9 829	–400	–	72 249	10 390	81 283	9 469		
1957 Q1	39 555	358	19 729	9 422	1 538	–	69 958	10 501	79 309	10 071		
Q2	42 535	366	18 978	9 375	850	–	71 568	10 401	80 667	9 664		
Q3	43 029	371	18 824	9 358	386	–	71 243	9 895	79 673	9 840		
Q4	45 315	373	18 906	10 102	–800	–	72 785	10 276	81 627	9 721		
1958 Q1	41 079	378	18 653	9 531	748	–	69 646	10 314	78 721	9 774		
Q2	43 336	381	18 542	9 338	113	–	70 999	9 841	79 382	9 659		
Q3	44 021	385	18 458	9 503	589	–	72 456	9 963	80 908	9 901		
Q4	46 740	381	18 829	10 198	–575	–	75 046	10 309	83 780	10 389		
1959 Q1	42 226	404	18 839	9 543	554	–	70 812	10 072	79 505	10 110		
Q2	45 671	415	18 927	10 069	355	–	74 969	10 412	83 848	10 716		
Q3	45 869	415	18 894	10 283	702	–	75 836	10 068	84 219	10 373		
Q4	48 931	428	19 163	11 579	31	–	80 048	10 977	89 347	11 152		
1960 Q1	44 789	442	19 301	10 887	1 488	–	76 654	11 149	86 381	11 776		
Q2	47 646	454	19 245	10 869	1 124	–	79 234	11 013	88 629	11 973		
Q3	47 614	460	19 163	11 267	1 479	–	80 055	10 463	88 691	11 655		
Q4	49 537	468	19 639	12 168	1 035	–	82 985	11 270	92 485	12 064		
1961 Q1	45 704	469	19 961	11 914	1 456	–	79 300	11 614	89 466	12 269		
Q2	48 695	472	19 910	12 073	1 231	–	82 398	11 398	92 098	11 937		
Q3	48 758	482	20 010	12 675	355	–	82 194	10 790	91 122	11 373		
Q4	50 506	483	20 277	12 795	–575	–	83 272	11 494	93 043	11 564		
1962 Q1	46 380	507	20 751	12 276	–185	–	79 045	11 437	88 998	12 146		
Q2	49 964	533	20 580	12 303	286	–	83 408	11 826	93 598	12 051		
Q3	49 603	550	20 469	12 603	408	–	83 465	11 013	92 604	11 781		
Q4	51 890	579	20 867	12 619	–428	–	85 229	11 792	95 265	12 163		
1963 Q1	47 435	812	21 166	11 235	137	–	80 078	12 075	90 752	12 047		
Q2	51 959	849	20 903	12 347	654	–	86 511	12 217	97 013	12 473		
Q3	52 888	818	20 734	13 033	121	–	87 451	11 575	97 104	12 591		
Q4	54 022	886	21 217	13 951	589	–	90 659	12 457	101 236	13 052		
1964 Q1	49 921	832	21 443	14 253	1 002	–	87 285	12 627	98 255	13 739		
Q2	53 301	816	21 290	14 081	1 880	–	91 562	12 717	102 412	13 914		
Q3	53 952	845	21 175	14 764	1 567	–	92 568	11 699	102 099	13 700		
Q4	55 470	1 001	21 609	15 550	1 720	–	95 714	12 871	106 531	14 190		
1965 Q1	50 754	963	21 313	15 681	859	–	89 594	12 405	100 163	13 171		
Q2	53 615	1 027	22 201	14 726	1 250	–	92 787	13 283	104 274	14 121		
Q3	54 706	1 064	21 949	15 101	1 496	–	94 480	12 888	105 385	14 761		
Q4	55 927	1 118	22 444	16 199	408	–	96 132	13 476	107 679	14 050		
1966 Q1	51 957	1 102	22 370	16 079	611	–	91 979	13 521	103 806	14 485		
Q2	55 485	1 084	22 471	15 046	1 022	–	95 110	13 249	106 429	14 402		
Q3	55 141	1 074	22 548	15 746	1 456	–	96 084	13 581	107 763	15 250		
Q4	56 124	1 144	23 120	16 505	–547	–	96 104	14 430	108 838	13 391		
1967 Q1	51 969	1 105	24 063	17 214	562	–	94 527	14 101	106 937	14 727		
Q2	55 550	1 153	23 630	16 997	769	–	98 010	14 206	110 362	15 498		
Q3	57 103	1 136	23 442	17 243	561	–	99 509	13 770	111 238	15 574		
Q4	59 229	1 192	24 463	17 611	121	–	102 496	13 051	113 170	15 764		
1968 Q1	55 813	1 181	24 593	18 504	–773	–	98 912	15 033	112 243	16 650		
Q2	56 187	1 197	23 807	17 039	1 582	–	99 876	15 223	113 391	16 294		
Q3	57 924	1 195	23 792	17 857	1 714	–	102 752	15 753	116 770	16 934		
Q4	60 211	1 239	23 942	19 640	684	–	106 069	16 034	120 257	16 325		
1969 Q1	54 410	1 232	24 214	17 878	785	–	98 339	15 654	112 473	17 043		
Q2	57 270	1 275	23 259	17 192	1 498	–	100 731	17 351	116 844	17 160		
Q3	58 366	1 240	23 339	18 330	758	–	102 293	17 486	118 490	17 265		
Q4	61 155	1 336	23 781	19 228	509	–	106 371	17 628	122 523	17 013		

See footnotes on page 22.

Sources: Office for National Statistics; Enquiries Column 1,2 020 7533 5998; Columns 4,6 020 7533 5926; Column 3 020 7533 5990; Column 5 020 7533 6009; Columns 7,9,11 020 7533 5944; Columns 8,10 020 7533 6078

1.3 Gross domestic product: by category of expenditure[1]

continued

£ million, 1995 prices, not seasonally adjusted [2]

	Domestic expenditure on goods and services at market prices											
	Final consumption expenditure			Gross capital formation								
	Households	Non-profit institutions [3]	General government	Gross fixed capital formation	Changes in inventories[4]	Acquisitions less disposals of valuables	Total	Total Exports	Gross final expenditure	*less* Total Imports	Statistical discrepancy (expenditure)[5]	Gross domestic product at market prices[5]
	ABPF	ABNU	NMRU	NPQR	ABMQ	NPJP	YBIK	KTMZ	ABME	KTNB		
1970 Q1	55 342	1 340	24 026	18 184	–584	–	97 998	17 139	113 996	16 662		
Q2	58 731	1 379	24 015	18 067	1 393	–	103 813	18 055	120 635	18 319		
Q3	60 694	1 370	23 931	18 566	1 337	–	106 297	17 400	122 170	18 128		
Q4	62 972	1 376	24 373	19 934	499	–	109 565	19 152	127 438	18 670		
1971 Q1	56 575	1 335	24 700	18 824	163	–	101 422	17 545	117 739	18 615		
Q2	60 475	1 379	24 683	18 462	258	–	105 278	19 884	124 293	19 143		
Q3	62 629	1 341	24 846	18 991	251	–	108 221	19 605	126 730	18 862		
Q4	65 750	1 411	25 115	19 965	169	–	112 770	19 676	131 122	19 020		
1972 Q1	60 273	1 333	26 037	19 218	–919	–	105 534	18 699	123 063	20 298		
Q2	64 311	1 410	25 508	18 413	506	–	110 260	19 915	129 044	20 822		
Q3	66 536	1 395	25 885	18 775	9	–	112 699	17 620	128 499	19 903		
Q4	70 157	1 491	26 446	19 806	394	–	118 646	21 301	138 699	22 119		
1973 Q1	65 859	1 498	27 117	21 268	2 056	–	118 496	20 564	137 670	23 088		
Q2	67 708	1 431	26 621	19 300	3 064	–	118 709	21 861	139 437	22 864		
Q3	69 779	1 521	26 836	19 733	2 667	–	121 080	21 933	141 782	22 937		
Q4	72 359	1 447	27 148	20 897	1 399	–	123 677	22 411	144 831	23 527		
1974 Q1	63 714	1 506	27 265	21 217	–730	–	113 039	22 181	134 422	23 068		
Q2	66 360	1 416	27 098	18 578	2 502	–	116 217	23 793	139 393	23 938		
Q3	68 654	1 499	27 327	19 318	2 437	–	119 590	23 850	142 675	23 325		
Q4	72 500	1 450	28 186	20 501	–59	–	122 471	23 307	144 764	23 015		
1975 Q1	64 709	1 522	29 458	20 340	–2 042	–	113 297	21 872	134 295	21 528		
Q2	66 999	1 463	28 648	18 593	–1 272	–	113 659	22 797	135 756	21 803		
Q3	68 038	1 520	28 512	19 584	–883	–	116 297	22 443	137 841	22 195		
Q4	70 675	1 495	29 520	19 591	–542	–	120 189	23 316	142 601	21 665		
1976 Q1	64 218	1 520	29 796	20 875	–696	–	115 388	23 263	137 964	21 554		
Q2	66 397	1 588	29 756	18 760	124	–	116 063	24 711	140 354	23 462		
Q3	68 645	1 550	29 260	19 613	1 145	–	120 087	25 099	144 655	23 328		
Q4	72 217	1 591	29 417	20 209	1 686	–	125 187	25 592	150 107	23 345		
1977 Q1	64 101	1 552	29 339	19 495	1 550	–	115 999	25 061	140 715	23 258		
Q2	65 465	1 569	29 240	18 738	1 900	–	116 810	26 286	142 965	24 143		
Q3	67 937	1 513	28 804	19 298	266	–	117 499	27 883	145 547	23 334		
Q4	72 931	1 576	29 191	20 709	1 042	–	125 497	26 196	151 131	22 717		
1978 Q1	67 945	1 553	29 862	20 763	322	–	120 365	25 489	145 406	24 221		
Q2	69 165	1 765	29 458	19 222	1 948	–	121 504	27 463	148 831	25 490		
Q3	72 436	1 608	29 455	19 825	1 076	–	124 230	27 457	151 434	24 343		
Q4	75 355	1 676	29 897	20 396	647	–	127 729	26 966	154 205	22 885		
1979 Q1	70 266	1 519	30 205	20 415	1 486	–	123 889	24 432	147 531	24 863		
Q2	75 036	1 658	30 349	19 284	1 064	–	126 959	29 344	156 279	27 131		
Q3	74 082	1 836	29 756	20 539	2 266	–	128 638	28 788	157 229	27 182		
Q4	78 069	1 726	30 281	22 069	–181	–	131 813	28 876	160 374	27 113		
1980 Q1	73 181	1 576	30 991	20 725	–895	–	125 015	28 439	153 347	27 588		
Q2	72 068	1 784	30 231	18 609	194	–	122 206	27 623	149 692	26 855		
Q3	75 269	1 671	30 402	19 176	–730	–	124 954	27 704	152 420	24 758		
Q4	76 738	1 799	30 847	19 888	–3 263	–	124 738	27 380	151 830	23 340		
1981 Q1	71 902	1 592	31 140	17 967	–1 703	–	119 599	26 105	145 401	22 432		
Q2	72 576	1 794	30 717	16 956	–1 549	–	119 048	27 020	145 955	24 505		
Q3	75 148	1 847	30 553	17 799	262	–	124 675	28 459	153 045	27 032		
Q4	77 611	1 976	30 272	18 729	–1 467	–	126 017	28 749	154 674	25 740		
1982 Q1	71 571	1 670	31 467	18 431	1 280	–	123 796	26 830	150 277	25 428		
Q2	72 345	1 981	30 644	17 657	780	–	122 597	27 975	150 483	27 239		
Q3	76 125	1 968	30 426	19 111	–671	–	126 109	27 849	153 697	26 521		
Q4	79 769	2 097	30 917	20 467	–3 173	–	128 885	28 611	157 257	25 429		
1983 Q1	74 812	1 803	31 835	20 056	621	–	128 575	27 471	155 608	26 640		
Q2	75 746	2 072	31 500	18 217	744	–	127 517	27 641	154 804	28 113		
Q3	80 220	2 115	31 052	19 527	1 433	–	133 831	28 604	161 981	28 450		
Q4	82 870	2 115	31 623	21 689	–908	–	136 754	29 519	165 869	28 288		
1984 Q1	76 514	2 082	32 815	21 641	621	–	133 234	29 379	162 345	29 084		
Q2	77 903	2 129	31 447	20 170	206	–	131 251	29 099	160 118	30 818		
Q3	79 965	2 164	31 359	21 728	751	–	135 620	29 999	165 365	30 822		
Q4	84 975	2 196	31 868	23 373	–68	–	142 001	32 216	174 116	31 827		

See footnotes on page 22.

Sources: Office for National Statistics; Enquiries Column 1 0171 533 5998; Columns 2,4,13,14 0171 533 5983; Column 3 0171 533 5985; Column 5 0171 533 6010; Columns 6,7,9,11,12,15 0171 533 5944; Columns 8,10 0171 533 6095

1.3 Gross domestic product: by category of expenditure[1]

continued

£ million, 1995 prices, not seasonally adjusted [2]

Domestic expenditure on goods and services at market prices

	Final consumption expenditure: Households	Final consumption expenditure: Non-profit institutions [3]	Final consumption expenditure: General government	Gross capital formation: Gross fixed capital formation	Gross capital formation: Changes in inventories[4]	Gross capital formation: Acquisitions less disposals of valuables	Total	Total Exports	Gross final expenditure	*less* Total Imports	Statistical discrepancy (expenditure)[5]	Gross domestic product at market prices[5]
	ABPF	ABNU	NMRU	NPQR	ABMQ	NPJP	YBIK	KTMZ	ABME	KTNB		
1985 Q1	78 734	2 242	33 342	24 195	127	–	138 398	30 859	169 048	31 489		
Q2	79 936	2 286	31 031	20 310	1 326	–	134 463	32 147	166 848	31 564		
Q3	83 896	2 329	31 186	22 253	858	–	140 223	31 719	171 823	31 077		
Q4	88 838	2 372	31 700	23 663	–1 168	–	144 911	33 176	178 044	31 517		
1986 Q1	83 021	2 248	33 417	23 656	694	–39	143 043	30 868	173 833	30 910		
Q2	86 025	2 300	31 761	20 361	1 073	49	141 092	33 712	174 765	34 300		
Q3	90 836	2 346	31 902	23 429	–229	–96	147 926	33 587	181 452	34 997		
Q4	93 949	2 389	32 164	24 884	–154	18	153 085	35 497	188 526	34 055		
1987 Q1	86 862	2 406	32 878	24 062	182	–87	146 278	33 842	180 067	32 693		
Q2	89 641	2 450	31 881	22 282	885	132	146 946	34 529	181 428	35 848		
Q3	95 799	2 505	32 193	26 268	1 680	–306	158 161	36 224	194 323	38 573		
Q4	100 299	2 567	32 299	27 908	–840	45	162 305	36 963	199 201	37 728		
1988 Q1	93 543	2 681	33 208	28 848	1 230	–42	159 937	34 123	193 971	37 267		
Q2	96 130	2 733	31 690	26 972	1 940	115	159 748	35 884	195 563	40 819		
Q3	103 821	2 769	31 801	29 293	1 008	–192	168 673	36 042	204 622	42 822		
Q4	106 933	2 788	32 582	30 249	1 705	157	174 633	36 377	210 902	42 465		
1989 Q1	97 977	2 749	32 948	31 801	805	8	167 009	35 482	202 396	42 315		
Q2	100 576	2 783	31 781	28 600	2 021	96	166 095	36 938	202 957	44 814		
Q3	106 119	2 813	32 700	30 614	1 011	–162	173 361	37 320	210 588	45 582		
Q4	108 826	2 857	32 895	31 143	–714	50	175 256	39 583	214 767	42 800		
1990 Q1	99 464	2 974	33 608	32 157	196	–33	169 079	37 680	206 683	43 656		
Q2	101 880	3 007	32 652	27 814	587	63	166 053	39 055	205 057	45 477		
Q3	106 263	3 040	33 437	29 376	122	–193	172 122	38 484	210 530	44 979		
Q4	108 181	3 058	33 923	30 021	–2 984	33	172 240	41 421	213 617	42 265		
1991 Q1	98 456	3 017	34 275	29 316	–1 667	–71	163 617	36 055	199 594	40 117		
Q2	98 837	3 054	34 338	25 179	–841	174	160 476	39 476	199 922	42 500		
Q3	104 218	3 067	34 399	26 556	–267	–110	167 602	39 415	206 965	43 007		
Q4	106 798	3 079	34 529	27 949	–2 574	–83	169 468	41 416	210 849	41 848		
1992 Q1	97 175	3 085	34 749	28 968	–937	–117	163 234	38 646	201 832	42 400		
Q2	99 663	3 098	34 292	25 153	–88	81	161 926	40 637	202 542	45 568		
Q3	105 406	3 123	34 445	26 954	422	–70	170 060	40 216	210 226	46 173		
Q4	107 782	3 139	34 723	27 171	–1 359	145	171 275	43 320	214 576	44 738		
1993 Q1	99 828	3 202	34 532	28 935	–1 713	26	165 013	40 861	205 845	44 391		
Q2	101 106	3 817	33 781	24 784	1 431	127	164 810	41 123	205 908	46 079		
Q3	108 275	3 844	34 266	26 929	471	–109	173 438	42 611	216 015	47 502		
Q4	110 872	3 860	34 458	28 479	171	–53	177 664	44 630	222 271	46 635		
1994 Q1	103 247	3 926	34 265	30 125	–841	–24	170 698	43 889	214 587	46 575		
Q2	104 354	3 951	34 695	25 710	3 025	31	171 766	45 222	216 988	49 472		
Q3	110 992	3 993	35 004	27 950	1 389	–73	179 255	46 841	226 096	49 031		
Q4	112 869	4 030	34 950	29 257	1 263	206	182 575	48 921	231 496	49 473		
1995 Q1	104 792	4 081	34 962	30 214	–1 061	29	173 017	49 278	222 295	47 887		
Q2	106 263	4 112	35 305	27 154	2 984	117	175 935	49 192	225 127	52 240		
Q3	112 283	4 134	35 221	29 054	1 545	–151	182 086	51 095	233 181	52 989		
Q4	115 115	4 154	35 587	29 938	1 044	–87	185 751	52 847	238 598	52 105		
1996 Q1	108 204	4 164	35 428	31 243	–610	–63	178 366	52 288	230 654	53 445		
Q2	110 022	4 165	36 034	28 829	1 430	12	180 492	53 204	233 696	56 285		
Q3	116 702	4 174	35 868	30 341	353	–97	187 341	54 573	241 914	57 141		
Q4	119 758	4 188	36 171	31 629	657	–38	192 365	57 535	249 900	57 090		
1997 Q1	111 764	4 202	35 029	32 409	150	–21	183 533	55 855	239 388	56 292		
Q2	114 866	4 241	35 418	30 963	2 638	49	188 175	58 639	246 814	62 081		
Q3	121 666	4 285	35 627	32 636	828	–	195 042	59 958	255 000	62 747		
Q4	124 405	4 327	35 421	35 238	146	–14	199 523	61 831	261 354	63 515		
1998 Q1	116 399	4 427	34 989	36 282	480	159	192 736	59 100	251 836	62 931		
Q2	119 766	4 500	35 801	34 489	1 716	59	196 331	60 386	256 717	66 763		
Q3	126 036	4 574	36 032	35 812	1 021	116	203 591	60 999	264 590	68 530		
Q4	129 177	4 611	36 231	37 854	1 012	123	209 008	62 013	271 021	68 003		
1999 Q1	121 501	4 625	36 448	38 672	–1 613	61	199 694	58 852	258 546	67 630		
Q2	125 545	4 605	36 918	36 751	–850	150	203 119	60 919	264 038	69 236		
Q3	130 024	4 648	36 787	37 716	1 780	–50	210 905	64 951	275 856	75 081		
Q4	135 794	4 674	37 160	40 133	–703	162	217 220	65 707	282 927	74 640		
2000 Q1	125 943	4 727	36 399	39 048	2 090	66	208 273	65 062	273 335	73 698		

See footnotes on page 22.

Sources: Office for National Statistics; Enquiries Column 1 0171 533 5998; Columns 2,4,13,14 0171 533 5983; Column 3 0171 533 5985; Column 5 0171 533 6010; Columns 6,7,9,11,12,15 0171 533 5944; Columns 8,10 0171 533 6095

1.3 Gross domestic product: by category of expenditure[1]

continued

£ million, 1995 prices, seasonally adjusted[2]

	Domestic expenditure on goods and services at market prices											
	Final consumption expend- iture			Gross capital formation								
	Households	Non-profit institutions [2]	General government	Gross fixed capital formation	Changes in inventories[3]	Acquisitions less disposals of valuables	Total	Total Exports	Gross final expenditure	*less* Total Imports	Statistical discrepancy (expenditure)[4]	Gross domestic product at market prices[4]
	ABJR	HAYO	NMRY	NPQT	CAFU	NPJR	YBIM	IKBK	ABMG	IKBL	GIXS	ABMI
1955 Q1	41 181	334	19 751	8 429	874	–	69 432	9 827	77 899	9 630	–755	68 710
Q2	41 389	341	19 674	8 611	–169	–	68 159	8 912	75 466	8 924	748	68 626
Q3	41 975	330	19 530	8 858	959	–	70 816	9 772	79 109	9 923	–661	69 675
Q4	41 700	334	19 301	8 966	808	–	70 261	9 785	78 611	9 732	–773	69 308
1956 Q1	41 809	336	19 227	8 953	885	–	70 445	9 865	78 892	9 720	–610	69 787
Q2	41 690	340	19 376	9 055	475	–	69 878	10 109	78 699	9 568	–672	69 737
Q3	41 715	347	19 444	9 135	282	–	69 742	9 951	78 356	9 612	–338	69 642
Q4	41 827	366	19 428	9 314	281	–	70 092	10 120	78 912	9 444	–941	69 876
1957 Q1	42 096	358	19 625	9 567	1 057	–	72 060	10 404	81 128	9 987	–1 267	71 138
Q2	42 406	366	19 092	9 610	628	–	71 428	10 279	80 370	9 664	–811	71 248
Q3	42 854	371	18 904	9 508	320	–	71 179	10 259	80 112	10 020	–492	70 778
Q4	43 078	373	18 816	9 572	–31	–	70 887	10 131	79 666	9 625	–597	70 766
1958 Q1	43 432	378	18 587	9 687	520	–	72 037	10 223	80 850	9 648	–775	71 791
Q2	43 306	381	18 638	9 575	–60	–	71 105	9 650	79 236	9 676	–656	70 165
Q3	43 811	385	18 539	9 616	569	–	72 395	10 410	81 427	10 211	–1 035	71 386
Q4	44 633	381	18 718	9 692	–154	–	72 610	10 144	81 287	10 188	–689	71 615
1959 Q1	44 663	404	18 746	9 714	221	–	73 166	9 948	81 556	10 110	–339	72 354
Q2	45 470	415	18 948	10 345	113	–	74 800	10 239	83 466	10 631	–444	73 571
Q3	45 690	415	19 053	10 364	554	–	75 670	10 529	84 657	10 515	–564	74 866
Q4	46 874	428	19 076	11 051	754	–	78 029	10 813	87 240	11 095	–867	76 515
1960 Q1	47 436	442	19 178	11 087	1 211	–	79 315	11 035	88 734	11 510	–162	78 245
Q2	47 182	454	19 268	11 163	909	–	78 839	10 807	87 993	11 955	528	77 555
Q3	47 486	460	19 343	11 279	1 348	–	79 896	10 958	89 180	11 947	283	78 576
Q4	47 482	468	19 559	11 662	1 658	–	80 878	11 095	90 279	12 056	–471	78 837
1961 Q1	48 342	469	19 804	12 101	1 283	–	82 038	11 498	91 889	12 138	–662	80 239
Q2	48 280	472	19 938	12 397	1 035	–	82 117	11 200	91 578	11 829	–485	80 502
Q3	48 507	482	20 214	12 634	260	–	81 902	11 288	91 490	11 640	–911	80 236
Q4	48 534	483	20 202	12 325	–111	–	81 107	11 310	90 772	11 536	–507	80 020
1962 Q1	48 894	507	20 565	12 401	–165	–	81 792	11 279	91 375	11 828	–222	80 551
Q2	49 668	533	20 623	12 644	–7	–	83 169	11 626	93 116	12 066	–989	81 306
Q3	49 338	550	20 693	12 549	316	–	83 159	11 548	93 006	12 172	–218	81 819
Q4	49 937	579	20 786	12 207	–63	–	83 027	11 615	92 968	12 075	–817	81 312
1963 Q1	50 152	814	20 972	11 273	46	–	82 724	11 871	93 001	11 896	–650	81 735
Q2	51 684	857	20 950	12 735	642	–	86 679	12 024	96 932	12 447	–352	85 455
Q3	52 290	839	20 969	13 015	43	–	86 914	12 111	97 263	12 818	248	85 938
Q4	52 178	855	21 129	13 543	770	–	88 382	12 318	98 909	13 002	–11	87 169
1964 Q1	52 802	836	21 236	14 209	962	–	90 067	12 424	100 634	13 653	–33	88 138
Q2	52 934	825	21 347	14 562	1 716	–	91 566	12 552	102 211	13 692	–273	89 499
Q3	53 226	867	21 432	14 792	1 411	–	91 873	12 273	102 155	14 005	431	89 752
Q4	53 682	966	21 502	15 085	2 080	–	93 623	12 665	104 297	14 193	180	91 507
1965 Q1	53 569	966	21 088	15 351	938	–	92 117	12 700	102 916	13 400	449	91 322
Q2	53 392	1 036	22 271	15 165	1 011	–	92 814	12 933	103 865	14 013	238	91 338
Q3	53 946	1 087	22 220	15 368	1 196	–	93 854	13 016	104 952	14 301	327	92 204
Q4	54 095	1 083	22 328	15 823	868	–	94 208	13 403	105 768	14 389	517	93 137
1966 Q1	54 781	1 106	22 096	15 664	810	–	94 523	13 445	106 118	14 714	681	93 261
Q2	55 275	1 090	22 585	15 626	737	–	95 286	13 235	106 579	14 292	179	93 768
Q3	54 317	1 097	22 835	15 975	1 148	–	95 351	13 763	107 296	14 743	382	94 158
Q4	54 334	1 111	22 993	16 111	–153	–	94 117	14 338	106 843	13 779	–513	93 993
1967 Q1	54 740	1 108	23 746	16 815	888	–	97 146	14 334	109 704	14 905	–1 039	95 052
Q2	55 434	1 155	23 781	17 562	433	–	98 235	13 841	110 121	15 167	–86	96 113
Q3	56 625	1 156	23 731	17 501	217	–	99 130	13 944	111 096	15 315	–878	96 156
Q4	57 052	1 167	24 340	17 187	475	–	100 031	13 009	110 786	16 176	834	96 469
1968 Q1	58 788	1 188	24 245	18 169	–340	–	101 924	15 194	115 292	16 622	–104	99 685
Q2	56 423	1 189	23 981	17 712	1 199	–	100 546	14 941	113 674	16 235	56	98 637
Q3	57 428	1 215	24 076	18 106	1 412	–	102 391	15 861	116 563	16 725	–631	100 358
Q4	57 496	1 220	23 832	19 053	936	–	102 748	16 047	117 132	16 621	–906	100 807
1969 Q1	57 312	1 242	23 866	17 664	1 267	–	101 467	16 078	115 958	17 215	1 007	100 752
Q2	57 813	1 265	23 437	17 814	1 034	–	101 572	16 933	117 120	17 019	458	101 662
Q3	57 877	1 261	23 588	18 525	554	–	101 967	17 506	118 206	16 951	–52	102 373
Q4	58 199	1 315	23 702	18 625	695	–	102 728	17 602	119 046	17 296	–1	102 870

1 Estimates are given to the nearest £ million, but cannot be regarded as accurate to this degree.

2 For years up to and including 1993, totals differ from the sum of the components because of the method used to rebase on 1995 prices.

3 Quarterly alignment adjustment included in this series. For description of adjustment see notes in the article on "UK National Accounts, second quarter 1992", *Economic Trends*, No.468, October 1992.

4 Gross Domestic Product is estimated in seasonally adjusted form only. No equivalent unadjusted estimates exist.

5 *Represents* Taxes on expenditure *less* Subsidies, both valued at 1990 prices.

Sources: Office for National Statistics; Enquiries Column 1 0171 533 5998; Columns 2,4,13,14 0171 533 5983; Column 3 0171 533 5985; Column 5 0171 533 6010; Columns 6,7,9,11,12,15 0171 533 5944; Columns 8,10 0171 533 6095

1.3 Gross domestic product: by category of expenditure[1]

continued

£ million, 1995 prices, seasonally adjusted[2]

	Domestic expenditure on goods and services at market prices											
	Final consumption expend- iture			Gross capital formation								
	Households	Non-profit institutions [2]	General government	Gross fixed capital formation	Changes in inventories[3]	Acquisitions less disposals of valuables	Total	Total Exports	Gross final expenditure	*less* Total Imports	Statistical discrepancy (expenditure)[4]	Gross domestic product at market prices[4]
	ABJR	HAYO	NMRY	NPQT	CAFU	NPJR	YBIM	IKBK	ABMG	IKBL	GIXS	ABMI
1970 Q1	58 348	1 356	23 675	18 015	–203	–	101 166	17 799	117 813	16 989	184	102 150
Q2	59 255	1 368	24 207	18 702	1 051	–	104 803	17 550	120 943	17 884	82	104 203
Q3	60 223	1 389	24 153	18 809	1 161	–	106 054	17 373	121 907	18 014	233	105 199
Q4	59 913	1 352	24 310	19 225	636	–	105 650	19 024	123 576	18 892	236	105 851
1971 Q1	59 672	1 351	24 355	18 477	522	–	104 467	18 177	121 405	18 416	590	104 529
Q2	61 026	1 373	24 865	19 139	–133	–	106 285	19 457	124 715	19 123	–481	106 036
Q3	62 181	1 357	25 052	19 330	245	–	108 290	19 587	126 773	18 777	–1 509	107 592
Q4	62 550	1 385	25 072	19 296	207	–	108 649	19 489	126 991	19 324	–1 034	107 613
1972 Q1	63 594	1 342	25 682	18 722	–225	–	109 036	19 209	127 009	20 116	–417	107 258
Q2	65 049	1 414	25 683	19 174	–9	–	111 412	19 311	129 383	20 503	577	110 251
Q3	66 095	1 400	26 111	19 108	64	–	112 847	17 762	128 816	19 980	924	110 658
Q4	66 539	1 473	26 400	19 208	160	–	113 844	21 253	134 097	22 543	988	113 043
1973 Q1	69 220	1 492	26 761	20 550	2 485	–	121 188	21 041	140 809	22 575	–483	118 646
Q2	68 711	1 453	26 782	20 215	2 536	–	120 306	21 486	140 506	22 691	–92	118 544
Q3	69 253	1 503	27 090	20 118	2 517	–	121 044	22 051	141 890	23 372	–301	118 845
Q4	68 521	1 449	27 089	20 315	1 648	–	119 424	22 191	140 515	23 778	361	117 443
1974 Q1	67 106	1 490	26 922	20 461	243	–	116 391	22 798	138 359	23 102	–1 222	114 510
Q2	67 453	1 441	27 233	19 599	1 710	–	117 692	23 527	140 477	23 666	–343	116 858
Q3	68 216	1 477	27 612	19 614	2 179	–	119 428	23 677	142 312	23 459	–1 438	118 037
Q4	68 453	1 463	28 109	19 940	18	–	117 806	23 129	140 106	23 119	–1 470	116 120
1975 Q1	67 961	1 509	29 123	19 651	–1 503	–	116 088	23 040	138 362	22 184	–510	116 548
Q2	68 134	1 483	28 741	19 764	–1 914	–	115 486	22 115	136 673	21 024	–2 067	114 842
Q3	67 504	1 505	28 842	19 589	–874	–	116 059	22 076	137 172	22 228	–820	114 892
Q4	66 822	1 503	29 432	19 104	–448	–	115 809	23 197	138 286	21 755	–1 502	116 092
1976 Q1	67 164	1 563	29 481	20 152	–195	–	117 862	23 718	140 870	21 467	–2 525	118 265
Q2	67 629	1 574	29 798	19 980	–468	–	118 047	24 605	142 116	23 229	–2 131	117 464
Q3	68 312	1 555	29 618	19 655	989	–	119 912	24 746	144 062	23 487	–2 682	118 638
Q4	68 372	1 557	29 332	19 670	1 933	–	120 904	25 596	146 032	23 506	–2 441	120 975
1977 Q1	66 907	1 682	29 035	18 955	2 007	–	118 429	25 719	143 823	23 319	–301	121 004
Q2	66 781	1 514	29 258	19 850	1 160	–	118 556	26 287	144 629	23 891	–706	120 642
Q3	67 665	1 498	29 171	19 434	234	–	117 685	27 245	144 955	23 272	–924	121 667
Q4	69 081	1 516	29 110	20 001	1 357	–	121 135	26 175	146 951	22 970	–1 912	123 263
1978 Q1	70 737	1 425	29 460	20 493	790	–	122 995	26 459	149 071	24 510	–1 191	124 140
Q2	70 514	1 759	29 561	20 239	1 299	–	123 286	26 950	149 931	24 655	–786	125 262
Q3	72 092	1 678	29 751	19 894	784	–	123 920	27 009	150 608	24 623	–247	126 546
Q4	71 558	1 740	29 900	19 580	1 120	–	123 627	26 957	150 266	23 151	–1 057	127 188
1979 Q1	72 732	1 495	29 781	20 148	1 490	–	125 679	24 911	149 811	24 736	757	126 581
Q2	76 697	1 696	30 450	20 368	499	–	129 306	29 509	158 722	26 867	–717	131 780
Q3	73 591	1 850	30 054	20 689	1 792	–	128 019	28 406	156 185	27 421	–360	128 811
Q4	74 433	1 698	30 306	21 102	854	–	128 295	28 614	156 695	27 265	–110	129 784
1980 Q1	75 719	1 677	30 521	20 402	–990	–	126 725	29 089	155 754	27 681	516	128 918
Q2	73 652	1 743	30 315	19 722	–397	–	124 403	27 883	152 104	26 651	526	126 388
Q3	74 703	1 661	30 725	19 349	–1 229	–	124 277	27 165	151 134	24 394	–1 711	125 913
Q4	73 182	1 749	30 910	18 925	–2 078	–	121 508	27 009	148 297	23 815	–904	124 472
1981 Q1	74 450	1 589	30 585	17 631	–1 947	–	120 901	26 805	147 475	22 833	–1 820	123 906
Q2	74 360	1 776	30 828	17 927	–1 913	–	121 604	27 094	148 490	24 096	–1 243	123 990
Q3	74 385	1 912	30 916	18 040	–400	–	123 823	28 306	152 049	26 814	169	125 772
Q4	74 042	1 932	30 353	17 853	–197	–	123 011	28 128	151 061	25 966	–25	125 591
1982 Q1	74 170	1 575	30 812	17 943	811	–	124 503	27 540	151 794	25 824	–819	125 735
Q2	74 139	2 027	30 785	18 834	602	–	125 734	28 148	153 692	26 923	–54	127 129
Q3	75 441	2 019	30 831	19 396	–1 325	–	125 419	27 556	152 690	26 091	183	127 344
Q4	76 060	2 095	31 026	19 493	–1 872	–	125 731	28 021	153 538	25 779	–398	128 031
1983 Q1	77 609	1 795	31 031	19 801	386	–	130 028	27 952	157 572	27 015	–494	130 627
Q2	77 840	2 071	31 733	19 405	678	–	131 066	27 905	158 505	27 714	–390	130 840
Q3	79 158	2 133	31 517	19 599	47	–	131 737	28 470	159 824	27 887	–229	132 165
Q4	79 041	2 106	31 729	20 684	779	–	133 846	28 908	162 361	28 875	–164	133 656
1984 Q1	79 408	2 238	31 883	21 363	102	–	134 485	29 635	163 845	29 223	80	135 019
Q2	79 970	2 068	31 754	21 643	697	–	135 736	29 543	164 927	30 520	105	134 566
Q3	79 383	2 110	31 882	21 807	114	–	134 832	30 439	165 144	30 772	201	134 575
Q4	80 596	2 155	31 970	22 099	597	–	137 053	31 076	168 028	32 036	222	136 042

See footnotes on page 26.

Sources: Office for National Statistics; Enquiries Column 1 0171 533 5998; Columns 2,4,13,14 0171 533 5983; Column 3 0171 533 5985; Column 5 0171 533 6010; Columns 6,7,9,11,12,15 0171 533 5944; Columns 8,10 0171 533 6095

1.3 Gross domestic product: by category of expenditure[1]

continued

£ million, 1995 prices, seasonally adjusted[2]

	Domestic expenditure on goods and services at market prices											
	Final consumption expend- iture			Gross capital formation								
	Households	Non-profit institutions [2]	General government	Gross fixed capital formation	Changes in inventories[3]	Acquisitions less disposals of valuables	Total	Total Exports	Gross final expenditure	*less* Total Imports	Statistical discrepancy (expenditure)[4]	Gross domestic product at market prices[4]
	ABJR	HAYO	NMRY	NPQT	CAFU	NPJR	YBIM	IKBK	ABMG	IKBL	GIXS	ABMI
1985 Q1	81 654	2 286	32 303	23 819	–547	–	139 180	31 440	170 493	32 119	–	138 292
Q2	82 145	2 267	31 432	21 902	1 263	–	138 722	32 718	171 594	31 270	–	140 496
Q3	83 353	2 309	31 742	22 273	–123	–	139 079	31 771	170 795	30 649	–	140 430
Q4	84 252	2 367	31 782	22 427	550	–	141 014	31 972	172 881	31 609	–	141 421
1986 Q1	86 647	2 248	32 515	22 733	–677	–23	143 201	32 826	175 971	32 485	–	143 467
Q2	88 505	2 300	32 257	22 152	800	–29	145 651	33 290	178 883	33 622	–	145 242
Q3	89 121	2 346	32 276	23 510	291	13	147 381	33 326	180 644	33 841	–	146 785
Q4	89 558	2 389	32 196	23 935	970	–29	148 913	34 222	183 078	34 314	–	148 745
1987 Q1	90 752	2 406	32 025	23 176	129	–62	148 149	35 092	183 197	33 934	–	149 242
Q2	92 147	2 450	32 442	24 091	902	40	151 898	34 762	186 600	35 633	–	150 950
Q3	93 897	2 505	32 496	26 242	409	–171	155 426	35 952	191 321	37 279	–	154 027
Q4	95 805	2 567	32 288	27 011	467	–23	158 217	35 752	193 901	37 996	–	155 891
1988 Q1	97 945	2 681	32 461	28 218	69	–16	161 553	35 164	196 635	38 515	–	158 103
Q2	98 825	2 733	32 253	28 714	629	13	163 427	35 921	199 269	40 121	–	159 135
Q3	101 214	2 769	32 023	29 140	1 356	–39	166 724	36 060	202 697	41 189	–	161 496
Q4	102 443	2 788	32 544	29 290	3 829	80	171 287	35 281	206 457	43 548	–	162 903
1989 Q1	102 889	2 749	32 329	30 950	727	37	170 109	37 137	207 161	44 218	–	162 938
Q2	103 282	2 783	32 313	30 434	1 524	–11	170 695	36 512	207 113	43 326	–	163 779
Q3	103 141	2 813	32 869	30 534	1 466	–16	171 189	37 406	208 510	44 344	–	164 161
Q4	104 186	2 857	32 813	30 240	–594	–18	169 728	38 268	207 924	43 623	–	164 296
1990 Q1	104 130	2 974	33 115	30 507	276	2	171 326	39 088	210 347	44 805	–	165 538
Q2	104 622	3 007	33 146	29 930	1 065	–47	171 972	39 101	211 004	44 664	–	166 335
Q3	103 715	3 040	33 542	29 657	–833	–61	169 244	38 931	208 113	43 852	–	164 254
Q4	103 321	3 058	33 817	29 274	–2 587	–24	166 952	39 520	206 423	43 056	–	163 359
1991 Q1	103 067	3 017	33 910	27 864	–653	–36	167 124	37 842	204 898	41 653	–	163 233
Q2	101 734	3 054	34 777	27 236	–2 333	62	164 390	39 391	203 738	41 504	–	162 223
Q3	101 997	3 067	34 453	26 787	–1 971	7	164 145	39 773	203 880	41 845	–	162 025
Q4	101 511	3 079	34 401	27 113	–392	–123	165 504	39 356	204 814	42 470	–	162 334
1992 Q1	101 237	3 085	34 530	27 220	–189	–87	165 740	39 977	205 677	43 440	–	162 231
Q2	102 482	3 098	34 624	27 219	–1 266	–21	166 005	40 880	206 854	45 035	–	161 818
Q3	103 008	3 123	34 462	27 258	–605	36	167 164	40 533	207 659	44 928	–	162 730
Q4	103 299	3 139	34 593	26 549	98	111	167 586	41 429	208 986	45 476	–	163 509
1993 Q1	103 892	3 202	34 447	27 106	–236	53	168 312	42 107	210 395	46 011	–	164 383
Q2	104 150	3 817	33 992	26 960	162	30	169 024	41 578	210 569	45 252	–	165 315
Q3	105 746	3 844	34 277	27 228	–25	–15	170 938	42 365	213 274	46 295	–	166 978
Q4	106 293	3 860	34 321	27 833	459	–77	172 651	43 175	215 801	47 049	–	168 751
1994 Q1	107 104	3 926	34 280	28 524	–247	–18	173 569	44 835	218 404	47 971	–	170 433
Q2	107 442	3 951	34 821	27 543	1 790	–55	175 492	45 550	221 042	48 456	–	172 586
Q3	108 064	3 993	34 863	28 329	1 258	21	176 528	46 570	223 098	48 047	–	175 051
Q4	108 852	4 030	34 950	28 646	2 035	192	178 705	47 918	226 623	50 077	–	176 546
1995 Q1	108 835	4 081	35 050	28 849	63	18	176 896	49 705	226 601	49 297	–	177 304
Q2	109 412	4 112	35 362	28 835	1 887	50	179 658	49 446	229 104	51 140	–	177 964
Q3	109 567	4 134	35 239	29 416	1 373	–67	179 662	51 230	230 892	52 097	–	178 795
Q4	110 639	4 154	35 424	29 260	1 189	–93	180 573	52 031	232 604	52 687	–	179 917
1996 Q1	112 399	4 164	35 559	30 181	933	–83	183 153	53 001	236 154	54 798	–	181 356
Q2	113 264	4 165	36 042	30 375	15	–49	183 812	53 799	237 611	55 315	–	182 296
Q3	113 909	4 174	35 911	30 719	486	–20	185 179	54 665	239 844	56 396	–	183 448
Q4	115 114	4 188	35 989	30 767	396	–34	186 420	56 135	242 555	57 452	–	185 103
1997 Q1	115 980	4 202	35 313	31 179	1 321	–15	187 980	57 345	245 325	58 288	–	187 037
Q2	117 803	4 241	35 296	32 742	767	–12	190 837	58 769	249 606	60 936	–	188 670
Q3	118 796	4 285	35 533	33 205	424	45	192 288	59 865	252 153	61 542	–	190 611
Q4	120 122	4 327	35 353	34 120	1 250	–4	195 168	60 304	255 472	63 869	–	191 603
1998 Q1	121 418	4 427	35 237	35 362	919	166	197 529	60 101	257 630	64 649	–	192 981
Q2	122 528	4 500	35 745	35 684	1 014	–43	199 428	61 039	260 467	66 178	–	194 289
Q3	123 242	4 574	35 949	36 526	878	267	201 436	61 013	262 449	67 263	–	195 186
Q4	124 190	4 611	36 122	36 865	1 418	67	203 273	60 345	263 618	68 137	–	195 481
1999 Q1	126 279	4 625	36 755	37 769	330	61	205 819	59 891	265 710	69 507	–92	196 111
Q2	127 569	4 605	36 759	38 209	–1 435	150	205 857	61 525	267 382	69 624	–114	197 644
Q3	128 544	4 648	36 845	38 427	–634	–50	207 780	64 952	272 732	72 994	–117	199 621
Q4	130 472	4 674	36 954	38 867	353	162	211 482	64 061	275 543	74 462	–91	200 990
2000 Q1	131 309	4 727	36 714	38 426	709	66	211 951	65 585	277 536	75 501	–42	201 993

See footnotes on page 26.

Sources: Office for National Statistics; Enquiries Column 1 0171 533 5998; Columns 2,4,13,14 0171 533 5983; Column 3 0171 533 5985; Column 5 0171 533 6010; Columns 6,7,9,11,12,15 0171 533 5944; Columns 8,10 0171 533 6095

1.4 Gross domestic product: by category of income[1]

£ million, current prices

	Compensation of employees	Gross operating surplus of corporations: Non-financial corporations: Public	Gross operating surplus of corporations: Non-financial corporations: Private[2]	Gross operating surplus of corporations: Financial corporations	Gross operating surplus of corporations: Total	Other income[3]	Gross value added at factor cost	Taxes on production *less* subsidies	Statistical discrepancy (income)[4]	Gross domestic product at market prices[4]
	HAEA	NRJT	NRJK	NQNV	CGBY	CGBW	CGCA	GCSC	GIXQ	YBHA
1946	5 778	17	..	..	..	..	..	..	..	..
1947	6 248	11	..	..	..	..	..	..	..	..
1948	6 807	85	2 159	..	..	..	..	1 285	125	11 797
1949	7 268	166	2 346	..	..	..	..	1 306	75	12 533
1950	7 650	180	2 263	..	..	..	..	1 419	111	13 072
1951	8 524	192	2 559	..	..	..	..	1 616	147	14 559
1952	9 131	297	2 979	..	..	..	..	1 674	134	15 768
1953	9 661	341	3 168	..	..	..	..	1 782	265	16 883
1954	10 313	362	3 365	..	..	..	..	1 847	240	17 869
1955	11 275	314	3 633	..	..	..	..	2 029	31	19 107
1956	12 299	354	3 727	..	..	..	..	2 155	119	20 541
1957	12 997	331	3 946	..	..	..	..	2 215	212	21 671
1958	13 506	367	4 035	..	..	..	..	2 290	250	22 585
1959	14 146	419	4 339	126	4 884	2 440	21 470	2 432	261	23 877
1960	15 197	560	4 818	510	5 888	2 046	23 131	2 471	24	25 494
1961	16 434	670	4 718	596	5 984	2 077	24 495	2 584	40	26 971
1962	17 338	786	4 726	656	6 168	2 139	25 645	2 772	–11	28 270
1963	18 232	883	5 158	685	6 726	2 282	27 240	2 915	68	30 223
1964	19 765	962	5 701	702	7 365	2 387	29 517	3 327	192	33 036
1965	21 346	1 030	5 965	805	7 800	2 823	31 969	3 713	91	35 773
1966	22 883	1 087	5 953	811	7 851	3 055	33 789	4 106	171	38 066
1967	23 840	1 188	6 235	888	8 311	3 274	35 425	4 400	269	40 094
1968	25 507	1 414	6 585	1 026	9 025	3 521	38 053	5 036	361	43 450
1969	27 280	1 476	7 193	1 044	9 713	3 868	40 861	5 993	–75	46 779
1970	30 613	1 432	7 481	1 096	10 009	4 381	45 003	6 520	–91	51 432
1971	33 555	1 546	8 653	1 525	11 724	4 966	50 245	6 645	477	57 367
1972	37 928	1 768	10 125	1 668	13 561	5 598	57 087	6 832	340	64 259
1973	43 953	2 054	11 774	2 409	16 237	6 390	66 580	7 224	189	73 993
1974	52 479	2 378	11 000	2 615	15 993	7 060	75 532	6 781	1 300	83 613
1975	68 605	2 890	12 392	2 978	18 260	9 214	96 079	8 289	1 131	105 499
1976	78 161	4 376	15 502	3 954	23 832	10 583	112 576	10 458	1 885	124 919
1977	86 722	5 024	22 718	4 657	32 399	11 801	130 922	13 798	759	145 479
1978	98 960	5 480	27 519	3 879	36 878	14 161	149 999	16 017	1 793	167 809
1979	115 948	5 452	31 464	5 048	41 964	16 276	174 188	21 641	1 590	197 419
1980	137 765	6 460	35 028	5 762	47 250	18 244	203 259	26 495	775	230 529
1981	149 654	8 209	38 242	5 068	51 519	20 324	221 497	30 947	808	253 252
1982	158 731	9 629	45 758	6 030	61 417	21 612	241 760	34 563	614	276 937
1983	169 679	10 539	53 584	8 587	72 710	23 280	265 669	37 054	–103	302 620
1984	181 197	9 048	61 951	6 736	77 735	25 471	284 403	38 694	1 052	324 149
1985	196 593	7 753	72 440	7 223	87 416	29 126	313 135	42 213	–	355 348
1986	212 060	8 638	70 616	10 049	89 303	31 979	333 342	48 481	–	381 823
1987	229 920	7 490	80 623	10 983	99 096	37 136	366 152	53 309	–	419 461
1988	256 790	7 906	92 771	9 484	110 161	40 835	407 786	59 976	–	467 762
1989	285 787	6 659	103 453	11 427	121 539	42 014	449 340	63 938	–	513 278
1990	315 208	4 110	107 132	11 711	122 953	49 623	487 784	68 433	–	556 217
1991	333 850	2 207	108 502	7 836	118 545	55 631	508 026	76 510	–	584 536
1992	347 036	2 237	108 460	15 657	126 354	56 884	530 274	77 891	–	608 165
1993	356 323	3 206	118 453	18 393	140 052	61 944	558 319	81 037	–	639 356
1994	369 960	3 627	133 237	23 616	160 480	60 603	591 043	86 551	–	677 594
1995	385 397	5 367	143 086	20 077	168 530	66 394	620 321	93 659	–	713 980
1996	404 521	5 114	158 805	18 970	182 889	70 231	657 641	98 417	–	756 058
1997	432 388	4 205	169 778	18 151	192 134	73 557	698 079	107 323	–	805 402
1998	463 044	4 054	174 421	19 126	197 601	77 124	737 769	113 885	–	851 654
1999	491 373	3 738	174 400	18 171	196 309	80 404	768 086	121 832	1 188	891 106

1 Estimates are given to the nearest £ million, but cannot be regarded as accurate to this degree.
2 Quarterly alignment adjustment included in this series.
3 Includes mixed income and the operating surplus of non- corporate sector less the adjustment for financial intermediation services indirectly measured (FISIM).
4 Gross domestic product is estimated in seasonally adjusted form only. No equivalent unadjusted estimates exist.

Sources: Office for National Statistics; Enquiries Column 1 020 7533 6005; Columns 2-7,9,10 020 7533 5944; Column 8 020 7533 5990

1.4 Gross domestic product: by category of income[1]

continued

£ million, current prices, not seasonally adjusted

	Compensation of employees	Gross operating surplus of corporations: Non-financial corporations: Public	Non-financial corporations: Private[2]	Financial corporations	Total	Other income[3]	Gross value added at factor cost	Taxes on production *less* subsidies	Statistical discrepancy (income)	Gross domestic product at market prices[4]
	HAEA	NRJT	NRJK	NQNV	CGBY	CGBW	CGCA	GCSC		
1955 Q1	2 726	..	..	..	..	..	..	468		
Q2	2 771	..	..	..	..	..	..	489		
Q3	2 842	..	..	..	..	..	..	517		
Q4	2 936	..	..	..	..	..	..	555		
1956 Q1	2 982	..	..	..	..	..	..	501		
Q2	3 040	..	..	..	..	..	..	525		
Q3	3 097	..	..	..	..	..	..	534		
Q4	3 180	..	..	..	..	..	..	595		
1957 Q1	3 192	..	..	..	..	..	..	531		
Q2	3 186	..	..	..	..	..	..	544		
Q3	3 275	..	..	..	..	..	..	543		
Q4	3 344	..	..	..	..	..	..	597		
1958 Q1	3 364	..	..	..	..	..	..	547		
Q2	3 317	..	..	..	..	..	..	559		
Q3	3 360	..	..	..	..	..	..	556		
Q4	3 465	..	..	..	..	..	..	628		
1959 Q1	3 455	119	..	32	..	583	..	582		
Q2	3 483	101	..	29	..	601	..	600		
Q3	3 543	92	..	32	..	616	..	584		
Q4	3 665	107	..	33	..	640	..	666		
1960 Q1	3 659	166	1 183	125	1 474	489	5 622	602		
Q2	3 755	144	1 221	127	1 492	503	5 750	607		
Q3	3 852	103	1 221	126	1 450	509	5 811	605		
Q4	3 931	147	1 193	132	1 472	545	5 948	657		
1961 Q1	3 977	174	1 152	142	1 468	527	5 972	604		
Q2	4 095	177	1 144	145	1 466	505	6 066	646		
Q3	4 139	145	1 223	151	1 519	437	6 095	620		
Q4	4 223	174	1 199	158	1 531	608	6 362	714		
1962 Q1	4 227	229	1 076	161	1 466	501	6 194	635		
Q2	4 305	209	1 225	163	1 597	549	6 451	697		
Q3	4 369	168	1 227	164	1 559	555	6 483	702		
Q4	4 437	180	1 198	168	1 546	534	6 517	738		
1963 Q1	4 383	247	1 064	169	1 480	541	6 404	635		
Q2	4 510	232	1 358	169	1 759	562	6 831	717		
Q3	4 599	185	1 315	170	1 670	567	6 836	753		
Q4	4 740	219	1 421	177	1 817	612	7 169	810		
1964 Q1	4 762	266	1 316	160	1 742	554	7 058	734		
Q2	4 884	251	1 480	170	1 901	583	7 368	826		
Q3	4 976	229	1 426	181	1 836	597	7 409	832		
Q4	5 143	216	1 479	191	1 886	653	7 682	935		
1965 Q1	5 122	292	1 449	194	1 935	679	7 736	880		
Q2	5 279	267	1 507	201	1 975	692	7 946	904		
Q3	5 375	221	1 480	203	1 904	703	7 982	919		
Q4	5 570	250	1 529	207	1 986	749	8 305	1 010		
1966 Q1	5 615	312	1 407	199	1 918	731	8 264	934		
Q2	5 727	278	1 443	204	1 925	755	8 407	1 001		
Q3	5 706	223	1 542	202	1 967	769	8 442	1 023		
Q4	5 835	274	1 561	206	2 041	800	8 676	1 148		
1967 Q1	5 716	318	1 547	212	2 077	787	8 580	1 025		
Q2	5 961	271	1 661	217	2 149	811	8 921	1 098		
Q3	5 971	232	1 478	223	1 933	826	8 730	1 113		
Q4	6 192	367	1 549	236	2 152	850	9 194	1 164		
1968 Q1	6 221	388	1 519	238	2 145	865	9 231	1 125		
Q2	6 320	314	1 608	252	2 174	866	9 360	1 192		
Q3	6 361	287	1 712	260	2 259	877	9 497	1 276		
Q4	6 605	425	1 746	276	2 447	913	9 965	1 443		
1969 Q1	6 610	452	1 774	250	2 476	918	10 004	1 344		
Q2	6 745	337	1 721	261	2 319	947	10 011	1 465		
Q3	6 777	304	1 734	265	2 303	988	10 068	1 540		
Q4	7 148	383	1 964	268	2 615	1 015	10 778	1 644		

See footnotes on page 29

Sources: Office for National Statistics; Enquiries Column 1 020 7533 6005; Columns 2-7,9,10 020 7533 5944; Column 8 020 7533 5990

1.4 Gross domestic product: by category of income[1]

continued

£ million, current prices, not seasonally adjusted

		Gross operating surplus of corporations								
		Non-financial corporations								
	Compensation of employees	Public	Private[2]	Financial corporations	Total	Other income[3]	Gross value added at factor cost	Taxes on production *less* subsidies	Statistical discrepancy (income)[3]	Gross domestic product at market prices[4]
	HAEA	NRJT	NRJK	NQNV	CGBY	CGBW	CGCA	GCSC		
1970 Q1	7 144	400	1 772	226	2 398	1 011	10 553	1 470		
Q2	7 626	366	1 734	255	2 355	1 069	11 050	1 617		
Q3	7 774	296	1 764	287	2 347	1 124	11 245	1 696		
Q4	8 069	370	2 211	328	2 909	1 177	12 155	1 737		
1971 Q1	7 942	390	2 023	365	2 778	1 194	11 914	1 529		
Q2	8 301	353	1 952	386	2 691	1 223	12 215	1 726		
Q3	8 496	353	2 107	388	2 848	1 258	12 602	1 665		
Q4	8 816	450	2 571	386	3 407	1 291	13 514	1 725		
1972 Q1	8 856	377	2 391	383	3 151	1 332	13 339	1 508		
Q2	9 360	419	2 342	395	3 156	1 369	13 885	1 740		
Q3	9 571	421	2 374	421	3 216	1 418	14 205	1 682		
Q4	10 141	551	3 018	469	4 038	1 479	15 658	1 902		
1973 Q1	10 273	517	3 176	530	4 223	1 561	16 057	1 727		
Q2	10 832	494	2 750	590	3 834	1 576	16 242	1 733		
Q3	11 160	433	2 609	632	3 674	1 613	16 447	1 855		
Q4	11 688	610	3 239	657	4 506	1 640	17 834	1 909		
1974 Q1	11 697	502	2 333	668	3 503	1 597	16 797	1 414		
Q2	12 460	550	2 714	658	3 922	1 681	18 063	1 885		
Q3	13 654	553	2 769	646	3 968	1 817	19 439	1 662		
Q4	14 668	773	3 184	643	4 600	1 965	21 233	1 820		
1975 Q1	15 959	578	2 924	685	4 187	2 116	22 262	1 475		
Q2	16 665	638	2 832	709	4 179	2 244	23 088	2 096		
Q3	17 809	560	2 854	762	4 176	2 379	24 364	2 277		
Q4	18 172	1 114	3 782	822	5 718	2 475	26 365	2 441		
1976 Q1	18 364	957	3 583	889	5 429	2 593	26 386	2 252		
Q2	19 295	985	3 360	953	5 298	2 606	27 199	2 430		
Q3	20 006	936	3 601	1 021	5 558	2 678	28 242	2 672		
Q4	20 496	1 498	4 958	1 091	7 547	2 706	30 749	3 104		
1977 Q1	20 722	1 293	5 085	1 213	7 591	2 723	31 036	2 598		
Q2	21 374	1 200	5 468	1 184	7 852	2 882	32 108	3 440		
Q3	21 989	1 125	5 624	1 144	7 893	3 024	32 906	3 709		
Q4	22 637	1 406	6 541	1 116	9 063	3 172	34 872	4 051		
1978 Q1	23 207	1 345	6 621	988	8 954	3 329	35 490	3 302		
Q2	24 470	1 335	6 599	938	8 872	3 472	36 814	3 883		
Q3	25 297	1 167	6 925	945	9 037	3 601	37 935	4 113		
Q4	25 986	1 633	7 374	1 008	10 015	3 759	39 760	4 719		
1979 Q1	26 598	1 482	6 794	1 134	9 410	3 880	39 888	4 256		
Q2	28 167	1 312	7 770	1 243	10 325	3 979	42 471	4 914		
Q3	29 887	1 033	7 846	1 320	10 199	4 137	44 223	5 967		
Q4	31 296	1 625	9 054	1 351	12 030	4 280	47 606	6 504		
1980 Q1	32 153	1 846	8 469	1 415	11 730	4 350	48 233	6 163		
Q2	34 066	1 283	8 990	1 459	11 732	4 471	50 269	6 345		
Q3	35 483	1 200	8 247	1 467	10 914	4 589	50 986	6 791		
Q4	36 063	2 131	9 322	1 421	12 874	4 834	53 771	7 196		
1981 Q1	35 941	1 993	8 406	1 325	11 724	4 889	52 554	6 666		
Q2	36 990	1 834	8 905	1 224	11 963	4 947	53 900	7 543		
Q3	38 098	1 768	9 746	1 220	12 734	5 126	55 958	8 223		
Q4	38 625	2 614	11 185	1 299	15 098	5 362	59 085	8 515		
1982 Q1	38 553	2 674	9 599	1 379	13 652	5 296	57 501	8 387		
Q2	39 516	2 177	11 499	1 415	15 091	5 314	59 921	8 111		
Q3	40 112	1 992	11 500	1 527	15 019	5 343	60 474	8 817		
Q4	40 550	2 786	13 160	1 709	17 655	5 659	63 864	9 248		
1983 Q1	40 974	3 119	11 865	2 076	17 060	5 598	63 632	8 871		
Q2	42 027	2 545	12 757	2 211	17 513	5 740	65 280	8 863		
Q3	42 946	1 843	13 633	2 212	17 688	5 875	66 509	9 427		
Q4	43 732	3 032	15 329	2 088	20 449	6 067	70 248	9 893		
1984 Q1	43 738	3 105	14 059	1 659	18 823	6 265	68 826	9 346		
Q2	44 752	2 054	14 504	1 557	18 115	6 321	69 188	9 180		
Q3	45 526	1 604	15 597	1 649	18 850	6 474	70 850	10 028		
Q4	47 181	2 285	17 791	1 871	21 947	6 411	75 539	10 140		

See footnotes on page 29

Sources: Office for National Statistics; Enquiries Column 1 020 7533 6005; Columns 2-7,9,10 020 7533 5944; Column 8 020 7533 5990

1.4 Gross domestic product: by category of income[1]

continued

£ million, current prices, not seasonally adjusted

	Compensation of employees	Gross operating surplus of corporations: Non-financial corporations: Public	Non-financial corporations: Private[2]	Financial corporations	Total	Other income [3]	Gross value added at factor cost	Taxes on production *less* subsidies	Statistical discrepancy (income)[4]	Gross domestic product at market prices [4]
	HAEA	NRJT	NRJK	NQNV	CGBY	CGBW	CGCA	GCSC		
1985 Q1	47 205	1 699	16 833	2 318	20 850	6 487	74 542	9 748		
Q2	48 555	1 820	18 100	881	20 801	7 957	77 313	9 724		
Q3	49 963	1 835	17 795	1 979	21 609	7 187	78 759	11 077		
Q4	50 870	2 399	19 712	2 045	24 156	7 495	82 521	11 664		
1986 Q1	51 123	2 589	17 784	2 278	22 651	7 488	81 262	11 327		
Q2	52 622	2 073	17 205	2 089	21 367	8 137	82 126	11 216		
Q3	53 576	1 521	16 895	2 805	21 221	7 996	82 793	12 661		
Q4	54 739	2 455	18 732	2 877	24 064	8 358	87 161	13 277		
1987 Q1	54 817	1 894	18 785	2 964	23 643	8 689	87 149	12 431		
Q2	56 683	1 726	18 783	2 421	22 930	9 450	89 063	12 058		
Q3	58 212	1 591	20 523	2 913	25 027	9 360	92 599	14 147		
Q4	60 208	2 279	22 532	2 685	27 496	9 637	97 341	14 673		
1988 Q1	61 016	1 910	22 057	2 200	26 167	10 067	97 250	13 840		
Q2	63 046	1 855	21 635	2 135	25 625	10 470	99 141	14 361		
Q3	65 099	1 751	23 347	2 795	27 893	9 873	102 865	15 760		
Q4	67 629	2 390	25 732	2 354	30 476	10 425	108 530	16 015		
1989 Q1	68 132	2 187	24 425	2 443	29 055	10 484	107 671	14 895		
Q2	70 327	1 458	25 112	2 709	29 279	10 320	109 926	15 542		
Q3	72 340	1 210	26 310	3 458	30 978	10 068	113 386	16 646		
Q4	74 988	1 804	27 606	2 817	32 227	11 142	118 357	16 855		
1990 Q1	76 111	1 522	25 654	2 625	29 801	11 670	117 582	16 385		
Q2	78 434	873	27 076	3 358	31 307	12 015	121 756	16 964		
Q3	79 809	654	26 328	3 578	30 560	12 548	122 917	17 686		
Q4	80 854	1 061	28 074	2 150	31 285	13 390	125 529	17 398		
1991 Q1	81 861	636	25 676	2 491	28 803	13 454	124 118	17 151		
Q2	83 019	585	26 137	1 459	28 181	14 234	125 434	18 701		
Q3	84 107	444	26 469	1 675	28 588	13 946	126 641	19 974		
Q4	84 863	542	30 220	2 211	32 973	13 997	131 833	20 684		
1992 Q1	85 908	436	26 207	2 972	29 615	14 386	129 909	19 140		
Q2	86 264	623	26 313	2 990	29 926	15 015	131 205	18 826		
Q3	87 127	463	25 981	4 835	31 279	13 945	132 351	19 489		
Q4	87 737	715	29 959	4 860	35 534	13 538	136 809	20 436		
1993 Q1	88 039	206	26 896	4 652	31 754	14 808	134 601	19 296		
Q2	88 369	1 082	28 402	4 770	34 254	15 526	138 149	19 536		
Q3	89 169	767	29 180	5 623	35 570	15 061	139 800	20 894		
Q4	90 746	1 151	33 975	3 348	38 474	16 549	145 769	21 311		
1994 Q1	91 405	324	31 774	6 266	38 364	14 788	144 557	20 721		
Q2	91 487	989	32 236	4 989	38 214	15 837	145 538	21 381		
Q3	92 650	997	32 420	6 911	40 328	14 854	147 832	21 939		
Q4	94 418	1 317	36 807	5 450	43 574	15 124	153 116	22 510		
1995 Q1	95 581	489	33 436	6 462	40 387	15 551	151 519	22 102		
Q2	95 711	1 629	34 115	3 923	39 667	17 895	153 273	23 822		
Q3	96 393	1 735	35 617	6 731	44 083	15 307	155 783	23 607		
Q4	97 712	1 514	39 918	2 961	44 393	17 641	159 746	24 128		
1996 Q1	100 002	1 169	37 032	4 450	42 651	17 733	160 386	23 860		
Q2	99 965	1 371	37 900	4 548	43 819	17 914	161 698	25 049		
Q3	101 140	1 269	38 822	5 934	46 025	17 248	164 413	24 728		
Q4	103 414	1 305	45 051	4 038	50 394	17 336	171 144	24 780		
1997 Q1	106 322	676	40 298	6 223	47 197	16 299	169 818	24 986		
Q2	106 538	1 046	40 902	3 676	45 624	19 826	171 988	26 932		
Q3	108 598	1 115	41 597	4 172	46 884	19 203	174 685	27 027		
Q4	110 930	1 368	46 981	4 080	52 429	18 229	181 588	28 378		
1998 Q1	114 474	873	42 599	7 037	50 509	16 694	181 677	26 461		
Q2	114 338	1 060	42 723	5 626	49 409	19 105	182 852	28 296		
Q3	115 718	1 029	43 282	5 100	49 411	19 534	184 663	29 263		
Q4	118 514	1 092	45 817	1 363	48 272	21 791	188 577	29 865		
1999 Q1	121 875	944	39 890	4 734	45 568	18 952	186 395	29 023		
Q2	120 936	1 017	40 491	2 653	44 161	22 773	187 870	29 767		
Q3	122 281	978	44 312	5 966	51 256	19 991	193 528	30 713		
Q4	126 281	799	49 707	4 818	55 324	18 688	200 293	32 329		
2000 Q1	129 974	907	44 026	4 392	49 325	19 742	199 041	31 015		

See footnotes on page 29

Sources: Office for National Statistics; Enquiries Column 1 020 7533 6005; Columns 2-7,9,10 020 7533 5944; Column 8 020 7533 5990

1.4 Gross domestic product: by category of income[1]

continued

£ million, current prices, seasonally adjusted

		Gross operating surplus of corporations								
		Non-financial corporations								
	Compensation of employees	Public	Private[2]	Financial corporations	Total	Other income [3]	Gross value added at factor cost	Taxes on production *less* subsidies	Statistical discrepancy (income)[4]	Gross domestic product at market prices [4]
	DTWM	CAEQ	CAER	NHCZ	CGBZ	CGBX	CGCB	CMVL	GIXQ	YBHA
1955 Q1	2 726	..	..	..	..	..	..	484	42	4 643
Q2	2 786	..	..	..	..	..	..	502	–43	4 682
Q3	2 854	..	..	..	..	..	..	527	4	4 849
Q4	2 909	..	..	..	..	..	..	516	28	4 933
1956 Q1	2 979	..	..	..	..	..	..	519	27	5 032
Q2	3 062	..	..	..	..	..	..	539	27	5 085
Q3	3 109	..	..	..	..	..	..	544	8	5 150
Q4	3 149	..	..	..	..	..	..	553	57	5 274
1957 Q1	3 188	..	..	..	..	..	..	550	73	5 279
Q2	3 210	..	..	..	..	..	..	556	27	5 359
Q3	3 288	..	..	..	..	..	..	553	51	5 465
Q4	3 311	..	..	..	..	..	..	556	61	5 568
1958 Q1	3 361	..	..	..	..	..	..	565	61	5 652
Q2	3 342	..	..	..	..	..	..	568	52	5 562
Q3	3 373	..	..	..	..	..	..	568	83	5 656
Q4	3 430	..	..	..	..	..	..	589	54	5 715
1959 Q1	3 459	..	..	32	..	..	..	600	32	5 763
Q2	3 505	..	..	29	..	..	..	607	95	5 961
Q3	3 554	..	..	32	..	..	..	600	44	5 968
Q4	3 628	..	..	33	..	..	..	625	90	6 185
1960 Q1	3 668	..	1 210	124	..	..	..	627	5	6 277
Q2	3 771	..	1 207	127	..	..	..	609	3	6 311
Q3	3 862	..	1 216	127	..	..	..	617	–26	6 388
Q4	3 896	..	1 200	132	..	..	..	618	42	6 518
1961 Q1	3 994	146	1 203	142	1 491	..	..	658	5	6 663
Q2	4 105	168	1 213	145	1 526	..	..	641	–4	6 643
Q3	4 147	173	1 205	152	1 530	..	..	614	52	6 866
Q4	4 188	183	1 152	157	1 492	..	..	671	–13	6 799
1962 Q1	4 253	198	1 134	161	1 493	..	..	693	–51	6 899
Q2	4 309	198	1 190	163	1 551	..	..	682	37	7 070
Q3	4 376	201	1 225	164	1 590	..	..	702	–23	7 134
Q4	4 400	189	1 225	168	1 582	..	..	695	26	7 167
1963 Q1	4 417	214	1 111	169	1 494	539	6 450	663	57	7 170
Q2	4 511	222	1 330	169	1 721	555	6 787	716	32	7 535
Q3	4 609	219	1 321	170	1 710	570	6 889	769	–21	7 637
Q4	4 695	228	1 396	177	1 801	618	7 114	767	–	7 881
1964 Q1	4 794	231	1 366	161	1 758	551	7 103	768	55	7 926
Q2	4 886	239	1 456	170	1 865	576	7 327	829	30	8 186
Q3	4 990	267	1 437	181	1 885	605	7 480	848	8	8 336
Q4	5 095	225	1 442	190	1 857	655	7 607	882	99	8 588
1965 Q1	5 149	254	1 496	196	1 946	677	7 772	921	52	8 745
Q2	5 263	249	1 484	201	1 934	687	7 884	907	20	8 811
Q3	5 415	263	1 496	203	1 962	711	8 088	934	–2	9 020
Q4	5 519	264	1 489	205	1 958	748	8 225	951	21	9 197
1966 Q1	5 643	273	1 444	201	1 918	725	8 286	979	45	9 310
Q2	5 710	262	1 436	204	1 902	752	8 364	1 009	80	9 453
Q3	5 752	266	1 564	201	2 031	777	8 560	1 038	5	9 603
Q4	5 778	286	1 509	205	2 000	801	8 579	1 080	41	9 700
1967 Q1	5 745	283	1 580	214	2 077	780	8 602	1 081	109	9 792
Q2	5 946	301	1 670	217	2 188	809	8 943	1 106	–7	10 042
Q3	6 022	278	1 501	222	2 001	827	8 850	1 119	109	10 078
Q4	6 127	326	1 484	235	2 045	858	9 030	1 094	58	10 182
1968 Q1	6 288	343	1 544	240	2 127	859	9 274	1 197	118	10 589
Q2	6 298	344	1 633	252	2 229	862	9 389	1 201	59	10 649
Q3	6 399	349	1 757	259	2 365	878	9 642	1 277	63	10 982
Q4	6 522	378	1 651	275	2 304	922	9 748	1 361	121	11 230
1969 Q1	6 686	401	1 788	252	2 441	916	10 043	1 434	–69	11 408
Q2	6 720	362	1 766	261	2 389	948	10 057	1 469	25	11 551
Q3	6 814	367	1 793	264	2 424	987	10 225	1 536	14	11 775
Q4	7 060	346	1 846	267	2 459	1 017	10 536	1 554	–45	12 045

1 Estimates are given to the nearest £ million, but cannot be regarded as accurate to thid degree.

2 Quarterly alignment adjustment included in this series.

3 Includes mixed income and the operating surplus of non-corporate sector less the adjustment for financial intermediation services indirectly measured (FISIM).

4 Gross domestic product is estimated in seasonally adjusted form only. No equivalent unadjusted estimates exist.

Sources: Office for National Statistics; Enquiries Column 1 020 7533 6005; Columns 2-7,9,10 020 7533 5944; Column 8 020 7533 5990

1.4 Gross domestic product: by category of income[1]

continued

£ million, current prices, seasonally adjusted

	Compensation of employees	Gross operating surplus of corporations: Non-financial corporations: Public	Non-financial corporations: Private[2]	Financial corporations	Total	Other income [3]	Gross value added at factor cost	Taxes on production *less* subsidies	Statistical discrepancy (income)[4]	Gross domestic product at market prices [4]
	DTWM	CAEQ	CAER	NHCZ	CGBZ	CGBX	CGCB	CMVL	GIXQ	YBHA
1970 Q1	7 235	370	1 777	228	2 375	1 016	10 626	1 581	–21	12 186
Q2	7 597	383	1 805	255	2 443	1 062	11 102	1 585	–9	12 678
Q3	7 812	351	1 840	286	2 477	1 117	11 406	1 689	–28	13 067
Q4	7 969	328	2 059	327	2 714	1 186	11 869	1 665	–33	13 501
1971 Q1	8 079	356	2 013	366	2 735	1 204	12 018	1 647	–20	13 645
Q2	8 258	386	2 061	386	2 833	1 225	12 316	1 689	114	14 119
Q3	8 509	417	2 215	388	3 020	1 261	12 790	1 661	161	14 612
Q4	8 709	387	2 364	385	3 136	1 276	13 121	1 648	222	14 991
1972 Q1	9 002	358	2 371	384	3 113	1 338	13 453	1 640	85	15 178
Q2	9 322	455	2 475	395	3 325	1 367	14 014	1 704	145	15 863
Q3	9 574	504	2 515	421	3 440	1 421	14 435	1 682	49	16 166
Q4	10 030	451	2 764	468	3 683	1 472	15 185	1 806	61	17 052
1973 Q1	10 432	557	3 153	531	4 241	1 574	16 247	1 893	29	18 169
Q2	10 796	534	2 900	590	4 024	1 560	16 380	1 692	7	18 079
Q3	11 144	540	2 766	633	3 939	1 593	16 676	1 841	44	18 561
Q4	11 581	423	2 955	655	4 033	1 663	17 277	1 798	109	19 184
1974 Q1	11 874	547	2 310	668	3 525	1 596	16 995	1 614	319	18 928
Q2	12 444	584	2 881	658	4 123	1 666	18 233	1 837	343	20 413
Q3	13 598	677	2 926	647	4 250	1 795	19 643	1 636	315	21 594
Q4	14 563	570	2 883	642	4 095	2 003	20 661	1 694	323	22 678
1975 Q1	16 209	610	2 944	685	4 239	2 142	22 590	1 741	108	24 439
Q2	16 633	706	2 995	709	4 410	2 222	23 265	2 050	465	25 780
Q3	17 691	694	2 991	763	4 448	2 354	24 493	2 223	192	26 908
Q4	18 072	880	3 462	821	5 163	2 496	25 731	2 275	366	28 372
1976 Q1	18 628	945	3 666	890	5 501	2 650	26 779	2 562	404	29 745
Q2	19 265	1 081	3 521	953	5 555	2 573	27 393	2 383	598	30 374
Q3	19 849	1 121	3 761	1 023	5 905	2 646	28 400	2 627	428	31 455
Q4	20 419	1 229	4 554	1 088	6 871	2 714	30 004	2 886	455	33 345
1977 Q1	20 992	1 228	5 275	1 213	7 716	2 820	31 528	2 947	50	34 525
Q2	21 344	1 320	5 498	1 185	8 003	2 823	32 170	3 427	139	35 736
Q3	21 811	1 364	5 704	1 147	8 215	2 978	33 004	3 652	197	36 853
Q4	22 575	1 112	6 241	1 112	8 465	3 180	34 220	3 772	373	38 365
1978 Q1	23 503	1 209	6 846	987	9 042	3 452	35 997	3 663	254	39 914
Q2	24 441	1 464	6 626	940	9 030	3 439	36 910	3 915	592	41 417
Q3	25 106	1 441	7 028	948	9 417	3 565	38 088	4 030	433	42 551
Q4	25 910	1 366	7 019	1 004	9 389	3 705	39 004	4 409	514	43 927
1979 Q1	26 943	1 306	7 076	1 132	9 514	4 014	40 471	4 649	–1	45 119
Q2	28 152	1 461	7 825	1 246	10 532	3 924	42 608	5 019	681	48 308
Q3	29 659	1 350	8 053	1 323	10 726	4 107	44 492	5 831	457	50 780
Q4	31 194	1 335	8 510	1 347	11 192	4 231	46 617	6 142	453	53 212
1980 Q1	32 593	1 623	8 807	1 412	11 842	4 463	48 898	6 561	–221	55 238
Q2	34 064	1 440	9 006	1 463	11 909	4 402	50 375	6 522	–236	56 661
Q3	35 189	1 620	8 341	1 470	11 431	4 550	51 170	6 601	797	58 568
Q4	35 919	1 777	8 874	1 417	12 068	4 829	52 816	6 811	435	60 062
1981 Q1	36 416	1 762	8 704	1 341	11 807	4 964	53 187	7 051	1 018	61 256
Q2	36 975	2 028	8 981	1 245	12 254	4 848	54 077	7 773	409	62 259
Q3	37 807	2 224	9 988	1 222	13 434	5 095	56 336	8 004	–331	64 009
Q4	38 456	2 195	10 569	1 260	14 024	5 417	57 897	8 119	–288	65 728
1982 Q1	39 004	2 351	9 921	1 390	13 662	5 325	57 991	8 683	528	67 202
Q2	39 516	2 358	11 655	1 454	15 467	5 235	60 218	8 394	–139	68 473
Q3	39 869	2 581	11 758	1 522	15 861	5 329	61 059	8 636	–8	69 687
Q4	40 342	2 339	12 424	1 664	16 427	5 723	62 492	8 850	233	71 575
1983 Q1	41 413	2 749	13 191	2 069	18 009	5 648	65 070	9 128	–127	74 071
Q2	42 038	2 774	12 320	2 287	17 381	5 664	65 083	9 207	–66	74 224
Q3	42 733	2 368	13 785	2 188	18 341	5 877	66 951	9 230	28	76 209
Q4	43 495	2 648	14 288	2 043	18 979	6 091	68 565	9 489	62	78 116
1984 Q1	44 081	2 685	14 516	1 613	18 814	6 301	69 196	9 553	241	78 990
Q2	44 817	2 293	15 643	1 692	19 628	6 218	70 663	9 677	251	80 591
Q3	45 394	2 159	15 440	1 591	19 190	6 555	71 139	9 788	290	81 217
Q4	46 905	1 911	16 352	1 840	20 103	6 397	73 405	9 676	270	83 351

See footnotes on page 33

Sources: Office for National Statistics; Enquiries Column 1 020 7533 6005; Columns 2-7 020 7533 5944; Column 8 020 7533 6013

1.4 Gross domestic product: by category of income[1]

continued

£ million, current prices, seasonally adjusted

	Gross operating surplus of corporations									
		Non-financial corporations								
	Compensation of employees	Public	Private[2]	Financial corporations	Total	Other income[3]	Gross value added at factor cost	Taxes on production *less* subsidies	Statistical discrepancy (income)[4]	Gross domestic product at market prices[4]
	DTWM	CAEQ	CAER	NHCZ	CGBZ	CGBX	CGCB	CMVL	GIXQ	YBHA
1985 Q1	48 042	1 313	17 439	2 245	20 997	6 530	75 569	9 969	–	85 538
Q2	48 630	2 054	18 743	1 043	21 840	7 841	78 311	10 317	–	88 628
Q3	49 401	2 413	17 944	1 889	22 246	7 292	78 939	10 770	–	89 709
Q4	50 520	1 973	18 314	2 046	22 333	7 463	80 316	11 157	–	91 473
1986 Q1	51 559	2 141	17 632	2 197	21 970	7 594	81 123	11 654	–	92 777
Q2	52 609	2 323	17 451	2 338	22 112	7 875	82 596	11 886	–	94 482
Q3	53 529	2 076	17 377	2 618	22 071	8 169	83 769	12 231	–	96 000
Q4	54 363	2 098	18 156	2 896	23 150	8 341	85 854	12 710	–	98 564
1987 Q1	55 304	1 747	19 111	3 057	23 915	8 641	87 860	12 938	–	100 798
Q2	56 691	1 841	19 927	2 543	24 311	9 286	90 288	12 683	–	102 971
Q3	58 151	1 942	20 604	2 564	25 110	9 684	92 945	13 608	–	106 553
Q4	59 774	1 960	20 981	2 819	25 760	9 525	95 059	14 080	–	109 139
1988 Q1	61 487	1 725	22 139	2 258	26 122	10 055	97 664	14 421	–	112 085
Q2	63 057	1 993	22 116	2 294	26 403	10 239	99 699	14 910	–	114 609
Q3	65 052	2 091	23 669	2 404	28 164	10 239	103 455	15 163	–	118 618
Q4	67 194	2 097	24 847	2 528	29 472	10 302	106 968	15 482	–	122 450
1989 Q1	68 561	2 113	25 499	2 582	30 194	10 365	109 120	15 521	–	124 641
Q2	70 334	1 558	25 813	2 878	30 249	10 044	110 627	15 905	–	126 532
Q3	72 303	1 438	26 301	2 968	30 707	10 513	113 523	16 091	–	129 614
Q4	74 589	1 550	25 840	2 999	30 389	11 092	116 070	16 421	–	132 491
1990 Q1	76 465	1 332	26 370	2 521	30 223	11 591	118 279	17 015	–	135 294
Q2	78 427	1 095	27 179	3 465	31 739	11 713	121 879	17 242	–	139 121
Q3	79 806	993	26 911	3 040	30 944	12 960	123 710	17 236	–	140 946
Q4	80 510	690	26 672	2 685	30 047	13 359	123 916	16 940	–	140 856
1991 Q1	82 101	593	26 977	2 298	29 868	13 481	125 450	18 006	–	143 456
Q2	83 017	584	26 992	1 550	29 126	13 927	126 070	19 049	–	145 119
Q3	84 169	567	27 040	1 212	28 819	14 238	127 226	19 593	–	146 819
Q4	84 563	463	27 493	2 776	30 732	13 985	129 280	19 862	–	149 142
1992 Q1	85 834	748	26 714	2 726	30 188	14 467	130 489	19 842	–	150 331
Q2	86 363	449	27 990	3 240	31 679	14 570	132 612	19 020	–	151 632
Q3	87 353	505	26 864	4 218	31 587	14 280	133 220	19 331	–	152 551
Q4	87 486	535	26 892	5 473	32 900	13 567	133 953	19 698	–	153 651
1993 Q1	87 857	623	28 559	4 258	33 440	15 037	136 334	19 957	–	156 291
Q2	88 581	853	28 879	5 121	34 853	14 990	138 424	19 637	–	158 061
Q3	89 410	771	30 549	4 890	36 210	15 386	141 006	20 372	–	161 378
Q4	90 475	959	30 466	4 124	35 549	16 531	142 555	21 071	–	163 626
1994 Q1	91 108	793	31 806	5 713	38 312	15 159	144 579	21 164	–	165 743
Q2	91 745	777	33 220	5 563	39 560	15 110	146 415	21 332	–	167 747
Q3	92 943	978	33 312	5 978	40 268	15 224	148 435	21 759	–	170 194
Q4	94 164	1 079	34 899	6 362	42 340	15 110	151 614	22 296	–	173 910
1995 Q1	95 141	897	34 972	5 728	41 597	16 103	152 841	22 653	–	175 494
Q2	95 995	1 513	34 696	4 541	40 750	17 123	153 868	23 515	–	177 383
Q3	96 775	1 657	35 919	5 816	43 392	15 604	155 771	23 470	–	179 241
Q4	97 486	1 300	37 499	3 992	42 791	17 564	157 841	24 021	–	181 862
1996 Q1	99 255	1 490	38 564	3 593	43 647	18 422	161 324	23 972	–	185 296
Q2	100 546	1 287	39 005	5 096	45 388	17 189	163 123	24 398	–	187 521
Q3	101 532	1 236	40 284	5 168	46 688	17 422	165 642	24 742	–	190 384
Q4	103 188	1 101	40 952	5 113	47 166	17 198	167 552	25 305	–	192 857
1997 Q1	105 502	1 099	42 080	5 161	48 340	17 204	171 046	25 908	–	196 954
Q2	107 161	980	41 463	3 979	46 422	19 095	172 678	26 600	–	199 278
Q3	108 926	988	42 770	3 654	47 412	19 249	175 587	27 127	–	202 714
Q4	110 799	1 138	43 465	5 357	49 960	18 009	178 768	27 688	–	206 456
1998 Q1	113 069	1 062	43 594	6 052	50 708	17 728	181 505	27 333	–	208 838
Q2	114 961	1 006	43 650	6 271	50 927	17 954	183 842	27 974	–	211 816
Q3	116 672	976	43 993	4 461	49 430	19 466	185 568	29 039	–	214 607
Q4	118 342	1 010	43 184	2 342	46 536	21 976	186 854	29 539	–	216 393
1999 Q1	120 343	1 094	42 069	3 875	47 038	19 903	187 284	29 747	275	217 306
Q2	121 719	991	43 216	3 208	47 415	21 608	190 742	30 000	315	221 057
Q3	123 457	935	44 452	5 552	50 939	19 685	194 081	30 714	320	225 115
Q4	125 854	718	44 663	5 536	50 917	19 208	195 979	31 371	278	227 628
2000 Q1	127 971	1 007	44 842	3 637	49 486	20 622	198 079	31 796	86	229 961

See footnotes on page 33

Sources: Office for National Statistics; Enquiries Column 1 020 7533 6005; Columns 2-7,9,10 020 7533 5944; Column 8 020 7533 5990

1.5 Income, product and spending per head

£

	At current prices				At 1995 prices		
	Gross national income at market prices	Gross domestic product at market prices	Household and NPISH final consumption expenditure	Households' gross disposable income	Gross domestic product at market prices	Household and NPISH final consumption expenditure	Real households' disposable income
	IHXS	IHXT	IHXU	IHXV	IHXW	IHXX	IHXY
1955	378	375	254	246	5 424	3 290	3 187
1956	404	402	264	262	5 452	3 291	3 251
1957	426	421	278	274	5 520	3 343	3 290
1958	443	437	292	286	5 516	3 421	3 337
1959	464	460	306	301	5 722	3 549	3 491
1960	491	487	319	322	5 981	3 655	3 692
1961	515	511	333	343	6 078	3 703	3 816
1962	535	531	349	356	6 097	3 753	3 827
1963	570	564	368	375	6 346	3 910	3 966
1964	620	612	393	402	6 647	4 003	4 109
1965	666	658	415	427	6 771	4 033	4 159
1966	702	697	437	452	6 865	4 083	4 232
1967	736	730	455	467	6 983	4 156	4 267
1968	793	787	488	496	7 235	4 256	4 325
1969	853	843	515	526	7 350	4 261	4 344
1970	935	924	561	576	7 503	4 371	4 492
1971	1 034	1 026	625	630	7 613	4 485	4 521
1972	1 155	1 146	706	726	7 865	4 757	4 886
1973	1 338	1 316	807	836	8 422	5 009	5 187
1974	1 510	1 487	929	970	8 278	4 928	5 134
1975	1 889	1 878	1 145	1 204	8 224	4 916	5 173
1976	2 242	2 222	1 331	1 389	8 455	4 940	5 153
1977	2 580	2 589	1 522	1 562	8 659	4 923	5 051
1978	2 987	2 987	1 756	1 835	8 957	5 190	5 425
1979	3 501	3 511	2 080	2 202	9 192	5 409	5 726
1980	4 063	4 093	2 411	2 596	8 978	5 399	5 811
1981	4 488	4 495	2 676	2 863	8 859	5 402	5 780
1982	4 904	4 917	2 931	3 098	9 023	5 460	5 770
1983	5 380	5 367	3 219	3 331	9 352	5 706	5 905
1984	5 769	5 736	3 440	3 619	9 560	5 803	6 105
1985	6 253	6 269	3 747	3 924	9 889	6 008	6 292
1986	6 737	6 715	4 143	4 247	10 275	6 386	6 546
1987	7 316	7 357	4 537	4 575	10 701	6 710	6 767
1988	8 150	8 183	5 111	5 044	11 224	7 196	7 103
1989	8 873	8 948	5 587	5 571	11 420	7 403	7 383
1990	9 563	9 661	6 043	6 206	11 456	7 433	7 632
1991	10 016	10 110	6 379	6 768	11 240	7 273	7 717
1992	10 446	10 484	6 688	7 324	11 209	7 283	7 975
1993	10 920	10 986	7 098	7 781	11 434	7 470	8 189
1994	11 683	11 603	7 440	8 028	11 894	7 660	8 266
1995	12 199	12 182	7 762	8 451	12 182	7 762	8 452
1996	12 928	12 856	8 269	8 879	12 451	8 016	8 607
1997	13 792	13 647	8 776	9 413	12 843	8 299	8 902
1998	14 558	14 376	9 315	9 614	13 131	8 600	8 876
1999	15 073	14 987	9 871	10 095	13 361	8 938	9 141

Source: Office for National Statistics; Enquiries 020 7533 5944

1.5 Income, product and spending per head

continued

£, seasonally adjusted

	At current prices				At 1995 prices		
	Gross national income at market prices	Gross domestic product at market prices	Household and NPISH final consumption expenditure	Households' gross disposable income	Gross domestic product at market prices	Household and NPISH final consumption expenditure	Real households'disposable income
	IHXS	IHXT	IHXU	IHXV	IHXW	IHXX	IHXY
1955 Q1	92	91	62	60	1 351	816	761
Q2	93	92	63	61	1 348	820	815
Q3	96	95	64	62	1 367	830	808
Q4	97	97	65	63	1 358	824	803
1956 Q1	99	99	65	65	1 366	825	787
Q2	100	99	66	65	1 363	822	820
Q3	101	101	66	66	1 360	821	815
Q4	104	103	67	66	1 363	823	829
1957 Q1	104	103	68	67	1 385	827	788
Q2	105	104	69	68	1 386	832	839
Q3	107	106	70	69	1 375	840	821
Q4	110	108	71	70	1 374	844	842
1958 Q1	111	110	72	71	1 392	850	811
Q2	109	108	72	71	1 359	846	842
Q3	111	109	73	72	1 381	855	836
Q4	112	110	75	72	1 384	870	848
1959 Q1	112	111	75	73	1 396	870	824
Q2	116	115	76	75	1 417	884	891
Q3	116	115	76	76	1 440	887	879
Q4	120	119	79	77	1 469	908	897
1960 Q1	121	120	80	78	1 499	917	871
Q2	122	121	79	80	1 482	910	936
Q3	123	122	80	81	1 499	915	931
Q4	125	124	80	83	1 501	913	954
1961 Q1	128	127	82	84	1 524	927	912
Q2	127	126	83	86	1 526	924	963
Q3	131	130	84	87	1 518	927	972
Q4	129	128	84	86	1 510	925	969
1962 Q1	131	130	86	87	1 516	930	914
Q2	134	133	88	88	1 527	943	954
Q3	135	134	87	90	1 533	935	967
Q4	135	134	88	91	1 521	945	992
1963 Q1	135	134	89	91	1 527	952	931
Q2	142	141	92	92	1 595	981	985
Q3	144	142	93	95	1 602	990	1 018
Q4	149	147	94	97	1 622	987	1 032
1964 Q1	150	147	96	98	1 637	996	988
Q2	154	152	97	99	1 659	997	1 024
Q3	156	154	99	102	1 661	1 001	1 038
Q4	160	159	101	103	1 690	1 009	1 059
1965 Q1	163	161	102	104	1 684	1 006	1 007
Q2	164	162	103	105	1 682	1 002	1 038
Q3	168	166	104	108	1 695	1 012	1 044
Q4	171	169	106	110	1 710	1 013	1 070
1966 Q1	172	171	108	115	1 710	1 025	1 075
Q2	175	173	110	111	1 717	1 032	1 051
Q3	177	176	109	112	1 722	1 013	1 040
Q4	178	177	110	114	1 716	1 013	1 066
1967 Q1	180	179	111	113	1 733	1 018	1 025
Q2	184	183	112	116	1 750	1 030	1 067
Q3	185	183	115	119	1 748	1 051	1 083
Q4	187	185	117	119	1 752	1 057	1 092
1968 Q1	194	192	122	122	1 808	1 088	1 080
Q2	195	193	119	125	1 787	1 044	1 091
Q3	200	199	122	123	1 817	1 062	1 070
Q4	204	203	125	126	1 823	1 062	1 084
1969 Q1	209	206	126	129	1 819	1 057	1 073
Q2	211	208	128	131	1 834	1 066	1 087
Q3	214	212	129	132	1 845	1 066	1 079
Q4	219	217	132	134	1 852	1 072	1 105

Source: Office for National Statistics; Enquiries 020 7533 5944

1.5 Income, product and spending per head

continued

£, seasonally adjusted

	At current prices				At 1995 prices		
	Gross national income at market prices	Gross domestic product at market prices	Household and NPISH final consumption expenditure	Households' gross disposable income	Gross domestic product at market prices	Household and NPISH final consumption expenditure	Real households'disposable income
	IHXS	IHXT	IHXU	IHXV	IHXW	IHXX	IHXY
1970 Q1	222	219	135	137	1 839	1 075	1 078
Q2	231	228	138	144	1 874	1 090	1 132
Q3	237	235	142	146	1 890	1 107	1 131
Q4	245	242	146	149	1 900	1 099	1 151
1971 Q1	247	244	148	149	1 873	1 093	1 081
Q2	255	253	155	157	1 897	1 116	1 130
Q3	263	261	159	160	1 922	1 135	1 137
Q4	269	268	163	164	1 921	1 141	1 173
1972 Q1	273	271	168	170	1 913	1 158	1 138
Q2	286	283	173	182	1 966	1 185	1 246
Q3	290	288	179	183	1 972	1 203	1 223
Q4	306	304	186	191	2 014	1 211	1 279
1973 Q1	326	323	196	198	2 112	1 259	1 240
Q2	328	322	198	206	2 109	1 248	1 314
Q3	335	330	203	211	2 113	1 258	1 313
Q4	349	341	210	221	2 088	1 244	1 320
1974 Q1	343	337	215	225	2 036	1 220	1 255
Q2	370	363	226	232	2 078	1 225	1 260
Q3	389	384	237	250	2 099	1 239	1 310
Q4	408	403	251	263	2 065	1 244	1 309
1975 Q1	439	435	267	286	2 073	1 236	1 313
Q2	461	459	284	293	2 043	1 238	1 286
Q3	481	479	292	308	2 043	1 227	1 299
Q4	508	505	302	317	2 065	1 215	1 275
1976 Q1	533	529	315	332	2 103	1 222	1 271
Q2	546	540	325	336	2 089	1 231	1 277
Q3	565	560	337	357	2 111	1 243	1 329
Q4	598	593	354	364	2 152	1 244	1 276
1977 Q1	614	614	363	370	2 153	1 220	1 216
Q2	633	636	373	379	2 147	1 215	1 241
Q3	653	656	386	395	2 165	1 231	1 271
Q4	680	683	400	418	2 194	1 257	1 323
1978 Q1	709	711	421	428	2 210	1 285	1 297
Q2	738	737	429	450	2 230	1 287	1 354
Q3	758	757	448	472	2 253	1 313	1 378
Q4	782	782	458	485	2 264	1 305	1 396
1979 Q1	803	803	476	504	2 252	1 321	1 376
Q2	855	859	517	524	2 344	1 394	1 419
Q3	903	903	529	561	2 290	1 341	1 421
Q4	940	946	558	613	2 306	1 353	1 510
1980 Q1	974	981	587	614	2 290	1 375	1 432
Q2	996	1 006	593	640	2 244	1 339	1 448
Q3	1 032	1 040	611	662	2 235	1 355	1 468
Q4	1 061	1 066	620	680	2 209	1 330	1 463
1981 Q1	1 085	1 087	645	699	2 198	1 349	1 459
Q2	1 104	1 105	661	705	2 200	1 351	1 444
Q3	1 132	1 136	676	716	2 232	1 354	1 433
Q4	1 167	1 167	694	743	2 229	1 348	1 444
1982 Q1	1 186	1 193	707	750	2 232	1 345	1 429
Q2	1 213	1 216	720	776	2 257	1 352	1 440
Q3	1 234	1 237	740	776	2 261	1 375	1 448
Q4	1 271	1 271	764	796	2 273	1 388	1 453
1983 Q1	1 319	1 315	781	807	2 318	1 409	1 445
Q2	1 314	1 317	794	831	2 321	1 418	1 476
Q3	1 361	1 351	818	839	2 344	1 441	1 485
Q4	1 386	1 384	826	854	2 369	1 438	1 499
1984 Q1	1 408	1 399	839	877	2 392	1 446	1 498
Q2	1 427	1 427	858	891	2 382	1 452	1 522
Q3	1 443	1 437	860	907	2 381	1 442	1 516
Q4	1 491	1 473	883	944	2 405	1 463	1 569

Source: Office for National Statistics; Enquiries 020 7533 5944

1.5 Income, product and spending per head

continued

£, seasonally adjusted

	At current prices				At 1995 prices		
	Gross national income at market prices	Gross domestic product at market prices	Household and NPISH final consumption expenditure	Households' gross disposable income	Gross domestic product at market prices	Household and NPISH final consumption expenditure	Real households'disposable income
	IHXS	IHXT	IHXU	IHXV	IHXW	IHXX	IHXY
1985 Q1	1 516	1 511	907	950	2 442	1 482	1 533
Q2	1 557	1 564	924	980	2 479	1 490	1 590
Q3	1 577	1 582	948	983	2 476	1 510	1 572
Q4	1 603	1 612	968	1 011	2 492	1 526	1 597
1986 Q1	1 640	1 633	999	1 025	2 526	1 565	1 603
Q2	1 668	1 662	1 031	1 065	2 555	1 598	1 649
Q3	1 690	1 688	1 049	1 070	2 581	1 608	1 647
Q4	1 739	1 732	1 064	1 087	2 613	1 615	1 647
1987 Q1	1 770	1 770	1 093	1 103	2 620	1 636	1 641
Q2	1 798	1 807	1 115	1 131	2 648	1 660	1 700
Q3	1 857	1 868	1 146	1 149	2 701	1 690	1 707
Q4	1 891	1 912	1 183	1 192	2 732	1 724	1 719
1988 Q1	1 950	1 963	1 225	1 211	2 769	1 762	1 734
Q2	2 000	2 006	1 254	1 252	2 785	1 777	1 793
Q3	2 072	2 074	1 301	1 270	2 824	1 818	1 787
Q4	2 128	2 140	1 331	1 311	2 846	1 839	1 789
1989 Q1	2 170	2 176	1 357	1 332	2 844	1 844	1 801
Q2	2 192	2 207	1 387	1 360	2 856	1 850	1 833
Q3	2 233	2 258	1 403	1 421	2 860	1 846	1 880
Q4	2 278	2 307	1 440	1 458	2 860	1 863	1 869
1990 Q1	2 325	2 353	1 467	1 494	2 880	1 863	1 891
Q2	2 390	2 418	1 508	1 533	2 891	1 871	1 913
Q3	2 431	2 447	1 523	1 572	2 852	1 854	1 922
Q4	2 417	2 443	1 545	1 607	2 833	1 845	1 906
1991 Q1	2 453	2 485	1 559	1 642	2 828	1 838	1 923
Q2	2 485	2 511	1 585	1 666	2 807	1 813	1 917
Q3	2 510	2 538	1 611	1 725	2 801	1 816	1 950
Q4	2 568	2 576	1 624	1 735	2 804	1 806	1 927
1992 Q1	2 582	2 594	1 638	1 773	2 800	1 800	1 936
Q2	2 598	2 615	1 669	1 834	2 790	1 821	2 010
Q3	2 623	2 629	1 682	1 851	2 804	1 829	2 011
Q4	2 643	2 646	1 699	1 866	2 815	1 833	2 018
1993 Q1	2 664	2 689	1 727	1 890	2 828	1 842	2 000
Q2	2 699	2 717	1 761	1 944	2 842	1 856	2 055
Q3	2 756	2 772	1 793	1 951	2 868	1 882	2 046
Q4	2 801	2 808	1 817	1 996	2 896	1 890	2 088
1994 Q1	2 866	2 842	1 830	1 982	2 922	1 904	2 049
Q2	2 881	2 874	1 850	1 985	2 957	1 908	2 063
Q3	2 929	2 913	1 867	2 013	2 996	1 918	2 068
Q4	3 007	2 974	1 893	2 048	3 019	1 930	2 086
1995 Q1	3 003	2 998	1 909	2 093	3 029	1 929	2 098
Q2	3 017	3 028	1 932	2 097	3 038	1 938	2 119
Q3	3 068	3 057	1 946	2 120	3 049	1 939	2 110
Q4	3 111	3 099	1 975	2 141	3 066	1 956	2 125
1996 Q1	3 170	3 155	2 026	2 198	3 088	1 985	2 112
Q2	3 223	3 190	2 051	2 211	3 101	1 998	2 171
Q3	3 239	3 236	2 079	2 222	3 118	2 007	2 154
Q4	3 296	3 275	2 113	2 248	3 144	2 026	2 170
1997 Q1	3 379	3 342	2 142	2 306	3 174	2 039	2 129
Q2	3 417	3 378	2 173	2 349	3 199	2 069	2 262
Q3	3 480	3 433	2 212	2 371	3 228	2 085	2 234
Q4	3 516	3 494	2 249	2 387	3 242	2 106	2 277
1998 Q1	3 558	3 530	2 282	2 393	3 262	2 127	2 080
Q2	3 606	3 577	2 316	2 381	3 281	2 145	2 280
Q3	3 696	3 621	2 343	2 398	3 293	2 157	2 206
Q4	3 698	3 648	2 374	2 442	3 295	2 171	2 310
1999 Q1	3 669	3 660	2 414	2 446	3 303	2 205	2 108
Q2	3 731	3 720	2 451	2 544	3 326	2 224	2 380 2 378
Q3	3 791	3 784	2 479	2 516	3 356	2 239	2 243
Q4	3 882	3 823	2 527	2 589	3 376	2 270	2 412
2000 Q1	3 857	3 859	2 546	2 567	3 390	2 283	2 160

Source: Office for National Statistics; Enquiries 020 7533 5944

1.6 Households'[1] disposable income and consumption

	£ million, current prices					£ million, 1995 prices		
	Households' income before tax		Gross households' disposable income[2]	Households' final consumption expenditure	Households' saving ratio[3] (percentage)	Real households' disposable income[4]	Households' final consumption expenditure	Index of real households' disposable income (1995=100)
	Total	*of which:* Wages and salaries						
	EWSB	QWLW	QWND	NSSG	RVGL	RVGK	NPSO	OSXR
1946	..	5 527	..	..	..	..	..	..
1947	..	5 937	..	..	..	..	..	..
1948	..	6 430	7 944	8 465	..	135 798	..	27.5
1949	..	6 825	8 346	8 823	..	139 138	..	28.1
1950	..	7 174	8 840	9 314	..	143 362	..	29.0
1951	..	8 010	9 552	10 060	..	141 473	..	28.6
1952	..	8 574	10 259	10 594	..	144 339	..	29.2
1953	..	9 051	10 987	11 300	..	151 248	..	30.6
1954	..	9 675	11 554	11 987	..	156 188	..	31.6
1955	..	10 570	12 520	12 920	..	162 396	167 320	32.8
1956	..	11 523	13 425	13 590	..	166 385	168 163	33.7
1957	..	12 159	14 104	14 332	..	169 167	171 626	34.2
1958	..	12 532	14 753	15 125	..	172 361	176 417	34.8
1959	..	13 116	15 666	15 925	..	181 361	184 046	36.7
1960	..	14 116	16 886	16 710	..	193 426	191 078	39.1
1961	..	15 232	18 107	17 570	..	201 546	195 233	40.7
1962	..	16 036	18 980	18 611	..	203 972	199 627	41.2
1963	..	16 813	20 111	19 826	4.5	212 683	208 902	43.0
1964	..	18 228	21 711	21 156	5.6	221 808	215 334	44.8
1965	..	19 598	23 240	22 532	6.0	226 061	218 233	45.7
1966	..	20 942	24 681	23 812	6.4	231 253	222 089	46.8
1967	..	21 737	25 694	25 032	5.6	234 478	227 375	47.4
1968	..	23 157	27 392	26 953	4.8	238 774	233 815	48.3
1969	..	24 805	29 171	28 610	4.9	240 917	235 112	48.8
1970	..	27 764	32 068	31 208	5.8	249 906	241 958	50.6
1971	..	30 397	35 270	34 991	4.2	252 896	249 683	51.1
1972	..	34 176	40 698	39 628	6.6	274 113	265 578	55.4
1973	..	39 406	46 976	45 360	7.5	291 634	280 114	59.0
1974	..	46 615	54 503	52 308	7.7	288 727	275 849	58.4
1975	..	60 342	67 732	64 368	8.5	290 867	275 165	58.9
1976	..	67 743	78 085	74 871	8.1	289 648	276 407	58.7
1977	..	74 933	87 717	85 500	6.9	283 817	275 240	57.5
1978	..	85 667	103 100	98 593	8.8	304 829	290 059	61.7
1979	..	100 477	123 853	116 996	10.2	322 020	302 731	65.2
1980	..	119 185	146 190	135 825	11.7	327 291	302 639	66.3
1981	..	128 086	161 349	150 796	11.5	325 752	302 987	65.9
1982	..	136 519	174 504	165 113	10.2	325 017	305 995	65.8
1983	..	145 803	187 789	181 478	8.3	332 942	320 124	67.4
1984	..	156 153	204 479	194 377	9.7	344 971	326 260	69.8
1985	..	170 451	222 478	212 420	9.1	356 762	338 918	72.2
1986	..	183 988	241 460	235 567	7.5	372 198	362 067	75.3
1987	385 983	200 189	260 878	258 669	5.5	385 796	381 462	77.9
1988	428 216	224 043	288 352	292 188	3.9	405 997	410 370	81.9
1989	474 620	250 141	319 581	320 479	5.6	423 510	423 832	85.5
1990	528 626	276 337	357 257	347 893	7.4	439 384	427 002	88.7
1991	573 576	291 905	391 316	368 881	9.4	446 102	419 599	90.1
1992	613 469	303 018	424 838	387 953	11.5	462 638	421 436	93.4
1993	639 781	310 252	452 810	413 089	11.0	476 613	433 939	96.2
1994	666 938	321 545	468 883	434 549	9.4	482 708	446 581	97.4
1995	705 589	335 589	495 337	454 934	10.3	495 337	454 171	100.0
1996	749 007	351 547	522 089	486 226	9.5	506 145	470 622	102.2
1997	788 914	375 643	555 518	517 909	9.3	525 321	488 936	106.1
1998	825 532	401 413	569 496	551 823	5.8	525 807	509 490	106.3
1999	874 094	426 347	600 259	586 906	5.0	543 507	531 416	109.9

1 All households' series include also Non-Profit Institutions Serving Households (NPISH).

2 Total households' income before tax *less* payments of income tax and other taxes, social contributions,and other current transfers.

3 Households' saving as a percentage of Total resources; the latter is defined as the sum of Gross household disposable income and the Adjustment for the net equity of the households in pension funds (D.8).

4 Gross households' disposable income revalued by the implied Household and NPISH final consumption expenditure deflator (1995 = 100).

Sources: Office for National Statistics;
Enquiries Columns 1,2,3,5,6,8 020 7 533 6003; Columns 4,7 020 7533 5998

1.6 Households'[1] disposable income and consumption

continued

Not seasonally adjusted

	£ million, current prices					£ million, 1995 prices		
	Households' income before tax		Gross households' disposable income[2]	Households' final consumption expenditure	Households' saving ratio[3] (percentage)	Real households' disposable income[4]	Households' final consumption expenditure	Index of real households' disposable income (1995=100)
	Total	*of which:* Wages and salaries						
	EWSB	QWLW	QWND	NSSG	RVGL	RVGK	NPSO	OSXR
1955 Q1	..	2 561	2 914	2 944	..	38 711	39 065	31.3
Q2	..	2 599	3 173	3 176	..	41 492	41 481	33.5
Q3	..	2 659	3 166	3 275	..	41 200	42 583	33.3
Q4	..	2 751	3 267	3 525	..	40 993	44 191	33.1
1956 Q1	..	2 795	3 155	3 125	..	40 181	39 752	32.5
Q2	..	2 847	3 394	3 384	..	41 953	41 782	33.9
Q3	..	2 902	3 373	3 410	..	41 753	42 159	33.8
Q4	..	2 979	3 503	3 671	..	42 498	44 470	34.4
1957 Q1	..	2 989	3 312	3 267	..	40 447	39 849	32.7
Q2	..	2 978	3 562	3 543	..	43 114	42 832	34.9
Q3	..	3 061	3 535	3 629	..	42 259	43 328	34.2
Q4	..	3 131	3 695	3 893	..	43 347	45 617	35.0
1958 Q1	..	3 134	3 525	3 494	..	41 811	41 384	33.8
Q2	..	3 073	3 722	3 742	..	43 469	43 642	35.1
Q3	..	3 112	3 690	3 790	..	43 221	44 331	34.9
Q4	..	3 213	3 816	4 099	..	43 860	47 060	35.5
1959 Q1	..	3 205	3 673	3 668	..	42 680	42 552	34.5
Q2	..	3 226	3 972	3 958	..	46 241	46 002	37.4
Q3	..	3 283	3 931	3 980	..	45 706	46 211	37.0
Q4	..	3 402	4 090	4 319	..	46 734	49 281	37.8
1960 Q1	..	3 395	3 923	3 902	..	45 474	45 153	36.8
Q2	..	3 486	4 275	4 197	..	48 993	48 017	39.6
Q3	..	3 579	4 251	4 185	..	48 831	47 991	39.5
Q4	..	3 656	4 437	4 426	..	50 128	49 917	40.5
1961 Q1	..	3 700	4 233	4 069	..	48 027	46 089	38.8
Q2	..	3 798	4 534	4 389	..	50 784	49 082	41.1
Q3	..	3 828	4 640	4 447	..	51 370	49 152	41.5
Q4	..	3 906	4 700	4 665	..	51 365	50 910	41.5
1962 Q1	..	3 906	4 444	4 292	..	48 543	46 802	39.2
Q2	..	3 983	4 750	4 723	..	50 781	50 401	41.1
Q3	..	4 042	4 814	4 678	..	51 607	50 059	41.7
Q4	..	4 105	4 972	4 918	..	53 041	52 365	42.9
1963 Q1	..	4 050	4 667	4 520	6.2	49 813	48 059	40.3
Q2	..	4 164	4 999	5 000	2.9	52 794	52 604	42.7
Q3	..	4 231	5 138	5 050	4.7	54 638	53 517	44.2
Q4	..	4 368	5 307	5 256	4.2	55 438	54 722	44.8
1964 Q1	..	4 384	5 092	4 859	7.7	53 178	50 587	43.0
Q2	..	4 503	5 390	5 282	5.1	55 215	53 941	44.6
Q3	..	4 589	5 502	5 376	5.3	56 072	54 594	45.3
Q4	..	4 752	5 727	5 639	4.4	57 343	56 212	46.3
1965 Q1	..	4 725	5 513	5 218	8.5	54 632	51 520	44.2
Q2	..	4 843	5 790	5 610	5.9	56 387	54 409	45.6
Q3	..	4 925	5 849	5 745	4.5	56 771	55 522	45.9
Q4	..	5 105	6 088	5 959	5.3	58 271	56 782	47.1
1966 Q1	..	5 144	6 147	5 560	12.4	58 640	52 801	47.5
Q2	..	5 249	6 106	6 018	4.3	57 376	56 310	46.4
Q3	..	5 211	6 090	6 017	3.8	56 877	55 967	46.0
Q4	..	5 338	6 338	6 217	5.0	58 360	57 011	47.2
1967 Q1	..	5 206	6 110	5 769	8.4	56 203	52 831	45.5
Q2	..	5 436	6 401	6 194	6.3	58 589	56 439	47.4
Q3	..	5 449	6 524	6 377	5.2	59 573	57 966	48.2
Q4	..	5 646	6 659	6 692	2.8	60 113	60 139	48.6
1968 Q1	..	5 656	6 664	6 377	7.7	59 530	56 722	48.2
Q2	..	5 733	6 868	6 542	7.7	60 214	57 103	48.7
Q3	..	5 765	6 815	6 816	3.1	59 082	58 831	47.8
Q4	..	6 003	7 045	7 218	0.8	59 948	61 159	48.5
1969 Q1	..	6 010	7 085	6 631	9.4	59 429	55 358	48.1
Q2	..	6 134	7 254	7 046	6.1	60 250	58 253	48.8
Q3	..	6 157	7 258	7 221	3.4	59 889	59 317	48.5
Q4	..	6 504	7 574	7 712	1.2	61 349	62 184	49.6

See footnotes on page 40.

Sources: Office for National Statistics;
Enquiries Columns 1,2,3,5,6,8 020 7533 6003; Columns 4,7 020 7533 5998

1.6 Households'[1] disposable income and consumption

continued

Not seasonally adjusted

	£ million, current prices					£ million, 1995 prices		
	Households' income before tax		Gross households' disposable income[2]	Households' final consumption expenditure	Households' saving ratio[3] (percentage)	Real households' disposable income[4]	Households' final consumption expenditure	Index of real households' disposable income (1995=100)
	Total	*of which:* Wages and salaries						
	EWSB	QWLW	QWND	NSSG	RVGL	RVGK	NPSO	OSXR
1970 Q1	..	6 471	7 495	7 087	8.3	59 917	56 381	48.5
Q2	..	6 924	7 993	7 632	7.5	62 923	59 790	50.9
Q3	..	7 042	8 093	7 975	4.5	62 952	61 754	50.9
Q4	..	7 327	8 487	8 514	3.1	64 114	64 033	51.9
1971 Q1	..	7 215	8 174	7 840	7.1	60 351	57 614	48.8
Q2	..	7 519	8 788	8 598	5.6	63 194	61 548	51.1
Q3	..	7 699	8 942	8 988	3.1	63 615	63 670	51.5
Q4	..	7 964	9 366	9 565	1.4	65 736	66 851	53.2
1972 Q1	..	7 978	9 251	8 928	7.4	63 811	61 294	51.6
Q2	..	8 442	10 238	9 627	9.9	69 867	65 395	56.5
Q3	..	8 622	10 241	10 134	5.1	68 623	67 592	55.5
Q4	..	9 134	10 968	10 939	4.3	71 812	71 297	58.1
1973 Q1	..	9 200	10 810	10 448	8.0	69 660	66 989	56.4
Q2	..	9 731	11 726	10 967	10.4	73 891	68 762	59.8
Q3	..	10 010	11 948	11 532	7.1	73 840	70 929	59.8
Q4	..	10 465	12 492	12 413	4.7	74 243	73 434	60.1
1974 Q1	..	10 397	12 414	11 456	12.1	70 575	64 904	57.1
Q2	..	11 114	13 137	12 543	8.0	70 886	67 466	57.4
Q3	..	12 114	14 132	13 438	7.8	73 673	69 850	59.7
Q4	..	12 990	14 820	14 871	3.6	73 593	73 629	59.6
1975 Q1	..	14 146	15 848	14 191	13.7	73 810	65 936	59.8
Q2	..	14 645	16 638	15 722	9.1	72 300	68 149	58.5
Q3	..	15 639	17 438	16 571	8.5	73 045	69 242	59.1
Q4	..	15 912	17 808	17 884	3.4	71 712	71 838	58.1
1976 Q1	..	16 024	18 466	16 966	12.2	71 455	65 424	57.9
Q2	..	16 698	19 032	17 997	9.2	71 799	67 664	58.1
Q3	..	17 306	20 288	19 044	10.0	74 681	69 861	60.5
Q4	..	17 715	20 299	20 864	1.3	71 713	73 458	58.1
1977 Q1	..	17 922	20 377	19 563	8.7	68 363	65 323	55.4
Q2	..	18 460	21 470	20 625	8.0	69 758	66 694	56.5
Q3	..	19 006	22 357	21 742	7.1	71 392	69 089	57.8
Q4	..	19 545	23 513	23 570	4.2	74 304	74 134	60.2
1978 Q1	..	20 036	23 813	22 700	9.2	72 882	69 148	59.0
Q2	..	21 218	25 425	23 699	11.2	76 071	70 578	61.6
Q3	..	21 922	26 463	25 301	8.5	77 420	73 677	62.7
Q4	..	22 491	27 399	26 893	6.4	78 456	76 656	63.5
1979 Q1	..	23 036	27 881	25 884	12.2	77 319	71 425	62.6
Q2	..	24 385	29 679	28 527	8.7	79 787	76 328	64.6
Q3	..	25 920	31 626	30 045	9.6	79 908	75 560	64.7
Q4	..	27 136	34 667	32 540	10.6	85 006	79 418	68.8
1980 Q1	..	27 903	34 304	31 799	11.9	80 619	74 392	65.3
Q2	..	29 491	36 128	32 704	13.9	81 557	73 502	66.1
Q3	..	30 702	37 475	34 861	12.0	82 682	76 574	67.0
Q4	..	31 089	38 283	36 461	9.4	82 433	78 171	66.8
1981 Q1	..	30 837	39 115	34 915	15.6	82 257	73 137	66.6
Q2	..	31 618	40 008	36 535	13.4	81 363	74 014	65.9
Q3	..	32 567	40 589	38 657	10.0	80 767	76 625	65.4
Q4	..	33 064	41 637	40 689	7.1	81 365	79 211	65.9
1982 Q1	..	33 097	42 236	38 419	14.4	80 475	72 868	65.2
Q2	..	33 968	43 411	39 752	12.5	81 124	73 955	65.7
Q3	..	34 550	44 071	42 170	9.4	81 570	77 704	66.0
Q4	..	34 904	44 786	44 772	4.9	81 848	81 468	66.3
1983 Q1	..	35 251	45 104	42 422	11.3	81 430	76 222	65.9
Q2	..	36 063	46 720	43 675	10.8	83 215	77 421	67.4
Q3	..	36 897	47 451	46 646	6.3	83 727	81 923	67.8
Q4	..	37 592	48 514	48 735	4.9	84 570	84 558	68.4
1984 Q1	..	37 620	48 994	45 533	12.2	84 548	78 191	68.4
Q2	..	38 538	50 949	47 418	11.2	85 969	79 621	69.6
Q3	..	39 250	51 109	48 976	8.7	85 683	81 711	69.3
Q4	..	40 745	53 427	52 450	6.8	88 771	86 737	71.8

See footnotes on page 40.

Sources: Office for National Statistics;
Enquiries Columns 1,2,3,5,6,8 020 7533 6003; Columns 4,7 020 7533 5998

1.6 Households'[1] disposable income and consumption

continued

Not seasonally adjusted

	£ million, current prices					£ million, 1995 prices		
	Households' income before tax							
	Total	*of which:* Wages and salaries	Gross households' disposable income[2]	Households' final consumption expenditure	Households' saving ratio[3] (percentage)	Real households' disposable income[4]	Households' final consumption expenditure	Index of real households' disposable income (1995=100)
	EWSB	QWLW	QWND	NSSG	RVGL	RVGK	NPSO	OSXR
1985 Q1	..	40 822	53 030	49 438	11.3	86 826	80 560	70.3
Q2	..	42 073	56 066	51 130	13.3	90 125	81 803	72.9
Q3	..	43 374	55 919	54 061	8.1	89 154	85 791	72.2
Q4	..	44 182	57 463	57 791	4.1	90 657	90 764	73.4
1986 Q1	..	44 309	58 041	54 333	11.5	91 043	85 024	73.7
Q2	..	45 631	60 473	56 961	10.7	93 724	88 073	75.8
Q3	..	46 508	60 898	60 549	5.7	93 673	92 912	75.8
Q4	..	47 540	62 048	63 724	2.4	93 758	96 058	75.9
1987 Q1	92 770	47 549	62 389	59 562	9.0	93 463	89 024	75.5
Q2	95 291	49 303	65 107	61 863	9.5	96 877	91 839	78.2
Q3	97 457	50 750	65 801	66 426	3.8	97 336	98 027	78.6
Q4	100 465	52 587	67 581	70 818	0.2	98 120	102 572	79.2
1988 Q1	102 786	53 248	68 723	66 758	7.5	98 993	95 979	79.9
Q2	105 439	55 009	72 373	69 806	8.3	102 433	98 616	82.7
Q3	107 944	56 801	72 985	76 099	1.3	102 163	106 320	82.5
Q4	112 047	58 985	74 271	79 525	–1.0	102 408	109 455	82.7
1989 Q1	113 087	59 600	75 813	73 998	8.0	103 153	100 515	83.3
Q2	116 245	61 505	78 917	77 587	7.5	105 086	103 154	84.0
Q3	121 231	63 332	81 930	82 673	5.0	107 907	108 709	87.1
Q4	124 057	65 704	82 921	86 221	2.0	107 364	111 454	86.7
1990 Q1	126 971	66 546	85 401	80 421	10.8	108 714	102 257	87.8
Q2	130 462	68 799	89 057	84 804	9.5	110 079	104 683	88.9
Q3	134 400	70 050	90 902	89 688	6.0	110 714	109 071	89.4
Q4	136 793	70 942	91 897	92 980	3.4	109 877	110 991	88.7
1991 Q1	139 418	71 480	94 011	85 907	12.5	110 987	101 261	89.6
Q2	141 804	72 562	97 259	89 427	11.7	110 756	101 679	89.4
Q3	145 854	73 592	99 989	95 068	8.4	112 779	107 043	91.1
Q4	146 500	74 271	100 057	98 479	5.0	111 580	109 616	90.1
1992 Q1	150 028	75 275	101 936	91 104	13.1	112 171	100 039	90.6
Q2	152 318	75 775	107 345	94 633	14.1	116 555	102 520	94.1
Q3	154 458	75 669	107 347	99 821	10.2	116 702	108 253	94.2
Q4	156 665	76 299	108 210	102 395	8.6	117 210	110 624	94.7
1993 Q1	156 432	76 474	108 807	96 399	13.1	116 274	102 773	93.9
Q2	159 209	77 175	114 048	100 107	14.0	119 517	104 750	96.5
Q3	160 147	77 783	113 704	106 996	8.6	119 131	111 910	96.2
Q4	163 993	78 820	116 251	109 587	8.1	121 691	114 506	98.3
1994 Q1	162 747	79 306	114 509	102 696	11.3	119 476	106 977	96.5
Q2	164 967	79 569	116 989	105 195	12.0	120 422	108 110	97.2
Q3	168 547	80 502	117 692	111 996	7.7	120 808	114 790	97.6
Q4	170 677	82 168	119 693	114 662	6.8	122 002	116 704	98.5
1995 Q1	172 266	83 112	120 884	107 124	12.8	122 826	108 680	99.2
Q2	175 643	83 402	124 165	110 379	13.4	124 128	110 183	100.2
Q3	178 053	83 876	124 694	117 323	8.6	123 699	116 227	99.9
Q4	179 627	85 199	125 594	120 108	6.5	124 684	119 081	100.7
1996 Q1	182 742	86 871	126 063	114 176	12.0	124 039	112 181	100.2
Q2	184 728	86 999	131 650	117 764	13.3	127 623	114 000	103.1
Q3	192 303	87 844	131 447	125 366	7.8	126 711	120 688	102.3
Q4	189 234	89 833	132 929	128 920	4.9	127 772	123 753	103.2
1997 Q1	192 064	92 354	131 387	121 445	9.8	125 444	115 768	101.3
Q2	197 700	92 559	140 724	125 605	14.0	133 427	118 902	107.7
Q3	199 064	94 352	139 993	133 692	7.6	131 871	125 744	106.5
Q4	200 086	96 378	143 414	137 167	5.9	134 579	128 522	108.7
1998 Q1	202 683	99 706	131 751	129 389	4.7	123 033	120 826	99.5
Q2	206 268 206 093	98 981	146 266	134 627	10.9	135 011	124 266	109.2
Q3	206 588 206 201	100 234	141 806	141 699	3.5	130 710	130 610	105.7
Q4	210 555	102 492	149 673	146 108	4.0	137 053	133 788	110.8
1999 Q1	211 418	105 963	136 876	137 964	2.0	125 143	126 126	101.2
Q2	222 373	105 095	156 448	144 082	11.3	141 334	130 150	114.3
Q3	217 045	106 059	147 511	148 914	2.2	133 416	134 672	107.9
Q4	223 258	109 230	159 424	155 946	3.9	143 614	140 468	116.2
2000 Q1	223 229	113 055	143 739	145 916	1.2	128 720	130 670	104.1

See footnotes on page 40.

Sources: Office for National Statistics;
Enquiries Columns 1,2,3,5,6,8 020 7533 6003; Columns 4,7 020 7533 5998

1.6 Households'[1] disposable income and consumption

continued

Seasonally adjusted

	£ million, current prices					£ million, 1995 prices		
	Households' income before tax		Gross households' disposable income[2]	Households' final consumption expenditure	Households' saving ratio[3] (percentage)	Real households' disposable income[4]	Households' final consumption expenditure	Index of real households' disposable income (1995=100)
	Total	*of which:* Wages and salaries						
	GDUT	ROYJ	RPHQ	RPQM	NRJS	NRJR	NPSP	OSXS
1955 Q1	..	2 561	3 043	..	..	40 091	41 447	32.4
Q2	..	2 614	3 101	..	..	40 653	41 656	32.9
Q3	..	2 671	3 178	..	..	41 176	42 245	33.3
Q4	..	2 724	3 198	..	..	40 476	41 972	32.7
1956 Q1	..	2 792	3 296	..	..	41 615	42 084	33.7
Q2	..	2 869	3 335	..	..	41 251	41 969	33.4
Q3	..	2 914	3 389	..	..	41 889	41 996	33.9
Q4	..	2 948	3 405	..	..	41 630	42 114	33.7
1957 Q1	..	2 985	3 457	..	..	42 062	42 389	34.0
Q2	..	3 002	3 502	..	..	42 310	42 703	34.2
Q3	..	3 074	3 554	..	..	42 364	43 153	34.3
Q4	..	3 098	3 591	..	..	42 431	43 381	34.3
1958 Q1	..	3 131	3 662	..	..	43 113	43 735	34.9
Q2	..	3 098	3 660	..	..	42 842	43 612	34.6
Q3	..	3 125	3 703	..	..	43 191	44 122	34.9
Q4	..	3 178	3 728	..	..	43 215	44 948	34.9
1959 Q1	..	3 209	3 807	..	..	44 003	44 987	35.6
Q2	..	3 248	3 911	..	..	45 443	45 801	36.7
Q3	..	3 294	3 945	..	..	45 745	46 032	37.0
Q4	..	3 365	4 003	..	..	46 170	47 226	37.3
1960 Q1	..	3 404	4 093	..	..	47 213	47 798	38.2
Q2	..	3 502	4 193	..	..	48 029	47 554	38.8
Q3	..	3 589	4 260	..	..	48 832	47 863	39.5
Q4	..	3 621	4 340	..	..	49 352	47 863	39.9
1961 Q1	..	3 717	4 411	..	..	49 840	48 725	40.3
Q2	..	3 808	4 529	..	..	50 631	48 667	40.9
Q3	..	3 836	4 584	..	..	50 670	48 902	41.0
Q4	..	3 871	4 583	..	..	50 405	48 939	40.8
1962 Q1	..	3 932	4 640	..	..	50 389	49 314	40.7
Q2	..	3 987	4 704	..	..	50 361	50 105	40.7
Q3	..	4 049	4 776	..	..	51 174	49 795	41.4
Q4	..	4 068	4 860	..	..	52 048	50 413	42.1
1963 Q1	..	4 084	4 862	4 786	4.5	51 778	50 773	41.8
Q2	..	4 165	4 930	4 953	2.6	52 299	52 338	42.3
Q3	..	4 241	5 113	5 014	5.1	54 180	52 940	43.8
Q4	..	4 323	5 206	5 073	5.6	54 426	52 851	44.0
1964 Q1	..	4 416	5 266	5 151	5.3	54 837	53 466	44.3
Q2	..	4 505	5 356	5 228	5.4	55 077	53 583	44.5
Q3	..	4 603	5 486	5 325	6.1	55 730	53 889	45.0
Q4	..	4 704	5 603	5 452	5.4	56 164	54 396	45.4
1965 Q1	..	4 752	5 650	5 509	5.4	55 873	54 332	45.2
Q2	..	4 827	5 725	5 561	5.6	55 946	54 194	45.3
Q3	..	4 965	5 883	5 673	6.2	56 973	54 785	46.1
Q4	..	5 054	5 982	5 754	6.7	57 269	54 922	46.3
1966 Q1	..	5 172	6 256	5 854	9.0	59 607	55 623	48.2
Q2	..	5 232	6 072	5 972	4.4	57 197	56 105	46.3
Q3	..	5 257	6 119	5 936	5.5	57 020	55 167	46.1
Q4	..	5 281	6 234	6 007	6.4	57 429	55 194	46.5
1967 Q1	..	5 235	6 213	6 060	5.1	57 162	55 600	46.3
Q2	..	5 421	6 364	6 164	6.0	58 319	56 325	47.2
Q3	..	5 500	6 555	6 319	6.5	59 824	57 508	48.4
Q4	..	5 581	6 562	6 444	4.8	59 173	57 942	47.9
1968 Q1	..	5 723	6 734	6 708	3.6	60 100	59 697	48.6
Q2	..	5 711	6 876	6 555	7.4	60 312	57 335	48.8
Q3	..	5 803	6 822	6 747	4.1	59 171	58 356	47.9
Q4	..	5 920	6 960	6 891	4.0	59 191	58 427	47.9
1969 Q1	..	6 086	7 162	6 985	5.3	59 914	58 263	48.5
Q2	..	6 109	7 262	7 078	5.5	60 491	58 789	48.9
Q3	..	6 194	7 298	7 148	4.8	60 258	58 848	48.8
Q4	..	6 416	7 449	7 343	4.2	60 254	59 212	48.8

See footnotes on page 40.

Sources: Office for National Statistics;
Enquiries Columns 1,2,3,5,6,8 020 7533 6003; Columns 4,7 020 7533 5998

1.6 Households'[1] disposable income and consumption

continued

Seasonally adjusted

	£ million, current prices					£ million, 1995 prices		
	Households' income before tax		Gross households' disposable income[2]	Households' final consumption expenditure	Households' saving ratio[3] (percentage)	Real households' disposable income[4]	Households' final consumption expenditure	Index of real households' disposable income (1995=100)
	Total	*of which:* Wages and salaries						
	GDUT	ROYJ	RPHQ	RPQM	NRJS	NRJR	NPSP	OSXS
1970 Q1	..	6 562	7 589	7 468	4.4	60 551	59 393	49.0
Q2	..	6 895	8 012	7 671	7.0	63 179	60 306	51.1
Q3	..	7 080	8 140	7 904	5.8	63 325	61 302	51.2
Q4	..	7 227	8 327	8 100	6.0	62 851	60 957	50.9
1971 Q1	..	7 352	8 319	8 267	3.4	61 288	60 714	49.6
Q2	..	7 476	8 799	8 641	5.0	63 415	62 097	51.3
Q3	..	7 712	8 962	8 905	4.1	63 823	63 233	51.6
Q4	..	7 857	9 190	9 110	4.2	64 370	63 639	52.1
1972 Q1	..	8 124	9 515	9 398	4.8	65 604	64 614	53.1
Q2	..	8 404	10 225	9 694	8.8	69 944	66 140	56.6
Q3	..	8 625	10 251	10 033	6.1	68 789	67 153	55.7
Q4	..	9 023	10 707	10 409	6.7	69 776	67 671	56.5
1973 Q1	..	9 359	11 129	11 004	5.2	71 348	70 336	57.7
Q2	..	9 695	11 555	11 085	7.9	72 963	69 774	59.1
Q3	..	9 994	11 874	11 384	7.7	73 623	70 395	59.6
Q4	..	10 358	12 418	11 763	9.1	73 700	69 609	59.7
1974 Q1	..	10 574	12 634	12 089	8.2	71 520	68 280	57.9
Q2	..	11 098	13 025	12 686	6.0	70 578	68 573	57.2
Q3	..	12 058	14 055	13 315	8.1	73 411	69 402	59.5
Q4	..	12 885	14 789	14 093	8.4	73 218	69 594	59.3
1975 Q1	..	14 362	16 101	14 966	10.0	74 537	69 195	60.4
Q2	..	14 630	16 484	15 913	6.9	71 917	69 283	58.2
Q3	..	15 534	17 346	16 369	9.0	72 919	68 699	59.0
Q4	..	15 816	17 801	16 959	8.2	71 494	67 988	57.9
1976 Q1	..	16 244	18 665	17 677	8.9	72 362	68 433	58.6
Q2	..	16 688	18 887	18 237	7.2	71 464	68 879	57.9
Q3	..	17 166	20 062	18 889	9.6	73 991	69 514	59.9
Q4	..	17 645	20 471	19 872	6.6	71 831	69 581	58.2
1977 Q1	..	18 150	20 772	20 325	6.2	69 923	68 112	56.6
Q2	..	18 452	21 282	20 919	5.8	69 309	68 003	56.1
Q3	..	18 843	22 173	21 624	6.7	70 744	68 831	57.3
Q4	..	19 488	23 490	22 402	8.8	73 841	70 294	59.8
1978 Q1	..	20 286	24 052	23 566	6.2	73 479	71 950	59.5
Q2	..	21 209	25 291	24 042	9.1	75 846	71 836	61.4
Q3	..	21 746	26 488	25 072	9.2	77 752	73 364	63.0
Q4	..	22 426	27 269	25 648	10.3	77 752	72 909	63.0
1979 Q1	..	23 329	28 352	26 707	10.3	78 673	73 954	63.7
Q2	..	24 390	29 444	28 987	6.4	79 511	77 981	64.4
Q3	..	25 709	31 555	29 672	10.3	80 103	75 055	64.9
Q4	..	27 049	34 502	31 320	13.4	83 733	75 741	67.8
1980 Q1	..	28 254	34 592	32 974	8.8	81 022	77 072	65.6
Q2	..	29 543	36 021	33 290	11.9	81 400	75 013	65.9
Q3	..	30 447	37 273	34 322	12.7	82 743	75 990	67.0
Q4	..	30 941	38 304	34 868	13.3	82 126	74 564	66.5
1981 Q1	..	31 211	39 406	36 229	12.4	82 469	75 678	66.8
Q2	..	31 661	39 713	37 170	11.3	81 117	75 761	65.7
Q3	..	32 316	40 350	37 978	10.8	80 835	75 941	65.5
Q4	..	32 898	41 880	39 014	11.3	81 331	75 607	65.9
1982 Q1	..	33 482	42 262	39 742	10.8	80 325	75 357	65.0
Q2	..	34 025	43 679	40 424	11.6	82 075	75 785	66.5
Q3	..	34 320	43 729	41 593	9.7	81 220	77 084	65.8
Q4	..	34 692	44 834	42 935	8.8	81 397	77 769	65.9
1983 Q1	..	35 625	45 496	43 884	8.4	82 118	78 999	66.5
Q2	..	36 128	46 830	44 675	8.9	83 561	79 505	67.6
Q3	..	36 694	47 297	46 017	7.1	83 356	80 885	67.5
Q4	..	37 356	48 166	46 471	8.6	83 907	80 735	67.9
1984 Q1	..	37 972	49 500	47 233	9.1	85 378	81 237	69.1
Q2	..	38 611	50 331	48 378	8.4	85 166	81 617	68.9
Q3	..	39 104	51 264	48 490	9.8	85 970	81 069	69.6
Q4	..	40 466	53 384	49 834	11.3	88 457	82 337	71.6

See footnotes on page 40.

Sources: Office for National Statistics;
Enquiries Columns 1,2,3,5,6,8 020 71 533 6003; Columns 4,7 020 7533 5998

1.6 Households'[1] disposable income and consumption

continued

Seasonally adjusted

	£ million, current prices					£ million, 1995 prices		
	Households' income before tax							
	Total	*of which:* Wages and salaries	Gross households' disposable income[2]	Households' final consumption expenditure	Households' saving ratio[3] (percentage)	Real households' disposable income[4]	Households' final consumption expenditure	Index of real households' disposable income (1995=100)
	GDUT	ROYJ	RPHQ	RPQM	NRJS	NRJR	NPSP	OSXS
1985 Q1	..	41 669	53 783	51 245	8.8	87 898	83 525	71.1
Q2	..	42 157	55 549	52 235	10.6	89 565	83 983	72.5
Q3	..	42 797	55 749	53 632	8.4	88 842	85 221	71.9
Q4	..	43 828	57 397	54 838	8.8	90 457	86 189	73.2
1986 Q1	..	44 767	58 202	56 618	7.6	91 183	88 633	73.8
Q2	..	45 655	60 537	58 473	8.2	93 810	90 541	75.9
Q3	..	46 448	60 854	59 552	7.0	93 268	91 205	75.5
Q4	..	47 118	61 867	60 428	7.1	93 937	91 688	76.0
1987 Q1	93 114	47 999	62 834	62 278	5.5	93 988	92 895	75.9
Q2	95 522	49 347	64 483	63 539	6.2	96 001	94 332	77.5
Q3	97 313	50 684	65 510	65 354	5.0	96 631	96 134	78.0
Q4	100 034	52 159	68 051	67 498	5.5	99 176	98 101	80.1
1988 Q1	103 115	53 698	69 175	69 979	3.7	99 464	100 360	80.3
Q2	105 652	55 049	71 531	71 640	4.8	101 398	101 298	81.9
Q3	107 813	56 742	72 601	74 405	3.0	101 456	103 725	81.9
Q4	111 636	58 554	75 045	76 164	4.2	103 679	104 987	83.7
1989 Q1	113 311	60 026	76 321	77 759	4.0	103 710	105 404	83.7
Q2	116 496	61 527	77 985	79 508	4.2	104 059	105 847	84.0
Q3	121 084	63 279	81 541	80 519	7.0	107 325	105 746	86.7
Q4	123 729	65 309	83 734	82 693	6.9	108 416	106 835	87.5
1990 Q1	127 193	66 920	85 863	84 309	7.1	109 100	106 900	88.1
Q2	130 820	68 786	88 216	86 766	6.7	109 449	107 412	88.4
Q3	134 123	70 025	90 508	87 726	7.6	110 162	106 535	89.0
Q4	136 490	70 606	92 670	89 092	8.1	110 673	106 155	89.4
1991 Q1	139 694	71 766	94 768	90 004	9.2	111 714	105 849	90.2
Q2	142 103	72 526	96 301	91 607	8.8	110 173	104 562	89.0
Q3	145 638	73 623	99 800	93 210	9.9	112 508	104 832	90.9
Q4	146 141	73 990	100 447	94 060	9.5	111 707	104 356	90.2
1992 Q1	150 345	75 272	102 721	94 926	10.4	112 892	104 082	91.2
Q2	152 549	75 810	106 342	96 762	11.5	116 037	105 325	93.7
Q3	154 363	75 854	107 406	97 610	12.0	116 786	105 867	94.3
Q4	156 212	76 082	108 369	98 655	11.8	116 923	106 162	94.4
1993 Q1	156 889	76 368	109 829	100 374	10.8	117 183	106 817	94.6
Q2	159 395	77 290	113 077	102 453	11.3	119 163	107 780	96.2
Q3	159 944	77 997	113 615	104 395	10.4	119 269	109 393	96.3
Q4	163 553	78 597	116 289	105 867	11.1	120 998	109 950	97.7
1994 Q1	163 248	79 107	115 613	106 754	9.2	120 244	110 834	97.1
Q2	165 072	79 712	115 890	107 980	8.7	119 553	111 198	96.5
Q3	168 199	80 753	117 588	109 093	9.6	120 783	111 862	97.5
Q4	170 419	81 973	119 792	110 722	10.0	122 128	112 687	98.6
1995 Q1	173 045	82 768	122 518	111 749	10.7	123 794	112 723	100.0
Q2	175 578	83 599	122 830	113 181	9.9	123 199	113 332	99.5
Q3	177 468	84 192	124 325	114 086	10.3	123 902	113 511	100.1
Q4	179 498	85 030	125 664	115 918	10.3	124 442	114 605	100.5
1996 Q1	183 732	86 312	129 094	118 987	10.7	126 456	116 376	102.1
Q2	184 559	87 330	129 955	120 557	9.6	126 575	117 242	102.2
Q3	191 301	88 200	130 707	122 284	8.9	126 209	117 895	101.9
Q4	189 415	89 705	132 333	124 398	8.6	126 905	119 109	102.5
1997 Q1	193 218	91 628	135 897	126 219	9.6	129 391	119 999	104.5
Q2	196 822	93 159	138 577	128 188	10.6	131 929	121 871	106.5
Q3	198 460	94 624	139 961	130 591	9.4	131 906	122 891	106.5
Q4	200 414	96 232	141 083	132 911	7.8	132 095	124 238	106.7
1998 Q1	205 940	98 257	141 547	135 013	7.7	131 929	125 830	106.7
Q2	205 442	99 378	140 985	137 156	5.2	130 568	127 036	105.6
Q3	207 834	101 109	142 097	138 846	5.0	130 803	127 816	105.8
Q4	210 977	102 669	144 867	140 808	5.3	132 507	128 808	107.2
1999 Q1	212 109	104 327	145 263	143 353	4.4	132 650	130 909	107.3
Q2	219 235	105 621	151 181	145 672	6.6	137 174	132 198	110.9
Q3	217 840	107 188	149 671	147 436	4.1	135 213	133 189	109.4
Q4	224 541	109 211	154 144	150 445	5.0	138 470	135 120	112.0
2000 Q1	224 488	110 868	152 985	151 714	3.8	137 176	136 036	110.9

See footnotes on page 40.

Sources: Office for National Statistics;
Enquiries Columns 1,2,3,5,6,8 020 7533 6003; Columns 4,7 020 7533 5998

1.7 Household final consumption expenditure-component categories[1]

£ million, current prices

	Durable goods	Food (Household expend-iture)[2]	Alcoholic drink and tobacco	Clothing and footwear	Energy products	Other goods	Rent, water and sewerage charges	Catering	Transport and communicat-ion	Financial services	Other services[3]	Total
	AEIT	CCDW	CDFH	CDDE	CCEC	ABZN	ABRG	CDEY	ABOZ	CEGK	ABOY	ABPB
1946	251	1 887	1 298	638	315	681	..	..	..	..	..	..
1947	343	2 166	1 415	736	341	769	..	..	..	..	..	..
1948	386	2 320	1 566	902	348	828	508	..	..	..	..	8 417
1949	454	2 508	1 508	1 013	367	879	522	..	..	..	..	8 771
1950	526	2 758	1 500	1 063	400	917	541	..	..	..	..	9 257
1951	597	3 022	1 574	1 116	445	1 001	562	..	..	..	..	9 998
1952	624	2 824	1 600	1 097	485	1 032	587	..	..	..	..	10 526
1953	770	3 122	1 632	1 115	522	1 074	625	..	..	..	..	11 226
1954	902	3 295	1 649	1 205	570	1 139	655	..	..	..	..	11 906
1955	1 007	3 585	1 713	1 297	634	1 243	678	..	..	..	..	12 832
1956	953	3 787	1 801	1 378	716	1 333	691	..	..	..	..	13 494
1957	1 077	3 928	1 887	1 439	748	1 414	751	..	..	..	..	14 227
1958	1 257	4 028	1 940	1 458	843	1 479	897	..	..	..	..	15 013
1959	1 471	4 157	1 981	1 525	867	1 559	966	..	..	..	..	15 802
1960	1 510	4 225	2 103	1 664	963	1 663	1 010	..	..	..	..	16 573
1961	1 457	4 366	2 292	1 729	1 041	1 781	1 072	..	..	..	..	17 422
1962	1 530	4 560	2 403	1 771	1 192	1 843	1 180	..	..	..	..	18 438
1963	1 730	4 689	2 518	1 873	1 309	1 922	1 322	1 164	1 144	294	1 600	19 565
1964	1 895	4 889	2 733	1 971	1 374	2 074	1 447	1 230	1 232	317	1 706	20 868
1965	1 916	5 059	2 927	2 099	1 546	2 206	1 621	1 301	1 344	340	1 792	22 151
1966	1 905	5 297	3 130	2 154	1 688	2 339	1 766	1 361	1 468	366	1 917	23 391
1967	2 054	5 485	3 251	2 219	1 804	2 466	1 912	1 392	1 582	425	1 989	24 579
1968	2 306	5 696	3 448	2 375	2 042	2 765	2 088	1 469	1 701	498	2 063	26 451
1969	2 250	6 035	3 723	2 505	2 225	2 910	2 312	1 559	1 849	533	2 153	28 054
1970	2 607	6 429	4 020	2 753	2 339	3 208	2 597	1 700	2 025	591	2 278	30 547
1971	3 331	7 105	4 284	2 990	2 547	3 600	2 931	1 871	2 320	708	2 563	34 250
1972	4 186	7 614	4 718	3 370	2 874	4 146	3 365	2 155	2 602	845	2 905	38 780
1973	4 597	8 751	5 361	3 860	3 129	4 725	3 937	2 539	3 169	907	3 385	44 360
1974	4 658	10 028	6 144	4 498	3 966	5 698	4 839	2 931	3 668	941	3 755	51 126
1975	5 872	12 313	7 583	5 206	5 119	6 769	5 882	3 600	4 709	1 192	4 636	62 881
1976	6 986	14 459	8 806	5 797	6 057	7 712	6 942	4 271	5 778	1 255	4 997	73 060
1977	7 754	16 596	10 173	6 630	6 895	8 946	7 873	5 107	6 682	1 512	5 336	83 504
1978	10 168	18 373	11 168	7 832	7 223	10 610	8 992	5 840	7 926	1 670	6 566	96 368
1979	13 087	20 988	12 899	9 168	8 846	12 583	10 599	6 874	9 355	2 017	8 042	114 458
1980	13 495	23 655	14 776	9 873	11 001	14 601	12 567	8 288	11 627	2 394	10 386	132 663
1981	13 942	24 946	16 667	10 155	13 422	15 803	15 201	8 820	13 128	2 792	12 244	147 120
1982	15 439	26 490	17 884	10 925	15 027	17 212	17 431	9 461	14 078	3 363	13 687	160 997
1983	18 250	28 061	19 479	12 120	16 220	18 764	19 049	10 928	15 242	4 215	14 553	176 881
1984	18 638	29 274	20 938	13 168	16 973	20 637	19 950	12 509	16 632	4 848	15 677	189 244
1985	20 166	30 657	22 657	14 912	18 578	23 054	21 621	13 875	18 622	5 621	16 837	206 600
1986	22 878	32 574	23 889	16 646	18 219	25 880	23 384	16 186	21 191	7 429	20 572	228 848
1987	26 322	34 402	25 116	17 848	18 628	28 890	25 357	17 885	23 835	9 260	23 600	251 143
1988	32 272	36 491	26 584	19 023	19 291	32 584	27 979	23 736	26 411	10 644	28 410	283 425
1989	35 283	39 143	27 755	19 847	20 460	36 313	31 295	27 359	28 321	12 457	32 260	310 493
1990	34 517	41 817	30 009	21 212	22 422	39 659	36 543	30 076	30 969	13 856	35 412	336 492
1991	32 867	44 044	32 680	22 209	24 955	42 171	42 411	30 671	32 843	14 549	38 385	357 785
1992	33 514	45 193	33 553	23 404	25 399	44 461	48 637	32 287	34 610	14 801	41 288	377 147
1993	35 374	46 334	34 865	24 777	26 136	46 738	52 405	35 154	37 840	16 316	43 169	399 108
1994	37 880	47 122	36 624	26 893	26 857	48 935	56 297	36 459	39 603	16 226	46 366	419 262
1995	39 496	49 274	37 456	28 347	27 118	51 947	59 798	37 727	41 360	16 784	49 146	438 453
1996	43 679	52 513	39 618	29 564	28 822	57 094	62 197	40 786	43 211	18 958	51 399	467 841
1997	49 925	53 188	40 858	31 115	28 593	61 921	66 421	42 652	46 247	21 461	55 926	498 307
1998	53 239	53 789	41 938	32 376	27 998	67 533	70 792	46 277	50 246	23 847	62 816	530 851
1999	54 867	54 862	44 611	33 530	28 861	72 867	77 916	48 708	54 390	25 917	67 840	564 369

1 More detailed estimates of Household Final Consumption Expenditure expressed in both current and constant prices appear in the ONS publication *Consumer Trends.* Any queries relating to Household Final Consumption expenditure should be addressed to the Office for National Statistics Consumers' Expenditure Branch on 0171 533 5998.

2 Before 1952 estimates for catering are included under Food; thereafter they are included under Other services.

3 Including the adjustments for international travel, etc.

Source: Office for National Statistics: Enquiries 020 7533 5998

1.7 Household final consumption expenditure-component categories[1]

continued

£ million, current prices, not seasonally adjusted

	Durable goods	Food (Household expend-iture)[2]	Alcoholic drink and tobacco	Clothing and footwear	Energy products	Other goods	Rent, water and sewerage charges	Catering	Transport and communicat-ion	Financial services	Other services[3]	Total
	AEIT	CCDW	CDFH	CDDE	CCEC	ABZN	ABRG	CDEY	ABOZ	CEGK	ABOY	ABPB
1955 Q1	237	851	357	262	170	271	168	..	..	..	..	2 923
Q2	238	896	414	332	155	285	169	..	..	..	..	3 154
Q3	243	878	462	301	145	315	170	..	..	..	..	3 253
Q4	289	960	480	402	164	372	171	..	..	..	..	3 502
1956 Q1	231	909	382	281	195	293	173	..	..	..	..	3 102
Q2	243	967	438	347	177	310	170	..	..	..	..	3 360
Q3	223	914	472	327	160	334	172	..	..	..	..	3 386
Q4	256	997	509	423	184	396	176	..	..	..	..	3 646
1957 Q1	230	929	407	297	196	319	178	..	..	..	..	3 242
Q2	274	977	464	368	182	324	182	..	..	..	..	3 517
Q3	271	978	489	340	168	352	186	..	..	..	..	3 602
Q4	302	1 044	527	434	202	419	205	..	..	..	..	3 866
1958 Q1	286	964	423	302	238	331	213	..	..	..	..	3 467
Q2	305	1 013	477	368	210	344	221	..	..	..	..	3 714
Q3	288	985	508	339	181	370	230	..	..	..	..	3 762
Q4	378	1 066	532	449	214	434	233	..	..	..	..	4 070
1959 Q1	325	1 008	418	309	254	342	240	..	..	..	..	3 639
Q2	382	1 039	481	388	208	370	238	..	..	..	..	3 928
Q3	347	1 015	522	348	186	385	243	..	..	..	..	3 949
Q4	417	1 095	560	480	219	462	245	..	..	..	..	4 286
1960 Q1	403	1 031	439	330	269	368	247	..	..	..	..	3 869
Q2	414	1 065	527	426	222	393	252	..	..	..	..	4 163
Q3	352	1 033	547	388	211	417	255	..	..	..	..	4 150
Q4	341	1 096	590	520	261	485	256	..	..	..	..	4 391
1961 Q1	358	1 056	477	358	294	392	262	..	..	..	..	4 033
Q2	409	1 094	562	428	243	421	266	..	..	..	..	4 353
Q3	353	1 091	602	404	229	451	270	..	..	..	..	4 410
Q4	337	1 125	651	539	275	517	274	..	..	..	..	4 626
1962 Q1	357	1 112	504	350	339	412	284	..	..	..	..	4 252
Q2	440	1 154	608	443	292	436	292	..	..	..	..	4 681
Q3	364	1 114	619	425	258	466	298	..	..	..	..	4 634
Q4	369	1 180	672	553	303	529	306	..	..	..	..	4 871
1963 Q1	396	1 143	508	364	395	416	317	245	248	71	353	4 456
Q2	472	1 183	638	457	305	474	333	301	288	79	406	4 936
Q3	434	1 150	663	453	282	490	333	345	330	68	436	4 984
Q4	428	1 213	709	599	327	542	339	273	278	76	405	5 189
1964 Q1	469	1 190	554	394	388	452	341	259	268	75	401	4 791
Q2	510	1 228	665	483	340	511	352	315	306	83	419	5 212
Q3	461	1 192	725	467	298	521	368	369	362	75	465	5 303
Q4	455	1 279	789	627	348	590	386	287	296	84	421	5 562
1965 Q1	519	1 217	602	427	432	488	393	275	284	78	416	5 131
Q2	501	1 261	720	513	382	541	403	333	336	88	438	5 516
Q3	456	1 246	773	505	345	556	409	387	394	79	496	5 646
Q4	440	1 335	832	654	387	621	416	306	330	95	442	5 858
1966 Q1	516	1 282	666	450	468	521	419	289	314	86	445	5 456
Q2	545	1 334	784	529	423	581	433	347	371	97	470	5 914
Q3	439	1 311	814	511	365	589	447	408	423	84	521	5 912
Q4	405	1 370	866	664	432	648	467	317	360	99	481	6 109
1967 Q1	474	1 327	697	461	498	537	467	298	349	92	461	5 661
Q2	510	1 370	807	530	438	599	474	353	398	111	492	6 082
Q3	516	1 370	845	531	387	620	482	414	457	101	539	6 262
Q4	554	1 418	902	697	481	710	489	327	378	121	497	6 574
1968 Q1	675	1 387	750	490	573	620	494	309	369	109	480	6 256
Q2	524	1 410	838	571	481	657	512	375	423	129	498	6 418
Q3	536	1 416	879	569	458	699	528	438	490	122	554	6 689
Q4	571	1 483	981	745	530	789	554	347	419	138	531	7 088
1969 Q1	545	1 461	782	507	644	638	562	331	397	127	504	6 498
Q2	592	1 504	909	618	500	701	573	400	462	139	511	6 909
Q3	556	1 493	967	597	466	736	582	454	544	120	566	7 081
Q4	557	1 577	1 065	783	615	835	595	374	446	147	572	7 566

See footnotes on page 47.

Source: Office for National Statistics: Enquiries 020 7533 5998

1.7 Household final consumption expenditure-component categories[1]

continued

£ million, current prices, not seasonally adjusted

	Durable goods	Food (Household expend-iture)[2]	Alcoholic drink and tobacco	Clothing and footwear	Energy products	Other goods	Rent, water and sewerage charges	Catering	Transport and communicat-ion	Financial services	Other services[3]	Total
	AEIT	CCDW	CDFH	CDDE	CCEC	ABZN	ABRG	CDEY	ABOZ	CEGK	ABOY	ABPB
1970 Q1	616	1 525	813	547	676	688	613	355	431	137	528	6 929
Q2	667	1 608	979	664	528	765	630	439	498	154	536	7 468
Q3	647	1 606	1 070	657	498	821	658	496	598	138	618	7 807
Q4	677	1 690	1 158	885	637	934	696	410	498	162	596	8 343
1971 Q1	744	1 656	877	591	699	764	706	399	488	151	588	7 663
Q2	808	1 776	1 053	739	588	857	732	484	583	183	611	8 414
Q3	888	1 796	1 116	709	547	914	741	539	676	175	699	8 800
Q4	891	1 877	1 238	951	713	1 065	752	449	573	199	665	9 373
1972 Q1	948	1 856	963	667	758	894	762	454	561	198	668	8 729
Q2	1 042	1 863	1 161	793	661	962	821	557	645	225	689	9 419
Q3	1 058	1 902	1 212	818	647	1 041	868	623	746	197	806	9 918
Q4	1 138	1 993	1 382	1 092	808	1 249	914	521	650	225	742	10 714
1973 Q1	1 275	2 048	1 058	823	850	1 046	925	536	676	212	762	10 211
Q2	1 049	2 141	1 318	896	717	1 088	956	683	803	236	835	10 722
Q3	1 119	2 246	1 398	907	676	1 176	1 004	731	890	215	915	11 277
Q4	1 154	2 316	1 587	1 234	886	1 415	1 052	589	800	244	873	12 150
1974 Q1	1 081	2 293	1 218	883	939	1 204	1 112	607	770	230	844	11 181
Q2	1 071	2 454	1 489	1 043	894	1 298	1 165	761	916	241	924	12 256
Q3	1 186	2 577	1 557	1 107	916	1 435	1 252	863	1 025	225	993	13 136
Q4	1 320	2 704	1 880	1 465	1 217	1 761	1 310	700	957	245	994	14 553
1975 Q1	1 388	2 772	1 438	1 099	1 310	1 483	1 377	754	939	285	1 009	13 854
Q2	1 485	3 043	1 810	1 246	1 168	1 586	1 436	919	1 177	307	1 186	15 363
Q3	1 509	3 221	2 008	1 249	1 128	1 675	1 493	1 079	1 340	291	1 196	16 189
Q4	1 490	3 277	2 327	1 612	1 513	2 025	1 576	848	1 253	309	1 245	17 475
1976 Q1	1 701	3 323	1 683	1 174	1 656	1 697	1 639	867	1 224	328	1 247	16 539
Q2	1 629	3 487	2 153	1 369	1 324	1 749	1 705	1 077	1 460	307	1 289	17 549
Q3	1 772	3 711	2 340	1 401	1 284	1 904	1 771	1 290	1 633	301	1 174	18 581
Q4	1 884	3 938	2 630	1 853	1 793	2 362	1 827	1 037	1 461	319	1 287	20 391
1977 Q1	1 975	3 883	2 045	1 326	1 879	1 935	1 871	1 048	1 445	364	1 307	19 078
Q2	1 759	4 129	2 517	1 479	1 611	2 017	1 952	1 280	1 694	357	1 337	20 132
Q3	2 032	4 159	2 612	1 641	1 496	2 233	1 992	1 536	1 923	391	1 225	21 240
Q4	1 988	4 425	2 999	2 184	1 909	2 761	2 058	1 243	1 620	400	1 467	23 054
1978 Q1	2 567	4 322	2 317	1 552	2 048	2 286	2 133	1 237	1 707	393	1 610	22 172
Q2	2 353	4 469	2 759	1 773	1 635	2 459	2 206	1 473	1 970	405	1 649	23 151
Q3	2 820	4 765	2 820	1 962	1 531	2 619	2 284	1 727	2 239	432	1 536	24 735
Q4	2 428	4 817	3 272	2 545	2 009	3 246	2 369	1 403	2 010	440	1 771	26 310
1979 Q1	3 127	4 793	2 522	1 784	2 390	2 619	2 467	1 380	1 915	475	1 815	25 287
Q2	3 696	5 104	3 117	2 158	1 864	2 929	2 595	1 684	2 335	502	1 930	27 914
Q3	3 165	5 482	3 349	2 234	2 002	3 118	2 713	2 071	2 721	503	2 045	29 403
Q4	3 099	5 609	3 911	2 992	2 590	3 917	2 824	1 739	2 384	537	2 252	31 854
1980 Q1	3 979	5 652	3 135	2 051	2 909	3 246	2 922	1 793	2 504	565	2 309	31 065
Q2	3 136	5 891	3 537	2 295	2 366	3 434	3 062	2 072	2 919	575	2 643	31 930
Q3	3 503	6 046	3 760	2 396	2 442	3 546	3 207	2 479	3 342	616	2 713	34 050
Q4	2 877	6 066	4 344	3 131	3 284	4 375	3 376	1 944	2 862	638	2 721	35 618
1981 Q1	3 708	5 894	3 427	2 153	3 480	3 572	3 547	1 958	2 828	660	2 814	34 041
Q2	3 314	6 095	4 096	2 308	2 998	3 723	3 733	2 222	3 381	693	3 067	35 630
Q3	3 664	6 417	4 265	2 395	2 934	3 830	3 882	2 585	3 815	706	3 228	37 721
Q4	3 256	6 540	4 879	3 299	4 010	4 678	4 039	2 055	3 104	733	3 135	39 728
1982 Q1	3 852	6 359	3 816	2 263	4 009	3 846	4 204	2 075	3 069	793	3 147	37 433
Q2	3 480	6 732	4 346	2 479	3 340	3 990	4 323	2 361	3 573	798	3 317	38 739
Q3	4 226	6 573	4 478	2 603	3 273	4 194	4 414	2 779	4 074	857	3 655	41 126
Q4	3 881	6 826	5 244	3 580	4 405	5 182	4 490	2 246	3 362	915	3 568	43 699
1983 Q1	4 738	6 477	4 151	2 449	4 518	4 152	4 724	2 297	3 366	1 004	3 447	41 323
Q2	4 164	6 887	4 637	2 805	3 783	4 396	4 751	2 702	3 814	1 040	3 563	42 542
Q3	5 006	7 210	4 956	2 921	3 427	4 564	4 761	3 250	4 423	1 068	3 895	45 481
Q4	4 342	7 487	5 735	3 945	4 492	5 652	4 813	2 679	3 639	1 103	3 648	47 535
1984 Q1	4 766	6 947	4 492	2 600	4 910	4 490	4 877	2 635	3 628	1 189	3 771	44 305
Q2	4 485	7 431	5 038	3 000	3 858	4 881	4 954	3 174	4 186	1 180	3 968	46 155
Q3	4 757	7 351	5 257	3 199	3 518	4 988	5 018	3 662	4 731	1 207	3 988	47 676
Q4	4 630	7 545	6 151	4 369	4 687	6 278	5 101	3 038	4 087	1 272	3 950	51 108

See footnotes on page 47.

Source: Office for National Statistics: Enquiries 020 7533 5998

1.7 Household final consumption expenditure-component categories[1]

continued

£ million, current prices, not seasonally adjusted

	Durable goods	Food (Household expend-iture)[2]	Alcoholic drink and tobacco	Clothing and footwear	Energy products	Other goods	Rent, water and sewerage charges	Catering	Transport and communicat-ion	Financial services	Other services[3]	Total
	AEIT	CCDW	CDFH	CDDE	CCEC	ABZN	ABRG	CDEY	ABOZ	CEGK	ABOY	ABPB
1985 Q1	5 082	7 157	4 831	2 981	5 281	4 991	5 227	2 965	4 155	1 314	4 072	48 056
Q2	4 606	7 636	5 415	3 431	4 276	5 427	5 345	3 528	4 566	1 356	4 116	49 702
Q3	5 560	7 788	5 652	3 607	3 967	5 615	5 470	4 064	5 279	1 414	4 166	52 582
Q4	4 918	8 076	6 759	4 893	5 054	7 021	5 579	3 318	4 622	1 537	4 483	56 260
1986 Q1	5 566	7 599	4 980	3 364	5 644	5 644	5 678	3 135	4 665	1 701	4 756	52 732
Q2	5 204	8 166	5 714	3 841	4 092	6 097	5 793	4 138	5 323	1 836	5 103	55 307
Q3	6 300	8 312	5 955	4 035	3 681	6 301	5 902	4 927	6 022	1 895	5 512	58 842
Q4	5 808	8 497	7 240	5 406	4 802	7 838	6 011	3 986	5 181	1 997	5 201	61 967
1987 Q1	6 318	7 920	5 228	3 570	5 654	6 236	6 142	3 760	5 277	2 138	5 535	57 778
Q2	5 836	8 505	5 980	4 084	4 056	6 781	6 297	4 480	5 915	2 231	5 853	60 018
Q3	7 422	8 808	6 244	4 300	3 810	7 047	6 401	5 162	6 772	2 411	6 137	64 514
Q4	6 746	9 169	7 664	5 894	5 108	8 826	6 517	4 483	5 871	2 480	6 075	68 833
1988 Q1	7 793	8 751	5 563	3 840	5 458	7 058	6 598	4 712	5 904	2 509	6 467	64 653
Q2	7 120	9 097	6 308	4 367	4 212	7 604	7 001	5 770	6 514	2 610	7 034	67 637
Q3	9 448	9 234	6 600	4 566	4 108	7 881	7 123	6 949	7 503	2 709	7 755	73 876
Q4	7 911	9 409	8 113	6 250	5 513	10 041	7 257	6 305	6 490	2 816	7 154	77 259
1989 Q1	8 979	9 130	5 797	4 149	5 420	7 985	7 417	5 919	6 462	2 955	7 532	71 745
Q2	8 117	9 907	6 633	4 658	4 814	8 463	7 807	6 671	6 965	3 061	7 974	75 070
Q3	9 940	9 806	6 873	4 730	4 283	8 641	7 956	7 944	7 933	3 190	8 803	80 099
Q4	8 247	10 300	8 452	6 310	5 943	11 224	8 115	6 825	6 961	3 251	7 951	83 579
1990 Q1	9 024	9 760	6 025	4 508	5 817	9 035	8 342	6 636	6 928	3 366	8 186	77 627
Q2	7 929	10 684	7 198	4 927	5 044	9 522	9 176	7 429	7 687	3 423	8 956	81 975
Q3	9 688	10 485	7 556	5 081	4 944	9 470	9 391	8 580	8 627	3 525	9 465	86 812
Q4	7 876	10 888	9 230	6 696	6 617	11 632	9 634	7 431	7 727	3 542	8 805	90 078
1991 Q1	8 540	10 369	6 502	4 625	6 820	9 478	9 778	6 856	7 345	3 612	9 102	83 027
Q2	7 018	11 172	7 880	5 103	5 793	10 154	10 683	7 584	8 100	3 639	9 577	86 703
Q3	9 595	11 076	8 326	5 349	5 188	10 088	10 867	8 766	9 082	3 658	10 333	92 328
Q4	7 714	11 427	9 972	7 132	7 154	12 451	11 083	7 465	8 316	3 640	9 373	95 727
1992 Q1	8 131	10 685	7 628	4 718	7 077	10 054	11 640	7 124	7 864	3 639	9 805	88 365
Q2	7 305	11 552	8 200	5 389	5 681	10 936	12 218	7 979	8 605	3 730	10 327	91 922
Q3	10 012	11 267	8 322	5 660	5 285	10 611	12 353	9 220	9 587	3 700	11 069	97 086
Q4	8 066	11 689	9 403	7 637	7 356	12 860	12 426	7 964	8 554	3 732	10 087	99 774
1993 Q1	8 715	11 201	7 906	5 001	7 220	10 669	12 469	7 780	8 462	3 934	10 154	93 511
Q2	7 381	11 645	8 555	5 612	5 858	11 330	13 102	8 653	9 322	4 004	10 907	96 369
Q3	10 705	11 456	8 694	5 913	5 498	11 185	13 267	10 175	10 592	4 192	11 597	103 274
Q4	8 573	12 032	9 710	8 251	7 560	13 554	13 567	8 546	9 464	4 186	10 511	105 954
1994 Q1	9 637	11 372	8 189	5 429	7 505	11 089	13 627	8 108	8 973	4 191	10 885	99 005
Q2	8 114	11 732	8 986	6 263	6 248	11 783	14 078	8 904	9 840	4 025	11 529	101 502
Q3	11 179	11 776	9 184	6 470	5 673	11 700	14 236	10 463	10 983	4 037	12 353	108 054
Q4	8 950	12 242	10 265	8 731	7 431	14 363	14 356	8 984	9 807	3 973	11 599	110 701
1995 Q1	9 882	11 886	8 486	5 667	7 849	11 456	14 713	8 489	9 410	4 005	11 715	103 558
Q2	8 398	12 338	9 294	6 542	6 092	12 355	15 040	9 242	10 292	4 019	12 677	106 289
Q3	11 922	12 434	9 384	6 675	5 570	12 368	15 118	10 713	11 345	4 365	12 796	112 690
Q4	9 294	12 616	10 292	9 463	7 607	15 768	14 927	9 283	10 313	4 395	11 958	115 916
1996 Q1	10 570	12 585	8 878	5 887	8 282	12 568	15 200	8 969	9 795	4 667	12 622	110 023
Q2	9 591	12 968	9 931	6 812	6 468	13 606	15 378	10 137	10 719	4 624	12 812	113 046
Q3	13 086	13 294	9 924	7 033	5 937	13 731	15 697	11 699	12 086	4 706	13 355	120 548
Q4	10 432	13 666	10 885	9 832	8 135	17 189	15 922	9 981	10 611	4 961	12 610	124 224
1997 Q1	11 612	12 917	9 347	6 240	8 173	13 820	15 897	9 521	10 292	5 096	13 560	116 475
Q2	10 897	13 206	10 210	7 187	6 448	14 934	16 586	10 538	11 456	5 266	14 120	120 848
Q3	15 164	13 073	10 239	7 369	6 093	14 858	16 846	12 093	13 000	5 473	14 530	128 738
Q4	12 252	13 992	11 062	10 319	7 879	18 309	17 092	10 500	11 499	5 626	13 716	132 246
1998 Q1	13 765	12 862	9 269	6 544	7 745	15 001	17 008	10 020	11 259	5 748	14 950	124 171
Q2	11 812	13 628	10 516	7 512	6 507	16 252	17 587	11 418	12 397	6 179	15 679	129 487
Q3	15 248	13 437	10 370	7 761	6 095	16 194	17 889	13 057	13 836	6 031	16 511	136 429
Q4	12 414	13 862	11 783	10 559	7 651	20 086	18 308	11 782	12 754	5 889	15 676	140 764
1999 Q1	14 247	13 161	9 626	6 852	7 901	16 293	18 889	10 953	12 220	6 394	16 249	132 785
Q2	13 220	14 178	11 071	7 806	6 583	17 501	19 260	12 014	13 443	6 513	16 923	138 512
Q3	14 441	13 743	11 093	7 975	6 276	17 510	19 727	13 430	14 886	6 364	17 768	143 213
Q4	12 959	13 780	12 821	10 897	8 101	21 563	20 040	12 311	13 841	6 646	16 900	149 859
2000 Q1	14 811	13 380	9 892	7 095	8 472	17 113	20 489	11 524	12 869	6 801	17 247	139 693

See footnotes on page 47.

Source: Office for National Statistics: Enquiries 020 7533 5998

1.7 Household final consumption expenditure-component categories[1]

continued

£ million, 1995 prices

	Durable goods	Food (Household expend-iture)[2]	Alcoholic drink and tobacco	Clothing and footwear	Energy products	Other goods	Rent, water and sewerage charges	Catering	Transport and communicat-ion	Financial services	Other services[3]	Total
	AEIV	CCBM	FCCA	FCCB	CCBS	ABZP	ABRI	CCHS	ABPD	CEGM	ABPC	ABPF
1948	3 002	32 737	24 047	5 911	9 373	10 091	..	..	..	..	..	142 958
1949	3 579	33 977	23 310	6 381	9 306	10 828	..	..	..	..	..	145 251
1950	3 995	35 572	23 548	6 612	9 702	11 222	..	..	..	..	..	149 082
1951	3 947	34 938	24 301	5 988	10 001	11 055	..	..	..	..	..	147 049
1952	3 840	30 760	24 425	5 896	9 904	11 148	..	..	..	..	..	147 017
1953	4 965	32 533	24 815	6 044	9 988	12 062	..	..	..	..	..	153 393
1954	5 921	33 210	25 041	6 479	10 410	12 922	..	..	..	..	..	159 716
1955	6 515	34 385	25 819	6 950	10 599	13 905	27 508	..	..	..	..	166 245
1956	5 748	34 941	26 179	7 226	11 010	14 210	28 014	..	..	..	..	167 041
1957	6 433	35 466	26 708	7 425	10 750	14 486	28 381	..	..	..	..	170 434
1958	7 472	35 893	27 118	7 455	11 486	15 325	28 924	..	..	..	..	175 182
1959	8 885	36 580	28 336	7 859	11 316	16 366	29 723	..	..	..	..	182 697
1960	9 137	37 366	29 607	8 465	12 318	17 492	30 517	..	..	..	..	189 586
1961	8 793	37 985	30 870	8 651	12 497	18 329	31 128	..	..	..	..	193 663
1962	9 212	38 366	30 542	8 612	13 729	18 870	32 190	..	..	..	..	197 837
1963	10 728	38 568	31 867	8 994	14 749	19 850	33 347	22 311	12 601	2 458	..	206 304
1964	11 599	39 041	32 709	9 372	15 035	20 651	33 771	22 651	13 089	2 662	..	212 644
1965	11 545	39 016	31 826	9 722	16 069	21 201	34 650	22 684	13 483	2 778	..	215 002
1966	11 360	39 445	32 919	9 718	16 792	21 864	35 554	22 375	13 977	2 939	..	218 707
1967	12 076	40 094	33 723	9 870	17 151	22 687	36 583	21 685	14 604	3 324	..	223 851
1968	12 897	40 303	34 761	10 411	18 119	23 481	37 714	21 725	14 951	3 565	..	230 135
1969	12 087	40 418	35 039	10 573	18 839	23 443	38 709	21 730	15 512	3 690	..	231 201
1970	13 096	40 824	36 573	11 032	19 225	23 737	39 644	22 263	16 043	4 023	..	237 739
1971	15 526	40 861	37 442	11 224	19 349	24 445	40 521	21 862	16 426	4 470	..	245 429
1972	18 872	40 789	40 089	11 838	20 634	26 870	41 468	23 129	17 443	4 839	..	261 277
1973	19 900	41 770	44 243	12 379	21 626	29 363	42 478	23 235	19 441	5 154	22 691	275 705
1974	17 430	41 038	44 678	12 226	21 542	30 007	43 298	22 789	19 463	5 304	21 792	271 228
1975	17 726	41 050	43 828	12 396	21 065	28 801	44 116	23 520	19 403	5 487	21 506	270 421
1976	18 600	41 484	43 709	12 470	21 530	28 728	44 974	23 795	19 676	4 984	19 883	271 477
1977	17 298	41 126	43 193	12 655	21 913	28 878	45 832	24 395	20 196	5 109	18 985	270 434
1978	19 788	41 879	44 417	13 832	22 433	30 941	46 677	24 183	21 477	5 278	21 754	284 901
1979	22 321	42 812	45 696	14 817	23 200	31 769	47 588	24 151	22 670	5 597	23 530	297 453
1980	21 278	42 866	44 008	14 655	22 893	31 009	48 294	24 240	23 117	5 798	26 393	297 256
1981	21 674	42 591	41 948	14 520	22 976	31 163	48 970	22 902	23 498	6 059	27 930	297 237
1982	22 796	42 694	40 200	15 054	23 096	31 856	49 772	22 384	23 346	6 607	28 203	299 810
1983	26 750	43 416	41 129	16 091	23 128	32 677	51 210	23 801	24 175	7 802	28 488	313 648
1984	26 557	42 676	41 217	16 946	23 575	34 033	51 831	24 923	25 587	8 572	28 755	319 357
1985	27 807	43 213	41 389	18 356	24 665	35 680	52 510	25 988	27 368	9 300	29 860	331 404
1986	30 704	44 572	41 167	19 975	26 165	38 513	53 237	28 504	29 999	11 463	33 638	353 831
1987	33 426	45 709	41 601	21 053	26 717	41 559	54 051	29 502	32 369	13 120	37 182	372 601
1988	38 552	46 745	42 181	21 654	27 464	45 053	54 848	36 084	34 325	14 627	42 427	400 427
1989	40 546	47 538	41 968	21 531	27 283	46 968	55 514	39 032	35 362	15 825	44 550	413 498
1990	38 101	47 055	41 654	22 105	27 389	47 995	56 127	39 539	36 320	16 603	45 466	415 788
1991	34 436	47 114	40 258	22 502	28 281	47 567	56 743	36 806	35 121	16 477	45 748	408 309
1992	34 474	47 664	38 415	23 683	27 961	47 817	57 191	36 279	35 704	16 202	46 543	410 026
1993	36 221	48 282	37 861	24 875	28 123	49 035	58 015	37 539	38 473	17 168	45 679	420 081
1994	38 583	48 931	38 441	26 928	27 754	50 119	58 862	37 319	40 011	16 397	48 117	431 462
1995	39 496	49 274	37 456	28 347	27 118	51 947	59 798	37 727	41 360	16 784	49 146	438 453
1996	42 701	50 931	38 007	29 773	28 210	55 419	60 344	39 704	42 188	18 034	49 375	454 686
1997	47 953	51 786	37 533	31 076	27 427	59 165	60 934	40 399	43 387	19 516	53 525	472 701
1998	51 797	51 627	36 467	32 544	27 106	63 419	61 555	42 609	45 865	20 191	58 198	491 378
1999	55 316	52 277	36 788	34 662	26 982	68 501	62 633	43 466	49 803	21 362	61 074	512 864

1 More detailed estimates of Consumers' Expenditure expressed in both current and constant prices appear in the ONS publication *Consumer Trends*. Any queries relating to Household Final Consumption Expenditure should be addressed to the Office for National Statistics Consumers' Expenditure Branch on 0171 533 5998.
2 Before 1952 estimates for catering are included under Food; thereafter they are included under Other services.
3 Including the adjustments for international travel, etc.
4 For the years before 1993, totals may not equal the sum of their components because of the method used in rebasing to 1995 prices.

Source: Office for National Statistics: Enquiries 020 7533 5998

1.7 Household final consumption expenditure-component categories[1]

continued

£ million, 1995 prices, not seasonally adjusted

	Durable goods	Food (Household expenditure)[2]	Alcoholic drink and tobacco	Clothing and footwear	Energy products	Other goods	Rent, water and sewerage charges	Catering	Transport and communication	Financial services	Other services[3]	Total
	AEIV	CCBM	FCCA	FCCB	CCBS	ABZP	ABRI	CCHS	ABPD	CEGM	ABPC	ABPF
1955 Q1	1 551	8 321	5 434	1 412	3 284	3 067	6 722	..	..	..	..	38 798
Q2	1 570	8 760	6 264	1 789	2 575	3 306	7 068	..	..	..	..	41 214
Q3	1 587	8 482	6 969	1 616	2 084	3 637	6 896	..	..	..	..	42 313
Q4	1 807	8 822	7 152	2 133	2 656	3 895	6 822	..	..	..	..	43 920
1956 Q1	1 396	8 563	5 703	1 479	3 324	3 214	6 871	..	..	..	..	39 476
Q2	1 468	8 848	6 385	1 820	2 698	3 368	7 162	..	..	..	..	41 503
Q3	1 350	8 441	6 807	1 718	2 154	3 670	7 040	..	..	..	..	41 878
Q4	1 534	9 089	7 284	2 209	2 834	3 958	6 941	..	..	..	..	44 184
1957 Q1	1 379	8 519	5 825	1 544	3 243	3 181	6 966	..	..	..	..	39 555
Q2	1 636	8 902	6 599	1 907	2 589	3 441	7 260	..	..	..	..	42 535
Q3	1 628	8 679	6 932	1 749	2 084	3 752	7 114	..	..	..	..	43 029
Q4	1 790	9 366	7 352	2 225	2 834	4 112	7 041	..	..	..	..	45 315
1958 Q1	1 667	8 742	5 980	1 546	3 551	3 461	7 094	..	..	..	..	41 079
Q2	1 797	8 998	6 632	1 872	2 863	3 598	7 398	..	..	..	..	43 336
Q3	1 715	8 816	7 090	1 739	2 121	3 917	7 263	..	..	..	..	44 021
Q4	2 293	9 337	7 416	2 298	2 951	4 349	7 169	..	..	..	..	46 746
1959 Q1	1 914	8 858	5 891	1 595	3 720	3 637	7 285	..	..	..	..	42 226
Q2	2 293	9 245	6 965	2 007	2 637	3 927	7 588	..	..	..	..	45 671
Q3	2 125	8 973	7 502	1 790	2 074	4 102	7 472	..	..	..	..	45 869
Q4	2 553	9 504	7 978	2 467	2 885	4 700	7 378	..	..	..	..	48 931
1960 Q1	2 415	9 155	6 339	1 682	3 855	3 895	7 473	..	..	..	..	44 789
Q2	2 478	9 438	7 406	2 185	2 762	4 185	7 814	..	..	..	..	47 646
Q3	2 138	9 155	7 709	1 978	2 377	4 431	7 682	..	..	..	..	47 614
Q4	2 106	9 618	8 153	2 620	3 324	4 981	7 548	..	..	..	..	49 537
1961 Q1	2 157	9 305	6 657	1 806	3 944	4 246	7 646	..	..	..	..	45 704
Q2	2 442	9 543	7 870	2 151	2 885	4 380	7 930	..	..	..	..	48 695
Q3	2 125	9 361	8 007	2 021	2 410	4 639	7 853	..	..	..	..	48 758
Q4	2 069	9 776	8 336	2 673	3 258	5 064	7 699	..	..	..	..	50 506
1962 Q1	2 125	9 470	6 461	1 730	4 442	4 310	7 854	..	..	..	..	46 380
Q2	2 620	9 619	7 640	2 159	3 302	4 557	8 193	..	..	..	..	49 964
Q3	2 188	9 295	7 974	2 050	2 546	4 825	8 118	..	..	..	..	49 603
Q4	2 279	9 982	8 467	2 673	3 439	5 178	8 025	..	..	..	..	51 890
1963 Q1	2 452	9 384	6 451	1 753	4 425	4 357	8 228	4 915	2 787	623	..	47 435
Q2	2 904	9 663	8 088	2 198	3 485	4 892	8 449	5 827	3 175	620	..	51 959
Q3	2 708	9 624	8 399	2 174	3 182	5 028	8 329	6 623	3 612	609	..	52 888
Q4	2 664	9 897	8 929	2 869	3 657	5 573	8 341	4 946	3 027	606	..	54 022
1964 Q1	2 881	9 711	6 972	1 884	4 233	4 583	8 361	4 997	2 912	675	..	49 921
Q2	3 095	9 773	8 030	2 296	3 769	5 086	8 403	5 930	3 281	661	..	53 301
Q3	2 831	9 511	8 503	2 249	3 304	5 197	8 480	6 728	3 752	659	..	53 952
Q4	2 792	10 046	9 204	2 943	3 729	5 785	8 527	4 996	3 144	667	..	55 470
1965 Q1	3 147	9 508	6 903	1 992	4 475	4 705	8 573	5 013	2 947	666	..	50 754
Q2	3 026	9 737	7 738	2 381	4 019	5 166	8 613	5 929	3 386	711	..	53 615
Q3	2 778	9 623	8 282	2 335	3 626	5 313	8 706	6 724	3 895	657	..	54 706
Q4	2 594	10 148	8 903	3 014	3 949	6 017	8 758	5 018	3 255	744	..	55 927
1966 Q1	3 097	9 726	7 101	2 057	4 688	4 927	8 787	4 927	3 064	724	..	51 957
Q2	3 241	9 840	8 339	2 395	4 261	5 408	8 876	5 848	3 540	767	..	55 485
Q3	2 617	9 746	8 515	2 303	3 629	5 511	8 917	6 646	3 965	675	..	55 141
Q4	2 405	10 133	8 964	2 963	4 214	6 018	8 974	4 954	3 408	773	..	56 124
1967 Q1	2 809	9 759	7 243	2 054	4 747	4 976	9 027	4 770	3 256	730	..	51 969
Q2	2 995	9 972	8 386	2 353	4 245	5 526	9 097	5 646	3 698	860	..	55 550
Q3	3 022	10 044	8 757	2 369	3 711	5 711	9 199	6 444	4 192	798	..	57 103
Q4	3 250	10 319	9 337	3 094	4 448	6 474	9 260	4 825	3 458	936	..	59 229
1968 Q1	3 904	9 942	7 766	2 165	5 170	5 479	9 324	4 795	3 337	812	..	55 813
Q2	2 913	10 029	8 464	2 513	4 302	5 521	9 400	5 678	3 763	923	..	56 187
Q3	2 965	10 007	8 836	2 491	4 060	5 882	9 469	6 447	4 276	874	..	57 924
Q4	3 115	10 325	9 695	3 242	4 587	6 599	9 521	4 805	3 575	956	..	60 211
1969 Q1	2 958	9 943	7 409	2 190	5 473	5 288	9 592	4 805	3 390	903	..	54 410
Q2	3 190	10 054	8 596	2 621	4 275	5 694	9 639	5 686	3 920	943	..	57 270
Q3	2 975	10 034	9 121	2 505	3 964	5 861	9 713	6 442	4 533	854	..	58 366
Q4	2 964	10 387	9 913	3 257	5 127	6 600	9 765	4 797	3 669	990	..	61 155

See footnotes on page 51.

Source: Office for National Statistics: Enquiries 020 7533 5998

1.7 Household final consumption expenditure-component categories[1]

continued

£ million, 1995 prices, not seasonally adjusted

	Durable goods	Food (Household expenditure)[2]	Alcoholic drink and tobacco	Clothing and footwear	Energy products	Other goods	Rent, water and sewerage charges	Catering	Transport and communication	Financial services	Other services[3]	Total
	AEIV	CCBM	FCCA	FCCB	CCBS	ABZP	ABRI	CCHS	ABPD	CEGM	ABPC	ABPF
1970 Q1	3 215	9 866	7 452	2 248	5 586	5 296	9 802	4 942	3 521	974	..	55 342
Q2	3 370	10 266	8 942	2 686	4 406	5 713	9 890	5 821	4 042	1 032	..	58 731
Q3	3 215	10 225	9 773	2 625	4 122	6 008	9 950	6 592	4 689	963	..	60 694
Q4	3 296	10 467	10 406	3 473	5 111	6 720	10 002	4 908	3 791	1 054	..	62 972
1971 Q1	3 528	9 965	7 726	2 272	5 470	5 355	10 016	4 830	3 586	1 050	..	56 575
Q2	3 721	10 286	9 182	2 803	4 476	5 821	10 109	5 723	4 156	1 162	..	60 475
Q3	4 132	10 156	9 744	2 657	4 123	6 119	10 175	6 486	4 733	1 074	..	62 629
Q4	4 145	10 454	10 790	3 492	5 280	7 150	10 221	4 823	3 951	1 184	..	65 750
1972 Q1	4 333	10 159	8 348	2 416	5 562	5 833	10 287	5 023	3 803	1 184	..	60 273
Q2	4 766	10 203	9 926	2 813	4 767	6 272	10 347	6 050	4 364	1 276	..	64 311
Q3	4 738	10 088	10 242	2 867	4 627	6 755	10 390	6 937	5 038	1 130	..	66 536
Q4	5 035	10 339	11 573	3 742	5 678	8 010	10 444	5 119	4 238	1 249	..	70 157
1973 Q1	5 678	10 081	8 835	2 780	5 872	6 701	10 558	5 305	4 339	1 257	5 415	65 859
Q2	4 659	10 383	10 929	2 937	5 071	6 866	10 596	6 296	4 966	1 300	5 710	67 708
Q3	4 799	10 659	11 552	2 881	4 818	7 285	10 639	6 680	5 428	1 261	6 027	69 779
Q4	4 764	10 647	12 927	3 781	5 865	8 511	10 685	4 954	4 708	1 336	5 539	72 359
1974 Q1	4 376	9 710	9 759	2 587	5 658	6 924	10 751	4 964	4 400	1 316	5 281	63 714
Q2	4 106	10 285	10 782	2 893	4 907	7 050	10 799	6 057	5 011	1 334	5 475	66 360
Q3	4 367	10 523	11 011	2 977	4 872	7 436	10 843	6 784	5 301	1 288	5 634	68 654
Q4	4 581	10 520	13 126	3 769	6 105	8 597	10 905	4 984	4 751	1 366	5 402	72 500
1975 Q1	4 625	9 845	9 586	2 725	5 850	6 786	10 937	5 165	4 359	1 452	5 213	64 709
Q2	4 521	10 148	10 717	3 025	4 844	6 847	11 005	6 134	4 969	1 422	5 565	66 999
Q3	4 381	10 483	11 001	2 940	4 548	6 995	11 045	7 192	5 430	1 295	5.335	68 038
Q4	4 199	10 574	12 524	3 706	5 823	8 173	11 129	5 029	4 645	1 318	5 393	70 675
1976 Q1	4 696	9 927	8 886	2 639	6 122	6 602	11 135	5 018	4 333	1 330	5 293	64 218
Q2	4 424	10 302	10 817	2 997	4 800	6 642	11 214	6 084	5 047	1 221	5 187	66 397
Q3	4 684	10 717	11 365	3 005	4 577	7 057	11 270	7 394	5 502	1 184	4 506	68 645
Q4	4 796	10 538	12 641	3 829	6 031	8 427	11 355	5 299	4 794	1 249	4 897	72 217
1977 Q1	4 613	9 745	9 087	2 647	6 103	6 597	11 375	5 255	4 466	1 318	4 893	64 101
Q2	3 952	10 219	10 692	2 890	5 061	6 576	11 426	6 216	5 092	1 228	4 786	65 465
Q3	4 412	10 224	10 857	3 098	4 815	7 122	11 469	7 438	5 723	1 286	4 243	67 937
Q4	4 321	10 938	12 557	4 020	5 934	8 583	11 562	5 486	4 915	1 277	5 063	72 931
1978 Q1	5 237	10 196	9 423	2 828	6 342	6 909	11 581	5 422	4 790	1 286	5 820	67 945
Q2	4 627	10 205	11 025	3 168	5 164	7 244	11 641	6 167	5 442	1 293	5 481	69 165
Q3	5 409	10 769	11 178	3 452	4 855	7 568	11 699	7 212	5 971	1 353	4 802	72 436
Q4	4 515	10 709	12 791	4 384	6 072	9 220	11 756	5 382	5 274	1 346	5 651	75 355
1979 Q1	5 645	10 144	9 698	3 031	6 952	7 163	11 820	5 238	4 934	1 410	5 887	70 266
Q2	6 566	10 590	11 587	3 603	5 258	7 721	11 874	6 201	5 835	1 420	5 760	75 036
Q3	5 078	11 065	11 422	3 529	4 880	7 619	11 926	7 183	6 418	1 349	5 683	74 082
Q4	5 032	11 013	12 989	4 654	6 110	9 266	11 968	5 529	5 483	1 418	6 200	78 069
1980 Q1	6 346	10 556	10 002	3 175	6 656	7 283	12 009	5 573	5 272	1 455	6 302	73 181
Q2	4 950	10 702	10 553	3 428	4 958	7 375	12 045	6 116	5 846	1 413	6 689	72 068
Q3	5 477	10 881	11 039	3 515	4 887	7 425	12 091	7 246	6 521	1 455	6 741	75 269
Q4	4 505	10 727	12 414	4 537	6 392	8 926	12 149	5 305	5 478	1 475	6 661	76 738
1981 Q1	5 844	10 357	9 473	3 103	6 515	7 214	12 178	5 355	5 167	1 501	6 959	71 902
Q2	5 205	10 498	10 246	3 317	5 197	7 393	12 215	5 784	6 083	1 507	7 103	72 576
Q3	5 674	10 884	10 468	3 421	4 790	7 491	12 264	6 678	6 719	1 516	7 035	75 148
Q4	4 951	10 852	11 761	4 679	6 474	9 065	12 313	5 085	5 529	1 535	6 833	77 611
1982 Q1	5 713	10 422	8 886	3 179	6 523	7 306	12 370	5 101	5 244	1 601	6 882	71 571
Q2	5 122	10 733	9 767	3 438	5 211	7 445	12 421	5 632	5 994	1 590	6 774	72 345
Q3	6 201	10 639	9 906	3 574	4 973	7 723	12 470	6 559	6 586	1 667	7 429	76 125
Q4	5 760	10 900	11 641	4 863	6 389	9 382	12 511	5 092	5 522	1 749	7 118	79 769
1983 Q1	7 106	10 291	9 073	3 311	6 548	7 483	12 742	5 177	5 458	1 918	6 891	74 812
Q2	6 123	10 697	9 830	3 742	5 418	7 666	12 783	5 919	6 042	1 936	7 015	75 746
Q3	7 334	11 074	10 413	3 868	4 851	7 870	12 825	7 052	6 819	1 945	7 597	80 220
Q4	6 187	11 354	11 813	5 170	6 311	9 658	12 860	5 653	5 856	2 003	6 985	82 870
1984 Q1	6 933	10 355	9 251	3 417	6 912	7 564	12 897	5 466	5 697	2 133	7 101	76 514
Q2	6 389	10 719	9 917	3 884	5 359	8 091	12 937	6 326	6 422	2 090	7 327	77 903
Q3	6 771	10 651	10 245	4 101	4 901	8 209	12 977	7 235	7 114	2 127	7 253	79 965
Q4	6 464	10 951	11 804	5 544	6 403	10 169	13 020	5 896	6 354	2 222	7 074	84 975

See footnotes on page 51.

Source: Office for National Statistics: Enquiries 020 7533 5998

1.7 Household final consumption expenditure-component categories[1]

continued

£ million, 1995 prices, not seasonally adjusted

	Durable goods	Food (Household expend-iture)[2]	Alcoholic drink and tobacco	Clothing and footwear	Energy products	Other goods	Rent, water and sewerage charges	Catering	Transport and communicat-ion	Financial services	Other services[3]	Total
	AEIV	CCBM	FCCA	FCCB	CCBS	ABZP	ABRI	CCHS	ABPD	CEGM	ABPC	ABPF
1985 Q1	7 153	10 178	9 146	3 760	7 139	7 918	13 063	5 720	6 223	2 235	7 304	78 734
Q2	6 361	10 795	9 917	4 266	5 587	8 437	13 103	6 619	6 762	2 252	7 300	79 936
Q3	7 634	11 012	10 248	4 435	5 225	8 638	13 146	7 546	7 563	2 352	7 427	83 896
Q4	6 659	11 228	12 078	5 895	6 714	10 687	13 198	6 103	6 820	2 461	7 829	88 838
1986 Q1	7 616	10 476	8 825	4 095	7 853	8 531	13 243	5 928	6 782	2 708	7 976	83 021
Q2	7 029	11 154	9 859	4 656	5 977	9 134	13 284	7 295	7 520	2 799	8 456	86 025
Q3	8 580	11 400	10 187	4 853	5 414	9 372	13 332	8 524	8 280	2 885	9 001	90 836
Q4	7 479	11 542	12 296	6 371	6 921	11 476	13 378	6 757	7 417	3 071	8 205	93 949
1987 Q1	8 233	10 566	8 731	4 247	7 993	9 176	13 447	6 267	7 296	3 148	8 712	86 862
Q2	7 473	11 308	9 963	4 837	5 813	9 842	13 488	7 437	8 110	3 195	9 253	89 641
Q3	9 461	11 806	10 352	5 127	5 497	10 125	13 534	8 590	8 975	3 374	9 787	95 799
Q4	8 259	12 029	12 555	6 842	7 414	12 416	13 582	7 208	7 988	3 403	9 430	100 299
1988 Q1	9 539	11 316	9 029	4 494	7 952	9 950	13 636	7 346	7 732	3 507	9 856	93 543
Q2	8 577	11 691	10 041	4 983	6 013	10 625	13 690	8 848	8 548	3 614	10 517	96 130
Q3	11 219	11 859	10 420	5 246	5 782	10 862	13 739	10 536	9 588	3 717	11 647	103 821
Q4	9 217	11 879	12 691	6 931	7 717	13 616	13 783	9 354	8 457	3 789	10 407	106 933
1989 Q1	10 448	11 312	8 921	4 639	7 499	10 620	13 825	8 621	8 170	3 834	10 720	97 977
Q2	9 341	12 145	10 127	5 051	6 319	10 989	13 855	9 598	8 829	3 940	11 087	100 576
Q3	11 421	11 951	10 363	5 167	5 662	11 067	13 894	11 292	9 712	4 038	12 104	106 119
Q4	9 336	12 130	12 557	6 674	7 803	14 292	13 940	9 521	8 651	4 013	10 639	108 826
1990 Q1	10 147	11 157	8 831	4 825	7 572	11 239	13 981	8 966	8 412	4 060	10 834	99 464
Q2	8 789	12 058	10 051	5 130	6 273	11 609	14 020	9 890	9 189	4 130	11 476	101 880
Q3	10 640	11 784	10 327	5 348	5 835	11 415	14 072	11 178	9 955	4 245	12 094	106 263
Q4	8 525	12 056	12 445	6 802	7 709	13 732	14 054	9 505	8 764	4 168	11 062	108 181
1991 Q1	9 136	11 176	8 610	4 828	8 109	11 064	14 136	8 569	8 082	4 147	11 157	98 456
Q2	7 386	11 945	9 638	5 128	6 541	11 507	14 173	9 187	8 788	4 128	11 451	98 837
Q3	9 916	11 894	10 045	5 499	5 699	11 277	14 198	10 327	9 579	4 166	12 268	104 218
Q4	7 998	12 099	11 965	7 047	7 932	13 719	14 236	8 723	8 672	4 036	10 872	106 798
1992 Q1	8 382	11 139	8 900	4 854	7 901	11 013	14 236	8 182	8 092	3 972	11 264	97 175
Q2	7 489	12 127	9 326	5 406	6 179	11 804	14 284	9 015	8 892	4 088	11 746	99 663
Q3	10 221	12 062	9 461	5 833	5 816	11 359	14 321	10 287	9 823	4 123	12 448	105 406
Q4	8 382	12 336	10 728	7 590	8 065	13 641	14 350	8 795	8 897	4 019	11 085	107 782
1993 Q1	9 028	11 590	8 858	5 153	7 915	11 345	14 418	8 466	8 627	4 178	10 792	99 828
Q2	7 525	12 131	9 228	5 596	6 195	11 957	14 487	9 285	9 586	4 226	11 534	101 106
Q3	10 846	11 954	9 269	6 010	5 832	11 751	14 531	10 817	10 683	4 442	12 370	108 275
Q4	8 822	12 607	10 506	8 116	8 181	13 982	14 579	8 971	9 577	4 322	10 983	110 872
1994 Q1	9 889	11 877	8 772	5 520	8 038	11 456	14 622	8 405	8 966	4 210	11 492	103 247
Q2	8 243	12 202	9 400	6 233	6 394	12 067	14 681	9 125	9 976	4 042	11 991	104 354
Q3	11 426	12 232	9 595	6 576	5 759	11 991	14 743	10 682	11 113	4 131	12 744	110 992
Q4	9 025	12 620	10 674	8 599	7 563	14 605	14 816	9 107	9 956	4 014	11 890	112 869
1995 Q1	9 994	12 025	8 662	5 779	7 882	11 630	14 865	8 593	9 374	4 038	11 950	104 792
Q2	8 394	12 359	9 271	6 486	6 060	12 383	14 935	9 275	10 354	4 015	12 731	106 263
Q3	11 903	12 369	9 356	6 786	5 562	12 319	14 976	10 674	11 248	4 379	12 711	112 283
Q4	9 205	12 521	10 167	9 296	7 614	15 615	15 022	9 185	10 384	4 352	11 754	115 115
1996 Q1	10 461	12 155	8 714	6 060	8 204	12 364	15 024	8 856	9 625	4 471	12 270	108 204
Q2	9 388	12 462	9 561	6 843	6 394	13 206	15 102	9 922	10 516	4 378	12 250	110 022
Q3	12 718	12 896	9 416	7 222	5 794	13 299	15 113	11 312	11 674	4 506	12 752	116 702
Q4	10 134	13 418	10 316	9 648	7 818	16 550	15 105	9 614	10 373	4 679	12 103	119 758
1997 Q1	11 220	12 564	8 770	6 380	7 912	13 300	15 139	9 074	9 746	4 735	12 924	111 764
Q2	10 362	12 962	9 406	7 132	6 210	14 264	15 216	10 076	10 906	4 812	13 520	114 866
Q3	14 474	12 731	9 293	7 481	5 692	14 161	15 261	11 443	11 980	4 938	14 212	121 666
Q4	11 897	13 529	10 064	10 083	7 613	17 440	15 318	9 806	10 755	5 031	12 869	124 405
1998 Q1	13 278	12 447	8 205	6 703	7 682	14 183	15 332	9 336	10 417	4 931	13 885	116 399
Q2	11 395	13 173	9 199	7 445	6 189	15 293	15 364	10 582	11 351	5 169	14 606	119 766
Q3	14 699	12 893	8 990	7 935	5 743	15 180	15 403	12 003	12 375	5 151	15 664	126 036
Q4	12 425	13 114	10 073	10 461	7 492	18 763	15 456	10 688	11 722	4 940	14 043	129 177
1999 Q1	14 205	12 338	8 058	7 164	7 858	15 218	15 523	9 882	11 298	5 424	14 533	121 501
Q2	13 117	13 484	9 128	7 967	6 081	16 410	15 610	10 766	12 383	5 306	15 293	125 545
Q3	14 486	13 261	9 073	8 359	5 599	16 457	15 703	11 977	13 359	5 260	16 490	130 024
Q4	13 508	13 194	10 529	11 172	7 444	20 416	15 797	10 841	12 763	5 372	14 758	135 794
2000 Q1	15 170	12 780	8 050	7 648	7 816	16 185	15 890	10 070	11 947	5 586	14 801	125 943

See footnotes on page 51.

Source: Office for National Statistics: Enquiries 020 7533 5998

1.7 Household final consumption expenditure-component categories[1]

continued

£ million, 1995 prices, seasonally adjusted

	Durable goods	Food (Household expend-iture)[2]	Alcoholic drink and tobacco	Clothing and footwear	Energy products	Other goods	Rent, water and sewerage charges	Catering	Transport and communicat-ion	Financial services	Other services[3]	Total
	AEIW	CCCA	FCCD	FCCE	CCCG	ABZQ	ABRJ	CCUU	ABJZ	CEGN	ABKR	ABJR
1955 Q1	1 648	8 559	6 239	1 724	2 670	3 368	6 870	..	..	..	..	41 181
Q2	1 546	8 669	6 404	1 733	2 641	3 482	6 870	..	..	..	..	41 389
Q3	1 647	8 611	6 650	1 733	2 684	3 543	6 871	..	..	..	..	41 975
Q4	1 674	8 546	6 526	1 760	2 604	3 512	6 897	..	..	..	..	41 700
1956 Q1	1 468	8 746	6 535	1 769	2 698	3 545	6 969	..	..	..	..	41 809
Q2	1 463	8 746	6 493	1 806	2 739	3 564	6 988	..	..	..	..	41 690
Q3	1 404	8 701	6 517	1 831	2 779	3 555	7 016	..	..	..	..	41 715
Q4	1 413	8 748	6 634	1 820	2 794	3 546	7 041	..	..	..	..	41 827
1957 Q1	1 481	8 714	6 657	1 882	2 603	3 482	7 041	..	..	..	..	42 096
Q2	1 605	8 812	6 707	1 840	2 641	3 626	7 087	..	..	..	..	42 406
Q3	1 683	8 918	6 642	1 866	2 709	3 670	7 114	..	..	..	..	42 854
Q4	1 664	9 022	6 702	1 837	2 797	3 708	7 139	..	..	..	..	43 078
1958 Q1	1 772	8 924	6 821	1 844	2 840	3 780	7 169	..	..	..	..	43 432
Q2	1 759	8 908	6 679	1 849	2 977	3 774	7 225	..	..	..	..	43 306
Q3	1 808	9 029	6 789	1 863	2 784	3 877	7 245	..	..	..	..	43 811
Q4	2 133	9 032	6 829	1 899	2 885	3 894	7 285	..	..	..	..	44 633
1959 Q1	1 989	9 040	6 822	1 926	2 918	3 978	7 379	..	..	..	..	44 663
Q2	2 218	9 146	7 001	1 978	2 783	4 092	7 397	..	..	..	..	45 470
Q3	2 231	9 164	7 175	1 934	2 773	4 060	7 472	..	..	..	..	45 690
Q4	2 447	9 230	7 338	2 021	2 842	4 236	7 475	..	..	..	..	46 874
1960 Q1	2 497	9 322	7 398	2 065	2 975	4 277	7 549	..	..	..	..	47 436
Q2	2 317	9 337	7 316	2 141	2 907	4 351	7 623	..	..	..	..	47 182
Q3	2 243	9 344	7 395	2 123	3 188	4 392	7 682	..	..	..	..	47 486
Q4	2 080	9 363	7 498	2 136	3 248	4 472	7 663	..	..	..	..	47 482
1961 Q1	2 212	9 438	7 773	2 193	3 020	4 618	7 721	..	..	..	..	48 342
Q2	2 255	9 470	7 784	2 165	3 043	4 515	7 737	..	..	..	..	48 280
Q3	2 212	9 567	7 655	2 141	3 199	4 599	7 836	..	..	..	..	48 507
Q4	2 114	9 510	7 658	2 152	3 235	4 597	7 834	..	..	..	..	48 534
1962 Q1	2 125	9 594	7 610	2 132	3 414	4 660	7 948	..	..	..	..	48 894
Q2	2 454	9 585	7 602	2 175	3 416	4 692	8 002	..	..	..	..	49 668
Q3	2 268	9 528	7 633	2 159	3 426	4 753	8 082	..	..	..	..	49 338
Q4	2 365	9 659	7 697	2 146	3 473	4 765	8 158	..	..	..	..	49 937
1963 Q1	2 377	9 552	7 513	2 147	3 881	4 848	8 234	5 569	..	..	..	50 152
Q2	2 679	9 650	8 193	2 231	3 499	4 965	8 458	5 577	..	..	..	51 684
Q3	2 808	9 767	8 096	2 282	3 629	5 019	8 317	5 579	..	..	..	52 290
Q4	2 864	9 599	8 065	2 334	3 740	5 018	8 338	5 586	..	..	..	52 178
1964 Q1	2 781	9 883	8 103	2 295	3 710	5 095	8 369	5 667	..	..	..	52 802
Q2	2 862	9 764	8 114	2 329	3 771	5 162	8 412	5 678	..	..	..	52 934
Q3	2 951	9 644	8 189	2 355	3 765	5 188	8 467	5 667	..	..	..	53 226
Q4	3 005	9 750	8 303	2 393	3 789	5 206	8 523	5 639	..	..	..	53 682
1965 Q1	3 005	9 672	7 998	2 406	3 915	5 224	8 581	5 690	..	..	..	53 569
Q2	2 845	9 741	7 813	2 419	4 024	5 255	8 623	5 675	..	..	..	53 392
Q3	2 909	9 746	7 989	2 447	4 141	5 310	8 693	5 662	..	..	..	53 946
Q4	2 786	9 857	8 026	2 450	3 989	5 412	8 753	5 657	..	..	..	54 095
1966 Q1	2 944	9 889	8 214	2 469	4 102	5 458	8 795	5 596	..	..	..	54 781
Q2	3 112	9 855	8 420	2 436	4 305	5 509	8 884	5 596	..	..	..	55 275
Q3	2 745	9 847	8 221	2 406	4 170	5 504	8 908	5 595	..	..	..	54 317
Q4	2 559	9 854	8 064	2 407	4 215	5 393	8 967	5 588	..	..	..	54 334
1967 Q1	2 645	9 925	8 396	2 458	4 145	5 513	9 033	5 414	..	..	..	54 740
Q2	2 898	9 995	8 478	2 407	4 343	5 662	9 103	5 402	..	..	..	55 434
Q3	3 140	10 129	8 470	2 492	4 282	5 719	9 191	5 426	..	..	..	56 625
Q4	3 393	10 045	8 379	2 513	4 381	5 793	9 256	5 443	..	..	..	57 052
1968 Q1	3 711	10 120	9 030	2 588	4 500	6 064	9 334	5 436	..	..	..	58 788
Q2	2 869	10 050	8 543	2 570	4 467	5 668	9 406	5 427	..	..	..	56 423
Q3	3 088	10 069	8 529	2 618	4 704	5 879	9 460	5 428	..	..	..	57 428
Q4	3 229	10 064	8 659	2 635	4 448	5 870	9 514	5 434	..	..	..	57 496
1969 Q1	2 848	10 178	8 667	2 622	4 781	5 843	9 599	5 433	..	..	..	57 312
Q2	3 160	10 015	8 696	2 674	4 536	5 873	9 639	5 426	..	..	..	57 813
Q3	3 063	10 062	8 837	2 644	4 616	5 872	9 707	5 422	..	..	..	57 877
Q4	3 016	10 163	8 839	2 633	4 906	5 855	9 764	5 449	..	..	..	58 199

See footnotes on page 51.

Source: Office for National Statistics: Enquiries 020 7533 5998

1.7 Household final consumption expenditure-component categories[1]

continued

£ million, 1995 prices, seasonally adjusted

	Durable goods	Food (Household expend-iture)[2]	Alcoholic drink and tobacco	Clothing and footwear	Energy products	Other goods	Rent, water and sewerage charges	Catering	Transport and communicat-ion	Financial services	Other services[3]	Total
	AEIW	CCCA	FCCD	FCCE	CCCG	ABZQ	ABRJ	CCUU	ABJZ	CEGN	ABKR	ABJR
1970 Q1	3 117	10 081	8 789	2 690	4 909	5 849	9 810	5 577	..	..	..	58 348
Q2	3 359	10 241	9 058	2 752	4 726	5 921	9 890	5 540	..	..	..	59 255
Q3	3 285	10 255	9 484	2 768	4 779	6 028	9 942	5 556	..	..	..	60 223
Q4	3 335	10 247	9 242	2 822	4 811	5 939	10 002	5 590	..	..	..	59 913
1971 Q1	3 445	10 203	9 133	2 719	4 842	5 898	10 020	5 443	..	..	..	59 672
Q2	3 730	10 280	9 290	2 876	4 839	6 076	10 108	5 431	..	..	..	61 026
Q3	4 191	10 156	9 482	2 795	4 757	6 163	10 169	5 478	..	..	..	62 181
Q4	4 160	10 222	9 537	2 834	4 911	6 308	10 224	5 510	..	..	..	62 550
1972 Q1	4 234	10 435	9 858	2 865	4 969	6 411	10 289	5 661	..	..	..	63 594
Q2	4 809	10 201	10 038	2 903	5 146	6 594	10 346	5 731	..	..	..	65 049
Q3	4 782	10 058	10 006	3 021	5 304	6 827	10 389	5 863	..	..	..	66 095
Q4	5 047	10 095	10 187	3 049	5 215	7 038	10 444	5 874	..	..	..	66 539
1973 Q1	5 537	10 426	10 449	3 241	5 275	7 317	10 558	5 962	..	..	..	69 220
Q2	4 757	10 406	11 103	3 041	5 487	7 247	10 595	5 946	..	..	..	68 711
Q3	4 845	10 530	11 369	3 009	5 504	7 368	10 641	5 629	..	..	..	69 253
Q4	4 761	10 408	11 322	3 088	5 360	7 431	10 684	5 698	..	..	..	68 521
1974 Q1	4 246	10 086	11 523	3 018	5 099	7 517	10 751	5 583	..	..	..	67 106
Q2	4 228	10 328	10 928	3 024	5 315	7 479	10 799	5 728	..	..	..	67 453
Q3	4 382	10 369	10 822	3 108	5 565	7 543	10 850	5 717	..	..	..	68 216
Q4	4 574	10 255	11 405	3 076	5 563	7 468	10 898	5 761	..	..	..	68 453
1975 Q1	4 451	10 250	11 278	3 166	5 259	7 339	10 939	5 817	..	..	..	67 961
Q2	4 682	10 199	10 839	3 166	5 269	7 287	11 005	5 807	..	..	..	68 134
Q3	4 362	10 295	10 840	3 045	5 217	7 108	11 052	6 075	..	..	..	67 504
Q4	4 231	10 306	10 871	3 019	5 320	7 067	11 120	5 821	..	..	..	66 822
1976 Q1	4 480	10 340	10 484	3 075	5 478	7 147	11 137	5 744	..	..	..	67 164
Q2	4 569	10 375	10 965	3 153	5 242	7 097	11 217	5 957	..	..	..	67 629
Q3	4 632	10 505	11 258	3 118	5 281	7 215	11 278	6 142	..	..	..	68 312
Q4	4 919	10 264	11 002	3 124	5 529	7 269	11 342	5 952	..	..	..	68 372
1977 Q1	4 342	10 145	10 697	3 100	5 382	7 157	11 381	5 988	..	..	..	66 907
Q2	4 074	10 312	10 813	3 067	5 532	7 027	11 427	6 078	..	..	..	66 781
Q3	4 339	10 010	10 756	3 211	5 561	7 312	11 475	6 178	..	..	..	67 665
Q4	4 543	10 659	10 927	3 277	5 438	7 382	11 549	6 151	..	..	..	69 081
1978 Q1	4 866	10 546	11 017	3 325	5 537	7 497	11 588	6 130	..	..	..	70 737
Q2	4 777	10 307	11 136	3 359	5 666	7 725	11 642	6 032	..	..	..	70 514
Q3	5 306	10 580	11 096	3 587	5 646	7 800	11 701	6 004	..	..	..	72 092
Q4	4 839	10 446	11 168	3 561	5 584	7 919	11 746	6 017	..	..	..	71 558
1979 Q1	5 145	10 457	11 247	3 563	6 058	7 762	11 825	5 876	..	..	..	72 732
Q2	6 789	10 698	11 733	3 832	5 810	8 199	11 876	6 092	..	..	..	76 697
Q3	4 911	10 870	11 371	3 672	5 718	7 865	11 928	6 011	..	..	..	73 591
Q4	5 476	10 787	11 345	3 750	5 614	7 943	11 959	6 172	..	..	..	74 433
1980 Q1	5 785	10 887	11 475	3 720	5 805	7 874	12 011	6 209	..	..	..	75 719
Q2	5 180	10 787	10 720	3 646	5 479	7 804	12 048	6 030	..	..	..	73 652
Q3	5 335	10 690	10 992	3 666	5 756	7 680	12 091	6 104	..	..	..	74 703
Q4	4 978	10 502	10 821	3 623	5 853	7 651	12 144	5 897	..	..	..	73 182
1981 Q1	5 336	10 681	10 771	3 648	5 671	7 798	12 181	5 930	..	..	..	74 450
Q2	5 479	10 577	10 477	3 550	5 734	7 815	12 215	5 711	..	..	..	74 360
Q3	5 448	10 710	10 441	3 590	5 661	7 769	12 264	5 645	..	..	..	74 385
Q4	5 411	10 623	10 259	3 732	5 910	7 781	12 310	5 616	..	..	..	74 042
1982 Q1	5 221	10 759	10 064	3 746	5 658	7 911	12 372	5 648	..	..	..	74 170
Q2	5 416	10 794	10 073	3 688	5 716	7 876	12 421	5 565	..	..	..	74 139
Q3	5 907	10 516	9 910	3 751	5 893	8 023	12 470	5 578	..	..	..	75 441
Q4	6 252	10 625	10 153	3 869	5 829	8 046	12 509	5 593	..	..	..	76 060
1983 Q1	6 779	10 777	10 239	3 958	5 585	8 164	12 742	5 750	..	..	..	77 609
Q2	6 617	10 706	10 259	4 008	5 903	8 070	12 783	5 848	..	..	..	77 840
Q3	6 691	10 925	10 435	4 032	5 788	8 201	12 825	6 034	..	..	..	79 158
Q4	6 663	11 008	10 196	4 093	5 852	8 242	12 860	6 169	..	..	..	79 041
1984 Q1	6 631	10 844	10 474	4 090	5 972	8 314	12 897	6 088	..	..	..	79 408
Q2	6 779	10 710	10 345	4 168	5 906	8 517	12 937	6 231	..	..	..	79 970
Q3	6 323	10 504	10 278	4 286	5 766	8 545	12 977	6 210	..	..	..	79 383
Q4	6 824	10 618	10 120	4 402	5 931	8 657	13 020	6 394	..	..	..	80 596

See footnotes on page 51.

Source: Office for National Statistics: Enquiries 0171 533 5998

1.7 Household final consumption expenditure-component categories[1]

continued

£ million, 1995 prices, seasonally adjusted

	Durable goods	Food (Household expend-iture)[2]	Alcoholic drink and tobacco	Clothing and footwear	Energy products	Other goods	Rent, water and sewerage charges	Catering	Transport and communicat-ion	Financial services	Other services[3]	Total
	AEIW	CCCA	FCCD	FCCE	CCCG	ABZQ	ABRJ	CCUU	ABJZ	CEGN	ABKR	ABJR
1985 Q1	6 875	10 682	10 443	4 490	6 109	8 714	13 061	6 387	..	..	..	81 654
Q2	6 801	10 826	10 367	4 578	6 187	8 868	13 104	6 514	..	..	..	82 145
Q3	7 051	10 772	10 330	4 625	6 188	8 992	13 149	6 488	..	..	..	83 353
Q4	7 080	10 933	10 249	4 663	6 181	9 106	13 196	6 599	..	..	..	84 252
1986 Q1	7 404	11 011	10 373	4 903	6 627	9 324	13 243	6 676	7 324	2 725	8 087	86 647
Q2	7 711	11 130	10 278	4 996	6 694	9 545	13 284	7 160	7 485	2 808	8 436	88 505
Q3	7 617	11 184	10 260	5 025	6 590	9 777	13 332	7 361	7 554	2 860	8 609	89 121
Q4	7 972	11 247	10 256	5 051	6 254	9 867	13 378	7 307	7 636	3 070	8 506	89 558
1987 Q1	8 006	11 102	10 303	5 088	6 780	10 012	13 447	7 060	7 900	3 161	8 874	90 752
Q2	8 182	11 255	10 388	5 206	6 510	10 263	13 488	7 334	8 072	3 209	9 198	92 147
Q3	8 435	11 616	10 455	5 322	6 702	10 559	13 534	7 391	8 151	3 343	9 273	93 897
Q4	8 803	11 736	10 455	5 437	6 725	10 725	13 582	7 717	8 246	3 407	9 837	95 805
1988 Q1	9 278	11 869	10 659	5 353	6 783	10 856	13 636	8 238	8 371	3 520	10 245	97 945
Q2	9 429	11 598	10 463	5 364	6 697	11 084	13 690	8 771	8 509	3 628	10 478	98 825
Q3	9 931	11 690	10 536	5 431	7 020	11 383	13 739	9 220	8 707	3 680	10 739	101 214
Q4	9 914	11 588	10 523	5 506	6 964	11 730	13 783	9 855	8 738	3 799	10 965	102 443
1989 Q1	10 161	11 876	10 543	5 473	6 574	11 572	13 825	9 593	8 851	3 874	11 220	102 889
Q2	10 279	12 004	10 534	5 423	6 951	11 527	13 855	9 530	8 781	3 933	11 051	103 282
Q3	10 009	11 818	10 468	5 326	6 769	11 692	13 894	9 920	8 833	3 996	11 062	103 141
Q4	10 097	11 840	10 423	5 309	6 989	12 177	13 940	9 989	8 897	4 022	11 217	104 186
1990 Q1	9 878	11 742	10 445	5 655	6 572	12 173	13 981	9 914	9 095	4 085	11 148	104 130
Q2	9 798	11 868	10 442	5 517	6 913	12 074	14 020	9 897	9 154	4 151	11 384	104 622
Q3	9 337	11 685	10 428	5 504	7 014	11 980	14 072	9 814	9 073	4 176	11 322	103 715
Q4	9 088	11 760	10 339	5 429	6 890	11 768	14 054	9 914	8 998	4 191	11 612	103 321
1991 Q1	9 008	11 725	10 194	5 649	7 067	11 963	14 136	9 455	8 696	4 202	11 515	103 067
Q2	8 420	11 764	10 015	5 549	7 246	11 888	14 173	9 183	8 774	4 129	11 456	101 734
Q3	8 707	11 833	10 116	5 670	6 874	11 875	14 198	9 084	8 767	4 106	11 442	101 997
Q4	8 301	11 792	9 933	5 634	7 094	11 841	14 236	9 084	8 884	4 040	11 335	101 511
1992 Q1	8 251	11 643	9 709	5 715	6 864	11 904	14 236	8 994	8 817	4 032	11 706	101 237
Q2	8 610	11 938	9 579	5 876	6 854	12 119	14 284	9 078	8 852	4 060	11 719	102 482
Q3	8 869	12 050	9 529	6 025	7 088	11 940	14 321	9 043	8 945	4 066	11 502	103 008
Q4	8 744	12 033	9 598	6 067	7 155	11 854	14 350	9 164	9 090	4 044	11 616	103 299
1993 Q1	8 852	12 053	9 736	6 103	6 808	12 234	14 418	9 331	9 442	4 245	11 110	103 892
Q2	8 754	12 000	9 413	6 099	6 913	12 259	14 487	9 377	9 548	4 255	11 408	104 150
Q3	9 229	11 962	9 321	6 224	7 157	12 332	14 531	9 448	9 704	4 371	11 714	105 746
Q4	9 386	12 267	9 391	6 449	7 245	12 210	14 579	9 383	9 779	4 297	11 447	106 293
1994 Q1	9 667	12 283	9 532	6 568	6 960	12 401	14 622	9 277	9 769	4 254	11 771	107 104
Q2	9 569	12 150	9 563	6 770	7 156	12 426	14 681	9 212	9 971	4 087	11 857	107 442
Q3	9 616	12 242	9 641	6 799	6 832	12 623	14 743	9 363	10 128	4 066	12 011	108 064
Q4	9 731	12 256	9 705	6 791	6 806	12 669	14 816	9 467	10 143	3 990	12 478	108 852
1995 Q1	9 830	12 426	9 402	6 918	6 824	12 662	14 865	9 510	10 205	4 092	12 101	108 835
Q2	9 750	12 330	9 355	7 060	6 850	12 844	14 935	9 332	10 321	4 070	12 565	109 412
Q3	10 038	12 370	9 369	7 077	6 641	13 028	14 976	9 336	10 229	4 319	12 184	109 567
Q4	9 878	12 148	9 330	7 292	6 803	13 413	15 022	9 549	10 605	4 303	12 296	110 639
1996 Q1	10 270	12 544	9 451	7 281	7 040	13 511	15 024	9 853	10 522	4 543	12 360	112 399
Q2	10 830	12 461	9 610	7 433	7 214	13 681	15 102	9 942	10 497	4 443	12 051	113 264
Q3	10 670	12 923	9 445	7 526	6 944	14 025	15 113	9 959	10 606	4 454	12 244	113 909
Q4	10 931	13 003	9 501	7 533	7 012	14 202	15 105	9 950	10 563	4 594	12 720	115 114
1997 Q1	10 931	12 972	9 528	7 621	6 929	14 473	15 135	9 980	10 604	4 686	13 121	115 980
Q2	11 805	12 935	9 411	7 736	6 928	14 678	15 211	10 013	10 892	4 848	13 346	117 803
Q3	12 380	12 750	9 367	7 769	6 740	14 935	15 266	10 236	10 934	4 947	13 472	118 796
Q4	12 837	13 129	9 227	7 950	6 830	15 079	15 322	10 170	10 957	5 035	13 586	120 122
1998 Q1	13 005	12 919	9 247	7 982	6 735	15 486	15 332	10 285	11 150	4 915	14 362	121 418
Q2	12 824	12 973	9 191	8 051	6 976	15 758	15 364	10 541	11 360	5 150	14 340	122 528
Q3	12 868	12 911	9 067	8 250	6 689	15 979	15 403	10 855	11 542	5 156	14 522	123 242
Q4	13 100	12 824	8 962	8 261	6 706	16 196	15 456	10 928	11 813	4 970	14 974	124 190
1999 Q1	13 493	12 767	9 139	8 499	6 803	16 601	15 523	10 837	12 081	5 406	15 130	126 279
Q2	13 726	13 256	9 139	8 627	6 829	16 891	15 610	10 764	12 385	5 265	15 077	127 569
Q3	13 934	13 270	9 184	8 702	6 601	17 346	15 703	10 847	12 504	5 275	15 178	128 544
Q4	14 163	12 984	9 326	8 834	6 749	17 663	15 797	11 018	12 833	5 416	15 689	130 472
2000 Q1	14 620	13 241	9 146	9 055	6 783	17 677	15 890	11 015	12 750	5 563	15 569	131 309

See footnotes on page 51.

Source: Office for National Statistics: Enquiries 0171 533 5998

1.8 Gross fixed capital formation

£ million, current prices

	Analysis by sector							Analysis by asset				
			Public corporations[2]		Private sector							
	Business investment[1]	General government	NHS trusts	Transfer costs of non-produced assets	Dwellings	Transfer cost of non-produced assets	Total	Transport equipment	Other machinery and equipment	Dwellings	Other building and structures[3]	Intangible fixed assets
	NPEM	NNBF	DLVG	DLXQ	DFDF	EQBY	NPQX	DLWZ	DLXI	DFDK	EQEC	DLXP
1948	..	512	–	..	52	..	1 502	261	531	344	363	3
1949	..	523	–	..	61	..	1 662	285	594	339	440	4
1950	..	556	–	..	58	..	1 799	275	679	338	502	5
1951	..	662	–	..	69	..	2 011	272	791	386	557	5
1952	..	800	–	..	120	..	2 265	280	838	513	628	6
1953	..	873	–	..	209	..	2 540	330	875	658	671	6
1954	..	805	–	..	255	..	2 741	354	971	674	736	6
1955	..	795	–	..	294	..	3 026	389	1 098	667	865	7
1956	..	831	–	..	325	..	3 315	449	1 202	662	995	7
1957	..	849	–	..	330	..	3 600	518	1 347	644	1 083	8
1958	..	821	–	..	352	..	3 724	550	1 390	616	1 160	8
1959	..	868	–	..	416	..	3 980	593	1 472	684	1 223	8
1960	..	897	–	..	490	..	4 368	660	1 591	761	1 347	9
1961	..	958	–	..	544	..	4 889	622	1 870	835	1 553	9
1962	..	1 068	–	..	581	..	5 049	541	1 887	925	1 688	8
1963	..	1 158	–	..	640	..	5 295	543	1 993	1 020	1 731	8
1964	..	1 433	–	..	769	..	6 279	649	2 293	1 283	2 046	8
1965	..	1 525	–	..	828	..	6 804	642	2 572	1 385	2 188	17
1966	..	1 719	–	..	837	..	7 261	594	2 846	1 489	2 299	33
1967	..	1 999	–	..	931	..	7 945	666	2 984	1 676	2 558	61
1968	..	2 197	–	..	1 089	..	8 728	835	3 140	1 907	2 803	43
1969	..	2 265	–	..	1 079	..	9 066	875	3 262	1 917	2 954	58
1970	..	2 457	–	..	1 069	..	10 036	1 002	3 773	1 870	3 282	109
1971	..	2 605	–	..	1 422	..	11 243	1 135	4 070	2 218	3 686	134
1972	..	2 776	–	..	1 748	..	12 347	1 364	4 157	2 566	4 090	170
1973	..	3 681	–	..	2 133	..	15 227	1 669	5 034	3 150	5 153	221
1974	..	4 395	–	..	2 310	..	18 134	1 845	5 851	3 786	6 331	321
1975	..	5 040	–	..	2 725	..	21 856	2 062	6 902	4 682	7 778	432
1976	..	5 506	–	..	3 151	..	25 516	2 375	8 558	5 450	8 595	538
1977	..	4 865	–	..	3 452	..	28 201	3 248	9 950	5 699	8 657	647
1978	..	4 889	–	..	4 091	..	32 208	4 112	11 709	6 325	9 481	581
1979	..	5 483	–	..	5 312	..	38 211	4 814	13 832	7 649	11 289	627
1980	..	6 036	–	..	6 115	..	43 238	4 741	15 301	8 674	13 680	842
1981	..	5 324	–	..	6 174	..	43 331	4 038	15 454	8 138	14 603	1 098
1982	..	5 235	–	..	6 850	..	47 394	4 511	16 734	8 920	15 730	1 499
1983	..	6 730	–	..	7 757	..	51 490	4 781	18 377	10 447	16 157	1 728
1984	..	7 780	–	..	9 186	..	58 698	5 938	20 782	11 932	17 817	2 229
1985	..	8 184	–	..	9 683	..	64 463	6 726	24 349	12 219	18 711	2 458
1986	43 229	9 094	–	–122	11 526	4 994	68 718	6 519	25 359	14 140	20 516	2 184
1987	50 158	9 184	–	–134	13 640	6 076	78 924	7 850	28 171	16 548	24 273	2 082
1988	60 348	8 468	–	–383	18 203	9 440	96 076	9 222	32 429	21 097	30 736	2 592
1989	72 421	11 617	–	–289	18 958	8 326	111 033	10 699	38 018	22 771	36 722	2 823
1990	75 575	14 563	–	–100	16 867	7 409	114 314	10 593	37 817	21 048	41 285	3 571
1991	69 040	14 062	104	168	15 577	5 729	104 680	8 668	35 075	18 339	38 535	4 063
1992	64 869	14 244	635	358	16 246	3 926	100 278	8 397	34 690	18 825	34 584	3 782
1993	63 886	13 722	1 033	376	17 124	5 089	101 230	9 594	35 566	19 892	32 530	3 648
1994	67 900	14 058	1 590	349	18 285	5 208	107 390	11 329	37 693	21 233	33 522	3 613
1995	76 437	14 005	1 786	126	18 784	5 222	116 360	11 055	44 464	21 588	35 314	3 939
1996	85 143	11 316	1 551	133	20 467	7 065	125 675	12 163	49 216	22 766	37 394	4 136
1997	93 023	9 872	1 327	314	22 018	7 599	134 153	13 186	52 206	23 927	40 585	4 249
1998	104 289	10 478	1 467	15	24 001	7 821	148 071	15 928	57 987	25 831	43 778	4 547
1999	110 965	10 186	1 449	164	25 996	9 612	158 372	17 297	59 564	27 599	49 442	4 470

1 Not including dwellings and costs associated with the transfer of ownership of non-produced assets.

2 Remaining investment by public corporations is included within business investment.

3 Including costs associated with transfer of ownership of non-produced assets.

Source: Office for National Statistics; Enquiries 020 7533 6010

1.8 Gross fixed capital formation

continued

£ million, current prices, not seasonally adjusted

	Analysis by sector							Analysis by asset				
			Public corporations[2]		Private sector							
	Business investment[1]	General government	NHS trusts	Transfer costs of non-produced assets	Dwellings	Transfer cost of non-produced assets	Total	Transport equipment	Other machinery and equipment	Dwellings	Other building and structures[3]	Intangible fixed assets
	NPEM	NNBF	DLVG	DLXQ	DFDF	EQBY	NPQX	DLWZ	DLXI	DFDK	EQEC	DLXP
1955 Q1	..	198	–	..	62	..	701	89	259	163	188	2
Q2	..	199	–	..	70	..	721	100	255	162	202	2
Q3	..	199	–	..	83	..	766	91	274	171	228	2
Q4	..	199	–	..	79	..	838	109	310	171	247	1
1956 Q1	..	205	–	..	75	..	787	107	298	153	227	2
Q2	..	208	–	..	83	..	799	104	278	171	244	2
Q3	..	208	–	..	85	..	823	109	290	171	251	2
Q4	..	210	–	..	82	..	906	129	336	167	273	1
1957 Q1	..	212	–	..	81	..	866	112	329	160	263	2
Q2	..	212	–	..	86	..	876	128	317	169	260	2
Q3	..	212	–	..	80	..	889	131	330	157	269	2
Q4	..	213	–	..	83	..	969	147	371	158	291	2
1958 Q1	..	205	–	..	81	..	921	139	355	148	277	2
Q2	..	205	–	..	85	..	903	137	328	156	280	2
Q3	..	205	–	..	91	..	915	124	340	155	294	2
Q4	..	206	–	..	95	..	985	150	367	157	309	2
1959 Q1	..	216	–	..	95	..	921	126	357	156	280	2
Q2	..	217	–	..	101	..	971	153	352	170	294	2
Q3	..	217	–	..	107	..	983	137	360	176	308	2
Q4	..	218	–	..	113	..	1 105	177	403	182	341	2
1960 Q1	..	225	–	..	113	..	1 038	155	387	179	315	2
Q2	..	224	–	..	124	..	1 040	163	355	194	326	2
Q3	..	224	–	..	126	..	1 102	158	407	193	342	2
Q4	..	224	–	..	127	..	1 188	184	442	195	364	3
1961 Q1	..	238	–	..	129	..	1 164	161	450	196	355	2
Q2	..	239	–	..	137	..	1 189	150	442	210	385	2
Q3	..	240	–	..	140	..	1 257	156	483	215	401	2
Q4	..	241	–	..	138	..	1 279	155	495	214	412	3
1962 Q1	..	266	–	..	139	..	1 228	137	483	214	392	2
Q2	..	266	–	..	149	..	1 245	138	453	237	415	2
Q3	..	267	–	..	151	..	1 277	127	463	243	442	2
Q4	..	269	–	..	142	..	1 299	139	488	231	439	2
1963 Q1	..	224	–	..	116	..	1 169	130	491	177	369	2
Q2	..	291	–	..	167	..	1 292	130	464	267	429	2
Q3	..	323	–	..	177	..	1 368	131	500	284	451	2
Q4	..	320	–	..	180	..	1 466	152	538	292	482	2
1964 Q1	..	341	–	..	176	..	1 508	159	574	297	476	2
Q2	..	351	–	..	194	..	1 507	161	533	328	483	2
Q3	..	370	–	..	199	..	1 586	160	567	328	529	2
Q4	..	371	–	..	200	..	1 678	169	619	330	558	2
1965 Q1	..	367	–	..	204	..	1 697	156	663	336	538	4
Q2	..	359	–	..	209	..	1 619	166	583	343	523	4
Q3	..	387	–	..	211	..	1 673	143	625	347	554	4
Q4	..	412	–	..	204	..	1 815	177	701	359	573	5
1966 Q1	..	412	–	..	201	..	1 803	152	731	356	556	8
Q2	..	404	–	..	215	..	1 713	151	656	363	535	8
Q3	..	429	–	..	215	..	1 821	140	706	383	584	8
Q4	..	474	–	..	206	..	1 924	151	753	387	624	9
1967 Q1	..	499	–	..	212	..	1 980	163	780	399	623	15
Q2	..	473	–	..	236	..	1 945	177	724	417	612	15
Q3	..	500	–	..	249	..	1 981	163	720	437	646	15
Q4	..	527	–	..	234	..	2 039	163	760	423	677	16
1968 Q1	..	591	–	..	239	..	2 151	180	809	451	700	11
Q2	..	513	–	..	256	..	2 029	194	710	447	667	11
Q3	..	532	–	..	286	..	2 158	209	746	496	696	11
Q4	..	561	–	..	308	..	2 390	252	875	513	740	10
1969 Q1	..	569	–	..	250	..	2 190	212	799	460	705	14
Q2	..	500	–	..	256	..	2 121	226	750	445	685	15
Q3	..	569	–	..	287	..	2 295	199	811	508	762	15
Q4	..	627	–	..	286	..	2 460	238	902	504	802	14

See footnotes on page 58.

Source: Office for National Statistics; Enquiries 020 7533 6010

1.8 Gross fixed capital formation

continued

£ million, current prices, not seasonally adjusted

	Analysis by sector							Analysis by asset				
			Public corporations[2]		Private sector							
	Business investment[1]	General government	NHS trusts	Transfer costs of non-produced assets	Dwellings	Transfer cost of non-produced assets	Total	Transport equipment	Other machinery and equipment	Dwellings	Other building and structures[3]	Intangible fixed assets
	NPEM	NNBF	DLVG	DLXQ	DFDF	EQBY	NPQX	DLWZ	DLXI	DFDK	EQEC	DLXP
1970 Q1	..	587	–	..	230	..	2 349	226	917	422	760	24
Q2	..	555	–	..	246	..	2 390	279	874	437	776	24
Q3	..	631	–	..	286	..	2 523	233	925	496	842	27
Q4	..	684	–	..	307	..	2 774	264	1 057	515	904	34
1971 Q1	..	696	–	..	290	..	2 664	264	1 010	482	877	31
Q2	..	577	–	..	343	..	2 676	303	944	539	858	32
Q3	..	631	–	..	394	..	2 847	275	1 018	595	925	34
Q4	..	701	–	..	395	..	3 056	293	1 098	602	1 026	37
1972 Q1	..	766	–	..	389	..	2 978	315	1 048	590	984	41
Q2	..	611	–	..	424	..	2 934	346	967	623	956	42
Q3	..	676	–	..	476	..	3 077	304	1 017	679	1 035	42
Q4	..	723	–	..	459	..	3 358	399	1 125	674	1 115	45
1973 Q1	..	1 009	–	..	462	..	3 739	402	1 282	706	1 297	52
Q2	..	768	–	..	562	..	3 528	386	1 125	793	1 171	53
Q3	..	925	–	..	515	..	3 748	385	1 232	784	1 290	57
Q4	..	979	–	..	594	..	4 212	496	1 395	867	1 395	59
1974 Q1	..	1 326	–	..	555	..	4 432	397	1 421	905	1 632	77
Q2	..	809	–	..	595	..	4 109	427	1 311	892	1 400	79
Q3	..	1 149	–	..	525	..	4 532	452	1 430	947	1 622	81
Q4	..	1 111	–	..	635	..	5 061	569	1 689	1 042	1 677	84
1975 Q1	..	1 367	–	..	674	..	5 249	509	1 664	1 147	1 827	102
Q2	..	1 119	–	..	744	..	5 095	474	1 571	1 206	1 738	106
Q3	..	1 188	–	..	655	..	5 628	501	1 804	1 108	2 105	110
Q4	..	1 366	–	..	652	..	5 884	578	1 863	1 221	2 108	114
1976 Q1	..	1 700	–	..	844	..	6 413	582	2 084	1 476	2 146	125
Q2	..	1 190	–	..	759	..	5 921	547	1 914	1 276	2 055	129
Q3	..	1 297	–	..	725	..	6 350	600	2 114	1 281	2 225	130
Q4	..	1 319	–	..	823	..	6 832	646	2 446	1 417	2 169	154
1977 Q1	..	1 558	–	..	802	..	6 762	755	2 342	1 454	2 075	136
Q2	..	1 000	–	..	816	..	6 623	786	2 243	1 312	2 117	165
Q3	..	1 128	–	..	866	..	7 045	839	2 529	1 399	2 105	173
Q4	..	1 179	–	..	968	..	7 771	868	2 836	1 534	2 360	173
1978 Q1	..	1 496	–	..	1 051	..	8 028	1 072	2 815	1 707	2 295	139
Q2	..	996	–	..	900	..	7 549	1 072	2 711	1 363	2 260	143
Q3	..	1 183	–	..	1 001	..	8 036	1 015	2 941	1 575	2 361	144
Q4	..	1 214	–	..	1 139	..	8 595	953	3 242	1 680	2 565	155
1979 Q1	..	1 573	–	..	1 124	..	8 833	1 134	3 232	1 742	2 578	147
Q2	..	1 069	–	..	1 170	..	8 717	1 306	3 112	1 646	2 510	143
Q3	..	1 395	–	..	1 256	..	9 642	1 213	3 449	1 856	2 966	158
Q4	..	1 446	–	..	1 762	..	11 019	1 161	4 039	2 405	3 235	179
1980 Q1	..	1 805	–	..	1 586	..	10 754	1 262	3 737	2 362	3 218	175
Q2	..	1 198	–	..	1 354	..	10 057	1 267	3 557	1 899	3 132	202
Q3	..	1 473	–	..	1 510	..	10 739	1 044	3 845	2 133	3 491	226
Q4	..	1 560	–	..	1 665	..	11 688	1 168	4 162	2 280	3 839	239
1981 Q1	..	1 875	–	..	1 453	..	10 755	963	3 807	2 044	3 722	219
Q2	..	1 112	–	..	1 622	..	10 242	1 054	3 530	2 055	3 336	267
Q3	..	1 123	–	..	1 656	..	10 862	910	3 806	2 130	3 713	303
Q4	..	1 214	–	..	1 443	..	11 472	1 111	4 311	1 909	3 832	309
1982 Q1	..	1 670	–	..	1 408	..	11 383	1 118	3 970	2 056	3 905	334
Q2	..	903	–	..	1 791	..	11 044	1 053	3 915	2 179	3 525	372
Q3	..	1 264	–	..	1 785	..	12 002	1 174	4 139	2 249	4 067	373
Q4	..	1 398	–	..	1 866	..	12 965	1 166	4 710	2 436	4 233	420
1983 Q1	..	2 418	–	..	1 426	..	12 816	1 226	4 533	2 418	4 203	436
Q2	..	1 059	–	..	1 978	..	11 647	1 116	4 160	2 426	3 552	393
Q3	..	1 567	–	..	2 137	..	12 729	1 089	4 447	2 730	4 033	430
Q4	..	1 686	–	..	2 216	..	14 298	1 350	5 237	2 873	4 369	469
1984 Q1	..	2 667	–	..	1 819	..	14 348	1 565	4 913	2 813	4 628	429
Q2	..	1 355	–	..	2 386	..	13 419	1 222	4 713	2 880	4 064	540
Q3	..	1 839	–	..	2 593	..	14 806	1 450	5 106	3 222	4 438	590
Q4	..	1 919	–	..	2 388	..	16 125	1 701	6 050	3 017	4 687	670

See footnotes on page 58.

Source: Office for National Statistics; Enquiries 020 7533 6010

1.8 Gross fixed capital formation

continued

£ million, current prices, not seasonally adjusted

	Analysis by sector							Analysis by asset				
			Public corporations[2]		Private sector							
	Business investment[1]	General government	NHS trusts	Transfer costs of non-produced assets	Dwellings	Transfer cost of non-produced assets	Total	Transport equipment	Other machinery and equipment	Dwellings	Other building and structures[3]	Intangible fixed assets
	NPEM	NNBF	DLVG	DLXQ	DFDF	EQBY	NPQX	DLWZ	DLXI	DFDK	EQEC	DLXP
1985 Q1	..	2 729	–	..	1 799	..	16 872	2 294	6 452	2 748	4 779	599
Q2	..	1 458	–	..	2 553	..	14 384	1 400	5 129	2 991	4 267	597
Q3	..	1 949	–	..	2 729	..	15 995	1 492	5 852	3 302	4 720	629
Q4	..	2 048	–	..	2 602	..	17 212	1 540	6 916	3 178	4 945	633
1986 Q1	10 808	3 259	–	–74	2 239	1 192	17 424	1 714	6 531	3 301	5 293	585
Q2	9 678	1 679	–	–28	2 615	1 083	15 027	1 451	5 488	3 030	4 521	537
Q3	10 865	2 032	–	–20	3 225	1 349	17 449	1 607	6 272	3 746	5 288	536
Q4	11 878	2 124	–	–	3 447	1 370	18 818	1 747	7 068	4 063	5 414	526
1987 Q1	11 211	3 219	–	28	2 658	1 365	18 481	1 754	6 751	3 672	5 849	455
Q2	11 328	1 550	–	–137	3 242	1 465	17 448	1 855	6 307	3 742	5 078	466
Q3	12 934	2 018	–	–24	4 097	1 606	20 631	2 111	7 062	4 741	6 182	535
Q4	14 685	2 397	–	–1	3 643	1 640	22 364	2 130	8 051	4 393	7 164	626
1988 Q1	13 925	3 523	–	–28	3 874	1 949	23 243	2 350	7 820	5 030	7 467	576
Q2	13 961	1 595	–	–103	4 744	1 949	22 146	2 219	7 106	5 240	6 949	632
Q3	15 550	1 497	–	–89	4 844	2 880	24 682	2 337	8 416	5 458	7 817	654
Q4	16 912	1 853	–	–163	4 741	2 662	26 005	2 316	9 087	5 369	8 503	730
1989 Q1	16 853	3 837	–	–141	4 826	2 503	27 878	2 700	9 204	6 016	9 281	677
Q2	17 210	1 862	–	–5	4 787	1 889	25 743	2 541	8 902	5 428	8 177	695
Q3	18 666	2 583	–	–69	5 000	1 984	28 164	2 733	9 619	5 846	9 282	684
Q4	19 692	3 335	–	–74	4 345	1 950	29 248	2 725	10 293	5 481	9 982	767
1990 Q1	18 739	5 793	–	–78	3 547	2 462	30 463	3 196	10 387	5 569	10 568	743
Q2	18 461	2 371	–	–43	4 186	1 624	26 599	2 430	8 889	4 802	9 619	859
Q3	18 976	2 932	–	17	4 656	1 697	28 278	2 551	9 193	5 401	10 215	918
Q4	19 399	3 467	–	4	4 478	1 626	28 974	2 416	9 348	5 276	10 883	1 051
1991 Q1	18 435	4 741	–	–2	3 400	1 731	28 305	2 519	9 338	4 509	10 981	958
Q2	16 469	2 563	30	55	3 856	1 313	24 286	2 148	7 990	4 357	8 767	1 024
Q3	16 394	3 287	30	59	4 255	1 400	25 425	1 738	8 392	4 794	9 499	1 002
Q4	17 742	3 471	44	56	4 066	1 285	26 664	2 263	9 355	4 679	9 288	1 079
1992 Q1	16 891	5 302	202	62	3 541	1 058	27 056	2 261	9 334	4 601	9 960	900
Q2	15 683	2 592	143	94	3 935	926	23 373	2 012	8 056	4 354	8 006	945
Q3	16 101	2 915	146	107	4 313	1 150	24 732	2 136	8 536	4 843	8 294	923
Q4	16 194	3 435	144	95	4 457	792	25 117	1 988	8 764	5 027	8 324	1 014
1993 Q1	16 087	5 691	148	130	3 488	978	26 522	2 936	8 874	4 632	9 189	891
Q2	14 899	2 419	294	61	4 369	1 009	23 051	1 891	8 258	4 794	7 239	869
Q3	16 128	2 806	296	94	4 587	1 253	25 164	2 512	8 858	5 148	7 727	919
Q4	16 772	2 806	295	91	4 680	1 849	26 493	2 255	9 576	5 318	8 375	969
1994 Q1	16 574	5 558	299	119	4 346	1 250	28 146	3 296	9 139	5 624	9 230	857
Q2	15 798	2 379	428	76	4 375	1 242	24 298	2 530	8 502	4 814	7 566	886
Q3	17 301	2 931	433	88	4 569	1 352	26 674	2 777	9 555	5 162	8 269	911
Q4	18 227	3 190	430	66	4 995	1 364	28 272	2 726	10 497	5 633	8 457	959
1995 Q1	17 571	5 354	435	81	4 515	1 570	29 526	2 834	10 648	5 663	9 460	921
Q2	18 124	2 406	449	6	4 819	1 183	26 987	2 990	10 008	5 260	7 773	956
Q3	20 028	2 908	453	23	4 582	1 263	29 257	2 811	11 467	5 110	8 919	950
Q4	20 714	3 337	449	16	4 868	1 206	30 590	2 420	12 341	5 555	9 162	1 112
1996 Q1	21 216	4 596	454	29	4 353	1 413	32 061	2 803	12 843	5 262	10 112	1 041
Q2	20 734	2 389	364	26	5 013	1 273	29 799	3 485	11 320	5 441	8 556	997
Q3	21 500	2 628	367	29	5 138	1 711	31 373	3 141	12 114	5 673	9 400	1 045
Q4	21 693	1 703	366	49	5 963	2 668	32 442	2 734	12 939	6 390	9 326	1 053
1997 Q1	22 120	4 023	369	97	4 957	1 597	33 163	3 765	12 308	5 821	10 219	1 050
Q2	22 328	1 208	284	71	5 354	2 270	31 515	2 985	12 549	5 658	9 197	1 126
Q3	23 491	2 178	349	76	5 305	1 905	33 304	3 365	12 930	5 677	10 281	1 051
Q4	25 084	2 463	325	70	6 402	1 827	36 171	3 071	14 419	6 771	10 888	1 022
1998 Q1	25 556	4 027	525	–27	5 401	1 763	37 245	4 086	14 456	6 088	11 551	1 064
Q2	25 350	1 347	290	–3	6 306	2 114	35 404	4 262	13 608	6 611	9 803	1 120
Q3	26 004	2 445	315	23	5 752	2 104	36 643	3 978	14 257	6 206	11 010	1 192
Q4	27 379	2 659	337	22	6 542	1 840	38 779	3 602	15 666	6 926	11 414	1 171
1999 Q1	27 377	3 654	495	38	5 825	2 275	39 664	4 720	15 096	6 395	12 358	1 095
Q2	27 126	1 488	265	54	6 637	2 139	37 709	4 537	14 233	6 864	10 962	1 113
Q3	27 638	2 415	351	64	6 245	2 660	39 373	4 233	14 596	6 683	12 737	1 124
Q4	28 824	2 629	338	8	7 289	2 538	41 626	3 807	15 639	7 657	13 385	1 138
2000 Q1	27 706	3 274	479	71	6 178	2 762	40 470	4 361	14 615	6 792	13 565	1 137

See footnotes on page 58.

Source: Office for National Statistics; Enquiries 020 7533 6010

1.8 Gross fixed capital formation

continued

£ million, 1995 prices

	Analysis by sector							Analysis by asset				
			Public corporations[2]		Private sector							
	Business investment[1]	General government	NHS trusts	Transfer costs of non-produced assets	Dwellings	Transfer cost of non-produced assets	Total	Transport equipment	Other machinery and equipment	Dwellings	Other building and structures[3]	Intangible fixed assets
	NPEN	EQDN	DLVH	EQDF	DFDP	EQCY	NPQR	DLWJ	DLWM	DFDV	DLWQ	EQDT
1948	..	..	–	..	..	..	23 396	..	..	7 735	..	..
1949	..	..	–	..	..	..	25 465	..	..	7 573	..	..
1950	..	..	–	..	..	..	26 838	..	..	7 413	..	..
1951	..	..	–	..	..	..	27 145	..	..	7 292	..	..
1952	..	..	–	..	..	..	27 596	..	..	8 785	..	..
1953	..	..	–	..	..	..	30 613	..	..	11 405	..	..
1954	..	..	–	..	..	..	33 124	..	..	11 771	..	..
1955	..	..	–	..	..	..	34 864	..	..	10 912	..	..
1956	..	..	–	..	..	..	36 457	..	..	10 444	..	..
1957	..	..	–	..	..	..	38 257	..	..	10 061	..	..
1958	..	..	–	..	..	..	38 570	..	..	9 578	..	..
1959	..	..	–	..	..	..	41 474	..	..	10 925	..	..
1960	..	..	–	..	..	..	45 191	..	..	12 142	..	..
1961	..	..	–	..	..	..	49 457	..	..	12 978	..	..
1962	..	..	–	..	9 489	..	49 801	..	..	13 936	..	..
1963	..	..	–	..	9 988	..	50 566	..	..	14 072	..	..
1964	..	..	–	..	11 675	..	58 648	..	..	17 358	..	..
1965	..	..	–	..	12 192	..	61 707	7 538	17 168	18 352	19 869	168
1966	..	..	–	..	11 859	..	63 376	6 813	18 271	18 958	20 031	316
1967	..	..	–	..	13 203	..	69 065	7 608	19 038	21 406	22 153	571
1968	..	..	–	..	14 571	..	73 040	9 321	19 423	23 109	23 269	395
1969	..	..	–	..	13 879	..	72 628	9 179	19 337	22 318	23 494	510
1970	..	..	–	..	12 717	..	74 751	9 747	20 747	20 259	24 334	1 034
1971	..	..	–	..	15 463	..	76 242	10 123	20 374	22 079	24 684	1 134
1972	..	..	–	..	16 876	..	76 212	11 365	19 623	22 709	24 126	1 306
1973	..	..	–	..	16 360	..	81 198	12 662	21 987	22 271	25 036	1 540
1974	..	..	–	..	14 307	..	79 614	12 151	22 621	20 977	23 933	1 917
1975	..	..	–	..	14 143	..	78 108	10 684	21 589	21 496	24 128	2 026
1976	..	..	–	..	14 315	..	79 457	10 358	22 319	22 179	24 216	2 170
1977	..	..	–	..	14 205	..	78 240	11 656	22 660	21 114	22 670	2 279
1978	..	..	–	..	15 158	..	80 206	12 774	24 233	21 283	22 322	1 890
1979	..	..	–	..	16 529	..	82 307	13 420	26 072	22 025	21 639	1 800
1980	..	..	–	..	15 621	..	78 398	11 351	26 040	20 402	20 607	2 057
1981	..	..	–	..	13 936	..	71 451	8 915	24 250	16 888	19 987	2 366
1982	..	..	–	..	14 845	..	75 666	9 169	24 543	17 963	21 998	2 926
1983	..	..	–	..	15 946	..	79 489	9 448	25 731	20 184	22 384	3 156
1984	..	..	–	..	17 016	..	86 912	11 070	28 187	21 055	24 374	3 807
1985	..	..	–	..	16 559	..	90 421	11 646	31 578	20 139	24 404	3 953
1986	..	9 964	–	–500	18 540	9 047	92 330	10 505	32 318	22 047	25 353	3 308
1987	61 744	9 945	–	–645	20 303	10 005	100 520	11 544	34 047	23 836	28 829	3 002
1988	72 036	9 171	–	–522	24 416	11 639	115 362	12 800	39 509	27 596	32 827	3 592
1989	80 671	11 152	–	–297	22 775	9 088	122 158	13 734	44 665	27 096	34 649	3 645
1990	80 626	13 277	–	–103	18 746	7 540	119 368	12 499	43 181	23 434	37 051	4 229
1991	73 526	13 339	90	182	16 603	5 716	109 000	9 656	39 086	19 587	36 301	4 474
1992	70 660	14 436	644	351	17 311	5 045	108 246	9 253	38 031	20 041	36 674	3 914
1993	68 449	15 043	1 118	368	18 353	5 821	109 127	10 589	36 958	21 491	36 284	3 677
1994	70 947	15 255	1 704	355	19 076	5 705	113 042	11 927	38 171	22 267	37 046	3 631
1995	76 437	14 005	1 786	126	18 784	5 222	116 360	11 055	44 464	21 588	35 314	3 939
1996	83 195	10 891	1 467	151	19 903	6 435	122 042	11 777	49 124	22 154	34 825	4 162
1997	93 006	9 691	1 238	327	20 824	6 160	131 246	12 982	54 241	22 669	37 251	4 103
1998	105 866	9 993	1 365	314	21 521	5 378	144 437	14 913	63 833	23 231	38 304	4 156
1999	113 899	10 038	1 322	376	22 109	5 528	153 272	16 256	68 701	23 522	40 805	3 988

See footnotes on page 58.

Source: Office for National Statistics; Enquiries 020 7533 6010

1.8 Gross fixed capital formation

continued

£ million, 1995 prices, not seasonally adjusted

	Analysis by sector							Analysis by asset				
				Public corporations[2]	Private sector							
	Business investment[1]	General government	NHS trusts	Transfer costs of non-produced assets	Dwellings	Transfer cost of non-produced assets	Total	Transport equipment	Other machinery and equipment	Dwellings	Other building and structures[3]	Intangible fixed assets
	NPEN	EQDN	DLVH	EQDF	DFDP	EQCY	NPQR	DLWJ	DLWM	DFDV	DLWQ	EQDT
1955 Q1	..	..	–	..	..	..	8 309	..	..	..	..	..
Q2	..	..	–	..	..	..	8 405	..	..	..	..	..
Q3	..	..	–	..	..	..	8 689	..	..	..	..	..
Q4	..	..	–	..	..	..	9 461	..	..	..	..	..
1956 Q1	..	..	–	..	..	..	8 819	..	..	..	..	..
Q2	..	..	–	..	..	..	8 837	..	..	..	..	..
Q3	..	..	–	..	..	..	8 972	..	..	..	..	..
Q4	..	..	–	..	..	..	9 829	..	..	..	..	..
1957 Q1	..	..	–	..	..	..	9 422	..	..	..	..	..
Q2	..	..	–	..	..	..	9 375	..	..	..	..	..
Q3	..	..	–	..	..	..	9 358	..	..	..	..	..
Q4	..	..	–	..	..	..	10 102	..	..	..	..	..
1958 Q1	..	..	–	..	..	..	9 531	..	..	..	..	..
Q2	..	..	–	..	..	..	9 338	..	..	..	..	..
Q3	..	..	–	..	..	..	9 503	..	..	..	..	..
Q4	..	..	–	..	..	..	10 198	..	..	..	..	..
1959 Q1	..	..	–	..	..	..	9 543	..	..	..	..	..
Q2	..	..	–	..	..	..	10 069	..	..	..	..	..
Q3	..	..	–	..	..	..	10 283	..	..	..	..	..
Q4	..	..	–	..	..	..	11 579	..	..	..	..	..
1960 Q1	..	..	–	..	..	..	10 887	..	..	..	..	..
Q2	..	..	–	..	..	..	10 869	..	..	..	..	..
Q3	..	..	–	..	..	..	11 267	..	..	..	..	..
Q4	..	..	–	..	..	..	12 168	..	..	..	..	..
1961 Q1	..	..	–	..	..	..	11 914	..	..	..	..	..
Q2	..	..	–	..	..	..	12 073	..	..	..	..	..
Q3	..	..	–	..	..	..	12 675	..	..	..	..	..
Q4	..	..	–	..	..	..	12 795	..	..	..	..	..
1962 Q1	..	..	–	..	2 324	..	12 276	..	..	3 301	..	..
Q2	..	..	–	..	2 479	..	12 303	..	..	3 641	..	..
Q3	..	..	–	..	2 435	..	12 603	..	..	3 613	..	..
Q4	..	..	–	..	2 251	..	12 619	..	..	3 381	..	..
1963 Q1	..	..	–	..	1 844	..	11 235	..	..	2 477	..	..
Q2	..	..	–	..	2 612	..	12 347	..	..	3 685	..	..
Q3	..	..	–	..	2 742	..	13 033	..	..	3 902	..	..
Q4	..	..	–	..	2 790	..	13 951	..	..	4 008	..	..
1964 Q1	..	..	–	..	2 705	..	14 253	..	..	4 038	..	..
Q2	..	..	–	..	2 959	..	14 081	..	..	4 437	..	..
Q3	..	..	–	..	2 994	..	14 764	..	..	4 428	..	..
Q4	..	..	–	..	3 017	..	15 550	..	..	4 455	..	..
1965 Q1	..	..	–	..	3 058	..	15 681	1 860	4 527	4 529	4 958	41
Q2	..	..	–	..	3 104	..	14 726	1 991	3 900	4 560	4 737	39
Q3	..	..	–	..	3 092	..	15 101	1 666	4 129	4 605	5 026	39
Q4	..	..	–	..	2 938	..	16 199	2 021	4 612	4 658	5 148	49
1966 Q1	..	..	–	..	2 890	..	16 079	1 770	4 815	4 593	4 964	78
Q2	..	..	–	..	3 057	..	15 046	1 769	4 232	4 648	4 679	77
Q3	..	..	–	..	3 022	..	15 746	1 565	4 507	4 842	5 027	76
Q4	..	..	–	..	2 890	..	16 505	1 709	4 717	4 875	5 361	85
1967 Q1	..	..	–	..	3 032	..	17 214	1 855	5 013	5 038	5 397	143
Q2	..	..	–	..	3 390	..	16 997	2 047	4 605	5 372	5 353	141
Q3	..	..	–	..	3 521	..	17 243	1 842	4 600	5 624	5 594	139
Q4	..	..	–	..	3 260	..	17 611	1 864	4 820	5 372	5 809	148
1968 Q1	..	..	–	..	3 272	..	18 504	2 084	5 147	5 624	5 960	101
Q2	..	..	–	..	3 450	..	17 039	2 186	4 382	5 439	5 579	99
Q3	..	..	–	..	3 817	..	17 857	2 303	4 556	5 958	5 718	98
Q4	..	..	–	..	4 032	..	19 640	2 748	5 338	6 088	6 012	97
1969 Q1	..	..	–	..	3 283	..	17 878	2 289	4 856	5 397	5 705	123
Q2	..	..	–	..	3 330	..	17 192	2 434	4 494	5 233	5 497	131
Q3	..	..	–	..	3 663	..	18 330	2 103	4 775	5 936	6 022	129
Q4	..	..	–	..	3 603	..	19 228	2 353	5 212	5 752	6 270	127

See footnotes on page 58.

Source: Office for National Statistics; Enquiries 020 7533 6010

1.8 Gross fixed capital formation

continued

£ million, 1995 prices, not seasonally adjusted

	Analysis by sector							Analysis by asset				
				Public corporations[2]	Private sector							
	Business investment[1]	General government	NHS trusts	Transfer costs of non-produced assets	Dwellings	Transfer cost of non-produced assets	Total	Transport equipment	Other machinery and equipment	Dwellings	Other building and structures[3]	Intangible fixed assets
	NPEN	EQDN	DLVH	EQDF	DFDP	EQCY	NPQR	DLWJ	DLWM	DFDV	DLWQ	EQDT
1970 Q1	..	..	–	..	2 831	..	18 184	2 312	5 275	4 690	5 823	252
Q2	..	..	–	..	2 974	..	18 067	2 774	4 856	4 800	5 839	257
Q3	..	..	–	..	3 366	..	18 566	2 216	5 022	5 320	6 179	256
Q4	..	..	–	..	3 546	..	19 934	2 445	5 594	5 449	6 493	269
1971 Q1	..	..	–	..	3 294	..	18 824	2 408	5 255	5 015	6 162	278
Q2	..	..	–	..	3 807	..	18 462	2 765	4 775	5 472	5 863	282
Q3	..	..	–	..	4 247	..	18 991	2 388	5 037	5 828	6 074	284
Q4	..	..	–	..	4 115	..	19 965	2 562	5 307	5 764	6 585	290
1972 Q1	..	..	–	..	3 972	..	19 218	2 735	5 098	5 504	6 137	323
Q2	..	..	–	..	4 198	..	18 413	2 903	4 614	5 634	5 770	324
Q3	..	..	–	..	4 544	..	18 775	2 505	4 760	5 926	6 041	327
Q4	..	..	–	..	4 162	..	19 806	3 222	5 151	5 645	6 178	332
1973 Q1	..	..	–	..	3 883	..	21 268	3 147	5 792	5 523	6 849	380
Q2	..	..	–	..	4 454	..	19 300	2 989	4 954	5 767	5 899	385
Q3	..	..	–	..	3 861	..	19 733	2 911	5 373	5 440	6 129	387
Q4	..	..	–	..	4 162	..	20 897	3 615	5 868	5 541	6 159	388
1974 Q1	..	..	–	..	3 691	..	21 217	2 892	5 895	5 482	6 803	494
Q2	..	..	–	..	3 775	..	18 578	2 943	5 254	5 069	5 397	490
Q3	..	..	–	..	3 171	..	19 318	2 879	5 391	5 101	5 930	477
Q4	..	..	–	..	3 670	..	20 501	3 437	6 081	5 325	5 803	456
1975 Q1	..	..	–	..	3 753	..	20 340	2 897	5 731	5 657	6 063	527
Q2	..	..	–	..	3 930	..	18 593	2 510	5 037	5 638	5 493	509
Q3	..	..	–	..	3 305	..	19 584	2 530	5 466	4 963	6 382	497
Q4	..	..	–	..	3 155	..	19 591	2 747	5 355	5 238	6 190	493
1976 Q1	..	..	–	..	3 976	..	20 875	2 784	5 771	6 193	6 199	529
Q2	..	..	–	..	3 468	..	18 760	2 444	5 103	5 225	5 880	531
Q3	..	..	–	..	3 305	..	19 613	2 523	5 454	5 225	6 228	526
Q4	..	..	–	..	3 566	..	20 209	2 607	5 991	5 536	5 909	584
1977 Q1	..	..	–	..	3 416	..	19 495	2 907	5 545	5 569	5 592	501
Q2	..	..	–	..	3 400	..	18 738	2 933	5 190	4 921	5 642	584
Q3	..	..	–	..	3 583	..	19 298	2 907	5 676	5 174	5 487	592
Q4	..	..	–	..	3 806	..	20 709	2 909	6 249	5 450	5 949	602
1978 Q1	..	..	–	..	3 998	..	20 763	3 431	6 052	5 891	5 665	469
Q2	..	..	–	..	3 464	..	19 222	3 388	5 670	4 743	5 481	474
Q3	..	..	–	..	3 701	..	19 825	3 090	6 036	5 293	5 502	464
Q4	..	..	–	..	3 995	..	20 396	2 865	6 475	5 356	5 674	483
1979 Q1	..	..	–	..	3 776	..	20 415	3 397	6 331	5 401	5 483	446
Q2	..	..	–	..	3 813	..	19 284	3 699	5 935	4 941	5 016	424
Q3	..	..	–	..	3 917	..	20 539	3 322	6 441	5 345	5 571	446
Q4	..	..	–	..	5 023	..	22 069	3 002	7 365	6 338	5 569	484
1980 Q1	..	..	–	..	4 342	..	20 725	3 147	6 626	5 959	5 275	460
Q2	..	..	–	..	3 559	..	18 609	3 063	6 125	4 589	4 863	506
Q3	..	..	–	..	3 822	..	19 176	2 460	6 467	4 959	5 146	545
Q4	..	..	–	..	3 898	..	19 888	2 681	6 822	4 895	5 323	546
1981 Q1	..	..	–	..	3 333	..	17 967	2 197	6 128	4 307	5 059	499
Q2	..	..	–	..	3 683	..	16 956	2 355	5 606	4 288	4 530	586
Q3	..	..	–	..	3 713	..	17 799	2 005	5 925	4 389	5 063	640
Q4	..	..	–	..	3 207	..	18 729	2 358	6 591	3 904	5 335	641
1982 Q1	..	..	–	..	3 095	..	18 431	2 332	5 965	4 191	5 454	675
Q2	..	..	–	..	3 917	..	17 657	2 116	5 770	4 412	4 937	730
Q3	..	..	–	..	3 858	..	19 111	2 375	5 999	4 521	5 717	725
Q4	..	..	–	..	3 975	..	20 467	2 346	6 809	4 839	5 890	796
1983 Q1	..	..	–	..	3 057	..	20 056	2 463	6 489	4 746	5 856	809
Q2	..	..	–	..	4 136	..	18 217	2 211	5 866	4 803	4 986	726
Q3	..	..	–	..	4 365	..	19 527	2 139	6 162	5 264	5 548	780
Q4	..	..	–	..	4 388	..	21 689	2 635	7 214	5 371	5 994	841
1984 Q1	..	..	–	..	3 533	..	21 641	3 003	6 778	5 112	6 384	759
Q2	..	..	–	..	4 629	..	20 170	2 286	6 408	5 304	5 633	933
Q3	..	..	–	..	4 650	..	21 728	2 682	6 911	5 541	6 032	1 003
Q4	..	..	–	..	4 204	..	23 373	3 099	8 090	5 098	6 325	1 112

See footnotes on page 58.

Source: Office for National Statistics; Enquiries 020 7533 6010

1.8 Gross fixed capital formation

continued

£ million, 1995 prices, not seasonally adjusted

	Analysis by sector							Analysis by asset				
				Public corporations[2]	Private sector							
	Business investment[1]	General government	NHS trusts	Transfer costs of non-produced assets	Dwellings	Transfer cost of non-produced assets	Total	Transport equipment	Other machinery and equipment	Dwellings	Other building and structures[3]	Intangible fixed assets
	NPEN	EQDN	DLVH	EQDF	DFDP	EQCY	NPQR	DLWJ	DLWM	DFDV	DLWQ	EQDT
1985 Q1	..	..	–	..	3 140	..	24 195	4 040	8 525	4 600	6 440	988
Q2	..	..	–	..	4 419	..	20 310	2 420	6 636	4 984	5 657	971
Q3	..	..	–	..	4 660	..	22 253	2 570	7 505	5 434	6 095	1 004
Q4	..	..	–	..	4 340	..	23 663	2 616	8 912	5 121	6 212	990
1986 Q1	..	3 648	–	–157	3 701	2 203	23 656	2 852	8 433	5 208	6 571	905
Q2	..	1 809	–	–108	4 310	1 989	20 361	2 343	7 019	4 845	5 598	824
Q3	..	2 225	–	–118	5 157	2 361	23 429	2 558	8 008	5 826	6 504	804
Q4	..	2 282	–	–117	5 372	2 494	24 884	2 752	8 858	6 168	6 680	775
1987 Q1	13 985	3 492	–	–91	4 092	2 549	24 062	2 686	8 205	5 419	7 186	666
Q2	13 919	1 643	–	–331	4 897	2 456	22 282	2 708	7 561	5 470	6 102	673
Q3	15 941	2 209	–	–140	6 023	2 538	26 268	3 076	8 585	6 769	7 303	772
Q4	17 899	2 601	–	–83	5 291	2 462	27 908	3 074	9 696	6 178	8 238	891
1988 Q1	16 955	3 822	–	–96	5 431	2 792	28 848	3 359	9 539	6 848	8 458	818
Q2	16 811	1 739	–	–153	6 498	2 517	26 972	3 088	8 639	6 990	7 590	886
Q3	18 458	1 677	–	–92	6 426	3 270	29 293	3 231	10 257	7 059	8 141	901
Q4	19 812	1 933	–	–181	6 061	3 060	30 249	3 122	11 074	6 699	8 638	907
1989 Q1	19 389	3 791	–	–163	6 001	2 932	31 801	3 567	11 087	7 400	9 197	902
Q2	19 333	1 813	–	3	5 822	2 076	28 600	3 271	10 510	6 510	7 821	913
Q3	20 612	2 466	–	–61	5 936	2 041	30 614	3 494	11 208	6 915	8 595	874
Q4	21 337	3 082	–	–76	5 016	2 039	31 143	3 402	11 860	6 271	9 036	956
1990 Q1	20 175	5 269	–	–84	4 043	2 595	32 157	3 869	11 970	6 292	9 492	912
Q2	19 675	2 156	–	–46	4 709	1 669	27 814	2 872	10 128	5 418	8 623	1 033
Q3	20 158	2 691	–	17	5 125	1 678	29 376	2 989	10 450	6 024	9 142	1 074
Q4	20 618	3 161	–	10	4 869	1 598	30 021	2 769	10 633	5 700	9 794	1 210
1991 Q1	19 515	4 371	–	1	3 649	1 735	29 316	2 844	10 477	4 828	10 043	1 077
Q2	17 461	2 411	26	60	4 144	1 315	25 179	2 369	8 928	4 667	8 159	1 139
Q3	17 561	3 155	26	64	4 521	1 370	26 556	1 912	9 357	5 117	9 039	1 094
Q4	18 989	3 402	38	57	4 289	1 296	27 949	2 531	10 324	4 975	9 060	1 164
1992 Q1	18 210	5 253	194	54	3 749	1 288	28 968	2 463	10 320	4 884	10 163	946
Q2	17 068	2 593	146	94	4 202	1 234	25 153	2 196	8 861	4 617	8 446	977
Q3	17 712	2 976	153	112	4 609	1 541	26 954	2 402	9 422	5 159	8 977	949
Q4	17 670	3 614	151	91	4 751	982	27 171	2 192	9 428	5 381	9 088	1 042
1993 Q1	17 365	6 091	157	129	3 719	1 125	28 935	3 254	9 331	5 063	10 220	902
Q2	16 027	2 636	317	54	4 725	1 188	24 784	2 094	8 551	5 182	8 078	873
Q3	17 159	3 125	323	94	4 915	1 422	26 929	2 758	9 164	5 541	8 605	924
Q4	17 898	3 191	321	91	4 994	2 086	28 479	2 483	9 912	5 705	9 381	978
1994 Q1	17 526	6 120	325	125	4 594	1 435	30 125	3 502	9 354	6 003	10 406	860
Q2	16 637	2 600	463	77	4 595	1 338	25 710	2 688	8 645	5 072	8 412	893
Q3	18 026	3 167	463	89	4 759	1 446	27 950	2 921	9 613	5 392	9 110	914
Q4	18 758	3 368	453	64	5 128	1 486	29 257	2 816	10 559	5 800	9 118	964
1995 Q1	17 897	5 508	450	83	4 600	1 676	30 214	2 880	10 703	5 781	9 931	919
Q2	18 222	2 422	453	5	4 856	1 196	27 154	3 011	10 001	5 298	7 889	955
Q3	19 936	2 874	448	23	4 552	1 221	29 054	2 802	11 481	5 074	8 749	948
Q4	20 382	3 201	435	15	4 776	1 129	29 938	2 362	12 279	5 435	8 745	1 117
1996 Q1	20 714	4 436	435	31	4 268	1 359	31 243	2 702	12 744	5 158	9 594	1 045
Q2	20 100	2 292	345	30	4 901	1 161	28 829	3 354	11 177	5 321	7 969	1 008
Q3	20 915	2 510	346	35	5 004	1 531	30 341	3 052	12 028	5 528	8 679	1 054
Q4	21 466	1 653	341	55	5 730	2 384	31 629	2 669	13 175	6 147	8 583	1 055
1997 Q1	22 010	3 915	344	98	4 750	1 292	32 409	3 570	12 768	5 592	9 451	1 028
Q2	22 359	1 233	265	74	5 088	1 944	30 963	3 362	12 539	5 381	8 593	1 088
Q3	23 562	2 136	325	80	5 008	1 525	32 636	3 176	13 688	5 365	9 400	1 007
Q4	25 075	2 407	304	75	5 978	1 399	35 238	2 874	15 246	6 331	9 807	980
1998 Q1	25 605	3 718	493	69	4 977	1 420	36 282	3 884	15 379	5 631	10 399	989
Q2	25 654	1 379	271	77	5 717	1 391	34 489	4 008	14 898	6 004	8 550	1 029
Q3	26 538	2 352	291	90	5 133	1 408	35 812	3 704	15 853	5 554	9 616	1 085
Q4	28 069	2 544	310	78	5 694	1 159	37 854	3 317	17 703	6 042	9 739	1 053
1999 Q1	28 113	3 584	452	91	5 057	1 375	38 672	4 389	17 221	5 570	10 514	978
Q2	27 853	1 638	243	102	5 665	1 250	36 751	4 334	16 389	5 866	9 175	987
Q3	28 228	2 318	322	107	5 273	1 468	37 716	4 068	16 700	5 656	10 314	978
Q4	29 705	2 498	305	76	6 114	1 435	40 133	3 465	18 391	6 430	10 802	1 045
2000 Q1	28 604	3 293	430	109	5 168	1 444	39 048	4 108	17 261	5 697	10 973	1 009

See footnotes on page 58.

Source: Office for National Statistics; Enquiries 020 7533 6010

1.8 Gross fixed capital formation

continued

£ million, 1995 prices, seasonally adjusted

	Analysis by sector							Analysis by asset				
			Public corporations[2]		Private sector							
	Business investment[1]	General government	NHS trusts	Transfer costs of non-produced assets	Dwellings	Transfer cost of non-produced assets	Total	Transport equipment	Other machinery and equipment	Dwellings	Other building and structures[3]	Intangible fixed assets
	NPEL	DLWF	DFTI	DLWH	DFEA	DLWI	NPQT	DLWL	DLWO	DFEG	DLWT	EQDO
1955 Q1	..	..	–	..	..	..	8 429	..	..	..	..	..
Q2	..	..	–	..	..	..	8 611	..	..	..	..	..
Q3	..	..	–	..	..	..	8 858	..	..	..	..	..
Q4	..	..	–	..	..	..	8 966	..	..	..	..	..
1956 Q1	..	..	–	..	..	..	8 953	..	..	..	..	..
Q2	..	..	–	..	..	..	9 055	..	..	..	..	..
Q3	..	..	–	..	..	..	9 135	..	..	..	..	..
Q4	..	..	–	..	..	..	9 314	..	..	..	..	..
1957 Q1	..	..	–	..	..	..	9 567	..	..	..	..	..
Q2	..	..	–	..	..	..	9 610	..	..	..	..	..
Q3	..	..	–	..	..	..	9 508	..	..	..	..	..
Q4	..	..	–	..	..	..	9 572	..	..	..	..	..
1958 Q1	..	..	–	..	..	..	9 687	..	..	..	..	..
Q2	..	..	–	..	..	..	9 575	..	..	..	..	..
Q3	..	..	–	..	..	..	9 616	..	..	..	..	..
Q4	..	..	–	..	..	..	9 692	..	..	..	..	..
1959 Q1	..	..	–	..	..	..	9 714	..	..	..	..	..
Q2	..	..	–	..	..	..	10 345	..	..	..	..	..
Q3	..	..	–	..	..	..	10 364	..	..	..	..	..
Q4	..	..	–	..	..	..	11 051	..	..	..	..	..
1960 Q1	..	..	–	..	..	..	11 087	..	..	..	..	..
Q2	..	..	–	..	..	..	11 163	..	..	..	..	..
Q3	..	..	–	..	..	..	11 279	..	..	..	..	..
Q4	..	..	–	..	..	..	11 662	..	..	..	..	..
1961 Q1	..	..	–	..	..	..	12 101	..	..	..	..	..
Q2	..	..	–	..	..	..	12 397	..	..	..	..	..
Q3	..	..	–	..	..	..	12 634	..	..	..	..	..
Q4	..	..	–	..	..	..	12 325	..	..	..	..	..
1962 Q1	..	..	–	..	2 480	..	12 401	..	..	3 501	..	..
Q2	..	..	–	..	2 420	..	12 644	..	..	3 569	..	..
Q3	..	..	–	..	2 324	..	12 549	..	..	3 490	..	..
Q4	..	..	–	..	2 265	..	12 207	..	..	3 376	..	..
1963 Q1	..	..	–	..	1 881	..	11 273	..	..	2 626	..	..
Q2	..	..	–	..	2 576	..	12 735	..	..	3 638	..	..
Q3	..	..	–	..	2 683	..	13 015	..	..	3 801	..	..
Q4	..	..	–	..	2 848	..	13 543	..	..	4 007	..	..
1964 Q1	..	..	–	..	2 851	..	14 209	..	..	4 230	..	..
Q2	..	..	–	..	2 898	..	14 562	..	..	4 399	..	..
Q3	..	..	–	..	2 898	..	14 792	..	..	4 300	..	..
Q4	..	..	–	..	3 028	..	15 085	..	..	4 429	..	..
1965 Q1	8 463	..	–	..	3 164	..	15 351	1 853	4 249	4 605	4 957	41
Q2	8 307	..	–	..	3 020	..	15 165	1 909	4 156	4 560	4 886	39
Q3	8 456	..	–	..	2 998	..	15 368	1 764	4 296	4 506	5 059	39
Q4	8 782	..	–	..	3 010	..	15 823	2 012	4 467	4 681	4 967	49
1966 Q1	8 625	..	–	..	2 996	..	15 664	1 762	4 498	4 681	4 928	78
Q2	8 566	..	–	..	2 974	..	15 626	1 689	4 552	4 658	4 877	77
Q3	8 792	..	–	..	2 938	..	15 975	1 683	4 673	4 745	5 011	76
Q4	8 755	..	–	..	2 951	..	16 111	1 679	4 548	4 874	5 215	85
1967 Q1	9 146	..	–	..	3 140	..	16 815	1 855	4 695	5 124	5 368	143
Q2	9 460	..	–	..	3 308	..	17 562	1 941	4 905	5 417	5 567	141
Q3	9 291	..	–	..	3 426	..	17 501	1 972	4 766	5 493	5 625	139
Q4	9 090	..	–	..	3 329	..	17 187	1 840	4 672	5 372	5 593	148
1968 Q1	9 445	..	–	..	3 390	..	18 169	2 084	4 873	5 721	5 931	101
Q2	9 354	..	–	..	3 353	..	17 712	2 119	4 705	5 483	5 839	99
Q3	9 527	..	–	..	3 723	..	18 106	2 440	4 727	5 818	5 734	98
Q4	10 165	..	–	..	4 105	..	19 053	2 678	5 118	6 087	5 765	97
1969 Q1	9 365	..	–	..	3 390	..	17 664	2 268	4 639	5 524	5 710	123
Q2	9 691	..	–	..	3 248	..	17 814	2 339	4 797	5 265	5 757	131
Q3	9 827	..	–	..	3 591	..	18 525	2 219	4 936	5 806	6 004	129
Q4	9 911	..	–	..	3 650	..	18 625	2 353	4 965	5 723	6 023	127

See footnotes on page 58.

Source: Office for National Statistics; Enquiries 020 7533 6010

1.8 Gross fixed capital formation

continued

£ million, 1995 prices, seasonally adjusted

	Analysis by sector							Analysis by asset				
			Public corporations[2]		Private sector							
	Business investment[1]	General government	NHS trusts	Transfer costs of non-produced assets	Dwellings	Transfer cost of non-produced assets	Total	Transport equipment	Other machinery and equipment	Dwellings	Other building and structures[3]	Intangible fixed assets
	NPEL	DLWF	DFTI	DLWH	DFEA	DLWI	NPQT	DLWL	DLWO	DFEG	DLWT	EQDO
1970 Q1	9 979	..	–	..	2 914	..	18 015	2 302	5 114	4 800	5 806	252
Q2	10 413	..	–	..	2 902	..	18 702	2 640	5 166	4 820	6 142	257
Q3	10 168	..	–	..	3 308	..	18 809	2 419	5 154	5 200	6 169	256
Q4	10 426	..	–	..	3 593	..	19 225	2 386	5 313	5 439	6 217	269
1971 Q1	10 111	..	–	..	3 378	..	18 477	2 396	5 050	5 082	6 053	278
Q2	10 282	..	–	..	3 747	..	19 139	2 679	5 106	5 504	6 132	282
Q3	10 307	..	–	..	4 222	..	19 330	2 601	5 148	5 765	6 134	284
Q4	10 078	..	–	..	4 116	..	19 296	2 447	5 070	5 728	6 365	290
1972 Q1	9 841	..	–	..	4 057	..	18 722	2 743	4 855	5 548	5 936	323
Q2	10 069	..	–	..	4 150	..	19 174	2 855	4 924	5 677	6 119	324
Q3	9 927	..	–	..	4 544	..	19 108	2 709	4 887	5 883	6 075	327
Q4	10 224	..	–	..	4 125	..	19 208	3 058	4 957	5 601	5 996	332
1973 Q1	10 994	..	–	..	3 950	..	20 550	3 091	5 537	5 482	6 540	380
Q2	10 733	..	–	..	4 433	..	20 215	3 002	5 328	5 857	6 255	385
Q3	10 825	..	–	..	3 887	..	20 118	3 107	5 510	5 450	6 203	387
Q4	11 132	..	–	..	4 090	..	20 315	3 462	5 612	5 482	6 038	388
1974 Q1	11 257	..	–	..	3 762	..	20 461	2 815	5 671	5 395	6 472	494
Q2	11 664	..	–	..	3 775	..	19 599	3 021	5 661	5 202	5 742	490
Q3	11 443	..	–	..	3 203	..	19 614	3 032	5 498	5 129	5 972	477
Q4	11 948	..	–	..	3 567	..	19 940	3 283	5 791	5 251	5 747	456
1975 Q1	11 527	..	–	..	3 836	..	19 651	2 855	5 440	5 523	5 866	527
Q2	11 191	..	–	..	3 956	..	19 764	2 596	5 465	5 858	5 884	509
Q3	11 795	..	–	..	3 317	..	19 589	2 588	5 554	4 973	6 261	497
Q4	11 258	..	–	..	3 034	..	19 104	2 645	5 130	5 142	6 117	493
1976 Q1	11 444	..	–	..	4 101	..	20 152	2 681	5 538	6 037	5 970	529
Q2	11 753	..	–	..	3 504	..	19 980	2 502	5 549	5 489	6 284	531
Q3	11 790	..	–	..	3 301	..	19 655	2 575	5 517	5 248	6 156	526
Q4	11 772	..	–	..	3 409	..	19 670	2 600	5 715	5 405	5 806	584
1977 Q1	11 229	..	–	..	3 567	..	18 955	2 773	5 384	5 412	5 432	547
Q2	12 157	..	–	..	3 469	..	19 850	2 925	5 643	5 225	5 953	593
Q3	11 759	..	–	..	3 547	..	19 434	2 965	5 751	5 193	5 490	583
Q4	12 248	..	–	..	3 622	..	20 001	2 993	5 882	5 284	5 795	556
1978 Q1	12 382	..	–	..	4 221	..	20 493	3 312	5 969	5 800	5 624	503
Q2	12 556	..	–	..	3 528	..	20 239	3 337	6 105	5 041	5 779	476
Q3	12 155	..	–	..	3 609	..	19 894	3 193	6 093	5 259	5 472	455
Q4	11 955	..	–	..	3 800	..	19 580	2 932	6 066	5 183	5 447	456
1979 Q1	12 485	..	–	..	3 988	..	20 148	3 250	6 310	5 290	5 427	473
Q2	12 668	..	–	..	3 896	..	20 368	3 614	6 391	5 259	5 361	425
Q3	12 845	..	–	..	3 850	..	20 689	3 474	6 540	5 329	5 528	441
Q4	12 606	..	–	..	4 795	..	21 102	3 082	6 831	6 147	5 323	461
1980 Q1	12 434	..	–	..	4 595	..	20 402	3 015	6 615	5 830	5 165	484
Q2	12 220	..	–	..	3 574	..	19 722	3 009	6 577	4 862	5 244	509
Q3	12 000	..	–	..	3 725	..	19 349	2 608	6 609	4 933	5 095	536
Q4	11 696	..	–	..	3 727	..	18 925	2 719	6 239	4 777	5 103	528
1981 Q1	11 149	..	–	..	3 496	..	17 631	2 057	6 106	4 191	4 939	526
Q2	11 123	..	–	..	3 698	..	17 927	2 328	6 001	4 491	4 869	593
Q3	11 252	..	–	..	3 658	..	18 040	2 168	6 098	4 389	5 016	630
Q4	11 217	..	–	..	3 084	..	17 853	2 362	6 045	3 817	5 163	617
1982 Q1	11 368	..	–	..	3 272	..	17 943	2 177	5 937	4 009	5 252	720
Q2	11 428	..	–	..	3 952	..	18 834	2 145	6 188	4 641	5 377	737
Q3	11 881	..	–	..	3 825	..	19 396	2 533	6 199	4 567	5 658	711
Q4	11 777	..	–	..	3 796	..	19 493	2 314	6 219	4 746	5 711	758
1983 Q1	11 519	..	–	..	3 956	..	19 801	2 270	6 331	5 116	5 588	856
Q2	11 598	..	–	..	3 898	..	19 405	2 346	6 369	4 847	5 441	732
Q3	11 558	..	–	..	3 937	..	19 599	2 273	6 401	4 986	5 508	767
Q4	12 413	..	–	..	4 155	..	20 684	2 559	6 630	5 235	5 847	801
1984 Q1	12 406	..	–	..	4 641	..	21 363	2 779	6 657	5 629	5 969	802
Q2	13 015	..	–	..	4 279	..	21 643	2 455	7 052	5 339	6 170	965
Q3	13 302	..	–	..	4 111	..	21 807	2 799	7 184	5 152	6 060	994
Q4	13 802	..	–	..	3 985	..	22 099	3 037	7 294	4 935	6 175	1 046

See footnotes on page 58.

Source: Office for National Statistics; Enquiries 020 7533 6010

1.8 Gross fixed capital formation

continued

£ million, 1995 prices, seasonally adjusted

	Analysis by sector							Analysis by asset				
			Public corporations[2]		Private sector							
	Business investment[1]	General government	NHS trusts	Transfer costs of non-produced assets	Dwellings	Transfer cost of non-produced assets	Total	Transport equipment	Other machinery and equipment	Dwellings	Other building and structures[3]	Intangible fixed assets
	NPEL	DLWF	DFTI	DLWH	DFEA	DLWI	NPQT	DLWL	DLWO	DFEG	DLWT	EQDO
1985 Q1	15 348	..	–	..	4 169	..	23 819	3 752	8 363	5 084	6 037	1 043
Q2	13 555	..	–	..	4 082	..	21 902	2 634	7 332	4 986	6 249	1 001
Q3	13 900	..	–	..	4 120	..	22 273	2 687	7 787	5 040	6 070	988
Q4	13 982	..	–	..	4 188	..	22 427	2 573	8 096	5 029	6 048	921
1986 Q1	14 046	2 583	–	–153	4 290	2 091	22 733	2 656	8 044	5 287	6 143	944
Q2	13 504	2 501	–	–106	4 208	2 163	22 152	2 505	7 794	5 036	6 164	841
Q3	14 232	2 476	–	–129	4 773	2 336	23 510	2 629	8 360	5 580	6 541	792
Q4	14 121	2 404	–	–112	5 269	2 457	23 935	2 715	8 120	6 144	6 505	731
1987 Q1	14 118	2 239	–	–69	4 671	2 407	23 176	2 506	8 083	5 494	6 620	690
Q2	14 738	2 357	–	–326	4 844	2 679	24 091	2 817	8 268	5 726	6 794	689
Q3	15 918	2 598	–	–160	5 633	2 482	26 242	3 096	8 620	6 508	7 424	777
Q4	16 970	2 751	–	–90	5 155	2 437	27 011	3 125	9 076	6 108	7 991	846
1988 Q1	17 256	2 489	–	–73	6 194	2 657	28 218	3 191	9 354	7 072	7 995	857
Q2	17 518	2 540	–	–152	6 382	2 746	28 714	3 199	9 321	7 167	8 278	905
Q3	18 358	2 091	–	–114	5 971	3 199	29 140	3 237	10 270	6 748	8 218	905
Q4	18 904	2 051	–	–183	5 869	3 037	29 290	3 173	10 564	6 609	8 336	925
1989 Q1	19 693	2 277	–	–139	6 789	2 759	30 950	3 344	10 791	7 670	8 662	946
Q2	20 164	2 630	–	1	5 695	2 271	30 434	3 445	11 271	6 695	8 504	920
Q3	20 477	2 953	–	–85	5 455	2 020	30 534	3 529	11 235	6 572	8 727	880
Q4	20 337	3 292	–	–74	4 836	2 038	30 240	3 416	11 368	6 159	8 756	899
1990 Q1	20 356	3 358	–	–57	4 591	2 420	30 507	3 584	11 529	6 202	8 831	963
Q2	20 508	3 180	–	–54	4 654	1 849	29 930	3 081	10 911	5 696	9 371	1 048
Q3	20 076	3 345	–	–7	4 759	1 665	29 657	3 032	10 526	5 834	9 342	1 097
Q4	19 686	3 394	–	15	4 742	1 606	29 274	2 802	10 215	5 702	9 507	1 121
1991 Q1	19 334	2 995	–	29	4 139	1 586	27 864	2 497	10 018	4 917	9 320	1 149
Q2	18 389	3 282	29	47	4 119	1 479	27 236	2 615	9 814	4 897	8 819	1 149
Q3	17 592	3 619	26	40	4 212	1 349	26 787	1 986	9 503	4 879	9 214	1 108
Q4	18 211	3 443	35	66	4 133	1 302	27 113	2 558	9 751	4 894	8 948	1 068
1992 Q1	18 144	3 514	207	27	4 208	1 190	27 220	2 156	9 934	4 994	9 212	992
Q2	17 843	3 622	131	119	4 175	1 356	27 219	2 440	9 636	4 849	9 207	1 011
Q3	17 693	3 506	152	106	4 356	1 508	27 258	2 419	9 565	4 984	9 177	958
Q4	16 980	3 794	154	99	4 572	991	26 549	2 238	8 896	5 214	9 078	953
1993 Q1	17 378	4 219	172	96	4 154	1 043	27 106	2 935	9 065	5 176	9 160	939
Q2	16 824	3 747	290	76	4 704	1 320	26 960	2 281	9 298	5 436	8 968	896
Q3	16 996	3 704	325	93	4 737	1 386	27 228	2 701	9 233	5 374	8 854	931
Q4	17 251	3 373	331	103	4 758	2 072	27 833	2 672	9 362	5 505	9 302	911
1994 Q1	17 618	4 207	311	100	4 973	1 315	28 524	3 414	9 023	5 852	9 349	886
Q2	17 190	3 726	492	91	4 586	1 458	27 543	2 533	9 455	5 332	9 321	902
Q3	17 892	3 631	454	92	4 778	1 482	28 329	2 862	9 753	5 530	9 267	917
Q4	18 247	3 691	447	72	4 739	1 450	28 646	3 118	9 940	5 553	9 109	926
1995 Q1	18 100	3 735	433	61	4 966	1 554	28 849	2 791	10 430	5 688	8 995	945
Q2	18 750	3 456	482	17	4 830	1 300	28 835	2 843	10 809	5 512	8 704	967
Q3	19 795	3 321	441	27	4 560	1 272	29 416	2 747	11 673	5 169	8 875	952
Q4	19 792	3 493	430	21	4 428	1 096	29 260	2 674	11 552	5 219	8 740	1 075
1996 Q1	20 902	2 995	419	9	4 620	1 236	30 181	2 653	12 354	5 166	8 937	1 071
Q2	20 568	3 217	368	42	4 909	1 271	30 375	3 146	12 015	5 536	8 666	1 012
Q3	20 877	2 839	341	39	5 044	1 579	30 719	2 941	12 407	5 641	8 678	1 052
Q4	20 848	1 840	339	61	5 330	2 349	30 767	3 037	12 348	5 811	8 544	1 027
1997 Q1	21 784	2 678	296	78	5 126	1 217	31 179	3 153	12 589	5 669	8 712	1 056
Q2	23 148	2 054	299	86	5 119	2 036	32 742	3 315	13 404	5 567	9 364	1 092
Q3	23 673	2 388	334	82	5 212	1 516	33 205	3 193	14 003	5 633	9 385	991
Q4	24 401	2 571	309	81	5 367	1 391	34 120	3 321	14 245	5 800	9 790	964
1998 Q1	25 625	2 521	396	58	5 423	1 339	35 362	3 574	15 305	5 839	9 655	989
Q2	26 116	2 128	333	83	5 543	1 481	35 684	3 671	15 665	5 984	9 335	1 029
Q3	26 751	2 616	306	86	5 346	1 421	36 526	3 737	16 252	5 803	9 649	1 085
Q4	27 374	2 728	330	87	5 209	1 137	36 865	3 931	16 611	5 605	9 665	1 053
1999 Q1	28 050	2 496	347	84	5 467	1 325	37 769	4 038	17 116	5 790	9 847	978
Q2	28 493	2 445	312	107	5 545	1 307	38 209	4 143	17 197	5 834	10 048	987
Q3	28 529	2 518	336	103	5 503	1 438	38 427	4 081	17 146	5 916	10 306	978
Q4	28 827	2 579	327	82	5 594	1 458	38 867	3 994	17 242	5 982	10 604	1 045
2000 Q1	28 611	2 470	321	102	5 508	1 414	38 426	3 715	17 243	5 859	10 600	1 009

See footnotes on page 58.

Source: Office for National Statistics; Enquiries 020 7533 6010

1.9 Gross value added at constant 1995 basic prices, by category of output[1,3]

1995 = 100

	Production						Service industries[4]					
	Agriculture, forestry, and fishing	Mining and quarrying inc oil & gas extraction	Manufacturing	Electricity gas and water supply	Total	Construction	Distribution; hotels and catering; repairs	Transport, storage and communication	Business services and finance	Government and other services	Total	Gross value added at basic prices
1995 weights[2]	*18*	*25*	*216*	*25*	*266*	*52*	*146*	*82*	*211*	*225*	*664*	*1 000*
	GDQA	CKYX	CKYY	CKYZ	CKYW	GDQB	GDQE	GDQH	GDQN	GDQU	GDQS	CGCE
1948	36.0	147.9	39.9	16.4	34.1	45.2	34.6	26.2	..	..	33.9	31.6
1949	38.6	152.5	42.8	17.5	36.4	47.3	35.9	27.6	..	..	34.0	32.9
1950	39.1	153.8	46.0	19.1	38.9	47.3	36.9	28.5	..	..	34.4	33.8
1951	40.1	158.5	47.4	20.4	40.1	45.5	36.4	29.8	..	..	34.8	34.6
1952	41.2	160.0	45.1	20.9	38.6	46.9	35.7	30.6	..	..	35.4	34.9
1953	42.0	159.8	48.3	22.0	41.0	50.2	38.0	31.6	..	..	36.1	36.2
1954	42.5	161.3	50.9	23.9	43.1	52.5	39.8	32.3	..	..	37.3	37.8
1955	42.1	157.8	54.1	25.2	45.5	52.6	41.7	33.1	..	..	38.4	38.9
1956	44.5	158.1	53.9	26.3	45.6	55.5	42.2	33.6	..	..	38.6	39.4
1957	45.5	157.3	55.2	27.3	46.6	55.4	43.2	33.6	..	..	39.3	40.1
1958	44.5	146.2	54.7	28.5	46.2	55.2	44.3	33.3	..	..	39.9	40.2
1959	46.3	140.6	57.9	29.3	48.4	58.3	46.8	34.8	..	..	41.6	41.8
1960	49.3	134.3	62.5	31.5	51.9	61.3	49.1	36.5	..	..	42.9	44.1
1961	49.6	130.6	62.7	32.9	52.1	66.1	50.0	37.4	..	..	44.0	45.3
1962	51.2	134.8	62.8	35.6	52.5	66.7	50.4	37.7	..	..	44.6	46.0
1963	53.2	134.3	65.1	37.3	54.3	66.5	52.4	38.9	..	..	46.1	48.3
1964	55.3	131.7	71.0	39.2	58.8	73.3	54.7	41.4	..	..	47.9	50.9
1965	56.7	125.8	73.0	41.9	60.4	76.7	55.8	42.3	..	..	49.1	52.3
1966	57.0	116.8	74.3	43.6	61.4	78.1	56.3	43.4	..	..	50.1	53.3
1967	58.8	114.4	74.8	45.2	61.8	81.3	56.7	44.0	..	..	51.2	54.4
1968	58.7	101.3	80.4	44.8	66.5	83.4	58.4	45.8	..	..	52.6	56.7
1969	58.6	93.4	83.4	47.7	68.8	82.7	58.8	47.6	..	..	53.4	57.9
1970	62.2	86.6	83.7	50.0	69.1	81.2	60.4	49.6	..	..	55.0	59.2
1971	65.5	84.8	82.9	52.5	68.8	82.6	61.7	50.9	..	..	56.4	60.5
1972	67.6	68.3	84.6	56.6	70.0	84.1	65.2	53.4	..	..	58.7	62.6
1973	69.7	76.4	92.5	60.2	76.3	86.1	68.2	57.4	..	..	61.2	66.7
1974	70.6	64.6	91.3	60.6	74.8	77.2	65.5	57.6	..	..	61.2	65.8
1975	65.1	72.9	85.0	61.7	70.7	73.1	63.2	56.9	..	..	61.9	65.5
1976	59.8	68.5	86.6	62.8	73.0	72.1	63.8	56.5	..	..	63.3	67.1
1977	67.6	66.6	88.3	65.4	76.8	71.8	63.4	58.2	..	..	64.2	68.6
1978	72.7	66.6	88.8	66.9	79.0	76.7	67.1	60.3	..	..	66.2	70.5
1979	71.5	80.1	88.6	69.6	82.0	77.2	69.1	62.7	..	..	68.1	71.9
1980	79.4	81.3	80.9	69.2	76.7	73.0	64.8	61.5	..	..	67.8	70.5
1981	81.5	84.9	75.9	70.8	74.2	67.3	63.8	61.6	..	..	68.0	69.8
1982	88.3	90.9	75.8	70.3	75.7	72.7	65.1	61.0	..	..	69.0	71.3
1983	83.5	91.7	77.5	72.7	78.4	77.3	67.9	62.8	67.6	80.1	71.3	73.9
1984	100.9	86.3	80.3	61.7	78.5	81.0	71.3	65.9	71.3	81.4	74.0	75.5
1985	95.6	94.9	82.6	74.9	82.8	81.2	74.3	68.6	74.2	82.7	76.3	78.7
1986	95.8	94.8	83.7	82.3	84.8	84.6	78.4	71.5	78.5	84.2	79.4	81.6
1987	93.5	94.8	87.7	84.5	88.2	94.5	84.0	76.6	81.4	85.6	82.7	85.1
1988	94.1	86.8	94.1	84.2	92.5	102.7	89.3	80.5	86.6	87.1	86.5	89.2
1989	99.2	76.7	97.9	84.3	94.4	108.2	92.2	84.1	87.7	87.8	88.3	91.1
1990	100.7	73.3	97.7	86.5	94.1	111.3	91.7	85.1	90.5	88.8	89.5	92.0
1991	105.7	76.7	92.8	91.4	91.0	102.3	88.7	82.7	90.1	91.7	89.3	90.9
1992	110.1	78.9	92.8	92.9	91.3	98.3	89.1	84.6	88.5	93.3	89.7	91.1
1993	101.2	84.2	94.1	96.8	93.3	97.1	93.6	87.3	90.7	95.4	92.5	93.2
1994	100.0	96.8	98.5	97.8	98.3	100.8	98.2	94.3	95.7	97.8	96.8	97.4
1995	100.0	100.0	100.0	100.0	100.0	100.0	100.0	100.0	100.0	100.0	100.0	100.0
1996	102.0	103.3	100.4	105.3	101.1	101.5	103.2	104.2	104.4	102.0	103.3	102.5
1997	103.5	102.1	101.7	105.7	102.1	104.7	106.5	113.4	111.2	103.5	107.8	106.0
1998	101.8	104.4	102.2	107.6	102.9	106.1	109.2	121.5	117.9	105.6	112.3	109.1
1999	103.1	108.0	102.2	109.3	103.4	106.4	111.3	130.8	122.3	106.5	115.6	111.4

1 Estimates cannot be regarded as accurate to the last digit shown
2 Weights may not sum to the totals due to rounding
3 Components of output are valued at basic prices, which excludes taxes and subsidies on production.
4 For a further breakdown of services, see Table 1.10

Sources: Office for National Statistics;
Enquiries Columns 1-11 020 7533 5972; Columns 12 020 7533 5944

1.9 Gross value added at constant 1995 basic prices, by category of output[1,3]

continued

1995 = 100, seasonally adjusted

	Production						Service industries[4]					
	Agriculture, forestry, and fishing	Mining and quarrying inc oil & gas extraction	Manufacturing	Electricity gas and water supply	Total	Construction	Distribution; hotels and catering; repairs	Transport, storage and communication	Business services and finance	Government and other services	Total	Gross value added at basic prices
1995 weights[2]	*18*	*25*	*216*	*25*	*266*	*52*	*146*	*82*	*211*	*225*	*664*	*1 000*
	GDQA	CKYX	CKYY	CKYZ	CKYW	GDQB	GDQE	GDQH	GDQN	GDQU	GDQS	CGCE
1948 Q1	36.0	149.1	39.1	16.1	33.5	45.2	34.6	26.2	..	..	33.9	..
Q2	36.0	145.2	39.4	16.3	33.7	45.1	34.6	26.2	..	..	33.9	..
Q3	36.0	148.2	40.4	16.6	34.4	45.2	34.6	26.2	..	..	33.9	..
Q4	36.0	149.1	40.8	16.8	34.8	45.1	34.6	26.2	..	..	33.9	..
1949 Q1	38.6	149.5	41.7	17.1	35.4	47.3	35.9	27.6	..	..	34.0	..
Q2	38.6	153.7	42.6	17.4	36.2	47.3	35.9	27.6	..	..	34.0	..
Q3	38.6	153.1	43.4	17.8	36.9	47.2	35.9	27.6	..	..	34.0	..
Q4	38.6	153.7	43.6	17.9	37.0	47.2	35.9	27.6	..	..	34.0	..
1950 Q1	39.1	150.3	44.6	18.5	37.6	47.4	36.9	28.5	..	..	34.4	..
Q2	39.1	154.8	45.7	19.0	38.6	47.4	36.9	28.5	..	..	34.4	..
Q3	39.1	155.8	47.0	19.6	39.6	47.1	36.9	28.5	..	..	34.4	..
Q4	39.1	154.5	46.9	19.4	39.6	47.2	36.9	28.5	..	..	34.4	..
1951 Q1	40.1	158.1	46.9	19.6	39.6	45.6	36.4	29.8	..	..	34.8	..
Q2	40.1	154.9	47.0	20.3	39.7	45.7	36.4	29.8	..	..	34.8	..
Q3	40.1	163.1	48.6	21.2	41.2	45.3	36.4	29.8	..	..	34.8	..
Q4	40.1	157.9	47.1	20.5	39.9	45.4	36.4	29.8	..	..	34.8	..
1952 Q1	41.2	154.0	45.8	20.1	38.9	46.8	35.7	30.6	..	..	35.4	..
Q2	41.2	160.3	44.5	20.5	38.1	46.9	35.7	30.6	..	..	35.4	..
Q3	41.2	168.2	43.8	21.0	37.9	46.8	35.7	30.6	..	..	35.4	..
Q4	41.2	157.6	46.1	22.1	39.4	46.9	35.7	30.6	..	..	35.4	..
1953 Q1	42.0	163.3	46.9	21.9	40.1	48.7	38.0	31.6	..	..	36.1	..
Q2	42.0	159.3	47.7	21.6	40.6	49.1	38.0	31.6	..	..	36.1	..
Q3	42.0	152.2	48.3	21.9	40.8	50.7	38.0	31.6	..	..	36.1	..
Q4	42.0	164.6	50.3	22.8	42.7	52.3	38.0	31.6	..	..	36.1	..
1954 Q1	42.5	162.9	49.6	23.6	42.2	52.5	39.8	32.3	..	..	37.3	..
Q2	42.5	160.9	50.5	23.5	42.9	52.4	39.8	32.3	..	..	37.3	..
Q3	42.5	158.6	51.1	24.2	43.3	52.8	39.8	32.3	..	..	37.3	..
Q4	42.5	162.8	52.2	24.3	44.2	52.3	39.8	32.3	..	..	37.3	..
1955 Q1	42.1	160.5	53.2	25.4	44.9	50.0	41.7	33.1	..	..	38.4	38.9
Q2	42.1	154.8	53.8	24.9	45.2	52.6	41.7	33.1	..	..	38.4	38.7
Q3	42.1	154.8	54.2	24.7	45.4	53.7	41.7	33.1	..	..	38.4	39.1
Q4	42.1	161.1	55.1	25.7	46.4	54.3	41.7	33.1	..	..	38.4	39.0
1956 Q1	44.5	157.6	54.4	26.2	45.8	53.0	42.2	33.6	..	..	38.6	39.3
Q2	44.5	159.2	54.2	26.2	45.7	56.7	42.2	33.6	..	..	38.6	39.4
Q3	44.5	157.8	53.5	26.4	45.3	56.2	42.2	33.6	..	..	38.6	39.4
Q4	44.5	157.9	53.7	26.6	45.4	56.2	42.2	33.6	..	..	38.6	39.4
1957 Q1	45.5	160.5	54.8	25.8	46.2	56.1	43.2	33.6	..	..	39.3	40.2
Q2	45.5	160.2	55.1	27.3	46.5	56.2	43.2	33.6	..	..	39.3	40.3
Q3	45.5	155.2	56.0	28.1	47.2	54.6	43.2	33.6	..	..	39.3	40.0
Q4	45.5	153.5	55.1	28.1	46.4	54.7	43.2	33.6	..	..	39.3	40.0
1958 Q1	45.0	149.2	55.3	28.1	46.6	55.0	43.9	33.4	..	..	39.8	40.6
Q2	45.0	147.1	54.5	28.6	46.0	54.9	43.4	32.7	..	..	39.3	39.5
Q3	44.2	143.9	54.1	28.6	45.7	55.1	44.4	33.3	..	..	40.2	40.3
Q4	43.9	144.8	55.1	28.8	46.4	55.9	45.3	33.7	..	..	40.4	40.3
1959 Q1	44.2	141.6	55.5	29.0	46.6	57.0	45.2	33.7	..	..	40.4	40.8
Q2	45.6	142.3	57.1	28.8	47.9	57.9	46.7	34.7	..	..	41.5	41.3
Q3	47.3	141.1	57.8	29.4	48.4	58.5	47.0	35.1	..	..	42.0	42.1
Q4	47.9	137.3	61.1	30.0	50.8	59.8	48.2	35.6	..	..	42.4	43.0
1960 Q1	48.6	138.5	62.3	30.6	51.7	60.9	48.9	36.0	..	..	42.7	44.0
Q2	48.9	133.7	62.4	30.6	51.6	60.9	49.1	36.3	..	..	42.8	43.7
Q3	49.4	132.8	62.4	32.4	51.8	60.7	49.1	36.7	..	..	43.2	44.3
Q4	50.2	132.2	63.1	32.5	52.4	62.9	49.1	37.1	..	..	43.1	44.5
1961 Q1	50.3	127.3	62.5	31.2	51.7	65.0	50.1	37.6	..	..	44.1	45.3
Q2	49.8	130.8	63.3	32.7	52.4	66.2	49.9	37.2	..	..	43.9	45.4
Q3	49.3	132.0	62.8	33.5	52.3	66.8	50.2	37.4	..	..	44.2	45.4
Q4	48.8	132.4	62.0	34.4	51.8	66.2	49.8	37.2	..	..	43.9	45.2
1962 Q1	49.0	133.0	62.0	34.6	51.8	67.0	49.9	37.4	..	..	44.2	45.6
Q2	50.7	135.2	63.1	35.4	52.7	67.6	50.3	37.6	..	..	44.6	46.0
Q3	52.0	136.9	63.5	35.9	53.1	67.8	50.6	37.8	..	..	44.9	46.2
Q4	52.9	134.2	62.8	36.4	52.5	64.3	50.8	37.8	..	..	44.9	46.0

See footnotes on page 69

Sources: Office for National Statistics;
Enquiries Columns 1-11 020 7533 5972; Columns 12 020 7533 5944

1.9 Gross value added at constant 1995 basic prices, by category of output[1,3]

continued

1995 = 100, seasonally adjusted

	Production						Service industries[4]					
	Agriculture, forestry, and fishing	Mining and quarrying inc oil & gas extraction	Manufacturing	Electricity gas and water supply	Total	Construction	Distribution; hotels and catering; repairs	Transport, storage and communication	Business services and finance	Government and other services	Total	Gross value added at basic prices
1995 weights[2]	*18*	*25*	*216*	*25*	*266*	*52*	*146*	*82*	*211*	*225*	*664*	*1 000*
	GDQA	CKYX	CKYY	CKYZ	CKYW	GDQB	GDQE	GDQH	GDQN	GDQU	GDQS	CGCE
1963 Q1	52.6	134.5	61.9	38.0	52.0	57.2	50.7	37.2	..	..	44.7	46.6
Q2	53.3	136.0	64.1	36.5	53.7	68.2	52.3	39.1	..	..	46.1	48.5
Q3	53.3	134.2	66.3	37.4	55.2	69.1	53.3	39.4	..	..	46.6	48.6
Q4	53.4	132.7	67.9	37.4	56.4	71.7	53.5	39.9	..	..	47.0	49.4
1964 Q1	53.9	137.2	70.1	38.5	58.2	72.4	53.8	40.7	..	..	47.1	50.3
Q2	55.0	129.2	70.1	38.9	58.0	73.7	54.5	41.6	..	..	47.7	50.7
Q3	55.9	130.4	70.9	39.2	58.7	72.9	54.9	41.6	..	..	48.0	50.8
Q4	56.2	130.1	72.8	40.3	60.2	74.3	55.5	41.7	..	..	48.6	51.7
1965 Q1	57.1	129.6	72.6	41.2	60.2	78.2	55.5	41.9	..	..	48.5	51.8
Q2	56.9	125.4	72.8	40.9	60.2	75.8	55.2	42.0	..	..	48.8	52.0
Q3	56.5	123.5	72.6	42.8	60.3	75.7	55.9	42.5	..	..	49.2	52.4
Q4	56.5	124.7	73.8	42.9	61.0	77.3	56.5	42.8	..	..	49.7	52.9
1966 Q1	57.8	117.6	75.1	42.3	61.7	77.0	56.5	42.8	..	..	49.7	53.0
Q2	57.1	120.5	74.7	43.4	61.6	77.9	56.7	42.6	..	..	50.2	53.2
Q3	56.2	111.5	75.0	44.2	61.8	78.6	56.2	44.0	..	..	50.2	53.5
Q4	56.6	117.5	72.6	44.6	60.3	79.1	55.7	44.4	..	..	50.3	53.5
1967 Q1	57.6	116.3	73.8	43.7	61.0	80.6	56.0	43.7	..	..	50.6	54.0
Q2	58.6	113.7	74.5	45.5	61.6	80.7	56.2	44.1	..	..	51.0	54.4
Q3	59.6	109.2	74.7	45.1	61.6	81.8	57.0	44.0	..	..	51.4	54.5
Q4	59.6	118.5	76.0	46.6	63.0	82.0	57.7	44.2	..	..	51.8	54.7
1968 Q1	60.8	105.3	79.3	42.6	65.6	83.7	59.5	45.7	..	..	52.9	56.4
Q2	59.6	102.1	80.0	45.9	66.4	83.2	57.6	45.3	..	..	52.3	56.2
Q3	57.9	99.4	80.9	46.3	67.0	83.3	58.3	45.8	..	..	52.6	57.0
Q4	56.7	98.4	81.5	44.3	67.2	83.4	58.3	46.4	..	..	52.7	57.1
1969 Q1	56.9	98.1	82.5	47.1	68.2	82.7	58.5	47.5	..	..	53.2	57.3
Q2	58.3	95.5	84.0	49.3	69.5	82.8	59.1	47.5	..	..	53.4	57.7
Q3	59.1	93.2	83.6	47.4	68.9	83.2	58.8	47.7	..	..	53.6	58.1
Q4	60.1	86.7	83.6	47.0	68.7	82.3	58.6	47.8	..	..	53.5	58.5
1970 Q1	60.7	91.2	83.0	50.8	68.8	79.0	60.2	48.6	..	..	54.5	58.0
Q2	61.8	88.7	83.8	48.4	69.1	81.6	60.5	49.5	..	..	54.9	59.1
Q3	62.7	87.2	83.7	49.9	69.2	82.8	60.6	49.9	..	..	55.2	59.4
Q4	63.5	79.2	84.3	51.2	69.5	81.2	60.5	50.5	..	..	55.3	60.3
1971 Q1	64.2	88.7	83.1	50.7	68.8	81.0	60.8	49.4	..	..	55.3	59.5
Q2	65.0	88.4	83.1	51.2	69.0	82.9	61.5	50.8	..	..	56.2	60.2
Q3	66.0	86.4	82.6	52.9	68.7	82.1	62.1	51.4	..	..	56.8	61.1
Q4	66.7	75.7	82.6	55.1	68.6	84.3	62.6	52.2	..	..	57.3	61.3
1972 Q1	67.6	32.5	80.3	52.9	65.3	84.0	63.6	51.6	..	..	57.8	60.8
Q2	67.5	80.3	84.4	56.8	70.3	85.8	64.8	53.1	..	..	58.6	62.4
Q3	67.6	80.0	85.2	58.4	71.0	83.4	65.5	54.0	..	..	58.8	62.9
Q4	67.6	80.3	88.5	58.4	73.4	83.1	66.7	54.9	..	..	59.5	64.4
1973 Q1	69.7	81.0	92.0	59.6	76.0	88.6	69.5	56.8	..	..	61.1	66.9
Q2	69.4	80.8	92.0	60.6	76.2	86.2	67.8	57.5	..	..	61.1	66.8
Q3	69.6	78.4	92.8	59.6	76.6	85.9	67.8	57.4	..	..	61.2	67.0
Q4	70.1	65.6	93.1	61.0	76.3	83.7	67.7	58.0	..	..	61.4	66.1
1974 Q1	70.9	39.2	88.3	55.1	70.9	80.1	65.5	56.5	..	..	60.9	64.7
Q2	71.6	71.8	94.1	60.5	77.1	78.9	65.5	58.1	..	..	61.1	65.8
Q3	70.9	74.2	93.3	63.6	77.0	76.8	65.8	58.1	..	..	61.5	66.9
Q4	68.9	73.0	89.4	63.1	74.1	73.1	65.3	57.7	..	..	61.5	65.7
1975 Q1	66.9	73.8	88.6	61.0	73.1	73.7	64.4	57.6	..	..	61.7	66.0
Q2	65.9	73.0	84.3	62.3	70.2	73.4	64.1	56.9	..	..	62.0	65.0
Q3	64.3	72.1	83.0	60.6	69.1	72.8	62.1	57.0	..	..	62.0	65.0
Q4	63.2	72.7	84.1	63.0	70.5	72.5	62.1	56.1	..	..	62.1	65.8
1976 Q1	60.6	69.7	85.1	63.0	71.3	73.5	63.1	55.7	..	..	62.6	67.0
Q2	58.2	69.1	86.3	62.9	72.7	71.5	63.9	56.0	..	..	63.2	66.3
Q3	58.7	67.5	86.2	61.1	72.6	70.5	63.9	56.7	..	..	63.4	67.0
Q4	61.8	67.6	88.7	64.3	75.5	72.9	64.3	57.9	..	..	64.0	68.2
1977 Q1	65.1	67.7	89.9	63.7	77.3	70.9	63.4	58.7	..	..	64.0	68.5
Q2	66.9	67.1	88.0	66.5	76.9	71.1	62.4	57.1	..	..	63.6	68.0
Q3	68.7	66.2	87.4	66.4	76.4	72.0	63.8	58.3	..	..	64.4	68.5
Q4	69.6	65.3	87.7	65.0	76.6	73.4	64.2	58.5	..	..	64.8	69.3

See footnotes on page 69

Sources: Office for National Statistics;
Enquiries Columns 1-11 020 7533 5972; Columns 12 020 7533 5944

1.9 Gross value added at constant 1995 basic prices, by category of output[1,3]

continued

1995 = 100, seasonally adjusted

	Production						Service industries[4]					
	Agriculture, forestry, and fishing	Mining and quarrying inc oil & gas extraction	Manufacturing	Electricity gas and water supply	Total	Construction	Distribution; hotels and catering; repairs	Transport, storage and communication	Business services and finance	Government and other services	Total	Gross value added at basic prices
1995 weights[2]	*18*	*25*	*216*	*25*	*266*	*52*	*146*	*82*	*211*	*225*	*664*	*1 000*
	GDQA	CKYX	CKYY	CKYZ	CKYW	GDQB	GDQE	GDQH	GDQN	GDQU	GDQS	CGCE
1978 Q1	71.3	60.9	87.6	66.9	76.9	74.4	65.4	60.0	..	..	65.3	69.8
Q2	73.2	65.1	89.4	68.0	79.3	78.3	66.6	60.2	..	..	65.8	70.2
Q3	73.5	68.0	89.8	67.5	79.9	77.6	67.8	60.0	..	..	66.5	70.8
Q4	72.7	72.2	88.4	65.1	79.8	76.6	68.7	60.8	..	..	67.1	71.1
1979 Q1	71.1	74.7	87.1	71.9	80.0	73.7	67.5	58.8	..	..	66.6	70.6
Q2	70.1	80.0	90.9	71.6	83.8	78.3	71.9	63.7	..	..	68.9	73.2
Q3	71.0	84.3	87.6	68.1	82.1	78.6	67.5	64.6	..	..	68.1	71.9
Q4	74.0	81.4	88.7	66.7	82.1	78.3	69.2	63.7	..	..	68.7	72.1
1980 Q1	77.3	81.9	86.5	70.4	80.8	76.6	67.1	63.7	..	..	68.4	71.4
Q2	79.6	79.8	82.7	69.0	77.7	74.1	65.5	62.1	..	..	67.9	70.7
Q3	80.6	80.3	78.9	68.2	74.9	73.4	63.8	60.5	..	..	67.5	70.4
Q4	80.3	83.0	75.7	69.2	73.2	67.9	63.0	59.8	..	..	67.3	69.3
1981 Q1	80.1	83.5	75.2	69.5	73.2	69.2	64.0	60.7	..	..	67.8	69.1
Q2	80.5	84.1	75.4	71.6	73.6	67.0	64.0	61.0	..	..	67.9	69.4
Q3	81.7	85.4	76.6	68.9	74.7	68.1	64.3	62.3	..	..	68.3	70.4
Q4	83.7	86.5	76.6	73.3	75.5	65.1	63.1	62.6	..	..	68.2	70.4
1982 Q1	86.5	85.6	76.3	70.5	74.9	70.6	64.4	61.0	..	..	68.6	70.4
Q2	89.3	91.6	76.4	70.1	76.2	71.8	64.5	61.5	..	..	68.7	71.4
Q3	89.5	94.4	75.6	69.9	76.2	73.4	65.5	60.4	..	..	69.0	71.5
Q4	88.0	92.1	74.9	70.8	75.5	74.8	66.0	61.4	..	..	69.7	71.8
1983 Q1	83.4	88.8	76.5	70.8	77.1	76.4	67.0	61.3	67.2	79.6	70.5	73.4
Q2	80.9	89.8	76.8	75.7	77.9	75.4	67.4	62.7	67.0	79.7	70.8	73.2
Q3	82.2	94.3	77.7	71.1	78.8	78.3	68.3	63.3	67.6	80.4	71.5	74.1
Q4	87.7	94.0	78.8	73.4	79.9	79.1	69.0	64.0	68.6	80.8	72.2	74.9
1984 Q1	96.5	91.5	80.1	75.2	80.5	80.1	71.3	64.6	69.9	81.2	73.3	75.6
Q2	102.7	83.7	79.9	64.6	77.9	81.2	70.7	65.3	70.6	81.2	73.5	75.1
Q3	103.7	82.7	80.6	52.6	77.2	81.8	71.1	66.4	71.5	81.5	74.1	75.2
Q4	100.7	87.3	80.6	54.2	78.2	80.7	72.2	67.3	73.1	81.9	75.1	76.2
1985 Q1	97.6	90.0	83.0	62.1	81.0	81.9	73.0	68.3	73.3	82.4	75.6	77.5
Q2	97.5	96.7	83.4	79.4	84.2	81.3	74.0	68.1	73.4	82.8	76.0	79.1
Q3	91.2	95.3	82.6	80.2	83.3	80.0	74.7	68.7	74.2	82.6	76.4	78.8
Q4	96.3	97.5	81.5	77.7	82.7	81.8	75.4	69.2	75.7	82.9	77.2	79.2
1986 Q1	94.9	86.1	82.9	83.1	83.3	78.3	76.0	70.1	77.4	83.9	78.2	80.1
Q2	95.3	98.9	82.7	83.6	84.6	84.4	77.8	70.6	78.3	83.8	79.0	81.3
Q3	96.8	99.3	83.2	82.4	84.9	86.8	79.3	71.4	79.0	84.3	79.7	82.0
Q4	96.1	94.7	86.0	79.9	86.4	88.9	80.4	73.9	79.3	84.8	80.7	83.1
1987 Q1	94.0	93.9	85.7	85.9	86.6	90.8	81.4	73.0	79.7	84.9	80.9	83.3
Q2	93.7	97.0	86.6	83.8	87.5	91.9	83.6	76.5	80.7	85.3	82.3	84.5
Q3	93.2	96.9	88.5	83.4	89.0	96.1	85.0	78.4	82.3	85.8	83.5	86.0
Q4	93.0	91.5	90.1	84.8	89.8	99.0	86.1	78.4	82.9	86.2	84.1	86.8
1988 Q1	93.4	89.1	92.1	81.9	90.9	101.2	88.1	80.3	85.0	86.7	85.6	88.1
Q2	93.5	89.8	92.7	83.1	91.5	101.9	88.1	79.3	86.0	86.9	85.9	88.5
Q3	93.9	85.2	95.4	86.9	93.6	102.7	89.8	80.2	87.5	87.2	86.9	89.8
Q4	95.5	83.2	96.3	84.7	93.9	104.9	91.1	82.3	87.9	87.5	87.7	90.6
1989 Q1	98.4	76.8	97.8	81.2	94.1	106.8	91.8	83.0	87.4	87.4	87.8	90.7
Q2	99.1	72.0	97.8	86.5	94.0	108.5	92.5	83.6	87.6	87.9	88.3	91.1
Q3	99.5	78.2	97.9	84.7	94.6	108.1	92.4	84.9	87.4	87.7	88.3	91.2
Q4	100.0	79.9	98.0	84.7	94.9	109.2	92.2	84.7	88.4	88.1	88.6	91.6
1990 Q1	98.8	74.1	98.2	81.4	94.1	112.6	92.9	85.9	90.8	88.5	89.8	92.2
Q2	100.2	77.8	98.8	86.9	95.5	112.8	92.6	85.3	90.7	88.5	89.7	92.6
Q3	101.7	70.4	97.6	88.3	93.9	110.6	91.3	84.7	90.1	88.7	89.2	91.7
Q4	102.2	71.0	96.4	89.4	93.0	109.1	89.7	84.4	90.4	89.5	89.1	91.4
1991 Q1	105.3	74.3	94.5	90.4	91.9	104.8	89.1	81.8	90.4	90.2	88.9	91.1
Q2	106.5	73.7	92.7	94.8	90.9	102.7	88.4	82.7	90.4	91.4	89.2	90.9
Q3	105.6	78.6	91.8	88.5	90.1	101.6	88.7	82.8	90.5	92.2	89.6	90.8
Q4	105.5	80.1	92.4	92.1	91.0	100.2	88.5	83.4	89.1	92.8	89.4	90.9
1992 Q1	111.2	78.5	92.7	91.3	91.0	99.5	87.7	84.1	88.0	93.3	89.2	90.8
Q2	110.8	75.6	92.7	89.9	90.6	98.2	88.7	84.3	88.1	93.3	89.4	90.7
Q3	110.5	78.7	93.0	93.8	91.5	98.1	89.5	84.3	88.9	93.1	89.8	91.2
Q4	108.0	82.7	92.7	96.5	92.0	97.3	90.4	85.8	89.2	93.6	90.5	91.7

See footnotes on page 69

Sources: Office for National Statistics;
Enquiries Columns 1-11 020 7533 5972; Columns 12 020 7533 5944

1.9 Gross value added at constant 1995 basic prices, by category of output[1,3]

continued

1995 = 100, seasonally adjusted

	Production						Service industries[4]					
	Agriculture, forestry, and fishing	Mining and quarrying inc oil & gas extraction	Manufacturing	Electricity gas and water supply	Total	Construction	Distribution; hotels and catering; repairs	Transport, storage and communication	Business services and finance	Government and other services	Total	Gross value added at basic prices
1995 weights[2]	*18*	*25*	*216*	*25*	*266*	*52*	*146*	*82*	*211*	*225*	*664*	*1 000*
	GDQA	CKYX	CKYY	CKYZ	CKYW	GDQB	GDQE	GDQH	GDQN	GDQU	GDQS	CGCE
1993 Q1	103.3	78.9	94.1	91.4	92.3	96.6	92.2	85.9	89.5	94.5	91.3	92.2
Q2	100.2	79.9	94.0	95.0	92.5	96.5	93.5	86.6	90.4	95.0	92.1	92.7
Q3	101.0	86.0	93.9	99.1	93.5	96.8	94.2	88.1	91.2	95.7	93.0	93.6
Q4	100.3	91.9	94.4	101.6	94.7	98.5	94.4	88.8	91.7	96.5	93.5	94.3
1994 Q1	98.9	94.7	96.5	96.8	96.3	99.8	97.3	88.9	93.3	96.8	94.8	95.5
Q2	98.4	98.3	98.0	98.3	98.1	100.7	97.7	93.5	94.9	97.5	96.2	96.9
Q3	100.7	97.2	99.3	97.9	98.9	100.9	98.8	95.8	97.1	98.1	97.7	98.1
Q4	101.9	97.2	100.3	98.0	99.8	101.8	99.1	99.0	97.6	98.7	98.5	99.0
1995 Q1	99.5	100.7	99.6	98.7	99.6	100.5	100.2	98.6	98.8	99.4	99.3	99.4
Q2	99.9	99.2	100.1	99.9	100.0	99.8	99.2	99.6	99.4	99.9	99.5	99.7
Q3	99.8	99.3	100.2	100.2	100.2	99.5	99.5	100.6	100.7	100.1	100.2	100.2
Q4	100.8	100.9	100.1	101.2	100.2	100.2	101.1	101.2	101.0	100.6	100.9	100.7
1996 Q1	104.9	102.2	100.4	104.7	101.0	100.5	101.2	103.0	102.9	101.2	102.0	101.6
Q2	99.7	103.6	99.9	105.9	100.8	100.6	103.2	103.2	104.0	101.6	102.9	102.1
Q3	101.8	104.2	100.3	105.8	101.2	101.6	103.9	104.2	104.7	102.2	103.6	102.8
Q4	101.4	103.4	100.9	104.8	101.5	103.2	104.6	106.6	105.9	102.9	104.7	103.6
1997 Q1	103.1	101.8	101.7	104.2	102.0	103.5	105.0	109.7	108.4	102.8	105.9	104.6
Q2	104.1	102.2	101.4	105.9	101.9	104.7	106.5	111.6	110.3	103.1	107.2	105.5
Q3	103.4	104.2	101.9	107.0	102.6	104.4	106.9	114.7	112.4	103.8	108.6	106.5
Q4	103.4	100.3	101.8	105.5	102.0	106.3	107.8	117.5	113.5	104.3	109.6	107.2
1998 Q1	101.5	101.0	102.3	103.7	102.3	109.0	108.8	118.4	115.3	104.9	110.7	108.1
Q2	102.2	105.0	102.7	107.7	103.4	105.3	108.9	120.0	118.0	105.5	112.0	109.1
Q3	101.8	105.4	102.4	109.3	103.3	105.0	109.5	122.7	119.0	105.9	112.9	109.6
Q4	101.7	106.0	101.4	109.5	102.6	105.1	109.6	124.8	119.4	106.1	113.4	109.7
1999 Q1	104.3	105.8	101.1	106.6	102.0	105.5	110.6	126.7	120.2	106.3	114.2	110.1
Q2	102.8	108.3	101.4	109.1	102.8	106.1	110.3	129.6	121.8	106.2	115.0	110.8
Q3	102.6	110.2	102.9	110.9	104.3	106.6	111.8	132.1	123.0	106.4	116.0	111.9
Q4	102.8	107.9	103.3	110.7	104.4	107.3	112.3	135.0	124.3	107.0	117.2	112.8
2000 Q1	101.6	106.0	102.8	107.7	103.6	110.5	113.4	136.6	124.8	107.6	117.9	113.3
Q2	..	..	..	..	..	..	113.8	..	..	..	119.1	..

See footnotes on page 69

Sources: Office for National Statistics;
Enquiries Columns 1-11 020 7533 5972; Columns 12 020 7533 5944

1.10 Index numbers of gross value added at constant 1995 basic prices: service industries

1995 = 100

	Distribution hotels and catering; repairs		Transport, storage and communication		Business services and finance			Government and other services					
	Motor trades; wholesale and retail trade; repairs	Hotels and restaurants	Transport and storage	Post and telecommunication	Financial intermediation[3]	Real estate, renting and business activities	Ownership of dwellings	PAD[1]	Education	Health and social work	Other services[2]	FISIM[4,5]	Total services
1995 weights	*117*	*29*	*54*	*29*	*67*	*111*	*72*	*61*	*56*	*65*	*43*	*-40*	*664*
	GDQC	GDQD	GDQF	GDQG	GDQI	GDQK	GDQL	GDQO	GDQP	GDQQ	GDQR	GDQJ	GDQS
1948	..	60.8	34.3	14.4	..	..	..	100.4	28.7	30.9	36.2	..	33.9
1949	..	58.2	36.2	14.9	..	..	..	97.1	30.4	33.8	34.9	..	34.0
1950	..	58.2	37.2	15.5	..	..	..	94.4	30.4	35.3	34.2	..	34.4
1951	..	59.0	39.0	16.0	..	..	..	99.3	31.2	36.0	34.2	..	34.8
1952	..	60.8	40.1	16.4	..	..	..	102.3	32.1	36.0	33.5	..	35.4
1953	..	62.5	41.4	16.9	..	..	..	103.0	32.9	36.0	33.5	..	36.1
1954	..	62.5	42.2	17.6	..	..	49.6	101.3	32.9	36.7	34.2	..	37.3
1955	..	65.2	43.1	18.3	..	..	50.7	99.7	34.6	37.5	34.2	..	38.4
1956	..	66.0	43.8	18.6	..	..	51.5	97.6	35.5	38.3	33.5	..	38.6
1957	..	67.8	43.7	18.6	..	..	52.3	95.4	36.3	39.0	34.2	..	39.3
1958	..	68.6	43.2	18.8	..	..	53.1	92.0	38.0	39.7	34.2	..	39.9
1959	..	71.2	45.1	19.7	..	..	54.0	90.2	38.9	40.4	34.2	..	41.6
1960	..	73.8	47.3	20.8	..	..	55.1	88.8	40.6	41.2	35.5	..	42.9
1961	..	75.6	48.1	21.7	..	..	56.3	89.3	42.2	41.9	36.8	..	44.0
1962	..	75.6	48.2	22.3	..	..	57.4	89.7	43.9	42.6	37.6	..	44.6
1963	..	76.5	49.6	23.5	48.4	..	58.4	91.6	45.6	43.4	38.2	19.3	46.1
1964	..	78.2	52.8	25.0	49.8	..	59.3	91.8	47.3	44.2	40.2	20.7	47.9
1965	..	78.2	53.4	26.6	51.3	..	60.9	92.9	49.8	45.6	40.9	22.1	49.1
1966	..	77.3	54.3	28.2	52.1	..	62.5	94.9	52.3	46.3	41.6	22.8	50.1
1967	..	75.6	54.4	29.7	52.3	..	64.3	97.8	54.8	47.8	41.6	26.9	51.2
1968	..	75.6	56.3	31.4	52.7	..	66.4	97.5	56.5	48.5	41.6	25.1	52.6
1969	..	75.6	58.4	32.8	52.9	..	68.2	96.2	58.2	47.1	42.2	26.0	53.4
1970	..	77.3	60.5	34.8	53.8	..	69.9	96.6	59.9	47.8	42.9	27.1	55.0
1971	..	77.3	62.4	35.3	53.5	..	71.4	98.5	63.3	49.3	43.6	29.2	56.4
1972	..	79.9	64.7	38.0	53.0	..	73.1	102.1	65.9	50.8	44.3	31.5	58.7
1973	64.4	79.9	69.5	41.0	55.3	..	74.8	104.8	69.2	51.5	45.6	34.7	61.2
1974	61.6	79.0	69.1	41.9	59.0	..	76.5	103.9	72.6	55.9	46.2	37.5	61.2
1975	59.4	77.3	67.9	41.6	62.0	..	78.3	106.1	75.2	61.1	47.6	37.0	61.9
1976	60.1	77.3	67.7	41.2	62.6	..	80.6	107.2	78.5	63.3	49.6	38.0	63.3
1977	59.6	77.3	69.1	43.0	62.3	..	82.5	106.1	79.4	64.0	51.6	38.8	64.2
1978	64.0	82.5	70.4	45.7	64.8	41.8	83.6	105.5	81.0	64.7	53.6	41.4	66.2
1979	66.2	84.2	72.3	48.7	68.2	44.8	85.1	105.9	83.5	66.2	54.9	44.8	68.1
1980	62.0	81.6	69.2	50.0	68.1	46.3	85.8	106.6	83.5	68.4	58.3	47.6	67.8
1981	61.0	79.9	68.6	51.1	68.6	47.8	87.0	106.9	82.7	70.6	57.6	49.9	68.0
1982	62.3	79.9	66.3	52.7	69.6	51.8	88.3	105.3	83.5	72.1	57.6	52.9	69.0
1983	65.4	80.1	67.9	54.8	70.1	57.0	89.0	105.3	83.8	73.2	59.8	57.2	71.3
1984	69.1	81.8	70.1	58.9	71.6	61.7	90.1	105.0	84.1	73.2	63.6	61.4	74.0
1985	71.7	86.9	73.6	60.3	72.2	66.9	91.1	105.0	84.4	73.6	67.0	65.2	76.3
1986	75.5	92.5	75.3	64.9	73.7	72.8	91.5	104.9	85.9	74.3	70.6	74.6	79.4
1987	81.1	98.2	81.4	68.2	82.1	76.4	91.5	103.1	85.7	76.1	77.0	83.4	82.7
1988	86.4	103.4	84.9	72.7	89.0	83.2	91.8	102.5	86.7	77.9	81.5	88.8	86.5
1989	89.4	106.1	88.2	76.8	92.3	84.1	92.1	102.2	87.8	79.7	81.1	91.7	88.3
1990	88.4	107.5	87.9	80.1	98.1	86.4	93.3	103.7	89.2	80.6	81.5	95.5	89.5
1991	86.3	100.4	84.4	79.6	98.7	84.1	94.8	105.6	92.2	86.1	81.4	94.0	89.3
1992	87.5	96.4	87.5	79.5	94.2	82.6	95.3	105.0	95.0	88.6	83.2	90.9	89.7
1993	92.5	98.5	89.3	83.6	96.3	84.7	96.5	102.9	95.0	92.6	90.1	91.6	92.5
1994	97.5	101.2	96.3	90.7	97.3	93.5	97.8	101.3	98.7	95.0	95.7	95.8	96.8
1995	100.0	100.0	100.0	100.0	100.0	100.0	100.0	100.0	100.0	100.0	100.0	100.0	100.0
1996	103.4	102.4	100.7	110.8	104.3	106.8	101.4	98.5	101.6	104.4	103.7	105.5	103.3
1997	107.3	103.6	106.5	126.2	109.9	117.6	103.5	96.7	103.0	108.3	106.7	112.8	107.8
1998	110.1	105.7	113.9	135.5	113.0	128.5	107.1	96.4	103.3	111.8	112.4	119.5	112.3
1999	112.2	107.5	117.2	156.1	112.5	135.7	110.3	96.2	103.8	114.5	112.7	121.3	115.6

1 Public administration and national defence; compulsory social security
2 Comprising sections O, P and Q of the SIC(92).
3 Comprises section J of the SIC(92). This covers activities of institutions such as banks, building societies, securities dealers, insurance companies and pension funds. It also covers institutions whose activities are closely related to financial intermediation but do not cover financial intermediation themselves. For example fund managers and insurance brokers.
4 The weight and proxy series for financial intermediation are calculated before the deduction of interest receipts and payments to provide a better indication of the underlying activity for this section (see note 3). However, this overstates the contribution to GDP because interest flows should be treated as transfer payments rather than final consumption. The financial services adjustment, which has a negative weight, corrects for this.
5 Financial Intermediation Services Indirectly Measured.

Source: Office for National Statistics; Enquiries 020 7533 5972

1.10 Index numbers of gross value added at constant 1995 basic prices: service industries

continued

1995 = 100, seasonally adjusted

	Distribution hotels and catering; repairs		Transport, storage and communication		Business services and finance			Government and other services					
	Motor trades; wholesale and retail trade; repairs	Hotels and restauran-ts	Transport and storage	Post and telecommu-nication	Financial intermedi-ation[3]	Real estate, renting and business activities	Ownership of dwellings	PAD[1]	Education	Health and social work	Other services[2]	FISIM[4,5]	Total services
1995 weights	*117*	*29*	*54*	*29*	*67*	*111*	*72*	*61*	*56*	*65*	*43*	*-40*	*664*
	GDQC	GDQD	GDQF	GDQG	GDQI	GDQK	GDQL	GDQO	GDQP	GDQQ	GDQR	GDQJ	GDQS
1948 Q1	..	..	34.3	14.4	..	..	..	100.4	..	..	..	..	33.9
Q2	..	..	34.3	14.4	..	..	..	100.4	..	..	..	..	33.9
Q3	..	..	34.3	14.4	..	..	..	100.4	..	..	..	..	33.9
Q4	..	..	34.3	14.4	..	..	..	100.4	..	..	..	..	33.9
1949 Q1	..	..	36.2	14.9	..	..	..	97.1	..	..	..	..	34.0
Q2	..	..	36.2	14.9	..	..	..	97.1	..	..	..	..	34.0
Q3	..	..	36.2	14.9	..	..	..	97.1	..	..	..	..	34.0
Q4	..	..	36.2	14.9	..	..	..	97.1	..	..	..	..	34.0
1950 Q1	..	..	37.2	15.5	..	..	..	94.4	..	..	..	..	34.4
Q2	..	..	37.2	15.5	..	..	..	94.4	..	..	..	..	34.4
Q3	..	..	37.2	15.5	..	..	..	94.4	..	..	..	..	34.4
Q4	..	..	37.2	15.5	..	..	..	94.4	..	..	..	..	34.4
1951 Q1	..	..	39.0	16.0	..	..	..	99.3	..	..	..	..	34.8
Q2	..	..	39.0	16.0	..	..	..	99.3	..	..	..	..	34.8
Q3	..	..	39.0	16.0	..	..	..	99.3	..	..	..	..	34.8
Q4	..	..	39.0	16.0	..	..	..	99.3	..	..	..	..	34.8
1952 Q1	..	..	40.1	16.4	..	..	..	102.3	..	..	..	..	35.4
Q2	..	..	40.1	16.4	..	..	..	102.3	..	..	..	..	35.4
Q3	..	..	40.1	16.4	..	..	..	102.3	..	..	..	..	35.4
Q4	..	..	40.1	16.4	..	..	..	102.3	..	..	..	..	35.4
1953 Q1	..	..	41.4	16.9	..	..	..	103.0	..	..	..	..	36.1
Q2	..	..	41.4	16.9	..	..	..	103.0	..	..	..	..	36.1
Q3	..	..	41.4	16.9	..	..	..	103.0	..	..	..	..	36.1
Q4	..	..	41.4	16.9	..	..	..	103.0	..	..	..	..	36.1
1954 Q1	..	..	42.2	17.6	..	..	49.6	101.3	..	..	..	..	37.3
Q2	..	..	42.2	17.6	..	..	49.6	101.3	..	..	..	..	37.3
Q3	..	..	42.2	17.6	..	..	49.6	101.3	..	..	..	..	37.3
Q4	..	..	42.2	17.6	..	..	49.6	101.3	..	..	..	..	37.3
1955 Q1	..	..	43.1	18.3	..	..	50.7	99.7	..	..	..	..	38.4
Q2	..	..	43.1	18.3	..	..	50.7	99.7	..	..	..	..	38.4
Q3	..	..	43.1	18.3	..	..	50.7	99.7	..	..	..	..	38.4
Q4	..	..	43.1	18.3	..	..	50.7	99.7	..	..	..	..	38.4
1956 Q1	..	..	43.8	18.6	..	..	51.5	97.6	..	..	..	..	38.6
Q2	..	..	43.8	18.6	..	..	51.5	97.6	..	..	..	..	38.6
Q3	..	..	43.8	18.6	..	..	51.5	97.6	..	..	..	..	38.6
Q4	..	..	43.8	18.6	..	..	51.5	97.6	..	..	..	..	38.6
1957 Q1	..	..	43.7	18.6	..	..	52.3	95.4	..	..	..	..	39.3
Q2	..	..	43.7	18.6	..	..	52.3	95.4	..	..	..	..	39.3
Q3	..	..	43.7	18.6	..	..	52.3	95.4	..	..	..	..	39.3
Q4	..	..	43.7	18.6	..	..	52.3	95.4	..	..	..	..	39.3
1958 Q1	..	..	43.2	18.8	..	..	52.7	92.5	..	..	..	..	39.8
Q2	..	..	43.2	18.8	..	..	53.0	92.3	..	..	..	..	39.3
Q3	..	..	43.2	18.8	..	..	53.3	91.9	..	..	..	..	40.2
Q4	..	..	43.2	18.8	..	..	53.3	91.4	..	..	..	..	40.4
1959 Q1	..	..	45.1	19.7	..	..	53.8	90.9	..	..	..	..	40.4
Q2	..	..	45.1	19.7	..	..	53.8	90.6	..	..	..	..	41.5
Q3	..	..	45.1	19.7	..	..	54.0	90.1	..	..	..	..	42.0
Q4	..	..	45.1	19.7	..	..	54.3	89.2	..	..	..	..	42.4
1960 Q1	..	..	47.3	20.8	..	..	54.6	88.8	..	..	..	..	42.7
Q2	..	..	47.3	20.8	..	..	54.9	88.6	..	..	..	..	42.8
Q3	..	..	47.3	20.8	..	..	55.4	89.0	..	..	..	..	43.2
Q4	..	..	47.3	20.8	..	..	55.7	88.8	..	..	..	..	43.1

See footnotes on page 74.

Source: Office for National Statistics; Enquiries 020 7533 5972

1.10 Index numbers of gross value added at constant 1995 basic prices: service industries

continued

1995 = 100, seasonally adjusted

	Distribution hotels and catering; repairs		Transport, storage and communication		Business services and finance			Government and other services					
	Motor trades; wholesale and retail trade; repairs	Hotels and restauran-ts	Transport and storage	Post and telecommu-nication	Financial intermedi-ation[3]	Real estate, renting and business activities	Ownership of dwellings	PAD[1]	Education	Health and social work	Other services[2]	FISIM[4,5]	Total services
1995 weights	*117*	*29*	*54*	*29*	*67*	*111*	*72*	*61*	*56*	*65*	*43*	*-40*	*664*
	GDQC	GDQD	GDQF	GDQG	GDQI	GDQK	GDQL	GDQO	GDQP	GDQQ	GDQR	GDQJ	GDQS
1961 Q1	..	..	48.1	21.7	..	..	55.9	88.9	..	..	..	..	44.1
Q2	..	..	48.1	21.7	..	..	56.2	89.4	..	..	..	..	43.9
Q3	..	..	48.1	21.7	..	..	56.4	89.5	..	..	..	..	44.2
Q4	..	..	48.1	21.7	..	..	56.4	89.5	..	..	..	..	43.9
1962 Q1	..	..	48.2	22.3	..	..	57.0	89.3	..	..	..	..	44.2
Q2	..	..	48.2	22.3	..	..	57.2	89.5	..	..	..	..	44.6
Q3	..	..	48.2	22.3	..	..	57.5	89.8	..	..	..	..	44.9
Q4	..	..	48.2	22.3	..	..	57.8	90.3	..	..	..	..	44.9
1963 Q1	..	..	49.6	23.5	..	..	58.0	91.3	..	..	..	17.7	44.7
Q2	..	..	49.6	23.5	..	..	58.3	91.8	..	..	..	18.4	46.1
Q3	..	..	49.6	23.5	..	..	58.5	91.7	..	..	..	19.8	46.6
Q4	..	..	49.6	23.5	..	..	58.7	91.5	..	..	..	21.2	47.0
1964 Q1	..	..	52.8	25.0	..	..	58.9	91.5	..	..	..	20.4	47.1
Q2	..	..	52.8	25.0	..	..	59.1	91.7	..	..	..	21.1	47.7
Q3	..	..	52.8	25.0	..	..	59.5	91.8	..	..	..	20.6	48.0
Q4	..	..	52.8	25.0	..	..	59.7	92.2	..	..	..	21.0	48.6
1965 Q1	..	..	53.4	26.6	..	..	60.5	92.2	..	..	..	21.2	48.5
Q2	..	..	53.4	26.6	..	..	60.6	92.5	..	..	..	21.6	48.8
Q3	..	..	53.4	26.6	..	..	61.0	93.1	..	..	..	22.8	49.2
Q4	..	..	53.4	26.6	..	..	61.4	93.6	..	..	..	22.6	49.7
1966 Q1	..	..	54.3	28.2	..	..	61.8	94.1	..	..	..	22.8	49.7
Q2	..	..	54.3	28.2	..	..	62.4	94.6	..	..	..	22.4	50.2
Q3	..	..	54.3	28.2	..	..	62.7	95.0	..	..	..	22.2	50.2
Q4	..	..	54.3	28.2	..	..	63.1	95.8	..	..	..	23.9	50.3
1967 Q1	..	..	54.4	29.7	..	..	63.5	96.8	..	..	..	28.0	50.6
Q2	..	..	54.4	29.7	..	..	64.2	97.8	..	..	..	26.3	51.0
Q3	..	..	54.4	29.7	..	..	64.5	98.3	..	..	..	26.9	51.4
Q4	..	..	54.4	29.7	..	..	64.9	98.4	..	..	..	26.5	51.8
1968 Q1	..	69.5	56.0	31.6	..	..	65.7	98.1	..	..	..	25.5	52.9
Q2	..	76.5	55.3	31.5	..	..	66.2	98.2	..	..	..	24.7	52.3
Q3	..	85.1	56.4	31.3	..	..	66.7	97.3	..	..	..	25.2	52.6
Q4	..	73.8	57.3	31.4	..	..	67.2	96.6	..	..	..	24.9	52.7
1969 Q1	..	68.6	58.5	32.3	..	..	67.4	96.5	..	..	..	25.7	53.2
Q2	..	77.3	58.6	32.4	..	..	68.0	96.1	..	..	..	25.8	53.4
Q3	..	84.2	58.5	33.0	..	..	68.4	96.0	..	..	..	26.5	53.6
Q4	..	74.6	58.2	33.6	..	..	68.9	96.1	..	..	..	25.8	53.5
1970 Q1	..	70.3	59.2	34.2	..	..	69.0	96.4	..	..	..	26.9	54.5
Q2	..	79.0	60.4	34.6	..	..	69.7	96.4	..	..	..	26.4	54.9
Q3	..	85.9	60.9	34.9	..	..	70.2	96.6	..	..	..	27.8	55.2
Q4	..	76.5	61.5	35.5	..	..	70.6	97.0	..	..	..	27.3	55.3
1971 Q1	..	69.5	61.7	32.7	..	..	70.6	97.8	..	..	..	27.3	55.3
Q2	..	78.2	62.0	35.5	..	..	71.3	98.1	..	..	..	28.7	56.2
Q3	..	84.2	62.6	36.1	..	..	71.7	98.9	..	..	..	30.1	56.8
Q4	..	77.3	63.2	37.2	..	..	72.1	99.2	..	..	..	30.6	57.3
1972 Q1	..	71.2	62.4	36.9	..	..	72.3	101.7	..	..	..	31.4	57.8
Q2	..	80.8	64.2	37.9	..	..	72.9	102.1	..	..	..	32.1	58.6
Q3	..	87.8	65.6	38.2	..	..	73.3	102.4	..	..	..	31.2	58.8
Q4	..	79.9	66.6	38.9	..	..	73.9	102.4	..	..	..	31.1	59.5
1973 Q1	65.8	80.8	69.1	40.1	..	..	73.6	104.8	68.4	50.8	..	33.5	61.1
Q2	64.0	79.9	69.7	40.9	..	..	74.3	105.2	69.2	51.5	..	34.0	61.1
Q3	63.9	80.8	69.3	41.2	..	..	75.1	104.6	70.1	51.5	..	35.2	61.2
Q4	63.9	79.9	69.9	41.7	..	..	76.2	104.6	70.1	51.5	..	36.3	61.4

See footnotes on page 74.

Source: Office for National Statistics; Enquiries 020 7533 5972

1.10 Index numbers of gross value added at constant 1995 basic prices: service industries

continued

1995 = 100, seasonally adjusted

	Distribution hotels and catering; repairs		Transport, storage and communication		Business services and finance		Government and other services						
	Motor trades; wholesale and retail trade; repairs	Hotels and restaurants	Transport and storage	Post and telecommunication	Financial intermediation[3]	Real estate, renting and business activities	Ownership of dwellings	PAD[1]	Education	Health and social work	Other services[2]	FISIM[4,5]	Total services
1995 weights	*117*	*29*	*54*	*29*	*67*	*111*	*72*	*61*	*56*	*65*	*43*	*-40*	*664*
	GDQC	GDQD	GDQF	GDQG	GDQI	GDQK	GDQL	GDQO	GDQP	GDQQ	GDQR	GDQJ	GDQS
1974 Q1	61.4	79.9	67.9	40.9	..	..	76.4	104.7	70.1	55.2	..	37.1	60.9
Q2	61.5	79.0	69.9	41.9	..	..	76.4	103.8	71.8	55.9	..	37.5	61.1
Q3	62.0	79.9	69.6	42.3	..	..	76.3	103.6	73.5	55.9	..	37.6	61.5
Q4	61.4	79.0	68.8	42.3	..	..	76.7	103.6	74.3	56.6	..	37.7	61.5
1975 Q1	60.6	79.0	69.1	41.7	..	..	77.2	104.5	74.3	58.8	..	37.2	61.7
Q2	60.3	78.2	67.3	42.2	..	..	78.0	105.9	74.3	61.1	..	37.1	62.0
Q3	58.3	77.3	68.2	41.6	..	..	78.7	106.8	75.2	62.5	..	36.8	62.0
Q4	58.3	77.3	67.2	40.8	..	..	79.2	107.2	76.0	62.5	..	37.0	62.1
1976 Q1	59.4	75.6	67.0	40.2	..	..	79.7	107.5	78.5	63.3	..	37.6	62.6
Q2	60.1	77.3	67.0	40.8	..	..	80.3	107.2	78.5	63.3	..	37.9	63.2
Q3	60.0	78.2	67.4	41.7	..	..	80.8	107.1	77.7	63.3	..	38.5	63.4
Q4	60.6	78.2	69.2	42.2	..	..	81.6	107.0	79.4	63.3	..	38.2	64.0
1977 Q1	59.5	77.3	71.3	41.6	..	..	82.0	106.3	79.4	64.0	..	38.0	64.0
Q2	58.5	77.3	67.9	42.1	..	..	82.4	106.3	79.4	64.0	..	38.5	63.6
Q3	59.9	78.2	68.9	43.6	..	..	82.8	106.0	78.5	64.0	..	39.1	64.4
Q4	60.5	78.2	68.3	44.6	..	..	82.9	105.9	80.2	64.7	..	39.7	64.8
1978 Q1	62.0	81.6	71.0	44.5	..	..	83.3	105.1	81.0	64.0	..	40.0	65.3
Q2	63.6	80.8	70.1	45.9	..	..	83.0	105.3	81.0	64.7	..	40.8	65.8
Q3	65.1	82.5	69.8	45.9	..	..	83.9	105.6	81.8	65.4	..	41.8	66.5
Q4	65.4	85.1	70.7	46.6	..	..	84.2	106.1	82.7	65.4	..	42.8	67.1
1979 Q1	64.5	84.2	65.8	48.3	..	..	85.0	105.2	82.7	65.4	..	43.1	66.6
Q2	69.6	85.1	73.9	49.0	..	..	84.7	106.0	82.7	67.0	..	44.5	68.9
Q3	64.7	82.5	75.9	48.4	..	..	85.3	106.3	84.4	67.0	..	45.3	68.1
Q4	66.0	85.1	73.8	49.1	..	..	85.3	106.2	83.5	67.0	..	46.3	68.7
1980 Q1	63.9	86.9	72.8	50.5	..	..	85.8	106.0	83.5	67.7	..	46.6	68.4
Q2	62.4	82.5	70.5	49.7	..	..	85.3	106.3	83.5	67.7	..	47.3	67.9
Q3	61.3	79.9	67.3	50.2	..	..	85.9	106.8	83.5	68.4	..	47.7	67.5
Q4	60.3	79.9	66.4	49.7	..	..	86.2	107.3	82.7	69.1	..	48.6	67.3
1981 Q1	61.3	80.8	67.4	50.5	..	..	86.8	107.3	82.7	70.6	..	49.1	67.8
Q2	60.9	81.6	67.7	50.9	..	..	86.5	107.0	82.7	70.6	..	49.4	67.9
Q3	61.0	82.5	69.3	51.6	..	..	87.3	106.8	82.7	70.6	..	50.1	68.3
Q4	60.7	76.5	70.0	51.5	..	..	87.6	106.4	82.7	70.6	..	50.8	68.2
1982 Q1	61.3	79.9	66.6	52.2	..	..	88.3	106.1	83.5	72.1	..	51.5	68.6
Q2	61.6	79.9	67.5	52.1	..	..	87.9	105.4	82.7	71.3	..	52.2	68.7
Q3	62.7	80.8	65.1	52.8	..	..	88.5	105.0	82.7	72.1	..	53.4	69.0
Q4	63.5	80.8	66.2	53.6	..	..	88.5	104.8	83.5	72.1	..	54.5	69.7
1983 Q1	64.6	79.2	66.7	52.9	..	..	88.6	105.1	83.7	73.6	..	55.5	70.5
Q2	65.1	79.7	67.5	54.9	..	..	88.9	105.3	83.6	72.8	..	56.5	70.8
Q3	65.9	80.3	68.7	54.8	..	..	89.1	105.5	83.6	73.4	..	57.3	71.5
Q4	66.4	81.5	68.6	56.4	..	..	89.4	105.4	84.1	73.3	..	59.4	72.2
1984 Q1	69.2	81.3	68.7	57.6	..	..	89.8	105.8	84.1	73.2	..	61.4	73.3
Q2	68.5	81.2	69.4	58.4	..	..	90.0	105.0	84.2	72.7	..	62.1	73.5
Q3	68.6	82.9	70.3	59.7	..	..	90.2	104.7	84.3	72.9	..	61.0	74.1
Q4	70.0	82.3	72.0	59.7	..	..	90.3	104.6	83.6	74.5	..	61.3	75.1
1985 Q1	70.7	83.9	73.1	60.3	..	..	90.6	104.5	85.1	73.3	..	61.3	75.6
Q2	71.5	86.1	73.8	59.1	..	..	90.9	105.2	84.7	73.6	..	63.9	76.0
Q3	72.0	87.8	73.5	60.8	..	..	91.3	105.1	84.1	73.6	..	66.6	76.4
Q4	72.6	89.6	74.2	61.0	..	..	91.8	105.1	84.0	73.6	..	68.9	77.2
1986 Q1	73.2	89.9	74.2	62.8	69.7	71.7	91.5	105.9	86.1	73.4	69.0	70.7	78.2
Q2	75.0	91.7	74.2	64.2	72.8	72.6	91.5	104.9	85.8	73.9	69.5	73.4	79.0
Q3	76.2	94.0	75.0	65.1	75.1	73.5	91.5	105.0	85.8	74.3	71.0	76.4	79.7
Q4	77.5	94.4	77.6	67.4	76.8	73.6	91.6	104.0	85.8	75.7	73.0	77.7	80.7

See footnotes on page 74.

Source: Office for National Statistics; Enquiries 020 7533 5972

1.10 Index numbers of gross value added at constant 1995 basic prices: service industries

continued

1995 = 100, seasonally adjusted

	Distribution hotels and catering; repairs		Transport, storage and communication		Business services and finance			Government and other services					
	Motor trades; wholesale and retail trade; repairs	Hotels and restaurants	Transport and storage	Post and telecommunication	Financial intermediation[3]	Real estate, renting and business activities	Ownership of dwellings	PAD[1]	Education	Health and social work	Other services[2]	FISIM[4,5]	Total services
1995 weights	*117*	*29*	*54*	*29*	*67*	*111*	*72*	*61*	*56*	*65*	*43*	*-40*	*664*
	GDQC	GDQD	GDQF	GDQG	GDQI	GDQK	GDQL	GDQO	GDQP	GDQQ	GDQR	GDQJ	GDQS
1987 Q1	78.8	94.0	77.5	65.2	79.4	73.9	91.5	103.5	85.5	75.7	74.0	80.4	80.9
Q2	80.4	99.3	81.8	67.2	81.3	75.4	91.5	103.1	85.6	75.9	76.2	82.6	82.3
Q3	82.1	99.4	83.6	69.3	83.8	77.1	91.6	103.0	85.7	76.1	78.3	83.7	83.5
Q4	83.3	100.2	82.6	70.9	83.9	79.2	91.6	102.9	86.0	76.6	79.6	86.8	84.1
1988 Q1	85.2	102.1	84.7	72.6	87.1	81.1	91.8	102.8	86.3	77.3	80.5	87.9	85.6
Q2	85.1	102.5	83.5	71.9	88.0	82.6	91.8	102.7	86.4	77.5	81.4	88.4	85.9
Q3	87.0	103.5	84.7	72.2	89.5	84.7	91.8	102.5	86.8	78.1	81.8	89.3	86.9
Q4	88.2	105.4	86.9	74.2	91.1	84.6	91.8	102.2	87.1	78.7	82.2	89.7	87.7
1989 Q1	89.0	105.5	87.9	74.4	90.0	84.0	91.9	102.1	87.0	79.3	81.0	89.2	87.8
Q2	89.6	106.9	87.6	76.6	92.1	84.0	92.0	101.9	87.9	79.9	81.5	91.4	88.3
Q3	89.4	107.4	89.1	77.6	92.8	83.6	92.2	102.1	88.2	79.4	80.8	92.5	88.3
Q4	89.5	104.9	88.3	78.4	94.3	84.9	92.5	102.7	88.3	80.0	81.1	93.8	88.6
1990 Q1	89.9	107.9	89.0	80.5	98.1	86.9	93.0	103.4	88.9	80.0	81.4	95.3	89.8
Q2	89.3	109.1	88.3	80.1	97.8	86.8	93.1	103.6	88.7	79.9	81.8	94.8	89.7
Q3	88.0	107.8	87.2	80.2	97.8	85.8	93.4	103.8	89.2	80.5	81.0	95.3	89.2
Q4	86.5	105.5	87.1	79.4	98.8	86.1	93.8	104.2	89.8	81.9	81.8	96.7	89.1
1991 Q1	86.2	103.5	82.8	79.9	99.7	85.1	94.2	105.1	90.7	83.5	80.6	95.9	88.9
Q2	85.7	101.3	84.2	79.9	99.2	84.5	94.7	105.4	91.6	85.9	81.4	94.5	89.2
Q3	86.6	98.7	85.0	78.9	98.8	84.4	95.0	106.0	92.5	87.0	81.6	93.7	89.6
Q4	86.5	98.3	85.5	79.4	97.1	82.4	95.3	105.9	94.1	87.8	81.8	92.1	89.4
1992 Q1	85.9	95.8	86.6	79.6	94.2	81.3	95.3	105.8	95.0	88.6	82.1	90.1	89.2
Q2	87.0	97.1	87.0	79.5	94.4	81.7	95.2	105.3	95.3	88.6	81.9	90.9	89.4
Q3	88.0	96.1	87.3	79.1	94.3	83.6	95.3	104.8	94.8	88.4	83.1	92.0	89.8
Q4	89.0	96.5	89.1	79.9	93.8	83.7	95.3	104.2	94.8	88.6	85.7	90.6	90.5
1993 Q1	91.1	97.2	88.3	81.5	95.4	83.2	95.7	103.9	94.5	90.5	88.0	90.9	91.3
Q2	92.4	98.3	88.6	82.9	95.9	84.3	96.3	103.1	94.6	92.2	88.8	91.1	92.1
Q3	93.0	100.0	90.1	84.3	96.5	85.2	96.8	102.4	95.0	93.5	90.9	91.4	93.0
Q4	93.4	98.6	90.4	85.8	97.4	85.9	97.1	102.3	96.1	94.2	92.4	92.9	93.5
1994 Q1	96.5	100.3	90.1	86.8	96.9	88.9	97.1	101.7	97.7	93.5	93.8	94.3	94.8
Q2	97.1	100.0	95.7	89.3	96.5	92.4	97.4	101.4	98.6	94.3	95.5	94.9	96.2
Q3	98.0	102.1	98.0	91.8	97.8	96.0	98.0	101.1	99.0	95.4	96.6	96.8	97.7
Q4	98.2	102.6	101.4	94.8	97.8	96.7	98.6	101.0	99.4	97.0	96.9	97.2	98.5
1995 Q1	99.3	103.8	100.2	95.7	98.4	98.7	99.3	100.9	100.0	98.0	98.7	98.7	99.3
Q2	99.1	99.4	100.3	98.2	99.8	98.9	99.9	100.0	99.8	99.6	100.2	99.5	99.5
Q3	99.8	98.7	100.2	101.4	100.8	100.8	100.3	99.7	100.0	100.4	100.3	100.1	100.2
Q4	101.8	98.2	99.3	104.7	101.1	101.7	100.4	99.4	100.2	102.0	100.9	101.7	100.9
1996 Q1	101.6	99.6	101.0	106.8	103.7	104.0	100.6	98.8	100.8	103.0	102.7	103.2	102.0
Q2	102.9	104.6	100.3	108.5	103.2	106.5	101.1	98.8	101.3	103.9	102.6	104.2	102.9
Q3	104.4	101.8	100.1	111.8	104.0	107.8	101.7	98.4	101.9	104.7	104.2	106.5	103.6
Q4	104.8	103.8	101.4	116.3	106.3	108.8	102.2	98.0	102.6	106.1	105.3	107.9	104.7
1997 Q1	105.7	102.2	104.2	119.8	106.6	113.3	102.7	97.2	102.4	106.9	105.3	108.6	105.9
Q2	107.2	103.3	104.1	125.4	109.6	116.4	103.1	96.9	102.9	107.7	105.2	113.1	107.2
Q3	107.5	104.2	106.9	129.2	110.5	119.4	103.6	96.6	103.3	108.8	107.2	112.9	108.6
Q4	108.6	104.5	110.7	130.2	112.6	121.1	104.4	96.2	103.2	109.7	109.2	116.6	109.6
1998 Q1	109.9	104.6	111.6	131.2	113.0	123.6	105.6	96.5	103.2	110.3	111.1	117.0	110.7
Q2	109.9	105.1	113.1	132.7	113.2	128.2	106.9	96.5	103.3	111.7	112.1	118.2	112.0
Q3	110.3	106.0	115.1	136.8	114.2	130.5	107.4	96.4	103.3	112.4	112.9	122.3	112.9
Q4	110.2	107.0	116.0	141.1	111.5	131.7	108.6	96.2	103.4	112.9	113.5	120.5	113.4
1999 Q1	111.2	108.2	115.6	147.2	112.4	132.0	109.6	96.2	103.6	113.6	113.4	120.8	114.2
Q2	111.5	105.8	116.3	154.1	113.2	134.4	110.3	96.3	103.6	113.8	112.5	121.7	115.0
Q3	112.7	108.1	118.1	158.0	111.9	137.1	110.6	96.0	103.8	114.8	111.9	121.1	116.0
Q4	113.4	108.0	118.7	165.3	112.6	139.5	110.6	96.4	104.1	115.8	112.9	121.7	117.2
2000 Q1	114.7	108.3	120.3	166.8	114.8	140.0	111.2	96.3	104.0	116.6	114.9	125.5	117.9

See footnotes on page 74.

Source: Office for National Statistics; Enquiries 020 7533 5972

1.11 Summary capital accounts and net lending/net borrowing

£ million, not seasonally adjusted

	Non-financial corporations				Financial corporations				General Government			
	Gross saving[1]	Capital transfers (net receipts)	Gross capital formation[2]	Net acquisition of non-financial assets	Gross saving[1]	Capital transfers (net receipts)	Gross capital formation[2]	Net acquisition of non-financial assets	Gross saving[1]	Capital transfers (net receipts)	Gross capital formation[2]	Net acquisition of non-financial assets
	NRJD	GZQV	FCCZ	FCFY	NQOL	GZQD	NHEG	NHEI	NNAU	GZQT	NNBI	NNBJ
1987	50 671	953	47 277	485	6 528	–	3 616	–31	2 104	–1 772	8 686	–582
1988	53 170	1 562	58 964	774	5 202	–	6 756	160	12 626	–2 508	8 146	–866
1989	46 000	1 495	67 409	858	7 073	–	8 267	165	18 290	–2 884	11 454	–842
1990	41 452	8 349	66 846	391	7 908	–	6 783	66	15 926	–10 260	14 719	–605
1991	45 850	3 519	57 901	–39	3 196	–	6 249	–8	4 216	–6 702	14 213	–396
1992	47 111	3 317	58 157	41	10 593	–	4 969	–49	–19 559	–6 170	14 227	–312
1993	62 014	3 187	60 727	254	9 407	–88	3 748	–203	–30 952	–6 985	13 698	–497
1994	74 870	3 275	65 671	214	16 695	–518	5 566	86	–26 700	–5 929	13 807	–485
1995	71 810	4 882	74 132	301	13 534	–	4 984	–77	–20 402	–7 097	13 851	–143
1996	81 354	3 599	79 538	117	11 474	–	5 212	–1	–16 854	–5 040	11 482	–467
1997	82 843	2 459	89 945	195	11 803	–	5 087	–39	–2 744	–3 910	10 012	–372
1998	90 732	1 505	97 798	723	11 229	–	9 411	–4	16 936	–3 229	10 585	–688
1999	81 044	1 660	99 797	726	7 384	–	7 773	26	24 637	–3 580	9 918	–696
1987 Q1	9 679	322	10 557	103	1 165	–	628	–17	2 417	–583	3 015	–125
Q2	12 543	154	11 052	113	2 169	–	665	–15	–3 003	–345	1 503	–135
Q3	13 832	234	12 937	126	1 812	–	892	–6	706	–435	1 968	–150
Q4	14 617	243	12 731	143	1 382	–	1 431	7	1 984	–409	2 200	–172
1988 Q1	9 979	360	13 412	163	–10	–	1 332	23	5 312	–728	3 443	–195
Q2	13 217	159	14 029	185	1 814	–	1 582	37	–167	–373	1 538	–214
Q3	15 016	745	14 687	205	1 677	–	1 958	47	3 316	–957	1 403	–226
Q4	14 958	298	16 836	221	1 721	–	1 884	53	4 165	–450	1 762	–231
1989 Q1	9 676	478	15 905	230	–129	–	1 969	50	7 729	–814	3 777	–228
Q2	13 730	259	17 253	227	2 653	–	1 424	45	684	–488	1 814	–219
Q3	11 730	402	17 486	213	2 415	–	2 144	38	3 148	–786	2 533	–205
Q4	10 864	356	16 765	188	2 134	–	2 730	32	6 729	–796	3 330	–190
1990 Q1	8 015	3 396	17 602	155	101	–	1 434	25	7 177	–3 914	5 795	–175
Q2	12 783	925	17 427	117	2 797	–	1 687	19	787	–1 446	2 389	–159
Q3	10 394	1 657	17 031	78	2 793	–	1 583	14	4 039	–2 110	2 990	–143
Q4	10 260	2 371	14 786	41	2 217	–	2 079	8	3 923	–2 790	3 545	–128
1991 Q1	6 174	1 564	15 468	11	276	–	1 517	3	6 162	–2 409	4 809	–116
Q2	14 215	573	14 232	–10	937	–	1 582	–2	–3 035	–1 235	2 620	–104
Q3	11 412	637	14 583	–20	254	–	1 418	–4	–378	–1 445	3 292	–93
Q4	14 049	745	13 618	–20	1 729	–	1 732	–5	1 467	–1 613	3 492	–83
1992 Q1	8 017	905	14 700	–13	1 907	–	1 458	–2	1 591	–1 822	5 296	–73
Q2	13 464	665	14 361	1	2 290	–	1 331	–4	–9 588	–1 238	2 594	–72
Q3	11 531	771	15 117	17	3 572	–	1 380	–13	–6 748	–1 392	2 897	–78
Q4	14 099	976	13 979	36	2 824	–	800	–30	–4 814	–1 718	3 440	–89
1993 Q1	9 996	1 010	13 525	54	2 368	–	1 066	–50	–4 129	–2 584	5 746	–104
Q2	16 007	748	15 176	65	3 399	–88	576	–60	–11 862	–1 502	2 497	–119
Q3	15 650	675	15 541	70	2 742	–	660	–56	–7 425	–1 407	2 767	–132
Q4	20 361	754	16 485	65	898	–	1 446	–37	–7 536	–1 492	2 688	–142
1994 Q1	16 188	1 011	15 047	57	4 842	–	1 065	–3	–4 670	–1 877	5 504	–145
Q2	20 195	737	16 768	50	4 138	–283	2 017	24	–11 038	–1 263	2 317	–137
Q3	17 558	754	16 540	50	4 513	–99	1 251	36	–6 297	–1 358	2 894	–117
Q4	20 929	773	17 316	57	3 202	–136	1 233	29	–4 695	–1 431	3 092	–86
1995 Q1	13 193	2 858	15 013	71	3 839	–	1 486	6	–2 157	–3 584	5 269	–50
Q2	20 808	667	19 817	80	1 790	–	798	–18	–8 854	–1 026	2 394	–28
Q3	19 095	654	19 479	80	4 654	–	1 330	–32	–6 325	–1 259	2 873	–24
Q4	18 714	703	19 823	70	3 251	–	1 370	–33	–3 066	–1 228	3 315	–41
1996 Q1	15 641	1 397	18 324	47	1 718	–	1 425	–20	347	–2 064	4 595	–76
Q2	24 394	726	20 469	33	3 230	–	1 425	–4	–11 268	–916	2 445	–111
Q3	20 149	662	19 422	24	3 274	–	1 090	9	–5 261	–842	2 688	–135
Q4	21 170	814	21 323	13	3 252	–	1 272	14	–672	–1 218	1 754	–145

1 Before providing for depreciation, inventory holding gains.
2 Comprises gross fixed capital formation and changes in inventories and acquisitions less disposals of valuables.

Sources: Office for National Statistics; Enquiries Column 1 020 7533 6039; Columns 2,6,9-12 020 7533 5983; Columns 3,4 020 7533 6013; Columns 5,8 020 7533 6052; Column 7 020 7533 5926

1.11 Summary capital accounts and net lending/net borrowing

continued

£ million, not seasonally adjusted

	Non-financial corporations				Financial corporations				General Government			
	Gross saving[1]	Capital transfers (net receipts)	Gross capital formation[2]	Net acquisition of non-financial assets	Gross saving[1]	Capital transfers (net receipts)	Gross capital formation[2]	Net acquisition of non-financial assets	Gross saving[1]	Capital transfers (net receipts)	Gross capital formation[2]	Net acquisition of non-financial assets
	NRJD	GZQV	FCCZ	FCFY	NQOL	GZQD	NHEG	NHEI	NNAU	GZQT	NNBI	NNBJ
1997 Q1	18 989	955	20 883	39	2 583	–	1 043	3	3 073	–1 639	4 049	–119
Q2	22 507	616	23 715	54	4 277	–	1 164	–7	–8 583	–907	1 280	–98
Q3	23 522	311	22 464	51	883	–	1 190	–15	–1 997	–586	2 214	–81
Q4	17 825	577	22 883	51	4 060	–	1 690	–20	4 763	–778	2 469	–74
1998 Q1	19 751	606	23 520	343	2 493	–	2 238	18	13 020	–1 420	4 089	–264
Q2	26 098	404	24 284	209	3 195	–	2 406	2	–5 540	–792	1 427	–190
Q3	25 163	192	24 822	125	3 849	–	1 480	–10	3 232	–423	2 440	–132
Q4	19 720	303	25 172	46	1 692	–	3 287	–14	6 224	–594	2 629	–102
1999 Q1	22 923	736	23 696	84	–2 625	–	1 341	–10	14 721	–1 456	3 615	–112
Q2	13 715	262	23 859	159	5 107	–	2 078	–1	–2 828	–452	1 446	–145
Q3	24 060	334	26 931	196	883	–	1 849	12	6 107	–726	2 347	–193
Q4	20 346	328	25 311	287	4 019	–	2 505	25	6 637	–946	2 510	–246
2000 Q1	23 068	451	27 749	78	–2 928	–	2 146	–10	20 307	–1 166	3 274	–112

1 Before providing for depreciation, inventory holding gains.
2 Comprises gross fixed capital formation and changes in inventories and acquisitions less disposals of valuables.

Sources: Office for National Statistics;
Enquiries Column 1 020 7533 6039; Columns 2,6,9-12 020 7533 5983; Columns 3,4 020 7533 6013; Columns 5,8 020 7533 6052; Column 7 020 7533 5926

1.11 Summary capital accounts and net lending/net borrowing

continued

£ million, not seasonally adjusted

	Households & NPISH				Net lending(+)/net borrowing(-)[3]					
	Gross saving[1]	Capital transfers (net receipts)	Gross capital formation[2]	Net acquisition of non-financial assets	Non-financial corporations	Financial corporations	General government	Households & NPISH	Rest of the world[4]	Statistical Discrepancy[5]
	NSSH	GZQH	NSSX	NSSY	EABO	NHCQ	NNBK	NSSZ	NHRB	RVFE
1987	15 134	1 152	20 441	128	3 862	2 943	–7 772	–4 283	5 250	–
1988	11 923	1 181	26 592	–68	–5 006	–1 714	2 838	–13 420	17 302	–
1989	18 865	1 659	26 589	–181	–20 772	–1 359	4 794	–5 884	23 221	–
1990	27 602	2 408	24 053	148	–17 436	1 059	–8 448	5 809	19 016	–
1991	38 031	3 473	21 304	443	–8 493	–3 045	–16 303	19 757	8 084	–
1992	50 150	3 274	21 024	320	–7 770	5 673	–39 644	32 080	9 661	–
1993	50 463	4 195	23 377	446	4 220	5 774	–51 138	30 835	10 309	–
1994	44 911	3 205	26 190	185	12 260	10 525	–45 951	21 741	1 425	–
1995	52 093	2 749	27 813	–81	2 259	8 627	–41 207	27 110	3 211	–
1996	50 687	2 163	31 029	337	5 298	6 263	–32 909	21 484	–136	–
1997	53 301	2 289	33 536	250	–4 838	6 755	–16 294	21 804	–7 427	–
1998	34 042	2 245	35 225	17	–6 284	1 822	3 810	1 045	–393	–
1999	31 074	2 716	39 284	–36	–17 819	–415	11 835	–5 458	10 205	1 652
1987 Q1	5 869	375	4 237	39	–659	554	–1 056	1 968	–351	–453
Q2	6 459	212	5 036	37	1 532	1 519	–4 716	1 598	1 561	–1 494
Q3	2 636	287	5 903	30	1 003	926	–1 547	–3 010	1 900	728
Q4	170	278	5 265	22	1 986	–56	–453	–4 839	2 143	1 219
1988 Q1	5 432	415	5 737	9	–3 236	–1 365	1 336	101	3 780	–616
Q2	6 317	227	6 595	–8	–838	195	–1 864	–43	4 035	–1 485
Q3	973	250	7 187	–26	869	–328	1 182	–5 938	4 051	164
Q4	–799	289	7 073	–43	–1 801	–216	2 184	–7 540	5 436	1 937
1989 Q1	6 465	476	7 080	–52	–5 981	–2 148	3 366	–87	5 378	–528
Q2	6 268	296	6 961	–53	–3 491	1 184	–1 399	–344	6 483	–2 433
Q3	4 348	381	6 598	–46	–5 567	233	34	–1 823	7 244	–121
Q4	1 784	506	5 950	–30	–5 733	–628	2 793	–3 630	4 116	3 082
1990 Q1	9 750	743	5 754	–5	–6 346	–1 358	–2 357	4 744	6 510	–1 193
Q2	8 888	555	5 883	23	–3 836	1 091	–2 889	3 537	6 524	–4 427
Q3	5 683	512	6 463	51	–5 058	1 196	–918	–319	4 292	807
Q4	3 281	598	5 953	79	–2 196	130	–2 284	–2 153	1 690	4 813
1991 Q1	12 237	854	4 987	102	–7 741	–1 244	–940	8 002	3 756	–1 833
Q2	11 827	776	5 205	116	566	–643	–6 786	7 282	1 609	–2 028
Q3	8 743	851	5 692	117	–2 514	–1 160	–5 022	3 785	2 820	2 091
Q4	5 224	992	5 420	108	1 196	2	–3 555	688	–101	1 770
1992 Q1	13 653	1 043	4 619	88	–5 765	451	–5 454	9 989	2 685	–1 906
Q2	15 556	684	5 058	75	–233	963	–13 348	11 107	3 538	–2 027
Q3	11 322	721	5 548	74	–2 832	2 205	–10 959	6 421	2 748	2 417
Q4	9 619	826	5 799	83	1 060	2 054	–9 883	4 563	690	1 516
1993 Q1	14 509	1 669	4 745	100	–2 573	1 352	–12 355	11 333	2 902	–659
Q2	16 249	844	6 064	114	1 514	2 795	–15 742	10 915	4 453	–3 935
Q3	10 038	846	6 557	118	714	2 138	–11 467	4 209	2 485	1 921
Q4	9 667	836	6 011	114	4 565	–511	–11 574	4 378	469	2 673
1994 Q1	13 012	1 113	6 184	91	2 095	3 780	–11 906	7 850	546	–2 365
Q2	14 260	612	5 989	63	4 114	1 814	–14 481	8 820	2 672	–2 939
Q3	9 337	652	6 608	31	1 722	3 127	–10 432	3 350	–231	2 464
Q4	8 302	828	7 409	–	4 329	1 804	–9 132	1 721	–1 562	2 840
1995 Q1	15 762	1 017	6 393	–27	967	2 347	–10 960	10 413	–1 652	–1 115
Q2	16 992	424	7 312	–34	1 578	1 010	–12 246	10 138	3 833	–4 313
Q3	10 974	653	6 873	–24	190	3 356	–10 433	4 778	1 307	802
Q4	8 365	655	7 235	4	–476	1 914	–7 568	1 781	–277	4 626
1996 Q1	15 517	921	6 687	43	–1 333	313	–6 236	9 708	328	–2 780
Q2	18 017	303	7 438	79	4 618	1 809	–14 518	10 803	1 410	–4 122
Q3	10 572	436	7 973	103	1 365	2 175	–8 656	2 932	105	2 079
Q4	6 581	503	8 931	112	648	1 966	–3 499	–1 959	–1 979	4 823

See footnotes 1 and 2 on page 79.

3 This balance is equal to gross saving *plus* capital transfers *less* gross fixed capital formation, *less* Net acquisition of non-financial assets, *less* changes in inventories.

4 Equals the current balance of payments accounts, *plus* capital transfers.

Sources: Office for National Statistics; Enquiries Columns 1,3,4,6,9 020 7533 6039 ; Columns 2,7 020 7533 5983; Columns 5,10 020 7533 5944; Column 8 020 7533 6032

1.11 Summary capital accounts and net lending/net borrowing

continued

£ million, not seasonally adjusted

	Households & NPISH				Net lending(+)/net borrowing(-)[3]					
	Gross saving[1]	Capital transfers (net receipts)	Gross capital formation[2]	Net acquisition of non-financial assets	Non-financial corporations	Financial corporations	General government	Households & NPISH	Rest of the world[4]	Statistical Discrepancy[5]
	NSSH	GZQH	NSSX	NSSY	EABO	NHCQ	NNBK	NSSZ	NHRB	RVFE
1997 Q1	13 218	912	7 432	89	–978	1 537	–2 496	6 609	–2 872	–1 800
Q2	20 457	375	8 347	67	–646	3 120	–10 672	12 418	–900	–3 320
Q3	10 996	473	8 312	50	1 318	–292	–4 716	3 107	–1 997	2 580
Q4	8 630	529	9 445	44	–4 532	2 390	1 590	–330	–1 658	2 540
1998 Q1	6 322	836	8 149	–62	–3 506	237	7 775	–929	162	–3 739
Q2	16 460	359	9 055	–9	2 009	787	–7 569	7 773	739	–3 739
Q3	5 107	477	8 984	34	408	2 379	501	–3 434	–1 586	1 732
Q4	6 153	573	9 037	54	–5 195	–1 581	3 103	–2 365	292	5 746
1999 Q1	2 839	705	9 300	44	–121	–3 956	9 762	–5 800	3 914	–3 799
Q2	18 444	468	9 490	15	–10 041	3 030	–4 581	9 407	1 698	487
Q3	3 416	638	9 829	–25	–2 733	–978	3 227	–5 750	3 994	2 240
Q4	6 375	905	10 665	–70	–4 924	1 489	3 427	–3 315	599	2 724
2000 Q1	1 776	933	9 525	44	–4 308	–5 064	15 979	–6 860	4 006	–3 753

See footnotes 1 and 2 on page 79.

3 This balance is equal to gross saving *plus* capital transfers *less*gross fixed capital formation,*less* Net acquisition of non-financial assets, *less*changes in inventories.

4 Equals the current balance of payments accounts, *plus* capital transfers.

Sources: Office for National Statistics;
Enquiries Column 1,3,4,6,9 020 7533 6039 ; Columns 2,7 020 7533 5983; Columns 5,10 020 7533 5944; Columns 8 020 7533 6032

1.11 Summary capital accounts and net lending/net borrowing

continued

£ million, seasonally adjusted

	Non-financial corporations				Financial corporations				General Government			
	Gross saving[1]	Capital transfers (net receipts)	Gross capital formation[2]	Net acquisition of non-financial assets	Gross saving[1]	Capital transfers (net receipts)	Gross capital formation[2]	Net acquisition of non-financial assets	Gross saving[1]	Capital transfers (net receipts)	Gross capital formation[2]	Net acquisition of non-financial assets
	RPJV	GZQW	RQBA	RQAX	RPPS	GZQE	RPYP	RPYO	RPQC	GZQU	RPZF	RPZE
1987 Q1	12 328	247	10 577	103	2 033	–	718	–17	171	–462	1 902	–125
Q2	12 128	216	11 221	113	1 579	–	808	–15	87	–430	2 116	–135
Q3	13 107	235	12 232	126	1 418	–	877	–6	1 300	–450	2 348	–150
Q4	13 108	255	13 247	143	1 498	–	1 213	7	546	–430	2 320	–172
1988 Q1	12 892	266	12 793	163	793	–	1 464	23	2 734	–585	2 202	–195
Q2	11 966	245	13 238	185	1 345	–	1 737	37	3 222	–482	2 273	–214
Q3	14 299	745	15 315	205	1 273	–	1 973	47	4 186	–962	1 817	–226
Q4	14 013	306	17 618	221	1 791	–	1 582	53	2 484	–479	1 854	–231
1989 Q1	13 642	302	16 016	230	931	–	2 170	50	4 768	–589	2 203	–228
Q2	12 062	331	17 037	227	2 130	–	1 582	45	4 574	–583	2 648	–219
Q3	9 933	432	18 199	213	2 024	–	2 147	38	4 630	–821	3 060	–205
Q4	10 363	430	16 157	188	1 988	–	2 368	32	4 318	–891	3 543	–190
1990 Q1	11 276	2 319	17 879	155	1 218	–	1 538	25	4 086	–2 805	3 668	–175
Q2	10 086	1 438	18 302	117	2 014	–	1 850	19	5 277	–1 975	3 520	–159
Q3	9 868	2 028	16 683	78	2 302	–	1 638	14	5 090	–2 488	3 720	–143
Q4	10 222	2 564	13 982	41	2 374	–	1 757	8	1 473	–2 992	3 811	–128
1991 Q1	10 313	1 123	16 199	11	973	–	1 542	3	3 036	–1 893	3 296	–116
Q2	12 130	833	13 544	–10	239	–	1 724	–2	1 855	–1 521	3 571	–104
Q3	11 044	742	13 151	–20	–43	–	1 450	–4	150	–1 568	3 797	–93
Q4	12 363	821	15 007	–20	2 027	–	1 533	–5	–825	–1 720	3 549	–83
1992 Q1	10 705	590	15 050	–13	2 197	–	1 368	–2	–1 023	–1 448	3 531	–73
Q2	12 998	826	14 112	1	1 506	–	1 444	–4	–5 635	–1 432	3 629	–72
Q3	11 850	854	14 109	17	3 191	–	1 442	–13	–6 563	–1 482	3 436	–78
Q4	11 558	1 047	14 886	36	3 699	–	715	–30	–6 338	–1 808	3 631	–89
1993 Q1	14 437	716	14 709	54	1 764	–	914	–50	–6 584	–2 184	3 961	–104
Q2	13 956	880	14 745	65	3 118	–88	674	–60	–7 952	–1 687	3 552	–119
Q3	16 444	779	15 112	70	2 339	–	757	–56	–7 775	–1 531	3 321	–132
Q4	17 177	812	16 161	65	2 186	–	1 403	–37	–8 641	–1 583	2 864	–142
1994 Q1	18 665	734	15 411	57	4 503	–	1 038	–3	–7 924	–1 465	3 725	–145
Q2	18 619	803	15 898	50	3 764	–283	2 051	24	–6 556	–1 395	3 342	–137
Q3	17 333	898	16 086	50	4 277	–99	1 387	36	–5 849	–1 538	3 337	–117
Q4	20 253	840	18 276	57	4 151	–136	1 090	29	–6 371	–1 531	3 403	–86
1995 Q1	17 722	2 530	15 875	71	3 446	–	1 440	6	–6 106	–3 127	3 518	–50
Q2	17 570	714	19 391	80	2 077	–	829	–18	–3 649	–1 126	3 400	–28
Q3	17 909	821	19 831	80	4 635	–	1 442	–32	–5 427	–1 465	3 327	–24
Q4	18 609	817	19 035	70	3 376	–	1 273	–33	–5 220	–1 379	3 606	–41
1996 Q1	19 797	1 160	19 759	52	1 374	–	1 397	–20	–5 427	–1 652	3 089	–76
Q2	22 342	657	19 752	28	3 397	–	1 471	–4	–6 320	–910	3 400	–111
Q3	18 996	883	20 016	25	4 216	–	1 221	9	–3 441	–1 125	3 048	–135
Q4	20 219	899	20 011	12	2 487	–	1 123	14	–1 666	–1 353	1 945	–145
1997 Q1	22 562	741	21 501	31	3 242	–	969	3	–3 367	–1 412	2 754	–119
Q2	18 914	590	22 329	48	3 358	–	1 113	–7	–1 851	–903	2 169	–98
Q3	22 654	460	22 433	53	1 350	–	1 374	–15	–670	–729	2 469	–81
Q4	18 713	668	23 683	63	3 853	–	1 631	–20	3 144	–866	2 620	–74
1998 Q1	21 139	438	23 782	332	2 672	–	2 229	18	1 933	–1 197	2 774	–264
Q2	23 638	404	23 898	202	2 845	–	2 320	2	3 350	–814	2 229	–189
Q3	23 686	323	25 143	126	4 438	–	1 841	–10	5 129	–568	2 706	–131
Q4	22 269	340	24 975	63	1 274	–	3 021	–14	6 524	–650	2 876	–104
1999 Q1	26 424	511	25 235	75	–3 001	–	1 283	–10	4 346	–1 199	2 428	–112
Q2	11 450	237	23 816	148	4 463	–	2 117	–1	8 583	–441	2 450	–145
Q3	20 579	560	24 964	201	2 263	–	2 082	12	7 096	–961	2 540	–193
Q4	22 591	352	25 782	302	3 659	–	2 291	25	4 612	–979	2 500	–246
2000 Q1	23 699	295	26 506	87	–1 901	–	2 061	–10	9 099	–967	2 436	–112

1 Before providing for depreciation, inventory holding gains.

2 Comprises gross fixed capital formation and changes in inventories and acquisitions and disposals of valuables.

Sources: Office for National Statistics;
Enquiries Columns 1,3-5,7-9,11,12 0171 533 6039;
Columns 2,6,10 0171 533 5986

1.11 Summary capital accounts and net lending/net borrowing

continued

£ million,seasonally adjusted

	Households & NPISH				Net lending(+)/net borrowing(-)[3]				
	Gross saving[1]	Capital transfers (net receipts)	Gross capital formation[2]	Net acquisition of non-financial assets	Non-financial corporations	Financial corporations	General government	Households & NPISH	Rest of the world[4]
	RPQL	GZQI	RPZV	RPZU	RQAW	RPYN	RPZD	RPZT	RQCH
1987 Q1	3 593	310	4 521	39	1 895	1 332	–2 068	–657	–584
Q2	4 190	250	5 091	37	1 010	786	–2 324	–688	1 115
Q3	3 405	312	5 494	30	984	547	–1 348	–1 807	1 630
Q4	3 946	280	5 335	22	–27	278	–2 032	–1 131	3 089
1988 Q1	2 718	348	6 216	9	202	–694	142	–3 159	3 509
Q2	3 623	265	6 572	–8	–1 212	–429	681	–2 676	3 636
Q3	2 266	268	6 734	–26	–476	–747	1 633	–4 174	3 764
Q4	3 316	300	7 070	–43	–3 520	156	382	–3 411	6 393
1989 Q1	3 241	412	7 706	–52	–2 302	–1 289	2 204	–4 001	5 388
Q2	3 475	334	6 844	–53	–4 871	503	1 562	–2 982	5 788
Q3	6 071	400	6 142	–46	–8 047	–161	954	375	6 879
Q4	6 078	513	5 897	–30	–5 552	–412	74	724	5 166
1990 Q1	6 434	700	6 226	–5	–4 439	–345	–2 212	913	6 083
Q2	6 175	586	5 870	23	–6 895	145	–59	868	5 941
Q3	7 152	533	6 121	51	–4 865	650	–975	1 513	3 677
Q4	7 841	589	5 836	79	–1 237	609	–5 202	2 515	3 315
1991 Q1	9 133	773	5 462	102	–4 774	–572	–2 037	4 342	3 041
Q2	8 823	816	5 232	116	–571	–1 483	–3 133	4 291	896
Q3	10 225	882	5 342	117	–1 345	–1 489	–5 122	5 648	2 308
Q4	9 850	1 002	5 268	108	–1 803	499	–6 011	5 476	1 839
1992 Q1	11 058	982	5 104	88	–3 742	831	–5 930	6 848	1 993
Q2	12 587	729	5 025	75	–289	66	–10 623	8 216	2 630
Q3	13 270	739	5 291	74	–1 422	1 762	–11 403	8 644	2 419
Q4	13 235	824	5 604	83	–2 317	3 014	–11 688	8 372	2 619
1993 Q1	12 162	1 564	5 319	100	390	900	–12 626	8 307	3 029
Q2	12 988	908	6 050	114	26	2 416	–13 071	7 732	2 897
Q3	12 086	875	6 321	118	2 041	1 638	–12 495	6 522	2 294
Q4	13 227	848	5 687	114	1 763	820	–12 946	8 274	2 089
1994 Q1	10 795	984	6 742	91	3 931	3 468	–12 974	4 946	629
Q2	10 252	684	6 010	63	3 474	1 406	–11 152	4 863	1 409
Q3	11 526	694	6 550	31	2 095	2 755	–10 607	5 639	118
Q4	12 338	843	6 888	–	2 760	2 896	–11 218	6 293	–731
1995 Q1	13 414	899	6 950	–27	4 306	2 000	–12 711	7 390	–985
Q2	12 396	479	7 235	–34	–1 187	1 266	–8 141	5 674	2 388
Q3	13 041	696	6 952	–24	–1 181	3 225	–10 195	6 809	1 342
Q4	13 242	675	6 676	4	321	2 136	–10 160	7 237	466
1996 Q1	14 274	746	7 146	43	1 146	–3	–10 092	7 831	1 114
Q2	12 769	366	7 503	79	3 219	1 930	–10 519	5 553	–181
Q3	11 909	498	8 013	103	–162	2 986	–7 479	4 291	365
Q4	11 735	553	8 367	112	1 095	1 350	–4 819	3 809	–1 434
1997 Q1	13 454	899	8 170	89	1 771	2 270	–7 414	6 094	–2 720
Q2	15 169	397	8 284	67	–2 873	2 252	–4 825	7 215	–1 769
Q3	13 511	467	8 273	50	628	–9	–3 787	5 655	–2 487
Q4	11 167	526	8 809	44	–4 365	2 242	–268	2 840	–451
1998 Q1	11 228	781	8 657	–62	–2 537	425	–1 774	3 414	472
Q2	7 587	381	9 059	–9	–58	523	496	–1 082	121
Q3	7 310	491	8 998	34	–1 260	2 607	1 986	–1 231	–2 102
Q4	7 917	592	8 511	54	–2 429	–1 733	3 102	–56	1 116
1999 Q1	6 578	673	9 869	44	1 625	–4 274	831	–2 662	4 103
Q2	10 306	482	9 513	15	–12 277	2 347	5 837	1 260	2 390
Q3	6 304	647	9 803	–25	–4 026	169	3 788	–2 827	2 444
Q4	7 886	914	10 099	–70	–3 141	1 343	1 379	–1 229	1 268
2000 Q1	6 021	890	10 059	44	–2 599	–3 952	5 808	–3 192	3 801

See footnotes 1 and 2 on page 83.

3 This balance is equal to gross saving *plus* capital transfers *less*gross fixed capital formation,*less* Net acquisition of non-financial assets, *less*changes in inventories.

4 Equals the current balance of payments accounts, *plus* capital transfers.

Sources: Office for National Statistics; Enquiries Columns 1,3-9 020 7533 6029; Column 2 020 7533 5986

1.12 Private Non-financial Corporations : Allocation of Primary Income Account

£ million, not seasonally adjusted

	Resources							Uses				
	Gross Operating Surplus							Property income payments				
	Gross trading profits											
	UK Continental shelf companies	Others	Rental of buildings	*less* Inventory holding gains	Gross operating surplus	Property income receipts	Total resources[1]	Total payments	*of which* Dividends	*of which* Interest	Gross balance of primary incomes	Share of gross national income(%)
	CAGJ	CAGK	FCBW	-DLQZ	NRJK	FACV	FCFQ	FCFR	NETZ	DSZV	NRJM	NRGZ
1987	10 342	71 203	3 407	–4 329	80 623	21 220	101 843	43 914	17 822	12 117	57 929	13.9
1988	8 065	86 272	4 077	–5 643	92 771	26 642	119 413	57 714	24 634	15 914	61 699	13.3
1989	8 012	96 938	4 996	–6 493	103 453	36 403	139 856	79 585	30 562	26 107	60 271	11.9
1990	8 752	98 304	5 648	–5 572	107 132	38 421	145 553	87 006	29 772	33 333	58 547	10.7
1991	8 322	94 969	6 947	–1 736	108 502	34 505	143 007	81 811	30 171	31 496	61 196	10.6
1992	8 345	93 641	8 285	–1 811	108 460	32 661	141 121	82 320	33 403	28 583	58 801	9.7
1993	9 312	102 082	9 451	–2 392	118 453	31 738	150 191	77 442	33 727	22 229	72 749	11.5
1994	10 654	117 351	9 062	–3 830	133 237	38 422	171 659	84 289	38 549	21 408	87 370	12.8
1995	12 018	126 313	9 244	–4 489	143 086	45 458	188 544	101 066	48 671	24 528	87 478	12.3
1996	15 538	134 776	9 449	–958	158 805	48 272	207 077	106 892	54 793	23 661	100 185	13.2
1997	13 786	146 576	9 777	–361	169 778	51 333	221 111	113 301	59 253	26 042	107 810	13.3
1998	11 208	151 584	10 876	753	174 421	52 457	226 878	113 679	55 173	31 232	113 199	13.1
1999	13 602	150 837	11 483	–1 522	174 400	50 401	224 801	124 571	64 107	30 334	100 230	11.1
1987 Q1	2 957	16 047	802	–1 021	18 785	5 147	23 932	10 330	3 250	2 962	13 602	13.8
Q2	2 287	16 920	827	–1 251	18 783	5 401	24 184	10 952	4 634	2 899	13 232	13.5
Q3	2 495	18 208	866	–1 046	20 523	5 122	25 645	10 252	3 988	3 110	15 393	14.4
Q4	2 603	20 028	912	–1 011	22 532	5 550	28 082	12 380	5 950	3 146	15 702	14.0
1988 Q1	2 478	19 729	953	–1 103	22 057	5 570	27 627	12 168	4 410	3 210	15 459	14.2
Q2	1 929	20 271	996	–1 561	21 635	6 203	27 838	13 679	6 175	3 435	14 159	12.8
Q3	1 819	21 850	1 038	–1 360	23 347	6 691	30 038	14 085	5 121	4 267	15 953	13.4
Q4	1 839	24 422	1 090	–1 619	25 732	8 178	33 910	17 782	8 928	5 002	16 128	12.8
1989 Q1	2 096	23 107	1 160	–1 938	24 425	7 806	32 231	16 707	5 134	5 500	15 524	12.8
Q2	1 768	24 110	1 236	–2 002	25 112	10 194	35 306	20 041	7 845	6 164	15 265	12.7
Q3	1 794	24 300	1 287	–1 071	26 310	8 101	34 411	20 347	6 727	6 829	14 064	10.9
Q4	2 354	25 421	1 313	–1 482	27 606	10 302	37 908	22 490	10 856	7 614	15 418	11.2
1990 Q1	2 545	23 638	1 328	–1 857	25 654	7 933	33 587	19 503	5 094	8 120	14 084	10.8
Q2	1 634	25 504	1 373	–1 435	27 076	8 744	35 820	20 446	6 297	8 339	15 374	11.8
Q3	1 886	24 663	1 430	–1 651	26 328	9 880	36 208	22 535	7 317	8 450	13 673	9.7
Q4	2 687	24 499	1 517	–629	28 074	11 864	39 938	24 522	11 064	8 424	15 416	10.4
1991 Q1	2 430	22 511	1 608	–873	25 676	7 504	33 180	20 855	5 754	8 613	12 325	9.1
Q2	1 567	23 627	1 692	–749	26 137	8 728	34 865	18 724	6 570	7 923	16 141	11.6
Q3	1 838	22 890	1 785	–44	26 469	8 218	34 687	20 858	7 561	7 487	13 829	9.3
Q4	2 487	25 941	1 862	–70	30 220	10 055	40 275	21 374	10 286	7 473	18 901	12.3
1992 Q1	2 451	22 686	1 955	–885	26 207	7 898	34 105	21 043	7 096	7 770	13 062	9.0
Q2	1 613	23 139	2 042	–481	26 313	7 972	34 285	19 414	7 480	7 208	14 871	10.2
Q3	1 642	22 151	2 110	78	25 981	7 752	33 733	19 939	7 698	7 082	13 794	8.9
Q4	2 639	25 665	2 178	–523	29 959	9 039	38 998	21 924	11 129	6 523	17 074	10.8
1993 Q1	2 589	23 380	2 302	–1 375	26 896	6 951	33 847	18 458	6 234	5 979	15 389	10.2
Q2	1 701	24 783	2 370	–452	28 402	7 469	35 871	19 008	8 802	5 420	16 863	11.2
Q3	2 000	25 033	2 398	–251	29 180	7 049	36 229	18 509	6 933	5 473	17 720	10.9
Q4	3 022	28 886	2 381	–314	33 975	10 269	44 244	21 467	11 758	5 357	22 777	13.4
1994 Q1	2 784	27 377	2 323	–710	31 774	8 491	40 265	18 843	7 167	5 421	21 422	13.2
Q2	2 496	28 233	2 269	–762	32 236	9 091	41 327	19 898	8 075	5 310	21 429	13.2
Q3	2 222	28 838	2 237	–877	32 420	8 705	41 125	20 921	8 690	5 215	20 204	11.6
Q4	3 152	32 903	2 233	–1 481	36 807	12 135	48 942	24 627	14 617	5 462	24 315	13.4
1995 Q1	3 528	29 680	2 264	–2 036	33 436	8 834	42 270	22 220	8 352	5 824	20 050	11.7
Q2	2 572	30 760	2 301	–1 518	34 115	10 208	44 323	22 375	8 926	6 073	21 948	13.0
Q3	2 387	31 844	2 332	–946	35 617	10 499	46 116	24 819	11 108	6 135	21 297	11.7
Q4	3 531	34 029	2 347	11	39 918	15 917	55 835	31 652	20 285	6 496	24 183	12.7
1996 Q1	4 106	31 760	2 349	–1 183	37 032	10 622	47 654	23 950	9 938	6 015	23 704	13.1
Q2	3 305	32 178	2 350	67	37 900	12 859	50 759	25 424	12 866	5 761	25 335	13.9
Q3	3 362	33 082	2 363	15	38 822	10 813	49 635	26 047	12 363	5 863	23 588	12.2
Q4	4 765	37 756	2 387	143	45 051	13 978	59 029	31 471	19 626	6 022	27 558	13.6

1 Total resources equals total uses.

Source: Office for National Statistics; Enquiries 020 7533 6013

1.12 Private Non-financial Corporations : Allocation of Primary Income Account

continued

£ million, not seasonally adjusted

	Resources							Uses				
	Gross Operating Surplus							Property income payments				
	Gross trading profits											
	UK Continental shelf companies	Others	Rental of buildings	*less* Inventory holding gains	Gross operating surplus	Property income receipts	Total resources[1]	Total payments	*of which* Dividends	*of which* Interest	Gross balance of primary incomes	Share of gross national income(%)
	CAGJ	CAGK	FCBW	-DLQZ	NRJK	FACV	FCFQ	FCFR	NETZ	DSZV	NRJM	NRGZ
1997 Q1	4 380	33 963	2 373	–418	40 298	10 685	50 983	24 423	10 751	6 020	26 560	13.7
Q2	2 788	35 284	2 423	407	40 902	12 621	53 523	29 113	16 252	6 311	24 410	12.4
Q3	2 820	36 394	2 468	–85	41 597	14 469	56 066	28 055	14 711	6 546	28 011	13.4
Q4	3 798	40 935	2 513	–265	46 981	13 558	60 539	31 710	17 539	7 165	28 829	13.5
1998 Q1	3 407	36 595	2 563	34	42 599	13 079	55 678	28 905	13 860	7 498	26 773	13.1
Q2	2 584	37 538	2 686	–85	42 723	12 529	55 252	28 104	13 411	7 528	27 148	13.1
Q3	2 282	37 767	2 785	448	43 282	13 109	56 391	27 388	11 908	8 146	29 003	13.1
Q4	2 935	39 684	2 842	356	45 817	13 740	59 557	29 282	15 994	8 060	30 275	13.2
1999 Q1	2 870	34 452	2 802	–234	39 890	8 885	48 775	21 173	8 035	7 501	27 602	13.1
Q2	2 726	35 510	2 832	–577	40 491	14 606	55 097	40 049	25 655	7 066	15 048	6.8
Q3	3 381	38 464	2 885	–418	44 312	12 845	57 157	28 785	12 785	7 584	28 372	12.4
Q4	4 625	42 411	2 964	–293	49 707	14 065	63 772	34 564	17 632	8 183	29 208	12.3
2000 Q1	4 769	36 602	2 983	–328	44 026	13 725	57 751	27 955	11 551	8 929	29 796	13.3

1 Total resources equals total uses.

Source: Office for National Statistics; Enquiries 020 7533 6013

1.12 Private Non-financial Corporations : Allocation of Primary Income Account

continued

£ million, seasonally adjusted

	Resources								Uses				
	Gross Operating Surplus								Property income payments				
	Gross trading profits												
	UK Continental shelf companies	Others[1]	Rental of buildings	*less* Inventory holding gains	Gross operating surplus[1]	Property income receipts[1,2]	Total resources[1,2]	Total payments	*of which* Dividends	*of which* Interest	Gross balance of primary incomes[1]	Share of gross national income[1] (%)
	CAGD	CAED	FCBW	-DLRA	CAER	RPBM	RPBN	RPBP	RVFT	ROCG	RPBO	NRJL
1987 Q1	2 540	16 640	802	–871	19 111	5 528	24 639	10 780	4 327	2 972	13 859	13.8
Q2	2 621	17 588	827	–1 109	19 927	5 286	25 213	11 096	4 852	2 957	14 117	13.8
Q3	2 741	18 205	866	–1 208	20 604	5 398	26 002	10 636	4 786	3 083	15 366	14.5
Q4	2 440	18 770	912	–1 141	20 981	5 008	25 989	11 402	3 857	3 105	14 587	13.6
1988 Q1	2 112	19 999	953	–925	22 139	6 146	28 285	12 728	5 658	3 217	15 557	14.0
Q2	2 196	20 376	996	–1 452	22 116	6 020	28 136	13 688	6 244	3 504	14 448	12.7
Q3	2 017	22 113	1 038	–1 499	23 669	7 118	30 787	14 590	5 964	4 244	16 197	13.7
Q4	1 740	23 784	1 090	–1 767	24 847	7 358	32 205	16 708	6 768	4 949	15 497	12.8
1989 Q1	1 782	24 386	1 160	–1 829	25 499	8 738	34 237	17 747	6 941	5 483	16 490	13.3
Q2	2 033	24 457	1 236	–1 913	25 813	9 791	35 604	19 969	7 794	6 267	15 635	12.5
Q3	2 031	24 195	1 287	–1 212	26 301	8 575	34 876	20 948	7 576	6 809	13 928	10.9
Q4	2 166	23 900	1 313	–1 539	25 840	9 299	35 139	20 921	8 251	7 548	14 218	10.9
1990 Q1	2 158	24 495	1 328	–1 611	26 370	8 598	34 968	20 220	6 815	8 043	14 748	11.1
Q2	1 958	25 088	1 373	–1 240	27 179	8 819	35 998	21 116	6 772	8 459	14 882	10.9
Q3	2 206	25 193	1 430	–1 918	26 911	10 703	37 614	23 127	8 315	8 450	14 487	10.4
Q4	2 430	23 528	1 517	–803	26 672	10 301	36 973	22 543	7 870	8 381	14 430	10.4
1991 Q1	2 034	23 937	1 608	–602	26 977	8 289	35 266	21 459	7 385	8 493	13 807	9.8
Q2	1 993	23 902	1 692	–595	26 992	8 805	35 797	19 489	7 175	8 031	16 308	11.4
Q3	2 162	23 406	1 785	–313	27 040	9 011	36 051	21 421	8 516	7 509	14 630	10.1
Q4	2 133	23 724	1 862	–226	27 493	8 400	35 893	19 442	7 095	7 463	16 451	11.1
1992 Q1	2 014	23 330	1 955	–585	26 714	8 759	35 473	21 969	9 014	7 645	13 504	9.0
Q2	2 045	24 169	2 042	–266	27 990	7 892	35 882	19 925	7 862	7 304	15 957	10.6
Q3	1 997	23 094	2 110	–337	26 864	8 546	35 410	20 511	8 686	7 115	14 899	9.8
Q4	2 289	23 048	2 178	–623	26 892	7 464	34 356	19 915	7 841	6 519	14 441	9.4
1993 Q1	2 144	25 087	2 302	–974	28 559	7 677	36 236	18 613	7 351	5 889	17 623	11.4
Q2	2 140	24 728	2 370	–359	28 879	7 688	36 567	20 134	9 846	5 498	16 433	10.5
Q3	2 431	26 281	2 398	–561	30 549	7 680	38 229	19 042	7 895	5 501	19 187	12.0
Q4	2 597	25 986	2 381	–498	30 466	8 693	39 159	19 653	8 635	5 341	19 506	12.0
1994 Q1	2 262	27 664	2 323	–443	31 806	9 523	41 329	19 881	9 137	5 362	21 448	12.9
Q2	3 004	28 866	2 269	–919	33 220	9 358	42 578	20 808	8 926	5 382	21 770	13.0
Q3	2 674	29 510	2 237	–1 109	33 312	9 366	42 678	21 609	9 843	5 245	21 069	12.3
Q4	2 714	31 311	2 233	–1 359	34 899	10 175	45 074	21 991	10 643	5 419	23 083	13.1
1995 Q1	2 920	31 526	2 264	–1 738	34 972	9 876	44 848	23 465	10 544	5 790	21 383	12.2
Q2	3 074	30 909	2 301	–1 588	34 696	10 687	45 383	23 741	10 224	6 147	21 642	12.3
Q3	2 920	31 848	2 332	–1 181	35 919	12 030	47 949	26 426	13 194	6 179	21 523	12.0
Q4	3 104	32 030	2 347	18	37 499	12 865	50 364	27 434	14 709	6 412	22 930	12.6
1996 Q1	3 440	33 575	2 349	–800	38 564	11 747	50 311	25 486	12 271	6 017	24 825	13.4
Q2	3 889	32 868	2 350	–102	39 005	13 106	52 111	26 475	13 890	5 827	25 636	13.6
Q3	4 095	34 034	2 363	–208	40 284	11 776	52 060	27 765	14 482	5 871	24 295	12.8
Q4	4 114	34 299	2 387	152	40 952	11 643	52 595	27 166	14 150	5 946	25 429	13.1
1997 Q1	3 757	35 973	2 373	–23	42 080	11 817	53 897	26 134	13 156	6 049	27 763	14.0
Q2	3 325	35 476	2 423	239	41 463	12 840	54 303	30 008	17 132	6 397	24 295	12.1
Q3	3 431	37 377	2 468	–506	42 770	15 818	58 588	29 765	16 774	6 536	28 823	14.0
Q4	3 273	37 750	2 513	–71	43 465	10 858	54 323	27 394	12 191	7 060	26 929	12.9
1998 Q1	3 026	37 834	2 563	171	43 594	14 785	58 379	32 027	17 261	7 486	26 352	12.5
Q2	2 992	38 019	2 686	–47	43 650	12 695	56 345	28 312	13 555	7 687	28 033	13.1
Q3	2 678	38 322	2 785	208	43 993	12 630	56 623	27 739	12 607	8 138	28 884	13.2
Q4	2 512	37 409	2 842	421	43 184	12 347	55 531	25 601	11 750	7 921	29 930	13.6
1999 Q1	2 549	36 912	2 802	–194	42 069	9 112	51 181	21 905	8 809	7 473	29 276	13.4
Q2	3 130	37 726	2 832	–472	43 216	15 209	58 425	40 202	25 822	7 244	18 223	8.2
Q3	3 971	38 068	2 885	–472	44 452	12 397	56 849	30 728	15 039	7 565	26 121	11.6
Q4	3 952	38 131	2 964	–384	44 663	13 683	58 346	31 736	14 437	8 052	26 610	11.5
2000 Q1	4 246	37 938	2 983	–325	44 842	14 595	59 437	30 901	14 468	8 878	28 536	12.4

1 Quarterly alignment adjustment included in this series.
2 Total resources equals total uses.

Source: Office for National Statistics; Enquiries 020 7533 6013

1.13 Private Non-financial Corporations: Secondary Distribution of Income Account

£ million, not seasonally adjusted

	Resources				Uses				
	Gross balance of primary income	Social contributions	Other current transfers	Total Resources	Current taxes on income	Social benefits	Other current transfers	Gross disposable income	Total uses
	NRJM	EWRT	FDBA	FDBC	FCCP	EWRT	FCCN	NRJQ	FDBC
1987	57 929	445	4 877	63 251	12 212	445	5 004	45 590	63 251
1988	61 699	394	5 229	67 322	14 011	394	5 393	47 524	67 322
1989	60 271	232	6 420	66 923	18 696	232	6 659	41 336	66 923
1990	58 547	975	8 564	68 086	19 558	975	8 805	38 748	68 086
1991	61 196	2 332	10 464	73 992	16 112	2 332	10 702	44 846	73 992
1992	58 801	2 814	11 147	72 762	12 752	2 814	11 387	45 809	72 762
1993	72 749	2 965	9 834	85 548	12 660	2 965	10 106	59 817	85 548
1994	87 370	3 443	9 286	100 099	14 331	3 443	9 597	72 728	100 099
1995	87 478	3 030	10 287	100 795	19 022	3 030	10 630	68 113	100 795
1996	100 185	2 695	10 121	113 001	20 991	2 695	11 576	77 739	113 001
1997	107 810	2 604	9 538	119 952	27 655	2 604	9 940	79 753	119 952
1998	113 199	2 845	9 934	125 978	24 970	2 845	10 293	87 870	125 978
1999	100 230	3 090	10 967	114 287	21 205	3 090	11 335	78 657	114 287
1987 Q1	13 602	135	1 208	14 945	5 060	135	1 238	8 512	14 945
Q2	13 232	105	1 206	14 543	1 804	105	1 236	11 398	14 543
Q3	15 393	104	1 217	16 714	2 702	104	1 249	12 659	16 714
Q4	15 702	101	1 246	17 049	2 646	101	1 281	13 021	17 049
1988 Q1	15 459	111	1 218	16 788	6 564	111	1 255	8 858	16 788
Q2	14 159	96	1 276	15 531	2 217	96	1 314	11 904	15 531
Q3	15 953	95	1 336	17 384	2 282	95	1 378	13 629	17 384
Q4	16 128	92	1 399	17 619	2 948	92	1 446	13 133	17 619
1989 Q1	15 524	63	1 460	17 047	7 413	63	1 515	8 056	17 047
Q2	15 265	63	1 543	16 871	2 460	63	1 604	12 744	16 871
Q3	14 064	57	1 646	15 767	3 130	57	1 709	10 871	15 767
Q4	15 418	49	1 771	17 238	5 693	49	1 831	9 665	17 238
1990 Q1	14 084	294	1 944	16 322	6 951	294	2 004	7 073	16 322
Q2	15 374	232	2 072	17 678	3 120	232	2 132	12 194	17 678
Q3	13 673	224	2 206	16 103	3 568	224	2 266	10 045	16 103
Q4	15 416	225	2 342	17 983	5 919	225	2 403	9 436	17 983
1991 Q1	12 325	629	2 468	15 422	5 974	629	2 527	6 292	15 422
Q2	16 141	567	2 580	19 288	2 339	567	2 640	13 742	19 288
Q3	13 829	570	2 672	17 071	2 677	570	2 731	11 093	17 071
Q4	18 901	566	2 744	22 211	5 122	566	2 804	13 719	22 211
1992 Q1	13 062	602	2 870	16 534	5 021	602	2 930	7 981	16 534
Q2	14 871	553	2 869	18 293	1 820	553	2 929	12 991	18 293
Q3	13 794	921	2 760	17 475	2 356	921	2 820	11 378	17 475
Q4	17 074	738	2 648	20 460	3 555	738	2 708	13 459	20 460
1993 Q1	15 389	895	2 590	18 874	5 063	895	2 658	10 258	18 874
Q2	16 863	636	2 475	19 974	1 829	636	2 543	14 966	19 974
Q3	17 720	711	2 339	20 770	2 363	711	2 407	15 289	20 770
Q4	22 777	723	2 430	25 930	3 405	723	2 498	19 304	25 930
1994 Q1	21 422	827	2 433	24 682	4 648	827	2 510	16 697	24 682
Q2	21 429	889	2 451	24 769	2 122	889	2 529	19 229	24 769
Q3	20 204	863	1 995	23 062	3 010	863	2 073	17 116	23 062
Q4	24 315	864	2 407	27 586	4 551	864	2 485	19 686	27 586
1995 Q1	20 050	774	2 373	23 197	6 213	774	2 455	13 755	23 197
Q2	21 948	756	2 584	25 288	2 688	756	2 666	19 178	25 288
Q3	21 297	751	2 616	24 664	3 350	751	2 698	17 865	24 664
Q4	24 183	749	2 714	27 646	6 771	749	2 811	17 315	27 646
1996 Q1	23 704	719	2 725	27 148	6 968	719	3 809	15 652	27 148
Q2	25 335	652	2 731	28 718	2 307	652	2 865	22 894	28 718
Q3	23 588	660	2 345	26 593	4 179	660	2 459	19 295	26 593
Q4	27 558	664	2 320	30 542	7 537	664	2 443	19 898	30 542

Source: Office for National Statistics; Enquiries 020 7533 6013

1.13 Private Non-financial Corporations: Secondary Distribution of Income Account

continued

£ million, not seasonally adjusted

	Resources				Uses				
	Gross balance of primary income	Social contributions	Other current transfers	Total Resources	Current taxes on income	Social benefits	Other current transfers	Gross disposable income	Total uses
	NRJM	EWRT	FDBA	FDBC	FCCP	EWRT	FCCN	NRJQ	FDBC
1997 Q1	26 560	667	2 451	29 678	7 141	667	2 551	19 319	29 678
Q2	24 410	495	2 461	27 366	2 980	495	2 585	21 306	27 366
Q3	28 011	730	2 233	30 974	5 182	730	2 322	22 740	30 974
Q4	28 829	712	2 393	31 934	12 352	712	2 482	16 388	31 934
1998 Q1	26 773	669	2 821	30 263	6 815	669	2 910	19 869	30 263
Q2	27 148	702	2 548	30 398	2 157	702	2 637	24 902	30 398
Q3	29 003	716	2 142	31 861	4 456	716	2 232	24 457	31 861
Q4	30 275	758	2 423	33 456	11 542	758	2 514	18 642	33 456
1999 Q1	27 602	755	2 590	30 947	4 385	755	2 684	23 123	30 947
Q2	15 048	874	2 675	18 597	2 311	874	2 769	12 643	18 597
Q3	28 372	773	2 253	31 398	4 953	773	2 348	23 324	31 398
Q4	29 208	688	3 449	33 345	9 556	688	3 534	19 567	33 345
2000 Q1	29 796	617	2 795	33 208	6 336	617	2 859	23 396	33 208

Source: Office for National Statistics; Enquiries 020 7533 6013

1.13 Private Non-financial Corporations: Secondary Distribution of Income Account

continued

£ million, seasonally adjusted

	Resources				Uses				
	Gross balance of primary income	Social contributions	Other current transfers	Total Resources	Current taxes on income	Social benefits	Other current transfers	Gross disposable income	Total uses
	RPBO	EWRT	FDBA	RPKY	RPLA	EWRT	FCCN	RPKZ	RPKY
1987 Q1	13 859	135	1 208	15 202	2 631	135	1 238	11 198	15 202
Q2	14 117	105	1 206	15 428	3 185	105	1 236	10 902	15 428
Q3	15 366	104	1 217	16 687	3 595	104	1 249	11 739	16 687
Q4	14 587	101	1 246	15 934	2 801	101	1 281	11 751	15 934
1988 Q1	15 557	111	1 218	16 886	3 698	111	1 255	11 822	16 886
Q2	14 448	96	1 276	15 820	3 848	96	1 314	10 562	15 820
Q3	16 197	95	1 336	17 628	3 434	95	1 378	12 721	17 628
Q4	15 497	92	1 399	16 988	3 031	92	1 446	12 419	16 988
1989 Q1	16 490	63	1 460	18 013	4 451	63	1 515	11 984	18 013
Q2	15 635	63	1 543	17 241	4 552	63	1 604	11 022	17 241
Q3	13 928	57	1 646	15 631	4 898	57	1 709	8 967	15 631
Q4	14 218	49	1 771	16 038	4 795	49	1 831	9 363	16 038
1990 Q1	14 748	294	1 944	16 986	4 329	294	2 004	10 359	16 986
Q2	14 882	232	2 072	17 186	5 470	232	2 132	9 352	17 186
Q3	14 487	224	2 206	16 917	5 187	224	2 266	9 240	16 917
Q4	14 430	225	2 342	16 997	4 572	225	2 403	9 797	16 997
1991 Q1	13 807	629	2 468	16 904	3 675	629	2 527	10 073	16 904
Q2	16 308	567	2 580	19 455	4 442	567	2 640	11 806	19 455
Q3	14 630	570	2 672	17 872	3 875	570	2 731	10 696	17 872
Q4	16 451	566	2 744	19 761	4 120	566	2 804	12 271	19 761
1992 Q1	13 504	602	2 870	16 976	3 275	602	2 930	10 169	16 976
Q2	15 957	553	2 869	19 379	3 017	553	2 929	12 880	19 379
Q3	14 899	921	2 760	18 580	3 200	921	2 820	11 639	18 580
Q4	14 441	738	2 648	17 827	3 260	738	2 708	11 121	17 827
1993 Q1	17 623	895	2 590	21 108	3 523	895	2 658	14 032	21 108
Q2	16 433	636	2 475	19 544	3 053	636	2 543	13 312	19 544
Q3	19 187	711	2 339	22 237	3 144	711	2 407	15 975	22 237
Q4	19 506	723	2 430	22 659	2 940	723	2 498	16 498	22 659
1994 Q1	21 448	827	2 433	24 708	3 075	827	2 510	18 296	24 708
Q2	21 770	889	2 451	25 110	3 501	889	2 529	18 191	25 110
Q3	21 069	863	1 995	23 927	4 236	863	2 073	16 755	23 927
Q4	23 083	864	2 407	26 354	3 519	864	2 485	19 486	26 354
1995 Q1	21 383	774	2 373	24 530	4 062	774	2 455	17 239	24 530
Q2	21 642	756	2 584	24 982	5 051	756	2 666	16 509	24 982
Q3	21 523	751	2 616	24 890	4 813	751	2 698	16 628	24 890
Q4	22 930	749	2 714	26 393	5 096	749	2 811	17 737	26 393
1996 Q1	24 825	719	2 725	28 269	4 971	719	3 809	18 770	28 269
Q2	25 636	652	2 731	29 019	4 254	652	2 865	21 248	29 019
Q3	24 295	660	2 345	27 300	6 058	660	2 459	18 123	27 300
Q4	25 429	664	2 320	28 413	5 708	664	2 443	19 598	28 413
1997 Q1	27 763	667	2 451	30 881	5 883	667	2 551	21 780	30 881
Q2	24 295	495	2 461	27 251	6 012	495	2 585	18 159	27 251
Q3	28 823	730	2 233	31 786	6 795	730	2 322	21 939	31 786
Q4	26 929	712	2 393	30 034	8 965	712	2 482	17 875	30 034
1998 Q1	26 352	669	2 821	29 842	5 863	669	2 910	20 400	29 842
Q2	28 033	702	2 548	31 283	5 075	702	2 637	22 869	31 283
Q3	28 884	716	2 142	31 742	5 813	716	2 232	22 981	31 742
Q4	29 930	758	2 423	33 111	8 219	758	2 514	21 620	33 111
1999 Q1	29 276	755	2 590	32 621	3 448	755	2 684	25 734	32 621
Q2	18 223	874	2 675	21 772	7 308	874	2 769	10 821	21 772
Q3	26 121	773	2 253	29 147	6 150	773	2 348	19 876	29 147
Q4	26 610	688	3 449	30 747	4 299	688	3 534	22 226	30 747
2000 Q1	28 536	617	2 795	31 948	5 340	617	2 859	23 132	31 948

Source: Office for National Statistics; Enquiries 020 7533 6013

1.14 Financial corporations : Allocation of Primary Income Account[1]

£million, not seasonally adjusted

	Resources									Uses				
		Property income,received								Property income paid				
	Gross operating surplus	Interest	Distributed income of corporations	Reinvested earnings on direct foreign investment	Property income to insurance holders	Rent	Total	Adjustment for financial services	Total	Total	*of which* Distributed income of corporations	Balance of gross primary income	Total uses	Share of gross national income
	NQNV	NHCK	NHCL	NHEM	NHDG	NHDH	NHDF	-NSRV	NQNW	NHDI	NHCN	NQNY	NQNW	RVGH
1987	10 983	103 973	10 167	431	29	24	114 624	–13 288	112 319	104 637	6 013	7 682	112 319	1.8
1988	9 484	120 779	13 843	610	36	28	135 296	–14 455	130 325	124 292	8 716	6 033	130 325	1.3
1989	11 427	171 634	17 549	351	42	28	189 604	–18 588	182 443	175 258	9 836	7 185	182 443	1.4
1990	11 711	200 253	18 834	97	56	28	219 268	–19 347	211 632	204 575	10 796	7 057	211 632	1.3
1991	7 836	184 344	19 717	517	60	28	204 666	–15 828	196 674	194 954	11 061	1 720	196 674	0.3
1992	15 657	160 105	23 281	511	66	28	183 991	–20 997	178 651	169 116	12 347	9 535	178 651	1.6
1993	18 393	137 414	23 559	2 346	65	28	163 412	–20 025	161 780	152 478	15 019	9 302	161 780	1.5
1994	23 616	139 217	27 021	1 687	66	28	168 019	–26 410	165 225	147 547	16 443	17 678	165 225	2.6
1995	20 077	162 995	31 659	3 001	74	28	197 757	–25 499	192 335	177 647	18 871	14 688	192 335	2.1
1996	18 970	166 866	39 174	3 895	66	28	210 029	–25 557	203 442	189 559	22 808	13 883	203 442	1.8
1997	18 151	184 628	39 855	4 394	75	28	228 980	–25 678	221 453	205 529	23 453	15 924	221 453	1.9
1998	19 126	214 603	37 652	3 119	84	28	255 486	–27 732	246 880	227 695	22 676	19 185	246 880	2.2
1999	18 171	191 921	51 764	4 387	58	29	248 159	–30 411	235 919	219 107	32 547	16 812	235 919	1.9
1987 Q1	2 964	25 534	1 899	70	7	6	27 516	–3 550	26 930	25 210	1 015	1 720	26 930	1.7
Q2	2 421	25 428	2 747	159	7	6	28 347	–2 940	27 828	25 918	1 741	1 910	27 828	2.0
Q3	2 913	26 469	2 382	142	7	6	29 006	–3 452	28 467	26 437	1 327	2 030	28 467	1.9
Q4	2 685	26 542	3 139	60	8	6	29 755	–3 346	29 094	27 072	1 930	2 022	29 094	1.8
1988 Q1	2 200	26 415	2 208	139	8	7	28 777	–3 246	27 731	27 232	1 257	499	27 731	0.5
Q2	2 135	26 988	3 626	166	9	7	30 796	–3 270	29 661	28 258	2 321	1 403	29 661	1.3
Q3	2 795	32 025	3 490	78	9	7	35 609	–4 168	34 236	32 435	2 056	1 801	34 236	1.5
Q4	2 354	35 351	4 519	227	10	7	40 114	–3 771	38 697	36 367	3 082	2 330	38 697	1.8
1989 Q1	2 443	38 282	2 973	111	10	7	41 383	–4 161	39 665	38 996	1 394	669	39 665	0.6
Q2	2 709	41 684	4 862	117	10	7	46 680	–4 502	44 887	42 753	2 917	2 134	44 887	1.8
Q3	3 458	44 078	4 265	81	11	7	48 442	–5 278	46 622	44 354	2 202	2 268	46 622	1.8
Q4	2 817	47 590	5 449	42	11	7	53 099	–4 647	51 269	49 155	3 323	2 114	51 269	1.5
1990 Q1	2 625	48 579	3 392	–24	14	7	51 968	–4 583	50 010	49 606	1 456	404	50 010	0.3
Q2	3 358	50 221	4 745	–	14	7	54 987	–5 266	53 079	50 863	3 119	2 216	53 079	1.7
Q3	3 578	50 581	4 701	71	14	7	55 374	–5 321	53 631	51 073	2 359	2 558	53 631	1.8
Q4	2 150	50 872	5 996	50	14	7	56 939	–4 177	54 912	53 033	3 862	1 879	54 912	1.3
1991 Q1	2 491	49 923	3 472	54	15	7	53 471	–3 977	51 985	51 570	1 594	415	51 985	0.3
Q2	1 459	47 246	5 108	173	15	7	52 549	–3 476	50 532	50 333	3 394	199	50 532	0.1
Q3	1 675	44 230	4 670	112	15	7	49 034	–4 037	46 672	46 798	1 988	–126	46 672	–0.1
Q4	2 211	42 945	6 467	178	15	7	49 612	–4 338	47 485	46 253	4 085	1 232	47 485	0.8
1992 Q1	2 972	40 781	4 594	241	14	7	45 637	–4 554	44 055	42 220	1 929	1 835	44 055	1.3
Q2	2 990	39 578	5 625	118	15	7	45 343	–4 389	43 944	42 493	3 629	1 451	43 944	1.0
Q3	4 835	40 373	5 022	128	14	7	45 544	–5 802	44 577	41 341	2 019	3 236	44 577	2.1
Q4	4 860	39 373	8 040	24	23	7	47 467	–6 252	46 075	43 062	4 770	3 013	46 075	1.9
1993 Q1	4 652	35 974	4 232	659	16	7	40 888	–5 009	40 531	38 080	2 617	2 451	40 531	1.6
Q2	4 770	33 643	7 096	298	15	7	41 059	–4 856	40 973	38 293	4 858	2 680	40 973	1.8
Q3	5 623	33 796	5 164	867	18	7	39 852	–5 582	39 893	37 122	2 939	2 771	39 893	1.7
Q4	3 348	34 001	7 067	522	16	7	41 613	–4 578	40 383	38 983	4 605	1 400	40 383	0.8
1994 Q1	6 266	34 178	4 130	683	14	7	39 012	–6 539	38 739	33 348	2 204	5 391	38 739	3.3
Q2	4 989	32 999	6 980	464	14	7	40 464	–5 767	39 686	36 063	4 537	3 623	39 686	2.2
Q3	6 911	34 338	7 612	373	21	7	42 351	–7 003	42 259	37 853	4 295	4 406	42 259	2.5
Q4	5 450	37 702	8 299	167	17	7	46 192	–7 101	44 541	40 283	5 407	4 258	44 541	2.4
1995 Q1	6 462	39 215	5 081	–40	17	7	44 280	–7 166	43 576	39 519	2 435	4 057	43 576	2.4
Q2	3 923	40 373	6 995	854	21	7	48 250	–5 040	47 133	45 955	5 398	1 178	47 133	0.7
Q3	6 731	41 643	7 839	922	13	7	50 424	–7 823	49 332	44 590	4 535	4 742	49 332	2.6
Q4	2 961	41 764	11 744	1 265	23	7	54 803	–5 470	52 294	47 583	6 503	4 711	52 294	2.5
1996 Q1	4 450	41 080	7 394	854	16	7	49 351	–5 843	47 958	46 055	4 385	1 903	47 958	1.1
Q2	4 548	41 026	10 613	732	19	7	52 397	–5 683	51 262	48 487	6 803	2 775	51 262	1.5
Q3	5 934	41 802	9 329	1 136	17	7	52 291	–6 901	51 324	47 710	4 622	3 614	51 324	1.9
Q4	4 038	42 958	11 838	1 173	14	7	55 990	–7 130	52 898	47 307	6 998	5 591	52 898	2.8

1 Data not consolidated.

Source: Office for national Statistics; Enquiries 020 7533 6055

1.14 Financial corporations : Allocation of Primary Income Account[1]

continued

£ million, not seasonally adjusted

	Resources									Uses				
		Property income,received								Property income paid				
	Gross operating surplus	Interest	Distributed income of corporations	Reinvested earnings on direct foreign investment	Property income to insurance holders	Rent	Total	Adjustment for financial services	Total	Total	*of which* Distributed income of corporations	Balance of gross primary income	Total uses	Share of gross national income
	NQNV	NHCK	NHCL	NHEM	NHDG	NHDH	NHDF	NSRV	NQNW	NHDI	NHCN	NQNY	NQNW	RVGH
1997 Q1	6 223	42 493	6 830	1 161	21	7	50 512	7 777	48 958	45 229	3 163	3 729	48 958	1.9
Q2	3 676	43 720	12 815	1 256	22	7	57 820	4 947	56 549	53 115	7 686	3 434	56 549	1.7
Q3	4 172	46 736	9 142	1 438	21	7	57 344	5 744	55 772	53 655	5 608	2 117	55 772	1.0
Q4	4 080	51 679	11 068	539	11	7	63 304	7 210	60 174	53 530	6 996	6 644	60 174	3.1
1998 Q1	7 037	52 187	7 973	980	21	7	61 168	8 971	59 234	54 967	4 585	4 267	59 234	2.1
Q2	5 626	53 211	11 320	596	20	7	65 154	6 931	63 849	59 686	7 653	4 163	63 849	2.0
Q3	5 100	54 813	7 939	1 032	21	7	63 812	6 897	62 015	56 504	2 670	5 511	62 015	2.5
Q4	1 363	54 392	10 420	511	22	7	65 352	4 933	61 782	56 538	7 768	5 244	61 782	2.3
1999 Q1	4 734	49 490	5 977	1 136	14	7	56 624	8 237	53 121	53 242	6 320	–121	53 121	–0.1
Q2	2 653	45 285	22 027	1 188	16	7	68 523	4 676	66 500	60 173	12 273	6 327	66 500	2.9
Q3	5 966	45 294	9 694	1 022	8	7	56 025	8 046	53 945	51 088	5 594	2 857	53 945	1.3
Q4	4 818	51 852	14 066	1 041	20	8	66 987	9 452	62 353	54 604	8 360	7 749	62 353	3.3
2000 Q1	4 392	52 803	8 335	1 292	15	8	62 453	8 892	57 953	58 271	6 522	–318	57 953	–0.1

1 Data not consolidated.

Source: Office for National Statistics; Enquiries 020 7533 6055

1.14 Financial corporations : Allocation of Primary Income Account[1]

continued

£million, seasonally adjusted

	Resources									Uses				
		Property income,received								Property income paid				
	Gross operating surplus	Interest	Distributed income of corporations	Reinvested earnings on direct foreign investment	Property income to insurance holders	Rent	Total	Adjustment for financial services	Total	Total	*of which* Distributed income of corporations	Balance of gross primary income	Total uses	Share of gross national income
	NHCZ	ROWJ	ROWK	ROWL	ROWM	ROCO	ROWI	-RITO	ROWN	ROWP	ROWR	ROWO	ROWN	NRJI
1987 Q1	3 057	25 798	2 605	70	7	6	28 486	–3 634	27 909	25 528	1 627	2 381	27 909	2.4
Q2	2 543	25 699	2 506	159	7	6	28 377	–3 075	27 845	25 963	1 460	1 882	27 845	1.8
Q3	2 564	26 246	2 494	142	7	6	28 895	–3 102	28 357	26 605	1 495	1 752	28 357	1.7
Q4	2 819	26 230	2 562	60	8	6	28 866	–3 477	28 208	26 541	1 431	1 667	28 208	1.5
1988 Q1	2 258	26 689	3 032	139	8	7	29 875	–3 307	28 826	27 697	2 039	1 129	28 826	1.0
Q2	2 294	27 321	3 328	166	9	7	30 831	–3 451	29 674	28 281	2 002	1 393	29 674	1.2
Q3	2 404	31 789	3 673	78	9	7	35 556	–3 781	34 179	32 758	2 369	1 421	34 179	1.2
Q4	2 528	34 980	3 810	227	10	7	39 034	–3 916	37 646	35 556	2 306	2 090	37 646	1.7
1989 Q1	2 582	38 547	4 013	111	10	7	42 688	–4 331	40 939	39 378	2 289	1 561	40 939	1.3
Q2	2 878	42 125	4 525	117	10	7	46 784	–4 709	44 953	42 903	2 505	2 050	44 953	1.6
Q3	2 968	43 822	4 530	81	11	7	48 451	–4 812	46 607	44 725	2 552	1 882	46 607	1.5
Q4	2 999	47 140	4 481	42	11	7	51 681	–4 736	49 944	48 252	2 490	1 692	49 944	1.3
1990 Q1	2 521	48 686	4 542	–24	14	7	53 225	–4 744	51 002	49 766	2 283	1 236	51 002	0.9
Q2	3 465	50 797	4 411	–	14	7	55 229	–5 489	53 205	51 221	2 738	1 984	53 205	1.4
Q3	3 040	50 458	4 945	71	14	7	55 495	–4 879	53 656	51 618	2 822	2 038	53 656	1.5
Q4	2 685	50 312	4 936	50	14	7	55 319	–4 235	53 769	51 970	2 953	1 799	53 769	1.3
1991 Q1	2 298	49 986	4 632	54	15	7	54 694	–4 046	52 946	52 036	2 633	910	52 946	0.6
Q2	1 550	47 819	4 834	173	15	7	52 848	–3 687	50 711	50 720	3 024	–9	50 711	–
Q3	1 212	44 159	4 938	112	15	7	49 231	–3 717	46 726	47 223	2 336	–497	46 726	–0.3
Q4	2 776	42 380	5 313	178	15	7	47 893	–4 378	46 291	44 975	3 068	1 316	46 291	0.9
1992 Q1	2 726	40 894	6 222	241	14	7	47 378	–4 577	45 527	43 418	3 318	2 109	45 527	1.4
Q2	3 240	40 084	5 262	118	15	7	45 486	–4 748	43 978	42 432	3 017	1 546	43 978	1.0
Q3	4 218	40 493	5 299	128	14	7	45 941	–5 430	44 729	41 788	2 464	2 941	44 729	1.9
Q4	5 473	38 634	6 498	24	23	7	45 186	–6 242	44 417	41 478	3 548	2 939	44 417	1.9
1993 Q1	4 258	36 186	5 669	659	16	7	42 537	–4 879	41 916	40 050	4 445	1 866	41 916	1.2
Q2	5 121	34 163	6 707	298	15	7	41 190	–5 316	40 995	37 644	3 851	3 351	40 995	2.1
Q3	4 890	33 786	5 378	867	18	7	40 056	–5 228	39 718	37 301	3 360	2 417	39 718	1.5
Q4	4 124	33 279	5 805	522	16	7	39 629	–4 602	39 151	37 483	3 363	1 668	39 151	1.0
1994 Q1	5 713	34 409	5 677	683	14	7	40 790	–6 250	40 253	35 003	3 539	5 250	40 253	3.1
Q2	5 563	33 569	6 476	464	14	7	40 530	–6 436	39 657	35 490	3 756	4 167	39 657	2.5
Q3	5 978	34 260	8 090	373	21	7	42 751	–6 586	42 143	37 967	4 878	4 176	42 143	2.4
Q4	6 362	36 979	6 778	167	17	7	43 948	–7 138	43 172	39 087	4 270	4 085	43 172	2.3
1995 Q1	5 728	39 353	7 052	–40	17	7	46 389	–6 673	45 444	41 605	4 061	3 839	45 444	2.2
Q2	4 541	41 150	6 690	854	21	7	48 722	–5 778	47 485	45 199	4 564	2 286	47 485	1.3
Q3	5 816	41 433	8 311	922	13	7	50 686	–7 475	49 027	44 456	5 108	4 571	49 027	2.5
Q4	3 992	41 059	9 606	1 265	23	7	51 960	–5 573	50 379	46 387	5 138	3 992	50 379	2.2
1996 Q1	3 593	41 363	10 080	854	16	7	52 320	–5 187	50 726	49 086	6 618	1 640	50 726	0.9
Q2	5 096	41 827	9 638	732	19	7	52 223	–6 413	50 906	47 176	5 475	3 730	50 906	2.0
Q3	5 168	41 542	9 948	1 136	17	7	52 650	–6 658	51 160	46 971	5 037	4 189	51 160	2.2
Q4	5 113	42 134	9 508	1 173	14	7	52 836	–7 299	50 650	46 326	5 678	4 324	50 650	2.2
1997 Q1	5 161	43 010	9 154	1 161	21	7	53 353	–6 901	51 613	47 486	4 610	4 127	51 613	2.1
Q2	3 979	44 659	11 687	1 256	22	7	57 631	–5 713	55 897	51 911	6 515	3 986	55 897	2.0
Q3	3 654	46 406	10 039	1 438	21	7	57 911	–5 615	55 950	53 051	6 419	2 899	55 950	1.4
Q4	5 357	50 553	8 975	539	11	7	60 085	–7 449	57 993	53 081	5 909	4 912	57 993	2.4
1998 Q1	6 052	52 129	10 831	980	21	7	63 968	–7 966	62 054	57 261	6 328	4 793	62 054	2.3
Q2	6 271	54 401	9 297	596	20	7	64 321	–8 093	62 499	57 666	6 161	4 833	62 499	2.3
Q3	4 461	55 226	8 730	1 032	21	7	65 016	–6 927	62 550	56 303	3 618	6 247	62 550	2.9
Q4	2 342	52 847	8 794	511	22	7	62 181	–4 746	59 777	56 465	6 569	3 312	59 777	1.5
1999 Q1	3 875	49 315	8 523	1 136	14	7	58 995	–7 280	55 590	55 929	8 543	–339	55 590	–0.2
Q2	3 208	46 457	18 822	1 188	16	7	66 490	–5 802	63 896	56 918	10 111	6 978	63 896	3.1
Q3	5 552	45 813	11 666	1 022	8	7	58 516	–8 316	55 752	51 260	6 639	4 492	55 752	2.0
Q4	5 536	50 336	12 753	1 041	20	8	64 158	–9 013	60 681	55 000	7 254	5 681	60 681	2.5
2000 Q1	3 637	52 508	12 163	1 292	15	8	65 986	–7 987	61 636	60 525	8 370	1 111	61 636	0.5

1 Data not consolidated.

Source: Office for National Statistics; Enquiries 020 7533 6055

1.15 Financial corporations : Secondary Distribution of Income Account[1]

£ million,not seasonally adjusted

	Resources				Uses				
	Gross balance of primary income	Social contributions	Other current transfers	Total Resources	Current taxes on income	Social benefits	Other current transfers	Gross disposable income	Total uses
	NQNY	NQOA	NQOE	NQOH	NHDO	NHDQ	NHDT	NQOJ	NQOH
1987	7 682	29 097	12 311	49 141	1 121	16 211	12 344	19 465	49 141
1988	6 033	33 253	13 199	52 530	795	17 529	13 235	20 971	52 530
1989	7 185	38 973	16 205	62 388	67	19 221	16 250	26 850	62 388
1990	7 057	40 226	21 618	69 007	–897	22 085	21 664	26 155	69 007
1991	1 720	40 382	26 413	68 779	–1 496	25 044	26 433	18 798	68 779
1992	9 535	41 750	28 140	79 710	–1 106	28 764	28 188	23 864	79 710
1993	9 302	40 438	24 827	74 843	–162	29 973	24 884	20 148	74 843
1994	17 678	43 291	23 443	84 709	909	33 014	23 517	27 269	84 709
1995	14 688	46 768	25 967	87 679	1 089	35 336	26 032	25 222	87 679
1996	13 883	54 889	36 723	105 735	2 344	40 307	36 788	26 296	105 735
1997	15 924	61 172	24 587	101 939	4 055	45 738	24 653	27 493	101 939
1998	19 185	66 140	25 156	110 700	7 882	49 992	25 230	27 596	110 700
1999	16 812	69 246	27 659	113 939	9 525	51 577	27 734	25 103	113 939
1987 Q1	1 720	6 760	3 050	11 546	547	3 731	3 058	4 210	11 546
Q2	1 910	7 317	3 045	12 284	–267	4 111	3 053	5 387	12 284
Q3	2 030	7 429	3 072	12 543	210	4 177	3 080	5 076	12 543
Q4	2 022	7 591	3 144	12 768	631	4 192	3 153	4 792	12 768
1988 Q1	499	7 775	3 075	11 362	500	4 319	3 084	3 459	11 362
Q2	1 403	8 090	3 220	12 724	–420	4 349	3 229	5 566	12 724
Q3	1 801	8 472	3 372	13 656	115	4 393	3 381	5 767	13 656
Q4	2 330	8 916	3 532	14 788	600	4 468	3 541	6 179	14 788
1989 Q1	669	9 170	3 685	13 531	787	4 524	3 696	4 524	13 531
Q2	2 134	9 663	3 895	15 699	–531	4 729	3 907	7 594	15 699
Q3	2 268	9 988	4 155	16 417	–159	4 900	4 167	7 509	16 417
Q4	2 114	10 152	4 470	16 741	–30	5 068	4 480	7 223	16 741
1990 Q1	404	9 978	4 907	15 320	292	5 236	4 918	4 874	15 320
Q2	2 216	10 034	5 230	17 505	–593	5 422	5 242	7 434	17 505
Q3	2 558	10 055	5 570	18 208	–246	5 609	5 581	7 264	18 208
Q4	1 879	10 159	5 911	17 974	–350	5 818	5 923	6 583	17 974
1991 Q1	415	10 007	6 230	16 724	134	5 944	6 235	4 411	16 724
Q2	199	10 092	6 512	16 868	–743	6 161	6 517	4 933	16 868
Q3	–126	10 125	6 745	16 808	–385	6 366	6 750	4 077	16 808
Q4	1 232	10 158	6 926	18 379	–502	6 573	6 931	5 377	18 379
1992 Q1	1 835	9 521	7 245	18 665	–84	6 764	7 257	4 728	18 665
Q2	1 451	10 028	7 243	18 779	–851	7 240	7 255	5 135	18 779
Q3	3 236	10 476	6 968	20 772	–348	6 770	6 980	7 370	20 772
Q4	3 013	11 725	6 684	21 494	177	7 990	6 696	6 631	21 494
1993 Q1	2 451	9 949	6 539	19 026	69	7 936	6 553	4 468	19 026
Q2	2 680	10 046	6 248	19 033	–733	7 797	6 262	5 707	19 033
Q3	2 771	10 073	5 906	18 815	15	6 808	5 920	6 072	18 815
Q4	1 400	10 370	6 134	17 969	487	7 432	6 149	3 901	17 969
1994 Q1	5 391	9 361	6 141	20 966	531	8 237	6 159	6 039	20 966
Q2	3 623	10 620	6 189	20 509	–534	8 232	6 208	6 603	20 509
Q3	4 406	11 776	5 037	21 293	–125	8 208	5 055	8 155	21 293
Q4	4 258	11 534	6 076	21 941	1 037	8 337	6 095	6 472	21 941
1995 Q1	4 057	10 315	5 990	20 427	202	8 380	6 006	5 839	20 427
Q2	1 178	12 131	6 523	19 895	–628	8 988	6 539	4 996	19 895
Q3	4 742	12 448	6 604	23 858	72	8 909	6 620	8 257	23 858
Q4	4 711	11 874	6 850	23 499	1 443	9 059	6 867	6 130	23 499
1996 Q1	1 903	13 301	6 876	22 142	169	9 733	6 892	5 348	22 142
Q2	2 775	13 951	6 891	23 675	–471	9 877	6 907	7 362	23 675
Q3	3 614	14 022	17 094	34 789	324	9 590	17 110	7 765	34 789
Q4	5 591	13 615	5 862	25 129	2 322	11 107	5 879	5 821	25 129
1997 Q1	3 729	14 687	6 183	24 660	1 130	11 473	6 199	5 858	24 660
Q2	3 434	16 368	6 209	26 077	–860	11 096	6 226	9 615	26 077
Q3	2 117	15 874	5 634	23 690	1 218	11 244	5 650	5 578	23 690
Q4	6 644	14 243	6 561	27 512	2 567	11 925	6 578	6 442	27 512
1998 Q1	4 267	15 751	7 215	27 291	1 756	11 850	7 233	6 452	27 291
Q2	4 163	17 289	6 428	27 935	950	12 523	6 446	8 016	27 935
Q3	5 511	17 551	5 402	28 519	1 643	12 606	5 421	8 849	28 519
Q4	5 244	15 549	6 111	26 955	3 533	13 013	6 130	4 279	26 955
1999 Q1	–121	16 300	6 539	22 772	2 494	12 419	6 558	1 301	22 772
Q2	6 327	18 703	6 754	31 836	1 210	12 668	6 773	11 185	31 836
Q3	2 857	17 742	5 686	26 337	1 949	12 982	5 705	5 701	26 337
Q4	7 749	16 501	8 680	32 994	3 872	13 508	8 698	6 916	32 994
2000 Q1	–318	17 217	6 974	23 938	1 998	13 923	6 993	1 024	23 938

1 Data not consolidated.
2 Gross saving = gross disposable income.

1.15 Financial corporations : Secondary Distribution of Income Account[1]

continued

£ million, seasonally adjusted

	Resources				Uses				
	Gross balance of primary income	Social contributions	Other current transfers	Total Resources	Current taxes on income	Social benefits	Other current transfers	Gross disposable income	Total uses
	ROWO	NSBN	RPED	RPEH	RPEK	NROD	RPEO	RPEI	RPEH
1987 Q1	2 381	6 800	3 050	12 247	381	3 735	3 058	5 073	12 247
Q2	1 882	7 298	3 045	12 237	250	4 106	3 053	4 828	12 237
Q3	1 752	7 420	3 072	12 256	326	4 180	3 080	4 670	12 256
Q4	1 667	7 579	3 144	12 401	164	4 190	3 153	4 894	12 401
1988 Q1	1 129	7 825	3 075	12 042	322	4 319	3 084	4 317	12 042
Q2	1 393	8 069	3 220	12 693	43	4 342	3 229	5 079	12 693
Q3	1 421	8 460	3 372	13 264	140	4 397	3 381	5 346	13 264
Q4	2 090	8 899	3 532	14 531	290	4 471	3 541	6 229	14 531
1989 Q1	1 561	9 153	3 685	14 406	587	4 510	3 696	5 613	14 406
Q2	2 050	9 738	3 895	15 690	–65	4 717	3 907	7 131	15 690
Q3	1 882	9 971	4 155	16 014	–144	4 915	4 167	7 076	16 014
Q4	1 692	10 111	4 470	16 278	–311	5 079	4 480	7 030	16 278
1990 Q1	1 236	10 109	4 907	16 283	66	5 198	4 918	6 101	16 283
Q2	1 984	10 029	5 230	17 268	–120	5 405	5 242	6 741	17 268
Q3	2 038	10 024	5 570	17 657	–241	5 643	5 581	6 674	17 657
Q4	1 799	10 064	5 911	17 799	–602	5 839	5 923	6 639	17 799
1991 Q1	910	10 133	6 230	17 345	–103	5 869	6 235	5 344	17 345
Q2	–9	10 190	6 512	16 758	–273	6 145	6 517	4 369	16 758
Q3	–497	10 067	6 745	16 379	–391	6 427	6 750	3 593	16 379
Q4	1 316	9 992	6 926	18 297	–729	6 603	6 931	5 492	18 297
1992 Q1	2 109	9 892	7 245	19 310	–58	6 651	7 257	5 460	19 310
Q2	1 546	10 036	7 243	18 882	–120	7 233	7 255	4 514	18 882
Q3	2 941	10 353	6 968	20 354	–147	6 854	6 980	6 667	20 354
Q4	2 939	11 469	6 684	21 164	–781	8 026	6 696	7 223	21 164
1993 Q1	1 866	10 454	6 539	18 946	116	7 807	6 553	4 470	18 946
Q2	3 351	9 947	6 248	19 605	54	7 807	6 262	5 482	19 605
Q3	2 417	9 872	5 906	18 260	231	6 904	5 920	5 205	18 260
Q4	1 668	10 165	6 134	18 032	–563	7 455	6 149	4 991	18 032
1994 Q1	5 250	9 883	6 141	21 347	635	8 116	6 159	6 437	21 347
Q2	4 167	10 453	6 189	20 886	320	8 253	6 208	6 105	20 886
Q3	4 176	11 509	5 037	20 796	129	8 303	5 055	7 309	20 796
Q4	4 085	11 446	6 076	21 680	–175	8 342	6 095	7 418	21 680
1995 Q1	3 839	10 894	5 990	20 788	416	8 277	6 006	6 089	20 788
Q2	2 286	11 812	6 523	20 684	290	9 031	6 539	4 824	20 684
Q3	4 571	12 164	6 604	23 403	366	8 980	6 620	7 437	23 403
Q4	3 992	11 898	6 850	22 804	17	9 048	6 867	6 872	22 804
1996 Q1	1 640	13 981	6 876	22 559	478	9 648	6 892	5 541	22 559
Q2	3 730	13 425	6 891	24 104	497	9 931	6 907	6 769	24 104
Q3	4 189	13 739	17 094	35 081	634	9 635	17 110	7 702	35 081
Q4	4 324	13 744	5 862	23 991	735	11 093	5 879	6 284	23 991
1997 Q1	4 127	15 041	6 183	25 412	829	11 367	6 199	7 017	25 412
Q2	3 986	15 526	6 209	25 787	358	11 065	6 226	8 138	25 787
Q3	2 899	15 347	5 634	23 945	1 323	11 481	5 650	5 491	23 945
Q4	4 912	15 258	6 561	26 795	1 545	11 825	6 578	6 847	26 795
1998 Q1	4 793	16 273	7 215	28 339	1 816	11 925	7 233	7 365	28 339
Q2	4 833	16 107	6 428	27 423	1 951	12 423	6 446	6 603	27 423
Q3	6 247	16 857	5 402	28 561	1 823	12 820	5 421	8 497	28 561
Q4	3 312	16 903	6 111	26 377	2 292	12 824	6 130	5 131	26 377
1999 Q1	–339	16 868	6 539	23 122	2 550	12 348	6 558	1 666	23 122
Q2	6 978	17 230	6 754	31 014	2 216	12 765	6 773	9 260	31 014
Q3	4 492	17 146	5 686	27 376	2 180	13 160	5 705	6 331	27 376
Q4	5 681	18 002	8 680	32 427	2 579	13 304	8 698	7 846	32 427
2000 Q1	1 111	17 828	6 974	25 978	2 070	14 067	6 993	2 848	25 978

1 Data not consolidated.
2 Gross saving = gross disposable income.

Source: Office for National Statistics; Enquiries 020 7533 6055

1.16 Private Non-financial Corporations:Capital Account

£ million, not seasonally adjusted

	Changes in liabilities and net worth				Changes in assets					
	Gross Saving[1]	Capital transfers receivable	*less* capital transfers payable	Total change in liabilities and net worth	Gross fixed capital formation	Changes in inventories	Acquisitions less disposals of valuables	Acquisitions less disposal of non-produced non-financial assets	Net lending or borrowing[2]	Total change in assets
	NRJQ	AIBR	FCFX	NRMG	FDBM	DLQX	NPOV	FDCN	DTAL	NRMG
1987	45 590	511	276	45 825	40 456	1 783	–55	1 192	2 449	45 825
1988	47 524	1 019	288	48 255	49 294	4 293	–23	1 508	–6 817	48 255
1989	41 336	561	330	41 567	58 647	2 426	–35	1 484	–20 955	41 567
1990	38 748	513	325	38 936	63 350	–1 687	–62	781	–23 446	38 936
1991	44 846	512	220	45 138	58 339	–4 858	–51	341	–8 633	45 138
1992	45 809	435	121	46 123	54 418	–1 921	–23	305	–6 656	46 123
1993	59 817	415	191	60 041	55 223	238	–27	551	4 056	60 041
1994	72 728	535	126	73 137	56 453	3 904	–	533	12 247	73 137
1995	68 113	577	144	68 546	64 021	4 542	–49	440	–408	68 546
1996	77 739	590	162	78 167	72 901	1 651	–71	332	3 354	78 167
1997	79 753	712	188	80 277	81 616	3 731	–55	462	–5 477	80 277
1998	87 870	753	216	88 407	89 269	3 982	32	710	–5 586	88 407
1999	78 657	754	257	79 154	97 154	–1 575	–7	713	–17 131	79 154
1987 Q1	8 512	195	67	8 640	8 680	540	–18	256	–818	8 640
Q2	11 398	105	63	11 440	9 398	620	13	287	1 122	11 440
Q3	12 659	106	78	12 687	10 426	1 043	–49	313	954	12 687
Q4	13 021	105	68	13 058	11 952	–420	–1	336	1 191	13 058
1988 Q1	8 858	133	85	8 906	10 844	1 043	–13	354	–3 322	8 906
Q2	11 904	89	67	11 926	11 396	1 416	11	371	–1 268	11 926
Q3	13 629	657	68	14 218	12 831	523	–35	386	513	14 218
Q4	13 133	140	68	13 205	14 223	1 311	14	397	–2 740	13 205
1989 Q1	8 056	201	79	8 178	13 322	827	–7	402	–6 366	8 178
Q2	12 744	109	82	12 771	14 320	1 382	8	392	–3 331	12 771
Q3	10 871	116	85	10 902	15 209	697	–33	366	–5 337	10 902
Q4	9 665	135	84	9 716	15 796	–480	–3	324	–5 921	9 716
1990 Q1	7 073	180	105	7 148	15 955	338	–15	270	–9 400	7 148
Q2	12 194	112	72	12 234	15 691	643	2	216	–4 318	12 234
Q3	10 045	98	70	10 073	15 762	–175	–43	167	–5 638	10 073
Q4	9 436	123	78	9 481	15 942	–2 493	–6	128	–4 090	9 481
1991 Q1	6 292	168	88	6 372	15 362	–1 278	–22	104	–7 794	6 372
Q2	13 742	106	46	13 802	14 041	–842	24	88	491	13 802
Q3	11 093	112	35	11 170	13 954	–383	–27	78	–2 452	11 170
Q4	13 719	126	51	13 794	14 982	–2 355	–26	71	1 122	13 794
1992 Q1	7 981	150	58	8 073	13 998	–775	–29	66	–5 187	8 073
Q2	12 991	87	20	13 058	13 101	–197	7	68	79	13 058
Q3	11 378	86	21	11 443	13 449	275	–21	77	–2 337	11 443
Q4	13 459	112	22	13 549	13 870	–1 224	20	94	789	13 549
1993 Q1	10 258	124	21	10 361	13 518	–1 149	–1	117	–2 124	10 361
Q2	14 966	88	25	15 029	12 870	860	19	135	1 145	15 029
Q3	15 289	87	25	15 351	13 820	327	–27	148	1 083	15 351
Q4	19 304	116	120	19 300	15 015	200	–18	151	3 952	19 300
1994 Q1	16 697	159	30	16 826	13 840	11	–11	146	2 840	16 826
Q2	19 229	107	32	19 304	12 771	2 648	–	137	3 748	19 304
Q3	17 116	134	32	17 218	14 446	718	–20	128	1 946	17 218
Q4	19 686	135	32	19 789	15 396	527	31	122	3 713	19 789
1995 Q1	13 755	217	27	13 945	14 664	–834	–	118	–3	13 945
Q2	19 178	107	38	19 247	15 449	2 904	17	114	763	19 247
Q3	17 865	123	42	17 946	16 547	1 398	–37	108	–70	17 946
Q4	17 315	130	37	17 408	17 361	1 074	–29	100	–1 098	17 408
1996 Q1	15 652	221	34	15 839	17 543	–756	–20	86	–1 014	15 839
Q2	22 894	111	42	22 963	17 418	1 853	–6	83	3 615	22 963
Q3	19 295	117	43	19 369	18 418	–117	–27	84	1 011	19 369
Q4	19 898	141	43	19 996	19 522	671	–18	79	–258	19 996
1997 Q1	19 319	178	42	19 455	19 213	303	–15	107	–153	19 455
Q2	21 306	174	48	21 432	20 120	2 564	–4	121	–1 369	21 432
Q3	22 740	163	49	22 854	20 532	802	–15	117	1 418	22 854
Q4	16 388	197	49	16 536	21 751	62	–21	117	–5 373	16 536
1998 Q1	19 869	170	49	19 990	21 681	534	17	323	–2 565	19 990
Q2	24 902	175	55	25 022	21 821	1 426	–4	201	1 578	25 022
Q3	24 457	198	55	24 600	22 858	943	9	128	662	24 600
Q4	18 642	210	57	18 795	22 909	1 079	10	58	–5 261	18 795
1999 Q1	23 123	310	58	23 375	23 961	–1 679	–4	93	1 004	23 375
Q2	12 643	133	70	12 706	23 856	–918	14	161	–10 407	12 706
Q3	23 324	170	64	23 430	24 265	1 678	–30	189	–2 672	23 430
Q4	19 567	141	65	19 643	25 072	–656	13	270	–5 056	19 643
2000 Q1	23 396	176	64	23 508	24 430	2 149	–7	87	–3 151	23 508

1 Gross saving is equal to gross disposable income.
2 Net lending is positive, net borrowing is negative.

Source: Office for National Statistics; Enquiries 020 7533 6013

1.16 Private Non-financial Corporations:Capital Account

continued

£ million, seasonally adjusted

	Changes in liabilities and net worth				Changes in assets					
	Gross Saving[1]	Capital transfers receivable	*less* capital transfers payable	Total change in liabilities and net worth	Gross fixed capital formation	Changes in inventories	Acquisitions less disposals of valuables	Acquisitions less disposal of non-produced non-financial assets	Net lending or borrowing[2]	Total change in assets
	RPKZ	CIDZ	FCFX	RPXH	ROAW	DLQY	NPOX	RQBW	RQBV	RPXH
1987 Q1	11 198	186	67	11 317	9 114	303	–15	256	1 659	11 317
Q2	10 902	129	63	10 968	9 723	470	–1	287	489	10 968
Q3	11 739	91	78	11 752	10 447	361	–30	313	661	11 752
Q4	11 751	105	68	11 788	11 172	649	–9	336	–360	11 788
1988 Q1	11 822	124	85	11 861	11 353	89	–9	354	74	11 861
Q2	10 562	113	67	10 608	11 616	227	–5	371	–1 601	10 608
Q3	12 721	642	68	13 295	12 801	1 235	–13	386	–1 114	13 295
Q4	12 419	140	68	12 491	13 524	2 742	4	397	–4 176	12 491
1989 Q1	11 984	177	79	12 082	13 781	668	–2	402	–2 767	12 082
Q2	11 022	126	82	11 066	14 658	661	–10	392	–4 635	11 066
Q3	8 967	121	85	9 003	15 160	1 510	–11	366	–8 022	9 003
Q4	9 363	137	84	9 416	15 048	–413	–12	324	–5 531	9 416
1990 Q1	10 359	149	105	10 403	16 319	409	–9	270	–6 586	10 403
Q2	9 352	133	72	9 413	16 103	978	–18	216	–7 866	9 413
Q3	9 240	109	70	9 279	15 686	–385	–21	167	–6 168	9 279
Q4	9 797	122	78	9 841	15 242	–2 689	–14	128	–2 826	9 841
1991 Q1	10 073	135	88	10 120	15 443	–367	–15	104	–5 045	10 120
Q2	11 806	127	46	11 887	14 555	–2 245	2	88	–513	11 887
Q3	10 696	127	35	10 788	13 904	–1 786	–7	78	–1 401	10 788
Q4	12 271	123	51	12 343	14 437	–460	–31	71	–1 674	12 343
1992 Q1	10 169	115	58	10 226	14 039	–418	–23	66	–3 438	10 226
Q2	12 880	107	20	12 967	13 741	–1 070	–14	68	242	12 967
Q3	11 639	101	21	11 719	13 338	–623	–1	77	–1 072	11 719
Q4	11 121	112	22	11 211	13 300	190	15	94	–2 388	11 211
1993 Q1	14 032	89	21	14 100	13 624	–74	3	117	430	14 100
Q2	13 312	109	25	13 396	13 487	–123	–	135	–103	13 396
Q3	15 975	101	25	16 051	13 657	83	–9	148	2 172	16 051
Q4	16 498	116	120	16 494	14 455	352	–21	151	1 557	16 494
1994 Q1	18 296	109	30	18 375	13 987	213	–9	146	4 038	18 375
Q2	18 191	131	32	18 290	13 131	1 485	–17	137	3 554	18 290
Q3	16 755	156	32	16 879	14 340	418	–3	128	1 996	16 879
Q4	19 486	139	32	19 593	14 995	1 788	29	122	2 659	19 593
1995 Q1	17 239	154	27	17 366	14 905	–74	–4	118	2 421	17 366
Q2	16 509	136	38	16 607	15 902	2 015	3	114	–1 427	16 607
Q3	16 628	147	42	16 733	16 432	1 837	–21	108	–1 623	16 733
Q4	17 737	140	37	17 840	16 782	764	–27	100	221	17 840
1996 Q1	18 770	168	34	18 904	17 874	542	–25	91	422	18 904
Q2	21 248	139	42	21 345	17 710	784	–19	78	2 792	21 345
Q3	18 123	135	43	18 215	18 361	516	–12	85	–735	18 215
Q4	19 598	148	43	19 703	18 956	–191	–15	78	875	19 703
1997 Q1	21 780	138	42	21 876	19 228	1 128	–14	99	1 435	21 876
Q2	18 159	203	48	18 314	20 702	477	–16	115	–2 964	18 314
Q3	21 939	177	49	22 067	20 435	818	–6	119	701	22 067
Q4	17 875	194	49	18 020	21 251	1 309	–19	129	–4 650	18 020
1998 Q1	20 400	133	49	20 484	21 984	708	20	312	–2 540	20 484
Q2	22 869	192	55	23 006	22 083	662	–26	195	92	23 006
Q3	22 981	214	55	23 140	22 959	1 094	42	130	–1 085	23 140
Q4	21 620	214	57	21 777	22 243	1 518	–4	73	–2 053	21 777
1999 Q1	25 734	247	58	25 923	23 998	52	–4	84	1 793	25 923
Q2	10 821	155	70	10 906	24 292	–1 550	14	150	–12 000	10 906
Q3	19 876	198	64	20 010	24 396	–453	–30	194	–4 097	20 010
Q4	22 226	154	65	22 315	24 468	376	13	285	–2 827	22 315
2000 Q1	23 132	164	64	23 232	24 513	1 039	–7	96	–2 409	23 232

1 Gross saving is equal to gross disposable income.
2 Net lending is positive, net borrowing is negative.

Source: Office for National Statistics; Enquiries 020 7533 6013

1.17 Balance of payments: summary
Balances (net transactions)

£ million

	Current Account										
	Trade in goods	Trade in services	**Total goods and services**	Compensation of employees	Investment income	**Total income**	**Current transfers**	**Current balance**	Capital Account	Financial Account	Net errors & omissions
	LQCT	KTMS	KTMY	KTMP	HMBM	HMBP	KTNF	HBOG	FKMJ	HBNT	HHDH
1946	−101	−274	−375	−20	88	68	166	−141	−21	181	−19
1947	−358	−197	−555	−19	159	140	123	−292	−21	552	−239
1948	−152	−64	−216	−20	252	232	96	112	−17	−58	−37
1949	−137	−43	−180	−20	234	214	29	63	−12	−103	52
1950	−54	−4	−58	−21	426	405	39	386	−10	−447	71
1951	−692	32	−660	−21	365	344	29	−287	−15	426	−124
1952	−272	123	−149	−22	265	243	169	263	−15	−229	−19
1953	−244	123	−121	−25	238	213	143	235	−13	−177	−45
1954	−210	115	−95	−27	261	234	55	194	−13	−174	−7
1955	−315	42	−273	−27	175	148	43	−82	−15	34	63
1956	50	26	76	−30	237	207	2	285	−13	−250	−22
1957	−29	121	92	−32	257	225	−5	312	−13	−313	14
1958	34	119	153	−34	303	269	4	426	−10	−411	−5
1959	−116	118	2	−37	269	232	–	234	−5	−68	−161
1960	−404	39	−365	−35	235	200	−6	−171	−6	−7	184
1961	−144	51	−93	−35	259	224	−9	122	−12	23	−133
1962	−104	50	−54	−37	346	309	−14	241	−12	−195	−34
1963	−123	4	−119	−38	416	378	−37	222	−16	−30	−176
1964	−551	−34	−585	−33	420	387	−62	−260	−17	392	−115
1965	−263	−66	−329	−34	467	433	−66	38	−18	49	−69
1966	−111	44	−67	−39	413	374	−89	218	−19	16	−215
1967	−601	157	−444	−39	411	372	−117	−189	−25	172	42
1968	−708	341	−367	−48	357	309	−89	−147	−26	672	−499
1969	−214	392	178	−47	543	496	−120	554	−23	−838	307
1970	−18	455	437	−56	612	556	−82	911	−22	−864	−25
1971	205	590	795	−63	560	497	−51	1 241	−23	−1 441	223
1972	−736	665	−71	−52	518	466	−51	344	−35	462	−771
1973	−2 573	760	−1 813	−68	1 283	1 215	−316	−914	−39	971	−18
1974	−5 241	1 065	−4 176	−92	1 429	1 337	−340	−3 179	−34	3 162	51
1975	−3 245	1 393	−1 852	−102	706	604	−317	−1 565	−36	1 554	47
1976	−3 930	2 465	−1 465	−140	1 385	1 245	−507	−727	−12	420	319
1977	−2 271	3 219	948	−152	−120	−272	−469	207	11	−3 665	3 447
1978	−1 534	3 679	2 145	−140	386	246	−958	1 433	−79	−2 798	1 444
1979	−3 326	3 965	639	−130	540	410	−961	88	−103	−97	112
1980	1 329	3 717	5 046	−82	−1 346	−1 428	−452	3 166	−4	−3 238	76
1981	3 238	3 834	7 072	−66	−369	−435	−88	6 549	−79	−6 612	142
1982	1 879	3 069	4 948	−95	−461	−556	−285	4 107	6	−2 010	−2 103
1983	−1 618	3 941	2 323	−89	1 205	1 116	−140	3 299	75	−4 068	694
1984	−5 409	4 341	−1 068	−94	2 497	2 403	−126	1 209	107	−8 009	6 693
1985	−3 416	6 619	3 203	−120	132	12	−988	2 227	185	−2 902	490
1986	−9 617	6 505	−3 112	−156	3 028	2 872	−2 045	−2 285	135	−2 341	4 491
1987	−11 698	6 686	−5 012	−174	1 677	1 503	−2 074	−5 583	333	5 065	185
1988	−21 553	4 330	−17 223	−64	1 355	1 291	−1 605	−17 537	235	15 135	2 167
1989	−24 724	3 917	−20 807	−138	74	−64	−2 620	−23 491	270	19 024	4 197
1990	−18 707	4 010	−14 697	−110	−448	−558	−4 258	−19 513	497	17 529	1 487
1991	−10 223	4 471	−5 752	−63	−1 890	−1 953	−669	−8 374	290	9 990	−1 906
1992	−13 050	5 674	−7 376	−49	2 164	2 115	−4 821	−10 082	421	5 716	3 945
1993	−13 319	6 623	−6 696	35	650	685	−4 607	−10 618	309	9 447	862
1994	−11 091	6 528	−4 563	−170	7 940	7 770	−4 665	−1 458	33	−6 082	7 507
1995	−11 724	8 915	−2 809	−296	6 272	5 976	−6 912	−3 745	534	937	2 274
1996	−13 086	8 897	−4 189	93	8 018	8 111	−4 522	−600	736	1 781	−1 917
1997	−11 910	12 414	504	83	11 087	11 170	−5 051	6 623	804	−13 186	5 759
1998	−20 537	12 582	−7 955	−10	14 255	14 245	−6 370	−80	473	−4 677	4 284
1999	−26 767	11 538	−15 229	201	8 131	8 332	−4 084	−10 981	776	5 853	4 352

Source: Office for National Statistics; Enquiries 020 7533 6078

1.17 Balance of payments: summary
Balances (net transactions)

continued

£ million, not seasonally adjusted

	Current Account										
	Trade in goods	Trade in services	**Total goods and services**	Compensation of employees	Investment income	**Total income**	**Current transfers**	**Current balance**	Capital Account	Financial Account	Net errors & omissions
	LQCT	KTMS	KTMY	KTMP	HMBM	HMBP	KTNF	HBOG	FKMJ	HBNT	HHDH
1955 Q1	−96	14	−82	−7	56	49	20	−13	−4	−15	32
Q2	−95	27	−68	−7	57	50	13	−5	−3	−53	61
Q3	−84	−6	−90	−7	76	69	11	−10	−3	70	−57
Q4	−40	7	−33	−6	−14	−20	−1	−54	−5	32	27
1956 Q1	−12	8	−4	−6	50	44	2	42	−3	−158	119
Q2	21	22	43	−8	57	49	−5	87	−3	−141	57
Q3	−17	−6	−23	−8	78	70	7	54	−3	−82	31
Q4	58	2	60	−8	52	44	−2	102	−4	131	−229
1957 Q1	−36	40	4	−8	50	42	−1	45	−3	−102	60
Q2	−8	48	40	−9	63	54	4	98	−3	−99	4
Q3	−26	10	−16	−8	86	78	2	64	−3	114	−175
Q4	41	23	64	−7	58	51	−10	105	−4	−226	125
1958 Q1	31	50	81	−8	101	93	−8	166	−3	−220	57
Q2	19	31	50	−10	45	35	8	93	−2	−108	17
Q3	−5	8	3	−8	118	110	4	117	−2	−79	−36
Q4	−11	30	19	−8	39	31	–	50	−3	−4	−43
1959 Q1	−22	53	31	−9	65	56	−9	78	−1	−107	30
Q2	−1	23	22	−10	87	77	7	106	−1	18	−123
Q3	−56	11	−45	−9	99	90	−1	44	−1	−35	−8
Q4	−37	31	−6	−9	18	9	3	6	−2	56	−60
1960 Q1	−68	12	−56	−8	71	63	−6	1	−2	−95	96
Q2	−92	9	−83	−9	50	41	2	−40	−1	14	27
Q3	−147	−6	−153	−9	73	64	−2	−91	−1	52	40
Q4	−97	24	−73	−9	41	32	–	−41	−2	22	21
1961 Q1	−65	27	−38	−9	101	92	−8	46	−3	35	−78
Q2	−49	10	−39	−9	57	48	−5	4	−2	16	−18
Q3	−31	−12	−43	−8	94	86	–	43	−4	−35	−4
Q4	1	26	27	−9	7	−2	4	29	−3	7	−33
1962 Q1	−50	24	−26	−9	118	109	−13	70	−4	−114	48
Q2	15	5	20	−9	102	93	−2	111	−2	−43	−66
Q3	−60	−9	−69	−9	100	91	−1	21	−3	−65	47
Q4	−9	30	21	−10	26	16	2	39	−3	27	−63
1963 Q1	2	25	27	−10	121	111	−13	125	−4	−87	−34
Q2	–	−1	−1	−10	105	95	−6	88	−4	6	−90
Q3	−74	−35	−109	−9	130	121	−10	2	−5	12	−9
Q4	−51	15	−36	−9	60	51	−8	7	−3	39	−43
1964 Q1	−129	3	−126	−9	144	135	−25	−16	−5	4	17
Q2	−107	−12	−119	−8	104	96	−18	−41	−3	62	−18
Q3	−182	−43	−225	−8	96	88	−6	−143	−6	205	−56
Q4	−133	18	−115	−8	76	68	−13	−60	−3	121	−58
1965 Q1	−87	6	−81	−9	127	118	−24	13	−5	54	−62
Q2	−56	−10	−66	−9	121	112	−20	26	−4	−58	36
Q3	−94	−66	−160	−8	125	117	−18	−61	−5	133	−67
Q4	−26	4	−22	−8	94	86	−4	60	−4	−80	24
1966 Q1	−65	12	−53	−10	113	103	−26	24	−5	47	−66
Q2	−89	9	−80	−10	132	122	−30	12	−4	64	−72
Q3	−103	−28	−131	−9	115	106	−16	−41	−5	44	2
Q4	146	51	197	−10	53	43	−17	223	−5	−139	−79
1967 Q1	−77	60	−17	−11	122	111	−26	68	−6	−159	97
Q2	−91	32	−59	−9	89	80	−32	−11	−6	−65	82
Q3	−136	18	−118	−10	124	114	−29	−33	−7	155	−115
Q4	−297	47	−250	−9	76	67	−30	−213	−6	241	−22
1968 Q1	−214	47	−167	−14	98	84	−29	−112	−7	396	−277
Q2	−197	88	−109	−11	118	107	−26	−28	−7	156	−121
Q3	−195	94	−101	−12	117	105	−24	−20	−6	96	−70
Q4	−102	112	10	−11	24	13	−10	13	−6	24	−31
1969 Q1	−194	89	−105	−12	186	174	−36	33	−7	−213	187
Q2	−26	100	74	−12	147	135	−38	171	−6	−130	−35
Q3	−14	107	93	−12	131	119	−26	186	−5	−4	−177
Q4	20	96	116	−11	79	68	−20	164	−5	−491	332

Source: Office for National Statistics; Enquiries 020 7533 6078

1.17 Balance of payments: summary Balances (net transactions)

continued

£ million, not seasonally adjusted

	Current Account										
	Trade in goods	Trade in services	**Total goods and services**	Compensation of employees	Investment income	**Total income**	**Current transfers**	**Current balance**	Capital Account	Financial Account	Net errors & omissions
	LQCT	KTMS	KTMY	KTMP	HMBM	HMBP	KTNF	HBOG	FKMJ	HBNT	HHDH
1970 Q1	27	139	166	−12	173	161	−26	301	−6	−610	315
Q2	−56	115	59	−15	184	169	−23	205	−5	−20	−180
Q3	−100	105	5	−14	161	147	−18	134	−6	43	−171
Q4	111	96	207	−15	94	79	−15	271	−5	−277	11
1971 Q1	−162	127	−35	−15	176	161	−10	116	−6	−468	358
Q2	112	132	244	−15	163	148	−20	372	−5	−246	−121
Q3	146	150	296	−16	160	144	−15	425	−6	−183	−236
Q4	109	181	290	−17	61	44	−6	328	−6	−544	222
1972 Q1	−214	156	−58	−14	143	129	−20	51	−8	−175	132
Q2	−46	179	133	−12	168	156	−18	271	−8	204	−467
Q3	−338	142	−196	−13	144	131	−16	−81	−9	68	22
Q4	−138	188	50	−13	63	50	3	103	−10	365	−458
1973 Q1	−570	146	−424	−17	141	124	−55	−355	−8	101	262
Q2	−427	177	−250	−16	383	367	−123	−6	−12	308	−290
Q3	−653	207	−446	−17	311	294	−63	−215	−10	28	197
Q4	−923	230	−693	−18	448	430	−75	−338	−9	534	−187
1974 Q1	−1 335	195	−1 140	−21	397	376	−84	−848	−10	849	9
Q2	−1 398	224	−1 174	−21	416	395	−85	−864	−7	1 005	−134
Q3	−1 268	361	−907	−25	323	298	−79	−688	−9	482	215
Q4	−1 240	285	−955	−25	293	268	−92	−779	−8	826	−39
1975 Q1	−984	309	−675	−23	158	135	−40	−580	−9	374	215
Q2	−680	299	−381	−25	125	100	−95	−376	−10	642	−256
Q3	−986	395	−591	−25	193	168	−80	−503	−9	469	43
Q4	−595	390	−205	−29	230	201	−102	−106	−8	69	45
1976 Q1	−673	542	−131	−36	261	225	−128	−34	−5	−31	70
Q2	−1 042	485	−557	−36	338	302	−123	−378	−4	160	222
Q3	−1 166	774	−392	−33	418	385	−126	−133	−4	234	−97
Q4	−1 049	664	−385	−35	368	333	−130	−182	1	57	124
1977 Q1	−1 082	641	−441	−38	76	38	−146	−549	9	−411	951
Q2	−915	713	−202	−40	−123	−163	−94	−459	−4	−1 069	1 532
Q3	−134	1 037	903	−36	4	−32	−141	730	−6	−1 516	792
Q4	−140	828	688	−38	−77	−115	−88	485	12	−669	172
1978 Q1	−693	797	104	−37	41	4	−368	−260	−23	−282	565
Q2	−193	690	497	−37	83	46	−215	328	−22	−696	390
Q3	−466	1 169	703	−31	256	225	−270	658	−19	−471	−168
Q4	−182	1 023	841	−35	6	−29	−105	707	−15	−1 349	657
1979 Q1	−1 640	881	−759	−31	393	362	−317	−714	−28	−796	1 538
Q2	−578	770	192	−34	−79	−113	−204	−125	−27	201	−49
Q3	−511	1 182	671	−28	437	409	−255	825	−27	−86	−712
Q4	−597	1 132	535	−37	−211	−248	−185	102	−21	584	−665
1980 Q1	−678	898	220	−20	−269	−289	−127	−196	10	−1 153	1 339
Q2	−318	694	376	−24	−541	−565	−144	−333	−34	−106	473
Q3	855	1 005	1 860	−16	−239	−255	−237	1 368	−1	−280	−1 087
Q4	1 470	1 120	2 590	−22	−297	−319	56	2 327	21	−1 699	−649
1981 Q1	1 458	1 098	2 556	−21	27	6	285	2 847	−46	−4 065	1 264
Q2	1 088	751	1 839	−21	−25	−46	−354	1 439	−37	−2 363	961
Q3	−146	1 036	890	−9	−32	−41	−306	543	−33	−494	−16
Q4	838	949	1 787	−15	−339	−354	287	1 720	37	310	−2 067
1982 Q1	−30	1 067	1 037	−28	−321	−349	507	1 195	−14	−77	−1 104
Q2	−108	548	440	−30	−124	−154	−465	−179	−7	1 197	−1 011
Q3	530	567	1 097	−15	9	−6	−312	779	−3	−1 686	910
Q4	1 487	887	2 374	−22	−25	−47	−15	2 312	30	−1 444	−898
1983 Q1	−442	1 148	706	−29	425	396	315	1 417	5	−2 043	621
Q2	−951	786	−165	−29	−80	−109	−297	−571	–	182	389
Q3	−338	916	578	−12	775	763	−129	1 212	48	552	−1 812
Q4	113	1 091	1 204	−19	85	66	−29	1 241	22	−2 759	1 496
1984 Q1	−748	1 224	476	−41	394	353	101	930	52	−1 211	229
Q2	−1 834	847	−987	−30	456	426	−295	−856	−5	−2 098	2 959
Q3	−1 730	1 029	−701	−4	817	813	−292	−180	6	−1 279	1 453
Q4	−1 097	1 241	144	−19	830	811	360	1 315	54	−3 421	2 052

Source: Office for National Statistics; Enquiries 020 7533 6078

1.17 Balance of payments: summary
Balances (net transactions)

continued

£ million, not seasonally adjusted

	Current Account										
	Trade in goods	Trade in services	**Total goods and services**	Compensation of employees	Investment income	**Total income**	**Current transfers**	**Current balance**	Capital Account	Financial Account	Net errors & omissions
	LQCT	KTMS	KTMY	KTMP	HMBM	HMBP	KTNF	HBOG	FKMJ	HBNT	HHDH
1985 Q1	−2 101	1 477	−624	−54	195	141	−243	−726	58	−2 055	2 723
Q2	−749	1 583	834	−31	56	25	−208	651	16	−176	−491
Q3	−799	1 835	1 036	−11	443	432	−502	966	54	−4 893	3 873
Q4	233	1 724	1 957	−24	−562	−586	−35	1 336	57	4 222	−5 615
1986 Q1	−2 052	1 803	−249	−66	504	438	−225	−36	89	−738	685
Q2	−2 338	1 391	−947	−45	786	741	−359	−565	−52	−1 317	1 932
Q3	−3 202	1 429	−1 773	−17	1 128	1 111	−834	−1 496	76	2 624	−1 207
Q4	−2 025	1 882	−143	−28	610	582	−627	−188	22	−2 910	3 081
1987 Q1	−2 170	1 963	−207	−85	863	778	−331	240	114	503	−857
Q2	−3 139	1 650	−1 489	−56	353	297	−390	−1 582	21	3 020	−1 459
Q3	−3 546	1 562	−1 984	−15	734	719	−721	−1 986	86	−2 155	4 055
Q4	−2 843	1 511	−1 332	−18	−273	−291	−632	−2 255	112	3 697	−1 554
1988 Q1	−4 635	1 353	−3 282	−33	215	182	−727	−3 827	47	8 439	−4 659
Q2	−5 122	1 016	−4 106	−24	465	441	−383	−4 048	13	709	3 326
Q3	−6 065	871	−5 194	9	733	742	363	−4 089	38	1 205	2 846
Q4	−5 731	1 090	−4 641	−16	−58	−74	−858	−5 573	137	4 782	654
1989 Q1	−6 459	1 113	−5 346	−32	423	391	−563	−5 518	140	10 598	−5 220
Q2	−7 260	1 095	−6 165	−55	57	2	−387	−6 550	67	776	5 707
Q3	−7 345	734	−6 611	−7	134	127	−757	−7 241	−3	5 774	1 470
Q4	−3 660	975	−2 685	−44	−540	−584	−913	−4 182	66	1 876	2 240
1990 Q1	−6 409	1 404	−5 005	−54	−621	−675	−1 055	−6 735	225	8 475	−1 965
Q2	−5 774	768	−5 006	−14	−487	−501	−1 051	−6 558	34	1 521	5 003
Q3	−4 998	642	−4 356	−3	817	814	−809	−4 351	59	3 524	768
Q4	−1 526	1 196	−330	−39	−157	−196	−1 343	−1 869	179	4 009	−2 319
1991 Q1	−3 727	1 202	−2 525	−48	−1 139	−1 187	−53	−3 765	9	−520	4 276
Q2	−2 540	1 008	−1 532	−13	−597	−610	419	−1 723	114	−8 479	10 088
Q3	−3 257	1 007	−2 250	16	54	70	−683	−2 863	43	1 948	872
Q4	−699	1 254	555	−18	−208	−226	−352	−23	124	17 041	−17 142
1992 Q1	−3 472	1 688	−1 784	−48	150	102	−1 129	−2 811	126	−8 891	11 576
Q2	−3 443	1 248	−2 195	34	−179	−145	−1 309	−3 649	111	4 601	−1 063
Q3	−3 995	1 074	−2 921	−19	1 605	1 586	−1 513	−2 848	100	3 024	−276
Q4	−2 140	1 664	−476	−16	588	572	−870	−774	84	6 982	−6 292
1993 Q1	−3 468	2 169	−1 299	−92	−185	−277	−1 421	−2 997	95	−6 918	9 820
Q2	−4 102	863	−3 239	−9	−232	−241	−975	−4 455	2	8 150	−3 697
Q3	−3 914	1 404	−2 510	92	1 183	1 275	−1 364	−2 599	114	8 426	−5 941
Q4	−1 835	2 187	352	44	−116	−72	−847	−567	98	−211	680
1994 Q1	−3 114	2 089	−1 025	−29	1 916	1 887	−1 655	−793	247	−6 161	6 707
Q2	−3 514	1 066	−2 448	−43	1 376	1 333	−1 360	−2 475	−197	3 511	−839
Q3	−2 702	1 485	−1 217	−48	3 029	2 981	−1 482	282	−51	−1 247	1 016
Q4	−1 761	1 888	127	−50	1 619	1 569	−168	1 528	34	−2 185	623
1995 Q1	−939	2 858	1 919	−252	941	689	−1 247	1 361	291	1 657	−3 309
Q2	−4 413	1 516	−2 897	6	563	569	−1 570	−3 898	65	−588	4 421
Q3	−4 491	1 909	−2 582	22	2 964	2 986	−1 759	−1 355	48	−3 029	4 336
Q4	−1 881	2 632	751	−72	1 804	1 732	−2 336	147	130	2 897	−3 174
1996 Q1	−3 114	2 326	−788	24	1 146	1 170	−970	−588	260	−3 196	3 524
Q2	−4 904	1 636	−3 268	8	3 156	3 164	−1 422	−1 526	116	1 867	−457
Q3	−3 681	2 059	−1 622	53	2 402	2 455	−1 193	−360	255	−277	382
Q4	−1 387	2 876	1 489	8	1 314	1 322	−937	1 874	105	3 387	−5 366
1997 Q1	−1 925	3 250	1 325	−32	2 254	2 222	−891	2 656	216	−5 698	2 826
Q2	−4 066	2 722	−1 344	−18	3 307	3 289	−1 113	832	68	584	−1 484
Q3	−3 271	2 936	−335	78	3 981	4 059	−1 920	1 804	193	−4 433	2 436
Q4	−2 648	3 506	858	55	1 545	1 600	−1 127	1 331	327	−3 639	1 981
1998 Q1	−4 211	3 315	−896	−12	2 277	2 265	−1 518	−149	−13	−5 496	5 658
Q2	−5 628	2 960	−2 668	−23	2 937	2 914	−944	−698	−41	−1 204	1 943
Q3	−5 844	3 130	−2 714	28	5 516	5 544	−1 473	1 357	229	−3 783	2 197
Q4	−4 854	3 177	−1 677	−3	3 525	3 522	−2 435	−590	298	5 806	−5 514
1999 Q1	−7 488	3 199	−4 289	−36	993	957	−561	−3 893	−21	1 744	2 170
Q2	−6 282	2 817	−3 465	85	2 182	2 267	−750	−1 948	250	3 075	−1 377
Q3	−7 006	2 546	−4 460	108	1 868	1 976	−1 766	−4 250	256	3 278	716
Q4	−5 991	2 976	−3 015	44	3 088	3 132	−1 007	−890	291	−2 244	2 843
2000 Q1	−6 571	3 162	−3 409	−60	−419	−479	−336	−4 224	218	3 300	706

Source: Office for National Statistics; Enquiries 020 7533 6078

1.18 Balance of payments: current account

£ million

	Credits									
	Trade in goods	Trade in services	**Total goods and services**	Compensation of employees	Investment income	**Total income**	Central govt current transfers	Other sectors current transfers	**Total current transfers**	**Total current account**
	LQAD	KTMQ	KTMW	KTMN	HMBN	HMBQ	FJUM	FJUN	KTND	HBOE
1946	978	447	1 425	5	217	222	..	..	267	1 914
1947	1 200	447	1 647	7	286	293	..	..	226	2 166
1948	1 663	528	2 191	7	395	402	..	..	188	2 781
1949	1 891	598	2 489	8	385	393	..	..	107	2 989
1950	2 293	695	2 988	9	612	621	..	..	112	3 721
1951	2 779	860	3 639	11	607	618	..	..	124	4 381
1952	2 817	933	3 750	12	549	561	..	..	268	4 579
1953	2 729	948	3 677	12	543	555	..	..	239	4 471
1954	2 829	998	3 827	12	593	605	..	..	156	4 588
1955	3 127	1 039	4 166	15	567	582	..	..	156	4 904
1956	3 439	1 147	4 586	16	628	644	..	..	142	5 372
1957	3 573	1 250	4 823	17	639	656	..	..	139	5 618
1958	3 470	1 218	4 688	17	749	766	..	..	142	5 596
1959	3 587	1 249	4 836	17	722	739	..	..	141	5 716
1960	3 801	1 333	5 134	17	737	754	..	..	146	6 034
1961	3 967	1 399	5 366	19	742	761	..	..	155	6 282
1962	4 065	1 435	5 500	19	828	847	..	..	155	6 502
1963	4 395	1 457	5 852	20	925	945	..	..	142	6 939
1964	4 632	1 551	6 183	25	988	1 013	..	..	233	7 429
1965	4 983	1 613	6 596	24	1 105	1 129	..	..	235	7 960
1966	5 348	1 800	7 148	25	1 074	1 099	..	..	227	8 474
1967	5 329	2 041	7 370	24	1 100	1 124	..	..	252	8 746
1968	6 537	2 425	8 962	26	1 246	1 272	..	..	327	10 561
1969	7 373	2 691	10 064	33	1 510	1 543	..	..	351	11 958
1970	8 266	3 223	11 489	33	1 641	1 674	..	..	412	13 575
1971	9 190	3 700	12 890	39	1 687	1 726	..	..	482	15 098
1972	9 587	4 000	13 587	49	3 735	3 784	..	..	561	17 932
1973	12 091	4 936	17 027	59	5 405	5 464	..	..	709	23 200
1974	16 546	6 285	22 831	69	6 817	6 886	..	..	770	30 487
1975	19 451	7 352	26 803	88	7 204	7 292	..	..	1 010	35 105
1976	25 404	9 614	35 018	114	9 208	9 322	..	..	1 179	45 519
1977	32 041	11 169	43 210	139	9 675	9 814	..	..	1 670	54 694
1978	35 331	12 048	47 379	159	12 271	12 430	..	..	2 140	61 949
1979	40 849	13 955	54 804	176	19 213	19 389	..	..	3 070	77 263
1980	47 493	15 002	62 495	219	25 991	26 210	..	..	3 813	92 518
1981	51 034	16 281	67 315	238	41 189	41 427	..	..	4 863	113 605
1982	55 657	16 922	72 579	252	48 728	48 980	..	..	5 572	127 131
1983	60 984	18 767	79 751	290	46 591	46 881	..	..	6 213	132 845
1984	70 565	20 944	91 509	323	56 655	56 978	..	..	7 079	155 566
1985	78 291	23 635	101 926	344	57 083	57 427	..	..	7 508	166 861
1986	72 997	24 784	97 781	369	51 958	52 327	1 932	4 374	6 306	156 414
1987	79 531	26 906	106 437	413	52 684	53 097	4 118	4 412	8 530	168 064
1988	80 711	26 723	107 434	445	61 932	62 377	5 160	4 514	9 674	179 485
1989	92 611	29 272	121 883	476	81 799	82 275	4 924	5 161	10 085	214 243
1990	102 313	31 188	133 501	543	88 186	88 729	4 294	5 956	10 250	232 480
1991	103 939	31 426	135 365	551	84 419	84 970	6 746	7 493	14 239	234 574
1992	107 863	35 428	143 291	551	74 549	75 100	4 254	7 386	11 640	230 031
1993	122 039	40 039	162 078	595	78 825	79 420	5 306	7 958	13 264	254 762
1994	135 260	43 507	178 767	681	82 639	83 320	5 008	7 801	12 809	274 896
1995	153 725	48 687	202 412	887	97 086	97 973	4 845	8 518	13 363	313 748
1996	167 403	52 900	220 303	911	101 669	102 580	6 754	14 632	21 386	344 269
1997	171 783	57 543	229 326	1 007	106 898	107 905	5 979	9 326	15 305	352 536
1998	164 092	61 382	225 474	840	108 392	109 232	6 381	9 043	15 424	350 130
1999	165 667	63 982	229 649	960	108 139	109 099	9 464	8 814	18 278	357 026

Source: Office for National Statistics; Enquiries 020 7533 6078

1.18 Balance of payments: current account

continued

£ million

	Debits									
	Trade in goods	Trade in services	**Total goods and services**	Compensation of employees	Investment income	**Total income**	Central govt current transfers	Other sectors current transfers	**Total current transfers**	**Total current account**
	LQBL	KTMR	KTMX	KTMO	HMBO	HMBR	FJUO	FJUP	KTNE	HBOF
1946	1 079	721	1 800	25	129	154	..	..	101	2 055
1947	1 558	644	2 202	26	127	153	..	..	103	2 458
1948	1 815	592	2 407	27	143	170	..	..	92	2 669
1949	2 028	641	2 669	28	151	179	..	..	78	2 926
1950	2 347	699	3 046	30	186	216	..	..	73	3 335
1951	3 471	828	4 299	32	242	274	..	..	95	4 668
1952	3 089	810	3 899	34	284	318	..	..	99	4 316
1953	2 973	825	3 798	37	305	342	..	..	96	4 236
1954	3 039	883	3 922	39	332	371	..	..	101	4 394
1955	3 442	997	4 439	42	392	434	..	..	113	4 986
1956	3 389	1 121	4 510	46	391	437	..	..	140	5 087
1957	3 602	1 129	4 731	49	382	431	..	..	144	5 306
1958	3 436	1 099	4 535	51	446	497	..	..	138	5 170
1959	3 703	1 131	4 834	54	453	507	..	..	141	5 482
1960	4 205	1 294	5 499	52	502	554	..	..	152	6 205
1961	4 111	1 348	5 459	54	483	537	..	..	164	6 160
1962	4 169	1 385	5 554	56	482	538	..	..	169	6 261
1963	4 518	1 453	5 971	58	509	567	..	..	179	6 717
1964	5 183	1 585	6 768	58	568	626	..	..	295	7 689
1965	5 246	1 679	6 925	58	638	696	..	..	301	7 922
1966	5 459	1 756	7 215	64	661	725	..	..	316	8 256
1967	5 930	1 884	7 814	63	689	752	..	..	369	8 935
1968	7 245	2 084	9 329	74	889	963	..	..	416	10 708
1969	7 587	2 299	9 886	80	967	1 047	..	..	471	11 404
1970	8 284	2 768	11 052	89	1 029	1 118	..	..	494	12 664
1971	8 985	3 110	12 095	102	1 127	1 229	..	..	533	13 857
1972	10 323	3 335	13 658	101	3 217	3 318	..	..	612	17 588
1973	14 664	4 176	18 840	127	4 122	4 249	..	..	1 025	24 114
1974	21 787	5 220	27 007	161	5 388	5 549	..	..	1 110	33 666
1975	22 696	5 959	28 655	190	6 498	6 688	..	..	1 327	36 670
1976	29 334	7 149	36 483	254	7 823	8 077	..	..	1 686	46 246
1977	34 312	7 950	42 262	291	9 795	10 086	..	..	2 139	54 487
1978	36 865	8 369	45 234	299	11 885	12 184	..	..	3 098	60 516
1979	44 175	9 990	54 165	306	18 673	18 979	..	..	4 031	77 175
1980	46 164	11 285	57 449	301	27 337	27 638	..	..	4 265	89 352
1981	47 796	12 447	60 243	304	41 558	41 862	..	..	4 951	107 056
1982	53 778	13 853	67 631	347	49 189	49 536	..	..	5 857	123 024
1983	62 602	14 826	77 428	379	45 386	45 765	..	..	6 353	129 546
1984	75 974	16 603	92 577	417	54 158	54 575	..	..	7 205	154 357
1985	81 707	17 016	98 723	464	56 951	57 415	..	..	8 496	164 634
1986	82 614	18 279	100 893	525	48 930	49 455	1 261	7 090	8 351	158 699
1987	91 229	20 220	111 449	587	51 007	51 594	1 316	9 288	10 604	173 647
1988	102 264	22 393	124 657	509	60 577	61 086	2 226	9 053	11 279	197 022
1989	117 335	25 355	142 690	614	81 725	82 339	2 055	10 650	12 705	237 734
1990	121 020	27 178	148 198	653	88 634	89 287	1 995	12 513	14 508	251 993
1991	114 162	26 955	141 117	614	86 309	86 923	3 218	11 690	14 908	242 948
1992	120 913	29 754	150 667	600	72 385	72 985	3 506	12 955	16 461	240 113
1993	135 358	33 416	168 774	560	78 175	78 735	4 156	13 715	17 871	265 380
1994	146 351	36 979	183 330	851	74 699	75 550	4 795	12 679	17 474	276 354
1995	165 449	39 772	205 221	1 183	90 814	91 997	4 795	15 480	20 275	317 493
1996	180 489	44 003	224 492	818	93 651	94 469	5 056	20 852	25 908	344 869
1997	183 693	45 129	228 822	924	95 811	96 735	5 087	15 269	20 356	345 913
1998	184 629	48 800	233 429	850	94 137	94 987	6 585	15 209	21 794	350 210
1999	192 434	52 444	244 878	759	100 008	100 767	7 278	15 084	22 362	368 007

Source: Office for National Statistics ; Enquiries 020 7533 6078

1.18 Balance of payments: current account

continued

£ million

	Balances(credits less debits)									
	Trade in goods	Trade in services	**Total goods and services**	Compensation of employees	Investment income	**Total income**	Central govt current transfers	Other sectors current transfers	**Total current transfers**	**Total current account**
	LQCT	KTMS	KTMY	KTMP	HMBM	HMBP	FJUQ	FJUR	KTNF	HBOG
1946	−101	−274	−375	−20	88	68	..	..	166	−141
1947	−358	−197	−555	−19	159	140	..	..	123	−292
1948	−152	−64	−216	−20	252	232	..	..	96	112
1949	−137	−43	−180	−20	234	214	..	..	29	63
1950	−54	−4	−58	−21	426	405	..	..	39	386
1951	−692	32	−660	−21	365	344	..	..	29	−287
1952	−272	123	−149	−22	265	243	..	..	169	263
1953	−244	123	−121	−25	238	213	..	..	143	235
1954	−210	115	−95	−27	261	234	..	..	55	194
1955	−315	42	−273	−27	175	148	..	..	43	−82
1956	50	26	76	−30	237	207	..	..	2	285
1957	−29	121	92	−32	257	225	..	..	−5	312
1958	34	119	153	−34	303	269	..	..	4	426
1959	−116	118	2	−37	269	232	..	..	–	234
1960	−404	39	−365	−35	235	200	..	..	−6	−171
1961	−144	51	−93	−35	259	224	..	..	−9	122
1962	−104	50	−54	−37	346	309	..	..	−14	241
1963	−123	4	−119	−38	416	378	..	..	−37	222
1964	−551	−34	−585	−33	420	387	..	..	−62	−260
1965	−263	−66	−329	−34	467	433	..	..	−66	38
1966	−111	44	−67	−39	413	374	..	..	−89	218
1967	−601	157	−444	−39	411	372	..	..	−117	−189
1968	−708	341	−367	−48	357	309	..	..	−89	−147
1969	−214	392	178	−47	543	496	..	..	−120	554
1970	−18	455	437	−56	612	556	..	..	−82	911
1971	205	590	795	−63	560	497	..	..	−51	1 241
1972	−736	665	−71	−52	518	466	..	..	−51	344
1973	−2 573	760	−1 813	−68	1 283	1 215	..	..	−316	−914
1974	−5 241	1 065	−4 176	−92	1 429	1 337	..	..	−340	−3 179
1975	−3 245	1 393	−1 852	−102	706	604	..	..	−317	−1 565
1976	−3 930	2 465	−1 465	−140	1 385	1 245	..	..	−507	−727
1977	−2 271	3 219	948	−152	−120	−272	..	..	−469	207
1978	−1 534	3 679	2 145	−140	386	246	..	..	−958	1 433
1979	−3 326	3 965	639	−130	540	410	..	..	−961	88
1980	1 329	3 717	5 046	−82	−1 346	−1 428	..	..	−452	3 166
1981	3 238	3 834	7 072	−66	−369	−435	..	..	−88	6 549
1982	1 879	3 069	4 948	−95	−461	−556	..	..	−285	4 107
1983	−1 618	3 941	2 323	−89	1 205	1 116	..	..	−140	3 299
1984	−5 409	4 341	−1 068	−94	2 497	2 403	..	..	−126	1 209
1985	−3 416	6 619	3 203	−120	132	12	..	..	−988	2 227
1986	−9 617	6 505	−3 112	−156	3 028	2 872	671	−2 716	−2 045	−2 285
1987	−11 698	6 686	−5 012	−174	1 677	1 503	2 802	−4 876	−2 074	−5 583
1988	−21 553	4 330	−17 223	−64	1 355	1 291	2 934	−4 539	−1 605	−17 537
1989	−24 724	3 917	−20 807	−138	74	−64	2 869	−5 489	−2 620	−23 491
1990	−18 707	4 010	−14 697	−110	−448	−558	2 299	−6 557	−4 258	−19 513
1991	−10 223	4 471	−5 752	−63	−1 890	−1 953	3 528	−4 197	−669	−8 374
1992	−13 050	5 674	−7 376	−49	2 164	2 115	748	−5 569	−4 821	−10 082
1993	−13 319	6 623	−6 696	35	650	685	1 150	−5 757	−4 607	−10 618
1994	−11 091	6 528	−4 563	−170	7 940	7 770	213	−4 878	−4 665	−1 458
1995	−11 724	8 915	−2 809	−296	6 272	5 976	50	−6 962	−6 912	−3 745
1996	−13 086	8 897	−4 189	93	8 018	8 111	1 698	−6 220	−4 522	−600
1997	−11 910	12 414	504	83	11 087	11 170	892	−5 943	−5 051	6 623
1998	−20 537	12 582	−7 955	−10	14 255	14 245	−204	−6 166	−6 370	−80
1999	−26 767	11 538	−15 229	201	8 131	8 332	2 186	−6 270	−4 084	−10 981

Source: Office for National Statistics; Enquiries 020 7533 6078

1.18 Balance of payments: current account

continued

£ million,not seasonally adjusted

	Credits									
	Trade in goods	Trade in services	**Total goods and services**	Compensation of employees	Investment income	**Total income**	Central govt current transfers	Other sectors current transfers	**Total current transfers**	**Total current account**
	LQAD	KTMQ	KTMW	KTMN	HMBN	HMBQ	FJUM	FJUN	KTND	HBOE
1955 Q1	799	253	1 052	4	124	128	..	..	49	1 229
Q2	700	271	971	3	139	142	..	..	41	1 154
Q3	786	268	1 054	4	158	162	..	..	36	1 252
Q4	842	247	1 089	4	146	150	..	..	30	1 269
1956 Q1	850	280	1 130	4	136	140	..	..	37	1 307
Q2	883	296	1 179	4	153	157	..	..	32	1 368
Q3	801	298	1 099	4	175	179	..	..	38	1 316
Q4	905	273	1 178	4	164	168	..	..	35	1 381
1957 Q1	907	312	1 219	4	140	144	..	..	40	1 403
Q2	906	326	1 232	4	159	163	..	..	37	1 432
Q3	855	324	1 179	4	179	183	..	..	33	1 395
Q4	905	288	1 193	5	161	166	..	..	29	1 388
1958 Q1	896	295	1 191	4	203	207	..	..	34	1 432
Q2	838	307	1 145	4	147	151	..	..	38	1 334
Q3	850	326	1 176	4	212	216	..	..	35	1 427
Q4	886	290	1 176	5	187	192	..	..	35	1 403
1959 Q1	862	297	1 159	4	155	159	..	..	32	1 350
Q2	907	313	1 220	4	191	195	..	..	37	1 452
Q3	850	338	1 188	4	196	200	..	..	35	1 423
Q4	968	301	1 269	5	180	185	..	..	37	1 491
1960 Q1	985	309	1 294	4	175	179	..	..	35	1 508
Q2	961	328	1 289	4	165	169	..	..	36	1 494
Q3	883	370	1 253	4	194	198	..	..	37	1 488
Q4	972	326	1 298	5	203	208	..	..	38	1 544
1961 Q1	1 014	339	1 353	4	198	202	..	..	35	1 590
Q2	1 005	348	1 353	5	168	173	..	..	40	1 566
Q3	938	380	1 318	5	207	212	..	..	40	1 570
Q4	1 010	332	1 342	5	169	174	..	..	40	1 556
1962 Q1	1 002	340	1 342	4	220	224	..	..	40	1 606
Q2	1 054	357	1 411	5	212	217	..	..	40	1 668
Q3	961	391	1 352	5	207	212	..	..	37	1 601
Q4	1 048	347	1 395	5	189	194	..	..	38	1 627
1963 Q1	1 086	339	1 425	4	233	237	..	..	38	1 700
Q2	1 114	360	1 474	5	221	226	..	..	36	1 736
Q3	1 047	402	1 449	5	245	250	..	..	34	1 733
Q4	1 148	356	1 504	6	226	232	..	..	34	1 770
1964 Q1	1 168	356	1 524	5	271	276	..	..	59	1 859
Q2	1 188	384	1 572	6	254	260	..	..	60	1 892
Q3	1 073	429	1 502	7	236	243	..	..	58	1 803
Q4	1 203	382	1 585	7	227	234	..	..	56	1 875
1965 Q1	1 189	371	1 560	5	278	283	..	..	58	1 901
Q2	1 260	413	1 673	6	283	289	..	..	59	2 021
Q3	1 203	439	1 642	6	275	281	..	..	57	1 980
Q4	1 331	390	1 721	7	269	276	..	..	61	2 058
1966 Q1	1 348	402	1 750	5	271	276	..	..	55	2 081
Q2	1 274	449	1 723	6	291	297	..	..	58	2 078
Q3	1 270	507	1 777	7	263	270	..	..	55	2 102
Q4	1 456	442	1 898	7	249	256	..	..	59	2 213
1967 Q1	1 411	446	1 857	5	271	276	..	..	59	2 192
Q2	1 411	477	1 888	6	260	266	..	..	65	2 219
Q3	1 261	579	1 840	6	267	273	..	..	62	2 175
Q4	1 246	539	1 785	7	302	309	..	..	66	2 160
1968 Q1	1 609	526	2 135	5	301	306	..	..	79	2 520
Q2	1 591	595	2 186	7	340	347	..	..	81	2 614
Q3	1 597	698	2 295	7	328	335	..	..	79	2 709
Q4	1 740	606	2 346	7	277	284	..	..	88	2 718
1969 Q1	1 695	610	2 305	8	389	397	..	..	82	2 784
Q2	1 884	660	2 544	8	385	393	..	..	85	3 022
Q3	1 821	767	2 588	8	368	376	..	..	93	3 057
Q4	1 973	654	2 627	9	368	377	..	..	91	3 095

Source: Office for National Statistics; Enquiries 020 7533 6078

1.18 Balance of payments: current account

continued

£ million, not seasonally adjusted

	Debits									
	Trade in goods	Trade in services	**Total goods and services**	Compensation of employees	Investment income	**Total income**	Central govt current transfers	Other sectors current transfers	**Total current transfers**	**Total current account**
	LQBL	KTMR	KTMX	KTMO	HMBO	HMBR	FJUO	FJUP	KTNE	HBOF
1955 Q1	895	239	1 134	11	68	79	..	..	29	1 242
Q2	795	244	1 039	10	82	92	..	..	28	1 159
Q3	870	274	1 144	11	82	93	..	..	25	1 262
Q4	882	240	1 122	10	160	170	..	..	31	1 323
1956 Q1	862	272	1 134	10	86	96	..	..	35	1 265
Q2	862	274	1 136	12	96	108	..	..	37	1 281
Q3	818	304	1 122	12	97	109	..	..	31	1 262
Q4	847	271	1 118	12	112	124	..	..	37	1 279
1957 Q1	943	272	1 215	12	90	102	..	..	41	1 358
Q2	914	278	1 192	13	96	109	..	..	33	1 334
Q3	881	314	1 195	12	93	105	..	..	31	1 331
Q4	864	265	1 129	12	103	115	..	..	39	1 283
1958 Q1	865	245	1 110	12	102	114	..	..	42	1 266
Q2	819	276	1 095	14	102	116	..	..	30	1 241
Q3	855	318	1 173	12	94	106	..	..	31	1 310
Q4	897	260	1 157	13	148	161	..	..	35	1 353
1959 Q1	884	244	1 128	13	90	103	..	..	41	1 272
Q2	908	290	1 198	14	104	118	..	..	30	1 346
Q3	906	327	1 233	13	97	110	..	..	36	1 379
Q4	1 005	270	1 275	14	162	176	..	..	34	1 485
1960 Q1	1 053	297	1 350	12	104	116	..	..	41	1 507
Q2	1 053	319	1 372	13	115	128	..	..	34	1 534
Q3	1 030	376	1 406	13	121	134	..	..	39	1 579
Q4	1 069	302	1 371	14	162	176	..	..	38	1 585
1961 Q1	1 079	312	1 391	13	97	110	..	..	43	1 544
Q2	1 054	338	1 392	14	111	125	..	..	45	1 562
Q3	969	392	1 361	13	113	126	..	..	40	1 527
Q4	1 009	306	1 315	14	162	176	..	..	36	1 527
1962 Q1	1 052	316	1 368	13	102	115	..	..	53	1 536
Q2	1 039	352	1 391	14	110	124	..	..	42	1 557
Q3	1 021	400	1 421	14	107	121	..	..	38	1 580
Q4	1 057	317	1 374	15	163	178	..	..	36	1 588
1963 Q1	1 084	314	1 398	14	112	126	..	..	51	1 575
Q2	1 114	361	1 475	15	116	131	..	..	42	1 648
Q3	1 121	437	1 558	14	115	129	..	..	44	1 731
Q4	1 199	341	1 540	15	166	181	..	..	42	1 763
1964 Q1	1 297	353	1 650	14	127	141	..	..	84	1 875
Q2	1 295	396	1 691	14	150	164	..	..	78	1 933
Q3	1 255	472	1 727	15	140	155	..	..	64	1 946
Q4	1 336	364	1 700	15	151	166	..	..	69	1 935
1965 Q1	1 276	365	1 641	14	151	165	..	..	82	1 888
Q2	1 316	423	1 739	15	162	177	..	..	79	1 995
Q3	1 297	505	1 802	14	150	164	..	..	75	2 041
Q4	1 357	386	1 743	15	175	190	..	..	65	1 998
1966 Q1	1 413	390	1 803	15	158	173	..	..	81	2 057
Q2	1 363	440	1 803	16	159	175	..	..	88	2 066
Q3	1 373	535	1 908	16	148	164	..	..	71	2 143
Q4	1 310	391	1 701	17	196	213	..	..	76	1 990
1967 Q1	1 488	386	1 874	16	149	165	..	..	85	2 124
Q2	1 502	445	1 947	15	171	186	..	..	97	2 230
Q3	1 397	561	1 958	16	143	159	..	..	91	2 208
Q4	1 543	492	2 035	16	226	242	..	..	96	2 373
1968 Q1	1 823	479	2 302	19	203	222	..	..	108	2 632
Q2	1 788	507	2 295	18	222	240	..	..	107	2 642
Q3	1 792	604	2 396	19	211	230	..	..	103	2 729
Q4	1 842	494	2 336	18	253	271	..	..	98	2 705
1969 Q1	1 889	521	2 410	20	203	223	..	..	118	2 751
Q2	1 910	560	2 470	20	238	258	..	..	123	2 851
Q3	1 835	660	2 495	20	237	257	..	..	119	2 871
Q4	1 953	558	2 511	20	289	309	..	..	111	2 931

Source: Office for National Statistics; Enquiries 020 7533 6078

1.18 Balance of payments: current account

continued

£ million, not seasonally adjusted

	Balances(credits less debits)									
	Trade in goods	Trade in services	**Total goods and services**	Compensation of employees	Investment income	**Total income**	Central govt current transfers	Other sectors current transfers	**Total current transfers**	**Total current account**
	LQCT	KTMS	KTMY	KTMP	HMBM	HMBP	FJUQ	FJUR	KTNF	HBOG
1955 Q1	–96	14	–82	–7	56	49	..	..	20	–13
Q2	–95	27	–68	–7	57	50	..	..	13	–5
Q3	–84	–6	–90	–7	76	69	..	..	11	–10
Q4	–40	7	–33	–6	–14	–20	..	..	–1	–54
1956 Q1	–12	8	–4	–6	50	44	..	..	2	42
Q2	21	22	43	–8	57	49	..	..	–5	87
Q3	–17	–6	–23	–8	78	70	..	..	7	54
Q4	58	2	60	–8	52	44	..	..	–2	102
1957 Q1	–36	40	4	–8	50	42	..	..	–1	45
Q2	–8	48	40	–9	63	54	..	..	4	98
Q3	–26	10	–16	–8	86	78	..	..	2	64
Q4	41	23	64	–7	58	51	..	..	–10	105
1958 Q1	31	50	81	–8	101	93	..	..	–8	166
Q2	19	31	50	–10	45	35	..	..	8	93
Q3	–5	8	3	–8	118	110	..	..	4	117
Q4	–11	30	19	–8	39	31	..	..	–	50
1959 Q1	–22	53	31	–9	65	56	..	..	–9	78
Q2	–1	23	22	–10	87	77	..	..	7	106
Q3	–56	11	–45	–9	99	90	..	..	–1	44
Q4	–37	31	–6	–9	18	9	..	..	3	6
1960 Q1	–68	12	–56	–8	71	63	..	..	–6	1
Q2	–92	9	–83	–9	50	41	..	..	2	–40
Q3	–147	–6	–153	–9	73	64	..	..	–2	–91
Q4	–97	24	–73	–9	41	32	..	..	–	–41
1961 Q1	–65	27	–38	–9	101	92	..	..	–8	46
Q2	–49	10	–39	–9	57	48	..	..	–5	4
Q3	–31	–12	–43	–8	94	86	..	..	–	43
Q4	1	26	27	–9	7	–2	..	..	4	29
1962 Q1	–50	24	–26	–9	118	109	..	..	–13	70
Q2	15	5	20	–9	102	93	..	..	–2	111
Q3	–60	–9	–69	–9	100	91	..	..	–1	21
Q4	–9	30	21	–10	26	16	..	..	2	39
1963 Q1	2	25	27	–10	121	111	..	..	–13	125
Q2	–	–1	–1	–10	105	95	..	..	–6	88
Q3	–74	–35	–109	–9	130	121	..	..	–10	2
Q4	–51	15	–36	–9	60	51	..	..	–8	7
1964 Q1	–129	3	–126	–9	144	135	..	..	–25	–16
Q2	–107	–12	–119	–8	104	96	..	..	–18	–41
Q3	–182	–43	–225	–8	96	88	..	..	–6	–143
Q4	–133	18	–115	–8	76	68	..	..	–13	–60
1965 Q1	–87	6	–81	–9	127	118	..	..	–24	13
Q2	–56	–10	–66	–9	121	112	..	..	–20	26
Q3	–94	–66	–160	–8	125	117	..	..	–18	–61
Q4	–26	4	–22	–8	94	86	..	..	–4	60
1966 Q1	–65	12	–53	–10	113	103	..	..	–26	24
Q2	–89	9	–80	–10	132	122	..	..	–30	12
Q3	–103	–28	–131	–9	115	106	..	..	–16	–41
Q4	146	51	197	–10	53	43	..	..	–17	223
1967 Q1	–77	60	–17	–11	122	111	..	..	–26	68
Q2	–91	32	–59	–9	89	80	..	..	–32	–11
Q3	–136	18	–118	–10	124	114	..	..	–29	–33
Q4	–297	47	–250	–9	76	67	..	..	–30	–213
1968 Q1	–214	47	–167	–14	98	84	..	..	–29	–112
Q2	–197	88	–109	–11	118	107	..	..	–26	–28
Q3	–195	94	–101	–12	117	105	..	..	–24	–20
Q4	–102	112	10	–11	24	13	..	..	–10	13
1969 Q1	–194	89	–105	–12	186	174	..	..	–36	33
Q2	–26	100	74	–12	147	135	..	..	–38	171
Q3	–14	107	93	–12	131	119	..	..	–26	186
Q4	20	96	116	–11	79	68	..	..	–20	164

Source: Office for National Statistics; Enquiries 020 7533 6078

1.18 Balance of payments: current account

continued

£ million,not seasonally adjusted

	Credits									
	Trade in goods	Trade in services	**Total goods and services**	Compensation of employees	Investment income	**Total income**	Central govt current transfers	Other sectors current transfers	**Total current transfers**	**Total current account**
	LQAD	KTMQ	KTMW	KTMN	HMBN	HMBQ	FJUM	FJUN	KTND	HBOE
1970 Q1	1 993	697	2 690	8	401	409	..	..	96	3 195
Q2	2 103	768	2 871	8	445	453	..	..	107	3 431
Q3	1 886	927	2 813	8	389	397	..	..	99	3 309
Q4	2 284	831	3 115	9	406	415	..	..	110	3 640
1971 Q1	2 067	829	2 896	9	426	435	..	..	114	3 445
Q2	2 406	913	3 319	9	454	463	..	..	120	3 902
Q3	2 297	1 036	3 333	11	405	416	..	..	115	3 864
Q4	2 420	922	3 342	10	402	412	..	..	133	3 887
1972 Q1	2 288	902	3 190	11	908	919	..	..	132	4 241
Q2	2 478	964	3 442	12	957	969	..	..	143	4 554
Q3	2 019	1 101	3 120	13	933	946	..	..	134	4 200
Q4	2 802	1 033	3 835	13	937	950	..	..	152	4 937
1973 Q1	2 755	1 018	3 773	13	1 163	1 176	..	..	165	5 114
Q2	2 996	1 170	4 166	14	1 403	1 417	..	..	176	5 759
Q3	2 962	1 415	4 377	16	1 294	1 310	..	..	171	5 858
Q4	3 378	1 333	4 711	16	1 545	1 561	..	..	197	6 469
1974 Q1	3 628	1 360	4 988	16	1 757	1 773	..	..	201	6 962
Q2	4 233	1 526	5 759	16	1 735	1 751	..	..	186	7 696
Q3	4 197	1 818	6 015	18	1 616	1 634	..	..	165	7 814
Q4	4 488	1 581	6 069	19	1 709	1 728	..	..	218	8 015
1975 Q1	4 521	1 590	6 111	19	1 734	1 753	..	..	264	8 128
Q2	4 856	1 749	6 605	21	1 834	1 855	..	..	249	8 709
Q3	4 676	2 107	6 783	24	1 736	1 760	..	..	241	8 784
Q4	5 398	1 906	7 304	24	1 900	1 924	..	..	256	9 484
1976 Q1	5 685	1 940	7 625	25	2 113	2 138	..	..	279	10 042
Q2	6 305	2 244	8 549	27	2 276	2 303	..	..	298	11 150
Q3	6 218	2 859	9 077	31	2 336	2 367	..	..	284	11 728
Q4	7 196	2 571	9 767	31	2 483	2 514	..	..	318	12 599
1977 Q1	7 562	2 365	9 927	31	2 343	2 374	..	..	390	12 691
Q2	8 070	2 667	10 737	32	2 386	2 418	..	..	430	13 585
Q3	8 212	3 356	11 568	38	2 400	2 438	..	..	412	14 418
Q4	8 197	2 781	10 978	38	2 546	2 584	..	..	438	14 000
1978 Q1	8 276	2 611	10 887	35	2 685	2 720	..	..	470	14 077
Q2	9 199	2 817	12 016	38	3 076	3 114	..	..	493	15 623
Q3	8 572	3 615	12 187	43	3 118	3 161	..	..	527	15 875
Q4	9 284	3 005	12 289	43	3 392	3 435	..	..	650	16 374
1979 Q1	8 505	2 959	11 464	39	4 121	4 160	..	..	631	16 255
Q2	10 857	3 270	14 127	41	4 497	4 538	..	..	775	19 440
Q3	10 107	4 108	14 215	49	4 966	5 015	..	..	782	20 012
Q4	11 380	3 618	14 998	47	5 629	5 676	..	..	882	21 556
1980 Q1	12 007	3 374	15 381	48	6 195	6 243	..	..	946	22 570
Q2	11 946	3 595	15 541	50	6 946	6 996	..	..	974	23 511
Q3	11 452	4 367	15 819	61	6 240	6 301	..	..	823	22 943
Q4	12 088	3 666	15 754	60	6 610	6 670	..	..	1 070	23 494
1981 Q1	11 783	3 493	15 276	51	7 877	7 928	..	..	1 505	24 709
Q2	12 356	3 858	16 214	55	9 332	9 387	..	..	826	26 427
Q3	12 776	4 824	17 600	66	11 207	11 273	..	..	1 040	29 913
Q4	14 119	4 106	18 225	66	12 773	12 839	..	..	1 492	32 556
1982 Q1	13 291	3 839	17 130	54	11 364	11 418	..	..	1 946	30 494
Q2	13 836	4 132	17 968	57	12 463	12 520	..	..	1 007	31 495
Q3	13 531	4 806	18 337	71	12 265	12 336	..	..	1 166	31 839
Q4	14 999	4 145	19 144	70	12 636	12 706	..	..	1 453	33 303
1983 Q1	14 720	4 223	18 943	62	12 535	12 597	..	..	1 803	33 343
Q2	14 818	4 474	19 292	66	11 057	11 123	..	..	1 353	31 768
Q3	14 844	5 495	20 339	82	11 298	11 380	..	..	1 364	33 083
Q4	16 602	4 575	21 177	80	11 701	11 781	..	..	1 693	34 651
1984 Q1	16 905	4 639	21 544	68	12 641	12 709	..	..	1 869	36 122
Q2	16 890	4 979	21 869	73	13 090	13 163	..	..	1 484	36 516
Q3	16 765	6 057	22 822	93	14 842	14 935	..	..	1 464	39 221
Q4	20 005	5 269	25 274	89	16 082	16 171	..	..	2 262	43 707

Source: Office for National Statistics; Enquiries 020 7533 6078

1.18 Balance of payments: current account

continued

£ million, not seasonally adjusted

	Debits									
	Trade in goods	Trade in services	**Total goods and services**	Compensation of employees	Investment income	**Total income**	Central govt current transfers	Other sectors current transfers	**Total current transfers**	**Total current account**
	LQBL	KTMR	KTMX	KTMO	HMBO	HMBR	FJUO	FJUP	KTNE	HBOF
1970 Q1	1 966	558	2 524	20	228	248	..	..	122	2 894
Q2	2 159	653	2 812	23	261	284	..	..	130	3 226
Q3	1 986	822	2 808	22	228	250	..	..	117	3 175
Q4	2 173	735	2 908	24	312	336	..	..	125	3 369
1971 Q1	2 229	702	2 931	24	250	274	..	..	124	3 329
Q2	2 294	781	3 075	24	291	315	..	..	140	3 530
Q3	2 151	886	3 037	27	245	272	..	..	130	3 439
Q4	2 311	741	3 052	27	341	368	..	..	139	3 559
1972 Q1	2 502	746	3 248	25	765	790	..	..	152	4 190
Q2	2 524	785	3 309	24	789	813	..	..	161	4 283
Q3	2 357	959	3 316	26	789	815	..	..	150	4 281
Q4	2 940	845	3 785	26	874	900	..	..	149	4 834
1973 Q1	3 325	872	4 197	30	1 022	1 052	..	..	220	5 469
Q2	3 423	993	4 416	30	1 020	1 050	..	..	299	5 765
Q3	3 615	1 208	4 823	33	983	1 016	..	..	234	6 073
Q4	4 301	1 103	5 404	34	1 097	1 131	..	..	272	6 807
1974 Q1	4 963	1 165	6 128	37	1 360	1 397	..	..	285	7 810
Q2	5 631	1 302	6 933	37	1 319	1 356	..	..	271	8 560
Q3	5 465	1 457	6 922	43	1 293	1 336	..	..	244	8 502
Q4	5 728	1 296	7 024	44	1 416	1 460	..	..	310	8 794
1975 Q1	5 505	1 281	6 786	42	1 576	1 618	..	..	304	8 708
Q2	5 536	1 450	6 986	46	1 709	1 755	..	..	344	9 085
Q3	5 662	1 712	7 374	49	1 543	1 592	..	..	321	9 287
Q4	5 993	1 516	7 509	53	1 670	1 723	..	..	358	9 590
1976 Q1	6 358	1 398	7 756	61	1 852	1 913	..	..	407	10 076
Q2	7 347	1 759	9 106	63	1 938	2 001	..	..	421	11 528
Q3	7 384	2 085	9 469	64	1 918	1 982	..	..	410	11 861
Q4	8 245	1 907	10 152	66	2 115	2 181	..	..	448	12 781
1977 Q1	8 644	1 724	10 368	69	2 267	2 336	..	..	536	13 240
Q2	8 985	1 954	10 939	72	2 509	2 581	..	..	524	14 044
Q3	8 346	2 319	10 665	74	2 396	2 470	..	..	553	13 688
Q4	8 337	1 953	10 290	76	2 623	2 699	..	..	526	13 515
1978 Q1	8 969	1 814	10 783	72	2 644	2 716	..	..	838	14 337
Q2	9 392	2 127	11 519	75	2 993	3 068	..	..	708	15 295
Q3	9 038	2 446	11 484	74	2 862	2 936	..	..	797	15 217
Q4	9 466	1 982	11 448	78	3 386	3 464	..	..	755	15 667
1979 Q1	10 145	2 078	12 223	70	3 728	3 798	..	..	948	16 969
Q2	11 435	2 500	13 935	75	4 576	4 651	..	..	979	19 565
Q3	10 618	2 926	13 544	77	4 529	4 606	..	..	1 037	19 187
Q4	11 977	2 486	14 463	84	5 840	5 924	..	..	1 067	21 454
1980 Q1	12 685	2 476	15 161	68	6 464	6 532	..	..	1 073	22 766
Q2	12 264	2 901	15 165	74	7 487	7 561	..	..	1 118	23 844
Q3	10 597	3 362	13 959	77	6 479	6 556	..	..	1 060	21 575
Q4	10 618	2 546	13 164	82	6 907	6 989	..	..	1 014	21 167
1981 Q1	10 325	2 395	12 720	72	7 850	7 922	..	..	1 220	21 862
Q2	11 268	3 107	14 375	76	9 357	9 433	..	..	1 180	24 988
Q3	12 922	3 788	16 710	75	11 239	11 314	..	..	1 346	29 370
Q4	13 281	3 157	16 438	81	13 112	13 193	..	..	1 205	30 836
1982 Q1	13 321	2 772	16 093	82	11 685	11 767	..	..	1 439	29 299
Q2	13 944	3 584	17 528	87	12 587	12 674	..	..	1 472	31 674
Q3	13 001	4 239	17 240	86	12 256	12 342	..	..	1 478	31 060
Q4	13 512	3 258	16 770	92	12 661	12 753	..	..	1 468	30 991
1983 Q1	15 162	3 075	18 237	91	12 110	12 201	..	..	1 488	31 926
Q2	15 769	3 688	19 457	95	11 137	11 232	..	..	1 650	32 339
Q3	15 182	4 579	19 761	94	10 523	10 617	..	..	1 493	31 871
Q4	16 489	3 484	19 973	99	11 616	11 715	..	..	1 722	33 410
1984 Q1	17 653	3 415	21 068	109	12 247	12 356	..	..	1 768	35 192
Q2	18 724	4 132	22 856	103	12 634	12 737	..	..	1 779	37 372
Q3	18 495	5 028	23 523	97	14 025	14 122	..	..	1 756	39 401
Q4	21 102	4 028	25 130	108	15 252	15 360	..	..	1 902	42 392

Source: Office for National Statistics; Enquiries 020 7533 6078

1.18 Balance of payments: current account

continued

£ million, not seasonally adjusted

	Balances(credis less debits)									
	Trade in goods	Trade in services	**Total goods and services**	Compensation of employees	Investment income	**Total income**	Central govt current transfers	Other sectors current transfers	**Total current transfers**	**Total current account**
	LQCT	KTMS	KTMY	KTMP	HMBM	HMBP	FJUQ	FJUR	KTNF	HBOG
1970 Q1	27	139	166	–12	173	161	..	..	–26	301
Q2	–56	115	59	–15	184	169	..	..	–23	205
Q3	–100	105	5	–14	161	147	..	..	–18	134
Q4	111	96	207	–15	94	79	..	..	–15	271
1971 Q1	–162	127	–35	–15	176	161	..	..	–10	116
Q2	112	132	244	–15	163	148	..	..	–20	372
Q3	146	150	296	–16	160	144	..	..	–15	425
Q4	109	181	290	–17	61	44	..	..	–6	328
1972 Q1	–214	156	–58	–14	143	129	..	..	–20	51
Q2	–46	179	133	–12	168	156	..	..	–18	271
Q3	–338	142	–196	–13	144	131	..	..	–16	–81
Q4	–138	188	50	–13	63	50	..	..	3	103
1973 Q1	–570	146	–424	–17	141	124	..	..	–55	–355
Q2	–427	177	–250	–16	383	367	..	..	–123	–6
Q3	–653	207	–446	–17	311	294	..	..	–63	–215
Q4	–923	230	–693	–18	448	430	..	..	–75	–338
1974 Q1	–1 335	195	–1 140	–21	397	376	..	..	–84	–848
Q2	–1 398	224	–1 174	–21	416	395	..	..	–85	–864
Q3	–1 268	361	–907	–25	323	298	..	..	–79	–688
Q4	–1 240	285	–955	–25	293	268	..	..	–92	–779
1975 Q1	–984	309	–675	–23	158	135	..	..	–40	–580
Q2	–680	299	–381	–25	125	100	..	..	–95	–376
Q3	–986	395	–591	–25	193	168	..	..	–80	–503
Q4	–595	390	–205	–29	230	201	..	..	–102	–106
1976 Q1	–673	542	–131	–36	261	225	..	..	–128	–34
Q2	–1 042	485	–557	–36	338	302	..	..	–123	–378
Q3	–1 166	774	–392	–33	418	385	..	..	–126	–133
Q4	–1 049	664	–385	–35	368	333	..	..	–130	–182
1977 Q1	–1 082	641	–441	–38	76	38	..	..	–146	–549
Q2	–915	713	–202	–40	–123	–163	..	..	–94	–459
Q3	–134	1 037	903	–36	4	–32	..	..	–141	730
Q4	–140	828	688	–38	–77	–115	..	..	–88	485
1978 Q1	–693	797	104	–37	41	4	..	..	–368	–260
Q2	–193	690	497	–37	83	46	..	..	–215	328
Q3	–466	1 169	703	–31	256	225	..	..	–270	658
Q4	–182	1 023	841	–35	6	–29	..	..	–105	707
1979 Q1	–1 640	881	–759	–31	393	362	..	..	–317	–714
Q2	–578	770	192	–34	–79	–113	..	..	–204	–125
Q3	–511	1 182	671	–28	437	409	..	..	–255	825
Q4	–597	1 132	535	–37	–211	–248	..	..	–185	102
1980 Q1	–678	898	220	–20	–269	–289	..	..	–127	–196
Q2	–318	694	376	–24	–541	–565	..	..	–144	–333
Q3	855	1 005	1 860	–16	–239	–255	..	..	–237	1 368
Q4	1 470	1 120	2 590	–22	–297	–319	..	..	56	2 327
1981 Q1	1 458	1 098	2 556	–21	27	6	..	..	285	2 847
Q2	1 088	751	1 839	–21	–25	–46	..	..	–354	1 439
Q3	–146	1 036	890	–9	–32	–41	..	..	–306	543
Q4	838	949	1 787	–15	–339	–354	..	..	287	1 720
1982 Q1	–30	1 067	1 037	–28	–321	–349	..	..	507	1 195
Q2	–108	548	440	–30	–124	–154	..	..	–465	–179
Q3	530	567	1 097	–15	9	–6	..	..	–312	779
Q4	1 487	887	2 374	–22	–25	–47	..	..	–15	2 312
1983 Q1	–442	1 148	706	–29	425	396	..	..	315	1 417
Q2	–951	786	–165	–29	–80	–109	..	..	–297	–571
Q3	–338	916	578	–12	775	763	..	..	–129	1 212
Q4	113	1 091	1 204	–19	85	66	..	..	–29	1 241
1984 Q1	–748	1 224	476	–41	394	353	..	..	101	930
Q2	–1 834	847	–987	–30	456	426	..	..	–295	–856
Q3	–1 730	1 029	–701	–4	817	813	..	..	–292	–180
Q4	–1 097	1 241	144	–19	830	811	..	..	360	1 315

Source: Office for National Statistics; Enquiries 020 7533 6078

1.18 Balance of payments: current account

continued

£ million,not seasonally adjusted

	Credits									
	Trade in goods	Trade in services	**Total goods and services**	Compensation of employees	Investment income	**Total income**	Central govt current transfers	Other sectors current transfers	**Total current transfers**	**Total current account**
	LQAD	KTMQ	KTMW	KTMN	HMBN	HMBQ	FJUM	FJUN	KTND	HBOE
1985 Q1	20 026	5 335	25 361	72	16 116	16 188	..	..	2 085	43 634
Q2	20 272	5 789	26 061	78	14 669	14 747	..	..	1 714	42 522
Q3	17 973	6 835	24 808	99	13 491	13 590	..	..	1 708	40 106
Q4	20 020	5 676	25 696	95	12 807	12 902	..	..	2 001	40 599
1986 Q1	17 612	5 593	23 205	78	12 945	13 023	735	1 118	1 853	38 081
Q2	18 396	5 900	24 296	82	12 565	12 647	274	1 202	1 476	38 419
Q3	16 751	7 154	23 905	106	13 033	13 139	537	1 017	1 554	38 598
Q4	20 238	6 137	26 375	103	13 415	13 518	386	1 037	1 423	41 316
1987 Q1	19 433	5 997	25 430	85	13 205	13 290	1 129	1 347	2 476	41 196
Q2	19 366	6 605	25 971	92	13 133	13 225	969	1 216	2 185	41 381
Q3	19 340	8 083	27 423	120	13 198	13 318	957	1 011	1 968	42 709
Q4	21 392	6 221	27 613	116	13 148	13 264	1 063	838	1 901	42 778
1988 Q1	19 216	6 045	25 261	94	14 116	14 210	1 186	1 058	2 244	41 715
Q2	20 177	6 494	26 671	100	14 887	14 987	1 123	1 267	2 390	44 048
Q3	19 849	7 802	27 651	129	16 237	16 366	1 553	1 202	2 755	46 772
Q4	21 469	6 382	27 851	122	16 692	16 814	1 298	987	2 285	46 950
1989 Q1	21 355	6 445	27 800	100	18 892	18 992	1 194	1 415	2 609	49 401
Q2	22 819	7 243	30 062	106	20 436	20 542	1 252	1 392	2 644	53 248
Q3	22 064	8 739	30 803	141	20 138	20 279	1 171	1 126	2 297	53 379
Q4	26 373	6 845	33 218	129	22 333	22 462	1 307	1 228	2 535	58 215
1990 Q1	24 860	7 175	32 035	109	21 283	21 392	1 125	1 456	2 581	56 008
Q2	25 859	7 632	33 491	126	21 509	21 635	1 037	1 363	2 400	57 526
Q3	23 816	8 964	32 780	158	22 405	22 563	1 067	1 473	2 540	57 883
Q4	27 778	7 417	35 195	150	22 989	23 139	1 065	1 664	2 729	61 063
1991 Q1	23 924	6 740	30 664	125	21 450	21 575	1 844	2 107	3 951	56 190
Q2	26 343	7 835	34 178	115	21 889	22 004	2 351	1 872	4 223	60 405
Q3	25 237	9 248	34 485	163	20 803	20 966	1 457	1 661	3 118	58 569
Q4	28 435	7 603	36 038	148	20 277	20 425	1 094	1 853	2 947	59 410
1992 Q1	25 606	8 058	33 664	122	18 422	18 544	1 402	2 067	3 469	55 677
Q2	26 972	8 647	35 619	117	17 339	17 456	974	1 809	2 783	55 858
Q3	25 204	9 997	35 201	162	18 679	18 841	884	1 692	2 576	56 618
Q4	30 081	8 726	38 807	150	20 109	20 259	994	1 818	2 812	61 878
1993 Q1	30 153	9 047	39 200	85	20 452	20 537	1 326	2 038	3 364	63 101
Q2	29 919	9 345	39 264	103	18 995	19 098	1 377	2 166	3 543	61 905
Q3	29 260	11 662	40 922	206	20 193	20 399	1 343	1 793	3 136	64 457
Q4	32 707	9 985	42 692	201	19 185	19 386	1 260	1 961	3 221	65 299
1994 Q1	32 054	9 858	41 912	154	20 312	20 466	1 108	2 500	3 608	65 986
Q2	33 395	10 439	43 834	153	19 334	19 487	1 334	1 780	3 114	66 435
Q3	32 948	12 673	45 621	200	21 246	21 446	1 304	1 783	3 087	70 154
Q4	36 863	10 537	47 400	174	21 747	21 921	1 262	1 738	3 000	72 321
1995 Q1	37 886	11 049	48 935	136	22 217	22 353	1 300	2 788	4 088	75 376
Q2	37 558	11 644	49 202	224	24 011	24 235	1 259	1 821	3 080	76 517
Q3	37 105	13 977	51 082	301	25 169	25 470	1 121	2 018	3 139	79 691
Q4	41 176	12 017	53 193	226	25 689	25 915	1 165	1 891	3 056	82 164
1996 Q1	41 589	11 965	53 554	230	24 983	25 213	1 664	3 056	4 720	83 487
Q2	41 480	12 749	54 229	219	25 420	25 639	1 707	2 054	3 761	83 629
Q3	40 448	14 887	55 335	249	25 464	25 713	1 341	7 454	8 795	89 843
Q4	43 886	13 299	57 185	213	25 802	26 015	2 042	2 068	4 110	87 310
1997 Q1	42 074	12 963	55 037	145	25 107	25 252	1 801	3 195	4 996	85 285
Q2	43 152	13 936	57 088	215	26 790	27 005	1 321	2 216	3 537	87 630
Q3	41 790	16 351	58 141	360	27 956	28 316	1 453	1 792	3 245	89 702
Q4	44 767	14 293	59 060	287	27 045	27 332	1 404	2 123	3 527	89 919
1998 Q1	41 404	13 808	55 212	191	26 106	26 297	1 680	3 324	5 004	86 513
Q2	41 310	15 098	56 408	178	27 345	27 523	1 467	1 969	3 436	87 367
Q3	39 648	17 455	57 103	231	27 957	28 188	1 533	1 824	3 357	88 648
Q4	41 730	15 021	56 751	240	26 984	27 224	1 701	1 926	3 627	87 602
1999 Q1	38 890	14 717	53 607	147	25 924	26 071	3 038	3 062	6 100	85 778
Q2	39 768	16 017	55 785	254	25 979	26 233	2 088	2 085	4 173	86 191
Q3	42 164	18 025	60 189	309	26 367	26 676	2 142	1 663	3 805	90 670
Q4	44 845	15 223	60 068	250	29 869	30 119	2 196	2 004	4 200	94 387
2000 Q1	44 790	14 834	59 624	157	30 003	30 160	2 743	3 150	5 893	95 677

Source: Office for National Statistics; Enquiries 020 7533 6078

1.18 Balance of payments: current account

continued

£ million, not seasonally adjusted

	Debits									
	Trade in goods	Trade in services	**Total goods and services**	Compensation of employees	Investment income	**Total income**	Central govt current transfers	Other sectors current transfers	**Total current transfers**	**Total current account**
	LQBL	KTMR	KTMX	KTMO	HMBO	HMBR	FJUO	FJUP	KTNE	HBOF
1985 Q1	22 127	3 858	25 985	126	15 921	16 047	..	..	2 328	44 360
Q2	21 021	4 206	25 227	109	14 613	14 722	..	..	1 922	41 871
Q3	18 772	5 000	23 772	110	13 048	13 158	..	..	2 210	39 140
Q4	19 787	3 952	23 739	119	13 369	13 488	..	..	2 036	39 263
1986 Q1	19 664	3 790	23 454	144	12 441	12 585	473	1 605	2 078	38 117
Q2	20 734	4 509	25 243	127	11 779	11 906	242	1 593	1 835	38 984
Q3	19 953	5 725	25 678	123	11 905	12 028	266	2 122	2 388	40 094
Q4	22 263	4 255	26 518	131	12 805	12 936	280	1 770	2 050	41 504
1987 Q1	21 603	4 034	25 637	170	12 342	12 512	528	2 279	2 807	40 956
Q2	22 505	4 955	27 460	148	12 780	12 928	292	2 283	2 575	42 963
Q3	22 886	6 521	29 407	135	12 464	12 599	256	2 433	2 689	44 695
Q4	24 235	4 710	28 945	134	13 421	13 555	240	2 293	2 533	45 033
1988 Q1	23 851	4 692	28 543	127	13 901	14 028	693	2 278	2 971	45 542
Q2	25 299	5 478	30 777	124	14 422	14 546	339	2 434	2 773	48 096
Q3	25 914	6 931	32 845	120	15 504	15 624	276	2 116	2 392	50 861
Q4	27 200	5 292	32 492	138	16 750	16 888	918	2 225	3 143	52 523
1989 Q1	27 814	5 332	33 146	132	18 469	18 601	667	2 505	3 172	54 919
Q2	30 079	6 148	36 227	161	20 379	20 540	425	2 606	3 031	59 798
Q3	29 409	8 005	37 414	148	20 004	20 152	484	2 570	3 054	60 620
Q4	30 033	5 870	35 903	173	22 873	23 046	479	2 969	3 448	62 397
1990 Q1	31 269	5 771	37 040	163	21 904	22 067	759	2 877	3 636	62 743
Q2	31 633	6 864	38 497	140	21 996	22 136	514	2 937	3 451	64 084
Q3	28 814	8 322	37 136	161	21 588	21 749	299	3 050	3 349	62 234
Q4	29 304	6 221	35 525	189	23 146	23 335	423	3 649	4 072	62 932
1991 Q1	27 651	5 538	33 189	173	22 589	22 762	1 084	2 920	4 004	59 955
Q2	28 883	6 827	35 710	128	22 486	22 614	742	3 062	3 804	62 128
Q3	28 494	8 241	36 735	147	20 749	20 896	661	3 140	3 801	61 432
Q4	29 134	6 349	35 483	166	20 485	20 651	731	2 568	3 299	59 433
1992 Q1	29 078	6 370	35 448	170	18 272	18 442	1 326	3 272	4 598	58 488
Q2	30 415	7 399	37 814	83	17 518	17 601	818	3 274	4 092	59 507
Q3	29 199	8 923	38 122	181	17 074	17 255	733	3 356	4 089	59 466
Q4	32 221	7 062	39 283	166	19 521	19 687	629	3 053	3 682	62 652
1993 Q1	33 621	6 878	40 499	177	20 637	20 814	1 329	3 456	4 785	66 098
Q2	34 021	8 482	42 503	112	19 227	19 339	988	3 530	4 518	66 360
Q3	33 174	10 258	43 432	114	19 010	19 124	906	3 594	4 500	67 056
Q4	34 542	7 798	42 340	157	19 301	19 458	933	3 135	4 068	65 866
1994 Q1	35 168	7 769	42 937	183	18 396	18 579	1 953	3 310	5 263	66 779
Q2	36 909	9 373	46 282	196	17 958	18 154	1 058	3 416	4 474	68 910
Q3	35 650	11 188	46 838	248	18 217	18 465	1 088	3 481	4 569	69 872
Q4	38 624	8 649	47 273	224	20 128	20 352	696	2 472	3 168	70 793
1995 Q1	38 825	8 191	47 016	388	21 276	21 664	1 758	3 577	5 335	74 015
Q2	41 971	10 128	52 099	218	23 448	23 666	851	3 799	4 650	80 415
Q3	41 596	12 068	53 664	279	22 205	22 484	999	3 899	4 898	81 046
Q4	43 057	9 385	52 442	298	23 885	24 183	1 187	4 205	5 392	82 017
1996 Q1	44 703	9 639	54 342	206	23 837	24 043	1 770	3 920	5 690	84 075
Q2	46 384	11 113	57 497	211	22 264	22 475	1 220	3 963	5 183	85 155
Q3	44 129	12 828	56 957	196	23 062	23 258	844	9 144	9 988	90 203
Q4	45 273	10 423	55 696	205	24 488	24 693	1 222	3 825	5 047	85 436
1997 Q1	43 999	9 713	53 712	177	22 853	23 030	1 726	4 161	5 887	82 629
Q2	47 218	11 214	58 432	233	23 483	23 716	1 308	3 342	4 650	86 798
Q3	45 061	13 415	58 476	282	23 975	24 257	1 325	3 840	5 165	87 898
Q4	47 415	10 787	58 202	232	25 500	25 732	728	3 926	4 654	88 588
1998 Q1	45 615	10 493	56 108	203	23 829	24 032	2 192	4 330	6 522	86 662
Q2	46 938	12 138	59 076	201	24 408	24 609	1 005	3 375	4 380	88 065
Q3	45 492	14 325	59 817	203	22 441	22 644	1 495	3 335	4 830	87 291
Q4	46 584	11 844	58 428	243	23 459	23 702	1 893	4 169	6 062	88 192
1999 Q1	46 378	11 518	57 896	183	24 931	25 114	2 708	3 953	6 661	89 671
Q2	46 050	13 200	59 250	169	23 797	23 966	1 372	3 551	4 923	88 139
Q3	49 170	15 479	64 649	201	24 499	24 700	1 772	3 799	5 571	94 920
Q4	50 836	12 247	63 083	206	26 781	26 987	1 426	3 781	5 207	95 277
2000 Q1	51 361	11 672	63 033	217	30 422	30 639	2 201	4 028	6 229	99 901

Source: Office for National Statistics; Enquiries 020 7533 6078

1.18 Balance of payments: current account

continued

£ million, not seasonally adjusted

	Balances(credits less debits)									
	Trade in goods	Trade in services	**Total goods and services**	Compensation of employees	Investment income	**Total income**	Central govt current transfers	Other sectors current transfers	**Total current transfers**	**Total current account**
	LQCT	KTMS	KTMY	KTMP	HMBM	HMBP	FJUQ	FJUR	KTNF	HBOG
1985 Q1	−2 101	1 477	−624	−54	195	141	..	..	−243	−726
Q2	−749	1 583	834	−31	56	25	..	..	−208	651
Q3	−799	1 835	1 036	−11	443	432	..	..	−502	966
Q4	233	1 724	1 957	−24	−562	−586	..	..	−35	1 336
1986 Q1	−2 052	1 803	−249	−66	504	438	262	−487	−225	−36
Q2	−2 338	1 391	−947	−45	786	741	32	−391	−359	−565
Q3	−3 202	1 429	−1 773	−17	1 128	1 111	271	−1 105	−834	−1 496
Q4	−2 025	1 882	−143	−28	610	582	106	−733	−627	−188
1987 Q1	−2 170	1 963	−207	−85	863	778	601	−932	−331	240
Q2	−3 139	1 650	−1 489	−56	353	297	677	−1 067	−390	−1 582
Q3	−3 546	1 562	−1 984	−15	734	719	701	−1 422	−721	−1 986
Q4	−2 843	1 511	−1 332	−18	−273	−291	823	−1 455	−632	−2 255
1988 Q1	−4 635	1 353	−3 282	−33	215	182	493	−1 220	−727	−3 827
Q2	−5 122	1 016	−4 106	−24	465	441	784	−1 167	−383	−4 048
Q3	−6 065	871	−5 194	9	733	742	1 277	−914	363	−4 089
Q4	−5 731	1 090	−4 641	−16	−58	−74	380	−1 238	−858	−5 573
1989 Q1	−6 459	1 113	−5 346	−32	423	391	527	−1 090	−563	−5 518
Q2	−7 260	1 095	−6 165	−55	57	2	827	−1 214	−387	−6 550
Q3	−7 345	734	−6 611	−7	134	127	687	−1 444	−757	−7 241
Q4	−3 660	975	−2 685	−44	−540	−584	828	−1 741	−913	−4 182
1990 Q1	−6 409	1 404	−5 005	−54	−621	−675	366	−1 421	−1 055	−6 735
Q2	−5 774	768	−5 006	−14	−487	−501	523	−1 574	−1 051	−6 558
Q3	−4 998	642	−4 356	−3	817	814	768	−1 577	−809	−4 351
Q4	−1 526	1 196	−330	−39	−157	−196	642	−1 985	−1 343	−1 869
1991 Q1	−3 727	1 202	−2 525	−48	−1 139	−1 187	760	−813	−53	−3 765
Q2	−2 540	1 008	−1 532	−13	−597	−610	1 609	−1 190	419	−1 723
Q3	−3 257	1 007	−2 250	16	54	70	796	−1 479	−683	−2 863
Q4	−699	1 254	555	−18	−208	−226	363	−715	−352	−23
1992 Q1	−3 472	1 688	−1 784	−48	150	102	76	−1 205	−1 129	−2 811
Q2	−3 443	1 248	−2 195	34	−179	−145	156	−1 465	−1 309	−3 649
Q3	−3 995	1 074	−2 921	−19	1 605	1 586	151	−1 664	−1 513	−2 848
Q4	−2 140	1 664	−476	−16	588	572	365	−1 235	−870	−774
1993 Q1	−3 468	2 169	−1 299	−92	−185	−277	−3	−1 418	−1 421	−2 997
Q2	−4 102	863	−3 239	−9	−232	−241	389	−1 364	−975	−4 455
Q3	−3 914	1 404	−2 510	92	1 183	1 275	437	−1 801	−1 364	−2 599
Q4	−1 835	2 187	352	44	−116	−72	327	−1 174	−847	−567
1994 Q1	−3 114	2 089	−1 025	−29	1 916	1 887	−845	−810	−1 655	−793
Q2	−3 514	1 066	−2 448	−43	1 376	1 333	276	−1 636	−1 360	−2 475
Q3	−2 702	1 485	−1 217	−48	3 029	2 981	216	−1 698	−1 482	282
Q4	−1 761	1 888	127	−50	1 619	1 569	566	−734	−168	1 528
1995 Q1	−939	2 858	1 919	−252	941	689	−458	−789	−1 247	1 361
Q2	−4 413	1 516	−2 897	6	563	569	408	−1 978	−1 570	−3 898
Q3	−4 491	1 909	−2 582	22	2 964	2 986	122	−1 881	−1 759	−1 355
Q4	−1 881	2 632	751	−72	1 804	1 732	−22	−2 314	−2 336	147
1996 Q1	−3 114	2 326	−788	24	1 146	1 170	−106	−864	−970	−588
Q2	−4 904	1 636	−3 268	8	3 156	3 164	487	−1 909	−1 422	−1 526
Q3	−3 681	2 059	−1 622	53	2 402	2 455	497	−1 690	−1 193	−360
Q4	−1 387	2 876	1 489	8	1 314	1 322	820	−1 757	−937	1 874
1997 Q1	−1 925	3 250	1 325	−32	2 254	2 222	75	−966	−891	2 656
Q2	−4 066	2 722	−1 344	−18	3 307	3 289	13	−1 126	−1 113	832
Q3	−3 271	2 936	−335	78	3 981	4 059	128	−2 048	−1 920	1 804
Q4	−2 648	3 506	858	55	1 545	1 600	676	−1 803	−1 127	1 331
1998 Q1	−4 211	3 315	−896	−12	2 277	2 265	−512	−1 006	−1 518	−149
Q2	−5 628	2 960	−2 668	−23	2 937	2 914	462	−1 406	−944	−698
Q3	−5 844	3 130	−2 714	28	5 516	5 544	38	−1 511	−1 473	1 357
Q4	−4 854	3 177	−1 677	−3	3 525	3 522	−192	−2 243	−2 435	−590
1999 Q1	−7 488	3 199	−4 289	−36	993	957	330	−891	−561	−3 893
Q2	−6 282	2 817	−3 465	85	2 182	2 267	716	−1 466	−750	−1 948
Q3	−7 006	2 546	−4 460	108	1 868	1 976	370	−2 136	−1 766	−4 250
Q4	−5 991	2 976	−3 015	44	3 088	3 132	770	−1 777	−1 007	−890
2000 Q1	−6 571	3 162	−3 409	−60	−419	−479	542	−878	−336	−4 224

Source: Office for National Statistics; Enquiries 020 7533 6078

1.18 Balance of payments: current account

continued

£ million, seasonally adjusted

	Credits									
	Trade in goods	Trade in services	**Total goods and services**	Compensation of employees	Investment income	**Total income**	Central govt current transfers	Other sectors current transfers	**Total current transfers**	**Total current account**
	BOKG	IKBB	IKBH	IJAH	HBOK	HBOH	FHDM	FHIB	IKBN	HBON
1955 Q1	789	264	1 053	4	138	142	..	..	..	1 244
Q2	704	258	962	3	141	144	..	..	..	1 147
Q3	813	255	1 068	4	144	148	..	..	..	1 252
Q4	821	262	1 083	4	144	148	..	..	..	1 261
1956 Q1	835	291	1 126	4	152	156	..	..	..	1 319
Q2	876	282	1 158	4	155	159	..	..	..	1 349
Q3	854	286	1 140	4	160	164	..	..	..	1 342
Q4	874	288	1 162	4	161	165	..	..	..	1 362
1957 Q1	896	325	1 221	4	155	159	..	..	..	1 420
Q2	892	314	1 206	4	161	165	..	..	..	1 408
Q3	898	306	1 204	4	164	168	..	..	..	1 405
Q4	887	305	1 192	5	159	164	..	..	..	1 385
1958 Q1	885	304	1 189	4	221	225	..	..	..	1 448
Q2	817	304	1 121	4	148	152	..	..	..	1 311
Q3	901	302	1 203	4	194	198	..	..	..	1 436
Q4	867	308	1 175	5	186	191	..	..	..	1 401
1959 Q1	849	310	1 159	4	164	168	..	..	..	1 359
Q2	886	308	1 194	4	194	198	..	..	..	1 429
Q3	904	313	1 217	4	182	186	..	..	..	1 438
Q4	948	318	1 266	5	182	187	..	..	..	1 490
1960 Q1	971	325	1 296	4	179	183	..	..	..	1 514
Q2	937	324	1 261	4	167	171	..	..	..	1 468
Q3	941	338	1 279	4	181	185	..	..	..	1 501
Q4	952	346	1 298	5	210	215	..	..	..	1 551
1961 Q1	999	356	1 355	4	195	199	..	..	..	1 589
Q2	982	346	1 328	5	171	176	..	..	..	1 544
Q3	997	347	1 344	5	197	202	..	..	..	1 586
Q4	989	350	1 339	5	179	184	..	..	..	1 563
1962 Q1	984	364	1 348	4	211	215	..	..	..	1 603
Q2	1 031	355	1 386	5	215	220	..	..	..	1 646
Q3	1 024	354	1 378	5	199	204	..	..	..	1 619
Q4	1 026	362	1 388	5	203	208	..	..	..	1 634
1963 Q1	1 061	365	1 426	4	220	224	..	..	..	1 688
Q2	1 089	358	1 447	5	221	226	..	..	..	1 709
Q3	1 114	362	1 476	5	240	245	..	..	..	1 755
Q4	1 131	372	1 503	6	244	250	..	..	..	1 787
1964 Q1	1 142	380	1 522	5	257	262	..	..	..	1 843
Q2	1 167	382	1 549	6	251	257	..	..	..	1 866
Q3	1 147	388	1 535	7	236	243	..	..	..	1 836
Q4	1 176	401	1 577	7	244	251	..	..	..	1 884
1965 Q1	1 203	393	1 596	5	266	271	..	..	..	1 925
Q2	1 216	413	1 629	6	276	282	..	..	..	1 970
Q3	1 265	395	1 660	6	279	285	..	..	..	2 002
Q4	1 299	412	1 711	7	284	291	..	..	..	2 063
1966 Q1	1 310	427	1 737	5	262	267	..	..	..	2 059
Q2	1 274	448	1 722	6	282	288	..	..	..	2 068
Q3	1 347	456	1 803	7	269	276	..	..	..	2 134
Q4	1 417	469	1 886	7	261	268	..	..	..	2 213
1967 Q1	1 413	478	1 891	5	264	269	..	..	..	2 219
Q2	1 365	474	1 839	6	248	254	..	..	..	2 158
Q3	1 338	525	1 863	6	273	279	..	..	..	2 204
Q4	1 213	564	1 777	7	315	322	..	..	..	2 165
1968 Q1	1 595	564	2 159	5	295	300	..	..	..	2 538
Q2	1 553	593	2 146	7	323	330	..	..	..	2 557
Q3	1 679	632	2 311	7	339	346	..	..	..	2 736
Q4	1 710	636	2 346	7	289	296	..	..	..	2 730
1969 Q1	1 714	655	2 369	8	381	389	..	..	..	2 840
Q2	1 826	656	2 482	8	360	368	..	..	..	2 935
Q3	1 907	684	2 591	8	383	391	..	..	..	3 075
Q4	1 926	696	2 622	9	386	395	..	..	..	3 108

Source: Office for National Statistics; Enquiries 020 7533 6078

1.18 Balance of payments: current account

continued

£ million, seasonally adjusted

	Debits									
	Trade in goods	Trade in services	**Total goods and services**	Compensation of employees	Investment income	**Total income**	Central govt current transfers	Other sectors current transfers	**Total current transfers**	**Total current account**
	BOKH	IKBC	IKBI	IJAI	HBOL	HBOI	FLUD	FLUZ	IKBO	HBOO
1955 Q1	879	249	1 128	11	83	94	..	..	..	1 251
Q2	787	244	1 031	10	89	99	..	..	..	1 158
Q3	896	248	1 144	11	93	104	..	..	..	1 273
Q4	880	256	1 136	10	127	137	..	..	..	1 304
1956 Q1	845	281	1 126	10	100	110	..	..	..	1 271
Q2	849	274	1 123	12	100	112	..	..	..	1 272
Q3	851	279	1 130	12	106	118	..	..	..	1 279
Q4	844	287	1 131	12	85	97	..	..	..	1 265
1957 Q1	933	283	1 216	12	102	114	..	..	..	1 371
Q2	914	278	1 192	13	99	112	..	..	..	1 337
Q3	902	285	1 187	12	102	114	..	..	..	1 332
Q4	853	283	1 136	12	79	91	..	..	..	1 266
1958 Q1	851	264	1 115	12	118	130	..	..	..	1 282
Q2	820	274	1 094	14	108	122	..	..	..	1 246
Q3	891	278	1 169	12	105	117	..	..	..	1 319
Q4	874	283	1 157	13	115	128	..	..	..	1 323
1959 Q1	884	265	1 149	13	106	119	..	..	..	1 305
Q2	898	288	1 186	14	113	127	..	..	..	1 343
Q3	924	283	1 207	13	109	122	..	..	..	1 366
Q4	997	295	1 292	14	125	139	..	..	..	1 468
1960 Q1	1 021	321	1 342	12	122	134	..	..	..	1 513
Q2	1 052	318	1 370	13	123	136	..	..	..	1 540
Q3	1 064	325	1 389	13	134	147	..	..	..	1 577
Q4	1 068	330	1 398	14	123	137	..	..	..	1 575
1961 Q1	1 063	338	1 401	13	114	127	..	..	..	1 567
Q2	1 041	337	1 378	14	119	133	..	..	..	1 554
Q3	1 000	337	1 337	13	125	138	..	..	..	1 517
Q4	1 007	336	1 343	14	125	139	..	..	..	1 522
1962 Q1	1 015	350	1 365	13	119	132	..	..	..	1 544
Q2	1 041	348	1 389	14	117	131	..	..	..	1 561
Q3	1 066	337	1 403	14	117	131	..	..	..	1 575
Q4	1 047	350	1 397	15	129	144	..	..	..	1 581
1963 Q1	1 066	349	1 415	14	128	142	..	..	..	1 599
Q2	1 111	360	1 471	15	121	136	..	..	..	1 649
Q3	1 148	368	1 516	14	125	139	..	..	..	1 703
Q4	1 193	376	1 569	15	135	150	..	..	..	1 766
1964 Q1	1 285	396	1 681	14	140	154	..	..	..	1 910
Q2	1 270	393	1 663	14	152	166	..	..	..	1 905
Q3	1 293	395	1 688	15	151	166	..	..	..	1 924
Q4	1 335	401	1 736	15	125	140	..	..	..	1 950
1965 Q1	1 253	413	1 666	14	163	177	..	..	..	1 912
Q2	1 307	418	1 725	15	163	178	..	..	..	1 981
Q3	1 332	419	1 751	14	163	177	..	..	..	2 012
Q4	1 354	429	1 783	15	149	164	..	..	..	2 017
1966 Q1	1 388	440	1 828	15	170	185	..	..	..	2 081
Q2	1 353	435	1 788	16	159	175	..	..	..	2 050
Q3	1 402	446	1 848	16	162	178	..	..	..	2 104
Q4	1 316	435	1 751	17	170	187	..	..	..	2 021
1967 Q1	1 463	432	1 895	16	161	177	..	..	..	2 144
Q2	1 461	442	1 903	15	172	187	..	..	..	2 188
Q3	1 447	477	1 924	16	159	175	..	..	..	2 196
Q4	1 559	533	2 092	16	197	213	..	..	..	2 407
1968 Q1	1 772	525	2 297	19	218	237	..	..	..	2 628
Q2	1 782	500	2 282	18	217	235	..	..	..	2 625
Q3	1 845	524	2 369	19	233	252	..	..	..	2 730
Q4	1 846	535	2 381	18	221	239	..	..	..	2 725
1969 Q1	1 863	574	2 437	20	216	236	..	..	..	2 778
Q2	1 892	555	2 447	20	230	250	..	..	..	2 822
Q3	1 887	563	2 450	20	264	284	..	..	..	2 858
Q4	1 945	607	2 552	20	257	277	..	..	..	2 946

Source: Office for National Statistics; Enquiries 020 7533 6078

1.18 Balance of payments: current account

continued

£ million, seasonally adjusted

	Balances(credits less debits)									
	Trade in goods	Trade in services	**Total goods and services**	Compensation of employees	Investment income	**Total income**	Central govt current transfers	Other sectors current transfers	**Total current transfers**	**Total current account**
	BOKI	IKBD	IKBJ	IJAJ	HBOM	HBOJ	FNSV	FNTC	IKBP	HBOP
1955 Q1	–90	15	–75	–7	55	48	..	..	20	–7
Q2	–83	14	–69	–7	52	45	..	..	13	–11
Q3	–83	7	–76	–7	51	44	..	..	11	–21
Q4	–59	6	–53	–6	17	11	..	..	–1	–43
1956 Q1	–10	10	–	–6	52	46	..	..	2	48
Q2	27	8	35	–8	55	47	..	..	–5	77
Q3	3	7	10	–8	54	46	..	..	7	63
Q4	30	1	31	–8	76	68	..	..	–2	97
1957 Q1	–37	42	5	–8	53	45	..	..	–1	49
Q2	–22	36	14	–9	62	53	..	..	4	71
Q3	–4	21	17	–8	62	54	..	..	2	73
Q4	34	22	56	–7	80	73	..	..	–10	119
1958 Q1	34	40	74	–8	103	95	..	..	–3	166
Q2	–3	30	27	–10	40	30	..	..	8	65
Q3	10	24	34	–8	89	81	..	..	2	117
Q4	–7	25	18	–8	71	63	..	..	–3	78
1959 Q1	–35	45	10	–9	58	49	..	..	–5	54
Q2	–12	20	8	–10	81	71	..	..	7	86
Q3	–20	30	10	–9	73	64	..	..	–2	72
Q4	–49	23	–26	–9	57	48	..	..	–	22
1960 Q1	–50	4	–46	–8	57	49	..	..	–2	1
Q2	–115	6	–109	–9	44	35	..	..	2	–72
Q3	–123	13	–110	–9	47	38	..	..	–4	–76
Q4	–116	16	–100	–9	87	78	..	..	–2	–24
1961 Q1	–64	18	–46	–9	81	72	..	..	–4	22
Q2	–59	9	–50	–9	52	43	..	..	–3	–10
Q3	–3	10	7	–8	72	64	..	..	–2	69
Q4	–18	14	–4	–9	54	45	..	..	–	41
1962 Q1	–31	14	–17	–9	92	83	..	..	–7	59
Q2	–10	7	–3	–9	98	89	..	..	–1	85
Q3	–42	17	–25	–9	82	73	..	..	–4	44
Q4	–21	12	–9	–10	74	64	..	..	–2	53
1963 Q1	–5	16	11	–10	92	82	..	..	–4	89
Q2	–22	–2	–24	–10	100	90	..	..	–6	60
Q3	–34	–6	–40	–9	115	106	..	..	–14	52
Q4	–62	–4	–66	–9	109	100	..	..	–13	21
1964 Q1	–143	–16	–159	–9	117	108	..	..	–16	–67
Q2	–103	–11	–114	–8	99	91	..	..	–16	–39
Q3	–146	–7	–153	–8	85	77	..	..	–12	–88
Q4	–159	–	–159	–8	119	111	..	..	–18	–66
1965 Q1	–50	–20	–70	–9	103	94	..	..	–11	13
Q2	–91	–5	–96	–9	113	104	..	..	–19	–11
Q3	–67	–24	–91	–8	116	108	..	..	–27	–10
Q4	–55	–17	–72	–8	135	127	..	..	–9	46
1966 Q1	–78	–13	–91	–10	92	82	..	..	–13	–22
Q2	–79	13	–66	–10	123	113	..	..	–29	18
Q3	–55	10	–45	–9	107	98	..	..	–23	30
Q4	101	34	135	–10	91	81	..	..	–24	192
1967 Q1	–50	46	–4	–11	103	92	..	..	–13	75
Q2	–96	32	–64	–9	76	67	..	..	–33	–30
Q3	–109	48	–61	–10	114	104	..	..	–35	8
Q4	–346	31	–315	–9	118	109	..	..	–36	–242
1968 Q1	–177	39	–138	–14	77	63	..	..	–15	–90
Q2	–229	93	–136	–11	106	95	..	..	–27	–68
Q3	–166	108	–58	–12	106	94	..	..	–30	6
Q4	–136	101	–35	–11	68	57	..	..	–17	5
1969 Q1	–149	81	–68	–12	165	153	..	..	–23	62
Q2	–66	101	35	–12	130	118	..	..	–40	113
Q3	20	121	141	–12	119	107	..	..	–31	217
Q4	–19	89	70	–11	129	118	..	..	–26	162

Source: Office for National Statistics; Enquiries 020 7533 6078

1.18 Balance of payments: current account

continued

£ million, seasonally adjusted

	Credits									
	Trade in goods	Trade in services	**Total goods and services**	Compensation of employees	Investment income	**Total income**	Central govt current transfers	Other sectors current transfers	**Total current transfers**	**Total current account**
	BOKG	IKBB	IKBH	IJAH	HBOK	HBOH	FHDM	FHIB	IKBN	HBON
1970 Q1	2 051	755	2 806	8	390	398	..	..	..	3 300
Q2	2 019	767	2 786	8	412	420	..	..	..	3 313
Q3	1 968	832	2 800	8	410	418	..	..	..	3 317
Q4	2 228	869	3 097	9	429	438	..	..	..	3 645
1971 Q1	2 111	895	3 006	9	413	422	..	..	..	3 542
Q2	2 332	910	3 242	9	419	428	..	..	..	3 790
Q3	2 381	937	3 318	11	431	442	..	..	..	3 875
Q4	2 366	958	3 324	10	424	434	..	..	..	3 891
1972 Q1	2 312	974	3 286	11	876	887	..	..	..	4 305
Q2	2 375	957	3 332	12	883	895	..	..	..	4 370
Q3	2 140	998	3 138	13	997	1 010	..	..	..	4 282
Q4	2 760	1 071	3 831	13	979	992	..	..	..	4 975
1973 Q1	2 768	1 113	3 881	13	1 120	1 133	..	..	..	5 180
Q2	2 904	1 186	4 090	14	1 309	1 323	..	..	..	5 588
Q3	3 122	1 251	4 373	16	1 378	1 394	..	..	..	5 938
Q4	3 297	1 386	4 683	16	1 598	1 614	..	..	..	6 494
1974 Q1	3 662	1 471	5 133	16	1 706	1 722	..	..	..	7 057
Q2	4 152	1 546	5 698	16	1 649	1 665	..	..	..	7 548
Q3	4 347	1 621	5 968	18	1 713	1 731	..	..	..	7 865
Q4	4 385	1 647	6 032	19	1 749	1 768	..	..	..	8 017
1975 Q1	4 689	1 753	6 442	22	1 701	1 723	..	..	..	8 430
Q2	4 626	1 781	6 407	23	1 770	1 793	..	..	..	8 448
Q3	4 837	1 841	6 678	21	1 818	1 839	..	..	..	8 758
Q4	5 299	1 977	7 276	22	1 915	1 937	..	..	..	9 469
1976 Q1	5 634	2 138	7 772	28	2 094	2 122	..	..	..	10 174
Q2	6 204	2 308	8 512	29	2 216	2 245	..	..	..	11 054
Q3	6 465	2 493	8 958	27	2 423	2 450	..	..	..	11 692
Q4	7 101	2 675	9 776	30	2 475	2 505	..	..	..	12 599
1977 Q1	7 529	2 647	10 176	34	2 341	2 375	..	..	..	12 940
Q2	7 990	2 755	10 745	34	2 339	2 373	..	..	..	13 547
Q3	8 425	2 880	11 305	34	2 470	2 504	..	..	..	14 221
Q4	8 097	2 887	10 984	37	2 525	2 562	..	..	..	13 986
1978 Q1	8 393	2 905	11 298	39	2 700	2 739	..	..	..	14 515
Q2	8 864	2 916	11 780	41	3 023	3 064	..	..	..	15 334
Q3	8 921	3 101	12 022	38	3 197	3 235	..	..	..	15 785
Q4	9 153	3 126	12 279	41	3 351	3 392	..	..	..	16 315
1979 Q1	8 421	3 252	11 673	43	4 153	4 196	..	..	..	16 506
Q2	10 809	3 354	14 163	44	4 424	4 468	..	..	..	19 408
Q3	10 523	3 568	14 091	43	5 080	5 123	..	..	..	19 998
Q4	11 096	3 781	14 877	46	5 556	5 602	..	..	..	21 351
1980 Q1	11 984	3 736	15 720	53	6 195	6 248	..	..	..	22 910
Q2	11 955	3 706	15 661	54	6 976	7 030	..	..	..	23 682
Q3	11 774	3 749	15 523	54	6 321	6 375	..	..	..	22 729
Q4	11 780	3 811	15 591	58	6 499	6 557	..	..	..	23 197
1981 Q1	11 867	3 842	15 709	57	7 854	7 911	..	..	..	25 119
Q2	12 306	3 967	16 273	60	9 411	9 471	..	..	..	26 601
Q3	13 266	4 210	17 476	58	11 352	11 410	..	..	..	29 939
Q4	13 595	4 262	17 857	63	12 572	12 635	..	..	..	31 946
1982 Q1	13 414	4 182	17 596	61	11 255	11 316	..	..	..	30 848
Q2	13 853	4 264	18 117	62	12 638	12 700	..	..	..	31 873
Q3	13 939	4 164	18 103	62	12 397	12 459	..	..	..	31 737
Q4	14 451	4 312	18 763	67	12 438	12 505	..	..	..	32 673
1983 Q1	14 644	4 552	19 196	70	12 358	12 428	..	..	..	33 418
Q2	14 861	4 604	19 465	72	11 270	11 342	..	..	..	32 214
Q3	15 526	4 776	20 302	71	11 418	11 489	..	..	..	33 167
Q4	15 953	4 835	20 788	77	11 545	11 622	..	..	..	34 046
1984 Q1	16 650	5 001	21 651	77	12 392	12 469	..	..	..	35 982
Q2	17 084	5 119	22 203	80	13 386	13 466	..	..	..	37 209
Q3	17 947	5 250	23 197	81	14 972	15 053	..	..	..	39 720
Q4	18 884	5 574	24 458	85	15 905	15 990	..	..	..	42 655

Source: Office for National Statistics; Enquiries 020 7533 6078

1.18 Balance of payments: current account

continued

£ million, seasonally adjusted

	Debits									
	Trade in goods	Trade in services	**Total goods and services**	Compensation of employees	Investment income	**Total income**	Central govt current transfers	Other sectors current transfers	**Total current transfers**	**Total current account**
	BOKH	IKBC	IKBI	IJAI	HBOL	HBOI	FLUD	FLUZ	IKBO	HBOO
1970 Q1	1 967	619	2 586	20	239	259	..	..	..	2 957
Q2	2 091	647	2 738	23	250	273	..	..	..	3 141
Q3	2 059	718	2 777	22	254	276	..	..	..	3 174
Q4	2 167	784	2 951	24	286	310	..	..	..	3 392
1971 Q1	2 150	756	2 906	24	255	279	..	..	..	3 294
Q2	2 285	780	3 065	24	279	303	..	..	..	3 508
Q3	2 241	780	3 021	27	271	298	..	..	..	3 454
Q4	2 309	794	3 103	27	322	349	..	..	..	3 601
1972 Q1	2 418	802	3 220	25	752	777	..	..	..	4 133
Q2	2 472	782	3 254	24	747	771	..	..	..	4 187
Q3	2 473	845	3 318	26	864	890	..	..	..	4 366
Q4	2 960	906	3 866	26	854	880	..	..	..	4 902
1973 Q1	3 191	946	4 137	30	980	1 010	..	..	..	5 347
Q2	3 390	997	4 387	30	973	1 003	..	..	..	5 692
Q3	3 800	1 069	4 869	33	1 066	1 099	..	..	..	6 211
Q4	4 283	1 164	5 447	34	1 103	1 137	..	..	..	6 864
1974 Q1	4 888	1 253	6 141	37	1 293	1 330	..	..	..	7 734
Q2	5 551	1 301	6 852	37	1 267	1 304	..	..	..	8 432
Q3	5 653	1 312	6 965	43	1 386	1 429	..	..	..	8 646
Q4	5 695	1 354	7 049	44	1 442	1 486	..	..	..	8 854
1975 Q1	5 577	1 416	6 993	42	1 506	1 548	..	..	..	8 811
Q2	5 290	1 444	6 734	46	1 652	1 698	..	..	..	8 781
Q3	5 871	1 514	7 385	50	1 642	1 692	..	..	..	9 412
Q4	5 958	1 585	7 543	52	1 698	1 750	..	..	..	9 666
1976 Q1	6 177	1 538	7 715	61	1 798	1 859	..	..	..	9 919
Q2	7 232	1 773	9 005	63	1 861	1 924	..	..	..	11 364
Q3	7 683	1 856	9 539	65	2 038	2 103	..	..	..	12 079
Q4	8 242	1 982	10 224	65	2 126	2 191	..	..	..	12 884
1977 Q1	8 483	1 899	10 382	69	2 234	2 303	..	..	..	13 152
Q2	8 860	1 968	10 828	72	2 400	2 472	..	..	..	13 838
Q3	8 595	2 056	10 651	75	2 551	2 626	..	..	..	13 858
Q4	8 374	2 027	10 401	75	2 610	2 685	..	..	..	13 639
1978 Q1	8 947	2 027	10 974	72	2 637	2 709	..	..	..	14 428
Q2	8 982	2 120	11 102	75	2 851	2 926	..	..	..	14 764
Q3	9 435	2 127	11 562	75	3 056	3 131	..	..	..	15 528
Q4	9 501	2 095	11 596	77	3 341	3 418	..	..	..	15 796
1979 Q1	9 885	2 329	12 214	70	3 741	3 811	..	..	..	16 853
Q2	11 265	2 501	13 766	75	4 356	4 431	..	..	..	19 214
Q3	11 108	2 512	13 620	78	4 850	4 928	..	..	..	19 632
Q4	11 917	2 648	14 565	83	5 726	5 809	..	..	..	21 476
1980 Q1	12 435	2 800	15 235	68	6 468	6 536	..	..	..	22 716
Q2	12 142	2 902	15 044	74	7 551	7 625	..	..	..	23 836
Q3	10 920	2 809	13 729	78	6 621	6 699	..	..	..	21 537
Q4	10 667	2 774	13 441	81	6 697	6 778	..	..	..	21 263
1981 Q1	10 184	2 771	12 955	72	7 851	7 923	..	..	..	21 952
Q2	11 030	3 125	14 155	76	9 470	9 546	..	..	..	24 930
Q3	13 407	3 140	16 547	77	11 506	11 583	..	..	..	29 531
Q4	13 175	3 411	16 586	79	12 731	12 810	..	..	..	30 643
1982 Q1	13 149	3 209	16 358	82	11 609	11 691	..	..	..	29 357
Q2	13 726	3 590	17 316	87	12 756	12 843	..	..	..	31 662
Q3	13 399	3 518	16 917	88	12 547	12 635	..	..	..	31 083
Q4	13 504	3 536	17 040	90	12 277	12 367	..	..	..	30 922
1983 Q1	14 884	3 515	18 399	91	11 976	12 067	..	..	..	31 778
Q2	15 456	3 727	19 183	95	11 331	11 426	..	..	..	32 283
Q3	15 689	3 789	19 478	96	10 799	10 895	..	..	..	31 963
Q4	16 573	3 795	20 368	97	11 280	11 377	..	..	..	33 522
1984 Q1	17 115	3 913	21 028	109	12 056	12 165	..	..	..	34 777
Q2	18 485	4 174	22 659	102	12 887	12 989	..	..	..	37 437
Q3	19 499	4 144	23 643	99	14 425	14 524	..	..	..	40 013
Q4	20 875	4 372	25 247	107	14 790	14 897	..	..	..	42 130

Source: Office for National Statistics; Enquiries 020 7533 6078

1.18 Balance of payments: current account

continued

£ million, seasonally adjusted

	Balances(credits less debits)									
	Trade in goods	Trade in services	**Total goods and services**	Compensation of employees	Investment income	**Total income**	Central govt current transfers	Other sectors current transfers	**Total current transfers**	**Total current account**
	BOKI	IKBD	IKBJ	IJAJ	HBOM	HBOJ	FNSV	FNTC	IKBP	HBOP
1970 Q1	84	136	220	–12	151	139	..	..	–16	343
Q2	–72	120	48	–15	162	147	..	..	–23	172
Q3	–91	114	23	–14	156	142	..	..	–22	143
Q4	61	85	146	–15	143	128	..	..	–21	253
1971 Q1	–39	139	100	–15	158	143	..	..	5	248
Q2	47	130	177	–15	140	125	..	..	–20	282
Q3	140	157	297	–16	160	144	..	..	–20	421
Q4	57	164	221	–17	102	85	..	..	–16	290
1972 Q1	–106	172	66	–14	124	110	..	..	–4	172
Q2	–97	175	78	–12	136	124	..	..	–19	183
Q3	–333	153	–180	–13	133	120	..	..	–24	–84
Q4	–200	165	–35	–13	125	112	..	..	–4	73
1973 Q1	–423	167	–256	–17	140	123	..	..	–34	–167
Q2	–486	189	–297	–16	336	320	..	..	–127	–104
Q3	–678	182	–496	–17	312	295	..	..	–72	–273
Q4	–986	222	–764	–18	495	477	..	..	–83	–370
1974 Q1	–1 226	218	–1 008	–21	413	392	..	..	–61	–677
Q2	–1 399	245	–1 154	–21	382	361	..	..	–91	–884
Q3	–1 306	309	–997	–25	327	302	..	..	–86	–781
Q4	–1 310	293	–1 017	–25	307	282	..	..	–102	–837
1975 Q1	–888	337	–551	–20	195	175	..	..	–5	–381
Q2	–664	337	–327	–23	118	95	..	..	–101	–333
Q3	–1 034	327	–707	–29	176	147	..	..	–94	–654
Q4	–659	392	–267	–30	217	187	..	..	–117	–197
1976 Q1	–543	600	57	–33	296	263	..	..	–65	255
Q2	–1 028	535	–493	–34	355	321	..	..	–138	–310
Q3	–1 218	637	–581	–38	385	347	..	..	–153	–387
Q4	–1 141	693	–448	–35	349	314	..	..	–151	–285
1977 Q1	–954	748	–206	–35	107	72	..	..	–78	–212
Q2	–870	787	–83	–38	–61	–99	..	..	–109	–291
Q3	–170	824	654	–41	–81	–122	..	..	–169	363
Q4	–277	860	583	–38	–85	–123	..	..	–113	347
1978 Q1	–554	878	324	–33	63	30	..	..	–267	87
Q2	–118	796	678	–34	172	138	..	..	–246	570
Q3	–514	974	460	–37	141	104	..	..	–307	257
Q4	–348	1 031	683	–36	10	–26	..	..	–138	519
1979 Q1	–1 464	923	–541	–27	412	385	..	..	–191	–347
Q2	–456	853	397	–31	68	37	..	..	–240	194
Q3	–585	1 056	471	–35	230	195	..	..	–300	366
Q4	–821	1 133	312	–37	–170	–207	..	..	–230	–125
1980 Q1	–451	936	485	–15	–273	–288	..	..	–3	194
Q2	–187	804	617	–20	–575	–595	..	..	–176	–154
Q3	854	940	1 794	–24	–300	–324	..	..	–278	1 192
Q4	1 113	1 037	2 150	–23	–198	–221	..	..	5	1 934
1981 Q1	1 683	1 071	2 754	–15	3	–12	..	..	425	3 167
Q2	1 276	842	2 118	–16	–59	–75	..	..	–372	1 671
Q3	–141	1 070	929	–19	–154	–173	..	..	–348	408
Q4	420	851	1 271	–16	–159	–175	..	..	207	1 303
1982 Q1	265	973	1 238	–21	–354	–375	..	..	628	1 491
Q2	127	674	801	–25	–118	–143	..	..	–447	211
Q3	540	646	1 186	–26	–150	–176	..	..	–356	654
Q4	947	776	1 723	–23	161	138	..	..	–110	1 751
1983 Q1	–240	1 037	797	–21	382	361	..	..	482	1 640
Q2	–595	877	282	–23	–61	–84	..	..	–267	–69
Q3	–163	987	824	–25	619	594	..	..	–214	1 204
Q4	–620	1 040	420	–20	265	245	..	..	–141	524
1984 Q1	–465	1 088	623	–32	336	304	..	..	278	1 205
Q2	–1 401	945	–456	–22	499	477	..	..	–249	–228
Q3	–1 552	1 106	–446	–18	547	529	..	..	–376	–293
Q4	–1 991	1 202	–789	–22	1 115	1 093	..	..	221	525

Source: Office for National Statistics; Enquiries 020 7533 6078

1.18 Balance of payments: current account

continued

£ million, seasonally adjusted

	Credits									
	Trade in goods	Trade in services	**Total goods and services**	Compensation of employees	Investment income	**Total income**	Central govt current transfers	Other sectors current transfers	**Total current transfers**	**Total current account**
	BOKG	IKBB	IKBH	IJAH	HBOK	HBOH	FHDM	FHIB	IKBN	HBON
1985 Q1	19 940	5 771	25 711	82	15 765	15 847	..	..	..	43 635
Q2	20 568	5 947	26 515	86	15 004	15 090	..	..	..	43 372
Q3	18 973	5 908	24 881	86	13 610	13 696	..	..	..	40 289
Q4	18 810	6 009	24 819	90	12 704	12 794	..	..	..	39 565
1986 Q1	18 301	6 176	24 477	93	12 646	12 739	734	959	1 693	38 909
Q2	18 001	6 028	24 029	93	12 838	12 931	269	1 157	1 426	38 386
Q3	17 726	6 120	23 846	89	13 148	13 237	541	1 041	1 582	38 665
Q4	18 969	6 460	25 429	94	13 326	13 420	388	1 217	1 605	40 454
1987 Q1	19 744	6 595	26 339	100	13 231	13 331	1 121	1 197	2 318	41 988
Q2	19 413	6 762	26 175	103	13 115	13 218	972	1 229	2 201	41 594
Q3	20 434	6 913	27 347	103	13 343	13 446	962	1 084	2 046	42 839
Q4	19 940	6 636	26 576	107	12 995	13 102	1 063	902	1 965	41 643
1988 Q1	19 230	6 654	25 884	110	14 200	14 310	1 183	964	2 147	42 341
Q2	20 192	6 623	26 815	112	14 843	14 955	1 120	1 216	2 336	44 106
Q3	20 932	6 645	27 577	111	16 432	16 543	1 556	1 243	2 799	46 919
Q4	20 357	6 801	27 158	112	16 457	16 569	1 301	1 091	2 392	46 119
1989 Q1	21 798	7 113	28 911	117	19 045	19 162	1 195	1 267	2 462	50 535
Q2	22 412	7 375	29 787	120	20 399	20 519	1 247	1 384	2 631	52 937
Q3	23 457	7 474	30 931	121	20 415	20 536	1 175	1 184	2 359	53 826
Q4	24 944	7 310	32 254	118	21 940	22 058	1 307	1 326	2 633	56 945
1990 Q1	25 237	7 887	33 124	128	21 470	21 598	1 118	1 312	2 430	57 152
Q2	25 835	7 772	33 607	142	21 517	21 659	1 042	1 337	2 379	57 645
Q3	25 444	7 653	33 097	135	22 716	22 851	1 071	1 536	2 607	58 555
Q4	25 797	7 876	33 673	138	22 483	22 621	1 063	1 771	2 834	59 128
1991 Q1	25 055	7 214	32 269	147	21 612	21 759	1 844	1 899	3 743	57 771
Q2	26 040	8 037	34 077	135	21 980	22 115	2 349	1 867	4 216	60 408
Q3	26 632	8 115	34 747	135	21 057	21 192	1 459	1 761	3 220	59 159
Q4	26 212	8 060	34 272	134	19 770	19 904	1 094	1 966	3 060	57 236
1992 Q1	26 238	8 633	34 871	147	18 593	18 740	1 395	1 855	3 250	56 861
Q2	26 953	8 871	35 824	139	17 453	17 592	968	1 830	2 798	56 214
Q3	26 551	8 755	35 306	129	18 625	18 754	891	1 809	2 700	56 760
Q4	28 121	9 169	37 290	136	19 878	20 014	1 000	1 892	2 892	60 196
1993 Q1	30 246	9 747	39 993	105	20 570	20 675	1 316	1 795	3 111	63 779
Q2	29 875	9 716	39 591	122	19 215	19 337	1 349	2 136	3 485	62 413
Q3	30 612	10 191	40 803	175	19 973	20 148	1 359	1 895	3 254	64 205
Q4	31 306	10 385	41 691	193	19 067	19 260	1 282	2 132	3 414	64 365
1994 Q1	32 096	10 510	42 606	189	20 556	20 745	1 102	1 991	3 093	66 444
Q2	33 327	10 647	43 974	166	19 567	19 733	1 312	1 862	3 174	66 881
Q3	34 228	11 072	45 300	161	21 013	21 174	1 315	1 981	3 296	69 770
Q4	35 609	11 278	46 887	165	21 503	21 668	1 279	1 967	3 246	71 801
1995 Q1	37 332	11 797	49 129	177	22 580	22 757	1 281	2 198	3 479	75 365
Q2	37 406	11 972	49 378	254	24 259	24 513	1 249	1 963	3 212	77 103
Q3	38 987	12 189	51 176	243	24 836	25 079	1 128	2 245	3 373	79 628
Q4	40 000	12 729	52 729	213	25 411	25 624	1 187	2 112	3 299	81 652
1996 Q1	41 136	12 864	54 000	320	25 412	25 732	1 664	2 308	3 972	83 704
Q2	41 706	13 118	54 824	232	25 473	25 705	1 692	2 287	3 979	84 508
Q3	42 225	13 010	55 235	180	25 217	25 397	1 347	7 595	8 942	89 574
Q4	42 336	13 908	56 244	179	25 567	25 746	2 051	2 442	4 493	86 483
1997 Q1	42 652	13 940	56 592	215	26 202	26 417	1 826	2 326	4 152	87 161
Q2	42 967	14 255	57 222	254	26 638	26 892	1 331	2 443	3 774	87 888
Q3	43 079	14 559	57 638	280	27 544	27 824	1 516	2 111	3 627	89 089
Q4	43 085	14 789	57 874	258	26 514	26 772	1 306	2 446	3 752	88 398
1998 Q1	41 518	14 792	56 310	255	26 858	27 113	1 663	2 538	4 201	87 624
Q2	41 638	15 450	57 088	189	26 719	26 908	1 470	2 162	3 632	87 628
Q3	40 915	15 654	56 569	182	27 522	27 704	1 618	2 121	3 739	88 012
Q4	40 021	15 486	55 507	214	27 293	27 507	1 630	2 222	3 852	86 866
1999 Q1	39 023	15 851	54 874	192	26 689	26 881	3 014	2 231	5 245	87 000
Q2	40 206	16 219	56 425	280	25 144	25 424	2 093	2 324	4 417	86 266
Q3	43 503	16 162	59 665	255	25 893	26 148	2 260	1 972	4 232	90 045
Q4	42 935	15 750	58 685	233	30 413	30 646	2 097	2 287	4 384	93 715
2000 Q1	44 586	15 695	60 281	214	31 227	31 441	2 722	2 477	5 199	96 921

Source: Office for National Statistics; Enquiries 020 7533 6078

1.18 Balance of payments: current account

continued

£ million, seasonally adjusted

	Debits									
	Trade in goods	Trade in services	**Total goods and services**	Compensation of employees	Investment income	**Total income**	Central govt current transfers	Other sectors current transfers	**Total current transfers**	**Total current account**
	BOKH	IKBC	IKBI	IJAI	HBOL	HBOI	FLUD	FLUZ	IKBO	HBOO
1985 Q1	21 928	4 411	26 339	126	15 629	15 755	..	..	..	44 212
Q2	20 796	4 221	25 017	108	14 931	15 039	..	..	..	42 009
Q3	19 526	4 088	23 614	112	13 422	13 534	..	..	..	39 469
Q4	19 457	4 296	23 753	118	12 969	13 087	..	..	..	38 944
1986 Q1	19 887	4 334	24 221	144	12 196	12 340	280	1 615	1 895	38 456
Q2	20 178	4 552	24 730	127	12 055	12 182	327	1 605	1 932	38 844
Q3	20 629	4 650	25 279	123	12 262	12 385	327	2 118	2 445	40 109
Q4	21 920	4 743	26 663	131	12 417	12 548	327	1 752	2 079	41 290
1987 Q1	21 634	4 734	26 368	170	12 311	12 481	333	2 317	2 650	41 499
Q2	22 241	5 025	27 266	148	12 665	12 813	380	2 286	2 666	42 745
Q3	23 512	5 232	28 744	135	12 963	13 098	318	2 406	2 724	44 566
Q4	23 842	5 229	29 071	134	13 068	13 202	285	2 279	2 564	44 837
1988 Q1	23 589	5 469	29 058	127	13 879	14 006	492	2 323	2 815	45 879
Q2	25 004	5 520	30 524	124	14 251	14 375	430	2 441	2 871	47 770
Q3	26 579	5 549	32 128	120	16 070	16 190	338	2 078	2 416	50 734
Q4	27 092	5 855	32 947	138	16 377	16 515	966	2 211	3 177	52 639
1989 Q1	28 208	6 214	34 422	132	18 473	18 605	459	2 562	3 021	56 048
Q2	29 120	6 179	35 299	161	20 216	20 377	521	2 610	3 131	58 807
Q3	30 202	6 463	36 665	148	20 826	20 974	551	2 526	3 077	60 716
Q4	29 805	6 499	36 304	173	22 210	22 383	524	2 952	3 476	62 163
1990 Q1	31 317	6 655	37 972	163	21 838	22 001	542	2 934	3 476	63 449
Q2	31 238	6 846	38 084	140	21 852	21 992	612	2 947	3 559	63 635
Q3	29 460	6 725	36 185	161	22 584	22 745	371	3 004	3 375	62 305
Q4	29 005	6 952	35 957	189	22 360	22 549	470	3 628	4 098	62 604
1991 Q1	28 063	6 396	34 459	173	22 418	22 591	786	2 979	3 765	60 815
Q2	28 063	6 825	34 888	128	22 472	22 600	866	3 078	3 944	61 432
Q3	29 101	6 778	35 879	147	21 656	21 803	752	3 089	3 841	61 523
Q4	28 935	6 956	35 891	166	19 763	19 929	814	2 544	3 358	59 178
1992 Q1	28 906	7 371	36 277	170	18 191	18 361	997	3 342	4 339	58 977
Q2	29 904	7 383	37 287	83	17 337	17 420	975	3 286	4 261	58 968
Q3	29 866	7 325	37 191	181	17 762	17 943	854	3 302	4 156	59 290
Q4	32 237	7 675	39 912	166	19 095	19 261	680	3 025	3 705	62 878
1993 Q1	33 954	7 962	41 916	174	20 385	20 559	891	3 537	4 428	66 903
Q2	33 093	8 306	41 399	112	19 131	19 243	1 145	3 537	4 682	65 324
Q3	33 753	8 446	42 199	116	19 744	19 860	1 034	3 529	4 563	66 622
Q4	34 558	8 702	43 260	158	18 915	19 073	1 086	3 112	4 198	66 531
1994 Q1	35 250	8 931	44 181	174	18 168	18 342	1 404	3 394	4 798	67 321
Q2	35 866	9 326	45 192	197	18 033	18 230	1 251	3 430	4 681	68 103
Q3	36 688	9 260	45 948	255	18 965	19 220	1 264	3 411	4 675	69 843
Q4	38 547	9 462	48 009	225	19 533	19 758	876	2 444	3 320	71 087
1995 Q1	38 940	9 379	48 319	376	20 979	21 355	1 314	3 684	4 998	74 672
Q2	40 759	10 080	50 839	217	23 675	23 892	1 025	3 808	4 833	79 564
Q3	42 617	10 160	52 777	290	22 990	23 280	1 149	3 816	4 965	81 022
Q4	43 133	10 153	53 286	300	23 170	23 470	1 307	4 172	5 479	82 235
1996 Q1	44 882	10 869	55 751	206	23 530	23 736	1 544	4 043	5 587	85 074
Q2	45 273	11 067	56 340	211	22 622	22 833	1 292	3 982	5 274	84 447
Q3	45 134	10 987	56 121	196	23 947	24 143	867	9 061	9 928	90 192
Q4	45 200	11 080	56 280	205	23 552	23 757	1 353	3 766	5 119	85 156
1997 Q1	44 859	10 945	55 804	177	22 910	23 087	1 496	4 278	5 774	84 665
Q2	45 968	11 150	57 118	233	24 077	24 310	1 389	3 376	4 765	86 193
Q3	45 780	11 468	57 248	282	24 125	24 407	1 386	3 752	5 138	86 793
Q4	47 086	11 566	58 652	232	24 699	24 931	816	3 863	4 679	88 262
1998 Q1	45 951	11 867	57 818	203	23 852	24 055	1 774	4 447	6 221	88 094
Q2	46 365	12 014	58 379	201	24 580	24 781	1 147	3 407	4 554	87 714
Q3	46 364	12 189	58 553	203	22 625	22 828	1 521	3 235	4 756	86 137
Q4	45 949	12 730	58 679	243	23 080	23 323	2 143	4 120	6 263	88 265
1999 Q1	46 623	13 105	59 728	183	24 998	25 181	2 129	4 053	6 182	91 091
Q2	46 438	13 078	59 516	169	23 979	24 148	1 652	3 600	5 252	88 916
Q3	49 232	13 068	62 300	201	24 717	24 918	1 837	3 685	5 522	92 740
Q4	50 141	13 193	63 334	206	26 314	26 520	1 660	3 746	5 406	95 260
2000 Q1	51 140	13 188	64 328	217	30 369	30 586	1 827	4 190	6 017	100 931

Source: Office for National Statistics;Enquiries 020 7533 6078

1.18 Balance of payments: current account

continued

£ million, seasonally adjusted

	Balances(credits less debits)									
	Trade in goods	Trade in services	**Total goods and services**	Compensation of employees	Investment income	**Total income**	Central govt current transfers	Other sectors current transfers	**Total current transfers**	**Total current account**
	BOKI	IKBD	IKBJ	IJAJ	HBOM	HBOJ	FNSV	FNTC	IKBP	HBOP
1985 Q1	–1 988	1 360	–628	–44	136	92	..	..	–41	–577
Q2	–228	1 726	1 498	–22	73	51	..	..	–186	1 363
Q3	–553	1 820	1 267	–26	188	162	..	..	–609	820
Q4	–647	1 713	1 066	–28	–265	–293	..	..	–152	621
1986 Q1	–1 586	1 842	256	–51	450	399	454	–656	–202	453
Q2	–2 177	1 476	–701	–34	783	749	–58	–448	–506	–458
Q3	–2 903	1 470	–1 433	–34	886	852	214	–1 077	–863	–1 444
Q4	–2 951	1 717	–1 234	–37	909	872	61	–535	–474	–836
1987 Q1	–1 890	1 861	–29	–70	920	850	788	–1 120	–332	489
Q2	–2 828	1 737	–1 091	–45	450	405	592	–1 057	–465	–1 151
Q3	–3 078	1 681	–1 397	–32	380	348	644	–1 322	–678	–1 727
Q4	–3 902	1 407	–2 495	–27	–73	–100	778	–1 377	–599	–3 194
1988 Q1	–4 359	1 185	–3 174	–17	321	304	691	–1 359	–668	–3 538
Q2	–4 812	1 103	–3 709	–12	592	580	690	–1 225	–535	–3 664
Q3	–5 647	1 096	–4 551	–9	362	353	1 218	–835	383	–3 815
Q4	–6 735	946	–5 789	–26	80	54	335	–1 120	–785	–6 520
1989 Q1	–6 410	899	–5 511	–15	572	557	736	–1 295	–559	–5 513
Q2	–6 708	1 196	–5 512	–41	183	142	726	–1 226	–500	–5 870
Q3	–6 745	1 011	–5 734	–27	–411	–438	624	–1 342	–718	–6 890
Q4	–4 861	811	–4 050	–55	–270	–325	783	–1 626	–843	–5 218
1990 Q1	–6 080	1 232	–4 848	–35	–368	–403	576	–1 622	–1 046	–6 297
Q2	–5 403	926	–4 477	2	–335	–333	430	–1 610	–1 180	–5 990
Q3	–4 016	928	–3 088	–26	132	106	700	–1 468	–768	–3 750
Q4	–3 208	924	–2 284	–51	123	72	593	–1 857	–1 264	–3 476
1991 Q1	–3 008	818	–2 190	–26	–806	–832	1 058	–1 080	–22	–3 044
Q2	–2 023	1 212	–811	7	–492	–485	1 483	–1 211	272	–1 024
Q3	–2 469	1 337	–1 132	–12	–599	–611	707	–1 328	–621	–2 364
Q4	–2 723	1 104	–1 619	–32	7	–25	280	–578	–298	–1 942
1992 Q1	–2 668	1 262	–1 406	–23	402	379	398	–1 487	–1 089	–2 116
Q2	–2 951	1 488	–1 463	56	116	172	–7	–1 456	–1 463	–2 754
Q3	–3 315	1 430	–1 885	–52	863	811	37	–1 493	–1 456	–2 530
Q4	–4 116	1 494	–2 622	–30	783	753	320	–1 133	–813	–2 682
1993 Q1	–3 708	1 785	–1 923	–69	185	116	425	–1 742	–1 317	–3 124
Q2	–3 218	1 410	–1 808	10	84	94	204	–1 401	–1 197	–2 911
Q3	–3 141	1 745	–1 396	59	229	288	325	–1 634	–1 309	–2 417
Q4	–3 252	1 683	–1 569	35	152	187	196	–980	–784	–2 166
1994 Q1	–3 154	1 579	–1 575	15	2 388	2 403	–302	–1 403	–1 705	–877
Q2	–2 539	1 321	–1 218	–31	1 534	1 503	61	–1 568	–1 507	–1 222
Q3	–2 460	1 812	–648	–94	2 048	1 954	51	–1 430	–1 379	–73
Q4	–2 938	1 816	–1 122	–60	1 970	1 910	403	–477	–74	714
1995 Q1	–1 608	2 418	810	–199	1 601	1 402	–33	–1 486	–1 519	693
Q2	–3 353	1 892	–1 461	37	584	621	224	–1 845	–1 621	–2 461
Q3	–3 630	2 029	–1 601	–47	1 846	1 799	–21	–1 571	–1 592	–1 394
Q4	–3 133	2 576	–557	–87	2 241	2 154	–120	–2 060	–2 180	–583
1996 Q1	–3 746	1 995	–1 751	114	1 882	1 996	120	–1 735	–1 615	–1 370
Q2	–3 567	2 051	–1 516	21	2 851	2 872	400	–1 695	–1 295	61
Q3	–2 909	2 023	–886	–16	1 270	1 254	480	–1 466	–986	–618
Q4	–2 864	2 828	–36	–26	2 015	1 989	698	–1 324	–626	1 327
1997 Q1	–2 207	2 995	788	38	3 292	3 330	330	–1 952	–1 622	2 496
Q2	–3 001	3 105	104	21	2 561	2 582	–58	–933	–991	1 695
Q3	–2 701	3 091	390	–2	3 419	3 417	130	–1 641	–1 511	2 296
Q4	–4 001	3 223	–778	26	1 815	1 841	490	–1 417	–927	136
1998 Q1	–4 433	2 925	–1 508	52	3 006	3 058	–111	–1 909	–2 020	–470
Q2	–4 727	3 436	–1 291	–12	2 139	2 127	323	–1 245	–922	–86
Q3	–5 449	3 465	–1 984	–21	4 897	4 876	97	–1 114	–1 017	1 875
Q4	–5 928	2 756	–3 172	–29	4 213	4 184	–513	–1 898	–2 411	–1 399
1999 Q1	–7 600	2 746	–4 854	9	1 691	1 700	885	–1 822	–937	–4 091
Q2	–6 232	3 141	–3 091	111	1 165	1 276	441	–1 276	–835	–2 650
Q3	–5 729	3 094	–2 635	54	1 176	1 230	423	–1 713	–1 290	–2 695
Q4	–7 206	2 557	–4 649	27	4 099	4 126	437	–1 459	–1 022	–1 545
2000 Q1	–6 554	2 507	–4 047	–3	858	855	895	–1 713	–818	–4 010

Source: Office for National Statistics; Enquiries 020 7533 6078

1.19 Balance of payments: financial account

£ million

	Investment in the UK (net credits)				UK investment abroad (net debits)					Net transactions				
	Direct	Portfolio	Other	**Total**	Direct	Portfolio	Other	Reserve assets	**Total**	Direct	Portfolio	Other	Reserve assets	**Total**
	HJYU	HHZF	XBMN	HBNS	-HJYP	-HHZC	-XBMM	-LTCV	-HBNR	HJYV	HHZD	HHYR	LTCV	HBNT
1963	257	..	..	495	315	..	..	..	525	−58	..	..	..	−30
1964	193	..	..	925	397	..	..	..	533	−204	..	..	..	392
1965	249	..	..	794	464	..	..	..	745	−215	..	..	..	49
1966	309	..	..	301	386	..	..	..	285	−77	..	..	..	16
1967	354	..	..	535	399	..	..	..	363	−45	..	..	..	172
1968	501	..	..	1 772	492	..	..	..	1 100	9	..	..	..	672
1969	446	..	..	476	649	..	..	..	1 314	−203	..	..	..	−838
1970	621	..	..	550	699	..	..	125	1 414	−78	..	..	−125	−864
1971	730	..	..	2 317	817	..	..	1 536	3 758	−87	..	..	−1 536	−1 441
1972	482	..	..	1 330	808	..	..	−692	868	−326	..	..	692	462
1973	1 113	..	..	3 932	2 045	..	..	228	2 961	−932	..	..	−228	971
1974	1 886	..	..	5 946	1 883	..	..	105	2 784	3	..	..	−105	3 162
1975	1 521	..	..	3 133	1 329	..	..	−655	1 579	192	..	..	655	1 554
1976	1 657	..	..	4 313	2 423	..	..	−853	3 893	−766	..	..	853	420
1977	2 551	..	..	9 943	2 404	..	..	9 588	13 608	147	..	..	−9 588	−3 665
1978	1 967	..	..	1 504	3 527	..	..	−2 329	4 302	−1 560	..	..	2 329	−2 798
1979	3 037	..	..	39 407	5 902	..	..	1 059	39 504	−2 865	..	..	−1 059	−97
1980	4 365	..	..	39 460	4 876	..	..	291	42 698	−511	..	..	−291	−3 238
1981	2 939	..	..	43 291	6 018	..	..	−2 419	49 903	−3 079	..	..	2 419	−6 612
1982	3 034	..	..	28 888	4 099	..	..	−1 421	30 898	−1 065	..	..	1 421	−2 010
1983	3 393	..	..	25 792	5 428	..	..	−607	29 860	−2 035	..	..	607	−4 068
1984	−181	..	..	23 631	6 055	..	..	−908	31 640	−6 236	..	..	908	−8 009
1985	4 514	..	..	46 851	8 448	..	..	1 758	49 753	−3 934	..	..	−1 758	−2 902
1986	5 850	..	..	87 788	11 674	..	..	2 891	90 129	−5 824	..	..	−2 891	−2 341
1987	9 469	36 556	39 797	85 822	19 188	−4 950	54 507	12 012	80 757	−9 719	41 506	−14 710	−12 012	5 065
1988	12 034	30 269	30 176	72 479	20 893	11 768	21 922	2 761	57 344	−8 859	18 501	8 254	−2 761	15 135
1989	18 581	18 208	72 629	109 418	21 472	38 864	35 498	−5 440	90 394	−2 891	−20 656	37 131	5 440	19 024
1990	18 566	13 413	64 596	96 575	10 588	15 914	52 468	76	79 046	7 978	−2 501	12 128	−76	17 529
1991	9 086	10 987	13 516	33 589	9 059	32 361	−20 500	2 679	23 599	27	−21 374	34 016	−2 679	9 990
1992	9 213	9 371	56 125	74 709	11 061	28 683	30 656	−1 407	68 993	−1 848	−19 312	25 469	1 407	5 716
1993	10 326	28 411	124 556	163 293	17 895	89 568	45 685	698	153 846	−7 569	−61 157	78 871	−698	9 447
1994	6 103	33 221	−15 042	24 282	22 208	−21 799	28 910	1 045	30 364	−16 105	55 020	−43 952	−1 045	−6 082
1995	12 936	37 182	66 131	116 249	28 165	39 291	48 056	−200	115 312	−15 229	−2 109	18 075	200	937
1996	16 554	44 190	160 197	220 941	22 508	59 816	137 346	−510	219 160	−5 954	−15 626	22 851	510	1 781
1997	22 599	27 183	193 878	243 660	38 895	51 933	168 398	−2 380	256 846	−16 296	−24 750	25 480	2 380	−13 186
1998	38 433	17 909	63 392	119 734	71 943	36 714	15 918	−164	124 411	−33 510	−18 805	47 474	164	−4 677
1999	52 326	115 602	18 069	185 997	125 288	5 432	50 063	−639	180 144	−72 962	110 170	−31 994	639	5 853

Source: Office for National Statistics; Enquiries 020 7533 6078

1.19 Balance of payments: financial account

continued

£ million, not seasonally adjusted

	Investment in the UK (net credits)				UK investment abroad (net debits)					Net transactions				
	Direct	Portfolio	Other	**Total**	Direct	Portfolio	Other	Reserve assets	**Total**	Direct	Portfolio	Other	Reserve assets	**Total**
	HJYU	HHZF	XBMN	HBNS	-HJYP	-HHZC	-XBMM	-LTCV	-HBNR	HJYV	HHZD	HHYR	LTCV	HBNT
1963 Q1	53	..	..	91	79	..	..	..	178	–26	..	..	..	–87
Q2	63	..	..	66	74	..	..	..	60	–11	..	..	..	6
Q3	52	..	..	144	81	..	..	..	132	–29	..	..	..	12
Q4	89	..	..	194	81	..	..	..	155	8	..	..	..	39
1964 Q1	59	..	..	247	93	..	..	..	243	–34	..	..	..	4
Q2	38	..	..	219	108	..	..	..	157	–70	..	..	..	62
Q3	59	..	..	263	98	..	..	..	58	–39	..	..	..	205
Q4	37	..	..	196	98	..	..	..	75	–61	..	..	..	121
1965 Q1	14	..	..	280	126	..	..	..	226	–112	..	..	..	54
Q2	88	..	..	180	123	..	..	..	238	–35	..	..	..	–58
Q3	56	..	..	162	122	..	..	..	29	–66	..	..	..	133
Q4	91	..	..	172	93	..	..	..	252	–2	..	..	..	–80
1966 Q1	64	..	..	62	107	..	..	..	15	–43	..	..	..	47
Q2	86	..	..	118	116	..	..	..	54	–30	..	..	..	64
Q3	67	..	..	70	85	..	..	..	26	–18	..	..	..	44
Q4	92	..	..	51	78	..	..	..	190	14	..	..	..	–139
1967 Q1	106	..	..	25	101	..	..	..	184	5	..	..	..	–159
Q2	81	..	..	–44	107	..	..	..	21	–26	..	..	..	–65
Q3	46	..	..	206	82	..	..	..	51	–36	..	..	..	155
Q4	121	..	..	348	109	..	..	..	107	12	..	..	..	241
1968 Q1	74	..	..	714	145	..	..	..	318	–71	..	..	..	396
Q2	85	..	..	492	110	..	..	..	336	–25	..	..	..	156
Q3	242	..	..	258	69	..	..	..	162	173	..	..	..	96
Q4	100	..	..	308	168	..	..	..	284	–68	..	..	..	24
1969 Q1	164	..	..	126	170	..	..	..	339	–6	..	..	..	–213
Q2	88	..	..	235	147	..	..	..	365	–59	..	..	..	–130
Q3	92	..	..	176	152	..	..	..	180	–60	..	..	..	–4
Q4	102	..	..	–61	180	..	..	..	430	–78	..	..	..	–491
1970 Q1	221	..	..	–303	191	..	..	76	307	30	..	..	–76	–610
Q2	245	..	..	428	159	..	..	34	448	86	..	..	–34	–20
Q3	70	..	..	302	214	..	..	–52	259	–144	..	..	52	43
Q4	85	..	..	123	135	..	..	67	400	–50	..	..	–67	–277
1971 Q1	241	..	..	212	230	..	..	204	680	11	..	..	–204	–468
Q2	164	..	..	815	218	..	..	126	1 061	–54	..	..	–126	–246
Q3	172	..	..	364	155	..	..	576	547	17	..	..	–576	–183
Q4	153	..	..	926	214	..	..	630	1 470	–61	..	..	–630	–544
1972 Q1	128	..	..	593	199	..	..	191	768	–71	..	..	–191	–175
Q2	112	..	..	494	190	..	..	–46	290	–78	..	..	46	204
Q3	150	..	..	–519	197	..	..	–639	–587	–47	..	..	639	68
Q4	92	..	..	762	222	..	..	–198	397	–130	..	..	198	365
1973 Q1	185	..	..	695	387	..	..	72	594	–202	..	..	–72	101
Q2	349	..	..	1 257	470	..	..	380	949	–121	..	..	–380	308
Q3	203	..	..	351	431	..	..	–254	323	–228	..	..	254	28
Q4	376	..	..	1 629	757	..	..	30	1 095	–381	..	..	–30	534
1974 Q1	792	..	..	1 478	477	..	..	–33	629	315	..	..	33	849
Q2	351	..	..	1 569	252	..	..	116	564	99	..	..	–116	1 005
Q3	445	..	..	1 146	433	..	..	189	664	12	..	..	–189	482
Q4	298	..	..	1 753	721	..	..	–167	927	–423	..	..	167	826
1975 Q1	303	..	..	1 105	395	..	..	142	731	–92	..	..	–142	374
Q2	224	..	..	1 183	531	..	..	–410	541	–307	..	..	410	642
Q3	586	..	..	398	69	..	..	–170	–71	517	..	..	170	469
Q4	408	..	..	447	334	..	..	–217	378	74	..	..	217	69

Source: Office for National Statistics; Enquiries 020 7533 6078

1.19 Balance of payments: financial account

continued

£ million, not seasonally adjusted

	Investment in the UK (net credits)				UK investment abroad (net debits)					Net transactions				
	Direct	Portfolio	Other	**Total**	Direct	Portfolio	Other	Reserve assets	**Total**	Direct	Portfolio	Other	Reserve assets	**Total**
	HJYU	HHZF	XBMN	HBNS	-HJYP	-HHZC	-XBMM	-LTCV	-HBNR	HJYV	HHZD	HHYR	LTCV	HBNT
1976 Q1	554	..	..	1 738	531	..	..	178	1 769	23	..	..	–178	–31
Q2	262	..	..	1 085	603	..	..	–354	925	–341	..	..	354	160
Q3	387	..	..	1 085	580	..	..	–61	851	–193	..	..	61	234
Q4	454	..	..	405	709	..	..	–616	348	–255	..	..	616	57
1977 Q1	834	..	..	3 753	606	..	..	3 197	4 164	228	..	..	–3 197	–411
Q2	654	..	..	1 422	818	..	..	1 158	2 491	–164	..	..	–1 158	–1 069
Q3	584	..	..	2 448	509	..	..	3 227	3 964	75	..	..	–3 227	–1 516
Q4	479	..	..	2 320	471	..	..	2 006	2 989	8	..	..	–2 006	–669
1978 Q1	869	..	..	1 264	632	..	..	–46	1 546	237	..	..	46	–282
Q2	265	..	..	–1 443	554	..	..	–2 026	–747	–289	..	..	2 026	–696
Q3	307	..	..	918	937	..	..	54	1 389	–630	..	..	–54	–471
Q4	526	..	..	765	1 404	..	..	–311	2 114	–878	..	..	311	–1 349
1979 Q1	290	..	..	3 606	1 350	..	..	955	4 402	–1 060	..	..	–955	–796
Q2	1 126	..	..	9 966	1 420	..	..	68	9 765	–294	..	..	–68	201
Q3	829	..	..	15 074	1 843	..	..	152	15 160	–1 014	..	..	–152	–86
Q4	792	..	..	10 761	1 289	..	..	–116	10 177	–497	..	..	116	584
1980 Q1	1 306	..	..	12 999	1 584	..	..	457	14 152	–278	..	..	–457	–1 153
Q2	863	..	..	7 913	1 645	..	..	140	8 019	–782	..	..	–140	–106
Q3	943	..	..	4 339	628	..	..	–223	4 619	315	..	..	223	–280
Q4	1 253	..	..	14 209	1 019	..	..	–83	15 908	234	..	..	83	–1 699
1981 Q1	378	..	..	10 789	1 538	..	..	319	14 854	–1 160	..	..	–319	–4 065
Q2	1 184	..	..	6 026	1 331	..	..	–1 448	8 389	–147	..	..	1 448	–2 363
Q3	663	..	..	13 119	1 348	..	..	–1 167	13 613	–685	..	..	1 167	–494
Q4	714	..	..	13 357	1 801	..	..	–123	13 047	–1 087	..	..	123	310
1982 Q1	1 358	..	..	11 341	1 163	..	..	–11	11 418	195	..	..	11	–77
Q2	877	..	..	1 217	842	..	..	–699	20	35	..	..	699	1 197
Q3	530	..	..	16 422	1 033	..	..	288	18 108	–503	..	..	–288	–1 686
Q4	269	..	..	–92	1 061	..	..	–999	1 352	–792	..	..	999	–1 444
1983 Q1	637	..	..	8 569	1 962	..	..	–652	10 612	–1 325	..	..	652	–2 043
Q2	1 355	..	..	419	463	..	..	142	237	892	..	..	–142	182
Q3	1 194	..	..	11 885	1 571	..	..	33	11 333	–377	..	..	–33	552
Q4	207	..	..	4 919	1 432	..	..	–130	7 678	–1 225	..	..	130	–2 759
1984 Q1	1 295	..	..	12 699	1 679	..	..	–77	13 910	–384	..	..	77	–1 211
Q2	–2 946	..	..	6 660	647	..	..	–857	8 758	–3 593	..	..	857	–2 098
Q3	1 500	..	..	–671	1 850	..	..	–279	608	–350	..	..	279	–1 279
Q4	–30	..	..	4 943	1 879	..	..	305	8 364	–1 909	..	..	–305	–3 421
1985 Q1	2 744	..	..	14 177	3 360	..	..	–90	16 232	–616	..	..	90	–2 055
Q2	258	..	..	6 199	1 669	..	..	607	6 375	–1 411	..	..	–607	–176
Q3	1 037	..	..	10 049	1 983	..	..	49	14 942	–946	..	..	–49	–4 893
Q4	475	..	..	16 426	1 436	..	..	1 192	12 204	–961	..	..	–1 192	4 222
1986 Q1	1 309	..	..	14 494	832	..	..	580	15 232	477	..	..	–580	–738
Q2	1 414	..	..	13 363	1 731	..	..	296	14 680	–317	..	..	–296	–1 317
Q3	1 706	..	..	45 499	3 742	..	..	2 321	42 875	–2 036	..	..	–2 321	2 624
Q4	1 421	..	..	14 432	5 369	..	..	–306	17 342	–3 948	..	..	306	–2 910
1987 Q1	1 941	10 672	4 494	17 107	2 597	3 151	9 333	1 523	16 604	–656	7 521	–4 839	–1 523	503
Q2	700	4 037	23 323	28 060	5 776	–1 487	16 282	4 469	25 040	–5 076	5 524	7 041	–4 469	3 020
Q3	2 733	15 308	6 705	24 746	7 628	654	18 350	269	26 901	–4 895	14 654	–11 645	–269	–2 155
Q4	4 095	6 539	5 275	15 909	3 187	–7 268	10 542	5 751	12 212	908	13 807	–5 267	–5 751	3 697
1988 Q1	4 936	2 127	6 055	13 118	4 901	1 021	–1 896	653	4 679	35	1 106	7 951	–653	8 439
Q2	1 659	2 974	16 750	21 383	5 641	3 716	10 686	631	20 674	–3 982	–742	6 064	–631	709
Q3	1 987	6 432	15 656	24 075	3 922	947	17 006	995	22 870	–1 935	5 485	–1 350	–995	1 205
Q4	3 452	18 736	–8 285	13 903	6 429	6 084	–3 874	482	9 121	–2 977	12 652	–4 411	–482	4 782

Source: Office for National Statistics; Enquiries 020 7533 6078

1.19 Balance of payments: financial account

continued

£ million, not seasonally adjusted

	Investment in the UK (net credits)				UK investment abroad (net debits)					Net transactions				
	Direct	Portfolio	Other	**Total**	Direct	Portfolio	Other	Reserve assets	**Total**	Direct	Portfolio	Other	Reserve assets	**Total**
	HJYU	HHZF	XBMN	HBNS	-HJYP	-HHZC	-XBMM	-LTCV	-HBNR	HJYV	HHZD	HHYR	LTCV	HBNT
1989 Q1	5 248	3 610	30 310	39 168	6 861	5 463	16 748	–502	28 570	–1 613	–1 853	13 562	502	10 598
Q2	5 996	781	11 956	18 733	5 805	9 793	4 493	–2 134	17 957	191	–9 012	7 463	2 134	776
Q3	2 575	4 083	22 623	29 281	4 258	11 159	8 448	–358	23 507	–1 683	–7 076	14 175	358	5 774
Q4	4 762	9 734	7 740	22 236	4 548	12 449	5 809	–2 446	20 360	214	–2 715	1 931	2 446	1 876
1990 Q1	6 920	–4 744	24 011	26 187	1 987	1 191	14 662	–128	17 712	4 933	–5 935	9 349	128	8 475
Q2	3 958	6 264	–1 206	9 016	1 116	2 515	3 787	77	7 495	2 842	3 749	–4 993	–77	1 521
Q3	6 200	11 089	17 852	35 141	2 512	–41	28 713	433	31 617	3 688	11 130	–10 861	–433	3 524
Q4	1 488	804	23 939	26 231	4 973	12 249	5 306	–306	22 222	–3 485	–11 445	18 633	306	4 009
1991 Q1	3 572	5 225	2 178	10 975	4 821	7 854	–3 326	2 146	11 495	–1 249	–2 629	5 504	–2 146	–520
Q2	2 351	–3 260	–2 947	–3 856	3 552	7 456	–7 231	846	4 623	–1 201	–10 716	4 284	–846	–8 479
Q3	1 923	1 256	7 347	10 526	1 801	11 220	–4 306	–137	8 578	122	–9 964	11 653	137	1 948
Q4	1 240	7 766	6 938	15 944	–1 115	5 831	–5 637	–176	–1 097	2 355	1 935	12 575	176	17 041
1992 Q1	2 823	–6 513	2 015	–1 675	3 218	7 058	–3 374	314	7 216	–395	–13 571	5 389	–314	–8 891
Q2	922	6 128	5 530	12 580	1 479	5 002	1 169	329	7 979	–557	1 126	4 361	–329	4 601
Q3	2 785	2 743	36 106	41 634	2 970	4 961	32 337	–1 658	38 610	–185	–2 218	3 769	1 658	3 024
Q4	2 683	7 013	12 474	22 170	3 394	11 662	524	–392	15 188	–711	–4 649	11 950	392	6 982
1993 Q1	2 324	–6 550	33 112	28 886	4 197	26 931	5 139	–463	35 804	–1 873	–33 481	27 973	463	–6 918
Q2	3 790	12 027	28 491	44 308	3 606	10 313	21 491	748	36 158	184	1 714	7 000	–748	8 150
Q3	4 387	11 379	13 424	29 190	4 818	13 636	1 775	535	20 764	–431	–2 257	11 649	–535	8 426
Q4	–175	11 555	49 529	60 909	5 274	38 688	17 280	–122	61 120	–5 449	–27 133	32 249	122	–211
1994 Q1	1 594	5 804	–21 967	–14 569	3 716	–21 821	9 416	281	–8 408	–2 122	27 625	–31 383	–281	–6 161
Q2	2 522	8 923	–11 059	386	6 134	–13 354	3 809	286	–3 125	–3 612	22 277	–14 868	–286	3 511
Q3	2 964	12 743	6 124	21 831	5 292	3 760	13 824	202	23 078	–2 328	8 983	–7 700	–202	–1 247
Q4	–977	5 751	11 860	16 634	7 066	9 616	1 861	276	18 819	–8 043	–3 865	9 999	–276	–2 185
1995 Q1	2 866	3 999	39 935	46 800	6 423	13 331	26 216	–827	45 143	–3 557	–9 332	13 719	827	1 657
Q2	990	9 961	–7 035	3 916	8 529	–2 121	–2 486	582	4 504	–7 539	12 082	–4 549	–582	–588
Q3	2 653	6 631	32 470	41 754	4 919	14 970	24 554	340	44 783	–2 266	–8 339	7 916	–340	–3 029
Q4	6 427	16 591	761	23 779	8 294	13 111	–228	–295	20 882	–1 867	3 480	989	295	2 897
1996 Q1	3 194	9 022	37 353	49 569	9 385	–876	45 590	–1 334	52 765	–6 191	9 898	–8 237	1 334	–3 196
Q2	4 893	6 106	45 791	56 790	4 300	21 986	28 402	235	54 923	593	–15 880	17 389	–235	1 867
Q3	5 099	9 643	24 880	39 622	2 476	24 940	13 394	–911	39 899	2 623	–15 297	11 486	911	–277
Q4	3 368	19 419	52 173	74 960	6 347	13 766	49 960	1 500	71 573	–2 979	5 653	2 213	–1 500	3 387
1997 Q1	8 675	8 166	75 132	91 973	9 232	13 890	76 007	–1 458	97 671	–557	–5 724	–875	1 458	–5 698
Q2	4 869	9 182	49 029	63 080	4 662	36 374	21 235	225	62 496	207	–27 192	27 794	–225	584
Q3	3 532	9 598	14 614	27 744	18 628	–2 663	15 876	336	32 177	–15 096	12 261	–1 262	–336	–4 433
Q4	5 523	237	55 103	60 863	6 373	4 332	55 280	–1 483	64 502	–850	–4 095	–177	1 483	–3 639
1998 Q1	8 911	–3 301	39 677	45 287	5 757	23 777	22 247	–998	50 783	3 154	–27 078	17 430	998	–5 496
Q2	6 869	–9 732	34 990	32 127	6 500	–2 114	28 636	309	33 331	369	–7 618	6 354	–309	–1 204
Q3	11 034	682	38 133	49 849	19 354	4 906	29 059	313	53 632	–8 320	–4 224	9 074	–313	–3 783
Q4	11 619	30 260	–49 408	–7 529	40 332	10 145	–64 024	212	–13 335	–28 713	20 115	14 616	–212	5 806
1999 Q1	12 562	20 176	63 072	95 810	8 782	7 919	78 202	–837	94 066	3 780	12 257	–15 130	837	1 744
Q2	6 988	81 777	46 271	135 036	80 735	3 401	47 623	202	131 961	–73 747	78 376	–1 352	–202	3 075
Q3	13 263	9 210	–40 354	–17 881	12 205	12 492	–45 097	–759	–21 159	1 058	–3 282	4 743	759	3 278
Q4	19 513	4 439	–50 920	–26 968	23 566	–18 380	–30 665	755	–24 724	–4 053	22 819	–20 255	–755	–2 244
2000 Q1	9 891	104 731	133 963	248 585	125 251	–9 219	131 618	–2 365	245 285	–115 360	113 950	2 345	2 365	3 300

Source: Office for National Statistics; Enquiries 020 7533 6078

1.20 Balance of payments: international investment position
Balance sheets valued at end of year

£ billion

	UK assets					UK liabilities				Net international investment position				
	Direct	Portfolio	Other	Reserve assets	**Total**	Direct	Portfolio	Other	**Total**	Direct	Portfolio	Other	Reserve assets	**Total**
	HBWD	HHZZ	HLXV	LTEB	HBQA	HBWI	HLXW	HLYD	HBQB	HBWQ	CGNH	CGNG	LTEB	HBQC
1963	..	..	..	..	..	..	..	..	..	..	..	..	..	..
1964	..	..	..	..	..	..	..	..	..	..	..	..	..	..
1965	..	..	..	..	..	..	..	..	..	..	..	..	..	..
1966	6.5	..	..	..	17.0	3.1	..	..	15.8	3.3	..	..	..	1.3
1967	7.5	..	..	..	20.6	3.5	..	..	18.7	4.0	..	..	..	1.9
1968	8.0	..	..	..	25.5	3.9	..	..	23.9	4.1	..	..	..	1.6
1969	8.6	..	..	..	31.1	4.3	..	..	28.8	4.3	..	..	..	2.3
1970	9.1	..	..	1.2	34.9	5.0	..	..	31.8	4.2	..	..	1.2	3.1
1971	9.5	..	..	2.5	40.3	5.7	..	..	36.8	3.8	..	..	2.5	3.5
1972	10.5	..	..	2.4	51.8	6.3	..	..	46.3	4.1	..	..	2.4	5.5
1973	12.6	..	..	2.8	65.9	7.7	..	..	61.6	4.9	..	..	2.8	4.3
1974	15.5	..	..	3.0	75.5	10.3	..	..	74.5	5.1	..	..	3.0	1.0
1975	18.7	..	..	2.7	96.8	12.1	..	..	95.8	6.6	..	..	2.7	1.0
1976	23.7	..	..	2.5	128.4	13.7	..	..	125.7	9.9	..	..	2.5	2.7
1977	24.6	..	..	11.0	141.1	15.8	..	..	137.0	8.8	..	..	11.0	4.1
1978	28.4	..	..	10.4	164.4	17.9	..	..	153.6	10.4	..	..	10.4	10.7
1979	31.6	..	..	13.2	195.9	22.1	..	..	186.7	9.6	..	..	13.2	9.2
1980	33.5	..	..	13.3	227.0	26.5	..	..	212.6	7.0	..	..	13.3	14.4
1981	45.3	..	..	12.0	324.7	30.1	..	..	297.4	15.2	..	..	12.0	27.3
1982	52.4	..	..	12.9	409.0	32.4	..	..	372.2	20.0	..	..	12.9	36.8
1983	58.3	..	..	12.8	478.2	37.3	..	..	430.5	20.9	..	..	12.8	47.7
1984	75.7	..	..	13.2	613.1	40.2	..	..	544.9	35.5	..	..	13.2	68.2
1985	70.0	..	..	13.2	583.5	44.5	..	..	522.2	25.5	..	..	13.2	61.4
1986	81.3	..	..	17.4	708.5	51.9	..	..	620.5	29.4	..	..	17.4	88.0
1987	85.9	121.7	449.0	27.0	683.6	62.8	128.5	442.0	633.4	23.1	–6.8	7.0	27.0	50.3
1988	104.3	153.7	475.6	28.7	762.4	77.0	158.9	475.5	711.4	27.3	–5.2	0.1	28.7	51.0
1989	123.2	227.3	566.0	26.3	942.8	100.1	194.1	597.5	891.8	23.1	33.2	–31.5	26.3	51.0
1990	120.7	197.3	555.9	22.5	896.4	113.5	189.2	602.0	904.6	7.2	8.1	–46.0	22.5	–8.2
1991	126.2	253.0	533.6	26.0	938.8	121.0	208.8	605.9	935.7	5.2	44.2	–72.3	26.0	3.1
1992	149.7	316.9	650.0	28.3	1 144.9	123.1	247.0	752.2	1 122.3	26.6	69.9	–102.2	28.3	22.5
1993	170.3	456.4	694.7	29.7	1 351.2	128.2	306.9	879.7	1 314.8	42.1	149.5	–184.9	29.7	36.4
1994	173.9	414.4	719.0	30.7	1 337.9	122.6	320.0	873.1	1 315.6	51.3	94.4	–154.1	30.7	22.2
1995	200.9	487.2	819.5	31.8	1 539.4	137.9	386.4	1 007.5	1 531.8	63.0	100.8	–188.0	31.8	7.6
1996	207.8	535.1	864.2	27.3	1 634.4	147.6	429.6	1 059.1	1 636.3	60.2	105.5	–194.9	27.3	–1.9
1997	226.5	626.7	1 066.2	22.8	1 942.2	167.1	588.4	1 269.3	2 024.8	59.4	38.3	–203.1	22.8	–82.6
1998	301.1	685.5	1 102.6	23.3	2 112.5	192.8	686.7	1 351.2	2 230.7	108.3	–1.2	–248.5	23.3	–118.1
1999	418.5	771.6	1 130.9	22.2	2 343.2	243.1	882.9	1 365.4	2 491.4	175.4	–111.3	–234.5	22.2	–148.3

Source: Office for National Statistics; Enquiries 020 7533 6078

1.20 Balance of payments: international investment position
Balance sheets valued at end of year

continued

£ billion, not seasonally adjusted

	UK assets					UK liabilities				Net international investment position				
	Direct	Portfolio	Other	Reserve assets	**Total**	Direct	Portfolio	Other	**Total**	Direct	Portfolio	Other	Reserve assets	**Total**
	HBWD	HHZZ	HLXV	LTEB	HBQA	HBWI	HLXW	HLYD	HBQB	HBWQ	CGNH	CGNG	LTEB	HBQC
1963 Q1	..	..	..	..	..	..	..	..	..	..	..	..	..	..
Q2	..	..	..	..	..	..	..	..	..	..	..	..	..	..
Q3	..	..	..	..	..	..	..	..	..	..	..	..	..	..
Q4	..	..	..	..	..	..	..	..	..	..	..	..	..	..
1964 Q1	..	..	..	..	..	..	..	..	..	..	..	..	..	..
Q2	..	..	..	..	..	..	..	..	..	..	..	..	..	..
Q3	..	..	..	..	..	..	..	..	..	..	..	..	..	..
Q4	..	..	..	..	..	..	..	..	..	..	..	..	..	..
1965 Q1	..	..	..	..	..	..	..	..	..	..	..	..	..	..
Q2	..	..	..	..	..	..	..	..	..	..	..	..	..	..
Q3	..	..	..	..	..	..	..	..	..	..	..	..	..	..
Q4	..	..	..	..	..	..	..	..	..	..	..	..	..	..
1966 Q1	..	..	..	..	..	..	..	..	..	..	..	..	..	..
Q2	..	..	..	..	..	..	..	..	..	..	..	..	..	..
Q3	..	..	..	..	..	..	..	..	..	..	..	..	..	..
Q4	6.5	..	..	..	..	3.1	..	..	..	3.3	..	..	..	..
1967 Q1	7.5	..	..	..	..	3.2	..	..	..	4.3	..	..	..	..
Q2	7.5	..	..	..	..	3.3	..	..	..	4.2	..	..	..	..
Q3	7.5	..	..	..	..	3.4	..	..	..	4.1	..	..	..	..
Q4	7.5	..	..	..	..	3.5	..	..	..	4.0	..	..	..	..
1968 Q1	8.0	..	..	..	..	3.6	..	..	..	4.5	..	..	..	..
Q2	8.0	..	..	..	..	3.6	..	..	..	4.4	..	..	..	..
Q3	8.0	..	..	..	..	3.9	..	..	..	4.2	..	..	..	..
Q4	8.0	..	..	..	..	3.9	..	..	..	4.1	..	..	..	..
1969 Q1	8.6	..	..	..	..	4.1	..	..	..	4.5	..	..	..	..
Q2	8.6	..	..	..	..	4.2	..	..	..	4.4	..	..	..	..
Q3	8.6	..	..	..	..	4.2	..	..	..	4.4	..	..	..	..
Q4	8.6	..	..	..	..	4.3	..	..	..	4.3	..	..	..	..
1970 Q1	9.1	..	..	1.1	..	4.5	..	..	..	4.6	..	..	1.1	..
Q2	9.1	..	..	1.2	..	4.8	..	..	..	4.3	..	..	1.2	..
Q3	9.1	..	..	1.1	..	4.9	..	..	..	4.2	..	..	1.1	..
Q4	9.1	..	..	1.2	..	5.0	..	..	..	4.2	..	..	1.2	..
1971 Q1	9.5	..	..	1.3	..	5.2	..	..	..	4.3	..	..	1.3	..
Q2	9.5	..	..	1.4	..	5.3	..	..	..	4.1	..	..	1.4	..
Q3	9.5	..	..	2.0	..	5.5	..	..	..	4.0	..	..	2.0	..
Q4	9.5	..	..	2.5	..	5.7	..	..	..	3.8	..	..	2.5	..
1972 Q1	9.4	..	..	2.6	..	5.8	..	..	..	3.6	..	..	2.6	..
Q2	9.9	..	..	2.7	..	6.0	..	..	..	3.9	..	..	2.7	..
Q3	10.1	..	..	2.4	..	6.2	..	..	..	3.9	..	..	2.4	..
Q4	10.5	..	..	2.4	..	6.3	..	..	46.3	4.1	..	..	2.4	..
1973 Q1	10.8	..	..	2.7	..	6.6	..	..	48.5	4.2	..	..	2.7	..
Q2	11.4	..	..	3.2	..	7.0	..	..	49.8	4.4	..	..	3.2	..
Q3	12.4	..	..	2.7	..	7.3	..	..	55.4	5.2	..	..	2.7	..
Q4	12.6	..	..	2.8	..	7.7	..	..	61.6	4.9	..	..	2.8	..
1974 Q1	12.9	..	..	3.1	..	8.6	..	..	66.5	4.3	..	..	3.1	..
Q2	13.0	..	..	2.9	..	9.0	..	..	69.5	4.0	..	..	2.9	..
Q3	13.4	..	..	2.7	..	9.5	..	..	71.1	3.9	..	..	2.7	..
Q4	15.5	..	..	3.0	..	10.3	..	..	74.5	5.1	..	..	3.0	..
1975 Q1	15.7	..	..	2.5	..	10.7	..	..	77.1	5.0	..	..	2.5	..
Q2	17.7	..	..	2.7	..	11.0	..	..	84.5	6.7	..	..	2.7	..
Q3	17.6	..	..	3.3	..	11.7	..	..	91.4	5.9	..	..	3.3	..
Q4	18.7	..	..	2.7	..	12.1	..	..	95.8	6.6	..	..	2.7	..

Source: Office for National Statistics; Enquiries 020 7533 6078

1.20 Balance of payments: international investment position
Balance sheets valued at end of year

continued

£ billion, not seasonally adjusted

	UK assets					UK liabilities				Net international investment position				
	Direct	Portfolio	Other	Reserve assets	**Total**	Direct	Portfolio	Other	**Total**	Direct	Portfolio	Other	Reserve assets	**Total**
	HBWD	HHZZ	HLXV	LTEB	HBQA	HBWI	HLXW	HLYD	HBQB	HBWQ	CGNH	CGNG	LTEB	HBQC
1976 Q1	19.8	..	..	3.1	..	12.7	..	..	102.5	7.1	..	..	3.1	..
Q2	21.5	..	..	3.4	..	12.9	..	..	111.0	8.6	..	..	3.4	..
Q3	23.5	..	..	3.5	..	13.3	..	..	119.5	10.2	..	..	3.5	..
Q4	23.7	..	..	2.5	..	13.7	..	..	125.7	9.9	..	..	2.5	..
1977 Q1	24.0	..	..	5.6	..	14.4	..	..	129.2	9.6	..	..	5.6	..
Q2	25.1	..	..	6.7	..	15.0	..	..	134.5	10.2	..	..	6.7	..
Q3	25.3	..	..	10.2	..	15.4	..	..	138.7	9.9	..	..	10.2	..
Q4	24.6	..	..	11.0	141.1	15.8	..	..	137.0	8.8	..	..	11.0	4.1
1978 Q1	26.4	..	..	12.9	151.3	16.7	..	..	143.6	9.7	..	..	12.9	7.7
Q2	27.1	..	..	10.9	154.2	17.0	..	..	145.3	10.1	..	..	10.9	8.9
Q3	27.6	..	..	10.9	158.5	17.4	..	..	148.4	10.3	..	..	10.9	10.1
Q4	28.4	..	..	10.4	164.4	17.9	..	..	153.6	10.4	..	..	10.4	10.7
1979 Q1	28.8	..	..	11.3	166.1	18.5	..	..	156.4	10.3	..	..	11.3	9.7
Q2	28.9	..	..	11.2	169.6	19.9	..	..	160.0	9.1	..	..	11.2	9.6
Q3	31.1	..	..	12.3	186.6	21.0	..	..	176.3	10.1	..	..	12.3	10.3
Q4	31.6	..	..	13.2	195.9	22.1	..	..	186.7	9.6	..	..	13.2	9.2
1980 Q1	32.3	..	..	13.5	210.3	23.4	..	..	200.5	8.9	..	..	13.5	9.8
Q2	33.4	..	..	14.7	212.0	24.3	..	..	199.6	9.2	..	..	14.7	12.4
Q3	33.5	..	..	14.3	214.7	25.2	..	..	201.1	8.3	..	..	14.3	13.6
Q4	33.5	..	..	13.3	227.0	26.5	..	..	212.6	7.0	..	..	13.3	14.4
1981 Q1	35.8	..	..	13.7	251.2	27.0	..	..	232.4	8.8	..	..	13.7	18.7
Q2	39.8	..	..	13.0	285.5	28.4	..	..	261.8	11.5	..	..	13.0	23.7
Q3	44.7	..	..	12.9	317.9	29.2	..	..	289.3	15.5	..	..	12.9	28.6
Q4	45.3	..	..	12.0	324.7	30.1	..	..	297.4	15.2	..	..	12.0	27.3
1982 Q1	46.6	..	..	11.5	346.8	31.3	..	..	322.2	15.3	..	..	11.5	24.5
Q2	47.2	..	..	10.9	351.3	32.0	..	..	328.1	15.2	..	..	10.9	23.2
Q3	48.2	..	..	12.3	377.7	32.3	..	..	352.3	15.8	..	..	12.3	25.4
Q4	52.4	..	..	12.9	409.0	32.4	..	..	372.2	20.0	..	..	12.9	36.8
1983 Q1	57.5	..	..	13.0	451.9	33.4	..	..	407.9	24.1	..	..	13.0	44.0
Q2	54.5	..	..	12.7	437.4	35.1	..	..	396.0	19.3	..	..	12.7	41.4
Q3	56.3	..	..	12.9	457.3	36.7	..	..	415.3	19.5	..	..	12.9	42.0
Q4	58.3	..	..	12.8	478.2	37.3	..	..	430.5	20.9	..	..	12.8	47.7
1984 Q1	63.4	..	..	13.1	504.0	39.6	..	..	451.2	23.8	..	..	13.1	52.8
Q2	65.0	..	..	12.5	531.7	37.4	..	..	476.7	27.6	..	..	12.5	55.0
Q3	69.6	..	..	12.7	569.5	39.6	..	..	510.9	30.0	..	..	12.7	58.6
Q4	75.7	..	..	13.2	613.1	40.2	..	..	544.9	35.5	..	..	13.2	68.2
1985 Q1	72.3	..	..	12.8	597.2	42.5	..	..	534.8	29.8	..	..	12.8	62.4
Q2	69.3	..	..	12.5	571.6	43.0	..	..	515.4	26.3	..	..	12.5	56.2
Q3	68.9	..	..	12.2	566.6	43.7	..	..	508.6	25.2	..	..	12.2	58.0
Q4	70.0	..	..	13.2	583.5	44.5	..	..	522.2	25.5	..	..	13.2	61.4
1986 Q1	69.6	..	..	13.9	601.1	46.4	..	..	538.2	23.1	..	..	13.9	63.0
Q2	69.0	..	..	14.0	611.4	47.8	..	..	543.4	21.2	..	..	14.0	68.1
Q3	77.8	..	..	18.4	702.7	50.2	..	..	612.3	27.5	..	..	18.4	90.4
Q4	81.3	..	..	17.4	708.5	51.9	..	..	620.5	29.4	..	..	17.4	88.0
1987 Q1	79.1	152.0	449.5	18.4	699.0	53.9	122.2	440.6	616.7	25.2	29.8	8.9	18.4	82.2
Q2	82.9	152.3	460.3	23.1	718.6	55.3	130.9	463.1	649.2	27.6	21.4	–2.7	23.1	69.4
Q3	88.5	154.5	474.2	23.3	740.3	58.6	146.7	467.4	672.6	29.9	7.8	6.8	23.3	67.7
Q4	85.9	121.7	449.0	27.0	683.6	62.8	128.5	442.0	633.4	23.1	–6.8	7.0	27.0	50.3
1988 Q1	87.1	131.2	442.3	26.6	687.1	67.7	132.6	441.6	641.9	19.3	–1.4	0.7	26.6	45.2
Q2	99.0	141.9	480.0	28.6	749.5	70.9	143.0	483.7	697.6	28.0	–1.1	–3.6	28.6	51.9
Q3	102.6	144.0	497.9	29.2	773.7	73.7	149.1	499.7	722.5	28.9	–5.0	–1.9	29.2	51.2
Q4	104.3	153.7	475.6	28.7	762.4	77.0	158.9	475.5	711.4	27.3	–5.2	0.1	28.7	51.0

Source: Office for National Statistics; Enquiries 020 7533 6078

1.20 Balance of payments: international investment position
Balance sheets valued at end of year

continued

£ billion, not seasonally adjusted

UK assets

	Direct	Portfolio	Other	Reserve assets	**Total**
	HBWD	HHZZ	HLXV	LTEB	HBQA
1989 Q1	103.5	169.7	517.3	28.9	819.4
Q2	119.8	189.3	553.8	28.7	891.6
Q3	117.9	204.8	548.9	27.4	899.0
Q4	123.2	227.3	566.0	26.3	942.8
1990 Q1	120.9	207.5	565.3	25.0	918.6
Q2	118.7	208.9	547.4	23.5	898.4
Q3	115.9	181.8	558.1	23.2	879.0
Q4	120.7	197.3	555.9	22.5	896.4
1991 Q1	128.3	218.1	583.2	25.3	954.9
Q2	134.5	229.6	600.7	27.8	992.7
Q3	130.9	244.5	573.1	26.8	975.3
Q4	126.2	253.0	533.6	26.0	938.8
1992 Q1	130.8	259.4	547.3	26.9	964.2
Q2	123.8	262.0	521.0	23.0	929.9
Q3	131.7	284.6	596.8	26.0	1 039.1
Q4	149.7	316.9	650.0	28.3	1 144.9
1993 Q1	161.1	362.5	661.0	28.5	1 213.1
Q2	162.2	386.1	679.9	29.1	1 257.3
Q3	165.4	414.2	687.1	29.9	1 296.5
Q4	170.3	456.4	694.7	29.7	1 351.2
1994 Q1	170.1	436.0	716.0	30.7	1 352.8
Q2	170.8	415.4	707.4	30.5	1 324.0
Q3	171.9	412.3	714.6	30.3	1 329.0
Q4	173.9	414.4	719.0	30.7	1 337.9
1995 Q1	179.0	432.5	752.8	30.6	1 394.9
Q2	189.1	440.7	763.1	31.5	1 424.4
Q3	191.2	463.2	777.7	31.5	1 463.6
Q4	200.9	487.2	819.5	31.8	1 539.4
1996 Q1	210.8	491.4	869.0	30.5	1 601.6
Q2	210.8	509.5	876.3	29.7	1 626.3
Q3	212.3	530.1	887.8	28.6	1 658.9
Q4	207.8	535.1	864.2	27.3	1 634.4
1997 Q1	200.5	551.7	946.8	25.5	1 724.6
Q2	203.2	620.0	951.1	24.9	1 799.2
Q3	220.5	639.4	1 017.4	25.6	1 902.9
Q4	226.5	626.7	1 066.2	22.8	1 942.2
1998 Q1	223.0	660.8	1 047.6	21.3	1 952.6
Q2	229.8	659.2	1 083.3	21.8	1 994.2
Q3	250.3	614.5	1 125.0	22.4	2 012.2
Q4	301.1	685.5	1 102.6	23.3	2 112.5
1999 Q1	314.5	703.3	1 174.1	22.1	2 214.1
Q2	391.2	726.8	1 216.8	22.1	2 357.0
Q3	403.1	733.9	1 154.0	21.4	2 312.4
Q4	418.5	771.6	1 130.9	22.2	2 343.2
2000 Q1	539.1	767.0	1 254.7	21.5	2 582.3

UK liabilities

	Direct	Portfolio	Other	**Total**
	HBWI	HLXW	HLYD	HBQB
1989 Q1	83.8	174.0	530.2	788.0
Q2	91.8	180.3	568.3	840.4
Q3	95.2	186.2	577.1	858.5
Q4	100.1	194.1	597.5	891.8
1990 Q1	106.4	186.9	607.3	900.6
Q2	109.0	192.3	584.1	885.4
Q3	114.1	185.6	586.5	886.2
Q4	113.5	189.2	602.0	904.6
1991 Q1	117.3	211.1	634.8	963.3
Q2	120.2	213.6	652.4	986.2
Q3	121.8	213.4	638.1	973.4
Q4	121.0	208.8	605.9	935.7
1992 Q1	122.2	199.4	621.9	943.4
Q2	119.6	205.8	598.3	923.7
Q3	120.8	215.0	686.6	1 022.4
Q4	123.1	247.0	752.2	1 122.3
1993 Q1	124.1	255.4	791.8	1 171.3
Q2	126.7	270.4	813.0	1 210.1
Q3	129.8	277.0	833.2	1 240.0
Q4	128.2	306.9	879.7	1 314.8
1994 Q1	126.9	301.2	878.9	1 307.1
Q2	126.7	297.0	856.0	1 279.7
Q3	126.4	312.6	858.4	1 297.4
Q4	122.6	320.0	873.1	1 315.6
1995 Q1	125.8	325.7	928.9	1 380.4
Q2	127.8	345.2	936.0	1 409.0
Q3	130.8	360.1	953.3	1 444.1
Q4	137.9	386.4	1 007.5	1 531.8
1996 Q1	139.5	399.7	1 047.0	1 586.2
Q2	142.6	402.0	1 070.5	1 615.1
Q3	145.8	417.2	1 100.2	1 663.3
Q4	147.6	429.6	1 059.1	1 636.3
1997 Q1	153.0	489.8	1 134.0	1 776.8
Q2	158.0	529.8	1 160.3	1 848.0
Q3	161.7	583.0	1 227.0	1 971.8
Q4	167.1	588.4	1 269.3	2 024.8
1998 Q1	170.3	633.3	1 251.4	2 055.0
Q2	175.0	628.3	1 294.5	2 097.9
Q3	184.2	584.1	1 351.2	2 119.5
Q4	192.8	686.7	1 351.2	2 230.7
1999 Q1	205.0	745.5	1 404.5	2 355.1
Q2	211.9	831.2	1 455.2	2 498.3
Q3	224.8	812.3	1 413.9	2 451.0
Q4	243.1	882.9	1 365.4	2 491.4
2000 Q1	252.4	961.6	1 497.1	2 711.1

Net international investment position

	Direct	Portfolio	Other	Reserve assets	**Total**
	HBWQ	CGNH	CGNG	LTEB	HBQC
1989 Q1	19.7	–4.3	–12.9	28.9	31.4
Q2	28.1	9.0	–14.5	28.7	51.2
Q3	22.7	18.6	–28.2	27.4	40.5
Q4	23.1	33.2	–31.5	26.3	51.0
1990 Q1	14.5	20.6	–42.1	25.0	18.0
Q2	9.6	16.7	–36.7	23.5	13.1
Q3	1.9	–3.9	–28.4	23.2	–7.1
Q4	7.2	8.1	–46.0	22.5	–8.2
1991 Q1	10.9	7.0	–51.6	25.3	–8.4
Q2	14.3	16.0	–51.8	27.8	6.5
Q3	9.1	31.0	–65.0	26.8	1.9
Q4	5.2	44.2	–72.3	26.0	3.1
1992 Q1	8.6	60.0	–74.6	26.9	20.8
Q2	4.2	56.2	–77.3	23.0	6.2
Q3	11.0	69.5	–89.8	26.0	16.7
Q4	26.6	69.9	–102.2	28.3	22.5
1993 Q1	37.0	107.1	–130.7	28.5	41.8
Q2	35.5	115.7	–133.1	29.1	47.2
Q3	35.6	137.1	–146.1	29.9	56.5
Q4	42.1	149.5	–184.9	29.7	36.4
1994 Q1	43.2	134.8	–162.9	30.7	45.8
Q2	44.2	118.4	–148.6	30.5	44.4
Q3	45.4	99.7	–143.8	30.3	31.7
Q4	51.3	94.4	–154.1	30.7	22.2
1995 Q1	53.2	106.8	–176.1	30.6	14.5
Q2	61.3	95.5	–173.0	31.5	15.4
Q3	60.5	103.2	–175.6	31.5	19.5
Q4	63.0	100.8	–188.0	31.8	7.6
1996 Q1	71.3	91.6	–178.0	30.5	15.4
Q2	68.2	107.5	–194.2	29.7	11.2
Q3	66.5	112.9	–212.4	28.6	–4.4
Q4	60.2	105.5	–194.9	27.3	–1.9
1997 Q1	47.5	61.9	–187.1	25.5	–52.2
Q2	45.3	90.2	–209.2	24.9	–48.8
Q3	58.7	56.4	–209.6	25.6	–68.9
Q4	59.4	38.3	–203.1	22.8	–82.6
1998 Q1	52.7	27.5	–203.8	21.3	–102.3
Q2	54.9	30.9	–211.2	21.8	–103.6
Q3	66.1	30.4	–226.2	22.4	–107.3
Q4	108.3	–1.2	–248.5	23.3	–118.1
1999 Q1	109.5	–42.2	–230.4	22.1	–141.0
Q2	179.3	–104.4	–238.3	22.1	–141.3
Q3	178.2	–78.5	–259.9	21.4	–138.7
Q4	175.4	–111.3	–234.5	22.2	–148.3
2000 Q1	286.7	–194.5	–242.3	21.5	–128.7

Source: Office for National Statistics; Enquiries 020 7533 6078

1.21 Trade in goods (on a balance of payments basis)

1995 = 100

	Volume indices (seasonally adjusted)		Price indices (not seasonally adjusted)		
	Exports	Imports	Exports	Imports	Terms of trade[1]
	BQKU	BQKV	BQKR	BQKS	BQKT
1955	17.8	17.3	..	..	..
1956	19.0	17.3	..	..	..
1957	19.3	18.0	..	..	..
1958	18.7	18.1	..	..	..
1959	19.1	19.5	..	..	..
1960	20.1	21.8	..	..	..
1961	20.7	21.4	..	..	..
1962	21.0	21.9	..	..	..
1963	22.4	23.1	11.2	10.6	105.7
1964	23.1	25.8	11.3	10.9	103.7
1965	24.4	25.8	11.7	10.9	107.3
1966	25.4	26.4	12.1	11.1	109.0
1967	25.1	28.8	12.3	11.1	110.8
1968	28.6	31.6	13.3	12.5	106.4
1969	31.3	31.9	13.7	12.8	107.0
1970	32.6	33.8	14.6	13.3	109.8
1971	34.6	35.3	15.4	13.9	110.8
1972	34.6	39.4	16.3	14.5	112.4
1973	39.2	44.8	18.3	18.5	98.9
1974	41.9	45.0	23.3	27.0	86.3
1975	40.1	41.0	28.5	30.9	92.2
1976	44.1	43.5	34.2	37.8	90.5
1977	47.6	44.5	40.4	43.7	92.4
1978	48.7	46.4	44.4	45.4	97.8
1979	50.8	50.9	49.2	48.3	101.9
1980	51.3	48.2	56.6	53.2	106.4
1981	50.8	46.3	61.6	57.8	106.6
1982	52.2	48.8	65.9	62.7	105.1
1983	53.3	53.1	70.5	68.3	103.2
1984	57.6	59.1	76.1	74.5	102.1
1985	60.8	60.9	80.1	78.2	102.4
1986	63.4	65.4	72.2	74.6	96.8
1987	67.2	70.5	74.7	76.8	97.3
1988	68.6	79.9	75.5	76.0	99.3
1989	72.6	86.5	78.9	79.3	99.5
1990	77.2	86.5	81.7	81.2	100.6
1991	78.0	81.9	82.8	82.2	100.7
1992	79.9	87.3	84.5	82.9	101.9
1993	82.8	90.6	95.0	91.2	104.2
1994	91.3	94.6	96.9	94.3	102.8
1995	100.0	100.0	100.0	100.0	100.0
1996	107.7	109.1	100.8	100.1	100.7
1997	116.5	119.0	95.2	93.8	101.5
1998	117.9	129.1	90.3	88.0	102.6
1999	121.6	138.7	89.8	86.8	103.5

1 Price index for exports expressed as a percentage of price index for imports.

Source: Office for National Statistics; Enquiries 020 7533 6064

1.21 Trade in goods (on a balance of payments basis)

continued

1995 = 100

	Volume indices (seasonally adjusted)		Price indices (not seasonally adjusted)		
	Exports	Imports	Exports	Imports	Terms of trade[1]
	BQKU	BQKV	BQKR	BQKS	BQKT
1955 Q1	18.2	17.5	..	..	..
Q2	16.1	16.0	..	..	..
Q3	18.5	18.2	..	..	..
Q4	18.5	17.6	..	..	..
1956 Q1	18.5	17.4	..	..	..
Q2	19.3	17.3	..	..	..
Q3	18.8	17.4	..	..	..
Q4	19.2	17.0	..	..	..
1957 Q1	19.4	18.3	..	..	..
Q2	19.2	17.7	..	..	..
Q3	19.3	18.3	..	..	..
Q4	19.1	17.8	..	..	..
1958 Q1	18.9	17.6	..	..	..
Q2	17.5	17.4	..	..	..
Q3	19.5	18.7	..	..	..
Q4	18.7	18.6	..	..	..
1959 Q1	18.2	18.7	..	..	..
Q2	18.9	19.4	..	..	..
Q3	19.5	19.2	..	..	..
Q4	20.0	20.5	..	..	..
1960 Q1	20.5	21.0	..	..	..
Q2	19.7	22.1	..	..	..
Q3	20.0	21.9	..	..	..
Q4	20.1	22.1	..	..	..
1961 Q1	20.9	22.2	..	..	..
Q2	20.4	21.5	..	..	..
Q3	20.8	21.1	..	..	..
Q4	20.6	20.9	..	..	..
1962 Q1	20.3	21.3	..	..	..
Q2	21.4	21.9	..	..	..
Q3	21.3	22.5	..	..	..
Q4	21.2	22.0	..	..	..
1963 Q1	21.7	21.7	11.1	10.6	104.7
Q2	22.4	22.9	11.1	10.5	105.7
Q3	22.5	23.6	11.2	10.6	105.7
Q4	22.9	24.1	11.3	10.8	104.6
1964 Q1	23.0	25.2	11.2	10.9	102.8
Q2	23.5	25.3	11.3	10.9	103.7
Q3	22.6	26.1	11.4	10.9	104.6
Q4	23.4	26.6	11.4	11.0	103.6
1965 Q1	23.6	24.3	11.6	10.9	106.4
Q2	24.0	25.8	11.6	10.9	106.4
Q3	24.7	26.5	11.7	10.9	107.3
Q4	25.3	26.7	11.8	10.9	108.3
1966 Q1	25.1	27.0	11.9	11.0	108.2
Q2	24.2	26.1	12.1	11.2	108.0
Q3	25.5	27.3	12.2	11.0	110.9
Q4	26.8	25.4	12.2	11.1	109.9
1967 Q1	26.9	28.4	12.2	11.0	110.9
Q2	25.9	28.8	12.2	10.9	111.9
Q3	25.3	28.5	12.3	11.0	111.8
Q4	22.5	29.4	12.4	11.5	107.8
1968 Q1	28.4	31.5	12.9	12.3	104.9
Q2	27.4	31.3	13.1	12.4	105.6
Q3	29.1	32.0	13.5	12.6	107.1
Q4	29.4	31.6	13.5	12.7	106.3
1969 Q1	29.2	31.7	13.6	12.6	107.9
Q2	31.2	32.0	13.6	12.7	107.1
Q3	32.3	31.9	13.7	12.9	106.2
Q4	32.5	32.1	13.8	13.1	105.3

See footnotes on page 131.

Source: Office for National Statistics; Enquiries 020 7533 6064

1.21 Trade in goods (on a balance of payments basis)

continued

1995 = 100

	Volume indices (seasonally adjusted)		Price indices (not seasonally adjusted)		
	Exports	Imports	Exports	Imports	Terms of trade[1]
	BQKU	BQKV	BQKR	BQKS	BQKT
1970 Q1	33.0	32.3	14.3	13.2	108.3
Q2	32.2	34.1	14.4	13.3	108.3
Q3	30.7	33.5	14.7	13.3	110.5
Q4	34.6	35.2	14.8	13.4	110.4
1971 Q1	32.5	34.6	15.0	13.5	111.1
Q2	35.5	35.7	15.2	14.0	108.6
Q3	35.5	35.0	15.5	14.1	109.9
Q4	34.9	36.1	15.8	14.0	112.9
1972 Q1	34.2	37.9	15.9	14.0	113.6
Q2	34.6	38.9	16.0	14.1	113.5
Q3	30.5	37.4	16.5	14.7	112.2
Q4	38.9	43.4	16.7	15.2	109.9
1973 Q1	37.9	43.8	17.4	16.3	106.7
Q2	38.5	43.9	17.9	17.5	102.3
Q3	40.0	45.3	18.5	19.3	95.9
Q4	40.3	46.2	19.4	21.0	92.4
1974 Q1	41.3	44.7	21.1	24.4	86.5
Q2	42.6	45.7	22.8	27.1	84.1
Q3	42.7	45.2	24.0	27.9	86.0
Q4	41.2	44.2	25.1	28.8	87.2
1975 Q1	40.7	41.7	27.2	29.8	91.3
Q2	39.2	39.3	27.8	30.0	92.7
Q3	39.2	42.1	29.0	31.0	93.5
Q4	41.3	40.8	30.1	32.6	92.3
1976 Q1	42.5	40.6	31.4	34.2	91.8
Q2	44.5	44.2	33.1	36.7	90.2
Q3	43.9	44.7	35.0	38.7	90.4
Q4	45.5	44.7	37.1	41.6	89.2
1977 Q1	46.6	44.7	38.6	42.5	90.8
Q2	47.8	46.0	40.1	43.6	92.0
Q3	49.3	44.1	41.2	44.3	93.0
Q4	46.7	43.1	41.7	44.3	94.1
1978 Q1	47.7	47.1	43.4	44.2	98.2
Q2	49.6	47.3	43.7	45.1	96.9
Q3	48.7	47.3	44.9	45.7	98.2
Q4	48.9	44.1	45.6	46.6	97.9
1979 Q1	44.1	47.1	47.1	47.4	99.4
Q2	54.9	51.4	48.3	47.5	101.7
Q3	51.9	52.9	49.8	47.9	104.0
Q4	52.5	52.4	51.6	50.4	102.4
1980 Q1	54.0	52.9	54.4	52.3	104.0
Q2	51.4	50.3	56.7	53.3	106.4
Q3	49.8	45.5	57.7	53.2	108.5
Q4	50.1	44.1	57.5	53.8	106.9
1981 Q1	49.3	42.0	59.0	54.4	108.5
Q2	50.0	44.0	60.7	56.3	107.8
Q3	52.0	50.4	62.6	59.6	105.0
Q4	51.9	48.7	64.2	60.8	105.6
1982 Q1	51.1	48.3	64.8	61.4	105.5
Q2	52.8	50.0	64.8	62.1	104.3
Q3	51.8	48.5	66.4	62.9	105.6
Q4	52.9	48.3	67.4	64.5	104.5
1983 Q1	52.3	51.5	69.4	67.1	103.4
Q2	52.4	52.6	70.0	68.2	102.6
Q3	53.7	53.1	71.0	68.3	104.0
Q4	54.9	55.1	71.7	69.7	102.9
1984 Q1	56.3	55.7	73.6	71.6	102.8
Q2	56.3	58.6	75.2	73.5	102.3
Q3	58.5	59.7	76.3	75.4	101.2
Q4	59.4	62.3	79.2	77.5	102.2

See footnotes on page 131.

Source: Office for National Statistics; Enquiries 020 7533 6064

1.21 Trade in goods (on a balance of payments basis)

continued

1995 = 100

	Volume indices (seasonally adjusted)		Price indices (not seasonally adjusted)		
	Exports	Imports	Exports	Imports	Terms of trade[1]
	BQKU	BQKV	BQKR	BQKS	BQKT
1985 Q1	60.1	62.7	82.8	81.8	101.2
Q2	62.7	60.8	81.6	79.9	102.1
Q3	60.1	59.5	78.3	76.3	102.6
Q4	60.2	60.5	77.7	74.8	103.9
1986 Q1	61.8	62.8	73.2	74.8	97.9
Q2	63.4	65.3	71.3	73.2	97.4
Q3	63.2	66.4	71.1	73.4	96.9
Q4	65.3	67.3	73.1	76.8	95.2
1987 Q1	67.0	66.1	74.2	78.1	95.0
Q2	65.4	69.4	74.5	76.3	97.6
Q3	68.1	72.7	75.3	76.5	98.4
Q4	68.3	73.8	75.0	76.4	98.2
1988 Q1	67.3	74.2	74.8	76.0	98.4
Q2	69.2	78.3	75.0	75.3	99.6
Q3	69.9	81.6	76.9	76.6	100.4
Q4	68.0	85.6	75.4	76.3	98.8
1989 Q1	71.8	86.4	76.0	76.6	99.2
Q2	70.3	85.5	78.6	79.2	99.2
Q3	72.6	87.6	79.9	80.2	99.6
Q4	75.7	86.3	81.0	81.4	99.5
1990 Q1	76.9	88.5	81.3	82.2	98.9
Q2	77.5	88.0	81.6	81.7	99.9
Q3	77.0	85.7	81.8	79.8	102.5
Q4	77.4	83.8	82.1	81.1	101.2
1991 Q1	75.6	81.6	81.8	80.7	101.4
Q2	78.3	80.8	82.7	81.9	101.0
Q3	79.3	82.0	84.0	83.4	100.7
Q4	78.8	83.1	82.8	82.7	100.1
1992 Q1	78.5	83.9	83.6	82.2	101.7
Q2	80.1	87.7	84.3	81.7	103.2
Q3	79.4	88.0	84.0	81.0	103.7
Q4	81.7	89.5	86.1	86.6	99.4
1993 Q1	82.6	91.0	94.5	90.7	104.2
Q2	81.6	88.7	94.5	91.3	103.5
Q3	82.7	90.6	95.6	91.5	104.5
Q4	84.5	92.1	95.3	91.2	104.5
1994 Q1	88.6	93.5	95.6	92.3	103.6
Q2	89.8	94.1	97.5	93.5	104.3
Q3	91.5	93.2	97.9	95.9	102.1
Q4	95.2	97.5	96.7	95.3	101.5
1995 Q1	98.1	96.1	99.5	98.0	101.5
Q2	97.5	99.3	100.0	99.7	100.3
Q3	101.5	101.7	100.0	101.5	98.5
Q4	102.9	103.0	100.6	100.8	99.8
1996 Q1	104.8	107.0	102.1	101.7	100.4
Q2	106.6	107.8	101.5	101.8	99.7
Q3	108.8	110.2	100.7	99.2	101.5
Q4	110.5	111.2	99.1	97.7	101.4
1997 Q1	113.4	113.5	97.4	95.5	102.0
Q2	116.1	119.2	95.4	94.0	101.5
Q3	117.8	119.1	94.5	93.5	101.1
Q4	118.7	124.0	93.6	92.1	101.6
1998 Q1	117.7	125.0	91.7	89.7	102.2
Q2	119.0	128.7	90.6	88.6	102.3
Q3	118.1	130.9	89.8	87.2	103.0
Q4	116.9	131.8	89.0	86.4	103.0
1999 Q1	115.0	134.1	88.8	86.1	103.1
Q2	118.1	134.0	89.4	86.4	103.5
Q3	127.3	141.9	90.5	87.1	103.9
Q4	126.1	144.8	90.6	87.8	103.2
2000 Q1	130.7	146.9	90.9	88.6	102.6

See footnotes on page 131.

Source: Office for National Statistics; Enquiries 020 7533 6064

1.22 Measures of UK competitiveness in trade in manufactures

1990 = 100, BBKM and BBKM are 1995=100

	Summary measures						Export unit value index[1,6]				
	Relative export prices[6]	Relative wholesale prices[5,6]	IMF index of relative unit labour costs[6]: Actual	IMF index of relative unit labour costs[6]: Normalised	Import price competitiveness[2,4]	Relative profitability of exports[2,4]	United Kingdom	United States	Japan	France	Germany[3]
	CTPC	CTPD	CTPE	CTPF	BBKM	BBKN	CTPI	CTPJ	CTPK	CTPL	CTPM
1975	91.8	80.1	..	..	..	..	42.0	46.4	48.7	47.0	44.2
1976	88.1	74.7	..	..	..	..	40.7	49.5	47.8	46.7	44.3
1977	93.5	79.0	..	..	..	..	46.9	52.2	52.6	50.0	49.3
1978	98.1	82.6	79.1	81.3	..	..	56.2	56.0	64.8	58.2	57.6
1979	102.4	90.1	93.0	93.9	..	..	67.4	64.8	68.1	68.2	66.8
1980	112.4	102.8	113.2	112.7	..	..	81.8	71.0	72.2	75.6	73.6
1981	111.7	106.4	118.5	120.6	..	..	75.8	79.8	76.4	65.8	62.4
1982	106.2	104.4	111.4	114.8	..	..	70.6	84.6	71.0	61.9	61.0
1983	100.8	97.2	101.5	106.5	..	..	65.4	85.5	70.1	58.8	58.8
1984	98.7	93.8	98.0	102.3	..	..	62.1	86.7	70.2	56.7	54.6
1985	102.0	96.9	101.0	102.1	..	..	64.3	86.5	69.9	58.0	55.1
1986	98.0	92.1	93.4	94.7	90.7	105.4	73.9	86.6	84.0	74.2	72.6
1987	100.3	93.5	94.3	98.2	91.5	105.9	85.8	90.7	92.0	85.9	86.0
1988	106.5	100.3	100.5	102.8	94.1	105.5	96.0	95.9	101.1	89.5	88.5
1989	100.1	97.9	98.3	100.1	97.0	104.0	90.3	98.3	100.4	87.0	86.7
1990	100.0	100.0	100.0	100.0	100.0	100.0	100.0	100.0	100.0	100.0	100.0
1991	101.9	105.2	103.7	103.9	118.3	119.6	100.6	101.1	107.4	96.3	97.0
1992	100.3	103.5	99.0	104.0	114.4	114.3	102.9	102.1	114.6	100.5	102.4
1993	102.1	96.2	88.9	95.5	105.5	101.9	97.8	102.3	124.5	92.5	91.8
1994	104.2	97.6	91.2	96.2	102.6	100.1	102.5	103.1	134.3	96.0	92.8
1995	104.0	94.0	90.2	91.5	100.0	100.0	113.1	106.3	145.5	107.2	107.0
1996	106.5	98.3	92.9	93.7	101.0	100.0	112.1	105.6	133.3	103.8	99.5
1997	99.0	114.7	114.3	113.9	105.6	103.5	111.7	107.6	122.0	92.2	85.9
1998	..	..	124.8	125.5	108.6	105.0	110.6	107.6	113.7	..	..
1999	..	..	..	..	109.1	105.4	..	..	..	..	..

	Wholesale price index[1,6]					Unit labour costs index[1,6]				
	United Kingdom	United States	Japan	France	Germany[3]	United Kingdom	United States	Japan	France	Germany[3]
	CTPN	CTPO	CTPP	CTPQ	CTPR	CTPS	CTPT	CTPU	CTPV	CTPW
1975	36.5	49.5	41.4	46.1	43.9	38.9	56.4	41.4	51.7	40.2
1976	34.6	51.8	43.3	45.2	44.4	35.3	58.7	42.0	50.0	39.4
1977	39.8	55.0	48.7	47.1	49.5	38.1	61.3	49.2	52.2	45.4
1978	47.7	59.1	61.2	55.2	57.9	48.2	65.6	64.5	61.3	54.4
1979	58.9	66.2	62.3	64.8	66.5	62.9	72.7	60.9	70.4	61.3
1980	74.8	75.6	69.1	73.8	72.1	84.3	81.0	61.7	81.4	68.4
1981	72.2	82.7	71.6	63.7	62.5	80.9	88.2	65.6	71.0	57.3
1982	67.7	84.7	64.1	58.9	61.7	72.9	92.1	58.6	65.3	56.5
1983	62.4	85.5	66.2	55.4	59.5	62.9	91.6	62.4	60.9	53.5
1984	58.3	87.6	66.2	52.6	54.9	56.8	91.6	62.2	56.7	48.6
1985	60.1	88.0	65.2	54.0	54.3	58.3	93.0	59.9	57.6	47.8
1986	68.8	86.1	85.7	71.0	71.8	69.1	93.0	89.4	76.6	67.0
1987	79.6	88.4	96.5	83.3	84.6	81.8	93.1	101.1	89.9	85.9
1988	89.6	92.3	108.2	86.8	87.7	89.6	95.1	111.1	88.0	88.1
1989	86.5	96.8	103.1	84.2	84.5	84.9	97.9	103.8	82.5	83.6
1990	100.0	100.0	100.0	100.0	100.0	100.0	100.0	100.0	100.0	100.0
1991	104.5	100.0	107.2	97.3	99.7	106.2	103.0	109.2	98.8	100.6
1992	107.5	99.7	112.3	103.3	107.4	108.1	102.2	120,4	106.1	114.6
1993	95.1	100.8	124.3	96.1	101.5	92.1	102.9	142.8	101.3	113.8
1994	99.4	102.2	132.6	98.8	104.0	93.5	102.7	156.3	97.9	114.3
1995	106.5	105.1	143.0	111.7	119.8	99.2	101.2	162.2	105.9	132.1
1996	108.2	107.6	123.3	107.5	113.4	100.2	99.5	134.2	104.4	127.8
1997	114.6	107.9	112.2	93.9	99.4	109.0	98.4	119.5	87.8	107.2
1998	116.5	106.8	102.7	..	..	115.4	98.0	111.1	85.2	102.1
1999	115.1	108.4	114.1	..	..	..	97.7	128.3	..	..

1 All the indices are shown in US dollars.
2 Excludes erratics (ships, North sea installations, aircraft, precious stones and silver bullion).
3 Includes the former German Democratic Republic as from 1991 Q1.
4 These series are now calculated on a SIC 1992 basis and have been rebased to 1995 prices
5 This series is calculated using UK producer prices. All other country indices are wholesale price indices.
6 These figures fall outside the scope of National Statistics.

Sources: International Monetary Fund; Office for National Statistics; Enquiries 020 7533 5914

1.22 Measures of UK competitiveness in trade in manufactures

continued

1990 = 100, BBKM and BBKN are 1995=100

	Summary measures						Export unit value index[1,6]				
			IMF index of relative unit labour costs[6]								
	Relative export prices[6]	Relative wholesale prices[5,6]	Actual	Normalised	Import price competitiveness[2,4]	Relative profitability of exports[2,4]	United Kingdom	United States	Japan	France	Germany[3]
	CTPC	CTPD	CTPE	CTPF	BBKM	BBKN	CTPI	CTPJ	CTPK	CTPL	CTPM
1975 Q1	91.5	79.7	–	–	..	..	42.6	45.6	50.1	46.9	46.1
Q2	91.8	81.1	–	–	..	..	43.0	46.5	49.3	48.6	46.1
Q3	93.0	79.9	–	–	..	..	41.5	46.4	48.1	46.0	42.9
Q4	90.8	79.5	–	–	..	..	40.5	47.2	47.3	46.5	42.0
1976 Q1	91.9	80.5	–	–	..	..	41.2	48.3	46.5	46.6	42.4
Q2	87.6	74.2	–	–	..	..	39.6	49.0	46.8	46.3	43.3
Q3	89.2	73.9	–	–	..	..	41.2	49.6	48.3	46.6	44.5
Q4	83.5	70.2	–	–	..	..	40.1	51.1	49.5	47.0	47.3
1977 Q1	90.6	76.0	–	–	..	..	43.9	50.9	50.1	48.3	47.8
Q2	92.0	78.2	–	–	..	..	45.5	51.4	51.7	48.9	48.5
Q3	93.7	79.9	–	–	..	..	47.2	52.7	52.9	50.6	49.4
Q4	98.6	82.4	–	–	..	..	51.2	53.7	56.1	52.1	51.5
1978 Q1	101.4	85.2	78.7	81.5	..	..	54.9	54.1	57.6	54.0	55.2
Q2	94.8	80.6	76.8	79.9	..	..	52.6	54.8	65.4	56.5	55.4
Q3	97.9	82.7	79.2	81.9	..	..	56.9	56.3	69.1	60.3	57.8
Q4	99.0	82.2	81.7	82.1	..	..	60.4	58.6	68.9	62.4	62.5
1979 Q1	98.5	83.9	87.2	87.9	..	..	62.1	62.1	68.3	65.0	64.0
Q2	103.0	89.6	91.7	95.0	..	..	65.4	64.5	67.1	65.5	63.8
Q3	107.5	95.7	95.6	94.8	..	..	72.0	65.6	69.9	69.5	68.0
Q4	101.5	91.9	97.3	98.0	..	..	70.5	67.1	67.4	72.9	71.8
1980 Q1	106.5	97.5	104.3	105.9	..	..	75.7	67.6	67.4	74.4	73.9
Q2	112.1	101.6	111.5	111.7	..	..	80.6	69.4	71.5	75.0	73.4
Q3	114.1	104.2	115.2	114.1	..	..	84.9	72.1	74.0	78.4	75.8
Q4	118.3	109.1	121.8	118.9	..	..	86.0	74.8	76.7	74.7	71.3
1981 Q1	120.2	112.4	128.0	127.7	..	..	84.1	76.7	78.5	70.3	66.0
Q2	114.9	109.9	122.6	123.7	..	..	76.8	78.5	75.9	65.1	61.5
Q3	105.0	101.6	113.6	116.9	..	..	68.6	80.9	74.3	62.7	58.6
Q4	106.0	100.8	109.7	114.1	..	..	73.3	82.9	77.3	65.8	64.1
1982 Q1	107.7	103.2	113.4	116.2	..	..	73.4	84.9	74.8	65.2	62.0
Q2	105.2	102.4	111.6	114.5	..	..	70.6	84.5	71.2	63.2	62.0
Q3	108.0	104.1	111.4	115.4	..	..	70.4	84.0	69.6	59.4	60.1
Q4	104.5	102.0	109.1	113.1	..	..	67.9	84.7	68.7	60.1	59.9
1983 Q1	96.3	93.3	96.5	101.1	..	..	64.3	86.2	70.8	61.3	61.9
Q2	102.4	98.9	102.3	106.7	..	..	66.8	85.3	69.6	59.3	60.6
Q3	104.1	99.7	104.0	109.4	..	..	65.9	85.0	68.5	57.5	56.7
Q4	101.5	97.4	103.3	108.8	..	..	64.6	85.5	71.7	57.6	56.6
1984 Q1	100.0	96.2	99.0	105.1	..	..	64.2	86.4	72.2	58.3	56.6
Q2	99.2	95.0	98.3	103.2	..	..	63.9	86.9	71.8	58.8	56.6
Q3	98.8	93.3	98.2	102.3	..	..	61.1	86.7	68.7	55.8	53.7
Q4	96.6	90.8	96.4	98.8	..	..	58.7	86.6	68.4	54.4	52.1
1985 Q1	94.4	88.6	91.7	94.8	..	..	55.6	86.2	66.8	52.3	49.7
Q2	102.1	97.0	101.0	103.3	..	..	62.5	86.6	68.6	55.7	52.9
Q3	105.8	101.6	106.5	106.8	..	..	67.8	86.6	69.8	59.8	57.2
Q4	104.2	98.9	104.6	103.4	..	..	71.1	86.6	75.4	66.0	62.3
1986 Q1	98.1	94.0	96.4	97.4	93.2	104.1	70.9	86.5	79.5	72.0	68.4
Q2	102.9	96.6	99.1	99.5	93.1	105.1	75.8	86.2	83.8	72.2	70.3
Q3	97.5	91.2	92.5	93.4	90.3	107.1	75.0	86.5	87.3	75.5	75.0
Q4	94.2	87.1	85.4	88.6	87.6	108.1	73.9	87.3	86.1	77.4	77.6
1987 Q1	96.4	89.6	89.0	93.6	87.7	106.3	80.4	88.5	88.4	83.8	84.9
Q2	100.5	94.1	95.1	98.2	91.2	106.2	85.3	90.3	91.5	85.1	85.6
Q3	101.0	94.1	94.9	98.9	92.0	106.7	85.0	91.2	91.7	84.7	83.7
Q4	104.2	96.8	98.3	102.2	92.8	105.8	92.8	92.7	96.9	90.0	90.0

See footnotes on page 135.

Sources: International Monetary Fund; Office for National Statistics; Enquiries 020 7533 5914

1.22 Measures of UK competitiveness in trade in manufactures

continued

1990 = 100,BBKM and BBKN are 1995=100

	Wholesale price index[1,6]					Unit labour costs index[1,6]				
	United Kingdom	United States	Japan	France	Germany[3]	United Kingdom	United States	Japan	France	Germany[3]
	CTPN	CTPO	CTPP	CTPQ	CTPR	CTPS	CTPT	CTPU	CTPV	CTPW
1975 Q1	36.8	48.6	41.9	45.6	45.8	38.2	56.5	41.7	50.1	42.2
Q2	37.8	49.0	41.9	48.1	45.7	40.0	56.4	40.5	53.9	42.2
Q3	35.6	49.8	41.1	45.5	42.4	38.9	55.9	42.2	51.7	39.3
Q4	35.4	50.5	40.7	45.5	41.9	37.9	56.6	41.2	51.1	37.5
1976 Q1	36.2	50.8	41.6	45.6	42.7	38.0	57.6	41.6	51.3	37.8
Q2	33.8	51.5	42.7	45.3	43.6	34.8	58.5	40.6	50.5	38.3
Q3	34.3	52.1	44.6	44.9	44.6	35.4	59.2	42.9	49.4	39.9
Q4	33.7	52.7	44.5	44.8	47.1	32.9	59.5	43.0	49.1	41.6
1977 Q1	37.0	53.7	45.8	45.4	47.6	35.4	60.0	45.5	49.4	42.9
Q2	38.9	54.9	47.6	46.4	48.6	36.9	60.5	47.8	50.9	44.5
Q3	40.4	55.3	49.1	47.7	49.9	38.4	61.6	50.4	52.9	45.9
Q4	42.9	56.1	52.8	49.1	51.9	41.7	63.0	53.9	55.7	48.3
1978 Q1	46.6	57.2	54.6	50.8	55.6	45.7	64.5	58.6	56.5	51.6
Q2	45.1	58.6	58.7	53.4	55.9	45.4	64.7	61.6	59.0	53.7
Q3	48.5	59.6	66.4	57.4	58.0	49.0	65.8	69.4	64.3	54.1
Q4	50.5	61.0	66.9	59.7	62.5	52.7	67.4	70.3	65.8	58.4
1979 Q1	52.7	62.9	64.3	61.5	64.0	58.0	69.6	66.9	69.0	61.2
Q2	56.4	65.0	61.4	62.0	63.8	60.0	71.5	61.0	68.2	58.5
Q3	63.6	67.2	63.5	66.1	67.7	65.4	73.9	61.2	70.4	61.8
Q4	63.1	69.6	60.2	69.7	70.7	68.2	75.7	55.3	74.2	64.2
1980 Q1	69.4	73.0	62.7	72.3	72.2	74.5	77.1	55.0	76.7	67.0
Q2	73.3	74.7	67.8	73.4	72.2	82.2	80.3	58.9	80.6	68.1
Q3	77.6	76.6	72.0	76.6	74.2	89.2	82.6	65.6	85.1	71.1
Q4	79.2	78.3	74.8	72.8	70.1	91.9	83.9	68.4	83.2	67.3
1981 Q1	78.9	80.9	76.0	68.2	65.6	91.1	85.7	68.4	77.2	60.2
Q2	73.6	82.8	71.6	62.8	61.4	82.8	87.4	65.2	70.4	57.2
Q3	66.2	83.4	68.5	60.5	58.8	73.7	88.7	63.8	66.7	53.7
Q4	69.4	83.8	70.7	63.9	64.9	75.5	91.2	65.3	70.9	58.4
1982 Q1	69.7	84.4	68.1	62.6	62.9	76.3	91.7	60.5	69.6	56.9
Q2	68.1	84.3	65.2	61.2	62.7	73.7	91.6	59.6	67.2	56.7
Q3	67.2	84.9	61.8	56.2	60.7	72.0	92.0	57.3	63.2	56.7
Q4	65.5	85.0	61.7	56.2	60.5	69.6	93.0	57.4	62.1	55.9
1983 Q1	61.8	84.9	67.0	59.2	62.6	62.9	92.3	64.0	65.6	56.9
Q2	63.8	85.0	66.1	55.8	60.8	64.3	91.8	62.9	61.0	54.6
Q3	62.7	85.8	64.7	53.7	57.6	62.8	91.0	60.5	59.4	52.3
Q4	61.3	86.4	66.9	53.4	57.3	61.6	91.5	62.0	58.1	50.8
1984 Q1	60.9	87.1	67.9	53.9	57.2	59.4	91.0	64.4	58.0	52.0
Q2	60.6	87.8	68.3	54.7	57.5	59.0	91.2	64.8	60.2	51.0
Q3	56.9	87.7	64.7	51.8	53.6	55.6	91.7	60.4	55.7	46.9
Q4	54.3	87.8	64.0	50.2	51.7	52.8	92.6	59.3	53.4	44.9
1985 Q1	51.2	87.8	61.6	48.1	49.0	48.6	93.3	54.8	52.2	42.8
Q2	58.3	88.1	62.6	51.5	51.9	55.8	92.3	56.8	54.9	45.4
Q3	64.0	87.8	64.9	56.2	56.2	62.5	92.7	60.1	58.8	49.5
Q4	66.9	88.3	73.1	61.9	62.0	67.0	93.6	69.7	66.1	55.0
1986 Q1	67.4	87.1	79.2	68.2	67.7	67.3	93.0	79.9	74.5	60.8
Q2	70.6	85.8	85.5	68.7	69.7	71.6	92.6	88.9	73.6	64.3
Q3	69.8	85.5	91.4	72.4	74.5	70.6	93.2	96.9	77.9	70.4
Q4	67.6	85.9	87.8	74.9	76.1	66.9	93.3	94.0	80.7	73.7
1987 Q1	74.0	86.9	91.3	81.0	82.6	76.0	93.6	97.6	90.2	84.2
Q2	79.5	88.0	97.2	82.8	83.9	81.9	92.8	104.1	89.6	84.6
Q3	78.7	88.9	95.3	82.0	82.7	80.9	93.2	98.9	87.3	84.5
Q4	86.1	89.7	102.9	87.9	89.5	88.5	93.1	104.4	92.4	90.5

See footnotes on page 135.

Sources: International Monetary Fund; Office for National Statistics; Enquiries 020 7533 5914

1.22 Measures of UK competitiveness in trade in manufactures

continued

1990 = 100, BBKM and BBKN are 1995=100

	Summary measures						Export unit value index[1,6]				
			IMF index of relative unit labour costs[6]								
	Relative export prices[6]	Relative wholesale prices[5,6]	Actual	Normalised	Import price competitiveness[2,4]	Relative profitability of exports[2,4]	United Kingdom	United States	Japan	France	Germany[3]
	CTPC	CTPD	CTPE	CTPF	BBKM	BBKN	CTPI	CTPJ	CTPK	CTPL	CTPM
1988 Q1	105.5	97.9	96.9	99.5	93.1	105.4	95.7	94.0	99.8	91.8	90.8
Q2	108.9	101.9	102.5	104.1	95.0	104.6	98.7	95.8	101.5	91.2	90.2
Q3	106.5	100.2	99.9	102.7	94.3	106.7	92.8	96.8	99.1	85.4	83.7
Q4	106.0	101.7	102.8	105.0	95.4	103.8	96.9	97.1	104.2	89.9	89.9
1989 Q1	103.9	102.2	101.1	103.8	98.4	101.3	94.1	98.1	103.7	88.0	87.5
Q2	100.5	98.9	99.7	101.7	96.9	102.9	88.9	98.4	99.9	85.3	84.6
Q3	99.4	97.3	97.9	99.5	96.2	103.8	88.3	98.2	98.5	85.6	85.1
Q4	97.4	93.9	94.5	95.3	95.5	103.9	89.6	98.4	99.7	89.4	90.1
1990 Q1	96.6	95.1	95.5	95.5	97.4	102.1	92.8	99.0	98.4	95.5	95.6
Q2	98.1	97.2	95.8	96.9	98.4	101.4	95.0	99.0	95.8	96.8	96.7
Q3	103.1	103.8	104.4	104.0	101.5	99.5	104.0	100.4	100.6	101.4	101.3
Q4	102.2	103.9	104.4	103.7	102.7	97.0	108.0	101.6	106.2	107.2	107.2
1991 Q1	102.7	106.3	105.4	105.3	125.1	125.0	106.7	101.5	107.9	103.5	104.3
Q2	101.2	105.4	104.2	104.1	119.5	120.9	96.8	101.0	105.3	92.8	92.9
Q3	102.1	104.6	103.1	103.1	115.4	116.7	97.1	100.9	106.0	92.3	92.7
Q4	101.7	104.7	102.2	103.3	115.8	117.0	101.7	101.2	110.5	97.6	99.1
1992 Q1	102.5	105.4	103.7	107.3	114.8	114.7	102.7	101.4	112.7	97.6	98.8
Q2	103.6	108.3	104.1	108.2	116.7	115.2	104.4	102.0	113.0	98.9	99.7
Q3	102.4	106.7	100.9	106.4	118.1	116.6	110.0	102.6	116.4	106.2	109.3
Q4	93.0	93.9	87.3	94.0	108.1	111.8	94.1	102.3	116.5	99.8	102.5
1993 Q1	98.3	93.2	85.2	92.5	106.5	102.9	94.5	102.3	120.7	94.5	93.7
Q2	101.0	96.5	88.1	94.9	105.6	103.1	98.2	102.3	124.5	95.5	93.3
Q3	104.2	97.8	90.9	97.2	104.8	101.2	98.7	102.3	126.5	89.6	90.4
Q4	105.9	98.1	91.3	97.5	105.0	101.4	99.9	102.3	126.5	90.7	89.9
1994 Q1	104.5	99.1	90.8	96.0	104.4	101.0	98.4	102.3	132.4	90.4	87.9
Q2	103.9	97.6	90.4	95.1	103.8	100.4	100.4	102.3	132.7	93.7	91.4
Q3	104.1	96.5	90.6	95.7	101.9	100.5	104.4	103.3	134.9	99.6	95.4
Q4	104.9	97.9	93.1	98.1	102.3	101.6	106.8	104.3	137.3	101.0	97.0
1995 Q1	105.1	96.4	91.9	92.9	102.0	100.1	111.0	106.3	145.1	102.9	103.9
Q2	103.3	93.1	89.1	90.4	99.8	99.9	113.8	107.3	152.2	108.3	109.5
Q3	104.6	93.9	89.7	91.5	98.6	100.5	113.8	106.3	143.6	108.6	106.5
Q4	103.9	93.4	90.0	91.1	99.6	99.5	113.8	105.3	142.2	109.2	108.2
1996 Q1	103.3	94.9	87.5	88.9	99.9	98.9	111.0	105.3	140.0	106.4	103.9
Q2	105.6	96.7	90.5	91.3	99.6	99.6	110.4	106.3	133.5	103.4	98.1
Q3	106.3	97.8	93.2	93.3	101.8	99.8	111.5	105.3	131.5	103.3	99.7
Q4	112.1	105.0	100.5	101.1	103.6	102.6	115.6	105.3	128.4	102.0	96.5
1997 Q1	113.7	111.4	106.2	107.4	104.2	103.2	112.9	108.3	124.9	95.2	91.0
Q2	114.9	113.8	112.7	111.9	106.1	104.0	111.2	108.3	123.6	92.8	87.1
Q3	116.8	116.9	117.4	116.9	106.9	104.7	110.1	108.3	121.8	89.2	82.6
Q4	119.2	117.8	120.8	119.5	107.4	105.3	112.5	105.3	117.9	91.8	83.3
1998 Q1	117.1	120.6	126.4	125.9	108.9	105.5	110.3	108.3	117.5	89.2	83.0
Q2	117.2	121.4	125.8	126.7	109.4	104.7	110.4	107.3	110.4	90.7	85.0
Q3	..	..	126.0	126.8	109.5	104.7	110.3	107.3	109.5	92.0	..
Q4	..	..	121.2	122.8	110.0	105.1	111.4	107.3	118.3	..	..
1999 Q1	..	..	..	..	109.8	104.9	109.9	107.3	120.8	..	..
Q2	..	..	..	..	109.2	105.6	..	..	115.4	..	..
Q3	..	..	..	..	108.9	106.5	..	..	..	..	..
Q4	..	..	..	..	109.4	106.9	..	..	..	..	..
2000 Q1	..	..	..	..	109.5	108.3	..	..	..	..	..
Q2	..	..	..	..	108.3	107.1	..	..	..	..	..

See footnotes on page 135.

Sources: International Monetary Fund; Office for National Statistics; Enquiries 020 7533 5914

1.22 Measures of UK competitiveness in trade in manufactures

continued

1990 = 100, BBKM and BBKN are 1995=100

	Wholesale price index[1,6]					Unit labour costs index[1,6]				
	United Kingdom	United States	Japan	France	Germany[3]	United Kingdom	United States	Japan	France	Germany[3]
	CTPN	CTPO	CTPP	CTPQ	CTPR	CTPS	CTPT	CTPU	CTPV	CTPW
1988 Q1	88.9	90.4	108.3	90.0	91.1	88.8	94.4	111.5	92.3	92.6
Q2	92.4	91.9	110.1	89.0	89.9	93.3	94.7	112.8	90.4	90.2
Q3	85.8	93.1	104.2	82.4	82.7	85.0	95.1	106.6	83.3	82.8
Q4	91.3	93.9	110.6	86.5	87.5	91.4	96.2	113.8	86.6	87.4
1989 Q1	90.5	95.6	108.2	84.6	85.1	87.6	96.8	109.2	82.7	84.6
Q2	85.6	97.2	103.4	81.9	82.0	83.7	96.8	102.8	79.3	81.4
Q3	84.6	96.9	101.0	82.8	82.6	83.7	98.6	101.9	82.3	81.7
Q4	85.1	97.5	100.2	87.5	88.4	84.1	99.2	102.0	85.7	87.0
1990 Q1	90.4	98.4	97.8	94.5	94.8	89.9	98.7	97.5	92.5	94.1
Q2	93.4	99.0	93.6	96.3	96.1	92.8	100.3	94.8	96.0	97.7
Q3	105.1	100.2	99.6	102.0	101.6	105.8	99.9	98.4	102.7	101.2
Q4	111.6	102.5	110.6	108.2	108.6	112.0	101.0	110.8	110.2	107.9
1991 Q1	110.9	99.3	108.5	105.1	107.0	112.5	102.8	106.0	107.7	105.2
Q2	101.0	100.2	104.8	93.5	95.0	103.5	103.4	107.8	94.9	96.8
Q3	100.0	99.7	105.2	92.8	95.5	101.7	102.9	106.9	93.4	97.3
Q4	105.8	100.8	110.7	98.7	102.5	106.8	103.0	116.5	100.5	103.9
1992 Q1	106.5	99.3	111.2	99.4	103.1	108.8	102.4	114.5	100.7	105.8
Q2	110.1	99.8	109.6	100.7	104.2	110.9	102.3	119.3	103.0	108.8
Q3	116.3	99.6	113.8	110.2	114.9	116.5	102.2	120.4	112.8	125.2
Q4	97.0	100.0	114.8	103.7	108.3	96.1	102.1	127.5	108.7	119.9
1993 Q1	92.1	100.6	116.0	98.4	102.7	89.0	102.0	128.6	103.6	115.7
Q2	97.3	101.3	125.9	99.6	103.8	93.6	102.6	145.3	104.8	116.4
Q3	95.8	100.5	130.0	93.5	100.0	93.2	103.7	150.4	98.1	112.6
Q4	95.2	100.9	126.5	93.2	99.5	92.7	103.5	148.9	99.1	110.6
1994 Q1	95.7	101.3	126.8	93.2	97.6	91.0	103.6	152.9	96.1	111.6
Q2	97.3	101.9	131.3	96.3	101.3	91.3	102.3	159.6	95.5	111.3
Q3	100.8	102.6	136.3	102.4	108.0	94.6	102.3	154.7	100.9	117.8
Q4	103.7	103.0	136.7	103.9	110.0	97.2	102.4	158.2	99.6	116.8
1995 Q1	105.5	104.0	140.8	107.3	115.6	98.0	101.6	161.3	100.9	126.6
Q2	107.6	105.3	157.7	113.3	123.0	99.8	101.4	183.0	107.6	134.2
Q3	106.7	105.3	142.7	112.9	120.0	98.9	101.1	159.2	107.0	132.2
Q4	106.3	105.9	133.1	113.5	120.7	100.0	100.5	148.7	108.3	135.7
1996 Q1	105.6	106.5	127.6	110.2	116.2	96.3	100.4	139.9	106.7	134.7
Q2	105.6	107.6	124.7	106.9	111.9	97.3	99.9	138.0	104.0	126.8
Q3	107.6	107.8	122.5	107.5	113.9	100.5	99.0	133.4	104.1	126.8
Q4	114.1	108.4	118.6	105.6	111.8	106.6	98.7	126.1	103.0	123.1
1997 Q1	113.8	108.3	111.5	97.9	103.5	106.2	99.3	119.8	94.3	115.3
Q2	114.2	107.9	114.2	94.9	100.5	108.5	98.7	120.2	88.4	109.3
Q3	113.9	107.7	114.9	90.2	95.6	108.4	97.5	122.0	83.3	101.3
Q4	116.4	107.8	108.5	93.2	98.6	113.1	98.2	116.4	85.5	103.8
1998 Q1	115.5	106.8	105.8	89.8	94.9	113.6	98.0	112.2	82.6	97.6
Q2	116.5	106.9	99.7	90.9	96.1	114.7	98.4	108.9	83.5	100.4
Q3	116.3	106.7	96.7	92.1	97.5	115.6	98.2	103.7	85.0	101.1
Q4	117.5	106.8	110.0	..	..	117.9	97.4	121.2	89.9	110.0
1999 Q1	114.9	106.8	112.0	..	..	115.2	96.8	125.6	..	105.1
Q2	114.4	108.1	108.0	..	..	112.4	96.9	118.3	..	101.6
Q3	114.4	109.2	114.2	..	..	111.4	97.2	120.2	..	94.9
Q4	116.8	109.7	123.4	..	..	..	95.8	129.4	..	..

See footnotes on page 135.

Sources: International Monetary Fund; Office for National Statistics; Enquiries 020 7533 5914

2.1 Prices

Producer price index 1995 = 100, others 1985 = 100

	Producer price index (1995 = 100)		General index of retail prices[1]				Pensioner indices[2]		
	Materials and fuel purchased by manufacturing industry	Output: all manufactured products: home sales	All items	Total food	All items except food	All items except seasonal food	One-person households	Two-person households	Purchasing power of the pound[3]
	PLKW	PLLU	FRAG	FRAH	FRAI	FRAK	FRAL	FRAM	FJAK
1948	..	..	8.4	7.1	9.3	..	..	..	1 198
1949	..	..	8.6	7.5	9.4	..	..	..	1 166
1950	..	..	8.8	8.1	9.5	..	..	..	1 132
1951	..	..	9.6	9.0	10.2	..	..	..	1 038
1952	..	..	10.6	10.4	10.8	..	..	..	948
1953	..	..	10.9	11.0	10.9	..	..	..	921
1954	..	..	11.1	11.3	11.0	..	..	..	904
1955	..	..	11.6	12.1	11.3	..	..	..	866
1956	..	..	12.1	12.7	11.9	12.2	..	..	824
1957	..	..	12.6	13.0	12.4	12.7	..	..	795
1958	..	..	13.0	13.3	12.9	13.0	..	..	771
1959	..	..	13.0	13.4	12.9	13.1	..	..	767
1960	..	..	13.2	13.3	13.2	13.3	..	..	760
1961	..	..	13.6	13.5	13.7	13.7	..	..	734
1962	..	..	14.2	14.0	14.4	14.3	13.9	14.0	704
1963	..	..	14.5	14.4	14.6	14.6	14.2	14.3	691
1964	..	..	15.0	14.8	15.1	15.1	14.7	14.8	669
1965	..	..	15.7	15.3	15.9	15.8	15.3	15.4	639
1966	..	..	16.3	15.9	16.6	16.4	15.9	16.1	614
1967	..	..	16.7	16.3	17.0	16.8	16.3	16.4	599
1968	..	..	17.5	16.9	17.8	17.6	17.1	17.2	573
1969	..	..	18.4	18.0	18.8	18.5	18.0	18.1	543
1970	..	..	19.6	19.2	19.9	19.7	19.2	19.3	511
1971	..	..	21.4	21.4	21.7	21.6	21.2	21.3	467
1972	..	..	23.0	23.3	23.1	23.1	22.8	22.8	436
1973	..	..	25.1	26.8	24.8	25.0	25.0	25.2	399
1974	32.0	19.8	29.1	31.6	28.5	29.0	29.0	29.2	345
1975	35.3	24.3	36.1	39.6	35.3	36.0	36.5	36.6	278
1976	44.3	28.4	42.1	47.6	40.8	41.7	43.5	43.5	238
1977	50.5	33.8	48.8	56.6	46.9	48.4	50.7	50.8	205
1978	50.5	36.8	52.8	60.6	50.9	52.7	54.9	54.8	190
1979	59.0	41.1	59.9	67.9	58.0	59.7	61.3	61.4	167
1980	69.3	47.6	70.7	76.1	69.4	70.7	71.4	71.3	142
1981	78.5	52.8	79.1	82.5	78.3	79.1	79.5	79.5	127
1982	83.4	57.3	85.9	89.0	85.1	85.8	86.9	86.7	117
1983	88.1	61.0	89.8	91.8	89.4	89.8	90.8	90.7	111
1984	96.6	64.6	94.3	97.0	93.7	94.1	95.4	95.3	106
1985	96.6	68.6	100.0	100.0	100.0	100.0	100.0	100.0	100
1986	81.0	69.5	103.4	103.3	103.5	103.3	103.2	103.2	97
1987	82.6	71.9	107.7	106.4	108.0	107.6	105.6	105.8	93
1988	84.5	74.6	113.0	110.1	113.6	113.0	109.5	109.8	89
1989	89.1	78.2	121.8	116.4	122.9	121.9	115.4	115.8	82
1990	88.5	83.0	133.3	125.7	134.9	133.5	124.2	124.5	75
1991	86.6	87.4	141.1	132.2	143.0	141.3	133.0	133.5	71
1992	86.3	90.2	146.4	135.0	148.7	146.9	137.6	138.7	68
1993	90.2	93.8	148.7	137.5	150.9	149.3	140.5	142.4	67
1994	91.9	96.1	152.4	138.9	155.1	152.9	143.0	145.4	65
1995	100.0	100.0	157.6	144.2	160.2	158.0	146.9	149.5	63
1996	98.8	102.6	161.4	148.9	163.9	162.0	150.2	153.3	61
1997	90.6	103.6	166.5	149.0	169.9	167.4	151.8	155.8	60
1998	82.5	104.2	172.2	150.9	176.3	173.0	153.9	158.5	58
1999	83.7	105.4	174.8	151.4	179.3	175.5	156.2	161.2	57

1 The index numbers given here are for comparative purposes only and should not be regarded as accurate to the last digit shown. The official Retail Prices Index series is shown in Table 2.2.

2 All items except housing.

3 Movements in the purchasing power of the pound are based on movements in the General index of retail prices.

Sources: Office for National Statistics;
Enquiries Columns 1-2 01633 812106; Columns 3-9 020 7533 5874

2.1 Prices

continued

Producer price index 1995 = 100, others 1985 = 100

	Producer price index (1995 = 100)			Not seasonally adjusted						
	Materials and fuel purchased by manufacturing industry		Output: all manufactured products: home sales (not seasonally adjusted)	General index of retail prices[1]				Pensioner indices[2]		
	Seasonally adjusted	Not seasonally adjusted		All items	Total food	All items except food	All items except seasonal food	One-person households	Two-person households	Purchasing power of the pound[3]
	PLKZ	PLKW	PLLU	FRAG	FRAH	FRAI	FRAK	FRAL	FRAM	FJAK
1948 Q1	..	..	..	8.2	7.1	9.1	..	..	..	1 225
Q2	..	..	..	8.4	7.3	9.3	..	..	..	1 185
Q3	..	..	..	8.4	7.1	9.4	..	..	..	1 190
Q4	..	..	..	8.4	7.1	9.5	..	..	..	1 190
1949 Q1	..	..	..	8.4	7.1	9.5	..	..	..	1 185
Q2	..	..	..	8.5	7.4	9.4	..	..	..	1 172
Q3	..	..	..	8.6	7.7	9.4	..	..	..	1 158
Q4	..	..	..	8.7	7.9	9.4	..	..	..	1 149
1950 Q1	..	..	..	8.8	8.0	9.5	..	..	..	1 140
Q2	..	..	..	8.8	8.1	9.4	..	..	..	1 136
Q3	..	..	..	8.8	8.1	9.5	..	..	..	1 136
Q4	..	..	..	9.0	8.2	9.6	..	..	..	1 115
1951 Q1	..	..	..	9.2	8.4	9.8	..	..	..	1 091
Q2	..	..	..	9.5	8.8	10.2	..	..	..	1 049
Q3	..	..	..	9.8	9.2	10.4	..	..	..	1 017
Q4	..	..	..	10.0	9.5	10.6	..	..	..	997
1952 Q1	..	..	..	10.3	9.9	10.7	..	..	..	971
Q2	..	..	..	10.6	10.4	10.8	..	..	..	946
Q3	..	..	..	10.6	10.6	10.8	..	..	..	940
Q4	..	..	..	10.7	10.7	10.8	..	..	..	935
1953 Q1	..	..	..	10.8	10.8	10.8	..	..	..	929
Q2	..	..	..	10.9	11.1	10.9	..	..	..	917
Q3	..	..	..	10.9	11.1	10.9	..	..	..	917
Q4	..	..	..	10.9	10.9	11.0	..	..	..	920
1954 Q1	..	..	..	10.9	10.9	11.0	..	..	..	920
Q2	..	..	..	11.0	11.1	11.0	..	..	..	909
Q3	..	..	..	11.1	11.5	11.0	..	..	..	898
Q4	..	..	..	11.2	11.6	11.1	..	..	..	890
1955 Q1	..	..	..	11.3	11.7	11.2	..	..	..	885
Q2	..	..	..	11.5	12.0	11.2	..	..	..	872
Q3	..	..	..	11.6	12.2	11.3	..	..	..	862
Q4	..	..	..	11.8	12.6	11.5	..	..	..	845
1956 Q1	..	..	..	11.9	12.5	11.7	12.0	..	..	838
Q2	..	..	..	12.2	12.9	11.9	12.1	..	..	820
Q3	..	..	..	12.1	12.5	12.0	12.2	..	..	824
Q4	..	..	..	12.3	12.7	12.1	12.4	..	..	815
1957 Q1	..	..	..	12.4	12.8	12.3	12.6	..	..	806
Q2	..	..	..	12.5	12.9	12.3	12.6	..	..	802
Q3	..	..	..	12.7	13.2	12.4	12.6	..	..	789
Q4	..	..	..	12.8	13.0	12.8	12.9	..	..	781
1958 Q1	..	..	..	12.9	13.0	12.8	12.9	..	..	777
Q2	..	..	..	13.0	13.5	12.8	13.0	..	..	767
Q3	..	..	..	12.9	13.1	12.9	13.0	..	..	775
Q4	..	..	..	13.1	13.4	12.9	13.1	..	..	765
1959 Q1	..	..	..	13.1	13.5	13.0	13.2	..	..	763
Q2	..	..	..	13.0	13.4	12.8	13.1	..	..	769
Q3	..	..	..	13.0	13.3	12.9	13.1	..	..	771
Q4	..	..	..	13.1	13.4	13.0	13.2	..	..	765
1960 Q1	..	..	..	13.1	13.3	13.0	13.2	..	..	765
Q2	..	..	..	13.1	13.3	13.1	13.2	..	..	761
Q3	..	..	..	13.1	13.3	13.2	13.3	..	..	761
Q4	..	..	..	13.3	13.3	13.4	13.5	..	..	754
1961 Q1	..	..	..	13.4	13.3	13.4	13.5	..	..	746
Q2	..	..	..	13.5	13.6	13.6	13.6	..	..	739
Q3	..	..	..	13.7	13.6	13.8	13.8	..	..	730
Q4	..	..	..	13.9	13.6	14.1	14.0	..	..	721

1 The index numbers given here are for comparative purposes only and should not be regarded as accurate to the last digit shown. The official Retail Prices Index is shown in Table 2.2.

2 All items except housing.

3 Movements in the purchasing power of the pound are based on movements in the General index of retail prices.

Sources: Office for National Statistics;
Enquiries Columns 1-3 01633 812106; Columns 4-10 020 7533 5874

2.1 Prices

continued

Producer price index 1995 = 100, others 1985 = 100

	Producer price index (1995 = 100)			Not seasonally adjusted						
	Materials and fuel purchased by manufacturing industry		Output: all manufactured products: home sales	General index of retail prices[1]				Pensioner indices[2]		
	Seasonally adjusted	Not seasonally adjusted	(not seasonally adjusted)	All items	Total food	All items except food	All items except seasonal food	One-person households	Two-person households	Purchasing power of the pound[3]
	PLKZ	PLKW	PLLU	FRAG	FRAH	FRAI	FRAK	FRAL	FRAM	FJAK
1962 Q1	..	..	..	14.0	13.7	14.2	14.1	13.7	13.8	714
Q2	..	..	..	14.3	14.4	14.3	14.2	14.0	14.1	699
Q3	..	..	..	14.2	14.1	14.4	14.3	13.9	14.0	702
Q4	..	..	..	14.2	13.9	14.5	14.4	14.0	14.0	702
1963 Q1	..	..	..	14.4	14.5	14.5	14.5	14.3	14.3	693
Q2	..	..	..	14.5	14.6	14.6	14.5	14.3	14.3	690
Q3	..	..	..	14.4	14.1	14.7	14.6	14.1	14.1	694
Q4	..	..	..	14.5	14.3	14.7	14.7	14.3	14.4	688
1964 Q1	..	..	..	14.6	14.5	14.8	14.8	14.4	14.5	683
Q2	..	..	..	14.9	14.8	15.0	15.1	14.6	14.7	671
Q3	..	..	..	15.1	14.9	15.2	15.2	14.7	14.8	664
Q4	..	..	..	15.2	15.0	15.4	15.4	14.9	15.0	658
1965 Q1	..	..	..	15.3	15.1	15.5	15.5	15.1	15.2	652
Q2	..	..	..	15.7	15.4	16.0	15.8	15.2	15.4	638
Q3	..	..	..	15.8	15.4	16.1	15.9	15.3	15.5	634
Q4	..	..	..	15.9	15.4	16.2	16.0	15.5	15.7	630
1966 Q1	..	..	..	16.0	15.5	16.3	16.1	15.7	15.8	625
Q2	..	..	..	16.3	16.1	16.5	16.3	15.9	16.1	613
Q3	..	..	..	16.4	15.9	16.7	16.5	15.9	16.1	611
Q4	..	..	..	16.5	16.0	16.8	16.6	16.2	16.3	607
1967 Q1	..	..	..	16.6	16.1	16.9	16.7	16.3	16.4	602
Q2	..	..	..	16.7	16.5	16.9	16.8	16.3	16.5	598
Q3	..	..	..	16.6	16.1	17.0	16.8	16.1	16.3	601
Q4	..	..	..	16.8	16.3	17.2	17.0	16.5	16.6	595
1968 Q1	..	..	..	17.1	16.7	17.4	17.2	16.8	16.9	586
Q2	..	..	..	17.4	17.0	17.8	17.6	17.0	17.1	574
Q3	..	..	..	17.6	16.9	18.0	17.7	17.0	17.2	569
Q4	..	..	..	17.8	17.0	18.2	18.0	17.4	17.5	563
1969 Q1	..	..	..	18.1	17.6	18.5	18.3	17.7	17.9	552
Q2	..	..	..	18.4	18.2	18.7	18.4	17.9	18.1	542
Q3	..	..	..	18.5	18.0	18.8	18.6	17.9	18.1	542
Q4	..	..	..	18.7	18.2	19.0	18.8	18.3	18.4	535
1970 Q1	..	..	..	19.0	18.7	19.4	19.1	18.8	18.9	526
Q2	..	..	..	19.5	19.3	19.7	19.5	19.1	19.2	514
Q3	..	..	..	19.7	19.3	20.0	19.9	19.2	19.4	507
Q4	..	..	..	20.1	19.6	20.5	20.3	19.7	19.9	497
1971 Q1	..	..	..	20.6	20.3	21.0	20.8	20.3	20.5	485
Q2	..	..	..	21.4	21.4	21.6	21.5	21.0	21.2	466
Q3	..	..	..	21.7	21.7	21.9	21.9	21.4	21.5	461
Q4	..	..	..	22.0	22.0	22.2	22.2	21.8	21.9	455
1972 Q1	..	..	..	22.3	22.7	22.4	22.5	22.3	22.3	448
Q2	..	..	..	22.7	22.9	22.9	22.9	22.5	22.6	440
Q3	..	..	..	23.1	23.5	23.2	23.2	22.9	23.0	434
Q4	..	..	..	23.7	24.0	23.8	23.8	23.4	23.5	422
1973 Q1	..	..	..	24.1	25.2	23.9	24.1	24.0	24.2	415
Q2	..	..	..	24.9	26.4	24.6	24.7	24.8	25.0	402
Q3	..	..	..	25.2	26.9	24.9	25.2	25.0	25.2	396
Q4	..	..	..	26.1	28.5	25.6	26.0	26.1	26.3	383
1974 Q1	..	31.5	18.2	27.2	30.0	26.5	27.0	27.3	27.5	368
Q2	..	31.5	19.4	28.8	31.1	28.3	28.6	28.4	28.8	348
Q3	..	31.5	20.2	29.5	31.6	29.1	29.5	29.3	29.6	339
Q4	..	33.3	21.3	30.8	33.5	30.2	30.8	30.9	31.0	324
1975 Q1	..	33.6	22.8	32.7	36.3	31.9	32.6	32.8	32.9	306
Q2	..	33.7	24.1	35.8	39.6	34.9	35.6	36.3	36.5	280
Q3	..	35.4	24.8	37.3	40.6	36.6	37.2	37.6	37.8	268
Q4	..	38.4	25.7	38.6	42.1	37.9	38.5	39.2	39.3	259

1 The index numbers given here are for comparative purposes only and should not be regarded as accurate to the last digit shown. The official Retail Prices Index series is shown in Table 2.2.

2 All items except housing.

3 Movements in the purchasing power of the pound are based on movements in the General index of retail prices.

Sources: Office for National Statistics;
Enquiries Columns 1-3 01633 812106; Columns 4-10 020 7533 5874

2.1 Prices

continued

Producer price index 1995 = 100, others 1985 = 100

	Producer price index (1995 = 100)			Not seasonally adjusted						
	Materials and fuel purchased by manufacturing industry		Output: all manufactured products: home sales (not seasonally adjusted)	General index of retail prices[1]				Pensioner indices[2]		
	Seasonally adjusted	Not seasonally adjusted		All items	Total food	All items except food	All items except seasonal food	One-person households	Two-person households	Purchasing power of the pound[3]
	PLKZ	PLKW	PLLU	FRAG	FRAH	FRAI	FRAK	FRAL	FRAM	FJAK
1976 Q1	..	40.1	26.8	40.0	45.0	38.9	39.6	41.2	41.2	250
Q2	..	43.2	27.7	41.5	46.6	40.3	41.0	42.8	42.8	241
Q3	..	45.1	28.8	42.5	47.2	41.3	42.2	43.6	43.7	236
Q4	..	49.0	30.2	44.4	51.4	42.7	43.9	46.3	46.3	225
1977 Q1	..	50.8	32.0	46.7	54.9	44.6	46.0	48.4	48.7	214
Q2	..	51.3	33.5	48.7	56.8	46.8	48.1	50.5	50.7	205
Q3	..	50.3	34.5	49.5	57.1	47.7	49.3	51.6	51.5	202
Q4	..	49.6	35.0	50.2	57.5	48.5	50.1	52.5	52.3	199
1978 Q1	..	49.1	35.8	51.1	58.7	49.3	51.0	53.4	53.3	196
Q2	..	50.7	36.4	52.4	60.6	50.5	52.2	54.7	54.7	191
Q3	..	50.3	37.2	53.4	61.3	51.5	53.3	55.4	55.4	187
Q4	..	52.0	37.7	54.3	61.8	52.5	54.3	56.0	56.0	184
1979 Q1	..	54.7	38.7	56.0	65.1	53.8	55.7	58.1	58.1	179
Q2	..	57.3	40.2	58.0	67.0	55.9	57.6	59.6	59.7	172
Q3	..	59.2	42.2	61.9	68.9	60.3	61.9	62.7	62.9	162
Q4	..	64.8	43.3	63.6	70.5	62.0	63.6	64.8	64.9	157
1980 Q1	..	69.4	45.6	66.7	73.6	65.0	66.5	67.7	67.7	150
Q2	..	69.3	47.5	70.5	76.1	69.2	70.5	70.8	70.9	142
Q3	..	68.8	48.3	72.0	77.1	70.9	72.1	72.7	72.5	139
Q4	..	69.8	49.2	73.4	77.5	72.4	73.5	74.3	73.9	136
1981 Q1	..	73.8	50.6	75.1	79.9	74.0	75.2	76.5	76.3	133
Q2	..	77.5	52.4	78.8	82.4	78.0	78.8	78.9	79.0	127
Q3	..	80.5	53.4	80.2	82.9	79.5	80.3	80.3	80.4	125
Q4	..	82.2	54.6	82.1	84.9	81.5	82.1	82.3	82.4	122
1982 Q1	..	83.0	55.9	83.5	88.5	82.3	83.2	84.9	84.8	120
Q2	..	81.6	56.7	86.2	90.4	85.2	85.7	87.1	86.9	116
Q3	..	83.0	57.7	86.5	88.3	86.2	86.7	87.3	87.0	116
Q4	..	86.1	58.8	87.2	88.7	86.9	87.5	88.5	88.2	115
1983 Q1	..	88.3	59.7	87.6	89.8	87.1	87.8	89.5	89.1	114
Q2	..	85.7	60.8	89.4	91.1	89.1	89.5	90.3	90.2	112
Q3	..	87.4	61.5	90.6	92.3	90.2	90.5	91.1	91.0	110
Q4	..	90.8	61.8	91.6	94.1	91.0	91.4	92.5	92.4	109
1984 Q1	..	93.9	62.9	92.2	95.7	91.3	91.8	93.7	93.5	108
Q2	..	94.8	64.3	94.0	97.8	93.2	93.6	95.5	95.6	106
Q3	..	97.0	65.0	94.9	97.2	94.3	94.8	95.6	95.6	105
Q4	..	100.7	66.3	96.0	97.2	95.8	96.1	96.6	96.6	104
1985 Q1	..	105.9	68.0	97.2	99.0	96.9	97.2	98.1	98.1	103
Q2	..	97.3	68.6	100.6	100.9	100.5	100.4	100.4	100.4	99
Q3	..	91.8	68.9	100.8	99.8	101.1	101.0	100.3	100.3	99
Q4	..	91.4	69.0	101.3	100.3	101.6	101.4	101.2	101.2	99
1986 Q1	84.3	85.2	69.3	102.0	102.1	102.0	102.0	102.2	102.1	98
Q2	80.1	79.8	69.3	103.3	103.9	103.2	103.1	103.4	103.3	97
Q3	79.0	77.7	69.4	103.5	103.5	103.5	103.4	103.4	103.4	97
Q4	81.1	81.3	70.1	104.8	103.6	105.1	104.8	103.8	103.9	95
1987 Q1	81.9	82.4	71.1	106.0	105.8	106.2	105.9	104.7	104.8	94
Q2	81.8	81.7	71.7	107.7	107.1	107.8	107.4	105.7	105.9	93
Q3	84.1	82.8	72.1	107.9	105.8	108.4	107.9	105.4	105.7	93
Q4	83.2	83.4	72.7	109.1	107.0	109.6	109.1	106.5	106.9	92
1988 Q1	83.2	83.3	73.4	109.6	108.9	109.9	109.4	107.4	107.8	91
Q2	85.0	84.0	74.3	112.3	110.1	112.6	112.1	109.2	109.5	89
Q3	87.0	84.8	75.0	113.8	109.9	114.6	113.9	110.0	110.3	88
Q4	86.2	85.8	75.5	116.2	111.3	117.3	116.4	111.3	111.6	86
1989 Q1	88.3	88.1	76.7	118.1	113.5	119.0	118.1	112.8	113.1	85
Q2	90.5	89.6	77.9	121.5	116.0	122.6	121.5	114.9	115.4	82
Q3	90.2	88.0	78.5	122.6	116.5	123.9	122.9	115.9	116.3	82
Q4	90.5	90.7	79.5	125.0	119.4	126.2	125.3	118.2	118.5	80

1 The index numbers given here are for comparative purposes only and should not be regarded as accurate to the last digit shown. The official Retail Prices Index series is shown in Table 2.2.

2 All items except housing.

3 Movements in the purchasing power of the pound are based on movements in the General index of retail prices.

Sources: Office for National Statistics;
Enquiries Columns 1-3 01633 812106; Columns 4-10 020 7533 5874

2.1 Prices

continued

Producer price index 1995 = 100, others 1985 = 100

	Producer price index (1995 = 100)			Not seasonally adjusted						
	Materials and fuel purchased by manufacturing industry		Output: all manufactured products: home sales (not seasonally adjusted)	General index of retail prices[1]				Pensioner indices[2]		
	Seasonally adjusted	Not seasonally adjusted		All items	Total food	All items except food	All items except seasonal food	One-person households	Two-person households	Purchasing power of the pound[3]
	PLKZ	PLKW	PLLU	FRAG	FRAH	FRAI	FRAK	FRAL	FRAM	FJAK
1990 Q1	89.9	90.7	80.8	127.2	123.1	128.1	127.2	120.4	120.6	79
Q2	88.2	88.1	82.6	133.2	125.9	134.7	133.2	123.3	123.7	75
Q3	87.9	86.3	83.6	135.4	126.0	137.3	135.7	125.2	125.6	74
Q4	87.9	89.0	85.0	137.5	127.6	139.5	137.7	127.8	128.2	73
1991 Q1	86.9	87.7	86.0	138.3	130.4	139.9	138.4	129.3	129.3	72
Q2	86.8	87.1	87.6	141.2	132.8	142.9	141.3	133.0	133.8	71
Q3	86.4	85.1	87.9	141.8	132.3	143.7	142.1	134.2	134.7	71
Q4	86.3	86.5	88.3	143.2	133.2	145.2	143.4	135.7	136.3	70
1992 Q1	85.7	86.5	89.1	144.0	135.8	145.8	144.1	136.6	137.5	69
Q2	85.1	85.4	90.3	147.1	135.9	149.3	147.4	138.1	139.2	68
Q3	85.1	83.9	90.4	147.0	134.0	149.6	147.7	137.4	138.6	68
Q4	89.0	89.2	91.0	147.6	134.4	150.2	148.2	138.5	139.8	68
1993 Q1	91.4	92.2	92.4	146.6	137.0	148.5	147.1	139.5	140.8	68
Q2	90.7	91.0	93.9	148.9	138.4	151.1	149.4	141.0	143.0	67
Q3	89.9	88.7	94.3	149.4	138.1	151.7	150.1	140.8	143.0	66
Q4	88.8	89.0	94.6	149.9	136.3	152.5	150.7	140.9	143.1	66
1994 Q1	88.7	89.4	95.3	150.1	137.7	152.6	150.7	141.0	143.5	66
Q2	91.5	91.7	95.9	152.8	139.7	155.4	153.2	143.8	145.9	65
Q3	93.1	91.9	96.3	152.8	139.2	155.5	153.3	143.4	145.7	65
Q4	94.4	94.6	96.9	153.8	138.9	156.7	154.4	143.9	146.2	65
1995 Q1	97.8	98.6	98.8	155.2	142.1	157.8	155.5	145.2	147.8	64
Q2	100.8	101.0	99.8	158.0	144.2	160.7	158.3	146.9	149.5	63
Q3	101.4	100.1	100.4	158.4	145.2	161.1	158.8	147.2	150.0	63
Q4	100.0	100.2	100.9	158.6	145.2	161.3	159.2	148.0	150.7	63
1996 Q1	100.4	101.2	102.2	159.5	148.4	161.7	159.8	149.1	152.1	62
Q2	100.0	100.2	102.6	161.5	150.4	163.8	161.9	150.7	153.8	61
Q3	98.0	96.9	102.6	161.8	149.3	164.3	162.5	150.5	153.7	61
Q4	96.7	96.9	103.2	162.8	147.4	165.9	163.7	150.7	154.3	61
1997 Q1	93.7	94.5	103.4	163.8	148.0	166.9	164.7	150.8	154.5	61
Q2	90.3	90.4	103.4	165.9	149.0	169.1	166.7	151.9	155.7	60
Q3	90.3	89.2	103.8	167.5	149.7	170.9	168.3	152.1	156.2	59
Q4	88.2	88.3	103.9	168.8	149.3	172.6	169.7	152.5	156.9	59
1998 Q1	84.7	85.3	104.0	169.3	149.2	173.2	170.2	152.4	156.8	59
Q2	82.9	83.2	104.4	172.5	151.1	176.7	173.3	154.0	158.6	57
Q3	81.7	81.1	104.3	173.0	151.5	177.2	173.9	154.1	158.8	57
Q4	79.9	80.2	103.9	173.8	152.2	178.0	174.6	155.2	159.7	57
1999 Q1	79.9	80.3	104.2	173.1	153.3	176.9	173.8	155.5	160.2	57
Q2	81.8r	81.9	105.4	174.9	152.0	179.3	175.8	156.5	161.4	57
Q3	85.3	84.6	105.8	175.0	150.3	179.7	176.2	156.1	161.1	57
Q4	87.8	88.0	106.1	176.3	150.0	181.3	177.4	156.8	161.9	57
2000 Q1	90.1r	90.6	106.7r	177.1	150.1	182.1	178.2	156.7	161.9	57
Q2	91.3p	91.2p	108.1p	180.4	150.3	186.0	180.5	157.7	163.3	55

1 The index numbers given here are for comparative purposes only and should not be regarded as accurate to the last digit shown. The official Retail Prices Index series is shown in Table 2.2.

2 All items except housing.

3 Movements in the purchasing power of the pound are based on movements in the General index of retail prices.

Sources: Office for National Statistics;
Enquiries Columns 1-3 01633 812106; Columns 4-10 020 7533 5874

2.2 Tax and Price Index

	Tax and Price Index: January 1978 = 100								January 1987 = 100											
	1981	1982	1983	1984	1985	1986	1987	1988	1989	1990	1991	1992	1993	1994	1995	1996	1997	1998	1999	2000
January	140.4	162.3	170.7	177.9	184.7	192.9	198.0	101.4	107.1	113.9	123.6	128.1	128.7	132.1	137.2	141.6	143.6	147.1	150.5	152.7
February	141.9	162.4	171.6	178.8	186.4	193.7	..	101.8	108.0	114.7	124.3	128.8	129.6	132.9	138.2	142.3	144.2	147.9	150.8	153.7
March	144.3	164.0	171.9	179.4	188.4	194.0	..	102.3	108.5	115.9	124.9	129.3	130.2	133.4	138.8	143.0	144.6	148.4	151.2	154.6
April	151.3	166.0	171.8	178.8	190.2	192.5	..	101.4	109.8	118.2	125.4	129.6	131.3	135.3	140.3	141.7	143.8	149.7	151.2	155.7
May	152.4	167.4	172.6	179.6	191.2	192.9	..	101.9	110.5	119.4	125.8	130.2	131.8	135.8	141.0	142.0	144.4	150.6	151.7	156.3
June	153.5	168.0	173.1	180.1	191.7	192.8	..	102.3	110.9	119.9	126.5	130.2	131.7	135.8	141.2	142.1	145.0	150.5	151.7	156.7
July	154.2	169.0	174.2	179.9	191.3	192.1	..	102.4	111.1	120.0	126.2	129.6	131.4	135.1	140.4	141.5	145.0	150.1	151.1	..
August	155.5	169.0	175.1	181.8	191.8	192.9	..	103.7	111.4	121.4	126.5	129.7	132.1	135.8	141.3	142.2	146.0	150.8	151.5	..
September	156.6	168.9	176.0	182.2	191.7	194.0	..	104.3	112.2	122.7	127.0	130.3	132.7	136.1	142.0	143.0	146.9	151.5	152.3	..
October	158.2	169.9	176.7	183.5	191.4	194.3	..	105.4	111.7	123.8	127.5	130.8	132.6	136.4	141.2	143.0	147.1	151.6	152.6	..
November	160.1	170.9	177.5	184.1	192.1	196.3	..	106.0	112.8	123.4	128.1	130.6	132.4	136.5	141.2	143.1	147.2	151.5	152.8	..
December	161.2	170.5	178.0	183.9	192.4	197.1	..	106.3	113.1	123.3	128.2	130.1	132.7	137.2	142.1	143.6	147.6	151.5	153.4	..

	Retail Prices Index: January 1974 = 100								January 1987 = 100											
	1981	1982	1983	1984	1985	1986	1987	1988	1989	1990	1991	1992	1993	1994	1995	1996	1997	1998	1999	2000
January	277.3	310.6	325.9	342.6	359.8	379.7	394.5	103.3	111.0	119.5	130.2	135.6	137.9	141.3	146.0	150.2	154.4	159.5	163.4	166.6
February	279.8	310.7	327.3	344.0	362.7	381.1	..	103.7	111.8	120.2	130.9	136.3	138.8	142.1	146.9	150.9	155.0	160.3	163.7	167.5
March	284.0	313.4	327.9	345.1	366.1	381.6	..	104.1	112.3	121.4	131.4	136.7	139.3	142.5	147.5	151.5	155.4	160.8	164.1	168.4
April	292.2	319.7	332.5	349.7	373.9	385.3	..	105.8	114.3	125.1	133.1	138.8	140.6	144.2	149.0	152.6	156.3	162.6	165.2	170.1
May	294.1	322.0	333.9	351.0	375.6	386.0	..	106.2	115.0	126.2	133.5	139.3	141.1	144.7	149.6	152.9	156.9	163.5	165.6	170.7
June	295.8	322.9	334.7	351.9	376.4	385.8	..	106.6	115.4	126.7	134.1	139.3	141.0	144.7	149.8	153.0	157.5	163.4	165.6	171.1
July	297.1	323.0	336.5	351.5	375.7	384.7	..	106.7	115.5	126.8	133.8	138.8	140.7	144.0	149.1	152.4	157.5	163.0	165.1	..
August	299.3	323.1	338.0	354.8	376.7	385.9	..	107.9	115.8	128.1	134.1	138.9	141.3	144.7	149.9	153.1	158.5	163.7	165.5	..
September	301.0	322.9	339.5	355.5	376.5	387.8	..	108.4	116.6	129.3	134.6	139.4	141.9	145.0	150.6	153.8	159.3	164.4	166.2	..
October	303.7	324.5	340.7	357.7	377.1	388.4	..	109.5	117.5	130.3	135.1	139.9	141.8	145.2	149.8	153.8	159.5	164.5	166.5	..
November	306.9	326.1	341.9	358.8	378.4	391.7	..	110.0	118.5	130.0	135.6	139.7	141.6	145.3	149.8	153.9	159.6	164.4	166.7	..
December	308.8	325.5	342.8	358.5	378.9	393.0	..	110.3	118.8	129.9	135.7	139.2	141.9	146.0	150.7	154.4	160.0	164.4	167.3	..

Tax and Price Index

	1982	1983	1984	1985	1986	1987	1988	1989	1990	1991	1992	1993	1994	1995	1996	1997	1998	1999	2000
January	*15.6*	*5.2*	*4.2*	*3.8*	*4.4*	*2.6*	*1.4*	*5.6*	*6.3*	*8.5*	*3.6*	*0.5*	*2.6*	*3.9*	*3.2*	*1.4*	*2.4*	*2.3*	*1.5*
February	*14.4*	*5.7*	*4.2*	*4.3*	*3.9*	*2.7*	*1.3*	*6.1*	*6.2*	*8.4*	*3.6*	*0.6*	*2.5*	*4.0*	*3.0*	*1.3*	*2.6*	*2.0*	*1.9*
March	*13.7*	*4.8*	*4.4*	*5.0*	*3.0*	*2.8*	*1.6*	*6.1*	*6.8*	*7.8*	*3.5*	*0.7*	*2.5*	*4.0*	*3.0*	*1.1*	*2.6*	*1.9*	*2.2*
April	*9.7*	*3.5*	*4.1*	*6.4*	*1.2*	*2.5*	*1.7*	*8.3*	*7.7*	*6.1*	*3.3*	*1.3*	*3.0*	*3.7*	*1.0*	*1.5*	*4.1*	*1.0*	*3.0*
May	*9.8*	*3.1*	*4.1*	*6.5*	*0.9*	*2.4*	*2.1*	*8.4*	*8.1*	*5.4*	*3.5*	*1.2*	*3.0*	*3.8*	*0.7*	*1.7*	*4.3*	*0.7*	*3.0*
June	*9.4*	*3.0*	*4.0*	*6.4*	*0.6*	*2.5*	*2.5*	*8.4*	*8.1*	*5.5*	*2.9*	*1.2*	*3.1*	*4.0*	*0.6*	*2.0*	*3.8*	*0.8*	*3.3*
July	*9.6*	*3.1*	*3.3*	*6.3*	*0.4*	*2.8*	*2.7*	*8.5*	*8.0*	*5.2*	*2.7*	*1.4*	*2.8*	*3.9*	*0.8*	*2.5*	*3.5*	*0.7*	..
August	*8.7*	*3.6*	*3.8*	*5.5*	*0.6*	*2.6*	*3.7*	*7.4*	*9.0*	*4.2*	*2.5*	*1.9*	*2.8*	*4.1*	*0.6*	*2.7*	*3.3*	*0.5*	..
September	*7.9*	*4.2*	*3.5*	*5.2*	*1.2*	*2.4*	*3.9*	*7.6*	*9.4*	*3.5*	*2.6*	*1.8*	*2.6*	*4.3*	*0.7*	*2.7*	*3.1*	*0.5*	..
October	*7.4*	*4.0*	*3.8*	*4.3*	*1.5*	*2.9*	*4.5*	*6.0*	*10.8*	*3.0*	*2.6*	*1.4*	*2.9*	*3.5*	*1.3*	*2.9*	*3.1*	*0.7*	..
November	*6.7*	*3.9*	*3.7*	*4.3*	*2.2*	*2.4*	*4.4*	*6.4*	*9.4*	*3.8*	*2.0*	*1.4*	*3.1*	*3.4*	*1.3*	*2.9*	*2.9*	*0.9*	..
December	*5.8*	*4.4*	*3.3*	*4.6*	*2.4*	*1.9*	*4.8*	*6.4*	*9.0*	*4.0*	*1.5*	*2.0*	*3.4*	*3.6*	*1.1*	*2.8*	*2.6*	*1.3*	..

Retail Prices Index

	1982	1983	1984	1985	1986	1987	1988	1989	1990	1991	1992	1993	1994	1995	1996	1997	1998	1999	2000
January	*12.0*	*4.9*	*5.1*	*5.0*	*5.5*	*3.9*	*3.3*	*7.5*	*7.7*	*9.0*	*4.1*	*1.7*	*2.5*	*3.3*	*2.9*	*2.8*	*3.3*	*2.4*	*2.0*
February	*11.0*	*5.3*	*5.1*	*5.4*	*5.1*	*3.9*	*3.3*	*7.8*	*7.5*	*8.9*	*4.1*	*1.8*	*2.4*	*3.4*	*2.7*	*2.7*	*3.4*	*2.1*	*2.3*
March	*10.4*	*4.6*	*5.2*	*6.1*	*4.2*	*4.0*	*3.5*	*7.9*	*8.1*	*8.2*	*4.0*	*1.9*	*2.3*	*3.5*	*2.7*	*2.6*	*3.5*	*2.1*	*2.6*
April	*9.4*	*4.0*	*5.2*	*6.9*	*3.0*	*4.2*	*3.9*	*8.0*	*9.4*	*6.4*	*4.3*	*1.3*	*2.6*	*3.3*	*2.4*	*2.4*	*4.0*	*1.6*	*3.0*
May	*9.5*	*3.7*	*5.1*	*7.0*	*2.8*	*4.1*	*4.2*	*8.3*	*9.7*	*5.8*	*4.3*	*1.3*	*2.6*	*3.4*	*2.2*	*2.6*	*4.2*	*1.3*	*3.1*
June	*9.2*	*3.7*	*5.1*	*7.0*	*2.5*	*4.2*	*4.6*	*8.3*	*9.8*	*5.8*	*3.9*	*1.2*	*2.6*	*3.5*	*2.1*	*2.9*	*3.7*	*1.3*	*3.3*
July	*8.7*	*4.2*	*4.5*	*6.9*	*2.4*	*4.4*	*4.8*	*8.2*	*9.8*	*5.5*	*3.7*	*1.4*	*2.3*	*3.5*	*2.2*	*3.3*	*3.5*	*1.3*	..
August	*8.0*	*4.6*	*5.0*	*6.2*	*2.4*	*4.4*	*5.7*	*7.3*	*10.6*	*4.7*	*3.6*	*1.7*	*2.4*	*3.6*	*2.1*	*3.5*	*3.3*	*1.1*	..
September	*7.3*	*5.1*	*4.7*	*5.9*	*3.0*	*4.2*	*5.9*	*7.6*	*10.9*	*4.1*	*3.6*	*1.8*	*2.2*	*3.9*	*2.1*	*3.6*	*3.2*	*1.1*	..
October	*6.8*	*5.0*	*5.0*	*5.4*	*3.0*	*4.5*	*6.4*	*7.3*	*10.9*	*3.7*	*3.6*	*1.4*	*2.4*	*3.2*	*2.7*	*3.7*	*3.1*	*1.2*	..
November	*6.3*	*4.8*	*4.9*	*5.5*	*3.5*	*4.1*	*6.4*	*7.7*	*9.7*	*4.3*	*3.0*	*1.4*	*2.6*	*3.1*	*2.7*	*3.7*	*3.0*	*1.4*	..
December	*5.4*	*5.3*	*4.6*	*5.7*	*3.7*	*3.7*	*6.8*	*7.7*	*9.3*	*4.5*	*2.6*	*1.9*	*2.9*	*3.2*	*2.5*	*3.6*	*2.8*	*1.8*	..

Note: The purpose and methodology of the Tax and Price Index were described in an article in the August 1979 issue of *Economic Trends* . The purpose is to produce a single index which measures changes in both direct taxes (including national insurance contributions) and in retail prices for a representative cross-section of taxpayers. Thus, while the Retail Prices Index may be used to measure changes in the purchasing power of after-tax income (and of the income of non-taxpayers) the Tax and Price Index takes account of the fact that taxpayers will have more or less to spend according to changes in direct taxation. The index measures the change in gross taxable income which would maintain their after tax-income in real terms.

Source: Office for National Statistics; Enquiries 020 7533 5874

3.1 Labour Market Activity[1,6]

United Kingdom[5]

Thousands, seasonally adjusted[3]

	Employment categories[2]					ILO unemployed	Total economically active	Economically inactive	Total aged 16 and over	Employment rate: age 16-59/64[4]
	Employees	Self - employed	Unpaid family workers	Government training and employment programmes	Total employment[2]					
TOTAL										
	MGRN	MGRQ	MGRT	MGRW	MGRZ	MGSC	MGSF	MGSI	MGSL	MGSU
1995 Q1	22 232	3 370	137	294	26 033	2 542	28 575	17 037	45 612	71.2
Q2	22 345	3 361	143	288	26 136	2 488	28 625	17 031	45 656	71.4
Q3	22 489	3 345	126	266	26 226	2 493	28 719	16 982	45 702	71.6
Q4	22 634	3 338	131	263	26 366	2 403	28 769	16 983	45 752	71.9
1996 Q1	22 681	3 314	130	245	26 371	2 380	28 751	17 051	45 802	71.9
Q2	22 711	3 336	122	249	26 417	2 385	28 803	17 049	45 852	71.9
Q3	22 753	3 374	116	246	26 488	2 330	28 818	17 084	45 902	72.0
Q4	22 899	3 390	120	224	26 634	2 277	28 911	17 041	45 952	72.3
1997 Q1	23 131	3 371	119	222	26 843	2 124	28 967	17 036	46 003	72.7
Q2	23 285	3 357	116	224	26 982	2 087	29 068	16 984	46 053	73.0
Q3	23 358	3 355	122	220	27 055	1 988	29 043	17 062	46 105	73.1
Q4	23 467	3 330	109	211	27 117	1 908	29 025	17 136	46 160	73.2
1998 Q1	23 572	3 315	100	202	27 188	1 851	29 039	17 177	46 216	73.4
Q2	23 694	3 266	100	170	27 230	1 824	29 054	17 218	46 272	73.4
Q3	23 873	3 209	106	165	27 352	1 825	29 177	17 146	46 323	73.7
Q4	23 973	3 235	95	145	27 448	1 812	29 261	17 103	46 363	73.8
1999 Q1	24 051	3 226	106	157	27 540	1 819	29 358	17 045	46 404	74.0
Q2	24 100	3 230	100	163	27 592	1 770	29 362	17 082	46 444	74.0
Q3	24 222	3 216	97	160	27 696	1 739	29 434	17 049	46 483	74.2
Q4	24 316	3 184	102	167	27 769	1 733	29 502	17 018	46 520	74.3
2000 Q1	24 391	3 174	109	150	27 824	1 713	29 538	17 019	46 556	74.4
MALE										
	MGRO	MGRR	MGRU	MGRX	MGSA	MGSD	MGSG	MGSJ	MGSM	MGSV
1995 Q1	11 605	2 559	43	193	14 400	1 665	16 065	6 071	22 135	76.2
Q2	11 682	2 546	47	188	14 463	1 628	16 092	6 074	22 166	76.4
Q3	11 750	2 530	45	166	14 492	1 623	16 115	6 081	22 196	76.5
Q4	11 819	2 527	41	167	14 554	1 562	16 116	6 113	22 229	76.8
1996 Q1	11 843	2 491	42	155	14 531	1 589	16 120	6 141	22 261	76.6
Q2	11 863	2 507	39	154	14 563	1 567	16 130	6 163	22 294	76.7
Q3	11 876	2 542	38	158	14 614	1 521	16 135	6 191	22 326	76.8
Q4	11 968	2 547	40	137	14 691	1 450	16 142	6 216	22 358	77.1
1997 Q1	12 147	2 518	42	132	14 838	1 340	16 178	6 212	22 390	77.8
Q2	12 230	2 488	36	139	14 894	1 308	16 202	6 221	22 423	78.0
Q3	12 305	2 469	39	141	14 953	1 237	16 191	6 265	22 455	78.1
Q4	12 388	2 456	37	130	15 011	1 186	16 197	6 292	22 490	78.3
1998 Q1	12 442	2 444	29	136	15 051	1 140	16 191	6 333	22 524	78.5
Q2	12 523	2 404	30	111	15 067	1 112	16 180	6 379	22 558	78.4
Q3	12 621	2 357	33	102	15 113	1 130	16 243	6 347	22 589	78.6
Q4	12 652	2 376	34	93	15 155	1 125	16 280	6 335	22 615	78.8
1999 Q1	12 677	2 381	37	101	15 196	1 123	16 319	6 321	22 640	78.8
Q2	12 699	2 388	35	108	15 230	1 094	16 324	6 341	22 666	78.9
Q3	12 778	2 377	33	105	15 293	1 060	16 353	6 337	22 690	79.1
Q4	12 854	2 340	35	109	15 339	1 048	16 386	6 328	22 714	79.2
2000 Q1	12 912	2 316	36	95	15 359	1 028	16 386	6 352	22 738	79.3

1 Data are from the Labour Force Survey which uses the definitions recommended by the International Labour Organisation (ILO), an agency of the United Nations. For details see Labour Market Trends pp S3-4 (May 1998 onwards) or the Guide to Labour Market Statistics Releases.

2 Includes those who did not state whether they were employees or self-employed.

3 The seasonally adjusted estimates may be subject to revision as more quarterly data become available.

4 The employment rate equals those in employment aged 16-64 (male) and 16-59 (female), as a percentage of all in these age groups. The underlying data are available on request.

5 Data for Great Britain are no longer published but are available on request. The previously published series relating to seasonal quarters (for GB or UK) are also available on request.

6 Labour Force Survey data have been regrossed using new population figures and revised back to 1993. For further details please refer to the May 2000 edition of *Labour Market trends.*

Source: Office for National Statistics; Enquiries 020 7533 6094

3.1 Labour Market Activity[1,6]

United Kingdom[5]

continued

Thousands, seasonally adjusted[3]

	Employment categories[2]: Employees	Self - employed	Unpaid family workers	Government training and employment programmes	Total employment[2]	ILO unemployed	Total economically active	Economically inactive	Total aged 16 and over	Employment rate: age 16-59/64[4]
FEMALE										
	MGRP	MGRS	MGRV	MGRY	MGSB	MGSE	MGSH	MGSK	MGSN	MGSW
1995 Q1	10 627	811	94	101	11 633	877	12 510	10 967	23 477	65.7
Q2	10 663	814	96	100	11 673	860	12 533	10 957	23 490	65.9
Q3	10 739	815	80	100	11 734	870	12 604	10 902	23 505	66.1
Q4	10 814	811	90	96	11 812	841	12 653	10 870	23 523	66.5
1996 Q1	10 838	823	88	90	11 840	791	12 631	10 910	23 541	66.7
Q2	10 848	829	83	94	11 854	818	12 673	10 886	23 559	66.7
Q3	10 877	831	78	88	11 874	809	12 683	10 893	23 576	66.7
Q4	10 932	844	80	87	11 943	827	12 769	10 825	23 594	67.1
1997 Q1	10 984	853	78	90	12 004	784	12 789	10 824	23 612	67.2
Q2	11 054	869	80	85	12 088	779	12 867	10 764	23 630	67.5
Q3	11 054	886	83	79	12 102	750	12 852	10 797	23 649	67.6
Q4	11 079	874	72	81	12 106	721	12 827	10 843	23 671	67.7
1998 Q1	11 130	871	70	66	12 137	711	12 849	10 844	23 692	67.8
Q2	11 171	863	70	59	12 162	712	12 874	10 839	23 714	67.9
Q3	11 252	852	73	63	12 239	694	12 934	10 799	23 733	68.2
Q4	11 321	859	62	52	12 293	687	12 981	10 768	23 748	68.4
1999 Q1	11 375	845	69	55	12 343	696	13 039	10 724	23 764	68.7
Q2	11 401	841	65	55	12 362	675	13 038	10 741	23 779	68.7
Q3	11 444	839	64	54	12 402	679	13 081	10 712	23 793	68.9
Q4	11 462	843	67	58	12 430	686	13 115	10 690	23 805	68.9
2000 Q1	11 479	858	73	55	12 465	686	13 151	10 667	23 818	69.0

See footnotes on page 146.

Source: Office for National Statistics; Enquiries 020 7533 6094

3.2 Labour Market Activity[1,5]

United Kingdom[4]

Thousands, not seasonally adjusted

	Employment categories[2]					ILO unemployed	Total economically active	Economically inactive	Total aged 16 and over	Employment rate: age 16-59/64[3]
	Employees	Self - employed	Unpaid family workers	Government training and employment programmes	Total employment[2]					
TOTAL										
	MGTA	MGTD	MGTG	MGTJ	MGTM	MGTP	MGTS	MGTV	MGTY	MGUH
1995 Q1	22 083	3 359	130	299	25 871	2 556	28 426	17 186	45 612	70.7
Q2	22 301	3 348	144	286	26 079	2 463	28 542	17 114	45 656	71.2
Q3	22 638	3 356	129	255	26 378	2 583	28 961	16 740	45 702	72.0
Q4	22 666	3 348	133	270	26 416	2 349	28 766	16 986	45 752	72.0
1996 Q1	22 542	3 303	124	249	26 218	2 389	28 607	17 194	45 802	71.4
Q2	22 662	3 323	122	247	26 355	2 363	28 718	17 134	45 852	71.7
Q3	22 894	3 382	119	237	26 632	2 421	29 053	16 850	45 902	72.4
Q4	22 942	3 401	122	230	26 695	2 220	28 915	17 037	45 952	72.5
1997 Q1	22 999	3 361	114	224	26 698	2 131	28 829	17 173	46 003	72.4
Q2	23 229	3 346	116	222	26 912	2 066	28 978	17 075	46 053	72.8
Q3	23 498	3 359	125	212	27 195	2 075	29 270	16 835	46 105	73.5
Q4	23 520	3 342	112	215	27 189	1 847	29 036	17 124	46 160	73.5
1998 Q1	23 445	3 305	95	204	27 049	1 858	28 907	17 310	46 216	73.0
Q2	23 632	3 257	99	168	27 155	1 804	28 959	17 313	46 272	73.2
Q3	24 016	3 210	109	158	27 492	1 908	29 400	16 922	46 323	74.1
Q4	24 036	3 247	98	149	27 530	1 749	29 279	17 084	46 363	74.0
1999 Q1	23 926	3 217	102	158	27 403	1 827	29 230	17 174	46 404	73.6
Q2	24 031	3 222	98	161	27 512	1 748	29 261	17 184	46 444	73.8
Q3	24 369	3 215	100	153	27 838	1 819	29 656	16 827	46 483	74.6
Q4	24 386	3 196	105	171	27 857	1 667	29 524	16 996	46 520	74.6
2000 Q1	24 272	3 166	106	152	27 696	1 722	29 418	17 138	46 556	74.0
MALE										
	MGTB	MGTE	MGTH	MGTK	MGTN	MGTQ	MGTT	MGTW	MGTZ	MGUI
1995 Q1	11 506	2 548	40	196	14 290	1 673	15 963	6 173	22 135	75.6
Q2	11 665	2 533	48	184	14 430	1 621	16 050	6 115	22 166	76.2
Q3	11 861	2 543	47	160	14 611	1 665	16 276	5 920	22 196	77.2
Q4	11 819	2 537	41	172	14 568	1 534	16 102	6 127	22 229	76.9
1996 Q1	11 750	2 481	40	157	14 428	1 595	16 023	6 238	22 261	76.1
Q2	11 844	2 494	39	151	14 529	1 561	16 089	6 204	22 294	76.5
Q3	11 983	2 552	39	153	14 726	1 565	16 291	6 035	22 326	77.4
Q4	11 971	2 557	40	142	14 709	1 418	16 127	6 231	22 358	77.2
1997 Q1	12 059	2 509	40	133	14 741	1 346	16 087	6 303	22 390	77.3
Q2	12 208	2 477	36	137	14 858	1 302	16 160	6 263	22 423	77.8
Q3	12 410	2 475	40	137	15 062	1 281	16 343	6 113	22 455	78.7
Q4	12 396	2 466	38	133	15 033	1 150	16 184	6 306	22 490	78.5
1998 Q1	12 357	2 437	28	137	14 959	1 147	16 106	6 418	22 524	78.0
Q2	12 496	2 395	29	110	15 030	1 106	16 135	6 423	22 558	78.2
Q3	12 727	2 360	34	98	15 219	1 173	16 392	6 197	22 589	79.2
Q4	12 664	2 386	35	96	15 181	1 087	16 268	6 347	22 615	78.9
1999 Q1	12 594	2 375	36	102	15 107	1 132	16 238	6 402	22 640	78.3
Q2	12 668	2 382	34	107	15 191	1 087	16 277	6 388	22 666	78.6
Q3	12 886	2 379	33	101	15 400	1 101	16 501	6 190	22 690	79.7
Q4	12 871	2 349	37	111	15 369	1 008	16 376	6 338	22 714	79.4
2000 Q1	12 833	2 309	35	95	15 273	1 034	16 307	6 431	22 738	78.8

1 Data are from the Labour Force Survey which uses the definitions recommended by the International Labour Organisation (ILO), an agency of the United Nations. For details see Labour Market Trends pp S3-4 (May 1998 onwards) or the Guide to Labour Market Statistics Releases.

2 Includes those who did not state whether they were employees or self-emloyed.

3 The employment rate equals those in employment aged 16-64 (male) and 16-59 (female), as a percentage of all in these age groups. The underlying data are available on request.

4 Data for Great Britain are no longer published but are available on request. The previously published series relating to seasonal quarters (for GB or UK) are also available on request.

5 Labour Force Survey data have been regrossed using new population figures and revised back to 1993. For further details please refer to the May 2000 edition of *Labour Market trends.*

Source: Office for National Statistics; Enquiries 020 7533 6094

3.2 Labour Market Activity[1,5]

United Kingdom[4]

continued

Thousands, not seasonally adjusted

	Employment categories[2]					ILO unemployed	Total economically active	Economically inactive	Total aged 16 and over	Employment rate: age 16-59/64[3]
	Employees	Self - employed	Unpaid family workers	Government training and employment programmes	Total employment[2]					
FEMALE										
	MGTC	MGTF	MGTI	MGTL	MGTO	MGTR	MGTU	MGTX	MGUA	MGUJ
1995 Q1	10 577	811	90	102	11 580	883	12 463	11 013	23 477	65.4
Q2	10 636	815	97	102	11 650	842	12 492	10 998	23 490	65.7
Q3	10 777	814	82	95	11 767	918	12 685	10 820	23 505	66.3
Q4	10 847	811	92	97	11 848	816	12 664	10 859	23 523	66.7
1996 Q1	10 792	822	85	92	11 791	794	12 584	10 956	23 541	66.4
Q2	10 818	829	83	95	11 826	802	12 628	10 930	23 559	66.5
Q3	10 911	830	80	84	11 905	856	12 761	10 815	23 576	66.9
Q4	10 971	844	82	88	11 986	802	12 788	10 806	23 594	67.3
1997 Q1	10 940	852	74	91	11 957	785	12 742	10 870	23 612	66.9
Q2	11 021	869	80	85	12 054	764	12 818	10 812	23 630	67.3
Q3	11 088	884	85	75	12 133	794	12 927	10 722	23 649	67.8
Q4	11 125	876	73	82	12 156	697	12 853	10 818	23 671	67.9
1998 Q1	11 088	869	67	67	12 090	711	12 801	10 891	23 692	67.5
Q2	11 135	862	70	58	12 125	698	12 823	10 891	23 714	67.6
Q3	11 289	850	75	59	12 273	735	13 008	10 725	23 733	68.4
Q4	11 372	861	62	53	12 349	662	13 011	10 737	23 748	68.7
1999 Q1	11 332	842	66	56	12 296	695	12 992	10 772	23 764	68.4
Q2	11 363	840	65	54	12 322	662	12 983	10 795	23 779	68.4
Q3	11 483	836	67	52	12 438	718	13 156	10 637	23 793	69.1
Q4	11 514	846	68	60	12 488	660	13 147	10 658	23 805	69.2
2000 Q1	11 438	857	71	56	12 423	688	13 111	10 707	23 818	68.7

See footnotes on page 148.

Source: Office for National Statistics; Enquiries 020 7533 6094

3.3 Labour Market Activity by age[1,7]

United Kingdom[4]

Thousands, seasonally adjusted[6]

	Total aged 16 and over			Age groups[5]							
				16 - 24		25 - 49		50 - 59/64		60/65 and over	
	Total	Male	Female	Male	Female	Male	Female	Male	Female	Male	Female
In employment											
	MGRZ	MGSA	MGSB	MGUR	MGUS	MGUU	MGUV	MGUX	MGUY	MGVA	MGVB
1995 Q1	26 033	14 400	11 633	2 116	1 867	9 108	7 363	2 885	1 898	291	506
Q2	26 136	14 463	11 673	2 113	1 875	9 150	7 382	2 906	1 904	294	511
Q3	26 226	14 492	11 734	2 140	1 896	9 164	7 392	2 912	1 930	277	516
Q4	26 366	14 554	11 812	2 146	1 889	9 208	7 469	2 932	1 934	268	519
1996 Q1	26 371	14 531	11 840	2 111	1 898	9 203	7 510	2 954	1 929	263	503
Q2	26 417	14 563	11 854	2 104	1 887	9 231	7 526	2 964	1 949	264	492
Q3	26 488	14 614	11 874	2 090	1 866	9 258	7 544	2 997	1 956	269	509
Q4	26 634	14 691	11 943	2 081	1 879	9 293	7 601	3 050	1 971	268	492
1997 Q1	26 843	14 838	12 004	2 111	1 874	9 350	7 594	3 108	2 017	269	519
Q2	26 982	14 894	12 088	2 109	1 889	9 375	7 622	3 142	2 042	268	534
Q3	27 055	14 953	12 102	2 094	1 878	9 403	7 632	3 172	2 064	285	528
Q4	27 117	15 011	12 106	2 106	1 890	9 434	7 618	3 192	2 090	279	507
1998 Q1	27 188	15 051	12 137	2 097	1 870	9 463	7 639	3 221	2 124	270	504
Q2	27 230	15 067	12 162	2 091	1 869	9 452	7 639	3 252	2 156	272	499
Q3	27 352	15 113	12 239	2 112	1 884	9 451	7 652	3 289	2 194	261	509
Q4	27 448	15 155	12 293	2 078	1 873	9 480	7 675	3 332	2 216	265	529
1999 Q1	27 540	15 196	12 343	2 089	1 885	9 478	7 711	3 347	2 233	282	513
Q2	27 592	15 230	12 362	2 095	1 854	9 490	7 737	3 362	2 250	283	521
Q3	27 696	15 293	12 402	2 109	1 878	9 519	7 742	3 378	2 261	287	522
Q4	27 769	15 339	12 430	2 131	1 879	9 526	7 733	3 388	2 284	294	534
2000 Q1	27 824	15 359	12 465	2 127	1 875	9 551	7 743	3 391	2 301	290	547
ILO unemployed											
	MGSC	MGSD	MGSE	MGVG	MGVH	MGVJ	MGVK	MGVM	MGVN	MGVP	MGVQ
1995 Q1	2 542	1 665	877	479	286	886	482	292	98	..	10
Q2	2 488	1 628	860	480	271	856	483	283	93	..	13
Q3	2 493	1 623	870	455	292	867	480	290	87	10	11
Q4	2 403	1 562	841	447	270	827	470	276	88	13	13
1996 Q1	2 380	1 589	791	472	250	832	444	272	86	13	10
Q2	2 385	1 567	818	465	260	822	460	269	87	11	11
Q3	2 330	1 521	809	453	265	799	434	256	97	13	13
Q4	2 277	1 450	827	450	274	742	441	246	100	12	11
1997 Q1	2 124	1 340	784	420	263	679	423	228	85	14	13
Q2	2 087	1 308	779	408	265	662	413	228	91	10	11
Q3	1 988	1 237	750	395	251	613	402	222	86	..	12
Q4	1 908	1 186	721	371	250	595	389	212	73	..	..
1998 Q1	1 851	1 140	711	366	252	560	377	204	72	..	11
Q2	1 824	1 112	712	366	251	545	377	189	74	12	11
Q3	1 825	1 130	694	382	244	551	372	188	69	10	..
Q4	1 812	1 125	687	389	244	542	360	185	75	..	..
1999 Q1	1 819	1 123	696	382	243	546	365	186	79	..	..
Q2	1 770	1 094	675	364	230	536	359	185	75	..	11
Q3	1 739	1 060	679	346	234	524	359	180	74	10	12
Q4	1 733	1 048	686	341	239	514	361	185	72	..	14
2000 Q1	1 713	1 028	686	344	255	491	342	186	76	..	12
Economically inactive											
	MGSI	MGSJ	MGSK	MGVV	MGVW	MGVY	MGVZ	MGWB	MGWC	MGWE	MGWF
1995 Q1	17 037	6 071	10 967	804	1 094	685	2 689	1 272	1 154	3 310	6 030
Q2	17 031	6 074	10 957	788	1 084	699	2 687	1 272	1 167	3 315	6 018
Q3	16 982	6 081	10 902	771	1 028	702	2 699	1 271	1 161	3 337	6 013
Q4	16 983	6 113	10 870	758	1 042	727	2 654	1 278	1 170	3 349	6 004
1996 Q1	17 051	6 141	10 910	752	1 040	754	2 660	1 274	1 191	3 362	6 019
Q2	17 049	6 163	10 886	751	1 026	764	2 649	1 280	1 184	3 368	6 026
Q3	17 084	6 191	10 893	764	1 030	778	2 668	1 282	1 190	3 368	6 005
Q4	17 041	6 216	10 825	764	996	796	2 595	1 280	1 211	3 377	6 022
1997 Q1	17 036	6 212	10 824	751	1 001	799	2 611	1 280	1 219	3 381	5 992
Q2	16 984	6 221	10 764	753	973	787	2 585	1 287	1 226	3 393	5 978
Q3	17 062	6 265	10 797	772	991	807	2 579	1 301	1 244	3 384	5 984
Q4	17 136	6 292	10 843	780	976	795	2 599	1 322	1 259	3 396	6 010

1 See footnote 1 on table 3.2
4 See footnote on page 151
5 See footnote on page 151

6 The seasonally adjusted estimates may be subject to revision as more quarterly data becomes available.

Source: Office for National Statistics; Enquiries 020 7533 6094

3.3 Labour Market Activity by age[1,7]

United Kingdom[4]

continued

Thousands, seasonally adjusted[6]

	Total aged 16 and over			Age groups[5] 16 - 24		25 - 49		50 - 59/64		60/65 and over	
	Total	Male	Female	Male	Female	Male	Female	Male	Female	Male	Female
Economically inactive (continued)											
	MGSI	MGSJ	MGSK	MGVV	MGVW	MGVY	MGVZ	MGWB	MGWC	MGWE	MGWF
1998 Q1	17 177	6 333	10 844	788	991	801	2 583	1 333	1 254	3 411	6 015
Q2	17 218	6 379	10 839	790	990	828	2 578	1 348	1 248	3 413	6 024
Q3	17 146	6 347	10 799	750	979	822	2 562	1 342	1 241	3 432	6 017
Q4	17 103	6 335	10 768	776	992	797	2 544	1 327	1 232	3 434	6 000
1999 Q1	17 045	6 321	10 724	772	982	791	2 495	1 336	1 232	3 421	6 016
Q2	17 082	6 341	10 741	785	1 027	785	2 467	1 348	1 239	3 423	6 008
Q3	17 049	6 337	10 712	790	1 001	764	2 455	1 361	1 249	3 424	6 006
Q4	17 018	6 328	10 690	776	999	762	2 455	1 365	1 246	3 424	5 990
2000 Q1	17 019	6 352	10 667	780	990	757	2 457	1 381	1 243	3 434	5 977
Economic activity rate(per cent)[2]											
	MGWG	MGWH	MGWI	MGWK	MGWL	MGWN	MGWO	MGWQ	MGWR	MGWT	MGWU
1995 Q1	62.6	72.6	53.3	76.3	66.3	93.6	74.5	71.4	63.4	8.3	7.9
Q2	62.7	72.6	53.4	76.7	66.4	93.5	74.5	71.5	63.1	8.4	8.0
Q3	62.8	72.6	53.6	77.1	68.0	93.5	74.5	71.6	63.5	7.9	8.1
Q4	62.9	72.5	53.8	77.4	67.5	93.2	74.9	71.5	63.3	7.7	8.1
1996 Q1	62.8	72.4	53.7	77.4	67.4	93.0	74.9	71.7	62.9	7.6	7.9
Q2	62.8	72.4	53.8	77.4	67.7	92.9	75.1	71.6	63.2	7.6	7.7
Q3	62.8	72.3	53.8	76.9	67.4	92.8	74.9	71.7	63.3	7.7	8.0
Q4	62.9	72.2	54.1	76.8	68.4	92.6	75.6	72.0	63.1	7.7	7.7
1997 Q1	63.0	72.3	54.2	77.1	68.1	92.6	75.4	72.3	63.3	7.7	8.2
Q2	63.1	72.3	54.4	77.0	68.9	92.7	75.7	72.4	63.5	7.6	8.4
Q3	63.0	72.1	54.3	76.3	68.2	92.5	75.7	72.3	63.4	8.0	8.3
Q4	62.9	72.0	54.2	76.1	68.7	92.7	75.5	72.0	63.2	7.8	7.9
1998 Q1	62.8	71.9	54.2	75.8	68.2	92.6	75.6	72.0	63.7	7.6	7.9
Q2	62.8	71.7	54.3	75.7	68.2	92.4	75.7	71.9	64.1	7.7	7.8
Q3	63.0	71.9	54.5	76.9	68.5	92.4	75.8	72.2	64.6	7.3	7.9
Q4	63.1	72.0	54.7	76.1	68.1	92.6	76.0	72.6	65.0	7.4	8.2
1999 Q1	63.3	72.1	54.9	76.2	68.4	92.7	76.4	72.6	65.2	7.8	8.0
Q2	63.2	72.0	54.8	75.8	67.0	92.7	76.6	72.5	65.2	7.9	8.1
Q3	63.3	72.1	55.0	75.7	67.8	92.9	76.7	72.3	65.1	8.0	8.2
Q4	63.4	72.1	55.1	76.1	67.9	92.9	76.7	72.4	65.4	8.1	8.4
2000 Q1	63.4	72.1	55.2	76.0	68.3	93.0	76.7	72.1	65.7	7.9	8.5
ILO unemployment rate (per cent)[3]											
	MGSX	MGSY	MGSZ	MGWZ	MGXA	MGXC	MGXD	MGXF	MGXG	MGXI	MGXJ
1995 Q1	8.9	10.4	7.0	18.4	13.3	8.9	6.1	9.2	4.9	..	2.0
Q2	8.7	10.1	6.9	18.5	12.6	8.6	6.1	8.9	4.6	..	2.5
Q3	8.7	10.1	6.9	17.6	13.3	8.6	6.1	9.1	4.3	3.6	2.1
Q4	8.4	9.7	6.6	17.2	12.5	8.2	5.9	8.6	4.3	4.8	2.4
1996 Q1	8.3	9.9	6.3	18.3	11.6	8.3	5.6	8.4	4.3	4.6	2.0
Q2	8.3	9.7	6.5	18.1	12.1	8.2	5.8	8.3	4.3	4.0	2.1
Q3	8.1	9.4	6.4	17.8	12.4	7.9	5.4	7.9	4.7	4.8	2.5
Q4	7.9	9.0	6.5	17.8	12.7	7.4	5.5	7.5	4.8	4.4	2.2
1997 Q1	7.3	8.3	6.1	16.6	12.3	6.8	5.3	6.8	4.0	4.9	2.5
Q2	7.2	8.1	6.1	16.2	12.3	6.6	5.1	6.8	4.3	3.5	2.0
Q3	6.8	7.6	5.8	15.9	11.8	6.1	5.0	6.5	4.0	..	2.1
Q4	6.6	7.3	5.6	15.0	11.7	5.9	4.9	6.2	3.4	..	..
1998 Q1	6.4	7.0	5.5	14.9	11.9	5.6	4.7	5.9	3.3	..	2.1
Q2	6.3	6.9	5.5	14.9	11.8	5.5	4.7	5.5	3.3	4.3	2.1
Q3	6.3	7.0	5.4	15.3	11.5	5.5	4.6	5.4	3.0	3.6	..
Q4	6.2	6.9	5.3	15.8	11.5	5.4	4.5	5.3	3.3	..	..
1999 Q1	6.2	6.9	5.3	15.5	11.4	5.4	4.5	5.3	3.4	..	..
Q2	6.0	6.7	5.2	14.8	11.0	5.3	4.4	5.2	3.2	..	2.0
Q3	5.9	6.5	5.2	14.1	11.1	5.2	4.4	5.1	3.2	3.3	2.2
Q4	5.9	6.4	5.2	13.8	11.3	5.1	4.5	5.2	3.1	..	2.5
2000 Q1	5.8	6.3	5.2	13.9	12.0	4.9	4.2	5.2	3.2	..	2.1

1 See footnote 1 on table 3.2
2 The activity rate is the percentage of people in each age group who are economically active.
3 ILO unemployment rate is the percentage of economically active people who are unemployed using the ILO definition.
4 Data for Great Britain are no longer published, but are available on request. The previously published series relating to seasonal quarters (for GB or UK) are also available on request.
5 Data for more detailed age groups are published in *Labour Market Trends*.
7 Labour Force Survey data have been regrossed using new population figures and revised back to 1993. For further details please refer to the May 2000 edition of *Labour Market Trends*.

Source: Office for National Statistics; Enquiries 020 7533 6094

3.4 Jobs and Claimant Count[1]
United Kingdom

Thousands, not seasonally adjusted

	Workforce jobs[2,3,4]	Employee jobs[2,3,4] All industries	Manufacturing industries	Production industries	Service industries	Total claimant count, nsa, annual averages[5,6]	Job Centre vacancies[5,7]
	DYDA	BCAD	YEJG	YEJH	YEJI	BCJA	BCOM
1950	23 257	20 758	..	..	..	341.1	..
1951	23 603	20 970	..	..	..	281.4	..
1952	23 590	20 916	..	..	..	462.5	..
1953	23 703	21 041	..	..	..	380.0	191.6
1954	24 038	21 404	..	..	..	317.8	240.4
1955	24 298	21 702	..	..	..	264.5	280.6
1956	24 514	21 965	..	..	..	287.1	241.1
1957	24 543	22 058	..	..	..	347.2	185.6
1958	24 278	21 884	..	..	..	500.9	137.1
1959	24 402	21 421	..	..	..	512.1	157.7
1960	24 844	21 899	..	..	..	392.8	212.8
1961	25 132	22 233	..	..	..	376.8	214.0
1962	25 322	22 452	..	..	..	499.9	150.0
1963	25 358	22 509	..	..	..	612.3	144.9
1964	25 662	22 816	..	..	..	413.4	222.0
1965	25 929	23 085	..	..	..	359.7	266.9
1966	26 095	23 257	..	..	..	390.9	256.6
1967	25 741	22 813	..	..	..	599.1	175.1
1968	25 601	22 655	..	..	..	601.3	189.5
1969	25 635	22 624	..	..	..	580.9	202.0
1970	25 543	22 479	..	..	..	618.0	188.3
1971	25 213	22 139	..	..	..	792.1	130.9
1972	25 196	22 137	..	..	..	875.7	147.3
1973	25 786	22 679	..	..	..	618.8	306.9
1974	25 866	22 804	..	..	..	614.9	297.5
1975	25 779	22 723	..	..	..	977.6	156.6
1976	25 570	22 557	..	..	..	1 359.4	122.0
1977	25 596	22 631	..	..	..	1 402.7	154.5
1978	25 755	23 227	6 837	7 553	13 922	1 382.9	210.3
1979	26 149	23 618	6 809	7 526	14 314	1 295.7	241.3
1980	26 107	23 433	6 512	7 226	14 434	1 664.9	143.0
1981	25 140	22 314	5 840	6 529	14 148	2 520.4	97.0
1982	24 702	21 826	5 505	6 160	14 102	2 916.9	111.3
1983	24 422	21 473	5 190	5 811	14 129	3 104.7	145.1
1984	25 086	21 647	5 082	5 669	14 458	3 159.8	157.4
1985	25 390	21 837	5 037	5 596	14 733	3 271.2	161.7
1986	25 440	21 800	4 915	5 423	14 911	3 292.9	188.2
1987	25 958	22 002	4 847	5 315	15 204	2 953.4	234.9
1988	26 894	22 688	4 887	5 331	15 837	2 370.4	248.0
1989	27 747	23 100	4 877	5 302	16 248	1 798.7	219.5
1990	28 019	23 364	4 756	5 160	16 643	1 664.5	173.6
1991	27 118	22 702	4 342	4 720	16 525	2 291.9	117.9
1992	26 411	22 406	4 125	4 481	16 575	2 778.6	117.1
1993	26 059	22 032	3 944	4 241	16 518	2 919.2	127.8
1994	26 218	22 121	3 963	4 224	16 651	2 636.5	157.9
1995	26 514	22 454	4 064	4 301	16 964	2 325.6	182.8
1996	26 749	22 732	4 106	4 334	17 213	2 122.2	226.5
1997	27 247	23 268	4 162	4 390	17 604	1 602.4	283.9
1998	27 571	23 762	4 185	4 402	17 960	1 362.3	296.6
1999	27 849	24 025	4 041	4 257	18 367	1 263.0	..

1 Prior to October 1982, the claimant count consisted of those people registered at Jobcentres who were unemployed (the registrant count). From October 1982 onwards, the count of claimants of unemployment related benefits consisted of all people claiming JSI or NI credits at Employment Service local offices. From October 1996, it has consisted of those claiming Jobseeker's Allowance and or NI credits.

2 With the shift in concept of measuring 'jobs' rather than 'people' from the employer surveys, the **Workforce** component (summing the claimant count and Workforce in employment series- now called Workforce jobs) will no longer appear in this table. The Workforce jobs series have been revised due to the addition of second Self-employment jobs from 1994 onwards. The self-employment series now has a 'centred' reference period e.g. the December estimate would be based on the LFS period Nov to Jan. For further information please refer to *Labour Market Trends*- May 1998 pp 249-258.

3 For all dates, individuals with two jobs as employees of different employers are counted twice.

4 Annual estimates relate to mid-year. Figures for the four quarters relate to March, June, September and December.

5 Annual figures are averages over the 12 months of the year.

6 The unadjusted claimant count figures have been affected by changes in coverage. The seasonally adjusted figures, however, as given later in this table, are estimated on the current basis, allowing for discontinuities, and are therefore recommended for the purposes of assessing trends. The seasonally adjusted figures, which relate only to claimants aged 18 or over, have been revised, in order to maintain the consistent series, available back to 1971 (1974 for the regions). (See the December 1990 issue of *Employment Gazette* for further details. See also pages 397-400 of the November 1995 issue of *Labour Market Trends* for details of previous discontinuities taken into account). Only those discontinuities that affect the current series of claimant count figures are shown.

7 Vacancies notified to Jobcentres and remaining unfilled.

Sources: Office for National Statistics;
Enquiries; Columns 1-5 01633 812079; Columns 6,7 020 7533 6094

3.4 Jobs and Claimant Count[1]

United Kingdom

continued

Thousands, not seasonally adjusted

	Workforce jobs[2,3,4]	Employee jobs[2,3,4] All industries	Manufacturing industry	Production industry	Service industries	United Kingdom Total claimant count, nsa[5]	Job Centre vacancies[6,7]
	DYDA	BCAD	YEJG	YEJH	YEJI	BCJA	BCOM
1950 Q1	..	..	..	..	..	403.9	..
Q2	23 257	20 758	..	..	..	357.3	..
Q3	23 327	20 812	..	..	..	296.9	..
Q4	23 324	20 772	..	..	..	327.0	..
1951 Q1	23 461	20 850	..	..	..	366.6	..
Q2	23 603	20 970	..	..	..	280.6	..
Q3	23 673	21 028	..	..	..	209.7	..
Q4	23 601	20 950	..	..	..	289.8	..
1952 Q1	23 594	20 929	..	..	..	425.9	..
Q2	23 590	20 916	..	..	..	517.6	..
Q3	23 558	20 882	..	..	..	453.8	..
Q4	23 483	20 814	..	..	..	439.8	..
1953 Q1	23 525	20 857	..	..	..	503.3	169.9
Q2	23 703	21 041	..	..	..	415.5	200.4
Q3	23 791	21 131	..	..	..	307.4	211.2
Q4	23 828	21 182	..	..	..	339.5	184.9
1954 Q1	23 878	21 238	..	..	..	414.6	188.5
Q2	24 038	21 404	..	..	..	353.0	242.3
Q3	24 147	21 515	..	..	..	249.1	253.1
Q4	24 171	21 547	..	..	..	281.2	277.8
1955 Q1	24 203	21 586	..	..	..	335.7	245.9
Q2	24 298	21 702	..	..	..	296.4	303.1
Q3	24 438	21 856	..	..	..	215.8	311.0
Q4	24 452	21 882	..	..	..	241.2	262.5
1956 Q1	24 418	21 855	..	..	..	302.4	254.6
Q2	24 514	21 965	..	..	..	282.1	267.5
Q3	24 599	23 031	..	..	..	263.4	243.3
Q4	24 499	21 952	..	..	..	279.4	199.2
1957 Q1	24 406	21 902	..	..	..	422.5	169.1
Q2	24 543	22 058	..	..	..	379.2	198.3
Q3	24 502	22 046	..	..	..	274.2	204.8
Q4	24 400	21 967	..	..	..	304.4	170.1
1958 Q1	24 203	21 797	..	..	..	439.9	147.6
Q2	24 278	21 884	..	..	..	495.0	148.3
Q3	24 231	21 852	..	..	..	450.3	136.8
Q4	24 182	21 813	..	..	..	551.8	115.7
1959 Q1	24 219	21 862	..	..	..	666.5	118.1
Q2	24 402	21 832	..	..	..	568.1	154.8
Q3	..	..	..	..	..	429.3	184.2
Q4	..	..	..	..	..	452.0	173.6
1960 Q1	..	..	..	..	..	497.6	181.0
Q2	24 844	22 320	..	..	..	426.8	224.3
Q3	..	..	..	..	..	320.5	237.5
Q4	..	..	..	..	..	356.6	208.3
1961 Q1	..	..	..	..	..	458.0	201.7
Q2	25 132	22 660	..	..	..	375.4	241.8
Q3	..	..	..	..	..	292.5	236.8
Q4	..	..	..	..	..	401.2	175.6
1962 Q1	..	..	..	..	..	503.2	150.7
Q2	25 322	22 885	..	..	..	478.9	172.4
Q3	..	..	..	..	..	435.0	156.6
Q4	..	..	..	..	..	532.5	120.4

See footnotes 1-4 on page 152.

5 The unadjusted claimant count figures have been affected by changes in coverage. The seasonally adjusted figures, however, as given later in this table, are estimated on the current basis, allowing for discontinuities, and are therefore recommended for the purposes of assessing trends. The seasonally adjusted figures, which relate only to claimants aged 18 or over, have been revised, in order to maintain the consistent series, available back to 1971 (1974 for the regions). (See the December 1990 issue of *Employment Gazette* for further details. See also pages 397-400 of the November 1995 edition of *Labour Market Trends* for details of previous discontinuities taken into account.) Only those discontinuities that affect the current series of claimant count figures are shown. Quarterly claimant count figiures relate to the average of the three months in each quarter.

6 Vacancies notified to Jobcentres and remaining unfilled.

7 Quarterly vacancy figures relate to the average of the three months in each quarter.

Sources: Office for National Statistics;

Enquiries; Columns 1-5 01633 812079; Columns 6,7 020 7533 6094

3.4 Jobs and Claimant Count[1]

United Kingdom

continued

Thousands, not seasonally adjusted

		Employee jobs[2,3,4]				United Kingdom	
	Workforce jobs[2,3,4]	All industries	Manufacturing industry	Production industry	Service industries	Total claimant count, nsa[5]	Job Centres vacancies[6,7]
	DYDA	BCAD	YEJG	YEJH	YEJI	BCJA	BCOM
1963 Q1	..	..	..	..	..	861.0	114.3
Q2	25 358	22 942	..	..	..	644.8	148.2
Q3	..	..	..	..	..	484.9	158.1
Q4	..	..	..	..	..	506.8	158.9
1964 Q1	..	..	..	..	..	540.4	183.3
Q2	25 662	23 254	..	..	..	448.4	231.2
Q3	..	..	..	..	..	349.0	243.6
Q4	..	..	..	..	..	376.3	230.0
1965 Q1	..	..	..	..	..	409.1	234.7
Q2	25 929	23 528	..	..	..	373.9	289.5
Q3	..	..	..	..	..	309.8	286.4
Q4	..	..	..	..	..	344.4	257.1
1966 Q1	..	..	..	..	..	382.7	262.0
Q2	26 095	23 706	..	..	..	337.4	296.9
Q3	..	..	..	..	..	293.7	274.1
Q4	..	..	..	..	..	468.1	193.6
1967 Q1	..	..	..	..	..	641.1	169.7
Q2	25 741	23 252	..	..	..	610.3	182.5
Q3	..	..	..	..	..	535.4	179.0
Q4	..	..	..	..	..	598.5	169.4
1968 Q1	..	..	..	..	..	671.0	168.2
Q2	25 601	23 092	..	..	..	615.1	195.5
Q3	..	..	..	..	..	550.9	199.4
Q4	..	..	..	..	..	585.6	194.9
1969 Q1	..	..	..	..	..	635.8	190.0
Q2	25 635	23 061	..	..	..	594.5	214.1
Q3	..	..	..	..	..	550.8	211.1
Q4	..	..	..	..	..	607.8	192.9
1970 Q1	..	..	..	..	..	667.0	184.1
Q2	25 543	22 912	..	..	..	652.5	200.3
Q3	..	..	..	..	..	607.2	196.4
Q4	..	..	..	..	..	633.5	172.4
1971 Q1	..	..	..	..	..	682.8	139.4
Q2	25 213	22 565	..	..	..	714.7	138.9
Q3	..	..	..	..	..	711.7	130.0
Q4	..	..	..	..	..	815.6	115.3
1972 Q1	..	..	..	..	..	936.1	113.0
Q2	25 196	22 564	..	..	..	918.4	143.8
Q3	..	..	..	..	..	776.2	157.0
Q4	..	..	..	..	..	783.5	175.5
1973 Q1	..	..	..	..	..	776.6	218.8
Q2	25 786	23 117	..	..	..	656.8	302.2
Q3	..	..	..	..	..	541.5	344.6
Q4	..	..	..	..	..	513.1	362.1
1974 Q1	..	..	..	..	..	611.5	276.3
Q2	25 866	23 244	..	..	..	588.0	323.3
Q3	..	..	..	..	..	552.1	317.5
Q4	..	..	..	..	..	615.4	272.8
1975 Q1	..	..	..	..	..	771.8	198.4
Q2	25 779	23 162	..	..	..	845.0	168.7
Q3	..	..	..	..	..	990.1	142.4
Q4	..	..	..	..	..	1 147.3	116.9

See footnotes 1-4 on page 152.

See footnote 5 on page 153.

6 Vacancies notified to Jobcentres and remaining unfilled.

7 Quarterly vacancy figures relate to the average of the three months in each quarter.

Sources: Office for National Statistics;
Enquiries; Columns 1-5 01633 812079; Columns 6,7 020 7533 6094

3.4 Jobs and Claimant Count[1]
United Kingdom
continued

Thousands, not seasonally adjusted

		Employee jobs[2,3,4]				United Kingdom	
	Workforce jobs[2,3,4]	All industries	Manufacturing industry	Production indsutry	Service industries	Total claimant count, nsa[5]	Job Centre vacancies[6,7]
	DYDA	BCAD	YEJG	YEJH	YEJI	BCJA	BCOM
1976 Q1	..	..	..	..	..	1 303.2	99.1
Q2	25 570	22 993	..	..	..	1 281.1	123.7
Q3	..	..	..	..	..	1 463.5	133.5
Q4	..	..	..	..	..	1 377.1	131.6
1977 Q1	..	..	..	..	..	1 448.2	132.8
Q2	25 596	23 068	..	..	..	1 392.3	163.3
Q3	..	..	..	..	..	1 622.4	160.6
Q4	..	..	..	..	..	1 518.3	161.1
1978 Q1	..	..	..	..	..	1 548.5	172.4
Q2	25 755	23 227	6 837	7 553	13 922	1 451.8	216.0
Q3	25 904	23 372	6 870	7 584	14 007	1 585.8	221.8
Q4	26 067	23 535	6 865	7 578	14 187	1 335.8	231.2
1979 Q1	25 894	23 364	6 804	7 519	14 098	1 372.8	219.3
Q2	26 149	23 618	6 809	7 526	14 314	1 260.9	265.0
Q3	26 279	23 710	6 822	7 540	14 352	1 347.3	253.6
Q4	26 310	23 709	6 766	7 485	14 432	1 267.5	227.2
1980 Q1	26 050	23 413	6 628	7 346	14 303	1 373.7	180.3
Q2	26 107	23 433	6 512	7 226	14 434	1 418.1	172.5
Q3	25 920	23 206	6 347	7 060	14 351	1 736.5	123.9
Q4	25 610	22 861	6 145	6 851	14 290	1 916.4	95.2
1981 Q1	25 182	22 401	5 954	6 647	14 085	2 271.1	85.3
Q2	25 140	22 314	5 840	6 529	14 148	2 372.7	103.1
Q3	25 078	22 236	5 799	6 482	14 117	2 511.8	99.5
Q4	24 888	22 034	5 690	6 363	14 092	2 771.6	100.1
1982 Q1	24 662	21 797	5 597	6 262	13 988	2 896.3	98.9
Q2	24 702	21 826	5 505	6 160	14 102	2 818.5	121.0
Q3	24 637	21 748	5 447	6 097	14 055	2 852.5	114.0
Q4	24 452	21 550	5 331	5 972	14 005	3 049.0	111.3
1983 Q1	24 225	21 298	5 236	5 868	13 903	3 225.2	111.3
Q2	24 422	21 473	5 190	5 811	14 129	3 169.9	148.8
Q3	24 753	21 590	5 185	5 799	14 212	3 066.0	162.8
Q4	24 917	21 631	5 138	5 742	14 336	3 085.9	157.5
1984 Q1	24 839	21 482	5 083	5 676	14 281	3 176.3	137.0
Q2	25 086	21 647	5 082	5 669	14 458	3 073.9	165.8
Q3	25 267	21 758	5 106	5 689	14 503	3 166.7	167.4
Q4	25 372	21 843	5 089	5 667	14 637	3 222.4	159.6
1985 Q1	25 214	21 677	5 038	5 610	14 555	3 310.7	139.3
Q2	25 390	21 837	5 037	5 596	14 733	3 230.7	170.3
Q3	25 512	21 896	5 076	5 624	14 739	3 273.9	170.5
Q4	25 520	21 909	5 036	5 572	14 840	3 269.6	166.8
1986 Q1	25 273	21 679	4 962	5 480	14 734	3 371.1	149.5
Q2	25 440	21 800	4 915	5 423	14 911	3 275.1	183.5
Q3	25 597	21 840	4 921	5 419	14 924	3 297.5	207.5
Q4	25 686	21 883	4 887	5 374	15 034	3 227.7	212.2
1987 Q1	25 546	21 709	4 814	5 286	14 958	3 222.1	192.3
Q2	25 958	22 002	4 847	5 315	15 204	2 999.6	234.3
Q3	26 282	22 199	4 898	5 366	15 302	2 880.8	248.9
Q4	26 573	22 454	4 906	5 370	15 570	2 710.9	264.0
1988 Q1	26 583	22 434	4 876	5 329	15 593	2 659.9	227.0
Q2	26 894	22 688	4 887	5 331	15 837	2 434.6	261.0
Q3	27 195	22 881	4 938	5 382	15 950	2 309.6	254.1
Q4	27 438	23 003	4 937	5 377	16 098	2 077.4	249.8

See footnotes 1-4 on page 152.

See footnote 5 on page 153.

6 Vacancies notified to Jobcentres and remaining unfilled.

7 Quarterly vacancy figures relate to the average of the three months in each quarter.

Sources: Office for National Statistics;
Enquiries; Columns 1-5 01633 812079; Columns 6,7 020 7533 6094

3.4 Jobs and Claimant Count[1]

United Kingdom

continued

Thousands, not seasonally adjusted

		Employee jobs[2,3,4]				United Kingdom	
	Workforce jobs[2,3,4]	All industries	Manufacturing industry	Production industry	Service industries	Total claimant count, nsa[5]	Job Centre vacancies[6,7]
	DYDA	BCAD	YEJG	YEJH	YEJI	BCJA	BCOM
1989 Q1	27 540	22 984	4 884	5 315	16 142	2 017.6	204.6
Q2	27 747	23 100	4 877	5 302	16 248	1 809.7	228.8
Q3	27 866	23 201	4 932	5 351	16 261	1 738.5	229.0
Q4	28 016	23 359	4 888	5 304	16 502	1 629.1	215.5
1990 Q1	27 864	23 210	4 793	5 204	16 454	1 669.8	173.7
Q2	28 019	23 364	4 756	5 160	16 643	1 586.8	200.6
Q3	27 922	23 320	4 754	5 154	16 587	1 651.8	176.2
Q4	27 786	23 222	4 638	5 032	16 665	1 749.7	144.1
1991 Q1	27 319	22 809	4 455	4 840	16 489	2 049.1	118.6
Q2	27 118	22 702	4 342	4 720	16 525	2 217.8	120.0
Q3	26 854	22 546	4 308	4 679	16 416	2 417.8	116.1
Q4	26 738	22 496	4 244	4 619	16 528	2 483.2	117.2
1992 Q1	26 526	22 356	4 151	4 518	16 519	2 697.3	100.3
Q2	26 411	22 356	4 125	4 481	16 575	2 707.5	125.8
Q3	26 055	21 998	4 069	4 421	16 272	2 822.3	122.9
Q4	26 068	22 008	3 972	4 298	16 404	2 887.3	119.4
1993 Q1	25 899	21 884	3 933	4 249	16 363	3 033.8	104.3
Q2	26 059	22 032	3 944	4 241	16 518	2 927.4	131.3
Q3	26 100	22 076	3 956	4 246	16 534	2 933.8	134.3
Q4	26 242	22 155	3 953	4 235	16 672	2 781.9	141.5
1994 Q1	26 068	21 971	3 925	4 198	16 536	2 836.1	125.4
Q2	26 218	22 121	3 963	4 224	16 651	2 657.5	155.8
Q3	26 401	22 261	4 014	4 269	16 715	2 620.6	167.4
Q4	26 512	22 381	4 035	4 283	16 882	2 431.7	183.0
1995 Q1	26 327	22 230	4 036	4 278	16 783	2 453.5	157.8
Q2	26 514	22 454	4 064	4 301	16 964	2 310.7	186.6
Q3	26 542	22 439	4 091	4 326	16 903	2 326.2	189.7
Q4	26 739	22 691	4 145	4 384	17 118	2 212.2	197.2
1996 Q1	26 508	22 474	4 113	4 346	16 971	2 281.4	172.7
Q2	26 749	22 732	4 106	4 334	17 213	2 155.9	211.9
Q3	26 935	22 850	4 158	4 387	17 278	2 146.1	245.6
Q4	27 064	23 017	4 166	4 393	17 438	1 905.6	275.9
1997 Q1	26 936	22 923	4 132	4 359	17 384	1 826.9	250.1
Q2	27 247	23 268	4 162	4 390	17 604	1 619.5	278.9
Q3	27 409	23 388	4 168	4 389	17 643	1 559.3	300.4
Q4	27 626	23 697	4 190	4 409	17 891	1 404.0	306.1
1998 Q1	27 569	23 643	4 190	4 408	17 833	1 445.5	255.4
Q2	27 571	23 762	4 185	4 402	17 960	1 354.0	291.7
Q3	27 806	23 972	4 195	4 412	18 132	1 361.9	309.4
Q4	27 907	24 099	4 136	4 354	18 333	1 288.0	330.0
1999 Q1	27 668	23 882	4 067	4 284	18 229	1 370.7	274.0
Q2	27 849	24 025	4 041	4 257	18 367	1 280.2	..
Q3	27 943	24 203	4 032	4 245	18 514	1 250.3	..
Q4	28 106	24 378	4 017	4 226	18 690	1 150.9	..
2000 Q1	27 844	24 129	3 970	..	..	1 219.2	..
Q2	..	..	..	..	..	1 109.2	..

See footnotes 1-4 on page 152.

5 See footnote 5 on page 153.
6 Vacancies notified to Jobcentres and remaining unfilled.
7 Quarterly vacancy figures relate to the average of the three months in each quarter.

Sources: Office for National Statistics;
Enquiries Columns 1-5 01633 812079; Columns 6,7 020 7533 6094

3.4 Jobs and Claimant Count[1]

United Kingdom

continued

Thousands, seasonally adjusted

		Employee jobs[2,3,4]				United Kingdom	
	Workforce jobs[2,3,4]	All industries	Manufacturing industry	Production industry	Service industries	Total claimant count, sa[5]	Job Centre vacancies[6,7]
	DYDC	BCAJ	YEJA	YEJF	YEJC	BCJD	DPCB
1959 Q1	..	..	..	..	..	..	..
Q2	24 408	21 838	..	..	..	..	..
Q3	..	..	..	..	..	..	..
Q4	..	..	..	..	..	..	..
1960 Q1	..	..	..	..	..	..	..
Q2	24 845	22 321	..	..	..	..	..
Q3	..	..	..	..	..	..	..
Q4	..	..	..	..	..	..	..
1961 Q1	..	..	..	..	..	..	..
Q2	25 125	22 653	..	..	..	..	..
Q3	..	..	..	..	..	..	..
Q4	..	..	..	..	..	..	..
1962 Q1	..	..	..	..	..	..	..
Q2	25 309	22 872	..	..	..	..	..
Q3	..	..	..	..	..	..	..
Q4	..	..	..	..	..	..	..
1963 Q1	..	..	..	..	..	..	..
Q2	25 342	22 926	..	..	..	..	..
Q3	..	..	..	..	..	..	..
Q4	..	..	..	..	..	..	..
1964 Q1	..	..	..	..	..	..	..
Q2	25 645	23 237	..	..	..	..	..
Q3	..	..	..	..	..	..	..
Q4	..	..	..	..	..	..	..
1965 Q1	..	..	..	..	..	..	..
Q2	25 915	23 514	..	..	..	..	..
Q3	..	..	..	..	..	..	..
Q4	..	..	..	..	..	..	..
1966 Q1	..	..	..	..	..	..	..
Q2	26 082	23 693	..	..	..	..	..
Q3	..	..	..	..	..	..	..
Q4	..	..	..	..	..	..	..
1967 Q1	..	..	..	..	..	..	..
Q2	25 734	23 245	..	..	..	..	..
Q3	..	..	..	..	..	..	..
Q4	..	..	..	..	..	..	..
1968 Q1	..	..	..	..	..	..	..
Q2	25 589	23 080	..	..	..	..	..
Q3	..	..	..	..	..	..	..
Q4	..	..	..	..	..	..	..
1969 Q1	..	..	..	..	..	..	..
Q2	25 621	23 047	..	..	..	..	..
Q3	..	..	..	..	..	..	..
Q4	..	..	..	..	..	..	..
1970 Q1	..	..	..	..	..	..	..
Q2	25 529	22 898	..	..	..	..	..
Q3	..	..	..	..	..	..	..
Q4	..	..	..	..	..	..	..

See footnotes 1-4 on page 152.

See foornote 5 on page 153.

6 Vacancies notified to Jobcentres and remaining unfilled.

7 Quarterly vacancy figures relate to the average of the three months in each quarter.

Sources: Office for National Statistics;
Enquiries Columns 1-5 01633 812079; Columns 6,7 020 7533 6094

3.4 Jobs and Claimant Count[1]
United Kingdom

continued

Thousands, seasonally adjusted

		Employee jobs[2,3,4]				United Kingdom	
	Workforce jobs[2,3,4]	All industries	Manufacturing industry	Production industry	Service industries	Total claimant count, sa[5]	Job Centre vacancies [6,7]
	DYDC	BCAJ	YEJA	YEJF	YEJC	BCJD	DPCB
1971 Q1	..	..	..	..	..	553.1	..
Q2	25 205	22 557	..	..	..	632.0	..
Q3	..	..	..	..	..	670.3	..
Q4	..	..	..	..	..	740.4	..
1972 Q1	..	..	..	..	..	767.4	..
Q2	25 191	22 559	..	..	..	748.0	..
Q3	..	..	..	..	..	699.7	..
Q4	..	..	..	..	..	662.1	..
1973 Q1	..	..	..	..	..	579.4	..
Q2	25 785	23 116	..	..	..	538.3	..
Q3	..	..	..	..	..	487.5	..
Q4	..	..	..	..	..	440.1	..
1974 Q1	..	..	..	..	..	483.4	..
Q2	25 867	23 245	..	..	..	500.2	..
Q3	..	..	..	..	..	525.1	..
Q4	..	..	..	..	..	547.7	..
1975 Q1	..	..	..	..	..	612.9	..
Q2	25 779	23 162	..	..	..	730.7	..
Q3	..	..	..	..	..	847.2	..
Q4	..	..	..	..	..	967.2	..
1976 Q1	..	..	..	..	..	1 040.0	..
Q2	25 550	22 973	..	..	..	1 081.3	..
Q3	..	..	..	..	..	1 102.5	..
Q4	..	..	..	..	..	1 103.9	..
1977 Q1	..	..	..	..	..	1 108.8	..
Q2	25 584	23 056	..	..	..	1 128.9	..
Q3	..	..	..	..	..	1 178.7	..
Q4	..	..	..	..	..	1 185.2	..
1978 Q1	..	..	..	..	..	1 155.5	..
Q2	25 738	23 210	6 851	7 568	13 887	1 142.7	..
Q3	25 834	23 302	6 845	7 558	13 991	1 136.5	..
Q4	26 002	23 470	6 844	7 558	14 142	1 098.0	..
1979 Q1	26 039	23 509	6 831	7 546	14 193	1 101.7	..
Q2	26 134	23 603	6 824	7 541	14 280	1 070.3	..
Q3	26 206	23 637	6 796	7 514	14 334	1 042.7	..
Q4	26 251	23 649	6 747	7 466	14 391	1 039.9	..
1980 Q1	26 192	23 555	6 653	7 372	14 397	1 094.0	181.5
Q2	26 093	23 419	6 528	7 242	14 399	1 215.1	152.4
Q3	25 843	23 130	6 319	7 033	14 331	1 412.6	113.4
Q4	25 557	22 808	6 128	6 833	14 253	1 682.3	89.5
1981 Q1	25 319	22 538	5 978	6 670	14 177	1 912.6	88.7
Q2	25 118	22 302	5 857	6 546	14 112	2 105.3	83.4
Q3	24 990	22 158	5 771	6 454	14 096	2 242.6	90.2
Q4	24 828	21 984	5 674	6 347	14 059	2 349.3	102.1
1982 Q1	24 785	21 930	5 620	6 284	14 077	2 414.6	112.4
Q2	24 681	21 815	5 522	6 178	14 064	2 473.8	114.6
Q3	24 554	21 675	5 418	6 068	14 038	2 555.1	112.9
Q4	24 388	21 495	5 314	5 955	13 970	2 644.1	115.5
1983 Q1	24 346	21 429	5 258	5 890	13 991	2 704.7	124.0
Q2	24 403	21 464	5 209	5 829	14 091	2 758.7	134.1
Q3	24 654	21 524	5 157	5 771	14 201	2 781.5	144.7
Q4	24 834	21 568	5 119	5 724	14 294	2 802.6	146.5
1984 Q1	24 978	21 611	5 106	5 699	14 368	2 842.7	148.1
Q2	25 085	21 641	5 101	5 688	14 422	2 860.0	150.7
Q3	25 172	21 696	5 076	5 658	14 500	2 901.2	151.2
Q4	25 277	21 768	5 067	5 643	14 588	2 947.1	150.7

See footnotes 1-4 on page 152.

See footnote 5 on page 153.

6 Vacancies notified to Jobcentres and remaining unfilled.

7 Quarterly vacancy figures relate to the average of the three months in each quarter.

Sources: Office for National Statistics;
Enquiries Columns 1-5 01633 812079; Columns 6,7 5 020 7533 6094

3.4 Jobs and Claimant Count[1]

United Kingdom

continued

Thousands, seasonally adjusted

		Employee jobs[2,3,4]				United Kingdom	
	Workforce jobs[2,3,4]	All industries	Manufacturing industry	Production industry	Service industries	Total claimant count, sa[5]	Job Centre vacancies [6,7]
	DYDC	BCAJ	YEJA	YEJF	YEJC	BCJD	DPCB
1985 Q1	25 352	21 807	5 061	5 634	14 642	2 974.9	157.8
Q2	25 384	21 827	5 050	5 611	14 697	2 995.8	164.3
Q3	25 422	21 840	5 046	5 592	14 741	2 999.1	162.9
Q4	25 421	21 828	5 013	5 547	14 786	3 019.1	163.3
1986 Q1	25 408	21 807	4 986	5 506	14 819	3 061.3	170.8
Q2	25 432	21 790	4 928	5 438	14 876	3 082.2	177.9
Q3	25 513	21 790	4 890	5 387	14 931	3 083.2	199.4
Q4	25 588	21 801	4 863	5 348	14 980	3 039.9	207.1
1987 Q1	25 675	21 831	4 839	5 313	15 037	2 968.6	215.1
Q2	25 949	21 994	4 863	5 333	15 171	2 854.8	228.0
Q3	26 207	22 155	4 866	5 333	15 315	2 720.9	240.1
Q4	26 477	22 373	4 881	5 342	15 516	2 574.1	258.3
1988 Q1	26 702	22 549	4 902	5 356	15 663	2 447.9	250.9
Q2	26 887	22 685	4 907	5 353	15 806	2 317.1	254.3
Q3	27 126	22 840	4 907	5 350	15 966	2 182.5	245.7
Q4	27 349	22 928	4 912	5 350	16 049	2 064.9	243.6
1989 Q1	27 649	23 092	4 913	5 346	16 203	1 920.8	227.0
Q2	27 740	23 099	4 900	5 328	16 216	1 790.2	220.7
Q3	27 830	23 190	4 902	5 320	16 307	1 711.1	220.4
Q4	27 928	23 284	4 864	5 279	16 445	1 650.0	210.0
1990 Q1	27 939	23 303	4 825	5 235	16 501	1 595.7	194.5
Q2	28 013	23 353	4 780	5 186	16 601	1 574.0	192.3
Q3	27 913	23 318	4 726	5 125	16 640	1 640.9	168.3
Q4	27 696	23 153	4 618	5 010	16 612	1 782.0	139.5
1991 Q1	27 392	22 899	4 488	4 873	16 532	1 970.5	137.6
Q2	27 103	22 682	4 362	4 742	16 478	2 208.1	111.9
Q3	26 855	22 555	4 283	4 653	16 476	2 389.2	109.2
Q4	26 650	22 430	4 228	4 585	16 436	2 503.6	112.9
1992 Q1	26 596	22 443	4 182	4 532	16 525	2 603.2	117.8
Q2	26 406	22 335	4 137	4 481	16 500	2 690.9	118.6
Q3	26 063	22 007	4 046	4 383	16 298	2 772.9	117.3
Q4	25 964	21 937	3 961	4 285	16 340	2 899.2	114.8
1993 Q1	26 011	21 975	3 960	4 276	16 410	2 930.4	121.2
Q2	26 050	22 006	3 951	4 250	16 479	2 912.2	124.8
Q3	26 074	22 081	3 935	4 225	16 589	2 869.6	129.5
Q4	26 172	22 080	3 938	4 219	16 608	2 794.3	135.9
1994 Q1	26 173	22 074	3 946	4 219	16 598	2 737.4	142.2
Q2	26 198	22 084	3 967	4 231	16 603	2 651.3	150.1
Q3	26 359	22 251	3 988	4 240	16 764	2 557.1	163.1
Q4	26 434	22 298	4 018	4 264	16 813	2 448.6	176.6
1995 Q1	26 445	22 345	4 055	4 298	16 857	2 362.6	175.7
Q2	26 492	22 414	4 069	4 308	16 912	2 306.9	184.8
Q3	26 499	22 430	4 075	4 310	16 932	2 259.4	182.7
Q4	26 639	22 586	4 126	4 363	17 038	2 229.8	184.5
1996 Q1	26 614	22 582	4 128	4 360	17 048	2 194.2	192.2
Q2	26 769	22 728	4 110	4 339	17 192	2 152.9	210.4
Q3	26 858	22 799	4 138	4 368	17 277	2 076.7	239.7
Q4	26 925	22 877	4 145	4 370	17 327	1 926.1	257.2
1997 Q1	27 071	23 057	4 149	4 375	17 480	1 759.0	277.1
Q2	27 305	23 305	4 173	4 400	17 616	1 617.8	280.2
Q3	27 344	23 349	4 151	4 372	17 647	1 524.9	293.5
Q4	27 493	23 562	4 172	4 390	17 783	1 436.3	282.4
1998 Q1	27 696	23 768	4 206	4 424	17 923	1 384.3	282.2
Q2	27 625	23 798	4 194	4 410	17 972	1 351.5	296.0
Q3	27 751	23 941	4 180	4 397	18 141	1 332.4	302.6
Q4	27 781	23 968	4 121	4 338	18 229	1 323.0	302.4
1999 Q1	27 787	23 999	4 083	4 300	18 306	1 308.1	301.7
Q2	27 899	24 060	4 049	4 264	18 369	1 275.4	302.7
Q3	27 897	24 177	4 018	4 231	18 516	1 222.0	312.7
Q4	27 993	24 258	4 006	4 214	18 585	1 186.6	339.7
2000 Q1	27 958	24 240	3 985	4 191	18 544	1 152.8	344.5
Q2	..	..	..	..	..	1 108.5	355.3

See footnotes 1-4 on page 152.

See footnote 5 on page 153.

6 Vacancies notified to Jobcentres and remaining unfilled.

7 Quarterly vacancy figures relate to the average of the three months in each quarter.

Sources: Office for National Statistics;

Enquiries Columns 1-5 01633 812079; Columns 6,7 020 7533 6094

3.5 Regional claimant count rates [1,2,3]
by Government Office Region

Percentages, seasonally adjusted[6]

	North East[4]	North West[4,5]	Yorkshire and the Humber[4]	East Midlands[4]	West Midlands[4]	East[4]	London[4]
	DPDM	IBWC	DPBI	DPBJ	DPBN	DPDP	DPDQ
1965 Q1	..	..	1.0	0.7	0.6	..	..
Q2	..	..	1.0	0.8	0.6	..	..
Q3	..	..	1.1	0.9	0.7	..	..
Q4	..	..	1.0	0.9	0.6	..	..
1966 Q1	..	..	0.8	0.8	0.5	..	..
Q2	..	..	0.9	0.8	0.6	..	..
Q3	..	..	1.1	1.0	0.7	..	..
Q4	..	..	1.4	1.3	1.2	..	..
1967 Q1	..	..	1.5	1.4	1.4	..	..
Q2	..	..	1.8	1.6	1.7	..	..
Q3	..	..	1.9	1.7	1.9	..	..
Q4	..	..	2.1	1.7	2.0	..	..
1968 Q1	..	..	2.3	1.8	2.0	..	..
Q2	..	..	2.4	1.8	2.0	..	..
Q3	..	..	2.5	1.8	1.9	..	..
Q4	..	..	2.5	1.9	1.9	..	..
1969 Q1	..	..	2.5	1.9	1.7	..	..
Q2	..	..	2.5	1.9	1.7	..	..
Q3	..	..	2.5	1.9	1.7	..	..
Q4	..	..	2.6	1.9	1.8	..	..
1970 Q1	..	..	2.7	2.1	1.8	..	..
Q2	..	..	2.8	2.2	1.9	..	..
Q3	..	..	2.8	2.2	1.9	..	..
Q4	..	..	2.7	2.2	2.0	..	..
1971 Q1	..	..	3.0	2.4	2.2	..	..
Q2	..	..	3.3	2.7	2.5	..	..
Q3	..	..	3.8	2.9	2.9	..	..
Q4	..	..	4.2	3.0	3.3	..	..
1972 Q1	..	..	4.3	3.2	3.7	..	..
Q2	..	..	4.4	3.2	3.8	..	..
Q3	..	..	4.0	2.9	3.5	..	..
Q4	..	..	3.8	2.8	3.2	..	..
1973 Q1	..	..	3.4	2.5	2.8	..	..
Q2	..	..	2.9	2.1	2.3	..	..
Q3	..	..	2.7	2.0	2.1	..	..
Q4	..	..	2.4	1.8	1.8	..	..
1974 Q1[5]	..	..	2.5	1.9	2.0	..	..
Q2	..	..	2.0	1.6	1.7	..	1.2
Q3	..	..	2.0	1.6	1.6	..	1.2
Q4	..	..	2.1	1.8	1.8	..	1.3
1975 Q1	..	..	2.2	2.0	2.1	..	1.5
Q2	..	..	2.7	2.4	2.7	..	1.8
Q3	..	..	3.0	2.8	3.3	..	2.2
Q4	..	..	3.5	3.1	4.0	..	2.6
1976 Q1	..	..	3.8	3.3	4.3	..	3.0
Q2	..	..	3.9	3.4	4.3	..	3.2
Q3	..	..	3.9	3.5	4.3	..	3.3
Q4	..	..	3.8	3.4	4.1	..	3.4
1977 Q1	..	..	3.7	3.4	4.1	..	3.4
Q2	..	..	3.8	3.5	4.1	..	3.4
Q3	..	..	4.1	3.7	4.2	..	3.4
Q4	..	..	4.2	3.7	4.1	..	3.4
1978 Q1	..	..	4.1	3.6	3.9	..	3.2
Q2	..	..	4.2	3.6	4.0	..	3.1
Q3	..	..	4.2	3.6	4.0	..	3.0
Q4	..	..	4.1	3.5	3.9	..	2.9

1 The seasonally adjusted figures, now relate only to claimants aged 18 or over, in order to maintain the consistent series, available back to 1971 for Great Britain, Northern Ireland and the United Kingdom (1974 for Wales and scotland; 1986 for the Government Office Regions), allowing for the effect of the change in benefit regulations for under 18 year olds from September 1988. (See pages 398 - 400 of the November 1995 , *Labour Market Trends*). The denominators used to calculate claimant count rates are the sum of the appropriate mid-year estimates of employee jobs and the claimant count, the self-employed, HM Forces and participants in work-related Government training programmes. Recent figures are based on mid-1998 estimates.

2 Figures for the four quarters relate to January, April, July and October.

3 From April 1974, rates in this table apply to claimants of unemployment-related benefits at Jobcentres. Prior to April 1974 the rates apply to registrants at employment offices and career offices.

4 New geographical boundaries were introduced in May 1997 for UK regions. The standard statistical regions have been replaced by Government Office Regions.

5 Includes Merseyside.

6 The consistent seasonally adjusted series relating to regions started in 1974 and hence figures from after that date are not comparable with those before.

Source: Office for National Statistics; Enquiries 020 7533 6094

3.5 Regional claimant count rates [1,2,3]
by Government Office Region

continued

Percentages, seasonally adjusted[5]

	South East[4]	South West[4]	Wales[4]	Scotland[4]	Great Britain[4]	Northern Ireland[4]	United Kingdom[4]
	DPDR	DPBM	DPBP	DPBQ	DPAJ	DPBR	BCJE
1965 Q1	..	1.4	2.3	3.0	1.3	5.9	1.4
Q2	..	1.5	2.4	2.8	1.3	6.0	1.4
Q3	..	1.6	2.4	2.8	1.4	6.0	1.5
Q4	..	1.5	2.6	2.7	1.3	5.8	1.4
1966 Q1	..	1.5	2.5	2.5	1.2	5.4	1.3
Q2	..	1.5	2.5	2.5	1.2	5.5	1.3
Q3	..	1.7	2.7	2.7	1.4	5.9	1.5
Q4	..	2.2	3.3	3.1	1.7	6.5	1.8
1967 Q1	..	2.3	3.6	3.4	1.9	7.0	2.2
Q2	..	2.4	3.7	3.6	2.1	7.5	2.3
Q3	..	2.5	4.0	3.7	2.3	7.4	2.4
Q4	..	2.4	3.9	3.7	2.3	7.1	2.4
1968 Q1	..	2.5	4.0	3.9	2.4	6.7	2.4
Q2	..	2.5	3.9	3.7	2.3	7.0	2.5
Q3	..	2.4	3.9	3.7	2.4	7.0	2.4
Q4	..	2.5	3.8	3.6	2.3	7.2	2.4
1969 Q1	..	2.5	3.9	3.7	2.3	7.1	2.4
Q2	..	2.6	3.9	3.5	2.3	6.9	2.4
Q3	..	2.7	3.9	3.7	2.3	6.7	2.4
Q4	..	2.7	4.0	3.6	2.3	6.7	2.4
1970 Q1	..	2.7	3.9	3.8	2.4	6.5	2.5
Q2	..	2.8	3.9	3.9	2.5	6.5	2.5
Q3	..	2.7	3.7	4.1	2.5	6.7	2.6
Q4	..	2.7	3.6	4.4	2.5	6.7	2.6
1971 Q1	..	2.9	3.9	4.8	2.1	5.3	2.2
Q2	..	3.2	4.1	5.3	2.4	5.4	2.5
Q3	..	3.3	4.6	5.8	2.6	5.7	2.6
Q4	..	3.5	4.8	6.2	2.8	6.0	2.9
1972 Q1	..	3.7	5.0	6.5	2.9	6.0	3.0
Q2	..	3.6	5.0	6.6	2.9	6.0	2.9
Q3	..	3.3	4.7	6.1	2.7	5.5	2.8
Q4	..	3.1	4.5	6.0	2.5	5.2	2.6
1973 Q1	..	2.7	4.0	5.4	2.2	4.9	2.2
Q2	..	2.5	3.5	4.8	2.0	4.6	2.1
Q3	..	2.4	3.4	4.4	1.8	4.2	1.9
Q4	..	2.2	3.1	3.8	1.7	4.0	1.7
1974 Q1[5]	..	2.3	3.3	3.9	1.8	4.1	1.9
Q2	..	1.8	2.8	3.0	1.9	4.0	1.9
Q3	..	2.1	2.9	3.1	2.0	4.2	2.0
Q4	..	2.2	2.9	3.0	2.1	4.5	2.1
1975 Q1	..	2.6	3.2	3.1	2.3	4.6	2.4
Q2	..	3.1	3.8	3.4	2.7	5.2	2.8
Q3	..	3.7	4.4	4.0	3.2	5.7	3.3
Q4	..	4.0	4.9	4.4	3.6	6.5	3.7
1976 Q1	..	4.3	5.1	4.6	3.9	6.6	4.0
Q2	..	4.5	5.2	5.0	4.1	7.0	4.1
Q3	..	4.6	5.2	5.2	4.1	7.2	4.2
Q4	..	4.7	5.2	5.4	4.1	7.3	4.2
1977 Q1	..	4.7	5.2	5.5	4.1	7.4	4.2
Q2	..	4.7	5.3	5.7	4.2	7.6	4.3
Q3	..	4.9	5.6	6.0	4.4	7.8	4.5
Q4	..	4.9	5.8	6.1	4.4	7.9	4.5
1978 Q1	..	4.7	5.6	6.0	4.3	7.9	4.4
Q2	..	4.5	5.7	5.9	4.2	8.1	4.3
Q3	..	4.4	5.7	5.8	4.2	8.2	4.3
Q4	..	4.2	5.5	5.7	4.1	7.9	4.1

1 See footnote on page 160.
2 Figures for the four quarters relate to January, April July and October.
3 From April 1974 rates in this table apply to claimants of unemployment -related benefits at Jobcentres. Prior to April 1974 the rates apply to registrants at employment offices and careers offices.
4 New geographical boundaries were introduced in May 1997 for UK regions. The standard statistical regions have been replaced by Government Office Regions.
5 The consistent seasonally adjusted series relating to regions started in 1974 and hence figures from after that date are not comparable with those before.

Source: Office for National Statistics; Enquiries 020 7533 6094

3.5 Regional claimant count rates [1,2,3]
by Government Office Region

continued

Percentages, seasonally adjusted[6]

	North East[4]	North West[4,5]	Yorkshire and the Humber[4]	East Midlands[4]	West Midlands[4]	East[4]	London[4]
	DPDM	IBWC	DPBI	DPBJ	DPBN	DPDP	DPDQ
1979 Q1	..	..	4.2	3.4	3.9	..	2.8
Q2	..	..	4.0	3.2	3.9	..	2.7
Q3	..	..	3.9	3.1	3.9	..	2.5
Q4	..	..	3.9	3.2	4.0	..	2.5
1980 Q1	..	..	4.1	3.3	4.1	..	2.6
Q2	..	..	4.7	3.8	4.7	..	2.9
Q3	..	..	5.5	4.7	5.8	..	3.3
Q4	..	..	6.7	5.7	7.3	..	4.1
1981 Q1	..	..	7.8	6.6	8.6	..	4.6
Q2	..	..	8.6	7.2	9.7	..	5.2
Q3	..	..	9.1	7.5	10.3	..	5.7
Q4	..	..	9.5	7.9	10.9	..	6.1
1982 Q1	..	..	9.7	8.0	11.3	..	6.4
Q2	..	..	10.0	8.1	11.5	..	6.6
Q3	..	..	10.4	8.4	11.8	..	6.9
Q4	..	..	10.8	8.7	12.2	..	7.1
1983 Q1	..	..	11.1	9.1	12.5	..	7.4
Q2	..	..	11.3	9.3	12.8	..	7.7
Q3	..	..	11.3	9.4	12.7	..	7.9
Q4	..	..	11.3	9.5	12.6	..	8.1
1984 Q1	..	..	11.3	9.5	12.4	..	8.0
Q2	..	..	11.4	9.5	12.4	..	8.1
Q3	..	..	11.6	9.7	12.5	..	8.3
Q4	..	..	11.8	9.9	12.6	..	8.5
1985 Q1	..	..	11.7	9.7	12.6	..	8.6
Q2	..	..	11.8	9.7	12.6	..	8.7
Q3	..	..	11.8	9.6	12.6	..	8.7
Q4	..	..	12.0	9.7	12.6	..	8.8
1986 Q1	..	..	12.3	9.8	12.7	..	9.0
Q2	16.6	..	12.4	9.8	12.7	8.2	9.1
Q3	16.5	..	12.4	9.8	12.7	8.2	9.2
Q4	16.2	..	12.2	9.7	12.5	8.0	9.0
1987 Q1	15.9	..	11.9	9.4	12.1	7.8	8.7
Q2	15.6	..	11.5	9.1	11.6	7.3	8.3
Q3	15.0	..	11.0	8.6	11.0	6.8	8.0
Q4	14.3	..	10.4	8.1	10.3	6.2	7.5
1988 Q1	13.7	..	9.9	7.6	9.6	5.7	7.2
Q2	13.2	..	9.5	7.2	9.0	5.1	6.8
Q3	12.6	..	9.0	6.8	8.4	4.6	6.3
Q4	12.2	..	8.5	6.4	7.8	4.2	5.9
1989 Q1	11.9	..	7.9	5.8	7.1	3.6	5.5
Q2	11.1	..	7.3	5.4	6.5	3.3	5.1
Q3	10.5	..	7.1	5.1	6.1	3.2	4.9
Q4	9.9	..	6.8	5.0	5.9	3.2	4.7
1990 Q1	9.6	..	6.5	4.8	5.6	3.1	4.7
Q2	9.4	..	6.3	4.8	5.4	3.2	4.6
Q3	9.5	..	6.5	5.1	5.7	3.6	5.0
Q4	9.8	..	7.0	5.5	6.1	4.3	5.6
1991 Q1	10.3	..	7.7	6.1	7.0	5.1	6.6
Q2	11.0	..	8.5	6.9	8.1	6.1	7.7
Q3	11.4	..	9.0	7.6	8.9	6.8	8.5
Q4	11.5	..	9.2	8.0	9.4	7.3	9.1
1992 Q1	11.7	..	9.4	8.5	9.8	7.9	9.7
Q2	11.8	..	9.6	8.8	10.1	8.3	10.1
Q3	12.0	..	9.9	9.0	10.3	8.8	10.6
Q4	12.5	..	10.3	9.4	10.8	9.3	11.1

1 See footnote on page 160.

2 Figures for the four quarters relate to January, April, July and October.

3 From April 1974 rates in this table apply to claimants of unemployment- related benefits at Jobcentres. Prior to April 1974 the rates apply to registrants at employment offices and careers offices.

4 New geographical boundaries were introduced in May 1997 for UK regions. The standard statistical regions have been replaced by Government Office Regions.

5 Includes Merseyside.

6 The consistent seasonally adjusted series relating to regions started in 1974 and hence figures from after that date are not comparable with those before.

Source: Office for National Statistics; Enquiries 020 7533 6094

3.5 Regional claimant count rates [1,2,3]

by Government Office Region

continued

Percentages, seasonally adjusted[5]

	South East[4]	South West[4]	Wales[4]	Scotland[4]	Great Britain[4]	Northern Ireland[4]	United Kingdom[4]
	DPDR	DPBM	DPBP	DPBQ	DPAJ	DPBR	BCJE
1979 Q1	..	4.1	5.5	5.7	4.0	7.8	4.1
Q2	..	3.9	5.4	5.6	3.9	7.8	4.0
Q3	..	3.8	5.1	5.6	3.8	7.8	3.9
Q4	..	3.7	5.0	5.7	3.8	7.8	3.9
1980 Q1	..	3.6	5.4	6.0	4.0	8.0	4.1
Q2	..	3.9	6.1	6.5	4.4	8.5	4.5
Q3	..	4.6	7.2	7.1	5.1	9.6	5.2
Q4	..	5.3	8.4	8.1	6.1	11.0	6.2
1981 Q1	..	5.8	9.4	8.9	7.0	11.9	7.1
Q2	..	6.5	10.1	9.7	7.7	12.5	7.8
Q3	..	6.8	10.7	10.3	8.2	12.7	8.3
Q4	..	7.1	11.1	10.6	8.6	13.1	8.7
1982 Q1	..	7.3	11.5	10.9	8.9	13.5	9.0
Q2	..	7.4	11.7	11.1	9.1	14.0	9.2
Q3	..	7.7	12.1	11.4	9.4	14.3	9.5
Q4	..	8.0	12.4	11.7	9.7	15.0	9.9
1983 Q1	..	8.2	12.7	12.0	10.0	14.7	10.1
Q2	..	8.4	12.9	12.2	10.2	15.0	10.3
Q3	..	8.5	12.8	12.3	10.3	15.3	10.4
Q4	..	8.6	12.9	12.3	10.3	15.4	10.5
1984 Q1	..	8.4	12.7	12.4	10.2	15.4	10.4
Q2	..	8.5	12.9	12.4	10.3	15.5	10.4
Q3	..	8.7	13.1	12.5	10.4	15.4	10.6
Q4	..	8.9	13.4	12.6	10.6	15.4	10.7
1985 Q1	..	8.9	13.5	12.6	10.5	15.3	10.7
Q2	..	9.0	13.6	12.9	10.6	15.4	10.7
Q3	..	9.0	13.6	12.9	10.6	15.5	10.8
Q4	..	9.1	13.6	13.0	10.7	15.9	10.8
1986 Q1	..	9.1	13.8	13.1	10.8	16.3	10.9
Q2	7.0	9.2	13.7	13.2	10.9	16.7	11.0
Q3	7.0	9.2	13.5	13.4	10.9	17.0	11.0
Q4	6.8	9.0	13.1	13.5	10.7	17.1	10.9
1987 Q1	6.6	8.6	12.8	13.5	10.4	16.7	10.5
Q2	6.1	8.1	12.2	13.2	10.0	16.5	10.1
Q3	5.7	7.7	11.8	12.7	9.5	16.3	9.6
Q4	5.2	7.2	11.2	12.2	8.9	15.9	9.1
1988 Q1	4.6	6.7	10.5	11.8	8.4	15.3	8.6
Q2	4.2	6.2	10.1	11.3	8.0	15.1	8.1
Q3	3.8	5.7	9.5	10.8	7.5	14.9	7.7
Q4	3.5	5.3	9.1	10.5	7.1	14.6	7.3
1989 Q1	3.0	4.7	8.1	10.0	6.5	14.5	6.7
Q2	2.8	4.4	7.5	9.4	6.0	14.1	6.2
Q3	2.7	4.2	7.0	9.0	5.8	13.8	6.0
Q4	2.7	4.0	6.7	8.6	5.5	13.4	5.8
1990 Q1	2.6	3.8	6.6	8.3	5.3	12.9	5.5
Q2	2.7	3.9	6.4	8.0	5.3	12.8	5.5
Q3	3.0	4.3	6.6	7.9	5.5	12.6	5.7
Q4	3.6	4.9	7.2	8.1	6.0	12.7	6.2
1991 Q1	4.5	5.7	7.9	8.2	6.7	12.6	6.9
Q2	5.5	6.6	8.8	8.6	7.6	12.8	7.7
Q3	6.2	7.3	9.3	8.8	8.2	12.9	8.4
Q4	6.7	7.8	9.5	9.0	8.6	13.2	8.8
1992 Q1	7.3	8.5	9.6	9.0	9.0	13.5	9.1
Q2	7.7	8.9	9.8	9.2	9.3	13.7	9.5
Q3	8.1	9.3	9.9	9.3	9.6	13.8	9.7
Q4	8.6	9.7	10.3	9.6	10.1	13.8	10.2

1 See footnote on page 160.

2 Figures for the four quarters relate to January, April, July and October.

3 From April 1974, rates in this table apply to claimants of unemployment- related benefits at Jobcentres. Prior to April 1974 the rates apply to registrants at employment offices and careers offices.

4 New geographical boundaries were introduced in May 1997 for UK regions. The standard statistical regions have been replaced by Government Office Regions.

5 The consistent seasonally adjusted series relating to regions started in 1974 and hence figures from after that date are not comparable with those before.

Source: Office for National Statistics; Enquiries 020 7533 6094

3.5 Regional claimant count rates [1,2,3] by Government Office Region

continued

Percentages, seasonally adjusted[6]

	North East[4]	North West[4,5]	Yorkshire and the Humber[4]	East Midlands[4]	West Midlands[4]	East[4]	London[4]
	DPDM	IBWC	DPBI	DPBJ	DPBN	DPDP	DPDQ
1993 Q1	12.7	..	10.3	9.6	11.0	9.6	11.5
Q2	12.9	..	10.3	9.5	10.9	9.5	11.6
Q3	12.9	..	10.1	9.4	10.7	9.3	11.5
Q4	12.7	..	9.9	9.2	10.3	8.9	11.3
1994 Q1	12.7	10.5	9.9	9.0	10.4	8.6	11.1
Q2	12.4	10.2	9.7	8.8	10.0	8.2	10.8
Q3	12.1	9.8	9.4	8.5	9.6	7.8	10.5
Q4	11.9	9.4	9.2	8.2	9.1	7.3	10.1
1995 Q1	11.5	9.0	8.7	7.7	8.4	6.7	9.6
Q2	11.3	8.6	8.6	7.4	8.2	6.6	9.5
Q3	11.2	8.5	8.4	7.3	7.9	6.5	9.3
Q4	11.0	8.3	8.3	7.2	7.8	6.3	9.2
1996 Q1	10.8	8.1	8.2	7.1	7.6	6.3	9.0
Q2	10.6	8.0	8.1	6.9	7.4	6.1	8.7
Q3	10.1	7.8	7.8	6.6	7.1	5.8	8.5
Q4	9.4	7.5	7.3	6.1	6.6	5.3	7.9
1997 Q1	8.8	6.9	6.8	5.4	6.0	4.7	7.2
Q2	8.4	6.4	6.4	5.0	5.6	4.2	6.6
Q3	8.2	5.9	6.2	4.7	5.3	3.9	6.1
Q4	8.0	5.6	5.9	4.3	5.0	3.6	5.7
1998 Q1	7.8	5.4	5.6	4.1	4.8	3.4	5.5
Q2	7.5	5.3	5.5	4.0	4.7	3.3	5.4
Q3	7.4	5.2	5.5	4.0	4.7	3.3	5.2
Q4	7.5	5.2	5.4	4.0	4.7	3.2	5.1
1999 Q1	7.5	5.1	5.4	4.0	4.8	3.2	5.0
Q2	7.4	5.1	5.2	3.9	4.7	3.1	4.8
Q3	7.1	4.9	5.0	3.8	4.6	2.9	4.7
Q4	6.8	4.8	4.8	3.7	4.4	2.9	4.6
2000 Q1	6.9	5.6	4.8	3.6	4.3	2.7	4.3
Q2	6.7	5.4	4.6	3.5	4.2	2.5	4.1

1 See footnote on page 160.
2 Figures for the four quarters relate to January, April, July and October.
3 From April 1974, rates in this table apply to claimants of unemployment- related benefits at Jobcentres. Prior to April 1974 the rates apply to registrants at employment offices and careers offices.
4 New geographical boundaries were introduced in May 1997 for UK regions. The standard statistical regions have been replaced by Government Office Regions.
5 Includes Merseyside.
6 The consistent seasonally adjusted series relating to regions started in 1974 and hence figures from after that date are not comparable with those before.

Source: Office for National Statistics; Enquiries 020 7533 6094

3.5 Regional claimant count rates [1,2,3]
by Government Office Region

continued

Percentages, seasonally adjusted[5]

	South East[4]	South West[4]	Wales[4]	Scotland[4]	Great Britain[4]	Northern Ireland[4]	United Kingdom[4]
	DPDR	DPBM	DPBP	DPBQ	DPAJ	DPBR	BCJE
1993 Q1	8.8	9.7	10.3	9.7	10.3	13.9	10.4
Q2	8.7	9.5	10.2	9.7	10.2	13.7	10.3
Q3	8.6	9.3	10.2	9.6	10.1	13.6	10.2
Q4	8.2	9.0	10.0	9.4	9.8	13.4	9.9
1994 Q1	7.8	8.6	9.8	9.5	9.7	13.0	9.7
Q2	7.4	8.2	9.5	9.3	9.3	12.8	9.4
Q3	7.0	7.9	9.1	9.1	9.0	12.5	9.1
Q4	6.6	7.5	8.7	8.7	8.6	12.1	8.7
1995 Q1	6.1	7.0	8.5	8.2	8.1	11.6	8.2
Q2	6.0	6.8	8.4	7.9	7.9	11.3	8.0
Q3	5.8	6.7	8.4	7.7	7.8	11.1	7.9
Q4	5.7	6.6	8.3	7.7	7.7	11.0	7.8
1996 Q1	5.4	6.5	8.2	7.8	7.5	11.0	7.6
Q2	5.2	6.3	8.2	7.8	7.4	11.0	7.5
Q3	5.0	6.0	7.9	7.7	7.1	11.1	7.2
Q4	4.5	5.5	7.5	7.3	6.6	9.9	6.7
1997 Q1	3.9	5.0	7.0	7.0	6.0	8.8	6.1
Q2	3.5	4.5	6.5	6.5	5.6	8.2	5.6
Q3	3.2	4.1	6.2	6.2	5.2	7.9	5.3
Q4	3.0	3.8	5.9	5.9	4.9	7.7	5.0
1998 Q1	2.8	3.6	5.7	5.8	4.7	7.7	4.8
Q2	2.7	3.5	5.6	5.7	4.6	7.4	4.7
Q3	2.6	3.4	5.5	5.7	4.6	7.3	4.6
Q4	2.6	3.4	5.5	5.6	4.5	7.3	4.6
1999 Q1	2.6	3.3	5.5	5.6	4.5	7.2	4.5
Q2	2.5	3.2	5.4	5.5	4.4	6.8	4.4
Q3	2.4	3.0	5.0	5.2	4.2	6.3	4.2
Q4	2.3	2.9	4.9	5.1	4.1	5.9	4.1
2000 Q1	2.1	2.7	4.7	5.1	3.9	5.6	4.0
Q2	2.0	2.6	4.6	4.9	3.8	5.4	3.8

1 See footnote on page 160.

2 Figures for the four quarters relate to January, April, July and October.

3 From April 1974 unemployment rates apply to claimants at unemployment benefit offices. Prior to April 1974 the rates apply to registrants at employment offices and careers offices.

4 New geographical boundaries were introduced in May 1997 for UK regions. The standard statistical regions have been replaced by Government Office Regions.

5 The consistent seasonally adjusted series relating to regions started in 1974 and hence figures from after that date are not comparable with those before.

Source: Office for National Statistics; Enquiries 020 7533 6094

3.6 ILO unemployment rates [1,2]
by Government Office Region

Percentages, not seasonally adjusted

	North East	North West[3]	Yorkshire and the Humber	East Midlands	West Midlands	East	London	South East
	MGXK	YCZF	MGXN	MGXO	MGXP	MGXQ	MGXR	MGXS
1992 Q2	12.3	10.2	9.9	8.5	11.0	7.9	12.1	7.9
Q3	13.1	10.3	9.4	8.5	11.7	8.8	13.1	8.2
Q4	12.7	10.3	9.5	8.4	11.7	9.2	12.5	8.5
1993 Q1	12.8	11.5	10.2	9.5	12.3	9.2	13.5	8.6
Q2	12.6	10.6	10.4	9.1	11.7	9.1	13.2	8.0
Q3	13.7	10.6	10.6	8.8	11.6	9.4	14.2	8.3
Q4	12.2	10.2	10.2	7.9	11.4	8.8	14.4	7.8
1994 Q1	12.9	10.8	9.9	8.2	10.9	9.0	13.6	7.7
Q2	12.8	10.3	10.3	8.5	10.1	7.9	12.9	7.2
Q3	12.0	10.5	9.8	8.9	9.5	8.4	12.7	7.1
Q4	12.6	9.2	9.0	7.7	8.6	7.4	11.8	6.8
1995 Q1	11.9	9.1	9.1	7.8	8.8	7.8	11.7	7.2
Q2	11.7	9.1	8.4	7.3	8.6	7.4	11.8	6.3
Q3	11.4	9.6	8.9	6.9	9.2	7.9	12.3	6.7
Q4	10.8	8.3	7.7	6.9	8.2	6.9	11.6	6.1
1996 Q1	11.0	8.5	8.1	7.4	8.7	6.5	11.1	6.7
Q2	10.6	8.4	8.5	7.5	9.4	6.3	11.3	6.0
Q3	11.0	8.3	8.7	7.1	8.7	7.0	11.9	6.0
Q4	9.4	7.5	8.4	6.7	7.3	6.5	11.0	5.4
1997 Q1	10.0	7.0	8.1	6.2	7.3	6.1	10.0	5.3
Q2	10.1	7.1	7.6	6.0	6.8	6.3	9.0	5.1
Q3	8.9	7.7	7.6	5.2	7.6	5.8	9.7	4.9
Q4	8.0	6.8	6.8	5.0	6.2	5.2	9.1	4.3
1998 Q1	8.6	6.7	7.3	5.3	6.3	5.4	8.0	4.5
Q2	8.6	6.8	7.4	4.9	5.9	4.9	8.3	4.2
Q3	8.5	7.1	7.3	5.6	6.4	4.7	8.3	4.6
Q4	9.1	6.9	6.8	4.6	6.3	4.2	7.6	3.8

	South West	England	Wales	Scotland	Great Britain	Northern Ireland	United Kingdom
	MGXT	YCZG	MGXU	MGXV	MGYQ	MGXW	MGUK
1992 Q2	8.8	9.7	8.7	9.6	9.7	..	..
Q3	9.0	10.1	10.0	10.3	10.1	..	..
Q4	9.2	10.1	10.6	10.5	10.2	..	..
1993 Q1	10.1	10.8	10.7	10.5	10.7	..	..
Q2	9.0	10.3	9.9	10.4	10.3	..	..
Q3	8.6	10.5	9.8	10.0	10.4	..	..
Q4	8.4	10.1	10.1	9.7	10.1	..	..
1994 Q1	8.1	10.0	9.9	10.3	10.0	..	..
Q2	7.5	9.6	9.4	10.3	9.6	..	..
Q3	8.3	9.6	9.8	9.4	9.6	..	..
Q4	7.3	8.7	9.8	8.5	8.8	..	..
1995 Q1	8.1	8.9	9.6	8.6	8.9	11.2	9.0
Q2	7.6	8.5	8.5	9.0	8.6	10.9	8.6
Q3	7.5	8.9	8.5	9.3	8.9	10.7	8.9
Q4	7.0	8.1	8.0	8.7	8.1	10.3	8.2
1996 Q1	7.1	8.2	8.9	9.1	8.3	9.4	8.4
Q2	6.1	8.1	8.1	8.7	8.2	10.7	8.2
Q3	6.5	8.2	8.7	8.6	8.3	10.3	8.3
Q4	6.4	7.5	8.4	8.4	7.6	9.2	7.7
1997 Q1	5.9	7.2	8.2	8.7	7.4	8.7	7.4
Q2	5.7	6.9	8.1	8.8	7.1	8.0	7.1
Q3	5.3	6.9	7.7	8.3	7.0	8.7	7.1
Q4	5.0	6.2	6.8	7.0	6.3	8.7	6.4
1998 Q1	4.8	6.2	7.5	7.8	6.4	8.5	6.4
Q2	4.6	6.0	6.8	7.6	6.2	6.9	6.2
Q3	5.0	6.3	7.7	7.7	6.4	8.1	6.5
Q4	4.4	5.8	7.0	7.4	6.0	6.8	6.0

1 Government Office Regions came into effect in April 1994.It was decided that from May 1997 sub-national data should be published for these areas rather than standard statistical regions (SSRs). Data by standard statistical regions is available on request.

2 Data are from the Labour Force Survey. ILO unemployment rate is the percentage of economically active people who are unemployed on the ILO measure. Data relating to seasonal quarters are also available (for GB or UK) on request.

3 Includes Merseyside.

Source: Office for National Statistics; Enquiries 020 7533 6094

3.6 ILO unemployment rates [1,2]
by Government Office Region

continued

Percentages, seasonally adjusted

	North East	North West[3]	Yorkshire and the Humber	East Midlands	West Midlands	East	London	South East
	YCNC	YCND	YCNE	YCNF	YCNG	YCNH	YCNI	YCNJ
1992 Q2	12.3	10.3	9.6	8.4	11.0	8.2	12.4	8.1
Q3	12.9	10.0	9.2	8.4	11.5	8.5	12.7	8.1
Q4	13.0	10.6	9.7	8.8	12.0	9.2	12.5	8.6
1993 Q1	12.7	11.3	10.1	9.4	12.2	9.1	13.6	8.3
Q2	12.6	10.6	10.2	9.0	11.7	9.3	13.5	8.2
Q3	13.5	10.3	10.4	8.6	11.4	9.1	13.8	8.2
Q4	12.5	10.5	10.4	8.2	11.7	8.8	14.4	7.9
1994 Q1	12.8	10.7	9.8	8.0	10.8	8.9	13.8	7.4
Q2	12.8	10.3	10.1	8.3	10.1	8.1	13.2	7.4
Q3	11.8	10.2	9.5	8.8	9.2	8.0	12.3	7.0
Q4	13.0	9.4	9.2	8.0	8.9	7.5	11.8	6.9
1995 Q1	11.8	9.1	9.0	7.7	8.7	7.8	11.9	6.9
Q2	11.6	9.1	8.2	7.2	8.6	7.6	12.1	6.5
Q3	11.2	9.2	8.7	6.8	8.9	7.5	11.9	6.5
Q4	11.2	8.5	7.9	7.2	8.6	7.0	11.5	6.2
1996 Q1	10.9	8.5	7.9	7.3	8.6	6.5	11.3	6.4
Q2	10.4	8.5	8.4	7.3	9.4	6.4	11.6	6.1
Q3	10.8	7.9	8.4	7.0	8.3	6.7	11.5	5.8
Q4	9.8	7.7	8.6	7.0	7.7	6.6	11.0	5.5
1997 Q1	9.9	7.0	8.0	6.1	7.2	6.1	10.3	5.2
Q2	9.9	7.2	7.5	5.8	6.8	6.3	9.3	5.2
Q3	8.8	7.3	7.4	5.1	7.2	5.5	9.2	4.7
Q4	8.5	6.9	7.1	5.3	6.5	5.3	9.2	4.5
1998 Q1	8.5	6.8	7.1	5.2	6.2	5.4	8.2	4.3
Q2	8.4	6.9	7.3	4.8	5.9	4.9	8.6	4.3
Q3	8.3	6.8	7.2	5.4	6.0	4.5	7.8	4.5
Q4	9.7	7.1	7.1	4.9	6.6	4.3	7.7	4.0

	South West	England	Wales	Scotland	Great Britain	Northern Ireland[4]	United Kingdom
	YCNK	YCNL	YCNM	YCNN	YCNO	MGXW	MGSX
1992 Q2	9.0	9.8	9.1	9.5	9.8	..	9.8
Q3	8.9	9.9	10.0	10.3	9.9	..	10.0
Q4	9.4	10.3	10.4	10.9	10.4	..	10.4
1993 Q1	9.8	10.6	10.4	10.4	10.6	..	10.6
Q2	9.2	10.4	10.3	10.2	10.4	..	10.4
Q3	8.5	10.3	9.8	10.0	10.2	..	10.3
Q4	8.5	10.3	10.0	10.1	10.2	..	10.3
1994 Q1	7.8	9.9	9.7	10.2	9.9	..	10.0
Q2	7.7	9.7	9.8	10.1	9.7	..	9.7
Q3	8.2	9.3	9.8	9.3	9.3	..	9.4
Q4	7.4	8.9	9.7	8.9	8.9	..	9.0
1995 Q1	7.8	8.8	9.3	8.5	8.8	11.2	8.9
Q2	7.8	8.6	8.8	8.8	8.6	10.9	8.7
Q3	7.4	8.6	8.4	9.2	8.6	10.7	8.7
Q4	7.1	8.2	8.0	9.2	8.3	10.3	8.4
1996 Q1	6.9	8.2	8.6	9.0	8.2	9.4	8.3
Q2	6.3	8.2	8.3	8.6	8.2	10.7	8.3
Q3	6.4	8.0	8.6	8.5	8.0	10.3	8.1
Q4	6.5	7.7	8.5	8.9	7.8	9.2	7.9
1997 Q1	5.7	7.1	7.9	8.6	7.3	8.7	7.3
Q2	5.8	6.9	8.3	8.6	7.2	8.0	7.2
Q3	5.2	6.6	7.5	8.2	6.8	8.7	6.8
Q4	5.1	6.4	7.0	7.4	6.5	8.7	6.6
1998 Q1	4.6	6.1	7.2	7.7	6.3	8.5	6.4
Q2	4.8	6.1	6.9	7.5	6.3	6.9	6.3
Q3	4.9	6.0	7.5	7.6	6.2	8.1	6.3
Q4	4.5	6.0	7.2	7.8	6.2	6.8	6.2

See footnotes on page 166.

4 Estimates for Northern Ireland are not seasonally adjusted; the quarterly series starting in 1995 provides insufficient data to do this reliably.

Source: Office for National Statistics; Enquiries 020 7533 6094

3.6 ILO unemployment rates [1,2]
by Government Office Region

continued

Percentages, not seasonally adjusted

	North East	North West[3]	Yorkshire and the Humber	East Midlands	West Midlands	East	London	South East
	MGXK	YCZF	MGXN	MGXO	MGXP	MGXQ	MGXR	MGXS
1999 Q1	9.8	6.7	7.0	5.2	7.1	4.2	7.6	4.0
Q2	9.9	6.1	6.4	5.4	6.9	4.2	7.2	3.8
Q3	9.8	6.7	6.2	5.8	6.6	4.1	8.0	4.0
Q4	7.8	5.9	5.8	5.2	6.5	4.1	7.0	3.9
2000 Q1	9.2	6.0	6.6	5.2	6.2	3.9	7.5	3.6

	South West	England	Wales	Scotland	Great Britain	Northern Ireland	United Kingdom
	MGXT	YCZG	MGXU	MGXV	MGYQ	MGXW	MGUK
1999 Q1	5.0	6.0	7.4	7.6	6.2	7.2	6.2
Q2	4.3	5.7	7.4	7.3	5.9	7.6	6.0
Q3	4.5	5.9	7.5	7.1	6.1	7.3	6.1
Q4	4.1	5.4	7.2	6.8	5.6	6.6	5.6
2000 Q1	4.4	5.6	6.9	7.7	5.8	6.6	5.9

1 Government Office Regions came into effect in April 1994.It was decided that from May 1997 sub-national data should be published for these areas rather than standard statistical regions (SSRs). Data by standard statistical regions is available on request.

2 Data are from the Labour Force Survey. ILO unemployment rate is the percentage of economically active people who are unemployed on the ILO measure. Data relating to seasonal quarters are also available (for GB or UK) on request.

3 Includes Merseyside.

Source: Office for National Statistics; Enquiries 020 7533 6094

3.6 ILO unemployment rates [1,2]
by Government Office Region

continued

Percentages, seasonally adjusted

	North East	North West[3]	Yorkshire and the Humber	East Midlands	West Midlands	East	London	South East
	YCNC	YCND	YCNE	YCNF	YCNG	YCNH	YCNI	YCNJ
1999 Q1	9.7	6.7	6.8	5.1	7.0	4.2	7.8	3.9
Q2	9.6	6.3	6.3	5.3	6.9	4.2	7.4	3.9
Q3	9.7	6.3	6.1	5.6	6.3	4.0	7.5	3.8
Q4	8.4	6.0	6.1	5.6	6.8	4.2	7.1	4.1
2000 Q1	9.0	6.1	6.3	5.2	6.1	4.0	7.6	3.5

	South West	England	Wales	Scotland	Great Britain	Northern Ireland[4]	United Kingdom
	YCNK	YCNL	YCNM	YCNN	YCNO	MGXW	MGSX
1999 Q1	4.9	6.0	7.2	7.5	6.2	7.2	6.2
Q2	4.5	5.8	7.5	7.2	6.0	7.6	6.0
Q3	4.4	5.7	7.3	7.0	5.9	7.3	5.9
Q4	4.2	5.6	7.4	7.2	5.9	6.6	5.9
2000 Q1	4.3	5.5	6.8	7.5	5.8	6.6	5.8

See footnotes on page 166.

4 Estimates for Northern Ireland are not seasonally adjusted; the quarterly series starting in 1995 provides insufficient data to do this reliably.

Source: Office for National Statistics; Enquiries 020 7533 6094

3.7 Average earnings

1995 = 100, seasonally adjusted

	Average earnings (GB)[1]						
	Whole economy	Private sector	Public sector	Manufacturing industries	Production industries	Service industries	Private sector services
	LNMQ	LNKY	LNNJ	LNMR	LNMS	LNMT	JJGH
1990	79.5	79.5	79.4	75.7	75.4	80.8	81.3
1991	85.7	85.4	86.7	81.7	81.7	87.0	87.1
1992	90.8	90.0	93.6	87.1	87.2	92.1	91.4
1993	93.6	93.0	96.0	91.2	91.2	94.5	93.9
1994	97.0	96.7	98.2	95.8	95.7	97.5	97.3
1995	100.0	100.0	100.0	100.0	100.0	100.0	100.0
1996	103.6	103.7	103.0	104.3	104.3	103.4	103.6
1997	108.0	108.7	105.3	108.8	108.5	107.9	108.8
1998	113.5	114.7	108.8	113.7	113.4	113.4	115.3
1999	119.0	120.4	113.3	118.3	117.8	119.2	121.5
1990 Jan	75.9	75.9	75.9	72.4	72.0	77.2	77.8
Feb	76.4	76.5	75.9	73.0	72.6	77.6	78.5
Mar	76.3	76.3	76.5	72.2	72.4	78.1	77.8
Apr	77.9	78.0	77.6	75.0	74.2	79.2	80.1
May	78.6	78.8	78.3	74.8	74.5	80.1	80.8
Jun	79.6	79.7	79.1	76.0	75.6	80.9	81.6
Jul	80.2	80.2	79.3	76.4	76.1	81.4	82.4
Aug	80.5	80.5	80.9	76.7	76.6	81.8	82.5
Sep	81.2	81.1	81.6	77.6	77.3	82.4	82.8
Oct	81.7	81.5	82.2	77.6	77.4	83.0	83.3
Nov	82.3	82.2	82.5	78.2	77.9	83.8	84.1
Dec	82.8	83.1	82.7	78.9	78.6	84.0	84.5
1991 Jan	83.1	83.0	83.2	79.1	79.0	84.3	84.8
Feb	83.4	83.1	84.2	79.5	79.4	84.5	84.7
Mar	82.9	82.5	84.5	77.6	78.3	84.9	84.4
Apr	84.4	84.3	84.9	81.5	81.0	85.6	86.0
May	85.1	84.9	85.8	81.6	81.5	86.2	86.7
Jun	85.5	85.4	85.6	81.7	81.6	86.7	87.2
Jul	85.9	85.3	87.2	82.0	81.9	87.1	87.1
Aug	86.8	86.4	88.5	82.4	82.4	88.0	88.1
Sep	87.1	86.8	88.0	82.9	82.9	88.4	88.6
Oct	87.5	87.2	88.5	83.5	83.5	88.9	88.9
Nov	88.3	87.9	89.6	84.2	84.2	89.8	89.7
Dec	88.1	87.7	90.3	84.5	84.4	89.1	88.6
1992 Jan	89.0	88.5	90.8	85.0	85.0	90.4	90.3
Feb	89.5	89.0	91.1	85.4	85.4	90.8	90.7
Mar	89.9	89.4	92.2	86.1	86.6	91.3	90.6
Apr	89.6	88.7	93.0	85.5	85.6	91.2	90.6
May	90.3	89.6	93.1	86.5	86.6	91.5	90.9
Jun	90.7	89.8	93.8	87.0	87.0	92.0	91.2
Jul	90.9	90.0	94.0	87.3	87.3	92.1	91.4
Aug	91.1	90.4	93.8	88.0	87.9	92.3	91.7
Sep	91.7	90.8	95.0	88.0	88.0	92.9	92.1
Oct	92.2	91.3	95.4	88.4	88.4	93.6	92.6
Nov	92.0	91.2	95.2	89.0	89.0	93.2	92.2
Dec	92.4	91.8	95.3	88.9	89.0	93.6	92.9
1993 Jan	92.5	91.7	95.7	89.3	89.3	93.6	92.7
Feb	92.6	91.8	95.7	89.6	89.6	93.7	92.8
Mar	92.0	91.1	95.6	89.5	89.9	92.9	91.6
Apr	92.9	92.2	95.4	89.9	90.0	94.1	93.7
May	93.3	92.6	96.1	90.9	90.9	94.3	93.5
Jun	93.2	92.5	95.8	90.8	90.8	94.1	93.4
Jul	93.9	93.3	95.9	91.5	91.5	94.8	94.4
Aug	94.0	93.4	96.2	92.0	91.9	94.7	94.1
Sep	94.2	93.8	96.0	92.3	92.3	95.1	94.7
Oct	94.6	94.0	96.4	92.8	92.7	95.4	94.8
Nov	95.0	94.6	96.9	92.8	92.8	95.9	95.4
Dec	95.0	94.6	96.9	92.9	93.2	95.8	95.5
1994 Jan	95.3	94.9	97.0	93.7	93.7	96.0	95.6
Feb	96.1	95.9	97.2	93.6	93.7	97.0	97.0
Mar	95.8	95.4	97.6	95.0	95.0	96.5	95.8
Apr	95.7	95.2	97.5	94.2	94.2	96.4	96.2
May	96.5	96.2	97.9	95.0	95.0	97.2	97.0
Jun	97.0	96.8	98.1	95.5	95.5	97.6	97.5
Jul	97.2	96.9	98.4	95.9	95.7	97.7	97.5
Aug	97.7	97.4	98.6	96.2	96.2	98.2	98.0
Sep	97.7	97.4	98.8	96.8	96.7	98.0	97.7
Oct	98.2	98.0	98.5	97.3	97.2	98.5	98.5
Nov	98.2	98.1	98.6	97.6	97.6	98.5	98.4
Dec	98.6	98.3	100.0	98.4	98.3	98.7	98.3

1 From 1993, the index has been reclassified from SIC 1980 to SIC 1992, in common with other economic series in the national accounts.

Source: Office for National Statistics; Enquiries 01928 792442

3.7 Average earnings

continued

1995 = 100, seasonally adjusted

	Average earnings (GB)[1]						
	Whole economy	Private sector	Public sector	Manufacturing industries	Production industries	Service industries	Private sector services
	LNMQ	LNKY	LNNJ	LNMR	LNMS	LNMT	JJGH
1995 Jan	98.8	98.8	98.6	98.3	98.3	98.9	99.0
Feb	99.2	99.1	99.6	98.9	98.9	99.2	99.1
Mar	99.5	99.4	99.7	99.0	99.0	100.0	99.8
Apr	99.5	99.4	99.8	99.5	99.4	99.4	99.5
May	99.5	99.6	99.5	99.5	99.5	99.6	99.6
Jun	99.8	99.7	99.8	99.8	99.8	99.7	99.6
Jul	99.9	99.9	100.1	100.3	100.3	99.8	99.7
Aug	100.1	100.1	99.9	100.2	100.3	100.0	100.0
Sep	100.5	100.6	100.2	100.8	100.8	100.3	100.4
Oct	101.0	101.0	100.8	101.3	101.3	100.9	100.9
Nov	101.2	101.4	100.7	101.1	101.1	101.3	101.5
Dec	101.4	101.5	101.3	101.7	101.5	101.4	101.5
1996 Jan	101.6	101.6	101.5	102.3	102.2	101.5	101.5
Feb	102.4	102.6	101.9	102.6	102.6	102.1	102.3
Mar	102.3	102.3	102.2	103.3	103.2	102.2	102.1
Apr	102.8	102.9	102.8	103.6	103.4	102.6	102.8
May	102.6	102.6	102.8	103.6	103.6	102.5	102.4
Jun	103.4	103.4	103.0	104.1	104.1	103.2	103.1
Jul	103.7	103.8	103.2	104.5	104.5	103.4	103.5
Aug	103.9	104.2	102.8	104.7	104.7	103.7	104.0
Sep	104.7	104.9	104.0	105.2	105.2	104.5	104.8
Oct	104.7	105.0	103.7	105.3	105.5	104.6	105.0
Nov	105.2	105.5	103.8	106.0	106.0	104.9	105.4
Dec	105.7	106.1	104.1	106.6	106.4	105.4	105.9
1997 Jan	106.1	106.5	104.3	106.5	106.4	106.0	106.6
Feb	106.2	106.6	104.3	107.1	106.8	105.8	106.3
Mar	107.0	107.6	104.4	107.1	106.9	107.3	108.2
Apr	106.6	107.0	105.2	107.5	107.3	106.4	107.1
May	106.8	107.3	104.9	108.1	108.0	106.7	107.2
Jun	107.5	108.0	104.8	108.4	108.2	107.2	107.7
Jul	107.9	108.6	105.0	108.6	108.5	107.7	108.8
Aug	108.6	109.3	105.3	109.4	109.1	108.4	109.5
Sep	109.0	109.7	106.0	109.7	109.4	108.7	110.0
Oct	109.6	110.4	106.1	110.0	109.9	109.4	110.7
Nov	110.2	111.1	106.6	111.1	110.9	109.9	111.3
Dec	110.9	111.9	106.9	111.5	111.1	110.8	112.2
1998 Jan	111.3	112.4	107.0	111.7	111.5	111.2	112.6
Feb	111.7	112.8	107.1	112.4	112.0	111.4	113.2
Mar	112.3	113.5	107.3	112.8	112.6	112.4	114.7
Apr	112.7	114.0	107.4	112.9	112.8	112.7	115.0
May	113.2	114.5	108.1	113.1	112.9	113.6	115.5
Jun	113.1	114.1	108.7	113.5	113.2	112.9	113.8
Jul	113.8	115.0	109.1	114.0	113.7	113.7	115.5
Aug	114.0	115.0	109.6	114.3	114.0	113.8	115.4
Sep	114.5	115.7	109.8	114.5	114.3	114.4	116.4
Oct	114.8	116.0	110.0	115.0	114.8	114.6	116.6
Nov	115.2	116.4	110.6	115.0	114.7	115.1	117.2
Dec	115.4	116.8	110.4	115.1	114.6	115.5	117.3
1999 Jan	116.3	117.5	111.2	116.2	115.8	116.2	117.8
Feb	117.3	118.7	111.5	116.2	115.8	117.4	119.7
Mar	117.7	119.1	111.9	116.7	116.4	117.9	120.8
Apr	117.3	118.5	112.4	117.0	116.7	117.3	119.4
May	117.9	119.1	113.2	117.1	116.7	118.4	120.4
Jun	119.1	120.3	114.0	117.4	117.1	119.7	121.2
Jul	118.9	120.1	113.6	118.0	117.5	119.2	121.3
Aug	119.6	121.1	113.7	118.9	118.3	119.9	122.2
Sep	119.8	121.2	114.0	119.4	118.8	120.0	122.4
Oct	120.7	122.2	114.5	120.2	119.6	120.7	123.3
Nov	121.1	122.6	114.9	120.4	119.8	121.2	123.9
Dec	122.6	124.6	114.4	121.8	120.8	122.7	125.6
2000 Jan	123.8	125.6	116.2	122.7	122.0	124.1	126.6
Feb	123.7	125.6	116.4	121.6	121.1	124.0	127.1
Mar	123.9	125.8	116.1	121.9	121.2	124.3	128.1
Apr	122.7	124.0	117.3	122.2	121.3	122.8	125.2
May	122.6	124.1	117.0	123.1	122.1	122.6	124.7
Jun	123.6	124.9	118.0	122.6	122.1	123.7	125.1

1 From 1993, the index has been reclassified from SIC 1980 to SIC 1992, in common with other economic series in the national accounts.

Source: Office for National Statistics; Enquiries 01928 792442

3.8 Productivity and Unit Wage Costs[3]

United Kingdom

1995 = 100, seasonally adjusted

	Workforce jobs[1]			Output per filled job[2]			Unit wage costs	
	Whole economy	Total production industries	Manufacturing industries	Whole economy	Total production industries	Manufacturing industries	Whole economy	Manufacturing industries
	LNNM	LNOJ	LNOK	LNNN	LNNW	LNNX	LNNK	LNNQ
1960	94.3	..	..	46.8	..	..	8.9	..
1961	95.4	..	..	47.5	..	..	9.3	..
1962	95.8	..	..	48.0	..	..	9.7	..
1963	95.9	..	..	50.3	..	..	9.7	..
1964	97.3	..	..	52.3	..	..	9.9	..
1965	98.2	..	..	53.2	..	..	10.4	..
1966	98.6	..	..	54.1	..	..	10.9	..
1967	97.3	..	..	55.9	..	..	11.1	..
1968	96.8	..	..	58.5	..	..	11.4	..
1969	96.8	..	..	59.8	..	..	11.9	..
1970	96.5	..	..	61.4	..	..	13.1	..
1971	95.3	..	..	63.5	..	..	14.1	..
1972	95.7	..	..	65.5	..	..	15.3	..
1973	97.6	..	..	68.3	..	..	16.6	..
1974	98.0	..	..	67.1	..	..	19.9	..
1975	97.5	..	..	67.1	..	..	25.8	..
1976	96.7	..	..	69.4	..	..	28.2	..
1977	96.8	..	..	70.8	..	..	30.5	..
1978	97.5	..	..	72.3	..	..	33.9	..
1979	98.8	167.0	160.2	72.8	52.2	55.3	38.9	43.4
1980	98.2	159.6	151.4	71.8	51.0	53.4	47.4	53.0
1981	94.9	146.1	138.1	73.5	54.0	55.0	51.8	58.2
1982	93.0	137.7	130.1	76.6	58.4	58.3	54.4	66.7
1983	92.6	130.7	123.8	79.8	63.8	62.6	56.5	67.7
1984	94.7	128.4	122.1	79.8	64.9	65.8	60.0	70.0
1985	95.8	127.2	121.6	82.1	69.1	68.0	63.2	74.0
1986	96.1	123.7	119.1	85.0	71.5	70.3	66.2	76.9
1987	98.1	122.0	117.9	86.8	75.3	74.4	69.6	78.6
1988	101.6	122.9	119.5	87.8	78.8	78.8	74.8	80.8
1989	104.6	122.8	119.8	87.1	80.8	81.7	82.7	84.8
1990	105.3	119.4	116.7	87.4	82.7	83.8	90.4	90.4
1991	102.2	110.4	107.8	89.0	85.6	86.2	96.2	94.8
1992	99.3	103.5	101.2	91.8	90.8	91.7	99.0	95.0
1993	98.3	99.2	97.8	94.8	95.7	96.2	99.0	94.8
1994	99.1	98.6	98.0	98.3	99.7	100.5	98.5	95.3
1995	100.0	100.0	100.0	100.0	100.0	100.0	100.0	100.0
1996	101.0	101.2	101.4	101.5	99.9	99.0	101.7	105.4
1997	102.8	101.7	102.1	103.0	100.4	99.6	104.7	109.2
1998	104.5	102.3	103.0	104.5	100.6	99.2	107.8	114.6
1999	105.2	98.8	99.4	105.9	104.7	102.8	111.6	115.0
1960 Q1	93.7	..	..	46.9	..	..	8.6	..
Q2	94.1	..	..	46.4	..	..	8.9	..
Q3	94.4	..	..	47.0	..	..	9.0	..
Q4	94.9	..	..	46.9	..	..	9.0	..
1961 Q1	95.3	..	..	47.5	..	..	9.1	..
Q2	95.4	..	..	47.6	..	..	9.3	..
Q3	95.5	..	..	47.5	..	..	9.4	..
Q4	95.3	..	..	47.4	..	..	9.5	..
1962 Q1	95.6	..	..	47.7	..	..	9.6	..
Q2	95.9	..	..	48.0	..	..	9.6	..
Q3	95.9	..	..	48.2	..	..	9.7	..
Q4	95.7	..	..	48.1	..	..	9.8	..
1963 Q1	95.4	..	..	48.8	..	..	9.7	..
Q2	95.8	..	..	50.6	..	..	9.5	..
Q3	96.1	..	..	50.6	..	..	9.7	..
Q4	96.5	..	..	51.2	..	..	9.7	..
1964 Q1	96.7	..	..	52.0	..	..	9.7	..
Q2	97.0	..	..	52.3	..	..	9.8	..
Q3	97.4	..	..	52.1	..	..	10.0	..
Q4	97.8	..	..	52.9	..	..	10.1	..
1965 Q1	98.0	..	..	52.8	..	..	10.1	..
Q2	98.1	..	..	53.0	..	..	10.3	..
Q3	98.2	..	..	53.4	..	..	10.5	..
Q4	98.5	..	..	53.7	..	..	10.6	..
1966 Q1	98.7	..	..	53.7	..	..	10.8	..
Q2	98.7	..	..	53.8	..	..	10.9	..
Q3	98.7	..	..	54.2	..	..	10.9	..
Q4	98.1	..	..	54.5	..	..	10.9	..

1 Comprises employee jobs,self-employment jobs, HM Forces and government supported trainees.
2 The ratios do not take into account part-time working or hours of work.

Source: Office for National Statistics; Enquiries 01633 812766

3.8 Productivity and Unit Wage Costs[3]

United Kingdom

continued

1995 = 100, seasonally adjusted

	Workforce jobs[1]			Output per filled job[2]			Unit wage costs	
	Whole economy	Total production industries	Manufacturing industries	Whole economy	Total production industries	Manufacturing industries	Whole economy	Manufacturing industries
	LNNM	LNOJ	LNOK	LNNN	LNNW	LNNX	LNNK	LNNQ
1967 Q1	97.4	..	..	55.4	..	..	10.7	..
Q2	97.3	..	..	55.9	..	..	11.1	..
Q3	97.4	..	..	56.0	..	..	11.2	..
Q4	97.1	..	..	56.4	..	..	11.3	..
1968 Q1	96.9	..	..	58.2	..	..	11.3	..
Q2	96.8	..	..	58.1	..	..	11.3	..
Q3	96.8	..	..	58.9	..	..	11.3	..
Q4	96.8	..	..	58.9	..	..	11.5	..
1969 Q1	96.8	..	..	59.2	..	..	11.8	..
Q2	96.8	..	..	59.6	..	..	11.8	..
Q3	96.8	..	..	60.1	..	..	11.9	..
Q4	96.7	..	..	60.5	..	..	12.2	..
1970 Q1	96.7	..	..	60.0	..	..	12.6	..
Q2	96.5	..	..	61.2	..	..	13.0	..
Q3	96.3	..	..	61.7	..	..	13.3	..
Q4	96.2	..	..	62.7	..	..	13.4	..
1971 Q1	95.7	..	..	62.1	..	..	13.9	..
Q2	95.5	..	..	63.0	..	..	14.0	..
Q3	95.1	..	..	64.3	..	..	14.2	..
Q4	94.8	..	..	64.7	..	..	14.4	..
1972 Q1	95.2	..	..	63.9	..	..	15.0	..
Q2	95.5	..	..	65.4	..	..	15.1	..
Q3	95.7	..	..	65.7	..	..	15.4	..
Q4	96.3	..	..	66.9	..	..	15.7	..
1973 Q1	97.3	..	..	68.7	..	..	15.7	..
Q2	97.7	..	..	68.4	..	..	16.3	..
Q3	97.7	..	..	68.5	..	..	16.7	..
Q4	97.8	..	..	67.6	..	..	17.6	..
1974 Q1	97.8	..	..	66.2	..	..	18.3	..
Q2	97.9	..	..	67.3	..	..	18.9	..
Q3	98.2	..	..	68.1	..	..	20.2	..
Q4	98.1	..	..	66.9	..	..	22.0	..
1975 Q1	97.8	..	..	67.5	..	..	24.4	..
Q2	97.6	..	..	66.6	..	..	25.2	..
Q3	97.4	..	..	66.7	..	..	26.8	..
Q4	97.1	..	..	67.7	..	..	26.9	..
1976 Q1	96.9	..	..	69.2	..	..	27.1	..
Q2	96.7	..	..	68.6	..	..	28.2	..
Q3	96.7	..	..	69.3	..	..	28.6	..
Q4	96.7	..	..	70.5	..	..	28.9	..
1977 Q1	96.8	..	..	70.8	..	..	29.6	..
Q2	96.8	..	..	70.3	..	..	30.3	..
Q3	96.8	..	..	70.8	..	..	30.7	..
Q4	96.9	..	..	71.5	..	..	31.4	..
1978 Q1	97.1	..	..	71.9	..	..	32.5	..
Q2	97.3	..	161.3	72.1	..	55.4	33.7	37.1
Q3	97.6	167.8	161.2	72.6	50.6	55.7	34.3	38.0
Q4	98.1	167.7	161.2	72.5	50.5	54.8	35.2	39.8
1979 Q1	98.4	167.5	160.9	71.7	50.8	54.1	36.8	41.4
Q2	98.7	167.4	160.7	74.1	53.2	56.6	37.1	41.9
Q3	99.0	167.0	160.1	72.6	52.3	54.7	39.9	44.0
Q4	99.2	166.1	159.1	72.7	52.5	55.7	41.9	46.2
1980 Q1	99.1	164.5	156.9	72.0	52.2	55.1	44.3	47.7
Q2	98.8	162.0	154.1	71.6	51.0	53.6	46.8	52.1
Q3	98.0	158.1	149.4	71.9	50.4	52.8	48.5	55.4
Q4	96.9	153.7	145.0	71.5	50.6	52.2	50.2	56.8
1981 Q1	96.0	150.0	141.7	72.0	51.9	53.1	50.9	57.3
Q2	95.2	147.0	139.0	73.0	53.2	54.2	51.5	57.4
Q3	94.6	144.8	137.0	74.4	54.8	55.9	52.0	58.8
Q4	94.0	142.6	134.8	74.9	56.3	56.8	53.0	59.2
1982 Q1	93.7	141.0	133.6	75.2	56.4	57.2	53.9	65.9
Q2	93.3	139.0	131.4	76.5	58.2	58.2	54.1	66.5
Q3	92.9	136.7	129.0	77.0	59.2	58.6	54.5	66.9
Q4	92.3	134.2	126.6	77.8	59.7	59.2	55.0	67.7

See footnotes on page 172.

Source: Office for National Statistics; Enquiries 01633 812766

3.8 Productivity and Unit Wage Costs[3]

United Kingdom

continued

1995 = 100, seasonally adjusted

	Workforce jobs[1]			Output per filled job[2]			Unit wage costs	
	Whole economy	Total production industries	Manufacturing industries	Whole economy	Total production industries	Manufacturing industries	Whole economy	Manufacturing industries
	LNNM	LNOJ	LNOK	LNNN	LNNW	LNNX	LNNK	LNNQ
1983 Q1	92.0	132.5	125.3	79.8	61.8	61.1	55.3	66.7
Q2	92.0	131.2	124.2	79.5	63.1	61.8	56.3	67.9
Q3	92.8	130.0	123.2	79.8	64.5	63.0	56.8	67.8
Q4	93.6	129.0	122.5	80.1	65.9	64.4	57.5	68.3
1984 Q1	94.1	128.7	122.3	80.4	66.5	65.5	58.1	68.1
Q2	94.5	128.6	122.3	79.4	64.4	65.3	59.6	69.5
Q3	94.9	128.3	121.9	79.3	64.0	66.1	60.4	70.4
Q4	95.2	128.0	122.0	80.0	64.9	66.1	61.8	72.1
1985 Q1	95.6	127.8	121.8	81.1	67.3	68.1	62.6	71.3
Q2	95.7	127.6	121.8	82.7	70.1	68.5	62.1	73.0
Q3	95.9	127.2	121.6	82.2	69.6	67.9	63.4	74.7
Q4	95.9	126.4	121.1	82.6	69.5	67.3	64.6	76.9
1986 Q1	95.9	125.5	120.5	83.6	69.4	68.8	65.4	76.1
Q2	95.9	124.2	119.5	84.8	71.0	69.2	66.0	77.8
Q3	96.2	123.1	118.4	85.3	71.8	70.2	66.6	77.5
Q4	96.4	122.3	117.9	86.2	73.8	72.9	67.0	76.5
1987 Q1	96.8	121.6	117.3	86.1	74.0	73.0	68.0	77.3
Q2	97.6	121.8	117.7	86.6	74.8	73.5	69.1	78.7
Q3	98.5	122.1	118.1	87.3	76.0	74.9	69.9	78.8
Q4	99.5	122.3	118.6	87.2	76.6	76.0	71.4	79.5
1988 Q1	100.5	122.7	119.1	87.7	77.4	77.3	72.4	79.2
Q2	101.2	122.9	119.5	87.4	77.9	77.6	74.0	81.5
Q3	102.0	122.9	119.7	88.0	79.8	79.7	75.3	80.6
Q4	102.9	123.1	119.8	88.0	80.2	80.4	77.3	82.0
1989 Q1	103.9	123.1	120.0	87.2	80.7	81.5	79.5	81.7
Q2	104.5	123.0	119.9	87.1	80.7	81.6	81.5	84.4
Q3	104.9	122.8	120.0	87.0	80.8	81.6	83.7	86.0
Q4	105.2	122.2	119.3	87.0	81.1	82.1	86.0	87.0
1990 Q1	105.4	121.3	118.5	87.5	81.4	82.9	87.4	87.5
Q2	105.6	120.3	117.4	87.7	83.2	84.1	89.5	89.4
Q3	105.4	119.1	116.5	87.0	82.9	83.8	91.9	91.7
Q4	104.8	117.0	114.4	87.2	83.4	84.2	92.9	92.9
1991 Q1	103.7	114.2	111.6	87.8	83.9	84.6	94.7	93.1
Q2	102.6	111.3	108.7	88.6	85.0	85.3	95.8	95.6
Q3	101.6	109.0	106.2	89.3	85.8	86.4	97.1	95.4
Q4	100.8	107.2	104.5	90.1	87.8	88.4	97.3	95.1
1992 Q1	100.4	105.8	103.3	90.4	88.9	89.7	98.8	95.3
Q2	99.9	104.6	102.1	90.9	89.4	90.7	99.2	95.2
Q3	98.8	102.8	100.6	92.3	91.6	92.5	99.0	94.9
Q4	98.1	100.8	98.7	93.5	93.4	94.0	98.8	94.4
1993 Q1	98.1	99.8	97.9	94.0	94.8	96.1	98.7	93.1
Q2	98.2	99.4	97.7	94.3	95.0	96.2	99.2	94.1
Q3	98.3	98.9	97.8	95.1	96.1	96.1	99.0	95.7
Q4	98.6	98.6	97.8	95.6	97.1	96.5	99.2	96.2
1994 Q1	98.7	98.5	97.5	96.7	97.8	98.9	98.8	95.1
Q2	98.8	98.6	97.9	98.1	99.5	100.1	98.2	94.8
Q3	99.3	98.6	98.2	98.9	100.3	101.1	98.3	95.3
Q4	99.6	98.8	98.5	99.4	101.0	101.8	98.9	96.0
1995 Q1	99.8	99.3	99.2	99.7	100.3	100.4	99.5	98.3
Q2	99.9	99.8	99.9	99.8	100.2	100.2	99.9	99.4
Q3	100.0	100.0	99.8	100.2	100.1	100.5	100.1	99.9
Q4	100.3	101.0	101.1	100.4	99.3	99.0	100.5	102.4
1996 Q1	100.4	101.3	101.1	101.2	99.7	99.3	100.8	103.4
Q2	100.8	100.9	101.0	101.3	99.9	98.9	101.5	104.9
Q3	101.2	101.2	101.7	101.6	100.1	98.7	101.9	106.2
Q4	101.5	101.3	101.7	102.1	100.1	99.1	102.8	106.9
1997 Q1	102.0	101.4	101.6	102.6	100.6	100.1	103.7	106.8
Q2	102.7	101.7	102.2	102.7	100.1	99.2	104.4	108.9
Q3	103.1	101.7	102.1	103.3	100.9	99.8	104.9	109.5
Q4	103.5	101.8	102.6	103.6	100.2	99.2	105.7	111.7
1998 Q1	104.2	102.6	103.5	103.7	99.7	98.9	106.8	113.5
Q2	104.3	102.8	103.5	104.6	100.6	99.3	106.8	114.0
Q3	104.5	102.4	103.1	104.8	100.9	99.3	107.9	115.1
Q4	104.8	101.4	102.0	104.7	101.2	99.4	109.4	115.7
1999 Q1	104.8	100.1	100.7	105.0	102.0	100.4	110.7	115.9
Q2	105.1	99.1	99.6	105.4	103.7	101.8	111.3	115.0
Q3	105.2	98.3	98.8	106.4	106.2	104.1	111.6	114.1
Q4	105.5	97.7	98.3	106.9	106.8	105.0	112.7	115.0
2000 Q1	105.5	97.2	97.8	107.4	106.5	105.1	113.9	116.1

See footnotes on page 172.

Source: Office for National Statistics; Enquiries 01633 812766

3.9 UK public and private sector jobs by major categories (at mid-year)

Thousands

	Central government				Local government						
	HM Forces	National Health Service	Other	Total	Education[1]	Health and social services	Construction	Police and civilians	Other	Local authority community programme	Total
	BCAH	FHBR	FHBS	FHBT	FHBU	FHBV	FHBW	FHBX	FHBY	CUKE	DYBG
1960	518	..	..	..	..	..	..	..	..	..	1 821
1961	474	575	741	1 790	785	170	103	108	703	–	1 869
1962	442	598	745	1 785	840	179	108	111	701	–	1 940
1963	427	612	749	1 788	870	188	117	115	719	–	2 008
1964	424	627	743	1 794	925	200	124	116	724	–	2 088
1965	423	650	743	1 816	962	209	137	121	725	–	2 154
1966	417	676	749	1 842	1 013	228	133	126	758	–	2 259
1967	417	690	789	1 896	1 072	239	135	133	785	–	2 364
1968	400	710	799	1 909	1 132	249	135	138	791	–	2 444
1969	380	716	794	1 890	1 189	257	132	141	787	–	2 505
1970	372	741	818	1 931	1 241	265	128	145	781	–	2 559
1971	368	785	813	1 966	1 297	276	124	152	803	–	2 652
1972	371	821	814	1 971	1 365	295	128	159	824	–	2 771
1973	361	848	818	1 986	1 436	315	130	162	848	–	2 891
1974	345	911	885	2 115	1 453	272	135	160	762	–	2 782
1975	336	1 042	917	2 291	1 508	309	164	171	765	–	2 917
1976	336	1 092	939	2 366	1 521	319	165	175	776	–	2 956
1977	327	1 099	939	2 361	1 506	322	155	172	766	–	2 921
1978	318	1 120	932	2 370	1 512	334	155	170	761	–	2 932
1979	314	1 152	922	2 388	1 539	344	156	176	782	–	2 997
1980	323	1 174	897	2 394	1 501	346	152	181	776	–	2 956
1981	334	1 207	879	2 420	1 454	350	143	186	766	–	2 899
1982	324	1 227	850	2 401	1 434	352	132	186	761	–	2 865
1983	322	1 227	835	2 384	1 434	360	130	187	768	27	2 906
1984	326	1 223	810	2 359	1 430	368	126	187	773	58	2 942
1985	326	1 223	811	2 360	1 429	376	125	187	774	67	2 958
1986	322	1 215	800	2 337	1 452	387	125	188	770	88	3 010
1987	319	1 212	781	2 312	1 486	398	128	191	763	96	3 062
1988	316	1 228	779	2 323	1 504	405	125	194	764	89	3 081
1989	308	1 226	780	2 314	1 444	411	119	195	771	–	2 940
1990	303	1 221	776	2 300	1 431	417	114	199	806	–	2 967
1991	297	1 098	783	2 178	1 416	414	106	202	809	–	2 947
1992	290	917	801	2 008	1 390	410	97	204	797	–	2 898
1993	271	543	792	1 606	1 201	398	90	207	783	–	2 679
1994	250	177	758	1 185	1 176	408	87	206	768	–	2 645
1995	230	97	708	1 035	1 188	412	83	207	749	–	2 639
1996	221	84	612	917	1 191	406	76	207	744	–	2 624
1997	210	78	582	870	1 193	403	65	206	726	–	2 593
1998	210	77	581	868	1 204	395	61	207	712	–	2 579
1999	208	76	571	855	1 241	388	60	206	727	..	2 622

Note: Components may not add to totals due to separate rounding.

1 Excludes polytechnics from April 1989, when they were transferred to the private sector.

3 The revision to self-employment jobs in 1994 was due to the inclusion of second self-employment jobs.

2 Participants in the YTS who receive work experience, participants in the new JTS and some trainees on similar Northern Ireland schemes. Those with contracts of employment are included in the appropriate employment category.

Source: Office for National Statistics; Enquiries 01928 792501

3.9 UK public and private sector jobs by major categories (at mid-year)

continued

Thousands

		Public corporations					Private sector			
	General government	Nationalised industries including Post Office	NHS trusts	Other	Total	Public sector	Total	*of which:* Self-employment jobs[3]	Government supported trainees[2]	Workforce jobs[4]
	FHCA	FHCB	CGXN	FHCC	DYBH	FHCE	DYBI	BCAG	DYCZ	DYDA
1960	..	..	..	..	1 865	..	..	1 766	..	24 844
1961	3 659	2 152	..	48	2 200	5 859	19 273	1 758	..	25 132
1962	3 725	2 120	..	76	2 196	5 921	19 401	1 745	..	25 322
1963	3 796	2 010	..	126	2 136	5 932	19 426	1 731	..	25 358
1964	3 882	1 949	..	130	2 079	5 961	19 701	1 716	..	25 662
1965	3 970	1 894	..	131	2 025	5 995	19 934	1 696	..	25 929
1966	4 101	1 839	..	123	1 962	6 063	20 032	1 681	..	26 095
1967	4 260	2 030	..	134	2 164	6 424	19 317	1 762	..	25 741
1968	4 353	1 941	..	128	2 069	6 422	19 179	1 786	..	25 601
1969	4 395	1 916	..	125	2 041	6 436	19 199	1 853	..	25 635
1970	4 490	1 879	..	146	2 025	6 515	19 028	1 902	..	25 543
1971	4 618	1 856	..	153	2 009	6 627	18 586	2 026	–	25 213
1972	4 742	1 769	..	160	1 929	6 670	18 526	1 996	–	25 196
1973	4 877	1 731	..	159	1 890	6 764	19 022	1 907	–	25 786
1974	4 897	1 777	..	208	1 985	6 881	18 985	1 933	–	25 866
1975	5 208	1 816	..	219	2 035	7 249	18 530	1 996	–	25 779
1976	5 322	1 752	..	228	1 980	7 299	18 271	1 952	–	25 570
1977	5 282	1 866	..	223	2 089	7 364	18 232	1 907	–	25 596
1978	5 302	1 844	..	217	2 061	7 357	18 398	2 210	–	25 755
1979	5 385	1 849	..	216	2 065	7 449	18 700	2 216	–	26 149
1980	5 350	1 816	..	222	2 038	7 387	18 720	2 351	–	26 107
1981	5 319	1 657	..	210	1 867	7 185	17 955	2 492	–	25 140
1982	5 266	1 554	..	202	1 756	7 021	17 681	2 552	–	24 702
1983	5 290	1 465	..	198	1 663	6 952	17 470	2 611	16	24 422
1984	5 301	1 410	..	189	1 599	6 900	18 186	2 937	175	25 086
1985	5 318	1 131	..	120	1 251	6 569	18 821	3 051	176	25 390
1986	5 347	1 058	..	129	1 187	6 534	18 906	3 092	226	25 440
1987	5 374	864	..	121	985	6 359	19 599	3 326	311	25 958
1988	5 403	791	..	121	912	6 315	20 579	3 547	343	26 894
1989	5 253	719	..	112	831	6 084	21 663	3 877	462	27 747
1990	5 267	675	..	110	785	6 052	21 967	3 928	423	28 019
1991	5 125	497	124	102	723	5 848	21 270	3 766	353	27 118
1992	4 906	457	314	105	876	5 782	20 629	3 441	325	26 411
1993	4 285	437	662	93	1 192	5 477	20 582	3 445	311	26 059
1994	3 830	382	1 000	80	1 462	5 292	20 926	3 545	302	26 218
1995	3 674	345	1 089	107	1 541	5 215	21 299	3 604	225	26 514
1996	3 541	286	1 102	135	1 523	5 064	21 685	3 615	181	26 749
1997	3 463	231	1 121	125	1 477	4 940	22 307	3 609	159	27 247
1998	3 447	232	1 123	121	1 476	4 923	22 648	3 487	112	27 571
1999	3 477	237	1 131	122	1 490	4 967	22 882	3 513	102	27 849

See footnotes on page 175.

Source: Office for National Statistics; Enquiries 01928 792501

4 The employee jobs component of the workforce jobs series has been revised between June 1959 and June 1995 to remove an upward step that existed between June and Septenber 1995. the self-employment jobs component has also been revised between June 1959 and March 1984 to include an estimate of the number of self-employed people whose main job is as an employee. This too overcomes a step that used to exist at June 1984. For more information, please see the technical report in *Labour Market Trends* February 2000, pp 91-92.

Selected output and demand indicators

4.1 Output of production industries[1]

Average 1995 = 100

	Total production industries	Mining and quarrying	Electricity, gas and water supply	Total manufacturing industries	By market sector: Durable goods industries	Non-durable goods	Investment goods industries	Intermediate goods industries
1995 weights[2]	*1 000*	*96*	*92*	*812*	*54*	*213*	*181*	*552*
	CKYW	CKYX	CKYZ	CKYY	ERKM	ERKP	ERKT	ERKX
1948	34.1	147.9	16.4	39.9	..	..	..	..
1949	36.4	152.5	17.5	42.8	..	..	..	..
1950	38.9	153.8	19.1	46.0	..	..	..	..
1951	40.1	158.5	20.4	47.4	..	..	..	..
1952	38.6	160.0	20.9	45.1	..	..	..	..
1953	41.0	159.8	22.0	48.3	..	..	..	..
1954	43.1	161.3	23.9	50.9	..	..	..	..
1955	45.5	157.8	25.2	54.1	..	..	..	..
1956	45.6	158.1	26.3	53.9	..	..	..	..
1957	46.6	157.3	27.3	55.2	..	..	..	..
1958	46.2	146.2	28.5	54.7	..	..	..	..
1959	48.4	140.6	29.3	57.9	..	..	..	..
1960	51.9	134.3	31.5	62.5	..	..	..	..
1961	52.1	130.6	32.9	62.7	..	..	..	..
1962	52.5	134.8	35.6	62.8	..	..	..	..
1963	54.3	134.3	37.3	65.1	..	..	..	..
1964	58.8	131.7	39.2	71.0	..	..	..	..
1965	60.4	125.8	41.9	73.0	..	..	..	..
1966	61.4	116.8	43.6	74.3	..	..	..	..
1967	61.8	114.4	45.2	74.8	..	..	..	..
1968	66.5	101.3	44.8	80.4	..	..	..	..
1969	68.8	93.4	47.7	83.4	..	..	..	..
1970	69.1	86.6	50.0	83.7	..	..	..	..
1971	68.8	84.8	52.5	82.9	..	..	..	..
1972	70.0	68.3	56.6	84.6	..	..	..	..
1973	76.3	76.4	60.2	92.5	..	..	..	..
1974	74.8	64.6	60.6	91.3	..	..	..	..
1975	70.7	72.9	61.7	85.0	..	..	..	..
1976	73.0	68.5	62.8	86.6	..	..	..	..
1977	76.8	66.6	65.4	88.3	..	..	..	..
1978	79.0	66.6	66.9	88.8	..	..	..	..
1979	82.0	80.1	69.6	88.6	..	..	..	..
1980	76.7	81.3	69.2	80.9	..	..	..	..
1981	74.2	84.9	70.8	75.9	..	..	..	..
1982	75.7	90.9	70.3	75.8	..	..	..	..
1983	78.4	91.7	72.7	77.5	..	..	..	..
1984	78.5	86.3	61.7	80.3	..	..	..	..
1985	82.8	94.9	74.9	82.6	..	..	..	..
1986	84.8	94.8	82.3	83.7	82.3	86.2	82.6	85.5
1987	88.2	94.8	84.5	87.7	88.5	90.3	84.5	88.8
1988	92.5	86.8	84.2	94.1	101.0	93.9	92.5	91.2
1989	94.4	76.7	84.3	97.9	103.0	95.3	100.4	91.2
1990	94.1	73.3	86.5	97.7	99.3	96.5	100.7	90.4
1991	91.0	76.7	91.4	92.8	90.3	93.3	94.1	89.1
1992	91.3	78.9	92.9	92.8	89.4	95.1	91.9	89.8
1993	93.3	84.2	96.8	94.1	90.6	96.2	93.4	92.4
1994	98.3	96.8	97.8	98.5	98.0	99.5	98.2	98.0
1995	100.0	100.0	100.0	100.0	100.0	100.0	100.0	100.0
1996	101.1	103.3	105.3	100.4	104.8	100.5	102.4	100.5
1997	102.1	102.1	105.7	101.7	106.5	101.8	103.7	101.3
1998	102.9	104.4	107.6	102.2	109.0	100.0	107.8	101.8
1999	103.4	108.0	109.3	102.2	111.3	99.4	113.0	101.0

1 The figures contain, where appropriate, an adjustment for stock changes.
2 SIC(92) weights.

Source: Office for National Statistics; Enquiries 01633 812786

4.1 Output of production industries[1]

continued

Average 1995 = 100

	Total production industries	Mining and quarrying	Electricity, gas and water supply	Total manufacturing industries	By market sector: Durable goods industries	Non-durable goods industries	Investment goods industries	Intermediate goods industries
1995 weights[2]	*1 000*	*96*	*92*	*812*	*54*	*213*	*181*	*552*
Seasonally adjusted								
	CKYW	CKYX	CKYZ	CKYY	ERKM	ERKP	ERKT	ERKX
1948 Q1	33.5	149.1	16.1	39.1	..	..	..	..
Q2	33.7	145.2	16.3	39.4	..	..	..	..
Q3	34.4	148.2	16.6	40.4	..	..	..	..
Q4	34.8	149.1	16.8	40.8	..	..	..	..
1949 Q1	35.4	149.5	17.1	41.7	..	..	..	..
Q2	36.2	153.7	17.4	42.6	..	..	..	..
Q3	36.9	153.1	17.8	43.4	..	..	..	..
Q4	37.0	153.7	17.9	43.6	..	..	..	..
1950 Q1	37.6	150.3	18.5	44.6	..	..	..	..
Q2	38.6	154.8	19.0	45.7	..	..	..	..
Q3	39.6	155.8	19.6	47.0	..	..	..	..
Q4	39.6	154.5	19.4	46.9	..	..	..	..
1951 Q1	39.6	158.1	19.6	46.9	..	..	..	..
Q2	39.7	154.9	20.3	47.0	..	..	..	..
Q3	41.2	163.1	21.2	48.6	..	..	..	..
Q4	39.9	157.9	20.5	47.1	..	..	..	..
1952 Q1	38.9	154.0	20.1	45.8	..	..	..	..
Q2	38.1	160.3	20.5	44.5	..	..	..	..
Q3	37.9	168.2	21.0	43.8	..	..	..	..
Q4	39.4	157.6	22.1	46.1	..	..	..	..
1953 Q1	40.1	163.3	21.9	46.9	..	..	..	..
Q2	40.6	159.3	21.6	47.7	..	..	..	..
Q3	40.8	152.2	21.9	48.3	..	..	..	..
Q4	42.7	164.6	22.8	50.3	..	..	..	..
1954 Q1	42.2	162.9	23.6	49.6	..	..	..	..
Q2	42.9	160.9	23.5	50.5	..	..	..	..
Q3	43.3	158.6	24.2	51.1	..	..	..	..
Q4	44.2	162.8	24.3	52.2	..	..	..	..
1955 Q1	44.9	160.5	25.4	53.2	..	..	..	..
Q2	45.2	154.8	24.9	53.8	..	..	..	..
Q3	45.4	154.8	24.7	54.2	..	..	..	..
Q4	46.4	161.1	25.7	55.1	..	..	..	..
1956 Q1	45.8	157.6	26.2	54.4	..	..	..	..
Q2	45.7	159.2	26.2	54.2	..	..	..	..
Q3	45.3	157.8	26.4	53.5	..	..	..	..
Q4	45.4	157.9	26.6	53.7	..	..	..	..
1957 Q1	46.2	160.5	25.8	54.8	..	..	..	..
Q2	46.5	160.2	27.3	55.1	..	..	..	..
Q3	47.2	155.2	28.1	56.0	..	..	..	..
Q4	46.4	153.5	28.1	55.1	..	..	..	..
1958 Q1	46.6	149.2	28.1	55.3	..	..	..	..
Q2	46.0	147.1	28.6	54.5	..	..	..	..
Q3	45.7	143.9	28.6	54.1	..	..	..	..
Q4	46.4	144.8	28.8	55.1	..	..	..	..
1959 Q1	46.6	141.6	29.0	55.5	..	..	..	..
Q2	47.9	142.3	28.8	57.1	..	..	..	..
Q3	48.4	141.1	29.4	57.8	..	..	..	..
Q4	50.8	137.3	30.0	61.1	..	..	..	..
1960 Q1	51.7	138.5	30.6	62.3	..	..	..	..
Q2	51.6	133.7	30.6	62.4	..	..	..	..
Q3	51.8	132.8	32.4	62.4	..	..	..	..
Q4	52.4	132.2	32.5	63.1	..	..	..	..
1961 Q1	51.7	127.3	31.2	62.5	..	..	..	..
Q2	52.4	130.8	32.7	63.3	..	..	..	..
Q3	52.3	132.0	33.5	62.8	..	..	..	..
Q4	51.8	132.4	34.4	62.0	..	..	..	..
1962 Q1	51.8	133.0	34.6	62.0	..	..	..	..
Q2	52.7	135.2	35.4	63.1	..	..	..	..
Q3	53.1	136.9	35.9	63.5	..	..	..	..
Q4	52.5	134.2	36.4	62.8	..	..	..	..

See footnotes on page 177.

Source: Office for National Statistics; Enquiries 01633 812786

4.1 Output of production industries[1]

continued

Average 1995 = 100

	Total production industries	Mining and quarrying	Electricity, gas and water supply	Total manufacturing industries	By market sector: Durable goods industries	Non-durable goods industries	Investment goods industries	Intermediate goods industries
1995 weights[2]	*1 000*	*96*	*92*	*812*	*54*	*213*	*181*	*552*
Seasonally adjusted								
	CKYW	CKYX	CKYZ	CKYY	ERKM	ERKP	ERKT	ERKX
1963 Q1	52.0	134.5	38.0	61.9	..	..	..	..
Q2	53.7	136.0	36.5	64.1	..	..	..	..
Q3	55.2	134.2	37.4	66.3	..	..	..	..
Q4	56.4	132.7	37.4	67.9	..	..	..	..
1964 Q1	58.2	137.2	38.5	70.1	..	..	..	..
Q2	58.0	129.2	38.9	70.1	..	..	..	..
Q3	58.7	130.4	39.2	70.9	..	..	..	..
Q4	60.2	130.1	40.3	72.8	..	..	..	..
1965 Q1	60.2	129.6	41.2	72.6	..	..	..	..
Q2	60.2	125.4	40.9	72.8	..	..	..	..
Q3	60.3	123.5	42.8	72.6	..	..	..	..
Q4	61.0	124.7	42.9	73.8	..	..	..	..
1966 Q1	61.7	117.6	42.3	75.1	..	..	..	..
Q2	61.6	120.5	43.4	74.7	..	..	..	..
Q3	61.8	111.5	44.2	75.0	..	..	..	..
Q4	60.3	117.5	44.6	72.6	..	..	..	..
1967 Q1	61.0	116.3	43.7	73.8	..	..	..	..
Q2	61.6	113.7	45.5	74.5	..	..	..	..
Q3	61.6	109.2	45.1	74.7	..	..	..	..
Q4	63.0	118.5	46.6	76.0	..	..	..	..
1968 Q1	65.6	105.3	42.6	79.3	..	..	..	..
Q2	66.4	102.1	45.9	80.0	..	..	..	..
Q3	67.0	99.4	46.3	80.9	..	..	..	..
Q4	67.2	98.4	44.3	81.5	..	..	..	..
1969 Q1	68.2	98.1	47.1	82.5	..	..	..	..
Q2	69.5	95.5	49.3	84.0	..	..	..	..
Q3	68.9	93.2	47.4	83.6	..	..	..	..
Q4	68.7	86.7	47.0	83.6	..	..	..	..
1970 Q1	68.8	91.2	50.8	83.0	..	..	..	..
Q2	69.1	88.7	48.4	83.8	..	..	..	..
Q3	69.2	87.2	49.9	83.7	..	..	..	..
Q4	69.5	79.2	51.2	84.3	..	..	..	..
1971 Q1	68.8	88.7	50.7	83.1	..	..	..	..
Q2	69.0	88.4	51.2	83.1	..	..	..	..
Q3	68.7	86.4	52.9	82.6	..	..	..	..
Q4	68.6	75.7	55.1	82.6	..	..	..	..
1972 Q1	65.3	32.5	52.9	80.3	..	..	..	..
Q2	70.3	80.3	56.8	84.4	..	..	..	..
Q3	71.0	80.0	58.4	85.2	..	..	..	..
Q4	73.4	80.3	58.4	88.5	..	..	..	..
1973 Q1	76.0	81.0	59.6	92.0	..	..	..	..
Q2	76.2	80.8	60.6	92.0	..	..	..	..
Q3	76.6	78.4	59.6	92.8	..	..	..	..
Q4	76.3	65.6	61.0	93.1	..	..	..	..
1974 Q1	70.9	39.2	55.1	88.3	..	..	..	..
Q2	77.1	71.8	60.5	94.1	..	..	..	..
Q3	77.0	74.2	63.6	93.3	..	..	..	..
Q4	74.1	73.0	63.1	89.4	..	..	..	..
1975 Q1	73.1	73.8	61.0	88.6	..	..	..	..
Q2	70.2	73.0	62.3	84.3	..	..	..	..
Q3	69.1	72.1	60.6	83.0	..	..	..	..
Q4	70.5	72.7	63.0	84.1	..	..	..	..
1976 Q1	71.3	69.7	63.0	85.1	..	..	..	..
Q2	72.7	69.1	62.9	86.3	..	..	..	..
Q3	72.6	67.5	61.1	86.2	..	..	..	..
Q4	75.5	67.6	64.3	88.7	..	..	..	..
1977 Q1	77.3	67.7	63.7	89.9	..	..	..	..
Q2	76.9	67.1	66.5	88.0	..	..	..	..
Q3	76.4	66.2	66.4	87.4	..	..	..	..
Q4	76.6	65.3	65.0	87.7	..	..	..	..

See footnotes on page 177.

Source: Office for National Statistics; Enquiries 01633 812786

4.1 Output of production industries[1]

continued

Average 1995 = 100

	Total production industries	Mining and quarrying	Electricity, gas and water supply	Total manufacturing industries	By market sector: Durable goods industries	Non-durable goods industries	Investment goods industries	Intermediate goods industries
1995 weights[2]	*1 000*	*96*	*92*	*812*	*54*	*213*	*181*	*552*
Seasonally adjusted								
	CKYW	CKYX	CKYZ	CKYY	ERKM	ERKP	ERKT	ERKX
1978 Q1	76.9	60.9	66.9	87.6	..	..	..	..
Q2	79.3	65.1	68.0	89.4	..	..	..	..
Q3	79.9	68.0	67.5	89.8	..	..	..	..
Q4	79.8	72.2	65.1	88.4	..	..	..	..
1979 Q1	80.0	74.7	71.9	87.1	..	..	..	..
Q2	83.8	80.0	71.6	90.9	..	..	..	..
Q3	82.1	84.3	68.1	87.6	..	..	..	..
Q4	82.1	81.4	66.7	88.7	..	..	..	..
1980 Q1	80.8	81.9	70.4	86.5	..	..	..	..
Q2	77.7	79.8	69.0	82.7	..	..	..	..
Q3	74.9	80.3	68.2	78.9	..	..	..	..
Q4	73.2	83.0	69.2	75.7	..	..	..	..
1981 Q1	73.2	83.5	69.5	75.2	..	..	..	..
Q2	73.6	84.1	71.6	75.4	..	..	..	..
Q3	74.7	85.4	68.9	76.6	..	..	..	..
Q4	75.5	86.5	73.3	76.6	..	..	..	..
1982 Q1	74.9	85.6	70.5	76.3	..	..	..	..
Q2	76.2	91.6	70.1	76.4	..	..	..	..
Q3	76.2	94.4	69.9	75.6	..	..	..	..
Q4	75.5	92.1	70.8	74.9	..	..	..	..
1983 Q1	77.1	88.8	70.8	76.5	..	..	..	..
Q2	77.9	89.8	75.7	76.8	..	..	..	..
Q3	78.8	94.3	71.1	77.7	..	..	..	..
Q4	79.9	94.0	73.4	78.8	..	..	..	..
1984 Q1	80.5	91.5	75.2	80.1	..	..	..	..
Q2	77.9	83.7	64.6	79.9	..	..	..	..
Q3	77.2	82.7	52.6	80.6	..	..	..	..
Q4	78.2	87.3	54.2	80.6	..	..	..	..
1985 Q1	81.0	90.0	62.1	83.0	..	..	..	..
Q2	84.2	96.7	79.4	83.4	..	..	..	..
Q3	83.3	95.3	80.2	82.6	..	..	..	..
Q4	82.7	97.5	77.7	81.5	..	..	..	..
1986 Q1	83.3	86.1	83.1	82.9	79.0	85.5	82.8	83.0
Q2	84.6	98.9	83.6	82.7	81.7	85.8	81.3	85.6
Q3	84.9	99.3	82.4	83.2	83.3	85.6	81.5	86.1
Q4	86.4	94.7	79.9	86.0	85.1	87.7	84.7	87.2
1987 Q1	86.6	93.9	85.9	85.7	83.9	88.7	82.9	87.5
Q2	87.5	97.0	83.8	86.6	86.2	89.9	83.6	88.1
Q3	89.0	96.9	83.4	88.5	91.2	90.9	85.4	89.4
Q4	89.8	91.5	84.8	90.1	92.7	91.6	86.1	90.2
1988 Q1	90.9	89.1	81.9	92.1	95.6	92.8	89.8	90.2
Q2	91.5	89.8	83.1	92.7	100.3	93.1	90.0	90.8
Q3	93.6	85.2	86.9	95.4	104.2	94.9	93.6	92.2
Q4	93.9	83.2	84.7	96.3	103.7	95.0	96.6	91.7
1989 Q1	94.1	76.8	81.2	97.8	106.2	94.9	98.7	91.0
Q2	94.0	72.0	86.5	97.8	104.8	95.2	99.6	90.6
Q3	94.6	78.2	84.7	97.9	101.3	95.2	102.3	91.1
Q4	94.9	79.9	84.7	98.0	99.6	95.8	100.8	92.0
1990 Q1	94.1	74.1	81.4	98.2	97.8	97.2	100.8	90.2
Q2	95.5	77.8	86.9	98.8	100.7	97.0	102.4	92.0
Q3	93.9	70.4	88.3	97.6	99.9	96.2	100.6	90.1
Q4	93.0	71.0	89.4	96.4	98.8	95.5	99.1	89.4
1991 Q1	91.9	74.3	90.4	94.5	93.6	94.1	97.4	89.0
Q2	90.9	73.7	94.8	92.7	91.0	93.2	94.3	88.8
Q3	90.1	78.6	88.5	91.8	88.7	92.7	91.6	88.7
Q4	91.0	80.1	92.1	92.4	87.8	93.3	92.9	89.8
1992 Q1	91.0	78.5	91.3	92.7	90.9	94.0	91.7	89.7
Q2	90.6	75.6	89.9	92.7	90.4	95.2	90.5	88.9
Q3	91.5	78.7	93.8	93.0	88.4	95.8	92.0	90.0
Q4	92.0	82.7	96.5	92.7	87.9	95.4	93.3	90.6

See footnotes on page 177.

Source: Office for National Statistics; Enquiries 01633 812786

4.1 Output of production industries[1]

continued

Average 1995 = 100

	Total production industries	Mining and quarrying	Electricity, gas and water supply	Total manufacturing industries	By market sector: Durable goods industries	Non-durable goods industries	Investment goods industries	Intermediate goods industries
1995 weights[2]	*1 000*	*96*	*82*	*812*	*54*	*213*	*181*	*552*
Seasonally adjusted								
	CKYW	CKYX	CKYZ	CKYY	ERKM	ERKP	ERKT	ERKX
1993 Q1	92.3	78.9	91.4	94.1	87.9	96.3	94.1	90.4
Q2	92.5	79.9	95.0	94.0	90.5	95.7	94.0	91.0
Q3	93.5	86.0	99.1	93.9	91.4	96.1	92.9	93.0
Q4	94.7	91.9	101.6	94.4	92.9	96.7	92.4	95.1
1994 Q1	96.3	94.7	96.8	96.5	94.4	99.0	94.8	96.2
Q2	98.1	98.3	98.3	98.0	97.5	98.6	97.5	98.2
Q3	98.9	97.2	97.9	99.3	99.9	99.7	99.5	98.5
Q4	99.8	97.2	98.0	100.3	100.2	100.7	100.9	99.0
1995 Q1	99.6	100.7	98.7	99.6	102.6	99.8	98.6	99.5
Q2	100.0	99.2	99.9	100.1	101.0	100.9	98.9	100.0
Q3	100.2	99.3	100.2	100.2	98.8	99.8	100.4	100.2
Q4	100.2	100.9	101.2	100.1	97.6	99.5	102.1	100.3
1996 Q1	101.0	102.2	104.7	100.4	102.9	100.5	102.1	100.6
Q2	100.8	103.6	105.9	99.9	104.7	100.7	101.7	100.1
Q3	101.2	104.2	105.8	100.3	106.3	100.5	102.4	100.4
Q4	101.5	103.4	104.8	100.0	105.3	100.3	103.5	100.9
1997 Q1	102.0	101.8	104.2	101.7	106.6	103.0	104.0	100.5
Q2	101.9	102.2	105.9	101.4	105.0	101.0	103.9	101.3
Q3	102.6	104.2	107.0	101.9	106.2	101.5	103.9	102.2
Q4	102.0	100.3	105.5	101.8	108.0	101.5	103.0	101.3
1998 Q1	102.3	101.0	103.7	102.3	107.3	99.8	106.5	101.5
Q2	103.4	105.0	107.7	102.7	108.9	100.8	106.9	102.7
Q3	103.3	105.4	109.3	102.4	111.0	100.7	108.5	101.9
Q4	102.6	106.0	109.5	101.4	108.6	98.9	109.4	101.2
1999 Q1	102.0	105.8	106.6	101.1	108.5	97.8	111.4	100.0
Q2	102.8	108.3	109.1	101.4	108.9	99.3	112.2	100.4
Q3	104.3	110.2	110.9	102.9	112.4	100.2	114.0	102.0
Q4	104.4	107.9	110.7	103.3	115.3	100.4	114.5	101.6
2000 Q1	103.6	106.0	107.7	102.8	114.8	99.8	111.3	101.4

See footnotes on page 177.

Source: Office for National Statistics; Enquiries 01633 812786

4.2 Engineering and construction: output and orders

Volume index numbers except where stated in £ million

	Total engineering industries							Construction(GB)					
	Home market		Export		Total			Output[3]			Orders received		
	Orders on hand end of period (average 1995 = 100)	New orders[2] (1995 average monthly sales = 100)	Orders on hand end of period (average 1995 = 100)	New orders[2] (1995 average monthly sales = 100)	Turnover (1995 average monthly sales =100)	Orders on hand end of period (average 1995 = 100)	New orders[2] (1995 average monthly sales = 100)	£ million at current prices, not seasonally adjusted	At 1995 prices, seasonally adjusted £ million	At 1995 prices, seasonally adjusted 1995 = 100	£ million at current prices, not seasonally adjusted	At 1995 prices, seasonally adjusted £ million	At 1995 prices, seasonally adjusted 1995 = 100
	FGVU	FGVV	FGVX	FGVY	FGVT	FGWA	FGWB	FGAY	FGAZ	FEAQ	FHAA	FHAB	FEAZ
1955	..	..	..	..	..	..	..	1 734	..	..	..	..	..
1956	..	..	..	..	..	..	..	1 971	..	..	..	..	..
1957	..	..	..	..	..	..	..	2 059	..	..	1 502	17 614	..
1958	..	..	..	..	..	..	..	2 126	..	..	1 489	17 522	..
1959	..	..	..	..	..	..	..	2 306	..	..	1 783	22 351	..
1960	..	..	..	..	..	..	..	2 508	..	..	2 092	25 453	..
1961	..	..	..	..	..	..	..	2 794	..	..	2 178	25 078	..
1962	..	..	..	..	..	..	..	2 990	..	..	2 316	25 355	..
1963	..	..	..	..	..	..	..	3 144	..	..	2 619	28 069	..
1964	..	..	..	..	..	..	..	3 633	..	..	3 139	33 796	..
1965	..	..	..	..	..	..	..	3 954	..	..	3 055	31 852	..
1966	..	..	..	..	..	..	..	4 214	..	..	3 013	29 468	..
1967	..	..	..	..	..	..	..	4 502	..	..	3 547	34 060	..
1968	..	..	..	..	..	..	..	4 881	..	..	3 367	30 960	..
1969	..	..	..	..	..	..	..	5 046	..	..	3 309	28 418	..
1970	..	..	..	..	..	..	..	5 358	..	..	3 532	28 201	..
1971	..	..	..	..	..	..	..	5 930	..	..	4 243	30 229	..
1972	..	..	..	..	..	..	..	6 754	..	..	5 293	32 448	..
1973	..	..	..	..	..	..	..	8 614	..	..	6 933	31 438	..
1974	..	..	..	..	..	..	..	9 733	..	..	6 009	20 999	..
1975	..	..	..	..	..	..	..	11 081	..	..	6 375	21 283	..
1976	..	..	..	..	..	..	..	12 181	..	..	6 874	22 626	..
1977	..	..	..	..	..	..	..	13 314	..	..	7 182	20 295	..
1978	..	..	..	..	..	..	..	15 703	..	..	8 927	21 439	..
1979	..	..	..	..	..	..	..	18 870	..	..	10 024	19 442	..
1980	..	..	..	..	..	..	..	22 052	41 307	78.5	10 114	13 739	..
1981	..	..	..	..	..	..	..	21 547	37 275	70.8	10 722	14 182	..
1982	..	..	..	..	..	..	..	22 954	38 508	73.1	11 446	16 261	..
1983	..	..	..	..	..	..	..	25 511	41 795	79.4	13 517	19 128	..
1984	..	..	..	..	..	..	..	27 776	43 504	82.6	14 630	19 596	..
1985	..	..	..	..	..	..	..	29 663	44 034	83.6	15 343	19 056	..
1986	..	..	..	..	..	..	..	32 049	45 525	86.5	17 108	23 313	105.7
1987	..	..	..	..	..	..	..	37 528	50 629	96.2	22 118	27 501	124.6
1988	..	..	..	..	..	..	..	44 853	55 438	105.3	26 298	28 347	128.5
1989	..	..	..	..	..	..	..	52 150	58 137	110.4	27 142	26 559	120.4
1990	..	..	..	..	..	..	..	55 307	58 375	110.9	22 491	22 508	102.0
1991	96.8	85.7	103.4	85.0	86.9	99.4	85.4	51 115	54 133	102.8	19 455	21 201	96.1
1992	90.3	85.7	102.0	83.4	86.0	94.9	84.7	47 472	51 927	98.6	17 493	20 629	93.5
1993	91.9	92.5	101.3	80.6	87.3	95.7	87.6	46 323	50 980	96.8	19 965	23 105	104.7
1994	105.6	103.0	104.2	91.2	95.4	105.1	98.1	49 439	52 692	100.1	21 285	22 701	102.9
1995	100.0	98.3	95.9	97.7	100.0	98.3	98.0	52 643	52 643	100.0	22 065	22 065	100.0
1996	94.1	98.0	94.4	108.7	103.7	94.2	102.5	55 243	53 863	102.3	22 834	22 764	103.0
1997	97.6	101.9	96.5	114.6	106.3	97.1	107.2	58 532	55 468	105.4	24 806	23 643	107.0
1998	89.6	100.9	102.1	124.2	111.4	94.5	110.6	62 060	56 370	107.1	27 477	24 901	112.9
1999	103.7	113.2	108.9	126.8	115.6	105.7	118.9	65 262	56 903	108.1	26 079	22 604	102.4

1 Manufacture of machinery and equipment, electrical and optical equipment (SIC(92) classes 29, 30, 31, 32 and 33).
2 Net of cancellations
3 These series include new work and repair and maintenance, estimates of unrecorded output by small firms and self-employed workers and output of the direct labour departments of the public sector.
4 Includes UK element of contract for the Channel Tunnel.

Sources: Office for National Statistics; Enquiries Columns 1-7 01633 812125; ; Department of the Environment, transport and the Regions;; Enquiries Columns 8-13 020 7890 5583

4.2 Engineering and construction: output and orders

continued

Volume index numbers except where stated in £ million

	Total engineering industries							Construction(GB)					
	Home market		Export		Total			Output[3]			Orders received		
	Orders on hand end of period (average 1995 = 100)	New orders[2] (1995 average monthly sales = 100)	Orders on hand end of period (average 1995 = 100)	New orders[2] (1995 average monthly sales = 100)	Turnover (1995 average monthly sales =100)	Orders on hand end of period (average 1995 = 100)	New orders[2] (1995 average monthly sales = 100)	£ million at current prices, not seasonally adjusted	At 1995 prices, seasonally adjusted		£ million at current prices, not seasonally adjusted	At 1995 prices, seasonally adjusted	
									£ million	1995 = 100		£ million	1995 = 100
	FGVU	FGVV	FGVX	FGVY	FGVT	FGWA	FGWB	FGAY	FGAZ	FEAQ	FHAA	FHAB	FEAZ
1955 Q1	..	..	..	..	..	..	..	385	..	..	..	..	..
Q2	..	..	..	..	..	..	..	431	..	..	..	..	..
Q3	..	..	..	..	..	..	..	456	..	..	..	..	..
Q4	..	..	..	..	..	..	..	462	..	..	..	..	..
1956 Q1	..	..	..	..	..	..	..	447	..	..	..	..	..
Q2	..	..	..	..	..	..	..	504	..	..	..	..	..
Q3	..	..	..	..	..	..	..	510	..	..	..	..	..
Q4	..	..	..	..	..	..	..	510	..	..	..	..	..
1957 Q1	..	..	..	..	..	..	..	500	..	..	..	..	..
Q2	..	..	..	..	..	..	..	522	..	..	..	..	..
Q3	..	..	..	..	..	..	..	515	..	..	..	..	..
Q4	..	..	..	..	..	..	..	522	..	..	..	..	..
1958 Q1	..	..	..	..	..	..	..	509	..	..	396	..	..
Q2	..	..	..	..	..	..	..	532	..	..	360	..	..
Q3	..	..	..	..	..	..	..	539	..	..	356	..	..
Q4	..	..	..	..	..	..	..	546	..	..	377	..	..
1959 Q1	..	..	..	..	..	..	..	546	..	..	450	..	..
Q2	..	..	..	..	..	..	..	577	..	..	443	..	..
Q3	..	..	..	..	..	..	..	590	..	..	412	..	..
Q4	..	..	..	..	..	..	..	593	..	..	479	..	..
1960 Q1	..	..	..	..	..	..	..	587	..	..	535	..	..
Q2	..	..	..	..	..	..	..	627	..	..	516	..	..
Q3	..	..	..	..	..	..	..	642	..	..	506	..	..
Q4	..	..	..	..	..	..	..	652	..	..	536	..	..
1961 Q1	..	..	..	..	..	..	..	659	..	..	591	..	..
Q2	..	..	..	..	..	..	..	699	..	..	554	..	..
Q3	..	..	..	..	..	..	..	720	..	..	531	..	..
Q4	..	..	..	..	..	..	..	716	..	..	501	..	..
1962 Q1	..	..	..	..	..	..	..	714	..	..	577	..	..
Q2	..	..	..	..	..	..	..	756	..	..	590	..	..
Q3	..	..	..	..	..	..	..	778	..	..	588	..	..
Q4	..	..	..	..	..	..	..	742	..	..	561	..	..
1963 Q1	..	..	..	..	..	..	..	629	..	..	666	..	..
Q2	..	..	..	..	..	..	..	799	..	..	649	..	..
Q3	..	..	..	..	..	..	..	850	..	..	697	..	..
Q4	..	..	..	..	..	..	..	866	..	..	607	..	..
1964 Q1	..	..	..	..	..	..	..	854	..	..	756	7 666	..
Q2	..	..	..	..	..	..	..	910	..	..	794	8 019	..
Q3	..	..	..	..	..	..	..	919	..	..	780	8 586	..
Q4	..	..	..	..	..	..	..	950	..	..	809	9 525	..
1965 Q1	..	..	..	..	..	..	..	938	..	..	857	8 616	..
Q2	..	..	..	..	..	..	..	980	..	..	787	7 695	..
Q3	..	..	..	..	..	..	..	1 012	..	..	749	7 893	..
Q4	..	..	..	..	..	..	..	1 024	..	..	663	7 648	..
1966 Q1	..	..	..	..	..	..	..	982	..	..	795	7 240	..
Q2	..	..	..	..	..	..	..	1 057	..	..	771	7 438	..
Q3	..	..	..	..	..	..	..	1 091	..	..	760	7 640	..
Q4	..	..	..	..	..	..	..	1 084	..	..	687	7 150	..
1967 Q1	..	..	..	..	..	..	..	1 051	..	..	1 012	9 314	..
Q2	..	..	..	..	..	..	..	1 133	..	..	897	8 385	..
Q3	..	..	..	..	..	..	..	1 164	..	..	807	7 974	..
Q4	..	..	..	..	..	..	..	1 154	..	..	831	8 386	..
1968 Q1	..	..	..	..	..	..	..	1 154	..	..	899	7 920	..
Q2	..	..	..	..	..	..	..	1 225	..	..	853	7 525	..
Q3	..	..	..	..	..	..	..	1 259	..	..	792	7 407	..
Q4	..	..	..	..	..	..	..	1 243	..	..	824	8 109	..

See footnotes on page 182.

Sources: Office for National Statistics; Enquiries Columns 1-7 01633 812125; ; Department of the Environment, transport and the Regions;; Enquiries Columns 8-13 020 7890 5583

4.2 Engineering and construction: output and orders

continued

Volume index numbers except where stated in £ million

	Total engineering industries							Construction(GB)					
	Home market		Export		Total			Output[3]			Orders received		
	Orders on hand end of period (average 1995 = 100)	New orders[2] (1995 average monthly sales = 100)	Orders on hand end of period (average 1995 = 100)	New orders[2] (1995 average monthly sales = 100)	Turnover (1995 average monthly sales =100)	Orders on hand end of period (average 1995 = 100)	New orders[2] (1995 average monthly sales = 100)	£ million at current prices, not seasonally adjusted	At 1995 prices, seasonally adjusted: £ million	At 1995 prices, seasonally adjusted: 1995 = 100	£ million at current prices, not seasonally adjusted	At 1995 prices, seasonally adjusted: £ million	At 1995 prices, seasonally adjusted: 1995 = 100
	FGVU	FGVV	FGVX	FGVY	FGVT	FGWA	FGWB	FGAY	FGAZ	FEAQ	FHAA	FHAB	FEAZ
1969 Q1	..	..	..	..	..	..	..	1 188	..	..	848	7 114	..
Q2	..	..	..	..	..	..	..	1 278	..	..	840	6 915	..
Q3	..	..	..	..	..	..	..	1 312	..	..	794	7 013	..
Q4	..	..	..	..	..	..	..	1 268	..	..	827	7 375	..
1970 Q1	..	..	..	..	..	..	..	1 219	..	..	907	6 967	..
Q2	..	..	..	..	..	..	..	1 353	..	..	959	7 313	..
Q3	..	..	..	..	..	..	..	1 413	..	..	873	7 212	..
Q4	..	..	..	..	..	..	..	1 373	..	..	792	6 708	..
1971 Q1	..	..	..	..	..	..	..	1 356	..	..	1 025	7 228	..
Q2	..	..	..	..	..	..	..	1 493	..	..	1 143	7 530	..
Q3	..	..	..	..	..	..	..	1 534	..	..	1 036	7 519	..
Q4	..	..	..	..	..	..	..	1 547	..	..	1 040	7 954	..
1972 Q1	..	..	..	..	..	..	..	1 542	..	..	1 298	8 207	..
Q2	..	..	..	..	..	..	..	1 692	..	..	1 460	8 565	..
Q3	..	..	..	..	..	..	..	1 715	..	..	1 215	7 424	..
Q4	..	..	..	..	..	..	..	1 805	..	..	1 321	8 251	..
1973 Q1	..	..	..	..	..	..	..	1 945	..	..	1 747	9 215	..
Q2	..	..	..	..	..	..	..	2 113	..	..	1 804	7 895	..
Q3	..	..	..	..	..	..	..	2 277	..	..	1 815	7 675	..
Q4	..	..	..	..	..	..	..	2 279	..	..	1 568	6 654	..
1974 Q1	..	..	..	..	..	..	..	2 258	..	..	1 471	5 234	..
Q2	..	..	..	..	..	..	..	2 462	..	..	1 502	5 053	..
Q3	..	..	..	..	..	..	..	2 558	..	..	1 536	5 242	..
Q4	..	..	..	..	..	..	..	2 455	..	..	1 502	5 471	..
1975 Q1	..	..	..	..	..	..	..	2 532	..	..	1 479	4 948	..
Q2	..	..	..	..	..	..	..	2 775	..	..	1 654	5 172	..
Q3	..	..	..	..	..	..	..	2 910	..	..	1 732	5 690	..
Q4	..	..	..	..	..	..	..	2 864	..	..	1 512	5 472	..
1976 Q1	..	..	..	..	..	..	..	2 883	..	..	1 809	6 163	..
Q2	..	..	..	..	..	..	..	3 004	..	..	1 947	6 077	..
Q3	..	..	..	..	..	..	..	3 112	..	..	1 628	5 291	..
Q4	..	..	..	..	..	..	..	3 182	..	..	1 490	5 096	..
1977 Q1	..	..	..	..	..	..	..	3 045	..	..	1 640	4 896	..
Q2	..	..	..	..	..	..	..	3 281	..	..	1 893	5 024	..
Q3	..	..	..	..	..	..	..	3 484	..	..	1 857	5 081	..
Q4	..	..	..	..	..	..	..	3 504	..	..	1 791	5 295	..
1978 Q1	..	..	..	..	..	..	..	3 490	..	..	2 100	5 581	..
Q2	..	..	..	..	..	..	..	3 969	..	..	2 301	5 247	..
Q3	..	..	..	..	..	..	..	4 144	..	..	2 385	5 431	..
Q4	..	..	..	..	..	..	..	4 100	..	..	2 144	5 179	..
1979 Q1	..	..	..	..	..	..	..	3 949	..	..	2 173	4 633	..
Q2	..	..	..	..	..	..	..	4 618	..	..	2 764	5 153	..
Q3	..	..	..	..	..	..	..	5 094	..	..	2 578	4 902	..
Q4	..	..	..	..	..	..	..	5 209	..	..	2 509	4 754	..
1980 Q1	..	..	..	..	..	..	..	5 122	10 747	81.7	2 517	3 863	..
Q2	..	..	..	..	..	..	..	5 490	10 423	79.2	2 772	3 576	..
Q3	..	..	..	..	..	..	..	5 919	10 494	79.7	2 511	3 165	..
Q4	..	..	..	..	..	..	..	5 520	9 644	73.3	2 314	3 135	..
1981 Q1	..	..	..	..	..	..	..	5 278	9 551	72.6	2 591	3 431	..
Q2	..	..	..	..	..	..	..	5 399	9 277	70.6	2 911	3 400	..
Q3	..	..	..	..	..	..	..	5 652	9 494	72.1	2 800	3 755	..
Q4	..	..	..	..	..	..	..	5 217	8 953	68.0	2 421	3 597	..
1982 Q1	..	..	..	..	..	..	..	5 324	9 343	71.0	2 751	3 805	..
Q2	..	..	..	..	..	..	..	5 659	9 489	72.1	2 890	3 894	..
Q3	..	..	..	..	..	..	..	6 004	9 675	73.5	2 949	4 111	..
Q4	..	..	..	..	..	..	..	5 967	10 000	76.0	2 857	4 451	..
1983 Q1	..	..	..	..	..	..	..	5 919	10 192	77.4	3 311	4 832	..
Q2	..	..	..	..	..	..	..	6 097	10 208	77.6	3 384	4 571	..
Q3	..	..	..	..	..	..	..	6 798	10 660	81.0	3 541	4 985	..
Q4	..	..	..	..	..	..	..	6 696	10 735	81.6	3 281	4 740	..

See footnotes on page 182.

Sources: Office for National Statistics; Enquiries Columns 1-7 01633 812125; ; Department of the Environment, transport and the Regions;; Enquiries Columns 8-13 020 7890 5583

4.2 Engineering and construction: output and orders

continued

Volume index numbers except where stated in £ million

	Total engineering industries							Construction(GB)					
	Home market		Export		Total			Output[3]			Orders received		
	Orders on hand end of period (average 1995 = 100)	New orders[2] (1995 average monthly sales = 100)	Orders on hand end of period (average 1995 = 100)	New orders[2] (1995 average monthly sales = 100)	Turnover (1995 average monthly sales =100)	Orders on hand end of period (average 1995 = 100)	New orders[2] (1995 average monthly sales = 100)	£ million at current prices, not seasonally adjusted	At 1995 prices, seasonally adjusted: £ million	At 1995 prices, seasonally adjusted: 1995 = 100	£ million at current prices, not seasonally adjusted	At 1995 prices, seasonally adjusted: £ million	At 1995 prices, seasonally adjusted: 1995 = 100
	FGVU	FGVV	FGVX	FGVY	FGVT	FGWA	FGWB	FGAY	FGAZ	FEAQ	FHAA	FHAB	FEAZ
1984 Q1	..	..	..	..	..	..	..	6 496	10 687	81.2	3 527	4 795	..
Q2	..	..	..	..	..	..	..	6 873	10 975	83.4	3 896	5 019	..
Q3	..	..	..	..	..	..	..	7 363	11 022	83.7	3 686	4 819	..
Q4	..	..	..	..	..	..	..	7 044	10 821	82.2	3 522	4 963	..
1985 Q1	..	..	..	..	..	..	..	6 995	10 964	83.3	3 673	4 710	..
Q2	..	..	..	..	..	..	..	7 265	10 958	83.3	4 099	4 698	..
Q3	..	..	..	..	..	..	..	7 732	10 973	83.4	3 769	4 746	..
Q4	..	..	..	..	..	..	..	7 672	11 136	84.6	3 803	4 901	..
1986 Q1	..	..	..	..	..	..	..	7 270	10 717	81.4	3 996	5 514	99.9
Q2	..	..	..	..	..	..	..	7 839	11 304	85.9	4 472	5 809	105.3
Q3	..	..	..	..	..	..	..	8 481	11 626	88.3	4 567	6 131	111.2
Q4	..	..	..	..	..	..	..	8 460	11 878	90.3	4 073	5 860	106.2
1987 Q1	..	..	..	..	..	..	..	8 612	12 208	92.7	4 795	6 248	113.3
Q2	..	..	..	..	..	..	..	8 941	12 292	93.4	5 232	6 270	113.6
Q3	..	..	..	..	..	..	..	9 908	12 889	97.9	7 120	8 635	156.5
Q4	..	..	..	..	..	..	..	10 067	13 241	100.6	4 971	6 348	115.0
1988 Q1	..	..	..	..	..	..	..	10 443	13 779	104.7	6 541	7 347	133.2
Q2	..	..	..	..	..	..	..	10 923	13 799	104.9	6 441	6 612	119.8
Q3	..	..	..	..	..	..	..	11 529	13 673	103.9	6 479	6 887	124.8
Q4	..	..	..	..	..	..	..	11 958	14 187	107.8	6 837	7 502	136.0
1989 Q1	..	..	..	..	..	..	..	12 232	14 402	109.4	6 994	6 937	125.8
Q2	..	..	..	..	..	..	..	12 969	14 723	111.9	7 588	6 996	126.8
Q3	..	..	..	..	..	..	..	13 508	14 479	110.0	6 361	6 233	113.0
Q4	..	..	..	..	..	..	..	13 441	14 532	110.4	6 198	6 394	115.9
1990 Q1	..	..	..	..	..	..	..	13 594	14 833	112.7	6 139	5 910	107.1
Q2	..	..	..	..	..	..	..	13 850	14 775	112.3	6 241	5 944	107.8
Q3	..	..	..	..	..	..	..	14 175	14 451	109.8	5 363	5 476	99.3
Q4	..	..	..	..	..	..	..	13 688	14 316	108.8	4 748	5 178	93.9
1991 Q1	108.8	94.2	103.0	87.8	89.3	106.5	91.5	12 937	13 808	104.9	4 697	4 849	87.9
Q2	105.9	85.9	104.2	86.7	87.8	105.2	86.2	12 757	13 569	103.1	5 453	5 612	101.7
Q3	101.8	82.2	100.5	79.4	85.6	101.3	81.1	13 006	13 466	102.3	4 804	5 365	97.3
Q4	96.8	80.3	103.4	85.9	84.8	99.4	82.7	12 414	13 289	101.0	4 501	5 375	97.4
1992 Q1	98.3	89.1	100.4	80.0	85.6	99.1	85.3	11 946	13 190	100.2	4 919	5 546	100.5
Q2	97.9	86.3	101.9	84.7	85.2	99.5	85.6	11 764	12 976	98.6	4 196	4 792	86.9
Q3	90.9	78.9	100.1	81.3	85.7	94.5	79.9	12 102	12 933	98.3	4 459	5 391	97.7
Q4	90.3	88.4	102.0	87.5	87.6	94.9	88.0	11 661	12 825	97.5	3 918	4 900	88.8
1993 Q1	91.6	92.8	105.5	83.2	86.3	97.1	88.8	11 337	12 722	96.7	4 984	5 650	102.4
Q2	90.3	89.9	106.8	83.5	87.5	96.8	87.2	11 429	12 695	96.5	4 675	5 169	93.7
Q3	91.2	94.2	106.9	80.8	87.8	97.5	88.6	11 814	12 698	96.5	5 003	5 727	103.8
Q4	91.9	93.2	101.3	75.1	87.7	95.7	85.6	11 742	12 865	97.7	5 303	6 559	118.9
1994 Q1	93.2	97.5	103.4	89.6	92.4	97.3	94.2	11 812	13 057	99.2	5 600	5 952	107.9
Q2	95.6	101.0	104.0	89.7	94.3	98.9	96.3	12 156	13 168	100.1	5 594	5 933	107.6
Q3	103.0	109.3	103.1	90.6	96.6	103.1	101.5	12 683	13 216	100.4	5 436	5 709	103.5
Q4	105.6	104.2	104.2	95.2	98.1	105.1	100.4	12 789	13 251	100.7	4 654	5 107	92.6
1995 Q1	100.7	91.3	102.1	96.3	97.8	101.2	93.4	12 697	13 140	99.8	5 841	5 567	100.9
Q2	100.8	100.0	102.4	95.6	97.9	101.5	98.2	12 999	13 169	100.1	5 196	5 115	92.8
Q3	97.3	95.9	98.4	96.2	100.4	97.8	96.1	13 433	13 129	99.8	5 196	5 226	94.7
Q4	100.0	105.9	95.9	102.6	103.9	98.3	104.5	13 514	13 204	100.3	5 832	6 158	111.6
1996 Q1	95.2	94.7	100.7	111.9	103.0	97.4	101.9	13 349	13 294	101.0	5 753	5 464	99.1
Q2	99.1	104.4	95.8	105.2	104.2	97.8	104.7	13 560	13 352	101.5	5 633	5 562	100.8
Q3	98.3	97.9	97.8	111.2	103.2	98.1	103.4	14 083	13 552	103.0	5 538	5 607	101.7
Q4	94.1	94.8	94.4	106.7	104.3	94.2	99.8	14 251	13 665	103.8	5 911	6 131	111.1
1997 Q1	96.8	103.8	93.2	110.2	105.1	95.4	106.5	13 961	13 700	104.1	6 197	5 767	104.5
Q2	95.7	100.2	97.4	118.0	106.5	96.4	107.6	14 400	13 834	105.1	6 287	5 908	107.1
Q3	95.7	101.2	99.0	116.2	106.7	97.1	107.5	14 771	13 860	105.3	6 196	5 931	107.5
Q4	97.6	102.4	96.5	114.0	107.1	97.1	107.2	15 219	14 074	106.9	6 126	6 036	109.4

See footnotes on page 182.

Sources: Office for National Statistics; Enquiries Columns 1-7 01633 812125; ;
Department of the Environment, transport and the Regions;;
Enquiries Columns 8-13 020 7890 5583

4.2 Engineering and construction: output and orders

continued

Volume index numbers except where stated in £ million

	Total engineering industries							Construction(GB)					
	Home market		Export		Total			Output[3]			Orders received		
	Orders on hand end of period (average 1995 = 100)	New orders[2] (1995 average monthly sales = 100)	Orders on hand end of period (average 1995 = 100)	New orders[2] (1995 average monthly sales = 100)	Turnover (1995 average monthly sales =100)	Orders on hand end of period (average 1995 = 100)	New orders[2] (1995 average monthly sales = 100)	£ million at current prices, not seasonally adjusted	At 1995 prices, seasonally adjusted: £ million	At 1995 prices, seasonally adjusted: 1995 = 100	£ million at current prices, not seasonally adjusted	At 1995 prices, seasonally adjusted: £ million	At 1995 prices, seasonally adjusted: 1995 = 100
	FGVU	FGVV	FGVX	FGVY	FGVT	FGWA	FGWB	FGAY	FGAZ	FEAQ	FHAA	FHAB	FEAZ
1998 Q1	97.4	105.5	103.1	127.2	111.6	99.7	114.6	15 211	14 431	109.7	6 972	6 188	112.2
Q2	98.2	102.3	106.9	126.4	110.0	101.7	112.3	15 129	13 964	106.1	6 553	5 867	106.4
Q3	91.2	95.4	107.1	122.4	111.5	97.5	106.7	15 773	13 968	106.1	7 146	6 565	119.0
Q4	89.6	100.3	102.1	120.9	112.4	94.5	108.9	15 947	14 006	106.4	6 806	6 281	113.9
1999 Q1	91.5	110.2	104.8	125.4	113.9	96.8	116.6	15 638	14 106	107.2	6 736	5 707	103.5
Q2	91.8	108.7	101.4	119.5	114.6	95.6	113.2	16 032	14 174	107.7	6 759	5 757	104.4
Q3	96.5	116.2	106.1	130.1	116.5	100.3	122.0	16 658	14 256	108.3	6 352	5 497	99.7
Q4	103.7	117.7	108.9	132.1	117.4	105.7	123.7	16 933	14 367	109.2	6 233	5 642	102.3
2000 Q1	110.1	117.7	106.9	122.8	116.2	108.8	119.8	17 063	14 808	112.5	6 864	4 346	103.5

See footnotes on page 182.

Sources: Office for National Statistics; Enquiries Columns 1-7 01633 812125; ; Department of the Environment, transport and the Regions;; Enquiries Columns 8-13 020 7890 5583

4.3 Motor vehicle production[1] and steel production and consumption

	Passenger cars[2]		Commercial vehicles		Not seasonally adjusted[3]	
	Not seasonally adjusted		Not seasonally adjusted			
	Total production (thousands)	*of which* for export (thousands)	Total production (thousands)	*of which* for export (thousands)	Crude steel production (thousand tonnes)	Finished steel consumption (thousand tonnes)
	FFAA	FFAB	FFAC	FFAD	FFAF	FFAE
1946	18.3	8.3	12.2	4.0	..	..
1947	23.9	12.9	12.9	4.2	..	..
1948	27.9	19.7	14.8	7.1	..	..
1949	34.3	22.7	18.2	8.9	..	..
1950	43.5	34.1	21.9	13.8	16 554	..
1951	39.7	30.6	21.5	13.5	15 890	..
1952	37.3	23.0	20.1	10.4	16 366	..
1953	49.6	26.1	20.0	9.4	17 891	..
1954	64.1	33.2	22.4	10.9	18 817	..
1955	74.8	32.5	28.3	12.1	20 108	..
1956	59.0	29.7	24.8	10.9	20 990	..
1957	71.7	38.5	24.0	10.8	22 047	..
1958	87.6	43.5	26.1	10.1	19 505	..
1959	99.2	50.8	30.9	11.6	20 510	..
1960	112.7	48.0	38.2	14.0	24 695	15 154
1961	83.7	33.5	38.3	13.6	22 441	14 479
1962	104.1	45.9	35.5	13.0	20 820	13 895
1963	134.0	54.1	33.7	13.8	22 880	14 551
1964	155.6	58.8	38.7	14.9	26 185	16 450
1965	143.5	54.4	37.9	14.5	27 421	16 893
1966	133.6	52.1	36.5	14.9	24 686	16 466
1967	129.3	47.0	32.1	11.6	24 257	15 840
1968	151.4	66.9	34.1	12.5	26 255	16 835
1969	143.1	68.7	38.8	16.1	26 822	17 782
1970	136.8	60.2	38.1	15.9	28 291	17 637
1971	145.1	59.5	38.0	15.7	24 153	16 722
1972	160.1	51.1	34.0	11.3	25 293	16 750
1973	145.6	50.4	34.7	13.3	26 594	18 445
1974	127.8	49.7	33.5	14.2	22 323	17 548
1975	105.6	44.4	31.8	15.5	20 098	15 446
1976	111.1	47.1	31.0	15.8	22 274	15 804
1977	109.6	46.9	33.2	16.4	20 411	15 300
1978	101.9	41.2	32.0	14.1	20 311	15 710
1979	89.2	32.7	34.0	13.6	21 464	15 480
1980	77.0	29.1	32.4	13.0	11 277	12 696
1981	79.6	25.4	19.1	9.5	15 573	12 416
1982	74.0	18.8	22.4	7.7	13 704	12 240
1983	87.1	19.8	20.4	5.2	14 986	11 510
1984	75.7	16.0	18.7	4.1	15 121	11 340
1985	87.3	17.3	22.2	5.5	15 722	11 560
1986	84.9	15.6	19.1	4.2	14 725	11 840
1987	95.2	18.8	20.6	5.1	17 414	12 330
1988	102.2	17.8	26.4	7.0	18 950	14 480
1989	108.3	23.4	27.2	8.0	18 740	14 700
1990	108.0	33.8	22.5	8.0	17 841	14 070
1991	103.1	50.4	18.1	9.2	16 474	12 180
1992	107.7	49.1	20.7	10.9	16 212	11 450
1993	114.6	44.4	16.1	7.6	16 625	11 660
1994	122.2	51.6	19.0	8.0	17 286	12 650
1995	127.7	62.1	19.4	7.7	17 604	13 241
1996	140.5	75.7	19.9	9.4	17 992	12 918
1997	141.5	80.2	19.8	8.6	18 501	13 994
1998	145.7	85.1	18.9	8.6	17 315	14 594
1999	148.9	94.9	15.5	6.2	16 298	13 456

1 Monthly averages.
2 As from January 1981, certain passenger cars were reclassified from assembly to production. These are almost exclusively built for the home market. Further details are given in Business Monitor PM 3510 Car and commercial vehicle production.
3 These figures fall outside the scope of National Statistics.

Sources: Office for National Statistics: Enquiries Columns 1-4 01633 812963; ISSB Ltd; Enquiries Columns 5-6 020 7343 3900

4.3 Motor vehicle production[1] and steel production and consumption

continued

	Passenger cars				Commercial vehicles				Not seasonally adjusted[5]		Seasonally adjusted[3,5]	
	Not seasonally adjusted		Seasonally adjusted[2,4]		Not seasonally adjusted		Seasonally adjusted[2,4]					
	Total production (thousands)	*of which* for export (thousands)	Total production (thousands)	*of which* for export (thousands)	Total production (thousands)	*of which* for export (thousands)	Total production (thousands)	*of which* for export (thousands)	Crude steel production (thousand tonnes)	Finished steel consumption (thousand tonnes)	Crude steel production (thousand tonnes)	Finished steel consumption (thousand tonnes)
	FFAA	FFAB	FFAO	FFAP	FFAC	FFAD	FFAQ	FFAR	FFAF	FFAE	FFAM	FFAN
1946 Q1	9.8	4.8	10.0	5.0	10.2	3.3	11.0	3.0	..	..	..	..
Q2	17.9	8.4	17.0	8.0	12.8	4.3	12.0	4.0	..	..	..	..
Q3	19.0	8.3	20.0	9.0	11.8	4.0	12.0	4.0	..	..	..	..
Q4	26.3	11.7	27.0	12.0	13.9	4.4	13.0	4.0	..	..	..	..
1947 Q1	19.0	8.7	19.0	9.0	10.1	3.0	10.0	3.0	..	..	..	..
Q2	27.0	12.8	25.0	12.0	13.8	4.2	13.0	4.0	..	..	..	..
Q3	24.7	14.1	26.0	14.0	13.1	4.2	14.0	4.0	..	..	..	..
Q4	24.9	16.1	26.0	17.0	14.5	5.4	14.0	5.0	..	..	..	..
1948 Q1	27.0	18.8	27.0	19.0	13.9	6.4	14.0	6.0	..	..	..	..
Q2	29.7	22.0	28.0	20.0	14.2	6.6	14.0	7.0	..	..	..	..
Q3	28.2	19.9	29.0	21.0	14.6	7.6	15.0	8.0	..	..	..	..
Q4	26.8	18.2	27.0	19.0	16.4	7.8	16.0	8.0	..	..	..	..
1949 Q1	32.1	21.3	32.0	21.0	17.4	8.7	17.0	8.0	..	..	..	..
Q2	33.5	21.8	32.0	20.0	17.7	7.9	18.0	8.0	..	..	..	..
Q3	33.1	20.7	35.0	22.0	17.1	7.9	18.0	9.0	..	..	..	..
Q4	38.7	27.0	39.0	28.0	20.6	11.0	20.0	11.0	..	..	..	..
1950 Q1	43.8	35.2	43.0	34.0	22.2	14.1	22.0	13.0	..	..	..	..
Q2	43.7	35.1	42.0	32.0	22.7	14.5	23.0	14.0	..	..	..	..
Q3	41.2	32.2	44.0	35.0	20.4	12.9	22.0	14.0	..	..	..	..
Q4	45.4	34.0	45.0	35.0	22.2	13.5	21.0	13.0	..	..	..	..
1951 Q1	41.1	30.5	40.0	30.0	22.8	14.6	22.0	14.0	..	..	..	..
Q2	40.4	32.7	39.0	30.0	21.9	13.8	22.0	14.0	..	..	..	..
Q3	36.3	28.1	40.0	31.0	19.6	11.8	22.0	13.0	..	..	..	..
Q4	40.8	31.0	40.0	32.0	21.7	13.6	20.0	13.0	..	..	..	..
1952 Q1	37.8	27.6	37.0	27.0	21.3	12.4	20.0	12.0	..	..	..	..
Q2	38.2	26.6	37.0	24.0	20.2	11.6	20.0	11.0	..	..	..	..
Q3	32.1	18.9	35.0	21.0	17.7	8.9	20.0	10.0	..	..	..	..
Q4	41.2	18.7	40.0	20.0	21.4	8.9	20.0	9.0	..	..	..	..
1953 Q1	43.1	24.8	42.0	24.0	20.3	8.9	19.0	8.0	..	..	..	..
Q2	50.8	31.5	48.0	28.0	19.4	9.2	19.0	9.0	..	..	..	..
Q3	48.7	24.1	55.0	27.0	18.1	9.0	20.0	10.0	..	..	..	..
Q4	55.7	24.1	54.0	26.0	22.0	10.4	21.0	10.0	..	..	..	..
1954 Q1	61.1	31.4	60.0	30.0	21.5	11.0	20.0	10.0	..	..	..	..
Q2	65.4	37.0	61.0	32.0	21.0	10.6	21.0	10.0	..	..	..	..
Q3	56.6	30.4	62.0	34.0	19.6	9.8	22.0	11.0	..	..	..	..
Q4	73.3	33.8	74.0	37.0	27.4	12.0	26.0	12.0	..	..	..	..
1955 Q1	78.0	37.8	76.0	36.0	28.1	12.8	27.0	12.0	..	..	..	..
Q2	75.6	34.6	67.0	30.0	27.7	12.1	27.0	12.0	..	..	..	..
Q3	66.7	28.6	73.0	33.0	26.7	11.4	31.0	13.0	..	..	..	..
Q4	78.9	29.2	84.0	32.0	30.7	12.2	29.0	12.0	..	..	..	..
1956 Q1	71.8	33.2	70.0	31.0	31.5	13.1	30.0	12.0	..	..	..	..
Q2	65.9	34.9	56.0	31.0	27.9	12.3	27.0	12.0	..	..	..	..
Q3	45.6	24.2	50.0	28.0	18.7	9.0	21.0	10.0	..	..	..	..
Q4	52.6	26.4	60.0	28.0	20.9	9.1	20.0	9.0	..	..	..	..
1957 Q1	53.0	33.7	50.0	31.0	22.2	11.0	21.0	10.0	..	..	..	..
Q2	76.5	41.6	60.0	37.0	23.8	10.2	23.0	10.0	..	..	..	..
Q3	72.7	36.8	78.0	42.0	22.3	9.5	25.0	11.0	..	..	..	..
Q4	84.7	41.9	98.0	44.0	27.7	12.4	27.0	12.0	..	..	..	..
1958 Q1	92.8	47.9	50.0	45.0	28.8	11.8	27.0	11.0	..	..	..	..
Q2	90.8	45.5	60.0	41.0	26.3	10.3	25.0	10.0	..	..	..	..
Q3	77.4	38.2	78.0	45.0	21.5	8.3	24.0	9.0	..	..	..	..
Q4	89.5	42.4	98.0	44.0	27.7	10.0	27.0	10.0	..	..	..	..
1959 Q1	86.1	46.6	82.0	44.0	26.6	10.3	25.0	10.0	..	..	..	..
Q2	105.2	54.4	81.0	49.0	32.2	12.5	31.0	12.0	..	..	..	..
Q3	84.5	43.2	89.0	51.0	29.5	10.8	33.0	12.0	..	..	..	..
Q4	120.9	59.2	144.0	60.0	35.2	13.0	35.0	13.0	..	..	..	..
1960 Q1	130.9	66.5	129.0	63.0	38.3	13.8	36.0	13.0	6 340.0	3 882.0	..	3 739
Q2	135.1	59.4	112.0	55.0	40.2	14.0	39.0	14.0	6 245.0	3 974.0	..	3 844
Q3	103.9	34.5	114.0	41.0	34.5	12.8	39.0	14.0	5 694.0	3 512.0	..	3 809
Q4	81.0	31.4	96.0	33.0	39.7	15.4	39.0	15.0	6 416.0	3 786.0	..	3 762

1 Monthly averages.
2 Seasonally adjusted figures before 1968 are given to the nearest thousand.
3 The seasonally adjusted quarterly figures are not constrained to sum to the unadjusted annual totals.
4 See footnote 5 on page 191.
5 These figures fall outside the scope of National Statistics.

Sources: Office for National Statistics; Enquiries Columns 1-8 01633 812963; ISSB Ltd; Enquiries Columns 9-12 020 7343 3900

4.3 Motor vehicle production[1] and steel production and consumption

continued

	Passenger cars				Commercial vehicles				Not seasonally adjusted[5]		Seasonally adjusted[3,5]	
	Not seasonally adjusted		Seasonally adjusted[2,4]		Not seasonally adjusted		Seasonally adjusted[2,4]					
	Total production (thousands)	*of which* for export (thousands)	Total production (thousands)	*of which* for export (thousands)	Total production (thousands)	*of which* for export (thousands)	Total production (thousands)	*of which* for export (thousands)	Crude steel production (thousand tonnes)	Finished steel consumption (thousand tonnes)	Crude steel production (thousand tonnes)	Finished steel consumption (thousand tonnes)
	FFAA	FFAB	FFAO	FFAP	FFAC	FFAD	FFAQ	FFAR	FFAF	FFAE	FFAM	FFAN
1961 Q1	72.7	29.8	70.0	27.0	41.5	15.7	39.0	15.0	6 309.0	3 811.0	..	3 732
Q2	94.6	32.6	81.0	30.0	41.5	14.2	40.0	14.0	6 103.0	3 772.0	..	3 608
Q3	81.7	30.2	90.0	35.0	34.5	11.9	38.0	13.0	4 892.0	3 368.0	..	3 639
Q4	85.7	41.4	95.0	42.0	35.8	12.5	35.0	12.0	5 137.0	3 528.0	..	3 500
1962 Q1	109.1	49.6	104.0	45.0	37.3	13.7	36.0	13.0	5 304.0	3 565.0	5 121.0	3 439
Q2	110.6	48.3	97.0	45.0	35.2	13.1	34.0	13.0	5 492.0	3 602.0	5 316.0	3 493
Q3	96.4	42.6	108.0	50.0	32.3	11.9	36.0	13.0	4 827.0	3 303.0	5 357.0	3 562
Q4	100.4	43.1	108.0	44.0	37.0	13.2	36.0	13.0	5 197.0	3 425.0	5 076.0	3 401
1963 Q1	127.4	53.6	120.0	49.0	34.1	14.3	32.0	13.0	5 414.0	3 447.0	5 243.0	3 358
Q2	140.3	53.4	124.0	49.0	33.7	14.3	32.0	14.0	5 633.0	3 697.0	5 453.0	3 538
Q3	122.1	50.2	139.0	58.0	30.9	12.4	35.0	14.0	5 383.0	3 452.0	5 948.0	3 759
Q4	146.2	59.2	153.0	60.0	35.9	14.0	35.0	14.0	6 450.0	3 955.0	6 299.0	3 896
1964 Q1	172.7	68.2	163.0	63.0	41.2	15.8	39.0	15.0	6 455.0	4 130.0	6 263.0	4 026
Q2	172.6	64.3	153.0	60.0	40.4	15.7	38.0	15.0	6 833.0	4 295.0	6 626.0	4 084
Q3	125.6	44.5	148.0	53.0	32.6	12.9	37.0	15.0	5 959.0	3 765.0	6 543.0	4 075
Q4	151.7	58.2	157.0	58.0	40.6	15.4	40.0	15.0	6 938.0	4 260.0	6 896.0	4 265
1965 Q1	153.3	58.8	144.0	54.0	40.4	15.0	39.0	14.0	7 227.0	4 456.0	6 893.0	4 288
Q2	162.9	58.5	144.0	54.0	42.2	15.7	39.0	15.0	7 077.0	4 437.0	6 871.0	4 283
Q3	113.9	46.7	138.0	56.0	31.2	12.0	36.0	14.0	6 457.0	3 832.0	7 033.0	4 147
Q4	144.0	53.5	148.0	53.0	37.9	15.4	37.0	15.0	6 660.0	4 168.0	6 594.0	4 175
1966 Q1	154.1	56.1	146.0	52.0	40.1	14.9	39.0	14.0	6 565.0	4 348.0	6 274.0	4 182
Q2	161.4	58.3	141.0	53.0	41.2	15.8	38.0	15.0	6 455.0	4 346.0	6 320.0	4 196
Q3	111.4	42.6	137.0	52.0	32.3	13.6	37.0	16.0	5 884.0	3 918.0	6 448.0	4 230
Q4	107.6	51.4	109.0	57.0	32.6	15.1	32.0	14.0	5 782.0	3 854.0	5 766.0	3 858
1967 Q1	129.2	53.0	122.0	50.0	31.7	13.5	31.0	13.0	6 252.0	4 065.0	6 081.0	4 026
Q2	148.8	55.0	130.0	50.0	34.7	12.4	32.0	12.0	6 287.0	4 151.0	6 126.0	3 900
Q3	105.1	35.1	130.0	43.0	27.8	9.1	32.0	11.0	5 530.0	3 526.0	6 100.0	3 813
Q4	134.2	44.9	136.0	44.0	34.1	11.5	34.0	11.0	6 188.0	4 098.0	6 168.0	4 101
1968 Q1	155.9	65.9	147.6	62.1	34.8	12.4	34.1	12.1	6 330.0	4 246.0	6 165.0	4 078
Q2	163.0	75.0	148.5	66.3	34.8	12.6	31.9	11.6	6 835.0	4 299.0	6 626.0	4 147
Q3	129.9	58.1	158.3	71.3	29.5	10.6	35.0	12.7	6 143.0	3 992.0	6 676.0	4 308
Q4	156.6	68.6	150.9	67.9	37.3	14.4	35.4	13.6	6 947.0	4 298.0	6 878.0	4 302
1969 Q1	150.4	70.5	144.1	67.9	40.1	16.4	39.7	16.2	7 139.0	4 608.0	6 920.0	4 434
Q2	161.7	79.8	149.6	71.9	42.1	17.4	38.9	16.1	7 139.0	4 685.0	6 910.0	4 525
Q3	118.2	56.5	149.7	71.6	32.8	13.7	40.8	17.0	5 809.0	4 087.0	6 339.0	4 419
Q4	142.0	68.0	128.9	63.6	40.2	16.8	35.8	14.9	6 735.0	4 402.0	6 661.0	4 404
1970 Q1	145.5	66.4	143.2	64.9	38.4	15.5	39.2	15.9	7 112.0	4 626.0	6 910.0	4 514
Q2	156.7	69.0	141.0	60.6	44.1	18.0	39.5	16.0	7 182.0	4 582.0	6 949.0	4 364
Q3	92.4	40.0	116.7	50.5	25.0	10.5	31.3	13.1	6 485.0	4 133.0	6 882.0	4 463
Q4	152.4	65.5	146.0	64.9	45.0	19.4	42.5	18.3	7 013.0	4 296.0	7 090.0	4 296
1971 Q1	144.1	67.6	139.4	64.8	36.6	16.1	36.8	16.4	6 598.0	4 696.0	6 325.0	4 520
Q2	156.7	69.3	145.5	63.0	44.5	18.4	40.3	16.5	6 145.0	4 303.0	5 975.0	4 158
Q3	121.3	47.6	147.6	58.3	32.4	13.5	39.2	16.2	5 876.0	3 763.0	6 411.0	4 067
Q4	158.5	53.6	148.2	52.0	38.7	14.7	35.7	13.5	5 534.0	3 960.0	5 561.0	3 977
1972 Q1	160.1	55.9	154.5	53.8	31.6	10.5	32.2	10.9	5 428.0	4 029.0	5 228.0	3 933
Q2	171.4	55.9	160.4	51.4	37.2	13.2	34.1	12.0	6 781.0	4 246.0	6 519.0	4 043
Q3	132.1	39.7	161.3	48.1	26.8	9.1	32.3	10.7	6 209.0	3 958.0	6 732.0	4 275
Q4	176.9	53.0	164.3	51.2	40.4	12.4	37.5	11.6	6 875.0	4 517.0	6 875.0	4 499
1973 Q1	159.5	52.8	152.3	50.6	35.4	12.1	35.4	12.5	6 889.0	4 909.0	6 671.0	4 667
Q2	148.7	51.9	139.9	47.8	36.5	13.3	33.6	12.1	6 667.0	4 498.0	6 415.0	4 368
Q3	117.3	40.8	144.8	49.8	30.0	12.0	35.8	14.0	6 396.0	4 253.0	6 954.0	4 599
Q4	157.0	56.2	145.4	53.5	36.9	15.6	34.1	14.4	6 642.0	4 785.0	6 649.0	4 811
1974 Q1	129.3	50.2	123.4	47.9	29.8	12.3	29.2	12.3	5 335.0	4 579.0	5 218.0	4 357
Q2	146.5	54.7	136.9	50.1	36.4	15.4	33.9	14.0	5 936.0	4 689.0	5 784.0	4 560
Q3	102.2	40.4	127.1	50.1	30.0	13.3	35.7	15.6	5 376.0	3 929.0	5 763.0	4 252
Q4	133.4	53.4	124.1	50.6	38.0	15.8	35.4	14.9	5 676.0	4 351.0	5 599.0	4 379
1975 Q1	127.4	46.7	123.2	44.9	36.1	15.6	35.6	15.7	6 242.0	4 368.0	6 102.0	4 267
Q2	95.9	47.6	89.3	43.5	32.7	16.1	30.5	14.6	4 803.0	3 868.0	4 661.0	3 695
Q3	89.9	39.3	107.9	47.8	26.0	12.9	30.4	15.2	4 305.0	3 436.0	4 231.0	3 715
Q4	109.3	43.9	102.1	41.2	32.2	17.5	30.4	16.7	4 747.0	3 774.0	4 719.0	3 769

1 Monthly averages.
2 Seasonally adjusted figures before 1968 are given to the nearest thousand.
3 The seasonally adjusted quarterly figures are not constrained to sum to the unadjusted annual totals.
4 See footnote 5 on page 191.
5 These figures fall outside the scope of National Statistics.

Sources: Office for National Statistics; Enquiries Columns 1-8 01633 812963; ISSB Ltd; Enquiries Columns 9-12 020 7343 3900

4.3 Motor vehicle production[1] and steel production and consumption

continued

	Passenger cars				Commercial vehicles				Not seasonally adjusted[5]		Seasonally adjusted[3,5]	
	Not seasonally adjusted		Seasonally adjusted[2,4]		Not seasonally adjusted		Seasonally adjusted[2,4]					
	Total production (thousands)	*of which* for export (thousands)	Total production (thousands)	*of which* for export (thousands)	Total production (thousands)	*of which* for export (thousands)	Total production (thousands)	*of which* for export (thousands)	Crude steel production (thousand tonnes)	Finished steel consumption (thousand tonnes)	Crude steel production (thousand tonnes)	Finished steel consumption (thousand tonnes)
	FFAA	FFAB	FFAO	FFAP	FFAC	FFAD	FFAQ	FFAR	FFAF	FFAE	FFAM	FFAN
1976 Q1	119.6	49.6	116.1	48.2	31.3	16.3	29.5	15.2	5 625.0	4 284.0	5 480.0	4 076
Q2	116.5	47.9	109.6	44.9	32.6	17.1	29.6	15.2	5 885.0	3 994.0	5 731.0	3 887
Q3	84.6	36.1	106.8	45.9	25.3	13.1	32.0	16.2	5 089.0	3 499.0	5 375.0	3 785
Q4	123.8	54.7	97.1	49.4	34.9	16.7	32.9	16.6	5 676.0	4 027.0	5 650.0	4 056
1977 Q1	110.1	49.9	108.2	49.0	36.5	19.2	33.7	17.3	5 550.0	4 090.0	5 417.0	3 744
Q2	123.7	53.8	101.4	45.4	33.7	17.3	31.4	15.7	5 038.0	3 774.0	4 908.0	3 758
Q3	90.2	34.9	110.1	43.7	28.6	13.9	34.4	17.1	5 095.0	3 572.0	5 419.0	3 974
Q4	114.6	49.1	119.0	49.5	33.9	15.1	33.2	15.5	4 728.0	3 864.0	4 641.0	3 824
1978 Q1	119.5	49.3	108.9	45.9	34.6	16.2	30.4	14.7	5 092.0	4 466.0	4 957.0	4 139
Q2	120.9	46.3	103.1	41.6	37.4	16.8	31.6	14.8	5 423.0	4 122.0	5 278.0	4 124
Q3	87.1	33.6	100.2	40.1	27.4	11.5	30.6	13.2	4 470.0	3 543.0	4 757.0	3 838
Q4	80.1	35.6	95.4	37.2	28.8	11.8	35.6	13.7	5 326.0	3 579.0	5 245.0	3 609
1979 Q1	108.5	39.6	91.8	34.4	40.0	16.1	35.6	14.4	5 078.0	4 059.0	4 954.0	3 776
Q2	105.6	37.5	90.6	29.8	40.5	17.4	36.5	15.3	5 875.0	3 975.0	5 720.0	3 955
Q3	57.1	19.8	87.7	32.7	24.2	9.7	31.5	12.7	5 160.0	3 493.0	5 485.0	3 754
Q4	85.7	34.0	88.5	34.0	31.4	11.0	32.6	11.7	5 351.0	3 953.0	5 252.0	3 995
1980 Q1	99.4	39.3	87.8	35.1	41.1	14.2	38.2	13.4	784.0	3 336.0	764.0	3 115
Q2	83.8	35.9	83.9	35.2	37.3	13.9	35.4	13.8	4 205.0	3 499.0	4 098.0	3 460
Q3	60.5	22.2	73.2	27.1	26.4	11.4	31.5	12.8	3 225.0	2 928.0	3 498.0	3 146
Q4	64.2	19.1	63.1	19.1	25.0	12.6	24.7	11.7	3 062.0	3 007.0	3 027.0	3 049
1981 Q1	81.9	26.1	74.5	24.8	19.1	10.4	18.4	10.2	3 675.0	3 206.0	3 585.0	2 994
Q2	81.8	27.6	77.0	25.8	19.8	10.4	18.6	9.4	4 005.0	3 040.0	3 892.0	3 024
Q3	75.1	23.5	85.2	26.2	16.2	7.9	18.8	9.3	3 851.0	3 060.0	3 813.0	3 272
Q4	79.4	24.4	81.6	24.8	21.4	9.3	20.8	9.1	4 041.0	3 110.0	4 018.0	3 150
1982 Q1	85.8	21.0	79.9	19.2	23.2	8.8	22.1	8.7	4 137.0	3 450.0	4 030.0	3 210
Q2	76.2	21.4	73.5	20.6	23.1	9.0	22.2	8.4	3 949.0	3 200.0	3 840.0	3 210
Q3	58.5	15.1	68.9	18.0	19.6	6.6	22.3	7.5	2 880.0	2 750.0	3 054.0	2 950
Q4	75.5	17.8	73.5	17.6	23.7	6.4	23.0	6.2	2 738.0	2 840.0	2 720.0	2 870
1983 Q1	88.7	20.1	86.6	20.5	23.3	5.4	22.1	5.3	3 869.0	3 030.0	3 768.0	2 810
Q2	95.8	19.5	89.2	17.7	20.9	6.0	19.1	5.2	3 914.0	2 930.0	3 813.0	2 900
Q3	75.3	18.5	87.3	21.3	16.7	4.4	19.7	5.2	3 483.0	2 620.0	3 690.0	2 820
Q4	88.4	21.0	85.1	19.7	20.6	5.1	20.5	5.1	3 720.0	2 930.0	3 662.0	2 980
1984 Q1	90.9	21.8	73.9	19.5	23.3	5.3	21.3	5.1	4 068.0	3 090.0	3 963.0	2 850
Q2	78.0	16.1	72.3	16.1	19.7	3.9	19.1	3.5	3 701.0	2 790.0	3 604.0	2 720
Q3	65.5	9.8	72.6	11.8	14.9	3.4	17.4	4.0	3 517.0	2 690.0	3 743.0	2 910
Q4	68.5	16.4	84.1	16.8	17.0	3.9	17.2	4.1	3 837.0	2 850.0	3 766.0	2 860
1985 Q1	97.1	18.2	84.5	15.9	23.3	5.3	21.6	5.1	3 857.0	3 050.0	3 714.0	2 820
Q2	94.8	18.4	89.6	19.1	25.2	6.3	23.6	5.6	4 388.0	2 790.0	4 117.0	2 820
Q3	73.9	15.1	89.8	17.7	20.1	4.6	23.8	5.3	3 614.0	2 670.0	3 920.0	2 910
Q4	83.6	17.6	85.4	16.6	20.0	5.7	19.6	5.9	3 862.0	3 050.0	3 965.0	3 010
1986 Q1	84.6	18.5	83.8	16.5	18.1	4.8	17.9	5.0	3 949.0	3 200.0	3 787.0	2 950
Q2	89.0	14.1	83.1	14.9	21.0	4.9	19.5	4.2	3 493.0	2 960.0	3 256.0	3 010
Q3	73.5	13.6	83.7	16.3	16.4	3.2	18.6	3.6	3 158.0	2 730.0	3 436.0	2 960
Q4	92.6	16.3	89.0	14.8	20.7	3.7	20.3	3.8	4 125.0	2 950.0	4 244.0	2 890
1987 Q1	94.4	20.7	88.3	18.8	20.7	4.6	20.3	4.5	4 209.0	3 050.0	3 989.0	2 870
Q2	100.7	18.3	91.6	19.7	20.3	5.9	18.5	5.1	4 568.0	2 900.0	4 392.0	3 030
Q3	86.6	15.7	100.2	18.9	18.5	4.6	21.2	5.2	4 187.0	3 200.0	4 673.0	3 260
Q4	99.2	20.7	100.7	17.9	22.8	5.2	22.3	5.4	4 454.0	3 180.0	4 672.0	3 170
1988 Q1	102.0	17.7	104.8	15.9	21.6	5.6	21.8	5.8	4 908.0	3 840.0	4 751.0	3 580
Q2	107.4	14.8	99.7	16.5	28.0	8.0	25.6	7.0	4 839.0	3 560.0	4 694.0	3 630
Q3	85.6	15.6	98.9	19.3	24.2	6.4	29.8	7.8	4 316.0	3 340.0	4 675.0	3 570
Q4	114.0	23.2	105.6	19.6	32.1	8.1	28.6	7.6	4 888.2	3 740.0	4 727.3	3 700
1989 Q1	118.7	25.9	109.8	22.7	30.0	8.3	28.1	7.9	5 030.8	3 970.0	4 854.0	3 670
Q2	120.5	22.6	109.3	24.1	30.1	9.3	27.4	8.0	4 854.8	3 850.0	4 740.6	3 910
Q3	90.1	19.2	107.5	24.2	21.9	6.8	25.8	8.1	4 396.6	3 400.0	4 912.0	3 660
Q4	103.7	25.9	106.5	22.6	26.9	7.4	27.5	7.9	4 450.6	3 480.0	4 282.6	3 530
1990 Q1	108.9	29.6	108.7	27.0	23.0	6.7	26.3	6.6	4 666.2	3 850.0	4 539.8	3 600
Q2	109.0	21.9	98.2	24.5	27.6	9.6	24.3	8.4	4 707.5	3 730.0	4 543.9	3 680
Q3	91.4	28.2	106.9	35.7	19.9	7.2	21.4	8.4	4 269.1	3 210.0	4 758.5	3 460
Q4	122.5	55.6	118.1	48.1	19.6	8.4	18.1	8.5	4 202.5	3 280.0	4 075.7	3 330

1 Monthly averages.
2 Seasonally adjusted figures before 1968 are given to the nearest thousand.
3 The seasonally adjusted quarterly figures are not constrained to sum to the unadjusted annual totals.
4 See footnote 5 on page 191.
5 These figures fall outside the scope of National Statistics.

Sources: Office for National Statistics; Enquiries 01633 812963; ISSB Ltd; Enquiries 020 7343 3900

4.3 Motor vehicle production[1] and steel production and consumption

continued

	Passenger cars				Commercial vehicles				Not seasonally adjusted[6]		Seasonally adjusted[3,6]	
	Not seasonally adjusted		Seasonally adjusted[2,5]		Not seasonally adjusted		Seasonally adjusted[2,5]					
	Total production (thousands)	*of which* for export (thousands)	Total production (thousands)	*of which* for export (thousands)	Total production (thousands)	*of which* for export (thousands)	Total production (thousands)	*of which* for export (thousands)	Crude steel production (thousand tonnes)	Finished steel consumption (thousand tonnes)	Crude steel production (thousand tonnes)	Finished steel consumption (thousand tonnes)
	FFAA	FFAB	FFAO	FFAP	FFAC	FFAD	FFAQ	FFAR	FFAF	FFAE	FFAM	FFAN
1991 Q1	115.4	56.6	109.8	53.1	19.3	9.0	17.8	7.7	4 075.6	3 530.0	3 912.8	3 290
Q2	116.1	54.9	103.8	53.8	17.8	9.2	16.9	8.9	4 365.1	3 030.0	4 267.5	2 980
Q3	83.3	39.2	100.5	50.1	13.7	6.6	17.0	8.8	3 849.2	2 710.0	4 222.2	2 920
Q4	97.5	51.0	99.2	45.4	21.5	12.1	20.9	11.7	4 187.3	2 910.0	4 101.3	2 980
1992 Q1	114.4	48.1	110.9	46.1	22.3	13.3	20.8	11.6	4 245.7	3 300.0	4 134.0	3 060
Q2	114.5	41.4	107.0	43.3	24.0	12.9	23.3	12.6	4 284.7	2 930.0	4 078.1	2 870
Q3	91.8	41.3	107.7	50.9	18.6	8.9	22.4	11.6	4 061.8	2 780.0	4 353.2	3 020
Q4	109.9	65.6	108.3	58.0	17.9	8.4	16.9	7.8	3 618.3	2 440.0	3 650.6	2 490
1993 Q1	121.5	51.5	109.5	46.2	19.7	10.1	17.6	8.5	4 221.0	3 050.0	4 028.6	2 730
Q2	126.1	44.3	115.6	46.1	15.5	6.7	15.2	6.7	4 461.7	2 910.0	4 249.6	2 800
Q3	100.3	35.6	116.4	42.4	11.9	5.0	13.3	6.0	3 948.3	2 730.0	4 166.4	3 020
Q4	110.6	46.2	111.0	40.3	17.3	8.6	17.4	8.6	3 986.4	2 970.0	4 126.9	3 170
1994 Q1	120.8	46.2	111.5	41.0	20.1	9.1	18.3	7.8	4 234.0	3 130.0	4 061.8	2 910
Q2	129.7	51.2	118.9	52.8	18.8	7.5	17.6	7.3	4 532.9	2 990.0	4 285.2	2 960
Q3	107.8	42.2	129.7	52.6	16.2	6.4	19.3	7.9	4 014.9	3 220.0	4 270.2	3 390
Q4	130.6	66.7	128.9	59.8	20.9	8.9	20.8	8.8	4 004.3	3 310.0[4]	4 722.3	..
1995 Q1	140.5	75.0	131.0	68.3	21.7	9.4	19.3	7.8	4 493.4	3 353.0	4 390.8	..
Q2	138.9	60.7	129.9	62.7	22.0	9.2	20.7	8.7	4 706.7	3 489.0	4 427.7	..
Q3	103.9	46.2	124.6	57.3	17.5	7.3	21.3	9.5	4 230.3	3 105.0	4 508.2	..
Q4	127.3	66.4	125.1	59.9	16.4	4.8	16.3	4.8	4 174.0	3 294.0	4 247.4	..
1996 Q1	141.0	74.1	132.4	67.0	20.8	10.8	18.9	9.3	4 315.8	3 509.0	4 257.6	..
Q2	142.6	68.9	136.2	71.5	21.8	9.5	21.0	9.3	4 674.0	3 326.0	4 384.6	..
Q3	125.6	71.0	144.8	84.2	16.4	6.8	19.3	8.7	4 297.7	3 001.0	4 554.5	..
Q4	152.9	88.7	149.2	80.4	20.4	10.4	20.3	10.4	4 704.2	3 082.0	4 796.8	..
1997 Q1	145.4	86.9	143.0	82.4	20.6	9.5	19.9	8.6	4 611.2	3 924.0	4 586.2	..
Q2	147.2	78.9	138.0	79.8	19.9	8.7	18.7	8.0	4 836.9	3 735.0	4 553.0	..
Q3	123.2	67.7	137.4	78.0	17.5	7.4	19.9	9.1	4 495.3	3 179.0	4 745.9	..
Q4	150.2	87.1	143.4	78.3	21.2	8.8	20.3	8.4	4 556.0	3 156.0	4 636.3	..
1998 Q1	154.1	89.0	149.8	82.4	20.0	8.9	18.9	7.8	4 498.7	3 984.7	4 492.4	..
Q2	156.1	81.6	147.1	82.9	20.0	9.7	18.9	9.3	4 660.0	3 788.0	4 392.7	..
Q3	134.5	75.1	150.2	86.9	16.5	7.4	19.1	9.1	4 502.0	3 598.6	4 765.5	..
Q4	138.0	94.6	135.2	88.3	19.3	8.4	18.7	8.1	3 657.4	3 088.2	3 687.6	..
1999 Q1	153.5	97.6	..	..	17.8	7.5	..	..	4 126.5	3 427.0	4 050.9	..
Q2	149.6	97.7	..	..	16.8	6.7	..	..	4 376.8	3 808.8	4 098.8	..
Q3	135.9	76.7	..	..	12.1	4.4	..	..	4 054.8	3 281.5	4 243.5	..
Q4	156.5	107.5	..	..	15.3	6.4	..	..	3 739.6	2 938.7	3 847.2	..
2000 Q1	163.5	103.8	..	..	17.8	9.6	..	..	4 442.5	3 686.6	4 409.0	..
Q2	..	..	..	..	..	..	..	..	4 019.8	3 204.3	3 787.9	..

1 Monthly averages.
2 Seasonally adjusted figures before 1968 are given to the nearest thousand.
3 The seasonally adjusted quarterly figures are not constrained to sum to the unadjusted annual totals.
4 From 1994 Q3 consumption no longer includes stock changes at steel stockholders and merchants.
5 Seasonally adjusted estimates are not available beyond December 1998. The introduction of a new bi-annual registration system is expected to have a significant impact on the seasonal patterns of production. Since it is not possible to determine a seasonal pattern from one year's data, it has been decided to publish only unadjusted data until sufficient data are available to construct a new seasonally adjusted series.
6 These figures fall outside the scope of National Statistics.

Sources: Office for National Statistics; Enquiries 01633 812963; ISSB Ltd; Enquiries 020 7343 3900

4.4 Indicators of fixed investment in dwellings

	Fixed investment in dwellings (£ million)		Orders received by contractors for new houses (GB) (£ million)	Housing starts (GB) (thousands)			Housing completions (GB) (thousands)			Building societies (£ million)			
	Current prices	1995 prices	current prices	Private enterprise	Housing associations	Local authorities, new towns and government departments	Private enterprise	Housing associations	Local authorities, new towns and government departments	Commitments on new dwellings	Advances on new dwellings	Average price of new dwellings: mortgages approved[1,2]	Quarterly average price of new dwellings at mortgage completion stage[4]
	DFDK	DFDV	FGAU	FCAB	CTOR	CTOV	FCAD	CTOT	CTOX	AHLC	AHLH	FCAY	BBJV
1950	338	7 413	..	19.8	1.9	182.5	27.4	1.6	169.2	..	..	..	..
1951	386	7 292	..	27.1	2.2	189.9	22.6	1.8	170.5	..	..	..	..
1952	513	8 785	..	52.3	3.9	238.2	34.3	2.2	203.4	..	..	..	..
1953	658	11 405	..	83.2	16.5	248.4	62.9	7.9	247.9	..	..	..	..
1954	674	11 771	..	106.8	7.2	216.0	90.6	14.9	242.3	..	..	..	..
1955	667	10 912	..	127.5	2.5	182.8	113.5	4.6	199.4	..	..	..	..
1956	662	10 444	..	120.4	1.8	156.5	124.2	2.7	173.8	..	..	2 280	..
1957	644	10 061	562	125.6	1.2	149.2	126.5	2.0	172.6	..	..	2 330	..
1958	616	9 578	550	136.9	1.4	120.8	128.1	1.2	144.3	..	140	2 390	..
1959	684	10 925	732	169.4	1.7	146.5	150.7	1.1	124.8	..	182	2 410	..
1960	761	12 142	778	182.8	1.6	124.8	168.6	1.8	127.4	..	206	2 530	..
1961	835	12 978	788	189.4	1.7	121.2	177.5	1.6	116.9	..	207	2 770	..
1962	925	13 936	857	186.0	1.9	135.8	174.8	1.6	129.0	..	214	2 950	..
1963	1 020	14 072	1 040	199.4	5.5	163.1	174.9	2.0	122.1	..	255	3 160	..
1964	1 283	17 358	1 305	247.5	4.9	173.8	218.1	2.9	152.7	..	358	3 460	..
1965	1 385	18 352	1 303	211.1	3.0	178.4	213.8	4.0	164.5	..	369	3 820	..
1966	1 489	18 958	1 248	193.4	4.7	181.2	205.4	4.6	175.6	..	416	4 100	..
1967	1 676	21 406	1 532	233.6	6.1	207.8	200.4	5.0	198.9	..	461	4 340	..
1968	1 907	23 109	1 360	200.1	8.3	186.0	222.0	6.3	185.4	..	510	4 640	..
1969	1 917	22 318	1 166	166.8	10.0	166.6	181.7	7.3	177.8	..	451	4 880	..
1970	1 870	20 259	1 265	165.1	8.6	145.3	170.3	8.5	171.6	..	510	5 180	..
1971	2 218	22 079	1 456	207.4	11.0	125.8	191.6	10.7	148.3	..	713	5 970	..
1972	2 566	22 709	1 977	228.0	9.7	113.3	196.5	7.7	115.2	964	862	7 850	..
1973	3 150	22 271	2 509	215.7	11.1	101.7	186.6	8.9	98.6	816	903	10 690	..
1974	3 786	20 977	2 009	105.9	11.8	134.3	140.9	9.9	118.7	704	700	11 340	..
1975	4 682	21 496	2 662	149.1	19.6	154:1	150.8	14.7	147.6	994	945	12 406	..
1976	5 450	22 179	2 880	154.7	29.2	141.6	152.2	15.8	147.2	1 119	1 125	13 442	..
1977	5 699	21 114	2 627	134.8	28.3	103.9	140.8	25.1	137.4	1 260	1 175	14 768	..
1978	6 325	21 283	3 231	157.3	20.5	86.9	149.0	22.8	108.0	1 523	1 504	17 685	..
1979	7 649	22 025	3 321	144.0	15.9	65.3	140.5	17.8	86.2	1 498	1 519	22 728	..
1980	8 674	20 402	2 702	98.8	14.8	41.5	128.4	21.1	86.0	1 444[3]	1 406[3]	27 244	..
1981	8 138	16 888	2 685	117.4	11.6	26.0	115.0	19.3	65.5	1 427	1 456	28 028	..
1982	8 920	17 963	3 912	140.8	18.3	34.9	125.4	13.1	37.3	1 931	1 716	28 508	..
1983	10 447	20 184	5 063	172.4	14.3	34.6	148.1	16.1	35.1	2 419	2 330	31 678	..
1984	11 932	21 055	4 877	158.5	12.6	27.3	159.4	16.6	34.0	2 980	2 900	34 160	..
1985	12 219	20 139	5 290	165.6	12.4	22.0	156.5	13.1	27.2	2 963	2 900	37 304	..
1986	14 140	22 047	6 193	180.6	13.2	20.4	170.9	12.6	23.0	3 626	3 517	43 647	..
1987	16 548	23 836	7 343	196.8	12.9	19.9	183.8	12.6	20.1	3 697	3 494	51 290	..
1988	21 097	27 596	8 775	221.7	14.5	16.4	199.9	12.8	19.7	4 787	4 629	64 615	..
1989	22 771	27 096	7 370	169.9	16.0	15.2	179.6	13.9	17.7	4 389	4 130	73 820	..
1990	21 048	23 434	5 538	137.1	18.5	8.6	161.3	17.6	16.6	3 790	3 668	77 556	..
1991	18 339	19 587	5 427	136.7	22.4	4.3	154.1	20.3	10.3	3 879	3 643	75 989	..
1992	18 825	20 041	5 263	120.2	33.8	2.7	141.4	26.5	4.7	3 201	3 189	73 441	..
1993	19 892	21 491	6 542	140.4	41.8	2.2	141.0	35.5	2.6	3 117	3 043	76 143	73 229
1994	21 233	22 267	7 106	158.4	41.4	1.4	147.8	36.8	2.0	4 095	3 879	77 074	74 805
1995	21 588	21 588	6 087	134.2	33.0	1.1	150.9	38.4	2.1	3 965	3 880	78 983	79 274
1996	22 766	22 154	6 487	144.8	29.4	0.6	147.6	32.3	0.9	4 545	4 188	81 716	85 271
1997	23 927	22 669	7 248	162.1	26.4	0.4	152.5	27.5	0.4	3 021	2 759	88 123	93 196
1998	25 831	23 231	6 930	154.5	22.3	0.2	145.9	23.4	0.4	1 999	1 916	96 679	96 674
1999	27 599	23 522	6 869	157.1	20.8	0.3	148.9	20.2	0.2	2 573	2 485	109 733	112 088

1 Mortgages with building societies by private owners. The series covers only dwellings on which building societies have approved mortgages during the period. The cost of land is included.

2 From July 1989 the Abbey National building society changed its status to one of public limited company and is excluded from the series. From August 1995, Cheltenham and Gloucester building society excluded, from August 1996, National and Provincial building society excluded, from April 1997, Alliance and Leicester excluded, from June 1997, Halifax excluded, from July 1997 Woolwich and Bristol and West excluded, from October 1997, Northern Rock excluded.

3 See notes and definitions.

4 Series based on mortgage lending by all financial institutions rather than building societies only, as previously published. This is because of the mergers, takeovers and conversions to plc status affecting the building society sector. The series is based on the the Department of the Environment, Transport and the Regions' 5% survey of Mortgage Lenders (at completion stage) which now includes all mortgage lenders rather than building societies only.

Sources: Office for National Statistics;
Enquiries Columns 1, 2 020 7533 6010; Columns 10, 11 Bank of England; 020 7601 3743, Department of the Environment, Transport and the Regions;
Enquiries Column 3 020 7890 5583; Columns 4-9 0117 9878055;
Column 12 020 7890 3325;
Scottish Development Department;
Welsh Office;
Building Societies Association

4.4 Indicators of fixed investment in dwellings

continued

Not seasonally adjusted

	Fixed investment in dwellings (£ million)		Orders received by contractors for new houses (GB) (£ million): current prices	Housing starts (GB) (thousands)			Housing completions (GB) (thousands)			Building societies (£ million)		Average price of new dwellings: mortgages approved[1,2]
	Current prices	1995 prices		Private enterprise	Housing associations	Local authorities, new towns and government departments	Private enterprise	Housing associations	Local authorities, new towns and government departments	Commitments on new dwellings	Advances on new dwellings	
	DFDK	DFDV	FGAU	FCAB	CTOR	CTOV	FCAD	CTOT	CTOX	AHLC	AHLH	FCAY
1955 Q1	163	..	..	25.1	..	..	22.1	..	..	..	..	..
Q2	162	..	..	38.1	..	..	28.0	..	..	..	..	..
Q3	171	..	..	34.8	..	..	30.3	..	..	..	..	..
Q4	171	..	..	29.5	..	..	33.1	..	..	..	..	..
1956 Q1	153	..	..	26.6	..	..	26.5	..	..	..	..	2 240
Q2	171	..	..	37.0	..	..	31.8	..	..	..	..	2 280
Q3	171	..	..	29.7	..	..	32.1	..	..	..	..	2 300
Q4	167	..	..	27.2	..	..	33.8	..	..	..	..	2 280
1957 Q1	160	..	..	27.8	..	..	29.4	..	..	..	..	2 290
Q2	169	..	..	36.6	..	..	32.0	..	..	..	..	2 290
Q3	157	..	..	33.1	..	..	32.1	..	..	..	..	2 340
Q4	158	..	..	28.1	..	..	33.0	..	..	..	..	2 380
1958 Q1	148	..	130	28.3	..	..	28.2	..	..	..	30	2 360
Q2	156	..	127	38.4	..	..	30.7	..	..	..	34	2 400
Q3	155	..	134	35.4	..	..	33.8	..	..	..	36	2 410
Q4	157	..	159	34.7	..	..	35.5	..	..	..	40	2 390
1959 Q1	156	..	202	35.9	..	..	30.3	..	..	..	32	2 390
Q2	170	..	172	48.2	..	..	37.4	..	..	..	46	2 400
Q3	176	..	172	45.4	..	..	39.6	..	..	..	51	2 410
Q4	182	..	187	40.0	..	..	43.3	..	..	..	53	2 420
1960 Q1	179	..	205	41.3	..	..	35.3	..	..	..	46	2 430
Q2	194	..	186	54.9	..	..	43.4	..	..	..	51	2 480
Q3	193	..	186	46.6	..	..	44.2	..	..	..	55	2 560
Q4	195	..	202	40.0	..	..	45.8	..	..	..	54	2 640
1961 Q1	196	..	220	43.6	..	..	40.2	..	..	..	47	2 690
Q2	210	..	191	56.8	..	..	45.6	..	..	..	53	2 740
Q3	215	..	187	48.8	..	..	45.1	..	..	..	52	2 790
Q4	214	..	190	40.3	..	..	46.7	..	..	..	55	2 850
1962 Q1	214	3 301	229	41.5	..	..	38.5	..	..	..	42	2 910
Q2	237	3 641	207	50.7	..	..	44.6	..	..	..	52	2 930
Q3	243	3 613	211	49.1	..	..	44.9	..	..	..	57	2 950
Q4	231	3 381	210	44.6	..	..	46.8	..	..	..	63	3 010
1963 Q1	177	2 477	277	28.0	..	..	28.7	..	..	..	42	3 080
Q2	267	3 685	248	60.3	..	..	44.4	..	..	..	65	3 130
Q3	284	3 902	252	58.4	..	..	48.9	..	..	..	76	3 160
Q4	292	4 008	262	52.7	..	..	52.8	..	..	..	72	3 280
1964 Q1	297	4 038	323	54.6	..	..	46.6	..	..	..	75	3 370
Q2	328	4 437	319	66.5	..	..	53.8	..	..	..	87	3 420
Q3	328	4 428	321	62.9	..	..	56.3	..	..	..	99	3 520
Q4	330	4 455	342	63.5	..	..	61.4	..	..	..	97	3 600
1965 Q1	336	4 529	373	56.6	..	..	50.5	..	..	..	88	3 700
Q2	343	4 560	320	58.5	..	..	53.8	..	..	..	89	3 800
Q3	347	4 605	315	48.5	..	..	53.6	..	..	..	86	3 850
Q4	359	4 658	294	47.6	..	..	56.0	..	..	..	106	3 920
1966 Q1	356	4 593	325	45.1	..	..	45.7	..	..	..	95	4 010
Q2	363	4 648	327	59.8	..	..	53.0	..	..	..	109	4 080
Q3	383	4 842	307	51.4	..	..	53.6	..	..	..	113	4 210
Q4	387	4 875	290	37.1	..	..	53.0	..	..	..	99	4 150
1967 Q1	399	5 038	457	59.7	..	..	42.3	..	..	..	95	4 270
Q2	417	5 372	401	72.6	..	..	47.8	..	..	..	114	4 310
Q3	437	5 624	324	53.9	..	..	51.9	..	..	..	122	4 360
Q4	423	5 372	350	47.5	..	..	58.5	..	..	..	130	4 420
1968 Q1	451	5 624	396	50.5	..	..	52.6	..	..	..	141	4 510
Q2	447	5 439	349	55.4	..	..	54.8	..	..	..	130	4 700
Q3	496	5 958	314	49.5	..	..	56.4	..	..	..	127	4 690
Q4	513	6 088	302	44.6	..	..	58.2	..	..	..	112	4 710
1969 Q1	460	5 397	310	35.4	..	..	42.6	..	..	..	110	4 720
Q2	445	5 233	281	52.7	..	..	47.1	..	..	..	120	4 840
Q3	508	5 936	285	43.0	..	..	46.5	..	..	..	117	4 940
Q4	504	5 752	288	35.7	..	..	45.5	..	..	..	104	5 040

See footnotes on page 192.

Sources: Office for National Statistics;
Enquiries Columns 1, 2 020 7533 6010; Columns 10, 11 Bank of England;
020 7601 3743, Department of the Environment, transport and the Regions;
Enquiries Column 3 020 7890 5583; Columns 4-9 0117 9878055;
Column 12 020 7890 3325;
Scottish Development Department;
Welsh Office;
Building Societies Association

4.4 Indicators of fixed investment in dwellings

continued

Not seasonally adjusted

	Fixed investment in dwellings (£ million): Current prices	Fixed investment in dwellings (£ million): 1995 prices	Orders received by contractors for new houses (GB) (£ million): current prices	Housing starts (GB) (thousands): Private enterprise	Housing starts (GB) (thousands): Housing associations	Housing starts (GB) (thousands): Local authorities, new towns and government departments	Housing completions (GB) (thousands): Private enterprise	Housing completions (GB) (thousands): Housing associations	Housing completions (GB) (thousands): Local authorities, new towns and government departments	Building societies (£ million): Commitments on new dwellings	Building societies (£ million): Advances on new dwellings	Average price of new dwellings: mortgages approved[1,2]
	DFDK	DFDV	FGAU	FCAB	CTOR	CTOV	FCAD	CTOT	CTOX	AHLC	AHLH	FCAY
1970 Q1	422	4 690	314	29.6	2.1	27.2	37.1	2.0	41.0	..	100	5 000
Q2	437	4 800	341	47.4	2.4	44.1	41.4	2.2	42.4	..	127	5 180
Q3	496	5 320	323	46.6	1.7	39.8	45.2	2.0	42.5	..	138	5 300
Q4	515	5 449	287	41.4	2.3	34.2	46.6	2.3	45.6	..	145	5 230
1971 Q1	482	5 015	305	40.7	3.0	27.2	40.5	2.8	38.5	..	136	5 600
Q2	539	5 472	370	51.8	2.4	36.9	45.4	2.7	35.4	..	180	5 770
Q3	595	5 828	375	57.5	2.0	32.8	50.1	2.0	34.5	..	196	6 190
Q4	602	5 764	407	57.5	3.5	28.9	55.6	3.0	39.8	..	201	6 350
1972 Q1	590	5 504	457	46.1	2.9	27.2	45.5	1.4	34.3	254	198	6 650
Q2	623	5 634	538	64.8	2.5	32.5	49.7	2.1	30.4	273	225	7 380
Q3	679	5 926	497	60.6	2.1	27.0	49.3	1.5	23.2	222	216	8 680
Q4	674	5 645	485	56.6	2.3	26.8	51.9	2.2	27.1	215	223	9 440
1973 Q1	706	5 523	666	55.5	3.1	23.4	46.0	2.0	22.7	246	239	10 150
Q2	793	5 767	654	62.0	2.7	29.9	48.9	2.5	26.7	211	238	10 640
Q3	784	5 440	636	55.9	2.3	25.5	46.3	1.9	23.5	201	230	10 960
Q4	867	5 541	553	42.4	3.1	22.9	45.5	2.4	25.8	158	196	11 240
1974 Q1	905	5 482	495	29.7	2.3	27.2	41.1	2.2	26.6	142	159	11 230
Q2	892	5 069	515	29.2	3.7	41.6	31.6	2.1	28.0	158	148	11 160
Q3	947	5 101	517	24.8	2.3	35.9	31.8	2.2	30.6	207	186	11 450
Q4	1 042	5 325	483	22.2	3.4	29.9	36.4	3.5	33.7	197	207	11 490
1975 Q1	1 147	5 657	605	28.8	3.8	31.6	33.4	3.5	31.6	225	197	11 818
Q2	1 206	5 638	694	41.6	5.0	39.9	38.8	3.6	36.1	261	241	12 401
Q3	1 108	4 963	695	41.4	4.9	42.0	38.2	3.5	38.1	253	250	12 664
Q4	1 221	5 238	669	37.4	6.1	40.4	40.4	3.8	41.9	255	257	12 746
1976 Q1	1 476	6 193	831	37.2	6.9	37.2	37.1	3.6	35.4	296	238	12 942
Q2	1 276	5 225	824	46.5	8.4	42.2	37.0	3.7	38.2	302	297	13 385
Q3	1 281	5 225	674	42.8	8.1	38.9	38.8	4.2	36.4	282	303	13 682
Q4	1 417	5 536	551	28.1	6.0	23.1	39.2	3.8	37.1	239	287	13 831
1977 Q1	1 454	5 569	564	26.2	5.0	21.8	31.8	4.5	31.5	249	232	13 986
Q2	1 312	4 921	737	38.1	7.4	29.9	35.0	4.1	34.5	308	275	13 463
Q3	1 399	5 174	677	39.1	8.1	29.1	35.7	7.5	34.8	327	320	14 951
Q4	1 534	5 450	649	31.4	7.7	23.1	38.3	8.4	36.3	376	348	15 442
1978 Q1	1 707	5 891	734	30.4	5.0	17.9	35.3	4.2	25.7	427	340	16 185
Q2	1 363	4 743	908	46.5	5.8	29.1	38.7	5.5	28.0	381	415	17 115
Q3	1 575	5 293	872	41.3	4.9	22.7	35.5	5.6	26.4	352	373	18 389
Q4	1 680	5 356	718	39.1	4.9	17.2	39.5	5.7	27.8	363	376	19 550
1979 Q1	1 742	5 401	625	23.3	3.7	11.6	29.3	4.6	16.5	387	334	20 612
Q2	1 646	4 941	948	40.0	4.4	20.0	33.6	3.7	20.7	388	395	22 118
Q3	1 856	5 345	989	41.2	3.9	18.0	32.1	3.9	20.3	375	408	23 650
Q4	2 405	6 338	759	39.4	3.8	15.8	45.5	5.4	28.7	348	382	25 036
1980 Q1	2 362	5 959	717	24.7	3.5	11.8	32.7	5.1	19.7	356	326	26 191
Q2	1 899	4 589	779	29.5	4.0	12.7	31.5	5.6	21.1	347	343	27 208
Q3	2 133	4 959	666	23.7	4.3	10.3	31.6	5.0	22.1	373	355	27 715
Q4	2 280	4 895	540	20.9	3.0	6.7	32.6	5.5	23.2	368[3]	382[3]	27 952
1981 Q1	2 044	4 307	583	26.5	1.5	6.2	29.1	6.1	18.8	392	342	28 512
Q2	2 055	4 288	711	32.8	2.5	7.1	26.4	4.7	17.5	387	387	28 621
Q3	2 130	4 389	733	32.8	3.0	6.8	29.0	4.4	15.2	332	369	27 990
Q4	1 909	3 904	658	25.2	4.6	6.0	30.6	4.1	14.0	316	358	26 794
1982 Q1	2 056	4 191	816	32.0	4.7	8.4	28.6	3.9	10.2	387	291	27 123
Q2	2 179	4 412	1 041	38.5	5.1	9.0	29.3	2.4	9.4	498	421	28 391
Q3	2 249	4 521	1 075	38.0	4.7	8.2	30.6	2.8	8.8	468	438	28 594
Q4	2 436	4 839	981	32.4	3.8	9.3	36.9	4.1	8.8	578	566	29 605
1983 Q1	2 418	4 746	1 205	40.9	3.6	11.3	33.1	3.6	7.5	599	486	30 570
Q2	2 426	4 803	1 359	48.6	4.1	9.3	36.3	4.0	8.3	606	587	31 825
Q3	2 730	5 264	1 371	44.6	2.9	7.0	35.9	3.7	9.6	562	593	32 245
Q4	2 873	5 371	1 129	38.3	3.7	7.1	42.8	4.9	9.7	652	664	32 096
1984 Q1	2 813	5 112	1 223	38.2	3.2	9.1	39.1	4.3	7.1	738	578	33 086
Q2	2 880	5 304	1 330	45.1	4.1	7.3	36.7	4.1	8.6	878	760	34 345
Q3	3 222	5 541	1 289	41.4	2.9	6.0	39.7	3.9	8.9	671	780	34 906
Q4	3 017	5 098	1 035	33.8	2.4	5.0	43.9	4.3	9.4	693	782	34 338

See footnotes on page 192.

Sources: Office for National Statistics;
Enquiries Columns 1, 2 020 7533 6010; Columns 10, 11 Bank of England;
020 7601 3743, Department of the Environment, Transport and the Regions;
Equiries Column 3 020 7890 5583; Columns 4-9 0117 9878055;
Column 12 020 7890 3325;
Scottish Development Department;
Welsh Office;
Building Societies Association

4.4 Indicators of fixed investment in dwellings

continued

Not seasonally adjusted

	Fixed investment in dwellings (£ million)		Orders received by contractors for new houses (GB) (£ million):	Housing starts (GB) (thousands)			Housing completions (GB) (thousands)			Building societies (£ million)		
	Current prices	1995 prices	current prices	Private enterprise	Housing assoc-iations	Local author-ities, new towns and government depart-ments	Private enterprise	Housing assoc-iations	Local author-ities, new towns and government depart-ments	Commit-ments on new dwellings	Advances on new dwellings	Average price of new dwellings: mortgages approved[1,2]
	DFDK	DFDV	FGAU	FCAB	CTOR	CTOV	FCAD	CTOT	CTOX	AHLC	AHLH	FCAY
1985 Q1	2 748	4 600	1 148	35.1	3.2	5.4	37.1	3.4	6.7	708	580	35 658
Q2	2 991	4 984	1 387	45.9	3.5	5.9	38.3	3.2	7.2	743	751	36 556
Q3	3 302	5 434	1 408	45.3	2.6	5.5	37.4	2.9	6.7	710	724	37 625
Q4	3 178	5 121	1 346	39.4	3.1	5.2	43.6	3.5	6.6	802	845	39 458
1986 Q1	3 301	5 208	1 291	37.5	3.2	5.0	37.2	3.0	4.9	791	637	40 470
Q2	3 030	4 845	1 750	51.5	4.1	4.9	40.6	3.3	6.1	1 104	910	43 443
Q3	3 746	5 826	1 660	50.4	3.0	5.4	41.9	2.8	5.5	949	976	45 065
Q4	4 063	6 168	1 492	41.2	2.9	5.0	51.2	3.5	6.5	782	994	45 749
1987 Q1	3 672	5 419	1 700	45.2	2.7	5.6	43.5	2.6	4.3	807	663	47 460
Q2	3 742	5 470	1 915	52.2	3.9	5.4	44.1	3.5	4.8	974	881	49 604
Q3	4 741	6 769	1 948	54.0	3.2	4.4	45.1	3.3	5.3	946	936	52 428
Q4	4 393	6 178	1 780	45.4	3.1	4.4	51.2	3.2	5.7	970	1 014	55 474
1988 Q1	5 030	6 848	2 037	52.1	3.3	4.8	50.0	3.0	4.4	1 268	921	60 395
Q2	5 240	6 990	2 291	61.8	3.7	4.4	47.5	3.0	5.4	1 467	1 222	63 342
Q3	5 458	7 059	2 270	56.6	3.8	3.5	50.4	3.1	5.3	1 170	1 326	67 425
Q4	5 369	6 699	2 177	51.3	3.7	3.7	52.2	3.6	4.7	882	1 160	69 342
1989 Q1	6 016	7 400	2 037	47.0	4.3	4.0	46.8	3.5	4.1	955	818	71 828
Q2	5 428	6 510	2 121	50.0	4.4	4.2	43.9	3.0	4.3	1 284	1 111	75 213
Q3	5 846	6 915	1 643	40.3	3.8	3.8	43.0	3.7	4.6	1 112	1 011	74 019
Q4	5 481	6 271	1 568	32.6	3.4	3.2	45.9	3.6	4.7	1 038	1 190	73 855
1990 Q1	5 569	6 292	1 580	36.0	4.7	3.2	41.2	3.6	4.2	1 003	858	77 018
Q2	4 802	5 418	1 555	37.4	5.0	2.1	38.2	4.2	4.3	968	938	77 783
Q3	5 401	6 024	1 320	34.4	4.4	1.7	39.0	4.3	4.6	864	886	78 955
Q4	5 276	5 700	1 083	29.4	4.4	1.6	42.9	5.5	3.5	955	986	76 585
1991 Q1	4 509	4 828	1 283	32.1	5.9	1.6	36.4	4.8	2.8	831	703	74 842
Q2	4 357	4 667	1 523	38.4	5.4	1.1	38.1	5.5	3.1	1 107	950	76 680
Q3	4 794	5 117	1 429	36.6	5.5	0.8	38.1	5.6	2.4	976	937	76 826
Q4	4 679	4 975	1 192	29.7	5.6	0.8	41.4	4.5	1.9	965	1 053	75 388
1992 Q1	4 601	4 884	1 373	32.0	8.7	0.9	37.2	5.3	1.6	832	699	73 125
Q2	4 354	4 617	1 421	34.7	8.5	0.6	34.3	5.6	1.2	919	885	74 467
Q3	4 843	5 159	1 391	29.8	9.2	0.6	35.6	7.3	1.2	730	847	72 740
Q4	5 027	5 381	1 076	23.6	7.5	0.6	34.3	8.3	0.7	720	758	73 231
1993 Q1	4 632	5 063	1 575	34.9	12.9	0.7	34.4	8.7	0.5	754	614	75 159
Q2	4 794	5 182	1 783	38.7	10.8	0.5	33.3	8.6	0.8	887	803	77 597
Q3	5 148	5 541	1 667	36.0	9.0	0.6	34.3	8.7	0.8	695	782	75 640
Q4	5 318	5 705	1 517	30.8	9.1	0.4	39.0	9.5	0.6	781	844	75 945
1994 Q1	5 624	6 003	1 859	38.1	12.0	0.4	33.6	9.4	0.6	969	725	75 537
Q2	4 814	5 072	1 978	44.7	11.7	0.4	35.4	8.6	0.4	1 109	997	77 413
Q3	5 162	5 392	1 799	40.7	10.0	0.2	38.4	9.1	0.6	1 011	1 033	78 175
Q4	5 633	5 800	1 470	34.9	7.6	0.3	40.4	9.8	0.4	1 006	1 124	77 163
1995 Q1	5 663	5 781	1 729	35.4	9.7	0.4	37.0	9.8	0.7	1 012	849	77 441
Q2	5 260	5 298	1 686	39.2	9.0	0.3	38.7	10.1	0.4	1 204	1 117	79 752
Q3	5 110	5 074	1 466	33.7	7.7	0.3	37.1	9.7	0.5	802	916	79 523
Q4	5 555	5 435	1 205	26.0	6.5	0.2	38.1	8.8	0.5	947	998	79 236
1996 Q1	5 262	5 158	1 544	33.0	8.6	0.2	35.6	9.0	0.3	975	762	79 141
Q2	5 441	5 321	1 620	37.3	7.6	0.2	35.3	7.7	0.2	1 291	1 134	81 782
Q3	5 673	5 528	1 594	39.4	7.0	0.1	37.0	8.1	0.2	1 119	1 069	82 013
Q4	6 390	6 147	1 730	35.1	6.2	0.1	39.9	7.5	0.2	1 160	1 223	83 532
1997 Q1	5 821	5 592	1 848	41.8	8.3	0.1	34.0	6.9	0.1	961	829	86 096
Q2	5 658	5 381	1 820	42.4	7.4	0.1	39.0	7.6	0.2	1 015	899	88 839
Q3	5 677	5 365	1 780	41.5	5.7	0.1	37.7	6.5	0.1	622	521	89 792
Q4	6 771	6 331	1 800	36.5	5.0	0.1	41.8	6.5	–	423	510	89 560
1998 Q1	6 088	5 631	2 062	41.8	6.1	0.1	33.8	7.2	0.1	499	377	92 638
Q2	6 611	6 004	1 777	40.5	6.1	–	37.8	5.6	0.1	586	547	96 839
Q3	6 206	5 554	1 736	40.0	5.5	–	36.7	5.2	0.1	471	473	97 702
Q4	6 926	6 042	1 355	32.2	4.6	0.1	37.6	5.4	0.1	443	519	100 113
1999 Q1	6 395	5 570	1 828	40.5	5.7	–	32.6	5.8	–	658	457	106 330
Q2	6 864	5 866	1 647	41.0	6.1	0.2	36.5	4.6	0.1	818	756	110 051
Q3	6 683	5 656	1 722	40.6	4.6	0.1	39.5	4.8	–	616	641	111 849
Q4	7 657	6 430	1 672	34.9	4.4	–	40.4	4.9	0.1	481	631	111 027
2000 Q1	6 792	5 697	1 881	42.8	4.9	0.1	34.5	5.5	–	425	438	115 568

See footnotes on page 192.

Sources: Office for National Statistics;
Enquiries Columns 1, 2 020 7533 6010; Columns 10, 11 Bank of England;
020 7601 3743, Department of the Environment, Transport and the Regions;
Enquiries Column 3 020 7890 5583; Columns 4-9 0117 9878055;
Column 12 020 7890 3325;
Scottish Development Department;
Welsh Office;
Building Societies Association

4.4 Indicators of fixed investment in dwellings

continued

Seasonally adjusted

	Fixed investment in dwellings (£ million)		Orders received by contractors for new houses (GB) (£ million):	Housing starts (GB) (thousands)			Housing completions (GB) (thousands)			Building societies (£ million)	
	Current prices	1995 prices	1995 prices	Private enterprise	Housing associations	Local authorities, new towns and government departments	Private enterprise	Housing associations	Local authorities, new towns and government departments	Commitments on new dwellings	Advances on new dwellings[1]
	GGAE	DFEG	FCAS	FCAT	CTOQ	CTOU	FCAV	CTOS	CTOW	AHLO	AHLS
1955 Q1	170	..	..	29.2	..	..	25.7	..	..	..	..
Q2	158	..	..	31.7	..	..	27.6	..	..	..	..
Q3	169	..	..	33.5	..	..	29.1	..	..	..	..
Q4	170	..	..	33.1	..	..	31.1	..	..	..	..
1956 Q1	160	..	..	29.0	..	..	29.3	..	..	..	..
Q2	167	..	..	31.5	..	..	31.7	..	..	..	..
Q3	169	..	..	29.2	..	..	31.6	..	..	..	..
Q4	166	..	..	30.7	..	..	31.6	..	..	..	..
1957 Q1	167	..	..	31.2	..	..	32.9	..	..	..	..
Q2	165	..	..	31.3	..	..	31.7	..	..	..	..
Q3	155	..	..	31.9	..	..	31.1	..	..	..	..
Q4	157	..	..	31.2	..	..	30.8	..	..	..	..
1958 Q1	154	..	..	31.3	..	..	31.8	..	..	..	..
Q2	152	..	..	32.7	..	..	30.5	..	..	..	..
Q3	154	..	..	34.2	..	..	32.6	..	..	..	..
Q4	156	..	..	38.7	..	..	33.2	..	..	..	..
1959 Q1	162	..	..	40.5	..	..	35.0	..	..	..	..
Q2	166	..	..	40.6	..	..	36.8	..	..	..	..
Q3	174	..	..	43.8	..	..	38.4	..	..	..	..
Q4	182	..	..	44.5	..	..	40.5	..	..	..	..
1960 Q1	186	..	..	45.2	..	..	39.6	..	..	..	..
Q2	190	..	..	47.2	..	..	43.1	..	..	..	..
Q3	189	..	..	45.2	..	..	42.7	..	..	..	..
Q4	196	..	..	45.2	..	..	43.2	..	..	..	..
1961 Q1	205	..	..	47.8	..	..	45.0	..	..	..	..
Q2	206	..	..	49.0	..	..	45.0	..	..	..	..
Q3	209	..	..	47.5	..	..	43.6	..	..	..	..
Q4	215	..	..	45.1	..	..	43.9	..	..	..	..
1962 Q1	227	3 501	..	45.4	..	..	43.1	..	..	..	..
Q2	232	3 569	..	43.9	..	..	44.3	..	..	..	..
Q3	235	3 490	..	47.8	..	..	43.9	..	..	..	..
Q4	231	3 376	..	48.9	..	..	43.5	..	..	..	..
1963 Q1	188	2 626	..	30.8	..	..	33.0	..	..	..	..
Q2	263	3 638	..	53.2	..	..	44.9	..	..	..	..
Q3	277	3 801	..	57.1	..	..	47.7	..	..	..	..
Q4	292	4 007	..	58.3	..	..	49.3	..	..	..	..
1964 Q1	311	4 230	..	61.0	..	..	53.7	..	..	..	..
Q2	325	4 399	..	57.1	..	..	53.2	..	..	..	..
Q3	319	4 300	..	60.2	..	..	54.6	..	..	..	..
Q4	328	4 429	..	69.2	..	..	56.6	..	..	..	..
1965 Q1	341	4 605	..	62.3	..	..	56.8	..	..	..	..
Q2	345	4 560	..	50.7	..	..	53.7	..	..	..	..
Q3	339	4 506	..	46.8	..	..	51.7	..	..	..	..
Q4	360	4 681	..	51.3	..	..	51.6	..	..	..	..
1966 Q1	363	4 681	..	50.6	..	..	52.0	..	..	..	..
Q2	367	4 658	..	52.3	..	..	53.0	..	..	..	..
Q3	374	4 745	..	49.7	..	..	51.4	..	..	..	..
Q4	385	4 874	..	40.8	..	..	49.0	..	..	..	..
1967 Q1	406	5 124	..	65.0	..	..	47.2	..	..	..	..
Q2	427	5 417	..	63.2	..	..	47.6	..	..	..	..
Q3	424	5 493	..	52.7	..	..	50.7	..	..	..	..
Q4	419	5 372	..	52.7	..	..	54.9	..	..	..	..
1968 Q1	463	5 721	..	54.6	..	..	57.4	..	..	..	..
Q2	462	5 483	..	47.4	..	..	53.8	..	..	..	..
Q3	481	5 818	..	46.0	..	..	53.2	..	..	..	..
Q4	501	6 087	..	52.1	..	..	57.6	..	..	..	..
1969 Q1	474	5 524	..	40.3	..	..	47.2	..	..	..	..
Q2	463	5 265	..	46.7	..	..	47.5	..	..	..	..
Q3	495	5 806	..	41.3	..	..	45.1	..	..	..	..
Q4	485	5 723	..	38.5	..	..	41.9	..	..	..	..

1 There are no seasonally adjusted figures for the average price of new dwellings on which new building society mortgages were completed.
2 See notes and definitions.

Sources: Office for National Statistics;
Enquiries Columns 1, 2 020 7533 6010; Columns 10, 11 Bank of England;
020 7601 3743, Department of the Environment, Transport and the Regions;
Enquiries Columns 3 020 7890 5583; Columns 4-9 0117 9878055;
Scottish Development Department;
Welsh Office;
Building Societies Association

4.4 Indicators of fixed investment in dwellings

continued

Seasonally adjusted

	Fixed investment in dwellings (£ million)		Orders received by contractors for new houses (GB) (£ million): 1995 prices	Housing starts (GB) (thousands)			Housing completions (GB) (thousands)			Building societies (£ million)	
	Current prices	1995 prices		Private enterprise	Housing assoc- iations	Local authorities, new towns and government departments	Private enterprise	Housing assoc- iations	Local authorities, new towns and government departments	Commitments on new dwellings	Advances on new dwellings[1]
	GGAE	DFEG	FCAS	FCAT	CTOQ	CTOU	FCAV	CTOS	CTOW	AHLO	AHLS
1970 Q1	436	4 800	..	41.5	1.7	32.9	39.4	2.3	42.3	..	..
Q2	458	4 820	..	49.4	2.5	37.3	39.2	1.9	42.3	..	..
Q3	482	5 200	..	50.6	2.1	38.3	41.6	2.4	45.2	..	..
Q4	494	5 439	..	49.9	2.3	36.8	41.9	1.9	41.8	..	..
1971 Q1	492	5 082	..	52.4	2.5	31.7	42.0	3.3	38.7	..	..
Q2	532	5 504	..	49.2	2.7	31.5	43.5	2.5	36.2	..	..
Q3	593	5 765	..	57.5	2.4	31.1	46.5	2.3	37.0	..	..
Q4	601	5 728	..	65.0	3.5	31.5	48.1	2.6	36.7	..	..
1972 Q1	598	5 548	..	54.9	2.6	31.1	45.7	1.7	34.5	..	..
Q2	611	5 677	..	61.6	2.5	27.3	47.4	1.8	30.8	..	..
Q3	685	5 883	..	57.0	2.5	25.7	46.1	1.9	24.5	..	..
Q4	672	5 601	..	60.3	2.1	29.2	45.4	1.9	25.4	..	..
1973 Q1	704	5 482	..	63.5	2.9	26.5	45.3	2.3	23.1	..	..
Q2	778	5 857	..	56.5	2.6	25.7	46.1	2.4	27.1	..	..
Q3	800	5 450	..	51.8	2.6	24.5	43.3	2.2	24.5	..	..
Q4	868	5 482	..	45.7	3.1	25.0	39.8	2.1	23.9	..	..
1974 Q1	885	5 395	..	34.8	2.2	30.9	40.5	2.4	27.2	..	..
Q2	887	5 202	..	26.1	3.7	36.8	28.9	2.1	28.6	..	..
Q3	972	5 129	..	24.5	2.5	33.8	29.0	2.5	31.3	..	..
Q4	1 042	5 251	..	26.4	3.4	32.8	31.3	3.0	31.6	..	..
1975 Q1	1 095	5 523	..	36.6	4.1	37.4	33.5	3.8	34.2	219	225
Q2	1 223	5 858	..	39.5	4.7	33.7	36.3	3.6	36.0	256	232
Q3	1 150	4 973	..	41.7	5.1	38.3	35.5	3.4	38.5	260	241
Q4	1 214	5 142	..	42.1	5.8	44.7	35.0	3.4	38.9	259	247
1976 Q1	1 385	6 037	..	44.5	7.6	43.4	36.1	3.7	37.8	290	271
Q2	1 328	5 489	..	42.3	8.1	36.9	33.9	3.7	39.0	291	285
Q3	1 333	5 248	..	40.2	7.9	35.5	35.3	4.2	36.4	289	289
Q4	1 404	5 405	..	32.5	5.6	25.7	33.2	3.4	34.0	249	280
1977 Q1	1 345	5 412	..	32.2	5.7	26.0	31.2	4.9	34.8	243	265
Q2	1 395	5 225	..	34.3	7.3	25.8	32.6	5.5	35.1	293	265
Q3	1 449	5 193	..	35.8	7.8	26.0	32.5	7.0	34.5	333	307
Q4	1 510	5 284	..	34.0	7.4	26.1	32.3	7.4	33.0	391	338
1978 Q1	1 584	5 800	..	35.9	5.7	22.3	34.7	5.5	22.5	419	375
Q2	1 476	5 041	..	38.3	5.4	24.6	34.4	5.7	29.7	365	397
Q3	1 620	5 259	..	35.0	4.7	20.6	32.6	5.5	28.4	363	363
Q4	1 645	5 183	..	41.4	4.6	19.4	32.8	5.1	27.4	376	369
1979 Q1	1 602	5 290	..	26.6	4.2	13.1	27.8	4.6	18.3	384	374
Q2	1 830	5 259	..	32.1	4.3	16.5	30.8	4.2	21.3	372	381
Q3	1 935	5 329	..	36.7	3.8	16.2	28.4	4.0	20.4	385	394
Q4	2 282	6 147	..	41.1	3.5	19.5	38.4	4.8	26.2	357	370
1980 Q1	2 158	5 830	..	28.1	3.9	12.7	34.1	5.1	22.1	350	363
Q2	2 118	4 862	..	25.8	3.6	10.9	32.2	6.0	21.3	332	333
Q3	2 242	4 933	..	21.9	4.4	10.4	32.2	5.0	22.0	381	346
Q4	2 156	4 777	..	22.9	2.8	7.7	29.9	4.8	21.1	381[2]	364[2]
1981 Q1	2 025	4 191	..	29.7	1.6	6.4	30.0	6.1	20.6	388	385
Q2	2 085	4 491	..	28.4	2.1	6.4	27.2	4.9	17.9	368	371
Q3	2 052	4 389	..	31.0	3.0	6.8	30.0	4.4	14.7	345	362
Q4	1 976	3 817	..	28.1	4.5	6.5	28.2	3.6	12.7	324	310
1982 Q1	2 007	4 009	..	34.6	4.9	8.0	29.5	3.8	11.4	376	357
Q2	2 219	4 641	..	33.4	4.4	7.8	30.3	2.5	9.7	445	396
Q3	2 192	4 567	..	35.7	4.9	8.5	31.7	3.0	8.7	522	433
Q4	2 502	4 746	..	37.3	3.8	10.6	33.7	3.9	8.0	586	517
1983 Q1	2 568	5 116	2 629	44.2	3.7	10.3	34.1	3.5	8.5	590	566
Q2	2 467	4 847	2 504	42.7	3.4	8.6	37.6	4.3	8.5	550	554
Q3	2 599	4 986	2 583	42.3	3.0	7.4	37.1	3.9	9.4	617	583
Q4	2 813	5 235	2 451	43.2	3.8	8.2	39.2	4.5	9.0	660	610
1984 Q1	3 070	5 629	2 466	40.6	3.6	8.4	40.0	4.3	7.9	731	675
Q2	2 926	5 339	2 313	40.3	3.7	6.9	38.0	4.1	9.0	794	719
Q3	3 006	5 152	2 323	39.2	3.1	6.5	40.8	4.2	8.7	715	752
Q4	2 930	4 935	2 144	38.6	2.6	5.7	40.4	3.9	8.7	717	717

1 There are no seasonally adjusted figures for the average price of new dwellings on which new building society mortgages were completed.
2 See Notes and definitions.

Sources: Office for National Statistics; Enquiries Columns 1, 2 020 7533 6010; Columns 10, 11 Bank of England; 020 7601 3743, Department of the Environment, Transport and the Regions; Enquiries Column 3 020 7890 5583; Columns 4-9 0117 9878055; Scottish Development Department; Welsh Office; Building Societies Association

4.4 Indicators of fixed investment in dwellings

continued

Seasonally adjusted

	Fixed investment in dwellings (£ million): Current prices	Fixed investment in dwellings (£ million): 1995 prices	Orders received by contractors for new houses (GB) (£ million): 1995 prices	Housing starts (GB) (thousands): Private enterprise	Housing starts (GB) (thousands): Housing associations	Housing starts (GB) (thousands): Local authorities, new towns and government departments	Housing completions (GB) (thousands): Private enterprise	Housing completions (GB) (thousands): Housing associations	Housing completions (GB) (thousands): Local authorities, new towns and government departments	Building societies (£ million): Commitments on new dwellings	Building societies (£ million): Advances on new dwellings[1]	Quarterly average price of new dwellings at mortgage completion stage[3]
	GGAE	DFEG	FCAS	FCAT	CTOQ	CTOU	FCAV	CTOS	CTOW	AHLO	AHLS	BBJV
1985 Q1	3 033	5 084	2 197	36.9	3.3	5.1	37.7	3.6	7.7	725	713	..
Q2	2 997	4 986	2 296	41.1	2.9	5.6	40.2	3.2	7.2	647	708	..
Q3	3 066	5 040	2 450	43.3	2.6	6.1	38.3	3.3	6.4	739	686	..
Q4	3 123	5 029	2 541	44.4	3.3	5.6	40.1	3.1	5.8	847	771	..
1986 Q1	3 313	5 287	2 302	39.5	3.1	4.6	37.9	3.2	5.7	814	792	..
Q2	3 201	5 036	2 623	46.1	3.5	5.0	42.1	3.0	6.1	969	863	..
Q3	3 609	5 580	2 634	48.4	3.3	5.7	43.6	3.1	5.6	959	914	..
Q4	4 017	6 144	2 573	46.6	3.3	5.1	47.3	3.3	5.7	874	918	..
1987 Q1	3 668	5 494	2 727	46.6	2.5	5.0	44.3	2.8	4.5	841	845	..
Q2	3 949	5 726	2 591	46.6	3.3	5.5	46.1	3.4	4.7	826	835	..
Q3	4 599	6 508	2 807	52.0	3.5	4.9	46.3	3.4	5.4	954	877	..
Q4	4 332	6 108	2 706	51.6	3.6	4.4	47.1	3.0	5.5	1 089	938	..
1988 Q1	5 172	7 072	2 829	53.4	3.2	4.5	50.1	3.1	4.6	1 290	1 102	..
Q2	5 443	7 167	2 666	55.1	3.0	4.3	49.7	3.1	5.5	1 295	1 169	..
Q3	5 260	6 748	2 794	54.5	4.0	3.7	51.8	3.1	5.4	1 174	1 269	..
Q4	5 222	6 609	2 840	58.7	4.3	3.9	48.3	3.5	4.3	1 002	1 077	..
1989 Q1	6 179	7 670	2 450	48.2	4.4	3.5	46.9	3.5	4.4	1 002	1 011	..
Q2	5 625	6 695	2 192	44.6	3.8	4.1	45.9	3.0	4.2	1 140	1 066	..
Q3	5 602	6 572	1 862	39.5	3.9	4.3	44.0	3.9	4.5	1 126	985	..
Q4	5 365	6 159	1 938	37.6	3.9	3.3	42.8	3.6	4.6	1 109	1 081	..
1990 Q1	5 308	6 202	1 728	36.4	4.4	3.1	41.5	3.7	4.0	1 065	1 037	..
Q2	5 147	5 696	1 547	33.6	4.6	2.0	39.7	4.6	4.6	855	895	..
Q3	5 334	5 834	1 405	33.2	4.4	1.8	39.9	4.2	4.5	880	870	..
Q4	5 259	5 702	1 316	33.9	5.1	1.5	40.3	5.1	3.5	979	873	..
1991 Q1	4 575	4 917	1 386	31.5	5.1	1.6	36.3	4.5	3.0	903	875	..
Q2	4 627	4 897	1 498	34.9	5.2	0.9	39.6	5.6	3.0	1 017	908	..
Q3	4 613	4 879	1 519	35.8	5.7	1.0	38.9	5.8	2.2	1 006	923	..
Q4	4 524	4 894	1 466	34.5	6.3	0.8	39.4	4.5	1.9	977	952	..
1992 Q1	4 595	4 994	1 472	32.0	7.8	0.8	37.3	5.2	1.6	879	855	..
Q2	4 578	4 849	1 426	31.2	8.0	0.8	35.7	5.6	1.0	831	835	77 360
Q3	4 748	4 984	1 517	29.2	9.6	0.4	36.4	7.2	1.1	771	820	69 893
Q4	4 904	5 214	1 377	27.8	8.5	0.7	32.1	8.4	0.9	749	685	70 043
1993 Q1	4 607	5 176	1 654	34.8	11.5	0.6	35.2	8.4	0.5	774	764	72 700
Q2	5 042	5 436	1 746	34.3	10.0	0.5	34.4	9.1	0.8	773	736	73 289
Q3	5 116	5 374	1 761	35.0	9.4	0.7	34.6	8.9	0.7	760	759	73 285
Q4	5 127	5 505	1 861	36.3	11.0	0.4	36.7	9.1	0.6	827	780	73 460
1994 Q1	5 506	5 852	1 867	38.3	10.7	0.4	34.9	9.4	0.6	971	879	72 892
Q2	5 063	5 332	1 924	39.6	10.9	0.4	36.8	8.9	0.4	974	921	74 421
Q3	5 291	5 530	1 850	39.5	10.8	0.2	38.6	9.1	0.7	1 089	1 021	74 310
Q4	5 373	5 553	1 712	40.8	9.1	0.4	37.8	9.4	0.3	1 046	1 049	76 852
1995 Q1	5 578	5 688	1 642	35.5	8.0	0.3	38.4	9.7	0.6	1 028	1 012	74 752
Q2	5 483	5 512	1 590	34.9	8.6	0.3	39.1	10.5	0.4	1 039	1 019	78 330
Q3	5 206	5 169	1 498	32.9	8.6	0.4	37.3	9.7	0.8	892	932	81 183
Q4	5 321	5 219	1 357	31.0	7.9	0.1	36.0	8.5	0.5	987	918	82 388
1996 Q1	5 274	5 166	1 428	31.9	7.0	0.2	36.8	8.5	0.2	1 009	924	81 066
Q2	5 673	5 536	1 488	33.2	7.2	0.2	35.8	8.2	0.3	1 130	1 033	83 339
Q3	5 793	5 641	1 590	38.6	8.1	0.2	37.5	8.4	0.1	1 195	1 102	85 408
Q4	6 026	5 811	1 814	40.7	7.4	0.1	37.7	7.2	0.2	1 210	1 147	88 928
1997 Q1	5 958	5 669	1 650	43.2	7.7	0.1	37.8	6.9	0.1	996	972	92 139
Q2	5 831	5 567	1 585	36.9	6.8	0.1	39.0	7.8	0.2	853	783	92 370
Q3	5 788	5 633	1 669	40.0	6.1	0.1	38.2	6.8	0.1	681	560	92 896
Q4	6 350	5 800	1 808	41.3	5.8	0.1	37.6	6.1	–	506	466	92 726
1998 Q1	6 334	5 839	1 753	40.3	6.0	0.1	36.6	6.9	0.1	521	499	94 401
Q2	6 615	5 984	1 465	38.2	5.5	–	37.9	5.9	0.1	442	439	96 669
Q3	6 464	5 803	1 509	38.7	5.5	–	36.2	5.4	0.1	506	495	94 050
Q4	6 418	5 605	1 258	37.7	5.3	0.1	35.1	5.2	0.1	537	490	101 809
1999 Q1	6 683	5 790	1 338	37.8	5.7	0.1	35.1	5.8	–	671	573	106 469
Q2	6 814	5 834	1 292	38.8	5.0	–	36.3	4.9	–	668	639	112 110
Q3	6 983	5 916	1 339	38.6	5.2	–	37.8	5.0	–	636	649	112 616
Q4	7 119	5 982	1 456	40.1	5.0	–	37.7	4.7	0.1	589	619	116 114
2000 Q1	7 013	5 859	1 354	41.2	4.7	0.1	37.8	5.3	–	449	560	121 017
Q2	..	..	..	..	..	..	..	..	..	..	..	120 507

1 There are no seasonally adjusted figures for the average price of new dwellings on which new building society mortgages were completed.
2 See Notes and definitions.
3 See footnote 4 on page 192.

Sources: Office for National Statistics; Enquiries Columns 1, 2 020 7533 6010; Columns 10, 11 Bank of England; 020 7601 3743, Department of the Environment, Transport and the Regions; Enquiries Column 3 020 7890 5583, Columns 4-9 0117 9878055; Scottish Development Department; Welsh Office; Building Societies Association

4.5 Number of property transactions[1,2]

Thousands

	Number of property transactions	
	In England and Wales	In England, Wales and Northern Ireland
	FTAP	FTAR
1959	876	..
1960	903	..
1961	903	..
1962	855	..
1963	936	..
1964	1 036	..
1965	959	..
1966	915	..
1967	977	..
1968	1 050	..
1969	1 009	..
1970	1 095	..
1971	1 201	..
1972	1 343	..
1973	1 244	..

	Number of property transactions	
	In England and Wales	In England, Wales and Northern Ireland
	FTAP	FTAR
1974	968	..
1975	1 174	..
1976	1 190	..
1977	1 239	..
1978	1 365	1 391
1979	1 306	1 331
1980	1 267	1 292
1981	1 351	1 378
1982	1 542	1 574
1983	1 669	1 704
1984	1 760	1 796
1985	1 743	1 780
1986	1 801	1 839
1987	1 937	1 974

	Number of property transactions	
	In England and Wales	In England, Wales and Northern Ireland
	FTAP	FTAR
1988	2 148	2 187
1989	1 580	1 620
1990	1 398	1 437
1991	1 306	1 344
1992	1 136	1 176
1993	1 196	1 236
1994	1 274	1 318
1995	1 135	1 182
1996	1 242	1 283
1997	1 440	1 480
1998	1 347	1 384
1999	1 469	1 515

1 The figures are based on counts of the relevant administrative forms processed each month. Because of the time lags involved, the series above should be lagged one month to give a broad representation of transactions occurring in the month (details are given in the June 1991 edition of *Economic Trends*).
2 Over the period from 20 December 1991 to 19 August 1992, the stamp duty threshold was temporarily increased from £30,000 to £250,000.

Source: Board of Inland Revenue; Enquiries 020 7438 6314

4.5 Number of property transactions[1,2]

continued

Thousands, not seasonally adjusted

	In England and Wales	In England, Wales and Northern Ireland
	FTAP	FTAR
1959 Q1	197	..
Q2	201	..
Q3	247	..
Q4	231	..
1960 Q1	226	..
Q2	222	..
Q3	225	..
Q4	230	..
1961 Q1	216	..
Q2	223	..
Q3	247	..
Q4	217	..
1962 Q1	192	..
Q2	208	..
Q3	221	..
Q4	234	..
1963 Q1	195	..
Q2	216	..
Q3	249	..
Q4	277	..
1964 Q1	237	..
Q2	261	..
Q3	259	..
Q4	279	..
1965 Q1	245	..
Q2	235	..
Q3	235	..
Q4	244	..
1966 Q1	223	..
Q2	229	..
Q3	239	..
Q4	224	..
1967 Q1	208	..
Q2	253	..
Q3	253	..
Q4	262	..
1968 Q1	254	..
Q2	255	..
Q3	270	..
Q4	270	..
1969 Q1	239	..
Q2	255	..

	In England and Wales	In England, Wales and Northern Ireland
	FTAP	FTAR
Q3	256	..
Q4	258	..
1970 Q1	232	..
Q2	271	..
Q3	298	..
Q4	294	..
1971 Q1	243	..
Q2	297	..
Q3	323	..
Q4	339	..
1972 Q1	308	..
Q2	352	..
Q3	349	..
Q4	334	..
1973 Q1	330	..
Q2	313	..
Q3	312	..
Q4	289	..
1974 Q1	237	..
Q2	213	..
Q3	243	..
Q4	275	..
1975 Q1	258	..
Q2	302	..
Q3	315	..
Q4	299	..
1976 Q1	269	..
Q2	297	..
Q3	316	..
Q4	308	..
1977 Q1	262	..
Q2	301	307
Q3	333	341
Q4	343	351
1978 Q1	331	337
Q2	351	358
Q3	349	356
Q4	334	340
1979 Q1	306	312
Q2	314	320
Q3	345	351
Q4	341	348

	In England and Wales	In England, Wales and Northern Ireland
	FTAP	FTAR
1980 Q1	312	318
Q2	328	334
Q3	308	314
Q4	319	326
1981 Q1	288	293
Q2	328	334
Q3	351	358
Q4	384	392
1982 Q1	320	328
Q2	368	377
Q3	424	433
Q4	429	437
1983 Q1	403	411
Q2	411	419
Q3	431	440
Q4	424	433
1984 Q1	424	433
Q2	427	436
Q3	456	466
Q4	452	461
1985 Q1	404	413
Q2	434	444
Q3	462	472
Q4	442	452
1986 Q1	390	399
Q2	418	427
Q3	499	509
Q4	494	504
1987 Q1	429	438
Q2	439	448
Q3	534	543
Q4	535	545
1988 Q1	487	497
Q2	518	528
Q3	616	626
Q4	527	537
1989 Q1	407	416
Q2	405	415
Q3	390	401
Q4	378	388
1990 Q1	344	354

	In England and Wales	In England, Wales and Northern Ireland
	FTAP	FTAR
Q2	360	369
Q3	349	359
Q4	345	355
1991 Q1	314	323
Q2	324	334
Q3	353	363
Q4	315	325
1992 Q1	236	245
Q2	265	275
Q3	367	379
Q4	268	277
1993 Q1	239	248
Q2	279	289
Q3	347	357
Q4	331	342
1994 Q1	299	309
Q2	312	322
Q3	345	356
Q4	319	331
1995 Q1	284	295
Q2	280	291
Q3	298	311
Q4	272	285
1996 Q1	261	272
Q2	284	294
Q3	338	348
Q4	360	369
1997 Q1	324	335
Q2	351	360
Q3	387	398
Q4	377	387
1998 Q1	317	327
Q2	317	327
Q3	377	386
Q4	335	345
1999 Q1	316	325
Q2	342	354
Q3	414	428
Q4	397	407
2000 Q1	367	381
Q2	352	362

See footnotes 1 and 2 on page 199.

Source: Board of Inland Revenue; Enquiries 020 7438 6314

4.5 Number of property transactions[1,2]

continued

Thousands, not seasonally adjusted

	In England and Wales	In England, Wales and Northern Ireland
	FTAP	FTAR
1977 Apr	96	98
May	102	104
Jun	103	105
Jul	104	106
Aug	113	115
Sep	116	120
Oct	110	114
Nov	121	123
Dec	112	114
1978 Jan	111	114
Feb	106	108
Mar	114	116
Apr	117	120
May	115	118
Jun	118	120
Jul	116	117
Aug	122	125
Sep	111	113
Oct	113	116
Nov	123	126
Dec	97	99
1979 Jan	105	107
Feb	98	100
Mar	103	105
Apr	86	88
May	117	119
Jun	110	113
Jul	110	112
Aug	116	118
Sep	119	121
Oct	126	129
Nov	118	120
Dec	97	99
1980 Jan	113	115
Feb	99	101
Mar	100	102
Apr	126	128
May	95	97
Jun	107	109
Jul	110	112
Aug	93	95
Sep	105	107
Oct	113	115
Nov	102	104
Dec	105	107
1981 Jan	98	100
Feb	88	90
Mar	102	103
Apr	108	110
May	101	103
Jun	118	121
Jul	117	119
Aug	116	118
Sep	118	121
Oct	125	128
Nov	137	140
Dec	122	124
1982 Jan	104	107
Feb	98	101
Mar	117	120
Apr	123	125
May	113	116
Jun	132	135

	In England and Wales	In England, Wales and Northern Ireland
	FTAP	FTAR
Jul	147	150
Aug	136	139
Sep	141	144
Oct	137	140
Nov	155	158
Dec	137	140
1983 Jan	126	129
Feb	122	125
Mar	155	158
Apr	135	137
May	133	136
Jun	143	146
Jul	138	141
Aug	148	151
Sep	145	148
Oct	144	147
Nov	148	151
Dec	132	135
1984 Jan	145	148
Feb	134	137
Mar	145	148
Apr	134	137
May	141	144
Jun	152	155
Jul	155	158
Aug	158	161
Sep	143	146
Oct	163	167
Nov	162	165
Dec	128	130
1985 Jan	147	151
Feb	126	129
Mar	130	133
Apr	147	150
May	146	149
Jun	141	144
Jul	162	165
Aug	152	155
Sep	149	152
Oct	161	165
Nov	149	152
Dec	132	135
1986 Jan	154	157
Feb	125	128
Mar	111	114
Apr	143	146
May	131	134
Jun	144	147
Jul	168	172
Aug	154	158
Sep	176	180
Oct	185	188
Nov	159	162
Dec	150	154
1987 Jan	155	158
Feb	130	133
Mar	144	147
Apr	138	140
May	137	140
Jun	165	168
Jul	189	192
Aug	165	168

	In England and Wales	In England, Wales and Northern Ireland
	FTAP	FTAR
Sep	180	183
Oct	187	191
Nov	180	183
Dec	168	171
1988 Jan	168	171
Feb	155	158
Mar	165	168
Apr	154	157
May	170	173
Jun	194	197
Jul	198	201
Aug	220	223
Sep	198	202
Oct	194	197
Nov	188	191
Dec	145	148
1989 Jan	154	157
Feb	126	129
Mar	127	130
Apr	131	134
May	133	137
Jun	142	145
Jul	129	132
Aug	132	136
Sep	128	132
Oct	134	138
Nov	138	142
Dec	106	108
1990 Jan	128	132
Feb	101	104
Mar	115	118
Apr	120	122
May	123	126
Jun	117	121
Jul	121	124
Aug	117	120
Sep	111	114
Oct	120	124
Nov	125	129
Dec	100	102
1991 Jan	126	130
Feb	93	96
Mar	94	97
Apr	109	111
May	109	112
Jun	107	110
Jul	129	132
Aug	111	115
Sep	112	116
Oct	118	122
Nov	102	105
Dec	95	98
1992 Jan	80	83
Feb	74	77
Mar	83	86
Apr	86	89
May	82	85
Jun	97	100
Jul	107	111
Aug	118	123
Sep	143	146
Oct	103	106
Nov	82	85

	In England and Wales	In England, Wales and Northern Ireland
	FTAP	FTAR
Dec	83	86
1993 Jan	78	81
Feb	72	75
Mar	88	92
Apr	87	90
May	87	91
Jun	105	109
Jul	114	118
Aug	113	116
Sep	120	122
Oct	110	114
Nov	119	122
Dec	102	106
1994 Jan	106	110
Feb	89	92
Mar	104	107
Apr	97	100
May	101	104
Jun	114	117
Jul	112	116
Aug	120	123
Sep	113	117
Oct	110	114
Nov	114	119
Dec	95	99
1995 Jan	104	107
Feb	86	90
Mar	95	99
Apr	86	89
May	95	99
Jun	99	103
Jul	101	106
Aug	99	104
Sep	97	101
Oct	99	103
Nov	97	102
Dec	76	80
1996 Jan	104	108
Feb	80	83
Mar	77	81
Apr	90	94
May	97	101
Jun	96	100
Jul	116	119
Aug	109	112
Sep	113	116
Oct	128	133
Nov	122	125
Dec	109	111
1997 Jan	132	137
Feb	98	101
Mar	95	97
Apr	118	121
May	113	116
Jun	120	123
Jul	135	140
Aug	108	110
Sep	144	148
Oct	140	144
Nov	121	124
Dec	116	119

See footnotes 1 and 2 on page 199.

Source: Board of Inland Revenue; Enquiries 020 7438 6314

4.5 Number of property transactions[1,2]

continued

Thousands, not seasonally adjusted

	In England and Wales	In England, Wales and Northern Ireland		In England and Wales	In England, Wales and Northern Ireland
	FTAP	FTAR		FTAP	FTAR
1998 Jan	119	122	May	106	110
Feb	94	97	Jun	126	130
Mar	104	108			
Apr	103	106	Jul	140	144
May	96	99	Aug	134	139
Jun	117	121	Sep	140	145
			Oct	134	137
Jul	129	132	Nov	141	144
Aug	119	121	Dec	122	126
Sep	129	133			
Oct	119	122	2000 Jan	137	143
Nov	110	113	Feb	112	116
Dec	107	110	Mar	118	122
			Apr	99	102
1999 Jan	112	116	May	124	128
Feb	96	99	Jun	129	132
Mar	108	110			
Apr	110	114	Jul	127	130

See footnotes 1 and 2 on page 199.

Source: Board of Inland Revenue; Enquiries 020 7438 6314

4.5 Number of property transactions[1,2]

continued

Thousands, seasonally adjusted

	England and Wales[3]		England and Wales[3]		England and Wales[3]		England and Wales[3]
	FTAQ		FTAQ		FTAQ		FTAQ
1977 Q2	306	1983 Q1	431			Q4	315
Q3	322	Q2	422	1989 Q1	440		
Q4	331	Q3	411	Q2	410	1995 Q1	308
		Q4	408	Q3	372	Q2	288
1978 Q1	351			Q4	369	Q3	275
Q2	356	1984 Q1	453			Q4	264
Q3	337	Q2	440	1990 Q1	375		
Q4	320	Q3	432	Q2	367	1996 Q1	280
		Q4	435	Q3	326	Q2	299
1979 Q1	326			Q4	333	Q3	313
Q2	319	1985 Q1	431			Q4	350
Q3	333	Q2	451	1991 Q1	347		
Q4	326	Q3	435	Q2	332	1997 Q1	360
		Q4	425	Q3	322	Q2	361
1980 Q1	333			Q4	303	Q3	354
Q2	334	1986 Q1	418			Q4	365
Q3	297	Q2	433	1992 Q1	266		
Q4	306	Q3	469	Q2	271	1998 Q1	344
		Q4	475	Q3	333	Q2	333
1981 Q1	308			Q4	258	Q3	345
Q2	335	1987 Q1	463			Q4	325
Q3	338	Q2	452	1993 Q1	264		
Q4	367	Q3	502	Q2	286	1999 Q1	345
		Q4	516	Q3	317	Q2	360
1982 Q1	343			Q4	324	Q3	376
Q2	376	1988 Q1	530			Q4	388
Q3	407	Q2	528	1994 Q1	325		
Q4	412	Q3	583	Q2	321	2000 Q1	391
		Q4	505	Q3	317	Q2	373

See footnotes 1 and 2 on page 199.

3 The sum of seasonally adjusted components does not exactly match the unadjusted (definitive) annual total.

Source: Board of Inland Revenue; Enquiries 020 7438 6314

4.5 Number of property transactions[1,2]

continued

Thousands, seasonally adjusted

	England and Wales[3]
	FTAQ
1977 Apr	98
May	106
Jun	102
Jul	103
Aug	107
Sep	112
Oct	104
Nov	112
Dec	116
1978 Jan	113
Feb	118
Mar	120
Apr	119
May	120
Jun	117
Jul	114
Aug	117
Sep	107
Oct	106
Nov	114
Dec	100
1979 Jan	108
Feb	110
Mar	108
Apr	87
May	124
Jun	108
Jul	107
Aug	111
Sep	115
Oct	118
Nov	108
Dec	99
1980 Jan	115
Feb	113
Mar	105
Apr	128
May	102
Jun	104
Jul	106
Aug	89
Sep	101
Oct	106
Nov	94
Dec	107
1981 Jan	100
Feb	101
Mar	107
Apr	110
May	110
Jun	115
Jul	111
Aug	112
Sep	115
Oct	117
Nov	126
Dec	124
1982 Jan	106
Feb	114
Mar	123
Apr	126
May	122
Jun	129

	England and Wales[3]
	FTAQ
Jul	139
Aug	131
Sep	137
Oct	128
Nov	142
Dec	142
1983 Jan	127
Feb	141
Mar	163
Apr	139
May	143
Jun	140
Jul	129
Aug	142
Sep	140
Oct	134
Nov	136
Dec	139
1984 Jan	145
Feb	155
Mar	154
Apr	139
May	150
Jun	150
Jul	145
Aug	151
Sep	137
Oct	149
Nov	150
Dec	136
1985 Jan	147
Feb	145
Mar	140
Apr	155
May	156
Jun	140
Jul	150
Aug	145
Sep	140
Oct	144
Nov	139
Dec	142
1986 Jan	154
Feb	144
Mar	120
Apr	151
May	140
Jun	142
Jul	156
Aug	149
Sep	164
Oct	164
Nov	149
Dec	162
1987 Jan	155
Feb	151
Mar	156
Apr	145
May	146
Jun	161
Jul	175
Aug	159

	England and Wales[3]
	FTAQ
Sep	168
Oct	166
Nov	167
Dec	182
1988 Jan	167
Feb	182
Mar	181
Apr	162
May	178
Jun	188
Jul	185
Aug	212
Sep	186
Oct	174
Nov	173
Dec	158
1989 Jan	153
Feb	148
Mar	139
Apr	136
May	137
Jun	137
Jul	122
Aug	128
Sep	122
Oct	122
Nov	126
Dec	116
1990 Jan	127
Feb	118
Mar	127
Apr	122
May	124
Jun	113
Jul	114
Aug	113
Sep	107
Oct	110
Nov	114
Dec	111
1991 Jan	126
Feb	112
Mar	104
Apr	113
May	110
Jun	110
Jul	111
Aug	106
Sep	105
Oct	103
Nov	98
Dec	102
1992 Jan	81
Feb	93
Mar	92
Apr	90
May	91
Jun	90
Jul	91
Aug	111
Sep	131
Oct	94
Nov	78

	England and Wales[3]
	FTAQ
Dec	86
1993 Jan	82
Feb	88
Mar	93
Apr	91
May	96
Jun	99
Jul	102
Aug	107
Sep	108
Oct	108
Nov	109
Dec	108
1994 Jan	109
Feb	107
Mar	109
Apr	108
May	106
Jun	107
Jul	106
Aug	109
Sep	102
Oct	106
Nov	106
Dec	104
1995 Jan	103
Feb	104
Mar	101
Apr	99
May	95
Jun	95
Jul	94
Aug	90
Sep	91
Oct	89
Nov	88
Dec	88
1996 Jan	96
Feb	92
Mar	92
Apr	97
May	101
Jun	101
Jul	101
Aug	106
Sep	106
Oct	113
Nov	119
Dec	119
1997 Jan	124
Feb	118
Mar	117
Apr	120
May	121
Jun	120
Jul	117
Aug	116
Sep	121
Oct	124
Nov	121
Dec	121

See footnotes 1 and 2 on page 199.

3 The sum of seasonally adjusted components does not exactly match the unadjusted (definitive) annual total.

Source: Board of Inland Revenue; Enquiries 020 7438 6314

4.5 Number of property transactions[1,2]

continued

Thousands, seasonally adjusted

	England and Wales[3]		England and Wales[3]
	FTAQ		FTAQ
1998 Jan	114	May	120
Feb	114	Jun	121
Mar	116		
Apr	111	Jul	126
May	109	Aug	126
Jun	113	Sep	124
		Oct	129
Jul	113	Nov	130
Aug	117	Dec	129
Sep	115		
Oct	108	2000 Jan	134
Nov	105	Feb	130
Dec	112	Mar	127
		Apr	118
1999 Jan	113	May	129
Feb	116	Jun	126
Mar	116		
Apr	120	Jul	119

See footnotes 1 and 2 on page 199.

3 The sum of the seasonally adjusted components does not exactly match the unadjusted (definitive) annual total.

Source: Board of Inland Revenue; Enquiries 020 7438 6314

4.6 Changes in inventories[2]

£ million, current prices

		Manufacturing (revised definition)					Distribution			
	Mining and quarrying	Materials and fuel	Work in progress	Finished goods	Total	Electricity, gas and water supply	Wholesale[1]	Retail[1]	Other industries[3]	All industries
	FADC	FBDB	FBDC	FBDD	DHBA	FADD	FAJB	FBYB		ABMP
1946	..	..	..	..	..	..	..	..		..
1947	..	..	..	..	..	..	..	..		..
1948	..	..	..	..	..	..	..	..		175
1949	..	..	..	..	..	..	..	..		65
1950	..	..	..	..	..	..	..	..		–210
1951	..	..	..	..	..	..	..	..		575
1952	..	..	..	..	..	..	..	..		50
1953	..	..	..	..	..	..	..	..		125
1954	..	..	..	..	..	..	..	..		56
1955	..	111	69	61	269	..	..	34		300
1956	..	81	136	88	150	..	..	20		259
1957	..	18	75	48	–19	..	37	47		238
1958	..	–96	31	95	–152	..	10	16		111
1959	..	18	51	12	125	..	7	47		178
1960	..	217	89	171	532	..	48	35		562
1961	..	53	59	78	242	..	29	28		279
1962	5	–72	–4	33	19	2	16	4		–8
1963	–46	–3	63	27	162	–64	25	42		161
1964	–	199	233	66	461	47	94	50		700
1965	–2	–8	140	112	322	35	47	23		461
1966	–9	19	62	141	186	55	22	12		288
1967	50	–3	81	–31	20	50	10	41		286
1968	–3	89	89	53	166	71	78	68		452
1969	–53	83	27	189	381	–103	64	34		537
1970	–48	115	106	90	314	–18	111	–6		382
1971	29	–154	–102	94	–162	38	154	8		114
1972	–10	–43	25	–151	–169	1	114	18		25
1973	–10	494	263	–39	718	–22	312	264		1 529
1974	–39	363	253	469	1 086	–6	323	–152		1 045
1975	193	–904	–179	20	–1 063	98	–247	–91		–1 354
1976	–24	15	297	–529	349	73	182	271		901
1977	26	190	297	321	807	–88	544	51		1 824
1978	112	82	141	32	255	10	560	456		1 804
1979	–87	61	–273	556	359	–73	1 061	481		2 162
1980	302	–1 464	–732	–406	–2 546	135	–392	–429		–2 572
1981	–26	–1 393	–76	–649	–2 115	130	–260	190		–2 768
1982	108	–796	–715	–345	–1 855	441	–68	1		–1 188
1983	–101	–366	476	–78	–3	432	169	–35		1 465
1984	–41	120	323	346	836	–445	12	465		1 296
1985	–314	197	–637	–120	–493	373	–85	267		821
1986	–115	–12	–159	–384	–555	–28	237	720		682
1987	–34	77	–285	–126	–335	–93	586	755		1 228
1988	–11	327	176	368	873	36	971	791		4 333
1989	172	–47	–368	581	164	113	775	346		2 677
1990	–187	–283	–1 540	–129	–1 953	–128	–552	181		–1 800
1991	172	–869	–1 434	–1 466	–3 769	178	–646	–401		–4 927
1992	73	–235	–1 275	–34	–1 544	–136	96	230		–1 937
1993	–73	–19	–1 107	–384	–1 510	–253	843	411		329
1994	–260	275	566	404	1 245	–602	1 332	931		3 708
1995	–123	514	1 144	998	2 656	–205	597	811		4 512
1996	–33	37	–201	12	–152	15	677	647		1 771
1997	63	355	–1 457	309	–232	69	1 501	822		4 388
1998	184	705	–689	692	555	–155	–56	1 015		4 461
1999	–193	92	–209	–2 041	–1 458	–187	–739	686		–1 946

1 Wholesaling and retailing estimates exclude the motor trade.
2 Estimates are given to the nearest million but cannot be regarded as accurate to this degree.
3 Not estimated in current price unadjusted form.

Source: Office for National Statistics; Enquiries 01633 812019

4.6 Changes in inventories[2]

continued

£ million, current prices, not seasonally adjusted

		Manufacturing (revised definition)					Distribution			
	Mining and quarrying	Materials and fuels	Work in progress	Finished goods	Total	Electricity, gas and water supply	Wholesale[1]	Retail[1]	Other industries[3]	All industries
	FADC	FBDB	FBDC	FBDD	DHBA	FADD	FAJB	FBYB		ABMP
1955 Q1	..	33	67	26	145	..	..	41		165
Q2	..	1	25	31	73	..	..	–10		–23
Q3	..	64	5	–33	45	..	..	10		147
Q4	..	13	–28	37	6	..	..	–7		11
1956 Q1	..	–2	57	49	74	..	..	38		123
Q2	..	1	51	56	68	..	..	–11		91
Q3	..	55	13	–21	10	..	..	13		48
Q4	..	27	15	4	–2	..	..	–20		–3
1957 Q1	..	17	28	36	30	..	44	52		149
Q2	..	–41	65	42	21	..	27	3		103
Q3	..	32	24	–36	–7	..	9	–3		58
Q4	..	10	–42	6	–63	..	–43	–5		–72
1958 Q1	..	–27	28	73	31	..	3	25		92
Q2	..	–69	23	18	–77	..	–15	1		30
Q3	..	21	6	8	–20	..	45	7		68
Q4	..	–21	–26	–4	–86	..	–23	–17		–79
1959 Q1	..	–16	–26	38	–6	..	19	18		18
Q2	..	–6	44	–24	20	..	4	26		84
Q3	..	40	37	–56	40	..	22	4		73
Q4	..	–	–4	54	71	..	–38	–1		3
1960 Q1	..	44	25	22	135	..	17	64		146
Q2	..	30	50	26	123	..	8	–		141
Q3	..	105	8	5	113	..	44	–2		164
Q4	..	38	6	118	161	..	–21	–27		111
1961 Q1	..	31	21	35	105	..	43	47		157
Q2	..	15	39	2	66	..	18	28		53
Q3	..	60	8	–44	31	..	14	–17		132
Q4	..	–53	–9	85	40	..	–46	–30		–63
1962 Q1	–1	–49	–19	9	–24	–16	2	50		–30
Q2	–1	–23	37	–4	30	14	–6	–21		18
Q3	–	27	–3	–43	–15	10	49	–3		53
Q4	7	–27	–19	71	28	–6	–29	–22		–49
1963 Q1	–29	–42	–27	69	19	–34	–9	50		–19
Q2	6	–23	42	–21	25	–11	25	3		81
Q3	–4	46	20	–91	–2	–13	15	–13		–3
Q4	–19	16	28	70	120	–6	–6	2		102
1964 Q1	–12	31	36	9	89	–29	13	35		90
Q2	9	19	92	57	165	18	19	5		232
Q3	4	68	71	–61	63	24	54	8		172
Q4	–1	81	34	61	144	34	8	2		206
1965 Q1	–5	–128	70	43	91	–8	–2	47		119
Q2	7	28	32	65	109	29	–6	–17		141
Q3	4	74	51	–47	73	15	59	6		170
Q4	–8	18	–13	51	49	–1	–4	–13		31
1966 Q1	–20	–8	47	46	80	–6	–3	47		78
Q2	14	–32	35	44	36	18	–7	19		126
Q3	1	97	–	–3	85	30	63	–10		156
Q4	–4	–38	–20	54	–15	13	–31	–44		–72
1967 Q1	6	–4	44	–1	31	4	–6	25		61
Q2	25	–32	10	50	21	25	–	36		142
Q3	17	47	29	–73	–6	23	31	10		92
Q4	2	–14	–2	–7	–26	–2	–15	–30		–9
1968 Q1	–7	10	–7	–67	–68	–11	–12	49		–92
Q2	12	–26	40	85	75	31	24	25		212
Q3	1	78	69	–22	95	45	58	–2		238
Q4	–9	27	–13	57	64	6	8	–4		94
1969 Q1	–20	15	38	75	142	–56	–2	40		110
Q2	–10	15	2	72	106	–1	2	14		222
Q3	–9	35	17	–50	27	–7	64	–22		142
Q4	–14	18	–30	92	106	–39	–	2		63

See footnotes on page 206.

Source: Office for National Statistics; Enquiries 01633 812019

4.6 Changes in inventories[2]

continued

£ million, current prices, not seasonally adjusted

		Manufacturing (revised definition)					Distribution			
	Mining and quarrying	Materials and fuels	Work in progress	Finished goods	Total	Electricity, gas and water supply	Wholesale[1]	Retail[1]	Other industries[3]	All industries
	FADC	FBDB	FBDC	FBDD	DHBA	FADD	FAJB	FBYB		ABMP
1970 Q1	–26	–7	–	63	57	–37	–11	–5		–76
Q2	–11	29	81	24	134	19	24	6		208
Q3	–3	72	23	–72	24	24	78	–16		214
Q4	–8	21	2	75	99	–24	20	9		36
1971 Q1	–2	–49	–29	100	21	–5	2	–24		26
Q2	8	–79	–39	26	–91	35	46	5		2
Q3	20	–3	12	–102	–92	24	85	–6		47
Q4	3	–23	–46	70	–	–16	21	33		39
1972 Q1	–26	–46	6	–30	–70	–64	–1	–8		–144
Q2	3	–89	52	–39	–76	48	–	46		97
Q3	9	37	10	–134	–87	22	83	–32		38
Q4	4	55	–43	52	64	–5	32	12		34
1973 Q1	–10	96	125	65	287	–22	46	80		427
Q2	20	117	49	–26	140	31	39	33		322
Q3	–3	147	91	–123	116	16	143	49		478
Q4	–17	134	–2	45	175	–47	84	102		302
1974 Q1	–	146	13	–51	109	–75	12	–81		–167
Q2	–28	–13	205	183	376	24	126	37		640
Q3	–1	252	153	116	519	48	139	–81		601
Q4	–10	–22	–118	221	82	–3	46	–27		–29
1975 Q1	23	–400	58	184	–158	–6	–138	–141		–583
Q2	31	–188	21	–15	–181	67	–123	–130		–366
Q3	58	–204	–62	–204	–471	37	33	72		–227
Q4	81	–112	–196	55	–253	–	–19	108		–178
1976 Q1	–58	–161	62	104	74	–39	–17	22		–209
Q2	35	–92	40	–680	–154	72	–33	–44		34
Q3	–6	173	129	–244	–43	54	194	137		457
Q4	5	95	66	291	472	–14	38	156		619
1977 Q1	–23	71	255	138	466	–150	114	111		583
Q2	29	–34	61	255	281	42	230	–16		712
Q3	8	138	–60	–224	–147	36	114	–67		114
Q4	12	15	41	152	207	–16	86	23		415
1978 Q1	–45	–60	59	106	110	–32	147	21		208
Q2	87	–33	21	126	111	62	27	197		766
Q3	29	127	–51	–259	–182	35	350	145		475
Q4	41	48	112	59	216	–55	36	93		355
1979 Q1	34	–216	–36	197	–56	–264	279	114		766
Q2	–18	157	–	–76	84	24	375	138		458
Q3	–72	259	100	–160	205	140	264	307		1 054
Q4	–31	–139	–337	595	126	27	143	–78		–116
1980 Q1	51	–532	60	210	–256	–73	–81	–144		–366
Q2	57	–99	–193	310	24	86	–442	–154		–37
Q3	88	–294	–67	–560	–910	131	272	9		–366
Q4	106	–539	–532	–366	–1 404	–9	–141	–140		–1 803
1981 Q1	28	–443	–103	–227	–772	–58	–	162		–951
Q2	–15	–383	–101	–204	–687	53	–222	43		–946
Q3	–13	–103	138	–457	–422	171	257	11		61
Q4	–26	–464	–10	239	–234	–36	–295	–26		–932
1982 Q1	125	–165	–133	182	–114	–101	465	277		699
Q2	–90	180	60	–8	231	263	–108	30		436
Q3	53	–283	–80	–592	–955	287	140	–21		–324
Q4	20	–528	–562	73	–1 017	–8	–565	–285		–1 999
1983 Q1	–29	–293	395	120	215	20	–2	28		544
Q2	–13	–25	68	139	187	233	141	–241		526
Q3	–58	99	233	–654	–331	182	448	179		1 005
Q4	–1	–147	–220	317	–74	–3	–418	–1		–610
1984 Q1	–154	–130	229	384	502	–296	151	244		443
Q2	104	133	301	–102	363	–279	–189	–37		187
Q3	–31	350	95	–373	56	–12	421	–86		557
Q4	40	–233	–302	437	–85	142	–371	344		109

See footnotes on page 206.

Source: Office for National Statistics; Enquiries 01633 812019

4.6 Changes in inventories[2]

continued

£ million, current prices, not seasonally adjusted

	Mining and quarrying	Manufacturing (revised definition): Materials and fuels	Work in progress	Finished goods	Total	Electricity, gas and water supply	Distribution: Wholesale[1]	Retail[1]	Other industries[3]	All industries
	FADC	FBDB	FBDC	FBDD	DHBA	FADD	FAJB	FBYB		ABMP
1985 Q1	–71	63	–292	141	–59	–103	178	–17		159
Q2	–164	98	176	282	571	107	–45	81		857
Q3	–174	298	172	–724	–240	356	236	176		690
Q4	95	–262	–693	181	–765	13	–454	27		–885
1986 Q1	–152	126	–124	–62	–61	–293	576	131		415
Q2	29	129	196	184	509	–32	–301	169		563
Q3	15	–92	99	–756	–749	203	56	183		–103
Q4	–7	–175	–330	250	–254	94	–94	237		–193
1987 Q1	40	–85	–79	112	–52	–385	382	–1		11
Q2	–50	–3	169	69	236	130	–93	246		712
Q3	–	188	381	–607	–39	165	617	446		1 282
Q4	–24	–23	–756	300	–480	–3	–320	64		–777
1988 Q1	–90	89	64	140	294	–201	261	43		706
Q2	–17	165	237	455	857	106	63	167		1 511
Q3	39	8	78	–807	–720	146	868	123		691
Q4	57	65	–203	580	442	–15	–221	458		1 425
1989 Q1	52	27	3	414	444	31	400	–356		844
Q2	102	–65	37	514	486	53	–150	400		1 629
Q3	8	243	347	–705	–116	112	795	153		723
Q4	10	–252	–755	358	–650	–83	–270	149		–519
1990 Q1	–81	–181	54	–53	–180	–128	374	–352		148
Q2	2	16	–321	309	3	–6	–302	88		732
Q3	–64	209	19	–500	–274	114	59	168		–41
Q4	–44	–327	–1 292	115	–1 502	–108	–683	277		–2 639
1991 Q1	103	–467	–25	5	–487	–161	1	–673		–1 457
Q2	–3	–209	–477	–10	–695	219	–279	–182		–808
Q3	26	214	–10	–1 042	–838	159	183	257		–339
Q4	46	–407	–922	–419	–1 749	–39	–551	197		–2 323
1992 Q1	–63	–195	–814	454	–555	–10	45	–210		–872
Q2	60	123	363	245	731	–213	–495	–426		–106
Q3	55	221	128	–483	–134	50	349	382		278
Q4	21	–384	–952	–250	–1 586	37	197	484		–1 237
1993 Q1	–309	–276	–222	–152	–650	–24	112	–639		–1 465
Q2	157	142	104	767	1 013	–41	–312	–389		1 137
Q3	30	209	–314	–806	–911	–8	748	740		468
Q4	49	–94	–675	–193	–962	–180	295	699		189
1994 Q1	–229	–192	204	273	285	–207	–93	–495		–323
Q2	7	143	468	936	1 547	–154	336	–15		2 765
Q3	12	374	175	–788	–239	–76	647	783		690
Q4	–50	–50	–281	–17	–348	–165	442	658		576
1995 Q1	–244	–157	470	515	828	–228	–516	–959		–1 399
Q2	14	210	573	1 135	1 918	–14	2	–43		3 216
Q3	118	746	448	–752	442	85	671	919		1 445
Q4	–11	–285	–347	100	–532	–48	440	894		1 250
1996 Q1	–12	–109	96	453	440	–212	–248	–614		–966
Q2	–10	115	465	421	1 001	60	–14	–235		1 964
Q3	14	102	–38	–881	–817	141	321	636		–103
Q4	–25	–71	–724	19	–776	26	618	860		876
1997 Q1	46	–28	200	393	502	77	–119	–391		261
Q2	–7	266	144	662	923	79	491	–73		2 934
Q3	10	420	–238	–273	–443	37	–44	802		869
Q4	14	–303	–1 563	–473	–1 214	–124	1 173	484		324
1998 Q1	–47	107	–512	509	–12	–116	–104	–163		585
Q2	84	282	281	–142	427	–47	–647	–154		1 707
Q3	66	458	10	–657	–240	20	151	928		959
Q4	81	–142	–468	982	380	–12	544	404		1 210
1999 Q1	2	6	–388	–692	–899	–80	–602	–357		–1 777
Q2	–74	–42	281	–742	–328	–17	–296	28		–998
Q3	–78	212	684	–543	528	–31	–124	803		1 642
Q4	–43	–84	–786	–64	–759	–59	283	212		–813
2000 Q1	21	–186	475	–143	146	–34	1 072	278		2 157

See footnotes on page 206.

Source: Office for National Statistics; Enquiries 01633 812019

4.6 Changes in inventories[2]

continued

£ million, 1995 prices, not seasonally adjusted

	Mining and quarrying	Manufacturing (revised definition): Materials and fuels	Manufacturing: Work in progress	Manufacturing: Finished goods	Manufacturing: Total[1]	Electricity, gas and water supply	Distribution: Wholesale[3]	Distribution: Retail[3]	Other industries	All industries[1]
	FADO	FBID	FBIE	FBIF	DHBH	FADP	FAJM	FBYH	DLWV	ABMQ
1948	..	..	..	..	1 202	..	..	..	..	1 671
1949	..	..	..	..	432	..	..	..	..	601
1950	..	..	..	..	–1 325	..	..	..	..	–1 842
1951	..	..	..	..	2 966	..	..	..	..	4 125
1952	..	..	..	..	318	..	..	..	..	441
1953	..	..	..	..	649	..	..	..	..	902
1954	..	..	..	..	307	..	..	..	..	427
1955	..	772	421	405	1 969	35	..	217	..	2 472
1956	..	538	849	590	2 336	97	..	128	..	1 923
1957	..	107	457	350	1 009	201	..	285	..	1 974
1958	..	–663	207	635	86	116	..	101	..	875
1959	..	90	308	169	622	66	96	288	..	1 642
1960	..	1 478	536	1 032	3 823	73	432	212	..	5 126
1961	..	421	369	484	1 559	33	235	166	..	2 467
1962	..	–425	91	234	–168	–46	165	24	..	81
1963	–177	–50	452	86	630	–31	189	239	..	1 501
1964	24	1 166	1 325	494	3 599	254	674	278	..	6 169
1965	8	624	817	705	2 562	11	390	128	..	4 013
1966	–84	129	526	785	1 650	223	155	70	..	2 542
1967	195	–39	490	–213	121	229	96	213	..	2 013
1968	–19	526	451	305	1 466	213	493	342	..	3 207
1969	–228	448	120	955	1 933	–176	402	162	..	3 550
1970	–189	583	460	380	1 975	–278	623	–26	..	2 645
1971	95	–695	–349	473	–685	368	671	25	..	841
1972	–33	–424	318	–813	–902	–34	533	71	..	–10
1973	–30	2 253	1 247	24	4 099	–218	1 330	1 730	..	9 186
1974	–98	1 214	963	1 732	4 576	–344	1 109	–507	..	4 150
1975	319	–2 534	–552	–33	–3 588	704	–760	–290	..	–4 739
1976	–22	–279	725	275	846	125	402	624	..	2 259
1977	38	416	754	569	1 434	–160	1 221	118	..	4 758
1978	125	286	384	19	474	93	1 119	858	..	3 993
1979	–68	–67	–800	990	671	–220	2 071	837	..	4 635
1980	246	–2 083	–1 301	–609	–4 261	238	–635	–656	..	–4 694
1981	–25	–1 792	–152	–933	–3 354	169	–352	278	..	–4 457
1982	78	–917	–1 089	–468	–2 628	505	–7	19	..	–1 784
1983	–62	–408	684	–57	–11	255	194	–55	..	1 890
1984	–31	242	481	360	1 131	–676	43	583	..	1 510
1985	–174	172	–796	–45	–612	321	–102	317	..	1 143
1986	–95	–66	–199	–420	–686	195	309	828	..	1 384
1987	12	75	–342	–221	–486	–132	680	859	..	1 907
1988	17	349	249	393	991	105	1 066	867	..	5 883
1989	215	–51	–370	620	199	–62	851	352	1 149	3 123
1990	–103	–266	–1 511	–136	–1 913	–129	–552	181	716	–2 079
1991	170	–861	–1 358	–1 346	–3 565	200	–612	–404	–420	–5 349
1992	66	–211	–1 124	–47	–1 382	–100	117	216	–616	–1 962
1993	–45	20	–981	–320	–1 281	–270	802	368	738	360
1994	–267	433	639	548	1 102	–661	1 332	884	2 451	4 836
1995	–123	514	1 144	998	2 656	–205	597	811	776	4 512
1996	–47	–105	–217	6	–316	15	681	638	859	1 830
1997	55	403	–1 332	340	–589	103	1 499	799	1 895	3 762
1998	257	721	–588	367	500	–154	–16	987	2 655	4 229
1999	–191	170	–236	–1 103	–1 169	–180	–686	674	166	–1 386

1 Differences between totals and the sum of the constituent parts prior to 1994 are due to the method of rebasing to 1995 prices.
2 Estimates are given to the nearest million, but cannot be regarded as accurate to this degree.
3 Wholesaling and retailing estimates exclude the motor trade.

Source: Office for National Statistics; Enquiries 01633 812019

4.6 Changes in inventories[2]

continued

£ million, 1995 prices, not seasonally adjusted

	Mining and quarrying	Manufacturing (revised definition) Materials and fuels	Work in progress	Finished goods	Total[1]	Electricity, gas and water supply	Distribution Wholesale[3]	Retail[3]	Other industries	All industries[1]
	FADO	FBID	FBIE	FBIF	DHBH	FADP	FAJM	FBYH	DLWV	ABMQ
1955 Q1	..	159	426	152	839	–29	..	260	..	1 385
Q2	..	84	170	175	506	17	..	–59	..	–208
Q3	..	449	24	–190	414	32	..	59	..	1 162
Q4	..	80	–199	268	210	15	..	–43	..	133
1956 Q1	..	106	362	287	868	–12	..	239	..	1 042
Q2	..	22	504	439	1 131	42	..	–65	..	976
Q3	..	358	34	–144	317	69	..	80	..	305
Q4	..	52	–51	8	20	–2	..	–126	..	–400
1957 Q1	..	158	232	365	810	45	..	316	..	1 538
Q2	..	–160	480	201	574	77	..	18	..	850
Q3	..	194	106	–296	60	31	..	–18	..	386
Q4	..	–85	–361	80	–435	48	..	–31	..	–800
1958 Q1	..	–240	182	453	475	–2	..	154	..	748
Q2	..	–411	157	415	165	25	..	7	..	113
Q3	..	148	37	–245	–134	52	..	42	..	589
Q4	..	–160	–169	12	–420	41	..	–102	..	–575
1959 Q1	..	–123	–124	489	280	–65	117	112	..	554
Q2	..	–45	254	–419	–281	16	62	159	..	355
Q3	..	247	197	–257	205	29	205	23	..	702
Q4	..	11	–19	356	418	86	–288	–6	..	31
1960 Q1	..	262	124	242	868	–144	94	386	..	1 488
Q2	..	209	316	52	713	19	72	–	..	1 124
Q3	..	704	39	–34	899	97	378	–14	..	1 479
Q4	..	303	57	772	1 343	101	–112	–160	..	1 035
1961 Q1	..	193	148	225	728	–71	246	275	..	1 456
Q2	..	159	250	–5	472	27	164	165	..	1 231
Q3	..	390	60	–290	180	65	141	–104	..	355
Q4	..	–321	–89	554	179	12	–316	–170	..	–575
1962 Q1	..	–338	–60	82	–341	–154	18	287	..	–185
Q2	..	–115	256	–72	91	–46	–	–120	..	286
Q3	..	183	8	–241	–113	65	328	–20	..	408
Q4	..	–155	–113	465	195	89	–181	–123	..	–428
1963 Q1	–98	–216	–143	462	154	–282	–73	285	..	137
Q2	28	–156	274	–174	–45	110	187	17	..	654
Q3	–11	299	117	–518	–129	116	137	–74	..	121
Q4	–96	23	204	316	650	25	–62	11	..	589
1964 Q1	–45	191	168	210	744	–269	64	285	..	1 002
Q2	50	141	510	292	1 182	167	150	–57	..	1 880
Q3	24	436	388	–333	548	183	409	43	..	1 567
Q4	–5	398	259	325	1 125	173	51	7	..	1 720
1965 Q1	–16	24	300	260	727	–262	–44	253	..	859
Q2	34	210	162	331	841	188	4	–89	..	1 250
Q3	19	423	284	–211	554	125	434	32	..	1 496
Q4	–29	–33	71	325	440	–40	–4	–68	..	408
1966 Q1	–120	129	144	275	636	–161	–62	249	..	611
Q2	54	–152	179	244	275	154	–33	101	..	1 022
Q3	5	528	121	–49	769	217	431	–52	..	1 456
Q4	–23	–376	82	315	–30	13	–181	–228	..	–547
1967 Q1	26	196	60	–40	224	–58	–45	127	..	562
Q2	108	–170	43	238	135	165	5	189	..	769
Q3	61	275	153	–433	–74	188	222	51	..	561
Q4	–	–340	234	22	–164	–66	–86	–154	..	121
1968 Q1	–26	67	–22	–374	–417	–166	–76	248	..	–773
Q2	47	–122	209	465	626	164	165	123	..	1 582
Q3	–	409	336	–110	750	209	363	–11	..	1 714
Q4	–40	172	–72	324	507	6	41	–18	..	684
1969 Q1	–87	75	175	395	802	–380	–	190	..	785
Q2	–44	92	17	366	599	146	18	65	..	1 498
Q3	–39	151	86	–251	–10	135	378	–104	..	758
Q4	–58	130	–158	445	542	–77	6	11	..	509

See footnotes on page 210.

Source: Office for National Statistics; Enquiries 01633 812019

4.6 Changes in inventories[2]

continued

£ million, 1995 prices, not seasonally adjusted

		Manufacturing (revised definition)					Distribution			
	Mining and quarrying	Materials and fuels	Work in progress	Finished goods	Total[1]	Electricity, gas and water supply	Wholesale[3]	Retail[3]	Other industries	All industries[1]
	FADO	FBID	FBIE	FBIF	DHBH	FADP	FAJM	FBYH	DLWV	ABMQ
1970 Q1	–105	–23	20	306	384	–362	–68	–21	..	–584
Q2	–42	143	349	92	820	96	123	27	..	1 393
Q3	–13	361	91	–379	162	144	445	–70	..	1 337
Q4	–29	102	–	361	609	–156	123	38	..	499
1971 Q1	–	–260	–101	489	197	–70	–14	–101	..	163
Q2	24	–326	–123	136	–424	280	222	18	..	258
Q3	61	–12	56	–450	–485	205	412	–25	..	251
Q4	10	–97	–181	298	27	–47	51	133	..	169
1972 Q1	–77	–196	46	–102	–382	–406	–31	–32	..	–919
Q2	8	–387	220	–148	–381	236	–21	179	..	506
Q3	23	159	52	–563	–500	164	413	–123	..	9
Q4	13	–	–	–	361	–28	172	47	..	394
1973 Q1	–33	487	535	159	1 244	–108	175	302	..	2 056
Q2	60	564	282	67	1 059	245	185	854	..	3 064
Q3	–8	682	421	–511	1 053	83	643	189	..	2 667
Q4	–49	520	9	309	743	–438	327	385	..	1 399
1974 Q1	–2	514	118	–176	924	–593	100	–290	..	–730
Q2	–71	–82	736	734	1 407	96	417	123	..	2 502
Q3	–2	795	533	405	2 252	135	468	–259	..	2 437
Q4	–23	–13	–424	769	–7	18	124	–81	..	–59
1975 Q1	50	–1 178	118	585	–816	58	–436	–402	..	–2 042
Q2	58	–529	82	–52	–471	312	–386	–353	..	–1 272
Q3	93	–540	–139	–615	–1 391	201	112	190	..	–883
Q4	118	–287	–613	49	–910	133	–50	275	..	–542
1976 Q1	–92	–440	86	303	–191	–188	–39	53	..	–696
Q2	55	–277	167	–116	–232	244	–72	–107	..	124
Q3	3	280	325	–657	191	145	469	324	..	1 145
Q4	12	158	147	745	1 078	–76	44	354	..	1 686
1977 Q1	–21	117	557	266	894	–433	271	239	..	1 550
Q2	36	–50	166	512	449	158	532	–33	..	1 900
Q3	11	261	–84	–563	–355	127	222	–134	..	266
Q4	12	88	115	354	446	–12	196	46	..	1 042
1978 Q1	–60	2	142	183	103	–28	285	42	..	322
Q2	105	–24	47	265	294	157	47	375	..	1 948
Q3	25	207	–107	–523	–383	96	713	271	..	1 076
Q4	55	101	302	94	460	–132	74	170	..	647
1979 Q1	41	–385	–200	450	–348	–525	605	203	..	1 486
Q2	–15	207	–40	–167	203	44	704	240	..	1 064
Q3	–66	346	90	–322	508	229	482	522	..	2 266
Q4	–28	–235	–650	1 029	308	32	280	–128	..	–181
1980 Q1	44	–671	–33	330	–515	–94	–164	–233	..	–895
Q2	44	–188	–229	495	114	124	–708	–234	..	194
Q3	72	–417	–158	–886	–1 540	204	454	14	..	–730
Q4	86	–807	–881	–548	–2 320	4	–217	–203	..	–3 263
1981 Q1	18	–666	–283	–342	–1 260	–68	–8	236	..	–1 703
Q2	–17	–579	–124	–324	–1 066	59	–333	65	..	–1 549
Q3	–9	–37	266	–665	–652	223	389	20	..	262
Q4	–17	–510	–11	398	–376	–45	–400	–43	..	–1 467
1982 Q1	86	–238	–243	327	–184	–122	666	375	..	1 280
Q2	–56	133	66	–6	357	284	–136	42	..	780
Q3	36	–213	–89	–886	–1 368	344	214	–11	..	–671
Q4	12	–599	–823	97	–1 433	–1	–751	–387	..	–3 173
1983 Q1	–17	–371	545	210	291	–47	–29	37	..	621
Q2	–9	–14	100	276	264	133	197	–322	..	744
Q3	–35	43	312	–999	–475	182	575	226	..	1 433
Q4	–1	–66	–273	456	–91	–13	–549	4	..	–908
1984 Q1	–88	–132	283	500	672	–312	208	317	..	621
Q2	57	125	384	–154	464	–316	–215	–51	..	206
Q3	–17	354	164	–531	62	–38	511	–103	..	751
Q4	17	–105	–350	545	–67	–10	–461	420	..	–68

See footnotes on page 210.

Source: Office for National Statistics; Enquiries 01633 812019

4.6 Changes in inventories[2]

continued

£ million, 1995 prices, not seasonally adjusted

		Manufacturing (revised definition)					Distribution			
	Mining and quarrying	Materials and fuels	Work in progress	Finished goods	Total[1]	Electricity, gas and water supply	Wholesale[3]	Retail[3]	Other industries	All industries[1]
	FADO	FBID	FBIE	FBIF	DHBH	FADP	FAJM	FBYH	DLWV	ABMQ
1985 Q1	–39	35	–332	249	–72	–147	212	–20	..	127
Q2	–91	76	231	446	709	142	–54	96	..	1 326
Q3	–99	324	188	–974	–289	246	282	209	..	858
Q4	55	–263	–883	234	–960	80	–542	32	..	–1 168
1986 Q1	–142	108	–176	–47	–114 652	–242	703	145	..	694
Q2	53	145	252	257	654 182	66	–339	189	..	1 073
Q3	15	–130	120	–970	–980 951	281	51	216	..	–229
Q4	–21	–189	–395	340	–243 656	90	–106	278	..	–154
1987 Q1	43	–96	–116	84	–127 308	–384	455	–9	..	182
Q2	–50	–	212	61	272 572	95	–104	277	..	885
Q3	6	207	443	–749	–98 194	195	695	507	..	1 680
Q4	13	–36	–881	383	–533 761	–38	–366	84	..	–840
1988 Q1	–93	109	67	128	303	–53	307	42	..	1 230
Q2	–8	191	275	525	992	77	59	182	..	1 940
Q3	53	–2	116	–931	–818	147	936	138	..	1 008
Q4	65	51	–209	671	513	–66	–236	505	..	1 705
1989 Q1	53	23	10	444	477	–54	449	–393	..	805
Q2	112	–74	37	551	517	100	–150	424	..	2 021
Q3	21	257	366	–750	–127	55	836	162	..	1 011
Q4	29	–257	–783	375	–665	–163	–284	159	..	–714
1990 Q1	–65	–181	56	–57	–182	–203	374	–358	..	196
Q2	22	6	–323	308	–10	59	–305	93	..	587
Q3	–31	214	19	–496	–263	118	50	170	..	122
Q4	–29	–305	–1 263	109	–1 460	–103	–671	276	..	–2 984
1991 Q1	117	–466	–17	11	–473	–168	1	–648	..	–1 667
Q2	–18	–202	–446	1	–648	243	–259	–172	..	–841
Q3	23	217	–2	–958	–743	168	179	237	..	–267
Q4	48	–410	–893	–400	–1 702	–43	–533	179	..	–2 574
1992 Q1	–65	–171	–735	398	–508	32	40	–182	..	–937
Q2	46	132	355	230	715	–238	–472	–388	..	–88
Q3	54	222	123	–425	–80	42	353	359	..	422
Q4	31	–394	–867	–250	–1 511	64	196	427	..	–1 359
1993 Q1	–302	–251	–218	–142	–611	–48	88	–577	..	–1 713
Q2	166	152	115	698	965	–33	–243	–346	..	1 431
Q3	30	206	–261	–678	–731	–	687	679	..	471
Q4	61	–87	–617	–198	–901	–189	270	612	..	171
1994 Q1	–241	–472	75	298	234	–227	–28	–579	–	–841
Q2	6	234	420	930	1 399	–170	336	–37	1 491	3 025
Q3	19	556	253	–722	–173	–85	612	778	238	1 389
Q4	–51	115	–109	42	–363	–179	412	722	722	1 263
1995 Q1	–250	–13	507	560	1 054	–228	–514	–952	–171	–1 061
Q2	11	205	576	1 118	1 899	–14	11	–32	1 109	2 984
Q3	143	639	413	–746	306	85	664	961	–614	1 545
Q4	–27	–317	–352	66	–603	–48	436	834	452	1 044
1996 Q1	–24	–45	159	478	592	–212	–238	–566	–162	–610
Q2	10	–82	360	289	567	60	–3	–230	1 026	1 430
Q3	10	121	91	–761	–549	141	306	594	–149	353
Q4	–43	–99	–827	–	–926	26	616	840	144	657
1997 Q1	38	–10	203	389	582	106	–124	–383	–69	150
Q2	–6	278	154	653	1 085	96	488	–69	1 044	2 638
Q3	9	439	–206	–259	–26	44	–29	782	48	828
Q4	14	–304	–1 483	–443	–2 230	–143	1 164	469	872	146
1998 Q1	–42	102	–479	435	58	–116	–94	–156	830	480
Q2	78	297	304	–94	507	–45	–616	–147	1 939	1 716
Q3	110	490	39	–673	–144	25	163	905	–38	1 021
Q4	111	–168	–452	699	79	–18	531	385	–76	1 012
1999 Q1	2	12	–383	–395	–766	–87	–589	–340	167	–1 613
Q2	–84	–41	260	–491	–272	–10	–284	28	–228	–850
Q3	–72	260	647	–301	606	–20	–79	788	557	1 780
Q4	–37	–61	–760	84	–737	–63	266	198	–330	–703
2000 Q1	12	–162	467	–94	211	–45	1 028	285	599	2 090

See footnotes on page 210.

Source: Office for National Statistics; Enquiries 01633 812019

4.6 Changes in inventories[2]

continued

£ million, 1995 prices, seasonally adjusted

		Manufacturing (revised definition)					Distribution			
	Mining and quarrying	Materials and fuels	Work in progress	Finished goods	Total[1]	Electricity, gas and water supply	Wholesale[4]	Retail[4]	Other industries[3]	All industries[1,3]
	FAEA	FBNF	FBNG	FBNH	DHBM	FAEB	FAJX	FBYN	DLWX	CAFU
1955 Q1	..	284	360	−33	799	..	..	36	..	874
Q2	..	242	−17	−82	277	..	..	−4	..	−169
Q3	..	112	12	323	608	..	..	116	..	959
Q4	..	134	47	197	506	..	..	69	..	808
1956 Q1	..	238	329	66	776	..	..	17	..	885
Q2	..	176	296	197	936	..	..	−9	..	475
Q3	..	11	19	425	495	..	..	133	..	282
Q4	..	118	194	−98	390	..	..	−13	..	281
1957 Q1	..	274	221	94	640	..	..	104	..	1 057
Q2	..	5	262	39	426	..	..	69	..	628
Q3	..	−158	89	273	242	..	..	30	..	320
Q4	..	−10	−132	−56	−186	..	..	82	..	−31
1958 Q1	..	−124	205	163	244	..	..	−42	..	520
Q2	..	−262	−73	347	−1	..	..	50	..	−60
Q3	..	−195	21	344	96	..	..	87	..	569
Q4	..	−76	41	−219	−242	..	..	6	..	−154
1959 Q1	..	−19	−76	161	184	..	93	−94	..	221
Q2	..	103	21	−335	−345	..	42	196	..	113
Q3	..	−96	174	296	453	..	35	78	..	554
Q4	..	106	168	47	400	..	−74	108	..	754
1960 Q1	..	376	196	−41	1 120	..	76	152	..	1 211
Q2	..	337	78	215	765	..	44	40	..	909
Q3	..	359	31	532	1 047	..	192	64	..	1 348
Q4	..	411	223	326	1 320	..	120	−44	..	1 658
1961 Q1	..	310	224	−19	662	..	240	25	..	1 283
Q2	..	283	12	224	598	..	150	228	..	1 035
Q3	..	28	72	273	404	..	−64	−27	..	260
Q4	..	−201	41	6	70	..	−91	−60	..	−111
1962 Q1	..	−216	27	−126	−339	−82	37	33	..	−165
Q2	..	−11	38	137	136	−32	–	−47	..	−7
Q3	..	−157	24	323	21	33	118	47	..	316
Q4	..	−27	−1	−100	−4	35	10	−9	..	−63
1963 Q1	−56	−116	−62	280	−23	−90	−25	81	..	46
Q2	−29	−46	85	−30	48	46	190	84	..	642
Q3	−33	−32	127	34	148	13	−84	−43	..	43
Q4	−59	155	293	−198	528	–	108	117	..	770
1964 Q1	−11	267	247	83	633	−85	142	84	..	962
Q2	4	263	345	318	1 272	99	168	–	..	1 716
Q3	5	107	388	209	852	84	168	74	..	1 411
Q4	26	548	327	−116	1 246	156	196	120	..	2 080
1965 Q1	19	56	383	177	683	−77	55	63	..	938
Q2	−14	371	38	255	852	113	31	−52	..	1 011
Q3	2	74	254	332	769	22	168	65	..	1 196
Q4	1	134	150	−59	546	−47	136	52	..	868
1966 Q1	−91	131	202	243	672	28	49	78	..	810
Q2	16	30	102	62	199	71	–	112	..	737
Q3	−10	182	42	524	997	108	160	−7	..	1 148
Q4	–	−213	170	−44	−32	16	−54	−113	..	−153
1967 Q1	60	191	125	−47	258	145	72	−25	..	888
Q2	72	24	−27	−15	37	63	45	197	..	433
Q3	40	−56	67	166	42	61	−58	115	..	217
Q4	23	−218	345	−317	−202	−40	37	−74	..	475
1968 Q1	21	83	16	−384	−426	64	33	126	..	−340
Q2	10	61	145	233	592	34	205	126	..	1 199
Q3	−29	107	248	484	994	69	101	59	..	1 412
Q4	−21	254	46	−28	470	46	154	31	..	936
1969 Q1	−39	114	218	324	881	−141	132	100	..	1 267
Q2	−73	270	−74	189	541	−5	49	59	..	1 034
Q3	−67	−125	3	371	231	−12	119	−21	..	554
Q4	−49	163	–	71	497	−18	102	24	..	695

1 Differences between totals and the sum of the constituent parts prior to 1994 are due to the method of rebasing to 1995 prices.

2 Estimates are given to the nearest million, but cannnot be regarded as accurate to this degree.

3 Quarterly alignment adjustment included in this series. For a description of adjustment see notes in article "UK National Accounts, second quarter 1992," *Economic Trends*, No.468, October 1992.

4 Wholesaling and retailing estimates exclude the motor trade.

Source: Office for National Statistics; Enquiries 01633 812019

4.6 Changes in inventories[2]

continued

£ million, 1995 prices, seasonally adjusted

	Mining and quarrying	Manufacturing (revised definition): Materials and fuels	Work in progress	Finished goods	Total[1]	Electricity, gas and water supply	Distribution: Wholesale[4]	Retail[4]	Other industries[3]	All industries[1,3]
	FAEA	FBNF	FBNG	FBNH	DHBM	FAEB	FAJX	FBYN	DLWX	CAFU
1970 Q1	−72	46	36	159	259	−124	79	−64	..	−203
Q2	−61	303	245	−20	913	−75	158	21	..	1 051
Q3	−31	118	20	266	426	−13	187	17	..	1 161
Q4	−25	84	185	−25	598	−66	199	–	..	636
1971 Q1	26	−160	−119	274	−42	204	150	−109	..	522
Q2	11	−155	−252	97	−458	65	259	17	..	−133
Q3	40	−249	17	195	−95	−7	147	62	..	245
Q4	18	−139	35	−93	−167	106	115	55	..	207
1972 Q1	−50	−77	−6	−364	−613	−102	97	141	..	−225
Q2	−6	−235	82	−150	−282	−8	54	−14	..	−9
Q3	1	−63	22	57	−81	−79	181	−17	..	64
Q4	22	−4	214	−356	−27	155	201	−39	..	160
1973 Q1	−7	765	522	−118	1 109	129	301	464	..	2 485
Q2	47	436	86	71	1 235	30	273	678	..	2 536
Q3	−31	458	356	−55	1 350	−82	384	305	..	2 517
Q4	−39	489	356	126	865	−295	372	283	..	1 648
1974 Q1	21	933	29	−357	1 429	−433	223	−131	..	243
Q2	−87	−235	537	682	1 228	−48	517	−23	..	1 710
Q3	−14	532	471	878	2 452	29	186	−160	..	2 179
Q4	−18	−22	−63	529	−20	108	183	−193	..	18
1975 Q1	70	−801	−3	364	−795	244	−341	−290	..	−1 503
Q2	49	−629	−102	−102	−803	152	−296	−440	..	−1 914
Q3	77	−758	−150	−53	−1 281	72	−153	260	..	−874
Q4	123	−324	−306	−242	−1 111	236	30	180	..	−448
1976 Q1	−58	−125	−48	69	−79	24	21	128	..	−195
Q2	35	−347	20	−176	−518	79	11	−144	..	−468
Q3	−12	87	316	−95	353	−1	227	369	..	989
Q4	13	119	423	477	1 186	23	143	271	..	1 933
1977 Q1	10	409	422	33	1 180	−238	298	275	..	2 007
Q2	14	−110	50	420	27	30	618	−37	..	1 160
Q3	4	70	−100	108	−68	−7	−26	−122	..	234
Q4	10	68	360	8	456	55	331	2	..	1 357
1978 Q1	−28	244	22	−74	149	169	296	49	..	790
Q2	78	−60	−35	157	33	52	123	393	..	1 299
Q3	24	8	−151	183	−150	−75	477	265	..	784
Q4	51	121	531	−247	495	−53	223	151	..	1 120
1979 Q1	75	−177	−303	190	−305	−355	476	201	..	1 490
Q2	−51	173	−105	−279	−42	−45	831	258	..	499
Q3	−64	124	8	376	755	88	136	514	..	1 792
Q4	−28	−161	−395	703	338	92	628	−136	..	854
1980 Q1	58	−487	−141	84	−755	79	−298	−378	..	−990
Q2	23	−227	−271	323	−324	45	−554	−171	..	−397
Q3	77	−650	−302	−108	−1 437	43	85	−38	..	−1 229
Q4	88	−681	−564	−908	−2 223	71	132	−69	..	−2 078
1981 Q1	28	−526	−432	−604	−1 569	114	−142	57	..	−1 947
Q2	−37	−632	−137	−453	−1 518	−18	−167	145	..	−1 913
Q3	−2	−260	94	17	−586	52	−10	−32	..	−400
Q4	−14	−346	354	107	−57	21	−33	108	..	−197
1982 Q1	88	−150	−414	51	−545	76	513	171	..	811
Q2	−68	116	34	−173	125	217	60	157	..	602
Q3	43	−444	−282	−112	−1 286	159	−230	−44	..	−1 325
Q4	15	−426	−427	−234	−1 217	53	−350	−265	..	−1 872
1983 Q1	−17	−249	435	−112	36	197	−236	−115	..	386
Q2	−15	−164	−67	209	−106	44	376	−199	..	678
Q3	−29	−114	153	−268	−195	15	156	201	..	47
Q4	−1	120	163	114	252	−1	−102	58	..	779
1984 Q1	−87	−54	197	212	456	−71	−54	246	..	102
Q2	50	33	218	−249	132	−417	−60	45	..	697
Q3	−12	159	−46	216	446	−174	152	−164	..	114
Q4	18	104	112	181	224	−14	5	456	..	597

See footnotes on page 214.

Source: Office for National Statistics; Enquiries 01633 812019.

4.6 Changes in inventories[2]

continued

£ million, 1995 prices, seasonally adjusted

	Mining and quarrying	Manufacturing (revised definition) Materials and fuels	Work in progress	Finished goods	Total[1]	Electricity, gas and water supply	Distribution Wholesale[4]	Retail[4]	Other industries[3]	All industries[1,3]
	FAEA	FBNF	FBNG	FBNH	DHBM	FAEB	FAJX	FBYN	DLWX	CAFU
1985 Q1	–38	87	–273	26	–361	48	–20	–14	..	–547
Q2	–96	–20	–77	253	320	80	131	161	..	1 263
Q3	–97	160	–	–167	205	117	–99	144	..	–123
Q4	57	–55	–445	–157	–844	76	–114	26	..	550
1986 Q1	–140	106	–73	–201	–187	–11	391	294	..	–677
Q2	65	71	–93	–44	–73	5	–110	210	..	800
Q3	–14	–243	–213	–104	–623	105	–226	98	..	291
Q4	–6	–	180	–71	120	96	254	226	..	970
1987 Q1	56	–97	–122	–33	–280	–166	158	182	..	129
Q2	–51	–75	–60	–257	–436	23	215	292	..	902
Q3	–13	187	213	61	513	22	289	426	..	409
Q4	20	60	–373	8	–337	–11	19	–41	..	467
1988 Q1	–70	122	49	13	201	153	80	364	..	69
Q2	–17	195	52	221	522	–21	388	110	..	629
Q3	40	–133	–215	–115	–515	–21	366	40	..	1 356
Q4	64	165	363	274	894	–7	232	353	..	3 829
1989 Q1	86	81	–125	351	341	125	212	–25	..	727
Q2	94	–60	–87	167	22	1	91	370	..	1 524
Q3	12	64	12	62	153	–99	357	60	..	1 466
Q4	23	–136	–170	40	–296	–89	191	–53	..	–594
1990 Q1	–33	–59	–124	–202	–424	–58	131	92	..	276
Q2	7	14	–368	–48	–447	–32	–53	5	..	1 065
Q3	–39	–127	–466	171	–469	–7	–355	–19	..	–833
Q4	–38	–94	–553	–57	–787	–32	–275	103	..	–2 587
1991 Q1	147	–303	–120	–202	–695	–55	–178	–272	..	–653
Q2	–23	–272	–626	–310	–1 344	173	–14	–9	..	–2 333
Q3	11	–120	–416	–515	–1 169	79	–96	31	..	–1 971
Q4	35	–166	–196	–319	–757	3	–324	–154	..	–392
1992 Q1	15	10	–743	244	–544	136	–60	193	..	–189
Q2	26	–17	33	–236	–245	–290	–144	–86	..	–1 266
Q3	27	–73	–91	77	–97	–41	33	35	..	–605
Q4	–2	–131	–323	–132	–652	95	288	74	..	98
1993 Q1	–147	–67	–227	–321	–684	–4	126	–104	..	–236
Q2	139	34	–323	112	–197	–4	76	30	..	162
Q3	–43	–50	–329	–110	–544	–109	369	241	..	–25
Q4	6	103	–102	–1	–	–153	231	201	..	459
1994 Q1	–64	–217	–32	103	–146	–112	192	267	–384	–247
Q2	–61	97	146	217	460	–189	512	269	799	1 790
Q3	–67	238	187	251	676	–202	278	214	359	1 258
Q4	–75	315	338	–23	630	–158	350	134	1 154	2 035
1995 Q1	–171	245	388	351	984	–137	–372	–180	–61	63
Q2	–21	51	289	310	650	–24	185	275	822	1 887
Q3	88	318	341	200	859	–15	464	435	–458	1 373
Q4	–19	–100	126	137	163	–29	320	281	473	1 189
1996 Q1	36	228	111	228	567	–113	–63	204	302	933
Q2	–19	–274	–125	–501	–900	44	151	117	622	15
Q3	–41	–144	72	160	88	31	219	34	155	486
Q4	–23	85	–275	119	–71	53	374	283	–220	396
1997 Q1	86	121	187	40	348	159	294	316	118	1 321
Q2	–44	232	–162	186	256	104	670	308	–527	767
Q3	–6	137	–456	426	107	–70	–240	195	438	424
Q4	19	–87	–901	–312	–1 300	–90	775	–20	1 866	1 250
1998 Q1	–17	220	–355	–	–135	–60	471	454	206	919
Q2	78	182	–118	–254	–190	–71	–593	201	1 589	1 014
Q3	90	236	–141	–287	–192	–32	7	261	744	878
Q4	106	83	26	908	1 017	9	99	71	116	1 418
1999 Q1	24	132	–278	–664	–810	–40	–150	237	1 069	330
Q2	–79	–177	–147	–447	–771	–36	–249	394	–694	–1 435
Q3	–89	5	453	–100	358	–65	–189	117	–766	–634
Q4	–47	210	–264	108	54	–39	–98	–74	557	353
2000 Q1	27	–75	574	–671	–172	–5	763	376	–280	709

See footnotes on page 214.

Source: Office for National Statistics; Enquiries 01633 812019

4.7 Inventory ratios

Index numbers: seasonally adjusted

	Manufacturers' inventories[1] to manufacturing production				Retail inventories to retail sales[2,3]	Total inventories[1,4] to gross value added
	Materials and fuel	Work in progress	Finished goods	Total inventories		
	FAPG	FAPH	FAPI	FAPF	FAPC	FDCA
1984	126.8	171.1	132.8	143.8	..	..
1985	126.6	163.6	131.9	140.9	..	..
1986	125.8	157.0	125.7	136.2	..	104
1987	118.5	148.6	116.9	128.0	98.2	101
1988	114.0	137.6	110.4	120.6	98.0	98
1989	110.9	132.0	112.5	118.5	100.1	101
1990	109.0	125.7	112.1	115.7	100.7	100
1991	107.4	120.6	111.1	113.1	100.5	99
1992	104.2	110.7	106.5	107.2	100.2	96
1993	101.0	102.3	101.3	101.5	98.2	95
1994	97.3	96.9	98.5	97.6	100.2	100
1995	100.6	101.9	101.5	101.3	102.5	102
1996	100.7	103.2	102.3	102.1	104.5	103
1997	100.7	98.7	102.7	100.8	104.2	101
1998	103.7	90.8	102.0	98.8	105.0	99
1999	105.3	89.2	99.4	97.8	107.4	97
1984 Q1	125.6	170.1	133.4	143.3	..	..
Q2	126.3	172.4	131.1	143.5	..	..
Q3	127.0	170.5	132.3	143.5	..	..
Q4	128.2	171.5	134.2	144.9	..	..
1985 Q1	125.5	164.3	130.6	140.3	..	..
Q2	124.7	162.8	132.6	140.3	..	..
Q3	127.7	164.4	132.1	141.6	..	..
Q4	128.8	162.9	132.3	141.4	..	..
1986 Q1	127.8	159.5	127.9	138.5	..	105
Q2	128.9	159.2	127.8	138.6	96.5	104
Q3	125.4	156.4	125.9	136.0	96.1	103
Q4	121.3	152.8	121.1	131.8	96.5	102
1987 Q1	120.7	152.3	121.2	131.5	97.9	102
Q2	118.6	150.3	117.4	128.8	97.8	101
Q3	118.0	148.7	115.5	127.4	99.4	100
Q4	116.6	143.2	113.5	124.4	97.5	99
1988 Q1	115.2	140.5	111.2	122.2	98.7	98
Q2	116.4	139.9	112.5	122.9	98.0	98
Q3	111.9	134.4	108.3	118.1	96.9	97
Q4	112.4	135.8	109.7	119.3	98.4	99
1989 Q1	111.4	132.8	111.2	118.5	98.2	100
Q2	110.9	132.2	112.6	118.6	100.7	101
Q3	111.4	132.1	113.1	118.9	101.3	101
Q4	110.0	130.8	113.3	118.1	100.2	101
1990 Q1	109.2	129.7	111.3	116.8	99.8	100
Q2	108.7	126.3	110.2	115.1	100.1	100
Q3	108.8	124.6	113.1	115.6	100.4	101
Q4	109.2	122.2	114.0	115.3	102.4	100
1991 Q1	108.5	123.8	114.4	115.7	100.3	100
Q2	107.9	121.6	113.7	114.6	100.9	99
Q3	107.7	119.7	110.0	112.5	100.8	98
Q4	105.4	117.4	106.3	109.7	99.9	97
1992 Q1	105.1	111.5	108.2	108.4	101.4	97
Q2	105.0	111.8	106.0	107.6	99.6	96
Q3	103.9	110.7	106.4	107.1	100.0	96
Q4	102.9	108.7	105.5	105.8	99.7	95
1993 Q1	100.7	105.4	101.0	102.4	97.5	95
Q2	101.2	103.2	102.1	102.2	97.5	95
Q3	100.8	100.9	101.2	101.0	98.5	94
Q4	101.3	99.6	100.7	100.5	99.0	94
1994 Q1	97.7	97.3	99.0	98.0	99.3	99
Q2	96.8	96.6	98.6	97.4	100.1	100
Q3	97.0	96.3	98.6	97.4	100.3	99
Q4	97.9	97.2	97.5	97.5	101.1	100

1 Measured at 1995 prices; end-March 1995=100.
2 Measured at 1995 prices; 1st quarter 1995=100.
3 Classes 64-65 excluding activity headings 6510 and 6520, retail distribution of motor vehicles and parts, and filling stations.
4 Including quarterly alignment adjustment (see footnote on page 26).

Sources: Office for National Statistics; Enquiries Columns 1-5 01633 812019; Column 6 020 7533 6009

4.7 Inventory ratios

continued

Index numbers: seasonally adjusted

	Manufacturers' inventories[1] to manufacturing production				Retail inventories to retail sales[2,3]	Total inventories[1,4] to gross value added
	Materials and fuel	Work in progress	Finished goods	Total inventories		
	FAPG	FAPH	FAPI	FAPF	FAPC	FDCA
1995 Q1	100.0	100.0	100.0	100.0	100.0	100
Q2	99.8	101.1	101.1	100.7	101.3	101
Q3	101.6	102.8	102.0	102.1	103.7	102
Q4	101.1	103.6	102.8	102.5	104.9	103
1996 Q1	102.1	103.9	103.6	103.2	105.6	103
Q2	101.0	103.7	101.6	102.1	104.4	103
Q3	99.8	103.7	102.0	101.9	103.8	103
Q4	99.7	101.6	102.0	101.1	104.0	102
1997 Q1	99.4	101.8	101.4	100.9	104.3	101
Q2	101.1	101.2	102.6	101.7	104.4	101
Q3	101.4	98.3	104.2	101.4	104.8	101
Q4	101.0	93.6	102.7	99.1	103.2	101
1998 Q1	101.9	91.5	102.4	98.6	103.6	99
Q2	102.7	90.6	100.9	98.0	104.8	99
Q3	104.3	90.0	99.7	97.8	105.6	99
Q4	105.8	91.0	105.2	100.6	106.0	100
1999 Q1	106.9	89.8	102.2	99.5	107.4	98
Q2	105.5	88.8	99.6	97.8	108.4	97
Q3	104.1	89.9	97.8	97.1	107.8	97
Q4	104.9	88.2	97.9	96.8	105.6	96
2000 Q1	104.9	91.6	95.0	96.9	106.3	97

1 Measured at 1995 prices; end-March 1995=100.
2 Measured at 1995 prices; 1st quarter 1995=100.
3 Classes 64-65 excluding activity headings 6510 and 6520, retail distribution of motor vehicles and parts, and filling stations.
4 Including quarterly alignment adjustment (see footnote on page 26).

Sources: Office for National Statistics; Enquiries Columns 1-5 01633 812019; Column 6 020 7533 6009

4.8 Retail sales, new registrations of cars and credit business (Great Britain)

Not seasonally adjusted

	Volume of retail sales per week, nsa, (average 1995=100)[1,2]			Predominantly non-food stores										Net lending (£ million)[3]	
	Value of retail sales per week, nsa, total (average 1995=100)[1,2]	All retailers	Predominantly food stores	Total	Non-special stores	Textiles, clothing and footwear	Household goods stores	Other stores	Non-store and repair	New registrations of cars (monthly average, thousands)	New registrations of cars (quarterly total, thousands)	Total consumer credit: net lending (£ million)[3,4]	of which: credit cards	Credit business (narrower coverage): agreements with consumers[5]	Finance houses and other specialist credit grantors: agreements with business
Sales in 1995 £ million	*166 681*	*166 681*	*74 914*	*83 184*	*15 035*	*26 100*	*19 770*	*22 280*	*8 583*						
	EAFY	EAHC	EAGW	EAGX	EAHI	EAGY	EAGZ	EAHA	EAHB	FHCH	BCGT	-AIKL			FSBU
1955	..	..	..	..	..	..	..	..	..	41.8	500.9	..			..
1956	..	..	..	..	..	..	..	..	..	33.3	399.7	..			..
1957	..	..	..	..	..	..	..	..	..	35.3	423.0	..			..
1958	..	..	..	..	..	..	..	..	..	46.3	555.3	..			111
1959	..	..	..	..	..	..	..	..	..	54.0	647.7	..			299
1960	..	..	..	..	..	..	..	..	..	67.1	804.9	..			92
1961	..	..	..	..	..	..	..	..	..	61.9	742.7	..			–1
1962	..	..	..	..	..	..	..	..	..	65.4	784.7	..			–35
1963	..	..	..	..	..	..	..	..	..	84.1	1 008.5	63			83
1964	..	..	..	..	..	..	..	..	..	99.3	1 190.7	181			168
1965	..	..	..	..	..	..	..	..	..	93.5	1 122.5	126			121
1966	..	..	..	..	..	..	..	..	..	88.8	1 065.4	–99			–135
1967	..	..	..	..	..	..	..	..	..	93.0	1 116.6	–29			–30
1968	..	..	..	..	..	..	..	..	..	93.1	1 416.8	60			56
1969	..	..	..	..	..	..	..	..	..	82.3	987.4	2			–11
1970	..	..	..	..	..	..	..	..	..	91.4	1 097.1	83			92
1971	..	..	..	..	..	..	..	..	..	108.5	1 301.8	215			251
1972	..	..	..	..	..	..	..	..	..	138.6	2 130.5	285			438
1973	..	..	..	..	..	..	..	..	..	137.3	1 648.2	284			444
1974	..	..	..	..	..	..	..	..	..	102.8	1 233.9	24			–164
1975	..	..	..	..	..	..	..	..	..	98.6	1 182.6	–407			–13
														FSBS	FSBT
1976	..	..	..	..	..	..	..	..	..	106.5	1 278.5	333		188	47
1977	..	..	..	..	..	..	..	..	..	109.4	1 313.4	738		376	335
1978	..	..	..	..	..	..	..	..	..	131.6	1 579.4	1 493		843	328
1979	..	..	..	..	..	..	..	..	..	142.1	1 705.1	2 086		1 113	483
1980	..	..	..	..	..	..	..	..	..	126.6	1 519.2	1 661		939	155
1981	..	..	..	..	..	..	..	..	..	124.5	1 494.6	2 473		582	120
1982	..	..	..	..	..	..	..	..	..	132.1	1 584.5	2 634		1 118	440
1983	..	..	..	..	..	..	..	..	..	150.5	1 806.1	3 287		1 620	805
1984	..	..	..	..	..	..	..	..	..	146.6	1 759.1	3 097		1 551	748
1985	..	..	..	..	..	..	..	..	..	153.5	1 841.8	3 820		2 309	442
1986	59.3	81.0	80.1	78.7	84.6	79.1	71.6	82.0	103.3	156.9	1 883.0	4 386		2 385	822
												VZQC	VZQS	RLWF	RLWD
1987	64.1	85.1	82.4	84.3	88.1	83.4	79.6	87.9	109.0	168.0	2 016.3	6 301	798	3 837	1 253
1988	70.4	90.5	86.0	91.5	93.0	87.5	90.1	96.4	113.3	184.2	2 210.4	6 843	675	3 913	1 929
1989	75.3	92.4	88.0	93.5	94.0	88.5	91.3	100.9	111.8	192.1	2 304.7	6 764	540	3 165	1 712
1990	80.5	93.0	89.4	93.9	94.3	89.9	89.7	102.5	109.4	167.1	2 005.0	4 616	1 761	3 683	428
1991	84.1	91.8	90.4	91.0	92.9	88.0	87.0	97.1	105.7	133.3	1 600.3	2 318	774	1 060	–785
1992	87.3	92.4	93.1	90.3	93.6	89.1	86.5	93.8	103.8	133.3	1 599.1	484	138	367	–371
1993	92.0	95.3	95.0	94.2	97.0	92.3	92.2	96.7	105.0	148.0	1 776.5	2 653	719	3 042	626
1994	96.3	98.8	98.1	98.4	99.0	97.5	97.3	100.1	106.1	158.9	1 906.3	5 743	1 483	5 515	1 035
1995	100.0	100.0	100.0	100.0	100.0	100.0	100.0	100.0	100.0	161.5	1 938.2	8 234	2 103	..	..
1996	105.4	103.1	101.8	104.4	106.0	104.3	106.8	101.4	101.4	168.2	2 018.4	11 215	3 029	..	..
1997	112.0	108.5	105.9	111.2	111.5	111.2	117.2	105.7	105.7	179.7	2 157.0	12 013	3 507	..	..
1998	116.4	111.7	108.8	114.3	111.5	112.0	125.2	109.2	111.6	188.4	2 261.6	14 490	4 854	..	..
1999	120.3	115.6	110.8	119.9	114.7	117.1	135.2	113.2	115.2	..	..	14 507	5 258	..	..

1 Great Britain only. The motor trades are excluded.

2 During 1998, the retail sales index was rebased using detailed information from the 1995 annual retailing inquiry. The reference year is now set at 1995=100. The index is classified on to the Standard Industrial Classification of economic activities 1992, in line with the classification of series forming the national accounts. Details of the revised figures for January 1993 to August 1998, were published in ONS First Release (98) 348 on 21 October 1998.

3 Net lending equals changes in amounts outstanding adjusted to remove distortions arising from revaluations of debt such as write-offs. Prior to 1987, net lending equals changes in amounts outstanding.

4 Covers all institutions providing finance for customers; including loans by banks on personal accounts and on bank credit cards and charge cards, by insurance companies, non-bank credit companies, unsecured loans by building societies and retailers, but excluding loans for house purchase.

5 Since end 1985, covers lending by finance houses and other specialist credit grantors, on bank credit cards (VISA and Mastercard only) and unsecured loans by building societies (since the end of 1986). Before end 1985 excluded loans on bank credit cards and block discounted agreements with finance houses and other specialist credit grantors. Loans by retailers are included until 1987. Prior to January 1991 loans greater than £15 000 were excluded.

Sources: Office for National Statistics;
Enquiries Columns 1-9 01633 812600; Columns 11-14 01633 812782;
Department of the Environment, Transport and the Regions;
Enquiries Column 10 020 7890 3077

4.8 Retail sales, new registrations of cars and credit business (Great Britain)

continued

Not seasonally adjusted

	Value of retail sales per week, nsa, total (average 1995=100)[1,2]	Volume of retail sales per week, nsa, (average 1995=100)[1,2]								New registrations of cars (monthly average, thousands)	New registrations of cars (quarterly total, thousands)	Total consumer credit: net lending (£ million)[3,4]	Net lending (£ million)[3]	
				Predominantly non-food stores										
		All retailers	Predominantly food stores	Total	Non-specialised stores	Textiles, clothing and footwear	Household goods stores	Other stores	Non-store and repair				Credit business (narrower coverage): agreements with consumers[5]	Finance houses and other specialist credit grantors: agreements with business
Sales in 1995 £ million	*166 681*	*166 681*	*74 914*	*83 184*	*15 035*	*26 100*	*19 770*	*22 280*	*8 583*					
	EAFY	EAHC	EAGW	EAGX	EAHI	EAGY	EAGZ	EAHA	EAHB	FHCH	BCGT	-AIKL		FSBU
1955 Q1	..	..	..	..	..	..	..	..	..	41.4	124.1	..		..
Q2	..	..	..	..	..	..	..	..	..	45.7	137.2	..		..
Q3	..	..	..	..	..	..	..	..	..	40.0	120.0	..		..
Q4	..	..	..	..	..	..	..	..	..	39.9	119.6	..		..
1956 Q1	..	..	..	..	..	..	..	..	..	39.6	118.9	..		..
Q2	..	..	..	..	..	..	..	..	..	41.2	123.6	..		..
Q3	..	..	..	..	..	..	..	..	..	28.4	85.3	..		..
Q4	..	..	..	..	..	..	..	..	..	24.0	71.9	..		..
1957 Q1	..	..	..	..	..	..	..	..	..	27.0	81.0	..		..
Q2	..	..	..	..	..	..	..	..	..	41.0	123.0	..		..
Q3	..	..	..	..	..	..	..	..	..	38.0	114.0	..		..
Q4	..	..	..	..	..	..	..	..	..	35.0	105.0	..		..
1958 Q1	..	..	..	..	..	..	..	..	..	47.0	141.1	..		–
Q2	..	..	..	..	..	..	..	..	..	51.8	155.4	..		19
Q3	..	..	..	..	..	..	..	..	..	42.9	128.6	..		13
Q4	..	..	..	..	..	..	..	..	..	43.4	130.2	..		79
1959 Q1	..	..	..	..	..	..	..	..	..	49.0	147.0	..		59
Q2	..	..	..	..	..	..	..	..	..	61.9	185.6	..		91
Q3	..	..	..	..	..	..	..	..	..	46.5	139.4	..		78
Q4	..	..	..	..	..	..	..	..	..	58.6	175.7	..		71
1960 Q1	..	..	..	..	..	..	..	..	..	74.6	223.9	..		61
Q2	..	..	..	..	..	..	..	..	..	82.4	247.2	..		48
Q3	..	..	..	..	..	..	..	..	..	65.1	195.2	..		–2
Q4	..	..	..	..	..	..	..	..	..	46.2	138.6	..		–15
1961 Q1	..	..	..	..	..	..	..	..	..	68.9	206.8	..		–
Q2	..	..	..	..	..	..	..	..	..	80.0	239.9	..		24
Q3	..	..	..	..	..	..	..	..	..	57.6	172.9	..		–2
Q4	..	..	..	..	..	..	..	..	..	41.0	123.1	..		–23
1962 Q1	..	..	..	..	..	..	..	..	..	63.8	191.4	..		–42
Q2	..	..	..	..	..	..	..	..	..	82.5	247.6	..		2
Q3	..	..	..	..	..	..	..	..	..	60.7	182.2	..		7
Q4	..	..	..	..	..	..	..	..	..	54.5	163.5	..		–2
1963 Q1	..	..	..	..	..	..	..	..	..	77.8	233.4	–9		–5
Q2	..	..	..	..	..	..	..	..	..	107.7	323.0	25		34
Q3	..	..	..	..	..	..	..	..	..	80.2	240.5	24		28
Q4	..	..	..	..	..	..	..	..	..	70.5	211.6	23		26
1964 Q1	..	..	..	..	..	..	..	..	..	106.5	319.5	29		35
Q2	..	..	..	..	..	..	..	..	..	121.5	364.4	51		57
Q3	..	..	..	..	..	..	..	..	..	93.0	278.9	41		44
Q4	..	..	..	..	..	..	..	..	..	76.0	227.9	60		32
1965 Q1	..	..	..	..	..	..	..	..	..	120.2	360.7	10		15
Q2	..	..	..	..	..	..	..	..	..	109.1	327.2	54		57
Q3	..	..	..	..	..	..	..	..	..	79.3	237.8	20		15
Q4	..	..	..	..	..	..	..	..	..	65.6	196.8	42		34
1966 Q1	..	..	..	..	..	..	..	..	..	116.1	348.3	–12		–22
Q2	..	..	..	..	..	..	..	..	..	119.9	359.6	–1		2
Q3	..	..	..	..	..	..	..	..	..	71.0	213.0	–46		–60
Q4	..	..	..	..	..	..	..	..	..	48.2	144.5	–40		–55
1967 Q1	..	..	..	..	..	..	..	..	..	100.3	301.0	–62		–73
Q2	..	..	..	..	..	..	..	..	..	102.3	306.9	–23		–28
Q3	..	..	..	..	..	..	..	..	..	87.6	262.9	4		11
Q4	..	..	..	..	..	..	..	..	..	81.9	245.8	52		60

See footnotes on page 219.

Sources: Office for National Statistics;
Enquiries Columns 1-9 01633 812600; Columns 11-13 01633 812782;
Department of the Environment, Transport and the Regions;
Enquiries Column 10 020 7890 3077

4.8 Retail sales, new registrations of cars and credit business (Great Britain)

continued

Not seasonally adjusted

	Value of retail sales per week, nsa, total (average 1995=100)[1,2]	Volume of retail sales per week, nsa, (average 1995=100)[1,2]: All retailers	Predominantly food stores	Predominantly non-food stores: Total	Non-specialised stores	Textiles, clothing and footwear	Household goods stores	Other stores	Non-store and repair	New registrations of cars (monthly average, thousands)	New registrations of cars (quarterly total, thousands)	Total consumer credit: net lending (£ million)[3,4]	Net lending (£ million)[3]: Credit business (narrower coverage): agreements with consumers[5]	Net lending (£ million)[3]: Finance houses and other specialist credit grantors: agreements with business
Sales in 1995 £ million	*166 681*	*166 681*	*74 914*	*83 184*	*15 035*	*26 100*	*19 770*	*22 280*	*8 583*					
	EAFY	EAHC	EAGW	EAGX	EAHI	EAGY	EAGZ	EAHA	EAHB	FHCH	BCGT	-AIKL		FSBU
1968 Q1	..	..	..	..	..	..	..	..	..	129.7	689.2	7		10
Q2	..	..	..	..	..	..	..	..	..	88.1	264.3	–		–1
Q3	..	..	..	..	..	..	..	..	..	80.2	240.7	10		7
Q4	..	..	..	..	..	..	..	..	..	74.2	222.6	43		40
1969 Q1	..	..	..	..	..	..	..	..	..	89.3	268.0	–35		–40
Q2	..	..	..	..	..	..	..	..	..	94.4	283.2	9		5
Q3	..	..	..	..	..	..	..	..	..	83.3	249.9	–6		–9
Q4	..	..	..	..	..	..	..	..	..	62.1	186.3	34		33
1970 Q1	..	..	..	..	..	..	..	..	..	95.9	287.7	–25		–25
Q2	..	..	..	..	..	..	..	..	..	102.8	308.4	28		33
Q3	..	..	..	..	..	..	..	..	..	91.0	273.0	17		19
Q4	..	..	..	..	..	..	..	..	..	76.0	228.0	63		65
1971 Q1	..	..	..	..	..	..	..	..	..	102.7	308.1	–29		–21
Q2	..	..	..	..	..	..	..	..	..	105.1	315.4	34		40
Q3	..	..	..	..	..	..	..	..	..	117.9	353.8	94		101
Q4	..	..	..	..	..	..	..	..	..	108.2	324.5	116		131
1972 Q1	..	..	..	..	..	..	..	..	..	133.7	401.1	45		45
Q2	..	..	..	..	..	..	..	..	..	156.1	468.2	67		119
Q3	..	..	..	..	..	..	..	..	..	142.0	894.1	49		113
Q4	..	..	..	..	..	..	..	..	..	122.4	367.1	124		161
1973 Q1	..	..	..	..	..	..	..	..	..	159.8	479.5	76		126
Q2	..	..	..	..	..	..	..	..	..	142.2	426.6	46		90
Q3	..	..	..	..	..	..	..	..	..	146.8	440.5	42		96
Q4	..	..	..	..	..	..	..	..	..	100.5	301.6	120		132
1974 Q1	..	..	..	..	..	..	..	..	..	109.1	327.3	–61		–108
Q2	..	..	..	..	..	..	..	..	..	110.1	330.2	–7		–55
Q3	..	..	..	..	..	..	..	..	..	110.5	331.5	–6		–39
Q4	..	..	..	..	..	..	..	..	..	81.6	244.9	98		38
1975 Q1	..	..	..	..	..	..	..	..	..	116.9	350.8	–93		–65
Q2	..	..	..	..	..	..	..	..	..	97.0	290.9	–		3
Q3	..	..	..	..	..	..	..	..	..	110.1	330.4	–131		–18
Q4	..	..	..	..	..	..	..	..	..	70.2	210.5	–183		67
													FSBS	FSBT
1976 Q1	..	..	..	..	..	..	..	..	..	117.4	352.2	–17	–80	–2
Q2	..	..	..	..	..	..	..	..	..	111.5	334.5	99	53	46
Q3	..	..	..	..	..	..	..	..	..	108.4	325.2	34	56	–24
Q4	..	..	..	..	..	..	..	..	..	88.9	266.6	217	159	27
1977 Q1	..	..	..	..	..	..	..	..	..	118.8	356.5	–58	–32	34
Q2	..	..	..	..	..	..	..	..	..	108.3	325.0	248	99	103
Q3	..	..	..	..	..	..	..	..	..	123.4	370.2	195	76	72
Q4	..	..	..	..	..	..	..	..	..	87.2	261.7	353	233	126
1978 Q1	..	..	..	..	..	..	..	..	..	148.6	445.9	270	3	39
Q2	..	..	..	..	..	..	..	..	..	132.2	396.5	461	178	138
Q3	..	..	..	..	..	..	..	..	..	150.2	450.5	279	253	69
Q4	..	..	..	..	..	..	..	..	..	95.5	286.5	483	409	82
1979 Q1	..	..	..	..	..	..	..	..	..	154.6	463.9	318	31	9
Q2	..	..	..	..	..	..	..	..	..	182.2	546.7	757	316	154
Q3	..	..	..	..	..	..	..	..	..	126.4	379.2	455	268	142
Q4	..	..	..	..	..	..	..	..	..	105.1	315.3	556	498	178
1980 Q1	..	..	..	..	..	..	..	..	..	164.4	493.1	223	179	150
Q2	..	..	..	..	..	..	..	..	..	123.1	369.4	605	309	156
Q3	..	..	..	..	..	..	..	..	..	136.9	410.8	429	263	–148
Q4	..	..	..	..	..	..	..	..	..	82.0	245.9	404	188	–3

See footnotes on page 219.

Sources: Office for National Statistics;
Enquiries Columns 1-9 01633 812600; Columns 11-13 01633 812782;
Department of the Environment, Transport and the Regions;
Enquiries 020 7890 3077

4.8 Retail sales, new registrations of cars and credit business (Great Britain)

continued

Not seasonally adjusted

	Value of retail sales per week, nsa, total (average 1995=100)[1,2]	Volume of retail sales per week, nsa, (average 1995=100)[1,2]: All retailers	Predominantly food stores	Predominantly non-food stores: Total	Non-special stores	Textiles, clothing and footwear	Household goods stores	Other stores	Non-store and repair	New registrations of cars (monthly average, thousands)	New registrations of cars (quarterly total, thousands)	Total consumer credit: net lending (£ million)[3,4]	of which: credit cards	Net lending (£ million)[3]: Credit business (narrower coverage): agreements with consumers[5]	Finance houses and other specialist credit grantors: agreements with business
Sales in 1995 £ million	*166 681*	*166 681*	*74 914*	*83 184*	*15 035*	*26 100*	*19 770*	*22 280*	*8 583*						
	EAFY	EAHC	EAGW	EAGX	EAHI	EAGY	EAGZ	EAHA	EAHB	FHCH	BCGT	-AIKL		FSBS	FSBT
1981 Q1	..	..	..	..	..	..	..	..	..	138.8	416.3	328		–72	14
Q2	..	..	..	..	..	..	..	..	..	124.3	372.8	665		169	74
Q3	..	..	..	..	..	..	..	..	..	138.2	414.7	749		173	–36
Q4	..	..	..	..	..	..	..	..	..	96.9	290.8	731		312	68
1982 Q1	..	..	..	..	..	..	..	..	..	139.2	417.6	252		–1	99
Q2	..	..	..	..	..	..	..	..	..	122.8	368.3	548		224	150
Q3	..	..	..	..	..	..	..	..	..	158.3	475.0	849		470	–17
Q4	..	..	..	..	..	..	..	..	..	107.9	323.6	985		425	208
1983 Q1	..	..	..	..	..	..	..	..	..	165.6	496.8	458		225	109
Q2	..	..	..	..	..	..	..	..	..	141.5	424.4	851		240	289
Q3	..	..	..	..	..	..	..	..	..	183.2	549.5	974		526	98
Q4	..	..	..	..	..	..	..	..	..	111.8	335.4	1 004		629	309
1984 Q1	..	..	..	..	..	..	..	..	..	167.0	501.1	431		268	191
Q2	..	..	..	..	..	..	..	..	..	146.7	440.1	993		367	186
Q3	..	..	..	..	..	..	..	..	..	167.8	503.3	766		398	101
Q4	..	..	..	..	..	..	..	..	..	104.9	314.6	907		518	270
1985 Q1	..	..	..	..	..	..	..	..	..	167.3	501.8	496		213	203
Q2	..	..	..	..	..	..	..	..	..	144.7	434.1	1 006		393	230
Q3	..	..	..	..	..	..	..	..	..	187.5	562.6	1 212		817	–74
Q4	..	..	..	..	..	..	..	..	..	114.4	343.3	1 106		886	83
1986 Q1	53.2	73.8	76.6	67.9	71.6	65.1	64.5	72.5	98.6	167.0	501.0	582		248	318
Q2	56.3	76.9	78.6	72.3	75.9	73.3	65.6	75.9	99.3	151.3	454.0	1 241		215	208
Q3	57.9	79.0	78.5	76.5	79.7	77.2	70.5	79.8	99.3	192.8	578.4	1 628		977	–
Q4	70.2	94.8	86.8	98.8	112.1	101.8	86.4	100.6	116.6	116.5	349.6	935		945	296
												VZQC	VZQS	RLWF	RLWD
1987 Q1	57.2	76.8	77.9	72.0	73.4	67.2	72.0	76.8	104.6	174.7	524.1	806	–169	399	136
Q2	60.5	80.5	80.7	77.0	78.4	76.0	72.7	81.6	104.0	156.5	469.4	1 831	300	1 039	552
Q3	62.3	83.1	81.2	81.8	82.0	81.4	78.7	85.3	104.9	212.9	638.6	1 804	194	1 065	122
Q4	76.3	100.1	89.6	106.2	118.5	108.9	94.9	108.0	122.5	128.1	384.2	1 860	473	1 334	443
1988 Q1	63.2	82.8	82.1	79.8	79.3	72.6	83.1	85.0	108.0	192.8	578.5	1 278	–202	471	372
Q2	66.0	85.3	84.0	83.1	81.7	79.2	82.0	89.3	109.9	170.9	512.8	1 861	286	1 066	609
Q3	68.3	87.9	84.4	88.3	86.1	84.9	89.2	92.3	108.1	243.4	730.1	2 411	286	1 393	216
Q4	84.0	106.2	93.4	114.6	124.9	113.3	106.1	119.1	127.3	129.7	389.0	1 293	305	983	732
1989 Q1	68.0	85.5	82.8	84.5	82.5	75.9	88.4	91.3	109.8	209.4	628.1	1 274	–396	290	566
Q2	71.3	87.9	87.1	85.8	83.2	81.6	84.1	93.4	107.8	187.2	561.5	2 194	338	1 003	268
Q3	72.5	89.0	86.9	88.5	86.2	84.7	86.9	95.6	106.1	241.3	723.9	2 065	304	1 217	245
Q4	89.2	107.1	95.3	115.2	124.0	112.0	105.6	123.4	123.4	130.4	391.2	1 231	294	655	633
1990 Q1	73.3	86.8	84.7	85.9	82.2	77.8	88.6	94.4	107.1	193.2	579.5	753	–14	477	296
Q2	77.1	89.2	88.4	87.6	85.0	84.2	84.3	96.1	105.7	158.5	475.4	1 363	321	939	154
Q3	78.0	90.0	88.4	89.4	87.6	87.6	84.6	96.8	104.0	210.6	631.8	1 474	599	1 187	–140
Q4	93.6	106.1	96.1	112.9	122.6	109.9	101.1	122.7	120.7	106.1	318.3	1 026	855	1 080	118
1991 Q1	77.1	86.6	87.3	83.3	82.2	75.5	86.7	89.3	106.0	152.8	458.3	89	–631	–225	–138
Q2	80.7	87.5	89.4	83.8	83.4	81.3	80.0	90.6	101.2	113.1	339.2	942	493	588	–18
Q3	82.1	89.1	90.0	86.5	86.8	86.1	82.1	90.8	101.5	177.9	533.7	902	461	631	–373
Q4	97.2	104.4	95.3	111.0	120.2	110.3	99.4	118.4	114.0	89.7	269.1	385	451	66	–256
1992 Q1	80.2	85.6	89.1	79.7	80.5	72.3	83.2	84.4	104.8	134.7	404.1	–397	–477	–610	148
Q2	84.2	88.6	92.8	83.7	83.5	81.7	80.3	89.4	98.1	120.2	360.5	47	277	157	200
Q3	84.2	89.5	91.3	86.2	86.8	87.4	83.1	87.6	100.6	177.2	531.5	676	106	392	–549
Q4	100.7	106.1	99.0	111.6	123.5	114.8	99.3	113.9	111.5	101.0	303.0	158	232	428	–170
1993 Q1	84.3	88.3	91.4	82.8	83.9	75.3	87.7	86.1	107.4	150.0	449.9	–261	–473	–330	20
Q2	88.1	90.7	94.3	86.4	86.0	84.2	85.1	90.3	98.7	126.7	380.2	634	339	700	651
Q3	89.0	92.0	93.1	89.8	89.7	89.2	89.1	91.1	100.9	204.2	612.5	1 308	244	1 329	–258
Q4	106.5	110.1	101.1	117.7	128.6	120.6	106.9	119.3	112.8	111.3	333.9	972	609	1 343	213

See footnotes on page 219.

Sources: Office for National Statistics; Enquiries Columns 1-9 01633 812600; Columns 11-14 01633 812782; Department of the Environment, Transport and the Regions; Enquiries Column 10 020 7890 3077

4.8 Retail sales, new registrations of cars and credit business (Great Britain)

continued

Not seasonally adjusted

		Volume of retail sales per week, nsa, (average 1995=100)[1,2]												Net lending (£ million)[3]	
				Predominantly non-food stores											
	Value of retail sales per week, nsa, total (average 1995=100)[1,2]	All retailers	Predominantly food stores	Total	Non-special stores	Textiles, clothing and footwear	Household goods stores	Other stores	Non-store and repair	New registrations of cars (monthly average, thousands)	New registrations of cars (quarterly total, thousands)	Total consumer credit: net lending (£ million)[3,4]	of which: credit cards	Credit business (narrower coverage): agreements with consumers[5]	Finance houses and other specialist credit grantors: agreements with business
Sales in 1995 £ million	*166 681*	*166 681*	*74 914*	*83 184*	*15 035*	*26 100*	*19 770*	*22 280*	*8 583*						
	EAFY	EAHC	EAGW	EAGX	EAHI	EAGY	EAGZ	EAHA	EAHB	FHCH	BCGT	VZQC	VZQS	RLWF	RLWD
1994 Q1	88.4	91.2	93.9	86.7	86.0	79.4	93.8	88.5	105.9	174.4	523.1	332	–519	364	146
Q2	91.5	93.4	96.5	89.7	86.2	88.9	89.0	93.0	100.3	140.7	422.0	1 600	661	1 424	651
Q3	93.0	95.7	97.0	93.5	90.7	94.8	92.5	94.4	102.6	211.0	633.1	1 974	469	1 886	–5
Q4	112.1	114.9	105.0	123.6	132.9	126.9	113.9	124.4	115.7	109.4	328.1	1 837	872	1 841	243
1995 Q1	90.6	92.0	95.2	87.9	84.8	81.5	96.6	89.8	103.5	172.7	518.2	1 198	–299	..	..
Q2	95.5	95.4	99.8	91.9	87.7	92.8	91.4	94.0	92.3	139.8	419.3	1 754	766	..	..
Q3	96.6	96.6	98.7	94.8	91.0	96.5	94.5	95.6	95.8	214.6	644.0	2 614	514	..	..
Q4	117.3	116.0	106.3	125.4	136.5	129.3	117.5	120.6	108.4	118.9	356.7	2 668	1 122	..	..
1996 Q1	95.3	94.1	98.0	89.9	88.7	83.8	99.7	89.0	99.8	175.4	526.2	1 292	–311	..	..
Q2	101.2	98.4	100.7	96.9	93.0	97.3	97.6	98.3	93.4	153.9	461.7	2 630	986	..	..
Q3	102.5	100.4	100.7	100.2	98.5	101.9	101.9	97.8	99.0	218.4	655.1	4 026	815	..	..
Q4	123.5	120.3	108.2	131.8	144.9	135.8	128.4	121.4	113.7	125.1	375.4	3 267	1 539	..	..
1997 Q1	101.5	99.3	101.9	96.7	95.4	89.8	108.6	94.9	102.9	181.9	545.6	1 849	–262	..	..
Q2	106.9	103.4	104.6	102.8	97.4	103.5	108.6	100.4	99.1	164.2	492.7	3 383	979	..	..
Q3	108.4	105.1	104.8	105.7	102.7	107.3	111.5	100.7	101.5	239.6	718.7	2 786	912	..	..
Q4	131.1	126.4	112.4	139.7	150.6	144.0	139.9	127.0	119.3	133.3	400.0	3 995	1 878	..	..
1998 Q1	106.9	103.5	105.2	101.4	97.7	92.7	119.5	98.0	108.6	206.7	620.0	2 905	–59	..	..
Q2	112.2	107.1	109.0	105.8	97.7	103.5	115.7	105.1	103.6	170.9	512.7	3 714	1 442	..	..
Q3	112.7	108.2	107.0	109.4	102.7	109.6	119.2	104.9	107.4	237.5	712.7	4 181	1 320	..	..
Q4	134.0	128.0	114.1	140.6	147.9	142.1	146.5	128.7	126.9	138.7	416.2	3 690	2 151	..	..
1999 Q1	110.9	106.1	106.7	104.6	97.0	95.7	128.3	99.2	115.8	213.6	640.9	2 622	–155	..	..
Q2	115.0	109.7	109.0	110.6	99.1	108.3	123.6	109.4	107.6	185.7	557.2	3 811	1 557	..	..
Q3	116.2	112.0	109.2	114.9	105.9	113.9	129.0	109.6	109.0	213.8	641.4	3 929	1 316	..	..
Q4	139.1	134.5	118.3	149.7	156.8	150.6	159.8	134.8	128.4	..	..	4 145	2 540	..	..
2000 Q1	114.3	111.2	109.0	112.5	105.5	101.8	142.3	103.2	117.2	..	..	2 883	–205	..	..
Q2	119.0	114.4	112.9	116.4	105.8	113.7	135.0	110.2	108.7	..	..	3 865	1 905	..	..

See footnotes on page 219.

Sources: Office for National Statistics;
Enquiries Columns 1-9 01633 812600; Columns 11-14 01633 812782;
Department of the Environment, Transport and the Regions;
Enquiries Column 10 020 7890 3077

4.8 Retail sales, new registrations of cars and credit business (Great Britain)

continued

Seasonally adjusted

	Value of retail sales per week, sa, total (average 1995=100)[1,2]	Volume of retail sales per week, sa, (average 1995=100)[1,2]										Net lending (£ million)[3]	
				Predominantly non-food stores									
		All retailers	Predominantly food stores	Total	Non-special stores	Textiles, clothing and footwear	Household goods stores	Other stores	Non-store and repair	New registrations of cars (quarterly total, thousands)	Total consumer credit: net lending (£ million)[3,4]	Credit business (narrower coverage): agreements with consumers[5]	Finance houses and other specialist credit grantors: agreements with business
Sales in 1995 £ million	*166 681*	*166 681*	*74 914*	*83 184*	*15 035*	*26 100*	*19 770*	*22 280*	*8 583*				
	EAQV	EAPS	EAPT	EAPV	EAPU	EAPX	EAPY	EAPW	EAPZ	DKBY	-AIKM		FSBV
1955 Q1	..	..	..	..	..	..	..	..	..	..	..		..
Q2	..	..	..	..	..	..	..	..	..	..	..		..
Q3	..	..	..	..	..	..	..	..	..	..	..		..
Q4	..	..	..	..	..	..	..	..	..	..	..		..
1956 Q1	..	..	..	..	..	..	..	..	..	..	..		..
Q2	..	..	..	..	..	..	..	..	..	..	..		..
Q3	..	..	..	..	..	..	..	..	..	..	..		..
Q4	..	..	..	..	..	..	..	..	..	..	..		..
1957 Q1	..	..	..	..	..	..	..	..	..	84.0	..		..
Q2	..	..	..	..	..	..	..	..	..	108.0	..		..
Q3	..	..	..	..	..	..	..	..	..	123.0	..		..
Q4	..	..	..	..	..	..	..	..	..	122.0	..		..
1958 Q1	..	..	..	..	..	..	..	..	..	142.0	..		7
Q2	..	..	..	..	..	..	..	..	..	133.0	..		10
Q3	..	..	..	..	..	..	..	..	..	138.0	..		13
Q4	..	..	..	..	..	..	..	..	..	155.0	..		81
1959 Q1	..	..	..	..	..	..	..	..	..	143.0	..		68
Q2	..	..	..	..	..	..	..	..	..	152.0	..		79
Q3	..	..	..	..	..	..	..	..	..	145.0	..		77
Q4	..	..	..	..	..	..	..	..	..	219.0	..		75
1960 Q1	..	..	..	..	..	..	..	..	..	213.0	..		74
Q2	..	..	..	..	..	..	..	..	..	199.0	..		30
Q3	..	..	..	..	..	..	..	..	..	212.0	..		–5
Q4	..	..	..	..	..	..	..	..	..	200.0	..		–7
1961 Q1	..	..	..	..	..	..	..	..	..	199.0	..		11
Q2	..	..	..	..	..	..	..	..	..	194.0	..		5
Q3	..	..	..	..	..	..	..	..	..	189.0	..		–4
Q4	..	..	..	..	..	..	..	..	..	178.0	..		–13
1962 Q1	..	..	..	..	..	..	..	..	..	183.0	..		–32
Q2	..	..	..	..	..	..	..	..	..	193.0	..		–13
Q3	..	..	..	..	..	..	..	..	..	201.0	..		5
Q4	..	..	..	..	..	..	..	..	..	226.0	..		5
1963 Q1	..	..	..	..	..	..	..	..	..	217.0	–10		2
Q2	..	..	..	..	..	..	..	..	..	253.0	28		19
Q3	..	..	..	..	..	..	..	..	..	269.0	24		28
Q4	..	..	..	..	..	..	..	..	..	293.0	21		34
1964 Q1	..	..	..	..	..	..	..	..	..	287.0	29		41
Q2	..	..	..	..	..	..	..	..	..	293.0	55		40
Q3	..	..	..	..	..	..	..	..	..	319.0	40		45
Q4	..	..	..	..	..	..	..	..	..	320.0	57		42
1965 Q1	..	..	..	..	..	..	..	..	..	315.0	10		35
Q2	..	..	..	..	..	..	..	..	..	274.0	58		42
Q3	..	..	..	..	..	..	..	..	..	277.0	19		28
Q4	..	..	..	..	..	..	..	..	..	283.0	39		16
1966 Q1	..	..	..	..	..	..	..	..	..	303.0	–12		3
Q2	..	..	..	..	..	..	..	..	..	323.0	3		–11
Q3	..	..	..	..	..	..	..	..	..	254.0	–47		–54
Q4	..	..	..	..	..	..	..	..	..	211.0	–43		–73
1967 Q1	..	..	..	..	..	..	..	..	..	246.0	–63		–48
Q2	..	..	..	..	..	..	..	..	..	274.0	–20		–35
Q3	..	..	..	..	..	..	..	..	..	297.0	5		18
Q4	..	..	..	..	..	..	..	..	..	325.0	49		35

See footnotes on page 219.

Sources: Office for National Statistics;
Enquiries Columns 1-9 01633 812600; Columns 11-13 01633 812782;
Department of the Environment, Transport and the Regions;
Enquiries Column 10 020 7890 3077

4.8 Retail sales, new registrations of cars and credit business (Great Britain)

continued

Seasonally adjusted

	Value of retail sales per week, sa, total (average 1995=100)[1,2]	Volume of retail sales per week, sa, (average 1995=100)[1,2]: All retailers	Predominantly food stores	Predominantly non-food stores: Total	Non-special stores	Textiles, clothing and footwear	Household goods stores	Other stores	Non-store and repair	New registrations of cars (quarterly total, thousands)	Total consumer credit: net lending (£ million)[3,4]	Net lending (£ million)[3]: Credit business (narrower coverage): agreements with consumers[5]	Finance houses and other specialist credit grantors: agreements with business
Sales in 1995 £ million	*166 681*	*166 681*	*74 914*	*83 184*	*15 035*	*26 100*	*19 770*	*22 280*	*8 583*				
	EAQV	EAPS	EAPT	EAPV	EAPU	EAPX	EAPY	EAPW	EAPZ	DKBY	AIKM		FSBV
1968 Q1	..	..	..	..	..	..	..	..	..	332.0	4		38
Q2	..	..	..	..	..	..	..	..	..	251.0	3		−10
Q3	..	..	..	..	..	..	..	..	..	270.0	12		13
Q4	..	..	..	..	..	..	..	..	..	291.0	41		15
1969 Q1	..	..	..	..	..	..	..	..	..	240.0	−39		−11
Q2	..	..	..	..	..	..	..	..	..	271.0	11		−2
Q3	..	..	..	..	..	..	..	..	..	267.0	−2		−2
Q4	..	..	..	..	..	..	..	..	..	235.0	32		4
1970 Q1	..	..	..	..	..	..	..	..	..	265.0	−32		6
Q2	..	..	..	..	..	..	..	..	..	293.0	29		26
Q3	..	..	..	..	..	..	..	..	..	284.0	23		26
Q4	..	..	..	..	..	..	..	..	..	282.0	63		34
1971 Q1	..	..	..	..	..	..	..	..	..	291.0	−37		9
Q2	..	..	..	..	..	..	..	..	..	301.0	36		39
Q3	..	..	..	..	..	..	..	..	..	343.0	100		109
Q4	..	..	..	..	..	..	..	..	..	396.0	116		94
1972 Q1	..	..	..	..	..	..	..	..	..	381.0	31		76
Q2	..	..	..	..	..	..	..	..	..	453.0	74		122
Q3	..	..	..	..	..	..	..	..	..	415.0	57		121
Q4	..	..	..	..	..	..	..	..	..	452.0	123		119
1973 Q1	..	..	..	..	..	..	..	..	..	452.0	61		169
Q2	..	..	..	..	..	..	..	..	..	422.0	54		89
Q3	..	..	..	..	..	..	..	..	..	428.0	51		102
Q4	..	..	..	..	..	..	..	..	..	384.0	118		84
1974 Q1	..	..	..	..	..	..	..	..	..	305.0	−78		−59
Q2	..	..	..	..	..	..	..	..	..	320.0	2		−52
Q3	..	..	..	..	..	..	..	..	..	327.0	3		−28
Q4	..	..	..	..	..	..	..	..	..	310.0	97		−25
1975 Q1	..	..	..	..	..	..	..	..	..	300.2	−118		−6
Q2	..	..	..	..	..	..	..	..	..	284.1	9		9
Q3	..	..	..	..	..	..	..	..	..	324.4	−115		−9
Q4	..	..	..	..	..	..	..	..	..	285.5	−183		−7
												FSBN	FSBO
1976 Q1	..	..	..	..	..	..	..	..	..	302.1	107	32	11
Q2	..	..	..	..	..	..	..	..	..	324.0	4	43	12
Q3	..	..	..	..	..	..	..	..	..	304.5	81	46	13
Q4	..	..	..	..	..	..	..	..	..	360.4	141	67	11
1977 Q1	..	..	..	..	..	..	..	..	..	308.2	76	63	27
Q2	..	..	..	..	..	..	..	..	..	314.1	148	108	69
Q3	..	..	..	..	..	..	..	..	..	359.8	236	68	130
Q4	..	..	..	..	..	..	..	..	..	353.1	278	137	109
1978 Q1	..	..	..	..	..	..	..	..	..	384.8	421	120	39
Q2	..	..	..	..	..	..	..	..	..	385.4	357	184	84
Q3	..	..	..	..	..	..	..	..	..	424.0	307	260	135
Q4	..	..	..	..	..	..	..	..	..	388.9	408	279	70
1979 Q1	..	..	..	..	..	..	..	..	..	398.9	492	190	14
Q2	..	..	..	..	..	..	..	..	..	538.6	660	315	103
Q3	..	..	..	..	..	..	..	..	..	355.3	459	248	200
Q4	..	..	..	..	..	..	..	..	..	428.2	475	360	166
1980 Q1	..	..	..	..	..	..	..	..	..	439.5	429	365	152
Q2	..	..	..	..	..	..	..	..	..	378.5	523	305	84
Q3	..	..	..	..	..	..	..	..	..	360.3	400	219	−54
Q4	..	..	..	..	..	..	..	..	..	341.0	309	50	−27

See footnotes on page 219.

Sources: Office for National Statistics;
Enquiries Columns 1-9 01633 812600; Columns 11-14 01633 812782;
Department of the Environment, Transport and the Regions;
Enquiries Column 10 020 7890 3077

4.8 Retail sales, new registrations of cars and credit business (Great Britain)

continued

Seasonally adjusted

	Value of retail sales per week, sa, total (average 1995=100)[1,2]	Volume of retail sales per week, sa, (average 1995=100)[1,2]: All retailers	Predominantly food stores	Predominantly non-food stores: Total	Non-special stores	Textiles, clothing and footwear	Household goods stores	Other stores	Non-store and repair	New registrations of cars (quarterly total, thousands)	Total consumer credit: net lending (£ million)[3,4]	of which: credit cards	Net lending (£ million)[3]: Credit business (narrower coverage): agreements with consumers[5]	Finance houses and other specialist credit grantors: agreements with business
Sales in 1995 £ million	*166 681*	*166 681*	*74 914*	*83 184*	*15 035*	*26 100*	*19 770*	*22 280*	*8 583*					
	EAQV	EAPS	EAPT	EAPV	EAPU	EAPX	EAPY	EAPW	EAPZ	DKBY	-AIKM		FSBN	FSBO
1981 Q1	..	..	..	..	..	..	..	..	..	370.1	574		113	15
Q2	..	..	..	..	..	..	..	..	..	383.2	593		174	6
Q3	..	..	..	..	..	..	..	..	..	352.6	687		89	66
Q4	..	..	..	..	..	..	..	..	..	388.8	619		206	33
1982 Q1	..	..	..	..	..	..	..	..	..	370.2	539		174	102
Q2	..	..	..	..	..	..	..	..	..	380.2	485		249	76
Q3	..	..	..	..	..	..	..	..	..	394.3	749		307	91
Q4	..	..	..	..	..	..	..	..	..	439.7	861		388	171
1983 Q1	..	..	..	..	..	..	..	..	..	446.1	786		408	113
Q2	..	..	..	..	..	..	..	..	..	443.0	785		298	206
Q3	..	..	..	..	..	..	..	..	..	454.9	839		422	227
Q4	..	..	..	..	..	..	..	..	..	462.2	877		492	259
1984 Q1	..	..	..	..	..	..	..	..	..	452.5	802		485	186
Q2	..	..	..	..	..	..	..	..	..	459.3	911		446	204
Q3	..	..	..	..	..	..	..	..	..	411.7	604		265	160
Q4	..	..	..	..	..	..	..	..	..	435.8	780		355	198
1985 Q1	..	..	..	..	..	..	..	..	..	454.3	915		461	185
Q2	..	..	..	..	..	..	..	..	..	455.1	893		496	113
Q3	..	..	..	..	..	..	..	..	..	462.9	1 030		656	157
Q4	..	..	..	..	..	..	..	..	..	469.7	982		696	–13
1986 Q1	57.4	79.4	79.8	75.9	82.4	76.8	67.4	79.9	101.1	454.1	1 036		784	308
Q2	58.8	80.5	79.6	78.3	84.8	79.7	70.8	80.5	102.8	477.3	1 105		330	82
Q3	60.0	81.5	79.9	79.8	85.9	79.8	72.8	83.2	104.0	473.7	1 431		770	223
Q4	61.0	82.6	81.0	80.9	85.3	80.2	75.7	84.5	105.6	478.1	928		501	209
											RLMH	VZQX	RLMJ	RLMG
1987 Q1	61.6	82.6	81.2	80.5	85.0	79.9	74.8	84.5	107.3	476.9	1 322	177	939	144
Q2	63.3	84.6	81.9	83.6	88.1	83.1	78.7	86.9	107.9	495.4	1 610	193	1 065	410
Q3	64.8	86.0	82.7	85.7	88.8	84.4	81.7	89.4	109.8	516.7	1 408	117	828	384
Q4	66.5	87.4	83.8	87.3	90.5	86.3	83.2	90.9	111.0	527.2	1 949	247	1 000	315
1988 Q1	68.0	88.7	85.1	88.8	91.4	85.8	86.8	93.0	110.6	527.6	1 808	207	1 058	381
Q2	69.5	90.0	85.8	90.4	92.2	86.5	88.2	96.0	114.2	543.3	1 603	163	1 059	419
Q3	71.3	91.3	86.1	92.7	93.6	88.0	93.1	97.5	113.3	589.4	1 947	159	1 042	544
Q4	72.8	92.2	86.9	93.8	94.9	89.6	92.4	99.1	115.2	549.9	1 448	57	756	571
1989 Q1	73.7	92.2	86.7	94.3	95.5	89.6	92.2	100.9	112.9	577.1	1 839	101	973	608
Q2	74.6	92.3	88.3	93.0	93.3	88.8	90.7	99.8	112.1	598.3	1 918	219	965	113
Q3	75.4	92.1	88.4	92.9	93.4	87.4	90.5	101.1	110.9	576.7	1 602	131	839	284
Q4	77.3	92.8	88.8	93.8	93.8	88.4	91.7	101.9	111.2	552.4	1 341	13	471	623
1990 Q1	79.3	93.7	88.6	96.0	95.1	91.8	92.4	104.6	109.6	531.7	1 385	559	1 008	74
Q2	80.3	93.5	89.4	94.7	95.2	91.2	90.6	102.6	110.3	519.3	1 145	207	838	105
Q3	81.1	93.1	89.8	93.8	94.8	89.9	88.6	102.9	108.7	500.3	983	379	786	100
Q4	81.2	91.9	89.9	91.3	92.5	86.7	87.1	99.8	108.8	453.9	1 093	553	899	–56
1991 Q1	82.3	92.1	90.7	91.3	93.1	88.2	86.3	98.6	107.4	420.2	732	4	485	–121
Q2	83.8	91.5	89.7	91.0	93.2	88.2	87.6	96.5	105.8	373.0	794	358	474	–196
Q3	84.9	91.8	91.0	90.6	93.2	88.4	86.4	95.8	105.4	419.3	403	258	215	–84
Q4	85.5	91.6	90.4	90.9	92.2	87.4	87.7	97.3	103.8	387.7	381	147	–131	–311
1992 Q1	86.0	91.5	92.1	89.3	92.4	86.5	85.9	94.3	103.9	381.7	252	165	155	111
Q2	87.2	92.6	93.3	90.4	93.5	88.5	86.2	94.7	103.8	386.6	–35	91	13	–31
Q3	87.4	92.5	92.8	90.7	94.0	90.4	86.9	93.0	104.7	405.0	149	–47	–18	–248
Q4	88.8	93.2	94.2	91.0	94.3	90.9	86.9	93.5	102.6	424.7	131	–89	211	–194
1993 Q1	90.6	94.6	94.7	92.9	96.4	90.7	90.0	96.2	106.9	415.4	377	190	426	–22
Q2	91.3	94.8	94.7	93.5	96.8	91.4	91.7	95.8	105.1	428.8	528	88	534	393
Q3	92.5	95.4	94.7	94.8	97.5	92.6	93.5	97.1	104.7	461.9	880	170	959	60
Q4	93.5	96.2	95.8	95.5	97.5	94.6	93.4	97.6	103.2	470.4	946	246	1 120	213

See footnotes on page 219.

Sources: Office for National Statistics;
Enquiries Columns 1-9 01633 812600; Columns 11-14 01633 812782;
Department of the Environment, Transport and the Regions;
Enquiries Column 10 020 7890 3077

4.8 Retail sales, new registrations of cars and credit business (Great Britain)

continued

Seasonally adjusted

		Volume of retail sales per week, sa, (average 1995=100)[1,2]											Net lending (£ million)[3]	
				Predominantly non-food stores										
	Value of retail sales per week, sa, total (average 1995=100)[1,2]	All retailers	Predominantly food stores	Total	Non-special stores	Textiles, clothing and footwear	Household goods stores	Other stores	Non-store and repair	New registrations of cars (quarterly total, thousands)[6]	Total consumer credit: net lending (£ million)[3,4]	of which: credit cards	Credit business (narrower coverage): agreements with consumers[5]	Finance houses and other specialist credit grantors: agreements with business
Sales in 1995 £ million	*166 681*	*166 681*	*74 914*	*83 184*	*15 035*	*26 100*	*19 770*	*22 280*	*8 583*					
	EAQV	EAPS	EAPT	EAPV	EAPU	EAPX	EAPY	EAPW	EAPZ	DKBY	RLMH	VZQX	RLMJ	RLMG
1994 Q1	94.8	97.6	96.8	97.3	98.7	95.7	96.6	98.9	105.7	483.4	892	168	1 087	86
Q2	95.7	98.4	97.8	97.8	98.0	97.3	96.3	99.8	107.1	479.4	1 520	381	1 271	323
Q3	96.9	99.5	98.8	99.0	99.1	98.7	97.4	100.9	107.2	471.8	1 436	407	1 460	370
Q4	97.5	99.5	99.1	99.1	99.8	98.1	98.2	100.6	105.4	467.4	1 719	407	1 588	280
1995 Q1	98.4	99.5	99.3	99.4	98.0	99.4	99.5	100.5	103.1	480.6	1 932	507	..	..
Q2	99.4	99.9	100.0	99.8	100.0	100.3	99.4	99.2	99.5	478.3	1 682	489	..	..
Q3	100.5	100.1	100.4	99.8	99.9	99.6	99.5	100.3	100.2	480.7	2 082	465	..	..
Q4	101.7	100.5	100.4	101.0	102.1	100.7	101.6	100.0	97.2	498.5	2 374	521	..	..
1996 Q1	102.6	101.0	100.7	101.3	102.2	101.4	102.0	100.0	100.1	493.5	2 189	616	..	..
Q2	105.2	102.9	101.3	104.7	105.4	104.4	106.9	102.8	100.0	512.5	2 546	725	..	..
Q3	106.2	103.6	102.1	105.1	107.1	104.7	107.9	101.6	102.9	498.5	3 514	764	..	..
Q4	108.0	105.1	103.5	106.8	109.4	106.9	110.7	101.3	102.9	513.8	2 919	809	..	..
1997 Q1	109.3	106.6	104.9	108.5	109.1	108.9	111.5	105.1	102.4	513.1	2 796	779	..	..
Q2	111.4	108.3	104.7	111.7	111.6	111.8	118.9	105.5	106.0	540.5	3 220	738	..	..
Q3	112.7	109.0	106.9	111.3	112.1	110.6	118.2	105.4	106.1	544.1	2 439	856	..	..
Q4	114.7	110.6	107.5	113.5	113.6	113.3	120.7	107.4	108.7	559.4	3 600	1 004	..	..
1998 Q1	115.7	111.6	108.9	114.2	112.8	112.6	123.1	109.0	109.1	579.3	3 806	1 110	..	..
Q2	116.2	111.4	109.0	113.7	111.7	110.9	125.1	108.4	110.6	570.0	3 522	1 187	..	..
Q3	117.0	112.1	108.9	114.9	111.4	113.1	126.4	109.3	112.7	572.0	3 836	1 255	..	..
Q4	117.3	112.1	108.7	114.8	110.5	112.6	127.0	109.4	114.9	567.2	3 342	1 186	..	..
1999 Q1	118.7	113.4	109.3	116.9	111.4	114.9	131.0	110.4	115.7	..	3 510	1 236	..	..
Q2	119.5	114.6	109.5	119.2	113.6	116.0	134.3	113.3	115.0	..	3 593	1 260	..	..
Q3	120.4	115.8	110.7	120.6	114.7	116.7	137.0	114.4	115.5	..	3 681	1 243	..	..
Q4	121.7	117.5	112.5	122.3	117.4	119.5	138.7	114.3	115.3	..	3 769	1 441	..	..
2000 Q1	122.8	119.1	112.6	125.4	120.7	121.9	145.3	114.8	116.3	..	3 723	1 263	..	..
Q2	123.6	119.5	112.8	125.9	121.1	122.3	146.7	114.7	116.8	..	3 687	1 583	..	..

See footnotes 1 -5 on page 219.

6 Data beyond 1998 is unavailable at present since seasonal adjustment has ceased. This is because the existing seasonal adjustment model is not applicable to the new bi-annual registration system.

Sources: Office for National Statistics; Enquiries Columns 1-9 01633 812600; Columns 11-14 01633 812782; Department of the Environment, Transport and the Regions; Enquiries Column 10 020 7890 3077

4.9 Inland energy consumption

Annual rates, temperature corrected and seasonally adjusted

	Primary fuel input (million tonnes of oil equivalent)						
				Primary electricity[4]			
	Coal[1]	Petroleum	Natural gas[2]	Nuclear	Hydro[3]	Net imports[5]	Total
	FDAI	FDAJ	FDAK	FDAL	FDAM	FDAW	FDAH
1990	69.2	78.1	56.0	16.3	0.5	1.0	221.0
1991	67.4	78.4	53.7	17.4	0.4	1.4	218.8
1992	64.6	78.8	56.1	18.3	0.5	1.4	219.8
1993	55.9	79.1	64.3	21.4	0.4	1.4	222.7
1994	53.3	78.8	66.3	21.2	0.5	1.5	221.5
1995	51.2	77.2	72.2	21.3	0.5	1.4	223.7
1996	46.8	78.6	80.0	22.2	0.3	1.4	229.2
1997	42.8	77.0	86.8	23.0	0.4	1.4	231.7
1998	43.1	76.7	90.1	23.3	0.5	1.4	235.2
1999	44.1	76.5	90.2	23.5	0.5	1.1	235.9
1990 Q1	71.4	82.1	54.4	15.9	0.5	–	224.3
Q2	65.6	82.5	53.9	15.9	0.4	1.2	219.6
Q3	68.3	79.5	52.2	15.9	0.4	1.4	217.7
Q4	68.1	74.4	53.2	17.3	0.4	1.5	214.9
1991 Q1	68.0	75.4	54.4	18.1	0.3	1.5	217.7
Q2	69.6	78.4	56.2	15.9	0.4	1.3	221.8
Q3	67.0	79.1	51.8	18.3	0.4	1.4	218.1
Q4	66.0	78.5	53.1	17.4	0.5	1.5	216.9
1992 Q1	64.9	78.5	53.2	18.6	0.4	1.5	217.1
Q2	67.3	78.9	53.3	18.3	0.5	1.4	219.6
Q3	64.3	77.3	58.9	17.3	0.6	1.4	219.7
Q4	61.0	76.9	60.8	19.1	0.5	1.5	219.8
1993 Q1	58.1	78.0	61.1	21.4	0.5	1.5	220.5
Q2	56.3	78.3	62.5	20.5	0.4	1.4	219.3
Q3	55.0	79.0	62.7	21.1	0.4	1.4	219.7
Q4	54.0	79.6	68.8	22.4	0.3	1.5	226.6
1994 Q1	53.7	78.7	68.7	20.1	0.5	1.5	223.2
Q2	53.3	77.1	67.6	21.6	0.6	1.4	221.6
Q3	53.0	77.3	68.7	21.9	0.5	1.5	222.9
Q4	52.9	79.3	70.0	21.0	0.4	1.5	225.2
1995 Q1	53.8	76.5	73.5	19.0	0.5	1.5	224.8
Q2	51.9	74.9	72.6	21.5	0.4	1.4	222.7
Q3	50.5	76.8	71.8	22.7	0.3	1.5	223.6
Q4	49.0	76.7	78.3	22.3	0.4	1.1	227.7
1996 Q1	50.4	77.8	82.3	22.0	0.2	1.5	234.1
Q2	49.0	77.6	78.6	22.8	0.3	1.5	229.8
Q3	45.7	78.5	80.7	21.7	0.3	1.4	228.4
Q4	43.9	76.3	85.4	24.4	0.4	1.4	231.9
1997 Q1	44.5	77.4	88.2	23.7	0.4	1.5	235.7
Q2	41.1	77.1	86.7	23.9	0.3	1.4	230.5
Q3	43.0	75.0	87.5	22.7	0.4	1.4	230.0
Q4	45.1	75.3	90.3	21.7	0.3	1.5	234.1
1998 Q1	44.5	77.8	92.0	23.3	0.5	1.4	239.5
Q2	46.2	74.5	90.5	22.4	0.4	1.4	235.2
Q3	44.0	75.7	89.1	23.2	0.5	0.3	232.8
Q4	41.3	75.6	94.1	24.2	0.5	1.2	236.8
1999 Q1	39.5	76.2	99.5	23.7	0.5	1.2	240.7
Q2	39.8	74.0	93.7	23.3	0.5	1.3	232.5
Q3	39.1	74.1	94.3	22.3	0.5	1.1	231.4
Q4	38.8	73.6	99.9	20.8	0.5	1.2	234.9

1 Includes solid renewables (wood, straw, waste) and net foreign trade and stock change in other solid fuels.
2 Includes colliery methane, landfill gas and sewage gas. Excludes gas flared or re-injected and non-energy use of gas.
3 Includes generation at wind stations. Excludes generation from pump-storage stations.
4 Not temperature corrected.
5 Not seasonally adjusted.

Source: Department of Trade and Industry; Enquiries 020 7215 5187

Selected financial statistics

5.1 Sterling exchange rates and UK reserves[6]

	Sterling exchange rate against major currencies[1]								UK official reserves[2] at end of period ($ million)[3]	UK international reserves[5] at end of period (£ million)	Sterling exchange rate index 1990=100
	Japanese yen	US dollar	Swiss franc	Euro[4]	French franc	Italian lira	Deutsche-mark	Spanish peseta			
	AJFO	AJFA	AJFD	THAP	AJFE	AJFF	AJFH	AJFM	AIPI	THFE	AJHX
1945	..	4.0000	17.400	..	203.8000	..	..	..	2 476	..	..
1946	..	4.0000	17.400	..	480.0000	..	..	..	2 696	..	..
1947	..	4.0000	17.400	..	480.0000	..	..	..	2 079	..	..
1948	..	4.0000	17.400	..	879.7000	..	..	..	1 856	..	..
1949	..	3.7000	15.900	..	1 053.1000	..	..	..	1 688	..	..
1950	..	2.8000	12.300	..	980.0000	..	..	..	3 300	..	..
1951	..	2.8000	12.200	..	979.7000	..	..	..	2 335	..	..
1952	..	2.8000	12.200	..	981.5000	..	..	..	1 846	..	..
1953	..	2.8000	12.200	..	982.8000	..	..	..	2 518	..	..
1954	..	2.8000	12.200	..	981.6000	..	11.730	..	2 762	..	..
1955	..	2.8000	12.200	..	978.1000	1 751	11.700	..	2 120	..	..
1956	..	2.8000	12.200	..	982.7000	1 751	11.700	..	2 133	..	..
1957	..	2.8000	12.200	..	1 059.6000	1 752	11.700	..	2 273	..	..
1958	..	2.8000	12.200	..	1 177.5000	1 745	11.700	..	3 069	..	..
1959	..	2.8000	12.100	..	13.8000	1 744	11.700	..	2 736	..	..
1960	..	2.8000	12.100	..	13.8000	1 743	11.700	..	3 231	..	..
1961	..	2.8000	12.100	..	13.7000	1 740	11.300	..	3 318	..	..
1962	..	2.8000	12.100	..	13.8000	1 743	11.200	..	2 806	..	..
1963	..	2.8000	12.100	..	13.7000	1 740	11.200	..	949	..	..
1964	..	2.8000	12.100	..	13.7000	1 743	11.100	..	827	..	..
1965	..	2.8000	12.100	..	13.7000	1 747	11.200	..	1 073	..	..
1966	..	2.8000	12.100	..	13.7000	1 744	11.200	..	1 107	..	..
1967	..	2.8000	12.100	..	13.7000	1 741	11.100	..	1 123	..	..
1968	..	2.4000	10.300	..	11.9000	1 492	9.600	..	1 009	..	..
1969	..	2.4000	10.300	..	13.3000	1 499	8.800	..	1 053	..	..
1970	857.80	2.4000	10.300	..	13.2000	1 502	8.700	..	1 178	..	..
1971	884.60	2.4000	10.100	..	13.5000	1 511	8.500	..	2 526	..	..
1972	752.30	2.5000	9.600	..	12.6000	1 460	8.000	160.80	2 167	..	..
1973	664.60	2.5000	7.800	..	10.9000	1 426	6.500	138.50	2 237	..	..
1974	682.70	2.3000	7.000	..	11.2000	1 522	6.000	134.90	6 789	..	..
1975	658.06	2.2198	5.723	1.6966	9.5007	1 447	5.447	127.28	5 429	..	129.6
1976	535.33	1.8046	4.516	1.5110	8.6045	1 497	4.551	120.59	4 129	..	112.3
1977	467.63	1.7455	4.189	1.4377	8.5737	1 540	4.051	133.08	20 557	..	106.8
1978	402.60	1.9197	3.423	1.4336	8.6443	1 628	3.850	146.96	15 694	..	107.2
1979	465.57	2.1225	3.528	1.4786	9.0268	1 763	3.888	142.39	22 538	..	113.1
1980	525.56	2.3281	3.896	1.6244	9.8252	1 992	4.227	167.11	27 476	..	124.4
1981	444.57	2.0254	3.969	1.7847	10.9353	2 288	4.556	185.91	23 347	..	127.8
1982	435.21	1.7489	3.548	1.7674	11.4851	2 364	4.243	191.82	16 997	..	123.3
1983	359.89	1.5158	3.182	1.7058	11.5469	2 302	3.870	217.48	17 817	..	115.6
1984	316.80	1.3364	3.129	1.6970	11.6365	2 339	3.790	214.28	15 694	..	111.4
1985	307.08	1.2976	3.154	1.7099	11.5495	2 463	3.784	219.56	15 543	..	111.3
1986	246.80	1.4672	2.635	1.4820	10.1569	2 186	3.183	205.31	21 923	..	101.4
1987	236.50	1.6392	2.439	1.4041	9.8369	2 123	2.941	201.87	44 326	..	99.3
1988	227.98	1.7796	2.603	1.4989	10.5969	2 315	3.124	207.16	51 685	..	105.3
1989	225.66	1.6383	2.678	1.4691	10.4476	2 247	3.079	193.88	38 645	..	102.3
1990	257.38	1.7864	2.469	1.3733	9.6891	2 133	2.876	181.29	38 464	..	100.0
1991	237.56	1.7685	2.529	1.4004	9.9474	2 187	2.925	183.22	44 126	..	100.7
1992	223.72	1.7665	2.476	1.3325	9.3248	2 163	2.751	179.91	41 654	..	96.9
1993	166.73	1.5015	2.218	1.2616	8.5073	2 360	2.483	191.33	42 926	..	88.9
1994	156.40	1.5329	2.090	1.2724	8.4852	2 467	2.481	204.83	43 898	..	89.2
1995	148.37	1.5783	1.865	1.1908	7.8730	2 571	2.260	196.71	46 986	..	84.8
1996	170.00	1.5617	1.931	1.2097	7.9890	2 408	2.350	197.82	46 300	..	86.3
1997	198.12	1.6382	2.376	1.4493	9.5606	2 789	2.840	239.87	38 418	..	100.6
1998	216.75	1.6574	2.400	1.4887	9.7681	2 876	2.914	247.37	35 343	..	103.9
1999	183.94	1.6180	2.431	1.5192	..	..	..	..	34 084	26 322	103.8

1 Average of daily Telegraphic Transfer rates in London.

2 Apart from transactions, the level of official reserves is affected by changes in the dollar valuation of gold, Special Drawing Rights and convertible currencies. Since end-March 1979 these rates have been revised annually. These valuation changes are described in detail in the description of Table 1.2I in the *Financial Statistics Explanatory Handbook*, where the values of the annual changes are also shown.

3 Amounts outstanding are revalued at end-March each year.

4 Prior to January 1999, a synthetic Euro has been calculated by geometrically averaging the bilateral exchange rates of the 11 Euro-area countries using "internal weights" based on each country's share of the extra Euro-area trade.

5 International reserves data are alll valued at end-period market prices and exchange rates. They additionally include other reserve assets such as repos (sale and purchase agreeements) and derivatives. Full details are shown in Table 1.2I of *Financial Statistics*.

6 These figures fall outside the scope of National Statistics.

Source: Bank of England; Enquiries 020 7601 4342

5.1 Sterling exchange rates and UK reserves[6]

continued

Not seasonally adjusted

	Sterling exchange rate against major currencies[1]						UK official reserves[2] at end of period ($ million)[3]
	Japanese yen	US dollar	Swiss franc	French franc	Italian lira	Deutsche-mark	
	AJFO	AJFA	AJFD	AJFE	AJFF	AJFH	AIPI
1945 Q1	..	4.0300	17.350	..	..	..	2 430
Q2	..	4.0300	17.350	..	..	..	2 515
Q3	..	4.0300	17.350	..	..	..	2 430
Q4	..	4.0300	17.350	..	..	..	2 476
1946 Q1	..	4.0300	17.350	480.0000	..	..	2 384
Q2	..	4.0300	17.350	480.0000	..	..	2 301
Q3	..	4.0300	17.350	480.0000	..	..	2 682
Q4	..	4.0300	17.350	480.0000	..	..	2 696
1947 Q1	..	4.0300	17.350	480.0000	..	..	2 380
Q2	..	4.0300	17.350	480.0000	..	..	2 410
Q3	..	4.0300	17.350	480.0000	..	..	2 383
Q4	..	4.0300	17.350	480.0000	..	..	2 079
1948 Q1	..	4.0300	17.350	864.0000	..	..	2 241
Q2	..	4.0300	17.350	864.0000	..	..	1 920
Q3	..	4.0300	17.350	864.0000	..	..	1 777
Q4	..	4.0300	17.350	1 062.0000	..	..	1 856
1949 Q1	..	4.0300	17.350	1 062.0000	..	..	1 912
Q2	..	4.0300	17.350	1 097.0000	..	..	1 651
Q3	..	3.6200	15.610	1 058.0000	..	..	1 425
Q4	..	2.8000	12.250	980.0000	..	..	1 688
1950 Q1	..	2.8000	12.250	980.0000	..	..	1 984
Q2	..	2.8000	12.250	980.0000	..	..	2 422
Q3	..	2.8000	12.250	980.0000	..	..	2 756
Q4	..	2.8000	12.250	980.0000	..	..	3 300
1951 Q1	..	2.8000	12.250	980.0000	..	..	3 758
Q2	..	2.8000	12.250	980.0000	..	..	3 867
Q3	..	2.8000	12.250	980.0000	..	..	3 269
Q4	..	2.8000	12.250	978.9600	..	..	2 335
1952 Q1	..	2.7900	12.200	983.8900	..	..	1 700
Q2	..	2.8000	12.220	973.9400	..	..	1 685
Q3	..	2.7900	12.190	980.5800	..	..	1 685
Q4	..	2.8000	12.190	987.5000	..	..	1 846
1953 Q1	..	2.8200	12.190	987.5000	..	..	2 166
Q2	..	2.8100	12.190	985.4100	..	11.710	2 367
Q3	..	2.8100	12.170	977.6000	..	11.700	2 486
Q4	..	2.8100	12.210	980.5200	..	11.700	2 518
1954 Q1	..	2.8100	12.210	980.9100	..	11.700	2 685
Q2	..	2.8200	12.230	984.6300	..	11.750	3 017
Q3	..	2.8100	12.200	980.6700	..	11.730	2 901
Q4	..	2.8000	12.240	980.3500	..	11.760	2 762
1955 Q1	..	2.7900	12.260	976.2400	..	11.770	2 667
Q2	..	2.8000	12.250	979.8700	..	11.750	2 680
Q3	..	2.7900	12.170	970.0400	1 740	11.690	2 345
Q4	..	2.8000	12.230	982.2600	1 756	11.730	2 120
1956 Q1	..	2.8100	12.240	983.8100	1 754	11.720	2 277
Q2	..	2.8100	12.250	983.7300	1 754	11.720	2 385
Q3	..	2.7800	12.190	980.8600	1 745	11.690	2 328
Q4	..	2.7800	12.230	982.5500	1 753	11.710	2 133
1957 Q1	..	2.8000	12.270	986.2400	1 760	11.750	2 209
Q2	..	2.7900	12.250	985.5200	1 756	11.740	2 381
Q3	..	2.7900	12.180	1 086.3800	1 741	11.680	1 850
Q4	..	2.8000	12.260	1 180.3900	1 752	11.760	2 273
1958 Q1	..	2.8200	12.270	1 179.8101	1 749	11.770	2 770
Q2	..	2.8200	12.240	1 179.0699	1 745	11.710	3 076
Q3	..	2.8000	12.200	1 173.0699	1 739	11.690	3 119
Q4	..	2.8100	12.210	1 177.3600	1 745	11.690	3 069
1959 Q1	..	2.8100	12.130	13.7700	1 745	11.740	3 139
Q2	..	2.8100	12.160	13.8000	1 747	11.770	3 172
Q3	..	2.8100	12.120	13.7700	1 743	11.740	3 284
Q4	..	2.8000	12.150	13.7500	1 740	11.700	2 736

See footnotes on page 229.

Source: Bank of England; Enquiries 020 7601 4342

5.1 Sterling exchange rates and UK reserves[6]

continued

Not seasonally adjusted

	Sterling exchange rate against major currencies[1]							UK official reserves[2] at end of period ($ million)[3]
	Japanese yen	US dollar	Swiss franc	French franc	Italian lira	Deutsche-mark	Spanish peseta	
	AJFO	AJFA	AJFD	AJFE	AJFF	AJFH	AJFM	AIPI
1960 Q1	..	2.8030	12.150	13.7600	1 740	11.690	..	2 780
Q2	..	2.8060	12.130	13.7600	1 741	11.700	..	2 892
Q3	..	2.8100	12.110	13.7700	1 744	11.720	..	3 108
Q4	..	2.8110	12.110	13.7800	1 745	11.730	..	3 231
1961 Q1	..	2.8020	12.090	13.7300	1 741	11.520	..	3 021
Q2	..	2.7940	12.080	13.6900	1 734	11.090	..	2 772
Q3	..	2.8000	12.090	13.7500	1 738	11.170	..	2 553
Q4	..	2.8130	12.150	13.8100	1 746	11.250	..	3 318
1962 Q1	..	2.8130	12.175	13.7900	1 747	11.244	..	3 452
Q2	..	2.8120	12.171	13.7800	1 745	11.236	..	3 433
Q3	..	2.8040	12.114	13.7400	1 740	11.199	..	2 792
Q4	..	2.8020	12.100	13.7300	1 740	11.218	..	2 806
1963 Q1	..	2.8030	12.125	13.7300	1 740	11.187	..	1 005
Q2	..	2.8010	12.112	13.7200	1 740	11.162	..	969
Q3	..	2.8000	12.090	13.7200	1 740	11.148	..	977
Q4	..	2.7980	12.073	13.7100	1 741	11.122	..	949
1964 Q1	..	2.7980	12.092	13.7100	1 743	11.122	..	950
Q2	..	2.7980	12.078	13.7100	1 748	11.117	..	966
Q3	..	2.7870	12.040	13.6600	1 741	11.077	..	907
Q4	..	2.7870	12.025	13.6500	1 741	11.077	..	827
1965 Q1	..	2.7930	12.094	13.6900	1 745	11.108	..	832
Q2	..	2.7950	12.131	13.7000	1 746	11.141	..	997
Q3	..	2.7930	12.063	13.6900	1 745	11.196	..	984
Q4	..	2.8040	12.105	13.7400	1 751	11.217	..	1 073
1966 Q1	..	2.8010	12.136	13.7300	1 750	11.238	..	1 276
Q2	..	2.7920	12.060	13.6800	1 743	11.202	..	1 170
Q3	..	2.7980	12.058	13.6900	1 739	11.129	..	1 129
Q4	..	2.7910	12.074	13.8000	1 744	11.099	..	1 107
1967 Q1	..	2.7940	12.105	13.8300	1 746	11.104	..	1 164
Q2	..	2.7960	12.073	13.7600	1 746	11.118	..	1 012
Q3	..	2.7860	12.072	13.6600	1 737	11.145	..	976
Q4	..	2.6210	11.326	12.8400	1 631	10.451	..	1 123
1968 Q1	..	2.4060	10.447	11.8400	1 503	9.621	..	1 134
Q2	..	2.3920	10.337	11.8400	1 491	9.535	..	1 118
Q3	..	2.3900	10.277	11.8800	1 486	9.553	..	1 132
Q4	..	2.3870	10.262	11.8500	1 488	9.509	..	1 009
1969 Q1	..	2.3900	10.307	11.8400	1 496	9.591	..	1 029
Q2	..	2.3900	10.325	11.8700	1 499	9.559	..	1 018
Q3	..	2.3870	10.273	12.6400	1 500	9.505	..	1 014
Q4	..	2.3950	10.326	13.3500	1 501	8.867	..	1 053
1970 Q1	859.50	2.4040	10.354	13.3300	1 512	8.853	..	1 129
Q2	861.40	2.4030	10.353	13.2700	1 511	8.735	..	1 163
Q3	856.00	2.3880	10.277	13.1800	1 498	8.671	..	1 111
Q4	854.50	2.3900	10.323	13.1900	1 488	8.686	..	1 178
1971 Q1	863.10	2.4140	10.382	13.3200	1 504	8.770	..	1 382
Q2	864.30	2.4190	10.084	13.3600	1 507	8.622	..	1 508
Q3	845.80	2.4410	9.848	13.4600	1 509	8.344	..	2 089
Q4	815.80	2.5030	9.895	13.7300	1 523	8.279	..	2 526
1972 Q1	796.00	2.5980	10.044	13.2500	1 524	8.299	..	2 715
Q2	788.60	2.6000	9.987	13.0500	1 514	8.256	..	2 673
Q3	735.90	2.4460	9.236	12.2300	1 421	7.775	..	2 337
Q4	711.60	2.3650	8.960	11.9300	1 380	7.575	..	2 167
1973 Q1	677.50	2.4180	8.354	11.5800	1 392	7.267	..	2 085
Q2	701.80	2.5320	7.978	11.2000	1 496	6.916	..	2 422
Q3	657.30	2.4810	7.296	10.3800	1 423	5.938	..	2 204
Q4	653.70	2.3820	7.441	10.4500	1 397	6.052	..	2 237
1974 Q1	661.44	2.2806	7.299	11.2364	1 473	6.184	133.85	6 444
Q2	670.87	2.3987	7.133	11.6864	1 532	6.001	138.35	6 711
Q3	698.86	2.3512	7.004	11.2415	1 536	6.135	134.68	7 170
Q4	693.57	2.3298	6.413	10.8187	1 546	5.870	132.70	6 789

See footnotes on page 229.

Source: Bank of England; Enquiries 020 7601 4342

5.1 Sterling exchange rates and UK reserves[6]

continued

Not seasonally adjusted

	Sterling exchange rate against major currencies[1]								UK official reserves[2] at end of period ($ million)[3]	Sterling exchange rate index 1990=100
	Japanese yen	US dollar	Swiss franc	Euro[4]	French franc	Italian lira	Deutsche-mark	Spanish peseta		
	AJFO	AJFA	AJFD	THAP	AJFE	AJFF	AJFH	AJFM	AIPI	AJHX
1975 Q1	700.87	2.3909	5.960	1.7680	10.2420	1 525	5.586	134.01	7 117	135.9
Q2	679.44	2.3249	5.861	1.7063	9.5031	1 462	5.477	130.22	6 198	131.5
Q3	634.40	2.1296	5.672	1.6757	9.2632	1 415	5.429	123.95	5 859	127.2
Q4	619.89	2.0431	5.413	1.6400	9.0330	1 389	5.303	121.30	5 429	124.1
1976 Q1	603.38	1.9968	5.148	1.6433	9.0330	1 529	5.140	127.48	5 905	123.1
Q2	539.63	1.8049	4.502	1.5317	8.4859	1 554	4.618	122.04	5 312	113.4
Q3	513.94	1.7665	4.379	1.4985	8.6662	1 483	4.473	120.20	5 158	110.8
Q4	484.85	1.6507	4.036	1.3713	8.2282	1 424	3.976	112.67	4 129	102.1
1977 Q1	488.58	1.7138	4.324	1.4263	8.5301	1 513	4.107	117.94	9 618	105.9
Q2	473.07	1.7190	4.316	1.4221	8.5127	1 523	4.059	118.71	11 572	105.8
Q3	461.79	1.7354	4.162	4.4342	8.4871	1 532	4.005	144.58	17 171	106.4
Q4	447.45	1.8134	3.962	1.4676	8.7655	1 592	4.033	150.27	20 557	108.9
1978 Q1	458.04	1.9276	3.720	1.4875	9.1665	1 662	4.000	155.06	20 320	111.2
Q2	404.54	1.8354	3.516	1.4116	8.4480	1 583	3.813	147.28	16 542	105.3
Q3	371.93	1.9319	3.240	1.4325	8.4605	1 617	3.874	145.48	16 511	106.5
Q4	377.24	1.9838	3.224	1.4038	8.5133	1 649	3.717	140.18	15 694	105.7
1979 Q1	406.29	2.0160	3.377	1.4177	8.6011	1 692	3.740	139.90	21 947	107.5
Q2	453.16	2.0811	3.566	1.4900	9.1047	1 762	3.944	138.76	22 070	113.0
Q3	488.47	2.2338	3.664	1.5430	9.4599	1 825	4.058	147.65	22 692	118.1
Q4	513.80	2.1572	3.506	1.4644	8.9452	1 772	3.811	143.09	22 538	113.6
1980 Q1	548.43	2.2542	3.747	1.5335	9.3431	1 857	3.995	151.67	26 963	119.2
Q2	528.62	2.2862	3.841	1.5870	9.6126	1 943	4.132	161.96	28 172	122.1
Q3	523.19	2.3820	3.885	1.6275	9.8088	2 008	4.227	171.77	27 637	125.1
Q4	502.19	2.3872	4.107	1.7478	10.5267	2 159	4.550	182.73	27 476	131.4
1981 Q1	474.50	2.3095	4.376	1.8572	11.2148	2 313	4.814	193.86	28 212	135.9
Q2	456.51	2.0771	4.226	1.8438	11.2454	2 355	4.728	189.34	25 631	131.9
Q3	425.68	1.8387	3.852	1.7452	10.6605	2 234	4.468	179.97	23 696	123.1
Q4	422.60	1.8833	3.441	1.6964	10.6392	2 253	4.226	180.75	23 347	120.9
1982 Q1	431.68	1.8452	3.458	1.7553	11.0706	2 330	4.331	186.89	18 969	123.6
Q2	434.28	1.7792	3.552	1.7526	11.1810	2 350	4.232	188.80	17 703	122.7
Q3	446.43	1.7252	3.647	1.8010	11.9818	2 404	4.281	193.52	18 299	124.8
Q4	428.20	1.6495	3.532	1.7594	11.6785	2 369	4.130	197.83	16 997	122.0
1983 Q1	360.36	1.5303	3.085	1.5947	10.5423	2 143	3.684	199.14	17 337	110.6
Q2	369.20	1.5546	3.227	1.7054	11.6196	2 298	3.867	216.29	17 711	116.4
Q3	365.83	1.5091	3.241	1.7654	12.0160	2 376	3.989	226.92	17 902	118.5
Q4	344.27	1.4708	3.174	1.7558	11.9973	2 387	3.936	227.25	17 817	116.9
1984 Q1	331.08	1.4353	3.151	1.7363	11.9022	2 385	3.875	221.60	16 749	115.1
Q2	320.71	1.3960	3.136	1.6953	11.6301	2 339	3.784	213.53	15 505	112.4
Q3	316.16	1.2993	3.169	1.6942	11.6207	2 333	3.786	214.30	15 260	110.8
Q4	299.42	1.2178	3.061	1.6620	11.3929	2 300	3.716	207.65	15 694	107.4
1985 Q1	287.14	1.1155	3.068	1.6214	11.0924	2 253	3.628	200.60	13 528	103.7
Q2	315.17	1.2577	3.255	1.7426	11.8272	2 474	3.878	218.80	14 318	112.6
Q3	328.10	1.3758	3.231	1.7779	11.9532	2 603	3.920	229.86	14 176	116.3
Q4	297.64	1.4356	3.064	1.6968	11.3248	2 514	3.711	228.47	15 543	112.6
1986 Q1	270.79	1.4391	2.849	1.5545	10.3829	2 303	3.382	212.42	18 750	105.1
Q2	256.40	1.5090	2.813	1.5710	10.7712	2 322	3.387	215.48	19 188	106.5
Q3	232.27	1.4891	2.515	1.4555	10.1009	2 140	3.109	201.45	22 426	99.9
Q4	229.22	1.4304	2.378	1.3522	9.3934	1 986	2.868	192.43	21 923	94.1
1987 Q1	236.20	1.5431	2.385	1.3518	9.4501	2 015	2.837	198.95	27 039	95.6
Q2	234.14	1.6410	2.448	1.4150	9.8908	2 134	2.964	207.02	34 364	99.8
Q3	237.82	1.6184	2.467	1.4181	9.9197	2 152	2.974	201.61	34 808	99.8
Q4	237.69	1.7535	2.457	1.4310	10.0821	2 188	2.989	200.10	44 326	102.1
1988 Q1	230.03	1.7972	2.473	1.4455	10.1923	2 221	3.013	203.10	47 519	102.9
Q2	231.18	1.8390	2.611	1.5068	10.6374	2 334	3.142	207.96	48 519	106.5
Q3	226.76	1.6951	2.652	1.5184	10.7159	2 349	3.165	209.41	50 482	105.3
Q4	224.05	1.7915	2.675	1.5254	10.8460	2 356	3.175	208.17	51 685	106.7
1989 Q1	224.37	1.7477	2.762	1.5434	10.9948	2 370	3.233	201.88	46 931	107.2
Q2	224.29	1.6259	2.755	1.4959	10.6306	2 287	3.140	197.40	43 665	103.6
Q3	227.17	1.5971	2.649	1.4605	10.3854	2 212	3.071	192.48	42 876	101.4
Q4	226.77	1.5849	2.548	1.3780	9.7891	2 119	2.876	183.92	38 645	97.0

See footnotes on page 229.

Source: Bank of England; Enquiries 020 7601 4342

5.1 Sterling exchange rates and UK reserves[6]

continued

Not seasonally adjusted

	Sterling exchange rate against major currencies[1]								UK official reserves[2] at end of period ($ million)[3]	UK international reserves[5] at end of period (£million)	Sterling exchange rate index 1990=100
	Japanese yen	US dollar	Swiss franc	Euro[4]	French franc	Italian lira	Deutschemark	Spanish peseta			
	AJFO	AJFA	AJFD	THAP	AJFE	AJFF	AJFH	AJFM	AIPI	THFE	AJHX
1990 Q1	245.05	1.6565	2.494	1.3425	9.4982	2 078	2.800	180.71	39 295	..	96.8
Q2	260.04	1.6761	2.416	1.3389	9.4562	2 065	2.812	175.77	39 014	..	97.0
Q3	270.33	1.8617	2.487	1.4112	9.9425	2 190	2.965	183.53	39 060	..	103.1
Q4	254.23	1.9462	2.475	1.3990	9.8484	2 197	2.923	184.90	38 464	..	102.9
1991 Q1	255.26	1.9098	2.493	1.3984	9.9317	2 188	2.920	182.70	42 258	..	102.6
Q2	236.22	1.7094	2.517	1.4130	10.0290	2 197	2.961	183.52	44 264	..	100.7
Q3	229.80	1.6853	2.558	1.4049	9.9800	2 192	2.937	183.85	44 593	..	99.9
Q4	229.61	1.7733	2.544	1.3857	9.8504	2 170	2.885	182.79	44 126	..	99.8
1992 Q1	227.67	1.7713	2.576	1.3759	9.7511	2 155	2.866	180.86	45 027	..	99.4
Q2	235.41	1.8095	2.667	1.3968	9.8258	2 198	2.916	183.15	45 700	..	101.2
Q3	237.90	1.9043	2.482	1.3460	9.4420	2 155	2.786	181.16	42 677	..	99.4
Q4	194.24	1.5808	2.189	1.2140	8.3018	2 146	2.445	174.60	41 654	..	87.7
1993 Q1	178.38	1.4771	2.224	1.2145	8.1898	2 283	2.414	172.17	40 898	..	86.6
Q2	168.59	1.5340	2.241	1.2490	8.3783	2 306	2.484	186.28	41 897	..	88.7
Q3	159.00	1.5047	2.221	1.2892	8.7443	2 384	2.522	202.47	43 044	..	90.2
Q4	161.34	1.4914	2.189	1.2921	8.7019	2 463	2.510	203.67	42 926	..	90.2
1994 Q1	160.00	1.4887	2.160	1.3089	8.7164	2 505	2.563	209.66	42 915	..	90.7
Q2	155.38	1.5050	2.118	1.2753	8.5461	2 413	2.497	205.02	43 374	..	89.1
Q3	153.66	1.5515	2.032	1.2448	8.2896	2 436	2.421	200.54	43 476	..	87.9
Q4	156.62	1.5851	2.054	1.2615	8.3968	2 515	2.446	204.23	43 898	..	89.1
1995 Q1	151.76	1.5831	1.962	1.2289	8.1613	2 599	2.336	206.49	46 122	..	87.2
Q2	134.88	1.5958	1.844	1.1869	7.8546	2 658	2.230	196.22	46 643	..	84.3
Q3	147.99	1.5739	1.857	1.1811	7.7815	2 534	2.252	193.20	47 182	..	84.3
Q4	158.38	1.5610	1.795	1.1656	7.6909	2 495	2.222	190.83	46 986	..	83.5
1996 Q1	161.92	1.5314	1.822	1.1676	7.7085	2 408	2.248	189.39	44 971	..	83.5
Q2	163.79	1.5237	1.896	1.1927	7.8613	2 369	2.320	194.27	45 410	..	84.8
Q3	169.41	1.5546	1.901	1.1974	7.9183	2 365	2.328	196.75	44 075	..	85.5
Q4	184.58	1.6358	2.104	1.2805	8.4630	2 490	2.503	210.71	46 300	..	91.4
1997 Q1	197.33	1.6312	2.339	1.3793	9.1133	2 666	2.701	228.14	40 057	..	96.9
Q2	195.74	1.6358	2.364	1.4320	9.4527	2 765	2.803	236.74	40 559	..	99.6
Q3	191.69	1.6264	2.418	1.4962	9.8871	2 863	2.935	247.73	41 015	..	102.5
Q4	207.75	1.6593	2.378	1.4855	9.7614	2 855	2.914	246.13	38 418	..	103.1
1998 Q1	211.03	1.6464	2.430	1.5294	10.0362	2 951	2.995	253.88	34 219	..	105.4
Q2	224.66	1.6537	2.467	1.5149	9.9424	2 925	2.965	251.79	34 792	..	105.3
Q3	231.11	1.6531	2.428	1.4875	9.7616	2 873	2.911	247.16	35 282	..	104.4
Q4	200.25	1.6762	2.279	1.4247	9.3446	2 758	2.787	236.97	35 343	..	100.6
1999 Q1	190.36	1.6329	2.331	1.4574	..	..	..	..	33 834	..	101.1
Q2	194.03	1.6064	2.433	1.5209	..	..	..	..	34 270	–	104.1
Q3	181.34	1.6020	2.446	1.5271	..	..	..	..	32 950	21 684	103.8
Q4	170.41	1.6307	2.514	1.5712	..	..	..	..	34 084	26 322	105.9
2000 Q1	171.85	1.6054	2.617	1.6286	..	..	..	..	..	22 432	108.4
Q2	163.28	1.5305	2.563	1.6398	..	..	..	..	..	..	107.7

See footnotes on page 229.

Source: Bank of England; Enquiries 020 7601 4342

5.2 Monetary aggregates[1]

£ million

	M0					M4				
	Amount out-standing		Changes		Velocity of circulation	Amount out-standing		Changes		Velocity of circulation
	Not seasonally adjusted	Seasonally adjusted	Not seasonally adjusted	Seasonally adjusted	ratio (seasonally adjusted)	Not seasonally adjusted	Seasonally adjusted	Not seasonally adjusted	Seasonally adjusted	ratio (seasonally adjusted)
At end period										
	AVAD	AVAE	AVAI	AVAJ	AVAM	AUYM	AUYN	AUZI	AUZJ	AUYU
1963	..	..	..	..	..	14 969	14 751	1 480	1 102	..
1964	..	..	..	..	..	16 106	15 896	1 151	1 188	..
1965	..	..	..	..	..	17 616	17 406	1 520	1 528	..
1966	..	..	..	..	..	18 757	18 542	1 148	1 147	..
1967	..	..	..	..	..	21 158	20 893	2 314	2 244	..
1968	..	..	..	..	..	22 964	22 649	1 813	1 733	..
1969	3 993	3 917	..	..	..	24 123	23 770	1 178	1 103	..
1970	4 206	4 097	213	180	12.97	27 009	26 643	2 893	2 858	..
1971	4 425	4 289	219	191	13.38	31 400	30 976	4 405	4 320	..
1972	5 053	4 845	628	555	14.16	38 674	38 156	6 870	6 757	..
1973	5 593	5 339	540	494	14.54	47 119	46 544	8 544	8 505	..
1974	6 452	6 157	859	819	14.69	52 197	51 671	5 079	5 245	..
1975	7 186	6 872	709	689	16.21	58 383	57 943	6 229	6 428	..
1976	7 988	7 648	789	762	17.16	64 970	64 538	6 853	6 884	..
1977	9 122	8 651	1 147	1 017	18.03	74 595	74 074	9 625	9 448	..
1978	10 362	9 836	1 247	1 190	18.11	85 770	85 090	11 253	11 050	..
1979	11 620	11 013	1 268	1 188	18.82	98 131	97 339	12 363	12 289	..
1980	12 243	11 649	639	650	20.24	114 923	114 149	16 807	16 806	..
1981	12 555	11 925	626	589	21.26	138 363	137 837	15 953	16 085	..
1982	12 948	12 302	393	376	23.05	154 953	154 865	16 539	17 323	..
1983	13 849	13 038	921	755	23.82	175 367	175 385	19 698	20 143	1.83
1984	14 615	13 746	766	708	24.19	199 004	199 158	23 232	23 057	1.74
1985	15 161	14 266	546	520	25.32	224 899	225 144	25 874	26 255	1.68
1986	15 946	15 023	785	757	26.17	258 304	258 186	34 855	34 703	1.58
1987	16 633	15 666	687	643	27.44	304 948	304 708	43 585	43 495	1.49
1988	18 040	16 867	1 407	1 201	28.69	358 233	357 755	52 516	52 500	1.42
1989	19 006	17 825	1 015	1 007	29.76	426 322	425 731	64 746	64 894	1.32
1990	19 492	18 300	486	475	30.63	477 128	476 692	50 356	50 659	1.23
1991	20 085	18 857	593	557	31.43	504 113	503 822	27 941	28 584	1.19
1992	20 581	19 393	496	536	31.94	517 919	517 709	17 955	18 680	1.18
1993	21 729	20 561	1 148	1 168	32.06	544 097	543 253	23 931	23 991	1.21
1994	23 322	21 955	1 589	1 390	31.94	567 195	566 080	25 386	25 643	1.22
1995	24 539	23 177	1 217	1 222	31.76	623 542	622 016	55 957	55 839	1.21
1996	26 153	24 733	1 614	1 556	31.53	682 999	681 887	59 395	59 978	1.16
1997	27 802	26 326	1 649	1 593	31.62	722 199	720 452	80 273	79 911	1.13
1998	29 346	27 733	1 599	1 462	31.56	782 850	780 680	59 723	59 726	1.13
1999	32 736	31 013	3 390	3 280	30.89	812 862	809 878	30 796	30 539	1.12

1 These figures fall outside the scope of National Statistics.

Source: Bank of England; Enquiries 020 7601 5468

5.2 Monetary aggregates[1]

continued

£ million

	M0					M4				
	Amount out-standing		Changes		Velocity of circulation ratio (seasonally adjusted)	Amount out-standing		Changes		Velocity of circulation ratio (seasonally adjusted)
	Not seasonally adjusted	Seasonally adjusted	Not seasonally adjusted	Seasonally adjusted		Not seasonally adjusted	Seasonally adjusted	Not seasonally adjusted	Seasonally adjusted	
At end period										
	AVAD	AVAE	AVAI	AVAJ	AVAM	AUYM	AUYN	AUZI	AUZJ	AUYU
1963 Q1	..	..	..	..	..	13 650	13 917	154	130	..
Q2	..	..	..	..	..	14 080	14 139	432	340	..
Q3	..	..	..	..	..	14 309	14 391	231	268	..
Q4	..	..	..	..	..	14 969	14 751	663	370	..
1964 Q1	..	..	..	..	..	14 875	14 997	–87	267	..
Q2	..	..	..	..	..	15 295	15 335	423	345	..
Q3	..	..	..	..	..	15 623	15 673	330	347	..
Q4	..	..	..	..	..	16 106	15 896	485	229	..
1965 Q1	..	..	..	..	..	16 006	16 131	–97	242	..
Q2	..	..	..	..	..	16 465	16 515	461	389	..
Q3	..	..	..	..	..	16 853	16 892	390	379	..
Q4	..	..	..	..	..	17 616	17 406	766	518	..
1966 Q1	..	..	..	..	..	17 797	17 915	183	511	..
Q2	..	..	..	..	..	18 046	18 098	251	186	..
Q3	..	..	..	..	..	18 333	18 368	289	274	..
Q4	..	..	..	..	..	18 757	18 542	425	176	..
1967 Q1	..	..	..	..	..	18 852	18 987	97	444	..
Q2	..	..	..	..	..	19 515	19 579	664	589	..
Q3	..	..	..	..	..	20 229	20 276	715	692	..
Q4	..	..	..	..	..	21 158	20 893	838	519	..
1968 Q1	..	..	..	..	..	21 194	21 348	38	450	..
Q2	..	..	..	..	..	21 855	21 922	663	568	..
Q3	..	..	..	..	..	22 134	22 211	281	284	..
Q4	..	..	..	..	..	22 964	22 649	831	431	..
1969 Q1	..	..	..	..	..	22 848	23 003	–115	347	..
Q2	3 819	3 785	..	..	..	22 956	23 036	109	27	..
Q3	3 818	3 803	–1	18	12.42	23 274	23 385	320	340	..
Q4	3 993	3 917	175	114	12.52	24 123	23 770	864	389	..
1970 Q1	3 834	3 882	–159	–35	12.49	23 988	24 155	–130	382	..
Q2	3 943	3 915	109	33	13.01	24 967	25 011	980	849	..
Q3	4 045	4 042	102	127	13.13	25 734	25 875	766	861	..
Q4	4 206	4 097	161	55	13.24	27 009	26 643	1 277	766	..
1971 Q1	4 289	4 348	83	251	12.79	27 473	27 655	466	1 007	..
Q2	4 322	4 299	33	–49	13.19	28 419	28 470	947	810	..
Q3	4 307	4 314	–15	15	13.63	29 373	29 537	956	1 063	..
Q4	4 425	4 289	118	–26	13.92	31 400	30 976	2 036	1 440	..
1972 Q1	4 316	4 376	–109	87	14.04	32 812	33 016	1 003	1 624	..
Q2	4 583	4 564	267	188	14.18	34 893	34 960	2 085	1 939	..
Q3	4 638	4 655	55	91	14.08	36 238	36 426	1 345	1 465	..
Q4	5 053	4 845	415	189	14.35	38 674	38 156	2 437	1 729	..
1973 Q1	4 888	4 976	–165	131	14.83	39 855	40 062	1 274	2 003	..
Q2	5 096	5 088	208	113	14.38	42 013	42 168	2 162	2 115	..
Q3	5 187	5 200	91	111	14.36	44 479	44 655	2 466	2 492	..
Q4	5 593	5 339	406	139	14.58	47 119	46 544	2 642	1 895	..
1974 Q1	5 420	5 525	–173	187	13.92	47 603	47 815	485	1 289	..
Q2	5 575	5 586	155	61	14.71	48 562	48 735	959	950	..
Q3	5 886	5 882	311	296	15.07	49 465	49 554	903	855	..
Q4	6 452	6 157	566	275	15.08	52 197	51 671	2 732	2 151	..
1975 Q1	6 285	6 369	–167	211	15.73	53 030	53 353	833	1 719	..
Q2	6 528	6 541	240	170	15.96	54 818	54 994	1 817	1 701	..
Q3	6 702	6 686	167	138	16.34	56 831	56 796	2 013	1 824	..
Q4	7 186	6 872	469	170	16.82	58 383	57 943	1 566	1 184	..
1976 Q1	6 956	7 081	–234	204	17.12	59 250	59 635	1 133	1 971	..
Q2	7 279	7 272	320	188	16.98	61 338	61 463	2 088	1 836	..
Q3	7 534	7 511	255	239	16.98	63 683	63 603	2 345	2 142	..
Q4	7 988	7 648	448	131	17.56	64 970	64 538	1 287	935	..
1977 Q1	7 700	7 826	–277	189	17.84	65 227	65 697	257	1 148	..
Q2	8 139	8 127	440	302	18.00	68 077	68 140	2 850	2 422	..
Q3	8 256	8 280	125	162	18.08	70 626	70 605	2 549	2 437	..
Q4	9 122	8 651	859	364	18.22	74 595	74 074	3 969	3 441	..

See footnote on page 234.

Source: Bank of England; Enquiries 020 7601 5468

5.2 Monetary aggregates[1]

continued

£ million

	M0					M4				
	Amount out-standing		Changes		Velocity of circulation ratio (seasonally adjusted)	Amount out-standing		Changes		Velocity of circulation ratio (seasonally adjusted)
	Not seasonally adjusted	Seasonally adjusted	Not seasonally adjusted	Seasonally adjusted		Not seasonally adjusted	Seasonally adjusted	Not seasonally adjusted	Seasonally adjusted	
At end period										
	AVAD	AVAE	AVAI	AVAJ	AVAM	AUYM	AUYN	AUZI	AUZJ	AUYU
1978 Q1	8 898	8 949	–214	307	18.17	77 391	77 908	2 796	3 804	..
Q2	9 225	9 276	325	324	18.20	79 942	79 884	2 629	2 046	..
Q3	9 528	9 571	311	303	17.96	82 273	82 321	2 331	2 434	..
Q4	10 362	9 836	825	256	18.10	85 770	85 090	3 497	2 766	..
1979 Q1	9 989	10 136	–360	313	17.97	87 222	88 033	1 454	2 950	..
Q2	10 352	10 420	357	278	18.75	91 226	91 033	4 004	3 008	..
Q3	10 725	10 782	380	369	19.16	94 257	94 282	3 031	3 262	..
Q4	11 620	11 013	891	228	19.40	98 131	97 339	3 874	3 069	..
1980 Q1	10 994	11 151	–618	145	19.83	99 389	100 479	1 258	3 158	..
Q2	11 295	11 376	300	224	20.12	105 141	104 857	5 752	4 370	..
Q3	11 523	11 566	236	198	20.35	109 005	109 023	3 864	4 152	..
Q4	12 243	11 649	721	83	20.67	114 923	114 149	5 933	5 126	..
1981 Q1	11 755	11 946	–490	295	20.86	116 684	117 755	1 711	3 550	..
Q2	11 931	12 018	164	59	20.74	123 040	122 657	6 356	4 872	..
Q3	11 889	11 892	282	198	21.27	127 011	127 120	3 971	4 423	..
Q4	12 555	11 925	670	37	22.19	138 363	137 837	3 915	3 240	..
1982 Q1	11 728	11 911	–827	–14	22.50	140 488	141 245	2 125	3 365	..
Q2	11 960	11 993	232	81	23.04	145 719	145 220	5 180	3 864	..
Q3	12 155	12 143	195	150	23.19	149 560	149 950	3 841	5 418	1.89
Q4	12 948	12 302	793	159	23.45	154 953	154 865	5 393	4 676	1.88
1983 Q1	12 431	12 549	–517	247	23.87	161 379	161 050	5 839	5 722	1.88
Q2	12 678	12 702	267	172	23.52	166 519	165 499	5 161	4 658	1.82
Q3	12 830	12 850	152	148	23.83	169 654	170 001	3 135	4 487	1.82
Q4	13 849	13 038	1 019	188	24.07	175 367	175 385	5 563	5 276	1.81
1984 Q1	13 030	13 230	–819	192	24.07	180 133	179 795	4 763	4 179	1.78
Q2	13 339	13 401	309	172	24.27	187 430	186 246	7 289	6 371	1.76
Q3	13 575	13 591	236	189	24.09	191 957	192 115	4 540	6 094	1.72
Q4	14 615	13 746	1 040	155	24.32	199 004	199 158	6 640	6 413	1.70
1985 Q1	13 738	13 959	–877	213	24.69	205 382	205 030	6 367	5 953	1.69
Q2	14 023	14 093	285	134	25.27	211 919	210 728	6 537	5 586	1.71
Q3	14 090	14 083	67	–10	25.45	218 031	217 927	6 098	7 369	1.67
Q4	15 161	14 266	1 071	183	25.86	224 899	225 144	6 872	7 347	1.65
1986 Q1	14 305	14 460	–856	194	25.82	235 536	235 169	10 368	9 559	1.61
Q2	14 477	14 569	172	109	26.04	245 483	244 282	9 950	9 483	1.58
Q3	14 769	14 750	292	181	26.25	248 888	248 045	7 329	7 153	1.56
Q4	15 946	15 023	1 177	273	26.56	258 304	258 186	7 208	8 508	1.56
1987 Q1	14 809	15 105	–1 137	82	26.81	271 028	270 777	9 550	9 294	1.52
Q2	15 083	15 201	274	96	27.15	282 056	280 908	11 247	10 216	1.49
Q3	15 534	15 461	451	260	27.76	293 264	291 149	11 161	10 473	1.49
Q4	16 633	15 666	1 099	205	28.03	304 948	304 708	11 627	13 512	1.46
1988 Q1	15 751	15 981	–882	315	28.37	317 466	316 947	12 104	11 984	1.45
Q2	16 247	16 275	496	294	28.40	330 201	328 428	12 697	11 426	1.42
Q3	16 793	16 758	546	483	28.79	348 408	345 438	18 182	17 039	1.41
Q4	18 040	16 867	1 247	109	29.20	358 233	357 755	9 533	12 051	1.39
1989 Q1	16 815	16 973	–1 225	106	29.49	372 978	372 242	14 883	14 782	1.37
Q2	17 089	17 160	325	238	29.60	390 447 392 145	388 431 389 490	17 129	15 282	1.33
Q3	17 504	17 465	413	303	29.91	410 154	407 141	17 027	16 680	1.30
Q4	19 006	17 825	1 502	360	30.05	426 322	425 731	15 707	18 150	1.28
1990 Q1	17 600	18 013	–1 406	188	30.24	442 516	441 661	16 351	16 105	1.25
Q2	18 194	18 248	594	235	30.56	460 305	456 748	17 800	15 128	1.24
Q3	18 325	18 286	131	38	30.88	469 830	467 034	9 463	10 228	1.22
Q4	19 492	18 300	1 167	14	30.83	477 128	476 692	6 742	9 198	1.19
1991 Q1	18 178	18 457	–1 314	157	31.16	485 669	484 630	8 011	7 463	1.19
Q2	18 585	18 647	407	190	31.28	496 286	492 721	10 292	7 929	1.19
Q3	18 751	18 721	166	74	31.49	500 717	498 736	4 477	6 155	1.19
Q4	20 085	18 857	1 334	136	31.79	504 113	503 822	5 161	7 037	1.19
1992 Q1	18 411	18 847	–1 674	–10	31.98	510 168	508 612	6 996	5 804	1.19
Q2	18 847	18 943	436	96	31.95	517 402	514 290	7 276	5 909	1.19
Q3	19 230	19 144	383	201	31.97	521 229	519 956	3 419	5 399	1.18
Q4	20 581	19 393	1 351	249	31.87	517 919	517 709	264	1 568	1.18

See footnote on page 234.

Source: Bank of England; Enquiries 020 7601 5468

5.2 Monetary aggregates[1]

continued

£ million

	M0					M4				
	Amount out-standing		Changes		Velocity of circulation ratio (seasonally adjusted)	Amount out-standing		Changes		Velocity of circulation ratio (seasonally adjusted)
	Not seasonally adjusted	Seasonally adjusted	Not seasonally adjusted	Seasonally adjusted		Not seasonally adjusted	Seasonally adjusted	Not seasonally adjusted	Seasonally adjusted	
At end period										
	AVAD	AVAE	AVAI	AVAJ	AVAM	AUYM	AUYN	AUZI	AUZJ	AUYU
1993 Q1	19 305	19 695	–1 276	302	31.91	523 777	521 512	5 917	4 000	1.20
Q2	19 835	19 852	530	157	31.94	529 032	526 321	4 770	4 537	1.21
Q3	20 267	20 182	432	330	32.17	533 701	533 266	4 744	7 183	1.22
Q4	21 729	20 561	1 462	379	32.20	544 097	543 253	8 500	8 271	1.22
1994 Q1	20 564	20 822	–1 165	261	32.05	554 960	551 999	11 578	9 601	1.21
Q2	21 163	21 182	595	356	31.88	558 050	555 079	3 624	3 774	1.21
Q3	21 610	21 599	447	417	31.88	560 988	561 066	2 558	5 730	1.22
Q4	23 322	21 955	1 712	356	31.97	567 195	566 080	7 626	6 538	1.24
1995 Q1	21 880	22 312	–1 442	357	31.80	583 724	580 269	16 677	14 443	1.23
Q2	22 266	22 347	386	35	31.73	595 453	591 799	11 685	11 568	1.21
Q3	22 798	22 760	532	413	31.77	606 327	606 668	10 232	14 291	1.19
Q4	24 539	23 177	1 741	417	31.74	623 542	622 016	17 363	15 537	1.19
1996 Q1	23 124	23 564	–1 415	387	31.76	640 239	636 512	17 283	15 166	1.18
Q2	23 932	24 011	808	447	31.55	654 201	650 227	13 511	13 296	1.16
Q3	24 441	24 367	509	356	31.43	666 680	667 022	12 269	16 598	1.16
Q4	26 153	24 733	1 712	366	31.40	682 999	681 887	16 332	14 918	1.14
1997 Q1	24 773	25 064	–1 380	331	31.67	711 556	707 656	28 370	25 671	1.13
Q2	25 430	25 521	657	457	31.60	728 526	724 238	19 408	19 073	1.12
Q3	25 919	25 848	489	327	31.64	705 964	707 119	13 437	18 954	1.11
Q4	27 802	26 326	1 883	478	31.57	722 199	720 452	19 058	16 213	1.16
1998 Q1	26 159	26 700	–1 615	402	31.45	742 696	738 505	17 277	14 938	1.14
Q2	26 753	26 857	621	184	31.65	756 760	752 157	17 045	16 700	1.14
Q3	27 516	27 401	763	544	31.68	768 543	770 713	12 449	19 346	1.13
Q4	29 346	27 733	1 830	332	31.47	782 850	780 680	12 952	8 742	1.12
1999 Q1	27 830	28 156	–1 516	423	31.09	791 140	786 450	9 028	6 691	1.11
Q2	28 854	28 835	1 024	679	31.05	798 348	793 014	6 789	6 320	1.11
Q3	29 449	29 346	595	511	30.90	790 512	794 323	–8 059	1 281	1.13
Q4	32 736	31 013	3 287	1 667	30.50	812 862	809 878	23 038	16 247	1.14
2000 Q1	29 939	30 484	–2 797	–529	29.80	831 698	826 709	18 515	16 438	1.13

See footnote on page 234.

Source: Bank of England; Enquiries 020 7601 5468

5.3 Counterparts to changes in money stock M4[1, 4]

£ million, not seasonally adjusted

	Public Sector Net Cash Requirement[3]	Purchases by the M4[2] private sector of: Central government debt: British government stocks	Purchases by the M4[2] private sector of: Central government debt: Other	Purchases by the M4[2] private sector of: Other public sector debt	External and foreign currency financing of public sector: Purchase of British government stocks by overseas sector	External and foreign currency financing of public sector: Other	Banks' and Building Societies' sterling lending to the M4 private sector	External and foreign currency transactions of UK banks and building societies	Net non-deposit sterling liabilities of the banks and building societies	Domestic counterparts	Total external and foreign currency counterparts	M4
	1	2	3	4	5	6	7	8	9	10	11	12
	RURQ	AVBY	AVBU	AVBV	AVBZ	AQGA	AVBS	AVBW	AVBX	AVBN	AVBP	AUZI
1963	789	35	23	−382	..	..	..	−118	−136	..	..	1 480
1964	982	4	−119	−405	..	−656	1 503	−46	−106	1 959	−702	1 151
1965	1 128	46	51	−343	..	−94	891	−1	−153	1 769	−95	1 520
1966	987	62	181	−340	..	−415	701	241	−168	1 491	−174	1 148
1967	1 846	124	−185	−186	..	−503	1 334	72	−62	2 807	−431	2 314
1968	1 263	−48	262	−226	..	−1 138	1 398	304	−34	2 686	−834	1 813
1969	−527	81	−9	−178	..	587	1 211	167	−58	490	754	1 178
1970	−219	215	164	124	..	1 326	1 917	−292	−292	2 154	1 034	2 893
1971	1 196	372	−1 941	271	..	2 665	3 227	−720	−413	2 877	1 945	4 405
1972	1 829	−38	−819	−255	..	−1 579	7 725	606	−746	8 601	−973	6 870
1973	4 069	62	−1 344	−866	..	−767	7 971	77	−609	9 854	−690	8 544
1974	6 253	61	−797	−1 613	..	−2 564	4 925	−135	−1 178	8 967	−2 699	5 079
1975	10 015	−1 723	−6 685	387	..	−1 027	2 403	−507	−544	8 298	−1 494	6 229
1976	8 911	−5 037	−10 369	−416	..	−2 844	7 025	987	−1 339	10 177	−1 985	6 853
1977	5 596	−4 912	−12 046	530	..	6 519	7 288	−1 660	−352	6 103	3 874	9 625
1978	8 262	−4 673	−10 651	−129	..	−1 102	9 813	1 554	−1 358	12 046	568	11 253
1979	12 750	−8 003	−16 944	−989	..	1 816	13 856	−3 502	−1 250	16 477	−2 862	12 363
1980	11 412	−6 755	−15 107	212	..	1 505	15 746	−624	−1 938	19 392	−635	16 807
1981	10 573	−6 904	−17 737	257	..	−549	17 715	906	−1 637	17 646	−51	15 953
1982	5 347	−4 724	−14 216	203	..	−967	25 665	−1 595	−1 797	21 744	−2 918	16 539
1983	11 128	−7 111	−2 984	304	..	−628	23 035	−725	−2 423	23 312	−2 294	19 698
1984	10 197	−6 657	−3 613	50	..	−647	30 314	−2 019	−3 321	28 022	−3 635	23 232
1985	7 625	−6 272	−2 869	1 024	..	−222	34 028	519	−4 893	30 781	−2 623	25 874
1986	2 630	−4 773	−2 127	1 001	..	117	47 059	−597	−6 017	41 121	−2 653	34 855
1987	−1 172	−2 191	−2 716	690	4 542	11 701	53 865	−5 242	−6 614	48 284	1 915	43 585
1988	−11 462	4 086	−1 061	787	840	4 302	82 326	−11 939	−13 014	74 004	−8 476	52 516
1989	−9 131	11 801	602	330	−1 992	−5 377	89 050	−13 625	−10 754	92 510	−17 009	64 746
1990	−1 298	2 253	−1 883	−1 137	−3 445	−497	70 556	−12 248	−8 443	68 100	−9 301	50 356
1991	7 003	−4 498	−1 175	−12	6 057	2 999	37 092	1 199	−8 564	38 363	−1 858	27 941
1992	28 623	−15 630	−4 418	−220	3 686	−8 961	25 605	8 842	−12 013	33 775	−3 805	17 955
1993	43 202	−27 866	−3 515	582	13 433	2 665	22 685	14 305	−14 850	35 245	3 537	23 931
1994	39 342	−18 846	−4 493	−87	1 336	1 990	31 567	−7 692	−15 064	47 485	−7 038	25 386
1995	35 446	−16 656	−4 835	−197	3 313	−328	57 736	−3 521	−8 377	71 496	−7 161	55 957
1996	24 778	−14 998	−4 461	218	10 545	−340	59 129	17 917	−12 213	64 576	7 032	59 395
1997	11 851	−14 745	−2 071	695	3 365	872	68 311	24 922	−6 201	64 045	22 429	80 273
1998	−6 395	1 891	−1 153	779	4 399	−312	63 929	13 289	−7 900	59 046	8 579	59 723
1999	−1 751	−5 186	1 822	963	−5 903	1 283	78 045	−48 062	−2 240	73 913	−40 876	30 796
1963 Q1	−610	28	27	43	..	..	..	–	25	..	..	154
Q2	386	5	52	−156	..	19	303	−52	−120	592	−33	432
Q3	457	4	−81	−140	..	5	87	−98	1	327	−93	231
Q4	556	−2	25	−129	..	−101	278	32	−42	764	−69	663
1964 Q1	−410	10	41	−112	..	−12	482	−82	4	2	−94	−87
Q2	377	10	−35	−98	..	−83	352	−39	−44	596	−122	423
Q3	505	−1	−103	−36	..	−146	229	−89	−25	595	−235	330
Q4	510	−15	−22	−159	..	−415	440	164	−41	766	−251	485
1965 Q1	−478	9	115	−129	..	−99	506	−7	15	14	−106	−97
Q2	506	−15	−42	−168	..	3	264	20	−135	560	23	461
Q3	491	16	19	−38	..	−93	−70	18	26	444	−75	390
Q4	609	36	−41	−8	..	95	191	−32	−59	751	63	766
1966 Q1	−684	30	345	−34	..	73	524	−99	74	135	−26	183
Q2	474	25	−27	−96	..	−284	204	97	−90	537	−187	251
Q3	542	−9	31	−114	..	−290	−27	223	−71	430	−67	289
Q4	655	16	−168	−96	..	86	–	20	−81	389	106	425
1967 Q1	−505	41	−136	69	..	459	427	−290	72	−146	169	97
Q2	621	38	59	−156	..	−12	197	23	−55	716	11	664
Q3	823	23	−16	−31	..	−490	317	182	−52	1 080	−308	715
Q4	907	22	−92	−68	..	−460	393	157	−27	1 157	−303	838
1968 Q1	−330	−33	53	−25	..	−486	580	128	121	276	−358	38
Q2	537	−5	129	−153	..	−355	550	47	−80	1 060	−308	663
Q3	561	−11	−98	−43	..	56	−48	−48	−95	370	8	281
Q4	495	1	178	−5	..	−353	316	177	20	980	−176	831

For most periods the relationships between the columns are as follows:
11 = 5+6+8; 12 = 9+10+11. Due to the inclusion of the latest Public Sector Net Cash Requirement information, now on a ESA95 basis,
10 is not = 1 + 2 + 3 + 4 + 7 for all periods. The other relationships may not add exactly for more recent time periods.

1 A wider range of figures is published monthly in *Financial Statistics*.
2 The M4 private sector comprises all UK residents other than the public sector, banks and building societies.
3 Formerly called the Public Sector Borrowing Requirement.
4 Figures in columns 2-12 fall outside the scope of National Statistics.

Sources: Office for National Statistics; Enquiries Column 1 020 7533 5984; Bank of England; Columns 2-12 020 7601 5468

5.3 Counterparts to changes in money stock M4[1, 4]

continued

£ million, not seasonally adjusted

	Purchases by the M4[2] private sector of: Central government debt: Public Sector Net Cash Requirement[3]	British government stocks	Other	Other public sector debt	External and foreign currency financing of public sector: Purchase of British government stocks by overseas sector	Other	Banks' and Building Societies' sterling lending to the M4 private sector	External and foreign currency transactions of UK banks and building societies	Net non-deposit sterling liabilities of the banks and building societies	Domestic counterparts	Total external and foreign currency counterparts	M4
	1	2	3	4	5	6	7	8	9	10	11	12
	RURQ	AVBY	AVBU	AVBV	AVBZ	AQGA	AVBS	AVBW	AVBX	AVBN	AVBP	AUZI
1969 Q1	−1 217	4	302	−60	..	205	591	41	30	−386	246	−115
Q2	−87	47	13	8	..	54	212	−4	−75	143	50	109
Q3	211	−7	−163	−88	..	−99	200	170	93	158	71	320
Q4	566	37	−161	−38	..	427	208	−40	−106	575	387	864
1970 Q1	−1 458	104	−147	−8	..	851	730	−239	−27	−712	612	−130
Q2	136	9	139	10	..	135	755	−146	−37	1 039	−11	980
Q3	305	45	223	111	..	−94	178	104	−58	816	10	766
Q4	798	57	−51	11	..	434	254	−11	−170	1 011	423	1 277
1971 Q1	−584	116	−668	61	..	708	714	−39	150	−352	669	466
Q2	294	96	−165	35	..	402	586	−24	−170	750	378	947
Q3	590	77	−571	67	..	659	787	−228	−346	872	431	956
Q4	896	83	−537	108	..	896	1 140	−429	−47	1 607	467	2 036
1972 Q1	−930	68	−119	−41	..	−84	2 102	−122	77	1 136	−206	1 003
Q2	736	−87	−337	−8	..	−942	2 325	469	−146	2 715	−473	2 085
Q3	775	−29	−165	−111	..	−230	1 212	164	−294	1 711	−66	1 345
Q4	1 248	10	−198	−95	..	−323	2 086	95	−383	3 039	−228	2 437
1973 Q1	−310	−17	−202	−281	..	−7	2 227	−31	−105	1 423	−38	1 274
Q2	1 392	40	−494	−164	..	83	1 578	−138	−55	2 287	−55	2 162
Q3	1 610	52	−282	−263	..	−472	1 743	314	−165	2 793	−158	2 466
Q4	1 377	−13	−366	−158	..	−371	2 423	−68	−284	3 351	−439	2 642
1974 Q1	−142	−19	−175	−622	..	−460	1 603	170	43	736	−290	485
Q2	1 950	74	−568	−459	..	−383	1 498	−450	−652	2 459	−833	959
Q3	1 538	56	−422	−139	..	−433	1 064	−81	−689	2 110	−514	903
Q4	2 907	−50	368	−393	..	−1 288	760	226	120	3 662	−1 062	2 732
1975 Q1	1 446	213	−1 493	51	..	−520	926	−20	419	962	−540	833
Q2	2 852	96	−459	115	..	−541	654	−506	−304	3 191	−1 047	1 817
Q3	2 662	−585	−1 681	257	..	254	28	24	−241	1 853	401	2 013
Q4	3 055	−1 447	−3 052	−36	..	−220	795	−5	−418	2 292	−308	1 566
1976 Q1	1 488	−862	−2 150	182	..	−662	947	283	92	1 409	−368	1 133
Q2	2 550	−871	−1 973	−94	..	−1 450	2 038	413	−329	3 455	−1 038	2 088
Q3	2 418	−730	−1 489	−62	..	−592	1 670	273	−603	3 301	−353	2 345
Q4	2 455	−2 574	−4 757	−442	..	−140	2 370	18	−499	2 012	−226	1 287
1977 Q1	893	−1 687	−4 144	−185	..	1 405	910	−637	476	−800	581	257
Q2	1 869	−560	−1 823	176	..	297	2 166	104	−406	2 888	368	2 850
Q3	1 031	−1 492	−3 449	222	..	2 578	1 872	−471	−306	1 025	1 830	2 549
Q4	1 803	−1 173	−2 630	317	..	2 239	2 340	−656	−116	2 990	1 095	3 969
1978 Q1	1 002	−771	−1 821	−92	..	48	1 950	679	372	1 702	722	2 796
Q2	1 924	−1 675	−3 560	257	..	−1 549	3 213	1 287	−873	3 703	−201	2 629
Q3	2 618	−1 109	−2 598	−232	..	177	1 920	−302	−361	2 767	−72	2 331
Q4	2 718	−1 118	−2 672	−62	..	222	2 730	−110	−496	3 874	119	3 497
1979 Q1	1 583	−1 978	−4 795	−522	..	617	3 549	−924	−68	1 938	−413	1 454
Q2	3 456	−2 207	−4 833	30	..	559	4 018	−856	−503	4 872	−369	4 004
Q3	3 910	−1 875	−3 606	−171	..	184	2 990	−816	−690	4 983	−1 259	3 031
Q4	3 801	−1 943	−3 710	−326	..	456	3 299	−906	11	4 684	−821	3 874
1980 Q1	−1 187	−1 456	−2 839	−374	..	277	4 269	−127	−488	1 615	133	1 258
Q2	4 674	−1 579	−3 459	20	..	529	4 219	−20	−685	7 022	−585	5 752
Q3	3 829	−2 277	−4 846	259	..	376	3 876	−231	−1 151	5 362	−345	3 864
Q4	4 096	−1 443	−3 963	307	..	323	3 382	−246	386	5 393	162	5 933
1981 Q1	−341	−2 291	−5 415	16	..	147	3 840	700	308	568	833	1 711
Q2	7 926	−1 753	−5 175	17	..	−212	2 848	−431	−162	7 158	−638	6 356
Q3	2 484	−969	−2 219	158	..	−669	4 528	473	−1 705	5 910	−234	3 971
Q4	504	−1 891	−4 928	66	..	185	6 499	164	−78	4 010	−12	3 915
1982 Q1	−2 245	−1 344	−4 178	48	..	−21	7 057	−445	186	2 218	−283	2 125
Q2	2 914	−479	−1 389	−180	..	−545	5 627	−1 308	−137	7 267	−1 943	5 180
Q3	1 910	−2 315	−1 450	94	..	115	7 464	−640	−1 536	5 630	−253	3 841
Q4	2 768	−586	−1 376	241	..	−516	5 517	798	−310	6 629	−439	5 393
1983 Q1	1 414	−400	−787	−247	..	−713	5 347	321	440	5 017	−512	5 839
Q2	3 271	−1 812	−612	169	..	256	5 876	−251	−711	6 795	−647	5 161
Q3	3 664	−3 338	−717	164	..	−126	6 076	−168	−1 967	5 238	−514	3 135
Q4	2 779	−1 561	−868	218	..	−45	5 736	−627	−185	6 262	−621	5 563
1984 Q1	73	−1 295	−861	−2	..	−239	8 148	−291	−438	4 988	−876	4 763
Q2	4 778	−1 182	−751	−582	..	−317	6 857	−1 034	−248	9 013	−1 414	7 289
Q3	3 014	−2 147	−797	−138	..	−420	7 372	−112	−1 725	6 519	−736	4 540
Q4	2 433	−2 033	−1 204	772	..	329	7 937	−582	−910	7 502	−609	6 640

See footnotes on page 238.

Sources: Office for National Statistics; Enquiries Column 1 020 7533 5984; Bank of England; Columns 2-12 020 7601 5468

5.3 Counterparts to changes in money stock M4[1, 4]

continued

£ million, not seasonally adjusted

		Purchases by the M4[2] private sector of:			External and foreign currency financing of public sector							
		Central government debt										
	Public Sector Net Cash Require-ment[3]	British government stocks	Other	Other public sector debt	Purchase of British government stocks by overseas sector	Other	Banks' and Building Soc-ieties sterling lending to the M4 private sector	External and foreign currency trans-actions of UK banks and building soc-ieties	Net non-deposit sterling liabili-ties of the banks and building soc-ieties	Domestic counter-parts	Total external and foreign currency counter-parts	M4
	1	*2*	*3*	*4*	*5*	*6*	*7*	*8*	*9*	*10*	*11*	*12*
	RURQ	AVBY	AVBU	AVBV	AVBZ	AQGA	AVBS	AVBW	AVBX	AVBN	AVBP	AUZI
1985 Q1	19	−3 328	−836	−237	..	−275	10 285	2 052	−644	4 855	1 061	6 367
Q2	2 752	−1 224	−813	309	..	471	7 907	245	−1 793	8 111	−561	6 537
Q3	2 837	−1 225	−591	394	..	−44	7 307	−42	−2 039	7 681	−463	6 098
Q4	2 017	−495	−629	558	..	−374	8 529	−1 736	−417	10 134	−2 660	6 872
1986 Q1	−1 832	−558	−21	160	..	385	11 124	810	323	7 361	1 123	10 368
Q2	2 484	−1 054	−815	1 026	..	373	10 409	1 135	−2 786	11 038	741	9 950
Q3	3 607	−1 523	−905	−215	..	−455	10 616	−1 038	−2 202	11 679	−2 033	7 329
Q4	−1 629	−1 638	−386	30	793	−186	14 910	−1 504	−1 352	11 043	−2 484	7 208
1987 Q1	−913	578	−706	131	724	1 287	10 762	−51	−1 057	10 094	513	9 550
Q2	1 388	−1 409	−1 000	135	1 271	4 067	13 394	−1 057	−2 976	12 485	1 738	11 247
Q3	449	1 434	−553	402	2 332	314	14 811	−2 170	−1 109	16 459	−4 189	11 161
Q4	−2 096	−2 794	−457	22	215	6 033	14 898	−1 964	−1 472	9 246	3 853	11 627
1988 Q1	−2 955	−657	−452	−78	489	1 777	18 633	−2 885	−689	14 391	−1 598	12 104
Q2	−1 668	879	−198	372	524	619	21 487	−4 713	−3 557	20 871	−4 617	12 697
Q3	−2 133	1 421	−461	95	−56	1 101	22 694	315	−4 949	21 658	1 472	18 182
Q4	−4 706	2 443	50	398	−117	805	19 512	−4 656	−3 819	17 084	−3 733	9 533
1989 Q1	−5 964	4 440	206	−66	−417	−218	21 913	−4 743	−1 481	20 908	−4 544	14 883
Q2	−16	3 839	−512	297	−1 080	−2 113	20 295	−1 160	−4 556	23 878	−2 193	17 129
Q3	−306	3 240	592	99	615	−650	26 232	−7 640	−3 813	29 744	−8 904	17 027
Q4	−2 845	282	316	–	−1 110	−2 396	20 610	−82	−904	17 980	−1 368	15 707
1990 Q1	−3 738	971	200	−332	−1 351	299	23 327	−4 309	−899	19 909	−2 659	16 351
Q2	6 069	4	−941	−249	−600	−936	17 029	702	−4 431	21 866	366	17 800
Q3	−474	160	−524	−57	−215	−847	16 062	−1 830	−3 385	15 310	−2 463	9 463
Q4	−3 155	1 118	−618	−499	−1 279	987	14 138	−6 811	272	11 015	−4 545	6 742
1991 Q1	−3 226	−318	53	227	1 702	1 610	12 777	−1 685	290	9 498	−1 777	8 011
Q2	7 017	−372	−13	49	2 214	781	6 277	2 900	−4 050	12 876	1 467	10 292
Q3	3 543	−2 488	−835	−28	834	471	10 639	−2 950	−3 087	10 876	−3 313	4 477
Q4	−331	−1 320	−380	−260	1 307	137	7 399	2 934	−1 717	5 113	1 765	5 161
1992 Q1	3 627	1 247	−1 070	−309	3 752	346	5 803	2 141	−955	9 216	−1 265	6 996
Q2	10 533	−5 992	−1 592	−248	2 402	172	8 335	4 530	−6 093	11 070	2 300	7 276
Q3	7 954	−6 232	−1 055	555	−1 971	−13 609	7 521	8 270	−1 810	8 598	−3 368	3 419
Q4	6 509	−4 653	−701	−218	−497	4 130	3 946	−6 099	−3 155	4 891	−1 472	264
1993 Q1	11 184	−4 181	−1 152	66	1 386	2 134	4 522	−3 741	−1 513	10 423	−2 993	5 917
Q2	13 494	−10 668	−409	−4	3 330	274	3 830	10 069	−8 496	6 253	7 013	4 770
Q3	10 777	−7 420	−519	276	5 187	262	8 538	1 693	−3 851	11 827	−3 232	4 744
Q4	7 747	−5 597	−1 435	244	3 530	−5	5 795	6 284	−990	6 742	2 749	8 500
1994 Q1	14 144	−778	−966	43	4 199	2 305	2 864	1 982	−3 834	15 324	88	11 578
Q2	12 158	−6 025	−2 285	87	−1 606	362	4 165	−2 488	−3 948	8 091	−520	3 624
Q3	9 292	−7 599	−668	−158	−1 275	−606	10 767	−6 503	−3 241	11 632	−5 834	2 558
Q4	3 748	−4 444	−574	−59	18	−71	13 771	−683	−4 041	12 438	−772	7 626
1995 Q1	11 490	−6 581	−547	97	−751	546	14 854	−3 394	−540	19 314	−2 096	16 677
Q2	11 393	−2 599	−693	−256	2 400	−370	9 577	1 716	−4 682	17 420	−1 054	11 685
Q3	9 051	−3 329	−1 300	60	1 402	−120	14 915	−3 858	−3 782	19 394	−5 380	10 232
Q4	3 512	−4 147	−2 295	−98	262	−384	18 390	2 015	627	15 368	1 369	17 363
1996 Q1	7 529	−1 771	−230	−12	3 669	1 041	17 618	5	−3 239	23 145	−2 623	17 283
Q2	10 470	−5 951	−1 406	−61	2 451	−819	13 433	2 301	−2 001	16 481	−969	13 511
Q3	5 984	−6 421	−2 274	275	1 655	−70	14 651	6 963	−5 092	12 122	5 238	12 269
Q4	795	−855	−551	16	2 770	−492	13 427	8 648	−1 881	12 828	5 386	16 332
1997 Q1	5 479	−5 133	−639	155	2 522	945	24 694	7 636	−2 255	24 567	6 059	28 370
Q2	8 134	−6 635	438	314	824	−535	18 534	3 745	−3 760	20 782	2 386	19 408
Q3	613	−2 004	−788	69	−2 792	−600	8 625	8 432	−3 699	6 511	10 624	13 437
Q4	−2 375	−973	−1 082	157	2 811	1 062	16 458	5 109	3 513	12 185	3 360	19 058
1998 Q1	−5 260	−1 867	−591	−42	883	240	23 262	9 810	−7 392	15 503	9 167	17 277
Q2	5 435	2 731	−391	747	2 213	−221	13 868	−2 822	−80	22 381	−5 255	17 045
Q3	−2 806	645	−260	47	−1 055	−187	18 499	−1 031	−3 514	16 127	−163	12 449
Q4	−3 764	382	89	27	2 358	−144	8 300	7 332	3 086	5 035	4 830	12 952
1999 Q1	−5 825	3 130	−478	323	−989	410	21 385	−10 772	−131	18 533	−9 373	9 028
Q2	5 330	−4 967	179	304	790	513	18 347	−9 808	−2 321	19 195	−10 085	6 789
Q3	−3 190	−2 686	1 656	−21	−5 498	103	12 703	−12 675	−9 443	8 459	−7 074	−8 059
Q4	1 934	−663	465	357	−206	257	25 610	−14 807	9 655	27 726	−14 344	23 038
2000 Q1	−12 764	5 051	−1 255	−133	2 140	2 550	36 711	−3 336	−6 180	27 621	−2 925	18 515
Q2	−11 232	..	..	..	..	..	..	..	..	..	..	..

See footnotes on page 238.

Sources: Office for National Statistics; Enquiries Column 1 020 7533 5984; Bank of England; Columns 2-12 020 7601 5468

5.3 Counterparts to changes in money stock M4[1, 4]

continued

£ million, not seasonally adjusted

	Public Sector Net Cash Requirement[3]	Purchases by the M4[2] private sector of: Central government debt: British government stocks	Purchases by the M4[2] private sector of: Central government debt: Other	Purchases by the M4[2] private sector of: Other public sector debt	External and foreign currency financing of public sector: Purchase of British government stocks by overseas sector	External and foreign currency financing of public sector: Other	Banks' and Building Societies' sterling lending to the M4 private sector	External and foreign currency transactions of UK banks and building societies	Net non-deposit sterling liabilities of the banks and building societies	Domestic counterparts	Total external and foreign currency counterparts	M4
	1	2	3	4	5	6	7	8	9	10	11	12
	RURQ	AVBY	AVBU	AVBV	AVBZ	AQGA	AVBS	AVBW	AVBX	AVBN	AVBP	AUZI
1982 Jan	..	..	..	..	..	..	..	..	..	..	..	..
Feb	..	..	..	..	..	..	..	..	..	..	..	..
Mar	..	..	..	..	..	..	..	..	..	..	..	..
Apr	..	..	..	..	..	..	..	..	..	..	..	..
May	..	..	..	..	..	..	..	..	..	..	..	..
Jun	..	129	–145	..	..	..	..	..	..	..	..	–
Jul	..	–876	–380	85	..	49	2 975	–	–277	2 232	..	2 030
Aug	..	–744	–487	–73	..	28	1 373	–1	–624	1 190	..	722
Sep	..	–695	–583	106	..	38	3 116	–1	–1 274	2 208	..	1 092
Oct	..	145	–854	63	..	20	1 940	–1	–206	1 480	–235	1 232
Nov	..	–380	–281	568	..	11	1 440	–1	354	2 106	–204	1 616
Dec	..	–351	–241	53	..	–547	2 137	–1	340	3 043	–799	2 543
1983 Jan	..	–313	–202	143	..	–295	1 220	–	2 174	–916	–454	584
Feb	..	199	–274	–108	..	–87	1 926	1	424	2 637	–53	3 059
Mar	..	–286	–311	–1 182	..	–331	2 201	–	–1 837	3 296	–325	2 192
Apr	..	–599	–162	–508	..	216	697	–3	–30	635	–48	1 143
May	..	–930	–189	216	..	189	2 634	–2	–1 121	2 911	–153	1 450
Jun	..	–283	–261	392	..	–149	2 545	–3	–161	3 249	–195	2 571
Jul	..	–975	12	–85	..	40	1 258	–1	1 077	905	–122	1 977
Aug	..	–675	–300	–271	..	–15	933	–1	–1 603	1 379	–86	84
Sep	..	–1 688	–429	–15	..	–151	3 885	–1	–1 747	2 954	–139	1 063
Oct	..	–449	–400	10	..	144	1 417	2	568	834	92	1 569
Nov	..	–238	–358	470	..	–97	1 593	1	–888	2 847	92	1 665
Dec	..	–874	–110	–294	..	–92	2 726	2	–421	2 581	–183	2 317
1984 Jan	..	–511	–136	38	..	–56	2 419	–	1 775	–629	–271	805
Feb	..	176	–290	–99	..	10	2 172	–	–588	2 266	15	1 808
Mar	..	–960	–435	–1 060	..	–193	3 557	–	–1 924	3 351	–322	2 146
Apr	2 362	–1 028	–164	–927	..	11	1 412	–	–282	1 687	–266	1 877
May	1 359	465	–232	121	..	–177	2 225	–	–676	3 851	63	2 998
Jun	1 057	–619	–355	252	..	–151	3 220	–1	–378	3 475	–177	2 412
Jul	699	–1 217	–61	–251	..	–184	2 174	–5	727	1 192	–135	1 999
Aug	1 695	–867	–601	–554	..	–108	1 432	–5	–766	1 103	–228	679
Sep	620	–63	–135	121	..	–128	3 766	–4	–1 856	4 224	–261	1 849
Oct	320	–1 439	–872	223	..	280	2 598	1	390	1 097	310	1 914
Nov	1 762	–455	–101	263	..	–82	2 528	1	436	3 906	–233	4 047
Dec	351	–139	–231	–431	..	131	2 811	1	–2 359	2 499	–104	692
1985 Jan	–2 231	–1 021	–594	251	..	–214	2 952	–	3 491	–615	–458	2 075
Feb	–79	–1 211	254	–382	..	–222	1 765	–1	–837	349	–401	–536
Mar	2 329	–1 096	–496	–1 071	..	161	5 568	–	–1 143	5 121	–133	4 820
Apr	1 831	–634	–521	–796	..	155	1 502	–1	–1 270	1 390	–222	808
May	949	–119	19	–17	..	239	2 700	–	–648	3 532	–229	2 765
Jun	–28	–471	–311	340	..	77	3 705	–1	365	3 189	–351	2 961
Jul	447	–370	–403	–336	..	–30	2 577	–4	109	1 956	–221	2 378
Aug	1 222	–265	–176	–95	..	82	1 702	–4	–285	2 379	16	2 297
Sep	1 168	–590	–12	–209	..	–96	3 028	–3	–2 019	3 346	–216	1 424
Oct	–137	–75	–289	395	..	–87	3 180	3	22	3 090	–581	2 347
Nov	650	–778	–120	604	..	–120	2 397	3	25	2 713	39	2 335
Dec	1 504	358	–220	–262	..	–167	2 952	3	–2 208	4 331	–380	2 169
1986 Jan	–4 266	–531	602	–91	..	104	1 785	–	5 010	–2 512	–28	2 652
Feb	–423	471	–286	19	..	80	4 308	–1	–1 882	4 146	24	2 288
Mar	2 857	–498	–337	–1 224	..	201	5 031	–	–1 887	5 727	333	5 438
Apr	969	–846	–366	–711	..	183	1 481	–29	510	490	–435	1 682
May	938	922	–148	262	..	20	3 189	–28	–470	5 222	–6	4 889
Jun	577	–1 130	–301	435	..	170	5 739	–28	–1 774	5 326	62	3 379
Jul	–215	–352	–493	–	..	–150	4 273	–54	253	3 214	–770	2 628
Aug	1 636	–1 247	–447	–235	..	–68	3 512	–55	–2 342	3 217	–289	717
Sep	2 186	76	35	163	..	–237	2 831	–54	–1 146	5 248	63	3 975
Oct	–133	–1 175	–52	–118	240	–207	5 133	545	–340	3 654	98	3 412
Nov	72	–650	–374	330	254	2	4 724	168	–969	3 964	–84	2 911
Dec	–1 568	187	40	–181	299	19	5 054	–2 217	–42	3 425	–2 497	885

See footnotes on page 238.

Sources: Office for National Statistics; Enquiries Column 1 020 7533 5984; Bank of England; Columns 2-12 020 7601 5468

5.3 Counterparts to changes in money stock M4[1, 4]

continued

£ million, not seasonally adjusted

	Public Sector Net Cash Requirement[3]	Purchases by the M4[2] private sector of: Central government debt: British government stocks	Purchases by the M4[2] private sector of: Central government debt: Other	Purchases by the M4[2] private sector of: Other public sector debt	External and foreign currency financing of public sector: Purchase of British government stocks by overseas sector	External and foreign currency financing of public sector: Other	Banks' and Building Societies' sterling lending to the M4 private sector	External and foreign currency transactions of UK banks and building societies	Net non-deposit sterling liabilities of the banks and building societies	Domestic counterparts	Total external and foreign currency counterparts	M4
	1	*2*	*3*	*4*	*5*	*6*	*7*	*8*	*9*	*10*	*11*	*12*
	RURQ	AVBY	AVBU	AVBV	AVBZ	AQGA	AVBS	AVBW	AVBX	AVBN	AVBP	AUZI
1987 Jan	-3 800	194	114	-250	-152	258	2 946	-654	885	-515	-243	126
Feb	-261	-29	-425	216	108	64	3 477	-230	-193	2 986	-273	2 519
Mar	3 148	413	-395	165	768	965	4 338	833	-1 749	7 623	1 030	6 905
Apr	2 045	-944	-61	91	255	1 746	3 001	-1 268	-678	4 082	222	3 626
May	-236	-736	-432	183	-9	2 896	3 798	-601	-1 003	2 616	2 303	3 917
Jun	-421	271	-507	-139	1 025	-575	6 595	813	-1 295	5 787	-787	3 705
Jul	-470	870	-137	207	1 234	449	5 823	-1 807	1 513	6 217	-2 593	5 137
Aug	699	380	-158	390	495	-306	2 390	934	-545	3 616	133	3 204
Sep	220	184	-258	-195	603	171	6 599	-1 297	-2 076	6 626	-1 729	2 820
Oct	-902	-739	-25	-43	841	3 818	4 137	409	-48	2 307	3 385	5 645
Nov	-1 583	-1 687	-228	304	-743	-148	4 338	228	-771	1 117	823	1 169
Dec	389	-368	-204	-239	117	2 363	6 422	-2 601	-653	5 822	-356	4 814
1988 Jan	-6 394	-310	11	-374	278	471	6 296	-1 957	2 464	-868	-1 765	-168
Feb	-282	-835	-55	322	337	-12	3 814	-713	-705	2 796	-1 062	1 029
Mar	3 721	488	-408	-27	-126	1 318	8 523	-215	-2 448	12 463	1 229	11 244
Apr	-1 091	-686	-90	430	271	263	5 949	-1 939	-729	4 369	-1 946	1 694
May	-384	650	69	-158	-152	303	5 656	-318	-1 596	5 600	137	4 142
Jun	-193	915	-177	100	405	53	9 882	-2 456	-1 233	10 902	-2 808	6 861
Jul	-1 656	1 127	-274	116	185	613	9 006	594	-1 822	8 369	1 022	7 570
Aug	-1 549	522	-71	133	191	480	4 721	433	-1 171	3 741	722	3 292
Sep	1 072	-228	-116	-155	-432	8	8 967	-713	-1 956	9 548	-273	7 320
Oct	-2 231	1 825	-37	130	154	468	6 453	-2 734	-1 429	6 076	-2 420	2 228
Nov	107	696	-133	28	-68	410	5 479	-1 904	-1 644	5 613	-1 426	2 544
Dec	-2 582	-78	220	239	-203	-72	7 580	-19	-747	5 395	112	4 761
1989 Jan	-7 148	495	-13	-244	119	757	7 388	-1 477	1 836	892	-839	1 889
Feb	-1 098	2 953	114	221	33	-452	4 632	-2 851	-1 179	6 760	-3 336	2 245
Mar	2 282	992	105	-43	-569	-523	9 893	-415	-2 138	13 256	-369	10 749
Apr	-1 529	876	-100	-92	-757	31	5 093	-2 289	-1 342	4 916	-1 501	2 073
May	399	1 184	-75	368	-67	-604	5 978	-485	-1 442	7 599	-1 022	5 135
Jun	1 114	1 779	-337	21	-256	-1 540	9 224	1 614	-1 772	11 363	330	9 921
Jul	-1 441	521	-25	259	276	157	7 864	-2 768	-1 246	7 170	-2 887	3 037
Aug	783	2 047	280	-59	841	-331	6 751	-2 533	-206	9 831	-3 704	5 920
Sep	352	672	337	-102	-502	-476	11 618	-2 339	-2 360	12 743	-2 313	8 070
Oct	-2 775	1 413	-1	96	-101	-2 089	4 830	983	-140	3 503	-1 005	2 357
Nov	401	2	335	172	-418	-465	4 511	-278	-960	5 238	-325	3 953
Dec	-471	-1 133	-18	-269	-591	158	11 269	-787	197	9 239	-38	9 398
1990 Jan	-5 081	765	107	-50	-23	782	5 376	-179	1 564	1 164	626	3 355
Feb	-683	468	-96	12	-465	-164	6 753	-2 028	-1 400	6 128	-1 727	3 001
Mar	2 026	-262	189	-294	-863	-319	11 197	-2 103	-1 063	12 617	-1 559	9 995
Apr	2 176	-567	-522	-78	-542	-693	2 441	-417	-808	3 476	-568	2 100
May	1 521	293	-455	-176	-236	-3	5 502	784	-2 275	6 611	1 017	5 353
Jun	2 372	278	36	4	178	-240	9 086	334	-1 349	11 779	-84	10 347
Jul	-2 916	547	-288	-152	-204	152	4 064	-2 584	686	1 419	-2 228	-123
Aug	744	47	-240	167	120	303	3 491	588	-1 605	4 169	771	3 335
Sep	1 698	-434	4	-72	-131	-1 301	8 507	166	-2 467	9 722	-1 005	6 251
Oct	-2 310	1 240	-486	-234	-327	123	4 624	-3 633	393	2 784	-3 183	-5
Nov	848	578	-476	-287	-439	672	4 752	-1 057	-452	5 430	54	5 032
Dec	-1 693	-700	344	22	-513	193	4 762	-2 121	330	2 801	-1 415	1 716
1991 Jan	-5 643	251	70	393	492	921	3 312	-2 453	3 635	-1 733	-2 024	-123
Feb	-767	-725	73	263	721	448	3 900	-1 115	-213	2 748	-1 388	1 147
Mar	3 184	156	-90	-429	489	241	5 566	1 883	-3 131	8 483	1 635	6 987
Apr	2 060	89	87	-119	903	793	1 034	-877	72	3 111	-987	2 195
May	3 562	-888	250	74	211	-281	1 836	1 191	-1 877	4 744	699	3 566
Jun	1 395	427	-350	93	1 100	269	3 407	2 586	-2 245	5 021	1 755	4 531
Jul	-1 115	-1 654	-232	-177	-218	-365	2 631	-1 430	512	-605	-1 577	-1 670
Aug	1 778	-262	-465	16	266	669	2 199	-1 132	-1 730	3 267	-729	808
Sep	2 880	-572	-138	132	786	167	5 808	-388	-1 868	8 214	-1 007	5 339
Oct	-1 903	753	-275	-48	949	-35	268	21	59	-1 296	-963	-2 199
Nov	848	-1 091	172	-41	201	-701	4 149	684	-1 779	4 064	-218	2 067
Dec	724	-982	-277	-171	157	874	2 982	2 229	3	2 345	2 945	5 293

See footnotes on page 238.

Sources: Office for National Statistics; Enquiries Column 1 020 7533 5984; Bank of England; Columns 2-12 020 7601 5468

5.3 Counterparts to changes in money stock M4[1, 4]

continued

£ million, not seasonally adjusted

	Public Sector Net Cash Requirement[3]	Purchases by the M4[2] private sector of: Central government debt: British government stocks	Other	Other public sector debt	External and foreign currency financing of public sector: Purchase of British government stocks by overseas sector	Other	Banks' and Building Societies' sterling lending to the M4 private sector	External and foreign currency transactions of UK banks and building societies	Net non-deposit sterling liabilities of the banks and building societies	Domestic counterparts	Total external and foreign currency counterparts	M4
	1	2	3	4	5	6	7	8	9	10	11	12
	RURQ	AVBY	AVBU	AVBV	AVBZ	AQGA	AVBS	AVBW	AVBX	AVBN	AVBP	AUZI
1992 Jan	−3 750	212	−236	29	879	115	2 584	−1 842	2 452	−1 391	−2 606	−1 545
Feb	970	15	−187	172	1 397	187	708	1 907	−867	1 699	697	1 528
Mar	6 407	1 020	−647	−510	1 476	44	2 511	2 076	−2 540	8 908	644	7 013
Apr	3 569	−2 852	−575	136	798	23	2 324	1 510	−1 131	2 460	735	2 063
May	3 121	−2 237	−620	−24	854	−48	1 609	2 185	−1 545	1 863	1 283	1 600
Jun	3 843	−903	−397	−360	750	197	4 401	835	−3 417	6 747	282	3 613
Jul	882	−1 423	−694	71	282	−158	2 919	−1 351	870	1 585	−1 791	664
Aug	2 966	−2 069	−161	181	−1 577	−476	1 715	−1 458	−2 749	2 666	−357	−440
Sep	4 106	−2 740	−200	303	−676	−12 975	2 888	11 078	68	4 347	−1 221	3 195
Oct	1 725	−1 744	−404	167	−181	1 350	3 503	−3 314	−91	3 203	−1 783	1 329
Nov	1 784	−417	−128	−303	123	393	−514	−2 225	−1 470	620	−1 955	−2 806
Dec	3 000	−2 492	−169	−81	−439	2 387	957	−559	−1 594	1 068	2 267	1 741
1993 Jan	−3 699	−593	−719	337	−171	328	3 339	−4 199	1 341	−1 338	−3 700	−3 697
Feb	5 720	−3 324	−196	−31	321	−196	−169	−73	430	1 977	−590	1 817
Mar	9 163	−264	−237	−240	1 236	2 002	1 353	531	−3 283	9 784	1 297	7 798
Apr	4 779	−4 127	−272	−81	1 457	277	431	4 241	−2 713	720	3 061	1 068
May	4 910	−3 989	1	58	279	−47	1 450	2 615	−2 310	2 428	2 289	2 407
Jun	3 805	−2 552	−138	19	1 594	44	1 949	3 212	−3 473	3 105	1 662	1 294
Jul	1 342	−2 581	−25	18	2 191	314	2 465	3 289	−990	1 409	1 412	1 831
Aug	3 646	−1 700	−375	270	1 872	−219	2 209	−1 673	−155	4 027	−3 764	108
Sep	5 789	−3 139	−119	−12	1 124	167	3 865	76	−2 706	6 391	−881	2 804
Oct	2 709	−2 258	−593	232	1 692	−140	1 958	3 078	−292	2 041	1 246	2 994
Nov	3 017	−788	−737	43	141	−2	267	1 289	−1 556	1 799	1 146	1 389
Dec	2 021	−2 551	−105	−30	1 697	137	3 570	1 917	858	2 902	357	4 117
1994 Jan	−1 792	828	−392	5	1 480	163	867	772	−464	−477	−545	−1 486
Feb	4 701	548	−508	−159	1 839	1 184	−1 472	3 126	−2 327	3 115	2 471	3 260
Mar	11 235	−2 154	−66	196	880	958	3 469	−1 916	−1 044	12 686	−1 838	9 804
Apr	4 553	−3 486	−929	63	−364	538	−876	1 542	−1 367	−679	2 444	399
May	4 439	−54	−707	43	−291	−35	554	−2 204	−1 913	4 276	−1 948	415
Jun	3 166	−2 485	−649	−19	−951	−141	4 486	−1 825	−668	4 494	−1 015	2 810
Jul	1 570	−1 881	−195	118	26	−344	3 717	−1 577	−2 482	3 330	−1 947	−1 099
Aug	3 475	−2 540	−326	−253	−491	−415	1 806	−2 027	−129	2 166	−1 951	86
Sep	4 247	−3 178	−147	−23	−810	153	5 243	−2 899	−629	6 136	−1 936	3 571
Oct	−297	−3 039	−135	73	−36	−247	1 699	1 126	−445	−1 694	915	−1 224
Nov	3 696	−531	−351	−115	−89	−216	6 592	−1 951	−2 772	9 288	−2 078	4 437
Dec	349	−874	−88	−17	143	392	5 479	143	−824	4 844	392	4 412
1995 Jan	−3 744	−2 236	−81	190	−654	848	5 246	−3 828	648	−624	−2 326	−2 302
Feb	5 145	−919	−297	88	185	−226	720	1 143	−549	4 735	733	4 918
Mar	10 089	−3 426	−169	−181	−282	−76	8 887	−709	−639	15 203	−503	14 061
Apr	3 818	−1 831	−228	−199	923	−20	2 628	−2 332	−983	4 187	−3 275	−70
May	4 155	158	−296	24	320	−205	4 773	−1 397	−1 179	8 811	−1 922	5 709
Jun	3 420	−926	−169	−81	1 157	−145	2 177	5 445	−2 520	4 422	4 143	6 045
Jul	817	−1 304	−380	94	163	91	9 136	−181	−2 479	8 359	−253	5 627
Aug	4 636	285	−687	−24	551	−64	−154	1 110	−2 254	4 059	495	2 300
Sep	3 598	−2 310	−233	−10	688	−147	5 933	−4 787	951	6 976	−5 622	2 305
Oct	−780	−2 815	−383	−40	868	−444	5 613	1 662	302	1 600	350	2 252
Nov	3 562	−317	−20	21	−838	62	3 937	−603	200	7 182	297	7 679
Dec	730	−1 015	−1 892	−79	232	−2	8 840	956	125	6 586	722	7 433
1996 Jan	−4 774	1 725	−689	−222	1 960	1 336	6 625	−1 470	699	2 665	−2 094	1 270
Feb	2 664	−1 781	819	296	1 315	54	4 643	−850	−2 627	6 646	−2 111	1 907
Mar	9 639	−1 714	−360	−86	394	−349	6 350	2 325	−1 310	13 834	1 582	14 106
Apr	3 227	−2 498	−390	−202	1 393	−350	1 081	−1 111	1 700	1 215	−2 854	60
May	3 558	−2 030	−883	129	11	−455	5 901	1 546	−1 507	6 673	1 080	6 246
Jun	3 685	−1 423	−133	12	1 047	−14	6 451	1 866	−2 193	8 593	805	7 205
Jul	−1 746	−4 014	−883	145	259	57	7 192	2 110	−1 402	693	1 908	1 199
Aug	4 475	−601	−275	46	954	−296	2 194	990	−55	5 802	−260	5 487
Sep	3 255	−1 805	−1 116	84	442	169	5 265	3 863	−3 636	5 627	3 590	5 582
Oct	−4 268	−325	−746	47	2 864	−123	8 261	5 297	583	2 966	2 310	5 859
Nov	2 783	2 012	617	106	862	−638	8 634	−390	−1 255	14 150	−1 890	11 005
Dec	2 280	−2 542	−422	−137	−956	269	−3 468	3 741	−1 209	−4 288	4 966	−532

See footnotes on page 238.

Sources: Office for National Statistics; Enquiries Column 1 020 7533 5984; Bank of England; Columns 2-12 020 7601 5468

5.3 Counterparts to changes in money stock M4[1, 4]

continued

£ million, not seasonally adjusted

	Public Sector Net Cash Requirement[3]	Purchases by the M4[2] private sector of: Central government debt: British government stocks	Central government debt: Other	Other public sector debt	External and foreign currency financing of public sector: Purchase of British government stocks by overseas sector	External and foreign currency financing of public sector: Other	Banks' and Building Societies' sterling lending to the M4 private sector	External and foreign currency transactions of UK banks and building societies	Net non-deposit sterling liabilities of the banks and building societies	Domestic counterparts	Total external and foreign currency counterparts	M4
	1	2	3	4	5	6	7	8	9	10	11	12
	RURQ	AVBY	AVBU	AVBV	AVBZ	AQGA	AVBS	AVBW	AVBX	AVBN	AVBP	AUZI
1997 Jan	–6 685	–3 234	–475	–99	771	1 240	12 508	1 100	175	2 014	1 569	3 758
Feb	3 275	–1 069	–193	248	454	111	7 373	5 253	–4 197	9 638	4 910	10 351
Mar	8 889	–829	29	6	1 297	–406	4 813	1 282	1 766	12 915	–421	14 261
Apr	–529	–1 178	–349	352	641	308	528	–1 793	–1 452	–1 178	–2 126	–4 756
May	4 163	–1 660	402	–84	132	–423	11 254	2 085	–1 550	14 073	1 530	14 054
Jun	4 500	–3 796	385	46	51	–420	6 752	3 453	–758	7 887	2 982	10 110
Jul	–3 650	–800	–236	–29	–1 824	–22	4 436	2 607	–414	–278	4 409	3 717
Aug	1 362	3 022	–17	91	2 023	–411	–880	2 700	360	3 577	266	4 202
Sep	2 901	–4 227	–535	7	–2 991	–167	5 069	3 126	–3 645	3 212	5 950	5 517
Oct	–5 631	–188	–1 169	88	2 355	897	1 779	5 554	2 976	–5 120	4 096	1 952
Nov	2 386	1 161	–81	–18	–276	–73	11 287	–3 616	–1 304	14 736	–3 413	10 019
Dec	870	–1 946	168	87	732	238	3 392	3 171	1 841	2 569	2 677	7 086
1998 Jan	–10 171	–1 584	–559	40	22	71	7 501	2 290	–373	–4 775	2 339	–2 808
Feb	–2 300	–1 776	–36	–177	460	152	15 408	4 798	–6 004	11 120	4 490	9 607
Mar	7 211	1 494	4	95	401	17	354	2 721	–1 016	9 158	2 337	10 479
Apr	–3 103	1 241	–635	145	279	–18	4 755	–3 073	995	2 395	–3 370	20
May	2 559	407	189	123	1 274	–135	7 090	–1 479	957	10 366	–2 888	8 435
Jun	5 979	1 084	55	479	660	–68	2 023	1 731	–2 033	9 620	1 003	8 590
Jul	–5 680	–1 354	–192	16	756	440	10 884	6 460	–14	3 677	6 144	9 807
Aug	1 221	967	181	–116	482	–244	1 665	–9 205	1 010	3 917	–9 931	–5 004
Sep	1 653	1 031	–249	147	–2 293	–383	5 950	1 713	–4 510	8 533	3 623	7 646
Oct	–7 976	1 728	78	–70	2 345	–307	4 620	4 082	2 763	–1 622	1 430	2 570
Nov	1 056	–932	134	33	505	–103	3 683	–1 100	2 133	3 976	–1 708	4 401
Dec	3 156	–414	–123	64	–492	266	–3	4 351	–1 810	2 681	5 109	5 980
1999 Jan	–11 939	–1 075	–55	88	–1 601	356	8 083	–3 266	–216	–4 899	–1 309	–6 424
Feb	–1 313	278	414	5	–624	126	9 155	117	–924	8 537	867	8 480
Mar	7 427	3 927	–837	230	1 236	–73	4 148	–7 623	1 009	14 895	–8 932	6 972
Apr	–2 231	–55	720	405	500	–150	7 011	2 808	–2 600	5 852	2 158	5 410
May	1 693	–249	–223	–170	1 509	438	908	1 550	2 198	1 960	479	4 637
Jun	5 868	–4 663	–318	69	–1 219	225	10 428	–14 166	–1 919	11 383	–12 722	–3 258
Jul	–5 267	–963	1 664	36	–2 746	–73	861	–2 150	–1 229	–3 669	523	–4 375
Aug	173	1 587	–1 001	–69	–2 050	167	8 575	–10 246	–1 347	9 268	–8 029	–108
Sep	1 904	–3 310	993	12	–702	9	3 268	–280	–6 867	2 860	432	–3 576
Oct	–9 070	–685	170	228	–371	109	6 395	4 219	4 567	–2 948	4 699	6 318
Nov	1 846	33	49	229	–237	344	12 328	–12 473	3 348	14 487	–11 893	5 942
Dec	9 158	–12	246	–100	402	–195	6 887	–6 553	1 740	16 187	–7 150	10 777
2000 Jan	–17 044	–168	–749	10	905	1 055	2 892	5 436	–5 234	–15 056	5 586	–14 704
Feb	–2 687	1 454	48	26	–79	972	13 681	–7 671	2 045	12 524	–6 620	7 948
Mar	6 967	3 765	–554	–169	1 314	523	20 137	–1 100	–2 991	30 153	–1 891	25 271
Apr	–6 714	336	2 138	144	307	1 424	3 881	3 225	–234	–187	4 342	3 921
May	–12 132	–1 607	2 171	18	956	851	16 110	6 012	–4 194	4 848	5 907	6 561
Jun	7 614	..	..	..	..	..	..	..	..	..	..	..

See footnotes on page 238.

Sources: Office for National Statistics; Enquiries Column 1 020 7533 5984; Bank of England; Columns 2-12 020 7601 5468

5.4 General government receipts and expenditure

£ million

	General government expenditure[1]				General government receipts[2]							
	Current	Capital	Financial	Total	Gross operating surplus	Taxes on production	Taxes on income and wealth	Taxes on capital	National Insurance Contributions	Property income	Miscellaneous current transfers	Total
	ANLR	NNEX	NNEY	QYXR	-NMXV	-NMYE	-NMZL	-NMGI	-AIIH	-GZQR	-NMZX	-GZQS
1948	3 727	443	177	4 236	–354	–1 858	–1 762	–215	–335	–63	–	–4 476
1949	3 938	488	–51	4 260	–373	–1 832	–1 952	–254	–436	–80	–	–4 812
1950	4 007	452	64	4 407	–427	–1 895	–1 976	–190	–440	–73	–	–4 885
1951	4 449	919	74	5 318	–448	–2 086	–2 104	–194	–452	–94	–	–5 254
1952	4 932	935	126	5 865	–399	–2 095	–2 364	–159	–476	–116	–	–5 481
1953	5 154	1 004	309	6 336	–450	–2 148	–2 326	–165	–525	–114	–	–5 597
1954	5 368	779	51	6 068	–520	–2 270	–2 370	–183	–532	–122	–	–5 867
1955	5 545	832	160	6 312	–546	–2 386	–2 571	–184	–594	–146	–5	–6 299
1956	6 041	938	274	7 014	–598	–2 519	–2 656	–166	–642	–165	–6	–6 610
1957	6 326	924	580	7 580	–641	–2 628	–2 912	–176	–657	–174	–7	–7 048
1958	6 734	928	580	7 982	–699	–2 681	–3 064	–182	–859	–212	–8	–7 553
1959	7 148	976	863	8 715	–739	–2 806	–3 129	–212	–897	–257	–10	–7 897
1960	7 636	1 015	590	8 965	–788	–2 964	–3 129	–236	–913	–284	–10	–8 167
1961	8 324	1 108	568	9 713	–749	–3 177	–3 516	–259	–1 072	–357	–12	–8 985
1962	8 862	1 260	617	10 447	–760	–3 380	–3 941	–266	–1 197	–458	–13	–9 856
1963	9 113	1 765	115	10 993	–639	–3 484	–3 913	–308	–1 303	–425	–15	–10 087
1964	9 617	1 653	782	12 052	–697	–3 843	–4 168	–307	–1 444	–490	–17	–10 966
1965	10 824	2 311	425	13 560	–936	–4 284	–4 740	–287	–1 685	–543	–18	–12 330
1966	11 699	2 000	1 020	14 718	–1 002	–4 665	–5 309	–308	–1 804	–638	–20	–13 577
1967	13 117	2 515	1 327	16 958	–1 074	–5 201	–6 058	–317	–1 924	–681	–22	–15 107
1968	14 367	3 029	1 179	18 575	–1 206	–5 931	–6 749	–384	–2 161	–776	–27	–17 060
1969	15 093	4 489	–485	19 097	–1 344	–6 835	–7 570	–456	–2 242	–886	–29	–19 182
1970	16 654	3 642	833	21 131	–1 504	–7 404	–8 622	–409	–2 655	–987	–33	–21 415
1971	18 523	3 661	1 450	23 635	–1 650	–7 584	–9 334	–419	–2 826	–1 181	–37	–22 817
1972	21 469	4 106	898	26 473	–1 748	–7 992	–9 591	–493	–3 337	–1 297	–42	–24 269
1973	24 425	5 433	442	30 300	–2 045	–8 510	–10 965	–426	–3 937	–1 513	–51	–27 136
1974	31 559	5 708	1 944	39 212	–2 556	–9 674	–14 698	–382	–5 000	–1 934	–53	–33 995
1975	41 574	6 680	3 116	51 373	–3 124	–11 700	–19 222	–309	–6 848	–2 287	–69	–43 218
1976	49 396	7 181	1 811	58 385	–3 773	–13 542	–21 644	–391	–8 423	–2 786	–110	–50 273
1977	55 087	6 974	–195	61 866	–4 152	–16 404	–23 544	–409	–9 503	–3 161	–128	–56 885
1978	63 469	7 240	1 872	72 581	–4 639	–18 822	–26 005	–386	–10 101	–3 397	–142	–63 040
1979	74 100	7 560	3 314	84 974	–5 415	–24 313	–29 480	–456	–11 526	–4 176	–126	–74 987
1980	92 230	8 633	3 854	104 717	–6 467	–30 340	–36 419	–479	–13 939	–5 449	–158	–92 676
1981	106 617	11 242	–206	117 653	–7 157	–35 134	–42 494	–1 010	–15 916	–6 203	–166	–107 475
1982	117 457	9 208	2 119	128 784	–7 228	–37 502	–47 823	–701	–18 095	–7 377	–174	–118 241
1983	127 075	10 595	872	138 542	–6 894	–40 335	–51 160	–690	–20 780	–7 570	–208	–126 978
1984	137 140	11 725	–1 477	147 388	–6 853	–43 023	–54 920	–750	–22 322	–7 871	–203	–135 294
1985	147 412	11 544	–1 897	157 059	–7 756	–45 874	–60 854	–923	–24 210	–8 881	–213	–148 062
1986	153 987	11 202	–3 863	161 326	–8 001	–50 276	–62 609	–1 025	–26 165	–7 016	–241	–154 603
1987	162 978	10 965	–6 489	167 454	–8 030	–54 411	–67 064	–1 089	–27 663	–7 674	–240	–165 464
1988	171 437	10 895	–5 041	177 291	–8 649	–61 553	–75 337	–1 107	–30 682	–7 619	–223	–184 489
1989	183 290	14 678	–1 600	196 368	–9 789	–64 344	–84 927	–1 182	–33 333	–8 988	–199	–201 857
1990	199 271	25 695	–9 933	215 033	–10 539	–68 101	–93 134	–1 321	–34 457	–8 744	–222	–215 433
1991	220 127	21 783	–9 399	232 511	–10 662	–77 510	–91 924	–1 264	–36 216	–7 678	–353	–224 666
1992	243 480	21 313	–6 144	258 649	–10 619	–78 755	–90 521	–1 228	–36 975	–6 873	–178	–224 207
1993	258 009	21 464	–4 066	275 407	–10 720	–81 766	–88 826	–1 278	–39 267	–6 182	–296	–227 487
1994	272 138	20 690	–5 401	287 427	–11 167	–88 748	–96 484	–1 439	–42 086	–6 533	–420	–246 039
1995	284 976	22 246	–2 529	304 693	–11 570	–94 010	–106 982	–1 441	–44 371	–7 172	–469	–265 346
1996	296 008	17 692	–7 650	306 050	–12 305	–100 653	–112 087	–1 637	–46 400	–7 280	–429	–280 142
1997	303 756	15 151	–2 149	316 758	–12 476	–109 595	–121 209	–1 601	–50 606	–6 650	–476	–301 977
1998	312 779	14 920	307	328 006	–13 140	–114 938	–140 258	–1 794	–54 273	–6 713	–390	–329 691
1999	320 897	14 746	1 287	336 930	–13 101	–124 409	–145 413	–1 944	–56 402	–5 974	–269	–346 847

1 See National Accounts Blue Book table 11.3 for a more detailed breakdown.

2 Excludes receipts that are netted off in the definition of General Government Expenditure.

Source: Office for National Statistics; Enquiries 020 7533 5987

5.4 General government receipts and expenditure

continued

£ million, not seasonally adjusted

	General government expenditure[1]				General government receipts[2]							
	Current	Capital	Financial	Total	Gross operating surplus	Taxes on production	Taxes on income and wealth	Taxes on capital	National Insurance Contributions	Property Income	Miscellaneous current transfers	Total
	ANLR	NNEX	NNEY	QYXR	-NMXV	-NMYE	-NMZL	-NMGI	-AIIH	-GZQR	-NMZX	-GZQS
1961 Q1	2 047	263	161	2 401	–204	–750	–1 716	–69	–227	–80	–3	–3 010
Q2	2 045	278	66	2 317	–179	–790	–588	–74	–261	–96	–3	–1 951
Q3	2 105	279	174	2 486	–181	–773	–642	–59	–291	–85	–3	–1 995
Q4	2 127	288	167	2 509	–185	–864	–570	–57	–293	–96	–3	–2 029
1962 Q1	2 250	304	175	2 657	–188	–811	–1 927	–73	–299	–100	–3	–3 361
Q2	2 146	316	136	2 524	–184	–840	–625	–68	–296	–124	–3	–2 100
Q3	2 182	316	163	2 588	–193	–834	–736	–62	–302	–115	–3	–2 206
Q4	2 284	324	143	2 678	–195	–895	–653	–63	–300	–119	–4	–2 189
1963 Q1	2 283	267	101	2 651	–158	–788	–1 847	–79	–296	–106	–3	–3 277
Q2	2 212	328	15	2 555	–157	–878	–701	–78	–313	–61	–4	–2 192
Q3	2 295	366	216	2 877	–159	–875	–689	–78	–348	–171	–4	–2 324
Q4	2 323	804	–217	2 910	–165	–943	–676	–73	–346	–87	–4	–2 294
1964 Q1	2 435	399	183	3 017	–166	–867	–1 803	–86	–354	–137	–4	–3 417
Q2	2 334	400	72	2 806	–173	–948	–756	–76	–358	–81	–4	–2 396
Q3	2 415	424	269	3 108	–177	–951	–831	–73	–364	–180	–4	–2 580
Q4	2 433	430	258	3 121	–181	–1 077	–778	–72	–368	–92	–5	–2 573
1965 Q1	2 649	438	226	3 309	–228	–1 029	–1 954	–78	–371	–152	–4	–3 774
Q2	2 654	417	109	3 183	–229	–1 042	–923	–70	–422	–88	–4	–2 738
Q3	2 754	452	350	3 556	–236	–1 055	–973	–68	–441	–209	–5	–2 947
Q4	2 767	1 004	–260	3 512	–243	–1 158	–890	–71	–451	–94	–5	–2 871
1966 Q1	2 907	487	192	3 585	–248	–1 073	–2 272	–86	–441	–169	–5	–4 252
Q2	2 841	469	144	3 456	–250	–1 134	–1 014	–79	–441	–111	–5	–2 993
Q3	2 932	499	362	3 793	–251	–1 153	–1 054	–74	–466	–249	–5	–3 209
Q4	3 019	545	322	3 884	–253	–1 305	–969	–69	–456	–109	–5	–3 123
1967 Q1	3 306	582	289	4 175	–257	–1 217	–2 456	–84	–464	–172	–5	–4 612
Q2	3 134	576	190	3 901	–267	–1 288	–1 207	–84	–486	–139	–5	–3 433
Q3	3 300	636	553	4 489	–271	–1 300	–1 246	–73	–471	–271	–6	–3 597
Q4	3 377	721	295	4 393	–279	–1 396	–1 149	–76	–503	–99	–6	–3 465
1968 Q1	3 711	806	412	4 924	–290	–1 362	–2 472	–95	–515	–206	–6	–4 903
Q2	3 461	703	138	4 303	–299	–1 409	–1 350	–90	–546	–147	–7	–3 805
Q3	3 619	719	354	4 694	–305	–1 481	–1 470	–91	–551	–249	–7	–4 108
Q4	3 576	801	275	4 654	–312	–1 679	–1 457	–108	–549	–174	–7	–4 244
1969 Q1	3 860	803	216	4 876	–323	–1 544	–2 684	–161	–546	–239	–7	–5 459
Q2	3 570	709	33	4 314	–329	–1 668	–1 529	–102	–552	–213	–7	–4 356
Q3	3 811	795	223	4 830	–343	–1 746	–1 679	–94	–556	–222	–7	–4 601
Q4	3 852	2 182	–957	5 077	–349	–1 877	–1 678	–99	–588	–212	–8	–4 766
1970 Q1	4 107	816	257	5 176	–363	–1 679	–3 079	–133	–628	–251	–8	–6 093
Q2	4 019	763	66	4 850	–372	–1 837	–1 900	–81	–658	–246	–8	–5 054
Q3	4 225	861	426	5 515	–379	–1 916	–1 877	–94	–684	–246	–9	–5 155
Q4	4 303	1 202	84	5 590	–390	–1 972	–1 766	–101	–685	–244	–8	–5 113
1971 Q1	4 458	1 013	367	5 838	–405	–1 770	–3 227	–110	–633	–285	–8	–6 384
Q2	4 431	833	238	5 503	–408	–1 952	–2 019	–106	–711	–277	–10	–5 429
Q3	4 706	884	414	6 005	–415	–1 878	–2 086	–100	–707	–288	–9	–5 429
Q4	4 928	931	431	6 289	–422	–1 984	–2 002	–103	–775	–331	–10	–5 575
1972 Q1	5 365	1 029	289	6 679	–436	–1 851	–3 349	–146	–792	–345	–10	–6 873
Q2	5 082	829	208	6 120	–426	–2 001	–2 041	–116	–825	–300	–10	–5 662
Q3	5 342	923	282	6 548	–429	–1 970	–2 105	–108	–837	–360	–13	–5 764
Q4	5 680	1 325	119	7 126	–457	–2 170	–2 096	–123	–883	–292	–9	–5 970
1973 Q1	5 928	1 347	497	7 774	–469	–1 932	–3 518	–100	–947	–418	–11	–7 319
Q2	5 763	1 046	87	6 892	–492	–2 041	–2 269	–106	–948	–314	–13	–6 104
Q3	6 179	1 222	66	7 467	–529	–2 183	–2 530	–118	–996	–439	–14	–6 730
Q4	6 555	1 818	–208	8 167	–555	–2 354	–2 648	–102	–1 046	–342	–13	–6 983
1974 Q1	7 351	1 660	263	9 283	–592	–2 093	–4 038	–120	–1 116	–530	–9	–8 420
Q2	7 022	1 121	363	8 503	–626	–2 453	–3 074	–93	–1 125	–376	–14	–7 686
Q3	8 236	1 473	812	10 519	–653	–2 462	–3 724	–92	–1 313	–540	–17	–8 726
Q4	8 950	1 454	506	10 907	–685	–2 666	–3 862	–77	–1 446	–488	–13	–9 163
1975 Q1	9 879	1 782	1 139	12 801	–731	–2 412	–5 143	–83	–1 526	–613	–15	–10 448
Q2	9 823	1 371	631	11 832	–749	–2 886	–4 145	–66	–1 702	–506	–15	–9 987
Q3	10 727	1 549	777	13 051	–794	–3 101	–4 911	–75	–1 789	–637	–18	–11 236
Q4	11 145	1 978	569	13 689	–850	–3 301	–5 023	–85	–1 831	–531	–21	–11 547

1 See National Accounts Blue Book table 11.3 for a more detailed breakdown.

2 Excludes receipts that are netted off in the definition of General Government expenditure.

Source: Office for National Statistics; Enquiries 020 7533 5987

5.4 General government receipts and expenditure

continued

£ million, not seasonally adjusted

	General government expenditure[1]				General government receipts[2]							
	Current	Capital	Financial	Total	Gross operating surplus	Taxes on production	Taxes on income and wealth	Taxes on capital	National Insurance Contributions	Property income	Miscellaneous current transfers	Total
	ANLR	NNEX	NNEY	QYXR	-NMXV	-NMYE	-NMZL	-NMGI	-AIIH	-GZQR	-NMZX	-GZQS
1976 Q1	12 045	2 150	775	14 967	–895	–2 979	–5 802	–111	–1 851	–763	–27	–12 328
Q2	11 992	1 578	281	13 851	–917	–3 281	–5 057	–92	–2 136	–621	–27	–12 034
Q3	12 665	1 691	637	14 993	–974	–3 438	–5 192	–96	–2 192	–745	–29	–12 570
Q4	12 694	1 762	118	14 574	–987	–3 844	–5 593	–92	–2 244	–657	–27	–13 341
1977 Q1	13 571	2 086	198	15 855	–1 006	–3 330	–6 735	–90	–2 261	–867	–32	–14 215
Q2	13 407	1 448	–236	14 619	–1 026	–4 073	–5 529	–100	–2 367	–701	–34	–13 727
Q3	13 958	1 556	88	15 602	–1 057	–4 310	–5 713	–103	–2 400	–962	–37	–14 480
Q4	14 151	1 884	–245	15 790	–1 063	–4 691	–5 567	–116	–2 475	–631	–25	–14 463
1978 Q1	15 583	2 280	300	18 163	–1 111	–3 952	–7 216	–99	–2 509	–959	–35	–15 772
Q2	15 319	1 468	368	17 155	–1 140	–4 572	–6 036	–93	–2 454	–776	–38	–15 002
Q3	16 026	1 693	709	18 428	–1 172	–4 838	–6 067	–99	–2 524	–908	–37	–15 533
Q4	16 541	1 799	495	18 835	–1 216	–5 460	–6 686	–95	–2 614	–754	–32	–16 733
1979 Q1	17 474	2 147	599	20 220	–1 266	–4 860	–7 920	–96	–2 646	–1 113	–29	–17 808
Q2	17 973	1 587	644	20 204	–1 302	–5 616	–7 129	–107	–2 850	–960	–32	–17 873
Q3	18 943	1 876	877	21 696	–1 406	–6 632	–7 042	–117	–2 947	–1 139	–34	–19 189
Q4	19 710	1 950	1 194	22 854	–1 441	–7 205	–7 389	–136	–3 083	–964	–31	–20 117
1980 Q1	22 124	2 409	240	24 773	–1 532	–7 050	–10 025	–119	–3 140	–1 353	–40	–23 120
Q2	22 101	1 788	1 519	25 408	–1 599	–7 215	–7 392	–120	–3 528	–1 260	–41	–21 012
Q3	23 865	2 144	1 243	27 252	–1 634	–7 770	–9 685	–122	–3 612	–1 309	–40	–24 028
Q4	24 140	2 292	852	27 284	–1 702	–8 305	–9 317	–118	–3 659	–1 527	–37	–24 516
1981 Q1	25 999	2 591	594	29 184	–1 765	–7 836	–11 100	–504	–3 601	–1 535	–46	–26 234
Q2	26 012	1 581	1 004	28 597	–1 777	–8 447	–8 427	–99	–4 002	–1 443	–40	–24 085
Q3	27 553	1 756	958	30 267	–1 811	–9 128	–11 961	–218	–4 091	–1 602	–46	–28 706
Q4	27 053	5 314	–2 762	29 605	–1 804	–9 723	–11 006	–189	–4 222	–1 623	–34	–28 450
1982 Q1	29 070	2 490	1 151	32 711	–1 843	–9 255	–13 673	–224	–4 162	–1 857	–44	–30 898
Q2	28 684	1 397	198	30 279	–1 821	–8 726	–10 253	–143	–4 598	–1 831	–41	–27 249
Q3	29 813	1 973	1 085	32 871	–1 778	–9 446	–12 344	–159	–4 613	–1 839	–46	–30 058
Q4	29 890	3 348	–315	32 923	–1 786	–10 075	–11 553	–175	–4 722	–1 850	–43	–30 036
1983 Q1	31 791	3 527	1 126	36 444	–1 727	–9 801	–15 116	–157	–4 799	–2 082	–53	–33 568
Q2	31 165	1 808	–32	32 941	–1 719	–9 700	–10 357	–171	–5 239	–1 815	–53	–28 888
Q3	32 111	2 522	–10	34 623	–1 728	–10 364	–12 052	–172	–5 329	–1 813	–56	–31 350
Q4	32 008	2 738	–212	34 534	–1 720	–10 470	–13 635	–190	–5 413	–1 860	–46	–33 172
1984 Q1	34 603	3 816	–217	38 202	–1 699	–10 509	–15 471	–170	–5 355	–1 916	–51	–35 007
Q2	33 493	2 256	6	35 755	–1 696	–10 171	–11 474	–190	–5 512	–1 887	–53	–30 817
Q3	34 052	2 727	–116	36 663	–1 738	–11 098	–13 903	–166	–5 644	–2 047	–55	–34 488
Q4	34 992	2 926	–1 150	36 768	–1 720	–11 245	–14 072	–224	–5 811	–2 021	–44	–34 982
1985 Q1	37 922	3 770	–276	41 416	–1 975	–11 245	–17 462	–239	–5 781	–2 189	–55	–38 791
Q2	36 030	2 127	–1 805	36 352	–1 840	–10 629	–12 453	–191	–6 015	–2 340	–57	–33 367
Q3	36 044	2 810	54	38 908	–1 932	–11 608	–15 509	–253	–6 193	–2 174	–55	–37 560
Q4	37 416	2 837	130	40 383	–2 009	–12 392	–15 430	–240	–6 221	–2 178	–46	–38 344
1986 Q1	38 836	3 936	–470	42 302	–2 010	–12 082	–18 574	–240	–6 210	–1 864	–71	–40 870
Q2	37 631	2 283	–1 263	38 651	–1 957	–11 818	–13 618	–269	–6 517	–1 762	–55	–35 813
Q3	38 223	2 478	63	40 764	–2 028	–12 722	–13 917	–256	–6 655	–1 620	–65	–37 080
Q4	39 297	2 505	–2 193	39 609	–2 006	–13 654	–16 500	–260	–6 783	–1 770	–50	–40 840
1987 Q1	40 333	3 746	–545	43 534	–2 060	–13 063	–19 014	–273	–6 732	–1 823	–58	–42 841
Q2	39 995	1 989	–3 354	38 630	–1 930	–12 397	–13 954	–276	–6 736	–1 912	–63	–37 091
Q3	40 692	2 525	–1 518	41 699	–2 044	–14 119	–16 416	–272	–6 978	–1 787	–54	–41 493
Q4	41 958	2 705	–1 072	43 591	–1 996	–14 832	–17 680	–268	–7 217	–2 152	–65	–44 039
1988 Q1	43 022	4 254	631	47 907	–2 087	–14 444	–22 573	–278	–7 209	–1 947	–74	–48 446
Q2	41 460	1 976	–2 951	40 485	–2 187	–14 463	–15 313	–279	–7 567	–1 703	–60	–41 410
Q3	41 879	2 409	–1 440	42 848	–2 199	–16 143	–17 124	–275	–7 820	–1 864	–45	–45 301
Q4	45 076	2 256	–1 281	46 051	–2 176	–16 503	–20 327	–275	–8 086	–2 105	–44	–49 332
1989 Q1	44 636	4 659	213	49 508	–2 458	–15 324	–24 335	–296	–8 044	–2 164	–40	–52 449
Q2	44 917	2 378	–1 397	45 898	–2 312	–15 771	–17 082	–295	–8 388	–1 990	–58	–45 670
Q3	46 408	3 410	–196	49 622	–2 482	–16 700	–19 454	–296	–8 617	–2 238	–65	–49 623
Q4	47 329	4 231	–220	51 340	–2 537	–16 549	–24 056	–295	–8 284	–2 596	–36	–54 115
1990 Q1	48 268	9 865	–3 931	54 202	–2 603	–16 412	–25 482	–331	–8 230	–2 631	–87	–55 487
Q2	49 113	4 006	487	53 606	–2 612	–16 938	–19 871	–330	–8 556	–1 853	–70	–49 957
Q3	49 807	5 287	–2 449	52 645	–2 723	–17 597	–22 299	–330	–8 781	–2 401	–45	–53 908
Q4	52 083	6 537	–4 040	54 580	–2 601	–17 154	–25 482	–330	–8 890	–1 859	–20	–56 081

1 See National Accounts Blue Book table 11.3 for a more detailed breakdown.

2 Excludes receipts that are netted off in the definition of General Government Expenditure.

Source: Office for National Statistics; Enquiries 020 7533 5987

5.4 General government receipts and expenditure

continued

£ million, not seasonally adjusted

	General government expenditure[1]				General government receipts[2]							
	Current	Capital	Financial	Total	Gross operating surplus	Taxes on prodcution	Taxes on income and wealth	Taxes on capital	National Insurance Contributi-ons	Property income	Miscellane-ous current transfers	Total
	ANLR	NNEX	NNEY	QYXR	-NMXV	-NMYE	-NMZL	-NMGI	-AIIH	-GZQR	-NMZX	-GZQS
1991 Q1	51 703	7 419	–2 518	56 604	–2 625	–17 406	–26 416	–317	–8 779	–2 593	–46	–57 936
Q2	54 945	4 067	–2 131	56 881	–2 618	–18 807	–19 866	–316	–9 007	–1 495	–117	–51 969
Q3	55 843	4 960	–1 406	59 397	–2 723	–19 851	–21 547	–316	–9 163	–2 062	–119	–55 549
Q4	57 636	5 337	–3 344	59 629	–2 696	–21 446	–24 095	–315	–9 267	–1 528	–71	–59 212
1992 Q1	59 349	7 353	–1 169	65 533	–2 642	–19 498	–27 091	–308	–9 232	–2 354	–123	–61 003
Q2	60 874	4 067	–1 035	63 906	–2 646	–18 965	–19 115	–307	–9 244	–1 300	–16	–51 358
Q3	61 218	4 518	–2 688	63 048	–2 685	–19 508	–21 048	–307	–9 207	–1 994	–28	–54 544
Q4	62 039	5 375	–1 252	66 162	–2 646	–20 784	–23 267	–306	–9 292	–1 225	–11	–57 302
1993 Q1	63 337	8 546	–1 663	70 220	–2 610	–19 529	–25 605	–320	–9 243	–2 125	–96	–59 374
Q2	64 015	4 200	–857	67 358	–2 675	–19 574	–18 776	–320	–9 939	–1 108	–81	–52 247
Q3	63 526	4 362	–1 906	65 982	–2 658	–20 357	–21 070	–320	–10 062	–1 905	–49	–56 190
Q4	67 131	4 356	360	71 847	–2 777	–22 306	–23 375	–318	–10 023	–1 044	–70	–59 676
1994 Q1	67 123	7 596	–1 254	73 465	–2 835	–20 885	–26 069	–360	–10 118	–2 467	–79	–62 613
Q2	67 282	3 803	–583	70 502	–2 736	–21 550	–20 358	–360	–10 515	–983	–102	–56 401
Q3	67 432	4 495	–1 769	70 158	–2 777	–21 928	–23 565	–360	–10 734	–2 006	–125	–61 282
Q4	70 301	4 796	–1 795	73 302	–2 819	–24 385	–26 492	–359	–10 719	–1 077	–114	–65 743
1995 Q1	69 867	9 164	–2 842	76 189	–2 925	–22 125	–29 038	–361	–10 888	–2 592	–142	–67 927
Q2	70 187	3 753	305	74 245	–2 851	–23 770	–22 353	–361	–11 065	–1 185	–109	–61 534
Q3	70 909	4 469	58	75 436	–2 876	–23 483	–24 873	–361	–11 188	–2 051	–113	–64 769
Q4	74 013	4 860	–50	78 823	–2 918	–24 632	–30 718	–358	–11 230	–1 344	–105	–71 116
1996 Q1	72 130	6 993	–2 667	76 456	–2 941	–24 040	–30 902	–410	–11 492	–2 972	–130	–72 740
Q2	73 420	3 660	–2 395	74 685	–2 996	–25 090	–21 493	–410	–11 392	–1 108	–73	–62 400
Q3	73 864	3 805	–2 357	75 312	–3 197	–25 368	–26 342	–410	–11 673	–1 947	–76	–68 845
Q4	76 594	3 234	–231	79 597	–3 171	–26 155	–33 350	–407	–11 843	–1 253	–150	–76 157
1997 Q1	74 590	5 922	–535	79 977	–3 072	–25 314	–34 402	–353	–12 213	–2 445	–217	–77 854
Q2	75 368	2 504	–1 508	76 364	–3 099	–27 616	–22 349	–415	–12 577	–1 067	–77	–67 041
Q3	75 989	3 151	–613	78 527	–3 092	–27 631	–28 534	–432	–12 814	–1 821	–100	–74 268
Q4	77 809	3 574	507	81 890	–3 213	–29 034	–35 924	–401	–13 002	–1 317	–82	–82 814
1998 Q1	76 884	5 681	–327	82 238	–3 231	–26 987	–43 667	–436	–13 224	–2 631	–164	–90 340
Q2	77 204	2 470	23	79 697	–3 286	–28 781	–25 099	–441	–13 401	–1 032	–65	–72 105
Q3	77 933	3 216	–33	81 116	–3 337	–29 722	–32 637	–485	–13 680	–1 717	–72	–81 650
Q4	80 758	3 553	644	84 955	–3 286	–29 448	–38 855	–432	–13 968	–1 333	–89	–87 411
1999 Q1	77 242	5 404	–346	82 300	–3 261	–29 277	–42 736	–445	–14 114	–2 511	–64	–92 408
Q2	78 864	2 247	193	81 304	–3 221	–30 364	–27 575	–494	–13 935	–882	–51	–76 522
Q3	80 599	3 416	306	84 321	–3 321	–31 420	–36 358	–536	–14 096	–1 435	–86	–87 252
Q4	84 192	3 679	1 134	89 005	–3 298	–33 348	–38 744	–469	–14 257	–1 146	–68	–91 330
2000 Q1	80 184	4 874	–521	84 537	–3 371	–31 734	–48 214	–546	–14 402	–1 392	–120	–99 779

1 See National Accounts Blue Book 11.3 for a more detailed breakdown.

2 Excludes receipts that are netted off in the definition of General Government Expenditure.

Source: Office for National Statistics; Enquiries 020 7533 5987

5.5 Financial transactions of the public sector[1]

£ million, not seasonally adjusted

	Surplus on current budget[2]		Net investment		Net borrowing[4]		Net cash requirement	
	General Government	Public Sector[3]	General Government	Public sector	General government	Public sector	General Government	Public Sector
	ANLW	ANMU	-ANNV	-ANNW	NNBK	ANNX	RUUS	RURQ
1963	586	575	1 377	1 330	–791	–755	324	789
1964	938	906	1 242	1 790	–304	–884	412	982
1965	1 068	1 197	1 710	1 938	–642	–741	439	1 128
1966	1 406	1 464	1 359	2 257	47	–794	145	987
1967	1 491	1 518	1 846	2 915	–355	–1 398	709	1 846
1968	2 145	2 228	2 307	3 089	–162	–861	197	1 263
1969	3 485	3 496	3 705	2 963	–220	533	–1 213	–527
1970	4 084	3 864	2 766	3 137	1 318	729	–1 209	–219
1971	3 509	3 161	2 662	3 414	847	–252	7	1 196
1972	1 888	1 576	2 963	3 055	–1 075	–1 479	858	1 829
1973	1 634	1 343	4 045	3 974	–2 411	–2 631	2 898	4 069
1974	1 054	241	4 024	4 768	–2 970	–4 526	5 003	6 253
1975	–139	–1 322	4 556	5 974	–4 695	–7 293	7 743	10 015
1976	–1 224	–1 729	4 684	6 459	–5 908	–8 191	6 399	8 911
1977	–557	–1 112	4 203	4 771	–4 760	–5 883	4 029	5 596
1978	–3 087	–3 545	4 130	4 692	–7 217	–8 237	7 179	8 262
1979	–2 290	–3 674	3 878	4 749	–6 168	–8 423	8 939	12 750
1980	–3 541	–5 063	4 071	4 999	–7 612	–10 062	9 042	11 412
1981	–3 678	–4 549	6 101	2 903	–9 779	–7 452	10 671	10 573
1982	–3 894	–4 062	3 871	3 600	–7 765	–7 662	4 104	5 347
1983	–4 958	–4 121	5 075	6 195	–10 033	–10 316	10 089	11 128
1984	–6 919	–7 718	6 004	5 502	–12 923	–13 220	8 894	10 197
1985	–4 821	–5 275	5 424	5 066	–10 245	–10 341	8 003	7 625
1986	–5 238	–5 108	4 618	3 374	–9 856	–8 482	3 482	2 630
1987	–3 787	–4 600	3 985	1 759	–7 772	–6 359	–12	–1 172
1988	6 040	5 731	3 202	1 082	2 838	4 649	–9 580	–11 462
1989	10 617	8 995	5 823	4 018	4 794	4 977	–8 892	–9 131
1990	7 835	4 929	16 283	7 367	–8 448	–2 438	3 659	–1 298
1991	–3 792	–7 065	12 511	9 098	–16 303	–16 163	7 820	7 003
1992	–27 088	–29 732	12 556	11 026	–39 644	–40 758	28 213	28 623
1993	–38 217	–40 178	12 921	10 796	–51 138	–50 974	44 068	43 202
1994	–33 913	–36 198	12 038	9 740	–45 951	–45 938	40 271	39 342
1995	–28 174	–29 204	13 033	9 336	–41 207	–38 540	36 916	35 446
1996	–24 968	–25 514	7 941	5 451	–32 909	–30 965	27 678	24 778
1997	–11 242	–11 830	5 052	3 825	–16 294	–15 655	13 402	11 851
1998	8 253	7 385	4 443	4 273	3 810	3 112	–6 404	–6 395
1999	15 698	14 411	3 863	3 264	11 835	11 147	–2 117	–1 751
1963 Q1	899	912	172	232	727	678	–710	–610
Q2	–116	–50	232	329	–348	–376	383	386
Q3	–69	–175	268	390	–337	–566	231	457
Q4	–128	–112	705	379	–833	–491	420	556
1964 Q1	882	864	299	437	583	425	–548	–410
Q2	–40	18	298	420	–338	–402	333	377
Q3	62	–13	321	465	–259	–478	296	505
Q4	34	37	324	468	–290	–429	331	510
1965 Q1	1 020	1 049	291	504	729	541	–647	–478
Q2	–24	79	269	447	–293	–365	435	506
Q3	82	1	301	486	–219	–485	221	491
Q4	–10	68	849	501	–859	–432	430	609
1966 Q1	1 230	1 257	330	547	900	709	–835	–684
Q2	33	118	309	504	–276	–384	395	474
Q3	159	33	338	588	–179	–555	210	542
Q4	–16	56	382	618	–398	–564	375	655
1967 Q1	1 185	1 223	418	719	767	502	–684	–505
Q2	176	222	410	666	–234	–443	460	621
Q3	171	–26	469	735	–298	–761	301	823
Q4	–41	99	549	795	–590	–696	632	907
1968 Q1	1 060	1 087	631	874	429	208	–626	–330
Q2	208	255	524	719	–316	–463	418	537
Q3	353	247	537	747	–184	–498	197	561
Q4	524	639	615	749	–91	–108	208	495
1969 Q1	1 454	1 511	613	758	841	750	–1 341	–1 217
Q2	637	636	516	634	121	4	–148	–87
Q3	638	565	597	740	41	–174	–42	211
Q4	756	784	1 979	831	–1 223	–47	318	566

1 National Accounts entities as defined under the European System of Accounts 1995 (ESA95).
2 Net saving, plus capital taxes.
3 Gross fixed capital formation, plus payments less receipts, of investment grants less depreciation.
4 Net borrowing = surplus on current budget minus net investmment.

Source: Office for National Statistics; Enquiries 020 7533 5984

5.5 Financial transactions of the public sector[1]

continued

£ million, not seasonally adjusted

	Surplus on current budget[2]		Net investment		Net borrowing		Net cash requirement	
	General government	Public Sector	General Government	Public Sector	General Government	Public sector	General Government	Public Sector
	ANLW	ANMU	-ANNV	-ANNW	NNBK	ANNX	RUUS	RURQ
1970 Q1	1 825	1 798	607	730	1 218	1 064	–1 603	–1 458
Q2	867	847	547	712	320	137	–8	136
Q3	758	627	639	803	119	–173	–38	305
Q4	634	592	973	892	–339	–299	440	798
1971 Q1	1 742	1 639	775	1 007	967	632	–881	–584
Q2	806	715	587	735	219	–19	86	294
Q3	524	398	631	824	–107	–425	263	590
Q4	437	409	669	848	–232	–440	539	896
1972 Q1	1 295	1 118	760	839	535	275	–992	–930
Q2	358	302	550	711	–192	–408	430	736
Q3	190	44	633	746	–443	–701	476	775
Q4	45	112	1 020	759	–975	–645	944	1 248
1973 Q1	1 146	1 023	1 026	1 184	120	–159	–559	–310
Q2	81	86	707	838	–626	–756	1 264	1 392
Q3	273	49	865	1 005	–592	–956	1 205	1 610
Q4	134	185	1 447	947	–1 313	–760	988	1 377
1974 Q1	758	433	1 271	1 299	–513	–857	–296	–142
Q2	331	226	713	863	–382	–640	1 767	1 950
Q3	134	–195	1 042	1 275	–908	–1 472	1 040	1 538
Q4	–169	–223	998	1 331	–1 167	–1 557	2 492	2 907
1975 Q1	157	–354	1 295	1 671	–1 138	–2 024	679	1 446
Q2	–272	–499	853	1 198	–1 125	–1 690	2 350	2 852
Q3	52	–503	1 003	1 447	–951	–1 952	2 105	2 662
Q4	–76	34	1 405	1 658	–1 481	–1 627	2 609	3 055
1976 Q1	–213	–490	1 554	2 058	–1 767	–2 551	947	1 488
Q2	–477	–601	962	1 386	–1 439	–1 987	2 165	2 550
Q3	–633	–1 003	1 057	1 480	–1 690	–2 483	1 622	2 418
Q4	99	365	1 111	1 535	–1 012	–1 170	1 665	2 455
1977 Q1	83	–68	1 419	1 538	–1 336	–1 606	751	893
Q2	–261	–341	764	942	–1 025	–1 283	1 627	1 869
Q3	–76	–541	856	1 130	–932	–1 671	428	1 031
Q4	–303	–162	1 164	1 161	–1 467	–1 323	1 223	1 803
1978 Q1	–442	–651	1 540	1 494	–1 982	–2 145	1 055	1 002
Q2	–973	–1 000	705	933	–1 678	–1 933	1 911	1 924
Q3	–1 170	–1 571	904	1 133	–2 074	–2 704	1 958	2 618
Q4	–502	–323	981	1 132	–1 483	–1 455	2 255	2 718
1979 Q1	–395	–764	1 296	1 389	–1 691	–2 153	864	1 583
Q2	–869	–1 203	695	817	–1 564	–2 020	2 926	3 456
Q3	–568	–1 277	934	1 310	–1 502	–2 587	2 579	3 910
Q4	–458	–430	953	1 233	–1 411	–1 663	2 570	3 801
1980 Q1	77	–18	1 351	1 717	–1 274	–1 735	–940	–1 187
Q2	–2 063	–2 650	671	729	–2 734	–3 379	3 691	4 674
Q3	–863	–1 759	974	1 378	–1 837	–3 137	2 953	3 829
Q4	–692	–636	1 075	1 175	–1 767	–1 811	3 338	4 096
1981 Q1	–864	–1 173	1 339	1 406	–2 203	–2 579	1 294	–341
Q2	–3 056	–3 234	302	356	–3 358	–3 590	7 460	7 926
Q3	6	–656	458	637	–452	–1 293	1 936	2 484
Q4	236	514	4 002	504	–3 766	10	–19	504
1982 Q1	667	699	1 169	1 343	–502	–644	–3 003	–2 245
Q2	–2 600	–2 694	68	304	–2 668	–2 998	3 269	2 914
Q3	–926	–1 473	635	909	–1 561	–2 382	1 055	1 910
Q4	–1 035	–594	1 999	1 044	–3 034	–1 638	2 783	2 768
1983 Q1	581	1 008	2 164	2 499	–1 583	–1 491	822	1 414
Q2	–3 486	–3 210	433	785	–3 919	–3 995	3 630	3 271
Q3	–1 982	–2 539	1 137	1 445	–3 119	–3 984	3 391	3 664
Q4	–71	620	1 341	1 466	–1 412	–846	2 246	2 779
1984 Q1	–838	–479	2 410	2 236	–3 248	–2 715	66	73
Q2	–3 929	–4 317	837	455	–4 766	–4 772	5 169	4 778
Q3	–838	–1 632	1 290	1 249	–2 128	–2 881	2 781	3 014
Q4	–1 314	–1 290	1 467	1 562	–2 781	–2 852	976	2 433

1 National accounts entities as defined under the European System of Accounts 1995 (ESA95).
2 Net saving, plus capital taxes.
3 Gross fixedcapital formation, plus payments less receipts, of investment grants less depreciation.
4 Net borrowing = surplus on current budget minus net investment.

Source: Office for National Statistics; Enquiries 020 7533 5984

5.5 Financial transactions of the public sector[1]

continued

£ million, not seasonally adjusted

	Surplus on current budget[2]		Net investment[3]		Net borrowing[4]		Net cash requirement	
	General Government	Public Sector	General Government	Public Sector	General Government	Public Sector	General Government	Public sector
	ANLW	ANMU	-ANNV	-ANNW	NNBK	ANNX	RUUS	RURQ
1985 Q1	–461	–973	2 285	2 219	–2 746	–3 192	104	19
Q2	–4 019	–4 258	613	376	–4 632	–4 634	3 181	2 752
Q3	136	–17	1 266	1 391	–1 130	–1 408	3 082	2 837
Q4	–477	–27	1 260	1 080	–1 737	–1 107	1 636	2 017
1986 Q1	607	716	2 328	1 967	–1 721	–1 251	–1 812	–1 832
Q2	–3 270	–3 258	648	274	–3 918	–3 532	2 970	2 484
Q3	–2 619	–3 080	819	691	–3 438	–3 771	3 826	3 607
Q4	44	514	823	442	–779	72	–1 502	–1 629
1987 Q1	988	592	2 044	1 489	–1 056	–897	–536	–913
Q2	–4 455	–4 797	261	–491	–4 716	–4 306	1 862	1 388
Q3	–780	–1 040	767	458	–1 547	–1 498	698	449
Q4	460	645	913	303	–453	342	–2 036	–2 096
1988 Q1	3 754	3 448	2 418	2 026	1 336	1 422	–2 229	–2 955
Q2	–1 776	–1 928	88	–494	–1 864	–1 434	–1 375	–1 668
Q3	1 641	1 517	459	–21	1 182	1 538	–1 925	–2 133
Q4	2 421	2 694	237	–429	2 184	3 123	–4 051	–4 706
1989 Q1	5 895	5 937	2 529	2 186	3 366	3 751	–5 193	–5 964
Q2	–1 215	–1 813	184	–254	–1 399	–1 559	233	–16
Q3	1 197	482	1 163	678	34	–196	–1 122	–306
Q4	4 740	4 389	1 947	1 408	2 793	2 981	–2 810	–2 845
1990 Q1	5 172	4 603	7 529	3 906	–2 357	697	717	–3 738
Q2	–1 233	–2 095	1 656	312	–2 889	–2 407	5 940	6 069
Q3	2 010	988	2 928	1 326	–918	–338	184	–474
Q4	1 886	1 433	4 170	1 823	–2 284	–390	–3 182	–3 155
1991 Q1	4 146	2 851	5 086	3 738	–940	–887	–2 703	–3 226
Q2	–5 047	–5 664	1 739	1 047	–6 786	–6 711	6 806	7 017
Q3	–2 378	–3 084	2 644	2 000	–5 022	–5 084	3 727	3 543
Q4	–513	–1 168	3 042	2 313	–3 555	–3 481	–10	–331
1992 Q1	–330	–1 268	5 124	4 764	–5 454	–6 032	2 897	3 627
Q2	–11 481	–11 986	1 867	1 674	–13 348	–13 660	10 610	10 533
Q3	–8 616	–9 453	2 343	2 001	–10 959	–11 454	8 317	7 954
Q4	–6 661	–7 025	3 222	2 587	–9 883	–9 612	6 389	6 509
1993 Q1	–5 952	–7 233	6 403	5 571	–12 355	–12 804	11 261	11 184
Q2	–13 678	–13 670	2 064	1 703	–15 742	–15 373	13 338	13 494
Q3	–9 237	–9 923	2 230	1 913	–11 467	–11 836	11 092	10 777
Q4	–9 350	–9 352	2 224	1 609	–11 574	–10 961	8 377	7 747
1994 Q1	–6 444	–8 025	5 462	4 626	–11 906	–12 651	13 263	14 144
Q2	–12 825	–12 950	1 656	1 165	–14 481	–14 115	12 819	12 158
Q3	–8 107	–8 781	2 325	1 875	–10 432	–10 656	9 629	9 292
Q4	–6 537	–6 442	2 595	2 074	–9 132	–8 516	4 560	3 748
1995 Q1	–4 037	–5 779	6 923	4 211	–10 960	–9 990	11 088	11 490
Q2	–10 776	–10 341	1 470	1 090	–12 246	–11 431	11 713	11 393
Q3	–8 289	–8 249	2 144	1 924	–10 433	–10 173	9 771	9 051
Q4	–5 072	–4 835	2 496	2 111	–7 568	–6 946	4 344	3 512
1996 Q1	–1 642	–2 770	4 594	3 785	–6 236	–6 555	8 661	7 529
Q2	–13 287	–12 851	1 231	664	–14 518	–13 515	11 247	10 470
Q3	–7 305	–7 463	1 351	839	–8 656	–8 302	6 537	5 984
Q4	–2 734	–2 430	765	163	–3 499	–2 593	1 233	795
1997 Q1	952	–313	3 448	3 008	–2 496	–3 321	5 135	5 479
Q2	–10 665	–10 381	7	–432	–10 672	–9 949	8 669	8 134
Q3	–4 102	–4 231	614	585	–4 716	–4 816	1 488	613
Q4	2 573	3 095	983	664	1 590	2 431	–1 890	–2 375
1998 Q1	10 858	9 816	3 083	2 982	7 775	6 834	–6 437	–5 260
Q2	–7 720	–7 457	–151	–319	–7 569	–7 138	6 256	5 435
Q3	1 086	855	585	608	501	247	–2 462	–2 806
Q4	4 029	4 171	926	1 002	3 103	3 169	–3 761	–3 764
1999 Q1	12 483	11 341	2 721	2 704	9 762	8 637	–6 607	–5 825
Q2	–5 042	–4 897	–461	–682	–4 581	–4 215	5 588	5 330
Q3	3 910	3 739	683	573	3 227	3 166	–3 104	–3 190
Q4	4 347	4 228	920	669	3 427	3 559	2 006	1 934
2000 Q1	18 058	16 847	2 079	2 025	15 979	14 822	–14 189	–12 764

1 National accounts entities as defined under the European System of Accounts 1995 (ESA95).
2 Net saving, plus capital taxes.
3 Gross capital formation, plus payments less receipts, of investment grants less depreciation.
4 Net borrowing = surplus on current bbudget minus net investment.

Sources: Office for National Statistics; Enquiries 020 7533 5984;
Enquiries 020 7533 5984

5.6 UK banks' loans, advances and acceptances to UK residents[1,2,12]

£ million

	Manufacturing	Other production	Financial	Services	Persons	Total loans, advances and acceptances
Amounts outstanding						
	BALH	BALI	BALJ	BALK	BALL	BALG
1986 Dec	29 648	16 184	55 504	53 410	48 323	203 069
1987 Mar	30 205	16 952	60 279	54 886	50 331	212 654
Jun	29 001	18 441	66 195	57 844	53 838	225 319
Sep	29 597	18 025	69 046	60 086	58 370	235 124
Dec	29 900	17 480	69 532	63 132	62 854	242 899
1988 Mar	31 455	18 291	69 188	68 693	65 969	253 596
Jun	33 814	19 065	70 284	73 058	70 350	266 571
Sep	38 589	20 027	75 727	78 762	75 928	289 033
Dec	40 688	21 265	80 754	84 169	78 120	304 996
1989 Mar	42 112	22 799	88 828	93 027	80 324	327 089
Jun	45 139	24 048	93 926	99 823	84 396	347 332
Sep	49 728	26 308	97 982	107 622	114 462	396 101
Dec	51 175	26 653	103 654	115 252	116 929	413 663
1990 Mar	53 435	28 126	106 412	118 698	119 369	426 039
Jun	53 866	28 668	109 064	122 869	122 694	437 161
Sep	53 371	29 228	108 716	124 523	125 112	440 951
Dec	54 291	29 451	111 396	129 242	127 232	451 611
1991 Mar	54 115	30 495	116 222	131 952	128 173	460 957
Jun	53 942	30 289	122 653	132 647	129 787	469 318
Sep	52 357	29 973	122 365	131 139	132 474	468 308
Dec	51 586	30 279	130 296	130 856	133 659	476 677
1992 Mar	51 413	30 317	106 724	129 110	134 348	451 911
Jun	49 131	30 388	107 086	128 207	135 758	450 570
Sep	48 253	30 538	105 844	124 744	138 316	447 695
Dec	50 196	32 606	113 035	132 747	139 055	467 639
1993 Mar	47 431	31 379	118 039	130 358	140 755	467 962
Jun	45 226	30 392	121 656	128 758	143 188	469 220
Sep	44 169	30 584	124 342	126 390	146 498	471 983
Dec	44 215	29 881	132 767	124 024	148 530	479 415
1994 Mar	42 499	29 170	137 207	119 153	149 905	477 934
Jun	40 647	27 666	135 381	116 829	152 033	472 556
Sep	40 501	27 044	137 220	115 795	154 911	475 472
Dec	40 873	26 673	144 071	117 674	158 331	487 621
1995 Mar	48 457	27 174	148 500	116 691	160 300	501 122
Jun	45 500	25 508	150 450	119 110	163 369	503 937
Sep	45 467	26 210	150 243	121 448	183 559	526 927
Dec[3]	47 351	27 942	138 776	122 672	186 998	523 739
1996 Mar	48 829	28 950	139 991	125 322	188 743	531 835
Jun	49 833	27 889	140 681	125 906	191 998	536 307
Sep	50 412	29 210	145 674	126 807	205 947	558 050
Dec	50 697	28 946	145 017	128 902	210 099	563 662
1997 Mar	49 976	29 752	165 011	128 401	213 414	586 554

1 In these statistics lending flows are generally calculated as changes in reported amounts outstanding; they are thus potentially distorted by revaluations (eg write-offs). The Bank has used published data and certain other information provided by the banks to make adjustments to lending flows from 1986 to remove these distortions. Up to end-1992, these adjustments are believed to be broadly accurate on an annual basis but have been allocated to individual quarters purely by averaging the annual figure. Because the adjustments have **not** been carried through to all individual industrial categories, the sum of the individual categories does not add exactly to the total changes. 'Unallocated adjustments' overleaf account for the difference. The individual categories that have been adjusted for write-offs are *persons*; in Q3 1995 only, £0.4 bn of write-offs were additionally allocated to *financial*; and in Q4 1995 only, £0.3 bn of write-offs were additionally allocated to *services*. From 1993, the write-off adjustments are on quarterly data reported by the banks for broad sectoral categories.

2 For a more detailed breakdown of these figures see *Financial Statistics* Table 4.2E. The analysis which is not seasonally adjusted covers loans, advances and acceptances and holdings of sterling commercial paper in both sterling and foreign currencies (changes in the latter being adjusted for exchange rate movements) provided by banks to their customers and therefore does not include funds placed through the local authority money market or funds lent to banks. Lending under reverse repos is also excluded under this analysis. Acceptances are not granted to persons.

3 At end-December 1995, the reporting of data on sale and repurchasing agreements was changed to bring it into line with the internationally agreed conventions. The net effect was to deflate the outstanding amount of bank lending to *financial* covered in this analysis by £16.6 bn; the change in lending to this category in Q4 1995 has been adjusted to remove this effect. In Q1 1996, four discount houses each absorbed a Stock Exchange money broker ("SEMB"). This led to an inflation of the discount houses' balance sheets and to other banks reclassifying their lending to the four SEMBs from *financial* to *banks* (which latter are outside the scope of this analysis). The change in lending to *financial* in Q1 1996 has been adjusted by £1.1 bn to remove these effects.

Source: Bank of England; Enquiries 020 7601 5360

5.6 UK banks' loans, advances and acceptances to UK residents[1,2,12]

continued

£ million

	Manufacturing	Other production	Financial	Services	Persons	Total loans, advances and acceptances
Changes[4,5,6,7,8,9,10,11]						
	FRAB	FRAC	FRAD	FRAE	FRAF	FRAA
1986 Dec	1 193	–570	2 715	–6 555	57	146
1987 Mar	880	950	6 139	2 020	2 087	12 141
Jun	–976	1 614	6 999	3 366	3 583	14 664
Sep	571	–418	2 698	2 188	4 600	9 740
Dec	796	–265	3 217	4 010	4 575	12 386
1988 Mar	1 397	731	–1 145	5 234	3 190	9 507
Jun	2 507	863	1 982	4 695	4 468	14 582
Sep	4 311	785	3 736	4 879	5 644	19 464
Dec	2 603	1 419	5 223	6 252	3 789	19 344
1989 Mar	1 051	1 411	6 714	8 246	2 361	19 897
Jun	2 202	1 019	2 806	5 657	3 890	15 712
Sep	4 467	2 126	4 613	7 497	2 779	21 577
Dec	1 035	247	4 228	7 130	2 765	15 508
1990 Mar	3 215	1 720	5 151	4 600	2 611	17 579
Jun	286	507	2 331	4 020	3 454	10 921
Sep	929	911	3 098	3 179	2 330	10 726
Dec	1 046	256	2 979	4 837	2 349	11 782
1991 Mar	–301	996	4 467	2 573	1 228	9 755
Jun	–1 341	–547	3 393	–556	1 756	3 521
Sep	–1 745	–377	–743	–1 578	2 974	–678
Dec	–441	405	8 446	299	1 946	11 435
1992 Mar	269	87	2 522	–1 341	1 075	3 883
Jun	–1 803	248	1 613	–236	1 815	2 758
Sep	–338	326	414	–2 709	2 962	1 922
Dec	–632	813	1 903	4 694	688	8 520
1993 Mar	–2 888	–1 136	4 936	–2 319	2 042	2 125
Jun	–2 146	–958	3 713	–1 502	2 848	3 037
Sep	–1 150	165	2 486	–2 482	3 643	3 379
Dec	–840	–1 037	8 390	–2 917	2 146	6 990
1994 Mar	–1 464	–393	3 433	–4 769	1 738	–367
Jun	–1 402	–1 347	–788	–1 671	2 412	–1 201
Sep	–16	–554	2 264	–767	3 193	4 915
Dec	331	–390	4 944	1 812	3 354	10 915
1995 Mar	7 527	347	4 631	–835	2 155	14 626
Jun	–3 356	–228	908	531	3 328	1 839
Sep	102	715	1 520	2 472	3 917	9 522
Dec[3]	1 650	1 658	4 328	1 311	3 999	14 054
1996 Mar	1 413	983	1 139	2 386	2 145	8 614
Jun	988	–942	2 088	908	3 621	7 285
Sep	997	1 358	5 412	655	3 500	12 410
Dec	1 385	76	4 032	3 532	4 500	14 187
1997 Mar	–878	744	17 783	–664	3 329	20 931

Footnotes 1-3 as page 269.

4 Changes in total lending in the three months to end August 1989 exclude data from Abbey National plc and Abbey National Treasury Services plc which joined the reporting population at the beginning of July 1989. The levels for August 1989 include data for these two institutions.

5 At end-March 1993, the industrial analysis moved onto an end calendar quarter basis. The analysis of the period to end-March 1993 therefore covers four months and the changes are not directly comparable with those previously published.

6 New conditions for netting were introduced at the end of December 1993. The initial effect was to reduce the amount of netting (and so increase lending reported as outstanding at end-December to approximately £2.5 billion). Over the subsequent two quarters banks adjusted their practices to the new conditions and netting increased by approximately £1.7 billion. The flows in the appropriate sub-sectors of the categories affected have been adjusted.

7 Cheltenham and Gloucester plc became part of the Lloyds Bank Group on 1 August 1995. As a result of this, total bank lending was boosted by £17 billion. Flows in 1995 Q3 have been adjusted for the change in the sectors' population; levels have not been adjusted.

8 At end-December 1995, the reporting of data on sale and repurchase agreements was changed to bring it in line with internationally agreed national accounting conventions. The net effect was to deflate total bank lending to Financial institutions covered by this analysis by £16.6 billion. Flows data have been adjusted to remove the effects of these changes.

9 In 1996 Q1, four discount houses each absorbed a Stock Exchange money broker. This led to an inflation of the discount houses' balance sheets and to other banks reclassifying their lending to four SEMB's from financial to banks (which latter are outside the scope of this analysis). The 1996 Q1 flows for financial have been adjusted by £1.1 billion to remove these effects.

10 In 1996 Q3, the business of National & Provincial Building Society was transferred to Abbey National plc. Flows data have been adjusted to reflect this change to the banking sector and for other banks reclassifying lending to this institution.

11 In 1997 Q1, changes in the reporting population accounted for an increase of £2.9 billion in the level of total sterling lending. Of this, some £2.2 billion was attributed to the effects of initial group restructuring, which has been adjusted from the flows.

12 These figures fall outside the scope of National Statistics.

Source: Bank of England; Enquiries 020 7601 5360

5.7 Consumer credit and other household sector borrowing

£ million

	Consumer credit								
		of which							
	Total consumer credit[1]	credit cards[1,2]	other[1,2]	Banks[1]	Building Societies' Class 3 Loans	Other specialist lenders	Retailers	Insurance companies	Loans secured on dwellings (NSA[1])
Amounts outstanding: quarterly									
	VZRI	VZRJ	VZRK	VRVV	VZRG	VZRH	RLBO	VZQZ	AMWT
1987 Q1	31 692	5 215	26 477	25 190	10	3 744	1 906	842	159 861
Q2	33 067	5 375	27 692	26 277	10	3 971	1 959	850	166 974
Q3	34 480	5 496	28 984	27 453	15	4 114	2 010	888	175 281
Q4	36 290	5 832	30 458	28 944	81	4 275	2 076	914	183 520
1988 Q1	38 046	5 977	32 069	30 489	124	4 422	2 082	929	191 689
Q2	39 502	6 137	33 365	31 844	174	4 386	2 140	958	202 092
Q3	41 464	6 321	35 143	33 565	238	4 498	2 192	971	214 600
Q4	42 678	6 493	36 185	34 520	296	4 603	2 274	985	223 657
1989 Q1	44 392	6 472	37 920	36 056	381	4 678	2 279	998	231 122
Q2	46 104	6 688	39 416	37 474	453	4 870	2 291	1 016	239 784
Q3	47 708	6 873	40 835	38 768	531	5 059	2 323	1 027	248 893
Q4	48 598	7 027	41 571	39 429	592	5 237	2 292	1 048	257 746
1990 Q1	49 936	7 412	42 524	40 257	661	5 594	2 335	1 089	265 516
Q2	50 957	7 601	43 356	41 062	730	5 698	2 343	1 124	277 735
Q3	51 948	8 071	43 877	41 832	769	5 831	2 344	1 172	286 615
Q4	53 012	8 755	44 257	42 887	784	5 780	2 356	1 205	294 743
1991 Q1	53 043	8 576	44 467	42 879	767	5 784	2 389	1 224	301 025
Q2	53 525	8 910	44 615	43 347	755	5 768	2 411	1 244	308 068
Q3	53 823	9 264	44 559	43 863	736	5 595	2 383	1 246	315 080
Q4	54 026	9 495	44 531	43 750	735	5 876	2 393	1 272	320 252
1992 Q1	53 938	9 500	44 438	43 752	732	5 764	2 397	1 293	324 738
Q2	53 432	9 573	43 859	43 446	703	5 559	2 423	1 301	329 898
Q3	53 465	9 766	43 699	43 689	759	5 279	2 428	1 310	336 300
Q4	53 188	9 723	43 465	43 317	739	5 426	2 406	1 300	339 022
1993 Q1	51 615	9 866	41 749	41 683	729	5 454	2 406	1 343	342 832
Q2	51 718	9 795	41 923	41 536	722	5 686	2 390	1 384	348 671
Q3	52 235	9 908	42 327	41 518	777	6 077	2 440	1 423	353 243
Q4	52 974	10 224	42 750	41 535	769	6 736	2 469	1 465	357 338
1994 Q1	53 479	10 354	43 125	41 703	774	7 099	2 482	1 421	361 518
Q2	54 649	10 685	43 964	42 245	1 063	7 442	2 524	1 375	366 282
Q3	55 836	11 047	44 789	43 039	1 069	7 932	2 477	1 319	371 434
Q4	57 617	11 385	46 232	44 546	1 105	8 124	2 550	1 292	375 885
1995 Q1	62 150	12 091	50 059	45 924	1 139	11 270	2 527	1 290	379 385
Q2	63 594	12 573	51 021	46 973	1 192	11 630	2 492	1 307	383 500
Q3	65 379	12 717	52 662	47 989	1 160	12 394	2 513	1 323	388 261
Q4	67 624	13 207	54 417	49 493	1 240	13 145	2 414	1 332	390 441
1996 Q1	69 448	13 789	55 659	50 844	1 347	13 498	2 430	1 329	393 786
Q2	71 449	14 219	57 230	51 939	1 446	14 336	2 422	1 306	399 014
Q3	74 685	14 939	59 746	53 657	1 407	15 829	2 472	1 320	403 976
Q4	76 861	15 434	61 427	55 231	1 479	16 411	2 483	1 257	409 451
1997 Q1	79 348	16 160	63 188	57 234	1 527	16 859	2 482	1 246	414 973
Q2	82 108	16 841	65 267	60 760	350	17 248	2 506	1 244	420 902
Q3	84 169	17 366	66 803	62 271	258	17 882	2 525	1 233	426 124
Q4	87 490	18 159	69 331	64 629	234	18 740	2 630	1 257	430 612
1998 Q1	92 101	19 317	72 784	66 745	232	21 242	2 637	1 245	435 606
Q2	95 283	20 500	74 783	69 575	197	21 605	2 666	1 240	442 040
Q3	98 584	21 459	77 125	72 174	184	22 313	2 672	1 241	449 629
Q4	101 663	22 323	79 340	73 077	303	24 413	2 626	1 244	456 790
1999 Q1	105 600	28 223	77 377	75 520	300	25 865	2 668	1 247	463 366
Q2	108 122	29 557	78 565	77 628	321	26 268	2 673	1 232	472 798
Q3	111 513	30 642	80 871	80 320	332	26 997	2 679	1 185	484 409
Q4	114 867	32 041	82 826	82 726	309	27 957	2 710	1 165	493 967
2000 Q1	118 198	33 097	85 101	85 759	317	28 360	2 619	1 144	503 526
Q2	120 961	34 687	86 274	88 550	322	28 355	2 605	1 129	..

1 These figures fall outside the scope of National Statistics.
2 Data have been revised from January 1999 onwards due to the availability of a more accurate breakdown between credit card and 'other lending'.

Credit card lending by other specialist lenders can now be separately identified and is included for the first time within the credit card component. There has been a switch between credit card lending and 'other' consumer credit. Hence, data from January 1999 onwards are not directly comparable with earlier periods.

Sources: Bank of England; Enquiries Columns 1-5, 9 020 7601 5468; Office for National Statistics; Enquiries Columns 6-8 020 7 533 6046

5.8 Analysis of bank lending to UK residents[1,2,4] Amounts outstanding

£ million, not seasonally adjusted

	Manufacturing[3]	Other production	Financial	Services	Persons	Total loans, advances and acceptances
Total Loans, Advances, Acceptances and Sterling Commercial paper						
	TBSF	BCEX	BCFH	BCFR	TBTW	TBSA
1997 Q3	50 389	31 121	234 126	133 660	347 337	796 633
Q4	50 974	28 766	233 595	134 653	364 814	812 802
1998 Q1	52 421	29 601	248 332	136 168	367 342	833 864
Q2	54 797	29 647	238 439	135 964	374 536	833 383
Q3	55 272	29 742	244 302	138 672	381 811	849 799
Q4	58 479	29 358	222 519	142 214	387 217	839 787
1999 Q1	57 953	30 559	233 637	145 567	391 551	859 265
Q2	63 628	31 143	234 949	149 892	402 074	881 686
Q3	62 703	30 750	237 505	150 106	412 420	893 484
Q4	61 444	30 619	233 532	154 080	420 392	900 067
2000 Q1	60 058	33 855	269 246	164 099	428 065	955 323
Q2	62 421	34 376	278 982	173 819	438 552	988 150
Of which in sterling						
	TBUF	BCEY	BCFI	BCFS	TBVW	TBUA
1997 Q3	39 527	27 260	125 439	120 269	347 074	659 569
Q4	39 923	25 353	128 523	121 745	364 589	680 133
1998 Q1	40 493	25 958	142 119	123 247	367 142	698 959
Q2	40 626	26 088	135 996	122 710	374 338	699 758
Q3	40 191	26 230	139 833	125 000	381 613	712 866
Q4	41 566	25 429	134 407	127 245	387 022	715 670
1999 Q1	40 983	26 172	148 670	129 614	391 349	736 788
Q2	41 443	26 457	152 170	130 514	401 835	752 419
Q3	40 671	26 269	151 850	132 540	412 205	763 535
Q4	41 372	26 108	153 031	137 102	420 159	777 772
2000 Q1	40 862	29 120	162 888	145 212	427 747	805 830
Q2	42 012	29 221	166 012	154 157	438 221	829 623
Changes in total lending(sterling)						
	TBWF	BCEZ	BCFJ	BCFT	TBXW	TBWA
1997 Q4	630	–1 873	5 410	1 554	5 925	12 165
1998 Q1	564	637	10 552	2 013	3 590	17 804
Q2	134	412	1 378	–539	7 488	9 296
Q3	–435	142	4 736	2 171	7 582	14 601
Q4	1 465	–755	–8 994	2 841	7 355	2 289
1999 Q1	–573	741	14 488	2 405	4 663	21 989
Q2	460	287	243	–211	8 047	9 089
Q3	–773	–186	1 472	2 189	10 542	13 451
Q4	684	–160	2 587	3 971	8 280	15 623
2000 Q1	–499	3 011	9 653	8 106	7 865	28 378
Q2	1 134	102	2 296	9 010	10 889	23 674
Changes in total lending (foreign currencies)						
	TBYF	BCFA	BCFK	BCFU	TBZW	TBYA
1997 Q4	624	–327	12 436	–95	–30	12 610
1998 Q1	1 247	342	4 437	860	–17	6 883
Q2	2 170	–119	–4 183	215	–4	–1 858
Q3	747	–90	–49	261	–2	881
Q4	1 229	276	–20 211	752	–11	–17 950
1999 Q1	171	456	2 911	1 064	7	4 617
Q2	5 062	235	–1 940	3 261	36	6 663
Q3	351	–89	4 314	–1 381	–18	3 184
Q4	–1 946	–21	–4 464	–662	17	–7 066
2000 Q1	–623	234	28 524	–1 191	85	27 045
Q2	221	182	–1 115	–183	–1	–879

1 Comprises loans advances (including under reverse repos), finance leasing, acceptances, facilities and holdings of sterling commercial paper issued by UK residents, provided by reporting banks to their UK resident non-bank and non-building society customers. This analysis is based on Standard Industrial Classification of 1992 and excludes lending to residents in the Channel Islands and the Isle of Man which are classified as non-residents for statistical purposes from end-September 1997. Holdings of investments and bills and adjustments for transit items are not included. For a more detailed breakdown of this data, see *Financial Statistics* Table 4.5B.

2 Changes in the reporting population in the quarter to end-December 1997, including the entry of Northern rock plc, account for an increase of £12.8bn in total sterling lending. Other currency lending was unchanged. Changes data have been adjusted to reflect only the new business undertaken by Northern Rock plc during the quarter.

3 Includes lending under DTI special scheme for domestic shipbuilding.

4 These figures fall outside the scope of National Statistics.

Source: Bank of England; Enquiries 020 7601 5360

5.8 Analysis of bank lending to UK residents[1,2,4] Amounts outstanding

continued

£ million, not seasonally adjusted

	Manufacturing[3]	Other production	Financial	Services	Persons	Total loans, advances and acceptances
Facilities granted						
	TCAF	BCFB	BCFL	BCFV	TCBW	TCAA
1997 Q3	100 776	58 509	265 180	201 836	364 628	990 929
Q4	102 574	55 194	268 619	204 879	384 932	1 016 199
1998 Q1	104 897	57 529	280 378	205 169	388 716	1 036 689
Q2	108 851	56 274	273 710	203 572	398 991	1 041 398
Q3	108 953	58 615	277 483	204 845	403 501	1 053 397
Q4	109 229	54 901	255 227	205 120	409 791	1 034 268
1999 Q1	110 892	56 903	266 091	209 045	416 745	1 059 676
Q2	114 982	57 185	265 451	220 011	430 544	1 088 172
Q3	115 419	58 191	269 033	224 079	440 730	1 107 452
Q4	115 494	57 089	267 360	244 113	450 322	1 134 379
2000 Q1	116 279	59 594	305 086	250 778	459 937	1 191 674
Q2	121 909	61 916	314 352	272 479	470 280	1 240 935
Of which in sterling						
	TCCF	BCFC	BCFM	BCFW	TCDW	TCCA
1997 Q3	72 001	46 301	143 597	173 536	364 346	799 781
Q4	72 567	44 081	147 896	176 583	384 685	825 812
1998 Q1	72 078	46 311	161 185	178 465	388 501	846 540
Q2	71 922	45 333	155 751	176 750	398 762	848 518
Q3	70 263	46 777	160 001	177 440	403 291	857 771
Q4	68 074	43 159	154 553	176 704	409 565	852 055
1999 Q1	69 646	43 808	169 013	179 104	416 502	878 073
Q2	69 305	43 143	169 568	185 229	430 261	897 507
Q3	71 306	43 956	170 769	188 497	440 461	914 989
Q4	71 189	42 524	172 940	195 502	450 053	932 209
2000 Q1	73 068	45 856	184 816	205 770	459 575	969 085
Q2	70 774	45 660	187 658	213 652	469 829	987 573
Changes in sterling (facilities granted)						
	TCEF	BCFD	BCFN	BCFX	TCFW	TCEA
1997 Q4	790	–2 054	6 681	3 023	8 185	17 144
1998 Q1	–870	2 028	10 109	1 867	4 853	18 435
Q2	–156	–698	2 067	–1 715	10 552	10 473
Q3	–1 658	1 444	5 148	571	4 836	10 746
Q4	–1 039	–2 891	–8 329	1 217	8 235	–2 430
1999 Q1	1 571	649	14 481	2 402	7 359	26 839
Q2	–340	–663	554	6 126	11 320	17 260
Q3	2 003	813	2 994	3 431	10 372	19 514
Q4	–135	–1 518	3 580	6 500	9 919	18 607
2000 Q1	1 888	3 332	11 670	9 975	9 797	36 904
Q2	–2 309	–197	2 014	8 238	10 984	18 973
Changes in foreign currencies (facilities granted)						
	TCGF	BCFE	BCFO	BCFY	TCHW	TCGA
1997 Q4	2 708	–595	15 628	1 033	–28	18 748
1998 Q1	3 425	453	2 056	–331	–24	5 593
Q2	3 871	–383	–1 730	–128	12	1 705
Q3	1 327	771	–2 747	265	–21	–391
Q4	–75	–1 224	–22 269	–1 121	7	–24 667
1999 Q1	208	1 320	1 904	1 568	17	5 031
Q2	3 932	714	–1 232	4 418	37	7 878
Q3	–456	584	4 166	1 712	–6	6 007
Q4	–94	90	–3 325	12 762	–3	9 440
2000 Q1	–761	–844	28 503	–6 219	94	20 789
Q2	5 652	1 821	–1 990	11 083	70	16 653

See footnotes on page 255.

Source: Bank of England; Enquiries 020 7601 5360

5.9 Other interest rates, security prices and yields[6]

Percentage rate

	Last Friday						Last working day	Average of working days			
									Financial Times index of industrial ordinary shares 1 July 1935 = 100		
	Treasury bill yield[1]	Deposits with local authorities - 3 months[2]	Inter-bank 3 months bid rate[3]	Inter-bank 3 months offer rate[3]	Sterling certificates of deposit 3 months bid rate	Sterling certificates of deposit 3 months offer rate	Interest on US $ deposits in London 3 months	British government securities: long dated[4] - 20 years	Price index	Dividend yield	Earnings yield[5]
	AJRP	AJOI	HSAJ	HSAK	HSAL	HSAM	AJIB	AJLX	AJMT	AJMU	AJMV
1955	..	..	..	..	..	..	..	..	195.00	4.81	12.85
1956	..	..	..	..	..	..	..	..	180.60	5.87	15.92
1957	..	..	..	..	..	..	..	..	188.30	5.86	15.04
1958	..	..	..	..	..	..	..	..	181.90	6.27	14.96
1959	..	..	..	..	..	..	..	..	250.20	4.86	10.82
1960	..	..	..	..	..	..	..	..	318.60	4.26	9.02
1961	..	..	..	..	..	..	..	..	319.80	4.87	9.62
1962	..	..	..	..	..	..	..	..	285.50	5.49	8.88
1963	..	..	..	..	..	..	4.25	5.30	316.83	4.93	6.73
1964	..	..	..	..	..	..	4.56	5.80	346.73	4.95	7.35
1965	..	..	..	..	..	..	5.31	6.43	337.45	5.73	9.11
1966	..	..	..	..	..	..	6.56	6.91	332.11	5.98	8.52
1967	..	..	..	..	..	..	6.31	6.80	354.95	5.36	6.69
1968	..	..	..	..	..	..	7.13	7.54	463.11	4.05	4.99
1969	..	..	..	..	..	..	10.06	9.05	420.41	4.43	5.81
1970	..	..	..	..	..	..	6.56	9.21	363.25	4.75	6.54
1971	..	..	..	..	..	..	5.75	8.85	383.55	4.10	6.22
1972	8.48	..	..	..	..	..	5.91	8.90	503.92	3.25	4.97
1973	12.82	..	..	..	..	..	10.19	10.71	434.46	4.15	8.33
1974	11.30	..	..	..	..	..	10.06	14.77	251.22	8.23	21.47
1975	10.93	..	..	..	11.06	11.19	5.87	14.39	311.07	6.80	19.48
1976	14.09	..	..	..	14.06	14.19	5.06	14.43	368.13	5.96	17.61
1977	6.39	..	..	..	6.31	6.44	7.19	12.73	452.32	5.43	16.50
1978	11.91	12.44	12.50	12.63	12.44	12.56	11.69	12.47	479.41	5.65	16.47
1979	16.49	17.00	16.94	17.06	16.75	17.00	14.50	12.99	475.52	6.49	16.61
1980	13.45	14.88	14.81	14.88	14.63	14.84	17.75	13.78	464.47	7.62	18.14
1981	15.35	15.75	15.63	15.75	15.75	15.94	13.63	14.74	518.49	6.24	12.12
1982	9.96	10.63	10.88	10.94	10.63	10.69	9.25	12.88	574.63	5.30	10.82
1983	9.04	9.00	9.34	9.41	9.25	9.34	9.94	10.80	693.06	4.70	9.58
1984	9.33	10.00	10.00	10.06	9.75	9.88	8.69	10.69	854.80	4.66	10.76
1985	11.49	12.00	11.88	11.94	11.75	11.88	7.94	10.62	1 004.66	4.62	11.48
1986	10.94	11.00	11.34	11.44	11.19	11.31	6.31	9.87	1 286.95	4.25	10.16
1987	8.38	9.00	8.88	8.88	8.69	8.81	7.38	9.47	1 600.07	3.73	8.98
1988	12.91	13.19	13.00	13.00	12.88	12.94	9.25	9.36	1 448.73	4.62	11.72
1989	15.02	15.03	15.13	15.16	15.03	15.09	8.34	9.58	1 781.41	4.46	10.80
1990	13.50	14.00	14.00	14.00	13.81	13.88	7.53	11.08	1 749.43	5.29	11.70
1991	10.45	10.93	10.94	11.00	10.75	10.88	4.22	9.92	1 921.86	4.98	8.72
1992	6.44	7.00	7.19	7.25	7.09	7.13	3.37	9.12	1 951.91	4.68	6.75
1993	4.95	5.31	5.31	5.31	5.22	5.25	3.31	7.87	2 287.94	4.10	5.26
1994	6.00	6.50	6.53	6.56	6.41	6.44	6.44	8.05	2 445.18	4.07	5.52
1995	6.31	6.44	6.47	6.50	6.44	6.47	5.54	8.26	2 510.44	4.25	6.90
1996	6.26	6.38	6.38	6.44	6.34	6.41	5.50	8.10	2 784.07	4.00	..
1997	7.13	7.50	7.59	7.63	7.53	7.59	5.69	7.09	3 047.65	3.69	..
1998	5.63	6.13	6.28	6.31	6.22	6.28	5.00	5.45	3 542.10	3.07	..
1999	5.70	5.88	5.94	6.00	5.88	5.94	5.98	4.70	3 882.48	2.76	..

1 Average discount rate expressed as the rate at which interest is earned during the life of the bills.
2 For a minimum term of 3 months and thereafter at 7 days' notice.
3 Spread of rates over the day in the inter-bank sterling market; from June 1982 rates are the spread at 10.30 a.m.
4 Averages of Wednesdays until February 1980; from March 1980 figures are the average of all observations (3 a week); from January 1982 average of working days. Calculated gross redemption yields - see *Financial Statistics Explanatory Handbook*.
5 A change of basis of calculation of the Earnings yield occured on 25 February 1973 and is explained in *Financial Statistics Explanatory Handbook*. No meaningful average for the month of February 1973 is therefore available. It is discontinued from April 1995.
6 These figures fall outside the scope of National Statistics.

Sources: Bank of England;
HM Treasury;
Financial Times;
Institute of Actuaries;
Faculty of Actuaries;
Enquiries 020 7601 4342 (Bank of England)

5.9 Other interest rates, security prices and yields[6]

continued

Percentage rate

	Last Friday						Last working day	Average of working days			
									Financial Times index of industrial ordinary shares 1 July 1935 = 100		
	Treasury bill yield[1]	Deposits with local authorities - 3 months[2]	Inter-bank 3 month bid rate[3]	Inter-bank 3 month offer rate[3]	Sterling certificates of deposit 3 months bid rate	Sterling certificates of deposit 3 months offer rate	Interest on US $ deposits in London 3 months	British government securities: long dated[4] -20 years	Price index	Dividend yield	Earnings yield[5]
	AJRP	AJOI	HSAJ	HSAK	HSAL	HSAM	AJIB	AJLX	AJMT	AJMU	AJMV
1963 Jan	..	..	..	..	..	..	3.38	5.34	288.40	5.34	7.90
Feb	..	..	..	..	..	..	3.50	5.50	294.70	5.23	7.40
Mar	..	..	..	..	..	..	3.63	5.63	304.00	5.08	7.18
Apr	..	..	..	..	..	..	3.72	5.47	308.50	4.97	7.10
May	..	..	..	..	..	..	3.81	5.31	311.50	4.96	6.72
Jun	..	..	..	..	..	..	3.88	5.20	308.00	5.07	6.71
Jul	..	..	..	..	..	..	4.00	5.11	313.10	5.00	6.65
Aug	..	..	..	..	..	..	4.00	5.07	321.40	4.89	6.47
Sep	..	..	..	..	..	..	4.19	5.05	326.40	4.81	6.29
Oct	..	..	..	..	..	..	4.13	5.08	338.70	4.65	5.98
Nov	..	..	..	..	..	..	4.25	5.32	342.40	4.61	6.17
Dec	..	..	..	..	..	..	4.25	5.52	344.90	4.59	6.17
1964 Jan	..	..	..	..	..	..	4.06	5.53	336.70	4.74	6.43
Feb	..	..	..	..	..	..	4.19	5.66	330.80	4.86	6.61
Mar	..	..	..	..	..	..	4.25	5.68	337.80	4.76	6.57
Apr	..	..	..	..	..	..	4.19	5.70	346.50	4.73	6.79
May	..	..	..	..	..	..	4.25	5.79	343.30	4.93	7.13
Jun	..	..	..	..	..	..	4.31	5.83	343.50	5.09	7.62
Jul	..	..	..	..	..	..	4.25	5.80	354.60	5.01	7.57
Aug	..	..	..	..	..	..	4.25	5.84	361.00	4.87	7.52
Sep	..	..	..	..	..	..	4.44	5.84	367.20	4.84	7.54
Oct	..	..	..	..	..	..	4.53	5.87	361.80	4.94	7.62
Nov	..	..	..	..	..	..	5.00	5.90	345.00	5.22	8.18
Dec	..	..	..	..	..	..	4.56	6.15	332.60	5.45	8.66
1965 Jan	..	..	..	..	..	..	4.56	6.18	338.50	5.40	8.51
Feb	..	..	..	..	..	..	4.63	6.21	348.00	5.36	8.42
Mar	..	..	..	..	..	..	4.88	6.28	335.30	5.67	8.93
Apr	..	..	..	..	..	..	4.88	6.48	339.50	5.69	8.95
May	..	..	..	..	..	..	5.31	6.68	350.00	5.54	8.69
Jun	..	..	..	..	..	..	4.94	6.69	331.30	5.86	9.26
Jul	..	..	..	..	..	..	4.69	6.71	317.60	6.15	9.85
Aug	..	..	..	..	..	..	4.56	6.60	322.60	6.09	9.74
Sep	..	..	..	..	..	..	4.94	6.26	329.70	5.95	9.62
Oct	..	..	..	..	..	..	5.06	6.25	345.10	5.68	9.20
Nov	..	..	..	..	..	..	5.31	6.32	350.30	5.62	8.99
Dec	..	..	..	..	..	..	5.31	6.47	341.50	5.80	9.15
1966 Jan	..	..	..	..	..	..	5.38	6.53	345.40	5.78	9.00
Feb	..	..	..	..	..	..	5.41	6.56	355.00	5.65	8.69
Mar	..	..	..	..	..	..	5.81	6.70	347.90	5.82	8.66
Apr	..	..	..	..	..	..	5.78	6.73	345.50	5.88	8.50
May	..	..	..	..	..	..	5.84	6.78	363.30	5.51	7.82
Jun	..	..	..	..	..	..	6.09	6.89	368.40	5.35	7.66
Jul	..	..	..	..	..	..	6.44	7.29	346.40	5.63	8.22
Aug	..	..	..	..	..	..	6.84	7.41	308.00	6.33	9.16
Sep	..	..	..	..	..	..	7.06	7.29	305.60	6.37	8.89
Oct	..	..	..	..	..	..	7.06	6.96	300.40	6.49	8.78
Nov	..	..	..	..	..	..	7.13	6.97	293.80	6.63	8.62
Dec	..	..	..	..	..	..	6.56	6.78	305.60	6.36	8.18
1967 Jan	..	..	..	..	..	..	5.56	6.73	317.40	6.10	7.74
Feb	..	..	..	..	..	..	5.69	6.50	315.90	6.11	7.71
Mar	..	..	..	..	..	..	5.38	6.49	322.10	5.96	7.45
Apr	..	..	..	..	..	..	4.69	6.42	338.00	5.54	6.92
May	..	..	..	..	..	..	5.13	6.57	343.20	5.44	6.87
Jun	..	..	..	..	..	..	5.38	6.75	347.80	5.38	6.82
Jul	..	..	..	..	..	..	5.13	6.94	352.70	5.32	6.67
Aug	..	..	..	..	..	..	5.03	6.90	355.70	5.29	6.64
Sep	..	..	..	..	..	..	5.78	6.91	373.10	5.06	6.32
Oct	..	..	..	..	..	..	5.78	7.00	393.10	4.82	5.88
Nov	..	..	..	..	..	..	6.56	7.14	407.90	4.59	5.61
Dec	..	..	..	..	..	..	6.31	7.26	392.50	4.78	5.69

1 Average discount rate expressed as the rate at which interest is earned during the life of the bills.
2 For a minimum term of 3 months and thereafter at 7 days' notice.
3 Spread of rates over the day in the inter-bank sterling market; from June 1982 rates are the spread at 10.30 a.m.
4 Averages of Wednesdays until February 1980; from March 1980 figures are the average of all observations (3 a week); from January 1982 average of working days. Calculated gross redemption yields - see *Financial Statistics Explanatory Handbook*.
5 A change of basis of calculation of the Earnings yield occured on 25 February 1973 and is explained in *Financial Statistics Explanatory Handbook.* No meaningful average for the month of February 1973 is therefore available. It is discontinued from April 1995.
6 These figures fall outside the scope of National Statistics.

Sources: Bank of England; HM Treasury; Financial Times; Institute of Actuaries; Faculty of Actuaries; Enquiries 020 7601 4342 (Bank of England)

5.9 Other interest rates, security prices and yields[6]

continued

Percentage rate

	Last Friday						Last working day	Average of working days			
	Treasury bill yield[1]	Deposits with local authorities - 3 months[2]	Inter-bank 3 month bid rate[3]	Inter-bank 3 month offer rate[3]	Sterling certificates of deposit 3 months bid rate	Sterling certificates of deposit 3 months offer rate	Interest on US $ deposits in London 3 months	British government securities: long dated[4] -20 years	Financial Times index of industrial ordinary shares 1 July 1935 = 100: Price index	Financial Times index of industrial ordinary shares 1 July 1935 = 100: Dividend yield	Financial Times index of industrial ordinary shares 1 July 1935 = 100: Earnings yield[5]
	AJRP	AJOI	HSAJ	HSAK	HSAL	HSAM	AJIB	AJLX	AJMT	AJMU	AJMV
1968 Jan	..	..	..	..	..	..	5.44	7.26	401.20	4.71	5.59
Feb	..	..	..	..	..	..	5.66	7.25	412.90	4.58	5.51
Mar	..	..	..	..	..	..	6.38	7.29	413.30	4.53	5.49
Apr	..	..	..	..	..	..	6.66	7.28	447.70	4.10	5.04
May	..	..	..	..	..	..	7.16	7.36	464.20	4.00	4.98
Jun	..	..	..	..	..	..	6.88	7.60	466.40	4.00	4.99
Jul	..	..	..	..	..	..	6.31	7.70	481.30	3.88	4.80
Aug	..	..	..	..	..	..	6.16	7.62	491.40	3.80	4.65
Sep	..	..	..	..	..	..	6.25	7.63	509.10	3.67	4.52
Oct	..	..	..	..	..	..	6.59	7.63	488.20	3.81	4.77
Nov	..	..	..	..	..	..	6.94	7.83	488.70	3.78	4.75
Dec	..	..	..	..	..	..	7.13	8.09	493.00	3.76	4.77
1969 Jan	..	..	..	..	..	..	7.69	8.36	509.90	3.65	4.72
Feb	..	..	..	..	..	..	8.50	8.57	480.40	3.84	5.05
Mar	..	..	..	..	..	..	8.53	8.77	470.60	3.96	5.18
Apr	..	..	..	..	..	..	8.56	8.85	465.60	3.97	5.12
May	..	..	..	..	..	..	10.56	9.15	431.90	4.30	5.54
Jun	..	..	..	..	..	..	10.56	9.55	398.00	4.60	6.05
Jul	..	..	..	..	..	..	10.44	9.27	378.10	4.93	6.40
Aug	..	..	..	..	..	..	11.31	9.34	376.30	4.89	6.44
Sep	..	..	..	..	..	..	11.25	9.37	384.60	4.78	6.31
Oct	..	..	..	..	..	..	10.00	9.03	376.20	4.84	6.46
Nov	..	..	..	..	..	..	11.00	9.13	379.60	4.73	6.41
Dec	..	..	..	..	..	..	10.06	9.15	392.80	4.53	6.10
1970 Jan	..	..	..	..	..	..	9.59	9.03	414.00	4.24	5.73
Feb	..	..	..	..	..	..	9.44	8.79	402.70	4.40	5.96
Mar	..	..	..	..	..	..	8.63	8.75	393.20	4.55	6.21
Apr	..	..	..	..	..	..	8.69	8.94	384.70	4.44	6.16
May	..	..	..	..	..	..	9.19	9.40	343.10	4.96	6.82
Jun	..	..	..	..	..	..	9.06	9.58	335.50	5.02	6.90
Jul	..	..	..	..	..	..	8.50	9.33	340.70	4.93	6.75
Aug	..	..	..	..	..	..	8.00	9.19	340.70	4.90	6.71
Sep	..	..	..	..	..	..	8.50	9.28	347.60	4.81	6.63
Oct	..	..	..	..	..	..	7.72	9.15	390.00	4.57	6.33
Nov	..	..	..	..	..	..	7.25	9.51	335.40	5.06	7.16
Dec	..	..	..	..	..	..	6.56	9.62	331.40	5.11	7.14
1971 Jan	..	..	..	..	..	..	5.88	9.51	340.70	4.95	6.90
Feb	..	..	..	..	..	..	5.34	9.35	330.90	5.03	6.97
Mar	..	..	..	..	..	..	5.38	9.07	322.80	4.97	6.88
Apr	..	..	..	..	..	..	6.25	9.07	354.60	4.45	6.51
May	..	..	..	..	..	..	7.63	9.03	369.20	3.85	5.84
Jun	..	..	..	..	..	..	6.50	9.08	374.80	4.14	6.37
Jul	..	..	..	..	..	..	6.72	9.22	399.30	4.04	6.24
Aug	..	..	..	..	..	..	9.25	8.96	405.30	3.76	5.87
Sep	..	..	..	..	..	..	7.63	8.50	422.80	3.64	5.71
Oct	..	..	..	..	..	..	6.06	8.51	412.40	3.78	5.87
Nov	..	..	..	..	..	..	6.50	7.79	414.30	3.82	5.97
Dec	..	..	..	..	..	..	5.75	8.10	455.50	3.55	5.53
1972 Jan	4.40	..	..	..	..	..	5.06	7.93	488.60	3.34	5.20
Feb	4.41	..	..	..	..	..	4.97	7.90	495.10	3.30	5.01
Mar	4.36	..	..	..	..	..	5.53	8.16	506.70	3.21	4.69
Apr	4.31	..	..	..	..	..	5.00	8.26	522.30	3.14	4.58
May	4.35	..	..	..	..	..	4.63	8.60	533.70	3.13	4.61
Jun	5.72	..	..	..	..	..	5.31	9.32	499.60	3.33	4.93
Jul	5.85	..	..	..	..	..	5.66	9.23	502.70	3.23	4.92
Aug	5.91	..	..	..	..	..	5.50	9.36	524.40	3.12	4.77
Sep	6.74	..	..	..	..	..	5.94	9.54	492.40	3.32	5.09
Oct	7.01	..	..	..	..	..	6.03	9.46	481.50	3.40	5.35
Nov	7.06	..	..	..	..	..	6.00	9.45	491.60	3.33	5.36
Dec	8.48	..	..	..	..	..	5.91	9.62	508.40	3.21	5.17

1 Average discount rate expressed as the rate at which interest is earned during the life of the bills.
2 For a minimum term of 3 months and thereafter at 7 days' notice.
3 Spread of rates over the day in the inter-bank sterling market; from June 1982 rates are the spread at 10.30 a.m.
4 Averages of Wednesdays until February 1980; from March 1980 figures are the average of all observations (3 a week); from January 1982 average of working days. Calculated gross redemption yields - see *Financial Statistics Explanatory Handbook.*
5 A change of basis of calculation of the Earnings yield occured on 25 February 1973 and is explained in *Financial Statistics Explanatory Handbook.* No meaningful average for the month of February 1973 is therefore available. It is discontinued from April 1995.
6 These figures fall outside the scope of National Statistics.

Sources: Bank of England; HM Treasury; Financial Times; Institute of Actuaries; Faculty of Actuaries; Enquiries 020 7601 4342 (Bank of England)

5.9 Other interest rates, security prices and yields[6]

continued

Percentage rate

	Last Friday						Last working day	Average of working days			
									Financial Times index of industrial ordinary shares 1 July 1935 = 100		
	Treasury bill yield[1]	Deposits with local author-ities - 3 months[2]	Inter-bank 3 months bid rate[3]	Inter-bank 3 months offer rate[3]	Sterling certifi-cates of deposit 3 months bid rate	Sterling certifi-cates of deposit 3 months offer rate	Interest on US $ deposits in London 3 months	British government securities long dated[4] -20 years	Price index	Dividend yield	Earnings yield[5]
	AJRP	AJOI	HSAJ	HSAK	HSAL	HSAM	AJIB	AJLX	AJMT	AJMU	AJMV
1973 Jan	8.29	..	..	..	..	..	6.63	9.56	489.90	3.32	5.36
Feb	8.23	..	..	..	..	..	8.44	9.65	453.60	3.55	–
Mar	8.10	..	..	..	..	..	8.69	10.01	445.50	3.61	7.30
Apr	7.82	..	..	..	..	..	8.25	9.93	464.10	3.53	7.29
May	7.33	..	..	..	..	..	8.63	10.02	457.40	3.77	8.17
Jun	7.08	..	..	..	..	..	9.06	10.15	464.90	3.91	8.68
Jul	11.20	..	..	..	..	..	11.47	10.60	431.20	4.35	9.66
Aug	11.28	..	..	..	..	..	11.56	11.30	422.80	4.46	9.97
Sep	11.25	..	..	..	..	..	10.47	11.55	418.00	4.53	10.13
Oct	10.96	..	..	..	..	..	9.19	11.28	434.70	4.34	9.81
Nov	12.85	..	..	..	..	..	10.47	12.00	401.50	4.73	10.68
Dec	12.82	..	..	..	..	..	10.19	12.50	329.90	5.72	12.87
1974 Jan	12.40	..	..	..	..	..	8.88	12.89	324.80	5.83	13.30
Feb	12.18	..	..	..	..	..	8.63	13.50	316.50	5.84	13.77
Mar	12.35	..	..	..	..	..	10.00	13.68	297.50	6.17	15.15
Apr	11.82	..	..	..	..	..	11.69	14.21	290.00	6.40	16.33
May	11.53	..	..	..	..	..	11.88	13.80	296.60	6.67	17.21
Jun	11.56	..	..	..	..	..	13.50	14.38	267.50	7.49	19.35
Jul	11.51	..	..	..	..	..	13.56	14.88	254.80	7.81	20.74
Aug	11.57	..	..	..	..	..	13.94	15.29	222.90	8.91	23.94
Sep	11.29	..	..	..	..	..	12.19	14.95	203.50	9.86	26.37
Oct	11.19	..	..	..	..	..	10.12	15.68	199.40	10.12	27.16
Nov	11.29	..	..	..	..	..	10.62	16.75	181.00	11.09	30.10
Dec	11.30	..	..	..	..	..	10.06	17.18	160.10	12.59	34.19
1975 Jan	10.53	..	..	..	11.69	11.81	7.44	16.02	183.70	10.99	30.28
Feb	10.01	..	..	..	10.69	10.88	7.31	14.58	262.62	7.56	21.66
Mar	9.59	..	..	..	9.88	10.00	6.97	13.43	292.67	6.81	20.35
Apr	9.46	..	..	..	9.63	9.75	6.81	13.89	314.87	6.51	19.30
May	9.67	..	..	..	9.81	9.94	6.06	14.53	338.99	6.12	18.09
Jun	9.71	..	..	..	9.63	9.75	6.75	14.41	332.62	6.06	18.07
Jul	10.72	..	..	..	10.50	10.75	6.97	13.93	304.40	6.69	19.62
Aug	10.66	..	..	..	10.38	10.50	7.34	13.87	298.26	6.94	19.91
Sep	10.76	..	..	..	10.56	10.75	8.06	13.79	328.85	6.31	17.58
Oct	11.74	..	..	..	11.56	11.69	6.81	14.66	341.92	6.14	16.88
Nov	11.30	..	..	..	11.19	11.31	7.06	14.81	367.90	5.76	16.02
Dec	10.93	..	..	..	11.06	11.19	5.87	14.79	366.10	5.73	15.98
1976 Jan	9.52	..	..	..	9.38	9.56	5.37	13.79	397.04	5.30	14.91
Feb	8.81	..	..	..	8.69	8.81	5.62	13.46	404.19	5.17	14.99
Mar	8.60	..	..	..	8.50	8.63	5.59	13.88	404.68	5.12	15.01
Apr	10.20	..	..	..	9.81	9.94	5.53	13.77	406.38	5.12	15.17
May	11.31	..	..	..	11.31	11.56	6.62	13.59	406.60	5.26	15.19
Jun	11.30	..	..	..	11.13	11.31	6.00	14.09	378.60	5.70	16.14
Jul	11.17	..	..	..	11.13	11.25	5.78	14.16	383.79	5.75	16.44
Aug	11.25	..	..	..	11.13	11.25	5.62	14.33	368.04	6.03	17.55
Sep	12.74	..	..	..	12.50	12.63	5.81	14.79	343.96	6.52	19.23
Oct	14.97	..	..	..	15.13	15.31	5.44	16.03	294.01	7.62	23.07
Nov	14.54	..	..	..	14.53	14.69	5.19	15.79	301.71	7.28	22.66
Dec	14.09	..	..	..	14.06	14.19	5.06	15.48	328.61	6.66	20.91
1977 Jan	12.09	..	..	..	12.00	12.25	5.31	14.48	374.68	6.01	18.69
Feb	11.06	..	..	..	11.13	11.25	5.19	13.93	393.76	5.88	18.77
Mar	9.57	..	..	..	9.56	9.69	5.25	13.25	418.21	5.39	16.91
Apr	7.64	..	..	..	7.63	7.81	5.31	13.05	415.07	5.51	16.82
May	7.57	..	..	..	7.69	7.94	6.16	12.69	456.70	5.08	15.54
Jun	7.60	..	..	..	7.75	7.88	5.81	13.26	451.03	5.19	15.85
Jul	7.44	..	..	..	7.50	7.63	6.25	13.62	443.14	5.38	16.09
Aug	6.52	..	..	..	6.56	6.69	6.31	13.12	478.60	5.23	15.26
Sep	5.37	..	..	..	5.63	5.75	6.91	11.88	522.70	5.07	14.98
Oct	4.53	..	..	..	4.81	4.94	7.19	10.98	511.91	5.27	15.55
Nov	6.53	..	..	..	6.56	6.88	7.00	11.28	480.45	5.56	16.72
Dec	6.39	..	..	..	6.31	6.44	7.19	11.16	481.63	5.56	16.83

1 Average discount rate expressed as the rate at which interest is earned during the life of the bills.
2 For a minimum term of 3 months and thereafter at 7 days' notice.
3 Spread of rates over the day in the inter-bank sterling market; from June 1982 rates are the spread at 10.30 am.
4 Averages of Wednesdays until February 1980; from March 1980 figures are the average of all observations (3 a week); from January 1982 average of working days. Calculated gross redemption yields - see *Financial Statistics Explanatory Handbook.*
5 See footnote on page 257.
6 These figures fall outside the scope of National Statistics.

Sources: Bank of England; HM Treasury; Financial Times; Institute of Actuaries; Faculty of Actuaries; Enquiries 020 7601 4342 (Bank of England)

5.9 Other interest rates, security prices and yields[6]

continued

Percentage rate

	Last Friday						Last working day	Average of working days			
									Financial Times index of industrial ordinary shares 1 July 1935 = 100		
	Treasury bill yield[1]	Deposits with local authorities - 3 months[2]	Inter-bank 3 months bid rate[3]	Inter-bank 3 months offer rate[3]	Sterling certificates of deposit 3 months bid rate	Sterling certificates of deposit 3 months offer rate	Interest on US $ deposits in London 3 months	British government securities long dated[4] -20 years	Price index	Dividend yield	Earnings yield[5]
	AJRP	AJOI	HSAJ	HSAK	HSAL	HSAM	AJIB	AJLX	AJMT	AJMU	AJMV
1978 Jan	5.85	6.41	6.31	6.38	6.19	6.38	7.41	11.06	482.26	5.57	16.96
Feb	6.07	6.94	6.75	6.88	6.69	6.94	7.50	11.75	458.30	5.85	17.74
Mar	6.09	6.82	6.88	7.00	6.63	6.75	7.50	11.72	455.03	5.94	17.51
Apr	7.12	8.07	8.31	8.44	8.13	8.25	7.69	12.39	460.86	5.85	17.25
May	8.67	9.13	9.31	9.44	9.13	9.31	7.94	12.72	476.62	5.58	16.86
Jun	9.49	9.97	10.06	10.25	10.00	10.19	8.69	12.79	466.06	5.68	16.65
Jul	9.33	10.10	9.94	10.06	9.56	9.72	8.41	12.72	472.17	5.62	17.06
Aug	9.03	9.32	9.31	9.38	9.13	9.31	9.00	12.55	508.81	5.28	15.88
Sep	9.38	9.51	9.69	9.81	9.56	9.69	9.53	12.64	515.99	5.21	15.02
Oct	10.56	10.94	11.00	11.06	10.81	11.00	11.41	12.91	497.44	5.42	15.09
Nov	11.91	12.22	12.06	12.25	12.13	12.25	11.78	13.16	476.92	5.86	15.86
Dec	11.91	12.44	12.50	12.63	12.44	12.56	11.69	13.22	482.43	5.98	15.73
1979 Jan	12.46	13.12	13.00	13.13	12.94	13.13	10.44	13.68	474.05	6.10	16.01
Feb	12.61	12.50	12.88	13.00	12.63	12.75	10.62	13.94	460.24	6.18	16.16
Mar	11.78	12.25	12.06	12.19	11.69	11.88	10.66	12.35	511.51	5.55	14.54
Apr	11.61	11.87	11.75	11.88	11.50	11.69	10.87	11.68	537.42	5.38	14.31
May	11.79	11.87	11.81	11.94	11.75	11.88	10.56	11.94	528.50	5.56	14.90
Jun	13.79	13.87	14.00	14.13	13.88	14.00	10.59	12.69	489.45	5.93	15.82
Jul	13.81	14.12	14.00	14.06	14.06	14.19	11.34	12.25	468.34	6.60	16.92
Aug	13.80	14.12	14.19	14.31	14.13	14.25	12.22	12.30	467.19	6.95	17.46
Sep	13.82	14.12	14.13	14.19	14.06	14.19	12.87	12.60	468.37	6.95	17.75
Oct	13.94	14.56	14.69	14.81	14.63	14.81	15.41	13.16	465.41	7.09	17.55
Nov	16.77	16.75	16.81	16.94	16.81	16.94	14.31	14.54	415.88	7.88	19.07
Dec	16.49	17.00	16.94	17.06	16.75	17.00	14.50	14.72	419.82	7.70	18.78
1980 Jan	16.39	17.44	17.25	17.38	17.28	17.44	14.41	14.17	440.66	7.43	18.42
Feb	16.80	18.26	18.13	18.25	18.13	18.31	16.97	14.45	460.70	7.17	17.64
Mar	16.97	18.69	18.13	18.25	18.33	18.50	19.94	14.70	440.84	7.74	19.26
Apr	16.73	17.57	17.31	17.38	17.19	17.31	13.94	14.27	435.45	8.05	19.73
May	16.73	17.19	17.00	17.13	16.88	17.06	9.75	14.01	432.40	8.21	20.05
Jun	16.32	17.00	16.81	16.94	16.81	17.00	9.75	13.78	451.17	7.96	19.20
Jul	14.98	15.75	15.44	15.44	15.44	15.56	9.81	13.07	488.54	7.42	17.96
Aug	15.53	16.69	16.81	16.94	16.56	16.75	12.50	13.58	484.86	7.48	17.68
Sep	14.86	15.94	15.75	15.88	15.75	15.88	13.94	13.38	491.72	7.45	17.28
Oct	14.90	16.69	16.81	16.88	16.63	16.75	15.25	13.12	483.80	7.59	17.14
Nov	13.38	14.57	14.56	14.69	14.44	14.56	18.31	13.22	493.45	7.36	16.43
Dec	13.45	14.88	14.81	14.88	14.63	14.84	17.75	13.67	470.10	7.56	16.93
1981 Jan	13.02	13.85	13.75	13.81	13.25	13.44	17.38	13.96	459.67	7.78	17.44
Feb	11.93	12.69	12.56	12.69	12.50	12.69	16.63	13.89	487.04	7.43	16.38
Mar	11.87	12.69	12.63	12.75	12.38	12.50	14.63	13.68	497.38	6.77	14.39
Apr	11.57	12.56	12.31	12.38	12.25	12.38	17.00	13.64	559.18	5.89	11.57
May	11.78	12.57	12.44	12.56	12.41	12.53	18.06	14.31	557.82	5.91	11.59
Jun	12.24	12.57	12.50	12.63	12.44	12.56	17.63	14.57	545.03	5.92	11.73
Jul	14.29	14.69	14.63	14.75	14.44	14.50	18.75	15.14	528.23	6.02	11.70
Aug	13.63	14.16	14.00	14.13	13.88	14.00	18.88	15.09	553.87	5.52	9.83
Sep	15.72	16.69	16.00	16.13	16.38	16.50	17.88	15.59	525.01	5.76	9.99
Oct	16.30	16.57	16.31	16.63	15.63	15.81	15.63	15.95	474.86	6.27	10.85
Nov	14.24	15.00	14.81	14.94	14.75	14.88	12.00	15.44	511.09	5.85	9.92
Dec	15.35	15.75	15.63	15.75	15.75	15.94	13.63	15.65	522.76	5.77	10.05
1982 Jan	14.04	14.50	14.50	14.56	14.31	14.44	14.69	15.58	543.00	5.57	9.83
Feb	12.90	13.97	14.00	14.13	13.75	13.88	15.00	14.74	565.61	5.43	9.62
Mar	12.87	13.58	13.63	13.69	13.50	13.63	15.50	13.72	560.33	5.63	10.57
Apr	13.03	13.69	13.69	13.81	13.63	13.75	14.88	13.96	563.62	5.57	11.22
May	12.60	13.35	13.38	13.50	13.25	13.38	14.38	13.69	578.75	5.41	11.25
Jun	12.62	13.13	13.13	13.19	13.06	13.25	15.75	13.56	569.98	5.50	11.45
Jul	11.02	11.88	11.81	11.94	11.38	11.56	13.00	13.20	559.67	5.47	11.51
Aug	9.94	10.88	10.75	10.88	10.50	10.59	11.63	12.23	561.12	5.28	11.58
Sep	9.92	10.50	10.81	10.94	10.44	10.56	10.44	11.40	580.10	5.02	11.02
Oct	8.69	9.63	9.56	9.69	9.13	9.25	9.94	10.50	601.83	4.76	10.54
Nov	9.89	10.50	10.25	10.50	10.31	10.44	9.88	10.64	618.73	4.87	10.44
Dec	9.96	10.63	10.88	10.94	10.63	10.69	9.25	11.34	592.79	5.08	10.81

1 Average discount rate expressed as the rate at which interest is earned during the life of the bills.
2 For a minimum term of 3 months and thereafter at 7 days' notice.
3 Spread of rates over the day in the inter-bank sterling market; from June 1982 rates are the spread at 10.30 am.
4 Averages of Wednesdays until February 1980; from March 1980 figures are the average of all observations (3 a week); from January 1982 average of working days. Calculated gross redemption yields - see *Financial Statistics Explanatory Handbook*.
5 See footnote on page 257.
6 These figures fall outside the scope of National Statistics.

Sources: Bank of England; HM Treasury; Financial Times; Institute of Actuaries; Faculty of Actuaries; Enquiries 020 7601 4342 (Bank of England)

5.9 Other interest rates, security prices and yields[6]

continued

Percentage rate

	Last Friday						Last working day	Average of working days			
									Financial Times index of industrial ordinary shares 1 July 1935 = 100		
	Treasury bill yield[1]	Deposits with local authorities - 3 months[2]	Inter-bank 3 months bid rate[3]	Inter-bank 3 months offer rate[3]	Sterling certificates of deposit 3 months bid rate	Sterling certificates of deposit 3 months offer rate	Interest on US $ deposits in London (3 months)	British government securities long dated[4] -20 years	Price index	Dividend yield	Earnings yield[5]
	AJRP	AJOI	HSAJ	HSAK	HSAL	HSAM	AJIB	AJLX	AJMT	AJMU	AJMV
1983 Jan	11.24	12.00	11.50	11.63	11.50	11.63	9.38	11.60	613.60	4.88	10.50
Feb	11.15	11.00	11.25	11.56	11.13	11.25	8.81	11.50	646.29	4.82	10.34
Mar	10.49	11.00	10.75	10.88	10.81	10.94	9.69	10.97	659.54	4.87	10.25
Apr	9.92	10.00	10.19	10.25	10.00	10.19	8.88	10.56	685.94	4.60	9.36
May	9.93	10.00	10.25	10.31	10.13	10.25	9.44	10.65	690.27	4.59	9.04
Jun	9.51	10.00	9.75	9.81	9.63	9.69	9.69	10.39	716.64	4.47	8.88
Jul	9.62	10.00	9.94	10.00	9.81	9.94	10.25	10.95	697.90	4.60	9.12
Aug	9.56	10.00	9.81	9.94	9.75	9.84	10.25	11.07	724.40	4.60	9.27
Sep	9.17	10.00	9.63	9.69	9.44	9.50	9.50	10.67	704.31	4.81	9.59
Oct	9.03	9.00	9.31	9.38	9.13	9.25	9.69	10.61	693.57	4.87	9.67
Nov	9.06	9.00	9.25	9.31	9.09	9.25	9.81	10.29	724.80	4.70	9.50
Dec	9.04	9.00	9.34	9.41	9.25	9.34	9.94	10.35	759.48	4.62	9.47
1984 Jan	9.06	9.00	9.38	9.44	9.28	9.34	9.75	10.28	810.58	4.42	9.16
Feb	9.05	9.00	9.31	9.38	9.25	9.34	10.13	10.42	814.62	4.50	9.48
Mar	8.56	9.00	8.94	9.00	8.81	8.88	10.69	10.23	866.42	4.34	9.43
Apr	8.54	9.00	8.88	8.94	8.84	8.91	11.00	10.40	881.08	4.36	9.93
May	9.19	10.00	9.63	9.75	9.63	9.75	11.75	10.93	870.55	4.49	10.44
Jun	9.06	10.00	9.44	9.50	9.31	9.44	12.19	11.15	824.50	4.79	11.13
Jul	11.69	12.00	12.19	12.25	12.00	12.25	11.81	11.67	787.59	5.08	11.80
Aug	10.18	11.00	10.75	10.81	10.50	10.63	11.94	10.98	835.82	4.93	11.57
Sep	10.24	11.00	10.75	10.81	10.56	10.63	11.44	10.78	859.32	4.84	11.51
Oct	10.13	11.00	10.56	10.69	10.44	10.50	10.00	10.69	865.15	4.89	11.66
Nov	9.27	10.00	9.75	9.81	9.63	9.75	9.19	10.32	912.35	4.67	11.23
Dec	9.33	10.00	10.00	10.06	9.75	9.88	8.69	10.46	929.59	4.62	11.73
1985 Jan	11.86	13.00	12.25	12.31	13.75	14.00	8.50	10.96	977.05	4.42	11.15
Feb	13.91	14.00	14.13	14.19	13.88	14.00	9.44	11.06	979.27	4.41	11.01
Mar	12.75	13.00	13.06	13.25	12.94	13.06	9.06	10.90	987.45	4.56	11.32
Apr	12.27	13.00	12.69	12.81	12.38	12.50	8.69	10.68	968.97	4.70	11.79
May	12.16	13.00	12.50	12.56	12.38	12.50	7.75	10.88	1 003.78	4.58	11.52
Jun	12.33	13.00	12.50	12.56	12.31	12.44	7.75	10.70	980.38	4.72	11.83
Jul	11.30	11.00	11.88	11.94	11.19	11.31	8.25	10.44	935.22	4.96	12.38
Aug	11.31	12.00	11.62	11.69	11.38	11.50	8.06	10.37	973.60	4.82	11.88
Sep	11.32	11.00	11.50	11.56	11.28	11.38	8.13	10.39	1 002.83	4.73	11.61
Oct	11.45	12.00	11.56	11.63	11.47	11.59	8.00	10.22	1 034.23	4.63	11.35
Nov	11.33	12.00	11.50	11.56	11.25	11.44	8.13	10.37	1 099.30	4.40	10.87
Dec	11.49	12.00	11.88	11.94	11.75	11.88	7.94	10.45	1 113.89	4.45	11.04
1986 Jan	12.47	13.00	12.81	12.94	12.69	12.82	8.00	10.80	1 127.58	4.43	10.89
Feb	12.21	12.00	12.25	12.63	12.13	12.26	7.81	10.40	1 220.80	4.27	10.32
Mar	11.04	11.00	11.25	11.31	11.07	11.19	7.38	9.39	1 348.98	4.00	9.55
Apr	10.09	10.00	10.25	10.38	10.19	10.32	6.81	8.76	1 391.12	3.87	9.49
May	9.56	10.00	9.75	9.88	9.63	9.75	7.06	9.00	1 329.64	4.11	10.20
Jun	9.52	10.00	9.81	9.88	9.60	9.73	6.81	9.23	1 332.13	4.14	10.03
Jul	9.76	10.00	9.88	9.94	9.82	9.94	6.44	9.37	1 309.62	4.21	10.14
Aug	9.56	10.00	9.91	9.94	9.69	9.82	5.69	9.41	1 262.13	4.37	10.56
Sep	9.93	11.00	10.50	10.56	10.44	10.57	6.06	9.97	1 286.23	4.31	9.91
Oct	10.85	11.00	11.06	11.19	11.00	11.12	5.88	10.62	1 262.33	4.42	10.16
Nov	10.96	11.00	11.38	11.44	11.18	11.21	6.06	10.80	1 289.25	4.41	10.21
Dec	10.94	11.00	11.34	11.44	11.19	11.31	6.31	10.69	1 283.58	4.45	10.50
1987 Jan	10.85	11.00	11.00	11.06	10.88	11.01	6.19	10.05	1 392.63	4.11	9.68
Feb	10.46	11.00	10.78	10.81	10.53	10.66	6.38	9.84	1 529.61	3.72	8.72
Mar	9.54	10.00	9.69	9.81	9.50	9.62	6.56	9.16	1 596.26	3.67	8.48
Apr	9.39	9.00	9.63	9.69	9.44	9.57	7.06	9.11	1 554.78	3.77	8.58
May	8.68	9.00	8.81	8.94	8.63	8.75	7.31	8.82	1 674.07	3.44	8.23
Jun	8.96	9.00	9.06	9.13	8.94	9.07	7.13	8.90	1 759.78	3.25	7.83
Jul	9.14	9.00	9.25	9.38	9.22	9.28	6.94	9.23	1 855.23	3.10	7.52
Aug	10.12	10.00	10.38	10.44	10.13	10.26	7.13	9.92	1 758.27	3.28	8.11
Sep	10.02	10.00	10.13	10.19	10.00	10.13	8.31	9.98	1 801.84	3.25	7.98
Oct	9.07	9.00	9.19	9.31	8.88	9.00	7.69	9.88	1 645.30	3.75	9.22
Nov	8.67	9.00	8.88	9.00	8.75	8.88	7.88	9.20	1 296.04	4.78	11.83
Dec	8.38	9.00	8.88	8.88	8.69	8.81	7.38	9.57	1 337.02	4.67	11.58

1 Average discount rate expressed as the rate at which interest is earned during the life of the bills.
2 For a minimum term of 3 months and thereafter at 7 days' notice.
3 Spread of rates over the day in the inter-bank sterling market; from June 1982 rates are the spread at 10.30 am.
4 Averages of Wednesdays until February 1980; from March 1980 figures are the average of all observations (3 a week); from January 1982 average of working days. Calculated gross redemption yields - see *Financial Statistics Explanatory Handbook.*
5 See footnote 5 on page 257.
6 These figures fall ouside the scope of National Statistics.

Sources: Bank of England; HM Treasury; Financial Times; Institute of Actuaries; Faculty of Actuaries; Enquiries 020 7601 4342 (Bank of England)

5.9 Other interest rates, security prices and yields[6]

continued

Percentage rate

	Last Friday						Last working day	Average of working days			
									Financial Times index of industrial ordinary shares 1 July 1935 = 100		
	Treasury bill yield[1]	Deposits with local authorities - 3 months[2]	Inter-bank 3 months bid rate[3]	Inter-bank 3 months offer rate[3]	Sterling certificates of deposit 3 months bid rate	Sterling certificates of deposit 3 months offer rate	Interest on US $ deposits in London (3 months)	British government securities long dated[4] -20 years	Price index	Dividend yield	Earnings yield[5]
	AJRP	AJOI	HSAJ	HSAK	HSAL	HSAM	AJIB	AJLX	AJMT	AJMU	AJMV
1988 Jan	8.85	8.75	8.72	8.78	8.56	8.63	6.81	9.57	1 419.38	4.39	11.02
Feb	8.96	9.31	9.31	9.63	9.06	9.13	6.75	9.38	1 397.56	4.48	11.16
Mar	8.26	8.63	8.69	8.72	8.50	8.63	6.81	9.12	1 446.73	4.48	11.37
Apr	7.96	8.50	8.41	8.50	8.25	8.38	7.25	9.12	1 421.19	4.57	11.89
May	8.29	7.63	7.72	7.75	7.50	7.63	7.69	9.27	1 427.45	4.59	11.86
Jun	9.95	9.88	9.34	9.38	9.06	9.19	7.88	9.32	1 470.13	4.51	11.56
Jul	10.49	10.69	10.84	10.88	10.50	10.63	8.31	9.51	1 488.92	4.52	11.47
Aug	11.98	12.25	12.00	12.13	11.75	11.88	8.50	9.47	1 474.30	4.61	11.67
Sep	11.80	11.81	11.91	11.94	11.75	11.88	8.63	9.60	1 429.22	4.80	12.11
Oct	11.89	12.00	12.03	12.06	11.88	12.00	8.56	9.23	1 493.35	4.65	11.71
Nov	13.01	13.06	12.81	13.13	12.06	12.13	9.31	9.30	1 478.12	4.78	12.00
Dec	12.91	13.19	13.00	13.00	12.88	12.94	9.25	9.45	1 438.44	5.08	12.84
1989 Jan	12.70	12.94	13.00	13.13	12.94	13.06	9.34	9.35	1 543.53	4.76	11.96
Feb	12.91	13.38	13.06	13.09	13.06	13.19	10.28	9.15	1 676.23	4.37	10.90
Mar	12.79	13.00	13.03	13.06	12.88	13.00	10.28	9.26	1 710.70	4.45	10.83
Apr	12.62	12.94	12.88	12.94	12.75	12.88	9.91	9.52	1 700.63	4.55	11.03
May	13.72	14.25	13.81	13.88	13.69	13.81	9.53	9.52	1 775.56	4.43	10.79
Jun	14.10	14.12	14.19	14.25	13.94	14.06	9.34	9.88	1 779.72	4.50	10.77
Jul	13.69	13.81	13.81	13.88	13.78	13.84	8.53	9.53	1 863.30	4.34	10.16
Aug	13.81	13.75	13.88	13.94	13.81	13.88	8.97	9.37	1 960.27	4.05	9.66
Sep[7]	–	14.56	14.63	14.69	14.25	14.38	9.16	9.62	1 958.98	4.10	9.85
Oct[7]	–	15.31	15.63	15.75	15.56	15.69	8.66	9.81	1 786.75	4.60	11.06
Nov	14.98	15.06	15.03	15.06	14.97	15.03	8.47	9.99	1 758.02	4.75	11.42
Dec	15.02	15.03	15.13	15.16	15.03	15.09	8.34	9.96	1 863.28	4.57	11.14
1990 Jan	14.99	14.94	15.13	15.19	15.06	15.13	8.34	10.28	1 894.20	4.51	11.01
Feb	14.87	15.06	15.09	15.13	15.00	15.06	8.34	10.72	1 816.79	4.76	11.47
Mar	15.14	15.13	15.22	15.25	15.13	15.19	8.47	11.46	1 771.99	4.98	11.76
Apr	15.17	15.16	15.28	15.31	15.13	15.25	8.66	11.77	1 718.96	5.22	12.03
May	15.00	15.13	15.03	15.09	14.94	15.06	8.34	11.49	1 757.40	5.21	11.71
Jun	14.85	14.94	14.94	14.97	14.88	14.94	8.34	11.01	1 904.97	4.86	10.76
Jul	14.86	14.94	14.94	15.00	14.91	14.97	7.91	11.03	1 873.36	4.96	10.90
Aug	14.82	14.94	14.97	15.00	14.88	15.00	8.03	11.41	1 710.25	5.52	11.82
Sep	14.76	14.97	14.94	14.97	14.88	14.94	8.28	11.32	1 599.08	5.93	12.52
Oct	13.57	13.75	13.78	13.81	13.75	13.81	8.03	11.12	1 619.55	5.90	12.34
Nov	13.11	13.50	13.50	13.56	13.38	13.44	8.34	10.94	1 630.44	5.90	12.31
Dec	13.50	14.00	14.00	14.00	13.81	13.88	7.53	10.42	1 696.14	5.67	11.83
1991 Jan	13.23	13.88	13.97	13.97	13.81	13.88	7.03	10.22	1 653.17	5.82	12.07
Feb	12.44	12.75	12.75	12.88	12.75	12.81	6.84	9.89	1 803.59	5.33	11.07
Mar	11.90	12.88	12.25	12.38	12.19	12.31	6.34	10.06	1 953.94	4.96	9.25
Apr	11.49	11.63	11.78	11.81	11.69	11.75	6.03	9.99	1 983.19	4.87	8.80
May	11.04	11.38	11.38	11.41	11.25	11.28	6.03	10.15	1 952.19	4.91	8.68
Jun	11.04	11.63	11.31	11.31	11.13	11.19	6.16	10.34	1 951.73	4.88	8.57
Jul	10.72	11.13	11.13	11.13	10.94	11.00	6.03	10.10	1 953.22	4.84	8.47
Aug	10.33	10.81	10.78	10.81	10.63	10.69	5.66	9.89	2 027.33	4.68	7.81
Sep	9.94	10.31	10.19	10.25	10.13	10.19	5.59	9.54	2 053.95	4.64	7.49
Oct	10.24	10.44	10.50	10.56	10.41	10.44	5.22	9.62	1 979.08	4.74	7.48
Nov	10.34	10.63	10.59	10.63	10.50	10.53	4.97	9.68	1 920.39	5.03	7.46
Dec	10.45	10.93	10.94	11.00	10.75	10.88	4.22	9.56	1 830.52	5.03	7.54
1992 Jan	10.15	10.56	10.63	10.66	10.44	10.50	4.12	9.33	1 937.55	4.71	7.06
Feb	9.98	10.25	10.31	10.34	10.16	10.22	4.19	9.21	1 974.94	4.62	6.78
Mar	10.48	10.69	10.78	10.81	10.66	10.72	4.31	9.54	1 946.12	4.61	6.57
Apr	10.06	10.53	10.50	10.56	10.31	10.44	4.00	9.33	1 983.89	4.55	6.58
May	9.65	10.00	10.00	10.00	9.88	9.91	4.00	8.99	2 123.50	4.32	6.22
Jun	9.69	10.06	10.06	10.13	9.94	9.97	3.84	9.02	2 027.33	4.56	6.68
Jul	9.85	10.25	10.25	10.31	10.13	10.16	3.37	8.90	1 856.49	4.97	7.20
Aug[7]	–	10.50	10.56	10.63	10.31	10.44	3.44	9.13	1 741.10	5.20	7.50
Sep	8.40	8.88	9.25	9.25	9.00	9.13	3.19	9.12	1 794.52	4.95	7.17
Oct	6.87	7.44	7.56	7.63	7.25	7.31	3.50	9.24	1 899.13	4.73	6.80
Nov	6.56	7.25	7.25	7.31	7.00	7.06	3.94	8.84	2 023.15	4.55	6.38
Dec	6.44	7.00	7.19	7.25	7.09	7.13	3.37	8.84	2 115.20	4.40	6.03

1 Average discount rate expressed as the rate at which interest is earned during the life of the bills.
2 For a minimum term of 3 months and thereafter at 7 days' notice.
3 Spread of rates over the day in the inter-bank sterling market; from June 1982 rates are the spread at 10.30 am.
4 Averages of Wednesdays until February 1980; from March 1980 figures are the average of all observations (3 a week); from January 1982 average of working days. Calculated gross redemption yields - see *Financial Statistics Explanatory Handbook*.
5 See footnote on page 257.
6 These figures fall outside the scope of National Statistics.
7 Treasury bills were not tendered in September, October 1989 and August 1992.

Sources: Bank of England, HM Treasury, Financial Times; Institute of Actuaries, Faculty of Actuaries; Enquiries 020 7601 4342 (Bank of England)

5.9 Other interest rates, security prices and yields[6]

continued

Percentage rate

	Last Friday						Last working day	Average of working days			
									Financial Times index of industrial ordinary shares 1 July 1935 = 100		
	Treasury bill yield[1]	Deposits with local authorities - 3 months[2]	Inter-bank 3 months bid rate[3]	Inter-bank 3 months offer rate[3]	Sterling certificates of deposit 3 months bid rate	Sterling certificates of deposit 3 months offer rate	Interest on US $ deposits in London (3 months)	British government securities long dated[4] -20 years	Price index	Dividend yield	Earnings yield[5]
	AJRP	AJOI	HSAJ	HSAK	HSAL	HSAM	AJIB	AJLX	AJMT	AJMU	AJMV
1993 Jan	5.51	6.25	6.25	6.31	6.06	6.16	3.25	8.91	2 161.96	4.35	5.98
Feb	5.49	6.13	6.13	6.13	5.91	5.97	3.12	8.63	2 195.20	4.35	5.93
Mar	5.47	5.88	6.00	6.06	5.94	6.00	3.19	8.33	2 252.83	4.35	6.08
Apr	5.46	6.13	6.13	6.13	5.88	5.94	3.12	8.39	2 213.18	4.27	6.27
May	5.32	5.88	5.84	5.91	5.75	5.81	3.31	8.60	2 207.04	4.21	6.21
Jun	5.26	6.00	5.88	5.94	5.75	5.78	3.25	8.39	2 249.20	4.12	4.99
Jul	5.16	5.81	5.88	5.94	5.75	5.81	3.25	7.96	2 242.42	4.12	4.90
Aug	5.16	5.81	5.69	5.75	5.69	5.75	3.19	7.39	2 371.00	3.89	4.64
Sep	5.25	5.94	5.88	5.91	5.78	5.81	3.31	7.18	2 348.43	3.95	4.66
Oct	5.08	5.50	5.63	5.69	5.47	5.50	3.37	7.09	2 363.62	3.94	4.58
Nov	4.87	5.38	5.31	5.34	5.22	5.25	3.44	7.06	2 357.95	3.94	4.58
Dec	4.95	5.31	5.31	5.31	5.22	5.25	3.31	6.46	2 492.46	3.73	4.26
1994 Jan	4.91	5.38	5.41	5.44	5.28	5.34	3.19	6.41	2 620.12	3.56	4.03
Feb	4.77	5.00	5.19	5.19	5.06	5.13	3.69	6.83	2 615.71	3.54	4.04
Mar	4.99	5.25	5.22	5.25	5.13	5.19	3.87	7.47	2 523.40	3.67	4.96
Apr	4.91	5.09	5.19	5.19	5.06	5.13	4.25	7.83	2 485.27	3.88	5.31
May	4.86	5.13	5.09	5.16	5.03	5.09	4.56	8.23	2 455.02	4.07	5.52
Jun	4.98	5.13	5.09	5.13	5.03	5.06	4.81	8.55	2 343.28	4.29	5.72
Jul	5.68	5.38	5.38	5.44	5.25	5.31	4.75	8.41	2 370.69	4.24	5.67
Aug	5.43	5.44	5.44	5.50	5.38	5.42	4.94	8.52	2 485.86	4.08	5.68
Sep	5.55	5.75	5.81	5.85	5.66	5.72	5.44	8.72	2 404.62	4.27	6.13
Oct	5.51	5.88	5.91	5.97	5.81	5.88	5.56	8.63	2 342.27	4.40	6.29
Nov	5.80	6.06	5.97	6.00	5.88	5.91	6.12	8.53	2 367.99	4.38	6.37
Dec	6.00	6.50	6.53	6.56	6.41	6.44	6.44	8.44	2 327.92	4.49	6.57
1995 Jan	6.20	6.69	6.69	6.72	6.59	6.66	6.25	8.61	2 314.26	4.52	6.63
Feb	6.29	6.69	6.69	6.75	6.63	6.66	6.19	8.52	2 318.80	4.55	6.82
Mar	6.21	6.56	6.59	6.63	6.53	6.56	6.19	8.50	2 354.84	4.49	7.21
Apr	6.73	6.88	6.91	6.94	6.81	6.88	6.12	8.39	2 438.47	4.34	–
May	6.17	6.56	6.50	6.56	6.44	6.47	6.00	8.18	2 495.93	4.25	–
Jun	6.73	6.75	6.88	6.91	6.75	6.81	5.94	8.16	2 520.49	4.23	–
Jul	6.71	6.75	6.78	6.81	6.69	6.75	5.75	8.36	2 566.60	4.15	–
Aug	6.68	6.69	6.75	6.78	6.69	6.72	5.81	8.24	2 618.07	4.10	–
Sep	6.65	6.69	6.75	6.78	6.69	6.75	5.82	8.09	2 632.99	4.07	–
Oct	6.64	6.63	6.69	6.72	6.63	6.66	5.85	8.29	2 598.68	4.10	–
Nov	6.48	6.44	6.59	6.63	6.56	6.59	5.79	7.97	2 618.81	4.09	–
Dec	6.31	6.44	6.47	6.50	6.44	6.47	5.54	7.75	2 647.33	4.07	–
1996 Jan	6.10	6.19	6.22	6.25	6.19	6.22	5.25	7.79	2 749.65	3.95	..
Feb	6.02	6.03	6.13	6.16	6.09	6.13	5.19	8.10	2 748.04	3.84	..
Mar	5.88	6.00	6.00	6.06	6.00	6.02	5.57	8.34	2 759.32	3.92	..
Apr	5.88	5.97	5.97	6.00	5.94	5.97	5.44	8.30	2 827.87	3.90	..
May	5.92	6.00	6.03	6.06	5.97	6.00	5.40	8.35	2 800.40	3.97	..
Jun	5.61	5.75	5.75	5.78	5.69	5.72	5.47	8.36	2 762.43	4.03	..
Jul	5.59	5.72	5.72	5.78	5.69	5.72	5.54	8.25	2 721.55	4.12	..
Aug	5.59	5.69	5.69	5.72	5.66	5.69	5.50	8.16	2 801.45	4.07	..
Sep	5.63	5.75	5.84	5.88	5.81	5.84	5.52	8.16	2 823.96	4.03	..
Oct	5.71	6.13	5.97	6.00	5.91	5.94	5.42	7.88	2 844.23	3.99	..
Nov	6.23	6.25	6.31	6.34	6.25	6.31	5.45	7.81	2 790.12	4.09	..
Dec	6.26	6.38	6.38	6.44	6.34	6.41	5.50	7.71	2 779.80	4.12	..
1997 Jan	6.02	6.19	6.22	6.25	6.13	6.19	5.48	7.74	2 816.35	4.11	..
Feb	5.84	6.13	6.13	6.19	6.06	6.13	5.47	7.39	2 851.43	4.01	..
Mar	6.13	6.25	6.28	6.31	6.22	6.25	5.73	7.62	2 878.24	3.91	..
Apr	6.23	6.41	6.44	6.47	6.34	6.41	5.69	7.77	2 844.17	3.90	..
May	6.31	6.50	6.53	6.56	6.47	6.50	5.75	7.23	2 978.86	3.69	..
Jun	6.52	6.81	6.78	6.81	6.78	6.81	5.72	7.18	3 000.31	3.66	..
Jul	6.76	6.97	6.94	6.97	6.88	6.94	5.64	6.97	3 074.31	3.57	..
Aug	7.05	7.19	7.22	7.25	7.19	7.25	5.65	7.02	3 155.89	3.51	..
Sep	7.02	7.16	7.19	7.25	7.19	7.22	5.71	6.79	3 222.33	3.52	..
Oct	7.02	7.25	7.25	7.31	7.19	7.25	5.72	6.48	3 346.83	3.39	..
Nov	7.26	7.56	7.63	7.66	7.56	7.59	5.84	6.54	3 146.25	3.60	..
Dec	7.13	7.50	7.59	7.63	7.53	7.59	5.69	6.31	3 256.86	3.47	..

1 Average discount rate expressed as the rate at which interest is earned during the life of the bills.
2 For a minimum term of 3 months and thereafter at 7 days' notice.
3 Spread of rates over the day in the inter-bank sterling market; from June 1982 rates are the spread at 10.30 am.
4 Averages of Wednesdays until February 1980; from March 1980 figures are the average of all observations (3 a week); from January 1982 average of working days. Calculated gross redemption yields - see *Financial Statistics Explanatory Handbook.*
5 See footnote on page 257.
6 These figures fall outside the scope of National Statistics.

Sources: Bank of England, HM Treasury, Financial Times; Institute of Actuaries, Faculty of Actuaries; Enquiries 020 7601 4342 (Bank of England)

5.9 Other interest rates, security prices and yields[6]

continued

Percentage rate

	Last Friday						Last working day	Average of working days			
									Financial Times index of industrial ordinary shares 1 July 1935 = 100		
	Treasury bill yield[1]	Deposits with local authorities - 3 months[2]	Inter-bank 3 months bid rate[3]	Inter-bank 3 months offer rate[3]	Sterling certificates of deposit 3 months bid rate	Sterling certificates of deposit 3 months offer rate	Interest on US $ deposits in London (3 months)	British government securities long dated[4] -20 years	Price index	Dividend yield	Earnings yield[5]
	AJRP	AJOI	HSAJ	HSAK	HSAL	HSAM	AJIB	AJLX	AJMT	AJMU	AJMV
1998 Jan	6.84	7.44	7.44	7.47	7.41	7.44	5.56	6.07	3 316.29	3.35	..
Feb	7.09	7.44	7.47	7.50	7.41	7.47	5.60	5.99	3 466.66	3.11	..
Mar	7.22	7.44	7.50	7.50	7.44	7.50	5.66	5.87	3 704.62	2.97	..
Apr	7.12	7.38	7.38	7.44	7.34	7.41	5.65	5.70	3 805.78	2.88	..
May	7.18	7.31	7.41	7.44	7.34	7.38	5.62	5.75	3 874.65	2.84	..
Jun	7.50	7.72	7.72	7.75	7.69	7.72	5.62	5.54	3 829.91	2.90	..
Jul	7.30	7.59	7.69	7.72	7.63	7.69	5.59	5.56	3 872.48	2.82	..
Aug	7.37	7.50	7.56	7.59	7.53	7.56	5.56	5.46	3 556.16	3.03	..
Sep	6.87	7.25	7.28	7.31	7.22	7.25	5.27	5.06	3 199.89	3.34	..
Oct	6.66	7.06	7.09	7.13	7.00	7.06	5.18	4.98	3 043.19	3.49	..
Nov	6.34	6.81	6.81	6.81	6.69	6.75	5.22	4.85	3 398.12	3.11	..
Dec	5.63	6.13	6.28	6.31	6.22	6.28	5.00	4.54	3 437.49	3.04	..
1999 Jan	5.39	5.89	5.69	5.75	5.63	5.69	4.90	4.40	3 533.15	2.92	..
Feb	5.11	5.31	5.38	5.40	5.31	5.34	4.96	4.49	3 662.63	2.86	..
Mar	4.93	5.22	5.22	5.25	5.16	5.22	4.88	4.66	3 760.35	2.76	..
Apr	4.98	5.19	5.22	5.25	5.16	5.22	4.93	4.59	3 996.92	2.61	..
May	4.98	5.25	5.25	5.28	5.22	5.25	4.97	4.84	3 964.51	2.67	..
Jun	4.76	5.03	5.06	5.09	5.03	5.06	5.35	4.91	4 042.05	2.66	..
Jul	4.92	5.13	5.16	5.22	5.09	5.16	5.35	4.89	4 083.59	2.69	..
Aug	4.90	5.06	5.09	5.13	5.06	5.13	5.48	4.80	4 024.71	2.63	..
Sep	5.24	5.25	5.38	5.41	5.34	5.41	5.95	4.94	3 913.54	2.69	..
Oct	5.32	5.88	5.88	5.94	5.81	5.88	6.10	4.93	3 700.20	3.01	..
Nov	5.28	5.75	5.78	5.81	5.72	5.78	6.11	4.40	3 886.71	2.86	..
Dec	5.70	5.88	5.94	6.00	5.88	5.94	5.98	4.51	4 021.40	2.80	..
2000 Jan	5.85	6.25	6.06	6.13	6.00	6.06	6.05	4.82	3 894.87	2.88	..
Feb	5.93	6.06	6.16	6.19	6.09	6.13	6.08	4.71	3 583.41	3.10	..
Mar	5.93	6.13	6.16	6.22	6.13	6.16	6.29	4.56	3 667.74	2.87	..
Apr	6.05	6.22	6.25	6.31	6.22	6.25	6.44	4.63	3 638.75	2.80	..
May	6.04	6.13	6.16	6.22	6.13	6.16	6.82	4.69	3 634.60	2.76	..
Jun	5.93	6.06	6.13	6.16	6.06	6.13	6.76	4.63	3 705.09	2.72	..

1 Average discount rate expressed as the rate at which interest is earned during the life of the bills.
2 For a minimum term of 3 months and thereafter at 7 days' notice.
3 Spread of rates over the day in the inter-bank sterling market; from June 1982 rates are the spread at 10.30 am.
4 Averages of Wednesdays until February 1980; from March 1980 figures are the average of all observations (3 a week); from January 1982 average of working days. Calculated gross redemption yields - see *Financial Statistics Explanatory Handbook.*
5 See footnote on page 257.
6 These figures fall outside the scope of National Statistics.

Sources: Bank of England, HM Treasury, Financial Times; Institute of Actuaries, Faculty of Actuaries; Enquiries 020 7601 4342 (Bank of England)

5.10 Selected retail banks: interest rates[5]

Per cent per annum

Base rates	
Date of change	New rate
1985 Jan 11	10.50
Jan 14[1]	12.00
Jan 28	14.00
Mar 20	13.50-14.00
Mar 21	13.50
Mar 29	13.00-13.50
Apr 3	13.00-13.25
Apr 12	12.75-13.00
Apr 19	12.50-12.75
Jun 12	12.50
Jul 15	12.00-12.50
Jul 16	12.00
Jul 29	11.50-12.00
Jul 30	11.50
1986 Jan 9	12.50
Mar 19	11.50
Apr 8	11.00-11.50
Apr 9	11.00
Apr 21	10.50
May 23	10.00-10.50
May 27	10.00
Oct 14	10.00-11.00
Oct 15	11.00
1987 Mar 10	10.50
Mar 18	10.00-10.50
Mar 19	10.00
Apr 28	9.50-10.00
Apr 29	9.50
May 11	9.00
Aug 6	9.00-10.00
Aug 7	10.00
Oct 23	9.50-10.00
Oct 29	9.50
Nov 4	9.00-9.50
Nov 5	9.00
Dec 4	8.50
1988 Feb 2	9.00
Mar 17	8.50-9.00

Base rates	
Date of change	New rate
Mar 18	8.50
Apr 11	8.00
May 17	7.50-8.00
May 18	7.50
Jun 2	7.50-8.00
Jun 3	8.00
Jun 6	8.00-8.50
Jun 7	8.50
Jun 22	8.50-9.00
Jun 23	9.00
Jun 28	9.00-9.50
Jun 29	9.50
Jul 4	9.50-10.00
Jul 5	10.00
Jul 18	10.00-10.50
Jul 19	10.50
Aug 8	10.50-11.00
Aug 9	11.00
Aug 25	11.00-12.00
Aug 26	12.00
Nov 25	13.00
1989 May 24	14.00
Oct 5	15.00
1990 Oct 8	14.00
1991 Feb 13	13.50
Feb 27	13.00
Mar 22	12.50
Apr 12	12.00
May 24	11.50
Jul 12	11.00
Sep 4	10.50
1992 May 5	10.00
Sep 16[1]	12.00
Sep 17[1]	10.00-12.00
Sep 18	10.00
Sep 22	9.00
Oct 16	8.00-9.00

Base rates	
Date of change	New rate
Oct 19	8.00
Nov 13[1]	7.00
1993 Jan 26[1]	6.00
Nov 23[1]	5.50
1994 Feb 8[1]	5.25
Sep 12[1]	5.75
Dec 7[1]	6.25
1995 Feb 2[1]	6.25-6.75
Feb 3	6.75
Dec 13	6.50
1996 Jan 18	6.25
Mar 8	6.00
Jun 6	5.75
Oct 30	5.75-6.00
Oct 31	6.00
1997 May 6	6.25
Jun 6	6.25-6.50
Jun 9	6.50
Jul 10	6.75
Aug 7	7.00
Nov 6	7.25
1998 Jun 4	7.5
Oct 8	7.25
Nov 5	6.75
Dec 10	6.25
1999 Jan 7	6.00
Feb 4	5.50
Apr 8	5.25
Jun 10	5.00
Sep 8	5.25
Nov 4	5.50
2000 Jan 13	5.75
Feb 10	6.00

1 Minimum lending rate set at one day on these dates.
See footnote 5 on page 267.

Source: Bank of England; Enquiries 020 7601 4342

5.10 Selected retail banks: interest rates[5]

continued

	End of month observation								
	Basic rate mortgages[2]			Weighted deposit rates-branch accounts- gross interest					
				Instant access			Time deposits		
	Bank	Building society	Banks + Building societies[4]	Bank	Building societies	Bank + Building societies	Bank	Building societies	Bank + Building societies
	AJVR	AJVS	AJVT	THAI	THAJ	THAK	THAL	THAM	THAN
1996	7.08	7.00	7.03	2.14	2.21	2.17	4.14	4.06	4.09
1997	8.62	8.16	8.51	3.41	3.23	3.38	5.78	5.66	5.75
1998	8.09	7.75	8.01	2.36	3.11	2.51	4.97	5.38	5.09
1999	7.22	6.88	7.14	1.52	2.02	1.62	4.20	4.14	4.18
1995 Jan	..	..	..	3.23	3.60	3.43	5.17	5.37	5.31
Feb	..	..	..	3.35	3.68	3.53	5.42	5.52	5.49
Mar	..	..	..	3.51	3.76	3.64	5.42	5.54	5.50
Apr	..	..	..	3.51	3.76	3.64	5.42	5.54	5.51
May	..	..	..	3.52	3.72	3.63	5.42	5.52	5.49
Jun	..	..	..	3.50	3.72	3.62	5.42	5.51	5.49
Jul	..	..	..	3.50	3.72	3.61	5.42	5.50	5.48
Aug	..	..	..	3.50	3.69	3.60	5.42	5.45	5.44
Sep	..	..	..	3.39	3.72	3.54	5.33	5.31	5.32
Oct	..	..	..	3.04	3.31	3.16	4.87	4.96	4.93
Nov	..	..	..	3.04	3.34	3.17	4.87	4.96	4.93
Dec	..	..	..	3.04	3.34	3.17	4.87	4.89	4.88
1996 Jan	7.69	7.74	7.72	2.72	2.81	2.76	4.58	4.66	4.63
Feb	7.53	7.50	7.51	2.49	2.75	2.61	4.42	4.56	4.52
Mar	7.48	7.48	7.48	2.47	2.69	2.57	4.43	4.43	4.43
Apr	7.40	7.26	7.31	2.31	2.48	2.39	4.32	4.27	4.29
May	7.23	7.16	7.19	2.28	2.43	2.35	4.25	4.22	4.23
Jun	7.19	7.15	7.17	2.27	2.42	2.34	4.23	4.22	4.23
Jul	7.19	7.15	7.17	2.21	2.35	2.27	4.22	4.18	4.19
Aug	7.10	6.93	7.00	2.14	2.17	2.15	4.14	4.00	4.05
Sep	6.99	6.89	6.93	2.16	2.14	2.15	4.13	3.99	4.04
Oct	6.98	6.89	6.93	2.11	2.14	2.12	4.11	3.99	4.03
Nov	6.98	6.89	6.93	2.11	2.17	2.13	4.11	3.99	4.03
Dec	7.08	7.00	7.03	2.14	2.21	2.17	4.14	4.06	4.09
1997 Jan	7.20	7.19	7.20	2.26	2.35	2.30	4.25	4.26	4.26
Feb	7.26	7.20	7.22	2.26	2.36	2.31	4.28	4.27	4.27
Mar	7.26	7.19	7.22	2.33	2.40	2.36	4.28	4.30	4.30
Apr	7.26	7.19	7.22	2.41	2.39	2.41	4.42	4.55	4.50
May	7.33	7.22	7.27	2.41	2.42	2.41	4.50	4.62	4.58
Jun	7.71	7.56	7.66	2.52	2.61	2.55	4.90	4.69	4.83
Jul	8.01	7.60	7.88	2.98	2.66	2.90	5.33	4.96	5.22
Aug	8.25	7.97	8.17	3.15	2.96	3.11	5.57	5.15	5.44
Sep	8.45	8.13	8.36	3.37	3.12	3.32	5.81	5.57	5.74
Oct	8.45	8.15	8.38	3.31	3.23	3.29	5.69	5.60	5.67
Nov	8.46	8.15	8.38	3.33	3.23	3.31	5.71	5.60	5.68
Dec	8.62	8.16	8.51	3.41	3.23	3.38	5.78	5.66	5.75
1998 Jan	8.70	8.20	8.58	3.45	3.37	3.43	5.90	5.80	5.87
Feb	8.70	8.34	8.61	3.46	3.39	3.45	5.93	5.83	5.90
Mar	8.70	8.35	8.61	3.45	3.39	3.43	5.92	5.83	5.89
Apr	8.69	8.36	8.61	3.42	3.49	3.43	5.88	5.83	5.87
May	8.69	8.36	8.61	3.30	3.49	3.34	6.02	5.84	5.97
Jun	8.69	8.36	8.61	3.34	3.50	3.37	5.98	6.03	5.99
Jul	8.95	8.38	8.81	3.52	3.77	3.57	6.18	6.05	6.14
Aug	8.95	8.50	8.84	3.52	3.83	3.59	6.18	6.14	6.17
Sep	8.95	8.65	8.88	3.53	3.92	3.61	6.18	6.18	6.18
Oct	8.95	8.62	8.87	3.45	3.92	3.55	6.13	6.18	6.14
Nov	8.70	8.24	8.59	3.07	3.49	3.15	5.79	5.85	5.81
Dec	8.09	7.75	8.01	2.36	3.11	2.51	4.97	5.38	5.09

1 Minimum lending rate set for one day on these dates

2 These data represent the weighted average of the "headline" rate on individual reporter's standard variable mortgage rate loans. They have superseded the previous mortgage rates which were simple averages. No data is available for the new series prior to January 1996. The data for old series AJTO are available on request.

3 Following the acquisition of Birmingham Midshires by Halifax PLC in April, Birmingham Midshires are not recorded in the building society sector for end-month April data onwards.

4 Weighted average of rates shown in previous two columns.

5 These figures fall outside the scope of National Statistics.

Sources: Bank of England; Building Societies Commission; Enquiries 020 7601 4342 (Bank of England)

5.10 Selected retail banks: interest rates[5]

continued

	End of month observation								
	Basic rate mortgages[2]			Weighted deposit rates-branch accounts- gross interest					
				Instant access			Time deposits		
	Bank	Building society	Banks + Building societies[4]	Bank	Building societies	Bank + Building societies	Bank	Building societies	Bank + Building societies
	AJVR	AJVS	AJVT	THAI	THAJ	THAK	THAL	THAM	THAN
1999 Jan	7.69	7.39	7.62	2.08	2.54	2.18	4.62	4.81	4.67
Feb	7.45	7.08	7.36	1.75	2.34	1.87	4.32	4.58	4.39
Mar	6.99	6.66	6.91	1.53	1.85	1.59	3.97	4.06	4.00
Apr	6.99[3]	6.65	6.90	1.45	1.97	1.55	3.93	4.03	3.96
May	6.88	6.65	6.82	1.36	2.00	1.49	3.85	4.03	3.90
Jun	6.87	6.63	6.82	1.35	1.96	1.47	3.85	4.02	3.90
Jul	6.84	6.60	6.78	1.27	1.91	1.39	3.77	4.00	3.83
Aug	6.84	6.59	6.78	1.25	1.90	1.38	3.83	4.00	3.88
Sep	6.84	6.58	6.77	1.32	1.87	1.43	3.83	3.97	3.87
Oct	6.95	6.62	6.87	1.38	1.87	1.47	3.91	3.97	3.93
Nov	6.98	6.67	6.90	1.40	1.92	1.50	3.93	4.03	3.96
Dec	7.22	6.88	7.14	1.52	2.02	1.62	4.20	4.14	4.18
2000 Jan	7.23	6.92	7.15	1.55	2.08	1.66	4.21	4.14	4.19
Feb	7.48	7.15	7.40	1.66	2.14	1.76	4.33	4.25	4.31
Mar	7.72	7.44	7.65	1.82	2.36	1.93	4.50	4.51	4.50
Apr	7.72	7.44	7.65	1.83	2.36	1.94	4.50	4.51	4.51
May	7.72	7.44	7.65	1.83	2.36	1.93	4.50	4.51	4.51

1 Minimum lending rate set for one day on these dates

2 These data represent the weighted average of the "headline" rate on individual reporter's standard variable mortgage rate loans. They have superseded the previous mortgage rates which were simple averages. No data is available for the new series prior to January 1996. The data for old series AJTO are available on request.

3 Following the acquisition of Birmingham Midshires by Halifax PLC in April, Birmingham Midshires are not recorded in the building society sector for end-month April data onwards.

4 Weighted average of rates shown in previous two columns.

5 These figures fall outside the scope of National Statistics.

Sources: Bank of England;
Building Societies Commission;
Enquiries 020 7601 6342 (Bank of England)

5.11 A selection of asset prices

	Physical assets							Financial assets[5]		
	Producer price indices (1995 = 100)			Housing: DETR all lenders mix adjusted house price index (1993 = 100)				British government stocks		
	Plant and machinery bought as fixed assets by		Manufactured output				Average price of agricultural land in England (1995 = 100)[1]	Fixed interest (Dec 1975 =100)	Index linked (April 1982= 100)	Company securities: FT-Actuaries all ordinary shares (10 April 1962 = 100)
	Motor vehicle industry[2]	All manufacturing industries[2]	Motor vehicle industry[2]	New dwellings[3]	Secondhand dwellings[3]	All dwellings[3]				
Annual	PVJL	PVNO	PQIR	BBKO	BBKP	BBKQ	BAJI	AJJY	AJJZ	AJMA
1963	..	..	..	..	..	..	..	..	..	100.61
1964	..	..	..	..	..	..	..	..	..	104.66
1965	..	..	..	..	..	..	..	..	..	99.08
1966	..	..	..	..	..	..	..	..	..	100.52
1967	..	..	..	..	..	..	..	..	..	107.35
1968	..	..	..	..	..	..	..	..	..	150.96
1969	..	..	..	..	..	..	..	..	..	149.62
1970	..	..	..	..	..	..	..	..	..	135.01
1971	..	..	..	..	..	..	..	..	..	163.93
1972	..	..	..	..	..	..	..	..	..	213.93
1973	..	..	..	..	..	..	..	..	..	184.13
1974	..	..	..	..	..	..	..	..	..	106.75
1975	..	..	..	..	..	..	..	..	..	133.11
1976	..	..	..	..	..	..	..	101.79	..	153.04
1977	..	..	..	..	..	..	..	114.14	..	191.93
1978	..	..	..	..	..	..	..	113.54	..	216.68
1979	..	..	..	..	..	..	..	111.72	..	245.50
1980	..	..	..	..	..	..	..	108.80	..	271.33
1981	..	..	..	..	..	..	..	106.35	..	307.96
1982	..	..	..	..	..	..	..	117.95	102.20	342.24
1983	..	..	..	..	..	..	..	127.84	107.49	434.72
1984	..	..	..	..	..	..	..	127.32	104.65	516.60
1985	..	..	..	..	..	..	..	128.70	110.23	631.98
1986	..	..	..	..	..	..	..	134.06	112.77	782.24
1987	..	..	..	..	..	..	..	136.61	116.35	1 024.64
1988	..	..	..	..	..	..	..	135.19	121.86	931.67
1989	..	..	..	..	..	..	..	130.45	135.63	1 110.29
1990	..	..	..	..	..	..	..	121.92	138.14	1 092.37
1991	84.8	87.2	87.9	..	..	..	..	131.11	147.51	1 187.30
1992	87.1	87.4	89.2	..	..	..	..	136.48	155.60	1 224.23
1993	92.7	93.1	93.1	100.0	100.0	100.0	..	148.19	178.85	1 457.38
1994	96.2	97.2	96.2	100.1	102.9	102.5	..	140.59	176.25	1 574.48
1995	100.0	100.0	100.0	104.7	103.0	103.2	..	139.69	182.74	1 647.07
1996	102.9	101.4	103.1	109.7	106.5	106.9	..	142.86	189.71	1 894.73
1997	101.9	99.3	104.5	120.7	116.3	116.9	..	147.42	202.34	2 235.79
1998	100.0	96.3	106.5	128.3	129.9	129.7	..	158.30	231.01	2 626.22
1999	99.8	95.5	106.8	147.9	144.1	144.6	..	160.35	252.41	2 918.22

1 Please note that because of some changes in coverage, the revised series from Q1 1993 is not directly comparable with the old series. From Q1 1993 prices of all sales of of agricultural land exclude some transfers in order to come closer to estimates of market determined prices. However the new series does not represent exactly competitive open market values. Sales are now analysed and recorded on the basis of when the transactions actually took place. Further information is available on the MAFF Website (www.maff.gov.uk) accessible through the Internet and by a faxback facility (Fax No 0906 711 0340 charged at 50 pence per minute). Data prior to Q1 1993 remains on the previous basis.

2 These indices are now published under SIC 1992 classification.

3 Series based on mortgage lending by all financial institutions rather than building societies only, as previously published. This change has been made necessary because of the mergers, takeovers and conversions to plc status affecting the building society sector. The series is based on the Department of the Environment, Transport and the Regions' 5% survey of mortgage lenders (at completion stage) but now includes all mortgage lenders rather than building societies only.

4 Provisional estimates.

5 These figures fall outside the scope of National Statistics.

Sources: Office for National Statistics;
Enquiries Columns 1-2 01633 812106 or 813390 ;;
Department of the Environment, Transport and the Regions;
Enquiries Columns 3-5 020 7890 3325;
Ministry of Agriculture, Fisheries and Food; Enquiries Column 6 020 7270 8371.;
Bank of England; Enquiries Columns 7-9 020 7601 5484

5.11 A selection of asset prices

continued

	Physical assets							Financial assets[5]		
	Producer price indices (1995 = 100)			Housing: DETR all lenders mix adjusted house price index (1993 = 100)				British government stocks		
	Plant and machinery bought as fixed assets by		Manufactured output							
	Motor vehicle industry[2]	All manufacturing industries[2]	Motor vehicle industry[2]	New dwellings[3]	Secondhand dwellings[3]	All dwellings[3]	Average price of agricultural land in England (1995 = 100)[1]	Fixed interest (Dec 1975 =100)	Index linked (April 1982= 100)	Company securities: FT-Actuaries all ordinary shares (10 April 1962 = 100)
	PVJL	PVNO	PQIR	BBKO	BBKP	BBKQ	BAJI	AJJY	AJJZ	AJMA
1963 Q1	..	..	..	..	..	..	..	..	..	95.95
Q2	..	..	..	..	..	..	..	..	..	98.55
Q3	..	..	..	..	..	..	..	..	..	101.54
Q4	..	..	..	..	..	..	..	..	..	106.40
1964 Q1	..	..	..	..	..	..	..	..	..	104.16
Q2	..	..	..	..	..	..	..	..	..	104.78
Q3	..	..	..	..	..	..	..	..	..	108.13
Q4	..	..	..	..	..	..	..	..	..	101.58
1965 Q1	..	..	..	..	..	..	..	..	..	99.18
Q2	..	..	..	..	..	..	..	..	..	98.16
Q3	..	..	..	..	..	..	..	..	..	95.32
Q4	..	..	..	..	..	..	..	..	..	103.67
1966 Q1	..	..	..	..	..	..	..	..	..	106.36
Q2	..	..	..	..	..	..	..	..	..	107.41
Q3	..	..	..	..	..	..	..	..	..	96.98
Q4	..	..	..	..	..	..	..	..	..	91.32
1967 Q1	..	..	..	..	..	..	..	..	..	95.82
Q2	..	..	..	..	..	..	..	..	..	103.07
Q3	..	..	..	..	..	..	..	..	..	108.88
Q4	..	..	..	..	..	..	..	..	..	121.64
1968 Q1	..	..	..	..	..	..	..	..	..	126.89
Q2	..	..	..	..	..	..	..	..	..	148.54
Q3	..	..	..	..	..	..	..	..	..	163.59
Q4	..	..	..	..	..	..	..	..	..	164.80
1969 Q1	..	..	..	..	..	..	..	..	..	170.50
Q2	..	..	..	..	..	..	..	..	..	151.51
Q3	..	..	..	..	..	..	..	..	..	137.32
Q4	..	..	..	..	..	..	..	..	..	139.14
1970 Q1	..	..	..	..	..	..	..	..	..	146.47
Q2	..	..	..	..	..	..	..	..	..	128.64
Q3	..	..	..	..	..	..	..	..	..	129.18
Q4	..	..	..	..	..	..	..	..	..	135.77
1971 Q1	..	..	..	..	..	..	..	..	..	135.78
Q2	..	..	..	..	..	..	..	..	..	158.20
Q3	..	..	..	..	..	..	..	..	..	180.10
Q4	..	..	..	..	..	..	..	..	..	181.65
1972 Q1	..	..	..	..	..	..	..	..	..	205.89
Q2	..	..	..	..	..	..	..	..	..	219.48
Q3	..	..	..	..	..	..	..	..	..	216.42
Q4	..	..	..	..	..	..	..	..	..	213.92
1973 Q1	..	..	..	..	..	..	..	..	..	196.95
Q2	..	..	..	..	..	..	..	..	..	191.70
Q3	..	..	..	..	..	..	..	..	..	179.80
Q4	..	..	..	..	..	..	..	..	..	168.05
1974 Q1	..	..	..	..	..	..	..	..	..	139.30
Q2	..	..	..	..	..	..	..	..	..	121.46
Q3	..	..	..	..	..	..	..	..	..	94.04
Q4	..	..	..	..	..	..	..	..	..	72.20
1975 Q1	..	..	..	..	..	..	..	..	..	104.85
Q2	..	..	..	..	..	..	..	..	..	139.58
Q3	..	..	..	..	..	..	..	..	..	135.18
Q4	..	..	..	..	..	..	..	..	..	152.83

See footnotes on page 269.

Sources: Office for National Statistics; Enquiries Columns 1-2 01633 812106 or 813390 ;; Department of the Environment, Transport and the Regions; Enquiries Columns 3-5 020 7890 3325; Ministry of Agriculture, Fisheries and Food; Enquiries Column 6 020 7270 8371.; Bank of England; Enquiries Columns 7-9 020 7601 5484

5.11 A selection of asset prices

continued

	Physical assets							Financial assets[5]		
	Producer price indices (1995 = 100)			Housing: DETR all lenders mix adjusted house price index (1993 = 100)				British government stocks		
	Plant and machinery bought as fixed assets by		Manufactured output				Average price of agricultural land in England (1995 = 100)[1]	Fixed interest (Dec 1975 =100)	Index linked (April 1982= 100)	Company securities: FT-Actuaries all ordinary shares (10 April 1962 = 100)
	Motor vehicle industry[2]	All manufacturing industries[2]	Motor vehicle industry[2]	New dwellings[3]	Secondhand dwellings[3]	All dwellings[3]				
	PVJL	PVNO	PQIR	BBKO	BBKP	BBKQ	BAJI	AJJY	AJJZ	AJMA
1976 Q1	..	..	..	..	..	..	..	105.31	..	166.73
Q2	..	..	..	..	..	..	..	103.36	..	163.44
Q3	..	..	..	..	..	..	..	101.72	..	150.21
Q4	..	..	..	..	..	..	..	96.75	..	131.76
1977 Q1	..	..	..	..	..	..	..	107.97	..	167.48
Q2	..	..	..	..	..	..	..	111.49	..	183.86
Q3	..	..	..	..	..	..	..	116.15	..	201.88
Q4	..	..	..	..	..	..	..	120.98	..	214.52
1978 Q1	..	..	..	..	..	..	..	118.42	..	203.97
Q2	..	..	..	..	..	..	..	112.68	..	210.93
Q3	..	..	..	..	..	..	..	112.94	..	228.23
Q4	..	..	..	..	..	..	..	110.11	..	223.58
1979 Q1	..	..	..	..	..	..	..	111.08	..	234.57
Q2	..	..	..	..	..	..	..	115.70	..	264.34
Q3	..	..	..	..	..	..	..	114.72	..	246.93
Q4	..	..	..	..	..	..	..	105.36	..	236.16
1980 Q1	..	..	..	..	..	..	..	104.35	..	249.13
Q2	..	..	..	..	..	..	..	107.64	..	252.20
Q3	..	..	..	..	..	..	..	111.63	..	285.25
Q4	..	..	..	..	..	..	..	111.60	..	298.73
1981 Q1	..	..	..	..	..	..	88	111.20	..	293.72
Q2	..	..	..	..	..	..	87	109.28	..	319.74
Q3	..	..	..	..	..	..	83	103.04	95.38	317.90
Q4	..	..	..	..	..	..	84	101.89	96.16	300.47
1982 Q1	..	..	..	..	..	..	86	108.49	97.74	320.89
Q2	..	..	..	..	..	..	83	111.70	100.60	328.63
Q3	..	..	..	..	..	..	87	122.77	102.02	340.83
Q4	..	..	..	..	..	..	89	128.82	108.45	378.62
1983 Q1	..	..	..	..	..	..	92	125.33	112.04	402.88
Q2	..	..	..	..	..	..	95	129.36	107.16	436.11
Q3	..	..	..	..	..	..	90	126.50	104.12	449.29
Q4	..	..	..	..	..	..	96	130.16	106.63	450.61
1984 Q1	..	..	..	..	..	..	98	130.30	105.17	499.26
Q2	..	..	..	..	..	..	101	125.81	103.34	510.24
Q3	..	..	..	..	..	..	104	124.55	100.88	502.40
Q4	..	..	..	..	..	..	78	128.60	109.19	554.51
1985 Q1	..	..	..	..	..	..	104	125.60	109.64	613.75
Q2	..	..	..	..	..	..	97	127.79	110.27	625.55
Q3	..	..	..	..	..	..	87	130.95	111.15	619.96
Q4	..	..	..	..	..	..	98	130.46	109.86	668.64
1986 Q1	..	..	..	..	..	..	90	133.43	108.86	729.09
Q2	..	..	..	..	..	..	93	140.58	116.86	800.73
Q3	..	..	..	..	..	..	82	133.78	113.83	792.95
Q4	..	..	..	..	..	..	83	128.44	111.55	806.18
1987 Q1	..	..	..	..	..	..	82	136.02	119.28	943.82
Q2	..	..	..	..	..	..	73	140.54	118.13	1 063.65
Q3	..	..	..	..	..	..	78	132.50	113.63	1 174.51
Q4	..	..	..	..	..	..	81	137.38	114.36	916.60
1988 Q1	..	..	..	..	..	..	83	138.31	117.76	908.67
Q2	..	..	..	..	..	..	82	136.53	120.74	931.35
Q3	..	..	..	..	..	..	80	132.99	121.39	946.30
Q4	..	..	..	..	..	..	86	132.94	127.55	940.37

See footnotes on page 269.

Sources: Office for National Statistics; Enquiries Columns 1-2 01633 812106 or 813390 ;; Department of the Environment, Transport and the Regions; Enquiries Columns 3-5 020 7890 3325; Ministry of Agriculture, Fisheries and Food; Enquiries Column 6 020 7270 8371.; Bank of England; Enquiries Columns 7-9 020 7601 5484

5.11 A selection of asset prices

continued

	Physical assets							Financial assets[5]		
	Producer price indices (1995 = 100)			Housing: DETR all lenders mix adjusted house price index (1993 = 100)				British government stocks		
	Plant and machinery bought as fixed assets by		Manufactured output				Average price of agricultural land in England (1995 = 100)[1]			Company securities: FT-Actuaries all ordinary shares (10 April 1962 = 100)
	Motor vehicle industry[2]	All manufacturing industries[2]	Motor vehicle industry[2]	New dwellings[3]	Secondhand dwellings[3]	All dwellings[3]		Fixed interest (Dec 1975 =100)	Index linked (April 1982= 100)	
	PVJL	PVNO	PQIR	BBKO	BBKP	BBKQ	BAJI	AJJY	AJJZ	AJMA
1989 Q1	..	..	..	..	..	..	89	132.67	131.92	1 037.42
Q2	..	..	..	..	..	..	92	130.11	132.93	1 089.48
Q3	..	..	..	..	..	..	98	130.86	138.63	1 182.76
Q4	..	..	..	..	..	..	106	128.18	139.05	1 131.51
1990 Q1	..	..	..	..	..	..	107	121.49	135.43	1 148.95
Q2	..	..	..	..	..	..	113	119.27	135.88	1 119.66
Q3	..	..	..	..	..	..	98	121.32	138.09	1 081.98
Q4	..	..	..	..	..	..	105	125.62	143.15	1 018.89
1991 Q1	85.2	89.3	87.1	..	..	..	96	130.11	145.37	1 099.00
Q2	84.9	87.4	87.9	..	..	..	103	129.52	147.19	1 206.59
Q3	84.4	86.1	88.3	..	..	..	87	132.00	147.89	1 239.48
Q4	84.8	85.8	88.1	..	..	..	83	132.83	149.59	1 204.14
1992 Q1	86.2	86.8	88.8	..	..	..	93	133.14	149.62	1 206.94
Q2	86.8	87.2	89.8	103.6	101.4	101.7	88	136.24	152.78	1 265.39
Q3	86.2	86.4	89.9	97.7	102.7	102.0	87	134.35	152.18	1 147.78
Q4	89.2	89.3	88.2	96.6	98.3	98.1	77	142.20	167.82	1 276.83
1993 Q1	91.7	92.1	91.9	99.1	98.5	98.6	74	144.18	171.70	1 384.00
Q2	92.4	92.7	92.6	101.0	99.1	99.4	80	143.44	173.73	1 403.58
Q3	93.2	93.4	93.4	101.9	101.4	101.5	81	150.07	181.20	1 472.33
Q4	93.4	94.0	94.4	97.7	99.9	99.6	81	155.08	188.77	1 569.60
1994 Q1	95.2	96.0	95.3	99.9	100.9	100.7	81	150.02	183.63	1 679.75
Q2	95.9	96.9	95.8	98.7	102.6	102.1	85	139.41	174.41	1 546.26
Q3	97.0	98.2	96.5	99.5	104.4	103.8	85	136.04	172.54	1 554.39
Q4	96.8	97.5	97.1	102.6	103.2	103.1	99	136.88	174.40	1 517.51
1995 Q1	98.8	99.4	98.9	100.8	102.4	102.2	80	136.42	175.28	1 506.36
Q2	99.6	99.5	99.3	105.0	103.0	103.3	91	139.07	182.67	1 608.42
Q3	100.7	100.6	100.4	107.9	103.6	104.2	104	139.97	185.48	1 714.06
Q4	100.9	100.5	101.4	106.1	102.2	102.8	114	143.31	187.53	1 759.44
1996 Q1	103.1	102.2	102.5	107.7	103.8	104.3	104	142.89	187.01	1 831.51
Q2	104.1	103.1	102.8	108.7	103.7	104.4	117	141.22	186.54	1 885.83
Q3	102.6	100.6	103.4	109.7	108.3	108.5	136	142.60	189.37	1 894.17
Q4	101.9	99.6	103.8	119.4	109.0	110.4	135	144.72	195.90	1 967.42
1997 Q1	102.3	99.4	104.1	124.5	109.8	111.9	111	144.72	196.52	2 089.90
Q2	102.0	99.7	104.2	118.5	113.5	114.2	140[4]	145.26	195.98	2 167.79
Q3	101.9	99.5	104.6	120.5	119.9	120.0	157[4]	148.80	202.28	2 317.34
Q4	101.6	98.8	104.8	120.5	118.9	119.1	128[4]	150.88	214.56	2 368.12
1998 Q1	100.9	97.4	105.7	123.2	121.9	122.1	121[4]	153.46	217.63	2 606.58
Q2	100.2	96.7	106.4	127.5	128.7	128.6	115[4]	155.49	227.44	2 796.69
Q3	99.6	95.8	106.7	129.9	134.8	134.2	151[4]	159.30	234.28	2 599.90
Q4	99.3	95.3	107.1	136.1	133.2	133.6	130[4]	164.94	244.69	2 501.69
1999 Q1	100.0	96.0	107.5	138.8	133.7	134.4	127[4]	166.57	252.85	2 771.59
Q2	99.9	95.8	107.5	145.9	139.2	140.1	127[4]	160.86	254.10	2 964.95
Q3	99.8	95.2	106.1	149.9	148.1	148.3	145[4]	157.17	248.40	2 934.06
Q4	99.4	94.8	106.2	153.7	151.9	152.1	..	156.78	254.31	3 002.30
2000 Q1	100.1p	95.3p	105.2	154.0	156.3	156.0	..	155.48	253.52	3 048.44
Q2	100.4p	63.9p	104.9p	163.0	164.8	164.5	..	156.95	259.28	3 011.87

See footnotes on page 269.

Sources: Office for National Statistics; Enquiries Columns 1-2 01633 812106 or 813390 ;; Department of the Environment, Transport and the Regions; Enquiries Columns 3-5 020 7890 3325; Ministry of Agriculture, Fisheries and Food; Enquiries Column 6 020 7270 8371.; Bank of England; Enquiries Columns 7-9 020 7601 5484

Notes and definitions: Contents

NATIONAL INCOME AND EXPENDITURE: GENERAL NOTES

Economic Trends: Tables 2.1, 2.2, 2.3, 2.4, 2.5, 2.6, 2.7, 5.6, 5.7
Annual Supplement: Tables 1.1, 1.2, 1.3, 1.4, 1.5, 1.6, 1.7, 1.8, 4.6

The statistics of national income and expenditure given here are the key statistics from the United Kingdom national accounts. The long-run quarterly and annual time series complement the much larger set of series given, in the shorter-run annual form, in the 2000 edition of *United Kingdom National Accounts*: the ONS *Blue Book* (The Stationery Office, August 2000). Where appropriate, tables have a section giving seasonally adjusted estimates to assist in interpreting the original unadjusted estimates.

With effect from 24 September 1998 the UK national accounts were converted onto the European System of Accounts 1995 (ESA95). This change results in a number of changes to the terminology and methodology used in presenting and compiling the accounts. In addition, constant price estimates were rebased onto 1995 prices. A short description of the national accounts is given in the introduction to the 2000 edition of *United Kingdom National Accounts:* the ONS *Blue Book*. More detailed information is available in *United Kingdom National Accounts*: *Concepts, Sources and Methods* (The Stationery Office 1998) and an overview of the move to ESA95 is available in *Introducing the ESA95 in the United Kingdom* (The Stationery Office, 1998).

The national accounts present a highly complex and highly independent set of statistics. In many cases it is important that individual time series should be used only in the light of some understanding of their context (that is, of their relationship with other series) and of the limitations upon interpretation which may arise for the methods used in compilation.

NATIONAL ACCOUNTS AGGREGATES

Economic Trends: Table 2.1
Annual Supplement: Tables 1.1, 1.2, 1.3, 1.4

Gross domestic product (GDP) is the total of all economic activity taking place on the UK territory (no matter who owns the economically-productive assets) before providing for depreciation (that is capital consumption). Its measurement can be approached in three largely independent ways: as the total of all output, production or value added by all activities which produce goods and services; as the total of all incomes earned from producing goods and services; and as the total of all expenditures made either in consuming the finished goods and services or in adding to wealth (less expenditure on imports).

Use of three different methods which, as far as possible, use independent sources of information avoids sole reliance on one source and allows greater confidence in the overall estimation process.

The resulting estimates however, like all statistical estimates, contain errors and omissions: we obtain the best estimates of GDP (i.e. the published figure) by reconciling the estimates obtained from all three approaches. On an annual basis this reconciliation is carried out through the construction of the input-output balances for the years for which data are available, and for subsequent periods by carrying forward the level of GDP set by the annual balancing process by using the quarterly movements in output, income and expenditure totals.

For years in which no input-output balance has been struck a statistical discrepancy exists between estimates of the total expenditure components of GDP and the total income components of GDP after the balancing process has been carried out. This statistical discrepancy is made up of two components which are shown in the accounts, namely:

the *statistical discrepancy (expenditure adjustment)*, which is the difference between the sum of the expenditure components and the definitive estimate of GDP, plus

the *statistical discrepancy (income adjustment)*, which is the difference between the sum of the income components and the definitive estimate of GDP (with sign reversed).

To improve the coherence of the accounts, statistical adjustments are made to the quarterly estimates of both the expenditure and income measures of GDP from 1993 onwards. The adjustments which sum to zero annually, are attributed to the changes in inventories component of the expenditure measure of GDP and to gross operating surplus of non-financial corporations on the income measure, where accurate measurements are most difficult.

These quarterly adjustments modify the aggregates derived from expenditure or income components so that they better reflect the quarter to quarter growth rates suggested by the output-based approach method of GDP. For gross operating surplus the alignment adjustments are constrained within the likely error range attached to the estimated path of non-financial corporations gross operating surplus. The impact of this constraint on the quarterly path of GDP is small.

The output-based approach of gross domestic product is calculated, in index-number form, by combining indices of the output of individual industries valued at the prices of a base year, with weights proportional to the contribution of each industry to gross domestic product in that base year. From 1994 onwards, the weights relate to 1995. For earlier years, the index based on 1990 has been linked at 1994 by reference to the annual levels in that year on the 1990 and 1995 bases.

GDP is measured only at market prices in the new system of accounts Value added is now measured at basic prices which excludes taxes on products, such as VAT and excise duties, and subsidies. This aggregate is named Gross Value Added at basic prices. Gross national income at market prices measures the incomes distributed by producer units which are resident in the UK. So, in calculating GNI it is necessary to exclude that part of resident producers' income paid overseas, but includes incomes generated overseas but paid to resident units ie GNI equals GDP less employment, property and entrepreneurial incomes received from the rest of the world. Adjustments are also made for taxes on production less subsidies.

GROSS DOMESTIC PRODUCT BY CATEGORY OF EXPENDITURE

Economic Trends: Table 2.2
Annual Supplement: Tables 1.3

Final consumption expenditure is that on goods and services used for the direct satisfaction of individual or collective needs and wants.

Household final consumption expenditure

Household final consumption expenditure covers all personal expenditure on goods (durable and non-durable) and services, including the value of income in kind, imputed rents for owner-occupied dwellings and the purchase of second-hand goods *less* the proceeds of sales of used goods.

The following are not included: all business expenditure and expenses; the final consumption expenditure of non-profit institutions serving households; interest and other transfer payments; improvements to dwellings; and the purchase of land and dwellings (and associated costs). These last two items are treated as capital expenditure.

The component categories shown in *Economic trends* correspond to the commodity classification in Table 6.3 of *United Kingdom National Accounts*, 1999 Edition, described in more detail in *United Kingdom National Accounts:*

Concepts, Sources and Methods. A more detailed breakdown of household final consumption by commodity is available in *Consumer Trends*, available quarterly from The Stationery Office.

Gross Fixed Capital formation

This comprises expenditure on the replacement of and additions to existing fixed assets; expenditure on maintenance and repairs is excluded. Fixed assets include new dwellings, other buildings and structures, vehicles, other machinery and equipment and cultivated assets, intangible fixed assets, and costs associated with the transfer of ownership of non-produced assets.

The figures are described in detail in Chapter 12 of *United Kingdom National Accounts: Concepts, Sources and Methods* 1998 Edition.

Changes in inventories

The quarterly estimates for production, construction, motor trades, wholesale and retail are based on results of a quarterly survey to a sample of firms in these industries. Inventories information for other parts of the economy, which account for a relatively small part of total inventories held, are obtained from other sources including annual survey information. The quarterly survey is statutory and returns accounts for about 53% of inventories held in the industries covered.

The survey collects the level of inventories, by type of inventories where appropriate, at the beginning and end of each quarter at book value prices. The book value change is then calculated, aggregated and UK estimate by industry is obtained. Various deflators, including PPI and RPI, are used to calculate the change in inventories at constant price and current price. Sesaonal adjustment is also carried out at broad industry level.

The quarterly results are benchmarked each year when results for the Annual Business Inquiry becomes available with its larger and more representative sample. At this time, any late data is incorporated, any changes to deflators taken on and the series re-seasonally adjusted. These results are then fed into the *Blue Book*.

The figures are described in detail in Chapter 6 of *United Kingdom National Accounts: Concepts, Sources and Methods* 1998 Edition. The Standard Industrial Classification revised 1992 is used. Estimates for manufacturing cover Divisions 15 to 37, those for wholesaling cover Division 51 excluding Group 511, and those for retailing cover Division 52.

TRADE IN GOODS AND SERVICES

See note on page 280 (for Table 1.18)

GROSS DOMESTIC PRODUCT BY CATEGORY OF INCOME

Annual Supplement: Tables 1.4

Compensation of employees

Compensation of employees is defined as the total remuneration payable by enterprises in cash or in kind, and comprises not only wages and salaries but also the value of social contributions payable by the employer (including imputed contributions for unfunded benefits), but not taxes paid by the employer. It is recorded on an accrual basis; that is in respect of entitlement arising out of work done during the accounting period whether paid in advance, simultaneously, or in arrears. It does not cover unpaid work (including that done by household members within their own households) or the earnings of the self-employed.

The contribution of financial corporations to Gross Domestic Product is measured by the difference between their receipts for services rendered (represented by charges and commissions) and their management expenses (salaries and wages and payments for current expenses), which may be described as their operating surplus. Interest receipts and payments and profits from buying and selling financial instruments are not taken into account since these are regarded as transfer payments and capital gains, respectively.

Gross operating surplus of corporations

Gross operating surplus includes data from both the public and private sectors. It is made up of gross trading profits, rental income (not land), partnerships that were previously included with self-employment income, financial intermediation services and a deduction for holding gains.

For private non-financial corporations, see notes on page 278.

For financial corporations, see notes on page 279.

SHARES OF INCOME AND EXPENDITURE

Economic Trends: Table 2.3

See notes on page 276.

INCOME, PRODUCT AND SPENDING PER HEAD

Economic Trends: Table 2.4
Annual Supplement: Tables 1.5

For definition of the series see the general notes about sources for the data. *Per capita* is defined as per head of the UK home population.

HOUSEHOLDS AND NON-PROFIT INSTITUTIONS SERVING HOUSEHOLDS (NPISH) DISPOSABLE INCOME AND CONSUMPTION

Economic Trends: Table 2.5
Annual Supplement: Table 1.6

Households and NPISH income and saving

The households and NPISH sector consists mainly of households and individual residents in the United Kingdom together with Sole Traders, Non-profit institutions serving households and private trusts. The savings generated by the household and NPISH sector is obtained as the difference between its estimates of income and expenditure and is subject to a wide margin of error.

Households' final consumption expenditure

See note on page 276.

HOUSEHOLD FINAL CONSUMPTION EXPENDITURE - COMPONENT CATEGORIES

Economic Trends: Table 2.6
Annual Supplement: Table 1.7

See note on page 276.

GROSS FIXED CAPITAL FORMATION

Economic Trends: Table 2.7
Annual Supplement: Table 1.8

See note on gross fixed capital formation above.

INDEX NUMBERS OF OUTPUT AT 1995 BASIC PRICES

Economic Trends: Table 2.8
Annual Supplement: Table 1.9

Indices of the output of individual industries valued at the prices of a base year, are combined using weights proportional to the contribution of each industry to gross domestic product in that base year in order to derive an output-based estimate of GDP.

The estimates in Table 1.9 are produced only on a quarterly, seasonally adjusted basis, except for production industries which are available monthly, unadjusted and seasonally adjusted. More detailed annual information is published once a year in Table 2.4 of *United Kingdom National Accounts; the ONS Blue Book*. Additional constant 1995 price output indices are available from National Statistics on-line Services (telephone 020 7533 5675).

Detailed methodology is given in Chapter 11 of *United Kingdom National Accounts: Concepts, Sources and Methods*, 1998 Edition. Following recommendations for change and upgrading contained in various studies on economic statistics, the sources used in the compilation of these index numbers have been reviewed and updated. The 1995-based estimates of output in Tables 1.9 and 2.8 are classified using groups from the 1992 *Standard Industrial Classification* (SIC(92)).

INDEX NUMBERS OF OUTPUT AT 1995 BASIC PRICES - SERVICE INDUSTRIES

Economic Trends: Table 2.9
Annual Supplement: Table 1.10

See note above. Table 1.10 contains further detail regarding the service sector.

SUMMARY CAPITAL ACCOUNTS AND FINANCIAL SURPLUS OR DEFICIT

Economic Trends: Table 2.10
Annual Supplement: Table 1.11

Summary Capital Accounts and net lending/net borrowing
The capital account concerns the acquisition of non-financial assets (some of which will be income creating and others which are wealth only) such as fixed assets or inventories, financed out of saving, and capital transfers involving the redistribution of wealth. Capital transfers include, for example, capital grants from private corporations to public corporations (e.g. private sector contributions to the extension of the Jubilee line). This account shows how saving finances investment in the economy. In addition to new gross fixed capital formation and changes in inventories it shows the redistribution of capital assets between sectors of the economy and the Rest of the World. The balance on the capital account if negative is designated *net borrowing*, and measures the net amount a unit or sector is obliged to borrow from others; if positive the balance is described as *net lending*, the amount the United Kingdom or a sector has available to finance others. This balance is also referred to as the financial surplus or deficit and the net aggregate for the five sectors of the economy equals net lending/borrowing from the Rest of the World.

The institutional sectors
The system identifies two kinds of institutions, consuming units - mostly households - and production units, mainly corporations and non-profit institutions or government units. Units can own goods and assets, incur liabilities and engage in economic activities and transactions with other units in their own right. All units within the country are put in one of the sectors. Also, the Rest of the World is treated as a sector in respect of its dealings with the United Kingdom.

Non-financial corporations are those which exist to produce goods and non-financial services. They are, in the UK, mainly public limited companies, private companies and partnerships. They are mostly owned privately, but there are some public corporations, which are shown separately.

Financial corporations are those engaged primarily in financial activities, and are subdivided into monetary financial institutions, other financial intermediaries and financial auxiliaries, and insurance corporations and pension funds.

General government comprises central government and local government.

The Households sector contains all the resident people of the United Kingdom as receivers of income and consumers of products. It includes individuals such as prisoners as well as conventional family units. It also contains one person businesses where household and business accounts cannot be separated. This sector currently includes non-profit institutions serving households, which include productive units such as charities and universities.

The Rest of the World sector comprises those units that are not in the United Kingdom. The accounts for the Rest of the World only record transactions between units in the Rest of the World and units in the UK, and is equivalent to the balance of payments.

The tables in Chapters 3 to 7 are based on the sector classification detailed above. More detailed definitions of these sectors are given in the appropriate chapters of *United Kingdom National Accounts Concepts, Sources and Methods* and, in full detail in *United Kingdom Sector Classification for the National Accounts*, 1998 edition, available from The Stationery Office.

PRIVATE NON-FINANCIAL CORPORATIONS SECTOR: ALLOCATION OF PRIMARY INCOME ACCOUNT

Economic Trends: Table 2.11
Annual Supplement: Table 1.12

Private non-financial corporations comprise all corporate bodies other than banks and other financial institutions. They also include non-profit institutions serving corporations, such as trade associations, property companies and co-operative societies. Private financial corporations are, in the UK, mainly public limited companies, private companies and partnerships.

The allocation of primary income account shows the sector's contributions to gross national income.

Gross trading profits
These relate to trading profits arising from activities in the United Kingdom, before providing for inventory holding gains (formerly known as stock appreciation) and consumption of fixed capital and before deduction of tax and interest payments. Annual estimates for all but the latest year are sourced from tax data. Quarterly estimates, *plus* annual estimates for the most recent year, are based on returns from a sample of corporations.

Rental of buildings
Rent received by corporations from letting buildings.

Property income received
This consists of interest, distributed income of corporations (dividend receipts), reinvested earnings on direct foreign investment, property income attributed to insurance policy-holders, and rent received from the letting of land.

Property income payments
This consists of interest, distributed income of corporations (mainly dividend payments), reinvested earnings on direct foreign investment, and rent paid for land and sub-soil assets. The rent on sub-soil assets represents the royalties and licence fees paid to government for exploration and extraction of minerals or fossil fuels.

PRIVATE NON-FINANCIAL CORPORATIONS SECTOR: SECONDARY DISTRIBUTION OF INCOME ACCOUNT

Economic Trends: Table 2.12
Annual Supplement: Table 1.13

The Secondary Distribution of Income Account shows current transfers between sectors as the national income is redistributed.

Social contributions and benefits
These are redundancy payments, statutory sick pay, statutory maternity pay, and claims made on employers' insurance. The benefits, paid to the households sector, equal the contributions received by the employer.

Other current transfers, resources
These are non-life insurance claims.

Current taxes on income
These are mainstream corporation tax, advance corporation tax, tax on investment income, petroleum revenue tax, windfall tax and capital gains tax. Tax repayments and overspill relief are subtracted.

Other current transfers, uses
These are net non-life insurance premiums and payments to charities and households, including the rebate paid by regional electricity companies in 1996 when the National Grid was demerged.

FINANCIAL CORPORATIONS SECTOR: ALLOCATION OF PRIMARY INCOME ACCOUNT

Annual Supplement: Table 1.14

Financial corporations are all corporations and quasi-corporations which are principally engaged in financial intermediation and/or in auxiliary financial activities (financial auxiliaries).
Financial intermediation is the activity by which an institutional unit acquires financial assets and at the same time incurs liabilities on its own account by engaging in financial transactions on the market
Auxiliary financial activities are ones closely related to financial intermediation but are not financial intermediation themselves; financial auxiliaries only facilitate financial intermediation. For example management of investment funds on behalf of others or insurance broking.

The sector includes banks (including the Bank of England), building societies, securities dealers, insurance corporations and pension funds, mutual funds and unit trusts etc. and financial auxiliaries. The latter include security brokers, fund managers, investment advisers and insurance brokers etc.

Property income received
This is the income receivable by the owner of a financial asset or a tangible non-produced asset in return for providing funds to or putting the asset at the disposal of, another institutional unit. It has five components: interest, distributed income of corporations (dividends), reinvested earnings on direct foreign investment, attributed property income of insurance policy holders and rent.

Distributed income of corporations
This is dividends paid and received on shares and other equity during the accounting period.

Reinvested earnings on direct foreign investment
This equals the operating surplus of the direct foreign investment corporation plus any property incomes and current transfers receivable less any property incomes or current transfers payable. Reinvested earnings of direct investment received are a resource.

Property income of insurance policy holders
This is the net property income received from the investment of insurance technical reserves (owned by policyholders) held in financial assets, land and buildings. This transaction is imputed and does not occur in practice.

Rent is the income derived from land and sub-soil assets.

Financial Intermediation Services Indirectly Measured (FISIM)
This is an indirect measure of the value of services for which financial intermediaries do not explicitly charge, but obtain their reward from the difference between interest receivable and interest payable. It is the counterpart to the amount included in the production account of financial corporations and needs to be excluded from property income to avoid double counting.

Property income paid
This is the income payable. It consists of the same five components as property income received, but only Distributed income is shown separately in the table.

Distributed income paid
This includes dividends paid on their own issued share capital plus estimates of the value of shares issued to shareholders in lieu of dividend payments (scrip dividends).

FINANCIAL CORPORATIONS SECTOR: SECONDARY DISTRIBUTION OF INCOME ACCOUNT

Annual Supplement: Table 1.15

The secondary distribution of income account shows how the balance of primary incomes is transformed into its disposable income by the receipt and payment of current transfers.

Social contributions
These are the sums received by insurance corporations and pension funds.

Other current transfers (received)
These are net non-life insurance premiums. Net non-life insurance premiums comprise premiums receivable from policy holders plus imputed premium supplements attributed to insurance policy holders less the insurance service charge.

Taxes on income
These are taxes on profits including capital gains.

Social benefits
These are all social insurance benefits provided by financial corporations under private funded social insurance schemes. They are intended to provide for needs such as sickness, unemployment, retirement and housing. The largest component relates to pensions paid.

Other current transfers (paid)
Non-life insurance claims are the amounts payable in settlement of claims.

Miscellaneous current transfers are various different kinds of current transfers that take place between financial corporations and non-resident units.

Gross disposable income
This is the balancing item for the secondary distribution of income account.

PRIVATE NON-FINANCIAL CORPORATIONS SECTOR: CAPITAL ACCOUNT

Economic Trends: Table 2.13
Annual Supplement: Table 1.16

The Capital Account records acquisitions less disposals of non-financial assets and measures the change in the sector's net worth due to saving and capital transfers.

Gross saving
This is the same as the gross disposable income series which appears in the Secondary Distribution of Income Account.

Capital transfers receivable
Theses are investment grants from general government.

Capital transfers payable
These consist of the betterment levy, development land tax and contributions made to the capital expenditure costs of public corporations and local government.

Gross fixed capital formation
See paragraph on page 277.

Change in inventories
See paragraph on page 277.

Acquisition less disposals of valuables
Valuables in this context are such things as precious metals and stones, antiques and other art objects.

Acquisition less disposals of non-produced non-financial assets
This covers land transfers between sectors, fees paid by football clubs to transfer players in and out of the country, and cross-border royalties.

BALANCE OF PAYMENTS: SUMMARY

Annual Supplement: Table 1.17

Balance of payments
The UK balance of payments is a statistical statement designed to provide a systematic record of the UK's economic transactions with the rest of the world. It may be described as a system of consolidated accounts in which the accounting entity is the UK economy and the entries refer to economic transactions between residents of the UK and residents of the rest of the world (non-residents).

The balance of payments accounts are concerned not only with payments made but also any economic transactions during a period that give rise to a payment in an earlier or later period, e.g. goods may change ownership in one period, though payment may be made in an earlier period (pre-payment) or in a later period (trade credit). They also include transactions for which there may never be a payment, e.g. goods shipped under foreign aid or goods shipped between related enterprises. There is also more than one 'balance': the balance of payments is a system of accounts in which many balances can be derived, such as the balance of goods and services, the balance on current account, and the balance on capital and financial account.

Balance of payments statements cover a wide range of economic transactions which include:
(i) goods, services, income and current transfers; and
(ii) capital transactions, such as capital transfers, and financial transactions involving the UK claims on, and liabilities to, non-residents.
Category (i) is shown in the current account and category (ii) in the capital and financial account.

The UK's **international investment position** is a closely related set of statistics. It can be viewed as the balance sheet recording the UK's stock (or level) of foreign financial assets and liabilities at a particular date. The net international investment position is the difference between the stock of foreign financial assets and foreign liabilities at a particular date.

Classifications such as assets and liabilities, type of investment (direct, portfolio and other investment and reserve assets), and instrument of investment, are used consistently in both the balance of payments and the international investment position.

Double entry system
Conceptually, an economic transaction has two sides: something of economic value is provided and something of equal value is received. The double-entry recording system in the balance of payments reflects this. When an economic value is provided (e.g. the UK exports a car) a credit entry is made, and when an economic value is received (e.g. a payment for the car) a debit entry is made. For example, when an exporter sells (provides) goods to a non-resident, the exporter may receive cash (a financial asset) or another type of financial asset (e.g. a trade credit claim) in return. The export is represented by a credit entry and the financial asset acquired is represented by an offset debit entry.

Credit entries, changes in all economic resources provided by the UK to non-residents, including:
exports of goods and services income accruing on the resources to UK from non-residents financial liabilities of the UK to non-residents and transfers which are offsets to debit entries.

Debit entries, changes in all economic resources received by the UK from non-residents including:
imports of goods and services, income accruing on the resources to non-residents from UK, financial claims of UK on non-residents and transfers, which are offsets to credit entries.

Sign convention in balance of payments statistics
The sign convention used in presenting the UK balance of payments statistics is to give no sign (an implied positive sign) to an increase in either credit or debit entries and a minus sign to a decrease in credit or debit entries. Balances or items which are net credits have no sign, while balances which are net debits have a negative sign.

Errors and omissions
It follows that, in principle, under a double-entry accounting system, the difference between the sum of credit and debit entries must be zero. In practice, some transactions are not measured accurately (i.e. errors) and some are not measured at all (i.e. omissions). Data sources used to compile the accounts often measure the credit and debit sides from different data sources and may not always do so consistently. There could be many reasons why these sources may not measure the acquisition side of the share transaction and the corresponding payments, either in the same accounting period or at the same value. To restore the equality of credit and debit entries, a net errors and omissions item is included in the balance of payments accounts.

BALANCE OF PAYMENTS: CURRENT ACCOUNT

Economic Trends: Table 2.14
Annual Supplement: Table 1.18

The items in this table are more fully defined in *United Kingdom Balance of Payments*: the National Statistics *Pink Book*, 2000 edition (The Stationery Office, August 2000). The Overseas Trade Statistics of the United Kingdom are the basis of the balance of payments figures, but certain adjustments are made in respect of valuation and coverage. The principal adjustment figures of imports is the deduction of freight and insurance from the Trade Statistics.

Trade in goods
The goods account covers exports and imports of goods. Imports of motor cars from Japan, for example, are recorded as debits in the trade in goods account whereas exports of vehicles manufactured in the UK are recorded as credits. Trade in goods forms a component of the expenditure measure of Gross Domestic Product (GDP).

Trade in services
The services account covers exports and imports of services (eg, civil aviation). Passenger tickets for travel on UK aircraft sold abroad, for example, are recorded as credits in the services account whereas the purchases of airline tickets from foreign airlines by UK passengers are

recorded as debits. Trade in services, along with trade in goods, forms a component of the expenditure measure of Gross Domestic Product (GDP).

Income

The income account consists of compensation of employees and investment income and is dominated by the latter. Compensation of employees covers employment income from cross-border and seasonal workers which is less significant in the UK than in other countries. Investment income covers earnings (eg, profits, dividends and interest payments and receipts) arising from foreign investment and financial assets and liabilities. For example, earnings on foreign bonds and shares held by financial institutions based in the UK are recorded as credits in the investment income account, whereas earnings on UK company securities held abroad are recorded as investment income debits. Investment income forms a component of Gross National Income (GNI) but not Gross Domestic Product (GDP).

Current transfers

Current transfers are composed of central government transfers (eg, taxes and payments to and receipts from the European Union) and other transfers (eg, gifts in cash or kind received by private individuals from abroad or receipts from the EU where the UK government acts as an agent for the ultimate beneficiary of the transfer). Current transfers do not form a component either of Gross Domestic Product (GDP) or of Gross National Income (GNI). For example payments to the UK farming industry under the EU Agricultural Guarantee Fund are recorded as credits in the current transfers account while payments of EU agricultural levies by the UK farming industry are recorded as debits in the current transfers account.

BALANCE OF PAYMENTS: CAPITAL ACCOUNT

Capital account transactions involve transfers of ownership of fixed assets, transfers of funds associated with acquisition or disposal of fixed assets, and cancellation of liabilities by creditors without any counterparts being received in return. The main components are migrants transfers, EU transfers relating to fixed capital formation (regional development fund and agricultural guidance fund) and debt forgiveness. Funds brought into the UK by new immigrants would, for example, be recorded as credits in the capital account, while funds sent abroad by UK residents emigrating to other countries would be recorded as debits in the capital account. The magnitude of capital account transactions are quite minor compared with the current and financial accounts.

BALANCE OF PAYMENTS: FINANCIAL ACCOUNT

Annual Supplement: Table 1.19

While investment income covers earnings arising from overseas investments and financial assets and liabilities, the financial account of the balance of payments covers the flows of such investments. While earnings on foreign bonds and shares held by financial institutions based in the UK are, for example, recorded as credits in the investment income account, the acquisition of such foreign securities by UK based financial institutions are recorded as net debits in the financial account as portfolio investment abroad. Similarly the acquisitions of UK company securities held by foreign residents are recorded in the financial account as net credits as portfolio investment in the UK.

BALANCE OF PAYMENTS: INTERNATIONAL INVESTMENT POSITION

Annual Supplement: Table 1.20

While the financial account covers the flows of foreign investments and financial assets and liabilities, the International Investment Position records the levels of external assets and liabilities. The total holdings of foreign securities by UK based financial institutions are recorded as levels of UK external assets, and the holdings of UK company securities held by foreign residents are recorded as levels of UK liabilities.

TRADE IN GOODS

Economic Trends: Table 2.15
Annual Supplement: Table 1.21

Trade in goods on a Balance of Payments basis

All information in these tables is on a Balance of Payments (BoP) basis, with exports and imports valued 'fob' (free on board), ie excluding insurance premiums and freight. They are derived from data on an Overseas Trade Statistics basis, which values exports 'fob' and imports 'cif' (including insurance and freight). Other differences of valuation and coverage between the OTS and BoP figures are described below in *Adjustment of OTS Data.*

Trade in goods on an Overseas Trade Statistics basis

Detailed OTS figures appear in *Overseas Trade Statistics of the United Kingdom,* published monthly by The Stationery Office as OTS 1, which also contains further information about definition and coverage of data. This publication now relates only to non-EU trade. There are two publications showing EU trade. The first OTS 2 being a monthly summary showing data by country and by broad commodity group (SITC division), and the second OTS Q providing quarterly detailed commodity level tables. There is also an annual edition OTS A which combines the intra-EU and non-EU data.

Adjustment of OTS Data

The adjustments required to convert data from an OTS to a BoP basis are of two types. Firstly there are 'valuation adjustments', principally the deduction from the import figures of freight costs and insurance premiums. Secondly there are 'coverage adjustments' to allow for items not included in the OTS (for example the import of ships built and delivered abroad direct to UK owners) and to exclude items in the OTS where no change of ownership has occurred (such as goods coming back to the United Kingdom after repair overseas). Adjustments are also made to the level of all exports and EU imports to take account of estimated under-recording. The adjustments are set out and described in the annual *United Kingdom Balance of Payments;* the National Statistics *Pink Book.*

Price and Volume Indices

The indicators of price movement ("deflators") for individual commodities used in the calculation of price and volume indices are based where possible on export and import price indices derived from price information collected from UK manufacturers. Exports of manufactured goods for commodities where export price indices (EPIs) are not available are deflated by appropriate producer price indices (PPIs) adjusted by the relationship between EPIs and PPIs where both exist. Similarly imports of manufactured goods for commodities where import price indices (IPIs) are not available are deflated by appropriate PPIs adjusted by the relationship between IPIs and PPIs where both exist. For commodities that are traded on world markets, price information on these world markets are used to deflate both exports and imports. For other commodities outside of manufactures the indices are based on the value and quantity data provided by Customs.

Seasonal adjustment

Values of trade and volume indices are seasonally adjusted independently; this allows for the possibility of seasonal movements in prices. The seasonally adjusted series for total trade are derived by summing or weighting together the series for 14 major commodity components.

MEASURES OF UK TRADE COMPETITIVENESS

Economic Trends: Table 2.16
Annual Supplement: Table 1.22

The index of *relative export prices* is the unit value index (values expressed in $US) of UK exports of manufactured goods divided by a weighted average of competitors' export unit value indices for manufactures. The index is prepared by the Office for National Statistics using indices published by the International Monetary Fund (IMF) for the United Kingdom and the other main manufacturing countries. The weight given to each country reflects the relative importance of that country in the United Kingdom's overseas markets and is derived from 1990 data.

The index of *relative wholesale prices* is the UK producer price index (values expressed in $US) for home sales of manufactures (including products of the food, drink and tobacco industries) divided by a weighted average of the indices of competitors' output prices. The index is prepared by the Office for National Statistics using national indices made available by the IMF. Wherever possible, these indices approximate final product prices (eg 'industry selling prices' or 'finished' goods prices).

The indices of *relative unit labour costs* and *relative normal unit labour costs* are indices of labour costs per unit of output in the United Kingdom divided by a weighted geometric average of competitors' unit labour costs. The series relate to manufacturing industry and are calculated by the research department of the IMF. In producing the 'normalised' series the basic indices are first adjusted to allow for estimated short-term variations in productivity from its long-term trend. The advantage of such an adjustment is that the resulting measure of competitiveness should be unaffected by differences in the cyclical situation of countries being compared. However, both actual and normalised series are published because of uncertainties about the trend rates of productivity growth in different countries. The weighting used by the IMF in constructing the indices for relative normal unit labour costs is somewhat different from that used in the relative export price and relative wholesale price indices described above, in that it attempts to take account of competition with domestic production in particular markets as well as competition with third countries.

The index of *import price competitiveness* is the ratio of an import weighted index of United Kingdom producer prices of home sales of manufactures to the unit value of United Kingdom imports of manufactures. The latter excludes the more erratic items - ships, North Sea installations, aircraft, precious stones and silver - because either their prices are notoriously hard to measure (eg, ships and aircraft) or they feature atypically in the United Kingdom (eg, trade in precious stones). The index of *relative profitability of exports* is the ratio of the unit value of United Kingdom exports of manufactures (again excluding the more erratic items) to an export weighted index of United Kingdom producer prices of home sales of manufactures.

PRICES

Economic Trends: Table 3.1
Annual Supplement: Table 2.1

Index numbers of producer prices

The producer price index was published for the first time in 1983, replacing the former wholesale price index. Full details of the differences between the two indices were given in an article in *British Business*, 15 April 1983. The producer price index is compiled according to the same general methodology as the wholesale price index: a comprehensive guide to the method of calculation of the wholesale price index entitled *Wholesale price index: principles and procedures* is produced by the Government Statistical Service.

Producer Price Indices (PPIs) are a series of economic indicators that measure the price movement of goods bought and sold by UK manufacturers. It is a base weighted index working on the basket of goods concept. A wide range of representative products are selected and the prices of these goods collected each month. The movement in these prices are weighted to reflect the relative importance of the products in a chosen year (known as the base year) currently 1995. These are then aggregated for various sectors of industry to provide the published indices in the monitor.

The input PPIs measure changes in the price of materials and fuel bought by manufacturers for processing. The output PPIs indicate changes in the prices manufacturers charge for goods destined for the UK market as they leave the factory net of VAT and after discounts.

The Producer Price Indices are calculated from the price movements of around 9,000 closely defined materials and products purchased (including imports) and manufactured by UK industry. This price data is converted into a basic set of price indices from which broad series are built up. Products destined for sale in the UK are grouped in accordance with the Standard Industrial Classification 1992 with weighting patterns based on overall purchases and sales by manufacturers within those groupings. The indices published in this monitor are widely used by business in price escalation clauses in contracts and for monitoring price movements in the products they trade.

The high level Producer Prices are constructed on a net sector basis i.e. net sector indices exclude transactions between companies classified to the same manufacturing sector, all other indices are constructed on a gross sector basis i.e.all transactions are included in deriving the weighting patterns, including sales within the same industry.

The indices relate to average prices for a month. The full effect of a price change occurring part-way through any one month will only be reflected in the index for the following month. The index numbers are compiled exclusive of value-added tax. Excise duties (on cigarettes, manufactured tobacco, petroleum and alcoholic liquor) are included.

General index of retail prices

The general index of retail prices is compiled by the Office for National Statistics. It measures the change from month to month in the average level of prices of the goods and services purchased by all types of household in the United Kingdom with the exception of households with the top four per cent of the incomes and households of retired persons dependent mainly on state benefits. As with most indices of this kind, it is based on the price movements of a large and representative selection of goods and services. Approximately 120,000 separate price quotations are obtained near the middle of each month. Many of these, including those for food, are obtained in over 140 areas selected so as to secure an adequate representation of different types of areas throughout the country. The prices used are the prices actually charged in shops, including supermarkets, department stores and local branches of chain stores. As far as possible they relate to products of unchanged quality at successive dates.

The index measures price changes only; it is not a cost of living index. The expenditure on which it is based does not include income tax payments; national insurance contributions; life insurance premiums and payments to pension funds; church collections, etc; cash gifts; national lottery and other betting payments; and capital sums or instalments for house purchase or major structural alterations. Mortgage interest payments and owner occupiers' depreciation costs are, however, included.

People spend different amounts on various types of goods and services. Their relative importance is expressed quantitatively by the use of 'weights' by which their price indices are multiplied in the calculation of the average change in prices of a group of products. Since January 1962 the weights have been revised regularly each January on the basis of spending patterns according to the most recent results of the Family Expenditure Survey. The index is expressed in percentage form, the average level of prices at the base date being represented by 100.

Pensioner indices

Two special indices of retail prices are compiled for one-person and two-person pensioner households, excluding housing costs, and published as quarterly and annual averages. Pensioner households are defined as those in which at least three-quarters of the total income is derived from national insurance retirement or similar pensions and/or supplementary benefits paid in addition or instead of such pensions.

Purchasing power of the pound

Changes in the internal purchasing power of a currency may be defined as the 'inverse' of changes in the levels of prices; when prices go up, the amount which can be purchased with a given sum of money goes down. Movements in the internal purchasing power of the pound are based on the consumers' expenditure deflator (CED) prior to 1962 and on the general index of retail prices (RPI) from January 1962 onwards. The CED shows the movement in prices implied by the national accounts estimates of consumers' expenditure valued at current and at constant prices, whilst the RPI is constructed directly by weighting together monthly movements in prices according to a given pattern of household expenditure derived from the Family Expenditure Survey. If the purchasing power of the pound is taken to be 100p in a particular month (quarter, year), the comparable purchasing power in a subsequent month (quarter, year) is

$$100\text{p} \times \frac{\text{earlier period price index}}{\text{later period price index}}$$

where the price index used is the CED for years 1946-1961 and the RPI for periods after 1961.

TAX AND PRICE INDEX

Annual Supplement: Table 2.2

The purpose and methodology of the tax and price index (TPI) were described in an article in *Economic Trends,* No 310, August 1979 (HMSO 1979). The TPI measures the change in *gross* taxable income needed for taxpayers to maintain their purchasing power, allowing for changes in retail prices. The TPI thus takes account of changes to direct taxes (including employees' national insurance contributions) facing a representative cross-section of taxpayers as well as changes in the retail prices index (RPI). Non-taxpayers and people with high incomes are excluded from the TPI.

The information on the composition and distribution of gross taxable incomes needed to calculate the TPI is based on the Inland Revenue's Survey of Personal Incomes, updated using later aggregate data on incomes.

At the time of a Budget the movement of the TPI relative to the RPI depends on the changes made to direct taxes and employees' national insurance contributions. Between Budgets the TPI normally rises slightly faster than the RPI (a more than proportionate increase in gross income being needed to offset any rise in prices, since *all* the extra income is fully taxed). However, it is the changes over twelve months which are usually the focus of interest.

LABOUR FORCE SURVEY

Economic Trends: Tables 4.1, 4.2, 4.3, 4.5A
Annual Supplement: Tables 3.1, 3.2, 3.3, 3.6

Concepts and Definitions

Discouraged Workers - a sub-group of the economically inactive population, defined as those neither in employment nor unemployed (on the ILO measure) who said they would like a job and whose main reason for not seeking work was because they believed there were no jobs available.

Economically active - people aged 16 and over who are either in employment of ILO unemployed.

Economic activity rate - the percentage of people aged 16 and over who are economically active.

Economically inactive - people who are neither in employment nor unemployed on the ILO measure. This group includes, for example, all those who were looking after a home or retired. Although no estimates appear in this publication, for other LFS analyses, this group would also include all people aged under 16.

Employment - people aged 16 or over who did some paid work in the reference week (whether as an employee or self-employed); those who had a job that they were temporarily away from (on holiday, for example): those on government-supported training and employment programmes; and those doing unpaid family work.

Employees - the division between employees and self-employed is based on survey respondents' own assessment of their employment status.

Ethnic groups - defined using the 1991 Census of Population classification. People interviewed in the Labour Force Survey were asked to classify their own ethnic group by means of the question "To which of these groups do you ... belong:? White, Black-Caribbean, Black-African, Black-Other, Indian, Pakistani, Bangladeshi, Chinese or Other" Respondents who answered Black-Other or Other were asked for further details of ethnic origin. From spring 1996, Black-Other is replaced with Black-neither Caribbean nor African. The broad groups used here differ from the 1991 Census broad groups in that "Black-mixed" is included with "Other" rather than "Black".

Full-time - the classification of employees, self-employed, those on government work-related training programmes and unpaid family workers in their main job as full-time or part-time is on the basis of self assessment. People on Government-supported training and employment programmes who are at college in the survey reference week are classified, by convention, as part-time.

Full-time education - in the LFS this is defined to include those people over the age of 16 who state that they are still at school or in some other form of full-time education, including sandwich courses. People on part-time courses, day or block-release courses, or Government employment and training schemes are not included.

Government-supported training and employment programmes comprise all people aged 16 and over participating in one of the Government's employment and training programmes administered by Training and Enterprise Councils in England and Wales, or Local Enterprise Companies in Scotland.

Hours worked - respondents to the LFS are asked a series of questions enabling the identification of their usual hours and their actual hours.

ILO unemployment - the International Labour Office (ILO) measure of unemployment used in this publication refers to people without a job who were available to start work in the two weeks following their LFS interview and who had either looked for work in the four weeks prior to interview or were waiting to start a job they had already obtained. This definition of unemployment is in accordance with that adopted by the 13th International Conference of Labour Statisticians, further clarified at the 14th ICLS, and promulgated by the ILO in its publications.

ILO unemployment (rate) - the percentage of economically active people who are unemployed on the ILO measure.

ILO unemployment (duration) - defined as the shorter of the following two periods: (a) duration of active search for work; and (b) length of time since employment.

Industry - the classification of respondents' industry of employment is based on the *Standard Industrial Classification* 1992: SIC(92).

Manual and non-manual - occupations in the LFS are defined using the groupings recommended in the *Standard Occupational Classification.*

Occupation - the classification of respondents' occupations are based on the *Standard Occupational Classification* (SOC), introduced in 1991.

Part-time - see full-time.

Private and public sector employment in the LFS are defined using a separate question form that used to define the industry sector in which a person works.

Second jobs - jobs from which LFS respondents hold in addition to a main full-time or part-time job.

Self-employed - see employees.

Temporary employees - in the LFS these are defined as those employees who say that their main job is non-permanent in one of the following ways: fixed period contract; agency temping; casual work; seasonal work; other temporary work.

Unpaid Family Workers - the separate identification of this group in the LFS is in accordance with international recommendations. The group comprises persons doing unpaid work for a business they own or for a business that a relative owns.

Survey Methodology
Each quarter's LFS sample of 61,000 households comprises 5 "waves", each of approximately 12,000 private households. Each wave is interviewed in 5 successive quarters, such that in any one quarter, one wave is receiving their first interview, one wave their second, and so on, with one wave receiving their fifth and final interview. Thus there is an 80% overlap in the samples for successive quarters.

A systematic unclustered sample design is used for the survey and it is therefore representative of the whole of the United Kingdom. Each person in the survey is given a weight or "grossing factor" related to that person's age, sex and region of residence.

People's economic activity is established in the LFS by asking them about their paid work, job search and so on, during a specific reference period, normally a period of one week or four weeks (depending on the topic) immediately prior to the interview. In wave 1, where possible, each member of the household is separately interviewed but, if one or more members are unavailable for interview, "proxy" information relating to them may be provided by a related adult member of the same household.

Further details of the LFS sample design and methodology are given in the article "The quarterly LFS - a new dimension in labour market statistics", *Employment Gazette*, October 1992.

Seasonal adjustment
Some key statistical series have been seasonally adjusted using the X-11 Arima package developed by the US Bureau of the Census. For further information on LFS seasonal adjustment please contact the Office for National Statistics on 020 7533 6140.

Sampling variability
Non-sampling errors and sampling errors - Surveys are prone to errors arising from a number of sources and processes. Frequently a distinction is drawn between non-sampling errors and sampling errors. Non-sampling errors arise from, for example, incomplete or out-of-date sample frames, or inaccurate coding. Such errors (or biases) are impossible to quantify without a certain knowledge of the characteristics of the population which the survey is trying to measure, but can be minimised by a concentration on quality management to ensure that, for example, interviewers are trained to ask questions in a standard fashion, and to code responses accurately and uniformly. Sampling errors arise from the fact that the sample chosen is only one of a very large number of samples which might have been chosen. It follows from this that one quarter's estimate of, say, the number of people in employment, is only one of a large number of samples which might have been made. The issue that is of interest to most users of survey data is the precision of an estimate - that is to say, the extent or range of the estimates which would (probably) have arisen from the different samples which might have been drawn. Greater precision is associated with a relatively narrow range.

In order to indicate the degree of precision of LFS estimates, standard errors, relative standard errors (i.e. the standard error as a percentage of estimate) and 95% confidence intervals (i.e. estimate + 1.96 standard error) for the estimates are calculated. The 95% confidence intervals show in the table on the next page indicate the ranges either side of the LFS estimates and estimated changes which are 95% certain to include the true values of the quantities estimated.

Very approximate estimates of the 95% Confidence Intervals for an LFS estimate of M thousand and of an estimated change of C thousand in the estimate of M thousand are, respectively, (in thousands): M +/- (M x 1.4) and C +/- (M x 0.8).

Sampling variability of small estimates
It follows from the nature of sampling variability that the smaller the group whose size is being estimated, or from which an estimate is being derived, the (proportionately) less precise that estimate is. Users should note that an estimate of 10,000 (the smallest released) has an approximate 95% confidence interval of +/- 4,000. Particular care must be taken in using estimates of changes from period to period for these variables. While, typically, an estimated change is much smaller than the estimate itself, the standard error of the change is of comparable size to the standard error of the estimate.

Further information regarding the *LFS Quarterly Supplement* and LFS Questionnaire are available from the Office for National Statistics on 020 7533 6179.

Further information on the Labour Market Statistics *First Release* is available on 020 7533 6112.

Further information on the *LFS Historical Supplement* is available on 020 7533 6143.

JOBS AND CLAIMANT COUNT

Economic Trends: Table 4.4
Annual Supplement: Table 3.4

Workforce jobs
The number of jobs is mainly collected through postal employer surveys. The total number of Workforce jobs is calculated by summing employee jobs, self-employment jobs from the LFS, those in HM Forces and government - supported trainees. The main part of the estimate is the employee jobs total, which represents how many jobs there are; it excludes homeworkers and private domestic servants.

Employee jobs - A measure of the number of jobs of employee status from a range of ONS employer surveys. Figures on a *Standard Industrial Classification* 1992 basis are available from June 1978; prior to this date figures were produced using SIC 1980.

The *Annual Employment Survey* (AES) was conducted annually from September 1995 to September 1998. The latest published results relate to AES 98. This comprised 105,000 enterprises, which covered roughly 0.5 million local units (i.e. workplaces) and 15.5m employees out of a total of approximately 23 million employee jobs. It is anticipated that the AES will be superseded in 1999 by the new Annual Business Inquiry (ABI). The outputs from the ABI will parallel those previously derived from the AES.

Short-term employment & turnover surveys - are smaller surveys which are conducted quarterly in the case of service industries and monthly for production industries. Around 34,000 service enterprises are surveyed each quarter and around 9,000 production enterprises every month. (An enterprise is defined as a group of workplaces under common ownership.)

Both the AES and Short-term survey take a sample of businesses from the Inter-Departmental Business Register (IDBR). The IDBR holds details of all businesses that run a PAYE tax system or register for VAT.

Labour force survey - a survey of households, it uses definitions from the International Labour Organisation (ILO). In any three month period a sample of approximately 120,000 people aged 16 or over in around 61,000 households are interviewed. The construction series is provided by LFS each quarter and benchmarked using the Annual Employment Survey.

Self-employment jobs (formerly *self-employed persons*) - Self-employed people in their main job and also people who are employees in their main job and who are self-employed in their second job. The Self-employment series now has a 'centred' reference period e.g. the December estimate would be based on the LFS period Nov to Jan. All data supplied by LFS.

The Self-employment jobs series have been revised upwards by approximately 250,000 due to the addition of second Self-employment jobs from June 1984 onwards. Figures on an *Standard Industrial Classification* 1992 basis are available from June 1978. Prior to this date figures were produced using SIC 1980.

HM Forces figures, provided by the Ministry of Defence, represent the total number of UK service personnel, male and female, in HM Forces, wherever serving and including those on release leave.

Government supported trainees (formerly Work-related government supported training programmes) This category includes all participants on government training and employment programmes who are receiving some work experience on their placement but who do not have a contract of employment (those with a contract are included in the employee jobs series).

Claimant count

The current figures for the United Kingdom, Great Britain and Government Office Regions, relate to all people claiming unemployment-related benefits (ie; Jobseekers allowance or National Insurance credits) at Employment Service offices on the day of the monthly count, who on that day had signed on as unemployed and available to do any suitable work. (Students claiming benefits during a vacation, but who intend to return to full-time education, are excluded).

Seasonally adjusted claimant count

The seasonally adjusted claimant count series is adjusted to allow for discontinuities in coverage. In effect the series takes the current coverage and estimates the position as if that coverage had been in force since 1971. In order to maintain a consistent series the seasonally adjusted claimant count data relate to unemployed claimants aged 18 and over. (There are now very few under 18s remaining in the count following the change in benefit regulations for young people in September 1988.)

Vacancies unfilled

The vacancy figures shown do not represent all the vacancies in the economy but only those vacancies notified to Jobcentres and Careers Offices (including, since 1980, 'self-employed' opportunities created by employers) and remaining unfilled on the day of the count. It is estimated that nationally about a third of all vacancies are notified to Jobcentres.

Vacancies notified to Jobcentres are mainly for adults aged 18 or over, but include some that are suitable for young persons, while vacancies notified to Careers Offices are suitable for young persons but include some that are suitable for adults. Because of possible duplication the two series should not be added.

REGIONAL CLAIMANT COUNT

Economic Trends: Table 4.5
Annual Supplement: Table 3.5

Since 1988 the denominators used to calculate claimant count rates are the sum of the appropriate mid-year estimates of employee jobs, self-employment jobs, unemployment-related benefit claimants, members of HM Forces and Government-supported trainees.

AVERAGE EARNINGS

Economic Trends: Table 4.6
Annual Supplement: Table 3.7

Average earnings index

The monthly average earnings index measures the average weekly earnings of all employees (manual and non-manual, full-time and part-time) in Great Britain, based on information obtained directly from employers. Up to the second quarter of 1989 the series uses as a base, average earnings in 1985 and provides indices for 25 industry groups of the *Standard Industrial Classification* (SIC) 1980 and for the main industrial sectors - manufacturing, production industries, service industries and the whole economy. Seasonally adjusted versions of the sectoral indices are available and it is these which are shown in *Economic Trends* and this Supplement. The unadjusted indices are published in *Labour Market Trends* (formerly *Employment Gazette).* The twelve month increases in underlying average weekly earnings are shown in *Economic Trends* with a longer time series being published in *Labour Market Trends.* The underlying percentage increases are the actual average earnings increases adjusted for temporary factors such as industrial disputes, delays in the implementation of pay settlements and lump sum payments of arrears (back-pay) following retrospective pay increases. The analysis of underlying changes was described in *Employment Gazette,* November 1989, pages 606-612 and recent analyses appear quarterly in *Labour Market Trends* in the Statistical Update section.

In 1988 a new, restructured average earnings index was produced based on 1988=100. This series is published in *Economic Trends* and *Labour Market Trends* and described in the November 1989 article in *Employment Gazette* (pp 606-612).

In September 1993 the base year was changed to 1990=100, and from January 1993 the index was re-classified from SIC 1980 to SIC 1992, in common with other economic series in the national accounts. As a result of the re-classification, the definition of manufacturing industries has changed.

Manufacturing on an SIC 1992 basis now includes fuel processing and production, but excludes extraction of minerals and ores.

In April 1998 the underlying rate was replaced by the headline rate as a measure of change. The headline rate is still a three-month average of annual changes in average earnings but differs from the underlying rate in that it is based wholly on reported figures, the data is seasonally adjusted and it is published to one decimal place. An article describing the changes in detail can be found in the May 1998 edition of *Labour Market Trends* pages 259-263.

Between November 1998 and March 1999 the methodology underpinning the Average Earnings Index was revised. The subsequent index, rebased to 1995=100, is calculated according to the methodology described in a report published by Chambers and Holmes, which can be found on the ONS website at *www.statistics.gov.uk.* Further information on the background to the review can be found in a report also published in March 1999 by Turnbull/King which is available on the Treasury website at *www.hm-treasury.gov.uk.*

In April 1999 the presentation of the headline rate changed. Previously, the headline rate was centred on the middle month of the three under consideration. The new presentation aligns the average with the last month of the three under consideration.

PRODUCTIVITY AND UNIT WAGE COSTS

Economic Trends: Table 4.7
Annual Supplement: Table 3.8

For this series output for the economy as a whole is the gross value added at basic prices. Output per filled job includes employee jobs, self-employment jobs (with or without employees), including both full-time and part-time workers as full units, work related government-supported trainees, and HM Forces. The indices of workforce jobs for the whole economy have been adjusted to reflect estimated employment levels for the quarter as a whole rather than at the end of the quarter.

Index number of output per filled job are calculated by dividing an index of output by an index of the numbers employed.

Unit wage costs

In the whole economy series the wages and salaries totals in the numerator are adjusted to incorporate the earnings of the self-employed, based on the ratio of the employed labour force to the number of employees in employment and HM Forces. The denominator is the output measure of gross value added at basic prices. For further information see *Employment Gazette*, May 1986, page 172, and August 1988, page S6.

Unit wage costs in manufacturing industries is a monthly index prepared by the Office for National Statistics using monthly indices of average earnings, employment and output. The construction and significance of the figures are described on page 261 of the June 1982 issue of *Employment Gazette*. Quarterly and annual indices are derived from the monthly series.

UK PUBLIC SECTOR JOBS BY MAJOR CATEGORIES

Annual Supplement: Table 3.9

This table is prepared by National Statistics and published once a year in *Economic Trends*, most recently in the June 2000 issue, No. 559. The sources and definitions are shown in *Economic Trends*.

The sectors used in this table are those used for the national accounts. Details on the coverage of the sectors are given in *United Kingdom Sector Classification for the National Accounts* published in August 2000.

All numbers are on a headcount basis. Workforce jobs comprise Employee jobs, Self-employment jobs, HM Forces, Government-supported trainees. Estimates of these figures are supplied by Employment, Earnings & Productivity Division, Prices and Business Group within ONS and are published in *Labour Market Trends* each month.

Estimates of employment in Central Government are obtained from a number of sources. HM Forces from the MoD, National Health Service/NHS Trusts figures are obtained from the NHS Executive. Other Central Government consists largely of those employed in the Civil Service. These numbers are obtained from the Personnel Statistics Branch of the Cabinet Office. The remainder of Central Government employees are derived from the Cabinet Office Public Bodies publication.

Public Corporations are public trading bodies which have substantial degrees of financial independence from Central Government (e.g. The Post Office and Civil Aviation Authority). Data are derived from the Inter-Departmental Business Register (IDBR) and other regular surveys carried out by Prices Group, ONS.

Local Government data which covers Education, Social Services, Construction and Other Local Authority data are supplied on a quarterly basis by Prices Group. Local Authority data relating to Scotland is supplied by the Joint Staffing Watch, Scottish Office. Police data are obtained from the Home Office biannually.

INDEX OF OUTPUT OF THE PRODUCTION INDUSTRIES

Economic Trends: Table 5.1
Annual Supplement: Table 4.1

This index is prepared by the Office for National Statistics with the help of the statistics divisions of government departments. From October 1998 (July index) the index has been calculated with 1995 as the base year for each month from January 1994. In addition, from July 1995 (May index) all indices have been reclassified according to the 1992 revised *Standard Industrial Classification* (SIC(92)).

All series are available annually, quarterly and monthly from 1978. Requests for indices, whether on a regular or *ad hoc* basis, should be sent to National Statistics On-line Services, Zone B1/12, 1 Drummond Gate, London SW1V 2QQ. Tel: 020 7533 5675.

The index is intended to provide a general measure of monthly changes in the volume of output of the production industries which comprise Sections C, Mining and quarrying, D, Manufacturing and E, Electricity, gas and water supply of the SIC(92).

The index is a weighted average of around 250 separate indicators, each of which describes the activity of a small sector of industry. Data to compile the indicators are obtained monthly where possible but for a few industries, only quarterly data are available. Most of the information for manufacturing industry emanates from a comprehensive system of monthly production inquiries to industry undertaken by ONS. The estimates of sales for each activity derived from these inquiries are adjusted by the changes in work in progress and finished goods to calculate the value of production in the industry.

To combine the individual production series, each industry has been given a weight proportional to its value added in 1995 (the base year) derived from the 1995 input-output tables.

The level of production is expressed as a percentage of the average monthly production in 1995. All current value data are deflated to 1995 values using the appropriate producer price indices and export deflators. From January 1995, the export deflators have been calculated from directly-collected export price information. To ensure comparability between different months, adjustments have to be made (where the basic figures refer to calendar months) for variations in the number of days in each month, excluding for each industry those which are not normally working days. The seasonally adjusted series also exclude any changes in production resulting from public and other holidays and from seasonal factors. From July 1995, ONS has replaced the X-II variant of the Census method II Seasonal Adjustment Program with X-II ARIMA. The adjustments are designed to eliminate normal month to month fluctuations and thus to show the trend more clearly.

Industrial classification

The industrial analysis of the index at published group level is consistent with the *Standard Industrial Classification revised 1992* (HMSO 1992), to which reference should be made for a description of each industrial group.

Market sector analysis

This analysis combines the output of industries which meet broadly similar categories of demand. From July 1995, the Consumer goods sector has been replaced by Durable goods and non-durable goods sectors, in line with SOEU requirements.

CONSTRUCTION: OUTPUT AND ORDERS

Economic Trends: Table 5.2
Annual Supplement: Table 4.2

Output

The output series relates to work done by contractors, including estimates of unrecorded output by small firms and self-employed workers, and output by public sector direct labour departments classified to 'Construction' in the 1992 *Standard Industrial Classification.* The figures collected are at current values. These are revalued at constant (1995) prices, seasonally adjusted and converted into an index.

Output is defined as the amount chargeable to customers excluding VAT for building and civil engineering work done in the relevant period. Contractors are asked to include the value of work done on their own initiative on buildings such as dwellings or offices for eventual sale or lease; and of work done by their own operatives on the construction and maintenance of their own premises. The value of goods made by the contractors themselves and used in the work is also included.

Contractors. The Department of the Environment, Transport and the Regions maintains a statistical register of private contracting 'firms', from which samples are drawn for regular inquiries into orders, output and employment. These firms are strictly 'reporting units' as some large firms instead of reporting as single units, prefer to report separately the operations of parts of their companies, for example regional divisions, while, in other cases, a single return may be made covering associated companies each of which are legally separate firms. In 1972 there were about 70,000 reporting units on this register, but in 1973, as a result of special inquiries, 25,000 others (mostly very small) were added. By late 1977 the number on the register had declined to about 85,000; this was partly a reflection of the fall in construction activity and partly a result of the difficulty experienced in picking up new entrants to the industry. Arrangements were made to obtain names and addresses of firms newly registered for VAT purposes as construction firms and with this additional source of information, the statistical register expanded by 1983 to about 160,000. Most of the new additions are small firms, but the register will still not include some very small firms and self-employed workers. By 1991 there were about 207,000 firms on the register. In 1992, the VAT-based registers maintained by the then Department of the Environment and by the then Central Statistical Office were 'matched' so that the overall coverage was improved. Following this and the recession in the construction industry, the register fell to 763,000 firms in 1998. Estimation procedures have been used to avoid any discontinuities in the Department's published series.

Output, employment and orders statistics are adjusted to allow for changes made to the register in order to produce consistent series for the industry.

From the first quarter of 1977, a small number of firms, including firms producing steel platforms for off-shore oil production, were reclassified as 'structural steel fabricators' and were transferred to the appropriate register held by the Department of Industry.

To ease the burden on small firms, stratified sampling methods are used in all inquiries. The 'annual census of output and employment', which before October 1976 included all firms on the register, is now sent to about 30,000 firms including all those with eight or more total employment; smaller firms not included in the 'census', are required to complete a simpler 'register-proving' return. The 'census' covers third quarter output and October employment and for each of the other three quarters output and employment inquiries are sent to about 12,000 firms including all those with 60 or more employees and a sample of smaller firms.

Public Sector Direct Labour Departments. Government departments, local authorities, new towns, nationalised industries and certain other public authorities make quarterly returns in respect of work done by employees engaged on building and civil engineering work.

ENGINEERING: TURNOVER AND ORDERS

Economic Trends: Table 5.2
Annual Supplement: Table 4.2

These data are based upon the results of the Office for National Statistics monthly inquiries and provide seasonally adjusted volume index numbers of total turnover, total home and export orders-on-hand and net new orders of the industries classified to divisions 29, 30, 31, 32 and 33 of the Standard Industrial Classification 1992.

The basic data for the index numbers of total turnover, total orders-on-hand are divided into home and export markets. Seasonally adjusted total indices are obtained by combining the seasonally adjusted home and export series with indices for net new orders being derived from the turnover levels and changes in the orders-on-hand.

Index numbers and non-seasonally adjusted data for the Total Engineering Industries are initially published together with a commentary in an ONS *News Release.*

MOTOR VEHICLE AND STEEL PRODUCTION

Economic Trends: Table 5.3
Annual Supplement: Table 4.3

The latest month for which seasonally adjusted estimates of car and commercial vehicle production are available is December 1998. The introduction of a twice yearly change in age identifier (first letter or number plate) is expected to have a significant impact on the seasonal patterns of production.

Seasonal adjustment relies on being able to isolate the repeating pattern in data from other causes of movement in an economic time series. Since this is impossible to do in the first year of a new seasonal pattern, it has been decided to publish only unadjusted estimates of production until such time as there are sufficient data to construct a new seasonally adjusted series.

The production figures for passenger cars and commercial vehicles for individual months prior to 1996 are totals for periods of four or five weeks. From 1996 onwards they are totals for the calendar month.

Passenger cars

Taxis, estate cars and station wagons are included. Car kits delivered as such by manufacturers for assembly abroad are included where the kits' values constitute 50 per cent or more of the complete vehicle. As from 1981, certain passenger cars were transferred from assembly to production, being reported in output for the first time.

Commercial vehicles

The following types are included: vans, trucks, special purpose vehicles, power units for articulated vehicles (but excluding their tractors), buses and coaches. Chassis delivered as such are included. Battery-driven vehicles are also included.

Index numbers and non-seasonally adjusted data for motor vehicles are initially published in an ONS *News Release.*

Crude steel production

The total of usable ingots, usable continuously cast semi-finished products and liquid steel for castings.

Finished steel consumption

Total receipt by consuming industries from UK steel producers, from stockholders and from imports, *minus* stock-build by consuming industries.

INDICATORS OF FIXED INVESTMENT IN DWELLINGS

Economic Trends: Table 5.4
Annual Supplement: Table 4.4

Orders received by contractors for new houses

Orders for housing exclude improvements, extensions and alterations and house/flat conversions. Examples of the kind of work covered:

Public sector housing - new work: local authority housing schemes; hostels (except youth hostels); married quarters for the services and police; old people's homes; orphanages and children's remand homes; and the provision within housing sites of roads and services for gas, water, electricity, sewage and drainage.

Private sector housing work: all privately-owned buildings for residential use, such as houses, flats and maisonettes, bungalows, cottages, vicarages, and provision of services to new developments. Also included is speculative work where no contract or order is recorded.

Housing starts and completions

These figures relate to new permanent dwellings only; that is, dwellings which may be expected to maintain their stability indefinitely (60 years or more).

A dwelling is a self-contained unit of accommodation. Self containment is where all of the rooms (including the kitchen, bathroom and toilet) are behind a door which only that household can use.

Monthly figures for Scotland are not available; estimates are included in the Great Britain monthly figures.

Figures for Northern Ireland are available from the Department for Social Development, Northern Ireland and are also included in *Housing and Construction Statistics.*

Housing starts and completions for individual local authority areas in England and Wales are published in *Local Housing Statistics.*

Information by sector

The private sector includes:

Private enterprise - this includes dwellings built for owner-occupiers and private landlords, whether persons or companies.

Registered Social landlords includes housing associations registered or unregistered with the Housing Corporation, societies, bodies of trustees or companies established for the purpose of providing social housing accommodation on a non-profit-making basis.

The public sector includes:

Local authorities - in this context refers only to authorities which are local housing authorities under the Housing Acts. Dwellings built by local authorities for sale to private owners are included under this heading.

In England and Wales local housing authorities are unitary authorities, the district councils, the Council of the Isles of Scilly, the London Borough councils, the Common Council of the City of London and, until its abolition on 31 March 1986, the Greater London Council.

In Scotland local housing authorities are the unitary authorities. Scottish Homes (formerly the Scottish Special Housing Association), because it is a statutory body assisting local authorities in their housing programmes, is treated as a local authority for the purposes of these statistics.

Any housebuilding activity by Housing Action Trusts (HATs) are included with the local authority sector.

New towns - this term includes development corporations established under the New Towns Acts for the purpose of laying out and developing a new town. All new towns in England and Wales have now been wound up and their housing stock transferred to local authority or housing association ownership.

Government departments - the figures relate to dwellings provided or authorised by government departments for the families of police, prison staff, the armed forces and certain other services; also included are new dwellings provided by county councils in England and Wales and by other local government bodies acting in capacities other than as housing authorities (for example, for parks, welfare etc).

Stages of construction

Started. A house or flat is counted as started on the date work begins on the laying of the foundation, including 'slabbing' for houses that require it, but not including site preparation. Thus when foundation work commences on a pair of semi-detached houses, two houses are started, and when work begins on a block of flats all the dwellings which that block will contain are started. The starts of houses in building schemes are usually phased over a period of weeks or, in very large schemes, months.

Completed. A dwelling is regarded as completed when it becomes ready for occupation, whether it is in fact occupied or not.

Seasonally adjusted figures

The seasonally adjusted figures show the broad trend in these series. They are derived by estimating the normal fluctuations caused by seasonal influences and removing this element from the actual monthly figures.

The seasonally adjusted figures contain an element of random fluctuations together with any effects of variation in seasonal influences such as the weather, which depart from the normal levels for that month.

Figures for more recent periods are revised annually in the light of the previous year's experience.

Building societies

Up to end-1980 the statistics are based on returns from a sample of about 50 societies, with assets amounting to 90 per cent of total building society assets; the results are grossed up to represent all societies and each year the figures are reconciled with the annual statutory returns made to the Registrar of Friendly Societies by all building societies. From the beginning of 1981 the return was redesigned and the sample reduced to the largest 17 societies (16 societies from 1983) with assets amounting to over 80 per cent of the total.

Following the introduction of the 1986 Building Societies Act, a new monthly return was introduced in January 1987. In September 1992 and October 1998 updated building society returns were introduced. Currently the data are based on 25 societies reporting to the Building Societies Commission, whose assets amounts to 95 percent of building society assets, grossed up to represent all societies.

The pre-1965 statistics are based on annual and quarterly samples smaller than the sample now used, together with the annual statistics of the Registrar of Friendly Societies. There are breaks in series: at July 1989 as a consequence of Abbey National Building Society's conversion to a public limited company; in August 1995 when the Cheltenham and Gloucester Building Society joined the Lloyds Banking Group; in August 1996 when the National and Provincial Building Society transferred its business to Abbey National plc; in April 1997 when Alliance and Leicester Building Society converted to public limited company status; in June 1997 when Halifax Building Society converted to public limited company status; in July 1997 when Woolwich Building Society converted to public limited company status and Bristol and West Building Society joined the Bank of Ireland Group; in October 1997 when Northern Rock Building Society converted to public limited company status; and, in April 1999 when Birmingham Midshires Building Society joined the Halifax Group.

Average price of new dwellings: mortgages approved

Data are obtained from a group of Building Societies. Each society completes a return every month, showing the number and total purchase price of dwellings mortgaged. Separate figures are provided for new and other dwellings; and for mortgages at approval and completion stages. The approval stage figures provide the more up to date indicator of price trends, whereas information based on completions give more accurate figures for dwellings actually purchased because a small, but significant number of mortgages approved do not result in completed transactions.

From 1956 to 1974 quarterly returns were obtained from a panel of 80 building societies. A monthly return was introduced in early 1974. In 1981 the form was revised and the sample reduced to the largest 17 societies (16 by the end of 1982). By the end of 1999 the largest 4 societies were providing returns. Recent mergers, takeovers and change of status in the financial sector having reduced the numbers. These changes effectively removed the Abbey National (July 1989), Cheltenham & Gloucester (August 1995), National Provisional (August 1996), Alliance & Leicester (April 1997), Halifax (June 1997), Bristol & West (July 1997), Woolwich (July 1997), Northern Rock (October 1997) and Birmingham Midshires (April 1999).

Average price of new dwellings at mortgage completion stage

Information on dwelling prices at national and regional level is collected and published by the Department every quarter from a five per cent sample survey, the Survey of Mortgage Lenders (SML). Until the first quarter of 1992 the survey was based on a sample of Building Societies, but from the second quarter of 1992 the survey was extended to include all mortgage lenders who were members of the Council of Mortgage Lenders (CML).

NUMBER OF PROPERTY TRANSACTIONS

Economic Trends: Table 5.5
Annual Supplement: Table 4.5

The counts of the number of property transactions are based on administrative records of the number of 'particulars delivered' forms notified to Inland Revenue Stamp Offices or District Land Registries. These forms are completed whenever freehold land or property is transferred on sale, or a lease for seven years or more is granted, or such a lease is transferred on sale. Further details may be found in two articles:

i. *Number of Property Transactions in England and Wales* by Paul Heggs and Alan Holmans in *Economic Trends,* No 452, June 1991.

ii. *Seasonal Adjustment of the Number of Property Transactions in England and Wales* in *Economic Trends*, No 484, February 1994.

Part 1 of Table 4.5 gives a long run of quarterly counts of property transactions in England and Wales, and a shorter run of quarterly counts of property transactions in England, Wales and Northern Ireland. Part 2 gives monthly counts for the latter series. The series are unadjusted.

Further details of 1999 property transactions can be found in *Inland Revenue Statistics 2000* Tables 16.1-16.4, published in October 2000.

CHANGES IN INVENTORIES

Economic Trends: Table 5.6
Annual Supplement: Table 4.6

See note on 'Changes in inventories' on page 277.

INVENTORY RATIOS

Economic Trends: Table 5.7
Annual Supplement: Table 4.7

See note on 'Changes in inventories' on page 277, note on 'Gross domestic product' on page 276 and note on 'Retail sales' below.

RETAIL SALES, NEW REGISTRATIONS OF CARS AND CREDIT BUSINESS

Economic Trends: Table 5.8
Annual Supplement: Table 4.8

Retail sales

The monthly retail sales estimates cover the retail trades (excluding the motor trades) in Great Britain. Until the end of 1991, the statistics were based on returns from a voluntary panel of 3,500 retailers. However, as a part of a package of measures to improve economic statistics, the inquiry was made compulsory from January 1992 and the sample size was increased to approximately 5,000. The new inquiry provides more soundly-based estimates as it covers all large retailers and a random sample of smaller retailers. The use of statutory powers means that it has been possible to improve the sample design at the detailed level and reduce the sampling error associated with the results.

For each four or five week period contributors report their retail sales for all their outlets and by mail order. The statistics include VAT, and services to customers. Hire purchase and other instalment credit sales are valued at the credit price of the goods; that is including deposits and, where credit is provided by the shop, credit charges. Figures of credit sales relate only to the period during which the transactions took place; cash received from credit sales in previous periods is not included. Sales by chemists and opticians exclude receipts under the National Health Service.

The retail sales index is based on the results of the 1995 annual retailing inquiry. From September 1998, the monthly retail index was rebased using detailed information from the larger scale 1995 annual retail inquiry.

The main features of the series are:

- The reference year has been set at 1995 = 100.
- It is aligned to the final results of the 1995 annual retailing inquiry and uses them in the estimation of sales for later years.
- It incorporates revised price deflators for each SIC(92) class based on the pattern of trade shown by the 1995 retailing inquiry. These deflators are used to convert the value estimates on to a constant price or volume basis: most components of the retail sales index are deflated onto a volume basis using price data from the retail prices index.

The latest summary statistics are published each month by First Release; more disaggregated value indices (not seasonally adjusted) are published each month in the ONS publication SDM 28: *Retail Sales*, available from National Statistics Direct on 01633 812078.

The latest summary statistics are published each month by *First Release*; more disaggregated value indices (not seasonally adjusted) are published each month in the ONS publication SDM28: *Retail Sales*, available from National Statistics Direct on 01633 812078.

New registration of cars

The figures for months up to September 1974 were compiled from information received by the then Department of the Environment from all registration and licensing authorities (county, county borough and borough councils) in Great Britain which administer the Vehicles (Excise) Act, 1971 (and previous similar Acts). The figures from October 1974 onwards are obtained from the Driver and Vehicle Licensing Agency at Swansea which took over responsibility for new registrations from that date.

Up to and including the fourth quarter of 1974 new registrations relate to the taxation class 'private cars and vans'. This taxation class includes vehicles other than cars used privately, but excludes cars which are exempted from vehicle taxation. In October 1982 a change in taxation regulations meant that the private taxation class would also include all light goods vehicles less than 1,525 kilograms unladen weight. From this date the old 'private car and van' taxation class was modified to the new 'private and light goods' taxation class. The time series on new registrations of cars has been preserved by counting, from the first quarter of 1975 onwards, the total of body type cars regardless of how they are taxed. The old 'private car and van' series and the 'body type car' series are slightly different in coverage, but this is unlikely to distort movements in the estimates of the underlying trend. Given that the estimates are counts of *car bodies* regardless of how they are taxed, this is irrelevant.

Since August 1998, the sequence of prefix letters is changing at six monthly intervals.

This change is leading to a more even monthly spread of new vehicle registrations, as opposed to the traditional peak in August. As a result, the existing seasonal adjustment model is no longer valid and reliable estimates of seasonally adjusted figures will not be available for some time.

Consumer credit (Total)

The series is defined, in principle, as lending to consumers (ie the personal sector excluding unincorporated businesses and non-profit- making bodies serving persons) to finance current expenditure on goods and services, but excluding very short-term borrowing akin to trade credit. How the figures are compiled was described in an article in the September 1979 issue of *Economic Trends*. As it explains, the definition of the series cannot be met exactly in practice, but the figures are thought to be a reasonably good indicator of consumer credit. The figures comprise lending other than for house purchase to individuals and households by the banks' sector, trustee savings banks (which joined the banks' sector at the end of 1981), non-bank consumer credit companies (many of which also joined the banks' sector as licensed deposit takers at the end of 1981), insurance companies, unsecured loans by building societies and retailers. Figures have not been compiled on this basis for earlier than 1976 because the separation of bank lending to individuals and households from bank lending to the rest of the personal sector (mainly unincorporated businesses) is available only from then.

Please note the break in series of AIKL to VZQC. The new series are the broader coverage of the total consumer credit of which data for credit cards is also provided.

Credit business (Narrower coverage)

The statistics relate to credit granted by finance houses and other specialist credit grantors (ie cheque traders, money lenders, etc), building societies' class 3 unsecured loans permitted under the terms of the Building Societies Act, 1986, credit advanced on bank credit cards (VISA and Mastercard only), and until the end of 1986 the self-financed credit business of selected kinds of retailers. The kinds of retail businesses covered were co-operative societies (until end 1975), household goods retailers, food retailers, mixed business retailers, general mail order businesses and clothing retailers (from beginning 1976).

The credit business of high street banks, building societies (except for class 3 loans), insurance companies and businesses which lend to other companies only is outside the scope of these series. Charge accounts, that is accounts which have to be paid in full at the end of the month or other period worked to, are excluded. The series includes all other credit agreements.

The monthly estimates are derived by projecting the results of benchmark inquiries forward by means of monthly returns from stratified panels of finance houses and other specialist credit grantors. Data for bank credit cards are supplied by the British Bankers' Association.

There are three breaks in the series. The first is at the end of 1975. Before this the finance house statistics are based on the results of the 1965 Benchmark Inquiry to Finance Houses and from the beginning of 1976 onwards they are based on the 1976 Benchmark Inquiry to Consumer Credit Grantors. Before 1976 the figures exclude running-account agreements and non-instalment agreements. They include agreements which have been block-discounted by retailers.

There is also a break at the end of 1975 due to a change in definition. Before this amounts outstanding included unearned charges for credit (ie those charges for fixed-sum credit which are known at the outset of an agreement but which do not become payable until some time in the future). From the beginning of 1976 onwards unearned charges are excluded.

The second break, due to coverage, is at the end of 1985. Prior to this amounts outstanding excluded block-discounted agreements outstanding to finance houses and other specialist credit grantors, but included running-account agreements. Amounts outstanding on bank credit cards were also excluded.

Collection of data on the narrower coverage stopped in December 1994, when monthly data on the broader coverage/whole economy series became available.

Net lending

The third break occurs at the end of 1986 where the net lending series replaces the changes in amounts outstanding series. The new series are a better measure of the net amount of credit advanced. The previously published estimates of net lending were calculated as changes in the reported amounts outstanding at the beginning and end of each period. They were thus distorted by revaluations of the debt, for example those resulting from amounts written-off during the period. The net lending series are now adjusted to remove distortions caused by revaluations.

Detailed statistics are published each month in the Bank of England's *Monetary* and *Financial Statistics*, and in *Financial Statistics* (published monthly by The Stationery Office).

INLAND ENERGY CONSUMPTION

Economic Trends: Table 5.9
Annual Supplement: Table 4.9

Primary fuel input

Coal
Consumption by primary and secondary fuel producers *plus* colliery and opencast disposals and disposals of imports to final users *plus* (for all annual data and quarterly data prior to 1973) net foreign trade and stock change in other solid fuels. From 1988 annual data also include solid renewable sources (eg wood, waste).

Petroleum
Inland deliveries for energy use *plus* refinery fuel and losses with an adjustment from the beginning of 1979 for the difference between deliveries and actual consumption at power stations and gasworks.

Natural gas
Indigenous natural gas produced, *less* gas-flared or re-injected, *plus* colliery methane piped to the surface and consumed at collieries or sold, *plus* imported natural gas, with adjustment for the net amount of natural gas sent to storage. Natural gas supplied for non-energy purposes is included. From 1988 annual data also include gaseous renewable sources (landfill gas, sewage gas etc).

Primary electricity - nuclear
Electricity generated (net of electricity used on works) by nuclear power stations belonging to British Energy (the holding company for Nuclear Electric and Scottish Nuclear) and Magnox Electric, British Nuclear Fuel Plc. and (until 1994) the UK Atomic Energy Authority.

Primary electricity - hydro
Electricity generated (net of electricity used on works) by natural flow hydro stations owned by major generating companies and other generators (ie; excluding pumped storage stations). From 1988 annual data also include other renewable primary electricity resources (wind, etc).

Primary electricity - net imports
Electricity imported from, *less* electricity exported to, countries outside the United Kingdom.

Tonnes of oil equivalent
The data are shown in a common unit of measurement, the tonne of oil equivalent (toe), which enables different fuels to be compared and aggregated. The tonne of oil equivalent is defined as follows:

1 tonne of oil equivalent	=	10^7 kilocalories
		396.8 therms
		41.87 gigajoules
		11,630 kWh

Hydro Electricity and net imports of electricity are presented in terms of the energy content of the electricity produced. Primary inputs for nuclear electricity assume a thermal efficiency of 37 per cent at nuclear stations.

Electricity available - public supply
Electricity available from the major generating companies, ie; AES Electric Ltd, Anglian Power Generators, Barking Power Ltd, BNFL Magnox, British Energy plc, Cookeeragh Power Ltd, Corby Power Ltd, Derwent Cogeneration Ltd, Edison Mission Energy Ltd, Fellside Heat and Power Ltd, Fibrogen Ltd, Fibropower Ltd,Fibrothetford Ltd, Fife Power Ltd, Humber Power Ltd, Lakeland Power Ltd, Medway Power Ltd, Midlands Power (UK) Ltd, National Power plc, NIGEN, Peterborough Power Ltd, PowerGen plc, Premier Power Ltd, Regional Power Generators Ltd, Rocksavage Power Company Ltd, Sita Tyre recycling Ltd, Scottish Power plc, Seabank Power Ltd, SELCHP Ltd, South Western Electricity, Sutton Bridge Power Ltd,Teeside Power Ltd, TXU Europe, Europe Power Ltd.

Temperature corrections
The adjusted total inland energy consumption series includes temperature corrections for coal, petroleum and, from 1973 onwards, natural gas.

The corrections used per centigrade degree are:

Coal	2.1%
Petroleum	0.7% (June - August)
	1.8% (September - May)

Figures for natural gas are corrected using a method developed by British Gas Transco. Prior to 1990, the annual temperature adjustment applied by the DTI differed from that applied by British Gas due to the effects of seasonal adjustment of the monthly data. From 1990 onward, the DTI's annual adjustment to the gas figures for temperature is the same as that applied by British Gas Transco. Nuclear, hydro and net imports of electricity are not corrected for temperature.

STERLING EXCHANGE RATES AND UK RESERVES

Economic Trends: Table 6.1
Annual Supplement: Table 5.1

Exchange rates

The exchange rates in the table have been collated from the *Monthly Digest of Statistics* and *Financial Statistics.* Data for the deutschemark and the lira are only available back to January 1963, and for the yen are only available back to January 1970.

Data may not always be comparable because of revaluations, devaluations or other currency agreements. Readers requiring specific information about such events should refer to more detailed analyses of the currencies in which they are interested.

United Kingdom official reserves

These comprise gold and convertible currencies and, from 1 January 1970, Special Drawing Rights (SDRs) held in the Exchange Equalisation Account, together with, from July 1972, the reserve position in the International Monetary Fund, and, from July 1979, European Currency Units acquired from swaps with the European Monetary Co-operation Fund. Gold is valued at $35 per fine ounce until end-1970; then at $38 per fine ounce until end-1972; and at $42.2222 per fine ounce thereafter, up to the end of March 1979. SDRs are valued at SDR1 = $1 until end-1970; then SDR1 = $1.08571 until end-1972; and at SDR1 = $1.20635 thereafter, up to the end of March 1979. Non-dollar convertible currencies are converted to dollars at middle or central rates. From end-March 1979 up to end-1999, the rates at which the reserves are valued in dollars are revised annually, and are based upon the market rates prevailing at end-March or during the three months preceding that date.

United Kingdom international reserves

From July 1999 reserves data have been published on the basis of the IMF Data Template on International Reserves and Foreign Currency Liquidity. Assets are mark-to-market in sterling using end period prices and exchange rates. In addition to the change in valuation, the coverage of reserves data has been expanded to include off balance sheet items such as forwards and swaps.

MONETARY AGGREGATES

Economic Trends: Table 6.2
Annual Supplement: Table 5.2

In the 1980s there were a number of changes to the broad monetary aggregates. In 1987 the aggregate formerly known as £M3 was renamed M3 and that formerly known as M3 was renamed M3c. At the same time a new aggregate, M4 was introduced and is constructed in a similar fashion to M3, except that banks and building societies are treated as if they were a single group of institutions. The measure of private sector liquidity formerly known as PSL2 (which included, in addition to M4, private sector holdings of certain money market instruments, CTDs and some national savings instruments) was renamed M5. These changes are discussed in greater detail in an article entitled 'Measures of broad money' in the *Bank of England Quarterly Bulletin,* May 1987. In July 1989 M3 and M3c ceased to be published (along with M1) as a consequence of the breaks in series that were caused by Abbey National Building Society's conversion to a public limited company (see *Bank of England Quarterly Bulletin,* August 1989). Another new monetary aggregate, M4c, which was similar in composition to the old M3c except that it included private sector foreign currency deposits with building societies as well as banks, was constructed. In March 1990 the Bank of England published a statistical discussion paper 'Monetary aggregates in a changing environment'. As a result of this discussion paper it was decided to no longer publish NIB M1, M4c or M5. A new series of 'liquid assets outside M4' was introduced; see May 1991 edition of *Bank of England Quarterly Bulletin.* In December 1992 the definition of deposits which, along with notes and coin, comprise M2 was altered. As a result, M2 is no longer published. From this date to 1999 the only aggregates published were M0, and M4 (and a European harmonised aggregate, M3H, which is similar to M4). In 1999 publication of M3H was replaced by the nearest equivalent that could be constructed from the available data of the European Central Bank's Euro M3 measure. The main difference is that some of the specific maturity analyses pertaining to inclusion or exclusion from the Euro M3 are not collected in the UK and so an estimate of these has had to be made.

A number of breaks in series have occurred from time to time. New, more comprehensive statistical returns from the banks were introduced in May 1975 and resulted in a break in series at end-June 1975. This break has been eliminated from the changes figures with the help of partial information provided by the banks. The introduction of the monetary sector in November 1981 created a further break in series (at end-December 1981) as did the inclusion of new contributors at end-March 1983 following the completion of a review of banking statistics. The Banking Statistics Review at the end September 1997 reclassified the Channel Islands and Isle of man as non-resident (and therefore outside of M4) to be consistent with ESA95 resulting in a break in series.

In each of these cases, and, if appropriate in the case of other minor breaks that have occurred such as reporting institutions either joining or leaving the reporting population, the effects which have been excluded from the changes series ie any changes in banks' and building societies' liabilities arising from alterations in the composition of the reporting population, or from the use of new sources of information, are reflected only in the levels and not in the changes. As a result, changes shown in the tables may differ from those which can be calculated by comparing levels. (Further details on breaks in monetary series are described in *Technical Series Paper No 23* entitled *Breaks in Monetary Series* published by the Bank of England in February 1989, updated annually in Part 2 of the *Bank of England Statistical Abstract*.)

The narrow money aggregate M0 was introduced in March 1984 and is calculated as a basis the average of weekly levels as at each Wednesday during each month. Long runs of all the monetary aggregates are available in the *Bank of England Statistical Abstract,* Part 2, published in November 1999. This is also available in disk form from the Bank's Monetary and Financial Statistics Division or the internet at the Bank of England's web site.

COUNTERPARTS TO CHANGES IN M4

Economic Trends: Table 6.3
Annual Supplement: Table 5.3

The table sets out the accounting identities between the public sector borrowing requirement and changes in M4. The table, as it related to M3, was discussed in articles in the *Bank of England Quarterly Bulletin* in March 1977 and December 1981. The relationship between external and foreign currency flows and the money supply was described in articles in December 1978 and December 1983. Background to the table is given also in the *Financial Statistics Explanatory Handbook,* 2000 Edition (The Stationery Office, 1999).

Public sector net cash requirement

The public sector net cash requirement (PSNCR – was previously known as the Public Sector Borrowing Requirement (PSBR); the definition is unchanged) indicates the extent to which the public sector borrows from the other sectors of the economy and overseas to finance the balance of expenditure and receipts.

Part of the central government net cash requirement is needed to finance central government lending to the rest of the public sector (local government and public corporations). Consequently the PSNCR is built up from the net cash requirement of central government *plus* 'contributions' from local government and public corporations. The local government 'contribution' is equal to the local government net cash requirement *less* the direct non-market borrowing by local government from central government. Transactions in other public sector debt are netted off the local government net cash requirement, as are their transactions in bank deposits and other short-term assets. The public corporations' 'contribution' is defined in a similar way. See also the table *Financial transactions of the public sector*, (table 6.5 *Economic Trends*, table 5.5 *Annual Supplement.)*

The main counterpart to a change in M4 is monetary financial institutions (mfis') lending in sterling to the UK private sector, which consists of all UK residents other than the public sector and mfis.

External and foreign currency counterparts

The definition of external and foreign currency counterparts was changed in June 1985 to include changes in net non-deposit liabilities in foreign currency. These comprise the foreign currency component of capital, internal funds and reserves of all UK mfis, *less* their foreign currency investments in other UK mfis and other non-financial assets. Figures are published on this revised basis from 1985, Q3. Figures for earlier periods reflect the former definition, whereby net non-deposit liabilities in foreign currency were included in column 9, which was then entitled 'Non-deposit liabilities (net)'. The change was first introduced in the *Bank of England Quarterly Bulletin*, June 1985 and was incorporated in *Economic Trends* for the first time in July 1985.

In 1999 the main analysis of counterparts was changed from the above "public sector approach" to one based wholly on the aggregate balance sheet of MFI's. In this approach the counterparts, in addition to MFI's lending in sterling to the UK private sector, are net foreign currency lending to the UK private sector, net sterling and foreign currency lending to the UK public sector, net sterling and foreign currency lending to non-residents, and other net assets. This new approach is described in detail in an article "Monetary statistics and the monetary financial institutions' consolidated balance sheet" published in the July 1999 issue of Monetary and Financial Statistics.

Long runs of data

Long runs of data are available in the *Bank of England Statistical Abstract* Part 2, published in November 1999. This is also available on the Internet.

GENERAL GOVERNMENT RECEIPTS AND EXPENDITURE

Economic Trends: Table 6.4
Annual Supplement: Table 5.4

This table shows data from national accounts for the general government sector.

General Government Expenditure (GGE): a detailed breakdown of the components is shown in the *Blue Book* table 11.3.

Current GGE includes final consumption (expenditure on wages, goods and services, and depreciation), social benefits, interest, subsidies and other current grants.

Capital GGE consists of gross capital formation and net payment of investment grants and other capital transfers.

Financial GGE represents the acquisition less disposals of financial assets acquired for policy purposes (such as student loans and lending to support industry or house purchase).

In defining GGE some receipts are netted-off expenditure such as sales of goods and services, receipts of occupational pension contributions and payments by European Commission. These receipts are therefore excluded from the definition of General Government receipts shown in the second part of the table to ensure they are counted only once.

The *Gross Operating Surplus* includes the surplus on general government trading activities (mainly Local Government housing) and non-trading capital consumption.

Taxes on production include VAT, excise duties, other taxes on expenditure such as air passenger duty, insurance premium tax and landfill tax. It also includes certain taxes paid by business such as rates, motor vehicle duty, and some licence and regulation fees.

Taxes on income and wealth include income tax, corporation tax, capital gains tax, household rates, and motor vehicle duty paid by households.

Taxes on capital are mainly death duties.

Property income includes interest and oil royalties.

Miscellaneous current transfers are mainly court fines.

The current and capital components of GGE, less General Government Receipts, equals General Government net borrowing in Table 6.5.

FINANCIAL TRANSACTIONS OF THE PUBLIC SECTOR

Economic Trends: Table 6.5
Annual Supplement: Table 5.5

This table shows four key indicators of general government and public sector finances. The most recent quarterly figures are reported in the ONS *First Release* called Public Sector Accounts.

"Surplus on the current budget" is the ESA95 national accounts balance net saving (B.8n) plus receipts of capital taxes. It is the statistic used to monitor the "Golden Rule" for public finances. This says that over the economic cycle current expenditure should not exceed current receipts so that borrowing is only undertaken to finance net investment.

Net investment is gross capital formation (net expenditure on fixed assets, land, and changes in stocks), plus payments less receipts of investment grants and other capital transfers, less depreciation.

Net borrowing is the identity B.9 in national accounts under ESA95. General Government net borrowing is the measure used by the European Commission to judge excessive government deficits under the Maastricht treaty.

The Public Sector Net Cash Requirement (PSNCR) was previously known as the Public Sector Borrowing requirement (PSBR).

UK BANKS' LOANS, ADVANCES AND ACCEPTANCES TO UK RESIDENTS

Annual Supplement: Table 5.6

The revised analysis introduced in November 1983 resulted in a major break in the series. Figures for August 1983 and earlier dates are not comparable with those in the revised analysis and a breakdown is therefore given only for data for November 1983 and later dates.

The analysis is based as far as possible on the *Standard Industrial Classification 1980*: there are five broad headings of manufacturing, other production, financial, services and persons. Loans, advances and acceptances are classified by industry, irrespective of owner (that is, private, local authority or government); loans are classified according to the main activity of the borrower - if necessary within the residual groups provided under the broad divisions. Lending to unincorporated businesses, etc, is allocated according to the trade or profession.

The analysis covers loans, advances and acceptances in both sterling and foreign currencies provided by reporting institutions to their customers (changes in foreign currencies have been adjusted to remove the effect of exchange rate movements). Loans and advances include lending under the DTI special scheme for domestic shipbuilding, secured money placed with Stock Exchange money brokers and (until March 1996) gilt-edged market makers and sterling time deposits placed with, holdings of sterling certificates of deposit issued by, and investments in securities by, building societies. They do not, however, include funds placed through specialised financial markets such as the local authority money market or funds lent to monetary sector institutions or overseas residents, or lending under reverse repos.

There was a break in the series between November 1981 and February 1982 caused by the transition to the group of institutions formerly described as the monetary sector and known now as 'banks operating in the United Kingdom'. Further details of the break are set out in the December 1981 and March 1982 issues of the *Bank of England Quarterly Bulletin*. Further details of breaks in series are contained in the footnotes to the table, in *Bank of England Discussion Paper No 23, 'Breaks in monetary series'*, and the *Bank of England Statistical Abstract* published in November 1992.

No data were collected for 1997 quarter 2 as banks prepared for the implementation of the Banking Statistics Review in September 1997. From 1997 quarter 3 levels data are based on the Standard Industrial Classification 1992.

CONSUMER CREDIT AND OTHER HOUSEHOLD SECTOR BORROWING

Economic Trends Table 6.6
Annual Supplement Table 5.7

This table brings together data on consumer credit and other households borrowing. It's main purpose is to provide information on a measure of consumer credit defined, in principle, as borrowing by consumers (i.e. the household sector excluding sole proprietors, partnerships and non-profit making institutions serving households) to finance current expenditure on goods and services; and to show how it compares with total households borrowing. Short-term borrowing akin to trade credit is excluded.

The table is arranged to show credit extended by each of the main types of credit granting institutions. Information on the type of goods purchased via credit agreements is no longer collected. Monthly data on all the main components of consumer credit became available with effect from April 1993.

The table shows borrowing through credit cards as a separate memorandum item. The figures only cover cards issued by banks and, with effect from the third quarter of 1992, building societies. Borrowing through Trustcard, part of Visa, is only included from end-1981 when TSB joined the banks' sector. Some credit cards are issued by or on behalf of retailers. Borrowing through these cards is included in the table according to the type of institution financing the scheme. Some are banks, some are specialist consumer credit companies, and others are retailers who finance their own schemes.

Repayment of borrowing through charge cards i.e. through "travel and entertainment" cards such as Diners and American Express is normally made in full at the end of the month. This form of borrowing is more akin to trade credit than consumer credit as defined here. Strictly speaking it should be included in the 'other' column. However, in practice this is not possible. Some data are not available and others are indistinguishably included in data for credit cards.

As a result of an ONS review of consumer credit issued by non-bank credit grantors, data for other specialist lenders were improved and revised back to January 1995. As a result the total amount outstanding was revised (in August 1997) upwards by £2.6bn. Flows have been break adjusted.

Scope of headings

Consumer credit:

(a) *credit cards: total.* The series covers lending on all bank credit cards and, where these are indistinguishable, charge cards, including Mastercard and Visa (but excluding Trustcard before end-1981). From the third quarter of 1992 the series also cover a relatively small amount of lending on building societies' credit cards.

(b) *banks.* The series covers bank lending in sterling to persons, households and individual trusts but excluding bank loans secured on dwellings.

(c) *building societies'* unsecured lending to individuals. Including sterling personal loans and bridging loans (prior to October 1998 known as class 3 lending). Lending by building societies subsidiaries is included in *other specialist lenders.*

(d) *other specialist lenders.* The series covers unsecured lending to individuals by finance houses, building societies subsidiaries and other specialist non-bank credit grantors and a small amount of unsecured lending by specialist mortgage finance companies.

(e) *insurance companies.* The series relates to policy loans and other loans to individuals by life assurance and general insurance companies. Figures are based on advances and redemptions of premium.

(f) *retailers.* The series only covers consumer credit financed directly by retailers.

Loans secured on dwellings

Loans secured on dwellings is the total of Building societies, Banks, central government, local government, insurance companies and pension funds, miscellaneous financial institutions and public non-financial corporations. Full details are given in Table 3.2C of *Financial Statistics* with detailed notes in the *Financial Statistics Explanatory Handbook.*

ANALYSIS OF BANKS LENDING TO UK RESIDENTS: AMOUNTS OUTSTANDING

Economic Trends: Table 6.7
Annual Supplement: Table 5.8

This analysis is based on the ONS's *Standard Industrial Classification (SIC)* of 1992 and excludes lending to residents in the Channel Islands and the Isle of Man which are classified as non-residents for statistical purposes from end-September 1997. Reporting institutions submit these data quarterly to the Bank of England on the Form AL which contains forty-four categories (formerly Form Q3 containing thirty-seven categories) classified by industry, according to the main activity of the borrower, irrespective of ownership (i.e. private, local authority or government). In this table there are five broad headings of manufacturing, other production, financial, services and persons Lending to unincorporated businesses etc is allocated according to the appropriate trade or profession. Banks with balance sheet assets/liabilities over £600mn or eligible liabilities over £60mn report these data which are then adjusted to reflect lending by all UK banks.

The analysis, which is not seasonally adjusted, covers loans, advances (including lending under reverse repos), finance leasing, acceptances and facilities in both sterling and other currencies, and holdings of sterling commercial paper issued by UK residents, provided by reporting banks to their UK resident non-bank and non-building society customers. The figures for loans and advances also include, indistinguishably, amounts lent under the Department of Trade and Industry special scheme for domestic shipbuilding for UK buyers. It does not, however, include funds placed through the local authority money market or funds lent to UK banks, UK building societies or non-residents. The figures for acceptances are for bills accepted by reporting institutions under facilities granted to UK residents (other than UK banks or building societies) which are still outstanding; those discounted by the reporting institution itself are included under advances but not under acceptances. Facilities data consist of the total amount of overdraft, loan and acceptance facilities outstanding, both drawn and undrawn.

The institutions report their other currency advances and acceptances outstanding after translation into sterling at the middle market spot rate pertaining in the London market at 4pm London time on the last working day of the London market in the period covered by the report.

The main differences between the SIC 1992 total and banks' sterling lending to the M4 private sector (as defined in the counterparts to M4) are:

(i) the M4 lending counterpart includes banks' investments in securities issued by the M4 private sector and adjustments for transit items;
(ii) this analysis includes lending to the UK public sector;
(iii) in this analysis lending to unincorporated businesses and non-profit making bodies is included in the appropriate industrial category; whereas in the sectoral analysis of the M4 lending counterpart it is included in lending to the household sector;
(iv) this analysis will not be seasonally adjusted until a sufficient run of data are available.
(v) this analysis covers both sterling and other currencies.

INTEREST RATES, SECURITY PRICES AND YIELDS

Economic Trends: Table 6.8
Annual Supplement: Table 5.9

Bank of England's minimum lending rate

The minimum rate at which the Bank normally lent to members of the London Discount Market Association against security. These arrangements were discontinued from 20.03.81 being replaced by a bonded dealing system at which the Bank no longer published as 'stop rate'. This system subsequently became unworkable and was superseded on 03.03.97 by a repo rate. A full description of these changes to the Bank's open market operations can be found in BOE Annual Abstract of Statistics published each year.

Building societies: rate of interest on ordinary shares

The Building Societies' Association replaced its recommended rates of interest with advised basic rates in November 1983, leaving societies free to offer interest rates above or below the advised rates. In November 1984 the advised rates were withdrawn and not replaced.

Interest paid by building societies on shares is net of income tax, which until 6 April 1991 was paid by the societies at the agreed composite rate. The composite rates for recent fiscal years are as follows:

Per cent	
1959/60	25.62
1960/61	26.67
1961/62	27.08
1962/63	27.50
1963/64	27.08
1964/65	29.17
1965/66	30.83
1966/67	31.25
1967/68	31.25
1968/69	32.08
1969/70	32.25
1970/71	32.75
1971/72	31.00
1972/73	30.00
1973/74	23.50
1974/75	26.25
1975/76	27.75
1976/77	27.75
1977/78	24.25
1978/79	22.50
1979/80	21.00
1980/81	22.50
1981/82	25.50
1982/83	25.25
1983/84	25.00
1984/85	25.25
1985/86	25.25
1986/87	25.25
1987/88	24.75
1988/89	23.25
1989.90	21.75
1990/91	22.00

With effect from 6 April 1991 composite rate tax for banks and building societies was replaced by basic rate tax with exemptions for non-tax payers.

Selected retail banks' base rate

The base rates of Barclays Bank, Lloyds TSB Bank, HSBC Bank and National Westminster Bank only are used to compile the figures in this series.

Each of these banks has a single base rate, which may sometimes differ from those of the other banks. The rates of interest charged by the banks on much of their lending to customers are set at margins over their own base rates; the size of the margin depends on the nature and status of the customer. A change in base rate normally signifies a marked change in the level of short-term market rate; hence base rate is widely used as an indicator of the broad level of interest rates. Some bank lending is more closely related to money market rates which vary daily and some, for example to persons for house purchase, is at rates which vary more or less frequently than base rate. The only loans for which the banks charge uniform rates are those for ECGD guaranteed exports and for domestic shipbuilding.

British government securities: long dated (20-year) yields

The table shows the gross redemption yield for 20-year maturities derived from fitting observed yield-maturity curves to a mathematical model of the gilt-edged market. The model used (Svensson yield curve) was described in an article in the *Bank of England Quarterly Bulletin* (May 1995).

Financial Times' FT 30 Index (Index of industrial ordinary shares)

This is a geometric index, calculated and published by the *Financial Times* at hourly intervals during the day and at the close of Stock Exchange business for the day. Figures shown in the table are closing figures. The base date is 1 July 1935, which equals 100. Constituents of the index are thirty market leaders, representing a cross-section of British industry. Dividend and earnings yield calculations are also geometric. Earnings yield was replaced on 1 April 1995 by Net Dividend Cover which shows the ability of a company to meet dividend payments from its current earnings.

A fuller description of the composition and compilation of the index is given in *Guide to FT Statistics*, last published by the *Financial Times* in 1984.

SELECTED RETAIL BANKS; INTEREST RATES

Annual Supplement: Table 5.10

Base rates

The minimum lending rate was introduced on 13th October 1972 and represented the minimum rate at which the Bank, acting as lender of last resort, normally lent to members of the discount market against the security of Treasury bills, other approved bills or government stocks with five years or less to maturity. Following the cessation of the continuous posting of MLR 20 in August 1981, the retail banks base rates now fulfil this role.

The table shows the dates of changes in the base rates of Barclays, Lloyds TSB, HSBC and National Westminster Banks at close of business on the respective dates. A spread is shown where the rates of the four banks did not change on the same day. MLR has been invoked on subsequent dates (as indicated by the footnotes to the table), lapsing at close of business on the same day.

The rates of interest charged by the banks on much of their lending to customers are set at margins over their own base rates; the size of the margin depends on the nature and status of the customer. A change in base rate normally signifies a marked change in the level of short-term market rates; hence base rate is widely used as an indicator of the broad level of interest rates. However, some bank lending is at rates more closely related to money market rates which vary daily and some, for example to persons for house purchase, is at rates which vary less frequently than base rate.

Weighted Interest rates

Mortgage rates; these represent the end-month observations of variable rate mortgage for existing borrowers offered by Abbey National, Alliance and Leicester, Bank of Scotland, Barclays Bank, Bristol and West, Cheltenham and Gloucester, Halifax, HSBC Bank, National Westminster Bank, Northern Rock, Royal Bank of Scotland and Woolwich and are weighted by their corresponding balance sheet data.

Gross interest on instant access accounts (low balances) and 90 day accounts (medium balances); these are weighted averages of end-month observations of the rates paid by Abbey National, Alliance and Leicester, Barclays Bank, Bristol and West, Cheltenham and Glouster, Halifax, Lloyds TSB Bank, HSBC Bank, National Westminster Bank, Northern Rock, Royal Bank of Scotland and Woolwich on instant access and 90 day accounts. The rates are grossed up at the current rate of composite rate tax until March 1991 and thereafter at the standard rate of income tax. Small balances are defined as £500, pre-1999 and £1000 thereafter, medium balances as £10,000 and high balances as £25,000.

A SELECTION OF ASSET PRICES

Economic Trends Table 6.9
Annual Supplement Table 5.11

Producer price indices

For plant & machinery bought as fixed assets

Each index is made up from two elements:

(1) The UK produced element is made up of Producer price indices (PPIs) showing the trends in prices of goods sold by manufacturers – also see notes covering producer prices on page 271. The value and types of capital equipment are assigned to each industry using the pattern of expenditure derived from the base year. These indices show the price trends for the items of a constant level of quality i.e. of the same specification.

(2) Import adjustments are then made using separate estimates for the price movements of imported goods within overall capital expenditure. Index values of the base series are then adjusted by these results. The all manufacturing index is a base weighted combination of its components.

For manufactured output

The index for motor vehicles is for UK produced goods and shows the trends in prices at the factory gate. The series reflects prices of replacing a car with another of the same specification. Weights are calculated on a gross sector basis i.e. all transactions are included and exclude imports.

Housing: DETR all lenders mix adjusted house price index

The mix-adjusted (or weighted) house price series is based on mortgage completions. The mix of properties (of dwelling type, size, location and age) changes from one period to the next. Consequently a house price series that removes the effect of these changes is a better measure of true house price movement than an index based on the simple average price, which will reflect the property mix for that specific period. The mix-adjusted series excludes:

- all sitting tenant purchases (right-to-buy)
- dwellings purchased without a mortgage (about 25 per cent of all purchases)
- loans obtained from another source (eg lenders who are not members of CML).

Average price of agricultural land in England

The series up to 1992 reflected the prices of vacant land sold without buildings. Sales notified to the Inland Revenue in the period are thought to have taken place, on average, about nine months earlier. The series was revised from Q1 1993 and is not directly comparable with the old series. The most important changes introduced from Q1 1993 are: (1) sales are now analysed and recorded on the basis of when transactions actually took place. They should therefore more accurately reflect the position regarding transactions at a given time than the previous series which were collated on the basis of validation dates; (2) prices of all sales now exclude some transfers in order to come closer to estimates of market determined prices for agricultural land. However, the new series does not represent exactly competitive open market values. Further information on these changes is available on the MAFF website (http://www.maff.gov.uk/esg/statnot) and by a faxback facility (Fax No. 0906 711 0340 charged at 50 pence per minute).

British Government stocks: Financial times Actuaries indices

The data are for the last Fridays of the month and are taken from daily series that appear in the *Financial Times*. The indices for fixed interest stocks are based on December 1975=100 and the series started in January 1976. The *index-linked index* is based on April 1982=100 and the series starts in May 1981. Further details of the indices and their computation are given in *Financial Times Guide to using the Financial Pages* published by Pitman Publishing.

GENERAL NOTE

All publications listed in these notes as published by The Stationery Office are available from the Publications Centre on 0870 600 5522.

All publications published by the Office for National Statistics are available from National Statistics Direct on 01633 812078.

First Releases are available from the ONS Press Office on 020 7533 5707.

Index of sources

This index gives the titles of official publications or other sources containing statistics allied to those in the tables of this *Annual Supplement.* These publications provide more detailed analyses than are shown in the *Annual Supplement.* More detailed analyses of the annual data for many of the series may be found in the National Statistics publication *Annual Abstract of Statistics* (2000 edition published by The Stationery Office, ISBN 0 11 621270 5, price £39.50).

The National Statistics publications listed below are available from The Stationery Office Publications Centre. Telephone 0870 600 5522 or fax 0870 600 5533.

A free booklet *Government Statistics: A Brief Guide to Sources* is available detailing the source department for a wide variety of economic data. It is available from the National Statistics Library at Newport. Telephone 01633 812973 or fax 01633 812599.

	Table	*Source*	*Further statistics*
Advances and acceptance (see Banking)			
Asset prices	6.9	Office For National Statistics DETr MAFF Bank of England	Financial Statistics (for Financial assets)
Average earnings (see Earnings)			
Balance of Payments		Office for National Statistics	Financial Statistics UK Balance of Payments UK Economic Accounts Bank of England Statistical Abstract
Current account	1.18		
Financial account summary	1.19		
International investment position	1.20		
Investment transactions	1.19		
Invisible credits	1.18		
debits	1.18		
Reserve assets	1.19		
Summary	1.17		
Bank lending (see Banking)			
Banking		Bank of England	
Bank lending	5.3, 5.6, 5.8		Financial Statistics
Bank's loans, advances and acceptances	5.6, 5.8		Bank of England Statistical Abstract
Bank of England's minimum lending rate (see Interest rates)			
British government securities long-dated 20 years yield (see Interest rates)			
Building societies		Bank of England	Financial Statistics
Advances on new dwellings	4.4	Building Societies Association	
Average prices of new dwellings on mortgage (see Housing)			
Commitments on new dwellings	4.4		
Capital account summary, analysis by sector	1.11	Office for National Statistics	Financial Statistics UK National Accounts
Car registrations and production (see Motor vehicles)			
Claimant count		Office for National Statistics	Labour Market Trends Monthly Digest of Statistics
Regional claimant count	3.5		British Labour Statistics:
Total claimant count	3.4		Historical Abstract 1886-1968 Year Book (1976)
Coal (see Energy)			
Commercial vehicles, production (see Motor vehicles)			

	Table	*Source*	*Further statistics*
Energy			
Household final consumption expenditure on energy products	1.7	Office for National Statistics	Monthly Digest of Statistics UK Economic Accounts
Industrial production: index for gas, electricity and water industries	4.1		Monthly Digest of Statistics
Primary fuel input: total, coal, petroleum, natural gas, nuclear and hydro-electricity	4.9	Department of Trade and Industry	United Kingdom Energy Statistics
Public supply: electricity	4.9		Digest of United Kingdom Energy Statistics
Engineering industries	4.2	Office for National Statistics	Monthly Digest of Statistics
Sales and orders: total, home market and export			UK Balance of Payments
Exchange rates			
Major currencies against sterling	5.1	Bank of England	Financial Statistics
Sterling	5.1	HM Treasury	Financial Statistics
Expenditure (see Gross final expenditure)			
Exports			
Of goods (Credits)	1.18	Office for National Statistics	Monthly Digest of Statistics
Price indices	1.21		UK Balance of Payments
Unit value indices	1.22		UK Economic Accounts
Value	1.18		
Volume indices	1.21		
Of goods and services in relation to gross final expenditure	1.3		
Of passenger cars, commercial vehicles (see Motor vehicles)			
Orders; engineering industries (see Engineering industries)			
Relative prices (see Trade competitiveness, UK summary measures)			
Relative profitability (see Trade competitiveness, UK summary measures)			
Final expenditure (see Gross final expenditure)			
Financial corporations (see Corporations)			
Fixed investment		Office for National Statistics	Monthly Digest of Statistics
By Private non-financial corporations (see Corporations)			UK National Accounts
By sector and by type of asset	1.8		UK Economic Accounts
In dwellings (see Housing)			
In relation to total gross expenditure	1.3		
Gas natural (see Energy)			
General government			
Consumption of goods and services	1.3	Office for National Statistics	Monthly Digest of Statistics UK National Accounts UK Economic Accounts
Receipts and expenditure	5.4		Financial Statistics UK National Accounts
Gross fixed capital formation (see Fixed investment)			
Gross domestic product	1.1	Office for National Statistics	Monthly Digest of Statistics
and components of gross expenditure	1.3		UK National Accounts
By category of output	1.9		UK Economic Accounts
Category of income	1.4		
In relation to inventories	4.7		
Market prices	1.1, 1.2, 1.3		
Per head	1.5		
Gross national income		Office for National Statistics	Monthly Digest of Statistics
Per head	1.5		UK National Accounts
Gross operating surplus of corporations (see Corporations)			
Gross value added (GVA) at basic prices	1.1, 1.2	Office for National Statistics	Monthly Digest of Statistics UK National Accounts UK Economic Accounts

	Table	*Source*	*Further statistics*
Household final consumption expenditure		Office for National Statistics	Consumer Trends
Component categories	1.7		Monthly Digest of Statistics
In relation to Gross households' disposable income	1.6		UK National Accounts
In relation to Gross final expenditure	1.3		UK Economic Accounts
Per head	1.5		
Households' gross disposable income (see Incomes)			
Households' income before tax (see Incomes)			
Households' saving ratio	1.6	Office for National Statistics	UK National Accounts
			UK Economic Accounts
Gross saving, financial/non-financial corporations (see Corporations)			
GVA is Gross Value Added at Basic Prices			
Housing		Department of the Environment, Transport and the Regions	Housing and Construction Statistics
Average price of new dwellings on mortgage	4.4	Building Societies Association	
Commitments and advances on new dwellings (see Building Societies)			
Fixed investment in dwellings	1.8, 4.4	Office for National Statistics	Monthly Digest of Statistics
Orders received by contractors for new houses	4.4	Department of the Environment	Housing and Construction Statistics
Starts and completions	4.4	Transport and the Regions	Housing and Construction Statistics
		Scottish Development Department	
		Welsh Office	
Hydro-electricity (see Energy)			
ILO unemployment rates	3.6	Office for National Statistics	Labour Market Trends
			Monthly Digest of Statistics
Imports			
Of goods	1.18	Office for National Statistics	Monthly Digest of Statistics
Price indices	1.21		UK Balance of Payments
Value	1.18		UK Economic Accounts
Volume indices	1.21		
Of goods and services in relation to total gross expenditure	1.3	Office for National Statistics	Monthly Digest of Statistics
Price competitiveness (see Trade competitiveness, UK summary measures)			UK Economic Accounts
Incomes		Office for National Statistics	Monthly Digest of Statistics
Compensation of employees	1.4		UK National Accounts
(see also Wages: Earnings)			UK Economic Accounts
Households' gross disposable income	1.6		
Per head	1.5		
Households' income before tax	1.6		
Industrial production: index	4.1	Office for National Statistics	Monthly Digest of Statistics
By market sector	4.1		UK National Accounts
By selected industries	4.1		UK Economic Accounts
In relation to output			
In relation to inventories (manufacturing industries)	4.7		
Inter-bank 3-month rate (see interest rates)			
Interest rates		Office for National Statistics	Financial Statistics
Bank of England's base rate	5.10	Bank of England	Bank of England Statistical Abstract
British government securities long-dated		HM Treasury	
(20 years) yield	5.9	Institute of Actuaries	
Financial Times index of industrial ordinary shares	5.9	Financial Times	
Inter-bank 3-month rate	5.9		
Lending rate	5.10		
Local authorities 3-month deposit rate	5.9		
Savings rates - gross interest	5.10		
Sterling certificates of deposit	5.9		
Treasury bill yield	5.9		

	Table	Source	Further statistics
Inventories			
Changes by industry groups	4.6	Office for National Statistics	Monthly Digest of Statistics
Ratios: total inventories to GVA, manufacturers inventories to manufacturing production, retailers stocks to retail sales	4.8		UK National Accounts UK Economic Accounts
Total changes in relation to GVA	1.3		Monthly Digest of Statistics UK National Accounts
Invisibles (see Balance of payments)			
Investment transactions (see Balance of payments)			
Labour Force Survey (see Employees)			
Liquidity (see Monetary aggregates)			
Local authorities 3-month deposit rate (see Interest rates)			
Manufacturing industry (see Banking: Employees; Industrial production; Output per filled job; Inventories; Unit wage costs)			
Monetary aggregates	5.2	Bank of England	Financial Statistics Bank of England Statistical Abstract
Motor vehicles			
New car registrations	4.8	Department of the Environment, Transport and the Regions	
Production of passenger cars and commercial vehicles: total and for export	4.3	Office for National Statistics	Monthly Digest of Statistics
National disposable income	1.1	Office for National Statistics	UK National Accounts
Natural gas (see Energy)			
Non-financial corporations (see Corporations)			
Nuclear electricity (see Energy)			
Operating surplus (see Corporations)			
Orders received			
By construction industry (see Construction)			
By contractors for new houses	4.4	Department of the Environment, Transport and the Regions	Housing and Construction Statistics
By engineering industries (see Engineering)			
Output			
By construction industry (see Construction)			
By engineering industries (see Engineering)			
Index numbers by industry groups	4.1	Office for National Statistics	Monthly Digest of Statistics
Index numbers at constant factor cost	1.9, 1.10		UK Economic Accounts
Per filled job	3.8		UK National Accounts British Labour Statistics: Historical Abstract 1886-1968 Year Book (1976)
Overseas trade (see Exports; Imports; Trade competitiveness, UK summary measures; Visible trade)			
Pensioner price indices (see Prices)			
Petroleum (see Energy)			
Population			
Estimates *per capita*, income, product and spending	1.5	Office for National Statistics	

	Table	Source	Further statistics
Prices			
Asset prices	6.9	Office for National Statistics Department of the Environment, Transport and the Regions MAFF Bank of England	Financial Statistics (for Financial Assets)
Average price of new dwellings on mortgage (see Housing)			
Pensioner price indices	2.1	Office for National Statistics	Labour Market Trends British Labour Statistics: Historical Abstract 1886-1968 Year Book (1976)
Producer price indices	2.1,5.11	Office for National Statistics	Monthly Digest of Statistics
Relative prices, UK summary measures of competitiveness (see Trade competitiveness, UK summary measures)			
Retail price indices	2.1,2.2		Labour Market Trends Monthly Digest of Statistics British Labour Statistics: Historical Abstract 1886-1968 Year Book (1976)
Tax and price index	2.2	Office for National Statistics	Monthly Digest of Statistics
Private sector			
Capital account, financial surplus/deficit	1.11	Office for National Statistics	Financial Statistics
Employment in	3.9		Monthly Digest of Statistics
Gross fixed investment	1.8		UK Economic Accounts
Housing starts and completions (see Housing)			UK National Accounts
Liquidity (see Monetary aggregates)			
Productivity	3.8	Office for National Statistics	
Property Transactions	4.5	Board of Inland Revenue	
Producer prices			
Index (see Prices)			
Relative prices (see Trade competitiveness, UK summary measures)			
Production (see Industrial production: Motor vehicles: Steel)			
Public sector		Office for National Statistics	Financial Statistics
Employment in	3.9		UK National Accounts
Net lending/net borrowing	1.11		UK Economic Accounts
Financial transactions	5.5		
Gross fixed investment	1.8		
Housing starts and completions (see Housing)			
Index numbers of output	1.9		
Net-cash requirement	5.3, 5.5		
Purchasing power of the pound	2.1	Office for National Statistics	
Regional claimant count (see Claimant count)			
Reserve assets (see Balance of payments)			
Retail price index (see Prices)			
Retail sales			
Ratio of distributors' inventories to retail sales	4.7	Office for National Statistics	
Volume index numbers for various groups of retailers	4.8	Office for National Statistics	Monthly Digest of Statistics
Value index numbers	4.8		
Salaries (see Wages and salaries)			
Saving ratio, households'	1.6	Office for National Statistics	Monthly Digest of Statistics UK Economic Accounts
Services (see Balance of payments)			

	Table	Source	Further statistics
Service industries: index numbers of output	1.9, 1.10	Office for National Statistics	
Steel production and consumption	4.3	ISSB Ltd.	Monthly Digest of Statistics
Sterling certificates of deposit (see Interest rates)			
Sterling (see Exchange rates)			
Subsidies on production	1.4	Office for National Statistics	Monthly Digest of Statistics UK National Accounts UK Economic Accounts
Tax and price index	2.2	Office for National Statistics	Monthly Digest of Statistics
Taxes on Production	1.4	Office for National Statistics	Monthly Digest of Statistics UK National Accounts UK Economic Accounts
Taxes, payment by corporations	1.13, 1.15	Office for National Statistics	Financial Statistics UK National Accounts UK Economic Accounts
Terms of trade	1.21	Office for National Statistics	Monthly Digest of Statistics
Total gross expenditure on goods and services	1.3	Office for National Statistics	Monthly Digest of Statistics UK National Accounts UK Economic Accounts
Trade competitiveness	1.22	Office for National Statistics	
Export unit value index		International Monetary Fund	International Financial Statistics
Import price competitiveness			
Relative export prices			
Relative profitability of exports			
Unit labour costs index			
Wholesale price index			
Trade in goods (see Visible trade)			
Transfers (see Balance of payments)			
Treasury bill yield (see Interest rates)			
Unemployment - ILO	3.1, 3.2, 3.3	Office for National Statistics	Labour Market Trends Monthly Digest of Statistics
Unfilled vacancies	3.2	Office for National Statistics	Labour Market Trends Monthly Digest of Statistics British Labour Statistics: Historical Abstract 1886-1968 Year Book (1976)
Unit values of exports and imports (see Exports; Imports)			
Unit wage costs			
Manufacturing industry	3.8	Office for National Statistics	Labour Market Trends
Whole economy	3.8		Monthly Digest of Statistics British Labour Statistics: Historical Abstract 1886-1968 Year Book (1976)
Vacancies notified and remaining unfilled (see Unfilled vacancies)			
Visible trade (see also Exports; Imports; Trade competitiveness, UK summary measures)	1.18, 1.21	Office for National Statistics	Monthly Digest of Statistics UK Balance of Payments

	Table	Source	Further statistics
Wages and salaries			
In relation to households' income before tax	1.6	Office for National Statistics	Labour Market Trends Monthly Digest of Statistics British Labour Statistics Historical Abstract 1886-1968 Year Book (1976)
Per unit of output - see unit wage costs			
Workforce jobs	3.4	Office for National Statistics	Labour Market Trends Monthly Digest of Statistics

Printed in the United Kingdom by The Stationery Office Limited
TJ004337 11/00 560038 19585